# Get started with your **Connected eBook**

Redeem your code below to access the **ebook** with search, highlighting, and note-taking capabilities; **case briefing** and **outlining** tools to support efficient learning; and more.

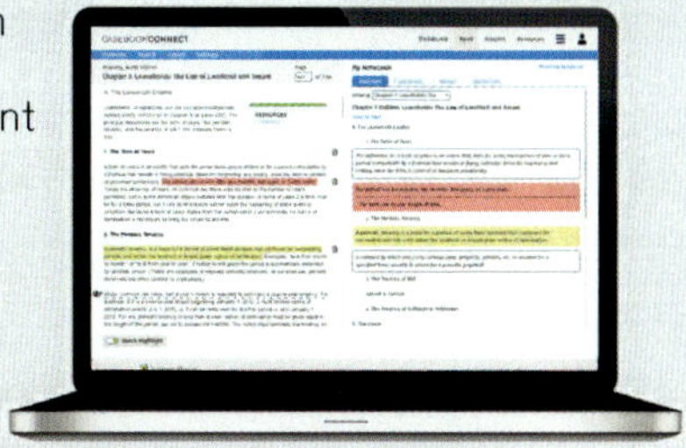

1. Go to www.casebookconnect.com
2. Enter your access code in the box and click **Register**
3. Follow the steps to complete your registration and verify your email address

**ACCESS CODE:**

Scratch off with care.

If you have already registered at CasebookConnect.com, simply log into your account and redeem additional access codes from your Dashboard.

Is this a used book? Access code already redeemed? Purchase a digital version at **CasebookConnect.com/catalog**.

If you purchased a digital bundle with additional components, your additional access codes will appear below.

"Being able to highlight and easily create case briefs was a fantastic resource and time saver for me!"

"I liked being able to search quickly while in class."

"I loved it! I was able to study on the go and create a more effective outline."

PLEASE NOTE: Each access code can only be used once. Access codes expire one year after the discontinuation of the corresponding print or bundle title and must be redeemed before then. We reserve the right to discontinue this program at any time for any business reason. For further details, please see the CasebookConnect End User License Agreement at CasebookConnect.com/terms.

**For technical support, please visit https://support.aspenpublishing.com**

9781543857894

# INTERNATIONAL INTELLECTUAL PROPERTY IN AN INTEGRATED WORLD ECONOMY

ASPEN CASEBOOK SERIES

# INTERNATIONAL INTELLECTUAL PROPERTY IN AN INTEGRATED WORLD ECONOMY

FIFTH EDITION


FREDERICK M. ABBOTT
*Edward Ball Eminent Scholar*
*Professor of International Law*
*Florida State University, Tallahassee*

THOMAS COTTIER
*Emeritus Professor of Law and Senior Research Fellow*
*World Trade Institute, University of Bern*

FRANCIS GURRY
*Former Director-General*
*World Intellectual Property Organization, Geneva*

RYAN B. ABBOTT
*Professor of Law and Health Sciences, University of Surrey School of Law, Guildford, UK*
*Adjunct Assistant Professor of Medicine, David Geffen School of Medicine at University of California Los Angeles*

MIRA BURRI
*Professor of International Economic and Internet Law*
*University of Lucerne, Switzerland*

HENNING GROSSE RUSE-KHAN
*Professor of Law, University of Cambridge*
*Fellow, King's College (Cambridge)*

MAEGAN McCANN
*Program Officer (National IP Strategies), IP and Innovation Ecosystems Sector*
*World Intellectual Property Organization*



ASPEN PUBLISHING

To contact Customer Service, e-mail customer.service@aspenpublishing.com, call 1-800-950-5259, or mail correspondence to:

Aspen Publishing
Attn: Order Department
1 Wall Street
Burlington, MA 01803

Printed in the United States of America.

1 2 3 4 5 6 7 8 9 0

ISBN 978-1-5438-5789-4

**Library of Congress Cataloging-in-Publication Data**

Names: Abbott, Frederick M., 1952- author. | Cottier, Thomas, 1950- author. | Gurry, Francis, 1951- author. | Abbott, Ryan B., author. | Burri, Mira, author. | Ruse-Khan, Henning Grosse, author. | McCann, Maegan, author.
Title: International intellectual property in an integrated world economy / Frederick M. Abbott, Thomas Cottier, Francis Gurry, Ryan B. Abbott, Mira Burri, Henning Grosse Ruse-Khan, Maegan McCann.
Description: Fifth edition. | Burlington : Aspen Publishing, 2024. | Includes index. | Summary: "Law school casebook on intellectual property in a global context"—Provided by publisher.
Identifiers: LCCN 2023059728 (print) | LCCN 2023059729 (ebook) | ISBN 9781543857894 (hardcover) | ISBN 9781543857900 (epub)
Subjects: LCSH: Intellectual property (International law)
Classification: LCC K1401 .A922 2024 (print) | LCC K1401 (ebook) | DDC 346.04/8—dc23
LC record available at https://lccn.loc.gov/2023059728
LC ebook record available at https://lccn.loc.gov/2023059729

# About Aspen Publishing

Aspen Publishing is a leading provider of educational content and digital learning solutions to law schools in the U.S. and around the world. Aspen provides best-in-class solutions for legal education through authoritative textbooks, written by renowned authors, and breakthrough products such as Connected eBooks, Connected Quizzing, and PracticePerfect.

The Aspen Casebook Series (famously known among law faculty and students as the "red and black" casebooks) encompasses hundreds of highly regarded textbooks in more than eighty disciplines, from large enrollment courses, such as Torts and Contracts, to emerging electives, such as Sustainability and the Law of Policing. Study aids such as the *Examples & Explanations* and the *Emanuel Law Outlines* series, both highly popular collections, help law students master complex subject matter.

**Major products, programs, and initiatives include:**

- **Connected eBooks** are enhanced digital textbooks and study aids that come with a suite of online content and learning tools designed to maximize student success. Designed in collaboration with hundreds of faculty and students, the Connected eBook is a significant leap forward in the legal education learning tools available to students.
- **Connected Quizzing** is an easy-to-use formative assessment tool that tests law students' understanding and provides timely feedback to improve learning outcomes. Delivered through CasebookConnect.com, the learning platform already used by students to access their Aspen casebooks, Connected Quizzing is simple to implement and integrates seamlessly with law school course curricula.
- **PracticePerfect** is a visually engaging, interactive study aid to explain commonly encountered legal doctrines through easy-to-understand animated videos, illustrative examples, and numerous practice questions. Developed by a team of experts, PracticePerfect is the ideal study companion for today's law students.
- The **Aspen Learning Library** enables law schools to provide their students with access to the most popular study aids on the market across all of their courses. Available through an annual subscription, the online library consists of study aids in e-book, audio, and video formats with full text search, note-taking, and highlighting capabilities.
- Aspen's **Digital Bookshelf** is an institutional-level online education bookshelf, consolidating everything students and professors need to ensure success. This program ensures that every student has access to affordable course materials from day one.
- **Leading Edge** is a community centered on thinking differently about legal education and putting those thoughts into actionable strategies. At the core of the program is the Leading Edge Conference, an annual gathering of legal education thought leaders looking to pool ideas and identify promising directions of exploration.

*For Devin and Ryan*
Fred

*For Elias, Emilie, Gerson, Margot and Sophie*
Thomas

*For Céline, Emma and Thomas*
Francis

*For Charlotte, Ryan and Theodora*
Ryan

*For Sophie and Alex*
Mira

*For Karima, Alia and Jasmin*
Henning

*For Jim and Carol*
Maegan

# SUMMARY OF CONTENTS

# CONTENTS

# PREFACE

We introduce this fifth edition by welcoming four new authors to this book project: Ryan Abbott, Mira Burri, Henning Grosse Ruse-Khan, and Maegan McCann. The new authors bring with them a range of experience in diverse aspects of international intellectual property (IP) law, representing a second generation of contributors. Ryan Abbott is Professor of Law and Health Sciences at the University of Surrey (United Kingdom), as well as Adjunct Assistant Professor of Medicine at the Geffen School, UCLA (USA). Most recently he is known for his pioneering work in the field of artificial intelligence (AI) and intellectual property. Mira Burri is Professor of International Economic and Internet Law at the University of Lucerne (Switzerland). She has focused recent attention on the role of copyright law in the digital environment, including the interface with data usage and protection, as well as digital trade. Henning Grosse Ruse-Khan is Professor of Law at the University of Cambridge and Fellow, Kings College, Cambridge (United Kingdom). He has published widely on the intersections of public international law, intellectual property and trade and investment regimes. Maegan McCann is Program Officer (National IP Strategies), IP and Innovation Ecosystems Sector at WIPO, following several years with the WTO Intellectual Property, Government Procurement and Competition Division (Switzerland). She was research assistant for the Second Edition of this book, and she prepared several major reports while at the WTO on matters such as the integration of IP in regional trading arrangements.

We are living in "interesting times". New technologies, most recently advances in AI, have raised a wealth of complex IP related questions. The most direct implications are so far in the areas patent and copyright. Yet, AI advances touch all forms of IP at some level. The international IP system has adapted itself to technological advance throughout its history. We are at the beginning of adapting to the proliferation of AI. This opens a window of opportunity for younger practitioners and academics in the IP field, but still demands knowledge of the fundamentals of IP law.

The long-anticipated Unitary Patent system has come into effect for the European Union (EU). This provides, on one hand, the opportunity for inventors to secure protection throughout a wider territory with a single instrument. This introduces, on the other hand, yet another level of complexity to the IP environment in Europe.

The COVID-19 pandemic of 2019-2023 illustrated the use of patented biotechnological inventions to address new and dangerous viruses, including through patent licensing arrangements. At the same time, concerns were expressed regarding whether IP rights were somehow delaying the production and distribution of vaccines and contributing to inequity. This was reminiscent of controversies from the late 1990s and early 2000s regarding access to HIV medicines, though the contexts were considerably different.

The challenge of climate change mitigation and adaptation calls for enhanced dissemination of technology to developing countries in line with the UNFCCC and the 2015 Paris Agreement. New avenues and approaches need to be found and developed in international IP law beyond compulsory licensing to address these contemporary demands.

We see new forms of challenges to fundamental principles of IP, such as the principle of independence, raised by conflicts over anti-suit injunctions that attempt to extend judicial control over national IP causes of action to a multi-country level.

This international IP system is equally challenged by political developments going to the continued viability of multilateral approaches to IP. What previously appeared to be a relatively stable long-term trend toward economic integration on a global level has given way to a fracturing that shows little immediate prospect of abating. While IP has played a role in this fracturing of relations, deeper concerns involving national and regional security interests are at play.

China and the United States have been at odds over IP protection since the early 1980s. Only recently, however, have these concerns escalated in consequence of China's emergence as a leading economic and military power. That emergence is perceived as threatening US, European, and other G7 interests. IP has gone from primarily an economic concern to a national and global security issue. This has implications for "legalization" at the multilateral level. Negotiations and movement toward a more integrated international IP system have stalled, and even rolled back. The WTO as an institution, and in particular its dispute settlement system, are functioning at a minimum level, and prospects for new IP initiatives at the WTO are dim. The focus of international attention seems to be shifting toward WIPO which may adapt to non-consensus decision-making. But this too has its limits.

There has been expanded "populist" political movement in various countries, and the populist phenomenon tends to manifest itself in favor of national interest and national solutions. This in turn de-prioritizes international focus. An example is the United Kingdom's withdrawal from the European Union, i.e., Brexit. The departure of one of the three leading EU economies has implications for the regional IP system in Europe. While the much-awaited Unitary European Patent is now reality, it does not cover the UK.

An expanding group of emerging market countries, starting with Brazil, China, India, Russia, and South Africa (BRICS), and recently adding several new participants, tries to shift the global balance of power away from the "Western" high income group. This may also have implications for international IP governance. While it is premature to identify specific IP-related developments, there is some parallel to the political power dynamic of the late 1960s that had a considerable focus on IP and technology transfer.

Notwithstanding the challenging international political environment, artists and inventors continue to create, businesses continue to make, sell, and trade, and the digital domain continues to expand. New pathogens emerge and demand innovative treatment. An international system that addresses the interests of creators and entrepreneurs remains necessary, even if it may be less "integrated". And this may give rise to new opportunities for practitioners and academics that can help navigate these choppy waters.

The first edition of this book was published by Aspen Publishers in 2007, but the true first edition was published by Aspen's predecessor, Kluwer International, in 1999 (as a two-volume set). We welcome that the second generation of authors provides a forward-looking perspective on the latest developments in this and future editions.

Frederick M. Abbott
Thomas Cottier
Francis Gurry
Ryan B. Abbott
Mira Burri
Henning Grosse Ruse-Khan
Maegan McCann

January 2024

# ACKNOWLEDGMENTS

For the fifth edition, the authors extend their appreciation to Elizabeth Dobkowski, Managing Editor, Aspen Publishing, for her support in bringing an exceptional group of new authors aboard, and to Kathy Langone, Senior Managing Editor, The Froebe Group, for orchestrating the copyediting and production of this work. The authors are grateful for assistance provided by Xavier Seuba, currently Principal Director, Patent Intelligence, at the European Patent Office, for his help in identifying important recent developments in the European patent space.

For the fourth edition, the authors extend their appreciation to Jeffrey Slutzky, Managing Editor, Legal Education, Wolters Kluwer Legal & Regulatory Solutions U.S. for his encouragement and support of this work, to Patrick Cline, Production Editor, The Froebe Group, for his outstanding supervision and work on integrating new materials, and to Kathy Langone, Director of Development, The Froebe Group, for important assistance with marketing aspects. The authors are grateful to Keriann Smith, student and research assistant at Florida State University College of Law, for her very capable work on this edition, including help in identifying sources of update materials.

For the third edition, the authors extend their appreciation to John Devins, Senior Managing Editor at Wolters Kluwer Law & Business for his continuing support of this work, and to Cindy Uh, Developmental Editor, and Suzanne Rapcavage, Copyeditor, at The Froebe Group for their superb assistance and close attention to detail.

For the second edition, the authors are grateful to Tetyana Payosova, doctoral student research fellow, and Andrea Kienast, junior research fellow, both at the Department of Economic Law and the World Trade Institute of the University of Bern for careful support and assistance. Both ardent students using the first edition, they offered valuable advice from a student's perspective in improving the book for teaching purposes. The authors are also grateful to Maegan McCann, Kelly Shaw, and Charles Whittington, students at Florida State University College of Law, for their able assistance with research, including their help in identifying recent judicial decisions of interest. The authors are indebted to faculty users of the first edition for their questions and comments that help refine the ongoing work. They also very much appreciate the commitment and effort of John Devins and Jessica Barmack, Assistant Managing Editor and Developmental Editor, respectively, at Aspen Publishers.

For the first edition, authors wish to thank the anonymous reviewers on behalf of Aspen Publishers who contributed to improving the organization of this book. They wish to thank Cathy Abbott, who has again demonstrated her excellent editing skills. They thank Leslie Jennings for her able assistance in securing permissions to reprint. Thomas Cottier acknowledges the research assistance of Christophe Germann with respect to his contribution. They also very much appreciate the commitment and effort of Richard Mixter and Eric Holt, the Acquisitions Editor and Managing Editor, respectively, at Aspen Publishers. The authors finally wish to thank Professor Jerry Reichman for his encouraging words.

The authors very much appreciate the assistance of The Froebe Group, who have coordinated the editing for all five editions.

In addition, we gratefully acknowledge permission to reprint materials from the following authors and publishers:

Abbott, Frederick M. Prosecuting Excessive Pricing of Pharmaceuticals Under Competition Law: Evolutionary Development, Columbia Science and Technology Law Review, Vol. 24, No. 2, pgs. 173-274 (2023). Reprinted by permission of Frederick Abbott.

Abbott, Ryan. Everything Is Obvious, 66 UCLA Law Review 2 (2019), adapted. Reprinted by permission of Ryan Abbott.

Beier, Freidrich-Karl. The European Patent System, 14 Vanderbilt Journal of International Law 1 (1981). Reprinted by permission of the Vanderbilt Journal of International Law.

Branstetter, Lee & Keith E. Maskus. Global Knowledge Flows, Absorptive Capacity, and Capability Acquisition: Old Ideas, Recent Evidence, and New Approaches, in Trade In Knowledge, p. 405 (A. Taubman & J. Watal, eds.). Cambridge University Press, 2022. Reprinted by permission of Lee Branstetter, Keith E. Maskus, and Cambridge University Press / Publishers' Licensing Services Limited.

Burri, Mira & Zaira Zihlmann. Intermediaries' Liability in Light of the Recent EU Copyright Reform, 11 Indian Journal of Intellectual Property Law 35 (2021). Reprinted by permission of Mira Burri.

Colangelo, Giuseppe & Valerio Torti. Anti-suit Injunctions and Geopolitics in Transnational SEPs Litigation, 14 European Journal of Legal Studies 45-84 (2023). Reprinted by permission of Giuseppe Colangelo.

Cottier, Thomas. The Agreement on Trade-Related Aspects of Intellectual Property Rights (TRIPs), in The World Trade Organization: Legal, Economic and Political Analysis, Vol. I 1040-1120, at 1082-1085 (Patrick F. J. Macroy, Arthur E. Appleton & Micheal G. Plummer, eds.). Springer: New York 2005. Reprinted by permission of Springer Publishing.

Cottier, Thomas. Industrial Property, International Law, http://www.mpepil.com/. Reprinted by permission of Max Planck Institute.

Cottier, Thomas. Inequality and Intellectual Property: Equity, Innovation and Creative Imitation, in Intellectual Property and Information Law series: Intellectual Property, Innovation, and Global Inequality (D. Benoliel, F. Gurry, K. Lee & P. Yu, eds.). Cambridge University Press, 2023. Reprinted by permission of Cambridge University Press.

Cottier, Thomas. The Legal Nature of Intellectual Property Rights in International Law, in 5 Kritika: Essays on Intellectual Property Ordering 23-47 (Gustavo Ghidini, Hanns Ullrich & Peter Drahos, eds.). Edward Elgar (Cheltenham, UK), 2022. Reprinted by permission of Edward Elgar Publishing.

Cottier, Thomas & Christophe Germann. Teaching Intellectual Property, Unfair Competition and Anti-Trust Law, at 130-166, in Teaching of Intellectual Property: Principles and Methods (Yo Takagi, Larry Allman & Mpazi A. Sinjela, eds.). Cambridge University Press, 2008. Reprinted by permission of Cambridge University Press.

Cottier, Thomas & Ana Jevtic. The Protection Against Unfair Competition in WTO Law: Status, Potential and Prospects, in Technology and Competition: Contributions in Honour of Hanns Ullrich (Josef Drexl, ed.). Larcier: Bruxelles, 2009, at 669-695.

Cottier, Thomas & Marion Panizzon. Legal Perspectives on Traditional Knowledge: The Case for Intellectual Property Protection, 7 Journal of International Economic Law 371-399 (2004). Reprinted by permission of Journal of International Economic Law.

Cottier, Thomas & Gabriela Wermelinger. Implementing and Enforcing Corporate Social Responsibility: The Potential of Unfair Competition Rules in International Law, at 81, 83-97, in Corporate Social Responsibility: Verbindliche Standards des Wettbewerbsrechts? (Reto M. Hilty & Frauke Henning-Bodewig, eds.). Springer: Berlin, Heidelberg, 2014. Reprinted by permission of Springer Publishing.

Gurry, Francis. Re-Thinking the Role of Intellectual Property, Speech at University of Melbourne, August 22, 2013. Reprinted by permission of Francis Gurry.

Helfer, Laurence R. Toward a Human Rights Framework for Intellectual Property, 40 U.C. Davis Law Review 971, 1017-1020 (2007). Reprinted by permission of U.C. Davis Law Review.

Kiewiet, Bart. Plant Variety Protection in the European Community, World Patent Information 27 (2005). Reprinted by permission.

Kuanpoth, Jakkrit. ASEAN IP Integration, in Emerging Markets and the World Patent Order (Frederick M. Abbott, Carlos M. Correa and Peter Drahos, eds.). Edward Elgar Publishing (Cheltenham UK and Northampton USA), 2013. Reprinted by permission of Edward Elgar Publishing.

Lessig, Lawrence. Open Source Baselines: Compared to What?, in Government Policy Toward Open Source Software (Robert W. Hahn, ed.). AEI-Brookings Joint Center: January 2003. Reprinted by permission of Lawrence Lessig.

Levine, David S. & Joshua D. Sarnoff. Compelling Trade Secret Sharing, 74 Hastings Law Journal 987 (2023). Reprinted by permission of David Levine and Joshua Sarnoff.

Maskus, Keith. Intellectual Property Rights in the Global Economy, Institute for International Economics (2000). Reprinted by permission of Keith Maskus.

Maskus, Keith. International Agreements on Intellectual Property Rights: TRIPS and Beyond. Prepared for the Routledge Handbook of International Trade Agreements (Robert Looney, ed.). Routledge, 2018. Reprinted by permission of Taylor & Francis Group.

Maskus, Keith E., & J. H. Reichman. The Globalization of Private Knowledge Goods and the Privatization of Global Public Goods, 7 Journal of International Economic Law 279 (2004). Reprinted by permission of Keith Maskus and Jerome Reichman.

Mondini, A. & P. Groz. New Developments in Swiss Patent Law, September 2009 Newsletter of law firm Schellenberg/Wittmer.

Moyer-Henry, Kari, Ph.D. Patenting Neem and Hoodia: Conflicting Decisions Issued by the Opposition Board of the European Patent Office, 27 Biotechnology Law Report 6-9 (2008). Reprinted by permission of Mary Ann Liebert, Inc.

Musungu, Sisule F., & Graham Dutfield. Multilateral Agreements and a TRIPS-Plus World: The World Intellectual Property Organization (WIPO), TRIPS Issues Papers 3, Quaker United Nations Office (QUNO), Geneva Quaker International Affairs Programme (QIAP), Ottawa. Reprinted by permission of Sisule F. Musungu and the Quaker United Nations Office.

Penrose, Edith. Economics of the International Patent System. 101-107, 162-169. Copyright © 1951 by The Johns Hopkins University Press. Reprinted by permission of The Johns Hopkins University Press.

Ricketson, Sam. The Birth of the Berne Union, The Centenary of The Berne Convention, Conference (Intellectual Property Law Unit, Queen Mary College, University of London and British Literary and Artistic Copyright Association London, April 17-18, 1986). Reprinted by permission of Sam Ricketson.

Samuelson, Pamela. The U.S. Digital Agenda at WIPO, 37 Virginia Journal of International Law 369 (1997). Reprinted by permission of Pamela Samuelson.

Stiglitz, Joseph E. Knowledge as a Public Good (1998). World Bank Group, www.worldbank.org. Reprinted by permission of Joseph Stiglitz.

Sykes, Alan O. Public Health and International Law: TRIPS, Pharmaceuticals, Developing Countries, and the Doha "Solution," 3 Chicago Journal of International Law 47 (2002). Reprinted by permission of the Chicago Journal of International Law.

UNCTAD/ICTSD Resource Book on TRIPS and Development. Cambridge University Press (2005). Reprinted by permission of Cambridge University Press.

Wendland, Wend, Director, Traditional Knowledge Division, WIPO and Secretary of the WIPO Intergovernmental Committee (IGC). Is an International Agreement on IP,

Genetic Resources and Associated Traditional Knowledge Finally in Sight? WIPO Magazine, February 2023. Licensed under an Attribution 4.0 International Creative Commons license (CC BY 4.0).

WIPO. 2023 PCT Yearly Review: Highlights, adapted from Patent Cooperation Treaty Yearly Review 2023: The International Patent System (2023). Licensed under an Attribution 4.0 International Creative Commons license (CC BY 4.0).

WIPO. The Hague Agreement Concerning the International Registration of Industrial Designs: Main Features and Advantages. WIPO Publication, No. 911(E). Reprinted by permission of the World Intellectual Property Organization.

WIPO. Intellectual Property and Genetic Resources, Traditional Knowledge and Traditional Cultural Expression, World Intellectual Property Organization (2022). Licensed under an Attribution 3.0 IGO Creative Commons license (CC BY 3.0 IGO).

WIPO. The Madrid Agreement Concerning the International Registration of Marks and the Protocol Relating to that Agreement, WIPO Intellectual Property Handbook (2006). Reprinted by permission of the World Intellectual Property Organization.

WIPO. PCT FAQS: Protecting Your Inventions Abroad: Frequently Asked Questions about the Patent Cooperation Treaty (PCT) (Status on July 2022). Licensed under an Attribution 4.0 International Creative Commons license (CC BY 4.0).

WIPO. Revised Issues Paper on Intellectual Property Policy and Artificial Intelligence (2020). Licensed under an Attribution 4.0 International Creative Commons license (CC BY 4.0).

WIPO. SCP Agrees on Future Work on Patent-Related Issues, WIPO Press release, Geneva, October 15, 2010. Licensed under an Attribution 4.0 International Creative Commons license (CC BY 4.0).

WIPO. Summary of the Convention Establishing the World Intellectual Property Organization (WIPO Convention), http://www.wipo.int (2006). Reprinted by permission of the World Intellectual Property Organization.

WIPO. Technical Study on Disclosure Requirements in Patent Systems Related to Genetic Resources and Traditional Knowledge, WIPO Intergovernmental Committee on Intellectual Property and Genetic Resources, Traditional Knowledge and Folklore, Study No. 3, Feb. 2004. Reprinted by permission of the World Intellectual Property Organization.

WIPO. The WIPO Copyright Treaty (WCT), WIPO Intellectual Property Handbook (2006). Reprinted by permission of the World Intellectual Property Organization.

WIPO Arbitration and Mediation Center. New Generic Top-Level Domains: Intellectual Property Considerations, http://www.wipo.int (2007). Reprinted by permission of the World Intellectual Property Organization.

Zhuang, Wei. Evolution of the Patent System in China, in Emerging Markets and the World Patent Order (Frederick M. Abbott, Carlos M. Correa & Peter Drahos, eds.). Edward Elgar Publishing (Cheltenham UK and Northampton USA), 2013. Reprinted by permission of Edward Elgar Publishing.

# INTERNATIONAL INTELLECTUAL PROPERTY IN AN INTEGRATED WORLD ECONOMY

## CHAPTER 1

# STRUCTURAL FRAMEWORK, BASIC PRINCIPLES, AND POLICIES

## I. INTRODUCTION

### A. International Intellectual Property as a Discipline

International trade, foreign investment, and technology have brought the international community closer together. The business sector functions globally, collecting and assembling inputs from factories and employees around the world, widely distributing products and services. Scientists and academicians continue to exchange ideas over the Internet and at international conferences, albeit security concerns have recently introduced some friction even among these communities. Social networking web sites and related forms of instantaneous distributed communication have changed the way individuals and communities interact locally and globally. Diseases show limited regard for national borders as pandemic and threats of pandemic challenge the global public health system. We collectively share a planetary environment that requires multilateral attention. In all this, intellectual property takes center stage. Fostering innovation, technological advances, and securing product differentiation way beyond national borders amounts to an important ingredient of international economic law.

Innovation is driving the global economy. Biotechnology is transforming agriculture and medicine. Materials and propulsion technologies are creating a new global transportation infrastructure in which outer space transportation and exploration systems are playing an increasing role. Developing and deploying environmentally friendly sources of energy is one of the great technological challenges of the twenty-first century. Artificial intelligence (AI) is part of the ever-changing innovation landscape, with autonomous machines and computer authors and inventors demanding attention in the field of intellectual property, as well as in many others. Less exotic innovation in areas such as supply-chain management has a profound effect on efficiencies of production and distribution.

Over the past decade it has become clear that a positive relationship between technological progress and human well-being cannot be taken for granted. New technologies that initially captured attention for their capacity to facilitate social interaction did not serve only as facilitators of the common good. They have also facilitated the expression of negative aspects of human nature. On a different front, concerns are increasingly raised regarding the risks associated with the deployment of new artificial intelligence (AI) systems. Technology itself may be "neutral" from a moral perspective, but its deployment and use involve decisions by human beings, often taken in situations of uncertainty.

Expression in the form of music, film, and video game provides content for new generations of personal entertainment technologies. Books are digitized and commonly read on portable electronic devices. New generations of digital products emerge with increasing frequency, with "wearable" computing devices and virtual reality headsets among the latest consumer enticement. Product design captured the imagination of consumers and attention to aesthetics is now a significant part of virtually every new product launch. And intellectual property secures that these products can be distinguished, among its other benefits to consumers and functioning markets.

The continued technological evolution of a series of frontier technologies promises to be radically disruptive to our society, economy, and legal systems including intellectual property law. This includes developments in AI, as well as the Internet of Things, distributed ledger technology, the metaverse, big data, and cloud computing. It also includes development in physical and biological technologies like autonomous driving and 3D printing, genetic engineering, human augmentation, and the brain-computer interface. For example, AI systems such as ChatGPT raise a set of IP-related concerns that hardly existed in the public consciousness a few years ago, while generative IP design systems are worrying design and artistic communities regarding the place of the human creator of expressive works.

A defining characteristic of technological development in the twenty-first century is acceleration in the rate of change. New technology markets develop rapidly, and technologies likewise "obsolesce" quickly. Intellectual property law struggles to keep pace. Whether the subject is a life or death matter, such as research, development, and access to drugs to treat disease, or one of personal entertainment, such as access to audio and video streams, the scope and terms of intellectual property protection are of great interest to the researcher, artist, producer, and consumer. And, because the market for drugs, entertainment, agricultural products, civilian aircraft, and energy is international, the lawyer should not, and really cannot, be satisfied with understanding only the nature of that protection in a single national market.

Yet, the nation-state continues to be the principal geographical and political entity around which the world community is organized. The critical role that national governments play in regulating political, economic, and social activity must be acknowledged. We have seen over the past several years something of a reversal of trends toward globalization and multilateralism toward an emphasis instead on national interests and priorities, with political agendas shifting toward the bilateral and unilateral. Protectionist U.S. trade policy as of 2017 or the decision of the United Kingdom in 2016 to leave the European Union have a real impact on IP governance worldwide.

Through the twentieth century and the start of the twenty-first, we could speak of interests in the international economic system, including the international IP system, as potentially affecting in different ways "developed," "developing," and "least developed" countries. These groups of countries were given differential treatment in the WTO TRIPS Agreement, and in several agreements and settings administered by WIPO. In 2023 this broad characterization of groups no longer represents economic or political reality. "Emerging market" refers to a number of dynamic country economies that reflect some, but not all, of the characteristics of high-income or developed economies. Even among this group, there are substantial differences and interests. A trend is emerging to identify countries along a spectrum from low income to low-middle income, to middle income, to high-middle income, and to high income.

In 2018, long-standing concerns expressed by the United States, as well as by the European Union and Japan, with China's approach to acquisition of technology—particularly requirements of technology transfer as a condition of approving foreign direct investment—emerged as the backdrop of a low intensity (for now) "trade war" between the United States and China. These disputes involve some complex interactions between investment, trade, and intellectual property rules that are explored in this book.

Perceptions regarding national and regional security interests are changing. Russia's invasion of the Ukraine challenged the late twentieth century notion that the rule of law had created a stable geopolitical order. China's political and military posturing in East Asia have raised sufficient concern regarding future global supply chain security that the multinational business community is moving toward "de-risking" or "decoupling".

In principle, the international legal treatment of each form of intellectual property right (IPR) can be studied as an extension of the domestic law applicable to that IPR. A course on patent law, for example, can include a component on patenting in foreign countries. But understanding the international regulatory framework that governs IPRs involves more than appreciating that the same IPR can or should be protected in more than one country. International institutions make law that governs IPRs, and they play a key role in administering that law. IP offices cooperate with each other, and that cooperation helps to shape how IP law is applied. The domestic IPR norms that all countries apply continue to be shaped, or at least constrained, by rules made in Geneva, Switzerland, at the World Trade Organization and the World Intellectual Property Organization, or in other international fora, whether by other multilateral institutions or by regional and bilateral treaty. The member states of the European Union adopted a new constitutional framework with the Lisbon Treaty that entered into force in December 2009, and that further consolidated the regulation of IPRs in regional institutions and rules.

When disputes arise concerning the application of these international and regional rules, they may be settled by dispute settlement mechanisms unique to these organizations.[3] Some of these dispute settlement mechanisms have been caught up in recent geopolitical tensions.

A technical understanding of how a patent application filed in the United States may also be filed in other countries does not fully convey an appreciation of how the international patent system affects the inventor. Moreover, each form of intellectual property is regulated differently in the international legal framework.

Many students of the international intellectual property system will go on to represent the intellectual property interests of large corporations with the money to take advantage of legal rules. Much of the time, their work may be devoted to seeking protection for and enforcing IP rights. But this is only part of what international intellectual property lawyers do. Businesses large and small have defensive, as well as offensive, interests in IP. The largest industrial (and digital) companies may wish to challenge claims to exclusive rights by their equally large competitors. IP lawyers may be contesting rights in IP—for example, by challenging the validity of patents—as well as seeking to protect them.

Public interest groups like Doctors without Borders (Médecins Sans Frontières) take a great interest in how the international IPRs system affects access to the medicines its patients desperately require. Multilateral organizations like the World Health Organization and the World Bank are concerned with the way that intellectual property affects public health and development. The COVID-19 pandemic raised again the relationship between IPRs and access to access to technologies, and whether patents and other IPRs somehow were impeding the development, manufacturing and supply of vaccines and other products. Questions surrounding the development of "green energy" technologies, their protection by IPRs, and providing access to them are debated in the United Nations Framework Convention

3. Intellectual property emerged as an important component of international trade regulation, addressing both trade in goods and services as well as the international law of international investment protection. It needs to be studied in close relation to these fields. For a comprehensive discussion, *see* Thomas Cottier & Matthias Oesch, International Trade Regulation: Law and Policy in the WTO, the European Union and Switzerland (2005).

on Climate Change.[4] The parties to the Convention on Biological Diversity are concerned with how patents may affect the preservation and exploitation of genetic resources. The Food and Agriculture Organization is concerned with how intellectual property rights affect the world food supply. Human rights institutions are taking a close look at how IPRs affect the rights and well-being of individuals and communities. To make a long story short, it is not only multinational corporations or business enterprises more generally that are concerned with international intellectual property rules and how they are applied. These rules affect everyone. Lawyers who understand the system are needed to represent the interests of all stakeholders in it.

## B. Trends in the International IP System

### *1. Harmonization, Integration, and Countervailing Trends*

The first major multilateral treaty regulating intellectual property was the Paris Convention for the Protection of Industrial Property concluded in 1883. During negotiation for that Convention, proposals were considered for a substantially harmonized international patent system. Owing to major differences between countries in the way that patents were granted and regulated, such proposals did not gain traction. The Paris Convention established a framework of basic principles and a mechanism for facilitating applications for patent and trademark in more than one country, but it did not create harmonized patent or trademark law. The Berne Convention for the Protection of Literary and Artistic Works, establishing international rules on copyright, was concluded in 1886. It established a higher level of substantive harmonization than the Paris Convention, and its rules provide much of the basis for international copyright protection today.

During the first half of the twentieth century, a number of revisions were made to the Paris and Berne Conventions, and several additional international agreements covering different forms of intellectual property were adopted. While the Paris and Berne Conventions were widely adopted (with the United States joining the latter convention only in 1986), other agreements achieved considerably less acceptance.

In the early 1970s, a new specialized agency of the United Nations was created—the World Intellectual Property Organization (or WIPO). The WIPO charter expressly envisioned the promotion of intellectual property rights. Administration of the Paris and Berne Conventions was transferred to and consolidated in WIPO. In 1977, the Patent Cooperation Treaty (PCT) was adopted under the auspices of WIPO with the objective of providing a more efficient means for inventors to secure patents in different countries. This was a significant step toward harmonization and integration of the international IP system, even though the PCT system does not establish an "international patent" or replace national patent offices.

In the late 1970s and early 1980s, two conflicting trends in IP were converging. Developing countries were demanding increased access to the technology owned and controlled by developed countries within the framework of their demands for a New International Economic Order. At the same time, industry interests in the United States, Europe, and Japan were growing increasingly frustrated with what they perceived as the misappropriation of their intellectual property interests in developing countries. Developing countries demanded reforms at WIPO intended to limit the scope of intellectual property protection, while developed countries demanded stronger rules. This produced a stalemate at WIPO.

4. *See, e.g.*, Wei Zhuang, Intellectual Property Rights and Climate Change: Interpreting the TRIPS Agreement for Environmentally Sound Technologies (2017).

The United States, the European Union, and Japan made a strategic decision to shift the focus of the intellectual property debate to another forum, the General Agreement on Tariffs and Trade (GATT). The GATT, up until the mid-1980s, was concerned with regulating international trade in goods, and took little interest in intellectual property matters. However, the trilateral group of industrialized parties perceived that pressure could be exerted on developing countries to accommodate demands for stronger IP protection within GATT because the developing countries were dependent on access to developed country markets for their exports. Thus, in 1986, the Uruguay Round of trade negotiations, including as one of its key components Trade-Related Aspects of Intellectual Property Rights (TRIPS), was launched. After seven years of highly contentious negotiations, the Agreement on Trade-Related Aspects of Intellectual Property Rights (TRIPS Agreement) was concluded in 1993, signed in 1994, and came into force on January 1, 1995. The TRIPS Agreement represented a sea change in the international regulation of IPRs, shifting the central forum for rulemaking to the newly created World Trade Organization (WTO) and transforming the substantive rules. For the time being, the TRIPS Agreement remains the furthest reach of multilateral harmonization efforts.

The results of the TRIPS negotiations were intensely controversial. We will be examining the basis for WTO controversy at various points throughout the book. There remains significant debate regarding the consequences of the adoption of higher levels of IP protection, notably for areas such as public health. In 2001, WTO Member countries adopted the Doha Declaration on the TRIPS Agreement and Public Health, which emphasized the right of governments to take measures to protect public health and expanded certain TRIPS Agreement flexibilities. More recently, during the COVID-19 pandemic a number of developing countries and NGOs pursued a "TRIPS waiver" at the WTO that was ultimately adopted in a much weaker form than was initially demanded.

The fact of controversy at the WTO did not ameliorate the concerns of industry in the United States, the European Union, Switzerland, and Japan, about the level of IP protection and its enforcement around the world. It seems unrealistic for these countries to seek to strengthen IP protection multilaterally under the auspices of the WTO, again for reasons we will examine.[3] IPRs rulemaking largely has shifted to bilateral and regional trade agreements, and to plurilateral efforts, involving like-minded groups of countries addressing common IPR substantive and procedural standards. Recently negotiated regional and bilateral trade agreements include detailed commitments on intellectual property rights that are significantly more stringent than TRIPS Agreement rules. Until recently these regional and bilateral trade agreements were mainly pursued by the United States and the European Union with many of their trading partners (including accession partners), and in most instances with success.[4] Twelve countries surrounding the Pacific region negotiated a Trans-Pacific Partnership (TPP) agreement that included strengthened IP protection, mainly to satisfy demands of the United States, particularly in favor of its originator pharmaceutical industry. After the negotiations concluded, the United States withdrew its signature. Following that, the remaining 11 countries elected to proceed with the agreement, but struck out a substantial part of the IP provisions that had been agreed based on U.S. demands. Subsequently, Canada, Mexico and the United States (joined in the meantime by the United Kingdom) reached agreement on a

3. While there was a recent effort at WIPO to negotiate a Substantive Patent Law Treaty (SPLT), which would have resulted in harmonization of the criteria of patentability, these negotiations made slow progress, and were suspended in 2006. Efforts to bridge the gaps and render IPRs more conducive to the interests of developing countries has been undertaken within the WIPO Development Agenda, so far with limited results.

4. The European Union and the United States attempted to launch negotiations on a Transatlantic Trade and Investment Partnership (TTIP) agreement that would have included new IP rules. These negotiations have stalled and are unlikely to resume.

revised NAFTA – the United States-Mexico-Canada Agreement (USMCA) – that incorporates various provisions from the "old" TPP text (and ACTA[5]), and includes some stronger elements of IP protection. Developments such as these add a level of uncertainty in predicting the course of future IP-related international negotiations and agreements.

Bilateral and regional trade agreements should be distinguished from another phenomenon, which is the establishment of regional systems for the grant and/or enforcement of IPRs. The most highly evolved such system is in Europe, where the European Patent Office reviews and grants patents. A new regulatory and infrastructure arrangement for an EU Unified Patent has recently entered into force both simplifying and complicating the patent system for Europe. The European Union has also created a European Union Trade Mark (EUTM) and harmonized rules across a broad spectrum of IP interests. The Lisbon Treaty extended the internal authority of the EU institutions in the field of IPRs. Somewhat less evolved regional systems are in place or under development elsewhere.

An important development in the field of international IP over the past 20 years has been the diffusion of economic and political power from the European Union and the United States toward emerging market countries like Brazil, China, India, Russia, and South Africa. China, in particular, has seen nothing short of spectacular growth in the number of patent filings and grants. While so far new Chinese patents may not consistently represent substantial innovations, it may be only a matter of time before the quality begins to match the quantity. And, while South Korea has for some time been considered among the developed country group, some of its major enterprises (e.g., Samsung) have more recently emerged as major patenting actors, challenging the dominance of European and U.S. companies in the innovation market.

As a general proposition, there is a broad historical trend toward harmonization, strengthening, and integration of the international intellectual property system at the multilateral level, but this trend has been slow-moving owing to differences among the interests of stakeholders in the system. So far, there are limited instances where countries have moved away from the broad trend, in favor of national autonomy. However, during the past several years we have seen a fairly significant pushback against the general idea of multilateralism. This pushback was led by a former champion of multilateralism, the United States, but seriously exacerbated by Russia's invasion of the Ukraine and by Chinese activity in the South China Sea, leading many multinational business enterprises to plan for a "less globalized" world. Whether this pushback is a short-term "political blip on the radar" or will ultimately reverse the broad historical trend toward globalization of IP governance is an open question.

In addition, there is a substantial interest among some stakeholders in expansion of the public domain. This has acted as a counterweight to the forces urging strengthening and integration of the international system and increases uncertainty about the speed and future direction of the trend. The current debate on intellectual property protection is characterized by the ongoing search for a proper balance between appropriation and the public domain in the process of shaping the public good of IPRs.

---

5. Concern among several high income countries (HICs) with a perceived lack of attention to IPRs enforcement in lower and middle income countries manifested itself in negotiations among a group of HICs on an Anti-Counterfeiting Trade Agreement (or ACTA) designed to make it easier to enforce IPRs at the border, as well as to enhance the role of government authorities (e.g., customs) in enforcement. Yet while the ACTA negotiations yielded a signed agreement, its ratification was defeated in the European Parliament through the efforts of a coalition of public interest groups. For almost all intents and purposes, the ACTA is dead. This suggests there may be more public pushback against adoption of strong IP rules than trade negotiators seem to anticipate. In any case, whether regional and bilateral agreements will serve as "precursors" to new multilateral rules at the WTO or WIPO is not clear.

### 2. *Stakeholder Interests*

Pressures have long been exerted by multinational industry to move the international system for the regulation of intellectual property toward harmonization and integration. Major multinational corporations assume that a globally harmonized and integrated intellectual property system will serve their interests by allowing them to more efficiently secure protection for their innovations and expressive works, and expand the geographic scope of their rights to exclude others from the market. These enterprises recognize that they are better able to take advantage of a fragmented system (because of their extensive financial resources) than some potential competitors, but this advantage would not seem to outweigh the value of a more integrated system. Major multinational corporations have been the primary driver for stronger intellectual property rights protection around the world.

Yet, even within this multinational stakeholder community concerns are arising about whether proliferation of IPRs and "overprotection" in fields such as computer software may, in fact, be stifling the capacity to innovate and to market new products. More thought is being given to restoring competitive working space. The multinational corporate community is not quite a one-way street in favor of stronger protection.

The IP-protection objectives of the major multinational companies may not be shared by competitors and potential competitors in diverse national markets who want to preserve their own positions on the market. A Korean, Taiwanese, Nigerian, or Chilean manufacturer may not be interested in the more efficient grant of patent rights to a German or American multinational corporation. National governments tend to promote the interests of enterprises owned and controlled by their own nationals. There are a number of reasons for this. One is that locally owned enterprises are more likely to contribute to national economic development by returning income and profits to the local economy, paying taxes, and employing local labor. There is a widely held belief, evidenced by national government policies around the world, that local ownership and control of business is preferable to foreign control from the standpoint of national economic development and security. Just as local business enterprises are not necessarily keen to further the interests of foreign national competitors by making it easier to protect innovation developed abroad, so the national government for its own economic reasons may not be interested in promoting the interests of foreigners. Also, domestically owned businesses are more likely to make contributions to and further the aspirations of local politicians. Government delegates represent the national constituency in multilateral negotiating fora, and they are likely to be advocating the interests of local national stakeholders on whom they depend for political support.

Yet, there is a counter pressure to acting on protectionist policies in favor of local industry. This is an era of global competition for investment capital, and failure to provide comparable levels of protection for foreign investors (and IP holders) may act as a disincentive to investment. China provides an example of a country with an internal market that is so large and dynamic that it was able to attract capital even with IPRs policies that to some extent may have favored the development of local industry. Most countries do not offer the same market opportunities, and in the competition for capital investment have an incentive for protecting IPRs. Research communities, including universities and government institutions, increasingly look to IPRs protection as a source of revenue and funding for their work, and take an international perspective. It is not only industrial enterprises that seek to maximize revenues from research and development (R&D), but parts of the public sector and individual researchers as well. The interest of research communities in maximizing revenues from innovation is not limited to the more highly developed countries. Research institutions in developing countries such as India are increasingly active in patenting their innovations in many countries.

There is a countervailing perspective regarding publicly funded R&D. Nongovernmental organizations and legislators are asking whether governments and supporting taxpayers are securing adequate benefits when the results of publicly funded research are not made more readily accessible.

There is also a substantial group of public intellectuals who argue that expansion of the "public domain" of knowledge may be preferable to further privatization and exclusion. Whether exclusive control of knowledge is exercised on behalf of government research institutions or the private sector does not change the negative impact of limiting the diffusion of knowledge.

NGOs with widely varying interests are taking an increasingly active role in the international intellectual property system. Whether the issue is protection of the environment, access to medicines, the rights of indigenous farmers, or more equitable distribution of global wealth, NGOs appreciate that the ownership of technology and its implementation may substantially influence their subject matter areas. Civil society is taking part in IP-related discussions and negotiations at multilateral fora in a very active way and acting to offset the narrower interests of industrialists.

The role of intellectual property lawyers should not be overlooked. Patent and trademark lawyers who represent clients before the local IP office do not necessarily have an interest in a "seamless electronically integrated international patent application and granting system." Much of the resistance to extension of the international trademark registration system is based on protecting the financial interests of local IP lawyers.

The foregoing factors, among others, exert pushes and pulls on the evolution of the international intellectual property system.

### *3. International Developments in Artificial Intelligence and Intellectual Property*

There is significant international debate and discussion about whether current IP systems are appropriate given the continued technological evolution of a host of frontier technologies, including first and foremost AI. For instance, while AI has been capable of generating creative and inventive works, to some degree, for decades, continued improvements in computing power, software designs, and the availability of big data needed to train many AI systems has meant these earlier capabilities now have commercial value and disruptive potential. For instance, the not-terribly-useful text generating system GPT-1 was released by OpenAI in 2018 to not much public interest. By contrast, the release of GPT-4 in 2023 resulted in a prominent group of AI thought leaders to call for a moratorium on the training of AI systems more powerful than GPT-4 out of concern it will pose "profound risks to society and humanity." https://futureoflife.org/open-letter/pause-giant-ai-experiments/.

AI is potentially disruptive to IP systems for many reasons. For instance, numerous generative AI systems are now publicly accessible and capable of generating valuable artwork or photographs at little to no cost for many users based on them proving simple text prompts. This phenomenon may be very disruptive to human creatives, either by causing technological unemployment or by democratizing creativity. It may also be used by bad actors to create and disseminate "deepfakes" for political disinformation, to defame individuals, or to appropriate the name, likeness, and image of people without their permission.

To put it in context, dealing with new technologies is nothing new for global intellectual property systems, whether this concerns the patentability of computer software or genetically engineered life forms in the case of patents, or liability for internet service providers in the case of copyright. Sometimes new technologies fit more or less seamlessly into existing laws, and sometimes new legal rules are needed. Of course, there is always a chance that this time will be different.

## Ryan Abbott*

### *Artificial Intelligence and Intellectual Property: An Introduction*

In 2020, the AI AlphaFold generated results that won a competition aimed at predicting the three-dimensional structure of proteins from two-dimensional amino acid sequences. That competition sounds much less interesting than one involving chess or Go, but unlike a board game, predicting protein folding structure can be a critical element of research and development. For example, if you are designing a new antibody to target a protein, or studying diseases that involve protein misfolding such as Alzheimer's, it may be necessary to understand what a protein looks like in three dimensions. DeepMind, which created AlphaFold, more recently used AI to predict the molecular structure of hundreds of thousands of proteins, including almost all those in the human body, and it published those results in an open access database.

AI is not just playing games and doing research; it is doing all sorts of basic activities which until recently could only be done by a person. These range from taking orders at a restaurant to driving a car. An AI still cannot safely drive a vehicle fully autonomously, but most of the time the AI is probably already safer than a human driver. It is likely that pretty soon, AI will be a better driver than most people all of the time. People, after all, set a low bar for driving—about 94 percent of motor vehicle accidents are caused by human error, which costs more than a million lives a year worldwide and more than 30,000 lives a year just in the United States. If AI, or rather when AI, outperforms average human drivers in the same way it outperforms people at board games, that will dramatically improve the way we live.

If functionally working for McDonalds or Uber is not impressive enough, AI is performing tasks that once required highly skilled professionals such as lawyers and doctors. The US Food and Drug Administration has approved AI that autonomously diagnoses certain conditions such as diabetic retinopathy and macular edema. AI is already used extensively in medical care, but largely as a decision support aid for a human doctor. For example, AI can analyze a patient's electrocardiogram and suggest that findings may be consistent with a heart attack, but ultimately that analysis is just something for a doctor to consider. Only a human physician can diagnose someone as having a heart attack. However, unlike a decision support aid, an AI that is autonomously diagnosing a patient is, in a limited context, essentially practicing medicine. There is evidence that this autonomous AI performs as well as or better than average doctors.

Some people are excited by the prospect of robot doctors, and some people are scared—but before getting scared, realize that human doctors and drivers have some unfortunate similarities. Medical error is one of the leading causes of death. To be sure, people are better off seeing doctors than not seeing doctors, but perhaps in a few years some of the AI that can autonomously diagnose will do a better job than most doctors. There is some low-hanging fruit to be had in healthcare.

None of this has escaped the attention of policy makers. In 2021, the UK government announced a ten-year plan to make the country a global AI superpower and noted that we are living in "the age of artificial intelligence." The report focuses on investments in planning, supporting the transition to an AI-enabled economy, and ensuring appropriate governance frameworks. The United Kingdom was late to the party by comparison to China, which released its AI strategy in 2017 and boldly planted a flag in the ground. China's

* Adapted from Research Handbook on Intellectual Property and Artificial Intelligence, Edward Elgar (Ryan Abbott ed., 2022).

strategy announced that the nation would become the world leader in AI by 2030, make AI a 30 billion dollar-a-year domestic industry, and make China a driving force for worldwide ethical norms and standards. Months later, Russian President Vladimir Putin declared that whoever becomes the leader in this sphere will become the ruler of the world.

At least someone took that seriously. According to the United States National Security Commission on AI, which was formed by Congress in 2018 and which published its report in March of 2021, China is winning the AI arms race (or at least the United States is falling behind). It is a 750-page report, but the gist is that the United States is not sufficiently prepared to defend or compete against China in the AI era. It proposes that America increases spending on non-defense AI R&D all the way up to 32 billion dollars a year in 2026—about what America now spends on biomedical research. The report also has a chapter on IP and notes that IP rules are important for national defense as well as industrial strategy. It even highlights some of the specific issues that need to be addressed for the United States to be successful at using and promoting AI—including my personal favorite, AI inventorship.

Different jurisdictions are not just competing in terms of technology and investment, they are also competing with respect to governance frameworks for AI. Having appropriate laws in place is not only a critical component of industrial strategy and economic competitiveness; more broadly, it is vital to ensuring that technology such as AI is developed and used in ways that promote social value and that limit harm. All technologies and activities can cause harm, and AI is no exception. AI has been used for political and social manipulation, it has caused flash crashes in the stock market, and some fairly prominent technologists think it may doom the human race. Governance is not all talk and reports—the European Commission recently came out with draft AI-specific regulations which propose a risk-based approach that completely prohibits certain uses of AI, such as for indiscriminate facial recognition in public places (with some exceptions) and for generating social scores of citizens. It proposes a variety of compliance mechanisms for high-risk AI systems and uses, and it takes a lighter approach to lower or minimal risk systems. This particular set of regulations does not focus directly on AI and IP, but AI and IP is a key part of the ongoing debate about appropriate legal frameworks. Just as rules that take AI into account are important generally so that we get the best possible outcomes, they are important specifically with respect to IP to make sure that IP systems can achieve their underlying goals. AI is going to be broadly economically and socially disruptive, and specifically disruptive to IP systems.

AI has been around for a long time, and to some extent so have the challenges it poses to IP rules. For instance, since the 1960s people have claimed to have developed computers capable of making music. In 1966 the United States Register of Copyright publicly questioned whether these works should be copyrightable and disclosed that the office had already received applications for at least partially computer-generated works including musical compositions. But that music was all terrible. Today's AI has come a long way since the 1960s, and OpenAI's music is now practically mediocre. The project's website has AI that makes music in the style of current and recently deceased artists, which raises another interesting set of IP issues.

As AI-generated music improves it is worth keeping in mind that it is only going to get better. At some point, we are going to have AI that can make music people want to hear. That is going to be incredibly disruptive because once you have AI that can make good music, you can have AI make a virtually unlimited amount of it at almost no marginal cost. That is going to be competition for human musicians in the way that self-driving Ubers are going to be competition for human drivers. But AI will not just replace people; it will change the way that music is made and consumed. AI will make personalized music for someone in real time, to improve their mood or accompany their workout.

Harold Cohen and his AI system AARON were making paintings in the 1970s that, for all I know, could have been made by an AI, one of the great modern artists of the twentieth century, or one of my toddlers. That probably says more about my lack of artistic sense than anything to do with AI, but as with AI musicians, the past few decades have been good for AI painters. Or, at least, their art is selling for more. Headlines were made in 2018 when Christie's became the first major auction house to offer an AI-generated artwork for sale. It went for $432,500 dollars. Now exhibits of AI-generated artwork are no longer remarkable.

If you are looking for shocking headlines in the art world, it is probably what people are paying for Non-Fungible Tokens (NFT). An NFT is basically data stored on a digital ledger that can represent things such as a photograph or a painting. Some of the NFTs now being exchanged for staggering sums of money were AI-generated. AI making art is going to be socially and economically disruptive just like AI making music, and it will also result in more business for copyright attorneys. Normally when a person makes a digital painting the work automatically attracts copyright protection more or less worldwide. That prevents someone else from copying or selling the work for the author's lifetime plus, in the United States and most large markets, 70 years. What if that author is an AI?

In fact, numerous legal questions are raised by these sorts of technological advances. With respect to AI generating historically copyrightable work: Can you get a copyright for an AI generated work? Who would own it? How long would copyright exist? Until recently these were basically academic questions because there was not much of a market for AI-generated content, but that is changing quickly given the speed at which AI is improving. These are, or will soon be, now commercially important questions. Similar considerations apply to AI making other sorts of IP historically protectable by patents, designs, and trademarks. For instance, AI is making trademarks, but perhaps more interesting is how AI can fundamentally alter how trademarks function. Trademarks are designed to indicate to consumers the source and origin of goods and services. What happens when commerce is online, and when AI is buying goods on your behalf? How does Alexa determine the source and origin of goods and services and what sort of competing signs would Alexa find confusing or deceptive? How do we apply infringement tests based on human consumers to AI-based purchases? What happens where AI is effectively both the buyer and the seller?

At the end of 2019, the United States Patent and Trademark Office (USPTO) put out a request for comments on AI and patents as well as a request for comments on AI and IP more generally. It published a report summarizing certain comments it received early last year. The United Kingdom Intellectual Property Office launched a similar consultation to the USPTO in 2020 and published its results in 2021. One of the most interesting outcomes was how different the UKIPO findings were from the USPTO findings—even with many of the same stakeholders providing submissions. Part of the difference may be the result of rapidly changing attitudes toward AI and IP. Again, these consultations are not just about AI making new IP—they are also about how AI is being developed using IP. For that matter, AI itself can be protected by IP rights.

On top of which, AI uses IP. Consider Clearview's AI, which has collected and trained on more than ten billion images from across the Internet. Clearview licenses this AI to law enforcement to use for facial recognition. Usually copying an image constitutes copyright infringement, but what if it is being copied to train an AI, or just to generate insights? Is that infringement? What if a bunch of machines are sending digital copies of images between each other and no one ever sees those copies? What if an AI is functionally infringing someone else's intellectual property but not in a way that is directly attributable to the person? Who would be responsible for that and on what basis?

Different jurisdictions already have different answers to some of these issues. For instance, there is a very broad exception to copyright infringement in Japan for text and data mining and a much narrower one in Europe. But there is not yet much case law exploring in what situations it would be infringement for a machine to do something that would be infringement for a person. As different jurisdictions come up with different answers to these questions another challenge will be presented because of the transnational nature of IP. A book that you write in the United States is protected in France, Brazil, and India. That is not now the case with a book written "by" an AI. World Intellectual Property Organization (WIPO), the UN agency most responsible for IP, has gotten in on the action by hosting a series of stakeholder discussions around IP and AI (recently broadened to IP and frontier technologies). In theory, an international treaty may come out of this work so that jurisdictions around the world can agree to a common set of rules involving IP and AI—but that is a slow process. Not oblivious to the time frames involved, WIPO is working on framing the debate and getting stakeholders to ask the right questions rather than proposing specific substantive solutions.

Getting consensus on definitions and language would be a good start, as it is remarkable that about 65 years after the term AI was coined it still lacks a widely accepted definition. Definitional problems are significant when laws are being written to regulate AI and some of the people debating these laws are talking about different things. If people cannot agree on what AI is, it will be hard for them to agree on the definition for an AI-generated work. Without a common understanding of an AI-generated work it becomes difficult to have harmonized IP rules.

Some of the WIPO conversations have focused on issues that have been debated for decades, such as whether you can patent software and whether someone should be able to "own" data. These are not new issues, but they are issues that are taking on newfound importance due to AI. Patents on new software architectures and uses may be more valuable now that AI can do more, and data ownership matters more given the importance of data for training AI, for AI using data to generate insights, and for AI generating new sorts of data. Some of these issues are more specific to advances in AI, such as deepfakes. Deepfakes are not new, in the sense that there have long been technologies that can be used for deception, but what is new is how easy it has become for just about anyone to use AI to make a realistic-appearing video. The law has long dealt with deception, but the evolution of technology means that some of our rules may need to be rethought.

People are also interested in AI in administrative decision making. Not only can AI make new IP or help people to make IP, but it can also file or help people to file for IP rights. For example, an application called Specifio can generate a patent application based on a single claim. It does not directly replace a patent attorney because the AI is not as good as a person, and a patent attorney needs to (or at least should) review and revise what the AI is generating—but if it takes that attorney half as much time to write an application with the help of the AI, then perhaps we only need half as many patent attorneys (or, at least, fewer junior attorneys). Perhaps we will still need all the lawyers but they will be more productive so we will have more IP filings. That suggests that IP offices may get busier and need to turn to AI for help. In fact, the USPTO is already using AI to classify incoming patent applications and determine who should review them. It may not be long before a patent application arrives at a patent office and AI classifies it, does a first pass at a prior art search, and then drafts an office action for a human examiner to review. Even without an AI replacing anyone, that is going to change the process of patent prosecution in all sorts of subtle and not-so-subtle ways.

The public is concerned about AI in decision making—not really with patent prosecution, because it is hard for the public to care about patent prosecution even with robots involved, but certainly with AI augmenting and automating administrative and even judicial decisions in other contexts. In part this is because of worries around impermissible biases and explainability and transparency. It would be bad to have AI making recommendations at criminal hearings without being able to explain the basis for those recommendations, particularly if its recommendations were based on protected characteristics.

## NOTES AND QUESTIONS

**1.** The example of AlphaFold winning a competition in 2020 seems like ancient history given how quickly AI is improving. How are policy makers supposed to stay head of developments in AI—or, should they? Historically, the law has often played catchup to technological developments. Is that how it should be done?

**2.** The EU AI Act referenced above is moving forward, but, at the time of writing, remains draft rules rather than legislation. It currently includes restrictions on the use of copyrighted material in the training of AI systems like GPT-4 and requires AI-generated content be labeled as such.

## C. A Brief Introduction to the Forms and Functions of Intellectual Property

Intellectual property is a defined set of the intangible products of creative activity.[6] Unlike real property and personal property, which is often protected by means of physical security devices (such as fences and other enclosures), intellectual property is mainly protected by sets of enforceable legal rights granted to "owners" or "holders." These legal rights are intended to solve the economic problem described by Kenneth Arrow as the "incomplete appropriability of knowledge."[7] Because intellectual property is intangible and typically easy to copy and transport, it is difficult for business enterprises to capture the full value of investments in it (i.e., competitors can easily appropriate it). Intellectual property rights are an effort to solve this incomplete appropriability problem.

Intellectual property is usually referred to by the form of "right" (or IPR) granted to the holder. So, for example, a "patent" is a set of legal rights granted to an inventor. It is not the invention itself. Historically, the patent and trademark were referred to as "industrial property rights," while the copyright and related rights were referred to as "authors' and artists' rights." However, with the advent of the protection of computer software by copyright, the line between industrial property rights and authors' and artists' rights blurred and this distinction is no longer particularly relevant.

Before we introduce the institutions and basic principles that govern the international IP system, it may be useful to briefly introduce or review the forms of IP and the functions they

6. In previous editions of this book, the term "human" preceded "creative activity." In recent years there has been growing attention to issues surrounding the potential for creative activity by nonbiologic entities (e.g., computer-based artificial intelligence, sophisticated data mining, etc.) and nonhuman biologic species (e.g., chimpanzees). Issues surrounding whether these sorts of nonhuman entities may create or own IPRs are complex and are only beginning to be explored in a serious way. By removing reference to "human" the authors do not express an opinion on these issues, but leave room for alternatives. Of course, it has long been the case that certain classes of nonhuman entities can create and own IPRs. In the U.S., for example, artificial persons largely in the form of corporations and governments can not only own copyright protected works, but they can also be authors for copyright purposes.

7. Kenneth J. Arrow, *Economic Welfare and the Allocation of Resources for Invention*, in THE RATE AND DIRECTION OF INVENTIVE ACTIVITY: ECONOMIC AND SOCIAL FACTORS 609 (Richard R. Nelson ed., 1962).

are intended to serve.[8] Bear in mind that these brief introductions are expanded upon in subsequent chapters of the book discussing patents, trademarks, copyright, unfair competition, and *sui generis* forms of protection. The nuances are not introduced here.

### *1. Patent*

The "patent" is a set of rights granted to the inventor of a product or process that is "new" (or "novel"), involves an "inventive step" (or is "nonobvious") and is "capable of industrial application" (or "useful").[9] The inventor must disclose the invention in the patent application in a way that enables others to make the invention without undue experimentation. The minimum term of a patent under the TRIPS Agreement is 20 years from the filing of the application. The holder of a patent may prevent others from making, using, offering for sale, selling, or importing for those purposes the invention during the patent term. As with other IPRs, the rights of the patent holder are qualified by certain important exceptions. The patent is typically referred to as a "hard" form of intellectual property because it generally excludes another person from using the invention without the consent of the patent holder even if the other person independently found the same invention.

The patent is intended to perform three functions: (1) to stimulate inventive activity; (2) to encourage investment in the products of inventive activity; and (3) to disseminate technical information to the public. The extent to which the patent effectively performs these functions has been the subject of long debate. The alternatives to using patents to stimulate inventive activity are reliance on trade secret protections (or confidential information) or other forms of IPR, other incentives such as market exclusivity or a first-mover advantage, government subsidy (or tax breaks), or the establishment of "prize funds". Economists generally believe that patents are a more efficient policy instrument than, for instance, government subsidies for promoting investment in innovation, while allowing that in certain circumstances subsidies can be more effective. There is recent concern that an over-proliferation of patents may impede inventive activity, at least in certain fields, as a "patent thicket" grows.

Patents have a cost to society in terms of allowing higher than competitive prices to be charged to consumers, and this cost must be weighed against their positive invention-encouraging effects. In some areas, the social cost of allowing market exclusivity may be quite high. By way of illustration, allowing the inventor of a new cancer drug to prevent others from making it may significantly increase its price and reduce patient access. To offset the social cost, the patent term is limited. After some years, generic producers are allowed to copy the drug and enter the market. Nonetheless, there is intense debate about the extent to which patents on pharmaceutical products should be permitted to restrict access to medicines. Prior to the TRIPS Agreement, many countries excluded pharmaceutical and food-related inventions from patenting, or sharply curtailed the rights granted to patent holders.

The social benefits and costs of patenting inventions in different fields of technology differ. High-definition television and cancer treatment serve different social functions, and limiting consumer access to these products has different social effects.

8. This section is excerpted from Frederick M. Abbott, *Intellectual Property Rights in World Trade*, in HANDBOOK OF INTERNATIONAL TRADE (A. Guzman & A. Sykes eds., 2007) (footnotes partly omitted).

9. The criteria of patentability are referred to by different words in European and American law. European law refers to new, involving an inventive step, and capable of industrial application, while American law refers to novel, nonobvious, and useful.

## 2. *Trademark*

A "trademark" is a sign or symbol that distinguishes the goods or services of one enterprise from another in commerce. Trademarks may consist of virtually any form of sign, including letters and words, designs, colors, shapes, sounds, and scents.[10] A trademark allows its holder to prevent others from using an identical or confusingly similar sign to identify its goods or services in commerce. Trademark rights may last as long as the right holder continues to use the mark in commerce. In civil law jurisdictions, trademark rights are most typically based on registration, although use in commerce may also establish trademark rights. In common law jurisdictions, trademark rights may be based either on registration or on use in commerce (the latter referred to as "common law" trademarks).[11] In some jurisdictions, trademark rights may extend beyond the prevention of consumer confusion to encompass the prevention of "dilution" of the trademark holder's interests, that is, third parties may be prevented from "tarnishing" or "blurring" the trademark.

It is generally believed that trademarks serve an efficiency-enhancing function by providing consumers with an easy way to identify products with preferred qualities or characteristics. Consumers come to identify certain "brands" that they prefer, and they make purchasing decisions based on brand identification (as a substitute for more costly and time-consuming product testing). Trademarks also provide a vehicle into which business enterprises can invest advertising dollars, stimulating brand identification and "goodwill." Economists are divided as to whether it is useful to encourage investments in goodwill since there is not necessarily a correlation between the usefulness and quality of products and the amount of advertising invested in them. This can lead to market distortions (in which consumers make purchases based on artificially stimulated demand).

## 3. *Copyright*

"Copyright" is granted to authors and artists to protect expressive works against unauthorized reproduction or distribution by third parties. Expressive works are broadly defined, and include such things as books, films, music recordings, and computer software. There is, in fact, no express limit on what material might be considered to embody protectable artistic expression. However, copyright does not extend to functional works or ideas. This principle is often referred to as the "idea-expression dichotomy," with the "idea" excluded from copyright protection. Under the TRIPS Agreement, the minimum term of copyright protection is the life of the author plus 50 years. However, in a number of places, including the United States and the European Union, the duration of copyright has been extended to the life of the author plus 70 years. Copyright also extends to the rights of performers in the fixation of their unfixed performances, and to rights of producers of sound recordings and broadcasters. These latter rights traditionally were protected as "neighboring rights" in European law, but as a consequence of more recent treaty developments are generally now considered the subject of copyright. Copyright also protects the "moral" rights of authors and artists, the extent of protection varying among jurisdictions. Moral rights include the right of the author to be identified with the work, and not to suffer from the mutilation or distortion of a work with which he or she is identified. Copyright is considered a "soft" form of IPR because it does not preclude independent creation by third parties.

---

10. Some jurisdictions impose limitations on the use of single colors as trademarks. The TRIPS Agreement does not mandate the acceptance of single colors, sounds, or scents as trademarks.

11. In both civil law and common law systems, trademark rights are dependent upon "use" of the mark, but registration affects presumptions in favor of the party asserting rights.

Copyright is intended to benefit the public by encouraging authors and artists to create and disseminate their works. As with other forms of IP, it is difficult to assess the economic effects of copyright protection. It is not easy to measure how much creative expression is gained (or lost) as a result of copyright, and the economic value of that expression. While movie and music producing companies routinely offer data regarding losses suffered as a result of inadequate enforcement of copyright protection, the figures typically do not reveal the extent to which the claimed losses—which usually refer to lost opportunity costs—should be offset by the economic and social benefit to consumers of unauthorized copies (such as students using unauthorized copies of word processing software) or even to economic gains/benefits to "pirates" (who may also be sources of employment).[12]

### 4. *Design Protection*

Designs are covered by various forms of IPRs, including design patent, copyright, trademark and trade dress, and *sui generis* registration systems. The protection of nonutilitarian designs has long been a problematic area for intellectual property law. The traditional "utility patent" is granted with respect to a useful or functional invention. It is not suited to nonfunctional aesthetic design. In a number of jurisdictions, this led to the creation of a separate "design patent" specifically granted to nonfunctional product elements. However, design patenting has a number of drawbacks, including that securing protection is time-consuming and costly. Copyright protection covers expressive works and in principle is suitable for design protection, but many designs include potentially functional elements, resulting in uncertainty at the enforcement stage. Trademark and trade dress also protect design. The design or shape of a product or its packaging may be distinctive and associated with a particular enterprise. However, as with copyright, trademark and trade dress offer protection only for nonfunctional design, and this aspect also creates enforcement uncertainty. To overcome problems with design protection by traditional forms of IP, jurisdictions such as the European Union have established design registration systems with somewhat more flexible standards than those associated with the traditional IPRs.

One of the industries most concerned with design protection is the textile or clothing industry. In this sector consumer preferences change very rapidly, and an expensive time-consuming process for securing protection would not be particularly helpful to the industry. The TRIPS Agreement acknowledges this and obligates Members not to impede the grant of protection by costly examination or publication requirements. The major economic issues associated with design protection arise when industries blur the line between form and function. For example, the most controversial issue in European design protection is the treatment of automobile spare parts, including body panels and motor parts.[13]

### 5. *Geographical Indication*

Geographical indications (GIs) are identifiers that associate a product with a place based on the quality or characteristics of the product or goodwill associated with the place.[14] The classic

12. In some low-income countries, for example, street vendors of pirated videos and CDs may form a significant part of the informal economy. Strong enforcement may push sales of copyrighted works into "legitimate" storefronts, but in a way unlikely to provide substitute employment for the displaced street vendors. Consumers in these countries may not be able to afford authorized copies.

13. In its 2001 Design Regulation, the European Union excluded engine components from design protection and put off for future negotiation a decision on whether automobile body parts were covered. Council Regulation (EC) No 6/2002 of 12 December 2001 on Community designs, at recitals 12-13.

14. A geographical indication is distinguished from a "mark of origin," which merely identifies the place where a good is produced. The latter is not intended to denote characteristics.

illustrative GI is "Champagne," that is, the name of a region in France known for producing quality sparkling wines by a specific method. GIs are protected in a variety of ways in different national jurisdictions. The United States protects them by collective and certification trademarks, as well as by a special labeling system for wines and spirits administered by the Treasury Department. The European Union protects them by special registration systems, which typically include elaborate monitoring of production methods. Many Latin American countries protect "appellations of origin" separately from trademarks. In addition, geographical indications are also protected by common and civil law unfair competition regimes.

GIs are controversial. The European Union was behind what is now a long-standing initiative at the WTO to increase the level of GI protection for agricultural products other than wines and spirits (which already enjoy comparatively high protection), but this has been resisted by the United States, among others. The European Union is a high-cost producer of specialized agricultural products and is seeking higher prices for those products based on GI protection. The United States is a low-cost producer of bulk agricultural products and is concerned about potential market access restrictions from stronger GI protection. Whether other countries support one or the other "camp" in this GIs debate has largely depended on whether they are efficient large-scale agricultural producers, on one hand, or are producers of specialized niche products, on the other. Countries within Asia and Africa have recently been focusing on the potential for promoting their locally-grown agricultural products through protection by geographical indications or other IP mechanisms.

### *6. Protection of Layout-Design of Integrated Circuits*

Integrated circuits (or semiconductors) (IC) are produced on the basis of three-dimensional maps or "mask works" that are used to direct sophisticated equipment that etches circuits on semiconductor materials. In the 1980s, it was unclear whether such mask works could be protected by copyright (since they perform a function), and patent protection is often unsuitable to incremental innovations in IC design. *Sui generis* (or unique) systems of IC layout protection were developed. Such systems can be given effect either through registration or automatic protection. There has been little enforcement activity based on *sui generis* IC layout-design protection, but it is the subject of TRIPS Agreement rules.

### *7. Protection of Undisclosed Information*

Undisclosed information is generally protectable if it is commercially valuable, undisclosed, and the business claiming rights takes reasonable steps to protect it. Protection of undisclosed information is generally (but not exclusively) synonymous with "trade secret" protection. Such protection is provided in a variety of ways, including by specific statute or by unfair competition law. Trade secret protection generally lasts as long as the relevant information remains secret. The TRIPS Agreement specifically requires protection of undisclosed data with respect to new chemical entities in pharmaceutical and agricultural chemical products that is submitted for government regulatory purposes, requiring protection against "unfair commercial use."

Trade secret protection enables businesses to develop and maintain production processes, customer lists, recipes, and other valuable information that provide advantages over competitors. Allowing businesses to protect such information encourages competition and is generally thought to be healthy from an economic standpoint. Trade secret protection can generate controversy when, for example, it is invoked to prevent employees from moving between companies in the same industry, and when it may be difficult to distinguish between company-specific secrets and general industry knowledge. The scope of protection of data submitted for regulatory purposes in the pharmaceutical and agricultural sector is highly controversial because the extent of protection helps to determine the speed at which copies (or "generic" versions of "originator" products) can be granted regulatory approval and brought to market.

### 8. *The Protection Against Unfair Competition*

All the different forms of intellectual property find a common and shared foundation in the idea of fairness and of protecting markets and people from unfair competition. We shall see that new and emerging forms of intellectual property, such as the protection of geographical indications or of undisclosed information, or the protection of tradition knowledge, refer to unfair competition and its foundations in Article 10*bis* of the Paris Convention and today being recognized as being part of the TRIPS Agreement and of WTO law. The broad principles against fair competition, safeguarding against consumer deception, free riding, and denigration of competing products offer a conceptual basis to address emerging challenges on a case-by-case basis, eventually and possibly leading to new forms of protection.

## D. The Legal Nature of Intellectual Property Rights

Intellectual property rights, in all their different forms, traditionally are conceived and understood to be private rights, as expressed in the preamble of the TRIPS Agreement: *Recognizing that intellectual property rights are private rights.* Intellectual property in the tradition of domestic law essentially pertains to commercial law and defines rights and obligations of private actors in relation to competitors. While the very fact of granting exclusive economic rights to private operators and thus monopoly rights, the close relationship to anti-trust rules and the existence of complex grant procedures clearly entails the dimension of public law, the nature of intellectual property so far has not been extended to dimension of public law in international adjudication on investment protection and at the WTO. However, the role of governments in restricting the use of intellectual property rights in the context of new challenges in particular in health policies beyond fair use, government use and compulsory licensing, requires clarifying the vertical relationship between right holders and the government. The following excerpt was inspired by the denial of the right to use intellectual property rights in vertical relations and the need to clarify the conditions for justifiable restrictions. Because international law does not make a distinction between private and public law, the characterization of intellectual property as private rights is misleading and does not offer the full and complex legal nature of intellectual property rights.

**Thomas Cottier***

---

## *The Legal Nature of Intellectual Property Rights in International Law*

. . .

### II The Heritage of Private Rights

The preamble of the TRIPS Agreement, defining intellectual property rights as private rights, expresses a long-standing tradition of perceiving such rights in purely horizontal terms. These rights essentially allow rightholders to prevent others from using protected information without

* In Gustavo Ghidini, Hanns Ulrich, Peter Dragos (eds.) 5 Kritika: Essays on Intellectual Property Ordering 23-47 (Cheltenham: Edward Elgar 2022).

their consent. They thus amount to an exclusive or monopoly right on the market. Transactions of intellectual property, such as sale or private licensing, equally pertain to such horizontal relations, all of which are subject to private law, in particular contract and tort law. Intellectual property, in the domestic realm, essentially pertains to the field and culture of the community of private and commercial law. And since intellectual property deals with exclusive rights exposed to anti-trust, that community also deals with competition law and its relationship of intellectual property and licensing and the abuse of dominant positions granted by means of such rights.

Traditionally, intellectual property thus is dealt with by a close epistemic community which is organised in learned societies and associations with very little or no contact to the field of public law, in particular constitutional and administrative law. The community also dealt with international law and treaties as an annex to the field, while intellectual property, prior to the TRIPS Agreement, was hardly recognised in the public international law discourse. Public international lawyers were not interested in the subject. IPRs, despite a close connotation to property, customary law of expropriation, and extensive treaty law amounting to the first multilateral economic law agreements in the 19th Century, does not prominently figure in treatises of public international law. The classical fragmentation of European law faculties and chairs in private and public law channelled education and prevented a fruitful dialog for many years, until and interestingly it was brought about by the internationalization of rules in European law and beyond. But the tradition of private law also translated into norm diffusion by international agreements. Other than tariffs and non-tariff barriers, imposed and addressed to governments, intellectual property was conceived to operate horizontally among traders in the market of information. Other than under GATT and GATS, it was a matter of exclusively protecting right-holders, and not goods and services, vis-à-vis government regulation. The inclusion of such rights in the multilateral trading system strongly and newly supported to argument of positive integration, as Ernst-Ulrich Petersmann repeatedly claims, constitutionalising international economic law and making it directly accessible to citizens and

## III The Public Law Angle

. . .

My angle, from the very beginning, was the angle of a public and international lawyer, mainly focusing the role of the state and government. It was evident to me, that intellectual property amounts to market regulation by government by granting exclusive of monopoly rights for a limited, and sometimes unlimited, period of time, in different shapes and forms. Obviously, procedures required to obtain rights, such as filing trademark and patent protection, including opposition procedures, pertain to the realm of public law. The same holds true for border measures dealing with imports. But it is equally true for substantive standards. At the heart of the legal demarche is the correction of market failures. As information is a public good, both non-excludable and non-rivalrous, it is open to free and undiminishing use by the public at large. This in return reduces incentives to invest time, money and personal efforts in creating such information and thus innovation in the first place. Governments and regulators thus intervene by granting exclusive rights and shape them in a manner conducive to provide optimal incentives to invest and create new information. Patent law, copyright, design, the protection of integrated circuits and trade secrets serve this purpose. Another strand is consumer protection which cannot be secured by non-excludable and non-rivalrous information. Consumers are not able to distinguish goods and services without the allocation of exclusive denominations of products. Trademarks, geographical indications, but also unfair competition rules, mainly serve such purposes. Efforts to protect traditional knowledge, finally, seek to bring about a better balance with the interests of rural and indigenous people interfacing with modern markets in preserving existing knowledge and thus contribute to important goals such as the preservation of cultural and biological diversity.

While shaped in the form of private law, intellectual property essentially forms part of economic policy defining market conditions. It is part of market regulation, as much as addressing tariffs, taxes and other non-tariff measures. As markets do not exist naturally, but are essentially constituted by law and depend upon rules, in particular contract and torts, intellectual property protection is an important ingredient in shaping market conditions for producers and consumers alike. It is all a matter of getting the policies right in the field of regulating information and innovation, balancing or the pertinent interests at stake. It has to be well calibrated. As Stiglitz observes: "If we do not design this legal framework properly, however, it may actually impede innovation."

From this angle, intellectual property is fully part of public law. Historically speaking, it would seem that this strand prevailed for a long time before the field was abandoned by public lawyers and adopted by the community of private and commercial lawyers, similar to competition law and policy which in its origin served the purpose of protecting democracy in the United States, as well as in Europe after World War II, before turning to consumer welfare analysis dominated by economists. Originally, the introduction of patent law was mainly motivated by an effort to control and curb exclusive, abusive and randomly granted monopolies and privileges (letters patent) issued by the crown to cronies in return for financial returns since patents first appeared in the city-state of Florence in 1421. In England, the Statute of Monopolies, adopted by Parliament in 1623, was one of the first acts establishing the supremacy of Parliament and thus at the heart of the process of constitutionalising the monarchy. The introduction of copyright protection by the Statute of Anne in 1710 – other than authors' rights in the French tradition following the Revolution – mainly served to break up the monopoly and censorship of the stationary guild in the Gutenberg age, to contribute to the promotion of works by introducing a 14 year copyright term for authors, but also to regulate foreign trade as a matter of public policy. It no longer emphasized the purpose to restrict freedom of expression and to control the public debate which, at times of religious wars, was perceived to be a threat to peace and security.

Yet, it would seem that the history of intellectual property was less perceived and written from a public law angle. It is only with the advent of anti-trust law and competition policy, that public interests have become fully apparent in disciplining excessive and abuse uses of intellectual property rights. As Hanns Ullrich observed "Knowledge does not fit neatly into the framework of analysis that treats property as either private or public". The borders between private and public law gradually disappeared in what became to be known, at least in the German speaking world, as economic law (*Wirtschaftsrecht*), although this process did not result in a uniform concept and notion of law. Private and public law pertain in respective areas, with fuzzy borders. The problem is essentially one of allocating appropriate procedures to settle disputes either in avenues of public or private law. As much as clear allocations no longer are possible in regulating mixed economies, ranging from agriculture to financial services, intellectual property today pertains both to private and public law alike. In fact, IP just belongs to the law as the traditional divide of private and public law in terms of legal philosophy and methodology no longer can be fruitfully made. Moreover, the field even entails provisions of penal law in the field of enforcement, in addition to administrative law regulating border controls and importation. The advent of international law as an important driver in the field put an end to distinguishing these different traditions and forms of the law also from a formal point of view.

## II. THE SOURCES AND CONTEXT OF INTERNATIONAL IP LAW

Intellectual property protection essentially relies on a combination of national, regional, and international law. While specific rights and obligations are mainly—and variably—defined and put into operation by national law (and increasingly also by regional law), international law provides the overarching framework for interfacing national and regional regulatory systems. It governs the transnational aspects of IPRs. It establishes basic principles for the international IPRs system, and it increasingly plays a role in harmonizing substantive and procedural rules in the process of globalization. The international law of intellectual property is one of the most advanced areas of law of global integration. Though often neglected in general courses on public international law, it offers an impressive body of international law reflected in a number of sources within and beyond those listed in Article 38 of the Statute of the International Court of Justice.[15]

> Article 38
>
> 1. The Court, whose function is to decide in accordance with international law such disputes as are submitted to it, shall apply:
>    a. international conventions, whether general or particular, establishing rules expressly recognized by the contesting states;
>    b. international custom, as evidence of a general practice accepted as law;
>    c. the general principles of law recognized by civilized nations;
>    d. subject to the provisions of Article 59 [which *inter alia* allows the Court to call witnesses and experts] judicial decisions and the teachings of the most highly qualified publicists of the various nations, as subsidiary means for the determination of rules of law.
> 2. This provision shall not prejudice the power of the Court to decide a case *ex aequo et bono*, if the parties agree thereto.

This list of sources still reflects the main contemporary sources of international law. At the same time, it may not adequately capture certain of the more recent evolutions in recognized principles of law. It is difficult, for example, to classify basic constitutional principles of international law such as the right to self-determination as purely matters of treaty or customary law. The same holds true for the concept of basic human rights. Moreover, Article 38 does not address the legal nature of recommendations and decisions of international organizations, nor does it capture the phenomenon of soft law. Finally, this list does not establish any formal hierarchy of sources. It leaves the relationship between treaty law and customary law open.

In the context of the international IPRs system, the uncertain relationship among different sources of international law has not so far raised serious difficulties since it has been predominantly grounded in treaty norms. Questions of interpretation and application of these norms have been addressed by reference to the law of treaties. In the future, other sources of international law—in particular "general principles of law" such as good faith—may play a more important role in the international IPRs system, especially as this system is now effectively open to quasi-judicial dispute settlement under the umbrella of the WTO.

## A. Treaty Law

Intellectual property protection in international law is essentially based upon treaty law, both multilateral and bilateral, and both global and regional. The bulk of multilateral agreements relating to intellectual property and administrated by WIPO are classified in terms of intellectual property treaties, global protection system treaties, and classification treaties. The WIPO

15. The text below is adapted from Thomas Cottier, *Industrial Property, International Law*, in Max Planck Encyclopedia of International Public Law, available at http://www.mpepil.com/updates.

web site offers a complete listing, including institutional arrangements and membership of the Convention Establishing the World Intellectual Property Organization, intellectual property protection treaties, and global protection system treaties.[16]

Major treaties are located outside WIPO. The TRIPS Agreement of the WTO establishes the modern backbone of international intellectual standards in all fields of intellectual property, including enforcement mechanisms with which Members of the WTO have to comply. The TRIPS Agreement refers to different treaties, such as the International Convention for the Protection of Performers, Producers of Phonograms and Broadcasting Organizations (Rome Convention) and the Treaty on Intellectual Property in Respect of Integrated Circuits (Washington Treaty). Most importantly, it incorporates the Paris and Berne Conventions (Articles 2 and 9(1), TRIPS Agreement). The TRIPS Agreement builds upon these Conventions, and substantially develops their standards. Incorporation—considered at the time as an act of unfriendly takeover by WIPO—was mainly undertaken in order to link the provisions of the Berne and Paris Conventions to the WTO dispute settlement and render them enforceable within the multilateral trading system. This puts the TRIPS Agreement, with its substantive and procedural standards, at the heart of multilateral and global law relating to intellectual property, although we can see in recent years a certain shifting of the "certain of gravity" back towards WIPO. The relationship of the Paris Convention and the TRIPS Agreement is found in the *U.S.-Havana Club* decision and the *Australia-Tobacco Plain Packaging* decision (discussed *infra*, in various chapters of this book). An introduction to the function and provisions of the TRIPS Agreement is presented later in this chapter (*infra*, pgs. [35-41]).

Many agreements, like the Convention on the Grant of European Patents (EPC),[17] administrated by the European Patent Office in Munich, and comparable systems under the Eurasian Patent Organization, the African Regional Intellectual Property Organization (ARIPO), the African Intellectual Property Organization (OAPI), and the Patent Office of the Cooperation Council for the Arab States of the Gulf (GCC Patent Office) are of major regional importance.

Numerous bilateral agreements complete what amounts to one of the most elaborate and complex fields of international law, albeit often neglected and hardly mentioned in general treatises and doctrine. We note that relevant treaty law is not limited to IPRs and trade agreements. An increasing number of agreements provide relevant context, ranging from human rights to environmental agreements. We address them later in this book. Finally, treaty law also encompasses the Vienna Convention on the Law of Treaties, which sets out the relevant provisions on treaty interpretation and also the interrelationship of different agreements.

Beyond treaty law, decisions, recommendations, guidelines, and other forms of soft law play an important role in administrating IPRs, in particular by international organizations such as WIPO or the European Patent Office. It is important to note the importance of reports and recommendations issued by policy-making bodies, such as the Organization for Economic Co-operation and Development (OECD) and the United Nations Conference on Trade and Development (UNCTAD). These instruments often amount to soft law and influence the shaping of national law and the interpretation of international agreements.

16. http://www.wipo.int/treaties/en/.

17. While the role of the EPC has been modified to a certain extent based on recent developments within the European Union, it nevertheless remains significant.

## B. Customary International Law

To date, the sources of international law other than treaty law, as expressed in Article 38 of the ICJ Statute, have been of much less importance to the international IPRs system than to the classical domains of international law. Indeed, it would appear that the link between international IP law and the full body of international law has not been fully established. This is not only because IP law has, for a long time, been highly specialized and contained. It is also because international lawyers, as a general proposition, have not exhibited interest in IPRs subject matter comparable to interest exhibited in other areas (e.g., regarding international security law or the law of natural resources), and interdisciplinary links between international lawyers and IP lawyers remain to be further developed in doctrine and practice.

Customary international law is defined both by evidence of state practice and by shared perceptions of law (*opinio iuris sive necessitatis*). Traditionally, rules of customary international law evolve over substantial periods of time as nations engage in more or less consistent patterns of conduct that reflect their shared perception of the required behavior in particular situations.

Nationally and internationally, regulation of IPRs has been a domain of legislation (including treaty). This "positivist" tradition in the IPRs field is likely to change. Regulation of IPRs is subject to the effects of rapid technological change and to interfaces with other regulatory areas. New problems often cannot be solved by recourse to positive rules relating to past technologies. But it may, for that matter, be quite difficult to resolve IP regulatory issues by traditional recourse to customary international law. Pace and circumstances are at odds with customary law, which by tradition has required longstanding practice, and an essentially stable societal and economic environment, to evolve. An example of modern forms of customary protection is the Uniform Domain Name Dispute Resolution Policy at WIPO established through the practice of a full-fledged dispute resolution system short of relying upon treaty law.

## C. Precedents and Doctrine

Judicial decisions provide a backbone for the IPRs system. Yet, almost all of the decisions we examine emanate either from national or regional courts, in particular the Court of Justice of the European Union. Outside the European Union, the field suffered from a lack of appropriate avenues of international dispute settlement. Until the inception of the WTO, the international IPRs system produced virtually no international legal precedents in the sense of decisions by international adjudicatory authorities. While the ICJ has jurisdiction to adjudicate matters relating to international IPRs conventions (Article 28, Paris Convention and Article 33, Berne Convention), no cases were brought before the Permanent Court of International Justice, and no cases have been brought so far before the ICJ, mainly due to their perceived weakness concerning the enforcement of decisions.

### *1. WTO Dispute Settlement*

With the advent of the TRIPS Agreement, disputes became subject to WTO dispute settlement. From 1995 to December 2022, a total of 283 panel reports and 167 Appellate Body reports were adopted. As of August 2023, 44 requests for consultations under the WTO DSU raised TRIPS issues. Only ten of these have ultimately resulted in adopted panel or Appellate Body decisions, the others having been subject to mutually agreed solutions, arbitration award or remaining in consultations.

While the decisions of the Dispute Settlement Body are binding, the reasoning of the panel or Appellate Body does not amount to *stare decisis*, as this concept is generally unknown in international law.[18] Future panels are obliged to consider the arguments and reasoning of past GATT panels and WTO panels and AB recommendations, but they may deviate, for good cause, from prior decisions. Since December 2019, the Appellate Body has not been able to hear further appeals due to the fact that Appellate Body members whose terms had expired have not been replaced due to resistance of the United States. As a result, 25 proceedings pending before the Appellate Body cannot be further advanced until new members are appointed. Parties may appeal into the void, essentially disrupting binding dispute settlement of the DSU. In the meantime, a number of countries, including the EU, Brazil, Canada, China, Mexico, and Switzerland, all accounting for two-thirds of WTO membership, introduced the plurilateral Multi-Party Interim Appeal Arbitration Arrangement pursuant to Article 25 of the DSU. Japan joined in 2023, and more members may follow in due course. The arrangement allows members to suspend the adoption of panel reports and to appeal and cross-appeal them to a pool of ten elected and permanent appeal arbitrations who sit on cases in divisions of three arbitrators appointed in turn by an undisclosed algorithm. As of 2023, two cases were settled under these proceedings, and several panel reports eligible for appeal were adopted without appealing them.

National and regional courts giving effect to decisions of WTO panels and the Appellate Body or the MPIA when such decisions specifically affect matters under their jurisdiction would substantially promote the rule of law in the international economic system. Even though not bound by them, national and regional courts should also take into account the reasoning and interpretations of panels and the Appellate Body. It is recommended to follow such reasoning and interpretations unless there are compelling reasons to do otherwise—and such compelling circumstances may indeed arise—since it is important to build a coherent system. Overall, the precedents set by the bodies of the WTO will be of more than a merely subsidiary character, as might appear contemplated by Article 38(1)(d) of the Statute of the ICJ.

### 2. *Domestic Court Decisions*

Today, most precedents of general importance in the IPRs field stem from national or regional courts. These rulings are not primary sources of international law under Article 38 of the Statute of the ICJ, though they are important in constituting the body of general principles of law and may be used as subsidiary sources. Core concepts, such as the doctrine of exhaustion, are primarily shaped and framed by national and regional courts, and it is important that courts make their decisions while fully informed about trends and developments in other jurisdictions. National and regional court precedents are of key importance to bringing about judicial coherence of the overall system. The international IPRs field could not have evolved without a strong comparativist approach, and such an approach will likely serve well in the future.

18. *Stare decisis* doctrine, as it is known in national legal systems, generally requires that legal rules be applied by one nation's courts in a consistent manner in equivalent sets of circumstances. Once a determination has been made as to the proper interpretation of a rule of law, that determination should be applied in comparable cases involving different parties. However, in international law each state is sovereign and, in recognition of this sovereignty, it is accepted that the method of application of a legal rule in one set of circumstances involving a sovereign entity (or entities) does not require an identical application of the same legal rule to an equivalent set of circumstances involving another sovereign entity. That is, judicial interpretations in respect of one sovereign entity do not automatically bind another sovereign entity.

### 3. *Doctrine*

Article 38 of the ICJ Statute refers to the writings of highly qualified jurists as a subsidiary or secondary source of international law. Recourse to the international academic community could be an important element in bringing about an overall coherence of the IPRs system. Yet, it is too early to tell what influence prominent authors will have in international IPRs adjudication. The WTO Appellate Body occasionally refers to leading authors. Common law courts (e.g., British and U.S. courts) refer to scholarly works, though this occurs much more frequently in the civil law tradition. The Swiss Federal Court, as example, frequently refers to scholars in order to explore different views, and to substantiate its own decisions.

## D. General Principles of Law

General principles apply extensively to national, regional, and international law, and they have the potential of substantially contributing to the coherence of the overall system. Beyond positive law, these principles are of paramount importance in the operation of intellectual property protection as in any other field of law. They assist in balancing the relationship between private rights and public domain as they are applicable to the conduct of private parties. As IPRs are mainly held and used by private operators, general principles of law are well suited to be applied to the IPRs field in order to assist in preventing and remedying the abuse of rights.

The term "general principles of law," as found in Article 38(1)(c) of the Statute of the ICJ, does not refer to principles of international law that are formally part of customary or treaty law (such as the principle that treaties should be performed in good faith), but refers instead to principles of law common to the different legal systems of the world. These general principles operate in all areas of the law, including IP regulation. They contain the most valuable general body of law—a record of human nature, experience, and wisdom, often essential to resolving difficult conflicts. It is not intended that national laws be adopted "lock, stock, and barrel," but the principles underlying such laws can be important in filling gaps and lacunae, and they may guide courts in the process of interpreting international and regional law.[19]

General principles of law, recognized in international law, comprise a considerable body of rules that are important to the interpretation and administration of IPRs. There are, to begin with, principles relating to good faith and equity.[20] Most importantly, the doctrines of abuse of rights (*abus de droit*, important in the relationship between IPRs and competition law[21]) and estoppel and acquiescence flow from the principle of good faith.[22] General principles of equity also include: "no one may transfer more than he has"[23] (arguably important in trademarks and

19. *See generally* Oscar Schachter, International Law in Theory and Practice 49-58 (1991); for a comprehensive classical analysis, *see* Wilfried Jenks, The Prospects of International Adjudication 316-427 (1964); B. Cheng, General Principles of Law Applied by International Courts and Tribunals (1953); Charles de Visscher, De L'Equité dans le Règlement Arbitral ou Judiciaire des Litiges de Droit International Public (1972).

20. For a comprehensive review and analysis, *see* Catherine Titi, The Function of Equity in International Law (2021); Ralph A. Newman, *The General Principles of Equity*, in Equity in the World's Legal Systems: A Comparative Study 599-604 (R.A. Newman ed., 1973); Thomas Cottier, Equitable Principles of Maritime Boundary Delimitation: The Quest for Distributive Justice in International Law (2015), with a general introduction to equity.

21. Doctrines regarding abuse of rights flow from the idea that legal entitlements do not confer unfettered discretion regarding the uses that may be made of such entitlements. *See infra.*

22. Closely related doctrines of estoppel and acquiescence refer to circumstances in which parties may as a consequence of their own conduct be precluded from asserting rights that might otherwise have been available to them. *See* Thomas Cottier & Jörg Paul Müller, *Estoppel*, in Encyclopedia of Public International Law, www.mpepil.com.

23. *Nemo plus iuris transfere potest quam ipse habet.*

parallel importation); the principle of *lex specialis;*[24] the latter in time rule;[25] the prohibition against retroactive laws;[26] and the principle of proportionality.[27] Equity also addresses concerns of distributive justice which has been a constant, underlying theme in defining the scope of IPRs, and exemptions therefore in particular in assessing the scope for use and imitation of innovation. Equity also stands for a particular, fact-intensive methodology in assessing and finding the law, balancing all pertinent interests at stake.[27a] Recent evolutions in the field of equity, address in particular the goals of sustainable development and human rights. However, concepts such as intergenerational equity are not yet part of general principles of law common to different legal systems. They will be addressed later in this book.

General principles have not figured prominently in IPRs adjudication, but some decisions have employed them extensively. For example, the decision of an EPO Technical Board of Appeal (*Procter & Gamble v. Unilever*, discussed below) in which general principles of law in relation to the doctrine of *res judicata* are used as a central source of law in interpreting the EPC. The advent of efficient dispute settlement under the umbrella of the WTO should also enhance the role of general principles.

### NOTES AND QUESTIONS

**1.** Some of the principles of equity may, at least initially, appear somewhat dated—or naive—in the present global business environment, in which the sharp operator is often applauded for taking advantage of opportunity. Yet, consider these principles from the standpoint of the arbitrator called upon to resolve a dispute between enterprises with an interest in maintaining long-term relations. Might the application of some of these principles of fairness help to fashion decisions that accommodate longer-term interests? These questions will lead us to consider the broader context within which intellectual property is embedded in public international law and how it relates to other regulatory areas of public international law throughout the textbook.

## III. THE MULTILATERAL IP INSTITUTIONS AND MAIN INSTRUMENTS

Governance of the international intellectual property system at the multilateral level is today principally shared by two institutions: the World Intellectual Property Organization (WIPO) and the World Trade Organization (WTO). The relationship between these two institutions and their respective subject matter authorities is not well defined.[28] The existence of

---

24. Specific rules take precedence over general rules. *Lex specialis derogat generalis.*

25. Absent an intervening rule, a law adopted later in time is presumed to take precedence over a law earlier in time to the extent of a conflict. (*Lex posterior derogat priori.*)

26. Laws should not impose new obligations or displace rights with respect to acts that have already occurred.

27. The rule that laws should not impose obligations in excess of those reasonably necessary to address circumstances that give rise to them. The doctrine of proportionality is a centerpiece of European Court of Justice jurisprudence.

27a. *See generally* Thomas Cottier et al., The Principle of Proportionality in International Law: Foundations and Variations, 18 Journal of World Investment & Trade 628-672 (2017); Thomas Cottier, Inequality and Intellectual Property: Equity, Innovation and Creative Imitation, in: D. Benoliel, F. Gurry, K. Lee & P. Yu (eds.), Intellectual Property, Innovation, and Global Inequality, Cambridge University Press, Intellectual Property and Information Law series (forthcoming 2024).

28. Recall that the WTO became involved in IPRs matters because U.S., European, and Japanese business groups grew frustrated with their inability to negotiate higher standards of protection at WIPO. During the GATT Uruguay Round, senior officials at WIPO were not anxious to see another institution assume major responsibility for IPRs subject matter, and there was not a good "spirit of cooperation" between the two institutions during the negotiations.

two fora with overlapping jurisdiction regarding the same subject matter presents possibilities for inconsistent rulemaking and oversight of implementation. It also raises room for "forum shopping" by all groups with interests in intellectual property matters. A group of countries may conclude that progress on a particular matter cannot be made at the WTO, and may look to WIPO as an alternative forum. WIPO presents the possibility for reaching agreements among a limited number of states. While its members also favor action by consensus where possible, it will conclude substantive agreements with acceptance by less than all its members. Negotiation at WIPO also has disadvantages. Governments are only negotiating about intellectual property and cannot offer "cross-concessions" in areas such as agricultural trade. In addition, WIPO agreements are not enforceable by withdrawal of trade concessions.

Despite the potential problems raised by the overlap of authority, there are some fairly clear distinctions between the roles of WIPO and the WTO. WIPO administers various treaties that facilitate the grant of IP rights in multiple jurisdictions. These include the Patent Cooperation Treaty and the Madrid Agreement and Protocol (on trademarks). The WTO does not perform a comparable administrative function. In addition, WIPO has substantially more staff devoted to IP matters than the WTO, and a substantial part of WIPO staff efforts are directed at training IP office personnel at the national level, as well as providing assistance with the drafting of national legislation. WIPO tends to engage in negotiations regarding more detailed "technical" aspects of IP regulation, such as defining the criteria for identification of well-known trademarks or on harmonization of patentability criteria. But this more technical facet of WIPO activity might also be undertaken at the WTO where, for example, governments have been negotiating on details concerning geographical indications and the potential for patent application disclosures regarding the source and origin of genetic resources. It perhaps should not be assumed that one of the two fora has a more extensive competence regarding rulemaking on "technical" IP matters than the other. (As a matter of geography, the headquarters of WIPO and the WTO are about a ten-minute walk from each other in Geneva. It is not so difficult for human technical expertise to move between the two organizations.)

We will examine the shared competence of WIPO and the WTO further after briefly introducing the two organizations.

## A. WIPO

### *1. Overview*

WIPO introduces its organizational structure and objectives in the following excerpt.

**(WIPO Convention) (1967)***

## *Summary of the Convention Establishing the World Intellectual Property Organization*

The WIPO Convention, the constituent instrument of the World Intellectual Property Organization (WIPO), was signed at Stockholm on July 14, 1967, entered into force in 1970 and was amended in 1979. WIPO is an intergovernmental organization that became in 1974 one of the specialized agencies of the United Nations system of organizations.

The origins of WIPO go back to 1883 and 1886 when the Paris Convention for the Protection of Industrial Property and the Berne Convention for the Protection of Literary and

* From http://www.wipo.int (visited June 18, 2023).

Artistic Works, respectively, were concluded. Both Conventions provided for the establishment of an "International Bureau". The two bureaus were united in 1893 and, in 1970, were replaced by the World Intellectual Property Organization, by virtue of the WIPO Convention.

WIPO's two main objectives are (i) to promote the protection of intellectual property worldwide; and (ii) to ensure administrative cooperation among the intellectual property Unions established by the treaties that WIPO administers.

In order to attain these objectives, WIPO, in addition to performing the administrative tasks of the Unions, undertakes a number of activities, including: (i) normative activities, involving the setting of norms and standards for the protection and enforcement of intellectual property rights through the conclusion of international treaties; (ii) program activities, involving legal and technical assistance to States in the field of intellectual property; (iii) international classification and standardization activities, involving cooperation among industrial property offices concerning patent, trademark and industrial design documentation; and (iv) registration and filing activities, involving services related to international applications for patents for inventions and for the registration of marks and industrial designs.

Membership in WIPO is open to any State that is a member of any of the Unions and to any other State satisfying one of the following conditions: (i) it is a member of the United Nations, any of the specialized agencies brought into relationship with the United Nations, or the International Atomic Energy Agency; (ii) it is a party to the Statute of the International Court of Justice; or (iii) it has been invited by the General Assembly of WIPO to become a party to the Convention. There are no obligations arising from membership of WIPO concerning other treaties administered by WIPO. Accession to WIPO is effected by means of the deposit with the Director General of WIPO of an instrument of accession to the WIPO Convention.

The WIPO Convention establishes three main organs: the WIPO General Assembly, the WIPO Conference and the WIPO Coordination Committee. The WIPO General Assembly is composed of the Member States of WIPO which are also members of any of the Unions. Its main functions are, *inter alia,* the appointment of the Director General upon nomination by the Coordination Committee, review and approval of the reports of the Director General and the reports and activities of the Coordination Committee, adoption of the biennial budget common to the Unions, and adoption of the financial regulations of the Organization.

The WIPO Conference is composed of the States party to the WIPO Convention. It is, *inter alia,* the competent body for adopting amendments to the Convention. The WIPO Coordination Committee is composed of members elected from among the members of the Executive Committee of the Paris Union and the Executive Committee of the Berne Union. Its main functions are to give advice to the organs of the Unions, the General Assembly, the Conference, and to the Director General, on all administrative and financial matters of interest to these bodies. It also prepares the draft agenda of the General Assembly and the draft agenda of the Conference. Where appropriate, the Coordination Committee nominates a candidate for the post of Director General for appointment by the General Assembly.

The principal sources of income of WIPO's regular budget are the fees paid by the users of the international registration and filing services, and the contributions paid by the governments of Member States. Each State belongs to one of 14 classes, which determines the amount of its contribution. . . .

The Secretariat of the Organization is called the International Bureau. The executive head of the International Bureau is the Director General who is appointed by the WIPO General Assembly and is assisted by two or more Deputy Directors General.

The headquarters of the Organization are in Geneva, Switzerland. The Organization has external offices in Algeria (Algiers), Brazil (Rio de Janeiro), China (Beijing), Japan (Tokyo),

Nigeria (Abuja), Russian Federation (Moscow), Singapore (Singapore) and a liaison office in the United States of America (at the United Nations in New York).

The Organization benefits from the privileges and immunities granted to international organizations and their officials in the fulfillment of its objectives and exercise of its functions, and has concluded a headquarters agreement with the Swiss Confederation to that effect.

## NOTES AND QUESTIONS

**1.** A number of developing countries and NGOs have expressed concern about the policy direction of WIPO. They argue that WIPO has been mainly concerned with promoting higher levels of IPRs protection, without adequately accounting for the different roles that IPRs play at varying levels of development. The efforts of these countries and NGOs resulted in the establishment at WIPO of a Provisional Committee on Proposals Related to a WIPO Development Agenda. The Fourth Session of the Provisional Committee on Proposals Related to a WIPO Development Agenda (PCDA) met on June 11-15, 2007. At that meeting, the PCDA approved a list of 45 proposals in a number of areas, including capacity building, technical assistance, norm-setting, and technology transfer, in addition to proposing establishment of a permanent Committee on Development and Intellectual Property at WIPO.[29] In October 2007, the proposal for the Committee was adopted by the WIPO General Assembly. The Committee on Development and Intellectual Property held its first meeting in Geneva from March 3-7, 2008.[30] This Committee has a broad mandate to study and make recommendations with respect to improving the intellectual property framework in order to better promote the development and use of technology, especially by developing countries. Documents with respect to the WIPO Development Agenda may be found at http://www.wipo.int. The thirtieth session of the Committee on Development and Intellectual Property was held April 24 to April 28, 2023. Under an agenda item on "Intellectual Property and Development", the Committee discussed "Women and IP" (as decided at its twenty-sixth session) and "IP and youth", among other topics. The Committee agreed that the next topic to be discussed under this agenda item at its thirty-first session is "Addressing Climate Change: IP Helps Achieve the Goals of Carbon Peaking and Carbon Neutrality". *See* Summary by the Chair, Thirtieth Session, Geneva, April 24 to 28, 2023, CDIP/30/SUMMARY, April 28, 2023, https://www.wipo.int/edocs/mdocs/mdocs/en/cdip_30/cdip_30_summary_by_the_chair.pdf. See also Director General's Report on the Implementation of the Development Agenda, Thirtieth Session, Geneva, April 24 to 28, 2023, CDIP/30/2, February 17, 2023 https://www.wipo.int/edocs/mdocs/mdocs/en/cdip_30/cdip_30_2.pdf.

**2.** Consider the relationship of industrialized and developing countries in WIPO and the role of emerging economies. Does the Development Agenda entail the return to blocs, or does it rather reflect a constellation of changing coalitions and variable geometry? What is the likely effect of an increasing interest of emerging economy industries in enhanced levels of protection? Where could be particular interests and potentials for developing countries with a large agricultural sector?

29. http://www.wipo.int/ip-development/en/agenda/pcda/pcda07_session4.html.

30. *New Body on Development and IP Wraps up Inaugural Meeting*, Geneva, March 10, 2008 PR/2008/540, WIPO Press Release, http://www.wipo.int/pressroom/en/articles/2008/article_0012.html.

### 2. *Substantive and Administrative Rules*

The WIPO Convention does not include substantive rules. The rules administered by WIPO are established in separate treaties or conventions between its members.[31] Some of those treaties, such as the Paris and Berne Conventions, principally codify substantive law applicable to the member states; others, such as the PCT, establish procedures for the review of patent applications. The Paris and Berne Conventions are widely adhered to by states, but most of the WIPO treaties, such as the Madrid Agreement on False Indications of Source, have significantly more limited membership. Of the administrative treaties, the PCT has wide membership, but other agreements, such as the Hague Convention on Industrial Design, have more limited membership.

Significant parts of the Paris and Berne Conventions are incorporated by reference in the WTO TRIPS Agreement, as are some references to the Rome Convention and the Treaty on Intellectual Property in Respect of Integrated Circuits.[32] This creates a concrete substantive link between WIPO and the WTO.

The rules of treaties and conventions administered by WIPO are examined throughout this book, so detailed treatment is not given here. The treaties and conventions share certain basic principles, which are discussed later in this chapter.

WIPO plays an active role in the negotiation of new intellectual property rules and agreements. This is typically done through the initial establishment of a committee of experts to analyze and make recommendations about the possibilities for such rules or agreements. This is followed by a drafting phase in which the WIPO members and observers periodically meet to make recommendations and review progress, and in which the Secretariat plays a major drafting role. If negotiations are sufficiently successful, a diplomatic conference will be convened to consider adoption of the proposed agreement.

### 3. *Dispute Settlement*

The WIPO treaties and conventions do not establish their own dispute settlement mechanisms. The Paris and Berne Conventions permit members to initiate dispute settlement before the International Court of Justice (a United Nations body). Up until 2023, no such claim had been brought before the ICJ. In the late 1990s, proposals were made for a stand-alone WIPO interstate dispute settlement mechanism, but these proposals did not move forward largely because of concerns with overlapping jurisdiction with the WTO dispute settlement mechanism. The lack of an internal state-to-state dispute settlement mechanism at WIPO without doubt reduces the possibilities for conflict with the WTO. At the same time, it may leave WIPO as a less attractive forum from an industry standpoint as the possibilities for rule enforcement are less than at the WTO.

There is, however, a robust arbitration mechanism established under the auspices of the WIPO Arbitration and Mediation Center. The initial focus of the Center was to serve as a dispute resolution service provider under the Internet Corporation for Assigned Names and Numbers (ICANN) Uniform Domain Name Dispute Resolution Policy (UDRP). The Center has enjoyed considerable success in this regard, being the leading provider of domain name dispute settlement services. More recently, the Center has increased attention to settlement of more traditional types of intellectual property disputes, such as patent and trademark

---

31. The full texts of all treaties administered by WIPO and up-to-date lists of the state parties to them are available at http://www.wipo.int.

32. The Treaty on Intellectual Property in Respect of Integrated Circuits has not come into force because it lacks sufficient ratification by signatories. Nonetheless, its rules are incorporated with modifications into the TRIPS Agreement.

infringement and licensing disputes, and its arbitration caseload is growing. The role of the Center is considered further in Chapter 3, in connection with domain name disputes, and in Chapter 6 regarding enforcement.

## B. WTO

### *1. Institutional Framework*

The World Trade Organization (WTO) is the primary multilateral institution regulating international trade.[33] It was established on January 1, 1995, by the Agreement Establishing the World Trade Organization (WTO Agreement). The WTO succeeded the General Agreement on Tariffs and Trade (GATT), established in 1947, also to regulate trade. The GATT 1947 was concerned almost exclusively with trade in goods and the various regulatory mechanisms, such as tariffs, quotas, and subsidies, which affect such trade. The WTO extends subject matter coverage to trade in services, such as banking and other financial services, and telecommunications. The WTO also extends subject matter coverage to trade-related aspects of intellectual property rights (TRIPS). This is accomplished by the incorporation of the TRIPS Agreement as one of the three "Multilateral Trade Agreements" (MTAs) (along with the GATT 1994 and the General Agreement on Trade in Services (GATS)) accepted by all WTO Members as part of their participation in the WTO Agreement.[34]

The WTO formally is a one country, one vote organization.[35] Under the WTO Agreement, the countries participating are referred to as "Members." As of June 2023, the WTO had 164 Members, with 24 countries at some stage of the process of accession. The WTO Agreement provides voting requirements for making various types of decisions, including majority voting on ordinary decisions[36] and three-quarter majority voting on waivers of compliance.[37] However, the WTO by customary practice (which is referred to in the WTO Agreement and derives from GATT 1947 practice) acts by "consensus" of its Members. Decisions are thus taken if none of the Members present formally objects to the motion.[38] There is an important reason for the consensus voting practice. Unlike the United Nations, which concentrates voting power in the Security Council, the WTO has no mechanism for weighting the vote of its Members, such as by aggregate volume of trade or gross domestic product. In principle, the United States or China has the same voting weight or power as Burundi or Ecuador. The great majority of WTO Members are developing (including emerging market) countries. Historically, the United States, the European Union, and other high-income economies were not willing to subject their trade policy to majority rule, particularly when they might regularly be outvoted by a bloc of developing countries. It is also doubtful that developing countries would be willing to subject themselves to majority rule in determining their trade interests. They are particularly concerned to protect their sovereignty.

The WTO Agreement obligates the Members to meet at least once every two years in a Ministerial Conference.[39] Since its inception, Ministerial Conferences have been held in

33. Information concerning the WTO, including a list of Members, texts of agreements, and dispute settlement decisions, as well as information concerning ongoing work programs and instructional aids, is available at http://www.wto.org.

34. Art. II:2, WTO Agreement.

35. Art. IX:1, *id.*

36. Art. IX:1, *id.*

37. Art. IX:3, *id.*

38. Footnote 1 to the WTO Agreement: "The body concerned shall be deemed to have decided by consensus on a matter submitted for its consideration, if no Member, present at the meeting when the decision is taken, formally objects to the proposed decision."

39. Art. IV:1, *id.*

Singapore, Seattle, Doha, Cancun, Hong Kong, Geneva, Bali, Nairobi, and Buenos Aires. As the name implies, the Ministerial Conference is a gathering of the trade ministers of the Members. The business of the WTO outside the Ministerial Conference is conducted by the General Council, which exercises the powers of the Ministerial Conference when it is not in session.[40] The General Council meets regularly at the headquarters of the WTO in Geneva. In addition to the General Council, there are subsidiary councils for each of the MTAs, including a Council for Trade-Related Aspects of Intellectual Property (TRIPS Council).[41] The TRIPS Council meets in regular session to oversee the implementation of the TRIPS Agreement and conduct other business, including negotiation further to an agenda "built in" to the TRIPS Agreement, and on proposals put forward by the Members. The TRIPS Council according to its rules of procedure acts only by consensus.[42] A matter that might be voted on other than by consensus must be referred to the General Council.

The consensus voting rule of the WTO and TRIPS Council has advantages and disadvantages. The advantages include that the interests of all Members need to be taken into account in decision making. The smallest and economically weakest country, at least in principle, can veto a decision. On the other hand, the requirement to achieve consensus means that decisions are very difficult to arrive at. It is not easy for 164 Members to agree on anything, much less highly complex international agreements. As the GATT has grown into the highly inclusive WTO, collective decision making has become one of the great challenges. It should not be surprising that there are proposals to reform the decision-making process to allow the possibility for action by less-than-consensus, with appropriate safeguards.

The WTO provides a forum for the Members to negotiate the progressive liberalization of barriers to trade in goods and services with the objectives of increasing global productivity, enhancing employment, encouraging development, and recognizing the importance of doing this in a sustainable way.[43] The WTO seeks to accomplish these objectives through "rounds" of trade negotiations, which are initiated with particular negotiating mandates, and which involve the exchange of offers of trade concessions among the various Members. Ultimately, the results of a round are embodied in new agreements and changes in schedules of commitments of Members in existing agreements.[44] The most recent round of negotiations was launched in November 2001 in Doha, Qatar, and is referred to as the Doha Development Round (DDR).[45] The DDR initially was proposed to be completed by 2005. Following the close of the Buenos Aires Ministerial in December 2017 it is unclear whether WTO Members consider the DDR to remain ongoing, or to have come to an inconclusive end. The prior GATT Uruguay Round lasted seven years (1986-1993).

Changes to the WTO Agreements can also take place outside the context of a negotiating round. For example, the first amendment to the TRIPS Agreement, relating to public health, was agreed upon by the Members in a session of the General Council in December 2005.[46]

40. Art. IV:2, *id.*

41. Art. IV:5, *id.*

42. Rules of Procedure for Meetings of the Council for TRIPS, Rule 33, WTO Doc. IP/C/1 (1995). In default of consensus in the TRIPS Council, the matter is referred to the General Council.

43. Preamble, *id.*

44. For example, the GATT 1994 incorporates an annex with the maximum tariff rate commitments or bindings of each Member. The conclusion of the DDR presumably will include revised (and reduced) tariff rate commitments by Members.

45. For a description of the issues at stake in the DDR, *see* 2006 Report of the Committee on International Trade Law of the International Law Association, available at http://www.ila-hq.org.

46. See discussion in Chapter 2, *infra.* The amendment effectively operates as a "waiver" until it is ratified by two-thirds of WTO Members. The waiver will continue in effect until the amendment is accepted by all WTO Members.

The administration of the WTO is carried out by the Secretariat, which is headed by a Director-General (DG), who is appointed by the Members.[47] The DG appoints several Deputy DGs and Directors of various Divisions, including the Intellectual Property, Government Procurement and Competition Division.

### 2. *Substantive Rules*

The WTO Agreements set forth the basic substantive rules governing international trade and the specific commitments of Members on trade liberalization. The entire network of rules regarding trade in goods, services, and TRIPS is extremely complex, reflecting the complexity of the modern global economy. That said, there are two basic principles that underlie the entire system. These are the principles of "most favored nation treatment" (MFN) and "national treatment." The MFN principle obligates each Member to extend the same trade concessions to all other Members.[48] The national treatment principle obligates each Member to treat goods imported from other Members the same way it treats domestically produced goods,[49] and to treat foreign services and service providers in covered sectors in the same way that domestic services and service providers are treated.[50] The MFN and national treatment principles also operate with respect to TRIPS, obligating Members to extend the same IP protection to all WTO Members (MFN)[51] and to treat foreign IP applicants and holders on the same basis as domestic applicants and holders (national treatment).[52] We will return to these principles later in this chapter.

In addition to the basic MFN and national treatment principles, the GATT 1994 provides for elimination of quotas (or quantitative restrictions) on trade in goods,[53] and provides for the binding of national tariffs.[54] There are special rules applicable to trade in agricultural products.[55] The WTO Agreements include obligations with respect to the application of anti-dumping and countervailing duty laws,[56] the application of sanitary and phytosanitary measures with respect to trade in food and agricultural products,[57] and the way that governments procure goods and services.[58] The TRIPS Agreement establishes minimum substantive standards of intellectual property rights protection and enforcement.

Throughout the WTO Agreements, special attention is given to the needs of developing countries, though there is considerable debate about how effective this attention is. As its name would indicate, one of the main objectives of the DDR was to address development-related issues.

### 3. *Dispute Settlement*

One of the main functions of the WTO is to settle disputes among its Members regarding compliance with its rules. The WTO Agreement incorporates the Dispute Settlement

47. Art. VI, WTO Agreement.
48. Art. I, GATT 1994, Art. II, GATS and Art. 4, TRIPS Agreement.
49. Art. III, GATT 1994.
50. Art. XVII, GATS.
51. Art. 4, TRIPS Agreement.
52. Art. 3, *id.*
53. Art. XI, GATT 1994.
54. Art. II, *id.*
55. *See, e.g.*, Agreement on Agriculture.
56. *See* Articles VI & XVI, GATT 1994, Agreement on Implementation of Article VI of the General Agreement on Tariffs and Trade 1994, and Agreement on Subsidies and Countervailing Measures.
57. Agreement on Sanitary and Phytosanitary Measures.
58. Agreement on Government Procurement.

Understanding (DSU) applicable to all Members.[59] The DSU provides for the appointment of "panels" to initially decide cases,[60] and establishes an Appellate Body (AB) to decide appeals on questions of law.[61] The decisions of panels and the AB must be formally adopted by Members sitting as the "Dispute Settlement Body" (DSB),[62] but because only a consensus against adoption (a so-called negative consensus) defeats the adoption of a panel or AB "report," for all practical purposes the panel and AB decisions are automatically adopted.[63]

The DSU applies to cases arising in relation to intellectual property rights. Before the adoption of the TRIPS Agreement, issues relating to intellectual property protection were litigated under the provisions of the GATT, and issues may continue to arise under all the WTO agreements. Today, the TRIPS Agreement is the main instrument addressing intellectual property rights and subject to dispute settlement,[64] although there are certain qualifications relating to complaints involving "nonviolation nullification or impairment" causes of action.[65] We will examine the non-violation complaint in Chapter 6, section II.

The DSU establishes rules of procedure relating to the establishment of panels, the powers of panels and the AB, and the time frame for decision making. In general, the time period from the initiation of a complaint by a Member to the rendering of a decision by the AB should not exceed two years.[66] Panels of three members are appointed by the agreement of the parties to a dispute, but if the parties cannot agree on the panelists (which is commonly the case), they are appointed by the Director-General of the WTO.[67] The panels hold hearings where the complaining and responding parties argue their cases and present evidence. Members other than the complainant and respondent may participate as third-party observers in the proceedings.[68] The panels issue preliminary and final reports that decide issues of law and fact and may make recommendations.[69] The usual form of recommendation is to request a Member whose law or practice is found to violate WTO law to bring its measures into conformity.[70] Panels do not typically make specific recommendations regarding changes to law or practice.

A complaining or responding party may request Appellate Body review of a panel decision.[71] The AB automatically accepts the case for review—it is not discretionary like the U.S. Supreme Court certiorari process—and examines the legal analysis of the panel. The AB is not expressly authorized to reexamine factual determinations, but as with domestic court processes it is often difficult to separate review of law and review of fact.

When the AB issues its report (or if the panel decision is not appealed), the DSB adopts it. A Member against which findings have been made has a reasonable period of time (rebuttably presumed to be a maximum of 15 months) to bring its measures into conformity.[72] If it fails to do this, the complaining Member is authorized to withdraw trade concessions up

59. Art. III:3, WTO Agreement, and Annex 2 (Understanding on Rules and Procedures Governing the Settlement of Disputes).

60. *E.g.*, Art. 6, DSU.

61. Art. 17, DSU.

62. Arts. 16 & 17.14, DSU.

63. In theory, the WTO membership could find some decision of a panel or the AB sufficiently offensive that even the party that won the case would object to its adoption.

64. Art. 64, TRIPS Agreement.

65. Art. 64.2-3, *id.*

66. Art. 20, DSU (including extensions).

67. Art. 8, *id.*

68. Art. 10, *id.*

69. Art. 11, *id.*

70. Art. 19, *id.*

71. Art. 17, *id.*

72. Art. 21, *id.*

to the level of harm it is suffering as a consequence of the noncompliance.[73] The withdrawal of concessions preferably is directed to the same category—goods, services, or IPRs—as the complained-against measure, but Members are allowed to withdraw "cross-concessions" when withdrawing a measure in the same category would not be effective. The questions of whether a Member has brought its measures into conformity or withdrawn an appropriate level of concessions are each subject to arbitration, generally by the same panel that decided the dispute.[74]

The possibility for enforcement of WTO dispute settlement decisions by withdrawal of trade concessions was one of the factors that motivated the United States, the European Union, and Japan to select the WTO as the alternative forum to WIPO. WTO dispute settlement has "teeth," although those teeth are more likely to favor strong economies. Small economies may find it very difficult to withdraw trade concessions against large economies with which they trade for at least two reasons. First, their imports tend to constitute only a small part of the exports of the larger economies, so the impact on the larger economies may be very minor. Second, by imposing higher tariffs or quotas on imports from their trading partners, small economies may damage their own producers and consumers, making the exercise counterproductive. On the other hand, when a country like the United States or an entity like the European Union withdraws concessions from a small economy country, the impact on the small economy country may be quite severe because it is dependent on exports to the country withdrawing concessions. Following success in separate dispute settlement actions, Ecuador threatened to withdraw TRIPS concessions from the European Union, and Brazil threatened to withdraw TRIPS concessions from the United States, and in each case the complaining developing country party appears to have achieved a favorable negotiated outcome.[75]

As of August 2023, the status of the dispute settlement system at the WTO is uncertain. Beginning during the Trump Administration, the United States has refused to approve the appointment of new Appellate Body members. This ultimately resulted in 2019 in the AB not being able to convene panels of members to hear appeals, and the work of the AB was suspended. The Biden Administration has not acted to remedy the situation. Since WTO Members have the right to appeal panel decisions, unless both parties to a panel decision agreed to forgo the right to an appeal, the decision of the panel cannot be considered final, thus leaving the parties "in limbo." To be clear, panels continue to be established and continue to render decisions, but the enforceability of such decisions through withdrawal of trade concessions is not available if the parties do not mutually adopt the report and have not foregone their right to appeal to the defunct Appellate Body. As a stopgap measure, the European Union proposed and about 50 WTO Members (including the EU member states) have agreed to participate in an arbitration mechanism as a substitute for the Appellate Body in disputes among themselves (the "Multi-Party Interim Appeal Arbitration Arrangement (MPIA)").[76] This arrangement is intended to allow appealed panel decisions to become final and enforceable at least among the members that have agreed to participate in the arrangement.

### 4. *The TRIPS Agreement*

The TRIPS Agreement performs a number of functions in the WTO legal system. First, the Agreement adopts certain generally applicable principles. These principles include national

73. Art. 22, *id.*

74. Art. 22.6-7, *id.*

75. *See* Frederick M. Abbott, *Cross-Retaliation in TRIPS: Options for Developing Countries*, ICTSD Programme on Dispute Settlement and Legal Aspects of International Trade, Issue Paper No. 8, April 2009, International Centre for Trade and Sustainable Development, Geneva. Antigua and Barbuda similarly won a WTO case against the United States and has threatened to withdraw concessions in TRIPS, but so far there is no settlement.

76. EU Press Release, Interim appeal arrangement for WTO disputes becomes effective, https://policy.trade.ec.europa.eu/news/interim-appeal-arrangement-wto-disputes-becomes-effective-2020-04-30_en.

treatment,[77] most favored nation (MFN) treatment,[78] and the right of each Member to determine its own policy and rules with respect to "exhaustion of rights."[79] These general principles are applicable to all forms of intellectual property covered by the Agreement, and are discussed in the next section.

Second, the TRIPS Agreement prescribes minimum substantive standards of IPRs protection for all WTO Members.[80] It does this by incorporating parts of the Paris, Berne, Rome, and Washington[81] Conventions[82] and by prescribing additional norms. It recognizes that Members may implement the substantive standards in accordance with their own customs and practices, leaving flexibility as to the manner in which the norms are translated into national law.[83] The Agreement refers to seven categories of intellectual property and its subject matter scope is generally limited to those categories.[84] However, because the Agreement incorporates rules of WIPO Conventions that refer to forms of IP not specifically mentioned in the TRIPS Agreement (e.g., Article 8 of the Paris Convention regulates "trade names," which are not specifically mentioned in the TRIPS Agreement), the scope of subject matter coverage is somewhat broader than would be ascertained by reference only to the TRIPS Agreement text.[85]

Third, the TRIPS Agreement requires that Members make provision for adequate and effective enforcement of IP rights, and it lays out a number of express requirements in terms of availability of administrative or judicial processes and remedies.[86] The Agreement also seeks to provide due process protection for those against whom IP claims are asserted. The preamble of the TRIPS Agreement indicates that intellectual property rights are "private" rights. This was included to reinforce that private holders of IPRs are expected to pursue enforcement of their rights in administrative and judicial proceedings, and that governments (with some limited exceptions spelled out in the Agreement) are not expected to "police" IPRs enforcement.

Fourth, the TRIPS Agreement recognizes the importance of maintaining competitive markets. It expressly authorizes Members to regulate IPRs by application of competition laws.[87] It also encourages cooperation among competition authorities.[88]

Fifth, the TRIPS Agreement gives special attention to the situation of developing and least developed countries.[89] For the most part, this was accomplished by incorporation of transitional arrangements that extended the time for compliance with various obligations. It is also reflected in the preamble and the provisions on objectives and principles.

Sixth, the TRIPS Agreement establishes institutional arrangements.[90] This includes defining the role of the TRIPS Council and making provision for further negotiations on prescribed subject matter (the "built-in" agenda) as well as subject matter put forward by the

---

77. Art. 3, TRIPS Agreement.

78. Art. 4, *id.*

79. Art. 6, *id.*

80. Part II, *id.*

81. The Treaty on Intellectual Property in Respect of Integrated Circuits was concluded in Washington, D.C., and is sometimes referred to as the "Washington Convention."

82. *E.g.*, arts. 2 & 9.1, TRIPS Agreement.

83. Art. 1.1, *id.*

84. Art. 1.2, TRIPS Agreement.

85. The WTO Appellate Body addressed this issue in respect to trade names in the *U.S.-Havana Club* decision, *infra* Chapter 3.

86. Part III, *id.*

87. *E.g.*, arts. 8.2 & 40, *id.*

88. Arts. 40.3-4, *id.*

89. *E.g.*, Preamble, arts. 7-8, 65-67, *id.*

90. Part VII, *id.*

Members.[91] The responsibilities of the TRIPS Council include review of the implementation of TRIPS commitments by the Members.

Seventh, the TRIPS Agreement incorporates dispute settlement under the DSU.[92] As noted earlier, this includes a moratorium on non-violation nullification or impairment complaints, which remains in effect at least until the 13th WTO Ministerial Conference (scheduled for February 2024).

The substantive and procedural rules of the TRIPS Agreement will be examined throughout the book.

Before doing so, the following excerpts address the relationship of the IP standards and traditional trade rules of the GATT and the WTO and the history of negotiations.

**Thomas Cottier***

## *The Agreement on Trade Related Aspects of Intellectual Property rights*

. . .

### From Tariffs to Intellectual Property

It is important to describe at the outset the inherent linkages between trade regulation and intellectual property protection and to understand the sequencing and the reasons thereof. The lack of appropriate protection of IPRs results in trade restrictions. This should be addressed in the proper context of what I call third generation trade barriers.

Trade policy in the early post-World War II era focused on the gradual reduction of tariffs and the elimination of preferential systems. Tariffs, the first generation of barriers, were high, stemming from the protectionist policies of the great depression of the 1930s. In addition, preferential tariffs existed within the colonial systems. After the failure to establish the International Trade Organization, based upon the Havana Charter, the 1947 General Agreement on Tariffs and Trade ("GATT") provided, in essence, a framework for a gradual and, as it turned out, successful process of tariff reductions. In seven rounds of multilateral negotiations, tariffs on manufactured goods, which averaged forty percent in 1947, were reduced by the conclusion of the Tokyo Round in 1979 to an average of 4.7 percent in the main industrialized nations. Further cuts were achieved in the Uruguay Round, the eighth round of multilateral trade negotiations, and the Round resulted in the decision of developing countries to bind many tariffs. Importantly, all quantitative restrictions were tariffied under the new Agreement on Agriculture. The average tariff reduction achieved by the 117 participants during the Uruguay Round negotiations amounted to forty percent.

The provisions of the GATT were designed to accompany tariff reductions and to prevent circumvention of tariff bindings by other means, in particular quantitative import restrictions, subsidies or discriminatory taxes on imports. Indeed, the gradual reduction (and even the elimination of tariffs within customs unions and free trade arrangements) increasingly shifted the emphasis in the negotiations to non-tariff measures, which began to replace tariffs as the main instrument of governmental trade policy in order to protect domestic industries and products. Quantitative

91. Art. 71, *id.*

92. Art. 64, *id.*

* In 1 The World Trade Organization: Legal, Economic and Political Analysis 1041-1120 (Patrick F.J. Macroy, Arthur E. Appleton & Michael G. Plummer eds., 2005) (footnotes omitted).

restrictions, export subsidies, anti-dumping measures, technical norms and standards, balance of payment measures, labeling requirements, import licensing, rules on government procurement, "voluntary" import obligations or export restrictions ("grey area" measures such as voluntary export restraints or "VERs," and orderly marketing arrangements or "OMAs") and other imaginative tools became widely-used instruments for economic and political ends, both in developing and industrialized countries. They form a second generation of barriers. Such non-tariff measures became, in addition to the classical process of tariff reductions, the main subject of trade negotiations in the Tokyo Round. The Tokyo Round agreements on non-tariff measures were further developed in the Uruguay Round, and new ones, in particular on safeguards (including a prohibition of grey area measures) and textiles were added.

As a result of the substantial tariff reductions and increasing legal disciplines in the field of non-tariff measures, a third generation of non-tariff barriers emerged during the 1980s. These barriers encompassed a number of issues, ranging from domestic farm support, to the restrictive regulation of service industries and investments, and finally, the protection of intellectual property. What do these subjects share in common? They stem from different fields of law, public and private, but the common trait is that they all are foremost part of *domestic* legal systems. They are not directly geared to border measures and classical international trade relations, but they have been affecting such relations more and more in terms of limiting market access while other barriers were gradually dismantled or at least legally disciplined. The great political difficulty in reaching final agreement on important issues in the Uruguay Round, such as the reduction of agricultural support, but also the failure to achieve substantial streamlining of conditions for investment, or to bring about significant liberalization of trade in services beyond binding existing levels of market access (a first and important step to establish a framework for liberalization), all stemmed from this development—turning more and more to areas of domestic law, beyond simple regulation of imports and exports.

The main difficulties to be settled in the area of intellectual property had similar roots. The patentability of pharmaceuticals, foodstuffs or living matter, i.e., how far exceptions to patentability should be allowed to go, or, in copyright, how the relationships of authors, producers, performers and users should be arranged, are primarily matters of domestic law and policy. At the same time, they are perhaps the most prominent examples of how far international negotiations and regulations have penetrated socially, ethically or culturally sensitive contemporary issues concerning the domestic political process.

International trade law has come a long way. It has left the area of mere transboundary action. More than ever before, international trade regulation now seeks to assure fair competition in a globalizing market economy. Foreign and domestic economic affairs can no longer be separated; and the increasing importance and attention paid to foreign policy in general is a natural effect of such developments. Today, efforts under the Doha Development Agenda aim, *inter alia*, at developing disciplines on anti-trust rules, on investment and enhanced transparency in government procurement.[89] These new areas continue the move towards the development of global rules on domestic conditions of competition beyond border measures, which essentially began in the Uruguay Round with the intellectual property and services negotiations.

The Uruguay Round mandate to negotiate on intellectual property resulted in what amounts to the most comprehensive instrument ever adopted in the field. Many consider it to be one of the main, if not the main, achievement of the Round. Others in hindsight, for

89. *Ministerial Declaration*, adopted on November 14, 2001 at the Ministerial Conference, Fourth Session, Doha, November 9-14, 2001, WT/MIN(01)/DEC/1, November 20, 2001, ¶¶20-26. The so-called Singapore issues also contain a future mandate on trade facilitation; *see* The Singapore Issues and the World Trading System: The Road to Cancun (Swiss State Secretariat of Economic Affairs and S. Evenett eds., 2003).

reasons already discussed, identify a fundamental and fatal error in placing IPRs under the umbrella of the WTO; it is argued that trade rules in favor of freer trade and market access are fundamentally at odds with the allocation of exclusive rights and monopolies under the very same instrument. Many economists fear that the balance tipped too much towards exclusive or monopoly rights, profoundly at odds with freer trade. For them, as mentioned before, the negotiating history suggests that many countries were forced into a strange agreement under the single undertaking approach of the Uruguay Round in return for other benefits expected, but without an inherent linkage to trade liberalization. The TRIPs Agreement is thus seen by some as an alien and misplaced body of law in the WTO.

Two counter-arguments should be made and stressed. First, the negative point of view ignores the fact that intellectual property is not the only field encompassing what was described above as a new generation of trade regulation. Other areas are in principle, equally structured and follow the patterns of positive or prescriptive integration. Rules relating to safeguards, dumping, subsidies, and agriculture are equally harmonizing, albeit setting maximum, and not minimum standards. To the extent that Members make use of such policy instruments, they are obliged to respect a set of well-defined disciplines aimed at excluding excessive recourse and use. Second, the contradiction between trade liberalization and exclusive rights is a formal one. In substance, there is no difference in principle between exclusive rights and freer trade. Intellectual property rights are an inherent part of the international trading system. The evolution of intellectual property disciplines in the European Communities both under free movement of goods and competition rules, despite the rule that property rights *per se* remain within the competence of the Member States, proves the point on an international level. Every rule-based trading system depends on intellectual property protection, to the extent that it presupposes property rights over traded goods and services. Whether or not the effects are beneficial or detrimental to national and global welfare depends on the balance achieved. Lack of, or insufficient protection amounts to *de facto* restrictions on market access, as exported products will be replaced by both generic and copied products that free-ride on research and development, investment in creative activities and in quality control and product differentiation undertaken elsewhere. On the other hand, lack of appropriate limitations on rights may unduly hamper the flow of goods and services. The real issue is one of balancing different policy goals. This is the core of the matter, upon which fruitful discussions between proponents and critics of intellectual property protection should focus. The proper debate is one of degrees and levels of protection, rather than protection *per se* or the existence of the TRIPs Agreement in the WTO.

## Uruguay Round Negotiations

The complexity and comprehensiveness of the TRIPs Agreement cannot be fully understood without recalling the negotiating process through which it was concluded. It may be described as one of the most successful operations in building coalitions, partnerships and, above all, creating a mutual learning process.

At the end of the Tokyo Round, the United States and the European Community launched negotiations on a draft Anti-Counterfeit Code. That effort ceased when intellectual property was included in the 1986 negotiating mandate for the Uruguay Round, which as a political compromise was limited to its "trade-related aspects." The initiative was eventually supported by U.S. estimates that its industries suffered losses of some 24 billion dollars in 1986 as a result of inadequate protection of intellectual property and related investments. At that time, no estimates were available for other countries, in particular for European industries. In the beginning, the European Community was reluctant to commit itself on the issue, but in the course of the negotiations, it gradually became one of the major *demandeurs*.

The seven-year negotiations went through three phases. A long process of fact-finding, which also worked as a tool for mutual education, led to comprehensive proposals by various contracting parties. In the second phase, intensive negotiations took place after the Montreal mid-term review (December 1989) and the April 1990 Ministerial Decision. The work was successfully concluded in December 1991, when the draft TRIPs Agreement was included in the "Dunkel text." During the last phase, efforts were aimed at preserving the results achieved and avoiding jeopardizing the results by counterproductive new IP proposals, as well as avoiding a deadlock in the negotiations on other IP issues, relating to agriculture or audiovisual services. Unlike the first two phases, the last phase was marked by conflicting interests between the United States and the EC on copyright issues (cultural aspects, levies on blank tapes, and national treatment of collecting societies).

The results were made possible by various factors, many of which are interesting for the purposes of a general assessment of the importance of intellectual property. To a great extent the results exceeded the initial expectations.

The educational process in the first phase led to a change in the attitude of a majority of developing countries toward the traditional UNCTAD approach of regarding higher protection of intellectual property as detrimental to the development of those countries. Negotiations were frank, and conducted by well-informed delegations. Complaints that many developing countries could not fully grasp the scope of obligations entailed by an IP agreement are not well founded, perhaps with the exception of complaints from some African States that were not prepared or able to make the necessary resources available during the negotiations. But there was a strong group of countries, including Brazil and India, which resolutely defended their interests, as well as those of small and often absent delegations. The efforts of these countries were reflected in key provisions, such as those relating to the recognition of social and developmental goals, compulsory licensing, and restrictive business practices.

The developing countries eventually recognized the importance of intellectual property protection as a prerequisite, albeit not the only one, for foreign direct investment and transfer of technology. In that respect, the decisive position in favor of IPRs maintained by the newly industrialized Asian economies, the political and economic transformation of Central and Eastern European countries, as well as the growing competition between those countries in order to make their markets more attractive, undoubtedly played an important role, within the context of a globalizing world economy, in reaching an agreement. Developing countries subsequently discovered the virtue of the multilateral system as a bulwark against unilateral pressure, in particular that of the United States (through the Super 301 procedure of the Trade Act). They also saw the TRIPs Agreement as a means to reinforce their position with respect to trade in goods: the potential of reprisals through the withdrawal of concessions in the field of intellectual property enhanced their negotiating power on market access to Europe and the United States. Last, there was a clear linkage, albeit not openly and formally stated as such, between the TRIPs negotiations and those in the fields of agriculture and textiles. No breakthrough on TRIPs would have been possible without middle and long-term prospects of better market access conditions for developing countries in those two areas.

## NOTES AND QUESTIONS

**1.** The negotiation of the TRIPS Agreement amounted to the first multilateral effort in standard setting and partial harmonization of domestic law. The negotiating experience is documented in a publication published at the twentieth anniversary of the WTO and provides important insights and lessons for future work on regulatory convergence beyond intellectual property rights. *See The Making of the TRIPS Agreement: Personal Insights from the Uruguay Round Negotiations* (Jayshree Watal & Anthony Taubman eds.), World Trade Organization 2015.

**2.** Following the Uruguay Round, the TRIPS Agreement compulsory licensing rules were amended to implement enhanced access to medicines. These changes will be discussed in Chapter 2. Other than that, the Doha Development Agenda (2011) has not produced additional changes and disciplines, even where Members were obliged to undertake further negotiations, in particular in the field of geographical indications. The shift to preferential trade agreements and TRIPS-plus obligations, discussed shortly, left the TRIPS Agreement of 1995 as the main foundation of intellectual property within the trading system.

**3.** It is important to note that the TRIPS Agreement is not the only instrument in the WTO addressing intellectual property rights. The provisions of GATT and other agreements may also be of relevance in assessing national IP-related regulations. Prior to the adoption of the TRIPS Agreement, important cases were dealt with under the rules of the General Agreement on Tariffs and Trade, which, *inter alia*, addresses the protection of IPRs in terms of an exception in Article XX(d).

**4.** IP-related cases decided under the GATT regime included *The United States Manufacturing Clause*, Report of the Panel adopted 15 June 1983, L/5609–31 S/74 (renewal of import restrictions for copyright protected works not consistent with the Provisional Protocol of Accession); and *United States–Section 337 of the Tariff Act of 1930*, Report by the Panel, adopted 7 November 1989, L/6439–36 S/345 (special administrative and judicial proceedings for imported patent protected products inconsistent with principle of national treatment under Article III and not justified under exceptions of GATT Article XX).

**5.** Consider whether the rules of GATT are still of relevance for IPRs, or whether all the pertinent issues today are absorbed by the TRIPS Agreement. The issue will be of particular relevance in the context of exhaustion of rights, which pertains both to the TRIPS Agreement and to GATT as a matter of import restriction under Article XI. Consider also the important role that GATT Article V prescribing freedom of transit may continue to play.

## C. Other Multilateral Institutions

WIPO and the WTO are the principal regulatory institutions for the international intellectual property system, but do not possess a shared monopoly (or duopoly) over the regulation of IPRs at the multilateral level. A substantial number of other multilateral institutions play a regulatory role. Ultimately, this raises questions of "coherence" among all of these legal regimes.

Coherence among rules systems is not a value that should be elevated at the expense of appropriate attention to institutional subject matter. For example, if the WTO were to adopt a trade rule that adversely affected public health interests, the WHO should not consider itself obligated to conform to the WTO rules. Rather, this would be an appropriate basis for conflict. Ultimately, coherence might result out of conflict, but it is not a superior value.

A significant number of United Nations agencies are active in IPRs regulation. UN human rights treaties, such as the UN Convention on Economic, Social, and Cultural Rights, address IPRs, and the UN Human Rights Commission has issued a number of reports on IPRs matters. The United Nations Conference on Trade and Development (UNCTAD) provides technical assistance and training in the IPRs area, as well as preparing analytic studies. The UN Development Programme (UNDP) and the UN Environment Programme (UNEP) each study the impact of IPRs on their respective area of competence. The World Health Organization (WHO) addresses IP related issues in the context of combatting pandemics and smoking. The Food and Agricultural Organization (FAO) deals with IP in the angle of plant genetic resources. UNESCO adopted in 2005 a Convention on the Protection of Cultural Diversity, which promotes the protection of national cultural institutions and may affect trade in intellectual property-protected goods and services. UNAIDS and UNICEF assist in supplying pharmaceutical products to developing countries and become involved in IPRs issues in this context.

The Food and Agriculture Organization (FAO) has addressed IPRs in its International Treaty on Plant Genetic Resources in Food and Agriculture.

The Convention on Biological Diversity (CBD) obligates bio-prospectors to obtain the prior informed consent of the host government before exploring for and/or removing genetic resources, and to make provision for the equitable sharing of benefits from their exploitation. These requirements are closely related to patenting of genetic resources. The more recently adopted Nagoya Protocol further addresses IPR issues relating to access and benefit sharing.

The World Health Organization (WHO) is considering mechanisms for promoting pharmaceutical research and development using mechanisms in addition to the patent, and has called attention to the potential conflict between trade-related intellectual property rules and access to medicines. Negotiations at the WHO for a potential Pandemic Accord and/or amendments to the International Health Regulations 2005 (IHR) are addressing the relationship between sharing of biological materials and information and the potential for patent-related complications arising out of such activities. This relationship was considered and addressed in the negotiating outcome of the Pandemic Influenza Preparedness Framework (PIP) negotiations culminating in 2011. These are further discussed in Chapter 2, Section V.C. (pp. 316-317).

The World Bank studies and provides guidance on intellectual property matters, including with respect to the use of bank funding to purchase medicines and the role of IPRs in transfer of technology for addressing climate change.

The Organization for Economic Cooperation and Development (OECD), which is limited in membership to developed countries, studies and reports on intellectual property issues.

We will revert to policy issues addressed by these various multilateral institutions throughout this book.

## IV. REGIONAL AND BILATERAL ARRANGEMENTS

There are different kinds of regional institutions relating to intellectual property. Some, like the European Patent Office, are specifically concerned with intellectual property matters. However, this is not the most common type of regional IP institution. Many, if not most, regional integration agreements—including customs unions and free trade areas—include chapters or provisions relating to intellectual property. These provisions may be implemented by regional institutions, or by national governments carrying out their regional obligations.

The role of regional and bilateral trade and investment agreements in establishing intellectual property standards must be emphasized. These limited membership agreements have dramatically grown in number and scope over the past decade. For the past several years, negotiations at the regional and bilateral level constituted the most dynamic part of IPRs rulemaking. WIPO conventions and the TRIPS Agreement do not alone provide a comprehensive sense of the rules governing the international IP system.

Representative terms of regional and bilateral agreements will be examined throughout the book. In the next section, we will consider how the regional and bilateral agreements fit (or fail to fit) within the context of a multilateral trading system based on most favored nation treatment, which is a principle of nondiscrimination among countries.

A significant number of recent regional and bilateral agreements have been negotiated in circumstances of asymmetric bargaining power. By this we mean that one country involved in the negotiations had a much larger economy than, and provided a major source of export revenue for, other countries involved in the negotiations. This gave the first country effective power to control the terms of the resulting agreement—a "take it or leave it" situation.

## A. Regional Integration Arrangements

Regional integration arrangements differ substantially in terms of their political, economic, and social objectives. Some regional integration efforts embody strong political commitments, including the creation of regional governing institutions. Others are principally directed toward more narrow trade objectives, such as elimination of regional tariffs. Furthest along among the former, in terms of institutional development, is the European Union, which now encompasses 27 member states and regional institutions including the Council, Parliament, Commission, and Court of Justice.

### *1. European Union*

The European Union or EU, as it is known today, is the most fully integrated among the many regional arrangements functioning around the world. The inception of the European Union generally can be traced to the entry into force of the Treaty of Rome in 1958 establishing the European Economic Community (EEC) among six European states. From the late 1950s until December 2009, the arrangement initially constituted by the Treaty of Rome was referred to by different names depending on which of the constitutive agreements and related institutions were being invoked (e.g., European Community, European Communities, or European Union). However, with the entry into force of the Lisbon Treaty in December 2009, the name "European Union" is now settled to identify the regional arrangement presently constituted by 27 member states in Europe.[93] There are three principal constituent instruments: the Treaty on the European Union (TEU), the treaty on the Functioning of the European Union (TFEU), and the Charter of Fundamental Rights of the European Union. The three Treaties have the same "legal value."[94] Although it is tempting to ascribe the TEU a more "political" character and the TFEU and the Charter a more legal or instrumental character, the distinction between the three Treaties is not so clear, and the use of three constitutive documents, as opposed to use of a single consolidated constitutional document, appears mainly to derive from historical factors.

We discuss the naming convention to help alleviate confusion by references in legislative and judicial decisions throughout the remainder of the book. Until 2010, the European Union was a Member of the WTO under the name "European Communities," and WTO dispute settlement decisions referred to the "EC." The European Court of Justice (ECJ), now referred to as the Court of Justice of the European Union (CJEU), mainly decided cases involving the "EC Treaty," but also some other instruments depending on the specific subject matter at issue. The history of the transformation from the EEC in 1958 to the European Union in 2009 is the subject of a voluminous literature. For present purposes, we focus on key developments and issues that affect regional and international IP law. Questions regarding how the European Union makes and implements internal IP law, and how EU IP policy is given effect internationally, remain very much alive. The evolution of the European Union has somewhat simplified matters regarding IP law, but not by very much.

The European Union is presently comprised of 27 member states, and there are procedures for accession of new members and withdrawal of existing members. (The United Kingdom has withdrawn, taking effect in 2020.) There are four principal institutions of the European Union: the European Council/Council, the European Parliament, the European Commission, and the CJEU. The European Council is comprised of the heads of state of the member states, but this body meets relatively infrequently, and day-to-day business from the member state perspective is conducted by the "Council" that is made up of senior

93. *See* Article 1, Treaty on European Union.

94. *Id.*

representatives of the member states that typically vary depending on the subject matter under consideration. The Council is essentially the EU institutional body of the governments of the member states. The Council plays a key role in legislating for the European Union, and at least through the late 1980s was principally responsible for promulgating EU legislation. The Council votes in different ways depending on the circumstances spelled out in the Treaties, whether by majority, qualified majority, or unanimity. Each member state has a single representative on the Council, yet the population and economic weight of the member states is quite different. "Qualified majority" assigns different weights to votes of the member states to take these differences into account.

The role of the European Parliament has grown steadily since the late 1980s. In early days of the European Union, the Parliament was largely a consultative body that did not have authority to control the adoption of legislation. With the entry into force of the Lisbon Treaty, the Parliament is now effectively a full partner with the Council in the adoption of EU legislation, and this has changed the dynamic of EU lawmaking considerably. The Parliament is composed of members (MEPs) directly elected by the citizens of the member states. The Parliament typically acts by majority vote of its members.

The Commission is the executive arm of the European Union, composed of "Directorates General" headed by "Commissioners." For purposes of international IP law, the most relevant Directorates are "Internal Markets" (responsible for internal EU IP law), "Trade" (responsible for external IP relations), and "Competition" (responsible for competition law), though certainly other Directorates can be and are important in some IP-related discussions. The Commission is responsible for proposing EU legislation to the Council and Parliament, and for overseeing the implementation of EU law. The Directorates and Directors General (DGs) are roughly analogous to the Cabinet-level Departments (or Executive Agencies) of the U.S. federal government (e.g., the Commerce, State, and Treasury Departments), and their "Secretaries."[95] In the European Union, legislative proposals must originate with the Commission (compare, for example, the United States, where the Congress is free to initiate legislation on its own).

The Court of Justice of the European Union, or CJEU, is responsible for the definitive interpretation of the EU Treaties. The CJEU is comprised of one judge from each member state, so presently 27 judges, though cases are typically heard by smaller panels or "chambers." The CJEU adopts decisions by a collegial process, and opinions are rendered by the Court. There are no "minority" or dissenting opinions. This collegial procedure was adopted early on to avoid even the appearance of potential bias based on the nationality of the judges that might have undermined the role of the Court. Most cases come before the CJEU as referrals or references from the courts of the member states that seek definitive interpretation of the EU Treaties. This is the procedure by which cases involving individuals (individual and corporate) come before the Court. The CJEU also hears challenges to the validity of EU legislation or implementing acts. The Council, Commission, Parliament, and member states may initiate claims before the CJEU, including against each other. There is a subsidiary body to the CJEU, the "General Court" (formerly known as the "Court of First Instance"). The General Court generally hears claims involving administrative actions taken at the EU level, and which are typically subject to further appeal to the CJEU. Important to the discussion of intellectual property, the TFEU includes a provision authorizing the establishment of specialized courts associated with the General Court (Article 257), and authorizes adoption of legislation conferring jurisdiction on the CJEU "in disputes relating to the application of acts

95. Bear in mind that in the United States, the conduct of external trade negotiations is the responsibility of the United States Trade Representative (USTR), also a Cabinet-level official.

adopted on the basis of the Treaties which create European intellectual property rights. These provisions shall enter into force after their approval by the Member States in accordance with their respective constitutional requirements" (Article 262). These provisions will be further addressed as we consider the EU Unitary Patent, the Agreement on a Unified Patent Court, and associated arrangements.

The EU institutions legislate with three formal types of acts: the "regulation," "directive," and "decision."[96] A "regulation" is a legislative act that is directly effective in the law of the member states. A "directive" is an instruction to the member states to achieve a specified result, but one that leaves the "form and methods" to accomplish the result to the member states to which it is addressed. A "decision" is an order binding on the particular persons to whom it is addressed. In addition to these formal types of acts, the Commission issues guidance documents to regulators that may not have a legally binding character, but that nevertheless influence the way EU law is implemented (a form of "soft law").

After the GATT Uruguay Round was concluded and it was time for countries to formally notify their ratification and acceptance, the Commission sought an advisory opinion from the CJEU regarding whether the European Union had the exclusive authority to formally enter into the WTO Agreements, including the TRIPS Agreement, or whether the member states must also become parties to the various agreements.[97] Referring to the common commercial policy (Article 113 of the EC Treaty, which subsequently became Article 133 of the EC Treaty and today is found in Article 207 of the TFEU), the CJEU refused to acknowledge exclusive competence of the Union governing organs in the field of IPRs on the basis of its *ERTA* decision.[98]

In said case, the Court held that if the European Union had adopted harmonizing measures in a particular area, then even in the absence of an express grant of exclusive competence in the EC Treaty, the European Union organs would assume exclusive competence for the conduct of external relations in that area to avoid conflict with the internal harmonizing measures. In this decision concerning the TRIPS Agreement, the Court said that the European Union had not yet achieved a sufficient level of harmonization in the IPRs area for the *ERTA* rationale to be applicable.

The Lisbon Treaty brought about some significant changes to the way intellectual property rights are treated in the EU Treaties, although to a certain extent these changes already were anticipated by developments in the European Union. First, Article 118 of the TFEU clarifies that EU institutions have the authority to regulate with respect to all forms of IPRs, including patents. It provides, in relevant part:

> In the context of the establishment and functioning of the internal market, the European Parliament and the Council, acting in accordance with the ordinary legislative procedure, shall establish measures for the creation of European intellectual property rights to provide uniform protection of intellectual property rights throughout the Union and for the setting up of centralised Union-wide authorisation, coordination and supervision arrangements.

This was important in the context of the creation of the EU Unitary Patent, a subject we will visit later.[99] From the inception of the European Union in 1958, there was controversy surrounding whether the powers of the European Union extended to legislating on internal IP matters, and especially with respect to patents. This accounted for the existence of a European

96. *See* Article 288, TFEU.

97. Opinion 1/94, *Re The Uruguay Round Treaties*, 1994 E.C.R. [1995] 1 C.M.L.R. 20515 (1994).

98. Case 22/70, *Commission of the European Communities v. Council of the European Communities*, 1971 E.C.R. 263 [1971] C.M.L.R. 335 (1971).

99. See *infra*, Chapter 2.

Patent Office and European Patent that are not part of the EU institutional or legislative structure.

Second, Articles 206 and 207 of the TFEU, which establish the "common commercial policy" that governs external trade relations of the European Union, addresses the institutional mechanisms for negotiating and concluding agreements concerning trade related aspects of intellectual property rights, as well as the implementation of those agreements. Since the 1990s, the CJEU has considered purely external trade aspects of IPRs to be within the exclusive jurisdiction of the European Union. However, because the member states retain authority to regulate internal IP matters, the general situation of IPRs was considered "mixed," dividing authority between the European Union and the member states.

Today, the European Union has the authority to harmonize internal IP legislation (per Article 118, above), and commercial aspects of IPRs are within the common commercial policy (per Article 207). These provisions concede important competences in relation to the conclusion and modification of international and bilateral trade agreements to the European Parliament and the Council. The member states' freedom to negotiate new agreements and amend existing ones is limited to a degree where the "mixed competence assumption" the CJEU has established may no longer be sustained.

However, much of EU IPRs regulation is undertaken by way of implementation at the member state level, and to what extent the controversy concerning the allocation of authority to legislate in the field of IPRs in ways that affect international trade persists remains to be seen.

Most recently, issues concerning the European Union as compared with member state competences led to the conclusion of the Agreement on a Unified Patent Court that required ratification by EU member states in the nature of an independent international agreement, as compared with EU legislation adopted on the basis of powers inherent in the TEU and TFEU.[100] It appears that issues concerning EU and member state competences may be with us for a very long time, even in the field of IP.

## NOTES AND QUESTIONS

**1.** As noted earlier, the European Union legislates in three different ways. The "directive" is a form of legislation at a more general level that instructs the member states to bring their own legislation into conformity as they see fit. The "regulation" is directly effective as law throughout the European Union and does not require member state legislation to be given effect. The "decision" is an order directed to a specific person(s). Some EU IPRs legislation takes the form of directive, such as the First Trade Marks Directive. The First Trade Marks Directive contemplated that each member state would maintain its own trademark law and trademark office, under general guidance from the European Union. EU IPRs legislation also takes the form of regulation, such as the European Union Trade Mark Regulation (EUTMR) (formerly, the Community Trade Mark Regulation or CTMR) and, more recently, the European Patent Regulation. The EUTMR established a single unitary trademark for the European Union that operates through a European Union Intellectual Property Office (EUIPO) (formerly the Office for Harmonization in the Internal Market or OHIM), and the

100. Illustrating the complexity of the process, as of May 2018, Germany's ratification of the Agreement on a Unified Patent Court is suspended pending resolution of a challenge brought before the Federal Constitutional Court. Complaint against the legislation enabling Germany to ratify the Agreement on a Unified Patent Court (UPC), case reference 2 BvR 739/17.

European Patent Office will now function as an EU institution as well as an institution established by the European Patent Convention.

**2.** Note that regional intellectual property law in Europe is not exclusively European Union law. The European Patent Convention is formally located outside the European Union and forms an international organization in its own right with membership beyond Members of the European Union.

**3.** Note that until recently the CJEU abbreviated the TRIPS Agreement as "TRIPs," as did other EU institutions. This is *not* the abbreviation used by the WTO, including its Appellate Body. The CJEU and other EU institutions appear to have changed their practice in favor of the WTO practice (i.e., TRIPS).

**4.** The status of the European Union and its member states as parties to the WTO, and their respective roles in the dispute settlement process, continues to be contentious. The European Union consistently takes the position that it alone is responsible for representing the interests of the member states in dispute settlement, notwithstanding that the member states are independently Members of the WTO. When a third country Member initiates consultations with an EU member state, it receives a letter from the EU WTO delegation indicating that the European Union will act as the sole representative in dispute settlement on behalf of the member state, and will be responsible for assuring implementation of any resulting decision. However, dispute settlement panels have been formed to include individual member states as named parties. In the *EU-Aircraft Subsidies* case, the panel made specific findings against individual EU member states and specifically recommended that they bring their measures into conformity.[101] In the subsequent decision on appeal, the Appellate Body maintained certain findings against individual member states and recommended that they bring their legislation into conformity.[102] In consultations initiated by India and Brazil with the European Union and the Netherlands regarding seizures of generic pharmaceuticals in transit, India and Brazil each named the Netherlands as a party to the consultations.[103] Consistent with the practice discussed above, the European Union notified India and Brazil that it is solely responsible for representing the interests of the member states in WTO dispute settlement. The Netherlands did not agree to participate in consultations, but it did send several representatives to the consultations held between India and Brazil and the European Union.

**5.** EU institutions and rules are further discussed throughout the book, including the status of the TRIPS Agreement within EU law.

## *2. Andean Community*

The Andean Community was created in 1969 pursuant to the Treaty of Cartegena.[104] The Andean Community (CAN) is comprised of Bolivia, Colombia, Ecuador, and Peru. Chile, Argentina, Brazil, Paraguay, and Uruguay are associate members. The CAN establishes a free trade area among its member countries and a common external tariff. It maintains common institutions, including a Council of Ministers, Presidential Council, Parliament, Commission, and Court of Justice. The Andean Community in the early 1970s adopted common provisions relating to intellectual property and transfer of technology, which sought to limit the influence

101. WT/DS316/R, 30 June 2010.

102. *European Communities and Certain Member States–Measures Affecting Trade in Large Civil Aircraft*, AB-2010-1, WT/DS316/AB/R, 18 May 2011, *e.g.*, at para. 1416.

103. *See* Request for Consultations by India, WT/DS408/1, G/L/921, IP/D/28, 19 May 2010 and Request for Consultations by Brazil, WT/DS409/1, IP/D/29, G/L/922, 19 May 2010.

104. Information regarding the Andean Community, including its constitutive texts, can be found at http://www.comunidadandina.org.

of foreign right holders in the regional economy. The legislation, principally Decisions 84 and 85 of the Andean Commission, required approval of technology licensing agreements and limited the royalty outflows that could be paid to foreign technology suppliers.[105] However, by the early 1990s, the Andean Community largely abandoned this experiment in rebalancing the terms of technology transfer with the adoption of Decision 344, which was superseded in 2000 by Decision 486. Noteworthy among Andean Community IP-related legislation is Decision 391, establishing the Common Regime on Access to Genetic Resources, adopted in 1996. Decision 391 is intended to implement the provisions of the Convention on Biological Diversity and, among other things, requires prospective bio-prospectors to obtain the prior informed consent of the host country before commencing their activities.[106]

### *3. ASEAN*

**Jakkrit Kuanpoth***

## *ASEAN IP Integration*

In 2003, ASEAN reached an agreement to establish by 2020 an ASEAN Economic Community (AEC). Four years later, ASEAN leaders adopted the AEC Blueprint bringing the deadline for completion of the ASEAN Community forward to 2015. [The AEC was formally established on December 31, 2015. — Eds.] The 2003 Agreement establishing the AEC envisages the conversion of ASEAN into a legal entity as a regional economic community and the transformation of ten ASEAN countries into a single market. The resulting single market means that goods, services, investments, capital and skilled labour will move freely among all the member countries. The AEC Blueprint committed member countries to work towards removing tariff and non-tariff barriers to trade and services as well as to harmonize and standardize trade and customs requirements. It is envisaged that the ASEAN single market will stimulate trade between member states and "will boost the development of production networks in the region and enhance ASEAN's capacity to serve as a global production centre to better meet the demands of the global supply chain."[1]

105. *See generally* Frederick M. Abbott, *Bargaining Power and Strategy in the Foreign Investment Process: A Current Andean Code Analysis*, 3 Syracuse J. Int'l L. & Com. 319 (1975).

106. Of the CAN member countries, Bolivia, Ecuador, and Peru are parties to the Nagoya Protocol (Protocol). Bolivia has established a National Focal Point (NFP) per Art. 13.1 of the Protocol but has not implemented related legislation. Ecuador has established an NFP and has implemented related legislation. In addition to its National Biodiversity Strategy 2015-2030, Ecuador has implemented the Standard that Regulates the Procedure for the Subscription of Framework Contracts for Access to Genetic Resources and the Regulation of the Common Regime on Access to Genetic Resources. Peru has established a far more comprehensive regime. In addition to its NFP, Peru has created several Competent National Authorities (CAN) and implemented legislation such as the Ratifican el Protocolo de Nagoya.

Of the CAN associate members, Argentina and Uruguay are party to the Protocol; both have formed a NFP and have written Interim National Reports on Implementation per Art. 29 of the Protocol. Neither country has implemented legislation. Country Profiles, The Access and Benefit-Sharing Clearing-House, https://absch.cbd.int/countries/status/party (visited July 8, 2018).

* In Emerging Markets and the World Patent Order 305, 306-08 (Frederick M. Abbott, Carlos M. Correa & Peter Drahos eds., 2013).

1. ASEAN Secretariat, "ASEAN Economic Community Handbook for Business," *ASEAN Secretariat*, Jakarta, 2011, p. xiii, http://www.scribd.com/doc/97536042/29/ASEAN-Collaboration-in-Intellectual-Property-Rights (accessed 13 July 2012).

In order to achieve the aim of economic integration, collaboration policies on IP must be established. Like the European Union (EU), ASEAN has expressed its intention to promote collaboration on IP issues. It is agreed that IP rights granted by member states must not act as a barrier to the movement of goods across national borders.[2] In 1995, the leaders of the member nations signed the ASEAN Framework Agreement on Intellectual Property Collaboration establishing the ASEAN Working Group on Intellectual Property Collaboration (AWGIPC). The AWGIPC acts as an IP consultative body and has played a key role in promoting regional collaboration on IP-related matters within ASEAN since 1996. It has held a number of workshops, seminars and symposia on various IP subjects. It has also worked to form strong networks among member countries' government officials.

The work of AWGIPC has been guided by the ASEAN IP Right Action Plan 2004–10, the ASEAN IP Rights Action Plan 2011–15, and the ASEAN Economic Blueprint.[104] [As of August 2023, the AEC Blueprint 2025 is operative[5]] These action plans and the Economic Blueprint were adopted in order to identify the end goals of the AEC and to set out the roles of IP in the AEC process.[3] They aim to achieve the following strategic goals on IP: (1) balancing the IP system for registration and enforcement, including establishing a regional filing system for designs; (2) accession to international agreements regarding designs, patents and trademarks; (3) enhancing IP awareness at all levels; (4) upholding active regional participation in the international IP community through consultations and information exchanges among national enforcement agencies on IP protection; (5) promoting capacity building for government officers, as well as regional collaboration on IP issues such as traditional knowledge, genetic resources and traditional cultural expressions.[4]

Two important works have been initiated by AWGIPC: (1) the establishment of the ASEAN Patent Examination Collaboration Program (ASPEC) and (2) the introduction of the ASEAN IP Portal. The ASPEC was operationalized in 2009. It provides accelerated patent examination procedures for corresponding applications filed in participating member countries. The patent offices of ASEAN countries have agreed to share information and allow examiners in another office to reuse their search and examination results.[5] The patent office of a member country is not obliged to follow the search and examination results of another country's patent office, but they can use the results if they wish to. Each country's office will decide separately whether to grant or reject an application on the basis of that country's own interests. All ASEAN members, excluding Brunei and Myanmar, have participated in the ASPEC. The other IP programme is called the ASEAN IP Portal, which is scheduled to enter into operation in 2012 [EDS – now operational[6]]. The programme will establish a single

2. A. Adcock and C. Gautier, "ASEAN: The Impact of Free Trade on IP," *Managing Intellectual Property*, 1 November 2010, http://www.managingip.com/Article/2710652/ASEAN-The-impact-of-free-trade-on-IP.html (accessed 13 July 2012).

104. [The work of the AWGIPC has also been guided by the more recent ASEAN IP Rights Action Plan 2016-2025, and by the AEC Blueprint 2025. *See Intellectual Property*, ASEAN Economic Community, ASEAN, http://asean.org/asean-economic-community/sectoral-bodies-under-the-purview-of-aem/intellectual-property/ (visited July 23, 2023) —Eds.]

5. https://asean.org/our-communities/economic-community/competitive-innovative-and-inclusive-economic-region/intellectual-property-rights/.

3. ASEAN Secretariat, "ASEAN Economic Community Handbook for Business," *ASEAN Secretariat*, Jakarta, 2011, p. xiii, http://www.scribd.com/doc/97536042/29/ASEAN-Collaboration-in-Intellectual-Property-Rights, (accessed 13 July 2012).

4. Department of Intellectual Property, Annual Report, Department of Intellectual Property, Bangkok, 2011.

5. ASEAN Secretariat, "ASEAN Intellectual Property Right Action Plan 2004–2010," *ASEAN Secretariat*, Jakarta, http://www.ecap3.org/resources/asean-ipr-action-plan-2004-2010.

6. ASEAN Intellectual Property Portal, https://www.aseanip.org/.

web-based database providing information in relation to ASEAN's progress and achievements on IP matters. Member countries' patent offices will be responsible for updating, managing and maintaining the database.

These arrangements aim to increase the efficiency of IP administration and reduce the costs of implementing IP laws. It is interesting to note that ASEAN does not envisage establishing a "unitary" regional IP system, whereby effective enforcement of IP rights is ensured throughout the ASEAN territory. IP rights are still issued or granted by competent national authorities, and national courts still have jurisdiction to determine infringement and validity of IP rights. The planned regional arrangements for IP protection may only be regarded as the beginning of a regional patent system if ASEAN deepens its economic integration towards a single economy.

The severe problem in creating a unitary IP system faced by ASEAN relates to the political dynamics in each member country. ASEAN has faced similar obstacles to those faced by the EU when trying to create a single IP system. Some ASEAN members appear unwilling to amend their national laws to assimilate to Western standards. Some aim to advance their own national interest in the ASEAN IP systems by preserving their national languages and national IP office, and some are demanding that they become the location for the central IP office.

In addition, the deeper the integration process amongst ASEAN members, the more developmental and technological gaps among its members appear. Among ASEAN nations, there is an obvious disparity in institutional capacity and skilled human resources among national IP offices. It is believed that regional policies like ASPEC and the IP Portal will help to bridge the gaps with less need to invest in physical infrastructure at each office. The AWGIPC also plans to accede to international IP treaties in order to strengthen institutional capacity and cross-border cooperation. It is expected that ASEAN as a group will join the following international agreements in the near future: the Hague Agreement Concerning the International Deposit of Industrial Designs, the Patent Cooperation Treaty (PCT), and the Protocol Relating to the Madrid Agreement Concerning the International Registration of Marks.

### *4. Mercosur*

Argentina and Brazil are large economy developing countries, which, together with Paraguay and Uruguay, formed the Mercosur in 1991.[107] The four founding countries still make up Mercosur's main body today; Venezuela acceded in 2012, but has since been permanently suspended. Bolivia, Chile, Colombia, Ecuador, Guyana, Peru and Suriname are "associated" members of the Mercosur, though Bolivia is in the process of accession. The Mercosur countries have made substantial progress toward reduction of traditional trade barriers between them. Harmonization or approximation of intellectual property rights rules has not so far been a priority.

There do not appear to have been significant IP-related developments since Law No. 17.052 of December 14, 1998, approving the Protocol of Harmonization of Intellectual Property in the Mercosur on Trademarks, Geographical Indications and Appellations of Origin.

An EU-Mercosur free trade agreement has been agreed upon,[108] though as of August 2023 it had not entered into force. The text includes a chapter on intellectual property that appears to focus on protection of geographical indications.[109]

107. https://www.mercosur.int/en/about-mercosur/mercosur-countries/, visited July 23, 2023.

108. EU Press Release, EU and Mercosur reach agreement on trade, June 28, 2019, https://ec.europa.eu/commission/presscorner/detail/en/IP_19_3396.

109. EU-Mercosur: Text of the agreement, https://policy.trade.ec.europa.eu/eu-trade-relationships-country-and-region/countries-and-regions/mercosur/eu-mercosur-agreement/text-agreement_en; IP chapter, https://circabc.europa.eu/ui/group/09242a36-a438-40fd-a7af-fe32e36cbd0e/library/0dd13d1e-528e-455e-941b-bc280753ca00/details.

### *5. USMCA (Formerly NAFTA)*

The North American Free Trade Agreement (NAFTA) between Canada, Mexico, and the United States entered into force on January 1, 1994. The NAFTA includes a detailed Chapter 17 on intellectual property. This chapter was negotiated at roughly the same time as the WTO TRIPS Agreement and is similar in most respects. However, there were some notable differences. These included "pipeline" patent protection for pharmaceutical and agricultural chemical products that could not previously be patented in Mexico,[110] and more restrictive protection of data submitted in connection with regulatory approval of pharmaceutical and agricultural products.[111] Outside of the IP chapter, Canada and Mexico insisted on measures allowing protection of local cultural institutions. Mexico, for example, limited foreign participation in its broadcast and film sectors.

In 2017, the United States requested that Canada and Mexico renegotiate the terms of the NAFTA, for among other purposes to "modernize" the agreement. The U.S. President threatened to terminate the NAFTA if U.S. demands were not met, although it is not clear that the president has constitutional authority within the United States to terminate a trade agreement without the consent of the Congress that approved and implemented it.

On September 30, 2018, the conclusion of a new agreement to take the place of the "old NAFTA" was announced among Canada, Mexico and the United States.[112] The new agreement is styled the "United States-Mexico-Canada Agreement" or "USMCA." Although President Trump referred to the TPP as a terrible deal for the United States, at least on the intellectual property side the USMCA essentially reproduces the IP provisions of the TPP, with some notable modifications. We will consider specific substantive provisions in subsequent chapters. We can note here that new features include: (1) requiring patent term extension in circumstances of unreasonable delay in the approval of new drugs; (2) requiring patent-regulatory approval "linkage" for pharmaceuticals; (3) requiring criminal penalties for willful trade secret misappropriation; (4) establishing rules against requirements for transfer of technology as a condition of foreign direct investment; (5) eliminating investor to state dispute settlement (ISDS) as between the United States and Canada, and sharply curtailing ISDS as between the United States and Mexico. Initially,the exception of the elimination or curtailment of ISDS, the Trump Administration essentially delivered the wish list of the U.S. originator pharmaceutical industry, virtually assuring higher pharmaceutical product prices in Canada and Mexico. However, in order to secure legislative approval for the USMC in the U.S. Congress, the Administration was forced to eliminate a requirement of ten years market exclusivity for newly approved biologic drugs, a change that was welcomed by Canada and Mexico. As with NAFTA, the USMCA) does not seek to integrate the political institutions of Canada, Mexico, and the United States. Just as when NAFTA was negotiated, none of the three country parties to the USMCA) has an interest in a quasi-federal polity in North America.

The following excerpt briefly explains the difference between the old NAFTA and EU institutional arrangements.

110. NAFTA, art. 1709(4).

111. NAFTA, art. 1711(6).

112. See Joint Statement from United States Trade Representative Robert Lighthizer and Canadian Foreign Affairs Minister Chrystia Freeland, Office of USTR Press Release, https://ustr.gov/about-us/policy-offices/press-office/press-releases/2018/september/joint-statement-united-states.

**Frederick M. Abbott***

## *The North American Integration Regime and its Implications for the World Trading System*

### I. The NAFTA Mutation of the EC Model Revisited

The NAFTA is a significantly different model of regional economic integration than the European Union. The EU is loosely based on the concept of a federal polity with an allocation of power between Union organs—the Council, Commission, Parliament and Court of Justice—on one side, and member state governments on the other side. The NAFTA is in the nature of a confederation among independent sovereigns, each maintaining autonomous political decision-making authority within constraints defined by agreement. The political decision-making apparatus of the NAFTA is closely circumscribed to roughly include within the boundaries of its central authority (the Free Trade Commission) the powers traditionally conferred upon trade ministers by their governments. The European Court of Justice has referred to the EC Treaty as a constitutional charter, and the Court has viewed its role as the guardian of that constitution. The NAFTA does not purport to serve as a constitution in the sense of altering the distribution of powers among its Parties.

The EC Treaty provides for the adoption of directives, regulations and decisions by the Union political organs. These enactments are customarily referred to as "secondary legislation" reflecting their status underneath the "primary legislation" of the EC Treaty. The relationship between primary and secondary Union legislation is similar to the traditional relationship between the constitution and parliamentary enactments of a national federal government. The EC Treaty and secondary legislation may have direct effect in the EU member states, meaning that this legislation may be relied on by individuals in the courts of the member states in appropriate circumstances.

The NAFTA political institutions are not empowered to enact secondary legislation except in very limited circumstances prescribed by the agreement (such as in adopting rules of procedure for NAFTA dispute settlement panels). There is no general legislative power allocated to the NAFTA political institutions. The NAFTA is in theory capable of direct effect within the national courts of its Parties. The United States has by legislation deprived the NAFTA of potential direct effect in U.S. courts.

The economic undertakings of the Parties were negotiated in detail. The results of these negotiations were expressed in the NAFTA text. The Parties have so far carried out the economic undertakings of the NAFTA substantially in accordance with its terms. Though a few matters are disputed, in the context of the overall undertaking, these disputes are modest.

The NAFTA prescribes mechanisms for the resolution of disputes between its Parties, and in limited circumstances for the resolution of disputes between the nationals of its Parties and Party governments. The general dispute settlement mechanism of the NAFTA is an arbitral procedure that refers determinations to Party governments for political resolution. This is consistent with the NAFTA's limited design in respect to intrusion on Party autonomy. The NAFTA's anti-dumping and countervailing duty dispute settlement apparatus directly binds Party governments.[9] Party nationals are entitled to pursue third party arbitration of

* IX:1 Collected Courses of the Academy of European Law: The EU, the WTO and the NAFTA 170 (J.H.H. Weiler ed., 2000).

9. The NAFTA includes a separate dispute settlement mechanism in respect to antidumping and countervailing duty (AD/CVD) related complaints (Chapter 19, NAFTA). The NAFTA contains no rules regarding the substance of the AD/CVD laws of the Parties, requiring only that each Party act in domestic AD/CVD actions in compliance with its own laws. In the AD/CVD dispute settlement system, arbitral panels constituted on a case-by-case basis make

investment-related claims at ICSID or under UNCITRAL rules.[10] Each of these dispute settlement mechanisms is operational.

The European Union is a customs union. The EC Treaty prescribes the elimination of tariffs and other restrictive regulations of commerce on trade between its member states, and prescribes the establishment of common tariffs applicable to goods originating outside EU territory. The EC Treaty prescribes that goods originating outside its territory are in free circulation within its territory following the payment of the applicable common tariff upon entry into any member state. The EC Treaty prescribes a common commercial policy which binds its member states to follow a coordinated trade policy program. The EC Treaty prescribes the free movement of services, capital and persons between its member states.

The NAFTA is a free trade area. The NAFTA prescribes the elimination of tariffs and other restrictive regulations of commerce between its Parties, but does not prescribe common tariffs applicable to goods originating outside NAFTA territory. Except in so far as goods originating outside the NAFTA are transformed within a Party(s) so as to assume a regional character, such third country goods are subject to the payment of tariffs upon entry into each NAFTA Party. The NAFTA prescribes the free movement of services and capital, and limited free movement of business persons, between its members. Except in so far as the Parties are limited in their relations with third countries by the terms of the NAFTA, the agreement does not mandate that the Parties pursue a common commercial policy.

## NOTES AND QUESTIONS

**1.** The NAFTA included Chapter 17 on Intellectual Property. When Mexico agreed to provide "pipeline" protection for pharmaceutical products that had been patented previously in the United States or Canada, but had not yet been patented or marketed in Mexico (NAFTA, art. 1709(4)), this raised concern for countries outside the NAFTA that were not entitled to MFN treatment by Mexico. It was this type of special treatment under a regional agreement that led countries to insist on an MFN provision in the TRIPS Agreement. We discuss the MFN treatment principle *infra*, at section VII.B.

**2.** Whether in the context of the NAFTA or the USMCA, what advantages would you see to harmonization of IPRs legislation among the United States, Canada, and Mexico? Do you think this would be a good idea?

**3.** Assuming for the sake of argument that the United States, Canada, and Mexico intended to harmonize their IP legislation, what should be the legislative process? Should the trade negotiators handle this and put the results before the legislatures of each country? How would this differ from the customary legislative process in the United States?

**4.** A notable development regarding the NAFTA investment and intellectual property chapters was the claim brought by the U.S.-based pharmaceutical company Eli Lilly against the government of Canada in 2012, which was rejected by a NAFTA-UNCITRAL arbitration

decisions as to whether a country Party has complied with its own AD/CVD laws in a particular action. The decisions of AD/CVD panels are directly binding on the country Parties. There are approximately 30 completed or active Chapter 19 panels reviewing AD/CVD decisions of Canadian, Mexican and U.S. administrative authorities. NAFTA Secretariat, www.nafta-sec-alena.org.

10. The NAFTA permits investors of Parties to pursue third party arbitration against a host government in the International Centre for the Settlement of Investment Disputes (ICSID) or under UNCITRAL rules. NAFTA, arts. 1115, *et seq.* . . . The NAFTA obligates the Parties to make adequate provision for the enforcement of resulting arbitral awards. Several proceedings based on NAFTA investment rules have been initiated in the ICSID by U.S. nationals against the government of Mexico, and claims both by U.S. nationals against the government of Canada and by Canadian nationals against the government of the United States have been initiated or threatened.

panel in early 2017.[113] Eli Lilly invoked the takings provisions in the NAFTA investment chapter as grounds for challenge of a determination of patent invalidity by Canadian federal courts regarding two Eli Lilly patents. The Eli Lilly complaint and subsequent proceedings against the government of Canada provided an illustration of why governments and other stakeholders have become increasingly concerned about the potential scope of ISDS obligations in trade and investment agreements. In fact, these concerns led Canada and the United States to eliminate ISDS from the USMCA.

## B. Legal and Economic Impact of IP Provisions in Regional Trade Agreements

The nearly 30 years following the creation of the WTO and entry into force of the TRIPS Agreement have witnessed a proliferation of regional trade agreements with IP provisions. Almost all of the modern preferential or cooperation agreements contain a chapter on intellectual property with varying levels of ambition. Main examples include the Comprehensive Economic and Trade Agreement between the EU and Canada (CETA), the Comprehensive and Progressive Agreement for Transpacific Partnership (CPTPP) between Australia, Brunei, Canada, Chile, Japan, Malaysia, Mexico, Peru, New Zealand, Singapore, Vietnam and the UK, the African Economic Community, the Sino-Swiss Free Trade Agreement and the Regional Comprehensive Economic Partnership (RCEP) between the Asia Pacific nations of Australia, Brunei, Cambodia, China, Indonesia, Japan, South Korea, Laos, Malaysia, Myanmar, New Zealand, the Philippines, Singapore, Thailand, and Vietnam. India, absent in these agreements, embarked in 2023 in negotiating a number of FTAs, in particular with the UK, Canada, and EFTA, with IPR among the most contentious issues. The African Continental Free Trade Area AfCFTA) of the African Union, eventually with 55 countries involved, has embarked on negotiations in Phase II. Overall, a 2020 study by the WHO, WIPO, and WTO notes that:

> Eighty-two per cent of the FTAs that entered into force after 2005 contain IP provisions. Among these, 20 per cent contain provisions that require the parties to implement more extensive protection and enforcement of IPRs than the standards provided for in the TRIPS Agreement. Such provisions are often referred to as "TRIPS plus". The non-discrimination principles under the TRIPS Agreement require parties to those FTAs to extend the application of any higher standards to all other WTO Members."

The increase of regional trade agreements with IP provisions has resulted in raised global standards for IP protection and enforcement. Higher IP standards of protection and enforcement potentially influence innovation and access to intellectual property. We recall that preferential trade or cooperation agreements are subject to the MFN clause of the TRIPs Agreement. Each of the provisions exceeding the minimal standards of the TRIPS Agreement can thus be invoked by all the Member states, even if not a member to the preferential agreement. Thus, these agreements rise the general standard of protection and contribute to what may be called the common law of intellectual property protection in international law. The excerpt below discusses the mixed empirical evidence regarding the role of raised global IP standards on encouraging innovation, technology transfer and access to new technologies.

---

113. *Eli Lilly v. Canada*, Final Award of the Arbitral Tribunal, ICSID Case No. UNCT/14/2 (March 16, 2017). For case documents, *see* http://www.international.gc.ca/trade-agreements-accords-commerciaux/topics-domaines/disp-diff/eli.aspx?lang=eng.

**Keith E. Maskus, Department of Economics, University of Colorado Boulder**

### *International Agreements on Intellectual Property Rights: TRIPS and Beyond*[10]

When negotiated, the TRIPS Agreement was, and remains, the most comprehensive global agreement covering standards of protection and enforcement norms in IPRs. Numerous developing and emerging nations implemented significant legal reforms over time, according to the allowable transition periods. At the same time, developed economies have continued to advance their own standards, particularly in the areas of digital protection, medical and biological patents, GIs, and trade secrets. Further, recent bilateral and regional PTAs with successively stronger IPRs chapters have ratcheted global protection upward. Together, these changes, despite the policy flexibilities inherent in TRIPS, have strongly increased the global scope of protection for patents, copyrights, and related rights.

Whether this new global regime has achieved an appropriate balance between incentives for innovation and licensing on the one hand, and the needs for access to new goods and information on the other, remains an open question. A positive note is that there is solid empirical evidence that this regime is encouraging the formal transfer of new technologies to emerging countries through enhanced trade and investment in high-technology sectors. Further, innovation seems to be growing in major emerging economies that have introduced markedly stronger patent laws, as measured by the development of new products, additional R&D investments, and foreign patenting. And the introduction of domestic patents is correlated with more rapid introduction of new global pharmaceuticals into developing markets. In this sense, TRIPS and the broader system seem to be improving the global landscape for technology transactions and the use of information.

However, there are reasons to remain cautious about the overall impacts of these policy shifts. First, there is little evidence to date that technology transfers, even through outsourcing within supply chains, are increasing to the poorest developing economies. It appears that reforming IPRs protection by itself is not particularly effective in connecting such countries to the global technological structure. Second, there is no indication that innovative enterprises in the advanced or emerging economies are investing more in products and technologies that would meet the specific needs of consumers and patients in poor countries. This is particularly unfortunate, for the development of such incentives was touted as a key reason for developing economies to support TRIPS in the first place. Put briefly, stronger international patent protection is not sufficient to overcome other market difficulties that may prevent such innovation and technology diffusion.

Perhaps most importantly, stronger IPRs raise fundamental, and as yet unanswered, concerns about the ability of governments and international organizations to procure needed public goods at reasonable cost. Private property rights in information do not seem to be an adequate global solution to such problems as procuring and distributing essential medicines, transferring green technologies, or diffusing scientific knowledge into the developing world. In this sense, the international system remains controversial and subject to further revisions.

## C. Regional IP Offices in Africa

While most countries outside of Europe exclusively rely upon national authorities and institutions, Africa shares a tradition of joint administration and of pooling resources.

10. Prepared for the Routledge Handbook of International Trade Agreements, ed. Robert Looney, 2018.

There are two principal regional IP institutions in Africa, ARIPO and OAPI. It was originally conceived that ARIPO would be constituted by English-speaking African states, and OAPI by the French-speaking, though this bifurcation is not rigid. Detailed information concerning the organizational structure and operation of ARIPO and OAPI may be found at their respective web sites, http://www.aripo.org and http://www.oapi.int/. Each of them provides a mechanism for securing patent protection across the regional territory of its membership, but with different procedural and substantive characteristics. ARIPO and OAPI signed a cooperation agreement in 2017 in an effort to harmonize their respective IP systems.[114]

In addition to the regional IP institutions of ARIPO and OAPI, there are a significant number of more general regional institutions in Africa, including the African Union, the New Partnership for Africa's Development (NEPAD), and the Southern African Customs Union (SACU). Each of these institutions includes some aspects of intellectual property regulation within its range of activities.

## D. Patent Office of the Cooperation Council for the Arab States of the Gulf (GCC Patent Office)

The GCC Patent Office is a regional patent office based in Riyadh, Saudi Arabia for the six-member Council for the Arab States of the Gulf (Gulf Cooperation Council or GCC), which consists of Bahrain, Kuwait, Oman, Qatar, Saudi Arabia, and the United Arab Emirates.[115] Established in 1992, the GCC Patent Office began accepting patent applications in 1998; a patent granted by the GCC Patent Office was valid in the six member states. Following a resolution of the Supreme Council in 2021, the GCC Patent Office suspended receiving new patent applications as of January 6, 2021; it will receive and conduct formal and/or substantive examination and the granting of patents only upon request from GCC Member States.[116] As of July 2023, Bahrain, Kuwait, and Qatar had requested the GCC Patent Office to receive, examine, and grant patent applications on their behalf.[117]

## E. Regional Consultation (APEC)

The Asia-Pacific Economic Cooperation forum (APEC) is essentially a consultative body among countries of the Pacific region, including the United States. Unlike the European Union or Mercosur, APEC does not establish governmental institutions or common legislation. It is rather a consultative body. It does, however, encourage transparency with respect to intellectual property rules and enforcement. An Intellectual Property Rights Experts Group (IPEG) was created in 1996 that coordinates and undertakes the work related to IPRs (*see* https://apec.org/Groups/Committee-on-Trade-and-Investment/Intellectual-Property-Rights-Experts-Group).

In addition to APEC, there are a number of regional institutions in Asia that include aspects of intellectual property regulation within the range of their activities, including ASEAN (see *supra*), AFTA, and SAFTA. *See generally* United Nations Economic and Social

114. *See* Hillary Muheebwa, *ARIPO, OAPI to Harmonise Practices on Intellectual Property in Africa*, IP-WATCH, Feb. 21, 2017, http://www.ip-watch.org/2017/02/21/aripo-oapi-harmonise-practices-issues-intellectual-property-africa/.

115. Patent Office at the Secretariat General for the Cooperation Council, https://www.gccpo.org/DefaultEn. Last visited: July 26, 2023.

116. Law Amending the Patent Law of the Cooperation Council for the Arab States of the Gulf. Available at: https://www.wipo.int/wipolex/en/legislation/details/21685. *See also*: PATENT OFFICE AT THE COOPERATION COUNCIL FOR THE ARAB STATES OF THE GULF (GCC-SG), https://inspire.wipo.int/system/files/gcc.pdf.

117. Patent Applications to Resume on Behalf of The State of Qatar from July 1, 2023, https://gccpo.org/AboutUsEn/ShowNews?id=69. Last visited: July 26, 2023.

Commission for Asia and the Pacific (UNESCAP), Asia-Pacific Trade and Investment Agreements Database (APTIAD), at http://www.unescap.org/tid/pta_app/.

## V. TRADE AND ECONOMIC COOPERATION AGREEMENTS

There is, at present, limited possibility for the United States or the European Union and other industrialized countries to negotiate higher standards of protection at the WTO or WIPO because a substantial number of developing countries consider that the standards already in place create administrative and economic burdens for them. Nonetheless, major industry groups in the United States perceive gaps in the TRIPS Agreement and place constant pressure on U.S. trade negotiators to remedy this situation. The result is the pursuit of a "second-best" solution (from an industry standpoint) of achieving higher standards in bilateral, regional, and more recently, "plurilateral" negotiations. They led to the inclusion of chapters on intellectual property in bilateral agreements spearheaded in the U.S.-Central America Free Trade Agreement (CAFTA), mainly increasing levels of protection beyond those of the WTO and WIPO Agreements: so-called TRIPS-plus obligations.[118] Another landmark to this effect was the 2014 Swiss-Sino Free Trade Agreement. In parallel, efforts to protect intellectual property by means of investment protection agreements have been prominent and opened a new field.

Given the difficulties on the multilateral level, the approach by way of preferential trade and economic cooperation agreements has been generalized. It is being pursued by all industrialized countries, in particular by the European Union and, to a lesser degree, by the EFTA. The Comprehensive and Progressive Agreement for Trans-Pacific Partnership (CPTPP), also known as TPP11, a signed trade agreement between Australia, Brunei, Canada, Chile, Japan, Malaysia, Mexico, New Zealand, Peru, Singapore, and Vietnam (minus the United States), and the UK in 2023 equally entails a comprehensive chapter on intellectual property, albeit deleting a number of standards particularly sought by the United States prior to leaving the project in 2017.[119] The United States achieved most of its intellectual property-related objectives in the text of the TPP it signed, but when the United States withdrew its signature, the remaining 11 TPP countries amended the text to remove the IP provisions that would have, *inter alia*, raised protection for pharmaceutical originator companies that (with the exception of Japan) they had provided only because of U.S. demands. Charlotte Greenfield & Colin Packham, *Final Version of Trans-Pacific Trade Deal Released, Rules Pushed by U.S. on Ice*, Reuters, Feb. 20, 2018.[120]

As of today, one of the most extensive and elaborate preferential trade agreements on intellectual property protection is the EU-Canadian Comprehensive Economic and Trade Agreement, signed October 30, 2016, and provisionally applied as of September 21, 2017 (with the provisional status continuing as of August 2023).[121] Following the structure of the

118. *See* Frederick M. Abbott, *The Evolution of Public Health Provisions in Preferential Trade and Investment Agreements of the United States* in Current Alliances in International Intellectual Property Lawmaking: The Emergence and Impact of Mega-Regionals, Global Perspectives for the IP System 45-63 (P. Roffe & X. Seuba eds., 4 CEIPI-ICTSD 2017), available at SSRN: https://ssrn.com/abstract=3032085.

119. The CPTPP was signed on February 3, 2016, and is not yet in force. *See* Rebecca Howard, *Trans-Pacific Partnership Trade Deal Signed, But Years of Negotiations Still to Come*, Reuters, Feb. 3, 2016. On January 23, 2017, President Trump signed an executive order withdrawing the United States signature. Ylan Q. Mui, *Withdrawal from Trans-Pacific Partnership Shifts U.S. Role in World Economy*, Wash. Post, Jan. 23, 2017.

120. https://www.reuters.com/article/us-trade-tpp/final-version-of-trans-pacific-trade-deal-released-rules-pushed-by-u-s-on-ice-idUSKCN1G50AP.

121. *Canada-EU Joint Statement: CETA at five years – the cornerstone of Canada/EU economic relations*, https://policy.trade.ec.europa.eu/news/joint-statement-ceta-five-years-cornerstone-canadaeu-economic-relations-2022-12-02_en.

TRIPS Agreement, chapter 20 contains 50 provisions addressing general provisions, specific forms of protection (including geographical indications), and enforcement. Moreover, the agreement protects intellectual property in investment protection in chapter 8 and addresses the relationship of intellectual property and investment protection in detail, as discussed below. *See* http://data.consilium.europa.eu/doc/document/ST-10973-2016-INIT/en/pdf (last visited July 24, 2023).

Negotiations between the United States and the European Union on the Transatlantic Trade and Investment Partnership Agreement (TTIP) were placed on hold by the United States, and the work on TRIPS-plus standards and perhaps other elements essential within a transatlantic free trade zone remains largely unexplored. The draft proposals published by the European Union essentially focused on geographical indications, adherence to existing international agreements, and law enforcement (*see* EU Commission, Directorate Trade, Intellectual Property (IP) and Geographical Indications, http://trade.ec.europa.eu/doclib/press/index.cfm?id=1230#market-access (visited July 23, 2018)).

Trade and economic cooperation agreements thus no longer are limited to addressing intellectual property in terms of legitimate restrictions of trade (e.g., Article XX(d) GATT 1947), but complement the set of rules of positive integration in intellectual property. These additional rules are of general importance as they are subject to the MFN obligations under the TRIPS Agreement. A country bilaterally or plurilaterally committing to higher levels of protection beyond the TRIPS Agreement is obliged by law to grant equal levels of protection to all Members of the WTO. Moreover, these agreements also venture into the field of investment protection and have begun to address the linkages between intellectual property and investment protection.

## A. The Advent of TRIPS-plus Standards

**Thomas Cottier***

### *Intellectual Property and Mega-Regional Agreements: Progress and Opportunities Missed*

#### I. The Common Law of Intellectual Property Protection

For industrialized countries and thus the EU, adequate protection of intellectual property (IP) is of paramount importance. The process of globalization increased division of labour and the importance of global value chains, calling for legal security in foreign trade and investment abroad. Products developed and engineered in Europe often are produced elsewhere, while marketing again takes place out of Europe, adding value and mainly service sector jobs. The effort to enhance international IP protection commenced by the US at the end of the General Agreement on Tariffs and Trade 1994 (GATT) Tokyo Round equally stimulated efforts on the part of the Commission and the EU ever since. It has been high on the agenda of external economic relations since the 1990s and has remained so, translating also into new powers to regulate IP in the internal market and in trade policy. It amounts to an important part of preferential trade agreements (PTAs) negotiated ever since in the wake of regime shifting, and thus also of emerging mega-regional agreements depicting the most recent development of a long history.

* In Mega-Regional Trade Agreements CETA, TTIP, and TISA: New Orientations for EU External Economic Relations 151-174 (Stefan Griller, Walter Oberwexer & Erich Vranes eds., 2017) (footnotes omitted).

. . . The chapters on IPRs in PTAs follow the structure of TRIPs, and build upon it, not necessarily in the same order. They are highly detailed and complex, culminating in the EU-Canadian Comprehensive Economic and Trade Agreement (CETA) concluded in 2015. The most recent phase of continued forum shifting relates to mega-regional agreements. Negotiations on the Trans-Pacific Trade Partnership (TPP) were concluded in the same year. Negotiations on the Transatlantic Trade and Investment Partnership Agreement (TTIP) and the China–ASEAN Regional Comprehensive Economic Partnership Agreement (RCEP) are under way. For TTIP, no comprehensive negotiating text on IPRs has been made available, either officially or informally. At the time of writing, outcomes for TTIP still remain a matter of speculation. Given the focus on the impact of the EU's commercial policy, we briefly compare the main IP provisions of CETA with TPP, taking into account also EU proposals on TTIP.

From the point of view of the EU, the most advanced agreement as of today in this respect is ch 22 of CETA, serving as a reference point for the state of the art in a world of fragmentation and varied standards. It is likely to influence TTIP negotiations, albeit results will not be identical due to diverging US concerns. These, in turn, are mainly reflected in TPP. Globally, ch 18 of this Agreement amounts to the most important recent document as it includes relations among industrialized as well as relations among and with developing countries.

Importantly, the new standards are not limited to the parties to these Agreements, but also benefit third parties. They globally raise levels of protection and enforcement. It is recalled that Art 3 of the TRIPs Agreement extended most-favoured nation (MFN) treatment to IP protection. Absent under the Berne and Paris Conventions, MFN obligations relate to any advantage and privilege granted to any other country, subject to certain exceptions. In other words, TRIPs+ obligations incurred under a PTA or mega-regional agreements are not limited to the parties to that agreement. They extend to all Members of the WTO. They create, subject to specific exceptions, equal conditions for all right-holders operating in a particular market. WTO Members negotiating PTAs and mega-regional agreements are aware that additional rights and obligations incurred provide the basis for domestic IPR law applicable erga omnes within the WTO Membership. While standards of protection within countries vary, they are equally applied to all 164 WTO Members (2016). Other WTO members thus benefit from spill-over effect, without reciprocal obligations.

To the extent that enhanced standards are granted to nationals on the basis of national treatment, these effects already result from the national treatment obligations of Art 3 TRIPs Agreement, Art 2 Paris Convention, and Art 5 para 1 Berne Convention. To the extent, however, that additional protection is granted to foreign right-holders, MFN triggers additional levels of protection. This is of particular importance in investment protection to the extent that it falls under the jurisdiction of the TRIPs Agreement. Overall, national treatment and the MFN clause of the TRIPs Agreement thus creates what may be called the common law of IPR protection, adding up layers of norms eventually created in different fora and instruments, from the Berne and Paris Conventions and related agreements under the auspices of the World Intellectual Property Organization (WIPO), the GATT, and the TRIPs Agreement of the WTO, to subsequent preferential trade and mega-regional agreements.

## II. Great Expectations

In the process of legal developments in different fora, one would expect that impending systemic problems are subsequently taken up and addressed. It would be expected that the mega-regionals, in particular TPP and TTIP and perhaps RCEP, while creating new standards of the common law, address problems identified and discussed post the adoption of the TRIPs Agreement and its remaining lacunae and issues. The IP system consists of many agreements, and their interrelationship awaits clarification on various and complex issues. Are they incorporated into agreements or merely referred to? The incorporation of IPRs into the multilateral trading system and the dispute settlement mechanism of the WTO is not a formality. It does not remain without implications in defining the relationship of exclusive rights, freer trade and market access, but also non-trade issues in particular human rights. These interfaces are expected to be addressed in subsequent agreements. There is no shortage of unresolved problems waiting to be addressed with a view to deepen and enhance the long-term legitimacy of international IP and trading and investment law. They in particular include the following issues, widely discussed in the literature over the last twenty years.

Parallel trade, that is, the lawful importation of IP-protected products lawfully placed on third markets, amounts to the most important trade-related issue of IPRs in a free trade context. Article 6 of the TRIPs Agreement leaves the matter essentially to WTO Member States. At the same time, parallel trade—depending on the origin of the product and not the right-holder—also falls under the disciplines of GATT 1994; restrictions call for particular justification. While leaving the regulation of parallel trade to domestic policy space—commensurate with industrial and economic conditions—is appropriate for patents and copyright, international exhaustion in trademarks and geographical indications (GIs) is appropriate in a system promoting and protecting free trade. The International Law Association adopted a report and resolution to this effect in 2000.

This issue also bears on the relationship of IPRs and competition law and investment protection and trade. The TRIPs Agreement is limited to setting minimum standards. Domestic law may, with limited exceptions on enforcement, freely adopt higher, more stringent levels of protection. Extending exclusive rights may unduly restrict competition and equal opportunities on the market. Yet, no disciplines exist in international economic law restraining the extension of protection domestically. In investment law, the contours and scope of protection of IPRs remains controversial and unsettled. What restrictions amount to regulatory taking? Do IPRs also oblige governments to allow usage, or are they limited to horizontal relations among competitors?

Much of the debate on IPRs relates to the needs of developing countries and emerging economies. While these countries generally opt for lower levels of protection, areas of genuine interests to them have remained underdeveloped. IP essentially is an offspring of industrialization. It has not catered to agriculture and rural populations. As up to 70 per cent of the population in developing countries relate to farming and rural life forms, an effort should be made to render the international IP system more beneficial to their economic and cultural interests. The promotion of GIs for specialized agricultural products and the protection of traditional knowledge (TK) and of genetic resources in the context of biodiversity are pressing needs. One would expect new rules on obligations to indicate the indication of origin of an invention, or efforts to catalogue TK electronically with a view to identify prior art. One would expect, beyond negative protection, the evolution of new types of IPRs addressing TK. This is less a matter of introducing appropriate disciplines in domestic law of developing countries, but much more an effort among industrialized countries to offer appropriate forms of protection which need coordination, if not harmonization, among themselves. Transfer of state-of-the-art technology and know-how and capacity building perhaps are the most urgent issues in the context of climate change mitigation and adaption. Governments are unable to honour even weak obligations as they do not possess the technology and cannot freely dispose of it. Companies, on the other hand, depend upon income, are interested to preserve first-mover advantages and thus are reluctant to license state-of-the-art technology. Particular efforts are required to bring about improvements. Again, this is primarily a matter among industrialized countries in keeping level playing fields among competitors. It requires coordination on tax incentives and subsidies; all matters to be addressed in international trade agreements with a view to bring first-hand technologies combating greenhouse gas emissions or facilitating climate change adaption to countries of production. We would expect answers to these fundamental questions in new agreements. To this effect, fundamental principles, objectives, and goals are expected to be further developed beyond the provisions of Arts 7 and 8 of the TRIPs Agreement, also in light of the experiences made with facilitating access to essential drugs under the 2001 Doha Declaration on the TRIPs Agreement and Public Health on access to essential drugs and its implementing instruments. One would expect efforts to graduate obligations at IP, commensurate with the level of social and economic development of countries and hence also the need to imitate technologies which has since been a major driver of development in economic history.

It will be seen that these issues are only partly and marginally addressed, if at all, in recent PTAs and mega-regional agreements. Great expectations of the kind indicated have barely been met and progress has been slow and arduous. Public policy interests in achieving an overall balanced, workable, and fully legitimate system are recognized, but hardly translate in operational terms. . . .

## NOTES AND QUESTIONS

**1.** In bilateral and regional settings, the industrial countries offer market access concessions in areas such as agriculture and textiles in exchange for tightening IP protection. This raises important public policy questions. For example, is it appropriate for developing countries to limit their possibility to lower domestic drug prices by preventing generic drugs from entering the market in exchange for improved access to the U.S. market for their agricultural producers? If poorer segments of developing country populations are unable to afford medicines, does providing owners of developing country agricultural exporting businesses remedy this?

## B. The Protection of IPRs Through Bilateral Investment Treaties (BITs)

As mentioned above, similarly as through FTAs, IPRs are increasingly also protected through disciplines of bilateral investment treaties (BITs). BITs have been concluded since 1959, as they emerged in a historical context of internationally diverging views on private property rights, ownership over national resources, and the sovereign right of states to regulate. At the time, Western market economies developed and negotiated BITs in order to broadly protect their investors' assets in those countries in which investors had to fear expropriation or unfair treatment.

BITs feature a number of broadly formulated treatment standards basically aiming to ensure that the treatment investors receive in a host country does not fall under a certain floor set in light of international law. Treatment standards that BITs enshrine today include standards on most favored nation treatment, national treatment, and fair and equitable treatment. Rules on expropriation in the agreements do not prohibit expropriation of investors or their investments as such, but condition it to the adherence to certain standards such as full and prompt compensation. The arguably most distinct feature of today's BITs, stipulated by the overwhelming majority of agreements, lies in their investor-state dispute settlement (ISDS) clauses, creating a dispute settlement system in which investors can sue the host countries of their investments directly before an international panel, in case they see their rights under the applicable BIT violated.

These features of investment agreements may also apply to investments taking the form of intellectual property rights, since the broadly formulated definitions of BITs may bring intangible assets such as IPRs under the scope of the agreements. Given that the protection clauses in BITs are usually formulated broadly, and clear evidence from case law on the matter is lacking, the precise level of protection offered by BITs for investments taking the form of IP is contested. However, in light of the fact that BITs have never been harmonized with the large body of international IP law such as the TRIPS Agreement, it cannot be excluded that protection standards for IPRs in investment agreements—particularly since they will be interpreted by a disparate group of arbitrators—will make available more stringent or more far-reaching protection for IPRs than dedicated, international intellectual property agreements. As such, there is a risk that protection of IPRs under investment agreements could place pressure on governments to allow in individual cases for higher IP protection standards "through the backdoor," meaning, via claims brought against the government of the host state by an investor. Recent IP-related claims brought under the investment chapters of trade and investment agreements have set off alarm bells, and started at least some governments rethinking the incorporation of IP within the scope of investor protection and related dispute settlement mechanisms.

## C. The EU-Canada Comprehensive Investment and Trade Agreement

The EU-Canada CETA Agreement has chapters both on intellectual property rights and investment protection. *See* http://data.consilium.europa.eu/doc/document/ST-10973-2016-INIT/en/pdf. Chapter 8 defines intellectual property to fall under the provisions of investment protection, but excludes lawful measures taken under the TRIPS Agreement from amounting to expropriation in Article 8.12 (5 and 6) if the measure is compatible with the TRIPS Agreement and Chapter 20 CETA on intellectual property protection, and further provides that inconsistency with the TRIPS Agreement does not establish an expropriation (though leaving the possibility that it might):

> 5. This Article does not apply to the issuance of compulsory licences granted in relation to intellectual property rights, to the extent that such issuance is consistent with the TRIPS Agreement.
>
> 6. For greater certainty, the revocation, limitation or creation of intellectual property rights, to the extent that these measures are consistent with the TRIPS Agreement and Chapter Twenty (Intellectual Property), do not constitute expropriation. Moreover, a determination that these measures are inconsistent with the TRIPS Agreement or Chapter Twenty (Intellectual Property) does not establish an expropriation.

The last paragraph shields restrictions of intellectual property compatible with TRIPS from challenges under investment protection brought by right holders against government. It stems from costly experiences made in the process of adjudicating the case *Eli Lilly and Company v. Government of Canada, supra.*

## NOTES AND QUESTIONS

**1.** Several sets of claims have been launched by private IPR holders against governments with respect to measures directly affecting public health. The first are the claims of the tobacco company Philip Morris against the governments of Australia and Uruguay under bilateral investment agreements. Philip Morris alleged, for example, that by adopting "plain packaging" requirements for tobacco products, the government of Australia unlawfully took its valuable trademark rights.[122] The U.S.-based pharmaceutical company Eli Lilly brought a claim under the investment chapter of the NAFTA alleging that the application by Canada's courts of the "promise doctrine" in the assessment of the patent criterion of utility constituted an expropriation of two patents (for which they sought $500 million compensation).[123] As pointed out in the previous edition of this book, both of these sets of claims were exceedingly weak from an IP law standpoint, and in each case the complaining IPR holder lost. The relevant decisions will be examined further in the patent and trademark chapters of this book. The cases seemed to confirm the worst fears of critics of including IP rights as part of protected investments in trade and investment agreements. Even though the claims did not succeed, they imposed substantial expense and created insecurity for the governments involved, which may have precisely been their objective.

**2.** In the wake of strong objections to investor to state arbitration, the European Union and Canada agreed to establish a standing tribunal and Appeal Tribunal in investment protection, Chapter 8.18 CETA Agreement. The system contemplated builds upon the WTO model of panels and the Appellate Body and should eventually result in a multilateral system. The European Union extended the system to its trade agreement with Vietnam, and other agreements will follow. It remains to be seen how investment protection under the new system will affect the interpretation of the TRIPS Agreement and of Article 20 CETA Agreement, the latter of which is subject to general dispute settlement under Article 27 CETA.

**3.** How do you think the relationship of IP and investment protection should evolve in the long run? Would you favor integrating them by means of a multilateral investment protection and cooperation agreement within the WTO, operating under a single and coherent dispute settlement mechanism?

## VI. INTERPRETATION AND STATUS OF IPR AGREEMENTS IN DOMESTIC LAW

International agreements in intellectual property protection pertain to the realm of international law and thus are subject to the customary rules of interpretation in accordance with Article 31 of the 1969 Vienna Convention on the Law of Treaties. The following case discusses the relevance of these rules for the interpretation of the TRIPs Agreement.

The TRIPS Agreement, at Article 1.1, provides flexibility for WTO Members regarding the manner in which they implement their obligations. The first WTO dispute settlement complaint under the TRIPS Agreement was brought by the United States against India. In its complaint, the United States alleged that India had failed to implement its obligation to provide a so-called mailbox for the filing of patent applications during India's ten-year transition period for providing protection for pharmaceutical products. The panel found that India had, in fact, failed to establish the mailbox. But in doing so, the panel emphasized the expectations of the United States and its private sector pharmaceutical constituency regarding the outcome of the Uruguay Round negotiations. The Appellate Body affirmed the panel's conclusion, but

122. All of the relevant documents in this matter are made available by the government of Australia at http://www.ag.gov.au/Internationallaw/Pages/Investor-State-Arbitration---Tobacco-Plain-Packaging.aspx.

123. *See* Notice of Arbitration, *Eli Lilly and Company, Claimant v. Government of Canada, Respondent*, In the Arbitration under the Arbitration Rules of the United Nations Commission on International Trade Law and the North American Free Trade Agreement, Sept. 12, 2013. The final award fully rejected the claim. *Eli Lilly and Company v. Government of Canada*, ICSID Case No UNCT/14/2, final award 16 March 2017; http://icsidfiles.worldbank.org/icsid/ICSIDBLOBS/OnlineAwards/C3544/DC10133_En.pdf (visited July 23, 2018).

took exception to its methodology. (We will further explore the substance of the patent "mailbox" system established by the TRIPS Agreement in Chapter 2.)

The following decision expounds the main principles of interpretation and assesses the role of domestic law in assessing compatibility with WTO obligations. It illustrates that the TRIPS Agreement establishes an overarching set of rules, but leaves WTO Members with discretion regarding the precise manner in which these rules are implemented and enforced.

## *WTO Appellate Body (1997)**

### India—Patent Protection for Pharmaceutical and Agricultural Chemical Products

43. In addition to relying on the GATT *acquis*, the Panel relies also on the customary rules of interpretation of public international law as a basis for the interpretative principle it offers for the *TRIPS Agreement*. Specifically, the Panel relies on Article 31 of the *Vienna Convention*, which provides in part:

> 1. A treaty shall be interpreted in good faith in accordance with the ordinary meaning to be given to the terms of the treaty in their context and in the light of its object and purpose.

44. With this customary rule of interpretation in mind, the Panel stated that:

> In our view, good faith interpretation requires the protection of legitimate expectations derived from the protection of intellectual property rights provided for in the Agreement.

45. The Panel misapplies Article 31 of the *Vienna Convention*. The Panel misunderstands the concept of legitimate expectations in the context of the customary rules of interpretation of public international law. The legitimate expectations of the parties to a treaty are reflected in the language of the treaty itself. The duty of a treaty interpreter is to examine the words of the treaty to determine the intentions of the parties. This should be done in accordance with the principles of treaty interpretation set out in Article 31 of the *Vienna Convention*. But these principles of interpretation neither require nor condone the imputation into a treaty of words that are not there or the importation into a treaty of concepts that were not intended.

46. In *United States—Standards for Reformulated and Conventional Gasoline*, we set out the proper approach to be applied in interpreting the *WTO Agreement* in accordance with the rules in Article 31 of the *Vienna Convention*. These rules must be respected and applied in interpreting the *TRIPS Agreement* or any other covered agreement. The Panel in this case has created its own interpretative principle, which is consistent with neither the customary rules of interpretation of public international law nor established GATT/WTO practice. Both panels and the Appellate Body must be guided by the rules of treaty interpretation set out in the *Vienna Convention*, and must not add to or diminish rights and obligations provided in the *WTO Agreement*.

47. This conclusion is dictated by two separate and very specific provisions of the DSU. Article 3.2 of the DSU provides that the dispute settlement system of the WTO:

> . . . serves to preserve the rights and obligations of the Members under the covered agreements, and to clarify the existing provisions of those agreements in accordance with customary rules of interpretation of public international law. Recommendations and rulings of the DSB cannot add to or diminish the rights and obligations provided in the covered agreements.

* AB-1997-5, WT/DS50/AB/R, 15 Dec. 1997.

Furthermore, Article 19.2 of the DSU provides:

> In accordance with paragraph 2 of Article 3, in their findings and recommendations, the panel and Appellate Body cannot add to or diminish the rights and obligations provided in the covered agreements.

These provisions speak for themselves. Unquestionably, both panels and the Appellate Body are bound by them.

48. For these reasons, we do not agree with the Panel that the legitimate expectations of Members *and* private rights holders concerning conditions of competition must always be taken into account in interpreting the *TRIPS Agreement*. . . .

57. . . . The Agreement takes into account, *inter alia*, "the need to promote effective and adequate protection of intellectual property rights." We believe the Panel was correct in finding that the "means" that the Member concerned is obliged to provide under Article 70.8(a) must allow for "the entitlement to file mailbox applications and the allocation of filing and priority dates to them." Furthermore, the Panel was correct in finding that the "means" established under Article 70.8(a) must also provide "a sound legal basis to preserve novelty and priority as of those dates." These findings flow inescapably from the necessary operation of paragraphs (b) and (c) of Article 70.8.

58. However, we do *not* agree with the Panel that Article 70.8(a) requires a Member to establish a means "so as to eliminate any reasonable doubts regarding whether mailbox applications and eventual patents based on them could be rejected or invalidated because, at the filing or priority date, the matter for which protection was sought was unpatentable in the country in question." India is *entitled*, by the "transitional arrangements" in paragraphs 1, 2 and 4 of Article 65, to delay application of Article 27 for patents for pharmaceutical and agricultural chemical products until 1 January 2005. In our view, India is obliged, by Article 70.8(a), to provide a legal mechanism for the filing of mailbox applications that provides a sound legal basis to preserve both the novelty of the inventions and the priority of the applications as of the relevant filing and priority dates. No more.

59. But what constitutes such a sound legal basis in Indian law? To answer this question, we must recall first an important general rule in the *TRIPS Agreement.* Article 1.1 of the *TRIPS Agreement* states, in pertinent part:

> . . . Members shall be free to determine the appropriate method of implementing the provisions of this Agreement within their own legal system and practice.

Members, therefore, are free to determine how best to meet their obligations under the *TRIPS Agreement* within the context of their own legal systems. And, as a Member, India is "free to determine the appropriate method of implementing" its obligations under the *TRIPS Agreement* within the context of its own legal system.

## NOTES AND QUESTIONS

**1.** Article 1.1 of the TRIPS Agreement is one of the provisions that establish that WTO Members enjoy "flexibility" in the manner in which they implement their obligations under the Agreement. This flexibility was later confirmed in the Doha Declaration on the TRIPS Agreement and Public Health (adopted by the WTO Ministerial Conference on November 14, 2001), which provides:

> 4. We agree that the TRIPS Agreement does not and should not prevent Members from taking measures to protect public health. Accordingly, while reiterating our commitment to the TRIPS Agreement, we affirm that the Agreement can and should be interpreted and

> implemented in a manner supportive of WTO Members' right to protect public health and, in particular, to promote access to medicines for all.
>
> In this connection, we reaffirm the right of WTO Members to use, to the full, the provisions in the TRIPS Agreement, which provide flexibility for this purpose.

**2.** Why do you think the Appellate Body was so intent on distinguishing a process of interpretation that relies on the express language of the Agreement, as opposed to a process that relies on the legitimate expectations of the parties? What is the practical difference between reliance on the wording, and reliance on legitimate expectations? Is the former an objective, and the later a subjective standard? How do you assess the role of good faith in treaty interpretation in accordance with Article 311(1) of the Vienna Convention?

**3.** The doctrine of protecting legitimate expectations derives from GATT practice of protecting legitimate expectations as to conditions of competition. It is an emanation of good faith and seeks to rely upon an interpretation that a party to an agreement is reasonably entitled to in light of the conduct exercised by the other party to an agreement. It is meant to be an objective standard. Did the Appellate Body fail to appreciate the panel's underlying reasoning in its so-called *India-Mailbox* decision?

**4.** The relationship of international law and domestic law within international fora and tribunals needs to be distinguished from the status of international law in domestic law. This relationship is dealt with *infra*, section VII.H.

## VII. BASIC PRINCIPLES OF INTERNATIONAL IP PROTECTION

All forms of IPRs embody certain cornerstones and shared concepts such as territoriality, ubiquity, exhaustion, and limited duration. The need to achieve some level of coherence and transnational uniformity resulted in various treaties, which in turn include important general principles like national treatment, most favored nation (MFN) treatment, and (in the context of registered rights) the right of priority. Addressing such features beforehand will help us navigate through the detailed provisions of the legal framework.

### A. National Treatment

It is appropriate to start with the principle of national treatment, which is one of the oldest organizing principles found in international trade and investment agreements. This was a core feature of nineteenth-century bilateral agreements, establishing the fundamental tenet of nondiscrimination: Foreign nationals or entitled subject matter (such as goods, services, or investment) shall not be treated less favorably than domestic nationals or subject matter. This principle, eventually enshrined in the GATT 1947 and the 1995 WTO agreements, including Article 3 of the TRIPS Agreement, is of paramount importance in bringing about level playing fields and fair conditions of competition for foreign products. It is equally a fundamental principle of political economy: As political systems tend to favor domestic constituencies and voters, it is the task of international agreements to bring about a proper rebalancing of these shortcomings. Mutual interest in furthering fair conditions of competition in foreign markets provides ample incentive for this rebalancing.

National treatment also effectively functions as a substitute for international harmonization. To the extent that states concentrate on national law, and progress in international law is slow (as it was after decolonization and before the Uruguay Round), the principle of national treatment allows the international community to automatically take advantage of improved standards in municipal law or regional law often introduced for the welfare (and at request) of domestic right holders.

In the field of IPRs, national treatment has been part of the international system from the very beginning. Articles 2 and 3 of the 1883 Paris Convention enshrined the principle, and ever since it has been part of all multilateral IPRs agreements.

2(1) Paris Convention [National Treatment for Nationals of Countries of the Union]

> Nationals of any country of the Union shall, as regards the protection of industrial property, enjoy in all the other countries of the Union the advantages that their respective laws now grant, or may hereafter grant, to nationals; all without prejudice to the rights specially provided by this Convention. Consequently, they shall have the same protection as the latter, and the same legal remedy against any infringement of their rights, provided that the conditions and formalities imposed upon nationals are complied with.

Article 3 of the TRIPS Agreement contains the most comprehensive statement of the principle and its exceptions under existing and partially incorporated international agreements. Its formulation is based on Article III of the GATT 1947 and requires member states to "accord to the nationals of other Members treatment no less favourable than that it accords to its own nationals with regard to the protection of intellectual property." The obligation extends to all parts of the Agreement, including the availability, acquisition, scope, maintenance, and enforcement of IPRs as well as those matters affecting the use of intellectual property rights specifically addressed in the Agreement.

Art. 3 TRIPS Agreement: National Treatment

> 1. Each Member shall accord to the nationals of other Members treatment no less favourable than that it accords to its own nationals with regard to the protection[3] of intellectual property, subject to the exceptions already provided in, respectively, the Paris Convention (1967), the Berne Convention (1971), the Rome Convention or the Treaty on Intellectual Property in Respect of Integrated Circuits. In respect of performers, producers of phonograms and broadcasting organizations, this obligation only applies in respect of the rights provided under this Agreement. Any Member availing itself of the possibilities provided in Article 6 of the Berne Convention (1971) or paragraph 1(b) of Article 16 of the Rome Convention shall make a notification as foreseen in those provisions to the Council for TRIPS.
>
> 2. Members may avail themselves of the exceptions permitted under paragraph 1 in relation to judicial and administrative procedures, including the designation of an address for service or the appointment of an agent within the jurisdiction of a Member, only where such exceptions are necessary to secure compliance with laws and regulations which are not inconsistent with the provisions of this Agreement and where such practices are not applied in a manner which would constitute a disguised restriction on trade.

The wording of the provision deviates from Article 2 of the Paris Convention, which requires equal treatment ("the same protection"). Differences between the two provisions are limited. While treatment no less favorable, in theory and practice, allows for reverse discrimination (discrimination à rebours) in favor of non-nationals, intellectual property laws normally provide, as abstract rules, for equal protection of all right holders alike and neither privilege nor disadvantage nationals, although exceptions to this finding exist. Moreover, Article 3 of the Paris Convention provides for equal protection also of resident nationals of non-members, thus extending protection beyond the TRIPS Agreement. Finally, national treatment obligations under Article III of the GATT also apply in regard to procedures affecting the importation of products protected by intellectual property rights.

3. For the purposes of Articles 3 and 4, "protection" shall include matters affecting the availability, acquisition, scope, maintenance and enforcement of intellectual property rights as well as those matters affecting the use of intellectual property rights specifically addressed in this Agreement.

In a case usually referred to as *U.S.-Havana Club*, the WTO Appellate Body has applied the national treatment principle. At the heart of the dispute were U.S. rules applied to trademarks nationalized by the government of Cuba in the 1960s. A more extensive excerpt from the decision appears in Chapter 3 with specific reference to the trademark law questions. Here the AB rigorously applies a standard that appears to preclude virtually any distinction between foreign and domestic national trademark applicants.

## *WTO Appellate Body**

United States — Section 211 Omnibus Appropriations Act of 1998

233. We turn now to the issue of national treatment. In this appeal we have been asked to address, for the first time, this fundamental principle of the world trading system as it relates to intellectual property. There are two separate national treatment provisions that cover trademarks as well as other intellectual property rights covered by the *TRIPS Agreement.* The European Communities claims, on appeal, that Sections 211(a)(2) and (b) violate both.

234. One national treatment provision at issue in this appeal is Article 2(1) of the Paris Convention (1967), which states:

> Nationals of any country of the Union shall, as regards the protection of industrial property, enjoy in all the other countries of the Union the advantages that their respective laws now grant, or may hereafter grant, to nationals; all without prejudice to the rights specially provided for by this Convention. Consequently, they shall have the same protection as the latter, and the same legal remedy against any infringement of their rights, provided that the conditions and formalities imposed upon nationals are complied with.

235. As we have already explained, the Stockholm Act of the Paris Convention, dated 14 July 1967, is but the most recent version of that important international intellectual property convention. Article 2(1) was part of the Paris Convention in 1883. Since that time, it has remained a treaty obligation of all the countries that have been party to the Paris Convention.

236. The parties to this dispute are not unacquainted with the national treatment obligation and other protections for trademarks and other forms of industrial property provided by the Paris Convention. Every one of the fifteen Member States of the European Union has long been a country of the Paris Union. Most of the current Member States of the European Union became party to the Paris Convention in the 1880's. The most recent did so in 1925 — seventy-seven years ago. Likewise, the United States has, from almost the very beginning, been a country of the Paris Union. The United States became a country of the Paris Union on 30 May 1887 — one hundred and fifteen years ago.

237. Thus, the national treatment obligation is a longstanding obligation under international law for all the countries directly involved in this dispute, as well as for many more countries of the Paris Union that, like the parties to this dispute, are also Members of the WTO. If there were no *TRIPS Agreement*, if there were no WTO, the parties to this dispute would be bound, nevertheless, under Article 2(1) of the Paris Convention (1967), to accord national treatment to other countries of the Paris Union.

238. As we have explained, what *is* new is that, as a consequence of the Uruguay Round, Article 2(1) of the Paris Convention (1967) was made part of the *WTO Agreement.* And, as we have previously explained, by virtue of Article 2.1 of the *TRIPS Agreement*, Article 2(1) of the Paris Convention (1967), as well as certain other specified provisions of the Paris Convention

* WT/DS176/AB/R, 2 Jan. 2002.

(1967), have been incorporated into the *TRIPS Agreement* and, thus, the *WTO Agreement.* Consequently, these obligations of countries of the Paris Union under the Paris Convention (1967) are also now obligations of all WTO Members, whether they are countries of the Paris Union or not, under the *WTO Agreement*, and, thus, are enforceable under the DSU.

239. In addition to Article 2(1) of the Paris Convention (1967), there is also another national treatment provision in the *TRIPS Agreement.* The other national treatment provision at issue in this appeal is Article 3.1 of the *TRIPS Agreement*, which states in relevant part:

> Each Member shall accord to the nationals of other Members treatment no less favourable than that it accords to its own nationals with regard to the protection [footnote 3] of intellectual property, subject to the exceptions already provided in, respectively, the Paris Convention (1967), the Berne Convention (1971), the Rome Convention or the Treaty on Intellectual Property in Respect of Integrated Circuits.
>
> Footnote 3: For the purposes of Articles 3 and 4, "protection" shall include matters affecting the availability, acquisition, scope, maintenance and enforcement of intellectual property rights as well as those matters affecting the use of intellectual property rights specifically addressed in this Agreement.

240. Thus, in drafting the *TRIPS Agreement*, the framers of the *WTO Agreement* saw fit to include an additional provision on national treatment. Clearly, this emphasizes the fundamental significance of the obligation of national treatment to their purposes in the *TRIPS Agreement.*

241. Indeed, the significance of the national treatment obligation can hardly be overstated. Not only has the national treatment obligation long been a cornerstone of the Paris Convention and other international intellectual property conventions. So, too, has the national treatment obligation long been a cornerstone of the world trading system that is served by the WTO.

242. As we see it, the national treatment obligation is a fundamental principle underlying the *TRIPS Agreement*, just as it has been in what is now the GATT 1994. The Panel was correct in concluding that, as the language of Article 3.1 of the *TRIPS Agreement*, in particular, is similar to that of Article III:4 of the GATT 1994, the jurisprudence on Article III:4 of the GATT 1994 may be useful in interpreting the national treatment obligation in the *TRIPS Agreement.*

243. As articulated in Article 3.1 of the *TRIPS Agreement*, the national treatment principle calls on WTO Members to accord no less favourable treatment to non-nationals than to nationals in the "protection" of trade-related intellectual property rights. The footnote to Article 3.1 clarifies that this "protection" extends to "matters affecting the availability, acquisition, scope, maintenance and enforcement of intellectual property rights as well as those matters affecting the use of intellectual property rights specifically addressed" in the *TRIPS Agreement*. . . .

---

### *1. National Treatment and Discrimination*

Several sets of issues tend to be raised in cases involving intellectual property and the national treatment principle. The national treatment principle is one of "nondiscrimination" between foreigners and domestic nationals. It is important at the outset to distinguish between "discrimination" and "differentiation." The national treatment principle does not prevent a government from establishing different rules that apply to foreigners and domestic nationals, that is, rules that take into account legitimate differences. What is prohibited are measures that adversely affect foreigners without justification, thereby creating an imbalance in conditions of competition. The WTO panel decision in the *EU-Geographical Indications* case, excerpted below, addresses various claims by the European Union regarding legitimate differentiation between the treatment of EU and foreign nationals. The possibility to differentiate between foreign and domestic nationals with respect to application procedures is expressly addressed in the relevant international agreements.

Another set of issues involves the distinction between *de jure* and *de facto* discrimination. Some legislation or regulation expressly addresses rights of foreigners in a way that is different from the way the rights of domestic nationals are addressed. Differences are stated as a matter of law or *de jure*. Some legislation or regulation does not make overt distinction between foreigners and domestic nationals, yet operates in a way that creates a difference that is discriminatory. This situation was addressed by a GATT panel in a 1989 case involving a European challenge to Section 337 of the U.S. Trade Act of 1930.[124] Section 337 allows holders of registered IP rights in the United States to seek remedies before the International Trade Commission (ITC) from imports that would infringe their rights. In 1989, the Section 337 procedures made it faster and easier for U.S. patent holders to block importation of infringing imports before the ITC than to obtain remedies for infringement in federal court. The Section 337 procedure was available to foreign nationals holding registered U.S. patents, and on its face did not differentiate between foreigners and domestic U.S. patent holders. However, the GATT panel did not think this *de jure* nondiscrimination insulated the legislation because imported products are preponderantly produced by foreigners.

If the term of copyright protection in two countries varies in duration (70 versus 50 years, the latter being a minimum standard under Article 12, TRIPS Agreement), the principle of national treatment generally would not allow the country with the longer term to accord only the shorter term to the other's nationals. IPRs holders would equally enjoy a term of 70 years in one country, and 50 years in the other. The Berne Convention deviates from the principle of national treatment in regard to the duration of copyright, stating that foreigners need only be accorded the term of their home country (Article 7, Berne Convention).

### *2. National Treatment and Reciprocity*

A national treatment obligation requires that a state grant to nationals of other states (enjoying protection) treatment equivalent to that which it grants its own nationals. Under WTO rules, the national treatment obligation is essentially unconditional. That is, once a WTO Member agrees to provide national treatment to another Member, it may not require any further "concession" in order to make that obligation operational.

Another potential approach to the treatment of foreign nationals is "material reciprocity" or "conditional national treatment." Under such an approach, a country would agree to provide national treatment to persons (or products) from foreign countries, but only on the condition that the foreign countries provide an equivalent level of protection as the first country. (Hypothetically, the United States might agree to provide the same form of "patent term extension" to foreign applicants as it provides to U.S. patent applicants, but only on the condition that the home countries of relevant foreign applicants provide equivalent patent term extension to U.S. national patent applicants.)[125]

Material reciprocity is not permitted under the TRIPS or GATT national treatment provisions. However, a number of IPRs in the field of copyright remain subject to the requirement of reciprocity. Here, national treatment of rights is only granted if applied mutually by both Parties. Such exceptions are referred to in Article 3.1 of the TRIPS Agreement. Corresponding

124. GATT Panel Report, *United States Section 337 of the Tariff Act of 1930*, adopted 7 November 1989, BISD 36S/345.

125. This is "hypothetical" because the United States does not restrict patent term extension to U.S. national patent applicants.

rules are contained in Articles 6.1 and 20 of the Berne Convention and Article 13.d and 16.1 of the Rome Convention. They essentially relate to the predominantly European system of collecting societies by which authors and performers obtain remuneration on the basis of membership and overall income from royalties, rather than on the basis of individual contracts.

Article 3.2 of the TRIPS Agreement qualifies those exceptions referred to in Article 3.1 that relate to judicial and administrative procedures, including the designation of an address for service or the appointment of an agent for foreign right holders (which does not exist for domiciled persons), thus facilitating intercourse with the authorities. Exceptions are only permitted where necessary to secure compliance with laws and regulations that are not inconsistent with the Agreement, and they must not be applied in a way that constitutes a disguised restriction on trade. The wording of these exceptions is very narrow. Obligations to appoint an agent for service are common in all fields of registered IPRs, such as trademarks or patents, and it is difficult to see why they should be limited to the exceptions set out in paragraph 1 of the provision. The text does not reflect the purpose of the provision and should be read in its overall context to encompass all rights that are subject to registration.

In a dispute over the treatment of geographical indications with the United States,[126] the European Union attempted to defend a provision in its legislation that made protection under its GIs legislation conditional upon an equivalent level of treatment being provided by third countries. The WTO dispute settlement panel rejected the EU approach, as discussed in the following excerpt.[127] The panel also rejected the European Union's claim that its regulations provided equivalent opportunity for non-nationals to register GIs for products produced within the territory of the European Union. The panel's decision was not appealed to the Appellate Body.

---

## *European Communities—Protection of Trademarks and Geographical Indications for Agricultural Products and Foodstuffs Complaint by the United States*

Report of the Panel*

### B. National Treatment Claims . . .

#### Less Favourable Treatment Accorded to the Nationals of Other Members

##### Less Favourable Treatment

7.131 The Panel now examines the second element of this claim which is whether the nationals of other Members are accorded less favourable treatment than the European Communities' own nationals. . . .

7.133 We recall that the Panel in *US—Section 211 Appropriations Act*, in a finding with which the Appellate Body agreed, found that the appropriate standard of examination under Article 3.1 of the TRIPS Agreement is that enunciated by the GATT Panel in *US—Section 337*. That GATT Panel made the following findings on the "no less favourable" treatment standard under Article III:4 of GATT 1947:

126. Australia brought a separate complaint against the European Union.

127. Another part of the EU-GIs WTO panel report, addressing the relationship between trademarks and GIs, appears in Chapter 3.

* WT/DS174/R, 15 Mar. 2005.

> "The words 'treatment no less favourable' in paragraph 4 call for effective equality of opportunities for imported products in respect of the application of laws, regulations and requirements affecting the internal sale, offering for sale, purchase, transportation, distribution or use of products. This clearly sets a minimum permissible standard as a basis."

Therefore, the Panel will examine whether the difference in treatment affects the "effective equality of opportunities" between the nationals of other Members and the European Communities' own nationals with regard to the "protection" of intellectual property rights, to the detriment of nationals of other Members. . . .

7.139 Although the parties disagree on whether the equivalence and reciprocity conditions in Article 12(1) of the Regulation discriminate in a manner inconsistent with the covered agreements, it is not disputed that those conditions accord less favourable treatment to persons with interests in the *GIs* to which those conditions apply.[172] The Panel considers that those conditions modify the effective equality of opportunities to obtain protection with respect to intellectual property in two ways. First, GI protection is not available under the Regulation in respect of geographical areas located in third countries which the Commission has not recognized under Article 12(3). The European Communities confirms that the Commission has not recognized any third countries. Second, GI protection under the Regulation may become available if the third country in which the GI is located enters into an international agreement or satisfies the conditions in Article 12(1). Both of those requirements represent a significant "extra hurdle" in obtaining GI protection that does not apply to geographical areas located in the European Communities.[173] The significance of the hurdle is reflected in the fact that currently no third country has entered into such an agreement or satisfied those conditions.

7.140 Accordingly, the Panel finds that the equivalence and reciprocity conditions modify the effective equality of opportunities with respect to the availability of protection to persons who wish to obtain GI protection under the Regulation, to the detriment of those who wish to obtain protection in respect of geographical areas located in third countries, including WTO Members. This is less favourable treatment. . . .

### Formally Identical Provisions

7.172 The issue for the Panel remains that of determining the treatment accorded to the nationals of other Members and to the European Communities' own nationals. On its face, the Regulation contains formally identical provisions vis-à-vis the nationals of different Members, with respect to the availability of GI protection.

7.173 It is well recognized that the concept of "no less favourable" treatment under Article III:4 of GATT 1994 is sufficiently broad to include situations where the application of formally identical legal provisions would in practice accord less favourable treatment. The GATT Panel in *US—Section 337*, which considered an intellectual property enforcement measure

---

172. . . . Note that the European Communities asserts only that the product specifications and inspection regimes for individual GIs do not constitute less favourable treatment. With respect to the equivalence and reciprocity conditions, it asserts that it does not apply them and that they do not depend on nationality, but *not* that they do not accord less favourable treatment where they apply: see its first written submission, paras. 113-126, and paras. 62-69. It also concedes that they constitute less favourable treatment for the purposes of Article III:4 of GATT 1994, but does not consider that the meaning of the phrase is necessarily the same as in Article 3.1 of the TRIPS Agreement: see its responses to Panel question Nos. 94(a) and 113.

173. This was also the approach of the Appellate Body in *US—Section 211 Appropriations Act* to an "extra hurdle" imposed only on foreign nationals: see para. 268 of its report.

prior to the conclusion of the TRIPS Agreement, interpreted the "no less favourable" standard under Article III:4 as follows:

> "On the one hand, contracting parties may apply to imported products different formal legal requirements if doing so would accord imported products more favourable treatment. On the other hand, it also has to be recognised that there may be cases where application of formally identical legal provisions would in practice accord less favourable treatment to imported products and a contracting party might thus have to apply different legal provisions to imported products to ensure that the treatment accorded them is in fact no less favourable.". . .

7.182 The Panel therefore considers it appropriate for the purposes of this claim to compare the effective equality of opportunities for the group of nationals of other Members who may wish to seek GI protection under the Regulation and the group of the European Communities' own nationals who may wish to seek GI protection under the Regulation. On this approach, there is no need to make a factual assumption that every person who wishes to obtain protection for a GI in a particular Member is a national of that Member.

. . .

7.189 The[se] provisions create a link between persons, the territory of a particular Member, and the availability of protection. The definition of a "designation of origin" requires that the applicant and users must produce, process and prepare the products covered by a registration in the relevant geographical area, whilst the definition of a "geographical indication" requires that the applicant and users must carry out at least one, or some combination, of these three activities in the geographical area, and must do so in accordance with a specification.

7.190 Accordingly, insofar as the Regulation discriminates with respect to the availability of protection between GIs located in the European Communities, on the one hand, and those located in third countries, including WTO Members, on the other hand, it formally discriminates between those persons who produce, process and/or prepare a product in accordance with a specification, in the European Communities, on the one hand, and those persons who produce, process and/or prepare a product in accordance with a specification, in third countries, including WTO Members, on the other hand. . . .

7.194 The Panel agrees that the vast majority of natural and legal persons who produce, process and/or prepare products according to a GI specification within the territory of a WTO Member party to this dispute will be nationals of that Member. The fact that there may be cases where such a person does not qualify as a national—and none has been brought to its attention—does not alter the fact that the distinction made by the Regulation on the basis of the location of a GI will operate in practice to discriminate between the group of nationals of other Members who wish to obtain GI protection, and the group of the European Communities' own nationals who wish to obtain GI protection, to the detriment of the nationals of other Members. This will not occur as a random outcome in a particular case but as a feature of the design and structure of the system. This design is evident in the Regulation's objective characteristics, in particular, the definitions of "designation of origin" and "geographical indication" and the requirements of the product specifications. The structure is evident in the different registration procedures.

7.195 Complete data on the persons who have actually availed themselves of protection under the Regulation is not available. . . . [T]here is no clear evidence that even a single person who has applied for or is entitled to use a registered GI is not one of the European Communities' own nationals. . . .

. . .

7.203 . . . Whilst the Regulation does not prevent a foreign national from producing goods within the territory of the European Communities which would be entitled to use a GI, the implications of its design and structure on the opportunities for protection are such that its different procedures will operate to accord different treatment to the European Communities' own nationals and to the nationals of other Members, to the detriment of the nationals of other Members.

7.204 Accordingly, the Panel's preliminary conclusion is that, with respect to the availability of protection, the treatment accorded to the group of nationals of other Members is different from, and less favourable than, that accorded to the European Communities' own nationals. . . .

## NOTES AND QUESTIONS

**1.** EU regulations governing geographical indications are extraordinarily complex, and for this reason (among others), the decision of the WTO panel in this case is also complex. However, the two aspects of the case presented above are not so difficult. First, the European Union argued that nationals of foreign countries would be treated the same as EU nationals with respect to recognition of their GIs, but only if the European Union decided that the foreign countries maintained GI protection systems equivalent to those in place in the European Union (such as by maintaining systems that monitored the production processes used for GI-protected products). In the alternative, a foreign country could negotiate an agreement with the European Union for the recognition of specific GIs. The panel said that the TRIPS Agreement national treatment provision did not allow the European Union to condition its provision of national treatment in these ways. Second, the European Union argued that foreigners were accorded the same *de jure* legal treatment as EU nationals according to the terms of its legislation, and were equally entitled to register GIs that met the requirements for protection within the European Union. The panel said that might be so, but was essentially beside the point. As a *de facto* matter, foreign applicants would almost exclusively seek to register GIs for products produced abroad, and the EU regulations effectively precluded that by imposing restrictive conditions. The only instances in which foreign nationals had become holders of EU-registered GIs involved foreign takeovers of existing EU businesses that had previously registered them. In sum, the European Union conferred the benefits of GI protection on its own nationals, and not on foreign nationals.

**2.** Assume that an American scientist invents a new chemical compound at a laboratory in California. The scientist files a patent application in the United States, and a U.S. patent is granted. The European Patent Office receives the same application and applies a (hypothetical) European Patent Convention rule that says that only inventive activity taking place in Europe can form the basis for a valid European patent. It says that it will grant patents to American inventors in Europe (so that it does not discriminate on the basis of nationality), but rejects the instant application because the invention was made in the United States. Is this permitted under the TRIPS Agreement national treatment rule?

**3.** The entire WTO negotiating process (save for exceptions in favor of developing countries) is based on the principle of reciprocity. (*See* Olivier Long, Law and Its Limitations in the GATT Multilateral Trading System (1987).) That is, no Member is expected to make a concession without receiving a concession from another Member in return. But, once the negotiating is complete, the agreements are drafted so as to make obligations unconditional. Why do WTO Members consistently reject establishing legal obligations based on the concept of reciprocity?

**4.** The EU Database Directive, discussed *infra* Chapter 4, similarly provides that nationals of third countries will only enjoy protection for their databases if their home countries provide equivalent protection for EU nationals. The European Union has sometimes attempted to defend this reciprocity condition on grounds that *sui generis* database protection is not the subject of the TRIPS Agreement, and therefore this part of the Database Directive is not subject to the TRIPS Agreement national treatment rule. In the *U.S.-Havana Club* case, excerpted *infra* Chapter 3, section II.D.2, the WTO Appellate Body discusses the scope of intellectual property subject matter covered by the TRIPS Agreement, though not this specific issue. Do you think the EU Database Directive condition is consistent with its TRIPS Agreement national treatment obligation?

**5.** The GATT 1994 addresses trade in goods, including agricultural products. It includes its own national treatment provision at Article III, which has a substantial history of interpretation in dispute settlement tracing all the way back to the formation of the GATT 1947. While the WTO Agreement takes precedence over its subsidiary agreements, such as GATT 1994 and the TRIPS Agreement, in the event of a conflict (Article XVI:4, WTO Agreement), it does not otherwise establish a hierarchy among these agreements. In parts of the text decision not reproduced here, the WTO panel in the text case analyzes the EU legislation under both national treatment rules. Why might it have done this?

**6.** While the national treatment principle is one of the bedrocks of international IP law, it is not a principle which is universally applied either as a matter of law or practice in some important areas of government regulation and trade. Article III:8 of the GATT 1994, for example, establishes a key exception to the rules on trade in goods that permit governments to discriminate in favor of nationals in the context of government procurement, not for commercial resale. Government procurement is a major source of expenditure in most countries across a large number of sectors. For example, governments are major purchasers of computer and electronic equipment used for an array of government purposes. When the Article III:8 exception was first adopted in the GATT 1947, the negotiating governments recognized that this was a significant area left uncovered by the national treatment discipline, but collectively were not willing to give up their ability to support local industry through government purchases. During the Tokyo Round which concluded in 1979, a Government Procurement Code was adopted by a select group of almost exclusively developed countries which placed some limits on use of the exception. The Agreement on Government Procurement (GPA) has been revised a number of times since then, most recently in 2012 through the negotiation of individual commitments by member governments to open up areas of procurement. But the GPA remains one of the few WTO "plurilaterals," and a number of important developing and emerging market countries remain outside (e.g., Brazil, China, India, and South Africa).[128] To take a hypothetical illustration, if a government that is not party to the GPA decides that it is going to install solar panels on all government facilities (but not to make them available for private commercial resale), it is free to buy them only from manufacturers located within the country, and to forgo purchasing from foreign sources, even if the prices from foreign sources are lower.[129]

128. WTO Parties and observers to the GPA, https://www.wto.org/english/tratop_e/gproc_e/memobs_e.htm (visited June 18, 2023).

129. It is important to note that the government procurement exception is narrowly construed, and that a system of preferences established by India encouraging the procurement of locally manufactured solar panels was successfully challenged at the WTO. *See India-Certain Measures Relating to Solar Cells and Solar Modules*, AB-2016-3, WT/DS456/AB/R, 16 Sept. 2016. It can certainly be argued that from a policy standpoint it would make sense to allow countries like India to build up their own capacity for alternative energy generation by establishing local production preferences, but this would require changes in WTO rules.

This is a way to stimulate local industry. Despite protestations to the contrary from trade negotiators, "buy national" regulations are a fairly common phenomenon. It is at least worth pondering whether governments can and should more actively use derogations from national treatment with respect to IP rights. You may well conclude they should not, but you should be able to explain why not.

## B. Most Favored Nation Treatment (MFN)

Most favored nation treatment (MFN) is a second mainstay of nondiscrimination in international trade and investment regulation. It has accompanied national treatment in many bilateral agreements, and it became the main conceptual and legal pillar of the GATT 1947. This classical principle prescribes in Article I, GATT 1994, that "any advantage, favour, privilege or immunity granted by any contracting party to any product originating in or destined for any other country shall be accorded immediately and unconditionally to the like product originating or destined for the territories of all other contracting parties." The MFN principle has been important to the successful reduction of tariff barriers during the last 50 years. Unlike national treatment, this cornerstone of the international trading system did not apply to intellectual property under the Paris and Berne Conventions. Neither of them contained comparable rights and obligations.

There was an important political motive for adoption of an unconditional MFN rule for the international trading system. In the pre-Second World War environment, trade concessions were widely used as an instrument of diplomacy. Political alliances were created and maintained through economic preferences. Since diplomatic decisions were often made for reasons apart from improving world prosperity, an economic system in which trade concessions were used as political instruments would be unlikely to generate a global welfare-optimizing result. The MFN principle was and is intended to de-politicize the international economic system so as to reduce the chances of breakdown into a system of diplomacy-based alliances. The net effect should be to distribute the benefits of trade widely. The MFN principle was the key multilateralism provision in the GATT 1947, and it remains a cornerstone of the WTO system, including in the TRIPS context.

So far as the Paris and Berne Conventions were concerned, the MFN principle appeared to be dispensable as nondiscrimination could be largely achieved on the basis of national treatment in the regulatory context of IPRs. As all foreign national IPRs holders are entitled to equal treatment with nationals, discrimination among foreign IPRs holders was unlikely to arise. In the 1980s and early 1990s, however, the United States pursued bilateral and regional agreements to obtain IPRs protection that went beyond national standards, particularly in the field of patent "pipeline" protection for pharmaceutical and chemical products.[130] This raised concerns during the Uruguay Round, and led to the introduction of the MFN principle in the international IPRs system—Article 4 of the TRIPS Agreement. An intention to maintain consistency within the WTO system also played a role in the adoption of Article 4.

Article 4 of the TRIPS Agreement establishes the obligation of most favored nation treatment. This obligation reflects the influence of GATT Article I and obliges all WTO members to extend privileges accorded to one Member immediately and unconditionally to all

130. "Pipeline" protection refers to several variations on a similar theme. Essentially, it connotes agreement by a country to provide patent (or equivalent) protection to products that already have been granted patent protection in a second country, or which are in the process of regulatory approval in that second country, even though patent (or equivalent) protection has not been available in the first country prior to expiration of the Paris Convention priority period.

other Members. Importantly, the provision is not limited to TRIPS obligations, but extends to all protection granted to intellectual property, with the exception of rights of performers, producers of phonograms, and broadcasting organizations not provided under the TRIPS Agreement. The MFN provision strengthens, in particular, the position of smaller IP-owner countries such as Switzerland vis-à-vis the large IP-owner trading powers in third markets. As a result of the TRIPS Agreement and its MFN clause, unilateral practices, or a bilateral agreement concluded between two Members, granting and providing greater protection (TRIPS-plus), or the improvement of registration procedures, may need to be extended to all Members, but this conclusion is controversial because of the potential adverse impact on non-IP-owner member exports.

Art. 4 TRIPS Agreement: Most-Favoured-Nation Treatment

> With regard to the protection of intellectual property, any advantage, favour, privilege or immunity granted by a Member to the nationals of any other country shall be accorded immediately and unconditionally to the nationals of all other Members. Exempted from this obligation are any advantage, favour, privilege or immunity accorded by a Member:
>
> (a) deriving from international agreements on judicial assistance or law enforcement of a general nature and not particularly confined to the protection of intellectual property;
> (b) granted in accordance with the provisions of the Berne Convention (1971) or the Rome Convention authorizing that the treatment accorded be a function not of national treatment but of the treatment accorded in another country;
> (c) in respect of the rights of performers, producers of phonograms and broadcasting organizations not provided under this Agreement;
> (d) deriving from international agreements related to the protection of intellectual property which entered into force prior to the entry into force of the WTO Agreement, provided that such agreements are notified to the Council for TRIPS and do not constitute an arbitrary or unjustifiable discrimination against nationals of other Members.

Article 4 thus provides for a number of enumerated exceptions to MFN, which relate to privileged, non-IPR-specific judicial assistance or law enforcement. Again, the provision refers to relevant privileges contained in the Berne Convention and the Rome Convention providing for reciprocity and that, logically not only exclude national treatment, but also MFN. Finally, privileges existing prior to the entry into force of the TRIPS Agreement in all areas of intellectual property are grandfathered to the extent that respective agreements were formally notified to the TRIPS Council and, in addition, do not amount to "arbitrary and unjustifiable discrimination" against nationals of other Members. The interpretation of this proviso will be influenced by the jurisprudence relating to the chapeau of GATT Article XX, which uses similar language. Special arrangements and practices therefore will only be lawful if they are based upon relevant factual differences between Members.

The TRIPS Agreement does not contain a "forward-looking" exception corresponding to Article XXIV of GATT and Article V of GATS allowing for privileges in the context of newly concluded free trade agreements, customs unions, and regional economic integration. Negotiators agreed that preferential treatment in terms of intellectual property protection was neither advisable, nor necessary. However, the agreements of customs unions and free trade areas in force when the TRIPS Agreement was adopted were notified to the TRIPS Council as falling under the Article 4(d) MFN exemption, and certain of the arrangements (including the EU) provided in the notification that the exemption from MFN would apply to future rules adopted by the customs union.

In the following brief excerpt, again from the *U.S.-Havana Club* case, the WTO Appellate Body stresses the importance of the MFN principle in TRIPS.

### *United States—Section 211 Omnibus Appropriations Act of 1998*

WTO Appellate Body*

297. Like the national treatment obligation, the obligation to provide most-favoured-nation treatment has long been one of the cornerstones of the world trading system. For more than fifty years, the obligation to provide most-favoured-nation treatment in Article I of the GATT 1994 has been both central and essential to assuring the success of a global rules-based system for trade in goods.* Unlike the national treatment principle, there is no provision in the Paris Convention (1967) that establishes a most-favoured-nation obligation with respect to rights in trademarks or other industrial property. However, the framers of the *TRIPS Agreement* decided to extend the most-favoured-nation obligation to the protection of intellectual property rights covered by that Agreement. As a cornerstone of the world trading system, the most-favoured-nation obligation must be accorded the same significance with respect to intellectual property rights under the *TRIPS Agreement* that it has long been accorded with respect to trade in goods under the GATT. It is, in a word, fundamental.

## NOTES AND QUESTIONS

**1.** Assume that you are representing a small developing country in trade negotiations with the European Union. The EU representative says that she would like your client country to provide EU national patent holders with a patent term of 25 years, instead of the 20 years your client country currently provides to all patent holders. In exchange, the European Union will allow duty and quota free access to the EU market for agricultural products produced in your client's country. This will provide a major competitive advantage for its exports. If your client extends an additional term of patent protection to EU nationals, can it refuse to extend it for U.S. nationals? Can your client require the United States to provide duty and quota free access for its agricultural products as a condition to extending patent protection for U.S. nationals? If not, how does the MFN treatment principle benefit your client country? Is it giving up something for nothing, or is there more to it than that?

**2.** How does a small developing country benefit from MFN? Does the principle serve different functions when applied to protection of patents than when applied to exports of bananas?

## C. Transparency

Transparency amounts to one of the fundamental and basic principles and equations of intellectual property protection. Exclusive rights are granted in return for the publication of inventions, which in return allows competitors to assess the state of the art and explore the possibilities of obtaining a voluntary license from the right holder. In addition, transparency assumes functions of legal security, which is essentially served by registration of IPRs. Conversely, the principles of transparency are not served in the field of copyright, which is not subject to registration and in the protection of undisclosed information. Trade secrets enjoy a growing importance. Unlike patents, they do not require publication. Yet, they also generally fail to benefit from legal security (except in some cases, such as where exclusive rights are granted on the basis of submission of confidential data to regulatory authorities). The principle of transparency therefore remains specific to different forms of IPRs. General rules of transparency, however, equally exist and follow the principles of WTO law.

* WT/DS176/AB/R, 2 Jan. 2002.

**Thomas Cottier***

## *The Agreement on Trade Related Aspects of Intellectual Property Rights (TRIPs)*

### Transparency and Good Governance

Transparency is one of the core principles of WTO law. Building upon the tradition of Article X GATT, Article 63 of the TRIPs Agreement contains important obligations in this regard. Members are obliged to publish not only laws and regulations, but also final judicial decisions and administrative rulings of general application, subject to the protection of undisclosed information affecting trade and commercial secrets of companies involved. Moreover, WTO notification requirements assist in ensuring that new legislation complies with TRIPs obligations. Members are obliged to notify the Council for TRIPs of their laws and regulations for the purpose of facilitating the Council's review of the operation of the TRIPs Agreement. In practice, some of these tasks are already fulfilled through WIPO's Collection of Laws for Electronic Access,[122] a database on the intellectual property-related legislation of most countries in English translation. In addition, under Article 63:3, each Member must be prepared to supply information on its relevant national rules and case law in response to a request from another Member. Article 63 aims at implementing transparency as a prerequisite for dispute prevention and settlement, and as a tool to assess the effectiveness of the TRIPs agreement.

A major portion of the work of the TRIPs Council in its first years consisted in exercising its review function and asserting a certain amount of peer pressure with a view to bringing about compliance. Further support for this effort is provided by regular trade policy reviews of Members under the Trade Policy Review Mechanism ("TPRM").[123] The TPRM reports reflect complaints of Members and responses to those complaints. They contain additional information on the state of play and problems relating to intellectual property protection in the concerned Members.

Perhaps more than any other agreement, the TRIPs Agreement promotes the doctrine of good governance through its rules on procedural standards in Part III of the Agreement.[124] . . . It is important to note that the many provisions in the Agreement on civil, administrative and penal procedures applicable to intellectual property protection not only benefit foreign right holders, but also domestic right holders as the benefit of these rules would normally be made available to them as well. Finally, we note that improvements in these procedures will not be limited to intellectual property, but will carry over to other areas of civil and administrative law enforcement. *De facto*, the TRIPs Agreement makes a general contribution to good governance in the field of judicial administration.

## D. Territoriality and Independence

### *1. Territoriality*

It is not infrequently said that intellectual property rights are "territorial" in nature. This is understood to mean that the grant of an IP right by a particular country has effect only within

* In 1 The World Trade Organization: Legal Economic and Political Analysis 1041 (Patrick F.J. Macrory, Arthur E. Appleton & Michael G. Plummer eds., 2005).

122. [This database has been renamed "WIPO Lex." For a detailed discussion see Thomas Cottier and Michelangelo Temmermann, *Transparency and Intellectual Property Protection in International Law*, in: Andrea Bianchi and Anne Peters (eds.). Transparency in International Law 197-220 (2013).—Eds.]

123. [See Chapter 6 of this book.—Eds.]

124. [*See* Thomas Cottier, *Emerging Doctrines of Good Governance: The Impact of the WTO and China's Accession*, in China in the World Trading System—Defining the Principles of Engagement 119 (Frederick M. Abbott ed., 1998).—Eds.]

the territory of that country (see, e.g., citations and references in *NTP v. Research in Motion*, below). Thus, for example, a patent granted within the United States is understood only to give the inventor rights within the United States to prevent enumerated acts (i.e., making, using, selling, offering for sale, and importing).

The concept of territoriality plays an enormously important role in the international IP system. In order to secure IPRs protection for one invention, expressive work, or indication of origin, the creator must obtain protection in each territory where protection is considered necessary. The grounding of the international IPRs system in the nation-state, and the principle of territoriality, was a logical consequence of the world political order of the late nineteenth century, when the Paris and Berne Conventions were negotiated and concluded. In that era, and to a large extent today, the sovereignty of each national government within its own territory was considered the paramount principle by which the international legal and political order was constituted.

To some extent, the notion of IP "territoriality" appears to be based on the Paris Convention rule of independence (see below), which prescribes that regulatory or judicial actions with respect to a patent or trademark in one country do not affect the validity or enforceability of a patent or trademark in another country. However, the blending of the concepts of "independence" and "territoriality" is not based on express terms of the Paris Convention. Neither the Paris nor Berne Convention uses the term "territorial" or "territoriality," nor do they expressly prescribe a jurisdictional limitation on the effect of the grant of a patent, trademark, or copyright.

Public international law, on the other hand, does impose limits on the jurisdictional reach of the laws and regulatory actions of countries. For the following, we use the United States as an example. The U.S. Congress does not ordinarily legislate for the territory of Canada or France, nor do U.S. courts ordinarily enforce Canadian or French law.[131] As a general rule, countries prescribe and enforce legislation with respect to conduct taking place within their own territories (the principle of "subjective territoriality"), to conduct that has a direct, foreseeable, and substantial effect within their own territories (the principle of "objective territoriality"), and to conduct of their nationals wherever those nationals may be located (the "nationality" principle).[132]

U.S. courts ordinarily refrain from enforcing French patents in American courts, and likewise French courts ordinarily refrain from enforcing U.S. patents. Each of these countries reserves to itself the right to determine whether a patent should be granted for its own territory and the terms under which it will enforce that patent. Moreover, the rule of "independence" prescribed by the Paris Convention prevents a U.S. court from directly applying a French administrative or judicial decision to invalidate or render unenforceable an American patent.

The observation that IPRs are territorial should not be understood categorically. There is some jurisprudence in the United States, particularly in the field of trademarks, which suggests that holders of rights in one nation (e.g., the United States) may on that basis assert rights to protect against injury suffered in other nations or regions. Doctrines asserting so-called extraterritorial IPRs are controversial, and to date have been used in very limited contexts. We could not from this limited experience generalize a departure from the accepted territorial nature of IPRs.

---

131. They may, however, more generally recognize and enforce judgments of Canadian and French courts on the basis of comity.

132. Two additional recognized bases of jurisdiction are the "protective" and "universal" principles, but those are of limited relevance to this discussion. *See generally* Restatement 3d Foreign Relations, Part IV.

*Microsoft v. AT&T* concerned the potential extraterritorial application of U.S. patent law. The decision of the Supreme Court reverses the Court of Appeals for the Federal Circuit. Microsoft exported a master disk incorporating its Windows program to a personal computer manufacturer in Taiwan. In order to install the Windows program on a substantial number of personal computers, the Taiwanese manufacturer made Windows CD copies from the master disk and installed the Windows program from the copies.

AT&T holds a patent on computer software used in voice recognition. Microsoft infringed that patent in the United States by incorporating the software in its Windows program.

An amendment to the U.S. Patent Act was adopted by Congress in 1984 to overturn a 1972 decision of the Supreme Court (*Deepsouth Packing Co. v. Laitram Corp.*, 406 U.S. 518 (1972)). In *Deepsouth Packing*, the Supreme Court held that it was not a violation of the Patent Act to collect and export components of a machine protected by a patent in the United States (along with instructions on their assembly) because the machine was not "made" in the United States. The Patent Act amendment established this type of activity as contributory infringement, providing, *inter alia:*

> Sec. 271(f)(1) Whoever without authority supplies or causes to be supplied in or from the United States all or a substantial portion of the components of a patented invention, where such components are uncombined in whole or in part, in such manner as to actively induce the combination of such components outside of the United States in a manner that would infringe the patent if such combination occurred within the United States, shall be liable as an infringer.

In *Microsoft v. AT&T*, the Supreme Court repeatedly stresses that the U.S. Patent Act is not intended to have extraterritorial effect, and that the amended Patent Act provision cited above is an exception to this general rule (that therefore should be construed narrowly). Applying this general principle to Microsoft's activities (that are not clearly prohibited by the statute), the Court held that it would not extend the statute to cover them. The factual basis for its ruling was that the "master disk" exported by Microsoft was not itself a component that was installed on a computer. Instead, CD copies were first made of the master disk, and those CD copies were used to install the program that infringed AT&T's software patent (in the United States). The decision turned on the definition of a "component" as used in the statute. The Court expressly refrained from deciding whether Microsoft would have violated AT&T's patent if it had directly exported the CD copies used to install the program on the computers.

## *Microsoft Corp. v. AT&T Corp.*
550 U.S. 437 (2007)

Justice Ginsburg for the Court:

Any doubt that Microsoft's conduct falls outside §271(f)'s compass would be resolved by the presumption against extraterritoriality, on which we have already touched. See *supra*. . . . The presumption that United States law governs domestically but does not rule the world applies with particular force in patent law. The traditional understanding that our patent law "operate[s] only domestically and d[oes] not extend to foreign activities," Fisch & Allen, [The Application of Domestic Patent Law to Exported Software: 35 U.S.C. §271(f), 25 U. Pa. J. Int'l Econ. L. 557, 565 (2004)] at 559, is embedded in the Patent Act itself, which provides that a patent confers exclusive rights in an invention within the United States. 35 U.S.C. §154(a)(1) (patentee's rights over invention apply to manufacture, use, or sale "throughout the United States" and to importation "into the United States"). See *Deepsouth*, 406 U.S., at 531, 92 S. Ct. 1700 ("Our patent system makes no claim to extraterritorial effect"; our legislation "d[oes] not, and [was] not intended to, operate beyond the limits of the United States, and we correspondingly reject the claims of others to such control over our markets." (quoting *Brown*, 19 How., at 195, 15 L. Ed. 595)).

As a principle of general application, moreover, we have stated that courts should "assume that legislators take account of the legitimate sovereign interests of other nations when they write American laws." *F. Hoffmann-La Roche Ltd. v. Empagran S.A.*, 542 U.S. 155, 164, 124 S. Ct. 2359, 159 L. Ed. 2d 226 (2004); see *EEOC v. Arabian American Oil Co.*, 499 U.S. 244, 248, 111 S. Ct. 1227, 113 L. Ed. 2d 274 (1991). Thus, the United States accurately conveyed in this case: "Foreign conduct is [generally] the domain of foreign law," and in the area here involved, in particular, foreign law "may embody different policy judgments about the relative rights of inventors, competitors, and the public in patented inventions." Brief for United States as *Amicus Curiae* 28. Applied to this case, the presumption tugs strongly against construction of §271(f) to encompass as a "component" not only a physical copy of software, but also software's intangible code, and to render "supplie[d] . . . from the United States" not only exported copies of software, but also duplicates made abroad.

AT&T argues that the presumption is inapplicable because Congress enacted §271(f) specifically to extend the reach of United States patent law to cover certain activity abroad. But as this Court has explained, "the presumption is not defeated . . . just because [a statute] specifically addresses [an] issue of extraterritorial application," *Smith v. United States*, 507 U.S. 197, 204, 113 S. Ct. 1178, 122 L. Ed. 2d 548 (1993); it remains instructive in determining the *extent* of the statutory exception. See *Empagran*, 542 U.S., at 161-162, 164-165, 124 S. Ct. 2359; *Smith*, 507 U.S., at 204, 113 S. Ct. 1178.

AT&T alternately contends that the presumption holds no sway here given that §271(f), by its terms, applies only to domestic conduct, *i.e.*, to the supply of a patented invention's components "from the United States." §271(f)(1). AT&T's reading, however, "converts a single act of supply from the United States into a springboard for liability each time a copy of the software is subsequently made [abroad] and combined with computer hardware [abroad] for sale [abroad.]" Brief for United States as *Amicus Curiae* 29; see 414 F.3d, at 1373, 1375 (Rader, J., dissenting). In short, foreign law alone, not United States law, currently governs the manufacture and sale of components of patented inventions in foreign countries. If AT&T desires to prevent copying in foreign countries, its remedy today lies in obtaining and enforcing foreign patents. See *Deepsouth*, 406 U.S., at 531, 92 S. Ct. 1700.[17]

## NOTES AND QUESTIONS

**1.** The Supreme Court limits the geographical scope of the U.S. Patent Act. As a matter of principle, it refuses to adopt an expansive interpretation of the statutory provision adopted by the Congress. In your view, does the fact that Microsoft is exporting a disk with embedded object code, which is copied onto a personal computer in a foreign country, provide a basis for placing the export outside the reach of Section 271(f)? What are the economic policy implications of the decision by the Supreme Court? Does it surprise you that Microsoft, which so actively campaigns against copyright piracy in China and Russia, is seeking to limit the geographic range of patent law?

17. AT&T has secured patents for its speech processor in Canada, France, Germany, Great Britain, Japan, and Sweden. App. in No. 04-1285 (CA Fed.), p. 1477. AT & T and its *amici* do not relate what protections and remedies are, or are not, available under these foreign regimes. Cf. Brief for Respondent 46 (observing that "foreign patent protections are *sometimes* weaker than their U.S. counterparts" (emphasis added)).

**2.** A recent U.S. Supreme Court patent decision, *WesternGeco LLC v. ION Geophysical Corp.*, 138 S. Ct. 2129 (2018), nominally adhered to the presumption against extraterritoriality. Damages suffered by a U.S. patent owner as a result of lost sales in foreign markets that flowed from patent infringement taking place within the United States were allowed.

**3.** Returning to the WTO consultations initiated by India and Brazil with the European Union and the Netherlands regarding transit seizures of generic pharmaceutical products based on patents only in the transit country (i.e., at the Dutch airport during transshipment), do you think the U.S. Supreme Court would be sympathetic to applying a U.S. patent to a pharmaceutical product shipment moving from India to Brazil solely on the basis of transit through a U.S. airport? Does it help to know that the United States is party to a GATT/WTO Article V obligation to allow "freedom of transit" through its ports and airports, and not to unreasonably interfere with such transit?

**4.** An issue related to the territorial scope of application of patents (and other IPRs) is whether the courts of one country should enforce judgments rendered by the courts of other countries. Should, for example, an award of damages for infringement of a patent rendered by a French court be enforceable in a U.S. court? We will examine this issue in Chapter 6.

The formation of regional institutions (such as the European Union), and the development of regional and multilateral mechanisms that facilitate the granting of IPRs on a multi-country basis, have not so far fundamentally altered the reliance of the international IPRs system on the principle of territoriality. The major area in which an evolution away from strict reliance on territoriality can be seen is in the European Union, where some forms of IPR are now granted and regulated on a Union-wide level. Note, however, that the European Union is somewhat exceptional in the sense of its organization as a quasi-federal polity. An evolution away from the strict nation-state IPRs territoriality principle in the European Union in some ways reflects a consolidation of that principle within a new and larger political unit.

Whether the principle of territoriality continues to serve well the international IPRs system, or the international economic and political systems, is another question. Challenges to territoriality are already present, and more are on the horizon. The inherent tension between territorially based IPRs, on one side, and the free movement of goods and services, on the other, is a subject that we address extensively in this book. Resolving this conflict may not necessarily involve a diminished stature for the basic principle of territoriality of IPRs, but may instead involve more adequately elaborating the goals that territoriality is expected to accomplish.

Another important challenge to the territoriality of IPRs is raised by the Internet and other forms of high-speed data transmission, as well as the concomitant evolution of global electronic commerce. As it has become possible to simultaneously and instantaneously transmit copyrighted works to all countries of the world, the utility of maintaining different rule systems and bundles of rights in each country is called into question. The Internet domain name is a globally employed identifier that has limited relevance as a creature of national law, and its regulation on a nation-to-nation basis raises a host of law and policy issues.

While the territorial basis of the international IPRs system may be under challenge, for present purposes the principle of the territorial nature of IPRs remains basic to the system. Neither the Paris, Berne, or Rome Conventions, nor any other instrument under the umbrella of WIPO, nor the TRIPS Agreement, creates a supranational system of IPRs protection. These international agreements are instruments to bring about minimum standards—to harmonize or approximate national and regional intellectual property law.

**Frederick M. Abbott***

## *The European Court of Justice Decision in the Joined* Philips/Nokia *Cases*

Toward the end of 2008, Indian pharmaceutical exporters became embroiled in disputes with originator pharmaceutical companies holding patents in the European Union (EU). Medicine produced generically (off-patent) in India and shipped to various developing countries was being seized by Dutch customs authorities while in transit through Schiphol Airport based on allegations of patent infringement in the Netherlands.

The government of India took up the cause of its exporters and initiated consultations with the EU and Netherlands pursuant to the World Trade Organization Dispute Settlement Understanding (DSU). India contended that the extension of local patents violated the fundamental GATT rule of "freedom of transit" for shipments through national territories. India argued that the seizures effectively amounted to extraterritorial extension of EU patents contrary to the principles of independence of patents and the territorial basis on which the international patent system is organized.

Dutch customs authorities and patent holders claimed that the seizures were authorized under Regulation 1383/2003 regarding intellectual property border measures. In particular, they referred to a provision that supposedly established a "manufacturing fiction" or "production fiction" that required administrative authorities and courts to treat goods in transit as if they had been manufactured within the EU member state in which an infringement action was brought.

As a consequence of consultations and negotiations between India and the EU, the parties reached an interim settlement in late 2010 under which the EU (and on behalf of its member states) undertook to refrain from further seizures of goods in transit based on local patents absent evidence of a substantial likelihood of diversion of the subject goods onto the EU market. The EU undertook to revise its border regulations to reflect this understanding.

While the foregoing events were unfolding, there was contemporaneously unfolding a pair of legal proceedings, *Philips v. Lucheng Meijing* and *Nokia v. HMRC*, that would place similar substantive subject matter before the European Court of Justice (ECJ) [(now CJEU)—EDS.]. Unlike the cases involving Indian pharmaceutical manufacturers, these Belgian and UK proceedings were concerned with copyright, design right and trademark. In the *Philips* case, electric shavers transiting through the port of Antwerp, Belgium were seized on the basis of alleged design rights and copyright. In the *Nokia* case, a shipment of mobile telephones and accessories transiting through London's Heathrow Airport was detained (pending further legal review by customs authorities) on the basis of alleged trademark rights. The ECJ was referred the questions whether and on what basis customs authorities were empowered to seize goods in transit based on suspicion of infringement of IP rights, and what standards might be applied in subsequent substantive proceedings.

In deciding the joined referrals,[127] the ECJ laid down fundamental principles of international intellectual property law that are important not only for Europe, but for the

---

* FSU College of Law, Public Law Research Paper, Jan. 2013, available at SSRN: https://ssrn.com/abstract=2246063.

127. *Koninklijke Philips Electronics NV v. Lucheng Meijing Industrial Company Ltd* and *Nokia Corporation v. Her Majesty's Commissioners of Revenue and Customs*, Joined Cases C?446/09 and C?495/09 [ECR 2011], ECJ Judgment, 1 Dec. 2011, available at http://curia.europa.eu/juris/celex.jsf?celex=62009CJ0446&lang1=en&type=NOT&ancre=.

continuing "respectful" evolution of the international intellectual property system. While *Philips/Nokia* directly involved copyright, design right and trademark subject matter, the ECJ in its decision drew no distinction among forms of IP, referring broadly to basic principles.

There was nothing surprising about the ECJ's decision in the sense that it confirmed what India had argued from the outset of its dispute with the EU and Netherlands concerning medicines in transit. The guidance provided by the ECJ for the EU, its member states and their customs authorities uses terms rather similar to those incorporated in the interim settlement resulting from the consultations with India.

A first key element of the ECJ's decision was acknowledgment that transit of goods through the territory of a country, without more, does not give rise to IP infringement. It referred to its precedent in *Commission v. France* [2000] ECR I-7653, stating that "The Court has repeatedly deduced . . . that goods placed under a suspensive customs procedure cannot, merely by the fact of being so placed, infringe intellectual property rights applicable in the European Union. . . ."

It confirmed that each country adopts and implements its own intellectual property norms, reminding "that imitations and copies coming from a non-member State and transported to another nonmember State may comply with the intellectual property provisions in force in each of those States." The IP law of the transit state does not govern goods merely passing through. Those goods instead are subject to the IP norms and rights in force in countries where they enter the stream of commerce, typically the countries of export (where produced) and destination. This reflects application of the principles of territoriality and independence of IP rights.

Critically, the Court grounded its decision in the EC Treaty and the Treaty on the Functioning of the European Union (TFEU), stating:

> In the light of the common commercial policy's main objective, set out in Article 131 EC and Article 206 TFEU and consisting in the development of world trade through the progressive abolition of restrictions on trade between States, it is essential that those goods be able to pass in transit, via the European Union, from one non-member State to another without that operation being hindered, even by temporary detention, by Member States' customs authorities.

The ECJ effectively acknowledged (though without expressly referring to it) Article V of the GATT regarding freedom of transit, and the role this provision plays in facilitating international trade.

The ECJ reference to the TFEU constrains EU options in the context of present efforts to amend the EU IP Border Regulation. The ECJ is the guardian of the TFEU. It is responsible for assuring that EU legislation is compatible with this constitutive charter. Because the ECJ has grounded its decision in *Philips/Nokia* in the TFEU, the Court has made clear that the legislative organs may not adopt revised IP border measures that are inconsistent with the fundamental reasoning of its holding without violating this constitutive charter of the EU.

### 2. *Patents with Cross-border Elements*

In the *NTP v. Research in Motion* case, decided before *Microsoft v. AT&T*, the U.S. Court of Appeals for the Federal Circuit examined whether a U.S. patent is infringed when part of the infringing action occurs in Canada. It also examined whether a U.S. process patent is infringed when part of the patented process is performed in Canada.

## *NTP v. Research In Motion*

418 F.3d 1282 (Fed. Cir. 2005), *rehearing en banc denied*

LINN, Circuit Judge. . . .

### 2. Section 271(a)

*Section 271(a)* of title 35 sets forth the requirements for a claim of direct infringement of a patent. It provides:

> Except as otherwise provided in this title, whoever without authority makes, uses, offers to sell, or sells any patented invention, within the United States or imports into the United States any patented invention during the term of the patent therefore, infringes the patent.

35 U.S.C. §271(a) (2000). The territorial reach of section 271 is limited. Section 271(a) is only actionable against patent infringement that occurs within the United States. . . .

Ordinarily, whether an infringing activity under section 271(a) occurs within the United States can be determined without difficulty. This case presents an added degree of complexity, however, in that: (1) the "patented invention" is not one single device, but rather a system comprising multiple distinct components or a method with multiple distinct steps; and (2) the nature of those components or steps permits their function and use to be separated from their physical location.

In its complaint, NTP alleged that RIM had infringed its patents by "making, using, selling, offering to sell and importing into the United States products and services, including the Defendant's BlackBerry TM products and their related software. . . ." According to RIM, the statutory requirement that the allegedly infringing activity occur "within the United States" was not satisfied because the BlackBerry Relay component of the accused system is located in Canada.[11] . . .

The district court declined to grant summary judgment in RIM's favor. . . .

RIM has . . . appealed whether any direct infringement, by it or its customers, can be considered "within the United States" for purposes of section 271(a). Citing the Supreme Court's decision in [*Deepsouth Packing Co. v. Laitram Corp.*, 406 U.S. 518 (1972)], RIM contends that an action for infringement under section 271(a) may lie only if the allegedly infringing activity occurs within the United States. RIM urges that, in this case, that standard is not met because the BlackBerry Relay component, described by RIM as the "control point" of the accused system, is housed in Canada. For section 271(a) to apply, RIM asserts that the entire accused system and method must be contained or conducted within the territorial bounds of the United States. RIM thus contends that there can be no direct infringement as a matter of law because the location of RIM's Relay outside the United States precludes a finding of an infringing act occurring within the United States. . . .

The question before us is whether the using, offering to sell, or selling of a patented invention is an infringement under section 271(a) if a component or step of the patented invention is located or performed abroad. . . . [I]t is unclear from the statutory language how the territoriality requirement limits direct infringement where the location of at least a part of the "patented invention" is not the same as the location of the infringing act.

---

11. There was a question below as to whether the Relay was also operated out of Virginia. This question appears to have been resolved in RIM's favor; on appeal, NTP does not contest the location of the BlackBerry Relay in Canada. For the purposes of our discussion, we assume that the BlackBerry Relay is located only in Canada. If, in fact, a Relay is also located in the United States, the need for this analysis would of course be obviated.

RIM argues that *Deepsouth* answers this question. However, *Deepsouth* did not address this issue. In *Deepsouth*, the Supreme Court considered whether section 271(a) prevented, as direct infringement, the domestic production of all component parts of a patented combination for export, assembly, and use abroad. 406 U.S. 518 at 527, 92 S. Ct. 1700, 32 L. Ed. 2d 273 (1972). The Court held that the export of unassembled components of an invention could not infringe the patent. *Id.* at 529. . . . In that case, however, both the act of making and the resulting patented invention were wholly outside the United States. By contrast, this case involves a system that is partly within and partly outside the United States and relates to acts that may be occurring within or outside the United States.

Although *Deepsouth* does not resolve these issues, our predecessor court's decision in *Decca Ltd. v. United States*, 210 Ct. Cl. 546, 544 F.2d 1070 (Ct. Cl. 1976), is instructive. In *Decca*, the plaintiff sued the United States for use and manufacture of its patented invention under 28 U.S.C. §1498. The claimed invention was a radio navigation system requiring stations transmitting signals that are received by a receiver, which then calculates position by the time difference in the signals. At the time of the suit, the United States was operating three such transmitting stations, one of which was located in Norway and thus was outside the territorial limits of the United States. Only asserted claim 11 required three transmitting stations. Thus, in considering infringement of claim 11, the court considered the extraterritorial reach of the patent laws as applied to a system in which a component was located outside the United States. The court recognized that *Deepsouth* did not address this issue. *Id.* at 1081. In analyzing whether such a system was "made" in the United States, however, the court focused on the "operable assembly of the whole" language from *Deepsouth* and concluded that "the plain fact is that one of the claimed elements is outside of the United States so that the combination, as an operable assembly, simply is not to be found solely within the territorial limits of this country." *Id.* at 1082. The court recognized that what was located within the United States was as much of the system as was possible, but the court reached no clear resolution of whether the accused system was "made" within the United States. Nevertheless, the court said, "Analyzed from the standpoint of a use instead of a making by the United States, a somewhat clearer picture emerges." *Id.* The court concluded that "it is obvious that, although the Norwegian station is located on Norwegian soil, a navigator employing signals from that station is, in fact, 'using' that station and such use occurs wherever the signals are received and used in the manner claimed." *Id.* at 1083. In reaching its decision, the court found particularly significant "the ownership of the equipment by the United States, the control of the equipment from the United States and . . . the actual beneficial use of the system within the United States." *Id.* Although *Decca* was decided within the context of section 1498, which raises questions of use by the United States, the question of use within the United States also was implicated because direct infringement under section 271(a) is a necessary predicate for government liability under section 1498. *Motorola, Inc. v. United States*, 729 F.2d 765, 768 n.3 (Fed. Cir. 1984).

*Decca* provides a legal framework for analyzing this case. As our predecessor court concluded, infringement under section 271(a) is not necessarily precluded even though a component of a patented system is located outside the United States. However, as is also evident from *Decca*, the effect of the extraterritorial component may be different for different infringing acts. In *Decca*, the court found it difficult to conclude that the system had been made within the United States but concluded that the system had been used in the United States even though one of the claim limitations was only met by including a component located in Norway. Not only will the analysis differ for different types of infringing acts, it will also differ as the result of differences between different types of claims. *See Minton v. Nat'l Ass'n of Sec. Dealers, Inc.*, 336 F.3d 1373, 1378 (Fed. Cir. 2003) ("It is not correct that nothing in §102(b) compels different treatment between an invention that is a tangible item and an invention that describes a series of steps in a process. The very nature of the invention may compel a difference." (quotation marks omitted)). Because the analytical frameworks differ, we will separately analyze the alleged infringing acts, considering first the system claims and then the claimed methods.

### A. "USES . . . WITHIN THE UNITED STATES"

The situs of the infringement "is wherever an offending act [of infringement] is committed." *N. Am. Philips Corp. v. Am. Vending Sales, Inc.*, 35 F.3d 1576, 1579 (Fed. Cir. 1994) ("[Section 271] on its face clearly suggests the conception that the 'tort' of patent infringement occurs where the offending act is committed and not where the injury is felt."). The situs of the infringing act is a "purely physical occurrence[]." *Id.* In terms of the infringing act of "use," courts have interpreted the term "use" broadly. In *Bauer & Cie v. O'Donnell*, 229 U.S. 1, 57 L. Ed. 1041, 33 S. Ct. 616, 1913 Dec. Comm'r Pat. 533 (1913), the Supreme Court stated that "use," as used in a predecessor to title 35, is a "comprehensive term and embraces within its meaning the right to put into service any given invention." *Id.* at 10-11. The ordinary meaning of "use" is to "put into action or service." Webster's Third New International Dictionary 2523 (1993). The few court decisions that address the meaning of "use" have consistently followed the Supreme Court's lead in giving the term a broad interpretation. E.g., *Roche Prods., Inc. v. Bolar Pharm. Co.*, 733 F.2d 858, 863 (Fed. Cir. 1984), superseded-in-part by 35 U.S.C. §271(e) (holding that testing is a "use").

The use of a claimed system under section 271(a) is the place at which the system as a whole is put into service, i.e., the place where control of the system is exercised and beneficial use of the system obtained. *See Decca*, 544 F.2d at 1083. Based on this interpretation of section 271(a), it was proper for the jury to have found that use of NTP's asserted system claims occurred within the United States. RIM's customers located within the United States controlled the transmission of the originated information and also benefited from such an exchange of information. Thus, the location of the Relay in Canada did not, as a matter of law, preclude infringement of the asserted system claims in this case.

RIM argues that the BlackBerry system is distinguishable from the system in *Decca* because the RIM Relay, which controls the accused systems and is necessary for the other components of the system to function properly, is not located within the United States. While this distinction recognizes technical differences between the two systems, it fails to appreciate the way in which the claimed NTP system is actually used by RIM's customers. When RIM's United States customers send and receive messages by manipulating the handheld devices in their possession in the United States, the location of the use of the communication system as a whole occurs in the United States. This satisfactorily establishes that the situs of the "use" of RIM's system by RIM's United States customers for purposes of section 271(a) is the United States. Therefore, we conclude that the jury was properly presented with questions of infringement as to NTP's system claims containing the "interface" or "interface switch" limitation; namely, claim 15 of the '960 patent; claim 8 of the '670 patent; and claims 28 and 248 of the '451 patent.

### 4. Section 271(g)

The next question is whether RIM can be said to "import[] into . . . or offer[] to sell, sell[], or use[] within the United States a product which is made by a process patented in the United States" and thus infringe under 35 U.S.C. §271(g). The district court held that "wireless electronic mail" specially formatted by a patented process can be a "product" under section 271(g). Section 271 Order at 13-14. The district court compared the breadth of "product" to the breadth of patentable subject matter, cited to *Diamond v. Chakrabarty*, 447 U.S. 303, 65 L. Ed. 2d 144, 100 S. Ct. 2204 (1980), and explained that specially formatted wireless email is not naturally occurring, an abstract idea, or a physical phenomenon. Section 271 Order at 14.

. . .

In *Bayer*, we considered whether research data from the performance of a method to identify substances, which inhibit or activate a protein affecting characteristics of the cell, was "a product which is made by a process." 340 F.3d at 1370. We held that "the production of information is not covered" by section 271(g), explaining that the process must be for the "manufacturing" of "a physical article." Id. at 1377. In this case, the relevant claims are directed to methods for the transmission of information in the form of email messages. . . . Because the "transmission of information," like the "production of information," does not entail the manufacturing of a physical product, section 271(g) does not apply to the asserted method claims in this case any more than it did in *Bayer.*

*AT&T, State Street Bank, Alappat,* and *Chakrabarty* do not command a different result because sections 101 and 271(g) are not coextensive in their coverage of process inventions. Although section 101 extends to "any process that applies an equation to a new and useful end," *AT&T*, 172 F.3d at 1357, section 271(g) does not cover every patented process and its purported result, *Bayer*, 340 F.3d at 1370. In *Bayer*, we expressed no doubt that a process producing research data is patentable under section 101. See 340 F.3d at 1371-78. However, we held that section 271(g) was inapplicable because research data is not a physical product. *Id.* at 1378. NTP's argument that the transformation of data and the manipulation of addresses qualify the asserted processes for section 271(g) protection is unpersuasive. The requirement that a process transform data and produce a "tangible result" was a standard devised to prevent patenting of mathematical abstractions. *AT&T*, 172 F.3d at 1359. We rejected this "tangible result" test for section 271(g) in *Bayer* when we held that research data—a "tangible result" for section 101 purposes—did not garner the protection of section 271(g).

For the foregoing reasons, the district court erred in not holding as a matter of law that §271(g) was inapplicable to the asserted method claims.

## NOTES AND QUESTIONS

**1.** We examine the subject of international exhaustion of IP rights throughout this book. In a recent case before the U.S. Supreme Court, *Impression Products, Inc. v. Lexmark Intern., Inc.*, 137 S. Ct. 1523 (2017), patent owners argued that the territorial nature of patent rights precluded an act taking place in a foreign country from affecting (i.e., exhausting) the rights of the patent owner in the United States. They argued, among other things, that the U.S. Congress intended patent owners to be able to secure a U.S. price for their products, regardless of the prices charged by the patent owners for the same products outside the United States. The Supreme Court rejected this reasoning, saying that a U.S. patent owner was not entitled to a particular price, whether or not a U.S. price. The act of placing a U.S.-patented product on the market anywhere in the world exhausts the U.S. patent owner's exclusive rights. We study this decision in more detail in Chapter 2.

### 3. *Independence*

The Paris Convention establishes a rule of "independence" of patents.

Article 4bis

Patents: *Independence of Patents Obtained for the Same Invention in Different Countries*

(1) Patents applied for in the various countries of the Union by nationals of countries of the Union shall be independent of patents obtained for the same invention in other countries, whether members of the Union or not.

(2) The foregoing provision is to be understood in an unrestricted sense, in particular, in the sense that patents applied for during the period of priority are independent, both as regards the grounds for nullity and forfeiture, and as regards their normal duration. . . .

(5) Patents obtained with the benefit of priority shall, in the various countries of the Union, have a duration equal to that which they would have, had they been applied for or granted without the benefit of priority.

The Paris Convention also establishes a rule of independence of trademarks.

Article 6

Marks: *Conditions of Registration; Independence of Protection of Same Mark in Different Countries*

. . . (3) A mark duly registered in a country of the Union shall be regarded as independent of marks registered in the other countries of the Union, including the country of origin.

The basic principle of independence states that a decision by the regulatory authorities or courts of any country with respect to the grant, denial, or invalidation of a patent or trademark does not have effects on corresponding patent or trademark proceedings or rights in any other country which is party to the Paris Convention. The reason for adoption of such a principle was fairly straightforward. There was concern that authorities in one country might use patent or trademark proceedings as a mechanism to gain commercial advantage by invalidating patents or trademarks of foreign owners. If the decisions were effective in other countries party to the Paris Convention, the interests of foreigners might be injured throughout the system. With the rule of independence, one country might behave "badly," but the effects on the right holder would be limited to that country.

Among the close-knit countries of the European Union, one of the major obstacles to establishing an EU-wide patent was determining what institutions would be sufficiently trustworthy to make decisions binding for all members of the European Union. The Paris Convention rule of independence of patents means that there is no mechanism for a "central attack" on either patents or trademarks under that Convention. That is, invalidating a patent or trademark in one national patent and trademark office will not invalidate parallel patents or trademarks in other national offices. (However, this observation has an exception under the Madrid Agreement Concerning the International Registration of Marks, which does provide a form of central attack with respect to trademarks (discussed in Chapter 3, *infra*).)

### *4. Independence in the Courts*

In the *Cuno v. Pall* decision that follows, a U.S. federal district court judge has occasion to give concrete effect to the principle of the *independence of patents* established by the Paris Convention. An English court had already ruled on the validity of various competing patent claims after prolonged litigation, and the U.S. federal court is in essence asked to repeat the process, but in a different national jurisdiction. The party that succeeded in England would for obvious reasons prefer that the U.S. judge decide that there is no point to reconsidering the same issues at what will undoubtedly be of considerable cost both in terms of money and wasted time. The U.S. judge seems to share this perspective, but must consider the relevant provisions of the Paris Convention.

## *Cuno, Inc. v. Pall Corporation*

729 F. Supp. 234 (E.D.N.Y. 1989)

Jack B. Weinstein, J.

The production of microporous nylon membrane filters generates hundreds of millions of dollars in worldwide revenues. It is vital to pharmaceutical, microchip and other industries requiring filtration of impurities the size of the smallest microbes. Plaintiff Cuno and defendants Pall and its associated companies are major competitors in this field. They press claims and counterclaims relating to the validity, infringement and enforceability of a number of key patents teaching methods of producing these filters.

Defendants move for partial summary judgment based on the collateral estoppel effect of factual findings made by a Justice of the United Kingdom Court of Chancery, Patent Division, in a prior adjudication between the parties. The European Patent Office's counterpart of defendants' United States patent at issue here was there found to be valid and non-infringing. Defendants argue that the findings of fact made by the foreign court are entitled to preclusive effect since the patent issued by the European Patent Office on behalf of the countries of the European Economic Community describes the same technological invention and makes claims that are in all material ways identical to those contained in defendants' United States patent.

Plaintiff argues that the traditional requirements for granting collateral estoppel are not present here and that the application of preclusive effect to findings made by a foreign court runs counter to policies underlying both domestic and foreign patent law. For the reasons noted below, the court denies defendants' motion.

### I. Facts . . .

On July 25, 1989 the British judge, Justice Falconer, ruled in Pall's favor, making extensive findings and construing critical terms in the claims made in Pall's EPC patent. In a 64-page opinion, he concluded, inter alia, 1) that Pall's patent was valid; 2) that Cuno's Zetapor membranes infringed claims in Pall's EPC patent; 3) that there was no merit to the anticipation defense raised by Cuno based on its United States Marinaccio patent; and 4) that there had been no invalidating prior public use when Pall utilized some of its filters in 1976 and 1977 in tests by prospective customers. An order enjoining Cuno from infringing the Pall EPC patent was entered on August 1, 1989. Shortly thereafter Cuno filed a notice of appeal.

Cuno continues to prosecute its opposition to the Pall EPC patent in the European Patent Office. It is unclear what, if any effect a decision revoking or modifying Pall's EPC patent would have on the British court's ruling should Cuno's opposition prove successful. The court's order contained a "liberty to apply" provision, which apparently allows either party to return to the court to make further applications in the event that matters are elicited "concerning or arising out of [Cuno's] Opposition in the [European Patent Office]." In any event, the parties have informed the court that the European Patent Office may not render a decision for years.

This court originally ordered a jury trial to begin in September. As a result of the United Kingdom decision, the court tentatively suggested that collateral estoppel might permit shortening of the trial. It became apparent, however, that the procedural and technical problems associated with a motion for application of collateral estoppel on the basis of findings made in the English judgment were so difficult and required so much further briefing and argument that it would be impossible to start the jury trial as scheduled.

In support and opposition to the motion for partial summary judgment, several days of hearings were conducted at which experts on patent and procedural law from the United States, the United Kingdom and Germany testified. Experts from both sides described the technology and development of a variety of patents in this field over the last 20 years. Extensive briefing and argument followed.

## II. Law . . .

Where the prior adjudication was by a foreign nation's court applying its patent law to its patents, the barriers to reliance on the foreign judgment for collateral estoppel purposes become almost insurmountable. Differences in the law of the two nations and in the detailed language of the patent are emphasized to avoid issue preclusion in a patent case pending in this country even where the invention, the technological and economic competition between the parties, and the consequences of the judgments are for all practical purposes the same. . . . As Chief Judge Markey remarked in *Stein Associates v. Heat and Control, Inc.*, 748 F.2d 653 (Fed. Cir. 1984):

> British law being different from our own, and British and United States courts being independent of each other, resolution of the question of whether the United States patents are valid could have no binding effect on the British court's decision.

*Id.* at 658. The converse is equally true.

Even if this court were to apply collateral estoppel to certain factual findings made by the British court—as opposed to importing its legal conclusions wholesale—it is not clear that trial time would be significantly shortened. Furthermore, the Federal Circuit's reluctance to give collateral estoppel effect to foreign judgments would seem to apply here to foreign findings of fact insofar as those findings involve mixed questions of fact and foreign law. It is a quiddity of our law that a well and thoroughly reasoned decision reached by a highly skilled and scientifically informed justice of the Patent Court, Chancery Division, in the High Court of Justice of Great Britain after four weeks of trial must be ignored and essentially the same issues with the same evidence must now be retried by American jurors with no background in science or patents, whose average formal education will be no more than high school. This curious event is the result of the world's chauvinistic view of patents.

The law's absurdity as revealed by this case lends force to recommendations for a universal patent system that recognizes that ours is a worldwide technological and economic community. *See, e.g.*, Note, International Patent Cooperation: The Next Step, 16 Cornell Int'l L.J. 229, 248-49, 252-68 (1983) (recommending unified international patent law); Beier, The European Patent System, Vand. J. Transnat'l L. 1, 14-15 (1981) (recommending greater cooperation along lines of European system). Obviously there are grave difficulties in devising a system that will not disadvantage the old fashioned single craftsman-inventor or citizens of countries with patent offices that are careful in investigating before issuing patents. But the European Patent Office furnishes a model that appears to be working. Perhaps paragraph (1) of Article 4*bis* of the Paris Convention, with its emphasis on nationality, needs to be reconsidered. It reads:

> (1) Patents applied for in the various countries of the Union by nationals of countries of the Union shall be independent of patents obtained for the same invention in other countries, whether members of the Union or not.

Convention of Paris for the Protection of Industrial Property, article 4*bis* (1), 21 U.S.T. 1583, 1635, T.I.A.S. No. 6923 (text), 24 U.S.T. 2140, T.I.A.S. No. 7727 (ratification).

There would appear to be no constitutional inhibition against a reconsideration of international patent policy. Clause 8 of Article I of the Constitution grants Congress power over patents. But, just as Congress delegates much of its patenting power to the patent office and the courts, the government may, under Article II, section 2, clause 2 of the Constitution, provide a role for international bodies through the treaty making powers. *See, e.g.*, 39 U.S.C. §407(a) (authorizing Postal Service, with consent of President, to negotiate and conclude postal treaties or conventions); *Universal Postal Union*, 16 U.S.T. 1291, T.I.A.S. 5881 (international treaty ratified and approved by United States Postmaster, approved by President). Cf. Casad, Issue Preclusion and Foreign Country Judgments: Whose Law?, 70 Iowa L. Rev. 53, 79-80 (1984) (suggesting treaty or exercise of federal common law power of Supreme Court to resolve issues of recognizing and enforcing foreign judgments).

### III. Other Grounds for Summary Judgment

As an alternative ground for summary judgment the court could rely on the evidence produced on the motion for summary judgment. It includes extensive affidavits, testimony before this court of scientific and legal experts, the transcript of the trial in Great Britain, patent files and extensive materials for judicial notice. Taken together this mass of evidence still depends somewhat on evaluation of the credibility of prospective witnesses. The issue must be left for the jury.

Should the jury decide in a way inconsistent with the United Kingdom court's decision or the record, the court could, after the trial, grant what would be in effect a delayed summary judgment motion. *See County of Suffolk v. Long Island Lighting Co.*, 710 F. Supp. 1387, 1393 (E.D.N.Y. 1989) (citing *DeRosa v. Remington Arms Co.*, 509 F. Supp. 762 (E.D.N.Y. 1981)).

### IV. Conclusion

The motion for summary judgment is denied. . . .

## NOTES AND QUESTIONS

**1.** Judge Weinstein says it is not clear what effect revocation of Pall's European patent would have on the British judge's finding of patent infringement in favor of Pall. Examine Articles 68 and 99 of the EPC and consider why the result may be unclear to Judge Weinstein. Is the result unclear to you?

**2.** Cuno claimed that Pall's patent was invalid because Pall had publicly used the patented product more than one year before applying for a patent in the United States. The rules in different jurisdictions vary on the extent to which an invention may be publicly disclosed prior to filing an application without undermining its patentability. In the United States, public disclosure within one year of filing does not affect patentability.[133] Under the EPC, public disclosure made within six months of an EPC filing does not affect novelty, but only in the limited cases of abuse in relation to the patent applicant or display at an officially recognized international exhibition.[134]

**3.** Judge Weinstein observes that it is a "quiddity" of U.S. patent law that the opinion of a specialized British judge must be ignored in favor of a decision by a jury with an average of high school education and no background in science. The question whether the U.S. patent system is adequately served by trying facts before a lay jury is a longstanding one. What do you think?

133. 35 U.S.C. §102(b).

134. EPC, Art. 55.

**4.** The key to Judge Weinstein's decision is Article 4*bis* of the Paris Convention. The drafters of the Paris Convention adopted the principle of independence, among other reasons, out of concern that national sentiment might cause administrators or courts in one country to refuse or revoke a foreigner's patent. The effects of such national sentiment would at least be limited if that decision applied only in one territory. Would such concerns about national sentiment be valid today? If so, how might a more efficient international patent system cope with such sentiment?

### *5. Independence at the WTO*

India and Brazil initiated dispute settlement consultations with the European Union and the Netherlands at the WTO on grounds that seizures of generic pharmaceuticals in transit between countries where there is no patent protection cannot be justified on the basis of a patent in the transit country. One of the legal grounds relied upon by India and Brazil was that extending the patent of a country where goods are merely passing through the airport to otherwise unpatented goods effectively deprived the exporting and importing countries of the right to make their own determinations regarding the grant or denial of patent protection, thereby interfering with the principle of independence. In fact, the Court of Justice of the European Union has strongly affirmed, in *Philips/Nokia*, *supra* page 84, footnote 127, that applying an IPR to goods based on "mere transit" interferes with the right of other countries to grant or deny IP rights.

## E. Ubiquity and Exhaustion of Rights

Intellectual property is characterized by a unique feature that clearly distinguishes it from real and tangible property. Ownership of IPRs is fundamentally different from ownership of a chair, a house, or a car. IPRs are of a "ubiquitous" nature. They exist independently of the specific material good in which they are incorporated. Yet, each and every copy of a protected product contains these IPRs. IPRs follow the product downstream and potentially control the use of the product. In an age in which goods increasingly contain IPRs-protected components (such as a refrigerator with a silicon chip), the potential effects of IPRs are extremely far-reaching.[135]

The question of when and where the rights of an intellectual property holder are "exhausted" is central to defining the economic effect of such rights.[136] An IPR is exhausted when the holder or owner may no longer exercise control over the use or movement of the good or service embodying that right. In the United States, exhaustion typically occurs upon the "first sale" of a good, and this principle is referred to as the "first sale rule." In other countries, exhaustion is typically referred to as occurring upon "placing the good on the market."[137] This is the "when" of exhaustion.

---

135. Perhaps the most telling example is in the field of biotechnology. The patented technical rule in this field is often an abstract idea. That idea is incorporated in each and every copy of a product that, moreover, may produce its own offspring. Logically, the patent right could expand endlessly, interfering in downstream markets infinitely. It therefore is necessary, at some point, to put an end to the effect on the market of IPRs. This concept is called "exhaustion of rights."

136. On the economics of exhaustion and parallel imports, *see, e.g.*, Keith Maskus, *Parallel Imports in Pharmaceuticals: Implications for Competition and Prices in Developing Countries*, Final Report to World Intellectual Property Organization (April 2001); Mattias Ganslandt & Keith E. Maskus, *Parallel Imports and the Pricing of Pharmaceutical Products: Evidence from the European Union*, Research Institute of Industrial Economics, Working Paper No. 622 (2004).

137. The answer to "when" exhaustion occurs is not necessarily clear even within a single country. A manufacturer may sell goods to the ultimate end-user through a distribution chain that involves a number of purchases and sales by intermediaries. It is certain that the manufacturer does not exercise control through an IP right once the good

To illustrate, consider the ubiquitous can of Coca-Cola. The Coca-Cola Company owns the trademark that it places on the can. It has the right to prevent third parties from making the first sale of the can under its trademark. Once it sells that can to a consumer, the consumer has the right to drink the soda inside it, and the right to sell or give the can of soda to someone else. That is, the Coca-Cola Company's right in its trademark has been "exhausted" by the sale. But, by purchasing the can of soda, the consumer does not acquire rights in the Coca-Cola trademark. It does not have the right to open a Coca-Cola bottling plant and to begin selling its own cans of Coca-Cola. That right remains with the trademark owner.

A country is free to decide whether exhaustion of an IPR takes place only upon the lawful first sale of a good within its own territory, a lawful first sale within a particular region, or a lawful first sale anywhere in the world. In other words, exhaustion may take place on a national, regional, or international basis. Moreover, a country may apply a different rule of the "where" of exhaustion to different forms of intellectual property. There are conceptual bases for treating different forms of IP differently from the standpoint of the applicable geographic rule of exhaustion, although the validity of the distinctions can be debated.

A rule of "national" exhaustion provides that the IP right holder's power to control movement of the good is only extinguished upon a first sale or placing on the market within the national territory. Using the Coca-Cola can to illustrate, the first sale of the product in New York will prevent the Coca-Cola Company from blocking a resale to California. On the other hand, a first sale of the product in Bangkok will not prevent the Coca-Cola Company from blocking importation into California.

A rule of "regional" exhaustion provides that the IP right holder's power to control movement of the good is only extinguished upon a first sale or placing on the market within the defined regional territory of an integration arrangement. The first sale of a can of Coca-Cola in Berlin will prevent the Coca-Cola Company from blocking import of the can into France or Poland (both EU member states). On the other hand, a first sale of the product in Bangkok will not prevent the Coca-Cola Company from blocking importation into any country of the European Union.

A rule of "international" exhaustion provides that the IP right holder's power to control movement of the good is extinguished upon a first sale or placing on the market anywhere in the world. The first sale of a can of Coca-Cola in New York, Bangkok, or Berlin will prevent the Coca-Cola Company from blocking importation into the United States, Germany, France, or Poland. In other words, after a first sale anywhere in the world, the good moves freely.

A rule of international exhaustion may be an important stimulant to achieving the benefit of open markets because it precludes producers from segmenting markets on the basis of IP rights.[138] Producers have to set their prices for the global market. This should exert downward pressure on those prices as producers seek to maximize global demand. In essence, a rule of international exhaustion is a tool for promoting competition and the efficient allocation of resources.

On the other hand, allowing producers to set different prices for different markets on the basis of IP rights increases their profit-making capacity, and some see benefits to greater

---

has been purchased by the end user. The case law is less definitive about the right of control through the intermediary chain. In EU law where the European Court of Justice refers to placing the goods on the market, it appears that exhaustion takes place when the goods are purchased outside the manufacturer's distribution chain.

138. *See, e.g.*, Frederick M. Abbott, *First Report (Final) to the International Trade Law Committee of the International Law Association on the Subject of Parallel Importation*, 1 J. INT'L ECON. L. 607 (1998), and *Second Report (Final) to the Committee on International Trade Law of the International Law Association on the Subject of the Exhaustion of Intellectual Property Rights and Parallel Importation*, presented in London, July 2000, at the 69th Conference of the International Law Association, rev. 1.1.

returns for IPRs holders.[139] It is also argued that consumers benefit because retailers who can charge higher prices will provide better service and support for products.

There are different factors that influence the choice of an exhaustion rule for different forms of IPR. Because trademark, copyright, and patent perform different economic and social functions, it may be possible to justify distinguishing how they are treated from the standpoint of an exhaustion rule. Some commentators believe that it is easier to justify market segmentation, for example, applying national exhaustion to patents,[140] while it is very difficult to justify that for trademarks,[141] and that copyright falls somewhere in between.[142] Because many countries have, in fact, adopted different rules of exhaustion for different IPRs subject matter, the arguments for different rules of exhaustion will be considered in the subject matter chapters on patents, trademark, and copyright. Suffice it to say at this stage that exhaustion rules are a subject of intense international debate.

It should be noted here that in November 2001, the WTO expressly confirmed, in paragraph 5(d) of the Doha Declaration on the TRIPS Agreement and Public Health, that the TRIPS Agreement permits Member countries to adopt their own policies and rules on the subject of exhaustion. Each WTO Member is free to choose international, regional, or national exhaustion without interference based on TRIPS Agreement rules.

The issue of exhaustion of rights is addressed in Article 6 of the TRIPS Agreement.

**Article 6: Exhaustion**

> For the purposes of dispute settlement under this Agreement, subject to the provisions of Articles 3 and 4 nothing in this Agreement shall be used to address the issue of the exhaustion of intellectual property rights.

In the final stages of the Uruguay Round, the GATT Contracting Parties were unable to address in great detail the complex issue of exhaustion of rights and to agree on a common standard. Whereas the scope and content of Article 6 appear to be simple, the provision is not devoid of normative content and poses a number of puzzling problems.

First, exhaustion rules are subject to the provisions of nondiscrimination, that is, national treatment and most favored nation treatment. While Members remain free to adopt whichever doctrine of exhaustion they wish (national, regional, or international), this has to be done on a consistent basis. The practical relevance of national treatment is limited in this context. For example, Members would be precluded from providing rules less favorable to foreign right holders than for nationals on the enforcement of contracts establishing marketing territories. The implications of MFN treatment are more important as Members are basically not allowed to treat other WTO Members differently in terms of exhaustion of rights of products originating from these countries. To what extent does MFN treatment affect and restrict the use of regional exhaustion?

---

139. *See, e.g.*, Alan O. Sykes, *TRIPS, Pharmaceuticals, Developing Countries, and the Doha "Solution,"* 3 Chi. J. Int'l L. 47-68 (2002).

140. *See* views of various commentators summarized in Second Report, *supra* note 133, and conclusions of ILA International Trade Law Committee.

141. Virtually all products traded on international markets are protected by trademark, and allowing producers to segment markets on the basis of those marks may severely inhibit trade and competition. There is limited social utility in dividing up markets on the basis of trademark rights.

142. Copyrighted expression presents some interesting issues in regard to exhaustion. Books, CDs, and DVDs are very much like traditional commodities traded on world markets, and there is limited reason to think that it is useful to divide up the world market based on the price of these products. Computer software has a significant utility function, and an argument can be made in favor of offering lower prices in less affluent markets.

Second, as noted above, customs territories and thus customs unions that were established before the TRIPS Agreement was adopted were grandfathered so as to be deemed single territorial entities for the purposes of the TRIPS Agreement. The use of regional exhaustion within such an entity therefore does not amount to a violation of MFN.

Third—and this is of importance to free trade agreements—differential treatment of parallel trade based upon exhaustion or other rules is dealt with primarily as a matter of trade in goods and thus falls under the GATT, as will be discussed below. The country of exportation, rather than the nationality of the right holder, is decisive in determining the exhaustion of rights in relation to the product at stake. For example, a product exported from Switzerland to the European Union will be subject to the doctrine of exhaustion applied by the European Union to third countries (or on the basis of specific bilateral treaty provisions) even if the right holder is a national of a member state of the European Union. MFN treatment as to the nationality of the right holder therefore does not exclude differential and preferential treatment of parallel imports based upon categories other than IPRs, in particular provisions relating to free movement of goods in trade agreements.

Finally, provisions other than national treatment and MFN are arguably exempted from invocation, in the context of Article 6, for purposes of WTO dispute settlement between Members. However, Article 6 does not preclude recourse to such other provisions of the Agreement in domestic dispute settlement for the purpose of construing national or regional law relating to exhaustion and parallel trade in accordance with WTO rules.

When it first proposed the Trade Marks Directive, the European Commission recommended that the European Union adopt a uniform rule of international exhaustion. However, EU industry strongly opposed this move. The Commission retreated to seemingly neutral ground in Article 7 of the directive, which appeared only to codify the rule of intra-Union exhaustion. Nevertheless, without a referral to the ECJ, the German Federal Supreme Court in the *Dyed Jeans*[143] case eliminated the longstanding German rule of international exhaustion for trademarks based on its interpretation of Article 7. This was followed by a referral from the Austrian Supreme Court to the CJEU in the *Silhouette* case (*Silhouette International Schmied GmbH & Co. KG v. Hartlauer Handelsgesellschaft mbH* (Case C-355/96), Court of Justice of the European Union [1998] 2 CMLR 953, 16 July 1998). The CJEU ruled that the possibility of disparate exhaustion rules among the EU member states would lead to practical problems as member states relying on national exhaustion would need to establish customs barriers with respect to goods coming from member states with international exhaustion, and that this approach was consistent with the language of Article 7. Disparate member state approaches to the international exhaustion question had not up until this decision seemed to pose notable practical trade problems within the European Union. Nonetheless, the CJEU relied on the opinion of its Advocate General Jacobs to the effect that they would.

## F. Duration of Intellectual Property Rights

The different disciplines of IPRs have in common that the duration of protection is—in general—limited. This principle is based, first, on the idea that IPRs are granted to allow the author or inventor to secure an appropriate return on investment, but that they should not unnecessarily impair the diffusion of knowledge. Second, limitations in time are motivated by competition policies that require a balancing of exclusive rights and open markets. Third, and related to the doctrine of exhaustion, IPRs inhering in products must at some point give way to legal security for the owner of the product.

143. *Urt. v. BGH,* 14.12.1995-1 ZR 210/93 (Stuttgart), NJW 1996, Heft 15, 994-997.

Exceptions to the principle of limited duration are found in trademarks and trade secrets. The protection of trademarks generally can be indefinitely extended if certain conditions are met. Trade secrets are protected as long as the conditions of secrecy are satisfied. The unlimited duration of trademarks relates to their prime function, which is to allow consumers to distinguish between products of competitors, and to identify their origin.

The duration of IPRs protection varies in different legal systems. Specific mechanisms for extending duration exist in the field of patents to offset time spent during government approvals and clinical trials.[144]

Efforts to harmonize the duration of protection at the international level have met with difficulty. The Paris Convention failed to regulate duration. The results achieved in the TRIPS Agreement were a major development, particularly in the fields of copyright and patent law, and have led to the substantial extension of protection in many countries.

Relevant provisions on minimal standards provided for different IPRs can be found in Articles 12, 18, 26(3), 33, and 38 of the TRIPS Agreement and Article 7 of the Berne Convention.

However, while the TRIPS Agreement has resulted in harmonization of minimum terms of protection, the TRIPS Agreement does not specifically prescribe, and it has not led to, harmonized maximum terms of protection. There has been a persistent trend within the European Union to extend the duration of IPRs protection beyond that mandated by the TRIPS Agreement and the United States has largely followed the European Union in this regard.

## NOTES AND QUESTIONS

1. Unlimited duration of trade secret protection is controversial. Some argue that it is not so apparent why the trade secret is more worthy of restriction on the diffusion of knowledge than other forms of IPR. On the other hand, unlimited duration seems inherent to the concept of trade secret since a trade secret exists as long as valuable information is not disclosed. Are trade secrets in practice really of unlimited duration? Why is the protection of intellectual property as undisclosed information a risky strategy?

## G. Right of Priority

The coexistence of national (or regional) systems of intellectual property, each based upon the principle of territoriality, requires appropriate tools of interconnection. One of the key instruments to bring about interconnection is the right of priority. Because the validity of IPRs generally depends on an intellectual step, filing and registration of rights theoretically should take place simultaneously in all countries where protection is sought. A failure to act simultaneously would risk that novelty, originality, or creativity would be lost, either as a later act of creation rendered the earlier act non-original, or as disclosure or public use of a covered product in one country undermined novelty in another.

The international IPRs system guards against the undermining of an intellectual step by means of the principle of right of priority. The principle prescribes the preservation of novelty, originality, and creativity upon the filing of an application for the grant of protection in one country of the Paris Union—for a limited period of time of twelve months (patents) and six

144. *See, e.g.*, Regulation (EC) No. 469/2009 of the European Parliament and of the Council of 6 May 2009 concerning the supplementary protection certificate for medicinal products, OJ L 152/1, 16.5.2009.

months (trademarks and industrial designs). During that limited period, a more recent invention, creation, or disclosure cannot legally destroy novelty, and the creator may file in other countries of the Paris Union based upon the priority date. This right of interconnection is contained in Article 4 of the Paris Convention:

**Article 4, Paris Convention (1967)**

**A.**

(1) Any person who has duly filed an application for a patent, or for the registration of a utility model, or of an industrial design, or of a trademark, in one of the countries of the Union, or his successor in title, shall enjoy, for the purpose of filing in the other countries, a right of priority during the periods hereinafter fixed.

(2) Any filing that is equivalent to a regular national filing under the domestic legislation of any country of the Union or under bilateral or multilateral treaties concluded between countries of the Union shall be recognized as giving rise to the right of priority.

(3) By a regular national filing is meant any filing that is adequate to establish the date on which the application was filed in the country concerned, whatever may be the subsequent fate of the application.

**B.**

Consequently, any subsequent filing in any of the other countries of the Union before the expiration of the periods referred to above shall not be invalidated by reason of any acts accomplished in the interval, in particular, another filing, the publication or exploitation of the invention, the putting on sale of copies of the design, or the use of the mark, and such acts cannot give rise to any third-party right or any right of personal possession. Rights acquired by third parties before the date of the first application that serves as the basis for the right of priority are reserved in accordance with the domestic legislation of each country of the Union.

The right of priority is more or less unknown in the copyright field since copyright adheres upon the creation of an expressive work, and, according to the Berne Convention, without the necessity of complying with formalities. Copyright adheres in countries throughout the Berne Union simultaneously.

While the right of priority is of paramount importance to the daily operation of the international IPRs system, the basic concept has rarely raised controversy or been the subject of court decision.

## H. Direct Effect and Consistent Interpretation

When a nation enters into an international agreement, it may assume obligations that require implementation in national law. The way this implementation takes place is defined by the national Constitution, which acts as the interface between international law and domestic law. For countries following a so-called monist tradition, an international agreement (including a treaty or convention) automatically becomes part of domestic law without further action by the national parliament or legislature. For countries following a so-called dualist tradition, an international agreement only becomes part of domestic law when it is implemented by the national legislature. Some countries determine whether an international agreement has direct effect or must be implemented into national law on a case-by-case basis.

Under EU law, as interpreted by the Court of Justice of the European Union, the determination whether an international agreement has direct effect is made on a case-by-case basis. This is also the case under the U.S. Constitution. Although the Constitution expressly provides that treaties are the supreme law of the land, the Supreme Court has long interpreted this to mean that international agreements will be given direct or "self-executing" effect depending on a number of factors. In India, which follows the Commonwealth constitutional tradition, treaties are not given direct effect. For a relevant treaty provision to be applied by the courts, it must first have been transformed by the Parliament into national law.

### *1. In EU Law*

In the following case, *Parfums Christian Dior v. Tuk*, the CJEU examines whether the WTO TRIPS Agreement is directly effective in EU law. If it is, private parties may rely on its provisions in courts within the European Union. If it is not, private parties may only rely on EU- or member state-implementing legislation. But note that the Court also discusses what is called the doctrine of consistent interpretation. Even if direct effect is lacking, courts are obliged to construe domestic law as far as possible in accordance with international law.

## *Parfums Christian Dior SA v. TUK Consultancy BV*

Judgment of the Court of Justice of the European Communities
14 Dec. 2000 in Joined Cases C-300/98 and C-392/98

REFERENCES to the Court under Article 177 of the EC Treaty (now Article 234 EC) by the Arrondissementsrechtbank's-Gravenhage (Netherlands) (C-300/98) and the Hoge Raad der Nederlanden (Netherlands) (C-392/98) for preliminary rulings in the proceedings pending before those courts. . . .

### Direct Effect of Article 50(6) of TRIPs

41. By the second question in Case C-392/98 and the only question in Case C-300/98, the national courts seek in essence to ascertain whether, and to what extent, the procedural requirements of Article 50(6) of TRIPs have entered the sphere of Community law so that, whether on application by the parties or of their own motion, the national courts are required to apply them.

42. It is settled case-law that a provision of an agreement entered into by the Community with non-member countries must be regarded as being directly applicable when, regard being had to the wording, purpose and nature of the agreement, it may be concluded that the provision contains a clear, precise and unconditional obligation which is not subject, in its implementation or effects, to the adoption of any subsequent measure (see, in that regard, Case 12/86 *Demirel* v *Stadt Schwäbisch Gmünd* [1987] ECR 3719, paragraph 14, and Case C-162/96 *Racke* v *Hauptzollamt Mainz* [1998] ECR I-3655, paragraph 31).

43. The Court has already held that, having regard to their nature and structure, the WTO Agreement and the annexes thereto are not in principle among the rules in the light of which the Court is to review measures of the Community institutions pursuant to the first paragraph of Article 173 of the EC Treaty (now, after amendment, the first paragraph of Article 230 EC) (see Case C-149/96 *Portugal* v *Council* [1999] ECR I-8395, paragraph 47).

44. For the same reasons as those set out by the Court in paragraphs 42 to 46 of the judgment in *Portugal* v *Council*, the provisions of TRIPs, an annex to the WTO Agreement, are not such as to create rights upon which individuals may rely directly before the courts by virtue of Community law.

45. However, the finding that the provisions of TRIPs do not have direct effect in that sense does not fully resolve the problem raised by the national courts.

46. Article 50(6) of TRIPs is a procedural provision intended to be applied by Community and national courts in accordance with obligations assumed both by the Community and by the Member States.

47. In a field to which TRIPs applies and in respect of which the Community has already legislated, as is the case with the field of trade marks, it follows from the judgment in *Hermès*, in particular paragraph 28 thereof, that the judicial authorities of the Member States are required by virtue of Community law, when called upon to apply national rules with a view to ordering provisional measures for the protection of rights falling within such a field, to do so as far as possible in the light of the wording and purpose of Article 50 of TRIPs.

48. On the other hand, in a field in respect of which the Community has not yet legislated and which consequently falls within the competence of the Member States, the protection of intellectual property rights, and measures adopted for that purpose by the judicial authorities, do not fall within the scope of Community law. Accordingly, Community law neither requires nor forbids that the legal order of a Member State should accord to individuals the right to rely directly on the rule laid down by Article 50(6) of TRIPs or that it should oblige the courts to apply that rule of their own motion.

## NOTES AND QUESTIONS

**1.** The CJEU decides that the TRIPS Agreement is not directly effective as a matter of EU law, but this is not the end of the matter. First, the Court expounds the doctrine of consistent interpretation. Both authorities and courts of the EU and of member states are obliged to construe EU law to the utmost extent possible in accordance with WTO law (*supra*, at section VII.H.1). Moreover, member states, and their Courts, are free to give direct effect to TRIPS provisions in areas that have not been fully harmonized and where Members retain regulatory powers. What is the difference between the doctrine of consistent interpretation and the doctrine of direct effect?

**2.** The Court generally excludes direct effect of the TRIPS Agreement. In *Portugal v. Council* [1999] ECR I-8395, the Court also referred to the lack of granting direct effect to WTO law in major trading partners, by which it mainly addressed the United States (see below). Are reasons based upon reciprocity convincing? Is it convincing to exclude direct effect on the level of EU law, but to allow for it within national law, by referring to the nature and structure of the WTO Agreements?

**3.** Many provisions of the TRIPS Agreement are suitable for direct effect as they deal with matters that pertain to the provinces of the courts and of case law. Instead of denying direct effect in general terms, might it be more appropriate to assess whether a particular provision is justiciable in a particular context? Could such an approach be reconciled with constitutional traditions?

**4.** Direct effect is suitable for so-called monist countries, which consider international law to be part of the law of the land, applicable without further transformation. It is not suitable, unless prescribed by an international agreement or domestic legislation, in countries with a dualist tradition. These countries generally require transformation of international agreements to domestic law prior to their application by domestic authorities and courts in a domestic context. The approach of the U.S. Supreme Court falls between the monist and dualist traditions because direct effect is permitted in some circumstances, and not in others.

**5.** Novartis, a multinational originator pharmaceutical company, sued the government of India in the courts of India alleging that a provision of the amended Indian Patent Act violated India's obligations under the TRIPS Agreement. Article 3(d) of the Indian Patent Act requires that applicants for drug patents based on modifications of existing chemical compounds demonstrate that the claimed inventions result in a significant enhancement in efficacy. Novartis contended that this adds an additional criterion for patentability not provided for in the TRIPS Agreement, and discriminates against the pharmaceutical sector.[145] However, India's constitutional structure is based on the dualist Commonwealth model, which denies direct effect to treaties such that Novartis could not base a claim under Indian law on the TRIPS Agreement. Not surprisingly, the Indian courts rejected Novartis' claim based on the lack of direct effect of the TRIPS Agreement (*see* decision of the Madras High Court, *Novartis v. India*, W.P. Nos. 24759 of 2006 and 24760 of 2006, decided Aug. 6, 2007 excerpted regarding a constitutional/delegation issue in Chapter 2, section IV.B *infra*). Knowledgeable observers both within and outside India remain perplexed as to what prompted Novartis to pursue a cause of action that clearly could not succeed in India, spending a great deal of money on legal fees to do so. Why do you think Novartis might have pursued a claim that it could not win? Is it possible that Novartis' entire team of lawyers was unfamiliar with Indian constitutional law? That does seem unlikely, doesn't it?

### *2. In U.S. Law*

U.S. law allows for the possibility of direct or "self-executing" effect for international agreements, including trade agreements. However, since 1979 when Congress approved the results of the GATT Tokyo Round, it has included language in implementing legislation for trade agreements that expressly deprives them of self-executing effect. This means that the agreements do not change federal law unless Congress expressly does so through legislation. It also means that individuals may not directly rely on the agreements in court. Congress apparently wants to carefully control any impact international commitments have in the domestic legal sphere. The following excerpt describes the situation as it applies to the intellectual property provisions of bilateral and regional trade agreements of the United States.

**Frederick M. Abbott***

## *Intellectual Property Provisions of Bilateral and Regional Trade Agreements in Light of U.S. Federal Law*

. . . Under the U.S. Constitution, treaties and other international agreements may be "self-executing" in domestic law. Whether an international agreement is self-executing depends on its terms and context. When the provisions of an international agreement are self-executing, they do not require additional implementing legislation to have effect in national law, and they may be directly relied on by private parties in the courts as a source of law. Congress approves the FTAs in legislation which also implements the agreements in domestic law to the extent deemed appropriate. Congress has made a practice of expressly denying self-executing effect to the FTAs in its implementing legislation. Section 102 of the Dominican Republic-Central America-United States Free Trade Agreement Implementation Act is typical of the provisions denying self-executing effect:

145. An excerpt of the *Novartis* case relating to the introduction of the efficacy standard is reprinted in Chapter 2, section IV.B.

* UNCTAD-ICTSD Project on IPRs and Sustainable Development, Issue Paper No. 12, February 2006, available at www.iprsonline.org.

**SEC. 102. RELATIONSHIP OF THE AGREEMENT TO UNITED STATES AND STATE LAW.**

(a) RELATIONSHIP OF AGREEMENT TO UNITED STATES LAW.—
  (1) UNITED STATES LAW TO PREVAIL IN CONFLICT.—No provision of the Agreement, nor the application of any such provision to any person or circumstance, which is inconsistent with any law of the United States shall have effect.
  (2) CONSTRUCTION.—Nothing in this Act shall be construed—
    (A) to amend or modify any law of the United States, or
    (B) to limit any authority conferred under any law of the United States, unless specifically provided for in this Act.

(b) RELATIONSHIP OF AGREEMENT TO STATE LAW.—
  (1) LEGAL CHALLENGE.—No State law, or the application thereof, may be declared invalid as to any person or circumstance on the ground that the provision or application is inconsistent with the Agreement, except in an action brought by the United States for the purpose of declaring such law or application invalid.
  (3) DEFINITION OF STATE LAW.—For purposes of this subsection, the term "State law" includes—
    (A) any law of a political subdivision of a State; and
    (B) any State law regulating or taxing the business of insurance.

(c) EFFECT OF AGREEMENT WITH RESPECT TO PRIVATE REMEDIES.—No person other than the United States—
  (1) shall have any cause of action or defense under the Agreement or by virtue of congressional approval thereof; or
  (2) may challenge, in any action brought under any provision of law, any action or inaction by any department, agency, or other instrumentality of the United States, any State, or any political subdivision of a State, on the ground that such action or inaction is inconsistent with the Agreement. Based on this type of implementing legislation, the FTAs do not change existing federal law unless specifically mandated by Congress. An individual may not directly invoke the provisions of an FTA in a court of the United States. To the extent that FTAs may impose obligations on the United States that are inconsistent with existing federal law, this is not relevant for domestic legal purposes (even if the United States may incur international legal liability).

U.S. practice with respect to the treatment of international agreements in domestic law is not unusual. Many countries do not directly apply treaties in domestic law, requiring implementing legislation to give them local effect. The European Court of Justice has denied direct effect to the WTO Agreement in EU law. It is nonetheless useful for developing countries to be aware that a provision in an FTA negotiated with the United States does not automatically become the domestic law of the United States.

For developed countries and regions, allowing international trade agreements to have direct effect may facilitate the process of integration by allowing private operators to challenge government conduct inconsistent with the agreements. Developing countries must recognize that directly effective international agreements allow private operators to challenge preexisting legislation that is inconsistent with them. If a government wants to control the terms of implementation of the agreement, it must be prepared to adopt implementing changes to domestic law that are consistent with the agreement. Also, for developing countries, allowing direct effect presents risks because large multinational companies often have substantially greater access to legal resources than even the national government. Governments may find themselves faced with court challenges based on international agreements which are given direct or self-executing effect. Even though governments may also be challenged on the basis of ordinary domestic legislation, the terms of domestic law typically will not have been negotiated with a foreign government.

USTR has expressly advised Congress that it may adopt subsequent legislation inconsistent with the terms of an FTA. USTR has advised Congress that decisions of dispute settlement panels under the FTAs do not affect U.S. federal law unless those decisions are expressly given effect by the Congress.

This is consistent with U.S. constitutional practice. Congress may adopt legislation inconsistent with prior international agreements. This is referred to as the "last in time" rule; meaning that the later-adopted of a statute or international agreement will govern. Also, the terms of the FTAs do not strictly obligate the parties to implement the decisions of dispute settlement panels. They may instead elect to offer compensation. In any case, most countries will not give direct effect to the decisions of dispute settlement panels of FTAs (or, for that matter, of the WTO (including the Appellate Body)). In order to give domestic effect to a dispute settlement decision, government implementing action is required.

The legislatures of U.S. FTA partners whose constitutions allow subsequent domestic legislation to conflict with the terms of an international agreement (i.e., those which do not follow a so-called "monist" approach), may also legislate inconsistently with the terms of the FTA. In doing so, they may breach an international obligation to the United States. Because of the large imbalance in effective political and economic power between the United States and its FTA partners, countries other than the United States may find the breach of such obligations problematic. The economy of the United States is significantly dependent on only a few foreign countries, meaning that the United States can afford to strain its political and economic relations with almost all other countries. For many smaller and developing country economies, denial of access to the U.S. market would create very serious adverse effects. Therefore, it is likely that the legislatures of most U.S. FTA partners will be significantly more reluctant to legislate inconsistently with an FTA than the U.S. Congress.

## NOTES AND QUESTIONS

**1.** Do you think it is a good idea for the United States to limit the effect of its international agreements in national law? Does this help or hinder U.S. influence on foreign IP systems? What factors go into your analysis?

**2.** Assess the reasons why the U.S. Congress would rule out direct effect in U.S. courts. What is the implication of direct effect on the balance of power between the different branches of government?

**3.** Does denial of direct effect equally exclude the doctrine of consistent interpretation, which in the United States is called the *Charming Betsy* doctrine? (*Murray v. The Schooner Charming Betsy*, 6 U.S. (2 Cranch) 64 (1804).) The matter has not been settled for intellectual property. In the trade remedy area in the United States, there seems to be a contest between the *Charming Betsy* doctrine and the canon of interpretation deriving from the *Chevron* case (*Chevron U.S.A., Inc. v. Natural Res. Def. Council, Inc.*, 467 U.S. 837 (1984)), which divides the process of review into two stages: If the intention of Congress is clearly reflected in the statute, there is no room for interpretation. If a statute is ambiguous or incomplete, the court will defer to any agency interpretation that is reasonable. In the *Corus* case (*Corus Staal BV and Corus Steel USA Inc. v. United States Department of Commerce*, 259 F. Supp. 2d 1253 CIT (2003)), the Court of International Trade found that U.S. legislation neither requires nor prohibits the practice of zeroing and therefore the *Charming Betsy* doctrine was not relevant.

**4.** Abbott suggests that the same factors that might make direct effect a good idea for the United States or the European Union may not make this a good idea for Thailand or Ecuador. Why the distinction? How does the annual revenue of Google compare with the Gross Domestic Product (GDP) of Ecuador? Which legal entity has more money to spend on IP litigation?

**5.** In a decision reversed by the U.S. Supreme Court in 2017, the Court of Appeals for the Federal Circuit in *Lexmark Intern., Inc. v. Impression Products, Inc.*, 816 F.3d 721 (2016), said that adoption by the United States of a rule of international patent exhaustion would put it in breach of provisions in several free trade agreements that included obligations regarding remedies against importation of patented products, which the Federal Circuit (erroneously) considered required blocking of parallel imports. The important aspect for present purposes is that the free trade agreements were specifically precluded by U.S. legislation from having direct effect in U.S. law, so the Federal Circuit was attempting to give these agreements effect indirectly by expressing concern over the potential breach of the agreements. The Supreme Court refused to play along, and did not even mention the free trade agreements when it adopted international patent exhaustion for the United States. *Impression Products, Inc. v. Lexmark Intern., Inc.*, 137 S. Ct. 1523 (2017).

## VIII. POLICIES UNDERLYING THE INTERNATIONAL IPRS SYSTEM

The characteristics and scope of IPRs are defined by law. In adopting and implementing IP laws, government authorities are seeking to balance a wide range of interests. The legislator deals with a multidimensional problem set.

The legislator may seek to promote investments in creativity by inventors, authors, and artists by providing legal mechanisms that allow them to secure a reward in the marketplace. Although a substantial amount of research has been devoted to identifying the causal relationship between the grant of IPRs and the output of creative works, correlations remain elusive. The legislator is working under conditions of substantial uncertainty.

The beneficiaries of IPRs, such as inventors, authors, and artists, generally have an interest in maximizing the economic benefits they derive from their investments in creativity. Yet, the interest in maximizing economic returns will, for some inventors and artists, be tempered or overtaken by a personal desire to confer a public benefit by making their contribution widely accessible (i.e., at low cost).

The legislator may seek to promote the public welfare by making the results of creative efforts widely available. "Stronger" IP protection, whether in terms of precluding independent creation, extending the scope of claims, or extending the duration of protection, may limit public access by enhancing pricing power. "Weaker" IP protection may allow greater dissemination to the public, but the legislator also considers whether underprotection may reduce the quantity of new creative works.

Questions about the characteristics and scope of IP protection take on different sensitivities depending on the field of regulation. The question of whether a new audio recording will be protected against free downloading from the Internet is much different than the question of whether a new anticancer drug will be protected against low-cost use by developing countries.

During most of the historical development of IP law, major decisions regarding the characteristics and scope of IPRs were made at the national level. In some areas, particularly copyright, international rules exercised an influence over the choices that the national legislature might make, yet, by and large the international system reserved wide discretion to each country in adopting and implementing IP law. With the entry into force of the TRIPS Agreement in 1995, that framework underwent a dramatic change, and the international IP system metamorphosed toward greater direct control at the multilateral level.

There was very little empirical or objective theoretical research concerning the possible effects of transforming the international IP regulatory system from one reserving substantial discretion to national authorities to one imposing a set of fairly comprehensive multilateral rules. Deeper inquiry into the implications of the TRIPS Agreement and the new multilateral "top down" regulatory system largely post-dated transformation of the rules, and is continuing.

As we examine the policies underlying IP protection at the international or multilateral level, a few basic questions might be kept in mind. Who is making the decisions regarding appropriate levels of IP protection? Where are these decisions being made? What are the objectives of the new rules? What are the interests at stake? Who is benefiting from the new rules? Who may be losing? Assuming that there are risks from underprotecting and overprotecting IP, and that decision makers are acting under conditions of uncertainty, on which side are risks better taken? Should we err on the side of underprotection or overprotection?

Without IP protection, information may be widely disseminated and used. It typically forms part of a "public commons." IP rules fence off parts of this public commons. In the first contribution, Joseph Stiglitz examines the rationale for building fences, and asks whether it is appropriate to build the same fences for the developed and developing countries.

## A. Public Welfare and Private Rights

**Joseph E. Stiglitz***

### *Knowledge as a Global Public Good*

Thomas Jefferson, the third President of the United States, described knowledge in the following way: "He who receives an idea from me, receives instruction himself without lessening mine; as he who lights his taper at mine, receives light without darkening me." In doing so, Jefferson anticipated the modern concept of a public good. Today, we recognize that knowledge is not only a public good, but a *global* or *international* public good. We have also come to recognize that knowledge is central to successful development. The international community, through institutions like the World Bank, has a collective responsibility for the creation and dissemination of one global public good—knowledge for development.

The purpose of this paper is to review the concept of global public goods, to explain the sense in which knowledge is a public good, and to explore the implications for *international* public policy that derive from the fact that knowledge is a global public good. In particular, I shall emphasize the role of knowledge for development, articulated forcefully in this year's World Development Report, and the consequences that follow.

#### I. Basic Concepts

This paper combines two concepts developed over the past quarter of century: the concept of global public goods and the notion of knowledge as a global public good.

A public good has two critical properties, non-rivalrous consumption—the consumption of one individual does not detract from that of another—and non-excludability—it is difficult if not impossible to exclude an individual from enjoying the good. Knowledge of a mathematical theorem clearly satisfies both attributes: if I teach you the theorem, I continue to enjoy the knowledge of the theorem at the same time that you do. By the same token, once I publish the theorem, anyone can enjoy the theorem. No one can be excluded. They can use

* Then-Senior Vice President and Chief Economist at the World Bank, presently professor at Columbia University. http://www.worldbank.org/knowledge/chiefecon/articles/undpk2/index.htm (1998).

the theorem as the basis of their own further research. The "ideas" contained in the theorem may even stimulate others to have an idea with large commercial value.

### Non-rivalrousness

The fact that knowledge is non-rivalrous — there is a zero marginal cost from an additional individual enjoying the benefits of the knowledge — has a strong implication. Even if one could exclude someone from enjoying the benefits of knowledge, it would be undesirable to do so because there are no marginal costs to sharing its benefits. If information is to be efficiently utilized, it cannot be privately provided as efficiency implies charging a price of zero — the marginal cost of another individual enjoying the knowledge. However, at zero price, only knowledge that could be produced at zero cost would be produced.

To be sure, to acquire and use knowledge, individuals may have to expend resources — just as they might have to expend resources to retrieve water from a public lake. That there may be significant costs associated with transmission of knowledge does not in any way affect the public good nature of knowledge itself: private providers can provide the "transmission" for a charge reflecting the marginal cost of transmission while at the same time, the good itself can remain free.

### Excludability

While its non-rivalrous property says that no one *should* be excluded from the enjoyment of a public good (since the marginal cost of benefiting from it is zero), non-excludability implies that no one *can* be excluded. This too has important implications: it means that knowledge cannot be provided privately. For assume someone produced, say, a theorem. Assume the theorem is valuable in providing insights into how to solve practical problems. But assume also that the theorem cannot be kept secret and must be immediately available. Then, since anyone can immediately enjoy the theorem, the individual could make no profit from it. Competition would drive its price to zero. At any positive price, it would pay someone to get the information (which by assumption he could do) and undercut the seller.

Some forms of knowledge are (or can be made) "excludable." For example, in some industries, such as metallurgy, trade secrets are used. To be sure, the firms run a risk: a competitor, observing the new alloy, could analyze its composition and infer the mix of metals (and with modern techniques, even the relative proportion of the atoms). The firm might have a hard time inferring precisely how the alloy is made, but there is no way that rivals can be excluded from knowledge of the chemical composition and the properties of the alloy. By the same reasoning, when a firm discovers that consumers love, say, yogurt, others cannot be excluded from using that knowledge to put on the market their own yogurts.

Patents provide the exclusive right to the inventor to enjoy the fruits of his innovative activity over a limited period of time [20 years], but in return, the inventor must disclose the details of his invention. The *fact* of the invention, let alone the details provided in the patent application, make an enormous amount of knowledge freely available. The development of rayon provided other researchers with enormous information: it demonstrated the feasibility of a synthetic fiber — knowledge which itself was of enormous commercial value and which enhanced incentives for others to look for other synthetic fibers. Indeed, research in chemicals often consists of looking for slight variations of the original chemical.

It is precisely because of the high value of the knowledge disclosed through the patent process (and the limited duration of the patent) that some firms prefer the seemingly less protective route of trade secrecy.

But because the returns to some knowledge can, to some extent, be appropriated (there is some degree of non-excludability) knowledge is often thought of as an *impure* public good.

## Global Public Goods

Shortly after [Paul] Samuelson articulated the general theory of pure public goods, it became recognized that the benefits of some public goods were limited geographically. These were called local public goods. Of course, the public goods earlier theory had focused on—such as national defense—were also limited geographically to a particular country. At the same time there are several public goods which are not so limited—the benefits of which accrue to everyone in the world. In my earlier paper, I identified five such global public goods: international economic stability, international security (political stability), the international environment, international humanitarian assistance, and knowledge.

Most knowledge is a global public good: a mathematical theorem is as "true" in Russia as it is in the United States, in Africa as it is in Australia. To be sure, there are some kinds of knowledge which are of value only or mostly to those living in the country, e.g. knowledge particular to a country's institutions, weather, or even geography. But scientific truths—including many of the propositions of the social sciences—are universal in nature. The problems with which economics deals, such as scarcity, are ubiquitous, and the "laws" of economics are accordingly universally applicable, even if idiosyncratic institutions exist within each country.

## The Role of the State

The central public policy implication of public goods is that the state must play some role in the provision of such goods; otherwise they will be undersupplied. If firms cannot appropriate the returns to producing knowledge, then they will have limited incentive to do so: in deciding how much to invest, they will only look at the return that they acquire, not the benefits that accrue to others. The benefits that have accrued from the development of the transistor, the laser, or the mathematical algorithms that underlay the modern computer have been enormous, extending well beyond benefits accruing to those who made or financed these innovations and discoveries.

Governments have pursued two different strategies in addressing these concerns. The first is to increase the degree of appropriability of the return to knowledge, by issuing patents and copyright protection. In doing so, governments are engaged in a careful balancing act: after all, one of the basic properties of knowledge as a public good is that the marginal cost of usage is zero (non-rivalrous consumption). Inventors obtain a return on their innovative activity, either through charging through the use of a patent (licensing) or by charging a monopoly price on the product. In either case, there is an inefficiency. The gain in *dynamic* efficiency, as a result of the greater innovative activity, is intended to balance out the losses from *static inefficiency*, from the underutilization of the knowledge, or the underproduction of the good protected by the patent.

One part of the "balancing" act is to limit the duration of the patent. A very short patent life would imply a low level of appropriability—such that the limited returns to innovative activity would imply low levels of innovation. A very long life to a patent would mean large losses in static efficiency; most of the fruits of the innovation would accrue to the innovator, with little passed on to consumers say in the form of lower prices, since the inventor would never be subjected to competitive pressure. Typically, patents last for [20] years, and as it turns out, in many cases, by the time the patent has expired, its value is limited, as new products and innovations have superseded it. This is *not* the case, however, for many drugs (partly because there may be a long testing period before the drug is actually marketed).

But there are other aspects of the patent system that play an important role in how the dynamic efficiencies are balanced with the static inefficiencies: the breadth and scope of a patent claim (whether a patent for a new genetically altered tomato covers all genetically altered vegetables, all genetically altered tomatoes, or only this particular genetically altered variety) can obviously have profound implications.

Initial knowledge is a key input into the production of further knowledge, and the design of the patent system can thus affect dramatically the overall pace of innovation. An excessively broad patent system (e.g. with long-lived patents of broad scope) can raise the price of one of the most vital inputs into the innovative process and thus reduce the pace of follow-on innovations, even as it may provide returns to those making the original innovation. As a result, the overall pace of technical progress may be slowed. Worries about the adverse effects of excessively strong intellectual property protection have been brought home by the recent anti-trust suit against Microsoft, which (it is alleged) has attempted to leverage the power associated with its control of the dominant operating system (itself a consequence of important network externalities which result in huge advantages associated with the establishment of an industry standard) to a broader dominance in application software. Many industry experts believe that in doing so, the overall pace of innovation in the industry may have been retarded.

These concerns are of particular importance to developing countries. New innovations (research and development expenditures) are even more concentrated in the advanced industrial countries than are incomes, and many of the advances in less developed countries consist of adapting the technologies of the more advanced countries to the circumstances of the developing world.

The second strategy for dealing with the appropriability problem entails direct government support. . . .

But there are some important situations where the costs of the improved appropriability strategy are high. This is particularly true in the case of basic research because its benefits are widespread and diffuse and because attempts to appropriate its returns may significantly slow the overall pace of innovation. Indeed, many advances in basic knowledge — such as mathematical theorems — are not patentable, in spite of their importance and their potential practical applications.

This discussion should have made clear one central point: the concept of "intellectual property" — the breadth, scope, and applicability of patent protection — is not just a technical matter. There are judgment calls and trade-offs, with different people and different countries all affected differently by alternative decisions. There are conflicts of interests between the developed and the less developed countries. But unfortunately, many of the key issues cannot even be summarized by a set of simply stated principles; in practice, decisions are made on a case-by-case approach.

The stance sometimes taken by the producers of knowledge, that we need "strong" intellectual property rights, masks this underlying debate. Strong, in this context, becomes equivalent to "good"; with the implication that the "stronger" the better. But I hope this discussion has brought out that issues are far more implicated [*sic*]: stronger, in the sense of "tighter" protection, could not only have large distributive consequences (between say developed and less developed countries), but also large efficiency consequences, with the pace of innovation actually impeded and living standards in less developed countries diminished.

Within some of the advanced industrialized countries there are effective competition policies, which work to mitigate the risks that results from the abuse of monopoly power associated with a patent. But most countries do not have comparably effective anti-trust policies. For instance, drug companies can, and have an incentive to, act like discriminating monopolists, charging higher prices where the consumer surplus is higher, and/or where they can extract more of the consumer surplus. Some European countries have policies that offset these monopolistic powers: given the large role of government in the health care sector, they can effectively exercise their monopsonistic powers. It is thus conceivable (and there are anecdotes supporting this possibility) that consumers in less developed countries be charged higher prices for drugs than consumers in far richer countries. (In doing so, it is the consumers in the less developed countries that, in effect, are paying the fixed cost of research; consumers in the more developed countries are partial free riders.) Within the United States, such price discrimination (not *fully* justified by differences in transactions costs) would probably be illegal. But there is no international competition policy which protects the poor country. Well-designed (not "excessively strong") intellectual property regimes can provide some protection. It is not clear the extent to which effective competition policies *within a country* might provide safeguards: presumably a country could pass a "most favored nation" provision—no firm, enjoying the benefit of intellectual property protection, could charge the consumers of that country a higher price than the price charged for the same good elsewhere in the world. [This is, in fact, a function of parallel trade. —Eds.]

There are other issues in the design of an intellectual property regime. Every innovation makes use of previously accumulated knowledge—it draws on the global commons of pre-existing knowledge. How much of the returns to the innovation should be credited to this use of the global commons? Current practice says zero—because it is a commons, there is no price. But this is not the way things need be. In many parts of the world, there is a recognition that charges can and should be imposed for the use of commons (whether they are forests, grazing lands, or fisheries). Such charges can be justified on both efficiency and equity grounds. The international community could similarly claim the right to charge for the use of the global knowledge commons. . . . [E]ven a rough rule of thumb, in which a certain fraction of the returns to innovations is used to finance a "replenishment" of the global knowledge commons, might be an improvement.

This issue of the use of the global knowledge commons has been brought home forcefully in the context of bio-diversity, where private firms have prospected for valuable drugs in natural settings. In many cases, local people have long recognized the value of these local drugs, though they have not identified the particular chemicals within the plants which give the desired effects.

The contrast between the way this unpatented knowledge is treated, and the way adaptations of innovations in developing countries of patented ideas from developed countries are treated could not be more stark. In the former case, all of the return is credited to the "discoverer," with none to the pre-existing knowledge; in the latter, the patent holder is allowed to act as a perfectly discriminating monopolist, regardless of the extent to which his own innovation built on pre-existing knowledge.

The effective use of knowledge developed in the advanced industrialized countries typically involves substantial elements of adaptation—combining global and local knowledge. Yet the intellectual property regime, as it has been evolving, assigns most of the bargaining power associated with how the fruits of these combinations are shared to the developed country, especially in larger developing countries, where there may be effective competition for the use of the patented idea.

*An international intellectual property regime, designed to facilitate the production and use of the global public good—knowledge—in a way that sustains high rates of growth and is consistent with broad notions of equity, must balance a variety of subtle concerns, including dynamic and static efficiency and the use of the global knowledge commons.*

## NOTES AND QUESTIONS

**1.** Joseph Stiglitz points out, and it should be emphasized, that patents are not the only mechanism by which governments can and do promote inventive activity. The principal alternative to the patent is the government "subsidy," that is, payment (direct or indirect) by the government to a person to support research.[146] Subsidies are frequently used to direct research in a particular direction, such as toward the development of a military application. Subsidies are also used when the government recognizes that the "market" does not offer an adequate incentive, such as in the development of a new vaccine to defend against a bioweapon threat. Moreover, governments use research and development subsidies to gain advantages in commercial sectors, for example, by promoting R&D in the large commercial aircraft sector. Stiglitz also notes that use of subsidies as a policy instrument for the promotion of invention has certain limitations or drawbacks. Who decides whether to grant a subsidy and under what conditions? Are government policymakers likely to be successful at predicting the most promising areas for research? Assuming that "neutral" policymakers might make good decisions, are there risks that government policymakers may be "captured" by special interests? Is it possible that patents may be a better policy instrument for encouraging research in some areas, and that subsidies may be a better policy instrument for encouraging research in others? In what fields of application do you think subsidies may be preferable?

**2.** In advanced industrial societies, competition or antitrust laws have played an essential role in maintaining the balance between the interests of IPRs holders and the general public. Until recently, few low- or middle-income countries had the resources to monitor, investigate, and prosecute competitive market abuses, so this vital part of the balancing equation was missing. This is changed fairly substantially over the past decade as competition authorities, particularly in the so-called emerging market countries, have become active in competition law enforcement. A number of international organizations, including the United Nations Development Program (UNDP) and the United Nations Conference on Trade and Development (UNCTAD), have been providing technical support for these efforts.[147] Still, for lower income countries with limited government resources, effective implementation of competition law remains a challenge. How would you suggest compensating for an imbalance in implementation and enforcement resources? Should low-income countries rely on competition authorities in the European Union or the United States to protect them? Do these authorities have developing country interests in mind?

**3.** At the conclusion of his essay (not reprinted above), Stiglitz notes a risk that some countries may prefer to "free ride" on investments in invention undertaken elsewhere, and that unchecked free riding could ultimately prevent the replenishment of the public commons. Might it be useful to draw distinctions between those countries that can afford to pay for new inventions and those that might be allowed to use inventions without contributing toward their development? In his article, *From Free Riders to Fair Followers*, Jerome Reichman explored this idea.[148] In section VIII.C *infra*, Keith Maskus's work on correlating levels of IP protection with stages of economic and social development may suggest some answers.

146. Perhaps the leading work on policy instruments for promoting invention is William D. Nordhaus, Invention, Growth and Welfare (1969). Another alternative mechanism for encouraging innovation is the "prize," which entails establishment of a reward for the person(s) who achieves a prescribed objective(s). There are many possible permutations of the prize formula. The prize mechanism does not in principle preclude the prize-winner from obtaining a patent. The prize might be variable and based on the long-run performance of the winning subject matter.

147. *See, e.g.*, Frederick M. Abbott, Sean Flynn, Carlos M. Correa, Jonathan Michael Berger & Natasha Nayak, UNDP, Using Competition Law to Promote Access to Health Technologies: A Guidebook for Low- and Middle-Income Countries, United Nations Development Program (F. M. Abbott ed., 2014). Available at SSRN: https://ssrn.com/abstract=2439416.

148. *See* J.H. Reichman, *From Free Riders to Fair Followers: Global Competition Under the TRIPs Agreement*, 29 N.Y.U. J. Int'l L. & Pol. 11 (1997).

## B. The Economics of the International Patent System

The seminal work on the economics of the patent system for an industrialized country was authored by Fritz Machlup as a report to the U.S. Senate in 1956.[149] We urge students who have not read Machlup's study as part of a course on patent law to do this. Machlup rejected a "natural rights" approach to patent protection since there was no way to resolve the philosophical question of entitlement to ownership of ideas, and since an answer did not in any case provide guidance to the appropriate design of a patent system. Machlup also discounted the view that patents are necessary to encourage invention since there was little empirical evidence to support such a correlation. Inventors do what they do with complex motives. In Machlup's view, the most persuasive economic case for the grant of patents was found in its encouragement of the commercialization of new products; that is, patents encourage investors to provide capital for manufacturing and distribution facilities because they believe that a patent ensures a better return. Machlup largely considered this effect a beneficial illusion since he thought investors tended to overvalue patents. Finally, Machlup discounted the importance of publication and disclosure to society because, *inter alia*, inventors seek patent protection precisely because their inventions can otherwise be copied.

Machlup was dismissive of the idea that a pharmaceutical company with an invention critical to public health—such as the polio vaccine—would be allowed to freely exploit it at monopoly prices. Is this a reflection of Machlup's naiveté, or have attitudes toward the virtues of the market shifted since the late 1950s?

Machlup's conclusion for the United States is well known: Based on what is known, if there were no patent system, he could not recommend creating one; yet, because the United States has a patent system and the economy appears to be functioning relatively well, based on what is known, he could not recommend getting rid of it.

Machlup limited his conclusion to a large industrial country such as the United States—it may *not*, he says, apply to "a small country and not [apply to] a predominantly nonindustrial country, where a different weight of argument might well suggest another conclusion."

Edith Tilton Penrose was a long-time colleague and collaborator with Fritz Machlup. Machlup observed in his foreward to her book, The Economics of the International Patent System (1951):

> The discussion of the economics of the international patent system, and in particular of the international patent [Paris] Convention, has been almost devoid of contributions by *bona fide* economists. The international patent Convention is now 67 years old and the literature on it is by no means small. But scrutinize it and you will find only a handful of economists writing on this subject, even as they address themselves more to peripheral issues than to the fundamental economic issue—the balance of costs and gains.
>
> The book by Dr. Edith Penrose is the first of its kind. . . . [T]he economic analysis of the international patent system is both novel and controversial. The parts of the study that deal with the economic evaluation of various provisions will undoubtedly draw fire, because several dogmas which legal experts have held in great respect are exposed to the bright searchlight of a skilled economic analyst and are shown to be untenable. One may safely predict that many members of the American patent bar, and especially international patent lawyers, will intensely dislike some of the views expressed and perhaps all of the suggestions contained in this book.

But the views and suggestions of Mrs. Penrose are not out of line with the current thinking of the more enlightened patent experts.

---

149. Fritz Machlup, *An Economic Review of the Patent System*, Subcomm. on Patents, Trademarks and Copyrights, of the Committee on the Judiciary, 85th Congress, 2d Sess. (excerpts *reprinted in* F. Abbott, T. Cottier & F. Gurry, The International Intellectual Property System: Commentary and Materials 224-46 (1999)).

Following are the Summary and Conclusions of the pioneering work by Edith Tilton Penrose. Her observations and questions from 1951 have not lost their relevance.

**Edith Tilton Penrose***

## *The Economics of the International Patent System*

### Chapter XI Summary and Conclusions

In this chapter I shall briefly recapitulate the argument of this study, the propositions I have tried to establish and the implications of the prevailing assumptions about the international extension of the patent system.

#### I.

The patent of invention is a monopoly privilege of ancient origin granted for the purpose of encouraging innovation. It was first systematically used in Venice in the 14th and 15th centuries and has today been adopted by nearly all countries. The only serious attack on the principle of the patent system took place in the 19th century under the influence of the free trade movement. It was defeated but it served to emphasize the economic effects of the restrictions on industry that are inherent in the patent system and that most countries try to reduce by placing specific limitations on the monopoly granted.

#### II.

The origin of the patent system is clearly economic. In the 19th century attempts were made to justify it by appealing to a "natural" property right in ideas and to an inventor's moral right to receive a reward for his services. Although vestiges of the latter still crop up in patent discussions, today the primary arguments for the patent system are economic. Patents are held to be necessary to persuade inventors to disclose their secrets and to encourage the making and introduction of inventions.[1]

#### III.

Theories of natural property rights, idealistic visions of a world drawn together in international unity, and pressures from manufacturers in industrial countries combined to advance the cause of the international protection of patentees. After a series of conferences the International Convention for the Protection of Industrial Property was signed in 1883 creating the International Union for the Protection of Industrial Property. Today forty countries are members of the Union.

The Convention is founded on two basic principles: 1) that foreigners should receive in each country the same treatment as the nationals of that country; and 2) that the first applicant for a patent on an invention in one country should have a right of priority over all other applicants to obtain patents on the same invention in other countries. Most countries have always felt, however, that the grant of unconditional patents to foreigners would retard their economic development and the most controversial issues in the international conferences have

* Economics of the International Patent System 101-07, 162-69 (1951)

1. I have not in this study attempted to appraise the influence of national patent systems on the rate of invention. Most countries have adopted some form of patent law under which patents are also granted on inventions already patented and worked in other countries and I am only concerned with the economics of this arrangement.

centered around the question of what restrictions a country should be permitted to place on its patents.

## IV.

Before the International Convention was created a patentee in one country could generally obtain patents on his invention in other countries, but he faced many special difficulties in those countries and was frequently discriminated against. The purpose of the Convention is to reduce the difficulties and eliminate the discrimination. It thus formally sanctions the principle that a patentee in one country ought to be able to obtain patents on his invention in all other countries with a minimum of difficulty. In other words, the Convention rests on the assumption that it is insufficient for a patentee to obtain a monopoly on his invention in one country only and that he ought to obtain a worldwide monopoly.

The deliberate adoption of this economic policy can be justified on economic grounds only if the gains that accrue to society from it exceed the costs incurred because of it. It is indeed awkward that the costs cannot be measured nor the gains counted. As a result the optimum limits of the patent system, whether with respect to time, space, patentability or restrictions on the use of the grant, must always remain a subject of controversy. There is no doubt, however, that the costs have been underestimated.

It is generally assumed that the economic justification for the international extension of the patent system lies in its effects upon the advance of technology and the development of industry. Upon analysis, however, it appears that if one were to rely on this justification one would have to conclude that on balance the social cost of extending the patent system internationally exceeds the gain to be derived from it for the world as a whole. Nearly all foreign patenting is done by already industrialized countries, and the question of the effect of the prospect of patents in foreign markets on the rate of invention is a question of the extent to which the expected increment of profit arising from the geographical extension of the limits of patent protection will stimulate additional invention. There are many factors to be taken into consideration: the size of the national market, the nature of national industry, the types of invention, the motivation of inventors and the methods of financing invention. I have concluded that on balance the effect on invention of a system in which patents in many countries can be obtained is probably negligible for the world as a whole although it may be important for some firms and for some inventions. With respect to the introduction of inventions, there is little evidence that business men in industrial countries require patent protection to encourage them to adopt inventions which have already been developed to a commercial stage elsewhere.

But whatever may be the effect of the international extension of the patent system on the rate of invention or innovation, a heavy social cost is incurred. The patent method of encouraging invention operates by restricting the use of new inventions in order that a monopoly rent may be earned by the patentees to recompense them for the expenses and risks of making or introducing new inventions. The social costs to which this restriction gives rise appear in the first instance as increased prices and royalty payments. The more fundamental and important cost, however, is the production lost through the less efficient use of resources when new techniques cannot be freely used and when monopoly power is extended by means of patent agreements.[5]

5. See discussion of the sources of costs and gains in an international extension of the patent system. . . . The costs with which we are concerned are not the costs of making the inventions but the social cost of the patent method of encouraging them.

### V.

A few individual countries may gain from the system in which foreign patents are permitted. Industrial exporting countries obtain monopoly profits resulting from the increased price of exports; in some instances patent protection may enable exporting countries to retain a market against competitors or to surmount tariff barriers. The majority of countries, however, probably lose, since the higher price of patented imports, royalty payments to foreign patentees and in particular the restriction on their own use of new techniques constitute a cost much greater than is generally realized and the benefit derived from patent protection in foreign countries is much less than is usually assumed.

Under these circumstances if individual countries weigh the costs and gains of granting patents on inventions already patented and primarily used in other countries, most of them could easily conclude that the costs exceed the gains and that it is not to their benefit to grant them. The reasons why any particular country has adopted a policy of granting such patents can, of course, be explained only in terms of its history and of the pressures that have influenced its government. These pressures include those of exporting firms who wish to obtain protection abroad, of patent lawyers, of spokesmen for "internationalism," and—of particular importance for many of the smaller countries—the pressure exerted by the larger industrial countries to persuade the smaller ones to adopt "suitable" patent laws. On the other hand, most countries have realized that the social costs of granting unrestricted patents on inventions primarily worked abroad would exceed any benefit to be obtained and have accordingly placed special restrictions on such patents.[9]

### VI.

From the point of view of the world economy and of the economies of individual countries, the usual justification for the establishment of an international patent system—that it promotes technological progress—is not convincing. But the mere existence of national laws creates an economic problem which can only be met by an international extension of patent protection. In order to show this clearly I have examined what would be the economic consequences of a prohibition of international patenting, that is, of a system in which a patentee could obtain a patent in one national market only. Such a system would have the effect of enabling producers of patented products to obtain as a result of their patents higher profits in one country than in other countries. The prospect of such profits, which are unrelated to the underlying economic factors, would, therefore, exert an uneconomic influence on the international location of industry.[10]

Let us assume for the moment that a patentee is permitted to obtain a patent on his invention only in the country in which he produces. There is nothing, however, to prevent him from deciding to produce only in the country in which he wants a patent; the choice of plant location in many industries is not independent of market considerations. If the location of a plant in one area would permit monopoly profits to be obtained which would be foregone if the plant were located in another area, an intelligent producer would include the possibility of obtaining these profits in his calculations regarding the most profitable location of his plant. Thus a strong incentive would be created for patentees to locate their plants in larger industrial countries merely because they could there obtain a monopoly profit greater than elsewhere. If the expected monopoly profits were very great, a producer might well find

9. This is particularly brought out in the Swiss controversy over the inauguration of patent protection. . . .

10. Because a short summary statement of the argument in this section would be misleading, I am giving a large part of the argument just as it appears in Chapter VI. . . .

it desirable to incur considerably higher costs of production in order to obtain the protected market. In addition, industrial research and technical innovations would tend to concentrate in these countries.

This tendency for patentees who wish to sell in the larger markets to take out their patents in those markets would have still other consequences. A patent has a double effect within the territory in which it is valid: it prevents others from producing or selling in that territory. But outside that territory the products or processes are free from the patent restrictions. Hence if an invention could only be patented in one country, there would be an incentive for firms who wished to use the invention, to establish plants outside the territory covered by the patent and there produce for the rest of the world. Thus the exporting industries of the countries in which the larger number of patents were taken out would suffer, since when one firm holds a patent on an important new process, all other firms producing competitive products in that industry are at a disadvantage. In industries where all firms produce largely for foreign markets and are in competition with foreign firms in foreign markets, the firms without access to new developments would not only be at a disadvantage compared with the firm holding the patent in the domestic market but also with respect to the rest of the world: firms in the rest of the world could freely use any of the new techniques. Not only is the monopolistic position of the patentee firm increased within the domestic industry, but for no sound economic reason the domestic industry, other than the patentee firm is handicapped in relation to foreign industry.[11]

If the patentee were not required to produce in the country in which he takes out his patent, the fear of losing and the hope of safeguarding his patent monopoly in this or that market would not enter into the calculations of the producer in determining the location of his plant. Yet the position of the countries containing the larger markets would be even more adversely affected. The tendency for patents to be concentrated in these markets would be strengthened and the restrictions on industry in these countries would consequently be increased. It is part of the purpose of the patent system to retard the development of competitors of the patentee in order to enable him to earn a reward for his innovating enterprise, but it is difficult to justify a discrimination between these competitors by which one group is retarded—the group unfortunate enough to be in the country selected for the patent—while all others are left free. The patentee firm may gain very little by this secondary effect since it may be selling in markets which would not be served by the restricted group of firms and the latter may suffer very much. If the patentee is not allowed to extend his monopoly over the greater part of his market, the patent, in securing protection to him against competitors, automatically discriminates between these competitors. This alone is sufficient to justify some international arrangement regarding foreign patents.

Because of the social costs of the international extension of patenting, however, any international arrangement regarding foreign patenting should meet three conditions: 1) It should prevent the exploitation of the weaker industrial countries by the stronger. 2) It should reduce the influence of patents on the location of industrial activity. 3) It should reduce the social cost to each country of granting patents on inventions developed and primarily worked abroad. The present International Convention has made considerable advances in all three directions but with respect to the third, much more needs to be done.

## VII.

Two methods of reducing the social costs to a country of granting patents on inventions developed and primarily worked abroad have been widely used. The oldest is compulsory

11. Foreign branch plants of domestic firms are of course here considered as part of "foreign industry."

working.[12] Most countries have at some time adopted compulsory working laws in order to ensure that all patents granted are worked in the country granting them. This method is not only ineffective and frequently nothing but a clumsy way of obtaining access to foreign inventions for domestic firms, but it also conflicts with the second of the functions of an international patent arrangement since it establishes an uneconomic influence on the location of industry of the sort discussed in the previous section. The efforts of the International Union for the Protection of Industrial Property to eliminate such requirements are therefore in the right direction.

## VIII.

The second method of reducing the cost of the patent monopoly is that of compulsory licensing.[14] This is by far the most effective and flexible method and enables the state to prevent most of the more serious restrictions on industry. It could be used very effectively to undermine the monopoly power of several of the more powerful international cartels whose position is largely based on their control of the patent rights to industrial processes in the larger industrial countries; and it could be used to ensure that patented new techniques developed abroad are available to domestic industries wishing to use them.

The International Convention places restrictions on the right of countries to subject patents to compulsory licensing. These restrictions should be eliminated and countries should be encouraged to use this device to break up some of the more serious of the monopolistic restrictions on the use of new techniques.

## IX.

The Convention has been attacked by those who are concerned about the rise of international monopolistic practices, especially of international cartels. Although it is true that the Convention is one-sided, being more concerned with the rights of patentees than with the public interest in these rights, and that undue restrictions are placed on the use of compulsory licensing, the Convention itself cannot be held responsible for the existing evils of international patent practices merely because it has not outlawed them, for, conversely, it certainly has not sanctioned them. The difficulty lies with the national patent laws and national policies existing independently of the Convention. So long as national patent laws exist, an international convention on patents is desirable, but the patent policies of national governments and their trade and monopoly policies have not been very well coordinated and this lack of coordination is reflected in the one-sided nature of the Convention.

The Convention has also been criticised by the friends of international patent protection because it does not establish uniformity of patent practice in administrative matters. The laws and practices of different countries are very different and it has not yet proved possible to obtain substantial agreement on any uniform provisions. This is indeed a real weakness of the Convention, for if international patenting is to be permitted, a reduction of legal and administrative difficulties is desirable not only from the point of view of patentees but also in the general interest. The more difficult and expensive international patenting is, the more the large, well financed, and legally equipped firms have an advantage over smaller firms. Indeed

---

12. Compulsory working means that the law requires a patentee or his licensee to produce under the patent in the country granting the patent, although a patentee is usually exempt from this requirement if he can produce "acceptable excuses" instead. Until recently revocation of the patent was the chief penalty for failure to work. Now compulsory licensing is becoming more commonly adopted.

14. Under compulsory licensing a patentee is required by law to license his patent to another producer who wishes to use it upon payment of a reasonable royalty. . . .

a single international patent valid in all Union countries, long the ideal of ardent supporters of international patenting, is a desirable, though far-distant goal, providing that the patented technique is made easily available at a reasonable royalty to all who wish to use it.

### X.

Although an international patent Convention between the industrial countries of the world is desirable, the non-industrial countries, few of whose nationals want patents in foreign countries, have nothing to gain from granting patents to foreign firms. In view of the desirability of encouraging the development of these countries and of the fact that foreign patents tend more to restrict than to advance their industrial techniques, such countries should be exempt from any international patent arrangements.

### XI.

Up to the present, the regime for the international protection of patent rights has been developed primarily in the interest of patentees. The gains to be derived from an extension of the patent system have been stressed, but the concomitant increase in social costs has been seriously neglected. So far as it goes, the International Convention has not been to any important extent incompatible with the best interests of the world economy. Nonetheless, the Convention in no way helps to alleviate the restrictions on trade and industrial activity which unregulated international patenting permits. A reconsideration of its provisions from this point of view is in order.

## NOTES AND QUESTIONS

**1.** Edith Tilton Penrose supports the early international patent system established by the Paris Convention mainly because it should prevent a distortion in the international allocation of productive resources. If inventors could effectively patent their inventions in only one country, they would be likely to locate their production facilities in densely populated industrialized countries where they could maximize their monopoly returns. Penrose explains that this would have a number of undesirable effects. It might well lead to a concentration of R&D activities in already well-off countries. It would also place domestic competitors of the patent holder that might otherwise export to other countries at a disadvantage vis-à-vis foreign producers of the same product, unhindered by patent.

**2.** Penrose sees little reason why developing countries should find it desirable to provide patent protection to foreign inventors, and proposes to exempt developing countries from any international patent arrangements.

**3.** Penrose introduces us to the concept of the compulsory patent license. A compulsory patent license is granted by a government without the consent of the patent holder, and it permits the exploitation of rights otherwise controlled by the patent holder. The license may be granted in favor of a private enterprise or in favor of the government itself. Compulsory licensing will be considered further in Chapter 2.

**4.** Penrose alerts us to the question whether international patent protection may foster higher levels of industrial concentration. Again, this question is probably more trenchant today than it was when Penrose raised it in 1951.

**5.** Penrose's perspective on the value of an international patenting system for developing countries is out of synch with current OECD industry views, and perhaps with the predominant current trend in opinion among international economists.

Nevertheless, Penrose returns us to the question of whether the same level of IPRs protection is appropriate for all countries.

## C. Intellectual Property Rights and International Trade

The most significant development in the regulation of IPRs since the conclusion of the Paris and Berne Conventions was the conclusion of the TRIPS Agreement and thus the incorporation of the international IP system in the World Trade Organizations and the rules of international trade.

**Lee Branstetter and Keith E. Maskus**

### *Global Knowledge Flows, Absorptive Capacity, and Capability Acquisition: Old Ideas, Recent Evidence, and New Approaches*[15]

#### 1.1 Technology Diffusion: Channels and the Role of IPRs

For most developing economies, accessing and deploying international technologies is the primary source of new information, productivity gains, and economic growth (Keller, 2004). International technology diffusion is therefore a major determinant of global technical change and increasing such flows is a critical part of development policy. It is equally vital to adapt technologies to local conditions and learn how to use and improve them. Countries seeking access to foreign technologies therefore build into their innovation systems the entire policy complex involving skill accumulation, investment, competition, R&D support, and intellectual property rights.

It has long been recognized that an important channel of acquiring technological information is trade in high-technology goods and services (Coe, et al, 1997). Imported capital goods and technical intermediate inputs can directly improve productivity by being placed into production processes. A second is foreign direct investment (FDI), by which multinational enterprises (MNEs) transfer to their subsidiaries newer and more productive technological information (Markusen, 2002). MNEs often indirectly increase local productivity through sharing with upstream suppliers best standards in producing intermediate inputs (Javorcik, 2004). Yet a third is technology licensing, which typically involves the transfer of production or distribution rights and the associated technical information and know-how. A fourth is the cross-border movement of engineers and technicians (Hovhanissyan and Keller, 2015).

One important factor determining how readily technologies may be diffused through these various channels is the scope of IPRs in recipient countries. On the one hand, patents, trademarks, and enforceable contracts for licensed trade secrets can reduce the information costs and uncertainty of technology transfer (Hoekman, et al, 2005). They can also limit the tendency of recipient firms to expropriate technology opportunistically (Antras, 2005). On the other hand, if patents have extensive scope, say through broad claims and a ban on experimental use, they can make it more costly for domestic firms to imitate foreign technologies.

Recent empirical evidence suggests that technology movements to emerging and middle-income economies are generally enhanced by IPR protection. For example, in the first study of the trade impacts of TRIPS reforms, Ivus (2010) analyzed the growth of high-technology exports from 24 OECD countries to 55 developing countries. Taking the 18 countries with larger policy reforms as the reference group, she found that high-technology exports to those nations grew significantly faster than low-technology exports. The stronger patent rights increased the value of OECD exports of patent-sensitive goods to those countries by 8.6 percent. More recent studies find strong evidence that such reforms also raise the exports of high-technology goods from middle-income economies (Delgado, et al, 2013 and in this volume).

15. In Trade in Knowledge, p. 405 (Ch. 13), eds. A. Taubman & J. Watal (Cambridge 2022).

This result suggests that such countries are able to incorporate foreign technical information into greater production of exportable goods. Maskus and Yang (2018) also found a pro-export impact and showed that potential sources of this learning include inward patent applications, incoming FDI, and intra-firm trade in high-technology intermediates.

Regarding FDI, recent evidence suggests that IPR reforms could affect multiple activities of MNEs. One prominent study analyzed the impacts on licensing of U.S. parents with affiliates after patent-law changes in 16 emerging economies (Branstetter, et al, 2006). The authors found that royalty payments to parents rose by 34 percent on average, mostly reflecting an increased volume of technology sold rather than higher royalty charges. There was also a significant increase in R&D investments at local subsidiaries. Both of these effects were much stronger in high-technology industries.

A related analysis found significantly positive increases after patent reforms in affiliate sales, net plant and equipment, and employee compensation among affiliates of U.S. MNEs (Branstetter, et al, 2011). Further, they found that value added in local firms rose significantly, especially in technology-intensive sectors. There was also strong evidence that firms in these countries expanded the range (or "extensive margin") of products exported to the United States after patent rights were broadened.

To summarize, the best available evidence supports the claim that patent reforms have positive effects on inward technology transfer through market-based channels. They raise imports of high-technology goods and may also stimulate export growth. Stronger IPRs expand the local activities of multinational firms, while increasing licensing to both affiliated and unaffiliated parties. They particularly stimulate such responses among high-technology firms.

While these are important benefits, they must be qualified. First, to date these impacts have been found only in larger and middle-income countries. There is little evidence of such effects in the poorest and smallest developing economies, where the limited amounts of technology transfer render patents of little relevance. Second, to date there are no serious studies of any potential restrictive impacts of IPR reforms in poor countries. Local firms may have to change product lines or close down if they cannot adapt to the new competitive environment post-reforms, a possibility about which systematic evidence is absent. Finally, the available measures of technology diffusion are indirect and may miss considerable amounts of formal and informal knowledge transfers.

Despite the flaws in data, it does seem that there has been little supply response in much of the developing world, even as developing countries have adopted stronger IPR protection. Put differently, formal technology markets are unresponsive to such reforms in poor countries, while updated legal regimes have had little detectable impact on domestic technology use or adaptation. This observation may puzzle advocates of strong global IPR protection but, as we argue later in the chapter, it largely reflects the lack of absorptive capacity and complementary human skills in such societies.

## NOTES AND QUESTIONS

**1.** The British Commission on Intellectual Property Rights examined the implications of the TRIPS Agreement for developing countries. *See Integrating Intellectual Property Rights and Development Policy*, Report of the Commission on Intellectual Property Rights, London, Sept. 2002.[150] That Commission concluded, *inter alia:*

150. http://www.iprcommission.org/graphic/documents/final_report.htm.

The difficulty for developing countries in this context is that they are "second comers" in a world that has been shaped by the "first comers." And because of that, it is a very different world from that in which the "first comers" developed. It is a cliché to say that we live in an age of globalisation, when the world economy is becoming more integrated. It is an article of faith in the international community that integration on appropriate terms into the world economy is a necessary condition for development. The question from our point of view is what are the appropriate terms for that integration in the field of IPRs. Just as the now-developed countries moulded their IP regimes to suit their particular economic, social and technological circumstances, so developing countries should in principle now be able to do the same.

We therefore conclude that far more attention needs to be accorded to the needs of the developing countries in the making of international IP policy. Consistent with recent decisions of the international community at Doha and Monterrey, the development objectives need to be integrated into the making of IP rules and practice. At Monterrey in March 2002, governments welcomed "the decisions of the World Trade Organization to place the needs and interests of developing countries at the heart of its work programme." They also acknowledged the concerns of developing countries, including:

> the lack of recognition of intellectual property rights for the protection of traditional knowledge and folklore; the transfer of knowledge and technology; the implementation and interpretation of the Agreement on Trade-Related Aspects of Intellectual Property Rights in a manner supportive of public health. . . ." [Monterrey Consensus, March 2002].

We believe this is a satisfactory but partial agenda. There is far more that needs to be thought about and done in considering the impact of the existing system upon developing countries. It is our contention that intellectual property systems may, if we are not careful, introduce distortions that are detrimental to the interests of developing countries. Very "high" standards of protection may be in the public interest in developed countries with highly sophisticated scientific and technological infrastructures (although we note, as above, that this is controversial in several respects), but this does not mean the same standards are appropriate in all developing countries. In fact we consider that developed countries should pay more attention to reconciling their own perceived commercial self-interest, with their own interest in the reduction of poverty in developing countries.

To achieve that end, so far as possible developing countries should not be deprived of the flexibility to design their IP systems that developed countries enjoyed in earlier stages of their own development, and higher IP standards should not be pressed on them without a serious and objective assessment of their development impact. We need to ensure that the global IP systems evolve so that they may contribute to the development of developing countries, by stimulating innovation and technology transfer relevant to them, while also making available the products of technology at the most competitive prices possible. We need to make sure that the IP system facilitates, rather than hinders, the application of the rapid advances in science and technology for the benefit of developing countries. (Report, at Introduction).

**2.** The final paragraph of the excerpt by Branstetter and Maskus points to an important issue. Assume for the sake of argument that stronger IP protection encourages foreign investors to transfer their technology to developing countries, and that this accelerates the establishment of local industry capacity. Yet the same stronger IP protection does not encourage local scientists and entrepreneurs to develop technological solutions. Does that merely cement an imbalance of technological power among countries? Thus, a question that has concerned development specialists for many years: What types of policies can and should be adopted by developing countries to assure that technology transfers will in fact improve the local R&D environment?

One of the major difficulties facing policymakers dealing with the TRIPS Agreement is the relative absence of reliable data and analysis concerning its present and future effects. Keith Maskus has played a lead role in seeking to close the information gap.

**3.** An IP system is only one factor that influences development. The ability of an economy to produce new technologies or absorb existing technologies depends not on the IP system alone, but on the broader local innovation ecosystem in which the IP system exists, and how well that local innovation ecosystem is connected to global networks. The Global Innovation Index (GII), a report co-published annually by WIPO, Cornell University and INSEAD, aims to track the performance of innovation in economies across the world (https://www.wipo.int/global_innovation_index/en/). The GII 2022 comprised around 80 indicators including measures on the political environment, education, infrastructure, and knowledge creation of 132 economies. The GII also tracks the socioeconomic impact of innovation in terms of labor productivity, life expectancy, and carbon dioxide emissions (https://www.wipo.int/edocs/pubdocs/en/wipo-pub-2000-2022-en-main-report-global-innovation-index-2022-15th-edition.pdf).

**Keith E. Maskus***

## *Intellectual Property Rights in the Global Economy*

### Chapter Four

#### EVIDENCE ON THE GLOBAL IMPACTS OF INTELLECTUAL PROPERTY RIGHTS: MEASURING WHAT CANNOT BE SEEN

***Determinants of Intellectual Property Rights***

It is obvious from the figures above [not reproduced here—Eds.] that the strength of IPRs tends to rise with levels of economic development and income. That optimal protection of intellectual property is an increasing function of income and technological capacity is easy to explain. As incomes rise the demand for higher-quality, differentiated products also rises, leading to growing preferences for protection of trademarks and copyrights or, in political economy terms, an increasing supply of IPRs. As an economy's technological sophistication increases, inventors and creators require stronger and deeper protection for their works, implying a rising demand for IPRs. Of course, causation may go both ways, with stronger property rights also contributing to growth in incomes. The latter point remains subject to debate and is not yet well understood in empirical terms. I elaborate these points in the following chapter on IPRs and economic development. . . .

Inspection of Figure 1.1 actually suggests that patent rights decline as incomes rise from low levels, then accelerate sharply at highest income levels. Thus, there seems to be a quadratic relationship between IPRs and GNP per capita. . . . This specification strongly suggests that countries tend to weaken their patent laws as incomes rise to some point and then strengthen them after that. This U-shaped curve is reminiscent of the so-called "environmental Kuznets curve," which indicated that countries reduce their environmental standards up to some level of per-capita income and then raise them continuously after that point (Grossman and Krueger, 1993). . . .

. . . I add further explanatory variables that account for other influences on patent rights. One of these is the economy's size, as measured by real GDP. It could be hypothesized that countries do not begin to provide strong IPRs until they reach a minimum size, because there are fixed costs in organizing and administering a patent system. In the regression . . . market size has no detectable impact on patent rights. This finding is potentially important in

* Institute for International Economics (2000).

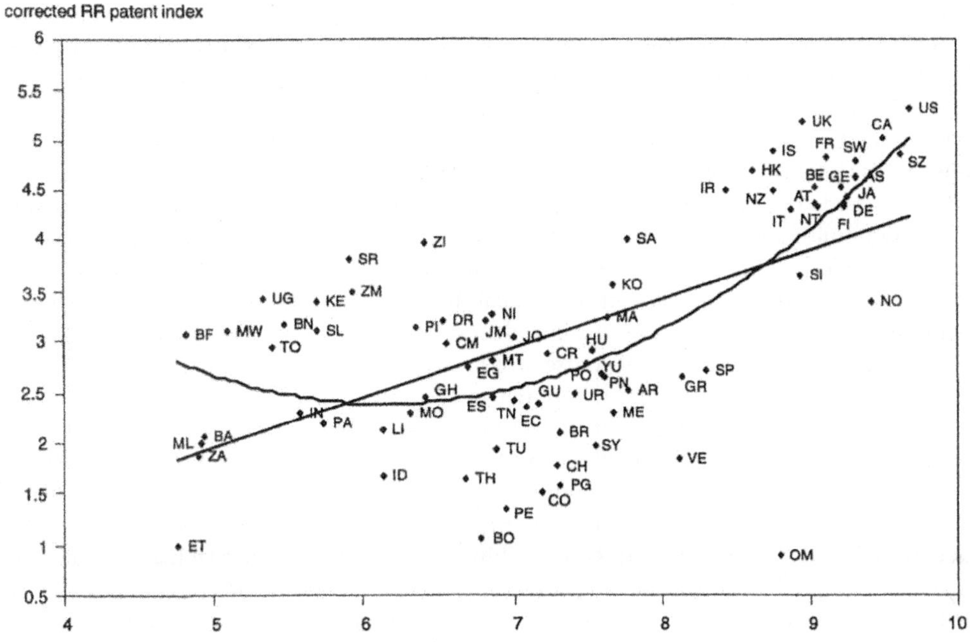


* = natural logarithm of per capita GNP.
*Note:* GNP measured in $1000s of 1984 US $s.
*Sources:* Maskus and Penubarti (1995) and author's calculations.

**Figure 1.1 Relationship Between Patent Rights and Per-Capita GNP**

policy terms. It suggests that the economy's GDP itself is not a determinant of IPRs reform, as opposed to per-capita income and economic development. Because U.S. trade authorities are concerned with the strength of IPRs protection in large but poor economies, such as India and China, they have mounted considerable pressure for change. This finding suggests that, despite such pressure, effective patent rights may remain limited until incomes grow well beyond current levels. Putting it differently, the higher standards required by TRIPS may well command limited enforcement attention in a wide swath of nations. . . .

## NOTES AND QUESTIONS

**1.** The data assembled by Keith Maskus highlights a phenomenon that is consistent with previous discussions of IP history and intuition. That is, as countries begin to move up the development curve, they borrow technology from more advanced countries to make their industries competitive. When a country reaches a certain point in its development, local interests in protecting new technologies begin to outweigh more diffuse interests in borrowing technologies, and the legislature is pressed to strengthen IP protection. The examples of the United States as "technology borrower" in the 1800s and early 1900s (the period of the "industrial revolution"), Japan in the 1950s through 1970s, and Taiwan in the 1980s and 1990s are commonly used to illustrate this phenomenon. The TRIPS Agreement is essentially an effort to eliminate that part of the development curve during which technology borrowing takes place. Yet, the consequences of eliminating the flexibility that the United States and other similarly situated countries enjoyed is unpredictable, and could be decidedly negative from the standpoint of developing countries. If local industries in these countries are precluded from using foreign technologies, and cannot afford to develop their own, they may find themselves in a perpetual circumstance of technological dependence. Foreign investors may dominate local industry as only they will be able to establish globally competitive businesses. In an alternative scenario, developing countries benefit from the introduction of foreign-owned technology as knowledge and training diffuses locally (through employment, leakage, etc.). Over the long term, as this diffusion results in greater local capacity for innovation, and as local entrepreneurs are able to access a more highly skilled labor force, developing country-based enterprises will become globally competitive. In another alternative scenario, since most multinational enterprises are publicly traded, and "ownership" can as well be vested in individuals from developed as well as developing countries, the whole notion of "local ownership" and control is irrelevant. Individuals in Bolivia and Tanzania can just as well own shares in Siemens and profit from the introduction of new technologies as individuals in the United States and Switzerland. Of course, this last scenario fails to identify how an individual in Bolivia or Tanzania would find the money to buy into Siemens, but it demonstrates how far one could go in attempting to rationalize technological dependence.

**2.** One of the principal difficulties in analyzing the role of IP in development involves the impracticability of disaggregating or isolating IP from other factors. China and Taiwan have experienced major inflows of foreign capital and high rates of economic growth while essentially ignoring foreign-held IPRs. But China has an enormous internal market that holds tremendous appeal for foreign investors, and Taiwan (during its low protection period in the 1980s and 1990s) excelled as a low-cost producer with a highly educated work force and proximity to major Asian markets. Would higher standards of IP protection have hurt either of these two economies? Would higher standards have helped? There is no "counter-factual" by which to test such hypotheses. What we do know is that low standards of IP protection did not create a "doomsday scenario" for these developing countries.

## D. Intellectual Property in a Digital Age

The invention of the microprocessor transformed the world in profound ways. The cost of building computers rapidly dropped, processing capacities expanded exponentially, and information became "digital." The Internet—a network of networks—connects the far reaches of the world community with vast information resources. A remote village today has a library resource capacity unthought of by even the greatest university libraries only decades ago.

It is a common axiom that intellectual property law continuously adapts to new technologies. Yet, intellectual property law has rarely been confronted with a challenge as complex as the Internet. If works protected by copyright can be uploaded to a server and accessed by individuals throughout the world instantaneously, the ability of copyright holders to control distribution of their work is challenged.

On one hand, the world has developed an information resource with incalculable capacity to disseminate information and promote understanding (though, as we know, information is not used only for "good" ends). On the other hand, the interests of copyright holders may be compromised (though copyright holders also have access to greatly expanded markets).

John Perry Barlow, a songwriter for the Grateful Dead and co-founder of the Electronic Frontier Foundation (EFF), was one of the first to suggest ways that the digitization of information and the Internet might challenge existing intellectual property paradigms. Barlow asks the reader to think of information in new ways—as a "living" entity whose characteristics fluctuate across time and space.

Barlow foresaw difficulties that would increasingly confront content providers and software developers, but likewise foresaw that enterprises would adapt their products to address new environments. His observations in 1994 anticipated to a large extent Microsoft's adaptation of its operating system technology (to ongoing interaction between the end-user and

Microsoft's server system, as well as Adobe's transition from a licensor of static software products to its continuous online update model).

He also suggested that legal rules might not provide the answers that content providers would seek. Copyright-dependent industries initiated major court battles against online distributors such as the original Napster. University administrators, at the insistence of copyright holders, pursued intrusive actions against their own students to punish them for taking advantage of materials readily accessible on the Internet. Where would this end? Would the inability of the copyright industries to protect their content lead to an Orwellian social order where access to information was strictly controlled by authorities? Would the Internet, hailed as a global good, become a tool of social control in the name of protecting against the downloading of rock and roll music? The music industry has again been transformed by streaming services. Without minimizing issues that may surround unauthorized downloading, relatively inexpensive access to a wide range of streamed music has certainly lessened interest in the downloading issue. A new technology has made concerns surrounding a recently new technology seem antiquated. Of course, we have a whole new set of issues surrounding access to personal data (and its misuse) that seems to be taking its place.

Bear in mind that Barlow's article was written about 30 years ago when the Internet was in its infancy.

**John Perry Barlow***

## *The Economy of Ideas: A Framework for Patents and Copyrights in the Digital Age. (Everything You Know about Intellectual Property is Wrong.)*

### . . . Interaction and Protection

Direct interaction will provide a lot of intellectual property protection in the future, and, indeed, already has. No one knows how many software pirates have bought legitimate copies of a program after calling its publisher for technical support and offering some proof of purchase, but I would guess the number is very high.

The same kind of controls will be applicable to "question and answer" relationships between authorities (or artists) and those who seek their expertise. Newsletters, magazines, and books will be supplemented by the ability of their subscribers to ask direct questions of authors. . . .

### Crypto Bottling

Cryptography, as I've said perhaps too many times, is the "material" from which the walls, boundaries—and bottles—of cyberspace will be fashioned.

Of course there are problems with cryptography or any other purely technical method of property protection. It has always appeared to me that the more security you hide your goods behind, the more likely you are to turn your sanctuary into a target. Having come from a place where people leave their keys in their cars and don't even have keys to their houses, I remain convinced that the best obstacle to crime is a society with its ethics intact.

While I admit that this is not the kind of society most of us live in, I also believe that a social over reliance on protection by barricades rather than conscience will eventually wither

* Wired 2.03, March 1, 1994.

the latter by turning intrusion and theft into a sport, rather than a crime. This is already occurring in the digital domain as is evident in the activities of computer crackers. . . .

But cryptography will not be used simply for making locks. It is also at the heart of both digital signatures and the aforementioned digital cash, both of which I believe will be central to the future protection of intellectual property.

I believe that the generally acknowledged failure of the shareware model in software had less to do with dishonesty than with the simple inconvenience of paying for shareware. If the payment process can be automated, as digital cash and signature will make possible, I believe that soft product creators will reap a much higher return from the bread they cast upon the waters of cyberspace.

Moreover, they will be spared much of the overhead presently attached to the marketing, manufacture, sales, and distribution of information products, whether those products are computer programs, books, CDs, or motion pictures. This will reduce prices and further increase the likelihood of noncompulsory payment.

But of course there is a fundamental problem with a system that requires, through technology, payment for every access to a particular expression. It defeats the original Jeffersonian purpose of seeing that ideas were available to everyone regardless of their economic station. I am not comfortable with a model that will restrict inquiry to the wealthy.

### An Economy of Verbs

The future forms and protections of intellectual property are densely obscured at this entrance to the Virtual Age. Nevertheless, I can make (or reiterate) a few flat statements that I earnestly believe won't look too silly in 50 years.

- In the absence of the old containers, almost everything we think we know about intellectual property is wrong. We're going to have to unlearn it. We're going to have to look at information as though we'd never seen the stuff before.
- The protections that we will develop will rely far more on ethics and technology than on law.
- Encryption will be the technical basis for most intellectual property protection. (And should, for many reasons, be made more widely available.)
- The economy of the future will be based on relationship rather than possession. It will be continuous rather than sequential.
- And finally, in the years to come, most human exchange will be virtual rather than physical, consisting not of stuff but the stuff of which dreams are made. Our future business will be conducted in a world made more of verbs than nouns.

## NOTES AND QUESTIONS

**1.** In a discussion of Lotus 1-2-3 and WordPerfect (each of which was the dominant program in its field of use "back in the day"), Barlow notes that software products generate increasing returns as they are more widely adopted and that to some extent piracy may serve a useful purpose from the creator's standpoint. Another side to the value of widespread adoption concerns a phenomenon known as "network effects." This phenomenon is the subject of considerable discourse in the antitrust field. Certain products, such as computer operating systems, are thought to generate increasing social returns as they are more widely adopted. It may be a mistake from a social welfare standpoint to inhibit the emergence of a dominant operating system since consumers benefit from the capacity of programmers to write to a single standard (thereby encouraging the creation of new applications), and they benefit from being able to more easily share their digital work. Would the conclusion that a single standard for computer operating systems is socially beneficial justify private monopoly control over that standard, or would it argue for the regulation of that standard as an "essential facility," access to which must be assured under defined terms and conditions? In the *Microsoft* case, the Court of Appeals for the District of Columbia Circuit considered Microsoft's argument that analysis of its behavior under the laws against monopolization should take into account network effects. The Court said:

> Whether or not Microsoft's characterization of the operating system market is correct does not appreciably alter our mission in assessing the alleged antitrust violations in the present case. As an initial matter, we note that there is no consensus among commentators on the question of whether, and to what extent, current monopolization doctrine should be amended to account for competition in technologically dynamic markets characterized by network effects. . . . Indeed, there is some suggestion that the economic consequences of network effects and technological dynamism act to offset one another, thereby making it difficult to formulate categorical antitrust rules absent a particularized analysis of a given market.
>
> Moreover, it should be clear that Microsoft makes no claim that anticompetitive conduct should be assessed differently in technologically dynamic markets. It claims only that the measure of monopoly power should be different. For reasons fully discussed below, we reject Microsoft's monopoly power argument.

*United States v. Microsoft*, 253 F.3d 34, 50 (D.C. Cir. 2001).

**2.** Barlow did not precisely anticipate the looming controversies surrounding file sharing and downloading of music and movies from the Internet. He did, however, anticipate through the intellectual property policies of the Grateful Dead one of the main economic arguments in favor of file sharing made by the original Napster in its much-publicized dispute with the recording industry—namely, that wide availability of free music on the Internet stimulates consumer demand for CDs, and therefore is not antithetical to recording industry interests. This argument did not particularly impress the district court or the Court of Appeals. *See A & M Records v. Napster*, 239 F.3d 1004, 1016-17 (9th Cir. 2001).

**3.** Barlow observed the fundamental problem that technology is enabling activities that interfere with rights in intellectual property as traditionally understood, and he suggested that technological measures may, in the long run, be more effective than law in controlling those activities. Yet Barlow knew then, and we know today, that envisioning technological controls and effectively implementing them are different matters. Since early days in California's Silicon Valley, computer software creators sought to protect their works against unauthorized duplication by technological means. No sooner had a new method of preventing access been encoded than methods of circumventing the code were found. Anticopying devices often made the ordinary use of programs difficult for authorized users, leading to frustration and dissatisfied customers. Are more sophisticated encryption technologies the answer to the problems faced by copyright holders?

**4.** As recently as 30 years ago, the distribution and sale of a copyright-protected work throughout the world was an expensive process that required the development and maintenance of a substantial physical distribution network. Today, a copyright-protected work can be sent or shared by an IPRs holder anywhere in the world virtually cost-free. Conceptually at least, the potential profit that can be obtained from global distribution vastly exceeds what was possible in the past. Should this potential windfall for copyright holders affect the level of protection their works are afforded?

**5.** Did Barlow anticipate Bitcoin and other cryptocurrencies? Or was his reference to "digital cash" more along the PayPal line?

## E. The Future of Global IP Policy

Few individuals have been so perceptively involved in the study of the relationship between intellectual property rights and economic development as Keith Maskus and Jerome Reichman. They here combine their experience and skills as economist and lawyer to assess the current state of the IP world and its implications for developed and developing countries. They make several important recommendations, a few of which are included within the following excerpt.

**Keith E. Maskus & J. H. Reichman***

### *The Globalization of Private Knowledge Goods and the Privatization of Global Public Goods*

#### . . . Technology Transfer After the TRIPS Agreement

The international flow of technological information and its successful integration into domestic production and management processes are central to the ability of firms in developing countries to compete in the global economy. Technological change is a principal source of sustained growth in living standards and is essential for the transformation and modernization of economic structures. In most instances, developing countries find it cheaper and faster to acquire foreign technologies than to develop them with domestic resources. Such technologies may "spill over" into wider improvements in productivity and follow-on innovation in the domestic economy.

International technology transfer (ITT) is a comprehensive term covering mechanisms for shifting information across borders and its effective diffusion into recipient economies. It refers to numerous complex processes, which range from innovation and international marketing of technology to its absorption and imitation. There are also many different channels through which technology may be transferred. One major conduit consists of trade in goods, especially capital goods and technological inputs. A second is foreign direct investment (FDI), which generally transfers technological information that is newer or more productive than that available from local firms. A third is technology licensing, which may occur either within firms or between unrelated firms. Licenses typically involve the purchase of production or distribution rights and the technical information and know-how required to exploit them.

There are also important non-market channels of ITT. Perhaps most significant is the process of imitation through product inspection, reverse engineering, and trial and error. A related mechanism is triggered when technical and managerial personnel leave a firm and start a rival firm based on information learned in the original location. Still another means is to study information available from patent applications. Thus, patents provide both a direct source of technology transfer, through FDI and licensing, and an indirect source through legally regulated disclosures. Indeed, "trade in ideas" is a significant factor in world economic growth, and developing economies could gain considerably more access to foreign technologies as international firms take out patents in their locations. Nevertheless, this benefit remains dependent on local abilities to learn from incoming technological information, and on the diffusion practices or strategies of technology-exporting firms.

Much knowledge appears to be transferred through the temporary migration of students, scientists, and managerial and technical personnel to universities, laboratories, and

* 7 J. Int'l Econ. L. 279 (2004).

conferences located mainly in the developed economies. Finally, technical information may be available from the public domain, making it free for taking, or from a research commons accessible with certain restrictions.

International markets for trading technologies are inherently subject to failure due to distortions attributable to concerns about appropriability, problems of valuing information by buyers and sellers, and market power, all strong justifications for public intervention at both the domestic and global levels. . . .

While the close and complex relationships between intellectual property rights and ITT cannot be fully discussed here, it is useful to consider some of the main impacts, both positive and negative, that stronger global IPRs may have on international information flows. First, the preponderance of econometric studies suggests that market-mediated flows of technology respond positively to the strengthening of patent laws across countries. This finding applies to international trade flows, especially in patent-sensitive industries and capital goods, as regards patents in middle-income and large developing countries. However, trade flows to poor countries seem unresponsive to patent laws. Similarly, recent studies of patents and inward FDI find positive impacts on more advanced and larger developing countries, but not on poor and small countries. Licensing volumes between U.S. firms and unrelated concerns in larger developing countries also expand with the rigor of local patent regimes.

A reasonable interpretation of these findings is that there are threshold effects in market-based licensing. Economies with low incomes and limited technological capacity present neither attractive markets nor a competitive imitation threat. Because their intellectual property regimes are not particularly important in attracting ITT, it seems unlikely that the standards implemented in compliance with TRIPS will encourage additional technology transfer to the poorest countries. However, at higher incomes and technological capacities, IPRs become an important factor in this regard, even though they are only one of a list of variables that influence ITT. Other important factors include effective infrastructure, efficient governance, market size and growth, and proximity to suppliers and demanders.

The literature also suggests that stronger patent rights may be expected to raise considerably the rents earned by international firms as patents become more valuable, with the result that firms in developing countries would pay more for the average inward protected technology. Expansion of breadth, scope, and length of patents would tend to amplify this result. Thus, there are countervailing impacts in middle-income countries: higher volumes of ITT but increased payments per unit of technology. Moreover, recipient countries are more likely to benefit where the supply of technologies is competitive and local firms are capable of adapting them effectively into production processes.

While the evidence supports the claim that TRIPS standards could enhance ITT (at least into the larger and more advanced developing economies) through better performing technology markets, it should be weighed against national historic experience. Few now-developed economies underwent significant technological learning and industrial transformation without the benefit of weak intellectual property protection. . . .

The extent to which the emerging global IP regime may be expected to enhance or impede ITT thus poses a complicated question. Answering it is made even harder because technology transfer across borders involves a mixture of private activities and public measures of encouragement (or discouragement). This mixture varies in cost and efficiency by sector, country, and over time, which suggests that globalized IP protection could have both complex and sub-optimal effects unless accompanied by appropriate complementary policy approaches.

The new system raises entry barriers for firms and competition in the poorest countries, while even the middle-income nations find their scope of action limited. Market distortions due to misuses of intellectual property rights may also be harder to detect or police in developing than in developed countries. Moreover, new or relatively untested forms of intellectual property protection that choke access to upstream information inputs—including scientific and technical data as such—could narrow access to the research commons and limit other transfer mechanisms, with incalculable long-term effects on ITT as it used to occur.

In our view, governments in developing countries need to be pro-active in ensuring that the net effect of expanded IP protection is to enhance access to technology and to encourage its domestic adaptation and diffusion. Potential gains in dynamic competition are reason enough for this approach. An additional important factor is that tightened protection raises significant questions regarding the ability to access international technology and information to improve the provision of broader public goods. In the rest of this article we explore these issues in more detail. . . .

## Instability and Loss of Balance in Developed Intellectual Property Regimes

The drive to stamp out free-riding practices thus tends to obscure serious problems engendered by the radical transformation of IP policies that has occurred in developed countries. This transformation constitutes a prolonged effort to strengthen the protection of investors in cutting-edge technologies, especially computer programs and biogenetically engineered products, which fit imperfectly within the classical patent and copyright paradigms.

Under the classical IP system, as implemented in the United States through the mid-1960s, for example, the strong legal monopolies of the patent law protected only a narrow layer of discontinuous inventions that fell outside the technical trajectories guiding the day-to-day application of normal scientific discoveries. . . . [V]igorously enforced antitrust laws, supplemented by a robust doctrine of patent misuse, rid the market of deleterious patent pools and other barriers to entry and, in the view of Professors Mowery and Rosenberg, by disciplining Bell Labs and IBM, paved the way for the technological leaps of the 1970s and 1980s.

This classical system of intellectual property protection obliged innovators to look to the public domain for the basic inputs of most technological development. . . .

If we now fast forward to a descriptive analysis of the current U.S. system, one could hardly imagine a starker contrast. The United States Court of Appeals for the Federal Circuit, entrusted by Congress to manage the patent system, has deliberately remolded that system to protect investment as such, rather than discontinuous technical achievements that elevate the level of competition. The patent system has accordingly degenerated to protecting incremental slivers of know-how applied to industry, including those very business methods that were formerly the building blocks of the free-enterprise economy.

The copyright system, expanding in the same direction, now confers virtually perpetual protection on computer software and digital productions of all kinds, and it encourages creators to surround even their unprotectible technical ideas and components with untouchable electronic fences. Once surrounded by these fences, even the underlying facts and data may be put off limits; while one-sided electronic adhesion contracts may override public interest exceptions favoring education and public research, and they may even prohibit reverse engineering by honest means.

As hybrid IP regimes multiply to fill still other perceived gaps in the system, there are virtually no products sold on the general products market that do not come freighted with a bewildering and overlapping array of exclusive property rights that discourage follow-on applications of routine technical know-how. Weak enforcement of antitrust laws then further reinforces the barriers to entry erected upon this thicket of rights, while the need to stimulate and coordinate investment in complex innovation projects justifies patent pools, concentrations of research efforts, and predatory practices formerly thought to constitute misuses of the patent monopoly.

The end results of this process, which James Boyle has felicitously called the Second Enclosure Movement, are not fully known, but the problems it is already causing for developed systems of innovation shed light on the larger problems facing the international economy. The availability of upstream data and scientific information from the public domain is shrinking at the very moment when advances in Internet technologies make it possible to link both centrally located and distributed data repositories as never before. A growing thicket of rights surrounds gene fragments, research tools, and other upstream inputs of scientific research, and the resulting transaction costs impede and delay research and development undertaken in both the public and private sectors. Lost research and competitive opportunities appear to be mushrooming as exchanges of even government funded research results become problematic. As well-known economists point out, complex research and development projects at every level—whether public or private—will become increasingly impracticable if too many owners of too many rights have to be tithed along the way.

Meanwhile, the sharing norms of science and the principle of open access to data have begun to break down as universities commercialize publicly funded research products. New intellectual property rights in collections of data—adopted in the EU and pending adoption in the U.S.—further undermine these norms by enabling scientists, universities and entrepreneurs to retain control of data and technical information even after the publication of research results in articles or after public disclosure for purposes of filing patent applications on such results.

These and other social disutilities cast light on the problems afflicting the international system and raise serious questions about its future prospects. They represent the unintended consequences of an excess of regulation and interference with market forces. In allowing large multinational firms to lock in temporary advantages, the IP system could discourage innovation by those same small and medium-sized firms that depend on access to public domain inputs for developing applications of new technologies.

In this environment, economists fear that the ratcheting up of intellectual property standards will boomerang against the capacity to innovate in developed countries. They ask whether the breakthrough inventions of the recent past would still be possible in a protectionist environment and in the presence of a shrinking public domain. They make us question whether future innovation will flourish in a dynamic, transnational system of innovation liberated from excessive governmental regulation or flounder in a re-regulated, ever more anticompetitive market that increasingly resembles the top-down economies that trailed behind U.S. high-tech industries in the past . . .

## NOTES AND QUESTIONS

**1.** As a general proposition, the academic community is substantially more skeptical of claims that strong intellectual property protection advances the interests of developing countries—or, for that matter, developed countries—than developed country business interests. What accounts for this difference in perspective? Are economists and law professors ignoring benefits conferred by the industrial community? Is the perspective of the business community too heavily shaped by narrow short-term interests in rent collection? What suggestions might you have for resolving the tension between the two perspectives?

**2.** When the international IPRs system was taking shape in the late 1800s, the possibilities for exploiting inventions and expressive works internationally were rather limited. A right to exclude others from practicing an invention or exploiting an expressive work on a global scale was in most cases a theoretical benefit. Does the fact that an inventive or expressive work can today *actually* be exploited among a very large base of consumers/end-users and earn large amounts of money affect how you think the balance should be struck between IPRs holders and the general public, or is it all the same?

**Francis Gurry***

## *Re-Thinking the Role of Intellectual Property*

The context in which intellectual property (IP) operates in the contemporary world is vastly different from the one in which IP was born. The new context has changed the position of IP both in the economy and in society. It calls equally for a change in the way in which we think about IP and its role.

### Traditional Explanations for IP

Let me start by recalling briefly the traditional explanations of why we have IP. There are four main reasons, applicable to varying degrees to all the rights that we characteristically consider to be IP rights.

One set of explanations arises from the non-rivalrous nature of knowledge and information. Knowledge and information are private goods in production. They cost human and financial resources to create. In contrast, they are public goods in consumption. Once available, they may be used by another without lessening their enjoyment by the producer. This characteristic of knowledge was noticed by Columcille in his defence against the charge by Finnian in Ireland in the Sixth Century that he had copied the illuminations of a bible that Finnian had lent to him. When called before King Diarmuid to answer to the charge of theft, Columcille protested that he had not stolen anything, since Finnian still had his drawings and "Finnian's book was none the worse for his copying from it." In dismissing the defence, the king ushered copyright into the world by pronouncing "To every cow her calf; and to every book its copy."[2]

IP creates a policy restriction, in the form of exclusive rights to commercial use, on the otherwise free availability of knowledge and information in order to compensate for the cost of production of the knowledge or information. It thereby creates an economic incentive to investment in knowledge creation and provides a safe passage through hostile terrain for the long and often lonely march of an idea from conception to commercial implementation as a new product, service or process. The exclusive rights, in effect, make access a saleable commodity and create the basis of markets for knowledge and technology.

This first set of explanations applies to those IP rights that cover new forms of knowledge,[3] namely, patents, plant variety rights, trade secret rights or rights in confidential information, industrial designs and copyright.

As suggested by the moral indignation of Finnian when he discovered that his drawings had been copied, IP also has an ethical basis. This is expressed in Article 27.2 of the Universal Declaration of Human Rights, which provides that "Everyone has the right to the protection of the moral and material interests resulting from any scientific, literary or artistic production of which he is the author." This ethical basis of IP applies to most IP rights. It has a long social history, as evidenced in the negative connotation of words in the ordinary language such as

* Speech at University of Melbourne, Aug. 22, 2013.

2. Royal Irish Academy MS 24 P 25. A copy of the page of the manuscript hangs at WIPO. See, also, Thomas Cahill, How the Irish Saved Civilization (1995, New York) 170. Thomas Jefferson made the same point when he wrote of an idea that ". . . no one possesses the less, because everyone possesses the whole of it. He who receives an idea from me, receives instruction himself without lessening mine; as he who lights his taper at mine, receives light without darkening me." (Letter to Isaac McPherson, August 13, 1813).

3. I am using "knowledge" (and "information") in a very general sense to cover also new creative expressions.

plagiarism, cheating or copying (or any of the last term's more pejorative derivations such as "copycat").

The other reasons for having IP apply more specifically to particular IP rights. A further reason, additional to the incentive to create new knowledge, for having a patent system is to get new knowledge into the open. A good example of this function of patents is the saxophone. The saxophone is the only instrument in the orchestra that was once patented. It was patented in 1846 in France by Adolphe Sax. Throughout the course of the next 70 or so years, another 14 patents were taken out in relation to the saxophone, some by Adolphe Sax and some by what we would now call competitors. These led to the mouthpiece that we now know, the alto sax, other different varieties of sax, and an improved mechanism for the saxophone itself. Much of that technology has been in the public domain for well over 100 years now, and anyone can make or use the saxophone. It is interesting and instructive to compare that with the evolution of the violin. In Cremona, in Italy, in the 17th and 18th centuries, the technology for making violins was family-based and secret. It was passed from generation to generation in secrecy. The result is that nobody, to this day, knows how the very best violins that the world has ever heard—by Stradivari, Guarneri and others—were made. The secret of their manufacture has been lost in time and in the secrecy of families and the methods by which they transmitted their knowledge.

The comparison of the transmission of knowledge concerning the saxophone with the retention of knowledge by luthiers is far from being the only example of the success of the disclosure function of the patent system. The Hollerith punched card, television, the jet engine, polymerization catalysts and the iPhone are all examples of major technologies or products published in the patent system years and, sometimes, decades[4] before the commercialization of the inventions. The patent system has been responsible for constructing the most complete, systematic and accessible record of humanity's technology.

In the case of trademarks, geographical indications and, depending on the jurisdiction, passing-off or unfair competition, the policy justification tends to be the maintenance of order in the marketplace. Messaging and signalling between producers and entrepreneurs, on the one hand, and consumers and the general public, on the other hand, are indispensable for ensuring correct information and the avoidance of deception and fraud in the market. Distributed markets in a globalized economy only reinforce this role of brands and identity presentation (trade dress).

These traditional explanations of the purpose of IP remain entirely valid. But much has changed in the world since they were first formulated. These changes do not undermine the traditional explanations, but they should cause us to add certain other responsibilities to the job description of IP in order to reflect better the position of IP in the contemporary economy and society. Let me describe briefly the main changes, which, I believe, consist in three major shifts—the economic shift from tangible to intangible, the geopolitical shift from West to East and the political shift from State to non-State.

### The Rise of Intangibles

Over the past few decades, the centre of wealth creation has been shifting from tangible assets or physical capital to intangible assets or intellectual capital or, as the OECD calls it, knowledge capital. There are many measures of this shift.[5] It is apparent in the asset distribution of

4. In the case of the iPhone, it was a few months. Enterprises tend to accord their new product announcements now with the publication of the corresponding patent application (18 months after the first filing).

5. For a general survey, see the publications relating to the two-year project of the OECD on *New Sources of Growth: Knowledge-based Capital,* particularly *New Sources of Growth: Knowledge-Based Capital: Key Analyses and Policy Conclusions—Synthesis* report. (OECD 2013)

the corporations in the S&P 500, which was 95% tangible assets and 5% intangible assets in 1978, but had become 20% tangible assets and 80% intangible assets by 2010. It is apparent in business investment trends. In a number of advanced economies, more is invested in knowledge based capital than in physical capital and the rate of increase in investment in knowledge based capital is consistently out-pacing the rate of increase in investment in physical capital.

This shift brings with it, naturally, a change in the focus of competition. Competition is increasingly targeted at the competitive advantage that is derived from knowledge based capital. That is why, after all, we are seeing increasing rates of investment in knowledge based capital. The competitive advantage conferred by knowledge based capital is expressed as innovation, innovation being increasingly understood in a comprehensive way as covering all the technological, design, organizational and marketing information that go into the commercialization of new products, services or processes. Innovation is the key to economic (and, by the way, military) success in the contemporary world for enterprises, industries and countries and is perceived as such by all those actors. This is why we see such emphasis placed on innovation. The Wall Street Journal last year did a survey of quarterly and annual reports filed with the Securities Exchange Commission and found that the word "innovation" had been used 33,528 times in those reports in the preceding year.[6]

IP captures and secures the competitive advantage conferred by innovation. This translates into enormous value for which IP is the custodian. In a study published last year by the United States Government,[7] it was estimated that, in 2010, $5.06 trillion in value added, or 34.8% of US GDP, and 27.1 million jobs, or 18.8% of all employment, were directly attributable to IP-intensive industries. Awareness of this value captured by IP also accounts for the rising demand for IP rights throughout the world. Between 1995 and 2011, worldwide the number of patent applications rose from 1.05 million to 2.14 million, the number of trademark applications from 2 million to 4.2 million and the number of design applications from around 245,000 to 775,000.

### The Geopolitical Shift from West to East

The second major shift informing the context in which IP operates is the geopolitical shift from West to East. The centre of economic gravity is moving and, with it, the centre of technological gravity. These are occurring at different speeds. Naturally, one may argue about how long this movement will continue for, where the centre will end up, whether there will be a centre or some other geometric configuration, and so forth. But it is undeniable that a shift, the likes of which we have not seen for several hundred years, is underway. Again, there are many measures of this shift. My concern here is the shift in the production of knowledge and technology. Let me cite three indicators of this, one relating to inputs to knowledge production and the other two relating to outputs.

Research and development (R&D) is one of the principal inputs to knowledge production. China is now the second largest investor in R&D, in absolute terms, in the world. The third largest, in absolute terms, is Japan. Asian countries represented 24% of global R&D in 1999, but accounted for 32% in 2009.[8]

6. *Wall Street Journal*, May 23, 2012.

7. U.S. Department of Commerce, *Intellectual Property and the U.S. Economy: Industries in Focus* (March 2012) available at http://www.uspto.gov/news/publications/IP_Report_March_ 2012.pdf.

8. National Science Board, *Science and Engineering Indicators 2012*, 4-5 (Arlington, Virginia: National Science Foundation (NSB 12-01)).

In terms of outputs, the rise of Asia is apparent in the production of scientific articles, where the first decade of the 21st Century saw the scientific production of a range of Asian countries increase at rates far greater than the rates of increase in the mature economies.[9] As a report of the Royal Society in 2011 stated, "The scientific league tables are not just about prestige — they are a barometer of a country's ability to compete on the world stage."[10] The picture is even clearer in the case of technology, as measured by the number of international patent applications filed under the Patent Cooperation Treaty (PCT). In 1994, Japan, China and the Republic of Korea accounted for 7.6% of all international patent applications. In 2012, they accounted for 38%, more than the shares of the EU or the USA.

### The Empowerment of Non-State Actors

The final shift is the diffusion of political power throughout society as a result of the empowerment brought about originally by the Internet and more recently by other forms of social media. The Internet has busted the State's monopoly on information, one of the bases on which it could claim the authority to make policy, and has facilitated the creation of networks of all conceivable varieties — social, political, economic, cultural, scientific and technological. It has, in short, created a shift in access to information and knowledge and in the capacity to use knowledge for all sorts of purposes.

There are many examples in the political, economic and social arenas that illustrate the application of this newfound empowerment. In the area of IP, the last two years have produced a number of major examples.

One of those was the coordinated action taken on January 18, 2012, to protest against the passage of certain IP legislation in the USA. The legislation was the Stop Online Piracy Act (SOPA) and the Protect Intellectual Property Act (PIPA). These bills enjoyed bipartisan support in Congress and their passage, ordinarily, seemed inevitable. But the protests caused them to be shelved. The protests involved 115,000 websites closing access to all or much of their content.

Participating websites included Wikipedia, which went dark, Google, which blacked out its logo, Reddit, Twitter and Tumblr. 162 million people experienced Wikipedia's blackout. Four and a half million people signed Google's online petition by 1.30pm PST on January 18. Nearly two and half million (2.4 million) SOPA-related tweets were sent in the first 16 hours of January 18. The top five trending terms on Twitter that day were "SOPA," "Stop SOPA," "PIPA," "Tell Congress" and "#factswithoutwikipedia." In addition (and I do not suggest that this was in any way part of the aforementioned coordinated action), the hacking group Anonymous stated that it had knocked out the websites of the FBI, the U.S. Department of Justice and several entertainment industry sites as retribution for anti-piracy efforts by both the government and the entertainment industry. The group said it was "the largest attack ever," with 5,635 participants involved in bringing down the sites. In addition to the Department of Justice and the FBI, the Recording Industry of America, Motion Picture Association of America, Universal Music and BMI websites were also reportedly attacked.[12] Other examples in the field of IP of the exercise of the power conferred by the Internet, social media and

---

9. Over that decade, the rate of increase in the number of published scientific articles was, on average, in the USA 1%, the EU 1.4% and Japan 1.1%, but was for China 16.8%, Republic of Korea 10.1%, Singapore 8.2%, India 6.9% (National Science Board, op. cit. 5-33).

10. Royal Society, Knowledge Networks and Nations. Scientific Collaboration in the 21st Century (2011).

12. Nbcnews.com, http://www.nbcnews.com/technology/anonymous-says-it-takes-down-fbi-doj-entertainment-sites-117735.

networking are the protests against the Anti-Counterfeiting Trade Agreement (ACTA)[13] and the re-configuration by Microsoft of its Xbox One Console.[14]

The three shifts outlined above have occurred against a backdrop of globalization, that is, the rise of free, open and interconnected markets and global value chains, driven by reduced trade barriers, improved transportation, telecommunications and communication devices. There are, of course, numerous by-products or consequences of the complex phenomenon of globalization. For present purposes, among the most important are the global awareness and use of consumer technologies (there are 6.8 billion mobile subscriptions in the world, for example), global fashions and trends and globalized consumption of culture and entertainment (as of July 28, 2013, the music video "Gangnam Style" by the Korean performer Psy had been viewed over 1.715 billion times on YouTube, having surpassed Justin Bieber's "Baby" as the site's most watched video).

Where does all this leave King Diarmuid and his cow? As mentioned above, I do not believe that any of these developments invalidate the traditional bases of IP. But we do need to recognize that the mission of IP is much larger and more sophisticated than any one of the individual bases alone might suggest. It is, in my view, really about the whole way in which knowledge and culture are produced, distributed and consumed in an economy in which knowledge is the basis of wealth generation and in a society with global habits of consumption of technology, culture and entertainment. Such a mission statement requires that we add two additional functions to the job description of IP.

## IP as a Regulator of Competitive Behaviour

The first additional function is for IP to be a mechanism for determining fair competition in relation to the resource base of the knowledge economy. Since innovation is increasingly the battleground for competition, and since IP captures the competitive advantage of innovation, IP will become, as the former Prime Minister of China, Wen Jiabao, said, the basis of competition in the future.

We can see the authenticity of this insight at the level of both countries and enterprises. More and more countries are adopting innovation strategies or plans or are explicitly making the capacity to innovate part of their industrial or technological strategy. Competition abounds with respect to most of the elements that go into constituting the capacity to innovate—for hosting R&D facilities, for positions on university league tables and for attracting human resources. In the USA, Mark Zuckerberg launched in April this year a lobbying group, FWD.us, to advocate immigration reform specifically to attract the talent necessary to support innovation through, for example, a simpler track for foreign science graduates to obtain residency and an increase in the quota for H-1B visas, the visa available to specialized temporary workers. The quota of 65,000 for H-1B visas was this year filled in five days in the USA. In 2007, Microsoft is reported to have opened a software development centre in Vancouver, Canada, to stow workers it was not yet able to bring to its Redmond headquarters. About half of science, technology, and engineering workers in Silicon Valley are foreign-born, compared to a quarter in the rest of the United States, according to the U.S. Bureau of Labor Statistics.

---

13. See, for example, "1.5 million signed a web petition calling on the European Parliament to reject ACTA" (http://www.nytimes.com/2012/02/06/technology/06iht-acta06.html) and "Global protests on February 11, 2012" (http://www.ibtimes.com/anti-acta-day-action-february-11-protest-details-where-when-how-join-worldwide-fight-407660.

14. John Gaudiosi, "Microsoft Xbox: The damage has been done—Anyone who questions the power of the crowd need only talk to Microsoft," *Fortune* Tech—Media Round-Up June 20, 2013, http://tech.fortune.cnn.com/2013/06/20/microsoft-xbox-the-damage-has-been-done/.

The darker side of this State-to-State competition is espionage (which, naturally, is also a feature of enterprise-to-enterprise competition). The intensity of the rhetoric on this subject has been rapidly escalating in the recent past. General Keith Alexander, Director of the National Security Agency and Commander of U.S. Cyber Command, called the loss of industrial information and intellectual property through cyber espionage "the greatest transfer of wealth in history." The Commission on the Theft of American Intellectual Property reported that "[t]he scale of international theft of American intellectual property . . . is unprecedented—hundreds of billions of dollars per year, on the order of the size of U.S. exports to Asia." The Commission's first recommendation was to "designate the national security advisor as the principal policy coordinator for all actions on the protection of American IP."

In the enterprise sector, IP similarly finds itself at the centre of competitive attention. As with State-to-State competition, there is a soft side and a hard side to this competition. The soft side is seen in the enhanced effort made by all firms to be innovative across all the stages of the conception, design, production and marketing of products and services and to protect through IP the advantage that their innovation confers. The hard side can be seen in sharp relief in the Smartphone patent wars. Here is an industry in which everything is wagered on innovation. Companies have been building patent arsenals to buy a stake at the table. Amongst the high-profile patent portfolio acquisitions in the past three years have been the acquisition by the so-called "Rockstar Group" (including Apple, Microsoft, Research in Motion and Sony) of the 6,000-patent portfolio of Nortel Networks for $4.5 billion; the acquisition by Google of Motorola Mobility, reportedly for its 17,000-patent portfolio, for $12.5 billion; the sale by Kodak of its digital imaging portfolio to a consortium of 12 licensees for $525 million; the sale by Microsoft of 650 patents to Facebook for $550 million; and the acquisition by Hewlett-Packard of 1,500 mobile technology patents from Palm for $1.2 billion.

There are multiple explanations for this behaviour. For the present purposes, I note just the focus of competitive behaviour sharpening on IP and that behaviour being frequently expressed through litigation. In the litigation wars, a terrorist has entered the ranks, effecting indiscriminate collateral damage. This is the patent troll, more politely known as a patent assertion entity (or a non-practicing entity). The problem, however, is that no one knows how to define this phenomenon and to say where the legitimate evolution of technology markets, with a wide and developing range of useful intermediaries, ends and where undesirable behaviour that puts innovation at risk commences. What we do know is that patent assertion entities share in common interest in the exclusion right that a patent confers and not in the underlying knowledge. We also know that the presence of such entities in the market is growing. Patent assertion entities filed 61% of new patent litigation in the USA in 2012. That translated into 3,054 patent infringement cases against 4,351 defendants. Some policy responses are now commencing in the USA, with the publication of the report *Patent Assertion and U.S. Innovation* by the Executive Office of the President of the USA.

## IP as the Mechanism for Finding Equilibrium among Competing Interests

I turn now to the second additional mission of IP. It is a function of the centrality of knowledge, creative works and entertainment in our economy and society and of the complexity of interests that result from that centrality. When King Diarmuid considered the issue that was brought before him, things were relatively simple—two disputants and a hand-produced bible. The ramifications of his decision were limited. It is true that, in a sense, they affected the whole monastic class, which constituted the literate class and the one responsible for most literary production. But the readership in the largely illiterate society of the time was small and the impact was local.

Compare this to a decision today on the legality of the settlement between publishers and Google over Google's plan to digitize all the books in the world, or a decision on the patentability of genetic information. There is a complexity that is born of the interconnectedness of societies and economies; the transparency, immediacy and universality that the Internet and technology has brought to the media and communications; and the central position of knowledge in the economy that requires us to consider IP differently. This complexity requires IP also to perform the function of finding the equilibrium point between the many and richly diverse interests that surround the acts of innovation and creation.

These interests include the interests of the individual innovator or creator, as against those of society in using the innovation or enjoying the experience of the creation; the interests of the producer, as against those of the consumer; the interests of encouraging investment in the production of new knowledge, as against those of sharing the social benefit of the new knowledge. A balancing act has to be performed in relation to the interests of all the individuals, enterprises, institutions, governments and the general public or civil society that coalesce around and claim a stake in an innovation or creation. In this world, where all those interests are capable of being expressed and communicated instantaneous around the world with the immediacy of the Internet or social media, it is increasingly anachronistic to consider IP as standing for one set of interests only. It provides the means to reconcile all those divergent interests and that is exactly what we are seeing with the vibrant public debate around IP.

In a sense, IP has always played this role.[24] The patent system is conceived as a bargain between the inventor and society, with society enticing the inventor to disclose the new invention in return for exclusive rights to commercial use for a limited period, beyond which the invention falls into the public domain and is available for use by all. But the new context requires the reconciliation of interests to be much more explicit and to be considered in relation to a range of issues and details at a much more granular level than that of the system itself.

### IP as a Financing Mechanism

I am tempted to add a third new role for IP, but I believe that it is more a new use of IP, rather than a mission statement. It arises from the increased appreciation and value of intangibles in the economy. The increased value of intangibles provides a means of leveraging or underwriting activities in the tangible economy that was not possible or, at least, not practiced, previously. Let me give you the example of sport. IP captures the commercial value of sport through the mechanisms of the spectacle and image or reputation.

Without a spectacle, there is no means of capturing anyone's attention. The spectacle provides the consumer experience. But the means of monetizing the spectacle is no longer through ticket sales. These can be important but are, perhaps, more important for creating the right atmosphere than for producing monetary returns. The real monetization of the spectacle is through broadcasting and the value of the broadcast depends on the capacity to

---

24. The opposition of interests and the implicit need to reconcile them is recognized in the two paragraphs of Article 27 of the Universal Declaration of Human Rights:

> "1. Everyone has the right freely to participate in the cultural life of the community, to enjoy the arts and to share in scientific advancement and its benefits.
>
> 2. Everyone has the right to the protection of the moral and material interests resulting from any scientific, literary or artistic production of which he is the author."

control access to it, for which IP is the gatekeeper. Thus, we find that 60% of the income of the International Olympic Committee comes from broadcasting rights that leverage a global audience and the advertising power that comes with such an audience. For the Beijing Olympics, it is estimated that $1.7 billion was paid by broadcasters for the exclusive rights to broadcast.

In addition to spectacle, there is image and reputation, which are captured by association with brands that, in turn, are protected by trademark law. Sporting teams now are sophisticated bearers of sandwich boards who also perform some ancillary form of sporting function. They are covered in marks and the revenue from the association with these marks provides, usually, the second major source of sport revenue after broadcasting rights. Roger Federer has won $77 million in prize money. But most of his money comes from sponsorships and endorsements. Last year he signed a five-year deal with Moët & Chandon for $30 million. It is reported that he also has deals with Rolex, Mercedes-Benz, Nike, Wilson, Lindt Chocolate, Jura, Gillette, Procter & Gamble, Credit Suisse and Netjets.

The analysis that I have given for sport could be equally applied to most forms of spectacles, including musical or theatrical performances or museum exhibitions.

The point is that IP provides a means of financing all these sporting and cultural manifestations in the tangible economy.

Having tried to describe the new role of IP, I would like to move to two final sets of considerations—what are the dominant themes and questions that are going to preoccupy us in the new world of IP, and how is this new context affecting the process of making policy for IP?

## Some Dominant Themes and Questions

I believe that there are three questions that are most likely to preoccupy us in the new context of IP. I shall call the first "entitlement." It relates to the function of IP as a regulator of competitive behaviour that I described above. The second and third questions relate to the function of IP as the keeper of the social and economic equilibrium in respect of the multiplicity of interests surrounding innovation or creation. I shall call them "appropriability" and "access." Each of these questions deserves a vastly more wide-ranging discussion than I am able to accord them here. I shall limit myself to sketching some highlights to provide an indication of why I believe that they are or will be the dominant questions in the new world of IP.

"Entitlement" is an age-old question. It is the question of the ownership of, or the right of control over, Finnian's illuminations. It is about who invented or created something first, what are the boundaries between legitimate inspiration from someone else's literary creation or design, on the one hand, and illicit imitation or slavish copying, on the other hand, and it has always animated the IP world. But it is likely to become even more animated, for three reasons.

The first reason is the enhanced values now involved as a consequence of the rise of the knowledge economy.

The second reason is the rise in importance of espionage and the illicit appropriation of trade secrets and confidential information. Technology has enabled espionage on a widespread basis in a way that was not possible previously. This development has coincided with the rise in value of the intangible assets that are the target of the espionage. At the same time, the movement of skilled persons from enterprise-to-enterprise on an international scale is now commonplace. This is not a form of espionage, but it does create a potential vulnerability for the knowledge assets of enterprises.

These developments underline the importance of that branch of IP that is the protection of confidential information or trade secrets. Worldwide it is in a poor condition. There is very little uniformity in approach, with the common law and the civil law traditions viewing the matter juridically in completely different ways. There are few multilateral provisions; those that exist are in the Paris Convention on the Protection of Industrial Property and the TRIPs Agreement. It is an area in great need of attention. But giving it multilateral attention will not be easy. It is a difficult sell to promote secrecy in an age of transparency. Even if this is an entirely superficial way of looking at the matter, this is the immediate reaction that one may expect and a great deal of care will need to be exercised in laying the basis for an international action.

The third reason for expecting greater animation over the question of entitlement is the silently growing tension between competition and cooperation. I have outlined the reasons why competition is heightening in the area of innovation and IP. At the same time, open innovation has become an increasingly important mode of behaviour in innovation. Open innovation may mean many things, but broadly it describes the tendency of a firm to look outside itself to partnerships and collaborations to satisfy its innovation needs, rather than relying on purely inside processes to generate innovation. As has been said, the advantages of cooperation are increasing. This tension between competition and cooperation is going to be a defining issue in the coming decades and IP will be the means of resolving the tension. This is why Samuel Palmisano, the former President and CEO of IBM, has said that "[i]ntellectual property will become one of the key geopolitical issues of the twenty-first century."

A second cluster of issues and questions will revolve around "appropriability," which is, of course, not a word. I use it to describe two things—whether something should be the subject of an IP right and whether something can be the subject of an IP right.

Whether something should be the subject of an IP right raises the question of what may be taken out of circulation and placed in the domain of private property. Theoretically, the position is clear. IP deals only with the new, the original and the distinctive. It only protects what did not previously exist and therefore does not involve any subtraction from the public domain. But in practice, the position is not so clear. The boundary between science and technology, or discovery and invention, is more and more difficult to draw, especially for lawyers, as the recent parliamentary and judicial attention given to gene patenting has shown.[30]

The question of what should be appropriated is not confined to scientific advances. It occurs equally with respect to the appropriation of words, signs and symbols through trademark law. Should colours be able to be the exclusive domain of one enterprise, for example?

A major challenge for IP here will be not to lose touch with the general public. As mentioned above, there is an increased social attention and focus on IP for a variety of reasons. If IP, whether through the legislature or the judiciary, takes decisions about appropriability that are not in consonance with the sentiment of the general public, it will lose the social credibility on which all good regulation depends.

Whether something is capable of being appropriated is an entirely different question that arises from the arrival of technologies of perfect and efficient imitation, notably the life sciences and digital technology. The problem that has emerged here is the disjunction between

30. See, e.g., IP Australia, Australian Government, *Patentable Subject Matter, Consultation on an Objects Clause and an Exclusion from Patentability* (July 2013); Centre for International Economics, *Economic Analysis of the Impact of Isolated Human Gene Patents: Final Report* (May 2013); Australian Government, *Response to Senate Community Affairs References Committee Gene Patents Report* (November 2011); Advisory Council on Intellectual Property, Australian Government, *Patentable Subject Matter, Final Report* (December 2010); Senate Standing Committee on Community Affairs, Parliament of Australia, *Inquiry into Gene Patents* (2010); Australian Law Reform Commission, *Genes and Ingenuity: Gene Patenting and Human Health, Report No 99* (2004); *Association for Molecular Pathology v Myriad Genetics Inc.*, 569 U.S. ___ (2013) (June 13, 2013); *Cancer Voices Australia v Myriad Genetics* [2013] FCA 65 (February 15, 2013).

the cost of production, on the one hand, and the cost of reproduction, on the other hand. In the case of a new pharmaceutical, the cost of production is estimated by industry to be in the vicinity of a billion dollars and to involve several years of work. Once available and disclosed, however, it can be reproduced by a competent graduate student in three months for a relatively meagre outlay. A new feature film may take two years to produce, involve several hundred persons and cost several hundred million dollars. But, once produced, it can be reproduced with perfect fidelity in a matter of seconds and for near zero cost. These developments are massive challenges for IP and, again, deserve much greater analysis than I am able to give them here.

The third issue that will occupy our attention in the new environment is access. As mentioned above, what IP does is to make access a saleable commodity. While this enables technology markets, it also creates social tension over the price of access and over the lack of access. We have seen this tension played out in relation to access to medicines and biomedical technologies, content on the Internet and climate change technologies, although the last area is more a theoretical debate than a full-scale political engagement that has seized the public's attention.

It is unlikely that the tension around access will subside. For policy-makers, the challenge will be to try to orchestrate an informed and reasonable public debate. For corporations, the challenge will be to balance being competitive and getting a financial return on investment, on the one hand, with management of a potentially hostile public response, on the other hand. There is a paradox at work here, of course. No one minds, it seems, someone making billions out of new social networking or media technology, but there is widespread social unease at someone making billions out of a new life-saving drug. Which outcome do we want to achieve in the innovation system?

## Policy-Making in the New Environment

Like the new context for IP, the environment for making policy for IP has changed considerably in the past two decades. The challenge before policy-makers is to produce answers as quickly as the speed of technological change is producing questions. There are very active IP policy agendas all over the world at all levels — national, bilateral, plurilateral, regional and multilateral. How do these all fit together?

It would be wonderful to say that there is a grand design. Regrettably, I think that reality is more opportunistic. We have moved from a multilateral world to a multispeed one. Given its competitive significance to the advanced economies, in particular, and given the social attention focussing on issues like appropriability and access, IP is pursued in every available arena by everyone who feels that they have a stake in it, which means governments, industry, the research community and all other concerned non-State actors. There are risks in this opportunism and I shall point to three.

The first is the maintenance of policy coherence in so many intersecting processes. Ideally, one level should fit into another like Russian dolls (with, presumably, the multilateral level being the biggest doll, not because it is the most important, but because all others should conform to it). What happens in practice is that there are, at any given moment, multiple processes taking place at multiple levels. There is a risk in this of the discussions in one process (for example, a plurilateral process like the Trans-Pacific Partnership talks) holding up discussions at another level (for example, the multilateral) because an issue is not ready for decision in the first process, while the second process is coming to a conclusion.

The second risk also arises from the complexity of managing policy processes occurring at multiple levels and involving so many diverse interests. This is the risk of non-delivery, with the consequences that policy is made by default by the private sector's actions and that the courts are called upon to make decisions that the legislature has not been able to make. The best example of this is the litigation in relation to the Google Books settlement, where a private law suit in the New York Southern District Court became the forum for international policy, with the sovereign States of France and Germany filing objections in an endeavour to preserve what they perceived to be the interests of internationally established principles.[32]

The final risk is that the capacity of the policy response is not equal to the size of the problem. We are seeing this happen in multilateral affairs more generally.

The capacity of the international community to reach agreement is limited, while the problems and challenges that confront the world are growing in dimension on a daily basis, with most of them, such as those arising out of the movement of persons, goods, arms, germs, pollution or cultural content, requiring international cooperation to provide an adequate policy response.

In WIPO, in the last two years, the Member States have bucked this trend by concluding two new treaties, the first, the Beijing Treaty,[33] directed at including actors and audiovisual performances within the international legal framework for copyright, and the second, the Marrakesh Treaty,[34] directed at improving access to published works for persons who are blind, visually impaired or otherwise print disabled. I believe that agreement was possible on these two treaties for a number of reasons,[35] but a prominent reason was that they dealt with specific and technical problems that were negotiated on their own merits and without making connections to interests in the wider IP or multilateral agenda. The new treaties constitute very welcome victories for actors, the visually impaired, IP, WIPO and multilateralism. But they also demonstrate that the road of adaptation of the IP policy to the new environment is a long one that needs to be constructed by a multiplicity of specific and technical solutions. At the back of our minds, however, we know that the world is moving very quickly and is, as it goes, throwing up major problems along the way that are going to require all the capacity that we are able to muster in order to provide solutions.

Here is the thought that I would like to leave you with. If you were in the 18th or the early 19th century, new wealth was being created, in new ways and on a rather massive scale, by physical capital and the process of industrialization. Industrialization spawned the great ideological debates and cleavages that shaped the world for the next 200 years—capitalism, Marxism, communism, socialism—and they all centered on property, the control of property and its use by the State and citizens. Now, in the early 21st century, new wealth is being created, in new ways and on a rather massive scale, by intellectual capital and virtualization. This is what we are seeing in what I have described—the contours of the new ideological battle lines that will shape our world for the foreseeable future.

## NOTES AND QUESTIONS

**1.** The potential of IP and intangible asset finance has gained ground in recent years. Estimates suggest that the global value of intangibles has increased tenfold over the last 25 years to reach approximately USD 74 trillion in 2021 (Brand Finance 2021, Global

32. *Authors Guild v Google*, No: 05 CV 8881, complaint filed on September 20, 2005, class action suit; and *McGraw-Hill et al v Google*, No: 05 CV 8136, complaint filed on October 19, 2005, civil action by five large publishers and the Association of American Publishers.

33. Beijing Treaty on Audiovisual Performances.

34. Marrakesh Treaty to Facilitate Access to Published Works for Persons who Are Blind, Visually Impaired or Otherwise Print Disabled.

35. For an analysis of the reasons, see my closing speech at the Marrakesh Diplomatic Conference, available at http://www.wipo.int/about-wipo/en/dgo/speeches/dg_dc2013_closing.html.

Intangible Finance Tracker—an annual review of the world's intangible value, https://brandirectory.com/reports/gift-2021). Further, small- and medium-sized enterprises (SMEs) make up around 90% of businesses worldwide – but they need access to capital to survive and scale. Without tangible assets, traditional financing may remain unattainable for many SMEs. WIPO launched an "Action Plan to move intangible asset finance from the margins to the mainstream" in 2022. The Action plan has three work streams: 1) raise the profile of intangible asset finance by, for example, convening a series of high-level conversations to raise awareness, and by establishing consultative groups; 2) reveal what is happening on the ground by developing country reports on IP-backed finance; and 3) equip participants in the finance and valuation ecosystems by building a toolkit to help borrowers and lenders. *See* the WIPO Intangible Asset Finance, Moving Intangible Asset Finance from the Margins to the Mainstream, https://www.wipo.int/edocs/mdocs/mdocs/en/wipo_hl_ip_ge_22/wipo_hl_ip_ge_22_disc.pdf.

## IX. INTELLECTUAL PROPERTY AND OTHER POLICY GOALS

Intellectual property rights form part of the larger body of economic law and of law in general, both domestically and in international relations. IPRs do not exist and stand in isolation. The discussion of the economics of intellectual property demonstrates a variety of policy goals pursued. They require coordination in law with other and related policy instruments and rules, ranging, *inter alia*, from international trade, competition, and investment to human rights and sustainable development. Much of the body of rules on intellectual property seeks to establish a proper balance between diverging and competing rules and interests: the limited scope of rights, the limited duration of rights, the proviso for exceptions, and so forth.

Yet, the balance within the system also has to take into account these extraneous but related policy concerns. The following excerpt expounds the interdependence of the law of intellectual property with other areas and the need to further embed intellectual property rights into the international legal order and to coordinate different components. The task still is at its infant stage and has become of increasing importance with increasing levels of protection due to preferential trade agreements in recent years.

**Thomas Cottier***

### *Embedding Intellectual Property in International Law*

. . .

#### IV. Human Rights

The fragmentation of public international law not only left trade outside of the core of public international law for decades, but also excluded closer interaction between trade and human rights. [See discussion in section IX.A, pp.172-184. —Eds.]

* In *Current Alliances in International Intellectual Property Lawmaking: The Emergence and Impact of Mega-Regionals* 15-44 (Pedro Roffe & Xavier Leuba eds., 2017) ICTSD-CEIPI, Global Perspectives and Challenges for the International Intellectual Property System, Issue Number 4 (footnotes omitted).

### A. Substantive and Procedural Standards

In interpreting and applying disciplines on IPRs in WTO law and preferential trade agreements, social and economic human rights will continue to be of paramount importance. Besides the right to health, the right to food and the right to life in general are of importance in assessing the scope and limitations of patents in pharmaceuticals, chemicals and foodstuffs. These rights may limit patent protection or undisclosed information, or copyright in view of the right to education and the right to information. They, however, may also foster protection to encourage research and development in genetic engineering, making available more efficient and drought resistant crops able to overcome hunger and malnutrition or disinformation in the internet age. The relationship of IPRs and human rights is not a one way street but must be considered case by case on the merits of the issue at hand.

Procedural human rights of due process, enshrined in Article 6 of the European Convention on Human Rights and other instruments are of importance in refining procedures granting patent, trademarks and design protection. They not only serve the protection of right holders, but also of competitors and consumers. Due process, and in particular the right to be heard of those affected, are important ingredients in refining procedures and securing that all sides have their day in court and are being heard. Finally, human rights are of importance in assessing unfair competition rules discussed above. Whether or not conduct of companies under CSR obligations is protected by freedom of speech, or whether it amounts to commercial speech subject to unfair competition, depends upon the interpretation of guarantees of freedom of speech and information enshrined in human rights instruments and constitutional law.

### B. Property and Human Rights

Embedding intellectual property also raises the question to what extent IPRs amount to human rights in their own rights. [See discussion in section IX.A following. — Eds.]

. . .

Importantly, in addressing such conflicts and tensions, human rights and property rights . . . are not on the same page and level. It is not simply a matter of balancing the two, but of adopting human rights as prime guidance in the process of shaping and applying intellectual property rights. Rather, in case of conflict and diverging interests, it is a matter of legal justification of intellectual property rights which restrict human rights, calling for appropriate legal foundations, compelling public interests and respect of proportionality. This essentially amounts to a constitutional approach, requiring adequate legal foundations, public interest and necessity (proportionality) of the regulation.

It is questionable whether the existing framework allows for sufficient flexibility to do so. Articles 7 and 8 of the TRIPs Agreement provide important doors of entry. However, the scope is limited as results must be compliant with the other provision of the TRIPs Agreement. General exceptions allowing recourse to public morals does not exist as in the field of trade in goods and services. As levels of protection increase, it is important to consider these elements in future treaty making and to provide for a clear basis which obliges legislators and adjudicators to consider human rights concerns in developing and assessing intellectual property standards and related procedures.

### C. The Missing Pieces

We shall briefly address below real property in the context of investment protection, the main purpose of which is to protect foreign direct investment in real estate, translating into activities of resource extractions, or building industries in the production of goods and services. Other than that, it is striking to observe that public international law hardly deals with real estate. Due to the principles of sovereignty over natural resources and territoriality, it is left to the nation state. It is not protected in binding universal human rights agreements. Regulations under the umbrella of international law range from capitalist to socialist, even communist models of ownership of means of production. Other than in the field of intellectual property, there are no transboundary transactions of real estate other than foreign direct investment.

At the same time, is should be recalled that the legal status of soil and real property plays an important role in international relations, ranging from fundamental geopolitical tensions to issues of social and economic development and thus efforts in private and official development assistance. Effort to enhance the livelihood of rural populations and local farmers cannot be detached from real estate law. The lack of land titles prevents farmers and indigenous people from defending their core interests in land use and management. It bars them from mortgaging real property and soil and thus impedes investment. Resources spent in ODA on rural development may fail due to lacking fundamentals which, however, cannot be addressed in terms of international law. No binding international rules exist on land registration and zoning, and efforts to support countries in that respect all depend upon domestic law and voluntary compliance with development programmes. Climate Change mitigation could be improved by binding land titles for indigenous peoples, beyond Art 26 of the 2007 UN Declaration on the Rights of Indigenous Peoples. Finally, from the point of view of sustainable development and international trade in agricultural products, soil quality and care are of utmost importance and an international concern. Countries depending upon food and feedstock imports have a stake and interest in sound soil management, preventing and remedying the deterioration of soil quality under principles of sustainable development. It is needless to emphasise that the issue is of particular importance in the age of climate change and the need to cope with climate change adaptation mainly affecting agricultural production.

International law has a long way to go in developing a human right to personally used property, both real and movable. The discrepancy to the level of intellectual property protection is striking. Developing appropriate tools of international disciplines on obligations at home, international cooperation and unilateral measures on soil and real property management under the emerging principle of common concern of humankind may also assist in addressing some of the imbalances which currently are unsuccessfully addressed in agricultural trade and intellectual property protection relating to genetic resources for food and agriculture, the protection of traditional knowledge and transfer of technology and know-how. We need to widen the option to avoid seeking property relating solutions exclusively by means of tools of intellectual property. Efforts should not merely focus on plant variety protection, farmers' rights and genetic resources in patent law, to GIs, labelling and trademark law and in the future to the protection of traditional knowledge. International law should also develop disciplines on land registration, sustainable soil management and the use of water resources in order to achieve an overall balance of interests at stake. Disciplines on virtual water in international trade will assist in implementing and enforcing such disciplines.

## V. Sustainable Development Goals

The 2015 Sustainable Development Goals, further developing the Millennium Development Goals enshrine the basic philosophy of balancing economic, social and ecological goals in different walks of life important to developing countries and society at large. To a large extent, the content of overlaps with social and economic human rights as enriched by environmental concerns not present when this generation of standards of justice and equity were drafted after World War II. The 2015 SDGs entail a wide field of human life and state ambitious goals:

> 1. No Poverty, 2. Zero Hunger, 3. Good Health and Well-being, 4. Quality Education, 5. Gender Equality, 6. Clean Water and Sanitation, 7. Affordable Clean Energy, 8. Decent Work and Economic Growth, 9. Industry, Innovation and Infrastructure, 10. Reduced Inequalities, 11 Sustainable Cities and Communities, 12. Responsible Consumption and Production, 13. Climate Action, 14. Life below Water, 15. Life and Land, 16. Peace Justice and Institutions, 17. Partnership for the Goals.

The difference to human right essentially is one of methodology and partly scope. While the implementation of political and civil rights mainly depends on courts, and social and economic rights primarily upon legislation and domestic programmes, sustainable development goals set out benchmarks and make available international tools allowing to measure and quantify progress made and identify shortcomings. SDGs not only are informed by efforts of civil society and non-governmental organizations supporting human rights and environmental goals, in particular mitigating climate change and adapting to climate change. They are essentially informed by working methods of the World Bank, UN Organizations and national development agencies funded by tax payers. From the point of view of international law, SDGs amount to soft law instruments which need to be taken into account in the interpretation of law. Compliance will depend upon specific programs and commitments made which may trigger legal obligations in good faith and the doctrine of estoppel. By and large, however, it will not be a matter of courts to secure implementation, but the political branches of government, national administrations and specialised international organizations.

Similar to human rights, SGD should be taken into account in shaping intellectual property and rights, in the process of interpretation and compliance. SDGs today provide the most important contemporary standards of justice and equity in international economic law. Again, Articles 7 and 8 of the TRIPs Agreement provide the basis to take SDGs into account. However, these provisions do not provide a basis to justify deviations from existing standards and rules, and the lack of general exceptions in the TRIPs Agreement may limit the possibility to effectively take into account SDGs. Agreement, to preferential trade agreements, amendments to the TRIPs Agreement, but also IPR Conventions should introduce appropriate foundations which allow taking into SDGs and human rights in specific regulatory areas. This is of importance in several areas relating to health, food and education and climate change. It goes beyond the scope of this paper to engage in a detailed analysis. It should be highlighted however that SDGs will be of utmost importance in developing new and effective disciplines on transfer of knowledge and technology on the basis of Articles 7 and 66(2) of the TRIPs Agreement in support of attaining the benchmarks defined by SDGs. Many of their goals cannot be achieved without enhancing the effort, and new tools need to be developed, such as tax incentives and framework rules of the operation of public private partnerships (PPP). Addressing intellectual property rights and PPPs has been one of the most difficult issues and has been left so far to a case-by-case approach, offering no transparency and sharing of mutual experience.

. . .

## VIII. Investment Protection

Intellectual property, for a long time, did not range prominently in international law of investment protection. Under customary law standards on compensation for lawful expropriation, it is unclear to what extent intellectual property forms part of protected property rights. In bilateral investment agreements, the issue is not dealt with uniformly. Some mention IPRs, some are silent and may or may not imply the inclusion of IPRs. For a long time, the issue was not addressed in private state arbitration. Recent developments clearly see the explicit inclusion of IPRs in investment protection, commensurate with the implied shift to investment protection in IPR standards discussed above. Contemporary issues relate to revocation of patents or strict limitations to trade mark protection in the health sector. The CETA agreement explicitly addresses intellectual property rights and renders them subject to fair and equitable treatment, regulatory taking and expropriation newly defined within the agreement. Moreover, these disciplines form part of the very same agreement which also contains rules on free trade and on intellectual property protection. The inclusiveness of all three areas raises interested issues of interaction. Should they be dealt with in isolation, or should the three components be applied and construed in combination, looking back and forth in the process of interpretation?

The CETA Agreement provides for a separate track in dispute settlement, and does not subject investment protection on IPRs to the dispute settlement system applicable to trade and IPRs protection. The remedies are different. While investment protection addresses financial compensation for past unlawful acts, WTO law (and RTAs) are forward looking and seek to adjust legislation and practices found to be incompatible with the treaty at hand. On substance, however, this does not exclude to take trade rules and IPRs standards into account in adjudicating issues of fair and equitable treatment or regulatory takings. For example in assessing restrictions the use of trademark rights by governments, Article 20 of TRIPs Agreement requires that the use of a trademark in the course of trade "shall not be unjustifiably encumbered by special requirements". This calls for taking into account standards developed on regulatory taking in investment protection. Vice-versa, assessing regulatory taking in investment protection arbitration requires taking into account Article 20 TRIPs. So far, this has not been the case in investment arbitration relating to plain packaging. It will be interesting to see to what extent WTO adjudication will establish the necessary bridges between trade and investment protection rules, also taking into account the increasing role of IPRs to foster and protect investment. Linkages to investment protection in this context are likely to enhance the level of protection of IPRs. This shift renders it necessary to also enhance the role and impact of non-trade concerns, in particular the consideration of human rights and sustainable development goals in the law of investment protection.

## IX. Progressive Regulation and Graduation of IPRs

Other than the rules on goods and services, which are subject to individual schedules defining market access rights, intellectual property rights establish standards and rules applying horizontally to all parties alike and Members alike, irrespective of levels of social and economic development and integration of a country in the world economy. True, the TRIPs Agreement in Part VI provides for a number of provisions on special and differential treatment for developing and least developing countries. Waivers exist in the field of patenting pharmaceutical and chemical products for least developing countries which have been extended. No such exceptions, however, exist in other core substantive and procedural obligations. The TRIPs agreement, for such reasons, has remained one of the most contentious agreements in the WTO, much more than the GATT and GATS Agreements or the plurilateral Government Procurement Agreement which countries are free to adhere to or to abstain from. Minimal TRIPs standards have a harmonizing effect. Moreover, TRIPs plus standards in preferential agreements apply across the board and increase levels of protection and requirements de facto for all countries alike. The agreement does not provide for progressive regulation and differentiated commitments.

The new Trade Facilitation Agreement, entered into force on 22 February 2017, provides for a number of options countries which may chose in taking commitments. While this approach leaves decisions on graduation to Members, another approach would trigger obligations within the agreement on the basis of economic thresholds and factors as defined ex ante. Other than under the TFA, Members would automatically graduate and incur obligations once these thresholds, for example on obligations to introduce patent protection for pharmaceuticals and chemicals, or an obligation to provide protection for integrated circuits, of geographical indications and designs are met. Art. 11 TRIPs Agreement provides a model to this effect. The introduction of protection of rentals, at the time (and no longer relevant due to information technology and online rentals) depended upon significant markets shares. It states: "A Member shall be excepted from this obligation in respect of cinematographic works unless such rental has led to the widespread copying of such works which is materially impairing the exclusive right or reproduction conferred in that Members on authors and their successors in title". The same idea can be found in Article 27(5) of the SCM Agreement which includes defined thresholds for specific countries. The provision states that "A developing country Member which has reached export competitiveness in any given product shall phase out its export subsidies for such product(s) over a period of two years". Annex VII of the Agreement defines the thresholds for Least Developed countries benefitting from a period of 8 years. It lists a number of countries and establishes a threshold of GDP $1000 per capita per annum.

This approach could also be developed and deployed in defining the kicking-in of specific provisions calling for the protection of intellectual property rights. It will be objected that negotiating such thresholds is complex. It is submitted that this in not more difficult than in other areas, such as agriculture. Progressive regulation in IPRs offers a predictable approach, for example in addressing the complex issue of pharmaceutical patents, while taking into account that primary needs of developing countries are not in the field of intellectual property rights and will be building up over time — not differently from the history of industrialised countries in the 19th and 20th Centuries.

## A. Intellectual Property and Human Rights

Worldwide attention to international human rights standards includes interest in whether — and the extent to which — the right to IPRs protection is part of the panoply of human rights that individuals enjoy. The protection of human creativity and the fruits of one's labor seem closely related to human rights concerns, and the question arises how the two fields are related. References to IPRs in human rights instruments are not extensive and, until recently, IPRs issues were rarely discussed by the human rights community. Efforts to bring about a better understanding of the relationship between human rights and intellectual property rights are currently underway. Also, it will be necessary to clarify their relationship to the principles set forth in Article 7 and 8 of the TRIPS Agreement. The following excerpt analyzes the relationship of intellectual property rights and human rights and elaborates on the nature of property rights as an institutional guarantee subject to powers of legislators and thus of change. The paper in particular addresses copyright, but the legal qualifications found of intellectual property also extend to other forms of protection. Today, human rights concerns are no longer limited to copyright and patent law, but may affect all areas of intellectual property protection.

**Thomas Cottier***

### *Copyright and the Human Right to Property: A European and International Law Approach*

#### I. Introduction

Ever since, International Law Courts have brought together different walks of life and different fields of law which, in domestic European jurisdictions, often are subject to specialised courts

* In Intellectual Property and the Judiciary (Christophe Geiger, Craig Nord & Xavier Seuba eds., 116-143, 2018); also in Thomas Cottier, *Copyright and Human Rights: The Impact of International and European Law*, 26 Annali Italiani di Diritto d'Autore, Della Cultura e Dello Spectacolo 518-537 (2017).

and separate silos and tracks of jurisprudence, with the exception of constitutional courts. This is particularly true for intellectual property, being exposed to disciplines of human rights before the European Court of Human Rights, or to disciplines of competition law and trade before the European Court of Justice, and more recently, also to international trade regulation before panels and the Appellate Body of the WTO. As both European and international law are not structurally organised along the division of private and public law, of commercial, competition and intellectual property law, they offer a timely laboratory with a view to interfacing different legal traditions and legal disciplines and to fully embed intellectual property law in European and international law. This in particular true for the relationship of copyright and human rights, a relationship of increasing importance in the digital age.

## II. Historical Background

Historically, monopoly rights granted for the purpose of printing precede the idea of human rights. . . .

## III. Legal Fragmentation

Throughout the 19th and early 20th Century, the evolution of copyright and human rights followed different and fragmented paths. A clear distinction between public law—to which fundamental and human rights pertained— and private law impeded integrated discussion in academia and the system of specialised courts in continental Europe. Intellectual property and copyright was adopted by, and assigned to, commercial law, and generally dealt with in common with corporate law, contracts and competition law. Human rights, on the other hand, became an almost exclusive prerogative of constitutional and international lawyers, developing their own methodology with a strong emphasis on case law, otherwise less prominent in continental European law. Private lawyers, for a long time, defended the view that human rights are limited to public law relations to the State and do not extend to horizontal among citizens and private operators. Matters relating to human rights and the protection of personality in copyright were dealt with by their own ways. The Italian initiative in the 1930s to include moral rights in the Berne Convention built on the traditions of personality protection in civil law. It was at a time when human rights in corporatist and fascist Europe were at a very dead end and could not be further apart.

In domestic law, legal cultures have largely remained fragmented until recent years. Commercial and private lawyers dealing with intellectual property as a matter of private rights would not connect to human rights primarily addressing government interventions and restrictions in the field of public law. Still today, and given the challenges of the digital age, copyright issues still are discussed by leading authors without strongly referencing constitutional law and the valuational impact of international human rights. Public lawyers, on the other hand, were not interested in IPRs and copyright as a matter of private law. Specialised associations, the structure of law faculties and specialisation of courts further impeded the interaction and cross-fertilization in Europe and beyond.

Bridging copyright and human rights only began after World War II, and is essentially due to international economic law and subsequently the process of European integration. In the last decade or so, scholars turned to exploring the relationship of international trade and human rights. They also began to analyse the relationship of human rights and intellectual property rights. The expansion of copyright to new areas of great economic importance following technological change and revolutions, in particular of electronic media (radio, television, internet) and the inclusion of computer programming to copyright protection in the TRIPs Agreement of the WTO brought about new transnational challenges and, eventually, the integration of copyright and economic law, in particular European community law and international economic law. Copyright (including related or neighbouring rights protecting performers) today forms an important part of international trade law. It is a key component of in global value chains together with other forms of protection, in particular patents, trade secrets and trademarks. Its disciplines are fully subject to WTO dispute settlement and legal enforcement by means of appropriate countermeasures, in particular additional surcharge tariffs and measures in case of failing compliance.

In Europe, the foundation of the European Economic Communities in 1957 with its four freedoms in goods, services, persons and capital and disciplines of competition law provided the groundwork for integrating copyright law in the process of integration. National territoriality of rights was overcome by means of disciplines of competition law and free movement of goods, inducing the doctrine of regional exhaustion. The early distinction between nationally defined property rights and the exercise of rights eventually made way to partial harmonization of rights in completing the common market. Eventually, shaping IPRs became a prerogative of the Union under Art. 18 TFEU. Today, it also forms part of the commercial policy under Article 207 TFEU. The Union is entitled to address IPRs and copyright in international agreements under sole powers. It no longer is a matter of shared competence required to be dealt with in mixed agreements. No longer is copyright dealt with in isolation, as a highly specialised subject matter, but dealt with in context of an overall legal framework, both in international and European law. While linkages to human rights still are embryonic in international economic law, they are strongly developing in European due recognition of unwritten fundamental rights by the European Court of Justice, inclusion on Articles 6 TEU and a binding Charter of Fundamental Rights of the European Union with the Lisbon Treaties of 2007.

## IV. The Recognition of Property Rights

This process and evolution also affected the relationship of copyright and human rights. It is essentially based upon the recognition of property as a fundamental right, entailing both tangible and intangible property. Different instruments vary. The United Nations law recognises the protection of material and moral interests resulting from scientific, literary and artistic works as addressed by copyright, it does not stipulate a proper guarantee of property rights, except for indigenous peoples protecting minorities. Binding rights to property exist in a regional context. In Europe, it is recognised by Protocol (1) of the European Convention for the Protection of Human Rights, in EU law and in particular the Charter of Fundamental Rights. In Africa, it forms part of the African Charter (Banjul) Charter of Human and Peoples' Rights. In international law, additional protection is granted by means of customary rules on investment protection and expropriation and bilateral investment protection agreement. While early texts do not explicitly include intellectual property, more recent instruments extend to intangible property rights. We briefly recall main human rights related texts.

### A. Treaty Texts

#### 1. United Nations

The Universal Declaration of Human Rights of December 10, 1948 enshrined protection of property and of intellectual property rights in Article 17(1):

1. Everyone has the right to own property alone as well as in association with others.
2. No one shall be arbitrarily deprived of his property.

Article 17(2) of the Declaration entails the protection of intellectual property:

> Everyone has the right to protection of moral and material interests resulting from any scientific, literary or artistic production of which he [or she] is the author.

While the Declaration expresses natural rights and has technically remained an instrument of soft law, the 1966 Covenant on Economic, Social and Cultural Rights embodies binding protection in Article 15 as a matter of progressive realization and implementation by law of development of science and culture.

The States Parties to the present Covenant recognize the right of everyone:

> . . .
>
> (c) To benefit from the production of the moral and material interests resulting from any scientific, literary and artistic production of which he [or she] is the author.
>
> 2. The steps to be taken by the States Parties to the present Covenant to achieve the full realization of this right shall include those necessary for the conservation, the development and diffusion of science and culture.

The 2007 Declaration on Rights of Indigenous Peoples provides the basis for future protection of traditional knowledge and traditional cultural expressions. It states in Article 31:

> 1. Indigenous peoples have the right to maintain, control, protect and develop their traditional cultural expressions, as well as the manifestations of their sciences, technologies and cultures, including human and genetic resources, seeds, medicines, knowledge of the properties of fauna and flora, oral traditions, literatures, designs, sports and traditional games and visual and performing arts. They also have the right to maintain, control, protect and develop their intellectual property over such cultural heritage, traditional knowledge, and traditional cultural expressions.
>
> 2. In conjunction with indigenous peoples, States shall take effective measures to recognise and protect the exercise of these rights.

### 2. Council of Europe

Due to the cold war, the UN Covenant does not entail a guarantee of private property rights. These are enshrined in regional instruments, in particular Protocol (1) to the European Convention on Human Rights.

> ARTICLE 1: PROTECTION OF PROPERTY
>
> Every natural or legal person is entitled to the peaceful enjoyment of his possessions. No one shall be deprived of his possessions except in the public interest and subject to the conditions provided for by law and by the general principles of international law.
>
> The preceding provisions shall not, however, in any way impair the right of a State to enforce such laws as it deems necessary to control the use of property in accordance with the general interest or to secure the payment of taxes or other contributions or penalties.

### 3. European Union

The Charter of Fundamental Rights of the European Union recognises intellectual property as a property in Article 17(2) and embeds protection in the overall protection of property rights by the legal order of the European Union:

> ARTICLE 16
>
> FREEDOM TO CONDUCT A BUSINESS
>
> The freedom to conduct a business in accordance with Community law and national laws and practices is recognised.

Article 17

Right to property

1. Everyone has the right to own, use, dispose of and bequeath his or her lawfully acquired possessions. No one may be deprived of his or her possessions, except in the public interest and in the cases and under the conditions provided for by law, subject to fair compensation being paid in good time for their loss. The use of property may be regulated by law in so far as is necessary for the general interest.

2. Intellectual property shall be protected.

### 4. African Union

Article 21 of the African Charter (Banjul) Charter of Human and Peoples' Rights entails protection of property (with a strong focus on natural resources): It does not specifically address intellectual property:

1. All peoples shall freely dispose of their wealth and natural resources. This right shall be exercised in the exclusive interest of the people. In no case shall a people be deprived of it.

2. In case of spoliation the dispossessed people shall have the right to the lawful recovery of its property as well as to an adequate compensation.

## B. Recognition in Case Law

In assessing the relationship of IPRs, copyright in particular, and human rights, legal guarantees of property rights are of utmost importance. Intellectual property being a form of property next to tangible, movable or immovable property, copyright benefits from guarantees of property protection in international and European human rights law.

Courts have recognised that intellectual property is protected by constitutional or international law guarantees of property rights. The former European Human Rights Commission recognised in 1990 in *Smith Kline v. the Netherlands* that a compulsory license of a patent granted by the Netherlands in order to allow the working of a dependent patent is subject to Protocol (1) of the Convention.[15] It was held to be justified under the exceptions allowing restricting private property rights. In *Anheuser Busch Inc. v. Portugal*, the Court in 2007 recognised a pending trade mark application as a matter pertaining to the Protocol (1) and thus protection under the Convention.[16] Property protection thus not only extends to established titles, but also to legitimate expectations in obtaining such titles. It thus can also benefit from the procedural guarantees of due process in Article 6 of the Convention.

There is no doubt that intellectual property and copyright today pertain to the property protection; the same holds true also for the European Union and the Court of Justice. Following the early recognition of unwritten property rights with a view to protect the primacy of Community law, these guarantees today are also extended to intellectual property and explicitly recognised in Article 17(2) of the Charter on Fundamental Rights. In *Promusica v. Téléphonica de España*, the Court clearly stated that the "fundamental right to property, which includes intellectual property rights such as copyright and the fundamental right to effective judicial protection constitute general principles of Community

15. ECommHR, *Smith Kline and French Laboratories Ldt v. the Netherlands*, No 12633/87, Commission decision of 4 October 1990.

16. ECtHR, *Anheuser Busch Inc. v Portugal* [GC] no 73040/0111 January 2007, ECJR 2007 I.

law."[17] Copyright protection as property right under EU law was confirmed in subsequent case law.[18]

The extension of property protection to IPRs finally can be observed in recent treaty practice in dispute settlement based upon bilateral investment protection agreements. Cases relating to restrictions on the use of trademarks for reasons of protecting public health (plain packaging of cigarettes) are assessed under the BITs.[19] The same applies to recent trade agreements. The Comprehensive Economic and Trade Agreement between the European Union and Canada explicitly includes intellectual property rights in investment protection[20], but also safeguards IP-related restrictions from performance requirements and compensation,[21] following the experience made in the *Lilly* case when denial of patent protection was challenged under the provisions of the North American Free Trade Agreement.[22]

## V. The Legal Nature of Property Rights

Given the protection of IPRs under the European Convention on Human Rights and the Charter on Fundamental Rights as well as the Art 15 of the Covenant on Economic, Social and Cultural Rights, further supported by the Universal Declaration of Human Rights, it has been argued that intellectual property and copy right in particular amount to human rights' guarantees on their own right. It provides the basis for the school of thought which assigns IPRs to the field of fundamental human rights, resulting thus in strong levels of protection which is essentially binding on legislators and subject to strict legal disciplines in restricting such rights, as generally applied for the restrictions of human rights. Courts thus would be obliged to strictly observe the rule of law, compelling public and respect of proportionality, all subject to full judicial review by constitutional and human rights courts. This perception implies that property rights are similar to human rights and enjoy the same level and intensity of protection.

Courts, however, throughout centuries, have dealt with property rights in a particular manner. Other than human rights, derived from natural law, property of land, assets and capital is assessed in terms of an institutional guarantee. Protection only exists to the extent that the legal order provides a system of property rights in positive law, either case law or statutory law or in a combination of both. In the words of David Hume, they are conventional

17. ECJ, Case C-275/06, *Productores de Música de Espanã (Promusicae) v. Telefónia de España SAU* [2008], Judgment of the Court (Grand Chamber) of 29 January 2008, ECR I-00271 (no obligation of internet provider to disclose identity of infringer in EU law).

18. CJEU, C-70/10, *Scarlet Extended NV v. Belgische Vereneging vn Auteurs, Componisten en Uitgevers, CVBA (SABAM)* [2011], Judgement of the Court (Third Chamber) of 24 November 2011, ECR I-1959; and CJEU, Case C-360/10, *Belgische Vereneging vn Auteurs, Componisten en Uitgevers, CVBA (SABAM) v. Netlog NV*, Judgement of the Court (Third Chamber) EU:C:2012:85 (MS must respect prohibition of general monitoring by IPS (E-Commerce Directive 2000/31 and of IP enforcement directive 2004/48: Filtering amounts to general monitoring prohibited).

19. *Philip Morris Asia Limited v. The Commonwealth of Australia, UNCITRAL*, PCA Case No. 2012-12; https://www.italaw.com/cases/851 (visited June 24, 2017); *Philip Morris Brands Sàrl, Philip Morris Products S.A. and Abal Hermanos S.A. v. Oriental Republic of Uruguay*, ICSID Case No. ARB/10/7 (formerly *FTR Holding SA, Philip Morris Products S.A. and Abal Hermanos S.A. v. Oriental Republic of Uruguay*); https://www.italaw.com/cases/460 (visited June 24, 2017).

20. Comprehensive Economic and Trade Agreement between Canada and the European Union, adopted February 15, 2017 by the European Parliament (not yet in force), Art. 8.1; http://ec.europa.eu/trade/policy/in-focus/ceta/ceta-chapter-by-chapter/ (visited June 24, 2017).

21. *Id.* Chapter 8.14(4); Chapter 13.10(6), Annex 8-D concerning Chapter 8.12(6).

22. *Eli Lilly and Company v. The Government of Canada*, UNCITRAL, ICSID Case No. UNCT/14/2; https://www.italaw.com/cases/1625 (visited June 24, 2017).

in nature.[23] Legislators and courts shape the property system in accordance with utilitarian concepts. This is true both for tangible and intangible property. Property law seeks to maximise welfare for the general public and society at large, rather than focussing on individual rights essentially protecting human dignity of the individual persons and right-holders. *Donaldson v. Beckett* laid such foundations in 1774 for intellectual property protection prior to the human rights movement. Ever since this case, as Peukert notes, "it has been widely accepted in both common law and civil law jurisdictions that copyrights, patents and other IP rights only exist under the statutes as 'creatures' of the legislature. For this reason, they are universally considered 'territorial in nature', bound to the territory of the public authority that granted them."

With a few exceptions invoking natural law, this approach has been consolidated over time by the main constitutional courts upon the establishment of human rights guarantees in domestic and international law.[24] Property is defined by legislation and subject to it; there is no predefined notion of property as a matter of natural law, except for personal items upon which we depend. Rather it is shaped in accordance with societal needs and changing with technological evolution. This also fits essential characteristics of intellectual property rights beyond territoriality: the limitation in time of copyright and patents. Or, the need to renew titles of protection periodically in trade mark law is incompatible with perceptions of pre-statal, natural law based human rights. The extension of patents and copyright to companies as main stakeholders in the system faces the problem that human rights—beyond procedural guarantees of due process and the right to do business—do not unequivocally pertain to juridical persons and large multinational companies in particular. Finally, the possibility to create new titles of protection such as related rights, GIs, integrated circuits, or the protection of undisclosed information and test data shows that the system is shaped and defined by legislation, practice, and precedents in the wake of social and economic change. It even could be abolished should it no longer serve welfare goals intended and pursued. At any rate, key issues, in particular the scope of rights, are constantly changing in light of technological advances and change.

### A. European Court on Human Rights

The structural difference of property rights explains why the European Court on Human Rights has treated alleged violations of intellectual property rights with considerable deference, even in cases affecting due process in the context of Article 6 ECHR. It exercises strong deferential standards towards domestic law and measures enforcing IPRs, including high fines.[25] This somewhat contrasts with rulings on unlawful blocking of Internet access as a violation of freedom of expression where copyright issues were not involved.[26]

23. David Hume, A Treatise on Human Rights (1739); see Online Library of Liberty, David Hume on Property as a convention which gradually emerges from society, http://oll.libertyfund.org/quotes/546 (accessed March 1, 2017).

24. Bundesverfassungsgericht Case 1 BvL 19/76 12 June 1979, BVerfG 52, 1 (Kleingarten); Bundesverfassungsgericht Case 1 BvR 987/58, 14 November 1962, BVerfG 15, 126 (Staatsbankrott); the same can be observed in the United States: *Golan v. Holder*, 132 S. Ct 873 (2012); *Eldred v. Ashcroft*, 537 U.S. 186 (2003) (Property is defined by legislation and subject to it; there is no predefined notion of property).

25. *See ECtHR, Dima v. Romania*, no 58472/00 (no copyright protection for created state emblems upheld); ECtHR, *Balan v. Moldova*, no 19247/03 (29 January 2008) (unreported) (no copyright for photos taken for official purposes upheld; *ECtHR, Ashby Donald and others v. France*, no 36769/08, 10 January 2013 (unreported) (restriction of freedom of press upheld and high penalities); *ECtHR Frederik Neij and Sunde Kolmisoppi v. Sweden*, no 40397/12, 19 February 2013 (free downloads protected by freedom of expression, but restrictions justified by copyright law, high penalties upheld).

26. *ECtHR, Ahmet Yildirim v Turkey*, no 3111/10, 18 December 2012, Reports of Judgments and Decisions 2012 (blocking of internet by Turkey incompatible with freedom of expression and information).

### B. Court of Justice of the European Union

The Court of Justice of the European Union takes a somewhat different approach due to a different perspective. The Court is mainly called upon to assess potential violations of secondary law in the field of intellectual property rights. In applying and interpreting IPR rules, the Court is obliged to take into account human rights enshrined in the Charter on Fundamental Rights. Human rights are introduced to balance interests and rights and are taken into account. In doing so, the Court seems to accept IPRs and human rights as on par and of similar standing and value. The case law is fact intensive, and consideration of human rights and balancing does not follow a particular methodology. *GS Media v. Sanoma Media*, discussed at the outset, reflects a constant pattern of the Court dedicated to balancing different interests at stake.[27] It remains unclear whether this implies an implicit recognition of property as a human right on par with other rights, in particular freedom of information and expression. At any rate, the approach differs from courts having property or human rights violations as their starting point, typical for constitutional courts and the European Court on Human Rights discussed above. The Charter on Fundamental Rights is not yet its starting point, but offers additional considerations which need to be taken into account in construing secondary legislation of the Union.,,,.

### C. Panels and the Appellate Body of the WTO

Again, the approach is yet a different one in WTO law. Panels and the Appellate Body are limited to assessing complaints relating to violation of WTO law. It is impossible to bring a complaint—other than before the European Court on Human Rights and the European Court of Justice, which are based upon the violation of human rights. Panels and the Appellate Body so far have not directly dealt with the relationship of human rights and intellectual property, and copyright and related rights in particular. A panel was called upon to assess fair use exemptions in copyright law, applying the three-step test for excessive restrictions on copyright and related rights imposed in restaurants and shopping malls.[28] The case indirectly relates to cultural rights of Irish musicians and freedom of information. Another panel addressed unlawful exclusions of prohibited works from copyright protection and allegedly insufficient enforcement of intellectual property rights in China.[29] The case indirectly touches upon freedom of information, securing that all works, independent of content, benefit from copyright protection. Connotations to the right to health exist in patent law and access to essential drugs. They are likely to be discussed in impending litigation on plain packaging relating to trademark law.

---

27. CJEU, C-314-12, *UPC Telekabel Wien GmbH v. Constantin Film Verleih GmbH, Wege Filmproduktionsgesellschaft mbH* [2014] Judgment of Court (Fourth Chamber) of 27 March 2014, EU:2014:192 (stresses freedom of expression in the Internet; injunctions taken on the basis of the Information Society Directive 2001/29 Art 8(3) must take human rights into account); CJEU, Case C 201/13 *Deckmyn and Vriheidsfonds VZW v. Vandersteen (. . .) and WPG Uitgevers België* [2014] Judgement of the Court (Grand Chamber) of 2 September 2014, EU:C:2014:2132 (Freedom of expression to be taken into account in assessing fair use exemptions leading to broad concept of parody); CJEU, Case C-117/13 *Technische Universität Darmstadt v. Eugen Ulmer KG* [2014], Judgement of the Court (Fourth Chamber) of 11 September 2014, EU:C:2014:2196 (publishers cannot restrict access to works under Art 5(3)(n) of the Information Society Directive 2001/29 and bar public libraries for the purpose of research and private study undertaken by individuals); CJEU, Case C 34/10, *Brüstle v. Greenpeace*, Judgement of the Court (Grand Chamber) of 18 October 2011 (importance to take human dignity into account in patent law).

28. United States – Section 110(5) of the US Copyright Act (WT/DS160, June 15, 2000).

29. China – Measures Affecting the Protection and Enforcement of Intellectual Property Rights (WT/DS/362/R, January 26, 2009).

One case, however, is of particular importance in the present context. In *China – Audiovisual Services*, the panel and the Appellate Body were called upon to assess the compatibility of Chinese law restricting copyright protection for censured works. Moreover, they were asked to assess whether the modalities of censorship exercised by state trading import monopolies controlled by the government are compatible with WTO law.[30] The panel and the Appellate Body found that censorship cannot exempt works from copyright protection. States, however, are free to operate censorship resulting in import restrictions, provided import restrictions are justified under Article XX GATT and the right to protect public morals. In this case, it was held for the first time that respondent does not meet the necessity test, and that less intrusive alternate ways and methods to exercise censorship are readily available. Censorship by state-trading companies is unlawful. If a state operates censorship, it must be operated by public authorities. Dispensing companies from such tasks render import monopolies unnecessary, and market access for foreign companies selling and import audio-visual goods and services, no longer must be denied.

It is important to note that neither the Parties, nor the Panel and the Appellate Body invoked human rights of freedom of information and expression, or cultural rights of citizens by denying access to certain foreign works. Yet, the need to transfer censorship operations to government authority inherently increases transparency and also open determinations to judicial review both mandatory under Article X GATT and the Protocol of Accession of the People's Republic of China. Indirectly, the ruling supports and protects human rights concern of unduly restricting freedom of information and expression.

The panel and the Appellate Body could have taken these rights into account under Article 31(3)(c) of the Vienna Convention on the Law of Treaties, in the process of applying and interpreting pertinent rules of the WTO, in particular the TRIPs Agreement and GATT 1994. While scholars have called for considering human rights in such a manner, Parties to the WTO, panels, and the Appellate Body so far have refrained from doing so. However, given the extensive experience of linking trade and environmental concerns, it is a matter of time until human rights will be introduced in litigation. Freedom of expression, in this particular case, could have a bearing on interpreting the notion of public morals in international law. It could have assisted in gradually improving freedom of information in China which, in my view, is an important ingredient of a market economy. Without freedom of information, markets cannot properly work.

**Laurence R. Helfer***

## *Toward a Human Rights Framework for Intellectual Property*

### Conclusion

The creation of a human rights framework for intellectual property is still in an early stage of development. During this gestational period, government officials, international jurists, NGOs, and commentators — many of whom have divergent views concerning the appropriate relationship between human rights and intellectual property — have a window of opportunity to influence the framework's substantive content and the procedural rules that mediate

30. *China – Measures Affecting Trading Rights and Distribution Services for Certain Publications and Audiovisual Entertainment Products* (WT/DS363/AB/R, Dec. 21, 2009).

* 40 U.C. Davis L. Rev. 971 (2007).

relationships among its component parts. In this conclusion, I briefly sketch three hypothetical futures for the framework and explain why each of these predictions is both plausible and likely to be contested by states and non-state actors.

### A. Using Human Rights to Expand Intellectual Property

One possible future relationship between human rights and intellectual property is an expansion of intellectual property protection standards at the expense of other human rights and the interests of licensees, users, and consumers. In this vision of the future (a dystopian one, to be sure), industries and interest groups that rely upon intellectual property for their economic well-being would invoke the authors' rights and property rights provisions in human rights treaties to further augment existing standards of protection. The fear of such expansions helps to explain why some commentators are skeptical of attempts to analyze intellectual property issues in human rights terms.

. . .

### B. Using Human Rights To Impose External Limits on Intellectual Property

Patent, trademark, and copyright owners who invoke the property rights and authors' rights provisions of human rights law to demand additional legal protections will likely face stiff resistance from user groups. These groups can draw upon other fundamental rights and freedoms to press for a competing version of the framework, one that relies on human rights law to restrict intellectual property. National courts in Europe are using the right to freedom of expression protected by the European Convention for precisely this purpose. "In particular, there have been a number of decisions in the field of copyright in which the freedom of expression has been invoked to justify a use that is not covered by an exception provided for in the law." These decisions rely on human rights law to overcome the "malfunctions" of the intellectual property system, using them as a "corrective when [intellectual property] rights are used excessively and contrary to their functions." In effect, these cases reach beyond intellectual property's own safety valves—such as fair use, fair dealing, and other exceptions and limitations—to impose external limits, or maximum standards of protection, upon rights holders.

. . .

### C. Achieving Human Rights Ends Through Intellectual Property means

The two future frameworks described above share a common strategy. They each take the existing baseline of intellectual property protection as a given and then invoke human rights law to bolster arguments for moving that baseline in one direction or the other.

A third human rights framework for intellectual property proceeds from a very different premise. It first specifies the minimum outcomes—in terms of health, poverty, education, and so forth—that human rights law requires of states. The framework next works backwards to identify different mechanisms available to states to achieve those outcomes. Intellectual property plays only a secondary role in this version of the framework. Where intellectual property laws help to achieve human rights outcomes, governments should embrace it. Where it hinders those outcomes, its rules should be modified (but not necessarily restricted, as I indicate below). But the focus remains on the minimum levels of human well-being that states must provide, using either appropriate intellectual property rules or other means.

A 2001 report by the U.N. High Commissioner for Human Rights analyzing the impact of TRIPS on the right to health exemplifies this outcome-focused, inductive approach. The report reviews the components of the right to health protected by article 12 of the ICESCR. According to a general comment issued by the CESCR Committee, the right to health includes an obligation for states to promote medical research and to provide access to affordable treatments, including essential drugs.

The High Commissioner's report analyzes how intellectual property affects these two obligations. It acknowledges that patents help governments promote medical research by providing an incentive to invent new medical technologies, including new drugs. But the report also asserts that pharmaceutical companies' "commercial motivation . . . means that research is directed, first and foremost, towards 'profitable' disease. Diseases that predominantly affect people in poorer countries . . . remain relatively under-researched." One way to remedy this market imperfection is to create incentives for innovation outside of the patent system.

A similar perspective informs the High Commissioner's discussion of access to essential medicines. The report states that patent protection decreases the affordability of drugs. But affordability also depends on factors unrelated to intellectual property, "such as the level of import duties, taxes, and local market approval costs." In light of these dual impediments, governments can improve access to patented pharmaceuticals in two ways. First, they can exploit the flexibilities already embedded in TRIPS, such as issuing compulsory licenses to manufacturers of generic drugs and importing cheaper drugs from other countries. Second, they can adopt affordability enhancing mechanisms outside of the intellectual property system, for example through differential pricing, "the exchange of price information, price competition and price negotiation with public procurement and insurance schemes." Strikingly, the efficacy of these mechanisms may require augmenting existing intellectual property protection rules, such as negotiating "drug licensing agreements with geographical restrictions[,] . . . so that cheaper drugs do not leak back to wealthier markets." It is too early to predict which of these three versions of the human rights framework for intellectual property, or others yet to be identified, will emerge as dominant. What is certain is that the rules, institutions, and discourse of international human rights are now increasingly relevant to intellectual property law and policy and that the two fields, once isolated from each other, are becoming ever more intertwined.

## NOTES AND QUESTIONS

**1.** Scholarly attention has increasingly turned to the relationship between the norm-system regulating international economic activity on one hand, and the norm-system regulating human rights, on the other. Two compilations that address this relationship in some detail are International Trade and Human Rights: Foundations and Conceptual Issues (F. Abbott, C. Breining-Kaufmann & T. Cottier eds., 2006), and Human Rights and International Trade (T. Cottier, J. Pauwelyn & E. Bürgi eds., 2006). IPRs are an important subset of the more general relationship between economic regulation and human rights. Several chapters of these books address IPRs and include references to the work of UN human rights organs on this subject.

**2.** Is the WTO Ministerial Conference, or are trade-negotiating rounds, suited to addressing human rights interests, particularly in light of the reciprocity-based character of the negotiations? Consider, for example, whether it is appropriate for Country *A* to exchange a concession on the terms of patent protection for pharmaceuticals with a concession by Country *B* to allow market access for textile products. Does the fact that higher pharmaceutical prices and limited access will result in a deterioration of public health conditions in Country *A* factor into these negotiations? How does the fact that improved market access for textiles may offset the price increase for pharmaceuticals affect this equation?

**3.** What is the relationship of the principles expounded in Article 7 and Article 8 of the TRIPS Agreement to the protection of human rights? Do these principles offer a door of entry for human rights consideration within the WTO and the TRIPS Agreement?

**4.** Does a multinational corporation have human rights? If an individual inventor has a human right to enjoy the fruits of his or her creative work, does that extend to the individual inventor's corporate patent assignee?

**5.** Additional references regarding the relationship between human rights and IPRs relevant to public health can be found in two biennial Reports of the Global Health Law Committee of the International Law Association, prepared in connection with the Johannesburg and Sydney Biennial Conferences.[151]

## B. Intellectual Property and Sustainable Development

With general objectives in Articles 7 and 8 of the TRIPS Agreement and human rights closely interacting with intellectual property rights, broad and somewhat elusive ideas of justice are equally important in shaping the international IPRs system. All laws and regulations, whatever the field, are grounded in (often unspoken) concepts and precepts of justice and equity. IPRs regimes evolved on the basis of utilitarian concepts, and justice was seen in furthering the common good by honoring investment and creativity.

Technological advances throughout the last century were facilitated by the emerging international IPRs system. Yet, to what extent did the system also contribute to the depletion of natural resources and to endangering the global environment and commons? Since adoption of the Stockholm principles in 1972, and the principles of the Rio Declaration in 1992, attention has been directed to the goals of sustainable development, and what the idea of intergenerational equity means to the international IPRs system. How should these concepts and principles affect the evolution of the IPRs system? How do they affect the field of biotechnology? It is important to observe in connection with sources of international law that the international IPRs system cannot be considered in isolation. It has to be responsive to prevailing concepts of justice. It has to adapt to the emerging aspirational norms of international law.

In a comparable manner to the relationship of intellectual property and human rights, the relationship of intellectual property and the principles of sustainable development in environmental law and policies of social and economic development amounts to a new issue that was also brought about by the process of globalization of lawmaking in the two fields. The 1992 Rio Summit on Sustainable Development, of Agenda 21, and foremost, the Convention on Biological Diversity (CBD), which was adopted at this time and which entered into force on December 29, 1993, evidenced the growing importance of the interconnection between the fields. Negotiations leading to the CBD were in the closing days of the negotiations of the TRIPS Agreement. Protection required for the plant varieties in the TRIPS Agreement was considered to be detrimental for the advancement of important goals of the CBD, in particular benefit sharing and access to technology. Intellectual property was also considered to be detrimental to achieving the protection of traditional knowledge of indigenous peoples and rural populations at large. Indeed, patenting genetically modified organisms that are based upon non-protectable traditional varieties or landraces risks creating a serious and inequitable balance. Moreover, it was felt that IPRs would seriously hamper the free flow of genetic material stored in gene banks, and this concern largely stimulated the efforts to bring about the new International Treaty on Plant Genetic Resources for Food and Agriculture adopted by the FAO Conference in 2001.

151. Int'l Law Ass'n, Glob. Health Law Comm., *First Report of the Committee* (2016); Int'l Law Ass'n, Glob. Health Law Comm., *Second Report of the Committee* (2018).

We should ask in a broader context: What is the relevance of patent or trademark laws for the creation and promotion of environmentally friendly products? Does sustainable development call for a "greening" of intellectual property? What, beyond the areas of traditional knowledge and genetic engineering, could be pertinent issues relating to other forms of IPR? What could and should be the impact of environmental law on the interpretation of intellectual property? Again, it is difficult to discuss these matters on a highly abstract level. It takes a particular context to advance insights and arguments.

The United Nations Framework Convention on Climate Change negotiations have included substantial attention to issues regarding technology transfer and the role that IP may play in facilitating or hindering the development and implementation of alternative energy resources and climate change adaptation and mitigation technologies, with a particular focus on developing countries.[152] Virtually all countries of the world are parties to the CBD, with the notable exception of the United States, which has signed but not ratified the agreement. One of the main reasons given by the United States for refusing to ratify the agreement is concern about the way in which provisions regarding intellectual property rights will be implemented. The TRIPS Agreement and the CBD were concluded at roughly the same time. Ever since, questions have been raised as to whether the two agreements are compatible. The following excerpt considers the objectives of the two agreements and how those objectives are sought to be accomplished.

**Frederick M. Abbott***

## *Preservation and Use of Genetic Resource Assets and the International Patent System*

Study for the Ministry of Foreign Affairs of Norway Draft of March 31, 2005 Hong Kong Ministerial Revision

. . . In 1992 the Convention on Biological Diversity (CBD) was adopted at the Rio Conference.[1] In 1994 the Agreement on Trade-Related Aspects of Intellectual Property Rights (TRIPS Agreement) was adopted in Marrakech.[2] From the outset, questions were raised as to whether there are conflicts or potential conflicts between the objectives and rules of these two international undertakings. These questions have been on the agenda of the WTO TRIPS Council and the Committee on Trade and Environment, they have been raised in the context of work programs and negotiations at the World Intellectual Property Organization (WIPO), they have been considered by the Conference of the Parties of the CBD, and they are the subject of numerous studies and reports by governments, intergovernmental and non-governmental organizations. This study attempts to clarify the issues at stake in analysis of the relationship between the TRIPS Agreement, related international patent system rules and the

152. *See* Wei Zhuang, Intellectual Property Rights and Climate Change: Interpreting the TRIPS Agreement for Environmentally Sound Technologies (2017).

* Full text available at http://papers.ssrn.com/sol3/papers.cfm?abstract_id=1924481.

1. Convention on Biological Diversity (CBD), adopted June 5, 1992, available at https://www.cbd.int/convention/text. As of March 26, 2005, there are 188 state parties to the CBD. The United States signed the CBD on June 4, 1993, but has not ratified the Convention. *See generally* Françoise Burhenne-Guilmin & Susan Casey-Lefkowitz, *The Convention on Biological Diversity: A Hard Won Global Achievement*, 3 (1992) YbIEL 43 (1993), and Edith Brown Weiss, *Introductory Note, United Nations Conference on Environment and Development*, 31 I.L.M. 814 (1992) (and agreement texts following, including Convention on Biological Diversity at 31 I.L.M. 818 (1992)).

2. Agreement Establishing the World Trade Organization, adopted April 15, 1994, available at http://www.wto.org/english/docs_e/legal_e/04-wto_e.htm. As of February 26, 2005, there are 148 Members of the WTO.

CBD. It examines the conflicts or potential conflicts between the objectives and rules of these international undertakings, and it makes certain recommendations regarding the promotion of complementarity among these systems. . . .

## III. The Goals of the Convention on Biological Diversity and Related Treaties Governing Genetic Resources

### *A. Preservation of Genetic Resource Stocks*

The first objective of the CBD is preservation of the diversity of genetic resources found in nature, including in animals and plants.[23] There are various reasons for promoting such preservation, including to allow continuity in the natural evolution of species (including adaptation to new environmental conditions), for use in research and development as a source of primary material for direct and recombinant use (taking advantage of natural development and adaptation of biological systems), and maintaining the quality of life from the presence of a diverse biological environment.

Determining the "economic value" of genetic resource stocks is a problematic exercise because it involves anticipating what technological capacities will evolve to exploit such resources, as well as what technological capacities will evolve as alternatives to the exploitation of genetic resources. The world community remains at early stages in assessing the economic value of genetic resource stocks and strong assumptions concerning their future value should be avoided. Anecdotal references to a comparatively small number of "biopiracy" cases are not a proper framework for evaluating the economic value of genetic resource stocks. The economic value of genetic resources may remain stable, or increase or decrease dramatically in the future. Notwithstanding caveats regarding indeterminacy in valuing genetic resources, there is a reasonable likelihood that such resources are of "material" value.

Developing countries are the preponderant owners of diverse genetic resources.[25] The special interest of the international community in encouraging development suggests that a presumption in favor of recognizing rights in genetic resources on the part of developing countries is appropriate. In other words, to the extent that developing countries are able to effectively exploit economic interests in genetic resources it is in the interests of the wider international community to support this.

### B. Recognizing Ownership and Control

#### 1. CBD-Based Rules

The second objective of the CBD is to recognize state ownership and control over genetic resources located within territorial boundaries. This basic objective has at least two grounds: first, to provide an economic incentive to countries for preserving genetic resources by assuring compensation for their use, and; second, to enhance economic welfare in countries that house existing stocks of genetic resources by assuring compensation for genetic assets.

These objectives are implemented by (i) broadly recognizing sovereignty over genetic resources,[26] (ii) requiring prior informed consent (PIC) of the host country as a condition of

23. *See, e.g.*, Secretariat of Convention on Biological Diversity, Sustaining Life on Earth, April 2000 ("CBD Secretariat Summary").

25. *See* FIC-Economic Development and Biodiversity, Table-Economic Development and Biodiversity, available at http://www.environment.gov.au/biodiversity/conservation/hotspots.

26. The CBD provides:

Article 15. Access to Genetic Resources

1. Recognizing the sovereign rights of States over their natural resources, the authority to determine access to genetic resources rests with the national governments and is subject to national legislation.

access to genetic resources,[27] and (iii) providing for the equitable sharing of benefits from the exploitation of such resources.[28]

Methods for implementation of PIC and equitable benefit sharing are elaborated in the Bonn Guidelines on Access to Genetic Resources and Fair and Equitable Sharing of the Benefits Arising Out of Their Utilization.

The CBD is implemented in national and regional legislation in various ways. Explicit legislation has been adopted by the Andean Community, Brazil, Costa Rica and India, among other countries. In addition, a number of countries through regulatory guidance offer some form of protection for genetic resources.

### 2. Public International Law

Because some countries are not parties to the CBD, and particularly from an economic standpoint the United States which has signed but not ratified the agreement, it is important to clarify that the principle of sovereignty of states over resources located within their territory did not arise in the CBD but was only codified in that agreement. The United States has in multilateral fora acknowledged its acceptance of this principle.[31] Therefore, to the extent that the rules of the international patent system are reviewed for promoting compliance with the objective of national sovereignty over genetic resource stocks, the review is not directed only to countries that are party to the CBD.

## IV. Complementarity and Potential Conflicts in Implementation of the CBD with the TRIPS Agreement and WIPO Conventions

### A. Complementarity and Its Limits

In adopting the CBD and in development of public international law states have decided that ownership and control over genetic resources is vested in the territory where those resources are located.[32] The CBD is intended to protect rights in genetic resources and promote the equitable sharing of benefits from the exploitation of such resources. The patent is an instrument that provides legal protection for intangible interests in inventive activity. It facilitates

---

27. The CBD provides:

Article 15. Access to Genetic Resources

5. Access to genetic resources shall be subject to prior informed consent of the Contracting Party providing such resources, unless otherwise determined by that Party.

28. The CBD provides:

Article 15. Access to Genetic Resources

7. Each Contracting Party shall take legislative, administrative or policy measures, as appropriate, and in accordance with Articles 16 and 19 and, where necessary, through the financial mechanism established by Articles 20 and 21 with the aim of sharing in a fair and equitable way the results of research and development and the benefits arising from the commercial and other utilization of genetic resources with the Contracting Party providing such resources. Such sharing shall be upon mutually agreed terms.

31. *See, e.g.*, Communication from the United States, Views of the United States on the Relationship between the Convention on Biological Diversity and the TRIPS Agreement dated 24 April 2001, IP/C/W/257, 13 June 2001 (implicitly acknowledging right of state to control access to genetic resources). *See also* U.S. statements in WIPO Intergovernmental Committee on Intellectual Property and Genetic Resources, Traditional Knowledge and Folklore.

32. An argument may be made in favor of treating genetic resources as the "common heritage of mankind" over which no state or person exercises ownership or control. Since the parties to the CBD have rejected that premise, this study does not analyze whether a regime based on common heritage may be preferable.

the commercialization of such interests. At a fundamental level the objectives of the CBD and international patent system are complementary. The international patent system should facilitate the objectives of the CBD by allowing states to legally protect their recognized interests in genetic resources, including inventions derived from genetic resources, including through commercialization.

However, to recognize that rule systems are conceptually complementary does not mean that they are properly aligned so as to achieve that complementarity. For example, if the international patent system as currently implemented facilitates circumvention of the CBD by allowing patent applicants to secure patents based on incomplete or misleading information, this may undermine the objectives of the CBD. Similarly, if the CBD is implemented in a way which adds an unnecessary level of insecurity to patent rights, this may undermine the commercial value of patents and incentives for the development of new products. The CBD and the international patent system have not been subject to "conscious alignment" and that is the reason for the present international dialogue.

The protection of genetic resource stocks presupposes the capacity of countries to enforce the sovereign right of ownership and control recognized by the CBD. The CBD adopts PIC and equitable benefit sharing as the mechanism for protecting and exploiting ownership interests. The commercial exploitation of genetic resources may (but does not necessarily) entail securing patent protection. With respect to patents, options for enforcing CBD-based rules include providing evidence of compliance with the requirements of that agreement as a condition of patentability.

## NOTES AND QUESTIONS

**1.** In the Doha Ministerial Declaration,[153] the TRIPS Council was instructed "to examine, *inter alia*, the relationship between the TRIPS Agreement and the Convention on Biological Diversity, the protection of traditional knowledge and folklore, and other relevant new developments raised by Members pursuant to Article 71.1."[154] At the Hong Kong Ministerial Conference, the WTO Director-General was directed to intensify consultations on this subject, among others. The General Council would "review progress and take any appropriate action no later than 31 July 2006."[155] Proposals by WTO Members to further the objectives of the CBD by mandating disclosure of the source and origin of genetic resources in patent applications, as well as by requiring evidence of compliance with prior informed consent (PIC) and equitable benefit sharing (EBS) requirements, remain controversial. The positions of WTO Members fall roughly into three categories:

a. A substantial group of developing countries argues that mandatory disclosure of source and origin is necessary to assure that patent examiners take into account information relevant to assessment of patentability (including novelty and inventive step), as well as in making determinations of inventorship. Evidence of compliance with PIC and EBS is argued to assure consistent implementation of TRIPS Agreement and CBD requirements. The penalty for failure to comply with mandatory disclosure and evidence requirements may include patent forfeiture.

b. A second group of countries sees merit in the proposal to impose a requirement to disclose the source and origin of genetic resources, but expresses concern with the potential remedy of patent forfeiture. Alternative remedies are suggested to include the civil assessment of

153. This note is adapted from the 2006 and 2010 Reports of the Committee on International Trade Law to the International Law Association.

154. Adopted 14 Nov. 2001, WT/MIN(01)/DEC/1 (20 Nov. 2001), at para. 19.

155. WT/MIN(05)/DEC (18 Dec. 2005), at para. 39.

compensation (e.g., royalties). Concern is also expressed with the potential bureaucratic complexities involved in evidencing compliance with PIC and EBS.

c. A third group of countries considers that complementarity between the TRIPS Agreement and CBD can be adequately addressed through contractual arrangements between countries housing genetic resource stocks and bio-prospecting enterprises and argues against the imposition of a mandatory disclosure and/or evidence requirement. This group argues that the source and origin of genetic resources are not relevant to determinations of patentability or inventorship, and that disclosure and/or evidence requirements would be unduly burdensome and create harmful uncertainty regarding the enforceability of patents.

d. Since the Hong Kong Ministerial, the Director-General of the WTO has convened a series of consultations with interested Members further to a request made there. The results of those consultations were reported by the Director-General at the Geneva March 2010 stocktaking of the Doha Round. He reported only that "while my consultations have not created convergence they have certainly shed clearer light on the divergences."[156] Although the constellation of Members supporting one or another position may have shifted over the past two years, there has been (as per the report of the Director-General) no material progress toward substantive agreement.

There does not appear to be much progress towards agreement. On April 21, 2011, the Director-General circulated a six-page report on his consultations:

"He concluded that members' views continue to diverge on both issues but that discussions underscore the benefits of understanding more fully how countries' own intellectual property systems work—the scope of protection for geographical indications in practice in various countries, and the 'practical and operational context' of the existing patent mechanisms for disclosing the origins of genetic material and any associated traditional knowledge used in inventions."

India has recently tried to revive the subject of TRIPS Agreement rules regarding source and origin of genetic resources. At the conclusion of the Buenos Aires Ministerial Conference in December 2017, WT/MIN(17)/57 entitled "Work programme on the relationship between TRIPS and the Convention on Biological Diversity (CBD)" was circulated. An International Conference on the TRIPS CBD Linkage was held in Geneva from June 7-8, 2018, although not under WTO auspices.

e. Progress, however, was achieved in addressing fair and equitable sharing of benefits under the Nagoya Protocol on Access to Genetic Resources and the Fair and Equitable Sharing of Benefits Arising from Their Utilization to the Convention on Biological Diversity, adopted October 29, 2010, and opened for signature. The Protocol entered into force on October 12, 2014. As of July 2018, 105 countries are party to the Protocol, with 107 ratifications and 92 signatures. The Protocol sets forth mechanisms to bring about fair and equitable benefit sharing with holders of traditional knowledge. It provides for clearing house mechanisms and funding, but does not address or alter intellectual property rights per se. In recognizing traditional knowledge, the Protocol will be of importance in further developing *sui generis* rights on plant genetic resources. As an illustration, the Protocol has been used as the backdrop to WIPO's intergovernmental Committee on Intellectual Property and Genetic Resources, Traditional Knowledge and Folklore (IGC) and the IGC's efforts in creating a legally binding instrument centered on genetic resources. IGC met for its 36th session from June 25-29, 2018. As a result of the session's discussions, a second revision (Rev2) of the original Consolidated Document Relating to Intellectual Property and Genetic Resource was created. Rev2 reflected a tentative consensus in several areas: the scope of the instrument's subject matter, disclosure requirements, and due

156. WTO, *Trade Negotiations Committee, Lamy Opens Stocktaking Week with Hope for Strong Signal on Concluding the Round*, 22 March 2010, available at http://www.wto.org/english/news_e/news10_e/tnc_dg_stat_22mar10_e.htm.

diligence. The debate surrounding the scope of the instrument's subject matter is particularly relevant to the Protocol. Some developing countries protested that the obligations under the Protocol required any potential instrument to incorporate IP rights beyond patents (e.g., plant variety protection), in contrast to developed countries' demands that the instrument exclusively address patents. Rev2 provided a package deal compromise by restricting the focus of the potential instrument to patents, but with the promise to review the instrument within four years of its enactment and to discuss expanding its scope to include other IP rights. Additionally, the discussions surrounding due diligence included reference to the Protocol by recommending any due diligence mechanisms conform with existing international obligations like the Protocol. Despite the session's progress, the United States, backed by Japan, prevented Rev2 from being formally recommended for the next IGC session, based largely on U.S. concern that such concessions will undermine the patent system. Rev2 was instead placed in the annex of the session's final decision document. Nonetheless, the session reflected positive movement in the development of *sui generis* rights on genetic resources and could further the IGC's efforts to garner consensus on the issues by fall 2019.[157]

**2.** As will be discussed further in Chapter 5, concerns regarding effective implementation of the goals of the Convention on Biological Diversity through disclosure of source and origin of genetic resources are proposed to be addressed in a WIPO International Legal Instrument Relating to Intellectual Property, Genetic Resources and Traditional Knowledge Associated with Genetic Resources. A Diplomatic Conference is proposed to be convened in 2024 following further sessions of meetings of the Inter-Governmental Committee (IGC) and the Preparatory Committee in September 2023. There is a Chair's draft of the proposed Instrument. The various documents are available at: https://www.wipo.int/diplomatic-conferences/en/genetic-resources/index.html#:~:text=On%20July%2021%2C%202022%2C%20the,Resources%20no%20later%20than%202024. This initiative bears the prospect of resolving the issues discussed at the WTO, but the extent of support for the diplomatic initiative among the various interested stakeholders is uncertain.

**3.** In the course of addressing climate change mitigation and climate change adaption, particular attention has been paid to the relevance of intellectual property rights. *See* UNEP, EPO, ICTSD, *Patents and Clean Energy: Bridging the Gap Between Evidence and Policy* (2010). The question arises as to whether combating climate change requires substantial changes in intellectual property protection in order to meet the challenges. While patents are of great importance in developing green technologies, main regulatory efforts need to address transfer of technology between developed and developing countries. The Clean Development Mechanism (CDM) within the Kyoto Protocol of the UN Framework Convention on Climate Change offers the potential to enhance transfer of climate change-related technology in coming years. As of August 2023, the CDM has registered approximately 8, 000 projects in 111 countries.[158] Participating countries have earned 2,337,571,050 certified emission reductions (CERs) issued for CDM project activities, which amounts to 2.3 billon tons of carbon reduced or avoided. The CDM's methods for reducing greenhouse emissions have largely

---

157. *See* Catherine Saez, *WIPO IP And Genetic Resources Committee Makes Progress Despite Block At End*, IP-Watch, July 2, 2018, http://www.ip-watch.org.proxy.lib.fsu.edu/2018/07/02/wipo-ip-genetic-resources-committee-makes-progress-despite-block-end/; *see also* Catherine Saez, *Disclosure, Sanctions – Still To Be Overcome In WIPO Genetic Resources Negotiations*, IP-Watch, June 28, 2018, http://www.ip-watch.org.proxy.lib.fsu.edu/2018/06/28/disclosure-sanctions-still-overcome-wipo-genetic-resources-negotiations/; Catherine Saez, *WIPO Genetic Resources Expert Group Ponders Disclosure Requirement, Databases*, IP-Watch, June 27, 2018, http://www.ip-watch.org.proxy.lib.fsu.edu/2018/06/27/wipo-genetic-resources-expert-group-ponders-disclosure-requirement-databases/.

158. Meeting report, CDM Executive Board 118th meeting, CDM-EB118, May 30-31, 2023, https://cdm.unfccc.int/UserManagement/FileStorage/AJ60BYNQOG159IM4KPEFXZV8T2SDW3.

been viewed as a success. Efforts to improve the CDM's methods now focus on integration with the recent Paris Climate Change Agreement.[159]

## C. Intellectual Property and Equality

At the very end of Chapter 1, we finally raise the question of the potential role of intellectual property in growing disparities of income and wealth distribution, within society, and among countries. The question informs much of the policy debate in the field, in particular between industrialized and developing countries. Intangible property possibly contributes to inequality, but causality is difficult to assess as inequality is due to a multitude of factors which cannot be isolated. The following excerpts discuss possible implications of equity as a legal methodology and focuses on the relationship of innovation and creative imitation, recognizing the latter as an important driver of development and contributing to decreasing inequality. A better balance between the two can be found by conceptualizing intellectual property as a means to stimulate and protect human investment. Exclusive rights and protection should be limited to appropriate returns and reasonable profits.

**Thomas Cottier***

### *Inequality and Intellectual Property: Equity, Innovation and Creative Imitation*

#### I. Introduction

. . .

Property and property rights are a major factor in income and wealth distribution. Most of it traditionally relates to movable capital (shares, assets and savings) and real estate. Between 1970 and 2016, the share of private capital significantly increased in industrialised countries at the expense of capital publicly owned. The role of intellectual property is more difficult to assess. In the same period, the value of intangible property surpassed the value of tangible property and became essential for global value chains. The number of registered titles constantly increased. While numbers are not conclusive for the value of such titles and thus wealth, the importance and impact of intellectual property clearly increased in the process of globalization. In the political and ideological debate, it is generally assumed that higher levels of protection increase income and wealth inequality. The view has fueled long standing resistance to effective protection prior to the TRIPS Agreement. It informs much of the debate on TRIPS-plus standards in bilateral and plurilateral cooperation agreements. Upon expounding in detail recent developments in international intellectual property treaty making, Carlos Correa assumes that they contribute to inequality: "IP provisions contained in FTAs are likely to aggravate current inequalities among and within countries, particularly low- and middle-income countries." The argument is supported by the general importance of property for income and wealth allocation. The more it is concentrated, the greater inequality between different percentiles of society. Yet, there are no econometric studies or models available showing that intellectual property protection conclusively causes, or contributed

159. *CDM Can Inspire, Inform, Outfit Any New Mechanism under Paris Agreement,* UN Framework Convention on Climate Change, May 3, 2018), https://unfccc.int/news/cdm-can-inspire-inform-outfit-any-new-mechanism-under-paris-agreement.

* Intellectual Property, Innovation, and Global Inequality, Cambridge University Press, Intellectual Property and Information Law series, eds. D. Benoliel, F. Gurry, K. Lee & P. Yu (forthcoming 2024).

to, international and domestic income and wealth inequality. Capital shares increased due to increased investment in intangible assets in companies' expenditure. According to Carsten Fink, one possible explanation is the effect on reduced competition due to concentration which may be caused, inter alia, by intellectual property rights, generating economic rents. Causality, however, is difficult to demonstrate, and a counterfactual under non-existing intellectual property protection does not exist. Even the impact of increased levels of protection is difficult to assess. Conclusions may be drawn from findings of increased concentration in IP-related industries and their push for high levels of protection, but there are many factors contributing to this effect. It is difficult to isolate the impact of intellectual property rights.

Given the empirical uncertainty of the impact of intellectual property on increasing income and wealth inequality internationally and domestically, this paper addresses the issue from the angle of law and legal methodology. Piketty, while an economist, stresses in his recent work the importance, in result, of constitutionalism and the importance of notions of property and thus of law for the allocation of income and wealth. Much depends upon the shape of the legal order and the directions it takes. The scope of intellectual property rights is critical, as well as the importance of competition and the avoidance of undeserved economic rents. Clearly, government policy and thus the law cannot possibly support such rents as they are not in the public interest and do not foster general welfare.

. . .

## II. The Impact of Intellectual Property Protection

. . .

The problem no longer is whether there should be protection or not, but how much, and at what levels. The devil is in the details in defining appropriate levels of commitment in international law and appropriate space for policies which may be affected by intellectual property protection and enforcement, such as health, education or culture. Article 7 and 8 of the TRIPS Agreement are of basic importance in expressing an appropriate balance. The commitment to transfer of technology and benefits to right holders and users and the reservation of essential policy interests, including competition policy, informs the interpretation of intellectual property rights and their scope, albeit these commitments are subject to the detailed provisions of the agreement and thus of limited practical effect.

Ever since the TRIPS Agreement was adopted, there is a basic consensus that intellectual property is a necessary component of domestic and international trade. All countries alike share an interest in protection trademarks and related forms of protection. All countries share an interest in protecting copyright and patents but vary on the proper scope of protection. Voices arguing that TRIPS does not belong to the WTO since the agreement juxtapose free trade by creating monopoly rights are largely a matter of the past. Both, the absence of protection and excessive protection of IPRs cause restrictions and distortions to trade. The debate today is much more about the adequacy of TRIPs-plus standards in bilateral and plurilateral agreements. While some of these provisions necessarily fill lacunae of the TRIPS Agreement (such as test data), others reflect predominant economic interests undermining the overall balance and putting the authority of intellectual property protection and enforcement of standards at risk. Foremost, these additional standards mainly reflect interests of industrialized countries and fail taking into account the interest of developing countries with much larger rural areas and thus an interest to protection traditional knowledge, grass root innovation and geographical indications. Overall, we assume the following effects.

Enhanced levels of IP protection certainly secure income in operating global value chains, but it also enables such chains and dislocation from which millions of workers have benefitted, albeit often under dire conditions. These in return triggered the effort to improve corporate social responsibility and corporate transparency and liability of multinational corporations. Trade volumes increased, and inequalities of income on national levels was reduced in the process of globalization between nations. Much of these effects are due to the rise of China, while other countries benefitted much less or even lost trading shares and income. Moreover, these results do not tell about domestic distributive effects which strongly depend upon constitutional and political arrangements and power relations.

Property protection, in a domestic context, raises fundamental questions of income and wealth distribution. Private property rights were the main target of communism which led to expropriation, state capitalism and power concentration, predominant today in China. Intellectual property was a non-issue in these systems and only become relevant with the turn to allowing and developing product markets under State capitalism. In the West and in market economies, it would seem that intellectual property in general offers and important foundation for competing industries, many of which are small and medium sized companies. The same holds true for the cultural and communication sector. They depend upon patent, copyright and trademark protection under price competition. Intellectual property thus is an instrument of horizontal balancing and power sharing. This does not exclude strong differences among sectors and depending upon the size of corporations. Many of the richest companies of the World depend upon intellectual property protection.

While intellectual property partly provides the foundation of legal protection of such wealth, income distribution would seem to be equally, if not predominantly, determined in the end by competition and fiscal and monetary policies. Taxation of intellectual property rights and licenses forms an important part of corporate tax, and the recent introduction of patent boxes significantly reduced tax burdens in a competitive environment. Exchange rates deploy an important effect on trade flows of IP protected goods and services. Much therefore depends upon the interaction with other policy areas and the ability to harness excessive accumulation of wealth due to intellectual property protection. It is a matter of achieving an overall fair balance between property rights and the interests of users of information. In doing so, it is important not to consider intellectual property in isolation, but in combination with other parts of international law, in particular trading rules, human rights and competition policy. If properly embedded in international and domestic law, excessive imbalances in wealth and income distribution can be avoided and properly harnessed by recourse to such policies and related rules. But all of this does not exempt us from revisiting existing intellectual property protection. The question is to what extent potential effects of unequal distribution can be potentially mitigated within the IP system itself. . . .

## IV. Innovation and Creative Imitation

Perhaps the most important issue, in the present context, is a discussion of innovation and imitation in shaping intellectual property law. It is a key to achieving an overall fair balance within legal system and thus potentially contributes to lessening inequality of income and wealth.

### A. The Conceptual Neglect of Creative Imitation

The focus and raison d'être of intellectual property very much been on innovation and the promotion and protection of it. In conventional thought, it is at the centre and heart of the field, in particular in patent law and copyright. Although other functions are being served, in particular product identification and consumer protection in trademarks and geographical indications, or the protection of existing information in the protection of trade secrets or data collections, innovation amounts to the main motivation and justification of granting exclusive monopoly rights. Imitation, on the other hand, is not equally recognised as a part of the equation. It is prohibited as counterfeiting and piracy and may in law amount to unfair competition. The scope for creative and lawful imitation indirectly enters through the door of defining the scope of rights, the duration of rights, in defining exceptions and finds expression in the goal of dissemination technology to the benefit of right holder and users expressed in Article 7 of the TRIPS Agreement. But there is no formal place for it in the legal system driving economic evolution. Creative imitation rather is a fact and tolerated to the extent that legal provisions allow for freedom to reproduce and imitate. The scope of creative imitation is defined by what is left to the information market, by what government intervention to correct market failures does not, or no longer, assigns to exclusivity. Imitation lawfully takes place to the extent that information is in the public domain and has become a public good. Imitation, in other words, takes place by default, to the extent that information is not protected by private intellectual property rights. Creative imitation is not a recognized goal or feature of the intellectual property system itself. It does not have a place of its own in the canon of values, but is rather looked upon with suspicion, like a grey area. We do not know a natural right to creative imitation. Developing countries took the matter up indirectly, first by refusing to renegotiate the Paris and Berne Conventions, and subsequent to the TRIPS Agreement by stressing the need for domestic policy space. TRIPS-plus developments discussed above reduce further reduce such policy space and thus reduce the potential for creative imitation. This in return may possibly contribute to inequality of income and wealth distribution by further reinforcing private property rights and concentration of economic power.

Upon reflection, the conceptual lack of recognition of creative imitation and the reduction to toleration within the overall system is somewhat astonishing. Much of our life is based upon imitation out of which new ideas, features and things evolve. Education and schooling of children and students are built upon it. We mainly learn by imitating. The acquisition of social skills and interaction is learned from looking at the behaviour and conduct of others. Societies require a large amount of imitation, repetition and reproduction in daily life in order to properly work and function. It is, in many respects, a prerequisite of innovation. Without imitation, innovation cannot occur.

These facts are also indirectly reflected in the evolution of nations in terms of social and economic development. The Netherlands or Switzerland, today's champions of strong intellectual property protection, strongly depended in the 19th Century upon imitation and were reluctant to adopt protection mainly of imported products. The evolution of the Berne and Paris Conventions of 1883 and 1886 was based upon national legislation and a set of bilateral agreements imposed by then dominating economies, in particular France and Germany, with a view to include neighbouring jurisdictions on equal terms of protection and conditions of competition. Japan strongly depended upon imitation after World War II and rose in reproducing western inventions at higher and better quality, for example cameras, TV sets and recording equipment. China followed suit and much of the present trade war with the United States in rooted in this stage of social and economic development. The claim of insufficient enforcement and even of "theft" of intellectual property within and by companies controlled by the state is mainly related to the phasing of economic and social development at a juncture where Chinese technology strongly competes with Western technology. Much of this "theft" is based upon agreed contractual arrangements of value chains and is lawful, while only espionage of trade secrets hold by unrelated companies clearly is illegal. The same holds true for developing countries in general, albeit the impact of imitation has been less felt on international markets and thus allows for what was called above the philosophy of benign neglect. And the same holds true domestically. Start-ups and new ventures depend upon ample space for creative imitation which may be curbed by existing monopoly rights. Many of the tensions arise because the relationship of creative innovation and creative imitation has not been properly addressed in intellectual property law and the legal order at large. It is submitted that both innovation and creative imitation should be recognised, and the case for exclusive rights fostering innovation needs particular attention and justification. It is submitted that focussing on incentives for investment plays a crucial role in balancing the two.

### B. Focusing on Investment

One way to approach and reconsider the equation is to put less emphasis on innovation, but to focus on stimulating and rewarding investment. The very reason to grant monopoly and exclusive rights on information is to foster and honor investment in creating such information, even though it may not always be original and new. The latter holds true for the fields of intellectual property which rely on product distinction (trademarks and GIs) or the protection of existing information (undisclosed information, data collections in particular big data) or the protection of traditional knowledge. Protection of trademarks and GIs, from an economic point of view, does not exhaust in product distinction, but also entails massive investment and advertising and promotion of such products. Protection of data collections, in particular Big Data and Traditional Knowledge, primarily protects the investment made in collecting, cultivating, arranging and using pre-existing information. So far, investment and investment protection has provided the foundation of sui generis data protection beyond copyright in EU law. It has not yet been recognized in law as general underpinning and justification of traditional intellectual property rights.

If we look at investment and what is needed to stimulate new information, creative imitation can be recognized next to innovation on equal footing. We recognize a right to creative imitation and leave a concept behind which treats creative imitation merely as an exception to innovation, but balance the two on par in defining the scope of protection, legal and compulsory licensing, and the duration of rights. It will remain necessary to draw a line between lawful and unlawful imitation for reasons of legal and business security. However, the overall equation may change upon the recognition of creative imitation as a proper goal of the overall system of fostering investment in the creation of new information and applications. It offers a check on monopoly rights. Conceptually, it will put an end to pressing for ever increasing levels of protection of innovation without due regard to the implications for creative imitation in the process of social and economic development, domestically and internationally. We argue below that the creation of exclusive rights warrants special justification and reasoning that market conditions and government funding in supporting innovation is not sufficient and intellectual property rights a necessity.

#### 1. Investment in Information as a Public Good

Human investment in capital, natural resources, time and human resources serves the production of goods and services. It serves the needs of society at large, also by shaping general framework conditions, including statehood and the legal order, the economy, culture and other fields of human life. The investment is based upon existing information and knowledge. We reiterate that people build upon experience. Much of it is dedicated to reproduction of existing goods and services essential in daily life. Out of this, incremental innovation and change result new ideas and new information, contributing to evolution. New information created falls into the public domain and is treated as a public good. Everybody can use it, and such use does not diminish the information. It is submitted to that reproduction and incremental creation of information is the normal state of play in human investment. It takes place under the umbrella of the general legal order an under policies of open source access. In market economies the framework is defined by the law of contracts, torts, fair competition and conduct prohibited by penal law. Or, it is supported by government policies, in particular education and research funding. The risks involved in such investments are reasonable as they deal with known information and experience. They take place in corresponding information markets.

### 2. Investment in Information as a Private Good and Property

Beyond the normal course of action of reproduction, imitation and incremental innovation in society, deliberate efforts at innovation are made in the process of human investment. They venture into new territory, based upon existing information. These efforts are financially risky as they cannot rely upon existing patterns and needs. Research and development beyond incremental change thus calls for a particular legal framework. For the private sector, this is where intellectual property protection enters the stage. Exclusive rights are necessary and granted to incentivize the production of products and ideas and to secure a fair return on the investment without which the effort would not be made in the first place by private operators. For the public sector, funding by the tax payer or charities of basic research, but also applied R&D, parallels the intellectual property system. Sometimes, the two are combined by means of private public partnerships (PPPs).

Intellectual property protection thus amounts to a lex specialis for the promotion and protection of financially risky investments in innovation. Exclusive rights, deviating from open access and use of information otherwise in the public domain, calls for particular justification in terms of state intervention and restrictions of freedom of commerce, whatever the form of law. It is not a given, and rules should respect the principal of proportionality. Generally speaking, measures need to be suitable, necessary, and not exceeding what is necessary to achieving a policy goal and overall appropriate taking into account all the interests at stake. That also informs the shaping of intellectual property law. Throughout history, there has been a debate on the usefulness of intellectual property as an expression of utilitarian philosophy. Some elevated it to the status of human rights. The European Convention for the Protection of Human Rights includes intellectual property as a right to property in Protocol I. There is no need to question the fundamentals here. The principles of intellectual property are deeply enshrined in legal orders and the world economy. However, attention is drawn to the fact that the scope of protection of rights and the relationship to public information requires particular and constant attention. The equation changes with changing technologies. Yet, additional standards, pressed for by vested interests, are not necessarily in the public interest. Ceilings of standards need to be considered in domestic and international law to establish a proper balance between investment in public goods and investment in private goods with a view to foster general welfare and the reduction of overall inequality in income and wealth, both influenced by property rights. The conventional approach of setting minimal standards in international law and the federalist approach focusing on national policy space does not sufficiently reflect the need to harness domestic law. It is not simply a matter of granting policy space to domestic legislation, but to equally contain in on the international level, commensurate with the doctrine of multilevel governance and vertical checks and balances. Intellectual property as a matter of non-tariff barriers is not different from other policy fields, such as promotion and facilitation of renewable energy or effective human rights protection.

It would be wrong to assume that human investment in imitation, reproduction and innovation can be neatly separated. Problems delineating protection and public domain thorough all forms of existing intellectual property protection exist. Disputes on patentability of inventions make the point. One may flow out of the other, as much as penicillin was discovered out of a reproduction process. It was not designed and intended in the first place. Yet, as investment turns to new territory and thus risks, the net of intellectual property rights offers adequate prospects of return if, and only if, the effort is successful. A substantial risk remains uncovered in case of failure and leaves little else than costs. It entails the option of bankruptcy under both models of public and private information alike.

### C. Appropriate Return of Capital and Reasonable Profits

The fundamental question is how far society, government and the law should enable return on capital in intellectual property protection beyond market rules and freedom of commerce, and to what extent this includes profits, and for how long. In the present context of increasing inequality of wealth and income, this is the crucial issue. From the point of public interest and thus intellectual property policy, it follows from the purpose of having exclusive rights in the first place that the investment made should be recovered with a fair share of profits to shareholders and stakeholders alike. It also follows, however, that the privilege of exclusivity should not include excessive profits to the detriment of ordinary investment in reproduction and incremental innovation. Of course, defining reasonable, non-excessive profits remains a matter of debate and uncertainty. But in principle there is no justification to grant exclusive rights in information beyond this point from a point of view of public interests. The scope of rights and the duration of exclusive rights are of crucial importance.

#### 1. The Scope of Rights

In defining the scope of intellectual rights, the importance of creative imitation taking place in and through the public domain must necessarily be considered. History shows a long record of gradually building levels of protection and exemptions thereof. These levels are outcomes of fierce political battles of different vested interests, prospects of private profits often prevailing over concerns of public welfare. International law of intellectual property protection today does not offer an effective balance. As indicated, it is essentially limited to minimal standards which countries can exceed, either unilaterally or by means of international agreements. Due to MFN obligations, higher standards are applied across the board and not limited to the parties of a preferential agreement. They lift all yachts with the tide. This open-ended approach raises problems of flexibility on, and of limitations, on the scope of protection.

The proper balance of creative imitation and innovation, however, much depends upon the state and process of social and economic development of a particular country. The needs for IP protection vary, and uniform minimal standards are not always suitable. While the TRIPS Agreement allows for flexibilities and is far from harmonization, there is need for more variable geometry on essential regulations. It could be realized by the approach of graduation as it can be found more recently in the Agreement on Trade Facilitation of the WTO. While international law defines standards of protection, the phasing in over time of such standards is made dependent upon the attainment of economic factors and indicators to be negotiated in advance. The approach, replacing traditional and rigid Special and Differential Treatment - offers predictability as to when a country, due to its share in world trade in a particular sector, will be obliged to assume specific additional obligations of intellectual property protection.

Except for rules on enforcement, the TRIPS Agreement and TRIPs-plus obligations in preferential trade agreements do not know ceilings of protection. Such ceilings are essentially left to domestic law, including competition law which is absent in international law.

The focus on promotion and protection of investment asks to what extent ceilings to levels of protection are required to protect creative imitation and to what extent investment necessarily depends upon sui generis intellectual property protection. A case needs to be made that protection is required to recuperate investment and to make a reasonable profit. The burden of persuasion lies with those seeking IP protection. Answers vary and depend upon technological advances. For example, the legal treatment of Big Data and Artificial Intelligence (IA) depends on the issue whether or not sufficient incentives to develop and collect data and to write algorithms exist under market conditions and open-source information. Appropriation of information should be only made if incentives for investment and adequate returns and reasonable profits otherwise cannot sufficiently materialise. The same holds true, for example, in assessing exclusivity of test data for pharmaceutical products, or qualification of essential standards of interconnection. The law should take into account the investment made and define reasonable profits up to which protection exists and elapses thereafter. The topical method of equity, described above, can be put to use to taking into account all relevant economic and financial factors in assessing such prospects. It can build upon the general principle of unjust enrichment which is based upon equity and recognised in domestic and international law. Ceilings in law should thus be formulated to the effect that the main purpose of protection is the promotion and recuperation of investment, including a reasonable, non-excessive profit. It should not exceed such bounds in formulating and applying intellectual property protection.

. . .

### 3. The Defense of Unjust Enrichment

Beyond temporal limitations of intellectual property rights, it conceivable to contemplate a defense and objection to alleged violations of intellectual property rights and exclusivity on the ground of excessive profits due to the dominant position granted. We recall the principle that lawful recourse to existing information and reliance upon it in the process of creative imitation would depend upon whether or not the costs of investment incurred to produce the information in the first place have been appropriately covered This entails an appropriate and reasonable margin of profit on return, which, however would be limited. Intellectual property protection, however, should stop here and not give rise to economic rents for which a public interest does not exist. Foundations to this effect can be found in the principle of unjust enrichment. The application of the principle is generally subject to positive law and thus of limited use, unless it is taken into account by negotiators and legislators in shaping the scope of intellectual property protection.

Based upon equity and topical jurisprudence the principle of unjust enrichment would grant objections and a defense to exclusivity, on a case by case basis, during the term of protection. The law would need to state just the principle of preventing economic rents, the prohibition of abuse of rights and of unjust enrichment. Again, the burden of persuasion and proof lies with the right holder claiming monopoly rights demonstrating that investment has not yet been recovered and reasonable profits were not yet made. Alternatively it could be made subject to stringent discovery rules. For example, the protection of a successful and highly profitable high-priced block buster patent, or of big data, or of a famous trade mark generating income and wealth independently of products for which it is used, or of a trade secret sold or licensed, would depend upon the issue whether the investment and effort made in the first place has been sufficiently recovered and thus no longer requires exclusive marketing rights. It thus may henceforth be open to imitation and to generic production in ordinary channels of market economy even during the term of protection. Non-economic aspects of intellectual property rights would not be affected, in particular moral rights or the protection of personality under human rights standards. Authors and successors in title remain entitled to defend the integrity of a work.

## D. Fostering Competition

This kind of thinking based upon investment, appropriate return and reasonable profit entails a fundamental shift in conceptualizing patent and copyright law and in particular to unending extension of trademark and trade secret protection. It would require holders of rights to make new efforts at innovation as existing information falls into the public domain once costs of creating the information and an appropriate profit allowing the development of new information in R&D are fully recuperated. Particular functions of IPRs in product differentiation and in particular securing safe products remain in place. As long as products are being produced, trademarks need to be attached and consumers protected from false and dangerous imitations. The regime, however, may at same point limit sale and exclusive licensing of independent rights, simply used to make profits into the IP portfolio. Information falls into the public domain and thus can be used for ordinary processes of creative imitation. International economic law should set appropriate parameters to this effect.

These effects foster competition, stimulate innovation, reduce dominant positions and concentration. They likely could make a contribution to more even distribution of income and wealth. Defenses to IP protection will mainly affect large corporations able to substantially profit from existing rights beyond appropriate return of investment and profits. Problems caused by excessive power, wealth and income on the basis of intellectual property rights no longer would need to be remedied ex post by means of often ineffective competition policy, combatting the abuse of dominant positions. Intellectual property law would make a contribution in curbing such positions in the first place.

. . .

## V. Conclusions

Squaring inequality and intellectual property rights is a difficult topic. There is a lack of empirical data demonstrating the relationship. It forms part of the larger debate on distributive justice among and within nations. It is at the heart of international economic law and thus includes intellectual property protection which has substantially increased contrary to the general trend of deregulation and trade liberalization under WTO rules. We know that enhanced property rights support the process of concentration which favors economic rents at the expense of competition. In line with general property theory, it is can be assumed that enhanced property rights at least indirectly contribute to increasing inequality of income and wealth. Recourse to equity, as developed in international law as a topical methodology, allows taking into account aspects of wealth and income distribution in the process of applying and interpreting existing intellectual property rights. Equity informs the interpretation of existing rules, and may even deny applications with a view to do justice in a particular case. Moreover, it is important to apply intellectual property in the context of all of international economic law, in particular the rules GATT. This is of particular importance in assessing bans on parallel importation and thus of price discrimination.

The topic, however, encourages reconsidering the relationship of innovation and imitation. An attempt is made to approach the issue by conceptualizing human investment in capital, natural resources, time and human resources in terms of imitation, reproduction and innovation all based upon existing information. For all activities alike, the legal order seeks allowing for appropriate returns on investment and fair profits. In areas of innovation, particular risks exist which public funding or intellectual property rights absorb in order to create incentives to invest human capital. Exclusive rights are justified only and to the extent as long as they secure such returns and reasonable profits. International economic law should thus set ceilings and adopt a timeframe including maximum periods of duration of patents, industrial designs and copyright. Rights unlimited in time, in particular trademarks, geographical indications should only be protected as long as they serve the purpose of distinguishing products and until investment is recuperated with a reasonable profit. The latter also should apply to trade secret protection. Recourse to unjust enrichment should be encouraged. The law must prevent exclusivity from being used for rent-seeking which contributes to inequality of wealth and income and does not respond to public interests in fostering human investment in reproduction, creative imitation and innovation alike.

## CHAPTER 2

# THE INTERNATIONAL PATENT SYSTEM

## I. THE PATENT AS INTELLECTUAL PROPERTY FORM

### A. Discovery and Invention

There is a fundamental distinction in patent law between the concepts of "discovery" of properties of nature or principles governing natural phenomena and of "invention," which presupposes technical intervention to make use of or alter natural things or phenomena.[1] The boundary line between these two types of activity may at times be blurred.

Imagine that a scientist discovers that a certain previously unknown form of magnetic wave strikes the earth's atmosphere from deep space, and that this kind of wave has an adverse effect on the transmission of data between the earth and communications satellites. Such a discovery may have enormous commercial implications, perhaps leading to the invention of a device that filters out the harmful effect of the wave. The inventor of the filtering device may be entitled to a patent. The discoverer of the magnetic wave cannot patent his or her discovery. Today, the distinction between discovery and invention is of particular importance in the fields of biotechnology and genetic engineering.

The U.S. Supreme Court acknowledged the discovery-invention distinction in a seminal decision on the patenting of life forms.*

---

1. The Fourth Edition referred to "human" intervention. In light of the evolving and increasingly recognized role of artificial intelligence (AI) in inventive activity, we have substituted "technical" for "human."

* In the United States there is a federal court system, and there are court systems for the separate states. Patents are the subject of federal legislation, and patent cases are exclusively subject to the jurisdiction of the federal courts. Patent cases may arise either in the form of appeals from determinations by the Patent and Trademark Office (PTO), or in the form of private civil litigation, such as private suits for patent infringement. Civil claims are brought in one of the many federal district courts located throughout the United States, depending upon the amenability of a defendant to suit in a particular location. While most decisions of federal district courts are appealed to one of twelve Circuit Courts of Appeal located in different regions of the country (the First through Eleventh Circuits and the District of Columbia Circuit), appeals from district court patent decisions may be heard only by the Court of Appeals for the Federal Circuit (CAFC), located in Washington, D.C. (a thirteenth appeals court). Decisions of the PTO (a federal agency) are directly and indirectly appealed to the CAFC. Also, the International Trade Commission (ITC) has initial jurisdiction over patent claims brought under Section 337 of the Trade Act of 1930, and appeals are taken to the CAFC. The federal court system as it applies to patent cases is therefore more centralized than it is in respect to most other kinds of cases. In most other areas of federal law, the various Courts of Appeal may divide on common questions, and a good portion of the Supreme Court's time is generally occupied with resolving splits among the Courts of Appeal. Since there is only one federal appeals court that decides patent appeals (the CAFC), the Supreme Court need not occupy itself with resolving splits among the Circuits on patent questions.

## *Diamond v. Chakrabarty*

447 U.S. 303 (1980)

Mr. Chief Justice BURGER[:] . . .

This is not to suggest that §101 [of the U.S. Patent Act] has no limits or that it embraces every discovery. The laws of nature, physical phenomena, and abstract ideas have been held not patentable. *See Parker v. Flook*, 437 U.S. 584 (1978); *Gottschalk v. Benson*, 409 U.S. 63, 67 (1972); *Funk Brothers Seed Co. v. Kalo Inoculant Co.*, 333 U.S. 127, 130 (1948); *O'Reilly v. Morse*, 15 How. 62, 112-121 (1854); *Le Roy v. Tatham*, 14 How. 156, 175 (1853). Thus, a new mineral discovered in the earth or a new plant found in the wild is not patentable subject matter. Likewise, Einstein could not patent his celebrated law that $E=mc^2$; nor could Newton have patented the law of gravity. Such discoveries are "manifestations of . . . nature, free to all men and reserved exclusively to none." *Funk, supra*, at 130.

Judged in this light, respondent's micro-organism plainly qualifies as patentable subject matter. His claim is not to a hitherto unknown natural phenomenon, but to a nonnaturally occurring manufacture or composition of matter—a product of human ingenuity "having a distinctive name, character [and] use." *Hartranft v. Wiegmann*, 121 U.S. 609, 615 (1887). The point is underscored dramatically by comparison of the invention here with that in *Funk*. There, the patentee had discovered that there existed in nature certain species of root-nodule bacteria which did not exert a mutually inhibitive effect on each other. He used that discovery to produce a mixed culture capable of inoculating the seeds of leguminous plants. Concluding that the patentee had discovered "only some of the handiwork of nature," the Court ruled the product nonpatentable:

> "Each of the species of root-nodule bacteria contained in the package infects the same group of leguminous plants which it always infected. No species acquires a different use. The combination of species produces no new bacteria, no change in the six species of bacteria, and no enlargement of the range of their utility. Each species has the same effect it always had. The bacteria perform in their natural way. Their use in combination does not improve in any way their natural functioning. They serve the ends nature originally provided and act quite independently of any effort of the patentee." 333 U.S., at 131.

Here, by contrast, the patentee has produced a new bacterium with markedly different characteristics from any found in nature and one having the potential for significant utility. His discovery is not nature's handiwork, but his own; accordingly it is patentable subject matter under §101.

## NOTES AND QUESTIONS

**1.** The Supreme Court distinguishes between the creation by Dr. Chakrabarty of a new bacterium and an earlier claim (in *Funk Brothers*) for use of existing root-nodule bacteria in combination to inhibit plant disease. The Court uses the latter to illustrate the unpatentable discovery of properties of nature. As we look further into patent claims for biotechnological inventions, consider them in light of the Supreme Court's distinction in *Diamond v. Chakrabarty* between the creation of new products and the use of known ones (as in *Funk Brothers*).

**2.** The decoding of the human genome raised the "discovery-invention" issue in a most profound way. For an introduction to the human genome and its various components, *see generally* JOHN SULSTON & GEORGINA FERRY, THE COMMON THREAD (2002). Questions regarding the basic information of the genetic code seemed largely resolved by the decision of the Wellcome Trust to place its work in the public domain, thereby preventing its competitor in the race to unravel the code (Celera Genomics) from patenting its raw information results (*see* the web site of the Wellcome Trust for information regarding public access to the human genome, http://www.wellcome.ac.uk). However, this represents only one subset of issues regarding the patentability of genetic information and materials.

While it might seem that sequencing (or mapping) the DNA of a material found in the human body involves "discovering" a property of nature, courts in the United States[2] (at least initially) and the European Union in its Biotechnology Directive[3] accepted that synthesizing the end product of a DNA sequence (using identical genetic information with previously known methods of synthesis) represented "invention" (*see Amgen v. Hoechst Marion Roussel*, 457 F.3d 1293 (Fed. Cir. 2006), *rehearing en banc denied*, 469 F.3d 1039 (Fed. Cir. 2006), *cert. denied*, 550 U.S. 953 (2007)). This decision seemed largely based on argument from the commercial biotechnology sector that investment in the discovery of new medicines and compounds would not take place in the absence of adequate financial incentive, and that patents for DNA-based products would provide that financial incentive. The "legal" approach adopted was that the act of reproducing naturally occurring substances via sequenced DNA through laboratory processes (e.g., purifying, isolating, and producing in quantity) involved human intervention, and therefore was inventive. The laboratory process was different than the "natural" process of creation.

One limit to the patenting of genetic information has been recognized in respect to expressed sequence tags (ESTs) used as genetic "markers" for research purposes based on an absence of specific utility (see criterion of utility, *infra*), *In re Fisher*, 421 F.3d 1365 (Fed. Cir. 2005).

2. *See, e.g.*, *Amgen v. Chugai Pharmaceutical*, 927 F.2d 1200 (Fed. Cir. 1991).

3. Directive 98/44/EC of the European Parliament and of the Council of 6 July 1998 on the legal protection of biotechnological inventions, OJ L 213, 30/07/1998 p. 0013-0021, provides:

> ARTICLE 5
>
> 1. The human body, at the various stages of its formation and development, and the simple discovery of one of its elements, including the sequence or partial sequence of a gene, cannot constitute patentable inventions.
>
> 2. An element isolated from the human body or otherwise produced by means of a technical process, including the sequence or partial sequence of a gene, may constitute a patentable invention, even if the structure of that element is identical to that of a natural element.
>
> 3. The industrial application of a sequence or a partial sequence of a gene must be disclosed in the patent application.

The EPO Guidelines for Examination, 5.2 (https://new.epo.org/en/legal/guidelines-epc/2023/g_ii_5_2.html) further expand on this:

> Although the human body, at the various stages of its formation and development, and the simple discovery of one of its elements, including the sequence or partial sequence of a gene, cannot constitute patentable inventions, an element isolated from the human body or otherwise produced by means of a technical process, which is susceptible of industrial application, including the sequence or partial sequence of a gene, may constitute a patentable invention, even if the structure of that element is identical to that of a natural element. Such an element is not *a priori* excluded from patentability since it is, for example, the result of technical processes used to identify, purify and classify it and to produce it outside the human body, techniques which human beings alone are capable of putting into practice and which nature is incapable of accomplishing itself (EU Dir. 98/44/EC, rec. 21).
>
> . . . The industrial application of a sequence or partial sequence must be disclosed in the patent application as filed.

In *Association for Molecular Pathology v. U.S. Patent and Trademark Office*, 702 F. Supp. 2d 181 (S.D.N.Y. 2010), a federal district court invalidated patents held by Myriad Genetics. The court noted that "the challenged patent claims are directed to (1) isolated DNA containing all or portions of the *BRCA1* and *BRCA2* gene sequence and (2) methods for 'comparing' or 'analyzing' *BRCA1* and *BRCA2* gene sequences to identify the presence of mutations correlating with a predisposition to breast or ovarian cancer." The court concluded that

> DNA's existence in an "isolated" form alters neither this fundamental quality of DNA as it exists in the body nor the information it encodes. Therefore, the patents at issue directed to "isolated DNA" containing sequences found in nature are unsustainable as a matter of law and are deemed unpatentable subject matter under 35 U.S.C. §101.

702 F. Supp. 2d at 185.

A divided panel of the Court of Appeals for the Federal Circuit, in *Association for Molecular Pathology v. United States Patent and Trademark Office*, 689 F.3d 1303, 1328 (C.A. Fed. 2012), reversed the district court. The U.S. Supreme Court then addressed whether unmodified information regarding gene sequences is patentable. The Supreme Court held that it is not—based on its precedents excluding from patentability the discovery of properties of nature or natural phenomenon. Justice Thomas, writing for a unanimous Supreme Court, in *Association for Molecular Pathology v. Myriad Genetics*, 133 S. Ct. 2107 (2013), said:

> It is undisputed that Myriad did not create or alter any of the genetic information encoded in the BRCA1 and BRCA2 genes. The location and order of the nucleotides existed in nature before Myriad found them. Nor did Myriad create or alter the genetic structure of DNA. Instead, Myriad's principal contribution was uncovering the precise location and genetic sequence of the BRCA1 and BRCA2 genes within chromosomes 17 and 13. The question is whether this renders the genes patentable.
>
> Myriad recognizes that our decision in Chakrabarty is central to this inquiry. Brief for Respondents 14, 23-27. In Chakrabarty, scientists added four plasmids to a bacterium, which enabled it to break down various components of crude oil. 447 U.S., at 305, and n.1, 100 S. Ct. 2204. The Court held that the modified bacterium was patentable. It explained that the patent claim was "not to a hitherto unknown natural phenomenon, but to a nonnaturally occurring manufacture or composition of matter—a product of human ingenuity 'having a distinctive name, character [and] use.'" Id., at 309-310, 100 S. Ct. 2204 (quoting *Hartranft v. Wiegmann*, 121 U.S. 609, 615, 7 S. Ct. 1240, 30 L. Ed. 1012 (1887); alteration in original). The Chakrabarty bacterium was new "with markedly different characteristics from any found in nature," 447 U.S., at 310, 100 S. Ct. 2204, due to the additional plasmids and resultant "capacity for degrading oil." Id., at 305, n.1, 100 S. Ct. 2204. In this case, by contrast, Myriad did not create anything. To be sure, it found an important and useful gene, but separating that gene from its surrounding genetic material is not an act of invention.
>
> Groundbreaking, innovative, or even brilliant discovery does not by itself satisfy the §101 inquiry. In *Funk Brothers Seed Co. v. Kalo Inoculant Co.*, 333 U.S. 127, 68 S. Ct. 440, 92 L. Ed. 588 (1948), this Court considered a composition patent that claimed a mixture of naturally occurring strains of bacteria that helped leguminous plants take nitrogen from the air and fix it in the soil. Id., at 128-129, 68 S. Ct. 440. The ability of the bacteria to fix nitrogen was well known, and farmers commonly "inoculated" their crops with them to improve soil nitrogen levels. But farmers could not use the same inoculant for all crops, both because plants use different bacteria and because certain bacteria inhibit each other. Id., at 129-130, 68 S. Ct. 440. Upon learning that several nitrogen-fixing bacteria did not inhibit each other, however, the patent applicant combined them into a single inoculant and obtained a patent. Id., at 130, 68 S. Ct. 440. The Court held that the composition was not patent eligible because the patent holder did not alter the bacteria in any way. Id., at 132, 68 S. Ct. 440 ("There is no way in which we could call [the bacteria mixture a product of invention] unless we borrowed invention from the discovery of the natural principle itself"). His patent claim thus fell squarely within the law of

> nature exception. So do Myriad's. Myriad found the location of the BRCA1 and BRCA2 genes, but that discovery, by itself, does not render the BRCA genes "new . . . composition[s] of matter," §101, that are patent eligible.

133 S. Ct. at 2116-2117.

The Supreme Court later drew a distinction between genetic information found in nature and genetic sequences created using the naturally occurring sequences, but modifying that information by removing certain parts (i.e., noncoding introns), stating:

> cDNA does not present the same obstacles to patentability as naturally occurring, isolated DNA segments. As already explained, creation of a cDNA sequence from mRNA results in an exons-only molecule that is not naturally occurring. Petitioners concede that cDNA differs from natural DNA in that "the non-coding regions have been removed." . . . They nevertheless argue that cDNA is not patent eligible because "[t]he nucleotide sequence of cDNA is dictated by nature, not by the lab technician." . . . That may be so, but the lab technician unquestionably creates something new when cDNA is made. cDNA retains the naturally occurring exons of DNA, but it is distinct from the DNA from which it was derived. As a result, cDNA is not a "product of nature" and is patent eligible under §101, except insofar as very short series of DNA may have no intervening introns to remove when creating cDNA. In that situation, a short strand of cDNA may be indistinguishable from natural DNA.

133 S. Ct. at 2119 (footnotes omitted).

The Supreme Court finally delineated what it was not deciding:

> It is important to note what is not implicated by this decision. First, there are no method claims before this Court. Had Myriad created an innovative method of manipulating genes while searching for the BRCA1 and BRCA2 genes, it could possibly have sought a method patent. But the processes used by Myriad to isolate DNA were well understood by geneticists at the time of Myriad's patents "were well understood, widely used, and fairly uniform insofar as any scientist engaged in the search for a gene would likely have utilized a similar approach," 702 F. Supp. 2d, at 202-203, and are not at issue in this case.
>
> Similarly, this case does not involve patents on new applications of knowledge about the BRCA1 and BRCA2 genes. Judge Bryson aptly noted that, "[a]s the first party with knowledge of the [BRCA1 and BRCA2] sequences, Myriad was in an excellent position to claim applications of that knowledge. Many of its unchallenged claims are limited to such applications." 689 F.3d, at 1349.
>
> Nor do we consider the patentability of DNA in which the order of the naturally occurring nucleotides has been altered. Scientific alteration of the genetic code presents a different inquiry, and we express no opinion about the application of §101 to such endeavors. We merely hold that genes and the information they encode are not patent eligible under §101 simply because they have been isolated from the surrounding genetic material.

133 S. Ct. at 2119.

The Supreme Court has made evident that not all questions raised by access to the human genetic code have been answered from a legal standpoint. Of course, they have not been answered from a scientific standpoint either.

## B. Patentable Subject Matter

An invention will involve a "subject matter," such as a machine or chemical compound. Generally speaking, the subject matter scope of patent protection is intended to be broad. Predetermining the subject matter scope of patent protection is inherently difficult since "invention" contemplates the doing of something not done before. Legislators are naturally constrained in their capacity to predict what will be invented and so to establish rules for things that have not been done. Yet, this does not preclude setting boundaries around patentable subject matter. For example, advances in reproductive technologies make it scientifically possible to modify the genetic structure of existing human beings such that "new" humans might be created through laboratory processes. It is generally accepted that such new humans, should they be made, will not be patentable subject matter.[4]

As with most areas of law, patentability tends to be formulated in terms of "rules" and "exceptions" to them. The TRIPS Agreement patent rules, which we examine closely in this chapter, initially establish a comprehensive scope of patentable subject matter.[5] The Agreement then permits each national government to adopt certain types of exception, such as to protect public order, and also includes a general provision addressing "limited exceptions."

In the first passages quoted below, the U.S. Supreme Court states the case for a broad scope of patent subject matter protection, invoking Thomas Jefferson, one of America's Founding Fathers (and an early "garage inventor").

## *Diamond v. Chakrabarty*

447 U.S. 303 (1980)

Mr. Chief Justice Burger [for the majority . . . ].

Guided by these canons of construction, this Court has read the term "manufacture" in §101 in accordance with its dictionary definition to mean "the production of articles for use from raw or prepared materials by giving to these materials new forms, qualities, properties, or combinations, whether by hand-labor or by machinery." *American Fruit Growers, Inc. v. Brogdex Co.*, 283 U.S. 1, 11 (1931). Similarly, "composition of matter" has been construed consistent with its common usage to include "all compositions of two or more substances and . . . all composite articles, whether they be the results of chemical union, or of mechanical mixture, or whether they be gases, fluids, powders or solids." *Shell Development Co. v. Watson*, 149 F. Supp. 279, 280 (DC 1957) (citing 1 A. Deller, Walker on Patents §14, p. 55 (1st ed. 1937)). In choosing such expansive terms as "manufacture" and "composition of matter," modified by the comprehensive "any," Congress plainly contemplated that the patent laws would be given wide scope.

The relevant legislative history also supports a broad construction. The Patent Act of 1793, authored by Thomas Jefferson, defined statutory subject matter as "any new and useful art, machine, manufacture, or composition of matter, or any new or useful improvement [thereof]." Act of Feb. 21, 1793, §1, 1 Stat. 319. The Act embodied Jefferson's philosophy that "ingenuity should receive a liberal encouragement." 5 Writings of Thomas Jefferson 75-76 (Washington ed. 1871). *See Graham v. John Deere Co.*, 383 U.S. 1, 7-10 (1966). Subsequent patent statutes in 1836, 1870, and 1874 employed this same broad language. In 1952, when the patent laws were recodified, Congress replaced the word "art" with "process," but otherwise left Jefferson's language intact. The Committee Reports accompanying the 1952 Act inform us that Congress intended statutory subject matter to "include anything under the sun that is made by man." S. Rep. No. 1979, 82d Cong., 2d Sess., 5 (1952); H.R. Rep. No. 1923, 82d Cong., 2d Sess., 6 (1952).[6] . . .

---

4. The "Harvard Mouse" cases made clear that the ethical question of patenting humans was one that needed to be addressed with some immediacy, not as a science fiction question. *See, e.g.*, EU Biotechnology Directive, at art. 5 (precluding patenting of the human body as such). Directive 98/44/EC of the European Parliament and of the Council of 6 July 1998 on the Legal Protection of Biotechnological Inventions, 1998 O.J. (L 213) 13-21.

5. TRIPS Agreement, art. 27.1 ("patents shall be available for any inventions, whether products or processes, in all fields of technology").

6. This same language was employed by P.J. Federico, a principal draftsman of the 1952 recodification, in his testimony regarding that legislation: "[Under] section 101 a person may have invented a machine or a manufacture, which may include anything under the sun that is made by man. . . ." Hearings on H.R. 3760 before Subcommittee No. 3 of the House Committee on the Judiciary, 82d Cong., 1st Sess., 37 (1951).

. . . A rule that unanticipated inventions are without protection would conflict with the core concept of the patent law that anticipation undermines patentability. *See Graham v. John Deere Co.*, 383 U.S., at 12-17. Mr. Justice Douglas reminded that the inventions most benefiting mankind are those that "push back the frontiers of chemistry, physics, and the like." *Great A. & P. Tea Co. v. Supermarket Corp.*, 340 U.S. 147, 154 (1950) (concurring opinion). Congress employed broad general language in drafting §101 precisely because such inventions are often unforeseeable.[10]

## NOTES AND QUESTIONS

**1.** In a later part of its opinion, the U.S. Supreme Court said that it was up to Congress (the U.S. legislative branch) to establish limits on the subject matter scope of patent protection. Generally speaking, a legislature or parliament is the branch of government considered to most directly reflect the "voice of the people." At the international level, patent rules are generally made by treaty. Treaties are typically negotiated by the executive branch of government, subject to subsequent approval by the legislative branch. Is there a difference in the democratic input into the two processes? What impact might these differences be expected to have on the outcome of the rulemaking?

Canada's Patent Act uses the same language as the U.S. Patent Act to define patentable subject matter. Yet, in a decision concerning the patentability of higher life forms, Canada's Supreme Court was able to discern limits without waiting for legislative intervention. The essence of the decision is that a higher life form is something greater than the sum of its parts.

### *Harvard College v. Canada (Commissioner of Patents)*

Supreme Court of Canada
2002 SCC 76 File No.: 28155
2002: May 21, 2002: December 5

BASTARACHE J.—

163. . . . the word "matter" captures but one aspect of a higher life form. As defined by the *Oxford English Dictionary*, *supra*, vol. IX, at p. 480, "matter" is a "[p]hysical or corporeal substance in general . . ., contradistinguished from immaterial or incorporeal substance (spirit, soul, mind), and from qualities, actions, or conditions." "*Matière*" is defined by the *Grand Robert de la langue française*, *supra*, vol. 4, p. 1260, as "[TRANSLATION] corporeal substance 'that is perceptible in space and has mechanical mass.' " Although some in society may hold the view that higher life forms are mere "composition[s] of matter," the phrase does not fit well with common understandings of human and animal life. Higher life forms are generally regarded as possessing qualities and characteristics that transcend the particular genetic material of which they are composed. A person whose genetic make-up is modified by radiation does not cease to be him or herself. Likewise, the same mouse would exist absent the injection of the oncogene into the fertilized egg cell; it simply would not be predisposed to cancer. The fact that it has this predisposition to cancer that makes it valuable to humans

10. Even an abbreviated list of patented inventions underscores the point: telegraph (Morse, No. 1,647); telephone (Bell, No. 174,465); electric lamp (Edison, No. 223,898); airplane (the Wrights, No. 821,393); transistor (Bardeen & Brattain, No. 2,524,035); neutronic reactor (Fermi & Szilard, No. 2,708,656); laser (Schawlow & Townes, No. 2,929,922). *See generally* Revolutionary Ideas, Patents & Progress in America, United States Patent and Trademark Office (1976).

does not mean that the mouse, along with other animal life forms, can be defined solely with reference to the genetic matter of which it is composed. The fact that animal life forms have numerous unique qualities that transcend the particular matter of which they are composed makes it difficult to conceptualize higher life forms as mere "composition[s] of matter." It is a phrase that seems inadequate as a description of a higher life form.

164. Lastly, I wish also to address Rothstein, J.A.'s assertion that "[t]he language of patent law is broad and general and is to be given wide scope because inventions are, necessarily, unanticipated and unforeseeable" (para. 116). In my view, it does not thereby follow that all proposed inventions are patentable. On the one hand, it might be argued that, in this instance, Parliament could foresee that patents might be sought in higher life forms. Although Parliament would not have foreseen the genetically altered mouse and the process of genetic engineering used to produce it, Parliament was well aware of animal husbandry or breeding. While the technologies used to produce a crossbred animal and a genetically engineered animal differ substantially, the end result, an animal with a new or several new features, is the same. Yet Parliament chose to define the categories of invention using language that does not, in common usage, refer to higher life forms. One might thus infer that Parliament did not intend to include higher life forms in the definition of "invention." . . .

166. Patenting higher life forms would involve a radical departure from the traditional patent regime. Moreover, the patentability of such life forms is a highly contentious matter that raises a number of extremely complex issues. If higher life forms are to be patentable, it must be under the clear and unequivocal direction of Parliament. For the reasons discussed above, I conclude that the current Act does not clearly indicate that higher life forms are patentable. Far from it. Rather, I believe that the best reading of the words of the Act supports the opposite conclusion—that higher life forms such as the oncomouse are not currently patentable in Canada.

## NOTES AND QUESTIONS

**1.** The decision by the Canadian Supreme Court is based on the express language of Canada's Patent Act. The Court appears to have left it open for the Parliament to allow for the patenting of higher life forms. Would such a decision by the Parliament be consistent with the Canadian Supreme Court's conception of patentable subject matter? If the Court is saying that higher life forms incorporate noncorporeal elements that are not encompassed by a "composition of matter," then on what would the Parliament be allowing patents? Perhaps what Canada's Supreme Court meant to say was, "We think it is wrong to allow for the patenting of higher life forms because these are creations of a divine spirit. We do not think that human beings should purport to own such creations. The patenting of higher life forms is inconsistent with the strong public policy of Canada." Why do you think Canada's Supreme Court chose to decide based on the language of the Patent Act? Was it attempting to force an ethical debate? As of July 2023, the Canadian Parliament has not legislated to change the outcome of the text decision. See Canada Manual of Patent Office Practice (MOPOP), 17.03.03 Higher life forms.

**2.** Justice Binnie of the Canadian Supreme Court noted in a dissenting opinion:

> "The oncomouse has been held patentable, and is now patented in jurisdictions that cover Austria, Belgium, Denmark, Finland, France, Germany, Greece, Ireland, Italy, Luxembourg, The Netherlands, Portugal, Spain, Sweden, the United Kingdom and the United States. A similar patent has been issued in Japan. New Zealand has issued a patent for a transgenic mouse that has been genetically modified to be susceptible to HIV infection. Indeed, we were not told of any country with a patent system comparable to Canada's (or otherwise) in which a patent on the oncomouse had been applied for and been refused." (at para. 2).

What consequences might flow from differential treatment of higher life forms in national patent laws?

**3.** The Technical Board of Appeal of the European Patent Office rejected an application by a Chinese inventor for producing a therapeutic pharmaceutical compound by inflaming the skin of rabbits through vaccination, then killing the rabbits and extracting the compound from their skin. Case No: T 1553/15 - 3.3.01, Decision of Technical Board of Appeal 3.3.01 of 28 September 2020, Appellant: VanWorld Pharmaceutical (Rugao) Company Limited. The invention was considered to contravene Article 53(a) of the EPC, which precludes patenting of subject matter deemed to be immoral or to contravene public order. Although the EPC does not exclude use of animals for experimentation, etc., in this case there were ample substitutes for the therapeutic compound being extracted from the rabbits, the production process required repetition, and there was no unique therapeutic benefit to humans as compared with available substitutes. The mechanism of action was understood. The Board contrasted a decision allowing creation of an oncomouse for cancer research purposes which involves only a small number of animals and substantial potential benefit.

The patent system, essentially developed for mechanics and chemistry, presents difficulties in fields other than genetic engineering. Established criteria also face difficulties when applied to business application software, which normally has been protected under copyright law. The U.S. Supreme Court considered the patentability of computer software used to perform "mental processes" in the following case.

## *Bilski v. Kappos [Director of the U.S. PTO]*

561 U.S. 593 (2010)

Justice Kennedy delivered the opinion of the Court . . . :[4]

The question in this case turns on whether a patent can be issued for a claimed invention designed for the business world. The patent application claims a procedure for instructing buyers and sellers how to protect against the risk of price fluctuations in a discrete section of the economy. Three arguments are advanced for the proposition that the claimed invention is outside the scope of patent law: (1) it is not tied to a machine and does not transform an article; (2) it involves a method of conducting business; and (3) it is merely an abstract idea. The Court of Appeals ruled that the first mentioned of these, the so-called machine-or-transformation test, was the sole test to be used for determining the patentability of a "process" under the Patent Act, 35 U.S.C. §101.

. . .

The Court of Appeals incorrectly concluded that this Court has endorsed the machine-or-transformation test as the exclusive test. It is true that *Cochrane v. Deener*, 94 U.S. 780, 788, 24 L. Ed. 139 (1877), explained that a "process" is "an act, or a series of acts, performed upon the subject-matter to be transformed and reduced to a different state or thing." More recent cases, however, have rejected the broad implications of this dictum; and, in all events, later authority shows that it was not intended to be an exhaustive or exclusive test. *Gottschalk v. Benson*, 409 U.S. 63, 70, 93 S. Ct. 253, 34 L. Ed. 2d 273 (1972), noted that "[t]ransformation and reduction of an article 'to a different state or thing' is the clue to the patentability of a process claim that does not include particular machines." At the same time, it explicitly declined to "hold that no process patent could ever qualify if it did not meet [machine or transformation] requirements." *Id.*, at 71, 93 S. Ct. 253. *Flook* took a similar approach,

4. [Justice Scalia did not join two parts of the majority opinion. See discussion *infra.*—Eds.]

"assum[ing] that a valid process patent may issue even if it does not meet [the machine-or-transformation test]." 437 U.S., at 588, n. 9, 98 S. Ct. 2522.

This Court's precedents establish that the machine-or-transformation test is a useful and important clue, an investigative tool, for determining whether some claimed inventions are processes under §101. The machine-or-transformation test is not the sole test for deciding whether an invention is a patent-eligible "process."

. . .

Section 101 similarly precludes the broad contention that the term "process" categorically excludes business methods. The term "method," which is within §100(b)'s definition of "process," at least as a textual matter and before consulting other limitations in the Patent Act and this Court's precedents, may include at least some methods of doing business. *See, e.g.*, Webster's New International Dictionary 1548 (2d ed. 1954) (defining "method" as "[a]n orderly procedure or process . . . regular way or manner of doing anything; hence, a set form of procedure adopted in investigation or instruction"). The Court is unaware of any argument that the " 'ordinary, contemporary, common meaning,' " *Diehr, supra*, at 182, 101 S. Ct. 1048, of "method" excludes business methods. Nor is it clear how far a prohibition on business method patents would reach, and whether it would exclude technologies for conducting a business more efficiently. *See, e.g.*, Hall, Business and Financial Method Patents, Innovation, and Policy, 56 Scottish J. Pol. Econ. 443, 445 (2009) ("There is no precise definition of . . . business method patents").

. . .

Even though petitioners' application is not categorically outside of §101 under the two broad and atextual approaches the Court rejects today, that does not mean it is a "process" under §101. Petitioners seek to patent both the concept of hedging risk and the application of that concept to energy markets. App. 19-20. Rather than adopting categorical rules that might have wide-ranging and unforeseen impacts, the Court resolves this case narrowly on the basis of this Court's decisions in *Benson, Flook*, and *Diehr*, which show that petitioners' claims are not patentable processes because they are attempts to patent abstract ideas. Indeed, all members of the Court agree that the patent application at issue here falls outside of §101 because it claims an abstract idea.

. . .

Today, the Court once again declines to impose limitations on the Patent Act that are inconsistent with the Act's text. The patent application here can be rejected under our precedents on the unpatentability of abstract ideas. The Court, therefore, need not define further what constitutes a patentable "process," beyond pointing to the definition of that term provided in §100(b) and looking to the guideposts in *Benson, Flook*, and *Diehr*.

And nothing in today's opinion should be read as endorsing interpretations of §101 that the Court of Appeals for the Federal Circuit has used in the past. *See, e.g., State Street*, 149 F.3d, at 1373; *AT & T Corp.*, 172 F.3d, at 1357. It may be that the Court of Appeals thought it needed to make the machine-or-transformation test exclusive precisely because its case law had not adequately identified less extreme means of restricting business method patents, including (but not limited to) application of our opinions in *Benson, Flook*, and *Diehr*. In disapproving an exclusive machine-or-transformation test, we by no means foreclose the Federal Circuit's development of other limiting criteria that further the purposes of the Patent Act and are not inconsistent with its text.

The judgment of the Court of Appeals is affirmed.

[Justice Scalia joined the majority of the Court, but did not join those parts of the opinion in which Justice Kennedy might be understood to question the utility of the machine-or-transformation test, which, in Justice Scalia's view, the CAFC had not suggested was the exclusive test of patentable process subject matter.

Justice Stevens, writing for a four-Justice minority, vigorously dissented, summarizing the view of the dissenting Justices:]

The Court correctly holds that the machine-or-transformation test is not the sole test for what constitutes a patentable process; rather, it is a critical clue. But the Court is quite wrong, in my view, to suggest that any series of steps that is not itself an abstract idea or law of nature may constitute a "process" within the meaning of §101. The language in the Court's opinion to this effect can only cause mischief. The wiser course would have been to hold that petitioners' method is not a "process" because it describes only a general method of engaging in business transactions—and business methods are not patentable. More precisely, although a process is not patent-ineligible simply because it is useful for conducting business, a claim that merely describes a method of doing business does not qualify as a "process" under §101.

## NOTES AND QUESTIONS

**1.** Justice Kennedy emphasizes that the world of the Internet is different than the world of brick and mortar, and suggests that more flexibility must be extended to the definition of patentable "processes" in this new environment. Justice Stevens is concerned that this will result in an unmanageable flood of patents on abstract ideas. Who is right?

**2.** In June 2014 the U.S. Supreme Court rendered a decision in *Alice v. CLS Bank Int'l*, 573 U.S. 208 (2014). Writing for a unanimous Court, Justice Thomas affirmed the holding in *Bilski* that abstract ideas are unpatentable (in this case, the idea of "intermediated settlement" used to mitigate settlement risk). Relying on its holding in *Mayo Collaborative Services v. Prometheus Laboratories, Inc.*, 566 U.S. (2013), the Court said that merely appending conventional steps, in this case implementing the abstract idea using software on a generic computer, did not transform the abstract idea into a patent-eligible invention. Three members of the Court (Justices Sotomayor, Ginsburg, and Breyer) concurred in the result, but would have gone further to hold that any claim that describes a method of doing business does not qualify for a process patent, as they also had proposed along with Justice Stevens (now retired) in *Bilski*. The combined holdings in *Mayo* and *Alice* resulted in a "presently conventional" two-step inquiry regarding whether subject matter is patentable. First, determine whether the claimed invention embodies a law of nature or abstract idea and is therefore presumptively non-patentable. If it does not, the subject matter challenge ends. If it does, proceed to step two and determine whether the putative inventor has sufficiently transformed the law of nature or abstract idea to distinguish it and justify patenting. If it is sufficiently transformed, it is patentable subject matter. This two-step *Mayo/Alice* test is sufficiently "non-informative" that it seems unlikely to stand the test of time, but for now this is the wisdom of the U.S. Supreme Court.

**3.** The U.S. Federal Circuit has recently rendered decisions which renew questions about the subject matter scope of method patenting, similar to the type of question raised in *Bilski*. *See, e.g.*, *Vanda Pharmaceuticals Inc. v. West-Ward Pharmaceuticals Int'l Ltd.*, 887 F.3d 1117 (Fed. Cir. 2018), in which a majority of Federal Circuit judges allowed claims directed toward a method for determining an appropriate drug regimen that was very similar to claims rejected by the Supreme Court in *Mayo v. Prometheus, id.*

4. In a case involving an application by Bentley Systems (UK) regarding Simulation of the Movement of an Autonomous Entity Through an Environment, the EPO Enlarged Board of Appeal addressed patenting of computer software employing a model that simulates potential activity in the real world, in this case pedestrian traffic inside a facility with various features of interest, and how a design might be implemented to facilitate movement within the facility (including, e.g., a railway station). Case G 0001/19 (Pedestrian simulation) of March 10,

2021.[5] The Enlarged Board found that for a computer software program to be patentable it does not need to produce a tangible effect in the real world, it can be directed to simulations of real-world activity, solving a technical problem such as how best to design a facility to accommodate people. Much of the decision deals with determining what is a technical solution to a problem, and therefore what is "technical." Could it include a value like pedestrian frustration with blocked movement? The Enlarged Board says that non-technical elements do not preclude patenting, but that mere data is not a technical solution. The decision brings to mind the distinction between U.S. cases such as *Diamond v. Diehr*, 450 U.S. 175 (1981), where software generates a tangible real-world effect, on one hand, and cases involving solution of a mathematical problem such as adjusting alarm limits, on the other, where software does not generate a real-world effect, *Parker v. Flook*, 437 U.S. 584. The EPO Enlarged Board also lays out a methodology for assessing inventive step in European law which is somewhat different than the series of steps for the U.S., including in particular solving a technical problem.

## C. Four Criteria

Establishing patentability is often framed in terms of satisfying three criteria: novelty, usefulness, and inventive step. However, enablement (i.e., disclosing means for producing the invention) is so fundamental to patentability that it should be considered a fourth basic criterion. The advance of science and technical skill during the past century, along with the proliferation of information, has made the application of the four criteria of patentability an enormously complex affair. This complexity is exacerbated by differences among national and regional patent laws, and the way in which they are applied by patent authorities (including patent offices and courts). There are political, social, economic, moral, and cultural dimensions to patents that transcend the domain of the patent law specialist.

Although the concept of invention is central to the law of patents, the U.K. House of Lords explains in *Biogen v. Medeva* that the determination of whether a product or process is patentable is nevertheless based on whether the applicant's claim(s) satisfies certain criteria.

In the United Kingdom, the House of Lords referred both to the upper chamber of the Parliament and to the highest judicial body of the land. Since October 1, 2009, jurisdiction of the House of Lords was transferred to the newly established Supreme Court, the highest appeal court of the United Kingdom.

### *Biogen, Inc. v. Medeva PLC*

House of Lords [1997] RPC 1 31 October 1996

Lord Hoffmann: . . .

#### 9. What Is an Invention?

The [U.K Patent Act] thus lays down various conditions, both positive . . . and negative . . . which an invention must satisfy in order to be a "patentable invention." This scheme might suggest that logically one should first decide whether the claimed invention can properly be described as an invention at all. Only if this question receives an affirmative answer would it be necessary to go on to consider whether the invention satisfies the prescribed conditions for being "patentable." In practice, however, I have no doubt that in most cases this would be a mistake and cause unnecessary difficulty.

5. https://www.epo.org/law-practice/case-law-appeals/recent/g190001ex1.html.

The Act does not define the concept of an invention. Section 1(1) was intended to reflect, "as nearly as practicable," article 52 of the European Patent Convention ("EPC"): *see* section 130(7) of the 1977 Act. Article 52 also has no definition of an invention. It seems that the parties to the EPC were unable to agree upon one: . . . But the reason why the parties were content to do without a definition was that they recognised that the question would almost invariably be academic. The four conditions in section 1(1) do a great deal more than restrict the class of "inventions" which may be patented. They probably also contain every element of the concept of an invention in ordinary speech. I say probably, because in the absence of a definition one cannot say with certainty that one might not come across something which satisfied all the conditions but could not be described as an invention. But the draftsmen of the Convention and the Act, as well as counsel at the bar, were unable to think of any examples. Just in case one should appear, section 1(5) gives the Secretary of State power to vary the list of matters excluded by paragraph (d) "for the purpose of maintaining them in conformity with developments in science and technology."

As the four conditions are relatively familiar ground, elucidated by definitions in the Act and the jurisprudence of the courts and the EPO, it will normally be more convenient to start by deciding whether they are satisfied. In virtually every case this will be the end of the inquiry. There may one day be a case in which it is necessary to decide whether something which satisfies the conditions can be called an invention, but that question can wait until it arises.

One can of course imagine cases in which the alleged subject-matter is so obviously not an invention that it is tempting to take an axe to the problem by dismissing the claim without inquiring too closely into which of the conditions has not been satisfied. So in Genentech Inc's Patent [1989] RPC 147, 264, Mustill LJ said, by reference to the ordinary speech meaning of "invention":

> You cannot invent water, although you certainly can invent ways in which it may be distilled or synthesised.

This is obviously right and in such a case it may seem pedantic to say that water fails the condition in paragraph (a) of section 1(1) because it is not new. Unfortunately, most cases which come before the courts are more difficult. Judges would therefore be well advised to put on one side their intuitive sense of what constitutes an invention until they have considered the questions of novelty, inventiveness and so forth. In the present case, I think that Medeva's counsel was right to resist the invitation of the Court of Appeal to make submissions on whether the claims constituted an invention.

## NOTES AND QUESTIONS

1. U.K. patent law accepts that the separate concept of "invention" is too broad to be analytically useful as the basis for assessing patentability. Yet, a number of countries expressly limit the subject matter of patentable "invention," even post-TRIPS Agreement. For example, in the European Patent Convention, at Article 52(2), "(c) schemes, rules and methods for performing mental acts, playing games or doing business, and programs for computers" are expressly excluded from the definition of "invention."[6] Decision 486 of the Andean

6. For Article 52, see *infra* section III. The European Patent Regulation and the Agreement on a Unified Patent Court supplement the provisions of the EPC, but do not supplant those provisions. *See, e.g.*, Article 24 of the Agreement on a Unified Patent Court. These relationships are discussed further *infra* section III.A.

Community, at Article 15, expressly excludes from the definition of "inventions": "(d) plans, rules, and methods for the pursuit of intellectual activities, playing of games, or economic and business activities; (e) computer programs and software, as such."[7] India, in Section 3 of the Patents Act, excludes business methods and computer software programs (as such) from the definition of "invention."[8]

It is important therefore to distinguish Lord Hoffmann's proposition that "invention" is not useful as a separate analytic criteria of patentability from a suggestion that "invention" may not be used to define patentable subject matter.

**2.** As we review the criteria of patentability in the following pages, consider whether there is something you would consider an "invention" that would not be captured by these criteria.

### *1. Novelty*

The first criterion and major qualification for a patent is that an invention be "new" or "novel." This means that the invention (product or process) has not been anticipated by prior art. In other words, the invention has not been disclosed or described before the date of the patent application filing. Although national patent rules differ regarding the form of disclosure that will be considered to anticipate an invention,[9] novelty will generally be defeated by an anticipating disclosure (in a covered form) anywhere in the world.[10] The patent applicant is usually obligated to identify prior art of which he or she is aware. One role of the patent examiner is to conduct a "prior art search" that attempts to identify relevant anticipating disclosure.

Naturally, there may be disagreement between an inventor and the patent examiner about whether a particular prior art disclosure in fact anticipates an invention. A prior inventor may have described a device similar, but not identical, to the subsequent inventor's device. The patent examiner must determine whether the second device is sufficiently different from the first device to be "new" or "novel" in the sense of not being encompassed by the prior art. Some inventions are considered "inherent" in the prior art, even if not specifically disclosed (*see, e.g., Abbott Labs. v. Baxter Pharms.*, 471 F.3d 1363 (Fed. Cir. 2006), *rehearing en banc denied*).

The European Patent Office (EPO) is established under the terms of the European Patent Convention (EPC) and issues patents with respect to 39 countries in Europe (not limited to EU countries).[11] A European Patent is granted with effect in EPC members that have been designated by an applicant, following an examination by the EPO. Once the patent is granted, it is governed by the law of the country in which it is practiced. In the EPC system, there is a post-grant opposition procedure that permits parties believing a patent should not have been

---

7. Andean Community, Decision 486—Common Provisions on Industrial Property (of September 14, 2000), available at WIPO Collection of Laws for Electronic Access (CLEA) database.

8. Section 3, as amended by the Patents (Amendments) Act, 2002, provides:

> The following are not inventions within the meaning of this Act,—(k) a mathematical or business method or a computer programme *per se* or algorithms.

9. Some countries, for example, require that a disclosure be in writing to constitute prior art, while for others oral disclosure will suffice.

10. The patent laws of a few countries limit anticipating disclosure to those that occur within their territory. This rule is largely a remnant of the colonial era and is generally being replaced.

11. As of November 2018, there are 38 EPO member states: Albania, Austria, Belgium, Bulgaria, Croatia, Cyprus, Czech Republic, Denmark, Estonia, Finland, France, Germany, Greece, Hungary, Iceland, Ireland, Italy, Latvia, Liechtenstein, Lithuania, Luxembourg, Former Yugoslav Republic of Macedonia, Malta, Monaco, Netherlands, Norway, Poland, Portugal, Romania, San Marino, Serbia, Slovakia, Slovenia, Spain, Sweden, Switzerland, Turkey, and the United Kingdom. *See* http://www.epo.org/about-us/epo/member-states.html.

granted to challenge the grant within a set time period. We examine the EPC/EPO arrangement in sections III.A-C, *infra*, as well as the new EU (Unitary) Patent System arrangements.

The following passage from a decision by the Technical Board of Appeal of the EPO in *Motorola v. Agence Spatiale Européenne* illustrates the issue of novelty. In this case, Motorola had been granted a patent by the EPO, but the patent was revoked by the Opposition Division. The opponent alleged that a document published before the initial filing (and priority date) of the patent application disclosed a means for controlling cellular telephone transmissions that included Motorola's claimed invention, at least insofar as Motorola's patent application described the invention. Motorola argued that the Opposition Division had not properly understood its claim. Motorola appealed the decision of the Opposition Division to the Technical Board, arguing that its claim was in fact new.

## *Motorola, Inc. v. Agence Spatiale Européenne, Alcatel Space Industries*

Satellite cellular telephone and data communication system T 0365/98
Technical Board of Appeal, Electricity I April 28, 1999

OPINION:

### SUMMARY OF FACTS AND SUBMISSIONS

**1. THIS IS AN APPEAL BY THE PROPRIETOR OF EUROPEAN PATENT NO. 0 365 885 AGAINST THE DECISION OF THE OPPOSITION DIVISION TO REVOKE THE PATENT. . . .**

III. The Opposition Division decided on the proprietor's main request (the patent as granted) and two auxiliary requests. The main request and the first auxiliary request were refused for lack of novelty with respect to E3. . . .

IV. On 26 March 1999 the appellant [Motorola] filed four new requests. . . .

### REASONS FOR THE DECISION

#### 1. construction of the invention

1.1. The invention is a satellite cellular system. This system comprises satellites in low-earth orbit, i.e. at a height at which satellites are not geostationary but have a period of perhaps a few hours. The satellites are capable of switching telephone calls from users on earth. Since the satellites are constantly moving, a communication link set up between two users needs generally to be redefined during the call. This process, a kind of dynamic re-routing, is referred to as handing-off. The handing-off can be between different "cells" — corresponding to different antenna beams — of one and the same satellite, or between two satellites. In the first case one speaks of intra-satellite handing-off, in the second case of inter-satellite handing-off. According to claim 1 (of all requests) the inter-satellite handing-off is performed by a "first means for handing-off" and the intra-satellite handing-off by "second means for handing-off."

1.2. A crucial point throughout the opposition proceedings has been how the term "handing-off" in claim 1 should be understood, taking into account the way it is used in the description. Briefly stated, the appellant [Motorola] is of the opinion that the expression not merely implies that the physical switching is performed in the satellites, but that the complete control of the handing-off process is located there. In particular, the invention comprises no external control on earth or in a geostationary satellite. The respondents, on the other hand, argue that there is no basis for such a restricted interpretation since the whole specification is silent on what kind of handing-off control is used and where it might be situated. . . .

1.6. . . . [T]he Board [cannot] see that an overall consideration of the specification supports the appellant's [Motorola's] understanding of the invention. It is true that there is no mention of any kind of switching control besides the satellites. It is also true that the appellant's interpretation is consistent with the teaching of the patent. This is however not conclusive. The fact that a controlling earth station is not described does not necessarily mean that there is none or could not be one — it may just as well be that the issue of handing-off control was never contemplated at the time the application was drafted. Nor is consistency sufficient — in fact, neither the appellant's nor the respondents' interpretations of the invention seem to contradict the patent specification in any way.

1.7. The Board thus finds that the invention as it has been disclosed concerns a satellite cellular system comprising satellites which are capable of establishing calls autonomously and which contain (some) means for intra-satellite and inter-satellite handing-off. The invention is however not limited . . . to a system in which the complete handing-off control is contained in the satellites.

### 2. The Appellant's Main Request

The closest prior art document, and the only one considered in the decision of the Opposition Division, is E3. It deals in particular with a system called MSS (Multiple Satellite System). This system comprises satellites which are in low earth orbits and employ packet switching technology, which implies that the satellites contain switching means. As to handing-off, it is said on page 1671 that when "a cell passes over, the user's receiving/transmitting antenna would adjust to its new frequency and an on-board computer in the satellite, perhaps under the direction of a traffic routing (and billing) ground station, would ensure that communication is not interrupted." The Board is satisfied that the skilled person would regard this statement as an indication that means for intra-satellite handing-off are present in the satellites. It is further said on page 1674 that "satellite changeover is required" as satellites move. This is regarded as referring to inter-satellite handing-off. Since, trivially, handing-off is not possible without "handing-off means" (of some kind) within the satellites, such means are also disclosed in E3. It is not clearly disclosed that the complete control of handing-off could be performed by the satellites, but this becomes irrelevant with the Board's understanding of the invention according to the patent in suit.

The Board thus concludes, as did the Opposition Division, that the subject-matter of claim 1 is not new. . . .

ORDER

For these reasons it is decided that:
The appeal is dismissed.

## NOTES AND QUESTIONS

**1.** In the text case, the Technical Board of Appeals has confirmed the revocation of Motorola's patent because the subject matter of the invention was disclosed prior to its application for the patent. Motorola was claiming that its invention was limited to a particular kind of "handing off" of signals within satellites, and Agence Spatiale was arguing that Motorola's patent claim was broader. The reason for these positions? If Agence Spatiale's broader construction was accepted, the invention had been disclosed earlier (and "anticipated").

2. One of the most controversial issues in respect to novelty concerns the availability of patent protection for "new uses" of existing products.[12] In terms of product patent subject matter, the inventor of a new use does not create a new manufacture or composition of matter. The invention has been disclosed and constitutes prior art in so far as the product "as such" is concerned. However, patent examiners and courts have been receptive to the argument that a new use for a known product may constitute an inventive process or method of use. While there is not unanimity among national jurisdictions on the patenting of new uses, the trend in decisions so far is largely to accept the novelty (and subject matter patentability) of new uses of known products.[13]

**3.** There are obvious practical difficulties associated with the patenting of new uses. Conceptually, the patent holder should not be able to prevent the manufacture, sale, or use of the compound outside the scope of the new use claim. In fact, the product for which a new use patent is granted may be patented by a third party and the new use patent holder may not make the product itself. But how does the new use patent holder address the situation in which a producer offers to sell its products for one purpose, yet buyers decide to use the product for the patented purpose? Should the patent holder be able to enjoin sales by the producer? Would not this extend patent protection beyond the scope of the claims? Should the way in which third-party producers advertise or promote their products matter?[14] See, e.g., the decision of the United Kingdom Supreme Court in *Warner-Lambert v. Mylan,* [2018] UKSC 56, dividing on the proper test for infringement liability.

**4.** A critical aspect of the new use question involves so-called second medical indication or second medical use patents. Regarding Swiss-type claims, jurisprudential and legislative development in the EU, *see Warner Lambert v. Mylan,* note 3, *id.* A compound or material that is known to be effective in the treatment of one medical condition or disease is found to be effective in the treatment of another condition or disease. The patenting of second medical uses has been allowed in a number of jurisdictions under the heading of "method of use" ("the use of compound *X* for the treatment of disease *Y*") or "Swiss claim" ("the use of compound *X* for the manufacture of a treatment for disease *Y*"). Such patenting has been rejected in some jurisdictions; for example, Section 3(d) of the India Patents Act (as amended 2005) provides:

> 3. What are not inventions
>
> The following are not inventions within the meaning of this Act,—
>
> *(d)* the mere discovery of a new form of a known substance which does not result in the enhancement of the known efficacy of that substance or *the mere discovery of any new property or new use for a known substance* or of the mere use of a known process, machine or apparatus unless such known process results in a new product or employs at least one new reactant.

---

12. The issue of "new use" might also be considered a question of patentable "subject matter" since it concerns whether a particular type of invention is patentable, or a question of inventive step since a new use may be obvious in light of prior art. *See* discussion of analytic possibilities in Chisum on Patents §1.03[8] (2002).

13. *See, e.g.*, U.S. cases collected, *id.*, at §1.03[8][c]. The "new use" of a known compound is considered by the Canadian Supreme Court in *Apotek v. Wellcome Foundation*, excerpted in the section on "Utility." In that case, the court assumed that a new use for an existing compound was patentable. The question was the point at which the patent applicant had in fact invented the new use.

14. *See, e.g., Warner-Lambert v. Apotexcorp.*, 316 F.3d 1348 (Fed. Cir. 2003), in which the holder of a method of use patent for a pharmaceutical compound asserted patent infringement based on a generic manufacturer's alleged inducement to doctors to prescribe for treatment of a medical condition outside the scope of the method of use claims. The U.S. Court of Appeals rejected the infringement claim for lack of proof of "specific intent" and "action to induce infringement."

> *Explanation.*—For the purposes of this clause, salts, esters, ethers, polymorphs, metabolites, pure form, particle size, isomers, mixtures of isomers, complexes, combinations and other derivatives of known substance shall be considered to be the same substance, unless they differ significantly in properties with regard to efficacy; . . . [italics added].

We examine a decision of the Indian High Court of Madras addressing the constitutionality of Section 3(d) later in this chapter.

**5.** If the premise of patentability of second medical indications is accepted (as in the United States and in the EU), an issue arises regarding what constitutes a new use. In *Perricone v. Medicis Pharmaceutical*, 432 F.3d 1368 (Fed. Cir. 2005), the CAFC permitted an inventor to claim a method of using the same pharmaceutical product for preventing sunburn as distinct from a claim for treating sunburn (432 F.3d at 1378-79).

6. The granting of second medical use patents on pharmaceutical products has important social and economic implications. On one hand, the discoverers of second medical uses argue that the expense of obtaining regulatory approval for new uses necessitates patent protection be granted to permit them to recover such expenses (e.g., in conducting clinical trials); otherwise, newly discovered uses would not make it to the market of doctors and patients. On the other hand, patents for new uses may be used as means to prevent the emergence of competition in the pharmaceutical market (and the lowering of prices) as patent holders place costly and time-consuming legal obstacles in the way of generic producers.[15] Pfizer's Viagra (sildenafil citrate) has been one of the most profitable medicines patented over the past decades. Pfizer's original patent for the compound disclosed its use in the treatment of cardiovascular disease. The property of treating erectile dysfunction was discovered as a "side effect" of cardiovascular treatment.[16] Pfizer did not discover a compound. It discovered that a known compound (on which it already held a product patent) possessed certain beneficial properties. Is this an "invention"?[17] An interesting discussion of the treatment of the Viagra patent in China can be found in Note, *Patent Law for New Medical Uses of Known Compounds and Pfizer's Viagra Patent*, 46 IDEA 283 (2006).

**7.** Viagra is sometimes referred to as a "lifestyle drug" since it does not involve a "life or death" medical condition. But the "new use" issue extends to many other compounds, including for the treatment of HIV/AIDS. Consider, for example, the discovery that combining certain known antiretroviral medicines into a triple combination therapy "cocktail" dramatically improves the effectiveness of treatment. Should the person who discovered that combining antiretroviral medicines results in more effective treatment of HIV/AIDS receive a patent on triple combination therapy?

## 2. *Inventive Step*

Inventive step or nonobviousness might be said to refer to the conceptual distance between prior art and invention. One way that legislators and courts have approached this criterion is to ask whether a claimed invention would have been obvious to a person reasonably skilled in the art practiced by the invention. However, this is not the only method by which inventive

15. *See Warner-Lambert, id.* The U.S. Federal Trade Commission has expressed concern about the ways that a range of patenting techniques are used to block generic competition (*see* FTC, Generic Drug Entry Prior to Patent Expiration: An FTC Study, July 2002).

16. *See Lilly Icos v. Pfizer*, 2002 WL 45115 (CA) (2002) 25(4) I.P.D. 25, 022, [2002] EWCA Civ 1, 23 Jan. 2002. Judgment by Lord Justice Aldous, at para. 59.

17. As it happens, Pfizer's second use patent for treatment of erectile dysfunction was invalidated in the United Kingdom on the basis of obviousness in light of prior art. That prior art included the suggestion published prior to submission of the patent application that the class of compounds of which sildenafil citrate is a part may be effective in the treatment of erectile dysfunction. *Id.*, at, e.g., para. 44.

step might reasonably be assessed. For example, in certain fields it may be possible to limit inventive step by excluding certain classes of "easy" manipulations of subject matter.

To illustrate the criterion, imagine that someone has been granted a patent on the clip that is used to keep ballpoint pens fastened to shirt pockets. Suppose that the patent application described a clip with a pointed tip, and that such clips as described in the application were soon found to tear holes in shirt pockets. A second person submits a patent application describing the same clip, but with a rounded end. The rounded end prevents shirt pockets from tearing. Such an invention may be new and useful, but it is probably too obvious to qualify for a patent (it lacks an inventive step).

The objective of the patent system is to reward invention. The patent grant allows its holder to exclude others from a range of activity with respect to the invention for a period of time. Because grants of exclusive rights in technology impose burdens on society, there is a need to limit such grants. The criterion of inventive step is intended to limit the grant of exclusive rights to those that have made a significant contribution to the development of new and useful technologies.

In *Biogen v. Medeva*, the U.K. House of Lords discussed the concept of inventive step in the complex environment of recombinant DNA research. What happens when many scientists share a general idea, but only one of them pursues concrete realization of that idea in the face of widely feared obstacles? Are the actions of the more determined scientist "inventive," or merely industrious?

## *Biogen, Inc. v. Medeva PLC*

House of Lords
[1997] RPC 1
31 October 1996

Lord Hoffmann: . . .

### 10. inventive step

I will therefore first consider the question of whether what Professor Murray did in 1978 involved, as at the date of Biogen 1, an inventive step. Section 3 says:

> An invention shall be taken to involve an inventive step if it is not obvious to a person skilled in the art, having regard to any matter which forms part of the state of the art by virtue only of section 2(2) above. . . .

Section 2(2) defines the state of the art:

> The state of the art in the case of an invention shall be taken to comprise all matter (whether a product, a process, information about either or anything else) which has at any time before the priority date of that invention been made available to the public (whether in the United Kingdom or elsewhere) by written or oral description, by use or in any other way.

The question is therefore whether what Professor Murray did was obvious having regard to all matter which had been made available to the public before 22 December 1978. Aldous J, after hearing expert evidence about what people skilled in the art of recombinant DNA technology would have thought and done at the time, held that it was not. I will summarise his reasoning. He followed the procedure suggested by Oliver LJ in *Windsurfing International Inc v Tabur Marine* (Great Britain) Ltd [1985] RPC 59, 73-74 by dividing the inquiry into four steps:

> The first is to identify the inventive concept embodied in the patent in suit. Thereafter, the court has to assume the mantle of the normally skilled but unimaginative addressee in the art at the priority date and impute to him what was, at that date, common general knowledge in the

> art in question. The third step is to identify what, if any, differences exist between the matter cited as being "known or used" and the alleged invention. Finally, the court has to ask itself whether, viewed without any knowledge of the alleged invention, those differences constitute steps which would have been obvious to the skilled man or whether they require any degree of invention.

Aldous J identified the inventive concept as "the idea or decision to express a polypeptide displaying HBV antigen specificity in a suitable host." The identification of the inventive concept is, as I have said, critical to this case and I shall have more to say about it later. At this stage I only observe that as formulated by Aldous J, the inventive concept means, in effect, having the idea of making HBV antigens by recombinant DNA technology.[18] But that seems to me to be putting the matter far too wide. The idea of making HBV antigens by recombinant DNA technology was shared by everyone at the Geneva meeting of Biogen in February 1978 and no doubt by others working in the field, just as the idea of flying in an heavier-than-air machine had existed for centuries before the Wright brothers. The problem which required invention was to find a way of doing it.

Aldous J then considered what would have been known to the man skilled in the art. I have already summarised what relevant information would have been available to the public in 1978. In particular, Aldous J considered the importance of the Villa-Komaroff paper and said:

> "It is accepted that once a decision [had] been made to try expression of the HBV genome, the technique set out in Villa-Komaroff would have been sufficient to enable it to be carried out. Thus the difference between the prior art and the inventive concept is the idea or decision to express a polypeptide displaying HBV antigen specificity in a suitable host." ([1995] RPC 25, 58.)

Again, I think that this is not a sufficiently specific way of stating the inventive concept. The general idea of expressing the gene for a polypeptide[19] displaying HBV antigen specificity in a suitable host was, as I have said, fairly widely entertained. The inventive concept was the notion that Professor Murray's method of achieving the goal—creating large fragments of genomic DNA, ligating them to pBR322 and introducing the hybrid molecule into E coli—would work.

Aldous J then considered what strategies would have been available in 1978 to a skilled man who wanted to achieve the goal of making HBV antigens by recombinant DNA technology. One (strategy A) was to try to find out more about HBV and its DNA. In particular, one would sequence the genome. This would provide the information upon which a decision could be made as to whether and if so how to express the relevant genes. The alternative (strategy B) was, as Professor Murray had done, to take the genomic DNA and try to express it in E coli. Biogen's case, as recorded by the judge, was that—"it was not until the sequence had been obtained, with the knowledge that introns would not be a problem, that the skilled man would seriously consider expression of HBV antigens." ([1995] RPC 25, 64.)

18. [Wilson & Gisvold's Textbook of Organic Medicinal and Pharmaceutical Chemistry (J. Delgado & W. Remers eds., 10th ed. 1998) says: "An antigen (Ag) is a substance that induces antibody formation, and then reacts with that antibody. Inherent in the definition is a chemical reaction" (154). Antigens are used in vaccines. *Id.* at 164-65.—Eds.]

19. [Remington, The Science and Practice of Pharmacy (20th ed. 2000), states: "Peptides are very small hydrolytic fragments of their original proteins. They contain from 2 to possibly 20 or so amino acids and commonly are subdivided into di-, tri-, etc., peptides according to the number of amino acid residues they contain. Collectively, the higher members are often termed *polypeptides*" (419).—Eds.]

The judge accepted this submission and held that strategy B would not have been obvious in 1978. He said:

> "In the present case, there is no evidence to suggest that anyone, other than Biogen, contemplated expression of the HBV antigen in December 1978, despite the fact that the skilled man must have read the Villa-Komaroff paper and there was an incentive to do so. The reason may well be that stated in the patent, namely the skilled man was put off by introns." ([1995] RPC 25, 65.)

He also rejected the argument that strategy A was an obvious way of making the antigens. The evidence showed only that sequencing might show that there were no introns[20] and that the gene could be expressed in bacteria but there was no ground for assuming that it would.

In the Court of Appeal, Hobhouse LJ held that strategy B was obvious. The decision to adopt it was a "matter of business judgment," a "mere commercial decision." Biogen had made a decision "to pursue an identified goal by known means." I think, with all respect to the closely-reasoned judgment of Hobhouse LJ, that the reference to a commercial decision is an irrelevancy. The fact that a given experimental strategy was adopted for commercial reasons, because the anticipated rewards seemed to justify the necessary expenditure, is no reason why that strategy should not involve an inventive step. An inventor need not pursue his experiment untouched by thoughts of gain. Most patents are the result of research programmes undertaken on the basis of hard-headed cost-benefit analysis. Nor do I think that the analogy of a bet is particularly helpful. In Genentech Inc's Patent [1989] RPC 147, 281, Mustill LJ said, in my opinion rightly, that "it cannot . . . be assumed that inventiveness must have been involved somewhere, just because a wager on success could have been placed at long odds." The question is not what the odds were but whether there was an inventive step.

Having said this, I do think that Hobhouse LJ was substantially correct in saying that Professor Murray had chosen to pursue an identified goal by known means. The goal of obtaining HBV antigens by recombinant DNA technology was obvious and the Villa-Komaroff method was by then part of the state of the art. If, therefore, the inventive concept was simply, as Aldous J said, "the idea or decision to express a polypeptide displaying HBV antigen specificity in a suitable host," I would agree with Hobhouse LJ that, so stated, the concept was obvious. It is however clear from the reasoning of Aldous J that in order to explain why he regarded the decision as involving an inventive step it is necessary to describe it with rather more particularity. A proper statement of the inventive concept needs to include some express or implied reference to the problem which it required invention to overcome. The reasons why the expert witnesses thought it was not obvious to try the expression of genomic HBV DNA in E coli were for the most part concerned with the uncertainties, in the absence of sequence information, about the presence of the HBV antigen genes in the Dane particle DNA, the perceived difficulties of expressing genomic eukaryotic DNA in a prokaryotic host, and, specifically, the problem of introns. It seems to me, therefore, that a more accurate way of stating the inventive concept as it appeared to Aldous J is to say that it was the idea of trying to express unsequenced eukaryotic DNA in a prokaryotic host.

The question of whether an invention was obvious had been called "a kind of jury question" (*see* Jenkins LJ in *Allmanna Svenska Elektriska A/B v The Burntisland Shipbuilding Co Ltd* (1952) 69 RPC 63, 70) and should be treated with appropriate respect by an appellate court. . . . Where the application of a legal standard such as negligence or obviousness involves no question of principle but is simply a matter of degree, an appellate court should be very cautious in differing from the judge's evaluation.

20. ["Introns" are portions of the DNA sequence that are presently thought not to code for proteins. *See, e.g.*, Wilson & Gisvold, *supra* note 18, and Sulston & Ferry, The Common Thread (2002). — Eds.]

In the present case I think that the reason why Hobhouse LJ differed from the judge on the question of obviousness was not because of any failure to give sufficient weight to the judge's evaluation of the evidence but because he took at face value the judge's statement of the inventive concept. On the other hand, if the concept is reformulated in accordance with the judge's reasoning as I have suggested, the argument for the existence of an inventive step is much stronger. If no question of principle were involved, I think it would be wrong to interfere with the judge's assessment. But the inventiveness alleged in this case is of a very unusual kind. It is said to consist in attempting something which a man less skilled in the art might have regarded as obvious, but which the expert would have thought so beset by obstacles as not to be worth trying. In *Raleigh Cycle Co Ltd v H Miller & Co Ltd* (1946) 63 RPC 113 the Court of Appeal was prepared to assume that it could be inventive to realise that a bicycle hub dynamo of conventional design could function satisfactorily even though it rotated at a lower speed than was previously thought essential. There may be a question of principle here but, like the Court of Appeal in that case, I shall not pursue the question of whether this amounts to an inventive step for the purposes of patent law because I am content to assume, without deciding, that what Professor Murray did was not obvious.

## NOTES AND QUESTIONS

**1.** The patent system is often justified as a stimulus to inventive activity through enhanced financial reward (or potential reward). If an invention is achieved by a commercial decision to invest capital in pursuit of a widely identified goal, can the patent grant be said to have stimulated inventive activity? Has it instead stimulated the investment of capital? Is there a difference?

**2.** The WIPO Secretariat has prepared reports on the implementation of the inventive step, a requirement in national jurisdictions in connection with the work program of the Standing Committee on the law of patents. *See, e.g.*, WIPO, Further Study on Inventive Step (Part III), Document prepared by the Secretariat, SCP/30/4l; Further Study on Inventive Step (Part II), Document Prepared by the Secretariat, SCP/29/4; Further Study on Inventive Step (Part I), Document prepared by the Secretariat, SCP/28/4, June 16, 2018;[21] Study on Inventive Step, Document prepared by the Secretariat, SCP/22/3, July 6, 2015.[22]

**3.** In *KSR v. Teleflex*, 550 U.S. 398 (2007), the U.S. Supreme Court addressed the test to be used in assessing the patent criteria of "nonobviousness" (referred to in most countries as the "inventive step" requirement). There is a long history of Supreme Court jurisprudence emphasizing the importance of granting patents only for genuinely creative inventions (those that would not be "obvious" to a person reasonably skilled in the art). In U.S. law, a patent examiner in making determinations regarding "novelty" may find that an invention has been "anticipated" only if the invention is disclosed in a single piece of prior art. In making a determination regarding nonobviousness, an examiner has more latitude because a number of prior art references may be combined to establish that a person reasonably skilled in the art would have considered the technical step as obvious. The Federal Circuit developed a "teaching, suggestion or motivation" (or "TSM") test for evaluating whether a combination of "prior art" represents a bar to a finding of nonobviousness. In the TSM test, the Federal Circuit said that at least one piece of combined prior art must have given some instruction to the reasonably skilled person that would direct him or her to combine the prior art. Unless

21. http://www.wipo.int/edocs/mdocs/scp/en/scp_28/scp_28_4.pdf.

22. http://www.wipo.int/edocs/mdocs/scp/en/scp_22/scp_22_3.pdf.

such a teaching, suggestion, or motivation was demonstrated, the reasonably skilled person would presumably not have thought to put together the prior art. This was a highly limiting requirement for disqualifying an invention on the basis of obviousness. It is often difficult to find an express teaching, suggestion, or motivation. *KSR v. Teleflex* involved combining prior art in the development of a digitally controlled truck accelerator pedal. The Supreme Court rejected the Federal Circuit's view that an explicit teaching, suggestion, or motivation to combine prior art must be demonstrated for a finding of obviousness. The Supreme Court said that a person reasonably skilled in the art should be assumed to be familiar with the general state of development in his or her field of technology, and should be understood to be capable of adapting technologies that are generally known, even if a specific suggestion to combine them is not found. Among the questions that the patent examiner may consider are whether it was "obvious to try" a combination of prior art (a question that the Federal Circuit said was not relevant). The Supreme Court therefore broadened in a very substantial way the factors that patent examiners may consider when assessing whether a claimed invention is obvious. This decision effectively makes it more difficult to secure a patent in the United States because it extends the grounds upon which patent examiners may reject applications.

**4.** It is sometimes suggested that patents should be granted only for "major" or "important" inventions since a proliferation of "minor" improvement patents does more to inhibit productivity and competition than to stimulate creative activity. The inventive step criterion in a limited way serves to distinguish between major and minor inventions. Development and application of a "major-minor" test for patentability presents some conceptual and practical issues, including how it might be applied across a broad spectrum of inventive subject matter and how to take into account uncertainty about the future value of inventions. Might a more rigorous application of the inventive step criterion be a useful way to address the problem of a proliferation of weak patents? *See* U.S. Federal Trade Commission, *To Promote Innovation: The Proper Balance of Competition and Patent Law and Policy*, ch. 3 (2003).

**5.** At least for some cases the argument can reasonably be made that patents on "foundational" inventions should be more difficult to obtain, or should perhaps be granted with different conditions, than less important inventions. For example, the mRNA vaccines developed to address the COVID-19 pandemic relied on two foundational inventions: the first involved substitution of the mRNA uracil nucleobase with a different nucleobase, N1-methylpseudouridine, that had the effect of reducing the immunogenicity of the vaccine; the second, a breakthrough in lipid nanoparticle (LNP) technology that allowed delicate mRNA to enter cells without breaking down.* As it happens, both of these patented technologies were out-licensed by their owners on a non-exclusive basis so that development of mRNA vaccines by third parties was not blocked. However, the technology of both inventions appears to be essential to the development of mRNA vaccines generally, and it might indeed be a problem if one or two inventors exclusively held that technology and refused to make it available more widely. Should we grant patents on the type of foundational technology that may be critical across a wide range of products essential to maintaining public health? Might there alternatively be a tweak to the patent system that would require such foundational technologies to be licensed non-exclusively? This perhaps is the role of compulsory licensing. That is, to provide a legal instrument to overcome potential critical blockages.

**6.** As suggested in the introduction to this inventive step criterion, alternatives to the case-by-case "person reasonably skilled in the art" approach may be feasible in some fields. For example, certain kinds of modifications to molecular structure may be sufficiently

* See Frederick Abbott, Intellectual Property and Technology Transfer for COVID-19 Vaccines: Assessment of the Record, Study for WIPO Global Challenges, https://www.wipo.int/publications/en/details.jsp?id=4684&plang=EN.

commonplace to warrant exclusion—or at least a strong presumption of exclusion—from inventiveness. This kind of approach has been suggested as a means to limit pharmaceutical patents for minor changes in chemical structure that may yield some patient benefit, but may not justify a new 20-year patent. This is one aspect of the approach taken by India in the adoption of Section 3(d) of the 2005 Patents Act Amendments and preclusion of patents on new forms of known substances that do not show a significant enhancement in efficacy over the known forms. The distance between the prior art and the claimed invention must be demonstrated through a secondary test, i.e., therapeutic efficacy. In other words, a showing that the result of applying the invention is to improve the treatment of the patient as compared with the existing forms of treatment. This is a way of establishing an objective test of inventive step that is less subjective than whether the reasonably skilled technician would regard the change as "obvious." Regarding Section 3(d), *see* the decision of the Supreme Court of India in *Novartis v. India*, *infra* section IV.B.

**7.** It has been suggested that the rapid evolution of artificial intelligence (AI) will inevitably lead to a change in the way inventiveness or nonobviousness is assessed. Computers implementing AI systems may eventually become better at problem-solving than human beings. What may be very difficult for the reasonably skilled-in-the-art human inventor may be commonplace or easy for an AI system. If that becomes the case, should patent examiners assess inventiveness by taking the reasonably skilled human as the baseline or benchmark, or should the new benchmark be the average or reasonably skilled AI system? And, where will we find patent examiners who can distinguish what may be "ordinary" from "inventive" when assessing the patent applications of AI systems?

**RYAN ABBOTT***

## *Everything Is Obvious*

What happens when inventive AI becomes a standard part of the inventive process? This is not a thought experiment. For instance, while the timeline is controversial, surveys of experts suggest that artificial general intelligence, which is a computer able to perform any intellectual task a person could, will develop in the next twenty-five years. Some thought leaders, such as Ray Kurzweil, one of Google's Directors of Engineering, predict computers will have human levels of intelligence in about a decade.

The impact of the widespread use of inventive AI will be tremendous, not just on innovation, but also on patent law. Right now, patentability is determined based on what a hypothetical, non-inventive, skilled person would find obvious. The skilled person represents the average worker in the scientific field of an invention. Once the average worker uses inventive AI, or inventive AI replaces the average worker, then inventive activity will be normal instead of exceptional.

If the skilled person standard fails to evolve accordingly, this will result in too lenient a standard for patentability. Patents have significant anticompetitive costs, and allowing the average worker to routinely patent their outputs would cause social harm. As the U.S. Supreme Court has articulated, "[g]ranting patent protection to advances that would occur in the ordinary course without real innovation retards progress and may . . . deprive prior inventions of their value or utility."

* Adapted from Ryan Abbott, *Everything Is Obvious*, 66 UCLA L. Rev. 2 (2019).

The skilled standard must keep pace with real world conditions. In fact, the standard needs updating even before inventive AI is commonplace. Already, computers are widely facilitating research and assisting with invention. For instance, computers may perform literature searches, data analysis, and pattern recognition. This makes current workers more knowledgeable and creative than they would be without the use of such technologies. The Federal Circuit has provided a list of nonexhaustive factors to consider in determining the level of ordinary skill: (1) "type[s] of problems encountered in the art," (2) "prior art solutions to those problems," (3) "rapidity with which innovations are made," (4) "sophistication of the technology," and (5) "educational level of active workers in the field." This test should be modified to include a sixth factor: (6) "technologies used by active workers."

This change will more explicitly take into account the fact that AI is already augmenting the capabilities of workers, in essence making more obvious and expanding the scope of prior art. Once inventive AI becomes the standard means of research in a field, the test would also encompass the routine use of inventive AI by skilled persons. Taken a step further, once inventive AI becomes the standard means of research in a field, the skilled person should be an inventive AI. Specifically, the skilled person should be an inventive AI when the standard approach to research in a field or with respect to a particular problem is to use an inventive AI (the "Inventive AI Standard").

To obtain the necessary information to implement this test, the Patent Office should establish a new requirement for applicants to disclose when an AI contributes to the conception of an invention, which is the standard for qualifying as an inventor. Applicants are already required to disclose all human inventors, and failure to do so can render a patent invalid or unenforceable. Similarly, applicants should need to disclose whether an AI has done the work of a human inventor. This information could be aggregated to determine whether most invention in a field is performed by people or AI. This information would also be useful for determining appropriate inventorship, and more broadly for formulating innovation policies.

Whether the Inventive AI Standard is that of a skilled person using an inventive AI or just an inventive AI, the result will be the same: The average worker will be capable of inventive activity. Conceptualizing the skilled person as using an inventive AI might be administratively simpler, but replacing the skilled person with the inventive AI would be preferable because it emphasizes that the AI is engaging in inventive activity, rather than the human worker.

Yet simply substituting an inventive AI for a skilled person might exacerbate existing problems with the nonobviousness inquiry. With the current skilled person standard, decisionmakers, in hindsight, need to reason about what another person would have found obvious. This results in inconsistent and unpredictable nonobviousness determinations. In practice, the skilled person standard bears unfortunate similarities to the "Elephant Test," or Justice Stewart's famously unworkable definition of obscene material: "I know it when I see it." This may be even more problematic in the case of inventive AI, as it is likely to be difficult for human decisionmakers to theoretically reason about what an AI would find obvious.

An existing vein of critical scholarship has already advocated for nonobviousness inquiries to focus more on economic factors or objective "secondary" criteria, such as long-felt but unsolved needs, the failure of others, and real-world evidence of how an invention was received in the marketplace. Inventive AI may provide the impetus for such a shift. Nonobvious inquiries utilizing the Inventive AI Standard might also focus on reproducibility, specifically whether standard AI could reproduce the subject matter of a patent application with sufficient ease. This could be a more objective and determinate test that would allow the Patent Office to apply a single standard consistently, and it would result in fewer judicially invalidated patents. A nonobviousness inquiry focused on either secondary factors or reproducibility may avoid some of the difficulties inherent in applying a "cognitive" inventive AI standard.

However the test is applied, the Inventive AI Standard will dynamically raise the current benchmark for patentability. Inventive AI will be significantly more intelligent than skilled persons and also capable of considering more prior art. An Inventive AI Standard would not prohibit patents, but it would make obtaining them substantially more difficult: A person or AI might need to have an unusual insight that other inventive AI could not easily recreate, developers might need to create increasingly intelligent AI that could outperform standard AI, or, most likely, invention will be dependent on specialized, non-public sources of data. The nonobviousness bar will continue to rise as AI inevitably become increasingly sophisticated. Taken to its logical extreme, and given there may be no limit to how intelligent AI will become, it may be that every invention will one day be obvious to commonly used AI. That would mean no more patents should be issued without some radical change to current patentability criteria.

## NOTES AND QUESTIONS

**1.** As discussed above, AI may impact or dramatically impact the nonobviousness standard. In what other areas of patent law do you think AI may have an impact?

**2.** Some of the areas people are concerned about include AI in IP administration (e.g., helping patent offices search prior art, or automate translations or examination activities), patent prosecution (e.g., drafting applications), and, as discussed further below, whether inventions "by" AI are patentable.

**3.** People are also concerned about patents "on" AI, namely certain "computer-implemented inventions," and whether these should be patentable. Patents on software as algorithms alone are generally not allowed, but where a computer is involved in a technical solution to a technical problem, this is generally allowed. People are also concerned about enablement and disclosure requirements for computer-implemented inventions, because of criticism that patents on AI that fail to disclose source code and training data, for example, cannot be replicated by skilled persons. In any event, these are longstanding concerns related to "software patents" rather than concerns about "AI-generated inventions".

**4.** A project called AllPriorArt (https://allpriorart.com/) is "attempting to algorithmically create and publicly publish all possible new prior art, thereby making the published concepts not patentable. The concept is to democratize ideas, provide an impetus for change in the patent system, and to preempt patent trolls. The system works by pulling text from the entire database of U.S.-issued and published (un-approved) patents and creating prior art from the patent language. While most inventions generated will be nonsensical, the cost to computationally create and publish millions of ideas is nearly zero – which allows for a higher probability of possible valid prior art. Further, a large institution could dedicate many servers to this task, along with developing more advanced techniques such as deep learning, to flood the prior art space. It is not unforeseeable with current technology (along with sufficient cash for fees) to flood the actual patent application process itself with sufficiently advanced patent applications based on this concept. A sister website called All The Claims is attempting the same thing, but with the use of claims and a more verbose alternative. Is this going to prevent applicants from getting patents?

### *3. Utility*

The third criterion for patenting is that an invention be "useful" or "capable of industrial application." Until fairly recently, it seemed that the requirement of utility was not terribly important to the patenting process since very few otherwise patentable inventions failed to meet this criterion. Some commercial use, it seemed, could be found for most anything.

However, developments in the fields of biotechnology and chemistry have made it possible for researchers to develop new materials, molecules, and compounds with relative ease, yet without, at least initially, any good idea whether these might be useful. The proliferation of artificial intelligence systems may lead to a similar proliferation of inventive concepts for which uses may not yet be foreseen. The question then arises to what extent patents should be granted on these "speculative" inventions, since a proliferation of patent grants might impede research by other persons. The criterion of utility has thus reemerged as a critical one in the evaluation of claims for inventions.

In *Apotex v. Wellcome Foundation*, the Supreme Court of Canada considered the point at which a concept turns from mere speculation to utility. If a scientist speculates that a certain substance might be useful in the treatment of a particular disease, does that speculation establish the usefulness of the substance? What objective evidence of effect, or at least potential effect, in the treatment of disease is needed to cross the utility barrier?

The *Apotex v. Wellcome* decision played an important role in a recently decided investor to state dispute settlement proceeding under the NAFTA, and was addressed subsequently in another decision by the Canadian Supreme Court involving a subsidiary utility doctrine that had evolved in the Canadian federal patent courts. These developments are discussed in the notes following the case excerpt.

## *Apotex, Inc. v. Wellcome Foundation Ltd.*

Supreme Court of Canada
2 002 SCC 77 File No.: 28287 2002:
February 14, 2002: December 5

BINNIE J.—

35. AZT has earned for the respondents hundreds of millions of dollars in worldwide sales since its usefulness was discovered for the treatment of HIV and AIDS. In the United States alone, it is estimated that AZT earned for the patent owner a profit of $592 million between 1987 and 1993: J. Yardley, "Industry Giant Owns Right to AIDS Drug? N.C. Trial to Decide," *Atlanta Constitution*, June 27, 1993 at p. 14, quoted in "Case Comment: *Burroughs Wellcome Co. v. Barr Laboratories, Inc.*" (1995), 108 *Harv. L. Rev.* 2053, at note 17.

36. It is not surprising that the appellants, being generic drug manufacturers, would like to obtain at least a percentage of the AZT market in Canada. To do so they must somehow have the patent declared invalid. Yet their challenge, understandably motivated by the hope of private profit, raises broader issues of public interest.

37. A patent, as has been said many times, is not intended as an accolade or civic award for ingenuity. It is a method by which inventive solutions to practical problems are coaxed into the public domain by the promise of a limited monopoly for a limited time. Disclosure is the *quid pro quo* for valuable proprietary rights to exclusivity which are entirely the statutory creature of the *Patent Act*. Monopolies are associated in the public mind with higher prices. The public should not be expected to pay an elevated price in exchange for speculation, or for the statement of "any mere scientific principle or abstract theorem" (s. 27(3)), or for the "discovery" of things that already exist, or are obvious. The patent monopoly should be purchased with the hard coinage of new, ingenious, useful and unobvious disclosures. The appellants' argument here is that the identification in March of 1985 of AZT as a treatment and prophylaxis for HIV/AIDS was a shot in the dark, a speculation based on inadequate information and testing, a lottery ticket for which the public in general and HIV and AIDS sufferers in particular have paid an exorbitant price. AZT works, but for reasons both unknown

and unknowable by Glaxo/Wellcome at the time it filed its patent application, the appellants argue. A lucky guess is not, they say, patentable.

38. Furthermore, if credit is to be given, the appellants argue, it should go to Drs. Broder and Mitsuya at the NIH who actually established the utility of AZT in human T-cells. If the patent on AZT was owned by the NIH or even by a co-ownership of Glaxo/Wellcome and the NIH, they say, the commercial history of AZT would have been vastly more oriented to the public interest.

39. The public interest arguments were not advanced in the U.S. just by advocates of rights for AIDS patients. The NIH itself in 1991 granted a non-exclusive licence to Barr Laboratories "to exploit any patent rights" the NIH "might have" in Glaxo/Wellcome's AZT patents. *See* Case Comment, *supra*, at p. 2054. *See also* "Agency Wants to End AIDS Drug Monopoly," *The New York Times*, May 29, 1991, p. A24. However, the U.S. patent owner successfully defeated this challenge in *Burroughs Wellcome v. Barr Laboratories, supra*, and *see* Case Comment, *supra*.

40. Under United States law, the Court of Appeals for the Federal Circuit said, it was irrelevant that Glaxo/Wellcome had no evidence of AZT's effectiveness against the HIV/AIDS virus in humans and no reasonable basis for believing that the invention would work (*Burroughs Wellcome Co. v. Barr Laboratories Inc., supra*, at p. 1921) until it subsequently received the NIH results. It was sufficient that on February 6, 1985, Glaxo/Wellcome scientists had a concept that was "definite and permanent" which could be applied by a person skilled in the art "without extensive research or experimentation" (p. 1919). In order for there to be an invention in the United States, U.S. law requires "reduction to practice." "Constructive reduction to practice" may occur when a patent application is filed in which an untested invention is adequately disclosed: *Travis v. Baker*, 137 F.2d 109, at p. 111. This seems to have some affinity with our doctrine of "sound prediction" discussed below. However, given the differences in our respective patent laws, the outcome of the U.S. litigation on this patent is of limited interest here. . . .

51. The *Patent Act* defines an "invention" as, amongst other criteria, "new and useful" (s. 2). If it is not useful, it is not an invention within the meaning of the Act.

52. It is important to reiterate that the only contribution made by Glaxo/Wellcome in the case of AZT was to identify a new use. The compound itself was not novel. Its chemical composition had been described 20 years earlier by Dr. Jerome Horwitz. Glaxo/Wellcome claimed a hitherto unrecognized utility but if it had not established such utility by tests or sound prediction at the time it applied for its patent, then it was offering nothing to the public but wishful thinking in exchange for locking up potentially valuable research turf for (then) 17 years. As Jackett C.J. observed in *Procter & Gamble Co. v. Bristol-Myers Canada Ltd.* (1979), 42 C.P.R. (2d) 33 (F.C.A.), at p. 39:

> By definition an "invention" includes a "new and useful process." A "new" process is not an invention unless it is "useful" in some practical sense. Knowing a new process without knowing its utility is not in my view knowledge of an "invention."

53. Glaxo-Wellcome says the invention was complete when the draft patent application was circulated internally on February 6, 1985. Its argument here, as in the United States, was that the written description identified the drug and its new use sufficiently to give the invention "definite and practical shape." It taught persons skilled in the art how the invention could be practised. This, however, misses the point. The question on February 6, 1985 was not whether or how the invention could be practised. The question was whether AZT did the job against HIV that was claimed; in other words, whether on February 6, 1985, there was *any* invention at all within the meaning of s. 2 of the *Patent Act*.

54. Canadian case law dealing with inventorship has to be read keeping the particular factual context in mind. In *Christiani v. Rice*, [1930] S.C.R. 443, this Court held, *per* Rinfret J. (as he then was), at p. 454:

> . . . for the purpose of section 7 [now s. 27] "it is not enough for a man to say that an idea floated through his brain; *he must at least have reduced it to a definite and practical shape* before he can be said to have invented a process." [Emphasis added.]. . .

55. In the present case, by contrast, if the utility of AZT for the treatment of HIV/AIDS was unpredictable at the time of the patent application, then the inventors had not made an invention and had offered nothing to the public in exchange for a 17-year monopoly except wishful thinking.

56. Where the new use is the *gravamen* of the invention, the utility required for patentability (s. 2) must, as of the priority date, either be demonstrated or be a sound prediction based on the information and expertise then available. If a patent sought to be supported on the basis of sound prediction is subsequently challenged, the challenge will succeed if, *per* Pigeon J. in *Monsanto Co. v. Commissioner of Patents*, [1979] 2 S.C.R. 1108, at p. 1117, the prediction at the date of application was not sound, or, irrespective of the soundness of the prediction, "[t]here is evidence of lack of utility in respect of some of the area covered." . . .

66. The doctrine of "sound prediction" balances the public interest in early disclosure of new and useful inventions, even before their utility has been verified by tests (which in the case of pharmaceutical products may take years) and the public interest in avoiding cluttering the public domain with useless patents, and granting monopoly rights in exchange for misinformation. . . .

70. The doctrine of sound prediction has three components. Firstly, as here, there must be a factual basis for the prediction. In *Monsanto* and *Burton Parsons*, the factual basis was supplied by the tested compounds, but other factual underpinnings, depending on the nature of the invention, may suffice. Secondly, the inventor must have at the date of the patent application an articulable and "sound" line of reasoning from which the desired result can be inferred from the factual basis. In *Monsanto* and *Burton Parsons*, the line of reasoning was grounded in the known "architecture of chemical compounds" (*Monsanto*, at p. 1119), but other lines of reasoning, again depending on the subject matter, may be legitimate. Thirdly, there must be proper disclosure. Normally, it is sufficient if the specification provides a full, clear and exact description of the nature of the invention and the manner in which it can be practised: H. G. Fox, *The Canadian Law and Practice Relating to Letters Patent for Inventions* (4th ed. 1969), at p. 167. It is generally not necessary for an inventor to provide a theory of *why* the invention works. Practical readers merely want to know that it does work and how to work it. In this sort of case, however, the sound prediction is to some extent the *quid pro quo* the applicant offers in exchange for the patent monopoly. Precise disclosure requirements in this regard do not arise for decision in this case because both the underlying facts (the test data) and the line of reasoning (the chain terminator effect) were in fact disclosed, and disclosure in this respect did not become an issue between the parties. I therefore say no more about it.

71. It bears repetition that the soundness (or otherwise) of the prediction is a question of fact. Evidence must be led about what was known or not known at the priority date, as was done here. Each case will turn on the particularities of the discipline to which it relates. In this case, the findings of fact necessary for the application of "sound prediction" were made and the appellants have not, in my view, demonstrated any overriding or palpable error.

72. On March 1, 1985, Glaxo/Wellcome received from the NIH the key results of the *in vitro* test of AZT against the HIV in a human cell line. This, taken together with Glaxo/Wellcome's own data on AZT, including the mouse tests, provided a factual foundation. Glaxo/Wellcome's knowledge of the mechanism by which a retrovirus reproduces, and the "chain terminator effect" of AZT, as disclosed in the patent, was found by the trial judge to provide a line of reasoning by which utility could be established as of the date of the U.K. patent application, March 16, 1985, which is also the priority date by which the invention must be evaluated for purposes of the Canadian patent. Although "sound prediction" was not the

precise approach followed by the trial judge, his reasoning as well as his ultimate ruling is entirely consistent with its application. . . .

76. Not all predictions, even sound ones, turn out to be correct. If the Glaxo/Wellcome prediction had subsequently been shown to be wrong, the patent would have been invalidated for want of utility. But, as Pigeon J. remarked in *Monsanto, supra*, at p. 1116, commenting on *Société des usines chimiques Rhône-Poulenc v. Jules R. Gilbert Ltd.*, [1968] S.C.R. 950, "while the substances without utility had not been tested, the true cause of the invalidity was the fact that they were without utility, not that they had not been tested before the patent was applied for."

77. The appellants take issue with the trial judge's conclusion. In their factum (though not in oral argument), they argue that utility must be demonstrated by prior human clinical trials establishing toxicity, metabolic features, bioavailability and other factors. These factors track the requirements of the Minister of Health when dealing with a new drug submission to assess its "safety" and "effectiveness." *See now*: *Food and Drug Regulations*, C.R.C., c. 870, s. C.08.002.(2) as amended by SOR/95-411, s. 4, which provides in part:

> A new drug submission shall contain sufficient information and material to enable the Minister to assess the safety and effectiveness of the new drug. . . .

The prerequisites of proof for a manufacturer who wishes to market a new drug are directed to a different purpose than patent law. The former deals with safety and effectiveness. The latter looks at utility, but in the context of inventiveness. The doctrine of sound prediction, in its nature, presupposes that further work remains to be done.

78. Glaxo/Wellcome contends that because AZT turned out to have both treatment and (limited) prophylactic properties, its prediction must necessarily have been sound, and the patent upheld on that basis. This argument presupposes that the critical date to establish utility is the state of knowledge when the patent is attacked, even though the attack may come years after its issuance, rather than as of the date the patent application is filed. The patent in this case was applied for in 1986, and issued in 1988. The trial did not occur until 1997, almost a decade after the grant of the AZT patent in Canada.

79. The "after-the-fact" validation theory was accepted by the Federal Court of Appeal, at para. 51:

> In other words, so long as an inventor can demonstrate utility or a sound prediction at the time a patent is attacked, the patent will not fail for lack of utility. The time at which usefulness is to be established is when required by the Commissioner of Patents or in court proceedings when the validity of the patent is challenged on that ground.

80. In my view, with respect, Glaxo/Wellcome's proposition is consistent neither with the Act (which does not postpone the requirement of utility to the vagaries of when such proof might actually be demanded) nor with patent policy (which does not encourage the stockpiling of useless or misleading patent disclosures). Were the law to be otherwise, major pharmaceutical corporations could (subject to cost considerations) patent whole stables of chemical compounds for all sorts of desirable but unrealized purposes in a shot-gun approach hoping that, as in a lottery, a certain percentage of compounds will serendipitously turn out to be useful for the purposes claimed. Such a patent system would reward deep pockets and the ingenuity of patent agents rather than the ingenuity of true inventors.

81. The Federal Court of Appeal was concerned that patents based on "instinct and intuition (and) gut reaction" might be invalidated in a case where the ignorance that passed at the time for "sound prediction" turned out to be wrong and the inventor eventually vindicated. An example was given of a hypothetical patent on the Wright brothers' airplane. Perhaps all the "experts" thought it would not fly, but it did. Would it not be illogical, it was asked, to

invalidate a hypothetical patent on a heavier-than-air flying machine because scientific opinion in the pre-flight era was wrong?

82. The hypothetical Wright brothers patent relates to a new and useful product, rather than (as here) to a new *use* for an old product, but all the same it illustrates, I think, the flaw in the Glaxo/Wellcome argument. The mere idea of a "heavier-than-air flying machine" is no more patentable than would be "*anything* that grows hair on bald men" (emphasis in original): *Free World Trust v. Electro Santé Inc.*, [2000] 2 S.C.R. 1024, 2000 SCC 66, at para. 32. The patent (even in this improbable scenario) would have to teach precisely *how* the machine could be made to fly. Section 34(1)(*b*) requires the applicant to set out in the specification "the method of constructing, making . . . or using a machine . . . in such full, clear, concise and exact terms as to enable any person skilled in the art . . . to make, construct . . . or use it." This means the Wright brothers' hypothetical patent would have to describe, amongst other things, how to design an air foil that creates "lift" by reducing the air pressure on the upper surface of the wing as the air rushes over it, as well as a suitable airborne method of forward locomotion. If the essentials of the heavier-than-air flying machine were set out with sufficient precision to allow the reader actually to make a flying machine that flies, it is hard to accept the "hypothetical" that experts would continue to insist, after it had flown, that the prediction was unsound. (Of course, if the prediction turned out to be wrong, the patent would be struck down for inutility. Leonardo da Vinci's elegant drawings showed exactly how to make a "bird man" machine but it never could, would or did sustain a person in flight.)

83. On the other hand, if the patent failed to disclose the essentials of a heavier-than-air flying machine, such that no one could "soundly predict" whether or not the ill-defined thing could get off the ground, then the patent would be rightly invalidated, even though the inventors had eventually flown some sort of machine in the meantime. It goes back to the same point. The public is entitled to accurate and meaningful teaching in exchange for suffering the patent monopoly. The patent claims must be supported by the disclosure. Speculation, even if it afterwards proves justified, does not provide valid consideration. As Lord Mustill pointed out in *Genetech Inc.'s Patent*, [1989] R.P.C. 147 (Eng. C.A.), at p. 275:

> Many years ago, an inventor could not have patented a heavier-than-air flying machine simply by writing down the concept, but equally the fact that the concept was capable of being written down in advance could not, in itself, exclude the rights of a person who had actually made one fly.

## NOTES AND QUESTIONS

**1.** The Canadian Supreme Court refers to an earlier decision on the same subject matter by the U.S. Court of Appeals for the Federal Circuit in *Burroughs Wellcome v. Barr Laboratories*, 40 F.3d 1223 (Fed. Cir. 1994), 32 U.S.P.Q. (2d) 1915 (1994). According to the Canadian Court, the CAFC said "it was irrelevant that Glaxo/Wellcome had no evidence of AZT's effectiveness against the HIV/AIDS virus in humans and no reasonable basis for believing that the invention would work . . . until it subsequently received the NIH results. It was sufficient that on February 6, 1985, Glaxo/Wellcome scientists had a concept that was 'definite and permanent' which could be applied by a person skilled in the art 'without extensive research or experimentation' (p. 1919)." The U.S. CAFC said in *Barr Laboratories*:

> Conception is the touchstone of inventorship, the completion of the mental part of invention. *Sewall v. Walters*, 21 F.3d 411, 415, 30 U.S.P.Q.2d (BNA) 1356, 1359 (Fed. Cir. 1994). It is "the formation in the mind of the inventor, of a definite and permanent idea of the complete and operative invention, as it is hereafter to be applied in practice." *Hybritech Inc. v. Monoclonal Antibodies, Inc.*, 802 F.2d 1367, 1376, 231 U.S.P.Q. (BNA) 81, 87 (Fed. Cir. 1986) (citation

> omitted). Conception is complete only when the idea is so clearly defined in the inventor's mind that only ordinary skill would be necessary to reduce the invention to practice, without extensive research or experimentation. *Sewall,* 21 F.3d at 415, 30 U.S.P.Q.2d (BNA) at 1359; *see also Coleman v. Dines,* 754 F.2d 353, 359, 224 U.S.P.Q. (BNA) 857, 862 (Fed. Cir. 1985) (conception must include every feature of claimed invention). Because it is a mental act, courts require corroborating evidence of a contemporaneous disclosure that would enable one skilled in the art to make the invention. *Coleman v. Dines,* 754 F.2d at 359, 224 U.S.P.Q. (BNA) at 862.
>
> Thus, the test for conception is whether the inventor had an idea that was definite and permanent enough that one skilled in the art could understand the invention; the inventor must prove his conception by corroborating evidence, preferably by showing a contemporaneous disclosure. An idea is definite and permanent when the inventor has a specific, settled idea, a particular solution to the problem at hand, not just a general goal or research plan he hopes to pursue. *See Fiers v. Revel,* 984 F.2d 1164, 1169, 25 U.S.P.Q.2d (BNA) 1601, 1605 (Fed. Cir. 1993); *Amgen, Inc. v. Chugai Pharmaceutical Co.*, 927 F.2d 1200, 1206, 18 U.S.P.Q.2d (BNA) 1016, 1021 (Fed. Cir. 1989) (no conception of chemical compound based solely on its biological activity). The conception analysis necessarily turns on the inventor's ability to describe his invention with particularity. Until he can do so, he cannot prove possession of the complete mental picture of the invention. These rules ensure that patent rights attach only when an idea is so far developed that the inventor can point to a definite, particular invention.
>
> But an inventor need not know that his invention will work for conception to be complete. *Applegate v. Scherer,* 51 C.C.P.A. 1416, 332 F.2d 571, 573, 141 U.S.P.Q. (BNA) 796, 799 (CCPA 1964). He need only show that he had the idea; the discovery that an invention actually works is part of its reduction to practice. *Id.; see also Oka v. Youssefyeh,* 849 F.2d 581, 584 n.1, 7 U.S.P.Q.2d (BNA) 1169, 1171 n.1 (Fed. Cir. 1988).

40 F.3d at 1227-28. The Canadian and U.S. courts follow different approaches in reaching the same result. The Canadian Supreme Court is principally concerned with whether Glaxo satisfied the criterion of utility by making a sound prediction. The CAFC is concerned with whether Glaxo (successor to Burroughs-Wellcome) had a definite and permanent idea. Are the decisions consistent? In what contexts do you think the approaches might yield different results?

**2.** The Canadian Supreme Court notes that the U.S. CAFC considered conception as of February 6, 1985 (para. 40). In Canada, analysis of sound prediction depended on Glaxo's knowledge as of the "priority date" of the U.K. patent application, March 16, 1985. Attention to these different dates in part reflects a difference between U.S. "first-to-invent" rules for determining inventorship, as compared with "first-to-file" rules prevailing in the rest of the world. As we will discuss in section D following, the United States has moved away from the first-to-invent rule.

**3.** Pharmaceutical Company *X* discovers a genetic sequence that causes "biological activity" to occur in human cells, but it cannot identify the function of that biological activity, including whether that activity might have some therapeutic effect generated by a medicine taking advantage of the sequence. Should the discovery of the "biological activity" be sufficient to meet the utility criterion?

**4.** The following excerpt from an article by Frederick Abbott describes legal events involving the *Apotex v. Wellcome* holding during the past several years:

### Legislative and Regulatory Takings of Intellectual Property: Early Stage Intervention Against a New Jurisprudential Virus

**Frederick M. Abbott***

The initiation by the US pharmaceutical company Eli Lilly of a claim for compensation against the government of Canada in the ISDS context under the North American Free

* In Intellectual Property, Technology Transfer and Investment: Understanding the Interfaces and Development Impact (In Honor of Pedro Roffe, Liber Amicorum Pedro Roffe) (C. Correa & X. Seuba eds., 2018).

Trade Agreement (NAFTA) broke new ground in originator pharmaceutical company attempts to protect patent exclusivity. Eli Lilly contended that the invalidation of two patents by Canadian federal patent courts based on failure to meet the utility requirement constituted a judicial expropriation of property within the meaning of the NAFTA investment chapter.

The basic thesis of the pharmaceutical company was that it had a legitimate expectation at the time it filed its patent applications regarding the way that Canadian patent law was interpreted and applied, and that by changing the parameters of judicial doctrine after its filings, the Canadian courts had defeated its legitimate expectations resulting in a denial of justice.

At the time the complaint was initiated, this theory of expropriation surprised knowledgeable observers, myself included, as several matters seemed apparent on their face. First, that the standards for a denial of justice under international law are very high, and whether one agreed with the details of the Canadian federal court decisions, they were a long juridical distance away from denial of justice. Second, that for those with a good understanding of patent law, and Canadian patent law, the judicial doctrines applied by the Canadian federal patent courts were perfectly reasonable, even if the courts of some other countries may have used other interpretations of patentability criteria. Third, NAFTA did not prescribe a fixed definition of patentability criteria, nor did the Agreement on Trade-Related Aspects of Intellectual Property Rights (TRIPS Agreement), and there was no basis to conclude that the Canadian federal patent courts had acted contrary to a NAFTA-prescribed standard. There were other flaws in the Eli Lilly jurisprudential hypothesis, sufficient taken altogether that I believe Eli Lilly should have been penalized for abuse of international legal process in pursuing the claim.

The arbitral tribunal established pursuant to the NAFTA investment chapter rejected the Eli Lilly claims, and the company was ordered to pay the legal fees of the Canadian government. Despite the largely comprehensive rejection of the claims, the arbitral tribunal nonetheless "for the sake of argument" examined the course of Canadian jurisprudence regarding interpretation and application of the utility criterion to determine whether there might be merit to Eli Lilly's claim that Canadian jurisprudence had undergone some major transformation since the time Eli Lilly undertook its "investments." This review of Canadian jurisprudence was an unfortunate detour by the arbitral panel since it implied that a major change in doctrine applicable to all patent owners, such as might result in the invalidation of pre-existing patents, may have constituted a prohibited judicial taking. Absent some showing that a change violated the terms of an international agreement, such as the NAFTA, or was discriminatorily directed against foreign nationals, a decision by the Canadian federal courts to adopt a substantial change in doctrinal approach to a criterion of patentability would not constitute an expropriation or defeat of legitimate expectations.

While the correct result was reached by arbitration tribunal, it did not close the door to future claims that judicial changes in doctrine may constitute a legislative taking. In this regard, governments that have begun to rethink and revisit ISDS provisions have another reason to do that. As the following sections of this paper illustrate, the originator pharmaceutical industry has seized upon legislative or regulatory taking as a "new frontier" in defending patent walls. It is a trend that warrants concern and close attention.

Several months following resolution of the NAFTA ISDS case, the Supreme Court of Canada took up the utility doctrine that had been applied by the Canadian federal patent courts to invalidate the subject patents, the so-called "promise doctrine." On June 30, 2017, in *AstraZeneca v. Apotex*, 2017 SCC 36, the Supreme Court rejected the promise doctrine, saying that it was not prescribed by the express text of the Canadian Patent Act. A patent applicant, according to the Court, was not required to demonstrate that its invention fulfilled promises made in its patent specification, such as a promise that a claimed drug compound—in the instant case a secondary patent based on a previously patented compound—would have a particular effect. The Supreme Court said that assessment of the utility criterion is limited to the terms of the patent claim(s), while confirming that at the time of application utility must be demonstrated, or there must be a sound prediction of utility. The Court said that only a scintilla of utility is required to support an application. This decision is arguably in line with prior decisions of the Supreme Court in so far as it maintains the "doctrine of sound prediction" that was set out in its previous major statement on the utility doctrine, *Apotex v. Wellcome*, 2002 SCC 77. However, because in its 2017 decision the Court sets a very low bar for the level of utility needing to be soundly predicted (i.e., a scintilla), it seems that this latest decision substantially diminishes the significance of the utility doctrine under Canadian patent law. This will naturally depend on the way the lower courts adapt to the new legal environment.

**5.** A NAFTA Chapter Eleven arbitral panel in *Glamis Gold v. USA*, decided June 8, 2009, identified the elements necessary to prove a breach of the minimum standard of treatment in violation of customary international law using these terms:

> to violate the customary international law minimum standard of treatment codified in Article 1105 of the NAFTA, an act must be sufficiently egregious and shocking—a gross denial of justice, manifest arbitrariness, blatant unfairness, a complete lack of due process, evident discrimination, or a manifest lack of reasons—so as to fall below accepted international standards and constitute a breach of Article 1105(1). The Tribunal notes that one aspect of evolution from Neer [Neer v. Mexico, 4 R. Int'l Arb. Awards, 60-62 (Oct. 15, 1926)] that is generally agreed upon is that bad faith is not required to find a violation of the fair and equitable treatment standard, but its presence is conclusive evidence of such. Thus, an act that is egregious or shocking may also evidence bad faith, but such bad faith is not necessary for the finding of a violation.

*Glamis Gold v. USA*, para. 616. Was it plausible that an arbitral panel would find that the Canadian doctrine of sound prediction constituted an egregious and shocking denial of justice? What might have motivated a large pharmaceutical company employing lawyers who should know what they are doing to pursue such a claim? What was the motive? What did they expect to accomplish? While Eli Lilly may have lost its ISDS claim, the subsequent decision of the Canadian Supreme Court to cut back the scope of the utility doctrine might reflect a reaction to pharmaceutical industry pressures, including that the U.S. Vice President was a former Senator from the state where Eli Lilly is based. Do external political pressures influence national courts?

### *4. Enablement*

The fourth criterion with respect to the grant of the patent is that an inventor shall have disclosed in the patent application either a means for enabling the practice of the invention (generally for most of the world), or the best known means for practicing the invention (for the United States).[23] One objective of this criterion is that persons other than the inventor should be able to benefit from the inventor's disclosure, and this is most likely to happen if others are well informed with respect to the means of making or using the invention. Another objective of this requirement is to distinguish true inventions from speculative concepts of would-be inventors about future possibilities. A claimed invention should function as described. Of course, many inventors would prefer to secure their patents without telling others just exactly how to go about making or using the invention. Third parties seeking to practice inventions based only on enabling disclosure made to the patent office not infrequently find this difficult.

The requirement of enabling disclosure played the decisive role in the decision of the U.K. House of Lords (now the Supreme Court) in *Biogen v. Medeva*. The patent applicant showed

23. Note that pursuant to the America Invents Act of 2011 the requirement to disclose the best mode remains intact in the United States, but failure to disclose best mode is no longer the basis for patent invalidation. *See* 35 U.S.C. 112(a), read with amended 35 U.S.C. 282.

that its invention would produce a specified result. Was this enough to exclude others from achieving the same result through a better means?

## *Biogen, Inc. v. Medeva PLC*

House of Lords [1997] RPC 1 31 October 1996

Lord HOFFMANN: . . .

I think that in concentrating upon the question of whether Professor Murray's invention could, so to speak, deliver the goods across the full width of the patent or priority document, the courts and the EPO allowed their attention to be diverted from what seems to me in this particular case the critical issue. It is not whether the claimed invention could deliver the goods, but whether the claims cover other ways in which they might be delivered: ways which owe nothing to the teaching of the patent or any principle which it disclosed.

It will be remembered that in Genentech I/Polypeptide expression the Technical Board spoke of the need for the patent to give protection against other ways of achieving the same effect "in a manner which could not have been envisaged without the invention." This shows that there is more than one way in which the breadth of a claim may exceed the technical contribution to the art embodied in the invention. The patent may claim results which it does not enable, such as making a wide class of products when it enables only one of those products and discloses no principle which would enable others to be made. Or it may claim every way of achieving a result when it enables only one way and it is possible to envisage other ways of achieving that result which make no use of the invention.

One example of an excessive claim of the latter kind is the famous case of *O'Reilly v Morse* (1854) 56 US (15 How) 62 in the Supreme Court of the United States. Samuel Morse was the first person to discover a practical method of electric telegraphy and took out a patent in which he claimed any use of electricity for "making or printing intelligible characters, signs, or letter, at any distances." The Supreme Court rejected the claim as too broad. Professor Chisum, in his book on Patents (vol 1, §1.03 [2]) summarises the decision as follows:

> Before Morse's invention, the scientific community saw the possibility of achieving communication by the "galvanic" current but did not know any means of achieving that result. Morse discovered one means and attempted to claim all others.

A similar English case is *British United Shoe Machinery Co Ltd v Simon Collier Ltd* (1908) 26 RPC 21. The patentee invented a piece of machinery for automatically trimming the soles of boots and shoes by means of a cam. One of the claims was in general terms for automatic means of trimming soles. Parker J said, at pages 49-50:

> (The) problem was simply how to do automatically what could already be done by the skill of the workman. On the other hand, the principle which the inventor applies for the solution of the problem is the capacity of a cam to vary the relative positions of two parts of a machine while the machine is running. Assuming this principle to be new, it might be possible for the inventor, having shown one method of applying it to the solution of the problem, to protect himself during the life of his patent from any other method of applying it for the same purpose, but I do not think that the novelty of the principle applied would enable him to make a valid claim for all means of solving the problem whether the same or a different principle were applied to its solution.

I return therefore to consider the technical contribution to the art which Professor Murray made in 1978 and disclosed in Biogen 1. As it seems to me, it consisted in showing that despite the uncertainties which then existed over the DNA of the Dane particle—in particular whether it included the antigen genes and whether it had introns—known recombinant techniques could nevertheless be used to make the antigens in a prokaryotic host cell. As I have said, I accept the judge's findings that the method was shown to be capable of making both antigens and I am willing to accept that it would work in any otherwise suitable host cell. Does this contribution justify a claim to a monopoly of any recombinant method of making the antigens? In my view it does not. The claimed invention is too broad. Its excessive breadth is due, not to the inability of the teaching to produce all the promised results, but to the fact that the same results could be produced by different means. Professor Murray had won a brilliant Napoleonic victory in cutting through the uncertainties which existed in his day to achieve the desired result. But his success did not in my view establish any new principle which his successors had to follow if they were to achieve the same results. The inventive step, as I have said, was the idea of trying to express unsequenced eukaryotic DNA in a prokaryotic host. Biogen 1 discloses that the way to do it is to choose the restriction enzymes likely to cleave the Dane particle DNA into the largest fragments. This, if anything, was the original element in what Professor Murray did. But once the DNA had been sequenced, no one would choose restriction enzymes on this basis. They would choose those which digested the sites closest to the relevant gene or the part of the gene which expressed an antigenic fragment of the polypeptide. The metaphor used by one of the witnesses was that before the genome had been sequenced everyone was working in the dark. Professor Murray invented a way of working with the genome in the dark. But he did not switch on the light and once the light was on his method was no longer needed. Nor, once they could use vectors for mammalian cells, would they be concerned with the same problem of introns which had so exercised those skilled in the art in 1978. Of course there might be other problems, but Biogen 1 did not teach how to solve them. The respondents Medeva, who use restriction enzymes based on knowledge of the HBV genome and mammalian host cells, owe nothing to Professor Murray's invention.

It is said that what Professor Murray showed by his invention was that it could be done. HBV antigens could be produced by expressing Dane particle DNA in a host cell. Those who followed, even by different routes, could have greater confidence by reason of his success. I do not think that this is enough to justify a monopoly of the whole field. I suppose it could be said that Samuel Morse had shown that electric telegraphy could be done. The Wright Brothers showed that heavier-than-air flight was possible, but that did not entitle them to a monopoly of heavier-than-air flying machines. It is inevitable in a young science, like electricity in the early nineteenth century or flying at the turn of the last century or recombinant DNA technology in the 1970s, that dramatically new things will be done for the first time. The technical contribution made in such cases deserves to be recognised. But care is needed not to stifle further research and healthy competition by allowing the first person who has found a way of achieving an obviously desirable goal to monopolise every other way of doing so. (*See* Merges and Nelson, On the Complex Economics of Patent Scope (1990) 90 Columbia Law Review 839.)

I would therefore hold that Biogen 1 did not support the invention as claimed in the European Patent and that it is therefore not entitled to the priority date of Biogen 1. As it is conceded that the invention was obvious when the patent application was filed, it is invalid.

## NOTES AND QUESTIONS

1. In the well-known *Star Trek* science fiction series, people (including alien people) are moved about from one point in space to another by means of the "transporter." The transporter has become so much a part of global culture that most of us likely assume it is only

a matter of time (even if a very long time) before people are "beaming" from one place to another. Should the producers of the *Star Trek* series have filed a patent application on the transporter before they first publicly introduced it? When it was introduced, was the concept of the transporter new?[24] When it was introduced, was the concept of the transporter capable of industrial application? When it was introduced, did the concept of the transporter involve an inventive step? If the *Star Trek* transporter were new, capable of industrial application, and involved an inventive step, why should not a patent examiner have recommended the grant of a patent? Could the producers of the *Star Trek* series have provided an enabling disclosure?

**2.** Many, if not most, patent licenses include an obligation on the part of the patent owner/licensor to provide technical "know-how" to the licensee in addition to rights to use the patented technology. "Know-how" is a general term that may encompass trade secrets, though it is not necessarily limited to information that is protected by some form of IPR. Among other things, it may include knowledge about a production process that has been acquired through years of implementation. Typically, covered know-how is expressly defined in the license agreement. The customary obligation to provide know-how reflects that the disclosure contained in a patent application may not be sufficient for making effective use of the covered technology, at least without considerable additional work, trial and error, etc. This does not mean that patent disclosures are unimportant. But, their importance must be understood in context.

**3.** See the recent decision of the UK Supreme Court in *Warner-Lambert v. Mylan* [2018] UKSC 56 addressing sufficiency of disclosure in relation to patents involving new uses of known pharmaceutical compounds ("plausibility" requires more than mere assertion, including reasonable scientific grounds though not necessarily experimentation results).

**4.** The US Supreme Court revisited the enablement requirement in the context of biotechnology in *Amgen v. Sanofi*, 598 U.S. ___ (2023). In this case, the pharmaceutical enterprise Amgen had developed an antibody treatment (marketed as "Repatha") to assist in lowering LDL cholesterol. It obtained several patents. Two of these went beyond the specific antibody used in Repatha, identifying 26 additional antibodies and their amino acid sequences, with two depicting three-dimensional structures. Amgen made claim to the entire genus of antibodies that performed the function ascribed to its patented drug (binding to specific amino acid residues on PCSK9 and blocking PCSK9 from binding to LDL receptors). There were potentially millions of antibodies that would perform these functions beyond the 26 that Amgen included in its specification, and Amgen provided little guidance as to how others might identify similarly functional antibodies other than to suggest that scientists develop and test additional antibodies to see whether they worked, or use antibodies known to perform the desired functions and substitute amino acids to create new ones, again testing to see whether they would work. Relying on a long line of cases establishing the proposition that an invention must be sufficiently enabled across the scope of the claims, including O'Reilly v. Morse, 15 How. 62 (1854)(Morse's telegraph) and The Incandescent Lamp Patent, 159 U. S. 465 (1895)(Edison's electric lamp). Amgen had, in effect, done nothing more than propose a research program. It had not provided sufficient guidance to enable the range of functional antibodies that it had claimed. Amgen's patent claims were invalidated under Section 112 of the US Patent Act for lack of sufficient enablement.

24. Staying within the science fiction genre, consider, for example, the teleportation device that played a prominent role in the 1958 science fiction film *The Fly*, with Vincent Price.

## D. Inventorship and Ownership

Inventorship laws vary widely by jurisdiction. In the U.S., the "inventor" of a new product or process is the individual that "conceived" of the invention. In the UK, the inventor is the "devisor" of the invention. Other jurisdictions, like the European Patent Office and Germany, have broader criteria for inventorship. Some jurisdictions, like Austria and Israel, do not require inventors to be listed in an application. The U.S. is an outlier in terms of the importance of inventorship designations, as inaccurate designation can render a patent invalid or unenforceable in the U.S. but not generally in other jurisdictions.

The "owner" of the patent is not necessarily, or even usually, the inventor. Patent rules generally allow ownership of the patent to be assigned, even before the invention is created. For example, researchers at corporations are typically required to execute agreements assigning any inventions made in the course and scope of their employment to the corporation. At the EPO, the application can be filed by a juridical entity (e.g., a corporation), although a corporation probably cannot be the named inventor (some EPO member states, Cypress and Monaco, have reported to EPO they do not restrict inventorship to natural persons). The United States has likewise changed its rules to allow a juridical entity to file an application, though as with the EPO a juridical entity cannot be named as an inventor.

What party or parties are considered the "inventor" is a matter of national (or regional) law. It is not a matter dictated by the Paris Convention or the TRIPS Agreement. If the inventor is an individual, and is the only person named as owner on the application, that person controls the rights conferred by the patent and is entitled to its corresponding financial benefits. As a general practice, if there is no contractual arrangement, ownership of an invention (and patent) will be jointly and equally shared by co-inventors. Each will be entitled to license patent rights to third parties, generally also being required to share the revenues from such licensing equally. Being "named" as an inventor on a patent application thus may have important financial consequences. However, as noted, many or most patents are assigned to a corporate or other juridical entity, and this transfers decision-making regarding a patent to that juridical entity, which may also include some royalty-sharing or its equivalent with the named inventor(s). It is not uncommon for disputes to arise regarding which individuals are entitled to be named as inventors in patent applications. These disputes can either be resolved in administrative proceedings at patent offices or in civil litigation, the fundamental question generally framed as which party or parties made substantial or meaningful contributions to the invention? There are also some jurisdictions, such as the UK, where inventors are entitled in certain circumstances to receive financial benefits from a patent regardless of underlying contractual arrangements.

### *1. AI-Generated Inventions*

Is an invention generated by an AI, in the absence of a traditional human inventor (an "AI-generated invention," although definitions in this space vary greatly), eligible for patent protection? The leading cases on the patentability of AI-generated inventions are being brought as part of the Artificial Inventor Project, led by one of this text's authors (Ryan Abbott). "The Artificial Inventor Project includes a series of pro bono legal test cases seeking intellectual property rights for AI-generated output in the absence of a traditional human inventor or author. It is intended to promote dialogue about the social, economic, and legal impact of frontier technologies such as AI and to generate stakeholder guidance on the protectability of AI-generated output." https://artificialinventor.com/.

Patents were filed for two AI-generated inventions in a total of 18 jurisdictions, with the AI listed as the inventor and the AI's owner listed as the patent applicant and owner of any resultant patents. As of the time of writing, the patents have been granted in South Africa and the designation of inventor allowed in Saudi Arabia. The patents have been denied on a final, non-appealable basis in the United States, Australia (after initially being allowed by the Federal Court of Australia), and Taiwan. In other jurisdictions, the applications either remain with patent offices or are in the process of judicial appeals.

These cases have been the subject of extensive international debate. The cases argue that inventorship is not intended to be a basis for denying patent protection (like novelty, inventive step, etc.), and that it would be antithetical to patent policy to deny the applications—but this very much depends on the specific language of patent legislation in different jurisdictions. In jurisdictions in which the patents have been denied, this has been on the basis that only a natural person can be an inventor, and patent applications failing to disclose a human inventor must be denied.

Of course, the debate and litigation do not concern whether an AI "owns" an invention or a patent. AIs do not have legal personality that would allow them to own property or property rights. So, if an AI invents something patentable, and if an AI inventor cannot own a patent, then who, if anyone, would own that patent if there's no human inventor to own it? Obvious options include the AI's programmers, owners, or users. The cases have argued that the AI's owner owning the AI's inventions is most consistent with general rules of property ownership, such that someone generally owns the tangible output of their property (e.g., a physical painting made by a 3D printer). AI inventorship is also relevant in the case of co-inventorship. For example, if an AI owned and out-licensed by a university is used by researchers at a pharmaceutical company to invent a new drug—both the university and the pharmaceutical company may end up jointly owning a patent on the new drug, or the drug may be unpatentable. This is a topic recently explored by the U.S. Patent and Trademark Office in a public request for comments. https://www.federalregister.gov/documents/2023/02/14/2023-03066/request-for-comments-regarding-artificial-intelligence-and-inventorship.

Also, naming an AI inventor may protect the integrity of the patent system and the moral rights of human inventors. That is, by ascribing inventorship to the true inventor, and not diluting the meaning of inventorship by including someone who has simply asked a machine to solve a problem.

These cases have resulted in a number of important judgments that have also shed light on the variability of inventorship standards with human beings. For example, at the time of writing, the United Kingdom Court of Appeal upheld, in a split decision, the UK Patent Office's rejection of these applications. This decision is currently under appeal to the UK Supreme Court with a decision expected in mid-late 2023.

Compare and contrast the following two judgments. In the United States, the Federal Circuit upheld a rejection of the applications based on the text of the U.S. Patent Act, and the U.S. Supreme Court subsequently declined to accept an appeal. In Australia, the patent office's denial was overturned by the Federal Court of Australia, although this was ultimately overturned on en banc appeal and the Australian High Court declined to accept a further appeal.

## *Thaler v. Vidal [Director of the USPTO]*

No. 21-2347 (Fed. Cir. 2022)

Stark, Circuit Judge.

This case presents the question of who, or what, can be an inventor. Specifically, we are asked to decide if an artificial intelligence (AI) software system can be listed as the inventor on a patent application. At first, it might seem that resolving this issue would involve an abstract inquiry into the nature of invention or the rights, if any, of AI systems. In fact, however, we do not need to ponder these metaphysical matters. Instead, our task begins – and ends – with consideration of the applicable definition in the relevant statute.

The United States Patent and Trademark Office (PTO) undertook the same analysis and concluded that the Patent Act defines "inventor" as limited to natural persons; that is, human beings. Accordingly, the PTO denied Stephen Thaler's patent applications, which failed to list any human as an inventor. Thaler challenged that conclusion in the U.S. District Court for the Eastern District of Virginia, which agreed with the PTO and granted it summary judgment. We, too, conclude that the Patent Act requires an "inventor" to be a natural person and, therefore, affirm.

. . .

## II. A.

The sole issue on appeal is whether an AI software system can be an "inventor" under the Patent Act. In resolving disputes of statutory interpretation, we "begin[] with the statutory text, and end[] there as well if the text is unambiguous." *BedRoc Ltd. v. United States*, 541 U.S. 176, 183 (2004). Here, there is no ambiguity: the Patent Act requires that inventors must be natural persons; that is, human beings.

The Patent Act expressly provides that inventors are "individuals." Since 2011, with the passage of the LeahySmith America Invents Act, the Patent Act has defined an "inventor" as "the individual or, if a joint invention, the individuals collectively who invented or discovered the subject matter of the invention." 35 U.S.C. §100(f) (emphasis added). The Act similarly defines "joint inventor" and "coinventor" as "any 1 of the individuals who invented or discovered the subject matter of a joint invention." §100(g) (emphasis added). In describing the statements required of an inventor when applying for a patent, the statute consistently refers to inventors and co-inventors as "individuals." *See* §115.

The Patent Act does not define "individual." However, as the Supreme Court has explained, when used "[a]s a noun, 'individual' ordinarily means a human being, a person." *Mohamad v. Palestinian Auth.*, 566 U.S. 449, 454 (2012) (internal alteration and quotation marks omitted). This is in accord with "how we use the word in everyday parlance": "We say 'the individual went to the store,' 'the individual left the room,' and 'the individual took the car,' each time referring unmistakably to a natural person." *Id.* Dictionaries confirm that this is the common understanding of the word. See, e.g., *Individual, Oxford English Dictionary* (2022) (giving first definition of "individual" as "[a] single human being"); *Individual,* Dictionary.com (last visited July 11, 2022), https://www.dictionary.com/browse/individual (giving "a single human being, as distinguished from a group" as first definition for "individual"). So, too, does the Dictionary Act, which provides that legislative use of the words "person" and "whoever" broadly include ("unless the context indicates otherwise") "corporations, companies, associations, firms, partnerships, societies, and joint stock companies, *as well as individuals*." 1 U.S.C. §1 (emphasis added). "With the phrase 'as well as,' the definition marks 'individual' as distinct from the list of artificial entities that precedes it," showing that Congress understands "individual" to indicate natural persons unless otherwise noted. *Mohamad*, 566 U.S. at 454.

Consequently, the Supreme Court has held that, when used in statutes, the word "individual" refers to human beings unless there is "some indication Congress intended" a different reading. *Id.* at 455 (emphasis omitted). Nothing in the Patent Act indicates Congress intended to deviate from the default meaning. To the contrary, the rest of the Patent Act supports the conclusion that "individual" in the Act refers to human beings.

For instance, the Act uses personal pronouns – "himself" and "herself" – to refer to an "individual." §115(b)(2). It does not also use "itself," which it would have done if Congress intended to permit non-human inventors. The Patent Act also requires inventors (unless deceased, incapacitated, or unavailable) to submit an oath or declaration. *See, e.g., id.* (requiring oath or declaration from inventor that "such individual believes himself or herself to be the original inventor or an original joint inventor of a claimed invention in the application"). While we do not decide whether an AI system can form beliefs, nothing in our record shows that one can, as reflected in the fact that Thaler submitted the requisite statements himself, purportedly on DABUS' behalf. Thaler directs us to several provisions of the Patent Act as supposed support for his position that "inventor" should be broadly read to include AI software, but each fails to persuade. First, Thaler points to the use of "whoever" in 35 U.S.C. §§101 and 271. Section 101 provides that "[w]hoever invents or discovers any new and useful process, machine, manufacture, or composition of matter, or any new and useful improvement thereof, may obtain a patent therefor, subject to the conditions and requirements of this title." As this very section makes clear, however, patents must satisfy the "conditions and requirements of" Title 35 of the U.S. Code, including its definition of "inventor." Section 271, in setting out what constitutes infringement, repeatedly uses "whoever" to include corporations and other non-human entities. That non-humans may infringe patents does not tell us anything about whether non-humans may also be inventors of patents. The question before us inevitably leads back to the Patent Act's definition of "inventor," which uses the word "individual" – and does not use "whoever." Furthermore, as we noted already, the Dictionary Act establishes that Congress uses "whoever" as a much broader term than "individual." *See* 1 U.S.C. §1.

Second, Thaler contends that AI software programs must qualify as inventors because otherwise patentability would depend on "the manner in which the invention was made," in contravention of 35 U.S.C. §103. Section 103 is not about inventorship. Instead, it provides, in relevant part, that inventions may still be nonobvious even if they are discovered during "routine" testing or experimentation. *See Honeywell Int'l Inc. v. Mexichem Amanco Holding S.A. de C.V.*, 865 F.3d 1348, 1356 (Fed. Cir. 2017); *see also Graham v. John Deere Co.*, 383 U.S. 1, 15 (1966) (explaining that second sentence of §103 was intended to clarify that "flash of creative genius" is unnecessary for patentability). This statutory provision relates to how an invention is made and does not trump a provision that specifically addresses who may be an inventor.

Third, Thaler emphasizes that the term "inventor" must be interpreted with attention to the "context in which that language is used[] and the broader context of the statute as a whole." *Yates v. United States*, 574 U.S. 528, 537 (2015) (internal quotation marks omitted). We have undertaken precisely this task. For the reasons explained above, the Patent Act, when considered in its entirety, confirms that "inventors" must be human beings.

---

## *Thaler v. Commissioner of Patents [Australia]*

[2021] FCA 879

Beach J:

1. The Deputy Commissioner of Patents has determined that patent application no. 2019363177 did not comply with reg 3.2C(2)(aa) of the *Patents Regulations 1991* (Cth). Reg 3.2C(2)(aa) requires that the applicant, who in this case is Dr Stephen Thaler, must provide the name of the inventor of the invention to which the application relates.

2. An artificial intelligence system, which has been described as a device for the autonomous bootstrapping of unified sentience (DABUS), was named as the inventor by Dr Thaler. But it has been determined by the Deputy Commissioner that such a system could not be an inventor.

3. The Deputy Commissioner considered that s 15(1) of the *Patents Act 1990* (Cth) is inconsistent with an artificial intelligence machine being treated as an inventor; so too reg 3.2C(2)(aa). It was also said that Dr Thaler's application and its deficiencies were incapable of remedy.

4. Further, it was determined that Dr Thaler had not complied with a direction under reg 3.2C(4), and that his application had lapsed.

5. Dr Thaler seeks judicial review of these decisions under s 5(1) of the *Administrative Decisions (Judicial Review) Act 1977* (Cth) and s 39B of the *Judiciary Act 1903* (Cth). He says that s 15, and the Act and the Regulations more generally, do not preclude an artificial intelligence system being treated as an inventor. He says that the Deputy Commissioner misconstrued s 15(1), and the Act and the Regulations more generally, as being inconsistent with an artificial intelligence system being treated as an inventor.

6. The underlying question for my determination is whether an "inventor" for the purposes of the Act and the Regulations can be an artificial intelligence system. As I have indicated, that question arises because reg 3.2C(2)(aa) requires that an applicant of a *Patent Cooperation Treaty* (Washington, 19 June 1970) (PCT) application must provide the name of the inventor of the invention to which the application relates.

7. The Deputy Commissioner held that an artificial intelligence system cannot be an inventor because "[s]ection 15(1) is clear, but not capable of sensible operation in the situation where an inventor would be an artificial intelligence machine as it is not possible to identify a person who could be granted a patent" (at [32]). The effect of his reasoning is that an artificial intelligence system can invent something that satisfies all of the requirements of patentability in terms of novelty, inventiveness and utility, but such an invention will be unpatentable because the Act requires a human inventor.

8. Now Dr Thaler is the owner of copyright in DABUS's source code. He is also the owner, is responsible for and is the operator of the computer on which DABUS operates. But Dr Thaler is not the inventor of the alleged invention the subject of the application. The inventor is identified on the application as "DABUS, The invention was autonomously generated by an artificial intelligence". DABUS is not a natural or legal person. DABUS is an artificial intelligence system that incorporates artificial neural networks.

9. The alleged invention is the output of DABUS' processes. Various products and methods are claimed concerning containers, devices and methods for attracting enhanced attention using convex and concave fractal elements.

10. In summary and for the following reasons, in my view an artificial intelligence system can be an inventor for the purposes of the Act. First, an inventor is an agent noun; an agent can be a person or thing that invents. Second, so to hold reflects the reality in terms of many otherwise patentable inventions where it cannot sensibly be said that a human is the inventor. Third, nothing in the Act dictates the contrary conclusion.

11. It follows that I reject the Deputy Commissioner's determination and the Commissioner's position before me.

12. First, that position confuses the question of ownership and control of a patentable invention including who can be a patentee, on the one hand, with the question of who can be an inventor, on the other hand. Only a human or other legal person can be an owner, controller or patentee. That of course includes an inventor who is a human. But it is a fallacy to argue from this that an inventor can only be a human. An inventor may be an artificial intelligence system, but in such a circumstance could not be the owner, controller or patentee of the patentable invention.

13. Second, on the Commissioner's logic, if you had a patentable invention but no human inventor, you could not apply for a patent. So by employing the Commissioner's device of using a procedural requirement in a subordinate instrument, you would substantively preclude the possibility of a patent grant for that invention. Nothing in the Act justifies such a result. And it is the antithesis of the s 2A object.

14. Third, in my view the Commissioner has not kept faith with the tenet that "[i]t is also of fundamental importance that limitations and qualifications are not read into a statutory definition unless clearly required by its terms or its context, as for example if it is necessary to give effect to the evident purpose of the Act" (*PMT Partners Pty Ltd (in liq) v Australian National Parks & Wildlife Service* (1995) 184 CLR 301 at 310 per Brennan CJ, Gaudron and McHugh JJ). Indeed the evident purpose of the Act, a proxy for which is s 2A, is at odds with the unreality of persisting with the notion that artificial intelligence systems cannot be inventors.

15. Fourth, much of the Commissioner's argument descended into dictionary definitions of "inventor." But more is required of me than mere resort to old millennium usages of that word. If words are only "pictures of ideas upon paper" (*Dodson v Grew* (1767) Wilm 272 at 278; 97 ER 106 at 108 per Wilmot CJ) and if, as Holmes J described it, they are not "crystal[s], transparent and unchanged, [but] the skin of a living thought and may vary greatly in colour and content according to the circumstances and the time in which [they] are used" (*Towne v Eisner*, 245 US 418, 425 (1918)), I need to grapple with the underlying idea, recognising the evolving nature of patentable inventions and their creators. We are both created and create. Why cannot our own creations also create?

## NOTES AND QUESTIONS

**1.** Why might you want, or not want, to protect AI-generated inventions? You'd want to if patents continue to act as an incentive for parties, and generally companies, to invest in the use and development of AI to generate useful inventions, to invest in commercializing new inventions, and to disclose new inventions rather than keep them as trade secrets. What might you want if patent law was purely to encourage inventive activity by persons?

**2.** Can an AI invent as a factual matter? Some critics have argued that behind every AI is a person, or at least enough human activity in any invention so that an AI cannot be considered an inventor.

**3.** What about non-traditional human inventorship? Should a human being be an inventor by virtue of having programmed an AI to invent? By virtue of having found a problem to solve? By virtue of owning or using an AI? By virtue of being the first person to recognize the utility of AI output?

**4.** What challenges does co-inventorship raise? If an invention requires joint conception by multiple parties in the United States, is it a problem if one of those parties is an AI? Does that render a patent, or certain claims, unprotectable?

**5.** There is an ongoing global battle regarding entitlement to patents on fundamental CRISPR (gene editing) technology. The contestants include individuals who were awarded the Nobel prize for CRISPR discoveries (Jennifer Doudna and Emmanuelle Charpentier) and business entities associated with them, and individuals associated with the Broad Institute, Harvard, and MIT. The biography of Jennifer Doudna by Walter Isaacson entitled *The Code Breaker* (2021) is an excellent introduction to the field and provides background to the disputes.

In the following case, the EPO Board of Appeal affirms rejection of a patent application from the Broad/Harvard/MIT group, deciding that it will continue to apply the "all applicants" rule. This rule requires that every inventor listed on an application the priority date of which is claimed must be included on the corresponding subsequent application. That is, all inventors on the first application must be inventors on the second application. Rejection of priority by the EPO allowed intervening prior art to defeat the subsequent application. The EPO confirms its longstanding practice.

### *T 0844/18 (CRISPR-Cas/Broad Institute) of 16.1.2020*

49. The Board . . . finds that the . . . objects and purposes actually highlight the question of who is the "applicant" whose interests are being safeguarded or facilitated. A feature of a priority right is that it comes into existence with the filing of one patent application but is exercised by the filing of another patent application, often in another country. So if A and B file the first patent application together, the appellants' interpretation of "any person" would allow A alone to file and own another patent application in another country claiming the same invention without involving B. This could of course result from an agreement between A and B, it could however equally result from more sinister circumstances, such as A trying to deprive B of its rights to a patent in another country. This second scenario can hardly be thought of as one that the law should seek to protect, and neither safeguards the interests of all of the patent applicants, nor assists the applicants in obtaining international protection. It is also to be borne in mind that an applicant can progress a patent application before the EPO without the active participation of the other applicants . . .

50. In the Board's view, the object and purpose of the Paris Convention cannot form the basis for favouring one or some persons to the detriment of all other persons who originally formed part of the group of persons that filed a patent application. Neither can they form a basis for exempting this person or persons from fulfilling any formal requirements. Indeed, this person or persons are defined by means of the action which they originally carried out, i.e. filing an application. Hence, if a group of persons decides together to carry out this act of filing, then they have decided to act as a unity for this purpose, thus implying that the "any person" is this group as such. . . .

117. For the reasons given above, the decision of the opposition division on the interpretation of the term "any person" in Article 87(1) EPC is to be confirmed. The interpretation is that of the so-called "all applicants" approach. The Board agrees with the EPO's long established practice on this issue.

118. A consequence of this is that priority has not been validly claimed from P1, P2, P5 and P11 and hence documents D3 and D4 become relevant prior art. The appellants have not provided any arguments, either before the opposition division or before the Board, as to why the claims of the patent in suit are novel over documents D3 and D4. The Board thus adopts the reasoning and decision . . . of the opposition division's decision."

## E. First to File

Since the very early days of patent law, patents were awarded in the United States to the "first and true inventor"—interpreted to mean the person who could demonstrate having first conceived the invention in a sufficiently fixed form. The statutory and regulatory language used to identify the first inventor varied over time, but the basic idea was that as long as the person who conceived the invention reduced it to practice without undue delay (and filing a patent application constituted "constructive reduction to practice"), that person would be entitled to the patent (as between competing claimants). Indeed, being the first person to file a patent application for the relevant subject matter gave the first applicant the benefit of a presumption of entitlement, but it could be rebutted by a subsequent applicant proving first conception and timely reduction to practice. As a matter of government policy, the United States asserted that the "first to invent" rule was the most fair to inventors, particularly to inventors with more limited resources, because it did not favor large enterprises with teams of patent lawyers that could rapidly file applications more or less irrespective of cost. The first to invent rule was argued to place inventors on an even footing, and moreover to represent fundamental fairness because a patent should be awarded to the person who conceived first.

The first to invent rule placed the United States out of harmony with the rest of the world that follows a "first to file" rule. Outside the United States, there is effectively a "race to the patent office." The person who files the first application for the relevant subject matter is entitled to the patent,[25] bearing in mind that account needs to be taken of "priority" based on Paris Convention rules. The first to file rule gives priority to the first application filed in any Paris country. The first application establishes on behalf of the applicant its "priority date," and this becomes the first to file date for all Paris countries.

The America Invents Act, adopted in 2011 but taking effect on various issues on a staggered timeline, changed the United States from a first to invent to a first to file country, bringing it into harmony with the rest of the world.[26] For larger enterprises, this was a relatively minor matter. They had long been living with first to file rules because of the reality of obtaining patents in many countries. While it might have been acceptable to move slowly in the United States, delay would jeopardize patenting everywhere else. An inventor could file late in the United States and subsequently prove it was the first and true inventor, but this would not entitle it to the patent everywhere else which relied on the initial filing date.

As a way to level the playing field for inventors with modest resources, the United States had in 1995 implemented a so-called "provisional application" that allows for the filing of an application that will establish a priority date under the Paris Convention, but does not require the submission of claims. The applicant must either file a corresponding nonprovisional application within one year of the initial filing date, or convert the provisional into a nonprovisional application within one year, at which time claims must be submitted. By filing a new corresponding application, the applicant has the benefit of a later filing date for purposes of U.S. law—and a longer effective patent term—while a converted application maintains the original filing date. Neither mechanism affects the priority date, which remains with the initial filing of the provisional application.[27] The change from "first to invent" to "first to file" has not eliminated the provisional application mechanism.

Although the shift from first to invent to first to file in the United States will eliminate certain patent office procedures used to determine who the legitimate first and true inventor is (e.g., the "interference" with respect to filing date), the practical effect of this shift is not very significant. If an inventor had any interest in patenting outside the United States, it would have been irresponsible for a patent attorney to suggest to the client that they delay filing a patent application in the United States because they could always demand their first to invent rights. This would risk losing the possibility for a patent everywhere else, and in the United States place an evidentiary burden on the tardy applicant that might be difficult to satisfy.

## F. Pre- and Post-Grant Opposition

The assessment whether a patent should be granted based on a filed application is entrusted to the national or regional patent office. That action may involve the WIPO Patent Cooperation Treaty studied later in this chapter. Some countries do not provide for substantive examination of patent applications by the patent office, but most countries with well-developed patent

25. It is very unlikely that two or more different patent applications will be filed by different inventors in precisely the same language. Necessarily patent offices need to assess whether different applications cover the same inventive concept in order to make a determination whether granting a patent on one application will preclude granting an application on another.

26. The date on which the first to file rule came into effect in the United States was March 16, 2013: http://www.uspto.gov/aia_implementation/faqs_first_inventor.jsp#heading-1.

27. One of the arguments put forward by the patent applicant in the "All Inventors" case at the EPO, supra pp. 217-218, was that some unique features associated with U.S. provisional application filings could preclude compliance with the "all applicants" rule at the EPO. This argument was rejected by the Board of Appeal on grounds that a conscientious provisional applicant could avoid such a result.

systems provide for such examination. The threshold question whether a patent applicant/inventor has satisfied the criteria of patentability will in the first instance typically be made by a patent examiner whose job it is to consider the various elements, including the relevant prior art, and who often will engage in a dialogue with the applicant that may result in changes to claims or other parts of the application. Interaction between patent examiners and applicants is reflected in a number of the judicial decisions set out in the preceding sections.

There is, however, an important role for the public to play with respect to patent applications and grants other than the possibility of civil court dispute over alleged infringement, counterclaims for invalidity, etc. Many countries provide in their patent law for a type of "opposition proceeding" that can be initiated at the patent office by a person other than the patent applicant seeking to prevent the grant of a patent (i.e., "pre-grant opposition") or challenging the decision of the patent office to grant the patent (i.e., "post-grant opposition"), as well as less elaborate provisions allowing third parties to submit prior art or observations to the patent office during the pendency of an application (i.e., third-party submissions).

The forms of pre- and post-grant opposition and third-party submission, and whether to make provision for such proceedings actions, are not controlled by a specific international legal rule or standard, though TRIPS Agreement general principles regarding the conduct of administrative proceedings may be relevant. These actions represent a way for the public to aid the patent office in assuring that only patents legitimately deserving to be granted are granted (or maintained).[28] The specific manner in which these procedures operate differs substantially among national patent offices. However, as a general matter, they are distinct from ordinary civil patent litigation that typically involves demand for injunction against future infringement, claims for damages, and counterclaims for invalidity. The opposition proceeding is limited to an assessment of the patent itself and whether it should, or should not, have been granted. The remedies are limited to denial of the patent grant, some modification to the patent, or patent revocation. These are all matters within the province of the patent office, although decisions may be appealable to the courts.

The European Patent Office has long operated a post-grant opposition procedure that is described later in this chapter. While the United States has maintained some limited forms of patent re-examination and challenge, only with the implementation of the America Invents Act in 2011 has it introduced a form of opposition proceeding involving a more or less full legal contest over patentability, with a route of appeal to the Court of Appeals for the Federal Circuit (CAFC).* At both the EPO and under the new U.S. Post-Grant Review (PGR) procedure, any interested person can initiate a challenge within nine months of the grant of the patent,** and in the United States, under the new Inter Partes Review (IPR) administrative challenges may be commenced after that. India maintains both pre- and post-grant opposition procedures.

Some governments have expressed concern that pre-grant opposition may result in unjustified delay in the granting of patents. The U.S. government, for example, has made elimination of pre-grant opposition a target of its intellectual property negotiating efforts. However,

---

28. T 1839/18 () of 19.3.2021: The EPO Board confirms that any person may file an opposition, regardless whether a "strawman," particularly because oppositions are intended to serve a public purpose of preventing maintenance of invalid patents, not to serve the interests of a particular party. The identity of the opponent is thus not material. Note that the Opposition Division is entitled to continue proceedings even if the opponent has withdrawn when it considers that the patent should be reviewed. Also serves the interest of patentee by assuring third parties of validity, and of promoting legal security.

* On the U.S. procedure, *see, e.g.*, http://www.uspto.gov/aia_implementation/faqs_post_grant_review.jsp.

** The U.S. PGR survived a constitutional challenge before the Supreme Court, *Oil States Energy Servs., LLC v. Greene's Energy Grp.*, 584 U.S. ___ (2018). *See, e.g.*, Brent Kendall, *Supreme Court Upholds New Process for Challenging Patents*, Wall St. J., April 24, 2018.

countries that maintain such systems argue that they operate to improve the integrity and quality of granted patents, and that the timing of pre-grant opposition procedures can be reasonably regulated. For a more detailed discussion of the various types of pre-grant and post-grant opposition, and third-party submission procedures, *see* a study on opposition systems prepared by the WIPO Secretariat for the Standing Committee on the Law of Patents (SCP/17/9, Oct. 31, 2011, as revised).[29]

## G. Term of Protection

The Paris Convention on the Protection of Industrial Property did not establish a minimum or maximum term of patent protection and, prior to the negotiation of the TRIPS Agreement, there was considerable variation among countries regarding the term of protection. The TRIPS Agreement (Article 33) prescribed a minimum patent term of 20 years from filing of the patent application, and did not prescribe a maximum term of protection.

The legislation of a number of countries provides for extension of the term of the patent on the occurrence of certain conditions. For example, the U.S. Patent Act provides for extension based on unreasonable delay by the Patent Office in processing applications,[30] and for pharmaceutical patents based on the length of the Food and Drug Administration (FDA) regulatory review process (at 35 U.S.C. §156). The latter provision is complex and subject to a substantial number of conditions and qualifications. The regulatory review is divided into two phases: (1) the phase during which the drug is subject to clinical testing (which is dated from authorization to test by the FDA) (the "testing" phase) and (2) the phase during which the FDA evaluates the test (and other) data (the "approval" phase). One half of the period of the testing phase plus the approval phase are subject to compensation (35 U.S.C. §156(c) & (g)). In no event may the duration of the extension exceed five years (35 U.S.C. §156(g)(6)(A)). The total period of effective patent protection may not exceed 14 years (the original patent term, shortened by the regulatory review period, plus the extension) (35 U.S.C. §156(c)(3)). There are a substantial number of additional conditions, including a limitation to the first commercial marketing of the product.

The European Union effectively extends the term of patents in the pharmaceutical sector, also based on the regulatory review period. However, it refers to this extension as the provision of a Supplementary Protection Certificate (SPC).[31] To further reinforce the harmonization of EU patent law and complement the Unitary Patent System (discussed further below), the European Commission proposed in April 2023 regulations on the unitary SPC for medicinal products and the SPC for plant protection products. Under the proposed regulation for medicinal products, unitary SPCs are only allowed on the basis of centralized marketing authorizations issued by the European Medicines Agency (EMA).

---

29. Available at http://www.wipo.int/edocs/mdocs/scp/en/scp_17/scp_17_9.pdf. *See also* WIPO - Opposition Systems, https://www.wipo.int/scp/en/revocation_mechanisms/opposition/index.html.

30. The U.S. Patent Act provides (at 35 U.S.C. §154) for extension of the patent term based on delay of the Patent Office, generally more than three years from the filing of the application. Unlike an extension based on drug regulatory approval, the extension based on delay of the Patent Office applies to all fields of technology. However, there are several important exceptions to the general rule of extension. Thus, for example, if an interference is declared under 35 U.S.C. §135(a) and a proceeding is held to determine the rightful claimant to a patent among competing claimants, the interference period is excluded from the processing time (as are appeals from decisions of the patent examiner). Likewise, delays based on national security review are excluded.

31. *See* Council Regulation (EEC) No. 1768/92 of 18 June 1992, Concerning the Creation of a Supplementary Protection Certificate for Medicinal Products. Available at http://eur-lex.europa.eu/LexUriServ/LexUriServ.do?uri=CELEX:31992R1768:EN:HTML.

In the negotiation of bilateral, regional, and plurilateral trade and investment agreements, the United States has been pressing other countries to provide for patent term extension as it is provided for in the United States.

In the WTO *Canada-Generic Pharmaceuticals* panel decision,[32] excerpted *infra* section II.B.1, the European Union unsuccessfully argued that a mechanism for patent term extension was a necessary element in laws that permit early working of patents for regulatory review purposes.

# II. THE MULTILATERAL PATENT AGREEMENTS

## A. The Paris Convention

### 1. Historical Perspective

As we have previously noted, efforts to create an international intellectual property rights (IPRs) system date back to the late 1800s, when two treaties that continue to form the backbone of the system were agreed upon—the Paris Convention for the Protection of Industrial Property (1883) and the Berne Convention for the Protection of Literary and Artistic Works (1886). The Paris Convention addresses patents, and we begin with a historical perspective on that Convention.

The Paris Convention has been subject to a series of revisions since its adoption in 1883. The most recent revision was undertaken at Stockholm in 1967 (and amended in 1979), and the Stockholm revision of the Paris Convention is the most widely adopted among its contracting parties.

As part of her economic analysis (recall the excerpt in Chapter 1), Edith Penrose described the negotiating history of the Paris Convention.

**Edith Tilton Penrose***

## *The Economics of the International Patent System*

## CHAPTER III

#### THE DEVELOPMENT OF THE INTERNATIONAL CONVENTION FOR THE PROTECTION OF INDUSTRIAL PROPERTY

As the patent system spread into one country after another in the 19th century, demands from various quarters for the adoption of international regulations increased. Commercial interests are no respecters of national boundaries and while the law of each country prevails only within the jurisdiction of that country, the interest of the patentees in the use of their inventions frequently extends beyond the jurisdiction of any one country. As might be expected, the patent laws adopted by the various countries, though designed broadly for the same purposes, varied considerably in their detailed provisions. Although few discriminated against foreigners specifically, the difficulty of complying with many different regulations made it almost impossible for a patentee to get protection in many countries.

32. *Canada—Patent Protection of Pharmaceutical Products*, Report of the Panel, WT/DS114/R, March 17, 2000 ("Canada-Generic Pharmaceuticals").

* Economics of the International Patent System 101-107, 162-169 (1951).

The definition of what was considered a patentable invention differed between the laws of different countries and consequently a patent might be obtained on an invention in some countries while in others the invention was excluded from patent protection. This was—and is—particularly true with regard to medicines, foods, drugs and chemical products. Novelty of the invention was required in most countries and an invention was frequently not considered new if it had been published or publicly used abroad. When an inventor applied for a patent in his own country he had to disclose the nature of his invention, and the publication of the specification attached to this patent application was held by a few other countries to destroy the newness of the invention for patent purposes. In applying for a patent in several countries an inventor had to draw up applications conforming to widely different and extremely detailed rules; he had strictly to observe complicated procedures, and he had to do all of these things within short periods of time. In the meantime, others might learn of his invention through the patent application in his own country and patent the invention themselves, if permitted. Or they might simply use it, thus either destroying its novelty for patent purposes or acquiring a legal right to its use which could not be touched even if the original inventor succeeded eventually in obtaining a patent. Taxes had to be paid on time or the patent would be forfeited. In many countries the invention had to be put into commercial use within a limited period of time. Thus, to obtain and maintain patents in foreign countries, a patentee was usually forced to incur the expense of obtaining and maintaining patent agents in each country to defend his interests.

Hence a patentee who wished to exploit his invention abroad, or to obtain a revenue from its exploitation abroad by others, or to prevent others from using his invention to compete with him in foreign markets, had a strong incentive to press for international agreements which would eliminate the difficulties of obtaining protection in countries other than his own. Patent lawyers, jurists and manufacturers joined in the demand for international legislation. The "rights of man" were freely invoked in the cause and at times the movement took on the tone of a religious crusade. One of the crusaders, for example, wrote:

> The striving of the individual human and the interest of the social organism join in a common cause to justify the juridical institution of the right of the inventor or of the creator. . . .But a right which has its source in a human aspiration as profound as that we have just revealed extends to the entire community of men who live and think. . . .How contain the explosion of a new principle in the narrow confines of a single country without permitting it to expand across the universe?

Nor was invention the only type of industrial property for which international arrangements were being asked. Trade marks, industrial designs and models were included. The only international protection existing when the International Convention for the Protection of Industrial Property was created in 1880 was such as had been written into bipartite treaties most of which were concerned primarily with other matters. Of these there were some 69 that included provisions affecting industrial property, but only two of them contained provisions for the protection of patents. This type of protection was generally considered to be unsatisfactory since it had no separate existence apart from the general commercial arrangements with which it was usually associated. Hence the protection was apt to be "*brève et précaire.*"

### *The Vienna Congress of 1873*

The first conference to consider the protection of inventors on an international scale met in Vienna in 1873. An international Exposition under the auspices of the Austria-Hungarian Government was to be held in that year and the inventors in some countries, particularly the United States, feared that their inventions would be inadequately protected under Austrian law. The United States took the lead in pressing Austria to protect more adequately inventions exhibited at the Exposition and, in addition, to revise her patent laws to give more complete protection to foreign patentees in general. Among those provisions of the Austrian law which met the disapproval of the United States was the compulsory working requirement, under which a patented article had to be manufactured in Austria within a year from the issue of the patent. The American Minister in Vienna even referred the Austrian Foreign Ministry to an article in the Scientific American which complained of Austrian treatment of American inventors and ended with a veiled threat of refusal to join in the Exposition if the Austrian law were not changed.

The Austrians passed a special law protecting exhibited inventions. In addition, on the suggestion of the United States, it was decided to hold an international conference on patent reform immediately after the Exposition. Thus, the first international conference on patents was held while the controversy between the patent and anti-patent forces throughout Europe was still lively and bitter. It was not an official conference although representatives from 13 countries were included among the 158 participants. The majority of those attending the conference were from Germany and the acute difference of opinion in Germany as to whether a patent law was desirable and whether Germany should adopt one was reflected in the debates of the conference.

The resolutions were very general but clearly endorsed the principle of patent protection. The first resolution, consisting of seven reasons why "the protection of inventions should be guaranteed by the laws of all civilized nations under the condition of a complete publication of the same," was violently debated but was adopted by a vote of 80 to 4. The second resolution, setting out the principles on which an "effective and useful patent law should be based" was even more controversial. The most notable decision of the conference was paragraph (f) of this resolution which recommended compulsory licensing of patents "in cases in which the public interest should require it." This principle was not again to be accepted by an international conference for 50 years but the anti-patent movement in the 19th century had created such an awareness of the possible monopolistic and restrictive effects of the patent system that some limitation of the patent monopoly had to be conceded by the patent advocates. The official United States position was strongly opposed to any concessions but the resolution was carried by a vote of 42 to 17.

Finally the conference resolved that it was "of pressing moment that governments should endeavor to bring about an international understanding upon patent protection as soon as possible" and empowered a preparatory committee "to continue the work commenced by this first international congress, and to use all their influence that the principles adopted be made known as widely as possible, and carried into practice." Five years later the conference that was to establish the basis of an international agreement was called.

### *The Paris Conference of 1878*

Under the auspices of the French Government, and again in connection with an international Exposition, a conference of nearly 500 participants, including eleven government delegates and delegates from 48 Chambers of Commerce and industrial and technical societies was called in Paris. Like the Vienna conference, this conference was an unofficial affair, although called by the French government and attended by some official delegates. More than three-fifths of the delegates were French industrialists and thus the French point of view completely dominated the conference. This is one of the reasons why the views of this conference in many respects contrasted strongly with those of the Vienna conference in which the German element was predominant. Malapert, a French jurist and patent authority, complained that, although invitations were widely sent out, the scope of the conference was so restricted by its promoters that people with a critical point of view did not attend:

> The acts of the organizing committee had restricted too much a field which ought to be open. There was no place where one could take account of the social position of different populations of the globe, although all were invited to engage in a common task. The radius of the circle was too short, the circumference inscribed a cell in which it was not possible to breathe. It was for this reason that many jurists and economists, expert in the study of patent laws, refrained from attending the conference where they would have nothing to learn and nothing to do or teach, since limits had been set outside of which it was forbidden to go.

The stenographic report of the conference shows clearly that critics of the operation of the patent system were not well received. "*Vice applandissements*" occur after speeches in which the strongest and most far-reaching claims were made for inventors' rights, while "*rumeurs*" are reported when remarks such as the following were made:

> Messieurs, after the eloquent words which you have just heard, it takes great temerity on my part to mount this platform; but I consider it my duty to arise here to tell you of the dangers and inconveniences which result from the monopoly of exploitation granted by the French law to patentees for fifteen years. (Murmurs)

It is not surprising, therefore, that the resolutions of the conference reflect almost exclusively the patentees' point of view. In addition to the exaltation of the rights of inventors was the exaltation of the spirit of international union. The dream of many who attended the conference was complete uniformity of the laws protecting industrial property in all nations. At this time the formation of unions of many kinds was being discussed in conferences all over Europe. The most important of these referred to postal matters, the telegraph, weights and measures, and literary and artistic property. A patent union analogous to these other unions, with a uniform international law, was the goal.

There were a few participants, however, who were aware of the social implications of the patent law and who felt that some recognition of the interest of society should be explicitly stated other than the general assertion that society benefitted because of the encouragement of invention. The very first debate of the conference was on the nature of the inventor's right and the proposition before the conference was as follows:

> The right of inventors and of industrial creators in their work, or of manufacturers and business men in their marks is a right of property, the civil law does not create it, it only regulates it.

M. Clunet, a French jurist, presented a "counter-proposition"[:]

> The right of inventors and of industrial creators is an equitable and useful creation of the civil law, which reconciles the rights of inventors and of society by the concession of a temporary monopoly.

The debate on this issue was heated and involved, but the conference came out decisively in favor of the first proposition. It adopted in effect the "natural property" theory of inventors' rights. Nonetheless, in spite of this extreme position, it was not possible for the participants in the discussions to escape the fact that at times there might be a serious interference with the welfare of society if this "most sacred of all property" was subject to no limitations. Hence it was proposed that "the principle of expropriation in the public interest is applicable to patents." The adoption of this proposal was opposed on the ground that it was not necessary; if a matter of public health or military necessity existed, the state obviously had the power to override private interests. The majority of the conference, however, felt it was worthwhile to make this principle explicit and adopted the proposal.

On the principle of expropriation in the public interest, the conference admitted the right of the state to revoke a patent if manufacture was not undertaken in the country in a specified time, at least if the patentee could not justify his inaction. In other words, the conference approved what is now known as compulsory working revocation of the patent if it was not worked. Even compulsory licensing as the sanction for failure to work was rejected. In later conferences, revocation of the patent was considered to be too harsh on the inventor, and its replacement by compulsory licensing was fought for and obtained. The Vienna conference had rejected the principle that a patent must be worked in the country granting it and had therefore not even proposed compulsory licensing as a sanction for non-working although it had approved compulsory licensing whenever the public interest required it. In both respects, the Vienna conference was far ahead of the times.

It seems curious, however, that in the 1878 conference, where the rights of inventors were upheld in the most extreme forms, the principle of compulsory licensing for failure to work was rejected in favor of outright revocation of the patent. This position was the direct result of the natural property theory of patents adopted by the conference. M. Charles Lyon-Caën, a prominent French lawyer, argued heatedly that compulsory licensing was a derogation of the right of property and compared the inventor subject to such licensing to a man who owned his house but was required to allow all who requested it, to live with him on the payment of a rental. Compulsory licensing only aided other private groups and could not be tolerated, although he would accept expropriation "*pour cause d'utilité publique*" if necessary:

> If one thinks that industry would have to suffer because of the monopoly, the remedy should not be to impose the obligation on the patentee to concede licenses, but to eliminate patents. . . . It is to completely misunderstand the absolute character of the right of property of the inventor to impose on him the obligation to concede licenses.

The conference accepted M. Lyon-Caën's point of view and approved the resolution that:

> Patents ought to assure, during their entire duration, to inventors or their assigns, the exclusive right to the exploitation of the invention and not a mere right to a royalty paid to them by third parties.

The conference adopted a number of other resolutions which were much more practical than those so far discussed. Some of them were subsequently taken over as the basis of the international Convention when it was finally agreed. These included the principle that foreigners should be treated equally with nationals in each country; that the laws of each country should apply to its colonies; that the importation of patented products by a patentee should not cause revocation of his patent; and that the rights acquired for the same invention in different countries should be independent of each others. It was also agreed that it should be possible for a patent claim to be made simultaneously at the appropriate national office and at the consulates of the various foreign nations in which a patent was desired.

When it came, however, to the problem of devising the framework of uniform legislation, the conference was obliged to recognize the realism of those who had insisted that uniformity was impossible in a world of national states with different interests, different legal structures and different economic histories, aspirations and ideologies. The participants contested vigorously over their different positions, but it soon became clear that the ideal of uniformity of legislation would have to give way to lesser goals. To the orators the ideal was good but the practical problems of achieving it were too great, since no state would admit that its own legal framework was not the best from which to take the international model.

The biggest obstacle to agreement on uniform patent laws was the question of the "previous examination" of the invention. Under the law of France and some other countries a patent was issued on the claim of the inventor, without examination of the merits or validity of his claim or of the novelty of the invention. Many other countries, on the other hand, required that the novelty, utility, patentability, etc. of the invention be scrutinized before the patent could be issued. Although most of the non-French delegates supported the latter system, the

French were in the majority and the conference passed a resolution that a patent should be delivered to all claimants at their own risk and thus without governmental examination.

Nor was there unanimous agreement on what products should be patentable. "*Batailles très chaudes*" took place on whether chemical products, pharmaceutical preparations and foodstuffs should be patentable and, although the conference decided in the affirmative, an important minority was left dissatisfied.

These various differences prevented the conference from coming to any final agreement on the nature of an international patent law, and it was decided to charge a permanent international commission with the task of carrying out the resolutions of the conference and of arranging an official international conference called by a government to lay the basis for uniform international legislation. In spite of the violent differences of opinion, the promoters of the conference had not yet lost hope of seeing such uniform legislation adopted.

### *The First Draft Convention*

The commission set up by the conference of 1878 set to work immediately after the conference was over and the French section, which formed the executive committee of the commission, produced a long draft which constituted in effect an extensive universal law. The French Minister of Commerce, to whom the draft was presented, recognized that such a far-reaching proposal could never command universal acceptance, and requested the section to draft a convention of more modest proportions. A "*Projet d'une Union Internationale pour la protection de la propriété industrielle*" was then drafted by the French delegate Jagerschmidt.

In the drafting of this project an eye was kept on existing national laws; uniform international legislation was no longer the goal and the convention was admittedly designed to encroach as little as possible on existing laws. Since the next step was a governmental one, it became necessary to produce specific proposals that would be politically viable. Thus the delegates had come down from the stars, and concentrated on provisions that they hoped would overcome the worst difficulties facing patentees with international interests, and would at the same time be politically practical. Gone was the talk of "natural property rights," or any attempt to define the nature of an inventor's right; gone were attempts to eliminate compulsory working, which was provided for in the laws of nearly all countries; and gone were attempts to impose a uniform standard of patentability devised in the interest of patentees. M. Jagerschmidt showed remarkable political acumen in the draft, most of the essentials of which were eventually accepted in the Convention.

### *The Conference at Paris in 1880*

The draft together with an invitation to an international diplomatic conference was sent by the French government to other governments. The response was favorable, and in 1880 the official conference met in Paris with representatives from 19 governments. The draft convention was adopted with some amendments and the amended draft was submitted to governments for their comment and approval. Provision was made for the protection of other forms of industrial property as well as for patents, for the organization of an International Bureau for the Protection of Industrial Property, for amendments to the Convention and for the adhesion of new member states.

The provisions on patents were confined to specific issues on which it was hoped sufficient agreement could be obtained to form a union. The important ones were as follows:

> Art. 2. The subjects or citizens of each of the contracting states shall enjoy, in all of the other States of the Union, so far as patents, industrial designs or models, trade marks, and commercial names are concerned, the advantages that their respective laws now grant, or may hereafter grant to their own nationals. Consequently they shall have the same protection as

the latter, and the same legal remedy against any infringement of their rights, provided they comply with the formalities and conditions imposed on nationals by the domestic legislation of each State.

Art. 3. The subjects of States not forming part of the Union who are domiciled or who have industrial or commercial establishments in the territory of one of the States of the Union are assimilated to the subjects or citizens of the contracting States.

Art. 4. Any person who has duly applied for a patent, the registration of an industrial design or model, or a trade mark in one of the contracting States, shall enjoy for the purpose of registration in other countries and subject to the rights of third parties, a right of priority during the periods hereinafter stated.

Consequently, subsequent filing in one of the other States of the Union, before the expiration of these periods shall not be invalidated through any acts accomplished in the interval, as, for instance, by another filing, by publication of the invention or the working thereof, by the sale of copies of the design or model, or by the use of the trade mark.

The above-mentioned periods of priority shall be six months for patents and three months for industrial designs or models and for trade marks they shall be increased by one month for countries overseas.

Art. 5. The introduction by the patentee into the country where the patent has been granted of objects manufactured in any of the countries of the Union shall not entail forfeiture. Nevertheless the patentee is subject to the obligation to work his patent in accordance with the laws of the country into which he introduces the patented articles.

### *The International Union for the Protection of Industrial Property*

In 1883 a brief conference was held at which the Convention was finally approved and signed. Ratifications were exchanged and in 1884 the International Union for the Protection of Industrial Property came into being. The Union was first composed of eleven countries, to which another twenty-nine were successively added.

Amendments to the Convention are made by Conferences of Revision, of which there have been six so far. These conferences meet periodically and are called when it seems desirable to the countries concerned. All amendments must have the unanimous approval of the members of the Union. If unanimity is not forthcoming Special Arrangements between the countries agreeing to the provisions under discussion may be adopted. The principle of special arrangements or "restricted unions" is not looked upon with favor, since it destroys the uniformity of the international regulations affecting members of the Union, and only three special arrangements have been established, none for patents.

The text of the Convention, as revised in the conferences of revision, comes into effect for each country when it deposits its ratification. The old text remains in force for countries that have not ratified the new text. Hence at any given time there may be several regimes in effect depending upon the progress of ratification of the latest revised texts.

## NOTES AND QUESTIONS

**1.** Edith Penrose discusses the factors that underlay the negotiation of the Paris Convention for the Protection of Industrial Property. She attributes the motivation for the negotiations to concerns surrounding the Austria-Hungarian International Exposition of 1873. What were American inventors concerned about? How could the display of an invention affect their economic rights? Generally speaking, disclosure of an invention would undermine its novelty, a critical element in determining patentability. Thus, disclosure of an invention in a country where a patent had not yet been granted may have prevented patent protection from ever being obtained there, or from being obtained in any other country whose patent office took into account foreign disclosures in determining novelty. If disclosure did not preclude patentability, someone other than the inventor may nevertheless have sought a patent on the invention before the original inventor. Some patent systems would have awarded a patent only to the true inventor, but it may not always have been easy to disprove another party's claim to inventive activity.

**2.** Edith Penrose notes that during the negotiation of the Paris Convention, there were some proposals to adopt a far more ambitious system of harmonized rules than those that eventually resulted. She observes that each country was persuaded that its own rules were the best, and that this made harmonization efforts difficult. Are matters so different today?

**3.** In the late 1800s many countries' patent systems did not provide for the pre-grant examination of patent applications (and some still do not, including the Swiss). These systems relied instead on post-grant opposition to patents by parties challenging the entitlement of the grantees. Such challenges may have taken the form of administrative or judicial proceedings seeking revocation of patents, or may have taken the form of defense against the enforcement of patents in civil litigation (claiming defects in the original patent grants). The absence of a pre-grant examination procedure reduces the *ex ante* cost of administering a patent system, but might impose substantial *ex post* costs, particularly on the general public, which may face a proliferation of product markets monopolized by patent holders.

**4.** The architects of the Paris Convention employed certain fundamental rules in the new international patent protection system. These were:

National treatment;
1. Independence of patents; and
2. Right of priority.

These fundamental principles continue to underlay the international patent protection system.

### *2. Paris Convention Rules*

WIPO administers the Paris Convention on behalf of the Paris Union. The WIPO Secretariat describes below the main features of the Convention.

## *The Paris Convention for the Protection of Industrial Property**

### PRINCIPAL PROVISIONS

5.9 The provisions of the Paris Convention may be sub-divided into four main categories:

- a first category contains rules of substantive law which guarantee a basic right known as the right to national treatment in each of the member countries;
- a second category establishes another basic right known as the right of priority;
- a third category defines a certain number of common rules in the field of substantive law which contain either rules establishing rights and obligations of natural persons and legal entities, or rules requiring or permitting the member countries to enact legislation following those rules;
- a fourth category deals with the administrative framework which has been set up to implement the Convention, and includes the final clauses of the Convention.

* From WIPO Intellectual Property Handbook (2004), at http://www.wipo.int.

## NATIONAL TREATMENT

5.10 National treatment means that, as regards the protection of industrial property, each country party to the Paris Convention must grant the same protection to nationals of the other member countries as it grants to its own nationals. The relevant provisions are contained in Articles 2 and 3 of the Convention.

5.11 The same national treatment must be granted to nationals of countries which are not party to the Paris Convention if they are domiciled in a member country or if they have a "real and effective" industrial or commercial establishment in such a country. However, no requirement as to domicile or establishment in the country where protection is claimed may be imposed upon nationals of member countries as a condition for benefiting from an industrial property right.

5.12 This national treatment rule guarantees not only that foreigners will be protected, but also that they will not be discriminated against in any way. Without this, it would frequently be very difficult and sometimes even impossible to obtain adequate protection in foreign countries for inventions, trademarks and other subjects of industrial property. . . .

5.14 This means furthermore, that any requirement of reciprocity of protection is excluded. Supposing that a given member country has a longer term of patent protection than another member country: the former country will not have the right to provide that nationals of the latter country will enjoy a term of protection of the same length as the term of protection is in the law of their own country. This principle applies not only to codified law but also to the practice of the courts (jurisprudence), and to the practice of the Patent Office or other administrative governmental institutions as it is applied to the nationals of the country.

5.15 The application of the national law to the national of another member country does not, however, prevent him from invoking more beneficial rights specially provided in the Paris Convention. These rights are expressly reserved. The national treatment principle must be applied without prejudice to such rights.

5.16 Article 2(3) states an exception to the national treatment rule. The national law relating to judicial and administrative procedure, to jurisdiction and to requirements of representation is expressly "reserved." This means that certain requirements of a mere procedural nature which impose special conditions on foreigners for purposes of judicial and administrative procedure, may also validly be invoked against foreigners who are nationals of member countries. An example is a requirement for foreigners to deposit a certain sum as security or bail for the costs of litigation. Another example is expressly stated: the requirement that foreigners should either designate an address for service or appoint an agent in the country in which protection is requested. This latter is perhaps the most common special requirement imposed on foreigners. . . .

## THE RIGHT OF PRIORITY

5.20 The right of priority means that, on the basis of a regular application for an industrial property right filed by a given applicant in one of the member countries, the same applicant (or its or his successor in title) may, within a specified period of time (six or 12 months), apply for protection in all the other member countries. These later applications will then be regarded as if they had been filed on the same day as the earliest application. Hence, these later applications enjoy a priority status with respect to all applications relating to the same invention filed after the date of the first application. They also enjoy a priority status with respect to all acts accomplished after that date which would normally be apt to destroy the rights of the applicant or the patentability of his invention. The provisions concerning the right of priority are contained in Article 4 of the Convention.

5.21 The right of priority offers great practical advantages to the applicant desiring protection in several countries. The applicant is not required to present all applications at home and in foreign countries at the same time, since he has six [for industrial designs and trademarks] or 12 [for patents and utility models] months at his disposal to decide in which countries to request protection. The applicant can use that period to organize the steps to be taken to secure protection in the various countries of interest in the particular case.

5.22 The beneficiary of the right of priority is any person entitled to benefit from the national treatment rule who has duly filed an application for a patent for invention or another industrial property right in one of the member countries.

5.23 The right of priority can be based only on the *first* application for the same industrial property right which must have been filed in a member country. It is therefore not possible to follow a first application by a second, possibly improved application and then to use that second application as a basis of priority. The reason for this rule is obvious: one cannot permit an endless chain of successive claims of priority for the same subject, as this could, in fact, considerably prolong the term of protection for that subject. . . .

5.26 The first application must be "duly filed" in order to give rise to the right of priority. Any filing, which is equivalent to a regular national filing, is a valid basis for the right of priority. A regular national filing means any filing that is adequate to establish the date on which the application was filed in the country concerned. The notion of "national" filing is qualified by including also applications filed under bilateral or multilateral treaties concluded between member countries.

5.27 Withdrawal, abandonment or rejection of the first application does not destroy its capacity to serve as a priority basis. The right of priority subsists even where the first application generating that right is no longer existent.

5.28 The effect of the right of priority is regulated in Article 4B. One can summarize this effect by saying that, as a consequence of the priority claim, the later application must be treated as if it had been filed already at the time of the filing, in another member country, of the first application the priority of which is claimed. By virtue of the right of priority, all the acts accomplished during the time between the filing dates of the first and the later applications, the so-called priority period, cannot destroy the rights which are the subject of the later application.

5.29 In terms of concrete examples, this means that a patent application for the same invention filed by a third party during the priority period will not give a prior right, although it was filed before the later application. Likewise, a publication or public use of the invention, which is the subject of the later application, during the priority period would not destroy the novelty or inventive character of that invention. It is insignificant for that purpose whether that publication is made by the applicant or the inventor himself or by a third party.

5.30 The length of the priority period is different according to the various kinds of industrial property rights. For patents for invention and utility models the priority period is 12 months, for industrial designs and trademarks it is six months. In determining the length of the priority period, the Paris Convention had to take into account the conflicting interests of the applicant and of third parties. The priority periods now prescribed by the Paris Convention seem to strike an adequate balance between them.

5.31 The right of priority as recognized by the Convention permits the claiming of "multiple priorities" and of "partial priorities." Therefore, the later application may not only claim the priority of one earlier application, but it may also combine the priority of several earlier applications, each of which pertaining to different features of the subject matter of the later application. Furthermore, in the later application, elements for which priority is claimed may be combined with elements for which no priority is claimed. In all these cases, the later application must of course comply with the requirement of unity of invention.

5.32 These possibilities correspond to a practical need. Frequently after a first filing further improvements and additions to the invention are the subject of further applications in the country of origin. In such cases, it is very practical to be able to combine these various earlier applications into one later application, when filing before the end of the priority year in another member country. This combination is even possible if the multiple priorities come from different member countries.

## PROVISIONS CONCERNING PATENTS

### *Independence of Patents*

5.33 Patents for invention granted in member countries to nationals or residents of member countries must be treated as independent of patents for invention obtained for the same invention in other countries, including non-member countries. The rule concerning the "independence" of patents for invention is contained in Article 4*bis*.

5.34 This principle is to be understood in its broadest sense. It means that the grant of a patent for invention in one country for a given invention does not oblige any other member country to grant a patent for invention for the same invention. Furthermore, the principle means that a patent for invention cannot be refused, invalidated or otherwise terminated in any member country on the ground that a patent for invention for the same invention has been refused or invalidated, or that it is no longer maintained or has terminated, in any other country. In this respect, the fate of a particular patent for invention in any given country has no influence whatsoever on the fate of a patent for the same invention in any of the other countries.

5.35 The underlying reason and main argument in favor of this principle is that national laws and administrative practices are usually quite different from country to country. A decision not to grant or to invalidate a patent for invention in a particular country on the basis of its law will frequently not have any bearing on the different legal situation in the other countries. It would not be justified to make the owner lose the patent for invention in other countries, on the ground that he or she lost a patent in a given country as a consequence of not having paid an annual fee in that country, or as a consequence of the patent's invalidation in that country, on a ground which does not exist in the laws of the other countries.

5.36 A special feature of the principle of independence of patents for invention is contained in Article 4*bis*(5). This provision requires that a patent granted on an application which claimed the priority of one or more foreign applications, must be given the same duration which it would have according to the national law if no priority had been claimed. In other words, it is not permitted to deduct the priority period from the term of a patent invoking the priority of a first application. For instance, a provision in a national law starting the term of the patent for invention from the (foreign) priority date, and not from the filing date of the application in the country, would be in violation of this rule.

### *The Right of the Inventor to Be Mentioned*

5.37 A general rule states that the inventor must have the right to be mentioned as such in the patent for invention. This is stated in Article 4*ter*.

5.38 National laws have implemented this provision in several ways. Some give the inventor only the right for civil action against the applicant or owner in order to obtain the inclusion of his name in the patent for invention. Others—and that tendency seems to be increasing—enforce the naming of the inventor during the procedure for the grant of a patent for invention on an *ex officio* basis. . . .

### *Importation, Failure to Work and Compulsory Licenses*

5.39 The questions of importation of articles covered by patents, of failure to work the patented invention and of compulsory licenses, are dealt with in Article 5A of the Convention.

5.40 With respect to importation, the provision states that importation by the patentee, into the country where the patent has been granted, of articles covered by the patent and manufactured in any of the countries of the Union will not entail forfeiture of the patent. This provision is quite narrowly worded, and hence only applies when several conditions are met. Consequently the countries of the Union have considerable leeway to legislate with respect to importation of patented goods under any of the circumstances which are different to those foreseen in this provision. . . .

5.44 With respect to the working of patents and compulsory licenses, the essence of the provisions contained in Article 5A is that each country may take legislative measures providing for which might result from the exclusive rights conferred by a patent for invention, for example failure to work or insufficient working.

5.45 Compulsory licenses on the ground of failure to work or insufficient working are the most common kind of coercive measure against the patent owner to prevent abuses of the rights conferred by the patent for invention. They are expressly dealt with by Article 5A.

5.46 The main argument for enforcing working of the invention in a particular country is the consideration that, in order to promote the industrialization of the country, patents for invention should not be used merely to block the working of the invention in the country or to monopolize importation of the patented article by the patent owner. They should rather be used to introduce the use of the new technology into the country. Whether the patent owner can really be expected to do so, is first of all an economic consideration and then also a question of time. Working in all countries is generally not economical. Moreover, it is generally recognized that immediate working in all countries is impossible. Article 5A therefore tries to strike a balance between these conflicting interests.

5.47 Compulsory licenses for failure to work or insufficient working of the invention may not be requested before a certain period of time has elapsed. This time limit expires either four years from the date of filing of the patent application or three years from the date of the grant of the patent for invention. The applicable time is the one which, in the individual case, expires last.

5.48 The time limit of three or four years is a minimum time limit. The patent owner must be given a longer time limit, if he can give legitimate reasons for his inaction—for example, that legal, economic or technical obstacles prevent working, or working more intensively, the invention in the country. If that is proven, the request for a compulsory license must be rejected, at least for a certain period. The time limit of three or four years is a minimum also in the sense that national law can provide for a longer time limit.

5.49 The compulsory license for non-working or insufficient working must be a non-exclusive license and can only be transferred together with the part of the enterprise benefiting from the compulsory license. The patent owner must retain the right to grant other non-exclusive licenses and to work the invention himself. Moreover, as the compulsory license has been granted to a particular enterprise on the basis of its known capacities, it is bound to that enterprise and cannot be transferred separately from that enterprise. These limitations are intended to prevent a compulsory licensee from obtaining a stronger position on the market than is warranted by the purpose of the compulsory license, namely, to ensure sufficient working of the invention in the country.

5.50 All these special provisions for compulsory licenses in Article 5A(4) are only applicable to compulsory licenses for non-working or insufficient working. They are not applicable to the other types of compulsory licenses for which the national law is free to provide. Such other types may be granted to prevent other abuses, for example, excessive prices or unreasonable terms for contractual licenses or other restrictive measures which hamper industrial development.

5.51 Compulsory licenses may also be granted for reasons of the public interest, in cases where there is no abuse by the patent owner of his rights—for example, in the fields of military security or public health.

5.52 There are also cases where a compulsory license is provided for to protect the public interest in unhampered technological progress. This is the case of the compulsory license in favor of the patent for invention granted to another person, then the owner of the dependent patent, in certain circumstances, may have the right to request a compulsory license for the use of that invention. If the owner of the dependent patent for invention obtains the compulsory license, he may in turn be obliged to grant a license to the owner of the earlier patent for invention.

5.53 All these other types of compulsory licenses can be grouped together under the general heading of compulsory licenses *in the public interest*. National laws are not prevented by the Paris Convention from providing for such compulsory licenses, and they are not subject to the restrictions provided for in Article 5A. This means in particular that compulsory licenses in the public interest can be granted without waiting for the expiration of the time limits provided for compulsory licenses that relate to failure to work or insufficient working.

5.54 It should be noted, however, that Article 31 of the TRIPS Agreement further provides a number of conditions with respect to the use of subject matter of a patent without the authorization of the right-holder.

***Grace Period for the Payment of Maintenance Fees***

5.55 Article 5*bis* provides for a grace period for the payment of maintenance fees for industrial property rights and deals with the restoration of patents for invention in case of non-payment of fees. . . .

***Patents in International Traffic***

5.58 Another common rule of substantive importance, containing a limitation of the rights of the patent owner in special circumstances, is contained in Article 5*ter*. It deals with the transit of devices on ships, aircraft or land vehicles through a member country in which such device is patented.

5.59 Where ships, aircraft or land vehicles of other member countries enter temporarily or accidentally a given member country and have on board devices patented in that country, the owner of the means of transportation is not required to obtain prior approval or a license from the patent owner. Temporary or accidental entry of the patented device into the country in such cases constitutes no infringement of the patent for invention. . . .

***Inventions Shown at International Exhibitions***

5.62 A further common rule of a substantive nature is the provision concerning temporary protection in respect of goods exhibited at international exhibitions, contained in Article 11 of the Convention.

5.63 The principle stated in Article 11 is that the member countries are obliged to grant, in conformity with their domestic legislation, temporary protection to patentable inventions, utility models, industrial designs and trademarks in respect of goods exhibited at official or officially recognized international exhibitions held in the territory of any member country. . . .

## NOTES AND QUESTIONS

**1.** In promoting the TRIPS Agreement, OECD country industries pointed to several weaknesses of the Paris Convention in respect to patents. One such weakness is that the Paris

Convention does not prescribe the subject matter areas or fields of invention for which a government must offer patent protection. Article 1(3) prescribes a broad scope of subject matter coverage for "industrial property," but this prescription does not extend specifically to patents. Why do you think that the drafters of the Paris Convention may have limited their subject matter definition to "industrial property"?

**2.** Note that the Paris Convention does not attempt to set forth any criteria of patentability. Edith Penrose has told us that efforts to harmonize substantive criteria for patenting proved too controversial. Do you think it is unusual to find a treaty (e.g., this one on "patents") that does not establish a definition for its most basic element? In fact, it is common for treaties to leave the meaning of basic terms open. The United Nations Charter allows the Security Council to take action after it has determined that a "threat to the peace" exists, but it does not attempt to define what a threat to the peace may be. Human rights treaties often (though certainly not always) refer to basic human rights in general terms. Reaching agreement on the specific content of rights may be quite difficult in a wide number of international contexts. Much of the Uruguay Round negotiations involved reducing broadly drafted GATT provisions to more precise rules.

**3.** Another provision of the Paris Convention criticized by OECD industry groups was the compulsory licensing provision. Article 5 refers only to preventing "abuses" of the patent right. There is no reference in Article 5 to compensation for the right holder.

**4.** Article 28 of the Paris Convention provides for dispute settlement before the International Court of Justice (ICJ). No complaint under the Paris (or Berne) Convention has ever been filed in the ICJ. In the TRIPS negotiations, OECD industry groups contended that referral to the ICJ is a "weak" means of settling IPRs-related disputes. Why is the ICJ perceived as weak? International dispute settlement bodies almost always rely on the persuasive force of their decisions (and not on gunboats) to assure compliance. ICJ judges are certainly as capable as WTO panel members of understanding the issues at stake in an IPRs-related dispute. Might the real concern of OECD industry groups with the Paris Convention have been that the ICJ would have too much flexibility in interpreting the Paris Convention since its provisions are rather broad? The real key to the perceived weakness of the Paris Convention perhaps lay more in its lack of substantive definition.

### 3. *Paris and the Independence of Patents*

See Chapter 1, section VII.D on the establishment of independence, including the *Cuno v. Pall* decision, as well as the recent dispute between India/Brazil and the European Union regarding seizures of pharmaceutical products in transit.

### 4. *Patent Exhaustion and the Free Movement of Goods*

We have previously introduced the subject of exhaustion of rights and parallel trade. Each country has the freedom to determine whether exhaustion of patent rights under its national law takes place when patented goods are first placed on the market anywhere in the world (i.e., international exhaustion), are first placed on the market within a regional territory (i.e., regional exhaustion), or are first placed on the market within that country (i.e., national exhaustion). We examine below the attitudes of the national courts of Japan and the United States, and a legislative provision from South Africa.

#### a. Japan

The Supreme Court of Japan in 1997 decided a case involving the parallel importation into Japan of a product patented both in Japan and Germany. The product was first sold in Germany with the consent of the German patent holder. A Japanese affiliate of the German patent holder held a license under a parallel patent in Japan. The Japanese patent holder/licensee thereafter attempted to block importation into Japan of the product first sold in Germany. The Supreme Court of Japan held that, pursuant to the Paris Convention principle of independence of patents, a first sale of the product in Germany did not exhaust the rights of the patent holder in Japan. However, it went on to hold that the close integration of the global economy leads to the presumption that a patent holder in Japan that consents to the placement of its product on the market in a foreign country does so with the expectation that such product may be exported to Japan or another third country. Consequently, unless the Japanese patent holder establishes a contractual obligation on the part of the first purchaser not to export the patented product to Japan, the Japanese patent holder may not block importation of the product into Japan. By entering into a restrictive agreement with the first purchaser, and by affixing a notice to the product itself declaring this restriction, the Japanese patent holder may apparently extend the restriction to subsequent purchasers. The Court says it is not relevant whether the product is patented in the country of first sale outside of Japan.

Following is an excerpt from the opinion of the Japanese Supreme Court in the *BBS* case.

## *BBS Kraftfahrzeugtechnik AG and BBS Japan, Inc. v. Rasimex Japan, Inc.*

Supreme Court Heisei 7(o) No. 1988 (July 1, 1997) J. of S. Ct., No. 1198 (July 15, 1997), 8-10*

The following is the summary of the Supreme Court decision in the *BBS* case, Part 3, Chapter 4, which, according to the translator, is translated as accurately as possible even at the sacrifice of ease of reading:

The Judgment is in favor of the importer (Rasimex) of a patented product (aluminum wheels) rejecting an appeal made by the patent holder (BBS). Part 1 of the Opinion relates the factual and procedural background of the case. Part 2 summarizes the arguments heretofore made by both parties. Part 3, occupying majority of pages of the decision, gives the opinion of the court in reaching the decision. Chapter 1 of Part 3 concludes that the present case should be decided only in light of the Japanese Patent Act and not by the Paris Convention or by the doctrine of territoriality. Chapter 2 states that the doctrine of exhaustion is based on Article 1 of the Japanese Patent Act ("The purpose of the Act is to promote invention and thereby to contribute to the development of industries"). Chapter 3 denies so-called international exhaustion, saying that patent rights in Japan and in the exporting country are different rights. Chapter 5 is the conclusion of the opinion.

Brackets [] are added for contextual clarity.

### 4

Now, considering the balance between the distribution of products in international trade and the right of a patentee, it is safely to be said that, in light of the situation that international trade is progressing extremely widely and highly in modern society, the highest degree of respect to the freedom of distribution of products including importation is required, even where a Japanese trader imports into Japan the product [first] sold in other countries and puts the same into distribution into the [Japanese] market. And whereas, even in economic transactions in other countries, a transaction is achieved on the basis that a seller generally transfers all of his rights in

* Translation with introductory synopsis by Tadayoshi Homma, Professor of Law, Chiba University, Japan.

the merchandise to the purchaser and the purchaser acquires all of the rights owned by the seller, it is naturally expected that, where a patentee has sold a patented product in other countries, the [first] purchaser or the third parties who purchased the same from the [first] purchaser may import into Japan, use or further sell to others as a business, in light of the abovementioned situation of international trade in modern society. Considering the above points, the patentee is not permitted to enforce his patent right in Japan [1] against the [first] purchaser of the product except where the patentee has agreed with the [first] purchaser to exclude Japan from the territories for sale or use or [2] against the third parties or subsequent purchasers who purchased the product from the [first] purchaser except where the patentee has agreed with the [first] purchaser as abovementioned and has explicitly indicated the same on the patented product. In other words, (1) in light of the abovementioned fact that a patented product sold in other countries is naturally expected to be imported into Japan subsequently, the sale of a product by the patentee in other countries without any reservation should be interpreted as a grant of rights to the [first] and subsequent purchasers to control the product in Japan without any patent restriction. (2) Focusing upon the right of the patentee on the other hand, it should be permitted for a patentee to make a reservation of right upon the sale of a patented product in other countries, to enforce his patent right in Japan, and where the patentee has agreed with the [first] purchaser and has explicitly indicated the same on the patented product, the subsequent purchasers can recognize the attached restriction to that effect even if third parties have intervened during the distribution of the product and can decide at his free will whether or not to purchase the product in the face of such restriction. (3) And the sale of the patented product in other countries by subsidiaries or affiliates who can be regarded as same as the patentee should be interpreted as the sale of the product by the patentee himself, and (4) the need to protect the belief in free trade of the purchaser of a patented product does not differ depending upon whether or not the patentee has a parallel patent right at the place of first sale of the patented product.

## NOTES AND QUESTIONS

**1.** The Japanese Supreme Court says that the rights of the Japanese patent holder are not exhausted by the first sale of the product outside Japan, but that the purchaser of the product outside Japan has a legitimate expectation that it will be able to resell the product in international commerce free of the patent restriction. Thus, the Court accepts a basic territorial nature for the patent grant, but seeks to limit the consequences of this territorial nature for the free movement of goods in world trade. What changes in business practices might you expect as a consequence of this decision? Might these changes add transparency to the effects of the international patent system? Are they likely to materially affect the flow of goods in world commerce?

**2.** As noted earlier, independence of patents should not be confused with a principle of territoriality (*see* Christopher Heath, *Parallel Imports and International Trade*, 28 IIC 623, 627-28 (1997)). The Japanese Supreme Court invokes independence as a ground for not expressly recognizing that exhaustion takes place when the products are placed on the German market. Yet, it reaches a conclusion consistent with the principle of international exhaustion. Japan was under some pressure from the United States not to accept international exhaustion of patents in this case. Might this help explain the Supreme Court's "interesting" reasoning?

### b. United States

In previous editions of this book we explained the tortuous history of the doctrine of international exhaustion of patents in the United States, and suggested that the Court of Appeals for the Federal Circuit got it wrong in its ruling in *Jazz Photo v. ITC*, 264 F.3d 1094 (Fed. Cir. 2001) when it announced that the United States followed a doctrine of national exhaustion. In May 2017, the Supreme Court overruled the Federal Circuit and affirmed a doctrine of international exhaustion of patents for the United States. The Supreme Court decision also overturned Federal Circuit precedent that had allowed patent-based post-sale use restrictions. That portion of the opinion is not included here, but briefly discussed in the Notes following.

## *Impression Products v. Lexmark International*

137 S. Ct. 1523 (2017)

Chief Justice Roberts delivered the opinion of the Court.

A United States patent entitles the patent holder (the "patentee"), for a period of 20 years, to "exclude others from making, using, offering for sale, or selling [its] invention throughout the United States or importing the invention into the United States." 35 U.S.C. §154(a). Whoever engages in one of these acts "without authority" from the patentee may face liability for patent infringement. §271(a).

When a patentee sells one of its products, however, the patentee can no longer control that item through the patent laws—its patent rights are said to "exhaust." The purchaser and all subsequent owners are free to use or resell the product just like any other item of personal property, without fear of an infringement lawsuit.

This case presents two questions about the scope of the patent exhaustion doctrine: First, whether a patentee that sells an item under an express restriction on the purchaser's right to reuse or resell the product may enforce that restriction through an infringement lawsuit. And second, whether a patentee exhausts its patent rights by selling its product outside the United States, where American patent laws do not apply. We conclude that a patentee's decision to sell a product exhausts all of its patent rights in that item, regardless of any restrictions the patentee purports to impose or the location of the sale.

. . .

Our conclusion that Lexmark exhausted its patent rights when it sold the domestic Return Program cartridges goes only halfway to resolving this case. Lexmark also sold toner cartridges abroad and sued Impression Products for patent infringement for "importing [Lexmark's] invention into the United States." 35 U.S.C. §154(a). Lexmark contends that it may sue for infringement with respect to all of the imported cartridges—not just those in the Return Program—because a foreign sale does not trigger patent exhaustion unless the patentee "expressly or implicitly transfer[s] or license[s]" its rights. Brief for Respondent 36–37. The Federal Circuit agreed, but we do not. An authorized sale outside the United States, just as one within the United States, exhausts all rights under the Patent Act.

This question about international exhaustion of intellectual property rights has also arisen in the context of copyright law. Under the "first sale doctrine," which is codified at 17 U.S.C. §109(a), when a copyright owner sells a lawfully made copy of its work, it loses the power to restrict the purchaser's freedom "to sell or otherwise dispose of . . . that copy." In *Kirtsaeng v. John Wiley & Sons, Inc.*, we held that this " 'first sale' [rule] applies to copies of a copyrighted work lawfully made [and sold] abroad." 568 U.S., at 525, 133 S. Ct. 1351. We began with the text of § 109(a), but it was not decisive: The language neither "restrict [s] the scope of [the] 'first sale' doctrine geographically," nor clearly embraces international exhaustion. Id., at 528–533, 133 S. Ct. 1351. What helped tip the scales for global exhaustion was the fact that the first sale doctrine originated in "the common law's refusal to permit restraints on the alienation of chattels." Id., at 538, 133 S. Ct. 1351. That "common-law doctrine makes no geographical distinctions." Id., at 539, 133 S. Ct. 1351. The lack of any textual basis for distinguishing between domestic and international sales meant that "a straightforward application" of the first sale doctrine required the conclusion that it applies overseas. Id., at 540, 133 S. Ct. 1351 (internal quotation marks omitted).

Applying patent exhaustion to foreign sales is just as straightforward. Patent exhaustion, too, has its roots in the antipathy toward restraints on alienation, see supra, at 1528–1533, and nothing in the text or history of the Patent Act shows that Congress intended to confine that borderless common law principle to domestic sales. In fact, Congress has not altered patent exhaustion at all; it remains an unwritten limit on the scope of the patentee's monopoly. See *Astoria Fed. Sav. & Loan Assn. v. Solimino*, 501 U.S. 104, 108, 111 S. Ct. 2166, 115 L. Ed. 2d 96 (1991) ("[W]here a common-law principle is well established, . . . courts may take it as given that Congress has legislated with an expectation that the principle will apply except when a statutory purpose to the contrary is evident" (internal quotation marks omitted)). And differentiating the patent exhaustion and copyright first sale doctrines would make little theoretical or practical sense: The two share a "strong similarity . . . and identity of purpose," *Bauer & Cie v. O'Donnell*, 229 U.S. 1, 13, 33 S. Ct. 616, 57 L. Ed. 1041 (1913), and many everyday products—"automobiles, microwaves, calculators, mobile phones, tablets, and personal computers"—are subject to both patent and copyright protections, see *Kirtsaeng*, 568 U.S., at 545, 133 S. Ct. 1351; Brief for Costco Wholesale Corp. et al. as Amici Curiae 14–15. There is a "historic kinship between patent law and copyright law," *Sony Corp. of America v. Universal City Studios, Inc.*, 464 U.S. 417, 439, 104 S. Ct. 774, 78 L. Ed. 2d 574 (1984), and the bond between the two leaves no room for a rift on the question of international exhaustion.

Lexmark sees the matter differently. The Patent Act, it points out, limits the patentee's "right to exclude others" from making, using, selling, or importing its products to acts that occur in the United States. 35 U.S.C. §154(a). A domestic sale, it argues, triggers exhaustion because the sale compensates the patentee for "surrendering [those] U.S. rights." Brief for Respondent 38. A foreign sale is different: The Patent Act does not give patentees exclusionary powers abroad. Without those powers, a patentee selling in a foreign market may not be able to sell its product for the same price that it could in the United States, and therefore is not sure to receive "the reward guaranteed by U.S. patent law." Id., at 39 (internal quotation marks omitted). Absent that reward, says Lexmark, there should be no exhaustion. In short, there is no patent exhaustion from sales abroad because there are no patent rights abroad to exhaust.

The territorial limit on patent rights is, however, no basis for distinguishing copyright protections; those protections "do not have any extraterritorial operation" either. 5 M. Nimmer & D. Nimmer, Copyright §17.02, p. 17-26 (2017). Nor does the territorial limit support the premise of Lexmark's argument. Exhaustion is a separate limit on the patent grant, and does not depend on the patentee receiving some undefined premium for selling the right to access the American market. A purchaser buys an item, not patent rights. And exhaustion is triggered by the patentee's decision to give that item up and receive whatever fee it decides is appropriate "for the article and the invention which it embodies." *Univis*, 316 U.S., at 251, 62 S. Ct. 1088. The patentee may not be able to command the same amount for its products abroad as it does in the United States. But the Patent Act does not guarantee a particular price, much less the price from selling to American consumers. Instead, the right to exclude just ensures that the patentee receives one reward—of whatever amount the patentee deems to be "satisfactory compensation," *Keeler*, 157 U.S., at 661, 15 S. Ct. 738—for every item that passes outside the scope of the patent monopoly.

This Court has addressed international patent exhaustion in only one case, *Boesch v. Graff*, decided over 125 years ago. All that case illustrates is that a sale abroad does not exhaust a patentee's rights when the patentee had nothing to do with the transaction. Boesch—from the days before the widespread adoption of electrical lighting—involved a retailer who purchased lamp burners from a manufacturer in Germany, with plans to sell them in the United States. The manufacturer had authority to make the burners under German law, but there was a hitch: Two individuals with no ties to the German manufacturer held the American patent to that invention. These patentees sued the retailer for infringement when the retailer imported the lamp burners into the United States, and we rejected the argument that the German manufacturer's sale had exhausted the American patentees' rights. The German manufacturer had no permission to sell in the United States from the American patentees, and the American patentees had not exhausted their patent rights in the products because they had not sold them to anyone, so "purchasers from [the German manufacturer] could not be thereby authorized to sell the articles in the United States." 133 U.S. 697, 703, 10 S. Ct. 378, 33 L. Ed. 787 (1890).

Our decision did not, as Lexmark contends, exempt all foreign sales from patent exhaustion. See Brief for Respondent 44-45. Rather, it reaffirmed the basic premise that only the patentee can decide whether to make a sale that exhausts its patent rights in an item. The American patentees did not do so with respect to the German products, so the German sales did not exhaust their rights.

Finally, the United States, as an amicus, advocates what it views as a middle-ground position: that "a foreign sale authorized by the U.S. patentee exhausts U.S. patent rights unless those rights are expressly reserved." Brief for United States 7-8. Its position is largely based on policy rather than principle. The Government thinks that an overseas "buyer's legitimate expectation" is that a "sale conveys all of the seller's interest in the patented article," so the presumption should be that a foreign sale triggers exhaustion. Id., at 32-33. But, at the same time, "lower courts long ago coalesced around" the rule that "a patentee's express reservation of U.S. patent rights at the time of a foreign sale will be given effect," so that option should remain open to the patentee. Id., at 22 (emphasis deleted).

The Government has little more than "long ago" on its side. In the 1890s, two circuit courts—in cases involving the same company—did hold that patentees may use express restrictions to reserve their patent rights in connection with foreign sales. See *Dickerson v. Tinling*, 84 F. 192, 194-195 (C.A.8 1897); *Dickerson v. Matheson*, 57 F. 524, 527 (C.A.2 1893). But no "coalesc[ing]" ever took place: Over the following hundred-plus years, only a smattering of lower court decisions mentioned this express-reservation rule for foreign sales. See, e.g., *Sanofi, S.A. v. Med–Tech Veterinarian Prods., Inc.*, 565 F. Supp. 931, 938 (D.N.J. 1983). And in 2001, the Federal Circuit adopted its blanket rule that foreign sales do not trigger exhaustion, even if the patentee fails to expressly reserve its rights. *Jazz Photo*, 264 F.3d, at 1105. These sparse and inconsistent decisions provide no basis for any expectation, let alone a settled one, that patentees can reserve patent rights when they sell abroad.

The theory behind the Government's express-reservation rule also wrongly focuses on the likely expectations of the patentee and purchaser during a sale. Exhaustion does not arise because of the parties' expectations about how sales transfer patent rights. More is at stake when it comes to patents than simply the dealings between the parties, which can be addressed through contract law. Instead, exhaustion occurs because, in a sale, the patentee elects to give up title to an item in exchange for payment. Allowing patent rights to stick remora-like to that item as it flows through the market would violate the principle against restraints on alienation. Exhaustion does not depend on whether the patentee receives a premium for selling in the United States, or the type of rights that buyers expect to receive. As a result, restrictions and location are irrelevant; what matters is the patentee's decision to make a sale.

. . .

The judgment of the United States Court of Appeals for the Federal Circuit is reversed, and the case is remanded for further proceedings consistent with this opinion.

It is so ordered.

**Frederick M. Abbott***

## *Comment on the US Supreme Court Decision "Impression Products v. Lexmark International" 35 U.S.C., §154(a)*

### 2.5 WHAT WAS UNSAID

The Supreme Court refers to several business sectors in its opinion, including automobile repair shops, semiconductor manufacturers and general retailers. Not once does the Court refer to the pharmaceutical sector. The originator pharmaceutical industry in the United States has been perhaps the most vocal opponent of international exhaustion, pharmaceutical industry groups submitted amicus briefs to the Supreme Court,[31] the Federal Circuit addressed questions to counsel during oral hearings concerning pharmaceuticals and referenced the sector in its opinion.[32] Cutting through the noise, the basic argument of the pharmaceutical originator industry was that international exhaustion and parallel imports would result in lower prices in the United States, which would adversely affect R&D investments by the companies, which would adversely affect the American public.[33] By this logic, any effort to control pharmaceutical prices is a negative.

This author submitted an amicus brief to the Supreme Court favoring international exhaustion and predominantly addressing pharmaceutical sector issues, though with a different perspective than the originator industry groups.[34] Allowing the originator companies to protect the US market against their own products sold more cheaply in foreign markets imposes a burden on US consumers. The interests of low and middle-income countries in pharmaceuticals provided under differential pricing programs can be protected in WTO-legitimate ways.[35]

The Supreme Court Justices were without doubt aware that the pharmaceutical industry in the United States was keenly interested in this case. The Justices knew that the industry finds the idea of price competition from parallel imports anathema. The case before the Court involved toner cartridges, and the Court did not need to venture into the pros and cons of parallel imported medicines. As the law stands following the Supreme Court's decision, parallel import of patented medicines into the United States is permitted, subject to compliance with FDA rules. Such medicines must be manufactured in facilities that have been inspected and approved by the FDA, and must be approved for marketing in the United States. The originator pharmaceutical industry will be lobbying for amendment to the Patent Act and/or the laws implemented by the FDA. Whether Congress will stand with the Supreme Court and the vast majority of US citizens for exerting downward pressure on domestic pharmaceutical prices, or will join with the pharmaceutical lobbyists, is an open question.

---

* IIC 48: 889-96 (2017).

31. *See, e.g.*, Brief for Pharmaceutical Research and Manufacturers of America as Amicus Curiae in Support of Respondent, S. Ct., No. 15-1189 (2017) ("PhRMA Brief"); Brief of Amici Curiae Biotechnology Innovation Organization and Croplife International in Support of Respondent, S. Ct., No. 15-1189 (Feb. 23, 2017)("BIO Brief").

32. *Lexmark International v. Impression Products*, 816 F.3d 721, 772 (Fed. Cir. 2016).

33. *See, e.g.*, PhRMA Brief at 9–19; BIO Brief at 24.

34. Brief of Amicus Curiae (Frederick M. Abbott) in Support of Petitioner in *Impression Products v. Lexmark International*, US Supreme Court, No. 15-1189, filed January 20, 2017. Available at SSRN: https://ssrn.com/abstract=2906967.

35. *Id.*, and; Frederick M. Abbott, Parallel Trade in Pharmaceuticals: Trade Therapy for Market Distortions, in: I. Calboli and E. Lee (eds.) Research Handbook on Intellectual Property Exhaustion and Parallel Imports, 145-65, (Edward Elgar Pub. 2016).

The Supreme Court ignored the Federal Circuit's references to avoiding contravention of free trade agreements. However, the fact that the Federal Circuit pursued this line of reasoning gives another reason for caution regarding the commitments made in such agreements.

### 3 FINAL NOTE

The US Supreme Court is looked to by judges and lawyers around the world as a source of sound jurisprudence. The decision in Impression Products stands as a strong affirmation of the right of WTO Members to adopt international exhaustion of patents. It confirms the stand taken by the government of South Africa in the late 1990s. It supports the free movement of goods in commerce, including those protected by intellectual property rights.

Of course, the decision still leaves some open questions regarding patent exhaustion. There are always open questions. For this moment, however, we can take the time to appreciate the categorical stance of the US Supreme Court in favor of international patent exhaustion and non-enforcement of post-sale patent restrictions.

## NOTES AND QUESTIONS

**1.** In *Quanta Computers v. LG Electronics*, 553 U.S. 617 (2008), the U.S. Supreme Court addressed the question of exhaustion of patent rights in the domestic context, specifically whether the sale of a product embodying a "method patent" exhausts the patent holder's rights in that method. The Supreme Court answered in the affirmative. LG Electronics licensed several method patents to Intel. The patented methods were used to improve the operation of Intel microprocessors. In its license agreement with Intel, LG Electronics required Intel to provide notice to third-party purchasers of Intel parts that they were not acquiring rights to practice LG's method patents when Intel products were combined with the products of third parties. Quanta Computers purchased microprocessors incorporating LG's method patents from Intel and incorporated those microprocessors in computers along with third-party parts. LG sued Quanta for violation of its method patents. LG argued that because the Intel microprocessors continued to use its method patents even after the purchase by Quanta, the sale to Quanta did not exhaust LG's patent rights (as might be anticipated if LG's patents covered a product). LG contended that method patents are not subject to traditional exhaustion because the purchaser practices the invention after the sale. The Supreme Court disagreed, holding that method patents involving processes incorporated in products are exhausted upon first sale, just as patented machine components would be. The Supreme Court noted that if method patents were permitted to escape the application of exhaustion doctrine, inventors would be encouraged to file patent applications in the form of method patents. The Supreme Court noted that LG was not in a contract relationship with the third-party purchasers from Intel. The third-party purchasers were entitled to expect they could use the Intel microprocessors without facing pass-through patent claims from LG. The Supreme Court in this case reversed the Federal Circuit, and in doing so limited the scope of rights that may be asserted by patent holders. This case was closely watched by product resellers in the United States. The resellers feared that an extension of the exhaustion doctrine would limit their ability to market products to end-users. The Supreme Court did not address "international" exhaustion issues in this decision.

**2.** You are advising the owner of a chain of pharmacies located in the United States. The owner tells you that popular cholesterol-lowering drugs are available in Canada at wholesale prices about half the wholesale prices of the same drugs available in the United States. The owner wants to know whether the pharmacy chain will face any patent-related problems if it purchases and imports the drugs from Canada for sale to U.S. consumers. How would you answer that question? What additional facts will be important to your analysis?

**3.** Article 69(1) of the 2008 China Patent Law prescribes a rule of international exhaustion of patent rights for China. Article 107A of the India Patents Act (as amended in 2005) adopts a rule of international exhaustion of patent rights for India.

### c. South Africa

Section 15C of South Africa's Medicines Amendments Act was the subject of threats by the European Union and the United States to impose trade sanctions for violation of the TRIPS agreement, and a lawsuit by 39 pharmaceutical companies.[33] The European Union and the United States eventually withdrew their objections, recognizing the TRIPS consistency of authorizing parallel imports. The pharmaceutical companies eventually withdrew their case and paid the legal fees of the South African government. This incident marked a low point for patent law as it had been used to threaten the legitimate interests of the South African government and people in the midst of the HIV/AIDS pandemic. The legitimacy of the international intellectual property system has yet to fully recover from this.

**Y. Tayler, ed.***

## *Parallel Imports in South Africa—Under the Rule of International Exhaustion*

South Africa has adopted legislation (Section 15C of the Medicines and Related Substances Control Amendment Act, No. 90 of 1997) pursuant to which its Minister of Health (through the Medicines Control Council) has issued regulations that establish the conditions for the parallel importation of medicines into the country. In addition to the regulations, the Council has issued a Guideline for Parallel Importation of Medicines in South Africa.

The regulations provide that: "parallel importation" means the importation into the Republic of a medicine protected under patent and/or registered in the Republic that has been put on to the market outside the Republic by or with the consent of such patent holder.

The regulations and guideline provide procedures under which a parallel importer must obtain a permit to undertake importation. These procedures are intended to assure that parallel import medicines are duly approved and registered by the Department of Health, and that the parallel importer will comply with requirements ordinarily imposed on vendors of medicine in South Africa, such as using an approved storage facility and having in place a recall procedure. The guideline also establishes that, "The parallel importer may use the proprietary name approved in South Africa as well as any trade marks applicable to the medicine in order to ensure the public health interests."

### d. Switzerland

Switzerland is not a member state of the European Union. However, it adapts its own laws to the Union's standards in specific sectors. In 2009, Switzerland unilaterally introduced the

33. *See* discussion in Frederick M. Abbott, *WTO TRIPS Agreement and Its Implications for Access to Medicines in Developing Countries*, prepared for the British Commission on Intellectual Property Rights (Study Paper 2a, Feb. 2002).

* World Bank, *Battling HIV/AIDS*, Annex 2, Box B.2.

concept of regional exhaustion for patents in relation to the EEA member states while keeping up national exhaustion for third countries.

**P. Groz & A. Mondini**

## *Switzerland: New Developments in Swiss Patent Law*

### 1.3 Present Exhaustion Regime in Swiss Intellectual Property Law

Until now, the exhaustion regime in Swiss copyright, trademark, and patent law was solely determined by case law. The Swiss Federal Court ruled that, under Swiss law, the principle of international exhaustion applies to copyrights (BGE 124 III 321, Nintendo) and to trademark rights (BGE 122 III 469, Chanel). However, patent rights were subject to national exhaustion (BGE 126 III 129, Kodak). No relevant Swiss Federal Court decision exists as yet concerning design rights.

Under the concept of national exhaustion, patent rights could be asserted to prevent parallel imports to Switzerland of patent-protected products first sold abroad, provided that the patent owner did not engage in a restriction of trade amounting to a violation of competition law. Since the Kodak judgment, the national exhaustion of patent rights has been the subject of much controversy.

On one hand it was argued, inter alia, that national exhaustion enables the patent holder to charge different prices in different countries depending on the demand. This allows further financing of research and development activities. A move away from the system of national exhaustion would harm Switzerland as a place for research. Similarly, with a transition to international exhaustion, there would be a danger that developing countries might no longer be supplied with drugs or other patent-protected products because of the fear that products sold in those countries at a lower price would then be re-imported to Switzerland.

On the other hand, it was broadly criticized that the restriction of intra-brand competition that follows from a system of national exhaustion is one of the main reasons that prices in Switzerland for some products are higher than in neighboring countries.

### 1.4 Regional Exhaustion in Patent Law since 1 July 2009

After a highly publicized political debate, the Swiss Parliament decided to amend the Patent Act (PatA) by introducing the regional exhaustion concept in relation to the contracting States of the European Economic Area. This patent law revision went into effect on 1 July 2009. This means that patented products first put on the market in the European Economic Area with the consent of the patent holder may now be imported into Switzerland without the patent holder's consent (Art. 9a PatA).

If a patented product is first put on the market outside the European Economic Area, the patent holder continues to be able to defend against possible parallel imports into Switzerland. The patent holder may not prevent the importation, however, where the patent in question does not pertain to the main function of the product (e.g., a perfume) to be imported, but is instead only of secondary importance (e.g., a patented closure on a perfume bottle, Art. 9a para 4 PatA).

It is noteworthy that the concept of national exhaustion continues to apply for patented goods with government-administered prices (particularly pharmaceuticals) in Switzerland or in the country of sale (Art. 9a para 5 PatA). This exception (introduced as a result of the efforts of the strongly-represented Swiss pharmaceutical industry) is of great practical relevance. First, patent protection is of fundamental importance to the pharmaceutical industry. Second, the price of pharmaceuticals differs greatly among European countries due to national regulations.

It should finally be noted that, exceptionally, international (not just regional) exhaustion applies to agricultural means of production and investment goods.

### 1.5 Simplified Approval of Parallel-Imported Drugs

The Swiss Therapeutic Products Act provides for a simplified marketing authorization procedure for parallel-imported drugs that are already approved in Switzerland. Previously, simplified approval was not possible as long as the already-approved therapeutic product (i.e., the original preparation) was still patent-protected. The first applicant was allowed to assert its patent rights during the marketing authorization procedure for the parallel-imported drug before the Swiss Agency for Therapeutic Products (Swissmedic).

With the revision of patent law effective 1 July 2009, the Therapeutic Products Act was also amended. It is no longer possible to claim patent protection in the administrative marketing authorization procedure for a parallel-imported drug. This results in a shortening and simplification of the marketing authorization procedure for parallel-imported drugs.

In the future, the owner of the original preparation will only be able to assert its patent rights against a parallel importer in civil court proceedings.

## NOTES AND QUESTIONS

**1.** How would you classify Switzerland's new exhaustion policy in the context of the multilateral trading system? Do you see any issues arising in connection with the nondiscrimination provisions of the TRIPS Agreement? Which parties could be subject to *de facto* discrimination and how likely is it that they are going to challenge Switzerland's new policy?

**2.** In an advisory opinion for the Swiss Federal Institute of Intellectual Property, Thomas Cottier and Rachel Liechti produced evidence that the exhaustion rules applied by Switzerland, which provide for regional exhaustion in connection with EU countries with simultaneous maintenance of national exhaustion toward other countries, result in a *de lege* discrimination of parallel exports from third countries under the GATT Agreement.[34] What are the prospects of justifying the Swiss patent exhaustion policy under Articles XXIV and XX(d) of GATT?

**3.** Thomas Cottier in a recent work, *Parallel Trade and Exhaustion of Intellectual Property in WTO Law Revisited*,* argues that Article 6 of the WTO TRIPS Agreement does not exclusively govern the field of parallel trade from a WTO law standpoint, and that rules of the GATT and GATS, which were not superseded by adoption of Article 6, remain applicable. He suggests that restrictions on parallel imports may be inconsistent with GATT rules such as Article XI (prohibiting the imposition of quotas) and Article III (prohibiting discrimination based on national origin). He posits that some IP owners might attempt to justify restrictions on parallel trade based on Article XX(d) of the GATT that allows GATT-inconsistent provisions necessary to protect intellectual property, but he concludes that such restrictions

34. Thomas Cottier & Rachel Liechti, *Ist die einseitig statuierte regionale Erschöpfung im schweizerischen Patentrecht mit dem WTO-Recht vereinbar?*, in Schweizerisches Jahrbuch für Europarecht/Annuaire suisse de droit européen (2007/2008) (Astrid Epiney & Tamara Civitella eds., 2007); available at https://www.ige.ch/fileadmin/user_upload/andere/Juristische_Infos/d/j10071d.pdf (accessed January 23, 2019).

* In Axel Metzger, Henning Grosse Ruse-Khan (eds.) Intellectual Property Ordering Beyond Borders 189-234 Oxford: Oxford University Press 2022.

generally would not be "necessary" within the meaning of that provision, with some possible exceptions. Prof. Cottier has long been concerned with the EU limitation of exhaustion to goods placed on the market only within the EU (i.e. regional exhaustion). He supports a general rule of international exhaustion.

#### e. The Doha Declaration

The WTO Doha Declaration on the TRIPS Agreement and Public Health, discussed in section II.B.1.c, *infra*, expressly confirms the right of each WTO Member to determine its own policy and rules with respect to exhaustion of rights and thus whether to permit parallel importation of medicines.

## B. The WTO TRIPS Agreement

We have previously examined the factors that brought about negotiation and conclusion of the TRIPS Agreement. Pharmaceutical and agricultural chemical producers were among the leading lobbying groups advocating higher standards of patent protection. Prior to the TRIPS Agreement, a substantial number of developing countries did not provide patent subject matter protection for pharmaceutical and food-related products. The TRIPS Agreement changed that: Articles 27 to 34 of the Agreement specifically address patents, in addition to incorporating the substantive provisions of the Paris Convention. The international system thus prescribes minimal standards requiring that, *inter alia*, patents be granted in all fields of technology, including chemicals and pharmaceutical products, both product and process patents (the latter with the burden of proof reversed); the minimum term of protection is 20 years from the filing of the application; and that the invention be sufficiently disclosed.

**Frederick M. Abbott[*]**

### *Intellectual Property Rights in World Trade*

The most significant changes to the international IP regulatory system brought about by the TRIPS Agreement were in the field of patents. The Paris Convention provides rules regarding the mechanisms by which patents are granted, and prescribes national treatment. It does not, however, define the subject matter scope of patent protection, the criteria of patentability or the term of patent protection. It includes a limited set of rules applicable to the compulsory licensing of patents.

The TRIPS Agreement provides that patents should be available for products and processes in all fields of technology on the basis of the criteria of novelty, inventive step and capability of industrial application.[58] It also provides for sufficiency of disclosure.[59] Taken together, these criteria reflect the basic rules of developed country patent systems. The Agreement provides that patents rights shall be available and enjoyed without discrimination based on place of invention, field of technology, and whether products are imported or locally produced.[60] The TRIPS Agreement prescribes a minimum 20 year term of protection counted from the filing of the patent application.[61]

* In Research Handbook in International Economic Law (A. Guzman & A. Sykes eds., 2007).

58. Article 27, TRIPS Agreement.

59. Article 29, *id.*

60. Article 27, *id.*

61. Article 33, *id.*

The TRIPS Agreement allows for certain exclusions from patentability, such as for the protection of public order and for diagnostic or therapeutic procedures.[62] It permits Members to refuse patenting of animals and plants, but requires that some form of plant variety protection be provided.[63] This may be through patent or a *sui generis* form of protection. Also, the exclusion for animals and plants does not extend to non-biological and microbiological processes.

The TRIPS Agreement expands upon the compulsory licensing rules found in the Paris Convention, prescribing substantive and procedural conditions for the grant of such licenses.[64] However, it does not limit the grounds upon which compulsory licenses may be granted, and it provides for a waiver of procedural prerequisites in cases of national emergency, extreme urgency, or for public non-commercial use. In addition to the provision on compulsory licensing, the TRIPS Agreement incorporates a general provision concerning exceptions to patent rights.[65] This allows a Member to adopt limited exceptions that do not unreasonably conflict with the normal exploitation of the patent or the legitimate interests of patent holders, taking into account the legitimate interests of third parties. This general exception provision is the subject of an important panel decision to be discussed later.[66]

The requirement that countries subject inventions in all fields of technology to patent protection required a major change to the patent laws of many countries. Developing countries were granted a ten-year transition period in which to provide patent protection for subject matter areas not previously covered.[67] In respect to pharmaceutical and agricultural chemical product patents, special "mailbox" rules required developing Members to accept applications filed during the transition period and preserve them for review when protection became available. If and when a patent was eventually granted the term would be limited based on the original filing date of the mailbox application.[68] This rather complex system was the subject of the first AB decision concerning TRIPS.[69] [see *supra* Chapter 1, section VI.]

### 1. *Fair Use Under the TRIPS Agreement*

The grant of a patent involves a bargain between the inventor and society. In some circumstances, important social interests dictate an alteration to the "business as usual" patent bargain. National security interests typically are found to take precedence over individual inventor interests, and provisions are routinely made in patent laws to allow governments to keep security-related inventions secret, or to use them under compulsory license.

The field of public health raises difficult patent-related issues that in recent years have garnered considerable attention. The most visible issues involved the HIV/AIDS epidemic

62. Article 27.2-3(a), *id.*

63. Article 27.3(b), *id.*

64. Article 31, *id.*

65. Article 30, *id.*

66. Canada—Patent Protection of Pharmaceutical Products, WT/DS114, 17 Mar. 2000 ("Canada-Generic Pharmaceuticals").

67. The change would have a particularly significant effect in countries which did not provide patent protection for pharmaceutical products since bringing such products under patent protection would affect generic producers and almost certainly increase the price of medicines. Article 64.4, TRIPS Agreement.

68. Article 70.8, TRIPS Agreement.

69. India—Patent Protection for Pharmaceutical and Agricultural Chemical Products, WT/DS50, 5 Sept. 1997 ("India-Mailbox"). [India's amended Patents Act also incorporates a *sui generis* prior user right to permit the continued production of medicines on which patents are granted, conditional on payment of a reasonable royalty. For an overview of the situation in India, *see* Frederick M. Abbott, *The WTO Medicines Decision: World Pharmaceutical Trade and the Protection of Public Health*, 99 Am. J. Int'l L. 317, 320-22 (2005), and the excerpt *infra* section III.D from *TRIPS II, Asia and the Mercantile Pharmaceutical War.*—Eds.]

and the COVID-19 pandemic and efforts by developing countries to address this crisis in ways they can afford, as well as concerns among developed and developing countries regarding access to medicines for the treatment of avian bird flu. But there are systemic issues involving patents and public health that do not involve immediate crises and that will continue to be the source of debate.

The objective of the TRIPS Agreement negotiations was to require all WTO Member countries to adopt and enforce high levels of patent protection. Nonetheless, it was accepted that the TRIPS Agreement would need to accommodate exceptions to the broad right of patent holders to exclude others from making use of patented inventions. As with most aspects of the TRIPS Agreement negotiations, the scope of exceptions and safeguards was controversial.

### a. Article 30 (Exceptions)

In WTO-GATT jurisprudence, a provision that allows an "exception" acts to waive compliance with an otherwise applicable requirement. For example, in traditional GATT-WTO jurisprudence, restrictions placed on imports to protect public health were considered an "exception" from the general requirement to freely allow imports.[35]

Article 30 of the TRIPS Agreement is headed "Exceptions to Rights Conferred." It provides for "limited exceptions" to the rights of patent holders. Since the Paris Convention contained no antecedent to Article 30 of the TRIPS Agreement, WTO dispute settlement panels interpreting Article 30 find themselves in largely uncharted legal territory.[36] The WTO panel in the *Canada-Generic Pharmaceuticals* decision that follows described Article 30 as imposing a three-prong test. An exception (1) should be "limited"; (2) should "not unreasonably conflict with a normal exploitation of the patent"; and (3) should "not unreasonably prejudice the legitimate interests of the patent owner, taking account of the legitimate interests of third parties."

In the *Canada-Generic Pharmaceuticals* case,[37] the European Union complained against Canadian legislation that (1) allowed generic drug manufacturers to stockpile drugs prior to the expiration of patents (so that the generic drugs could immediately enter the market immediately after the expiration of patents), and (2) allowed use of patented technology for purposes of securing regulatory approval prior to the expiration of patent terms.

The WTO panel found that Canada's stockpiling legislation was inconsistent with its TRIPS obligations. Bulk stockpiling of generic pharmaceuticals did not constitute a limited exception to the rights of patent holders in the sense of Article 30. However, the panel found that the provisions allowing product testing and submission of data for regulatory approval was an allowable limited exception. Having made this finding, the panel was confronted with the European Union's argument that limited exceptions under Article 30 remain subject to the TRIPS Article 27.1 prohibition of discrimination as to "field of technology." The panel's response follows.

---

35. In its *EC-Asbestos* decision, the Appellate Body determined that the GATT does not require WTO Members to treat products posing health risks as being "like" products that do not pose such risks. Import barriers to unsafe imports may no longer be considered "exceptional." *European Communities—Measures Affecting Asbestos and Asbestos-Containing Products*, Report of the Appellate Body, AB-2000-11, WT/DS135/AB/R, 12 March 2001.

36. The three-pronged test has an antecedent in Article 9(2) of the Berne Convention dealing with copyright, and decisions of national courts under the Berne Convention might provide some guidance to panels considering the scope of exceptions to patent protection. However, patents and copyright serve substantially different functions and the utility of the analogies is uncertain.

37. *Canada—Patent Protection of Pharmaceutical Products*, Report of the Panel, WT/DS114/R, March 17, 2000 ("Canada-Generic Pharmaceuticals"). WTO dispute settlement decisions are often referred to by names that identify their essential subject matter in lieu of the formal titles.

## *Canada—Patent Protection of Pharmaceutical Products, Report of The Panel*

WT/DS114/R, March 17, 2000

### . . . (A) Applicability of Article 27.1 to Article 30 Exceptions

7.88 Canada took the position that Article 27.1's reference to "patent rights" that must be enjoyable without discrimination as to field of technology refers to the basic rights enumerated in Article 28.1 subject to any exceptions that might be made under Article 30. In other words, governments may discriminate when making the "limited" exceptions allowed under Article 30, but they may not discriminate as to patent rights as modified by such exceptions.

7.89 In support of this position, Canada argued that the scope of Article 30 would be reduced to insignificance if governments were required to treat all fields of technology the same, for if all exceptions had to apply to every product it would be far more difficult to meet the requirement that Article 30 exceptions be "limited." It would also be more difficult to target particular social problems, as are anticipated, according to Canada, by Articles 7 and 8 of the TRIPS Agreement. Conversely, Canada argued, requiring that exceptions be applied to all products would cause needless deprivation of patent rights for those products as to which full enforcement of patent rights causes no problem.

7.90 Canada acknowledged that there are certain textual difficulties with this position. It acknowledged that two of the primary purposes of Article 27.1 were to eliminate two types of discrimination that had been practised against pharmaceuticals and certain other products—either a denial of patentability for such products, or, if patents were granted, automatic compulsory licences permitting others to manufacture such products for a fee. Canada acknowledged that, in order to preclude discrimination as to compulsory licences, the non-discrimination rule of Article 27 was made applicable to Article 31 of the TRIPS Agreement, which grants a limited exception for compulsory licences under specified conditions. To defend its position, therefore, Canada was required to explain how Article 27.1 could apply to exceptions made under Article 31, but not to exceptions made under its neighbouring exception provision in Article 30. Canada argued that Article 31 was "mandatory" in character while Article 30 was "permissive," and that this distinction made it appropriate to apply the non-discrimination provision to the former but not the latter.

7.91 The Panel was unable to agree with Canada's contention that Article 27.1 did not apply to exceptions granted under Article 30. The text of the TRIPS Agreement offers no support for such an interpretation. Article 27.1 prohibits discrimination as to enjoyment of "patent rights" without qualifying that term. Article 30 exceptions are explicitly described as "exceptions to the exclusive rights conferred by a patent" and contain no indication that any exemption from non-discrimination rules is intended. A discriminatory exception that takes away enjoyment of a patent right is discrimination as much as is discrimination in the basic rights themselves. The acknowledged fact that the Article 31 exception for compulsory licences and government use is understood to be subject to the non-discrimination rule of Article 27.1, without the need for any textual provision so providing, further strengthens the case for treating the non-discrimination rules as applicable to Article 30. Articles 30 and 31 are linked together by the opening words of Article 31 which define the scope of Article 31 in terms of exceptions not covered by Article 30. Finally, the Panel could not agree with Canada's attempt to distinguish between Articles 30 and 31 on the basis of their mandatory/permissive character; both provisions permit exceptions to patent rights subject to certain mandatory conditions. Nor could the Panel understand how such a "mandatory/permissive" distinction, even if present, would logically support making the kind of distinction Canada was arguing.

In the Panel's view, what was important was that in the rights available under national law, that is to say those resulting from the basic rights and any permissible exceptions to them, the forms of discrimination referred to in Article 27.1 should not be present.

7.92 Nor was the Panel able to agree with the policy arguments in support of Canada's interpretation of Article 27. To begin with, it is not true that being able to discriminate against particular patents will make it possible to meet Article 30's requirement that the exception be "limited." An Article 30 exception cannot be made "limited" by limiting it to one field of technology, because the effects of each exception must be found to be "limited" when measured against each affected patent. Beyond that, it is not true that Article 27 requires all Article 30 exceptions to be applied to all products. Article 27 prohibits only discrimination as to the place of invention, the field of technology, and whether products are imported or produced locally. Article 27 does not prohibit bona fide exceptions to deal with problems that may exist only in certain product areas. Moreover, to the extent the prohibition of discrimination does limit the ability to target certain products in dealing with certain of the important national policies referred to in Articles 7 and 8.1, that fact may well constitute a deliberate limitation rather than a frustration of purpose. It is quite plausible, as the EC argued, that the TRIPS Agreement would want to require governments to apply exceptions in a non-discriminatory manner, in order to ensure that governments do not succumb to domestic pressures to limit exceptions to areas where right holders tend to be foreign producers.

7.93 The Panel concluded, therefore, that the anti-discrimination rule of Article 27.1 does apply to exceptions of the kind authorized by Article 30. We turn, accordingly, to the question of whether Section 55.2(1) of the Canadian Patent Act discriminates as to fields of technology.

### (B) Discrimination as to the Field of Technology

7.94 The primary TRIPS provisions that deal with discrimination, such as the national treatment and most-favoured-nation provisions of Articles 3 and 4, do not use the term "discrimination." They speak in more precise terms. The ordinary meaning of the word "discriminate" is potentially broader than these more specific definitions. It certainly extends beyond the concept of differential treatment. It is a normative term, pejorative in connotation, referring to results of the unjustified imposition of differentially disadvantageous treatment. Discrimination may arise from explicitly different treatment, sometimes called "*de jure* discrimination," but it may also arise from ostensibly identical treatment which, due to differences in circumstances, produces differentially disadvantageous effects, sometimes called "de facto discrimination." The standards by which the justification for differential treatment is measured are a subject of infinite complexity. "Discrimination" is a term to be avoided whenever more precise standards are available, and, when employed, it is a term to be interpreted with caution, and with care to add no more precision than the concept contains.

7.95 The European Communities acknowledged that the words of the regulatory review exception of Section 55.2(1) do not limit its application to pharmaceutical products. The terms of the exception protect potentially infringing conduct:

> solely for uses reasonably related to the development and submission of information required under any law [ . . . ] that regulates the manufacture, construction, use or sale of any product.

Applied literally, these words apply to any of a wide range of products that require regulatory approval for marketing. The EC itself mentioned agricultural chemicals, foodstuffs, cosmetics, automobiles, vessels and aircraft as products that often require regulatory approval.

7.96 The EC pointed out, however, that pharmaceuticals were the only products mentioned in Canada's 1991 legislative debates on the enactment of Sections 55.2(1). It also asserted that Section 55.2(1) was "in effect applied only to pharmaceuticals products." These assertions led to two distinct allegations of discrimination. The first claim of discrimination was the claim that the legislative history's concentration on pharmaceuticals actually governs the legal scope of the measure, so that, as a matter of law, Section 55.2(1) applied only to pharmaceuticals. If that is so, it could be said that Section 55.2(1) imposes *de jure* discrimination against pharmaceuticals. The second claim of discrimination was the claim that, whatever the *de jure* scope of Section 55.2(1), the actual effects of Section 55.2(1) are limited to pharmaceutical producers, and these differential effects amount to a case of de facto discrimination.

7.97 Canada denied that the *de jure* scope of Section 55.2(1) is limited to pharmaceuticals. It pointed to the words of that provision making the exception available to "any product" for which marketing approval was needed. . . .

7.98 In considering how to address these conflicting claims of discrimination, the Panel recalled that various claims of discrimination, *de jure* and de facto, have been the subject of legal rulings under GATT or the WTO. These rulings have addressed the question whether measures were in conflict with various GATT or WTO provisions prohibiting variously defined forms of discrimination. As the Appellate Body has repeatedly made clear, each of these rulings has necessarily been based on the precise legal text in issue, so that it is not possible to treat them as applications of a general concept of discrimination. Given the very broad range of issues that might be involved in defining the word "discrimination" in Article 27.1 of the TRIPS Agreement, the Panel decided that it would be better to defer attempting to define that term at the outset, but instead to determine which issues were raised by the record before the Panel, and to define the concept of discrimination to the extent necessary to resolve those issues.

7.99 With regard to the issue of *de jure* discrimination, the Panel concluded that the European Communities had not presented sufficient evidence to raise the issue in the face of Canada's formal declaration that the exception of Section 55.2(1) was not limited to pharmaceutical products. Absent other evidence, the words of the statute compelled the Panel to accept Canada's assurance that the exception was legally available to every product that was subject to marketing approval requirements. In reaching this conclusion, the Panel took note that its legal finding of conformity on this point was based on a finding as to the meaning of the Canadian law that was in turn based on Canada's representations as to the meaning of that law, and that this finding of conformity would no longer be warranted if, and to the extent that, Canada's representations as to the meaning of that law were to prove wrong.

7.100 The Panel then turned to the question of de facto discrimination. Although the EC's response to the Panel's questions indicated that it did intend to raise the issue of de facto discrimination, the EC did not propose a formal definition of de facto discrimination, nor did it submit a systematic exposition of the evidence satisfying the elements of such a concept.

7.101 As noted above, de facto discrimination is a general term describing the legal conclusion that an ostensibly neutral measure transgresses a non-discrimination norm because its actual effect is to impose differentially disadvantageous consequences on certain parties, and because those differential effects are found to be wrong or unjustifiable. Two main issues figure in the application of that general concept in most legal systems. One is the question of de facto discriminatory effect - whether the actual effect of the measure is to impose differentially disadvantageous consequences on certain parties. The other, related to the justification for the disadvantageous effects, is the issue of purpose - not an inquiry into the subjective purposes of the officials responsible for the measure, but an inquiry into the objective characteristics of the measure from which one can infer the existence or non-existence of discriminatory objectives.

## NOTES AND QUESTIONS

**1.** The *Canada-Generics* panel was chaired by Professor Robert Hudec, one of the world's most highly respected trade law experts, now deceased.[38] Although this was not an Appellate Body decision, it was bound to exercise an important influence on future WTO jurisprudence.

**2.** Do you find the logic in paragraph 7.92 of the panel report persuasive? The panel finds that Article 30 is subject to Article 27.1 because Article 27.1 applies the rule of nondiscrimination to the enjoyment of "patent rights," and Article 30 addresses "exceptions to the exclusive rights conferred by a patent." Does it follow that a limited exception to the exclusive rights conferred by a patent could not be defined in terms of a particular subject matter? Why? Is there some logical step missing?

**3.** The panel also finds that Article 30 is subject to Article 27.1 because the parties agree that Article 31 (compulsory licensing) is subject to Article 27.1. (This is based on Article 70.6, which limits retroactive application of Article 27.1 with respect to compulsory licenses granted before the TRIPS Agreement became known.) The panel says that no party provided it with a reason why Article 30 exceptions should be treated differently than Article 31 compulsory licensing. The parties agreed that Canadian legislation authorizing automatic compulsory licensing of pharmaceutical patents was intended by TRIPS negotiators to be prohibited by the Agreement. Does it follow that applying different rules to the compulsory licensing of pharmaceutical patents than to patents in other fields of technology cannot be justified? This seems a very doubtful result in light of the panel's subsequent indication that WTO Members may differentiate among patented products for *bona fide* reasons. What may TRIPS negotiators have found particularly objectionable about Canada's automatic compulsory licensing of pharmaceutical patents? Might the absence of a requirement for considering a compulsory license on its individual merits have been the failing of the Canadian legislation? If this is the case, how does the United States justify its government use legislation (28 U.S.C. §1498), which applies automatically to all patents? This legislation allows the U.S. federal government to use any patent and prohibits patent holders from obtaining injunctions. The only remedy is a suit for compensation before the Federal Court of Claims in Washington, D.C. It has, for example, been suggested that "effectively automatic" compulsory licenses of medicines can be successfully enabled within the terms of Article 31(a) of the TRIPS Agreement by, for example, designating medicines included on the WHO's Essential Medicines List as subject to such licensing, with the merits of such licenses having been duly considered. *See, e.g.*, Submission of the Global Health Law Committee of the International Law Association to the United Nations High-Level Panel on Access to Medicines, June 2016.

**4.** The panel's decision focuses on the term "discrimination" and makes clear that this means something other than "differentiation." The panel does not attempt to provide a general definition of "discrimination" or what elements must be demonstrated to prove it. It does say that the term is "pejorative in connotation, referring to results of the unjustified imposition of differentially disadvantageous treatment." The panel clearly leaves open the possibility that patented technologies may be treated differently for regulatory purposes if the differences are justified.

**5.** The panel draws a distinction between *de jure* and *de facto* discrimination, noting that a number of GATT-WTO panels have addressed this distinction. These panels have held that legislation that is nondiscriminatory on its face (and therefore *de jure* nondiscriminatory) may nevertheless discriminate in its "operational effect" (and therefore be *de facto* discriminatory).

---

38. *See* Frederick M. Abbott, *Bob Hudec as Chair of the Canada-Generic Pharmaceuticals Panel—The WTO Gets Something Right*, 6 J. Int'l Econ. L. 733 (2003).

*See, e.g., United States—Section 337 of the Tariff Act of 1930*, BISD 36S/345, Report by the Panel adopted Nov. 7, 1989.

**6.** In *Merck v. Integra Lifesciences*, 545 U.S. 193 (2005), the U.S. Supreme Court interpreted 35 U.S.C. §271(e) to allow the use of patented inventions for the purpose of conducting research with respect to drugs as to which there is some reasonable prospect that an application to the FDA may be submitted, regardless whether an application is, in fact, eventually submitted or successful. The relevant research may be conducted at the pre-clinical trial phase. The Supreme Court made clear that the regulatory review exception is not limited to the development by generic producers of information necessary to show bioequivalence in the abbreviated new drug application (ANDA) process. It said, among other things:

> Properly construed, §271(e)(1) leaves adequate space for experimentation and failure on the road to regulatory approval: At least where a drugmaker has a reasonable basis for believing that a patented compound may work, through a particular biological process, to produce a particular physiological effect, and uses the compound in research that, if successful, would be appropriate to include in a submission to the FDA, that use is "reasonably related" to the "development and submission of information under . . . Federal law." §271(e)(1).
>
> For similar reasons, the use of a patented compound in experiments that are not themselves included in a "submission of information" to the FDA does not, standing alone, render the use infringing. The relationship of the use of a patented compound in a particular experiment to the "development and submission of information" to the FDA does not become more attenuated (or less reasonable) simply because the data from that experiment are left out of the submission that is ultimately passed along to the FDA. 545 U.S. at 207.

The exception broadly allows third-party use of patented technology for research and experimentation toward the development of new drugs. In reaching this decision, the Supreme Court overruled a highly restrictive interpretation of the regulatory review exception adopted by the Court of Appeals for the Federal Circuit in the same case.[39] Article 271(e), interpreted by the Supreme Court in *Merck v. Integra Lifesciences*, applies only to drugs and to veterinary biological products. Does Article 271(e) discriminate as to field of technology, or does it constitute legitimate differentiation in the sense accepted by the *Canada-Generic Pharmaceuticals* panel? In 2002, the CAFC rendered a highly restrictive interpretation of the common law "experimental use exception" in *Madey v. Duke University*, 307 F.3d 1351 (Fed. Cir. 2002). It restricted experimental use to actions performed "for amusement, to satisfy idle curiosity, or for strictly philosophical inquiry" (citing *Embrex v. Service Engineering*, 216 F.3d 1343 (Fed. Cir. 2000)). It observed that universities are in the business of providing education and that as a consequence their activities are conducted with a commercial aim. For that reason, research activities conducted by universities do not generally fall under an experimental use exception. *Madey*, 307 F.3d at 1362. The common law "experimental use exception" interpreted by the CAFC in *Madey* is different than the statutory "regulatory review exception" interpreted by the Supreme Court in *Merck v. Integra*. For all intents and purposes, however, the Supreme Court has in the field of drug research and development created a broad experimental use exception that takes precedence over the narrow CAFC interpretation.

### b. Article 31 (Compulsory Licensing)

As noted earlier, compulsory licensing is a long-standing feature of the international IP system incorporated in the Paris Convention. Article 31 of the TRIPS Agreement was the subject of considerable attention during the Uruguay Round negotiations. The HIV epidemic that was wreaking havoc during the 1990s created substantial interest, particularly among

39. *Integra Lifesciences I v. Merck*, 331 F.3d 860 (Fed. Cir. 2003).

non- governmental organizations, regarding the potential use of compulsory licensing to overcome patent barriers to production of low-cost generic antiretroviral medicines. The HIV epidemic was distinguished from the more recent COVID-19 pandemic in that the antiretroviral medicines capable of treating – though not curing – HIV were small molecule chemical drugs that could be reverse engineered and produced by generic manufacturers without undue difficulty. Indian generic manufacturers were capable of producing generic HIV drugs, but they were not able to supply them to markets in Africa. In essence, the main obstacle to entry of generic producers onto the market were patents.

The COVID-19 pandemic was substantially more complex in terms of constraints on development and manufacture of vaccines, and particularly the newly emerging mRNA vaccines. Although there are patents on some of the core technologies underlying the mRNA vaccines, the use of those technologies to create and manufacture vaccines is much more difficult than manufacturing already-developed HIV drugs. The major suppliers of the mRNA vaccines, Pfizer/BioNTech and Moderna, spent years and invested heavily in use of lipid nanoparticle technology to create and manufacture their mRNA vaccines. For a follow-on manufacturer, access to the information in patent documents would not provide sufficient guidance to enable the manufacture of equivalent vaccines. In addition, there were limitations in the scaling up of the materials used to create the vaccines that would constrain third-party manufacturers. Notwithstanding the considerable difference in the circumstances surrounding HIV antiretrovirals and the vaccines used to prevent and/or reduce the severity of COVID-19, there was considerable pressure exerted at the WTO and elsewhere for addressing inequities in the distribution of vaccines as an IP problem. We might more realistically have said that addressing COVID-19 was a "technology transfer", as well as a financing, problem. This entailed a more "holistic" solution than compulsory patent licensing.

The following excerpt from the WHO-WIPO-WTO "Promoting Access to Medical Technologies and Innovation"* briefly explains the use of compulsory licensing under TRIPS Agreement rules.

> "TRIPS requirements for compulsory licences and government use
>
> Article 31 of the TRIPS Agreement sets out certain conditions regarding the way in which compulsory licences and government-use authorizations should be issued. Notably, each case must be considered on its individual merits (Article 31(a)); prior efforts to negotiate a voluntary licence are normally required; and the licence must ordinarily be limited to predominantly supplying the domestic market (Article 31(f)). There are limitations regarding scope and duration (Article 31(c)). The right to use the patent must not be exclusive (Article 31(d)); neither may it be assignable to any third party (Article 31(e)). The patent holder has normally a right to receive adequate remuneration based on the economic value of the authorization (Article 31(h)) and a right to apply for a judicial or administrative review that could lead to termination of the use or licence (Article 31(g)).
>
> The requirement that prior efforts be made to negotiate a voluntary licence for a reasonable period of time has been interpreted in different ways in national laws. The requirement to negotiate may be waived in situations of national emergency, in other circumstances of extreme urgency or in cases of public non-commercial use (Article 31(b)). The right holder is, however, entitled to receive notification about the use in these cases. In cases where the use of the patent is authorized without the consent of the patent holder, to remedy adjudicated cases of anti-competitive practices, WTO members are not obliged to apply these conditions (Article 31(k)). In such cases, the licence need not be predominantly for the supply of the domestic market (thus allowing exports of unlimited quantities) and the amount of remuneration can be different (i.e. it would generally be a lesser amount or nothing at all).

* WHO, WIPO & WTO, Promoting Access to Medical Technologies and Innovation Intersections between public health, intellectual property and trade, 2nd Ed. (2020), at p. 237, https://www.wto.org/english/res_e/booksp_e/who-wipo-wto-2020_e.pdf.

The limitation of compulsory licences and government use to predominantly for the supply of the domestic market, found in Article 31(f) of the TRIPS Agreement, was revised following the Doha Declaration to allow production of pharmaceutical products under a compulsory licence exclusively for export under certain terms and conditions. In effect, Article 31(f) limits the quantity that could normally be exported under a standard compulsory licence, which was identified as a potential problem for countries that had insufficient manufacturing capacity or no domestic manufacturing capacity in the pharmaceutical sector, and therefore wished to import such products. The entry into force of Article 31*bis* of the TRIPS Agreement made the Special Compulsory Licensing System (the System) a permanent part of the Agreement, providing a secure legal pathway for the production and export of generic medicines to other members that rely on the import of the needed medicines for the treatment of their patients."

## NOTES AND QUESTIONS

**1.** In section IV.B, *infra*, we will examine a decision by the Indian Controller of Patents granting a compulsory license on an anti-cancer drug, Nexavar, and appeal of that decision to the Indian courts. The decision and attendant political controversy illustrates that compulsory licensing has both legal and political dimensions. The Nexavar license concerned a "non-communicable disease" (NCD). Advocates of improved access to medicines for lower-income populations point out that NCDs are a global phenomenon affecting individuals at all income levels, and that it is important to make drugs available at affordable prices. The originator pharmaceutical industry expresses concern that focus on reduced prices will place downward pressure on the revenues that help fund R&D. This might also affect profits for shareholders and executive compensation for management.

### c. The Doha Declaration on the TRIPS Agreement and Public Health

The WTO Council for TRIPS held sessions in June and September 2001 specifically devoted to issues concerning access to medicines. A substantial group of developing countries submitted a detailed proposal for a declaration on TRIPS and Public Health to be adopted at the Doha Ministerial.[40] The United States and a small group of like-minded countries submitted an alternate proposal. Following extensive negotiations based on a compromise text prepared by the WTO Secretariat, Ministers in Doha adopted a Declaration on the TRIPS Agreement and Public Health (WT/MIN(01)/DEC/2).

**Frederick M. Abbott***

## *The Doha Declaration on the TRIPS Agreement and Public Health: Lighting a Dark Corner at the WTO*

### . . . III. The Legal Effects of the Doha Declaration

#### A. Paragraph-by-Paragraph Commentary

The discussion and analysis of the TRIPS Agreement that preceded the Doha Ministerial was itself of legal significance. The Members of the WTO evidenced a concrete interest in

40. Issues raised by developing countries in regard to the TRIPS Agreement and access to medicines were identified and analyzed in F.M. Abbott, *The TRIPS Agreement, Access to Medicines and the WTO Doha Ministerial Conference*, 5 J. World Intellectual Prop. 15 (2002), first published as Quaker United Nations Office Occasional Paper No. 7, Sept. 8, 2001.

* 5 J. Int'l Econ. L. 469 (2002).

addressing the complex set of issues surrounding the effects of the TRIPS Agreement on access to medicines. The expressions of interest represent action by states to direct implementation of the agreement along more particularized lines, and in this sense represent a form of state practice that may be taken into account when interpreting the agreement.

The title "Declaration on the TRIPS Agreement and Public Health" incorporates the language of the initial developing Member draft, and rejects narrower formulations directed at "intellectual property," "pandemics" and other limiting terms. This signals that the Declaration applies to a broad scope of public health concerns, and not to a limited set of special circumstances.

. . .

> 4. *We agree that the TRIPS Agreement does not and should not prevent Members from taking measures to protect public health. Accordingly, while reiterating our commitment to the TRIPS Agreement, we affirm that the Agreement can and should be interpreted and implemented in a manner supportive of WTO Members' right to protect public health and, in particular, to promote access to medicines for all. In this connection, we reaffirm the right of WTO Members to use, to the full, the provisions in the TRIPS Agreement, which provide flexibility for this purpose.*

Comment: The first important point regarding this paragraph is that it is stated in the form of an agreement (i.e., "we agree"). Since this statement was adopted by consensus of the Ministers, and since the operative language is in the form of an agreement, this may be interpreted as a "decision" of the Members under article IX:1 of the WTO Agreement. This decision of WTO Members would appear to constitute an agreement on the method of application of the agreement within the meaning of Article 31(3)(a) of the Vienna Convention on the Law of Treaties ("VCLT"), and to be the substantive equivalent of an interpretation of the TRIPS Agreement.

Although paragraph 4 is not an "interpretation" in the formal sense since it was not based on a recommendation of the TRIPS Council pursuant to article IX:2 of the WTO Agreement, a decision that states a meaning of the Agreement may be considered as a very close approximation of an interpretation and, from a functional standpoint, may be indistinguishable.

Ministers in Doha should be assumed to have acted with a purpose. The only apparent purpose for agreeing on a method of application of the TRIPS Agreement is to have an effect on the way in which the agreement is implemented by WTO Members.

There are different ways that paragraph 4 might be understood, and it is perhaps premature to venture interpretations in the absence of concrete cases. However, there is already one concrete case on the horizon, and a few words might be addressed to that.

Paragraph 6 of the Declaration, as discussed in further detail below, directs the TRIPS Council to seek a solution to the problem of use of compulsory licensing by Members with insufficient or no manufacturing capacity. This is a complex undertaking and is addressed in some detail by this author in another paper.[81]

. . .

> 5. *Accordingly and in the light of paragraph 4 above, while maintaining our commitments in the TRIPS Agreement, we recognize that these flexibilities include:*
>
> (a) *In applying the customary rules of interpretation of public international law, each provision of the TRIPS Agreement shall be read in the light of the object and purpose of the Agreement as expressed, in particular, in its objectives and principles.*

Comment: Paragraph 5(a) states an interpretative principle that has been enunciated by the panel in the *Canada-Generic Pharmaceuticals* case, and that would already be understood

81. *See* Frederick M. Abbott, *Compulsory Licensing for Public Health Needs: The TRIPS Agenda at the WTO After the Doha Declaration on Public Health*, Quaker United Nations Office—Geneva, Occasional Paper 9, February 2002, available at http://www.quno.org.

by operation of Article 31 of the Vienna Convention on the Law of Treaties. By particularizing reference to objective and principles, the Declaration appears indirectly to reference Articles 7 (Objectives) and 8 (Principles) of the TRIPS Agreement. This might to a certain extent elevate those provisions above the preamble of the TRIPS Agreement for interpretative purposes.

. . .

[EDS note: In the subsequent WTO disputes *Australia – Tobacco Plain Packaging*, involving tobacco plain packaging measures requiring tobacco products and their retail packaging to appear in a uniform manner, the panels were of the opinion that paragraph 5 of the Doha Declaration could be considered to constitute a subsequent agreement among Members to interpret each provision of the TRIPS Agreement in light of Articles 7 and 8. Although the Appellate Body did not address the legal status of the Declaration on appeal, it agreed that paragraph 5 reflects "the applicable rules of interpretation, which require a treaty interpreter to take account of the context and object and purpose of the treaty being interpreted". As the interpretative importance of Articles 7 and 8 TRIPS as expression of the agreement's object and purpose directly followed from Article 31(1) of the Vienna Convention on the Law of Treaties (which is commonly understood to codify the customary international law of treaty interpretation), the Appellate Body did not need to rely on paragraph 5 (a) of the Doha Declaration, and hence needed not rule on its legal status.]

. . .

(b) *Each Member has the right to grant compulsory licences and the freedom to determine the grounds upon which such licences are granted.*

Comment: Paragraph 5(b) states propositions that are clear from the text of Article 31 of the TRIPS Agreement, but which the pharmaceutical sector, among others, has attempted to put in doubt. There has been a great deal of misperception in the public press concerning the bases upon which compulsory licenses may be issued, and this inaccurate press reporting may influence national government officials who are not conversant with intellectual property law. For this reason, it is very helpful to have a direct and unequivocal statement regarding the right of Members to grant compulsory licenses.

(c) *Each Member has the right to determine what constitutes a national emergency or other circumstances of extreme urgency, it being understood that public health crises, including those relating to HIV/AIDS, tuberculosis, malaria and other epidemics, can represent a national emergency or other circumstances of extreme urgency.*

Comment: This is a strong statement of Member sovereignty in regard to implementation of the waiver of negotiation with patent holders prior to the grant of compulsory licenses. As such, it should act as a strong defense against any assertion in dispute settlement that a Member declared an emergency, etc., without justification. Framing the determination as one reserved to each Member ("can represent"), rather than as a joint determination, makes clear that the determination is a matter to be undertaken by each Member in its sovereign discretion.

(d) *The effect of the provisions in the TRIPS Agreement that are relevant to the exhaustion of intellectual property rights is to leave each Member free to establish its own regime for such exhaustion without challenge, subject to the MFN and national treatment provisions of Articles 3 and 4.*

Comment: This is an unequivocal recognition of the right of each Member to permit parallel importation of medicines. This should foreclose further argument from the U.S., Switzerland, and the pharmaceutical sector that while Article 6 of the TRIPS Agreement precludes TRIPS dispute settlement on the issue of exhaustion, Article 28 nonetheless prevents parallel importation of patented drugs. The formulation of paragraph 5(d) does not foreclose the interpretation advanced by some commentators that parallel importation may be based on compulsory licensing.

The EU and U.S. each proposed to incorporate in the Declaration on the TRIPS Agreement and Public Health a limit on international exhaustion to marketing with the consent of the patent holder. Such limitation was not included in the Doha Declaration. Instead, paragraph 5(d) leaves each Member "free to establish its own regime for such exhaustion without challenge." This appears to leave each Member with the discretion to determine whether it will recognize compulsory-licensed marketing or sale of a product in a country of export as exhausting the patent holder's rights in the country of import to consent to importation and resale.

Although the Doha Declaration appears to resolve the issue of exhaustion based on marketing under compulsory license, it may be useful to consider the legal issues in more detail since they are likely to be further discussed by Members.

There are circumstances under which patented products may be first sold or put onto the market under compulsion of government authority. This is typically through the grant to the government itself, or to a third party, of a compulsory license to make and dispose of the product. Such licenses may be authorized because the government determines that public interests will be met by the grants, including as a remedy for anticompetitive practices by patent holders.

When patent holders are required to license third parties to produce and dispose of patented drugs, and the licensees put the drugs on the market, buyers are entitled to use or dispose of those drugs just as if the drugs had been put onto the market by the patent holders. In other words, first sales by the licensees have the same effects (in the local market) as first sales by patent holders. The right of the patent holders to control subsequent sales or transfers is extinguished or exhausted by the licensees' acts.

The question has been raised whether drugs (or other patented products) put onto the market under compulsory license in one country may be parallel imported into another country without the consent of the patent holder in that other country.

. . .

. . . [A]lthough (as noted below) there is some case law in the developed country WTO Members holding that exhaustion of patent rights is based on the "consent" of the patent holder to placement of goods on the market, the Appellate Body is not under an international legal obligation to interpret the TRIPS Agreement to reflect the traditional practices of developed country Members. Practice in developing Members may well evolve in an alternative direction, provided that such practice is not inconsistent with the express terms of the TRIPS Agreement.

. . .

Developing countries that provide patent protection for medicines have limited potential supply of those drugs. They may be purchased locally at on-patent prices, or they may be purchased following placement on the market abroad by the patent holder (or its agent). Although parallel importation may allow price savings, these savings are not likely to be on the order of magnitude seen in the relationship between on-patent versus off-patent medicines.

. . .

It is clear that WTO Members may authorize parallel importation of patented medicines placed on the market by or with the consent of the patent holder. It is not clear whether the Appellate Body will construe exhaustion doctrine to authorize parallel importation of medicines placed on the market by compulsory licensees. It is likely that developed Members such as the U.S., EU and Switzerland will resist an interpretation of exhaustion doctrine that is not based on the consent of the patent holder. Paragraphs 4 and 5(d) of the Doha Declaration, however, support an interpretation that advances the interests of developing Members in obtaining low cost access to pharmaceutical supplies.

> 6. *We recognize that WTO Members with insufficient or no manufacturing capacities in the pharmaceutical sector could face difficulties in making effective use of compulsory licensing under the TRIPS Agreement. We instruct the Council for TRIPS to find an expeditious solution to this problem and to report to the General Council before the end of 2002.*

Comment: A substantial change to the TRIPS-imposed legal conditions in developing and least developed countries will occur on January 1, 2005 and January 1, 2016. Among the important consequences of this changed situation will be that developing countries with the present capacity to export off-patent drugs will lose that capacity in regards to newly-developed patented drugs (and drugs in the mailbox pipeline that come under patent). At this juncture, affordable access to on-patent medicines in developing and least developed countries will become increasingly dependent on compulsory licensing. If the prices of medicines offered by patent holders are too high, or if sustainable access is otherwise restricted or threatened, relief will be sought through the issuance of compulsory licenses.

Certain developing countries will have capacity to manufacture under compulsory license, but there will certainly be developing and least developed countries without that capacity. Moreover, developing countries will require a variety of medicines, and it may be important that production of different medicines be allocated among countries. Finally, it may well be that certain developed countries will wish to aid developing and least developed countries by producing under compulsory license to satisfy import requirements.

Article 31 of the TRIPS Agreement permits all WTO Members to grant compulsory licenses regarding, *inter alia*, pharmaceutical products and processes. The terms of Article 31 are in general permissive and flexible. As confirmed by paragraphs 5(b) and (c) of the Doha Declaration, Article 31 does not limit the grounds upon which licenses may be granted, and it permits each Member to determine in its own discretion what constitutes a national emergency or circumstances of extreme urgency (thereby establishing an exception from pre-grant negotiation). There is substantial flexibility in terms of the administrative processes that may be adopted to implement a compulsory licensing regime.

To date, developing countries have made limited use of compulsory licensing as a tool to address public health issues. This stems from a number of causes: (1) the TRIPS Agreement has only recently begun to increase the incidence of patent protection; (2) use has been opposed by developed country WTO Members and interested industry groups within them, and a strong political commitment to act in the face of this opposition is required; (3) some developing countries have expressed concern regarding a potential backlash from foreign direct investors; (4) developing country enterprises may find it easier to reach accommodation with foreign patent holders than to challenge them through the compulsory licensing process for various economic and administrative reasons and, as noted earlier; (5) effectively implementing compulsory licensing requires that certain preconditions relating to administrative, financial and technical capacity be met, and these conditions are often not met in developing countries.

Addressing the limited use by developing countries of the compulsory licensing tool will require that substantial attention be paid to putting into place appropriate legal infrastructure. In this regard, developing countries will need to seek advice and assistance from sources such as UNCTAD, WHO and non-governmental organizations (NGOs) attentive to their interests. Addressing the problem of limited use will also require access to and coordination of financial and technical resources. The solution to the limited use of compulsory licensing by developing countries requires addressing a number of important elements.

Recognizing the multi-dimensional nature of the problem, the TRIPS Agreement nevertheless establishes certain obstacles to effectively addressing access to medicines through compulsory licensing. The most widely noted of these potential obstacles is Article 31(f), which provides:

> (f) any such use shall be authorized predominantly for the supply of the domestic market of the Member authorizing such use;

Article 31(f) establishes a limitation: the terms of the compulsory license should include the condition that the licensee uses the patented invention predominantly to supply the domestic market of the Member granting the license.

The word "predominantly" would generally appear to refer to the major part or majority, and would generally suggest that more than fifty percent of the production by a compulsory licensee should be intended for supply of the domestic market of the Member granting the license.

The limitation imposed by Article 31(f) creates two inter-linked problems:

> 1. By restricting the availability of export drugs made under compulsory license, it limits countries that are not in a position to support manufacturing under compulsory license (or where patent protection is not in force) in the availability of supply of generic import drugs, and;
>
> 2. By requiring compulsory licensees to supply a predominant part of their production to the domestic market, it limits the flexibility of countries to authorize the export of compulsory-licensed drugs and thereby to exploit economies of scale.

Article 31(f) creates difficulties on the demand and supply side of the generic drug pipeline.

The demand side problem is self-evident. If a developing Member lacks manufacturing capacity for a particular drug, and there are no Members that are able to supply it by export under compulsory license (or exception), there may be no affordable supply of the drug. The supply side problem is identified because there are WTO Members, including developing Members, with the capacity to address the drug import needs of a wide range of developing Members under compulsory license, but that may be inhibited from undertaking this role because of the Article 31(f) limitation. . . .

### IV. FUTURE WORK PROGRAM

This issue of availability of low-priced medicines becomes more pressing as the transition timetables in the TRIPS Agreement draw to an end, and the available supply of generic (off-patent) pharmaceutical products is progressively reduced. If there are limited supplies made available for export, there are, by definition, limited supplies available for import. Article 31(f) appears to restrict the right of Members to grant compulsory licenses for export. Although there were several proposals made in advance of the Doha Ministerial to address this situation, including proposals in the developing Member draft Declaration, there was no political consensus to resolve it at that stage, and the matter has been set for further discussion.

[The Paragraph 6 issue was addressed through two years of negotiations at the WTO. The negotiations and result are described and analyzed in Frederick M. Abbott, *The WTO Medicines Decision: World Pharmaceutical Trade and the Protection of Public Health*, 99 AM. J. INT'L L. 317 (2005), and in section d, immediately following, which refers also to the adoption of a proposal for amendment.—EDS.]

> *7. We reaffirm the commitment of developed-country Members to provide incentives to their enterprises and institutions to promote and encourage technology transfer to least-developed country Members pursuant to Article 66.2. We also agree that the least-developed country Members will not be obliged, with respect to pharmaceutical products, to implement or apply Sections 5 and 7 of Part II of the TRIPS Agreement or to enforce rights provided for under these Sections until 1 January*

*2016, without prejudice to the right of least-developed country Members to seek other extensions of the transition periods as provided for in Article 66.1 of the TRIPS Agreement. We instruct the Council for TRIPS to take the necessary action to give effect to this pursuant to Article 66.1 of the TRIPS Agreement.*

Comment: This paragraph directs the TRIPS Council to authorize the extension until January 1, 2016 of the transition period for least developed Members (hereinafter "LDCs") to implement or enforce pharmaceutical patent protection. The terms of this extension are somewhat ambiguous in that it is not clear from the express text whether LDCs are required to implement mailbox and exclusive marketing rights provisions prior to the end of the transition deadline. There is some indication that paragraph 7 was understood by negotiators in Doha not to require that mailbox and exclusive marketing rights requirements be implemented or enforced.

## NOTES AND QUESTIONS

**1.** The WTO acted to implement paragraph 7 of the Doha Declaration. The implementing decisions are described by the WTO Secretariat as follows:

> Intellectual Property: TRIPS and Public Health Council approves LDC decision with additional waiver*
>
> The WTO council responsible for intellectual property, on 27 June 2002, approved a decision extending until 2016 the transition period during which least-developed countries (LDCs) do not have to provide patent protection for pharmaceuticals.
>
> The Council for Trade-Related Aspects of Intellectual Property Rights (TRIPS) also approved a waiver that would exempt least-developed countries from having to provide exclusive marketing rights for any new drugs in the period when they do not provide patent protection.
>
> The waiver is to be submitted to the WTO General Council for approval on 8 July 2002.
>
> Both decisions are part of WTO members' ongoing efforts to ensure that intellectual property protection supports and does not obstruct poorer countries' need to tackle serious public health problems.
>
> "I am pleased that WTO members have acted promptly to implement this important part of the Doha Declaration on TRIPS and public health, and have seen fit to go beyond the strict reading of that declaration by also approving a draft waiver on exclusive marketing rights," said WTO Director-General Mike Moore.

The TRIPS Council's decision formalized part of paragraph 7 of the Declaration on the TRIPS Agreement and Public Health, which WTO ministers adopted on 14 November 2001 at their conference in Doha, Qatar. The relevant part of paragraph 7 of the Doha declaration says: "We . . . agree that the least-developed country members will not be obliged, with respect to pharmaceutical products, to implement or apply Sections 5 and 7 of Part II of the TRIPS Agreement or to enforce rights provided for under these Sections until 1 January 2016, without prejudice to the right of least-developed country members to seek other extensions of the transition periods as provided for in Article 66.1 of the TRIPS Agreement. We instruct the Council for TRIPS to take the necessary action to give effect to this pursuant to Article 66.1 of the TRIPS Agreement." But countries making use of the extra period still had to allow inventors to submit patent applications during the period (Article 70.8, sometimes called the "mailbox" provision).

**2.** On November 6, 2015, the TRIPS Council further extended the decision exempting LDCs from implementing or enforcing patents with respect to pharmaceuticals until January

* WTO News: 2002 Press Releases, Press/301, 28 June 2002.

1, 2033, or when a particular country ceases to be an LDC, if earlier (IP/C/73, 6 Nov. 2015). On this occasion, the General Council also waived LDC obligations respecting both mailbox applications and exclusive marketing rights (WT/L/971, 2 Dec. 2015).

**3.** Article 66.1 of the TRIPS Agreement initially allowed LDC members an 11-year transition period, until 2006. This transition period has been extended three times in response to specific requests from the LDC Group. Most recently, in June 2021, the TRIPS Council extended the transition period further until 1 July 2034—or when a particular country ceases to be in the least developed category if that happens before 2034. Unlike the first extension, the two most recent extension Decisions did not include a so-called "no rollback" clause.

### d. The Special Compulsory Licensing System – WTO August 30, 2003 Decision and December 6, 2005 Amendment

The mandate for resolving the issue of effective use of compulsory licensing by countries with insufficient capacity in the pharmaceutical sector led to an additional two years of negotiations leading to the adoption of a waiver, and another two years of debate leading to adoption of the amendment of the TRIPS Agreement (Article 31*bis*) which entered into force following acceptance of two-thirds of WTO Members on January 23, 2017.[41] The Special Compulsory Licensing System (i.e., the waiver and amendment) is described in the following excerpt from a report of the International Law Association Committee on International Trade Law. The waiver continues to apply to WTO Members that have not yet accepted the amendment.

**The TRIPS Agreement and Public Health**

## *Report of the Committee on International Trade Law of the International Law Association at the 2006 Biennial Meeting, Toronto*

...

Developing country *demandeurs* of the Doha Declaration recognized that as of January 1, 2005, the world pharmaceutical supply market would change substantially as the 10-year TRIPS Agreement transition period for introducing pharmaceutical product patent protection ended. India has served as a major supplier of low-priced generic drugs to the developing world because, among other reasons, it did not provide product patent protection for pharmaceuticals. Up until January 1, 2005, a country seeking to import supplies of generic medicines generally could find them for export in India. Even if the product was patented in the importing country, the issuance of a compulsory license in that country would be adequate to permit the importation.

Following the end of the transition period, new drugs—and "older" drugs which are patentable pursuant to the mailbox system—could be protected by patent in all developing countries,[10] including India. Generic supplies would be restricted. If an importing country sought low-cost supplies from a country where products are under patent, the existing text of the TRIPS Agreement created a potential impediment. The exporting country could issue a

41. https://www.wto.org/english/tratop_e/trips_e/tripsfacsheet_e.htm.

10. This does not include least developed countries, which, further to the Paragraph 7 of the Doha Declaration and WTO implementing measures, have at least until January 1, 2016 to introduce or enforce pharmaceutical patent and data protection.

compulsory license and produce a generic version of the drug, but pursuant to Article 31(f) of the TRIPS Agreement it could only export a non-predominant portion of its production. This might significantly restrain export supply capacity.[11]

Article 31 *bis* authorizes the issuance of compulsory licenses predominantly for the supply of pharmaceutical products to export markets, thereby overcoming the potential obstacle presented by Article 31(f). It also provides that the obligation of Article 31(h) to provide adequate remuneration in the circumstances of the case is satisfied by the payment of remuneration in the exporting country, which should take into account the economic value of the authorization to the importing country.

There are various conditions associated with the grant of compulsory licenses for export under Article 31 *bis*. These include certain notifications to the TRIPS Council, a determination by the importing country that it lacks manufacturing capacity,[12] and identification of the exported products as supplied pursuant to the Article 31 *bis* system. The conditions have been the subject of considerable debate. A number of NGOs, generic producers and some developing countries argue that the conditions make the system overly difficult to use. Some developed countries and pharmaceutical industry constituencies argue that the system is too open-ended. These arguments may be better assessed once the system is used, or attempts have been made to use it.

A substantial number of developed and emerging market countries "opted out" of the system as importing countries, either wholly or by limiting their usage to certain circumstances. As the threat of an avian flu pandemic has emerged in 2005-06, and as there are shortages of patented antiviral drug therapy for the flu in many developed countries, question has been raised regarding the wisdom of opting out of a system that facilitates the importation of drugs necessary to protect public health.

Canada and Norway were the first countries to adopt legislation and regulations implementing the August 30 waiver decision. China, the European Union, India, South Korea and Switzerland each have adopted (or are soon to adopt) implementing legislation or regulations.

The Committee welcomes adoption of the Medicines Export Amendment. However, the Committee recognizes that effective use of the Amendment can be adversely influenced by political pressure from Members and their industry constituencies. It therefore urges WTO Members to refrain from seeking to prevent use of the Amendment by the application of political pressure. It also urges Members not to seek terms in bilateral and regional trade agreements which undermine the letter or spirit of the Amendment.

## NOTES AND QUESTIONS

**1.** The Canadian Commissioner of Patents issued the first compulsory license for export to Apotex, Inc., a Canadian manufacturer of pharmaceutical products, pursuant to Canada's Access to Medicines Regime (CAMR) on September 19, 2007. The license covers export to Rwanda, a least-developed African country, of a fixed dose combination of antiretroviral medicines used in the treatment of HIV/AIDS. The Apotex formulation, referred to as Apo-Triaver, combines 300 mg Zidovudine (AZT), 150 mg Lamivudine (3TC), and 200 mg Nevirapine. Canadian patents on the separate antiretroviral components were held by the Glaxo Group, Shire Biochem, and Boehringer Engelheim, respectively. The license authorized

11. Article 30 of the TRIPS Agreement on Exceptions to Rights Conferred may also provide the basis for third-party exports of patented pharmaceuticals. The Amendment reserves the position of Members on this question. Medicines Export Amendment, Article 31 *bis* (5).

12. Least developed countries are automatically determined to lack manufacturing capacity.

the manufacture of 15,600,000 Triaver tablets, and was initially valid for two years from the date of issuance. *See* Introductory Note to World Trade Organization Canada First Notice to Manufacture Generic Drug for Export, by Frederick M. Abbott, International Legal Materials, Nov. 2007.

**2.** As of July 2023, the August 30, 2003 waiver, or Article 31*bis*, has been used only once, and for this reason has been subject to criticism as being ineffective. However, this criticism may be premature or unwarranted for several reasons. First, one of the principal reasons the waiver/amendment was negotiated was to address the global pharmaceutical supply situation following India's implementation of pharmaceutical product patent protection. That protection was only initiated on January 1, 2005, and even then provided a transition mechanism that allowed generic drug makers to continue producing products that were already under production (and in which investment had been made) prior to the grant of a patent, upon payment of a reasonable royalty. Because India was still producing a wide range of generic drugs, need for the new system did not abruptly materialize. Second, when worries over an avian flu pandemic circulated and global demand for Roche's patented Tamiflu (oseltemovir) escalated, a number of countries indicated that they would produce the drug under compulsory license. Roche responded by offering to quickly negotiate voluntary licenses. While the August 30, 2003 waiver (Article 31*bis*) has been used only once, it provided important "background" for the announcements regarding compulsory licensing and almost certainly affected Roche's decision making. Third, NGOs have consistently criticized the Article 31*bis* mechanism as being unduly complicated, therefore constituting an impediment to its use. That criticism may to a certain extent be self-fulfilling in the sense that if governments perceive the mechanism as being too difficult to use, they may be dissuaded from trying to use it. For those familiar with the heavily regulated pharmaceutical industry, the level of complexity in the Article 31*bis* system seems hardly unusual. Fourth, many countries procure medicines through international procurement programs, such as those run by UNICEF (UNICEF is the largest single vaccine buyer in the world), the Global Fund, and Unitaid, among others; these programs may have other ways of leveraging lower prices. Fifth, it is unclear whether, and if so, in what circumstances, the use of the Special Compulsory Licensing System could have been appropriate, but did not occur.

**3.** The preceding discussion of patent rules affecting access to medicines reflects serious concern about the potential impact on developing countries, and supports recognizing exceptions to strong patent protection in order to promote lower-cost access. There are other points of view promoting the idea that stronger protection is better. *See* Harvey E. Bale Jr., *The Conflicts Between Parallel Trade and Product Access and Innovation: The Case of Pharmaceuticals*, 1 J. Int'l Econ. L. 637, 640 (1998); J.A. DiMasi, R.W. Hansen & H.G. Grabowski, *The Price of Innovation: New Estimates of Drug Development Costs*, 22 J. Health Econ. 151 (2003). The following is an excerpt from Alan O. Sykes, *Public Health and International Law: TRIPS, Pharmaceuticals, Developing Countries, and the Doha "Solution,"* 3 Chi. J. Int'l L. 47 (2002):

> The precise impact of the Doha Declaration on the policies of developing nations remains to be seen, but it seems likely that the Declaration will embolden them to enact measures that will reduce the returns to pharmaceutical patent holders, at least with respect to drugs that are used to treat certain diseases. Such measures will likely include the award of compulsory licenses for the production of patented medications (with minimal royalties payable to the patent holder), and the allowance of "parallel imports" of medications from nations where prices are lower. This essay will take a preliminary look at the merits of such policies from an economic perspective, and draw on this analysis to suggest some directions for the resolution of legal issues that remain on the table after Doha.

> The ultimate wisdom of measures that relax intellectual property protection for pharmaceuticals in developing countries turns on complex matters, including empirical issues about which one can only hazard an educated guess. It is conceivable that patent rights in the developing world have negligible impact on research incentives. They may simply raise prices on patented drugs, transferring rents to foreign pharmaceutical patent holders, and creating deadweight losses by pricing consumers out of the market who are willing to pay the marginal cost of medicines but not the monopoly markup charged by the patent holder.
>
> But there is another possibility, one which in my view better accords with what we know about the importance of patents to pharmaceutical research, and with the extraordinary value to consumers of medicines that successfully treat serious conditions. Developing nations have long had little intellectual property protection for pharmaceuticals, and we have concurrently witnessed an apparent dearth of research into diseases such as malaria and drug-resistant tuberculosis that are of particular importance to these nations. The lack of patent protection may have resulted, at least in part, from an acute collective action problem—developing nations reap the full benefits from lower prices when they do not create pharmaceutical patents, yet the costs in terms of diminished research incentives are largely externalized to the rest of the developing world. The WTO TRIPS agreement held out some promise of overcoming part of this problem. Yet, just as the obligations of developing nations under TRIPS are beginning to take hold, the Doha Declaration casts great doubt on the future credibility of patent rights for pharmaceuticals in developing nations. The result may be quite unfortunate for research incentives, especially those relating to particular diseases. *Id.*, at 48-49.

Many experts on pharmaceutical R&D disagree strongly with Sykes' suggestion that an absence of patent protection in developing countries is discouraging research on so-called neglected diseases. The main problem, instead, is an absence of "demand pull." That is, pharmaceutical companies simply will not invest in treatments for individuals who do not have the capacity to pay, especially when there is an abundance of patients in wealthier countries who will pay for costly treatments for diseases affecting them. The WHO Commission on Intellectual Property Rights, Innovation and Public Health agreed with that assessment, citing absence of demand pull as the key problem limiting research on neglected diseases. *See Public Health: Innovation and Intellectual Property Rights*, Report of the Commission on Intellectual Property Rights, Innovation and Public Health, April 2006, at 28-32.

**4.** The revised system allowing member states to grant compulsory licensing under Article 31(f) of TRIPS has not been widely used. Do you think issues connected with the patenting of pharmaceuticals have received too much public attention, or perhaps not enough? What do you think has been the main effect of the August 30, 2003 waiver (Article 31*bis*) on the conduct of right holders and research-based companies relating to the supply of drugs to least developed countries?

### e. The COVID-19 Pandemic and the MC12 TRIPS Waiver

The COVID-19 pandemic that started at the end of 2019 with an outbreak of the SAR-CoV-2 virus in Wuhan, China, had a tremendous impact on global public health and on the international economy. As this 5th edition of this casebook is being prepared, the director general of the WHO has recently declared an end to the emergency phase of the pandemic by removing its designation as a public health emergency of international concern (PHEIC).

From the outset, there was concern as to whether intellectual property rights might act as a barrier to the development, manufacture, and distribution of health products needed to address the rapidly expanding problem. Some scholars that had addressed issues connected with the HIV-AIDS epidemic proposed advance mechanisms to preempt these problems. For example, one of the co-authors of this book proposed the establishment of an international patent pooling arrangement that would entail the use by governments of their powers to compulsory license.* However, international political tensions were such that ideas for broad multilateral cooperation could not realistically be carried out. In addition, at the outbreak of the pandemic, it seemed reasonable to expect that therapeutic treatments along the lines of small molecule chemical antiviral drugs that had previously been developed to address the Avian Flu epidemic would emerge as the "therapeutic" options to address the virus-induced disease. But this is not how the scientific response played out. Vaccination emerged as the public health response of choice – or necessity – and this brought into play a substantially different type of technological response than would have been the case with antiviral therapies, which in fact emerged rather late.

Nonetheless, India and South Africa, supported by a number of NGOs, launched an initiative at the WTO for a waiver of the main provisions of the TRIPS Agreement, establishing substantive obligations with respect to protection of patents and undisclosed information (including trade secrets) among other IP rights, so as to allow WTO member countries to essentially ignore the multilateral norms in order to address the pandemic. For many IP experts that favored promoting access, the request for a waiver seemed unnecessary and unwise because WTO member governments already had authority to override IP rules built into the TRIPS Agreement and reinforced by the Doha Declaration. And beyond that, there is a national security provision, Article 73, of the TRIPS Agreement that would allow the governments to take whatever steps they considered necessary to protect their essential security interests in a time of an international emergency, that the pandemic seemed to fit.** And, putting aside fine legal niceties, what international dispute settlement body would impose penalties on a government for providing its citizens with the products needed to address a pandemic, and what might those penalties look like? The key problem was that India and South Africa had come to the WTO to ask for "permission" to take steps to address a global crisis, and a crisis within their own borders, knowing in advance that they would meet resistance from countries that had previously demanded strict compliance with IP rules.

It is no surprise that India and South Africa received a cool welcome from the European Union, the United States, Switzerland, Japan, and others that are home to the major multinational originator pharmaceutical companies. Though the United States claimed to support the idea of a waiver, the Biden Administration did so to forestall a rebellion from the liberal side of the Democratic Party, and its "support" for a waiver was for a strictly limited variety. The "waiver" that was ultimately agreed upon at the WTO Twelfth Ministerial Conference (MC12) in December 2022 made only one substantive concession, and this was to remove the restriction of Article 31(f) of the TRIPS Agreement on exporting more than a predominant part of products produced under a compulsory license—the same restriction that had already been addressed by Article 31*bis*—but which Article 31*bis* amendment, according to some NGOs, is difficult to navigate. Even the MC12 waiver of the Article 31(f) restriction is framed in a puzzling way since it does not even refer to Article 31*bis* which establishes conditions on compulsory licensing for export, so it is not clear what the new waiver is doing. Finally, the MC12 result is limited to COVID-19 vaccines. It does not address therapeutics and diagnostics negotiations for which were put off, with a deadline that was ignored as of July 2023.

* See Frederick M. Abbott & Jerome H. Reichman, *Facilitating Access to Cross-Border Supplies of Patented Pharmaceuticals: The Case of the COVID-19 Pandemic*, 23 J. Int'l Econ. L. 535 (Oxford 2020), at *doi.org/10.1093/jiel/jgaa022*

** See COVID-19 Pandemic: Access to Prevention and Treatment Is a Matter of National and International Security, Open letter from Carlos Correa, Executive Director of the South Centre, April 4, 2020, https://www.southcentre.int/wp-content/uploads/2020/04/COVID-19-Open-Letter-REV.pdf, and; Frederick M. Abbott, *The TRIPS Agreement Article 73 Security Exceptions and the COVID-19 Pandemic,* Research Paper 116, South Centre, Geneva (August 2020), at http://dx.doi.org/10.2139/ssrn.3682260.

The positive element of the failure of the waiver effort at the WTO may be to refocus the attention of public health advocates on more practical solutions to problems associated with lack of access to affordable medicines (including vaccines). Africa, for example, may benefit more from successfully establishing local infrastructure to produce and distribute medicines, and from encouraging efforts by regional scientists to develop R&D capacity. The same goes for other regions. It is inexpensive for a government to send one or two delegates to meetings in Geneva to debate about patents. Much more effort is required to build a local or regional pharmaceutical sector. IP may be a problem in certain contexts, but it is not the most difficult one to tackle.

## C. The Patent Cooperation Treaty

Securing a patent generally requires submitting an application that describes an invention to a governmental authority, an examination of that application by the authority in respect to formal requirements (such as mention of the inventor), an examination in respect to whether the claimed invention meets the criteria of patentability, publication of the application (in most countries and regions prior to the grant of a patent), and the grant (or denial) of a patent by the authority. These procedures may vary along a number of different lines among nations and regions. Formal requirements differ — some nations allow applications only by natural persons, others by both natural and legal persons. Some nations, such as South Africa and Switzerland, do not subject applications to pre-grant examination regarding the criteria of patentability (although the South African government on May 23, 2018, adopted the Intellectual Property (IP) Policy of the Republic of South Africa-Phase 1, which calls for implementation of pre-grant examination, pending legislative action).[42] Some nations, such as India, permit third parties to pursue pre-grant opposition.

The main instrument and innovation at the multilateral level concerning the grant of patents is the Patent Cooperation Treaty (PCT). The PCT is widely used by businesses seeking a broad territorial scope of patent protection for their inventions.

The Patent Cooperation Treaty represented the first major step following conclusion of the Paris Convention toward a truly internationalized patent system. First and foremost, it must be stressed that use of the PCT system does not result in the grant of an "international patent." Rather, the PCT facilitates the grant of national and regional patents, which remain substantively governed by national and regional patent laws. However, there are many reasons why use of the PCT system has grown dramatically over the past decade, and why its use has now become standard operating procedure among many, if not most, multinational enterprises.

Before the advent of the PCT, an inventor seeking to patent his or her invention in many countries would file a patent application in a first country. Assuming that this inventor was entitled to the benefits of the Paris Convention, this inventor would then have a 12-month priority period in which to file corresponding patent applications in all other countries in which he or she sought protection. Since filing a patent application in a foreign country would usually require the appointment of a foreign agent, translation of the patent application and compliance with a different set of formalities than applied to the first filed application, a great deal of time pressure was involved in the process, as well as a great deal of expense. After expiration of the priority period, the inventor faced a variety of risks that might result in loss of the ability to obtain a patent. If a third party had filed an application on the same invention during the priority period (and the inventor had not), that third-party application would now

42. *See* Cabinet Decision, http://www.thepresidency.gov.za/cabinet-statements/statement-cabinet-meeting-23-may-2018, and text of policy, http://www.thedti.gov.za/news2018/IP_Policy2018-Phase_I.pdf.

take precedence (in a first to file country). If the inventor had disclosed the invention during the priority period, novelty might be lost. For these reasons, the 12-month priority period was treated as something of an "all or nothing" proposition.

The PCT made dramatic changes to the old Paris Convention system. First, the patent applicant need comply with only one set of formal requirements when filing the PCT application, and only a limited number of national and regional formal requirements become applicable at subsequent stages in the process. The patent applicant generally files his or her PCT application in a Receiving Office (RO), which is a national or regional patent office where the first filing would ordinarily take place. The PCT also permits initial filing of a patent application with the International Bureau at WIPO (which filing results in a grant of priority under the Paris Convention). However, many countries (including the United States) do not allow patent applications for local inventions to be filed abroad until a national security review is completed. As a consequence, the first filing of patent applications with the International Bureau is not very common.

Before the end of the priority period, the RO transmits the application to the International Bureau at WIPO, and also transmits a copy to the International Search Authority (ISA). In its PCT application, the inventor specifies or "designates" the countries in which he or she will seek a patent. PCT fees are structured such that once a certain number of countries are designated, the applicant may designate all PCT countries with no additional designation fees payable.

One of the major advantages of the PCT procedure is that it delays decisions with respect to the payment of fees, preparation of translations (and so forth) up to 30 months from the priority date. This allows applicants to prepare their international strategies with more deliberation. When applications are ready to enter the National Phase, the applicant has a much better idea whether the invention will be commercialized (as will justify the expense of patenting in national offices), and whether a patent will, in fact, be granted.

---

## *WIPO PCT FAQs*
## *Protecting your Inventions Abroad: Frequently Asked Questions About the Patent Cooperation Treaty (PCT) (status on July 2022)*

**1) What is the Patent Cooperation Treaty (PCT)?**

...

The PCT procedure includes:

**Filing:** you file an international application with a national or regional patent Office or WIPO, complying with the PCT formality requirements, in one language, and you pay one set of fees.

**International Search:** an "International Searching Authority" (ISA) (one of the world's major patent Offices) identifies the published patent documents and technical literature ("prior art") which may have an influence on whether your invention is patentable, and establishes a written opinion on your invention's potential patentability.

**International Publication:** as soon as possible after the expiration of 18 months from the earliest filing date, the content of your international application is disclosed to the world.

**Supplementary International Search (optional):** a second ISA identifies, at your request, published documents which may not have been found by the first ISA which carried out the main search because of the diversity of prior art in different languages and different technical fields.

**International Preliminary Examination (optional):** one of the ISAs at your request, carries out an additional patentability analysis, usually on a version of your application which you have amended in light of content of the written opinion.

**National Phase:** after the end of the PCT procedure, usually at 30 months from the earliest filing date of your initial application, from which you claim priority, you start to pursue the grant of your patents directly before the national (or regional) patent Offices of the countries in which you want to obtain them.

**2) How do I protect my invention in several countries?**

Patents are territorially limited. In order to protect your invention in multiple countries you have a few options:

(a) Direct or Paris route: you can directly file separate patent applications at the same time in all of the countries in which you would like to protect your invention (for some countries, regional patents may be available) or, having filed in a Paris Convention country (one of the Member States of the Paris Convention for the Protection of Industrial Property), then file separate patent applications in other Paris Convention countries within 12 months from the filing date of that first patent application, giving you the benefit in all those countries of claiming the filing date of the first application (consult Question 11);

(b) PCT route: you can file an application under the PCT, directly or within the 12-month period provided for by the Paris Convention from the filing date of a first application, which has legal effect in all Contracting States of the PCT. . . .

---

## *WIPO 2023 PCT Yearly Review*

### Highlights

***About* 278,100 PCT applications were filed in 2022**

Approximately 278,100 international patent applications (PCT applications) were filed under WIPO's Patent Cooperation Treaty (PCT) in 2022. This represents a marginal growth of 0.3% compared to the previous year, and marks the slowest rate of increase since a decline in PCT applications in 2009.

Since the PCT System became operational in 1978, the PCT System has received about 4.82 million applications. Overall, PCT filings have grown consistently every year, exceptin2009, during the global financial crisis and the resultant economic downturn.

***Applicants from 134 countries filed PCT applications in 2022***

In 2022, the PCT had 157 member states and applicants from 134 countries filed PCT applications at 85 receiving offices (ROs). However, despite such a widespread geographical distribution, filing activity was heavily concentrated in a select number of economies.

Combined, the top 10 ROs accounted for 93.8% of applications filed in 2022. With 74,420 filings, the China National Intellectual Property Administration (CNIPA) received the most PCT applications. It was followed by the United States Patent and Trademark

Office (USPTO) (55,330), the Japan Patent Office (JPO) (48,826), the European Patent Office (EPO) (38,854), the Korean Intellectual Property Office (KIPO) (21,964) and the International Bureau (IB) of WIPO (13,713).

***The top five countries of origin accounted for over 72% of applications in 2022***

With 70,015 PCT applications, applicants residing in China filed the most applications in 2022. They were followed by applicants from the United States of America (US) (59,056) and Japan (50,345) (figure A7). Together with applicants from Germany and the Republic of Korea, these top five countries accounted for 78.7% of all PCT applications filed in 2022. Driven mainly by a rapid increase in filings by applicants from China, the combined share of the top five users of the PCT System has increased by 4.2 percentage points over the past decade.

The top 20 origins included 17 high-income countries – mostly European – and three middle-income economies, namely, China, India and Türkiye. Outside the top 20 origins, other large middle-income economies with notable numbers of PCT applications were Brazil, the Islamic Republic of Iran, the Russian Federation and South Africa, whose filings ranged between 200 and 900. Applicants from the Democratic People's Republic of Korea, Sudan, Syrian Arab Republic and Uganda accounted for most of the 14 applications filed by applicants residing in low-income countries.

Nine of the top 20 origins filed more PCT applications in 2022 compared to the previous year. 19 India (+25.4%), the Republic of Korea (+6.2%), France (+5.9%) and Singapore (+5.3%) saw the sharpest increases in filing. In contrast, the countries that experienced the steepest falls were Israel (–7.1%), Finland (–6.6%), Italy (–6.6%) and Spain (–6.5%). Among those large middle-income economies not to feature among the top 20 origins, Colombia (+23.5%), Mexico (+19.9%), Thailand (+19%) and Malaysia (+17.8%) underwent sharp growth in PCT filings (table A9). In contrast, Ukraine (–40.9%), the Russian Federation (–14.5%) and Brazil (–11%) all saw a marked contraction.

### *1. The PCT and Gender Considerations*

WIPO data from March 2023 estimates that only 16.2 percent of inventors named in international patent applications were women in 2022. While numbers are rising, progress is slow. WIPO estimates that, at current rates, parity among PCT-listed inventors will be reached only in 2061. Women's participation in patenting varies across world regions, sectors and industries. To help reduce these disparities and promote women's participation in the IP system, WIPO established in 2023 its first WIPO Intellectual Property and Gender Action Plan. https://www.wipo.int/export/sites/www/women-and-ip/en/docs/rn2023-1_ipgap.pdf/.

–

## NOTES AND QUESTIONS

**1.** An increasingly important part of the international framework for securing patent protection is found in a series of worksharing agreements entered into among a number of patent offices that allow applicants to request accelerated processing based on decisions made by one or more of the offices. The primary network of worksharing arrangements is known as the Patent Prosecution Highway (PPH), and five patent offices (the European Patent Office (EPO), the Japan Patent Office (JPO), the Korean Intellectual Property Office (KIPO), the State Intellectual Property Office of the People's Republic of China (SIPO), and the United States Patent and Trademark Office (USPTO)) have recently initiated a pilot program that substantially formalizes the network under the name IP5. *See, e.g., EPO Extends Fast-track Pilot Programmes with Four Countries*, Dec. 22, 2017, http://www.epo.org/news-issues/news/2017/20171222.html, and *Patent Prosecution Highway (PPH)—Fast Track Examination of Applications*, http://www.uspto.gov/patents/init_events/pph/index.jsp. Proposals have been made within WIPO to include formalized integration of the PPH with the PCT and other WIPO procedures, though so far these proposals have not progressed. A number of developing countries, in particular, are concerned that PPH-shared patent examination processes may exclude some of the flexible variations in assessment of patentability in use by these countries. *See, e.g.*, Catherine Saez, *At WIPO, Differences Remain on Global Priorities in Patent Law*, IP-WATCH, Sept. 28, 2013; http://www.jpo.go.jp/ppph-portal/index.htm; http://www.wipo.int/pct/en/filing/pct_pph.html.

## D. Substantive Patent Law Harmonization in WIPO

Discussion of case law at the outset of this chapter reveals that patent law, despite common foundations, largely varies among different jurisdictions. As noted earlier in the excerpt by Edith Penrose, differences among national approaches to patenting precluded any serious pursuit of harmonized patent law in the late 1800s. Common rules in the Paris Convention and the TRIPS Agreement are still far from constituting a harmonized international patent system. Following the adoption of the TRIPS Agreement, a new effort to make progress on harmonizing key concepts of patent law has been underway.

A work program for a draft Substantive Patent Law Treaty (SPLT) was initiated at the WIPO in 2000 under the auspices of the Standing Committee on the Law of Patents (SCP). The WIPO Secretariat (International Bureau) has prepared treaty drafts, as well as draft regulations and practice guidelines, along with explanatory notes. However, this work program generated substantial controversy. SPLT negotiations were put on hold in 2006.[43]

There was considerable resistance, particularly among some developing countries, to harmonizing national patent laws based closely on models employed by highly developed countries. There was a perception that this would act to solidify the dominance of developed country enterprises in the technology-dependent global economy. While developed countries have characterized their limited areas of harmonization interest as "technical" matters, the resistant developing countries argued this does not adequately characterize the potential welfare impact of the proposed rules. What was sought by developing countries is to maintain "flexibility" or "policy space." Some developing countries have insisted that the SPLT negotiations, if they are to be renewed, must not ignore subject matter of interest to them, including control of anticompetitive practices.

It is not only developing country resistance that blocked movement toward a more harmonized patent system. There remain some serious differences between the United States and the European Union on issues such as grace periods for disclosure.

The following excerpt expressed the viewpoint shared by a number of developing countries concerning the SPLT negotiations.

**Sisule F. Musungu & Graham Dutfield***

### *Multilateral Agreements and a TRIPS-Plus World: The World Intellectual Property Organisation (WIPO)*

... The negotiations on the SPLT, on the other hand, are aimed at initially creating uniform substantive patent law standards on prior art, novelty, utility and inventiveness,

43. http://www.wipo.int/policy/en/scp/.

* TRIPS Issues Papers 3, Quaker United Nations Office (QUNO), Geneva Quaker International Affairs Programme (QIAP), Ottawa.

requirements relating to sufficient disclosure and the drafting of claims and, possibly, to facilitate the mutual recognition of patent search and examination results. After this first phase of work, further harmonisation is envisaged in areas where the main players, the USA and the Europeans, do not agree such as the first to file versus first to invent principles and post grant opposition proceedings.

Harmonisation as proposed in the SPLT drafts is likely to result in TRIPS-plus standards for developing countries. While most of the proposed standards will benefit international industries, they will make it more difficult for developing countries to adapt their patent laws to local conditions and needs[,] including adapting their laws to take into account their critical public health and other needs. Such a result will undermine the achievements in Doha on public health and elsewhere on the other issues of intellectual property and development. One can conclude that the process of patent law harmonisation, coupled with various bilateral agreements that contain TRIPS-plus standards, will seriously compromise the ability of developing countries to use the various TRIPS flexibilities for development objectives.

Harmonised patent law standards will also make it more difficult for these countries to seek amendments to the TRIPS Agreement, for example, to introduce disclosure requirements with respect to genetic resources and traditional knowledge.

Some of the proposals in the SPLT negotiations that have implications for TRIPS flexibilities include those aimed at:

— reducing the flexibility of countries to define patentability requirements by, for example, eliminating the requirements for a technical character in inventions;
— introducing matters of equivalence in international patent rules; and
— prohibiting countries from imposing any further conditions, other than those specifically provided for in the treaty, on patent applicants.

The draft SPLT under article 12 seeks to harmonise the conditions for patentability. An important aspect of the draft deals with industrial applicability or utility. One proposed approach is to define industrially applicable inventions as those which "can be made or used for exploitation in any field of [commercial] [economic] activity." Considering that after the adoption of the SPLT contracting parties would not be allowed to impose any further conditions on applicants other than those specifically spelt out in the SPLT, if accepted, this proposal would mean that anything used in commercial and/or economic activity except mere discoveries, abstract ideas as such, scientific and mathematical theories and laws of nature as such and purely aesthetic creations, would be patentable. This would pave the way for the mandatory patenting of such things as business methods and software and eliminate the current flexibility under TRIPS which allows each country to define what an invention is, including requiring that inventions have a technical character. The possibility of introducing matters of equivalence under this treaty also poses TRIPS-plus risks. If, for example, equivalence for purposes of infringement proceedings, was harmonised based on the approach that a process or product would be considered as equivalent if it performs substantially the same function as the protected process or product, then the freedom under TRIPS to define equivalence so as to allow inventing around patented inventions would be eliminated.

## NOTES AND QUESTIONS

**1.** In October 2010, a compromise was reached that formed the basis for ongoing discussions of various patent law issues in the SCP. This does not constitute a resumption of negotiations on the SPLT. The WIPO press release announced:

SCP Agrees on Future Work on Patent-Related Issues

Geneva, October 15, 2010

PR/2010/666

The WIPO Standing Committee on the Law of Patents (SCP) agreed on late Friday at the close of its week-long session from October 11-15, 2010 to include a number of key substantive issues relating to patent law and practice in its future work. Delegations from 86 countries, 5 international organizations and 25 non-governmental organizations participated in the session of the Committee, which was characterized by a very positive and constructive atmosphere among member states that resulted in significant progress in the Organization's substantive agenda with respect to the further development of the international patent system.

WIPO Director General Francis Gurry expressed satisfaction about the progress achieved and highlighted the importance for WIPO to be able to offer a consensus-based and a multilateral forum to all member states for patent-related matters.

In summarizing the work of the Committee, SCP Chairperson Maximiliano Santa Cruz from Chile said the SCP decided to include the following issues into its future work:

(i) Exceptions and limitations to patent rights;
(ii) Quality of patents, including opposition systems;
(iii) Patents and health;
(iv) Client-patent advisor privilege;
(v) Transfer of technology.

The Committee also agreed that the non-exhaustive list of issues first identified at its June 2008 meeting will remain open for further elaboration and discussion at its next session, and that four more issues will be included in the list, namely, "Impact of the patent system on developing countries and LDCs," "Patents and food security," "Strategic use of patents in business" and "Enhancing IT infrastructure for patent processing."

**2.** Meetings of the SCP through 2022 have continued to focus on the elements listed above, with an array of reports on specific subjects, such as exceptions to patent rights. These reports and information regarding the work of the SCP can be found at http://www.wipo.int/policy/en/scp/.

**3.** A great deal of information concerning the SPLT negotiations, including draft texts and explanatory notes prepared by the Secretariat, can be found at the WIPO web site, at http://www.wipo.int. *See, e.g.*, WIPO International Bureau, Draft Substantive Patent Law Treaty, SCP/10/2, Sept. 30, 2003.

**4.** Assess the reasons why patent law harmonization is slow and meets resistance, looking back through this chapter. How do you assess differences in economic interests, rooted in the structure of different economies? Is it suitable to harmonize what perhaps is best left to the process of trial and error in case law and among different jurisdictions? Which are the elements that should be harmonized in addition to the TRIPS Agreement from the point of view of the international trading system?

**5.** Are developing countries right to be worried about solidifying developed country technological dominance? Does the patent system play a significant role in the global economic imbalance? Does the fact that the patent system is complex and expensive to use argue for or against harmonization from the standpoint of developing countries? Might developing country inventors gain from a harmonized system, which might reduce their transaction costs? Recall that today nothing prevents developing country inventors from filing patent applications in developed countries.

**6.** Some industry interests in the United States, Europe, and Japan suggest that because of the slow pace of harmonization efforts at WIPO, developed and "like-minded" developing countries should abandon that effort and undertake their own harmonization effort in a forum like the OECD. Do you think this is a useful suggestion? What would be the drawbacks?

## E. Territorial Reach

See Chapter 1, section VII.D, including the *Microsoft v. AT&T*, *Philips/Nokia*, and *NTP v. Research in Motion* decisions.

The question of the territorial reach of patents took on considerable significance in the context of seizures by customs authorities in the Netherlands of medicines in transit between India and other developing countries, where the medicines were not patented in the exporting or importing countries, but where Dutch customs authorities undertook seizures of the generic drugs based on claims under local Dutch patents. India and Brazil eventually initiated consultations with the European Union and the Netherlands pursuant to the WTO Dispute Settlement Understanding. On December 10, 2010, senior political officials of the European Union and India announced that this matter had been settled with an EU undertaking to change its relevant legislation to make clear detention/seizures of generic medicines in transit based on patents is not permitted, and committing the European Union to a cessation of the practice pending amendment of the legislation. India signaled that it would suspend further dispute settlement action at the WTO. *See EU and India Resolve Dispute over Generic Drugs*, REUTERS, December 10, 2010.

**Frederick M. Abbott***

### *Seizure of Generic Pharmaceuticals in Transit Based on Allegations of Patent Infringement: A Threat to International Trade, Development and Public Welfare*

The European Union amended its border control regulations in 2003 in a way that allegedly signaled permission to EU patent holders to demand seizure of goods in transit through EU ports and airports. The precise intention of the EU IP Border Regulation has been the subject of some controversy among European courts. What has generated intense controversy, however, is the use of the regulation as the basis for seizure of pharmaceutical products alleged to be infringing "local" patents on their way through European airports. Although the next steps at the inter-governmental level remain to be determined, the fundamental IP related issues raised by the seizures are worthy of attention because of their long-term implications for the international economic system, economic development and public welfare.

Implementation of the EU IP Border Regulation represents a challenge to fundamental ideas about the way the international intellectual property system operates. The Paris Convention on the Protection of Industrial Property incorporates "independence" of patents as a core principle. The principle is framed in terms of protecting national institutions and decision-making against intrusive determinations by foreign authorities. The principle of independence of patents preserves the sovereign authority of states to adopt and implement patent protections as they consider appropriate, within the framework of a general set of rules. Each member of the Paris Convention decides whether to grant or deny patent protection, and that determination is not dependent on decisions of foreign courts or administrative bodies. The principle of "independence" is corollary to the "act of state doctrine" in international law pursuant to which the courts in one country do not sit in judgment on the acts of foreign governments taken within their own territory based on considerations of comity and restraint.

* 1 W.I.P.O. J. 43 (2009).

The principle of independence is sometimes equated with a "territorial" nature of the international patent system. The Paris Convention does not prescribe the jurisdictional scope of patents, nor does it prescribe or define "territoriality." The scope, extension or limitation of patent jurisdiction is determined by national legislatures and courts within boundaries prescribed by public international law. Traditionally, national legislatures and courts have approached potential extraterritorial application of patent law with considerable caution, recognising the problems that would arise in attempting to extend local control to economic activity taking place (and fundamentally regulated by) foreign legislatures and courts. (A territorial nature of the international patent system is recognised in the WTO Decision of August 30, 2003, at para. 6(i), and in the corresponding TRIPS Agreement Amendment, at art. 31*bis*.3, each expressly referring to the "territorial nature of [ . . . ] patent rights.")

In recent years, some national courts have begun to move away from a rigid understanding of the "territoriality" of patent law. In the Blackberry case, the United States Court of Appeals for the Federal Circuit recognised that advances in technology may create situations in which an invention operates through actions carried out in more than one country, and that the issue of infringement within a country may not always be assessed only by examination of actions within that single national territory.

A modest extension into extraterritorial application of patent law in the Blackberry case was grounded in traditional international law concepts of jurisdiction whereby an act undertaken outside the territorial limits of a state that has a direct and substantial effect within that state may lead its courts to take cognisance of those acts. In cases such as Blackberry, the infringement affects most directly and substantially the country where the allegedly infringed patent is held. Following the US Supreme Court decision in *Microsoft v AT&T*, which stressed limitation of patent infringement to the national territory (and cautioned against extraterritorial extension), the Federal Circuit acknowledged a strong presumption against extraterritorial effect in excluding process patents from the scope of a US statutory prohibition on exporting infringement-capable components.

It is an axiom of public international law that sovereign nations exercise exclusive control over activities taking place within their own territory (although international human rights law challenges certain aspects of that axiom). The European Union bases its exercise of jurisdiction over pharmaceutical products moving in transit through EU airports on its right as sovereign to control activity taking place within EU (and Member State) territory. This extension of jurisdiction is said to be codified in EU customs regulations.

Yet a corollary of the axiom of sovereign control over activities within the national territory is that states have the right to cede elements of exclusive control through international agreement and custom. Thus, through a long history of international agreements and custom, states of the international community have adopted exceptions from exercise of jurisdiction in favor of immunity for diplomats, for naval vessels from in rem admiralty actions and for activities taking place on foreign operated military bases established under basing agreements.

Since 1947, Member States of the European Union have been members of the GATT, now the World Trade Organization (WTO). The EU is a Member of the WTO. The WTO provides the legal framework under which international trade is conducted. From its inception, the GATT/WTO has recognised in GATT art. V the principle of "freedom of transit" for goods moving through ports and airports in international trade. This fundamental principle has been so widely and consistently implemented that there has been virtually no controversy about it in the history of the GATT/WTO, despite the fact that goods are constantly moving in transit through its Members. It is simply a "given" in international trade law that the customs authorities of a country do not seize or detain goods passing through their ports and airports en route to foreign destinations without a good reason. GATT art. V prohibits Members from imposing unreasonable regulatory requirements on goods in transit.

The WTO TRIPS Agreement did not purport to modify the three core principles of the Paris Convention: national treatment, independence and right of priority. The TRIPS Agreement obligates WTO Members to extend patent subject matter coverage to all fields of technology. But the authority to grant or deny patent protection remains with national patent offices of Members based on relevant national legislation. An inventor may lack patent protection in a WTO Member for a number of reasons, including: (1) no patent was ever sought; (2) a patent has expired; (3) a patent application was rejected because the claimed invention was deemed not to meet the criteria of patentability; (4) the claimed invention did not constitute patentable subject matter under the law of the particular Member (e.g. computer software as such in Europe). India, as a case in point, was not required by the TRIPS Agreement to provide pharmaceutical product patent protection until January 1, 2005, and many pharmaceutical products patented in Europe are not patented in India.

. . .

The European Court of Justice in *Montex Holdings v Diesel* raised serious doubt whether seizure of IP protected goods in transit and not intended for the European internal market was permissible. The Court of Justice noted that violation of the 1994 IP Border Regulation (predecessor of the 2003 IP Border Regulation) was predicated upon infringement of an EU intellectual property right (in that case a trade mark), and that the Trademark Directive predicated trade mark infringement on entry into the EU stream of commerce. The ECJ said that unless direct evidence of third party action to place the goods into the EU stream of commerce was present, there could be no infringement under EU law; thus no seizure was authorised. The High Court of England and Wales recently affirmed this line of reasoning in *Nokia v UK Customs*, also with respect to trademarks, but on this occasion expressly interpreting the 2003 EU IP Border Regulation. Dutch authorities and pharmaceutical patent holders, on the other hand, have relied on a decision of the Court of The Hague in the Netherlands, *Sisvel v Sosecal*, grounded in recital 8 of the 2003 IP Border Regulation. The Court of The Hague interprets the recital to establish a "manufacturing fiction." Using this "fiction," an act of patent infringement takes place by "use" of the patent for manufacturing in the Netherlands, even though it is absolutely clear that no such manufacturing takes place. It is a truly remarkable theory under which Dutch law is deemed to be violated by actions taking place in another country, e.g. India, as if those actions had taken place in the Netherlands.

It is hard to imagine a greater departure from the principle of independence of patents than the "manufacturing fiction" that is said to support a finding of infringement of a Netherlands patent by an action in India. The absence of a patent in India where the manufacturing takes place (and which is independent of the Netherlands) is completely ignored. There is no direct or substantial effect on the Netherlands that might be deemed to constitute a reasonable substitute for actual manufacturing. There is no harm in or to the Netherlands unless one reaches to the farthest levels of attenuation (which the European Commission has soundly rejected in the area of competition law).

It is also difficult to imagine what the international legal system will be like if the "fictional acts" theory of jurisdiction becomes widely adopted. American manufacturers might be sued in Europe for violating EU environmental law standards when manufacturing in the United States in compliance with US environmental law. Chinese companies could be sued in the EU for failing to provide EU-standard paid vacation for their workers on the fiction that they were manufacturing in France. A doctor performing a legal abortion in Germany could be prosecuted in Ireland on the theory that the abortion would have been illegal if performed in Ireland. An 18-year-old student drinking beer in Germany could be prosecuted in Florida because 21 is the legal drinking age in Florida. The concept of national sovereignty would be completely meaningless in this new "fictional acts" environment.

. . .

It is neither the responsibility nor the right of WTO Members outside a country that has not granted patent protection to "cure" that situation in favor of a local patent holder by disregarding the decisions taken by authorities in the country that has not provided protection. The European Union has elected to disregard the sovereign rights of foreign WTO Members by refusing to give effect to their decisions as to patent status by the use of force—the seizure and detention by customs authorities of goods in transit. The allegations of infringement are purely for the convenience of a patent holder that happens to have chosen a particular transit country as a place to obtain a patent. This is a form of "long-arm" extension of jurisdiction that the European Union has claimed to abhor when adopted by US antitrust authorities.

While the threat to the international economic system and foundations of international law are serious enough, an even more important negative consequence of the EU policy with respect to the seizure of generic pharmaceuticals in transit is the breach of the understanding reached at the WTO regarding access to medicines as embodied in the Doha Declaration on the TRIPS Agreement and Public Health. There was a bargain reached at the conclusion of the GATT Uruguay Round of trade negotiations in 1993 that provided a 10-year transition period for countries such as India that did not provide pharmaceutical patent protection to institute that protection. That bargain acknowledged that public health systems and patients throughout the developing world relied on countries such as India to provide low-cost generic versions of pharmaceutical products on patent in the developed countries, and that a rapid transition to globalised patent protection would have significant adverse effects on public health. In good measure as a consequence of India's decision to take full advantage of the transition period, a significant part of the developing world can and does continue to rely on that country for the supply of low-cost generic medicines.

### NOTES AND QUESTIONS

**1.** You may wish to consult the requests for consultations transmitted by India and Brazil to the European Union and the Netherlands, available on the WTO web site (*European Union and a Member State—Seizure of Generic Drugs in Transit*, Request for Consultations by India, WT/DS408/1, G/L/921, IP/D/28, 19 May 2010 (initiated May 11, 2010); Request for Consultations by Brazil, WT/DS409/1, IP/D/29, G/L/922, 19 May 2010 (initiated May 12, 2010)). From the requests for consultations, can you identify the differences in approach between India and Brazil on the legal issues?

## III. REGIONAL SYSTEMS

### A. The New European Union Patent System

The long-awaited European patent with unitary effect arrived as of June 1, 2023. Fifty years after conclusion of the European Patent Convention (EPC) that has formed the framework for the granting of patents in Europe, there is a new regulation and an Agreement on a Unified Patent Court that brings about the eventual possibility of securing a single patent with effect throughout the European Union (excluding Croatia and Spain for the foreseeable future).*

* The texts of the Regulation (EU) No 1257/2012 of the European Parliament and of the Council implementing enhanced cooperation in the area of the creation of unitary patent protection, and Council Regulation (EU) No 1260/2012 implementing enhanced cooperation in the area of the creation of unitary patent protection with regard to the applicable translation arrangements, and others, can be found at https://link.epo.org/web/legal_texts_relation_to_the_unitary_patent_system_2023_en.pdf.

As of July 2023, several EU member states have yet to ratify the Agreement on a Unified Patent Court (UPC). Consequently, a Unitary Patent will presently take effect only in 17 EU member states, and coverage of a Unified Patent will not be retroactively extended to member states that had not yet ratified the UPC Agreement. In traditional European fashion, while the new system is intended to streamline the patent system, including the enforceability of patents, because of the "legacy" aspects (e.g., continued availability of national patents) and the presence of non-EU member states in the existing framework, the system is rather complex (and will remain so at least for the foreseeable future).

Putting a long history into a few words, the grant of patents in Europe up until recently was not under the jurisdiction of an EU institution because it was not clear that the European Union had competence to regulate in the field of patents. The EPC was adopted in 1973 (entering into force in 1977) as the best available substitute granting patents for Europe, but it did not provide for a unitary patent. Instead, it allowed applicants to obtain the grant of a European Patent from the European Patent Office (EPO), and to designate the European countries where the patent would be given effect (subject to validation under national law). The EPC prescribed rules with respect to the grant of patents, such as the criteria of patentability, but it was up to the national law to provide the rules and court procedures for enforcement. Also, it always remained a possibility to apply for a patent in the member state national offices, although the rules on the grant of patents were expected to be aligned with the EPC.

The Lisbon Treaty of 2009 resolved any lingering ambiguity as to whether the European Union had competence to regulate in the field of patents, and made clear that it would be possible to adopt a regulation prescribing the terms of a unitary patent for the European Union.[44] But, resolving the patent question still left doubts among at least some member states as to whether the EU constitutive documents (the Treaty on European Union (TEU) and Treaty on the Functioning of the European Union (TFEU)) authorized the EU institutions to create a new court structure that would in many circumstances supplant the existing member state courts in terms of patent law enforcement. As a consequence of these doubts, a separate Agreement on a Unified Patent Court was negotiated among EU member states, although not all of them have signed and/or ratified that agreement. That UPC Agreement entered into force on June 1, 2023, following receipt of sufficient notice of ratifications, though as noted at present only 17 member states have ratified.

With the advent of the new system for a European Patent with Unitary Effect (or Unitary Patent) there will now be three basic routes for obtaining patent protection in Europe. It remains available to apply for a patent in an individual member state (or states) directly to the national patent office. Alternatively, an applicant can opt to use the preexisting "classical" European Patent route, filing with the European Patent Office (EPO) and designating specific EPC member states where patent protection is wanted. There are currently 39 countries (including the EU member states) that are members of the EPC "legacy" system. Third, and the new route, the applicant applies to the European Patent Office and designates the Unitary Patent which will be applicable for all of the EU member states where the government has ratified the Agreement on a Unified Patent Court.[45] This essentially entails applying for and securing a patent at the EPO under the EPC system, and subsequently designating or requesting "unitary effect". An important development was the June 2016 referendum vote in the United Kingdom to withdraw from the European Union, initiating the so-called Brexit.

---

44. Although, this did not prevent Spain and Italy from challenging the authority of the EU institutions to pursue enhanced cooperation in the field of patents before the CJEU, a challenge that was rejected. ***Spain and Italy** v. Council*, Joined Cases C-274/11 and C-295/11 (Judgment of the Court (Grand Chamber), 16 April 2013.

45. https://www.unified-patent-court.org/en.

On March 29, 2017, the United Kingdom notified the European Union under Article 50 of the TEU of its intention to withdraw. The United Kingdom ceased to be a member of the European Union on January 31, 2020. Although there had been a good deal of speculation and writing about possible arrangements that might permit the UK to join the Unified Patent Court, no such arrangements emerged. Unitary Patents will not be available for or cover the UK. With that said, the United Kingdom remains part of the "legacy" European Patent Convention arrangement along with other non-EU state parties. U.K. inventors will be able to apply for Unitary Patents just as other non-EU-based inventors—but those Unitary Patents will not be effective in the United Kingdom.

The arrangement for dispute settlement under the new European Patent System represents a substantial break from the previous system. The new UPC arrangement is described by the EPO as follows:

> Twenty-five EU Member States signed an international agreement to establish the Unified Patent Court (UPC), to which seventeen are currently bound. This new court will deal with questions of infringement and validity of both Unitary Patents and European patents.
>
> The UPC:
>
> - is a new supranational court that allows the proprietors of Unitary Patents and European patents to enforce their rights – and third parties to have patents revoked – in all EU Member States having ratified the UPC Agreement
> - puts an end to the need for litigation before national courts in different countries
> - enhances legal certainty through harmonised case law in the area of patent infringement and validity
> - provides litigants with simpler, quicker and more efficient judicial procedures
> - harmonises substantive patent law relating to the rights conferred by Unitary Patents and European patents and the limitations of those rights as well as the remedies in cases of infringement
>
> . . .
>
> The UPC comprises
>
> - a Court of First Instance
> - a Court of Appeal
> - a Registry.
>
> The Court of First Instance is composed of a central division (with its seat in Paris and a section in Munich) and several local and regional divisions. The Court of Appeal is located in Luxembourg.
>
> . . .
>
> The UPC . . . will have exclusive competence for the settlement of disputes in respect of both "classic" European patents and Unitary Patents. This exclusive competence is however subject to exceptions with regard to European patents: cases may still be brought before national courts, and proprietors of European patents may opt out from the UPC's exclusive competence during a transitional period of seven years, which may be prolonged by up to a further seven years. The opt-out will be effective for the entire life of the European patent concerned. The UPC's rulings will have effect throughout the territories of those Member States that have already ratified the UPC Agreement (the contracting Member States) at the time they are issued. The UPC will not have any jurisdiction over national patents.[46]

The EPO-run European patent system has for a long time included a post-grant opposition mechanism that allows any interested person to oppose the grant of a European patent

46. https://www.epo.org/applying/european/unitary/upc.html/.

within nine months of publication of the grant.[47] This post-grant opposition mechanism is not generally modified by the introduction of the Unitary Patent or the creation of the UPC. Oppositions to Unitary Patents may be filed at the EPO within nine months of their grants. Decisions by the EPO Opposition Division may still be appealed to the Boards of Appeal. However, a final decision to revoke a patent will henceforth be appealable to the UPC.

## NOTES AND QUESTIONS

**1.** The Unitary Patent and the UPC are not open to non-members of the European Union, not even Members of the EEA Agreement (Norway, Iceland, and Liechtenstein). The CJEU rules out an international court based upon the European Patent Convention in Opinion 1/09 Unified Patent Litigation System, March 8, 2011, C2112, OJ 2011 C. 2112; *see* Matthew Parish, International Courts and the European Legal Order, 23 European Journal of Public International Law 141-153 (2012). How does this square with the broader membership of the European Patent Organization, discussed below? Switzerland opted to create its own patent court, seeking to attract international litigation.

**2.** Note that jurisdiction limited to member states of the European Union does not exclude private operators and right holders based in third countries from relying upon the Unitary Patent and to seek rulings of the UPC.

**3.** As will have become apparent from the discussion so far, the "European" patent system (in particular the EPC, discussed further in B. below) has, until the recent emergence of the Unitary Patent and the UPC, been primarily created and regulated *outside* the European Union (EU) legal order. There are, however, some aspects of EU patent law which are worth noting. For once, the EU "Bio-tech" Directive has harmonized patent protection for biotechnological inventions.[48] In addition, the extension of patent term for medicinal and other

47. https://www.epo.org/applying/european/oppositions.html:

Opposition can only be based on the grounds specified in Article 100 EPC:

- that the subject-matter of the patent is not patentable within the terms of Articles 52-57 EPC,
- that the invention is not disclosed clearly and completely enough for a person skilled in the art to carry it out,
- that the patent's subject-matter extends beyond the content of the application as filed.

Notice of opposition must be filed online or in writing with the EPO (Munich, The Hague or Berlin), and an opposition fee is payable (see the current "Schedule of fees and expenses"). Oppositions can be filed either online using EPO software or by submitting the EPO opposition form (Form 2300), which contains all the necessary information to ensure that the opposition is admissible.

There are three possible outcomes at the end of the proceedings:

- the opposition is rejected and the patent is maintained as granted,
- the patent is maintained in an amended form, in which case a new patent specification is published,
- the patent is revoked.

The opposition applies to all states designated in the European patent. As with any other final decision of first-instance divisions, decisions by opposition divisions can be appealed within two months from the date of notification of the decision.

. . .

An appeal can be filed against decisions of the departments of first instance of the European Patent Office (EPO). The appeal is filed with the EPO's Boards of Appeal in a judicial procedure in which a board acts as the department of final instance in grant, opposition, limitation and revocation procedures before the EPO.

48. DIRECTIVE 98/44/EC OF THE EUROPEAN PARLIAMENT AND OF THE COUNCIL of 6 July 1998 on the legal protection of biotechnological inventions, addressing in particular questions of patentability and scope of protection in relation to bio-technological inventions.

regulated products via so called "supplementary protection certificates" (SPCs) is provided via an EU Regulation.[49]

**4.** Most relevant for the present discussion, in April 2023, the EU introduced plans for an EU-wide compulsory licensing mechanism in form of a proposed EU Regulation (EUCL Reg) creating a compulsory license mechanism (EUCL).[50] The idea is that during a crisis or emergency in the EU (such as a pandemic), an EUCL facilitates cross-border supply of "crisis-relevant products" throughout the EU. An EUCL would cover patents, patent applications, and SPCs, as well as utility models, and is intended to be a last resort when efforts to reach a voluntary agreement to use the protected technology on reasonable terms have failed. Importantly, recital 14 makes clear that any test data protection that may exist in parallel must not stand in the way of an EUCL and should be restricted accordingly.

**5.** The EUCL Reg is essentially based on Art.31 TRIPS; however, prohibits any export (with the exception of a targeted export under the Art.31*bis* TRIPS system – discussed below). In this respect, the EU does not use the flexibility laid down in Art. 31(f) TRIPS, according to which supply under a compulsory license must be "predominantly" for the domestic market, hence allowing exports of anything less than the predominant part of the production. However, this is understandable against the background of the EUCL's objective of supplying the EU internal market with crisis products. Essentially, the EUCL mechanism extends the common market rationale from harmonizing standards of IP protection to the supply products benefitting from limits to IP protection. As a mechanism implementing Article 31 TRIPS, the EUCL Reg also contains valuable insights on what the EU considers TRIPS-compliant – in particular on the subject of the amount of compensation for the award of a compulsory license: Under Article 9 of the EUCL Reg, compensation must not exceed 4% of the licensee's total gross revenue generated by the license. This is likely to be of importance for developing countries with similar approaches to compensation when issuing a compulsory license, which could defend themselves against pressure for higher royalty rates from industry and other WTO Members by referring to the EU practice. The same applies to the relationship between compulsory licensing and test data protection.

**6.** With regard to the Article 31*bis* TRIPS mechanism for export under a compulsory license to developing countries without sufficient domestic manufacturing capacities, Article 23 EUCL Reg proposes an amendment to EU Regulation 816/2006 that introduced the EU mechanism implementing Art.31*bis* TRIPS. As confirmed by recital 37, this would create the possibility of applying for a single EU-wide compulsory license for export to third countries without sufficient domestic manufacturing capacities – an option that is likely to become particularly important if the respective production under a compulsory license for export requires cooperation between companies in different EU Member States.

**7.** Finally, the EUCL Reg proposal could be viewed as representing a model for the uniform regulation of compulsory licensing in any regional (trade or other economic cooperation)

49. REGULATION (EC) No 469/2009 OF THE EUROPEAN PARLIAMENT AND OF THE COUNCIL of 6 May 2009 concerning the supplementary protection certificate for medicinal products (setting out subject matter, conditions for and the effects of SPC protection, as well as the relevant procedural aspects for granting a SPC) and REGULATION (EU) 2019/933 OF THE EUROPEAN PARLIAMENT AND OF THE COUNCIL of 20 May 2019 amending Regulation (EC) No 469/2009 concerning the supplementary protection certificate for medicinal products (introducing an 'export exception', allowing the production of an otherwise SPC-protected medicinal product for the purpose of export to third countries). The EU recently announced plans for a comprehensive reform of the SPC regime; see: https://single-market-economy.ec.europa.eu/industry/strategy/intellectual-property/patent-protection-eu/supplementary-protection-certificates-pharmaceutical-and-plant-protection-products_en.

50. COM(2023)224 — Proposal for a regulation of the European Parliament and of the Council on compulsory licensing for crisis management and amending Regulation (EC) 816/2006 – see: https://single-market-economy.ec.europa.eu/publications/com2023224-proposal-regulation-compulsory-licensing-crisis-management_en.

context – and hence may also be of interest for developing countries. Regional trade agreements (RTAs) and related cooperation mechanisms such as Mercosur, SADC, the Andean Community, ASEAN, ECOWAS, CARIFORUM/CARICOM or the GCC could also consider creating a process for the uniform issuance of a compulsory license. This would, with regard to the members of the RTA, effectively circumvent the obstacle in Art. 31(f) TRIPS, according to which compulsory licensed products are to predominantly supply the domestic market. For the purpose of compliance with Article 31 TRIPS, this would raise further interesting questions: Is it only because of the EU's legal status as a WTO Member that it can create a supra-national compulsory licensing mechanism, despite all EU Member States being WTO Members in their own right? Or could other WTO Members also introduce cross-border compulsory licensing mechanisms as long as this is in the framework of a WTO-recognized RTA or a customs union?

## B. The "Legacy" of the European Patent Convention System

For constitutive and other reasons discussed above in relation to implementation of the new EU Patent System, arrangements for the grant of patents initially established in 1973 by the European Patent Convention ("EPC") will remain in place. Since EU Patents will not extend to the EPC members that are not EU member states (or have opted out of the EU Patent System), the "legacy" EPC system will remain as a mechanism for the grant of European Patents (distinguished from EU Patents). It is too early to tell what the impact of the partially overlapping systems will be, other than to note that the situation will be complicated. Moreover, the European Patent Office that was created as part of the EPC system will serve as the granting authority for the new unitary Unitary Patents.

In the EPC system, the application for a patent is examined by the search authority of the EPO located in The Hague. The EPC establishes the criteria of patentability, which are that the invention be new, capable of industrial application, and involve an inventive step. The key provision, Article 52, provides:

> (1) European patents shall be granted for any inventions which are susceptible of industrial application, which are new and which involve an inventive step.
> (2) The following in particular shall not be regarded as inventions within the meaning of paragraph 1:
> (a) discoveries, scientific theories and mathematical methods;
> (b) aesthetic creations;
> (c) schemes, rules and methods for performing mental acts, playing games or doing business, and programs for computers;
> (d) presentations of information.
> (3) The provisions of paragraph 2 shall exclude patentability of the subject-matter or activities referred to in that provision only to the extent to which a European patent application or European patent relates to such subject-matter or activities as such.
> (4) Methods of treatment of the human or animal body by surgery or therapy and diagnostic methods practiced on the human or animal body shall not be regarded as inventions which are susceptible of industrial application within the meaning of paragraph 1. This provision shall not apply to products, in particular substances or compositions, for use in any of these methods.

If an EPC patent is granted, the inventor obtains a separate bundle of patent rights in each EPC country that was designated in the application. There are a number of differences in the process by which patents are granted as between the United States and EPC-Europe. The EPC establishes an administrative and judicial system for resolving disputes that may arise throughout the patenting process, from the time the application is submitted until any opposition has run its course (and even after). At each stage, decisions of bureaucrats may be appealed to various Boards of Appeal.

We begin with an excerpt from Friedrich-Karl Beier introducing the basic rules of the EPC concerning patentability and the application procedure.

**Friedrich-Karl Beier***

## *The European Patent System*

### . . . IV. The Munich Patent Convention

#### b. conditions of patentability

Part II of the Munich Convention contains the provisions of substantive patent law of which the chapter on patentability is the most important one. Under article 52(1), European patents shall be granted for inventions which are new, involve an inventive step, and are susceptible of industrial applications. Since the basic provisions on patentability mention only these four criteria, namely: invention, novelty, inventive step or nonobviousness, and industrial applicability, and are to be understood as containing an exhaustive enumeration, no other criteria of patentability can be applied to European patent applications, in particular the requirement that the invention achieve technical progress as was required in the Federal Republic of Germany and is still required in many other countries. At first glance, it seems contrary to the basic philosophy of patent protection to abandon the very requirement of technical progress whose promotion is the main purpose of the patent system. We must admit, however, that the requirement of technical progress as a separate object of examination, in addition to novelty and nonobviousness, is of minor importance in practice and that its proof in some fields leads to practical difficulties. It is, therefore, no great loss if European patent law relinquishes the requirement of technical progress as an independent examination criterion and proceeds from the general presumption that an invention which is susceptible of industrial application and which is not obvious to the average man skilled in the art constitutes an enrichment of technology and thus contributes to technical progress, without the applicant's having to prove in each case that the invention is more advantageous than all other known technical solutions. This does not mean, however, that we should totally forget that patents are granted to advance the art, stimulating not only technical but also economic and social progress. If, therefore, the invention actually achieves such progress, it should be taken into consideration as a positive criterion for patentability, be it as a general rule derived from the main objective of patent protection or as the most important indicia in proving an inventive step.

The Munich Convention avoids the questionable attempt to give a positive definition to the term "invention." Article 52(2) gives only a negative, non-exhaustive enumeration of subjects which should not be considered inventions. Excluded are discoveries, scientific theories, mathematical methods, aesthetic creations, presentations of information, and, in particular, non-technical mental processes, including computer programs. With that provision, the contracting states have, under the motto of "no experiments," adopted a very conservative concept of patentable inventions which leaves little room for the future adaptation of the European patent system to new scientific and technical developments. This is, in my opinion, a shortsighted view which can only be explained, not justified, by the administrative consideration

* 14 Vand. J. Transnat'l L. 1 (1981).

that the newly-created EPO should not be burdened with additional and difficult problems of substantive patent law and search.

Much more forward looking is article 53, containing the other exceptions to patentability. The catalogue is, fortunately, very small. Only inventions whose publication or exploitation would be contrary to the *ordre public* or morality and inventions in the area of plant cultivation and animal breeding are excluded. The latter exclusion does not, however, apply to microbiological processes and the products thereof. Thus, the patentability of microbiological inventions, which play an important role in the field of antibiotics, is expressly acknowledged. Rule 28 of the Implementing Regulations contains specific provisions concerning the disclosure of such inventions and regulating the details of microorganism deposit, culture collection, and the release of samples to the public. Although the content of rule 28 was improved during the Munich Diplomatic Conference, the pharmaceutical industry was not completely satisfied. It therefore urged a further amendment, which, after an interesting discussion, was recently adopted by the Administrative Council.

The most important feature of article 53, however, is that it does not exclude or restrict patent protection for chemical and pharmaceutical inventions, foods, or agricultural products. This is a complete deviation from the existing national law of many contracting states, which, for reasons of economic, health, or agricultural policy, have restricted patent protection in these fields to the manufacturing process only or even, for pharmaceutical inventions, have granted no protection at all, as in Italy. In all these fields, full patent protection will be available at the end of a transition period. Exceptions may be claimed by the contracting states by way of reservation. Up to now, only Austria has used that possibility to maintain provisionally its existing restrictions for chemical products, medicines, and foods.

With respect to novelty, the basic patentability criterion, the French law concept of absolute novelty has been adopted. According to article 54, an invention is considered new if it does not belong to the state of the art. The state of the art comprises everything made available to the public before the priority date through written or oral description, use, or any other method. All substantive, temporal, and territorial limitations of the novelty concept, which are known from various national patent laws, have become obsolete. The European novelty examination is based on the strictest worldwide novelty standard.

According to article 64(3), the content of prior applications, which on the priority date of a later publication have not yet been published, will also belong to the state of the art. . . .This solution constitutes a reasonable compromise which facilitates the granting procedure and meets the demands of patent practice.

Unfortunately, the same cannot be said with respect to article 55 dealing with non-prejudicial disclosures. In contrast to the German, Japanese, and United States patent laws, which provide a grace period of six or twelve months during which the inventor or his legal successor is protected against the anticipatory effects of his own disclosures, article 65 restricts that protection to disclosures by third parties which may be considered as evident abuse. This very narrowly defined exception, together with the introduction of the absolute novelty concept and the requirement of nonobviousness, will certainly lead to great disadvantages for independent inventors, scientists, and small and medium-sized enterprises which are used to test, exhibit, or give other information on their inventions before filing a patent application. The grace period accorded them sufficient time to evaluate the technical and economic value of the invention, and, if necessary, to improve the invention without fear of losing patent protection. If these possibilities no longer exist, serious disadvantages for many inventors will be the consequence. A more liberal solution which should preferably be an international, worldwide solution would be highly desirable.

My final comments on patentability concern the concept of nonobviousness, for which the Munich Convention utilizes the somewhat unfortunate expressions "inventive step," "*activité inventive*," and "*erfinderische Tätigkeit*" adopted by the Strasbourg Patent Convention of 1963. These terms, at least the German and French versions, are unfortunate since they mis-state the real meaning of this important criterion of patentability. It is not the activity of inventing which is decisive to the concept, but rather the product of that activity, the invention, and its distance from the state of the art. It is nevertheless a welcome development that this judge-made condition of patentability, whose practical importance is much greater than that of novelty, is now firmly anchored in the European patent law. According to the legal definition in article 56, an invention shall be considered to involve an inventive step if, having regard to the state of the art it is not obvious to a person skilled in the art. This definition corresponds to the definitions developed by United States and German courts for nonobviousness or *Erfindungshöhe* respectively. It is to be hoped that this criterion, upon which the quality of future European patent examination will largely depend, will find reasonable interpretation by the European Patent Office and the national courts. After thorough discussions within interested circles, the European Patent Office recently announced its intention to follow the middle line practiced by the German Patent Office rather than the too liberal English or too strict Dutch standard of evaluating nonobviousness.

### V. The European Granting Procedures

Most of the remaining articles of the Munich Patent Convention deal with the European patent granting procedure. It is not possible in this article to comment on the details of that procedure. It will be sufficient to say that the European Patent Office will practice one of the most elaborate, modern examination procedures based on the experiences of large, national patent offices and provide all the necessary legal guarantees for the patent applicant as well as for competitors and the general public. This procedure contains the following steps:

(1) The filing of a European patent application designating the member states for which protection is sought, in one of the three official languages, English, French, or German;
(2) the examination on filing and formal requirements;
(3) the drawing up of a search report revealing the relevant state of the art;
(4) the publication of the application, together with the search report, eighteen months after the date of priority;
(5) the examination of the published patent application as to patentability, dependent on a written request by the applicant which can be filed within six months after publication; otherwise the application will be deemed to be withdrawn;
(6) the grant of the European patent or its refusal, with the possibility of appeal; and
(7) a post-grant opposition procedure to give third parties the opportunity to raise objections against patentability; if the opposition is successful, the patent will be revoked, with retroactive effect; if the opposition fails or no opposition is raised during the nine month period after publication of the grant, the European patent will be given full effect within the territories of all contracting states for which it has been granted.

## NOTES AND QUESTIONS

**1.** In *Biogen*,[51] the UK Supreme Court observed the conceptual difficulties surrounding attempts to define "invention" beyond the requirements of newness, industrial applicability, and inventive step. Note that the drafters of the EPC did not overcome these conceptual difficulties.

51. See *supra* section I.C.2.

**2.** The EPC expressly excludes computer software from the scope of patentable subject matter. The EPO has nevertheless found some room for patenting computer software that forms part of an otherwise patentable invention (see, e.g., EPO decision in Bentley, supra pp. 185-186 (note 4). This is consistent with the approach that the U.S. Supreme Court adopted in *Diamond v. Diehr*.[52] The U.S. Patent and Trademark Office today grants, and the CAFC confirms, patents on computer software standing alone.

**3.** Debate over the grant of patents on computer software has been going on within the European Union for a number of years. The European Commission submitted a proposal to allow such patenting to the Council and Parliament. (*See* Proposal for a Directive of the European Parliament and of the Council on the patentability of computer-implemented inventions, Brussels, 20.02.2002, COM(2002) 92 final.) On July 6, 2005, the European Parliament rejected the proposal after intensive discussion and lobbying from various stakeholder groups.

**4.** Friedrich-Karl Beier is quite critical of the EPC rule on nonprejudicial disclosures, suggesting that it will substantially disadvantage small and medium-sized businesses. Recall that the U.S. Patent Act provides a broad one-year grace period for prior public disclosure. At least part of the patent bargain between inventors and the public at large is that inventors receive a grant of exclusivity in exchange for disclosing their inventions to the public. If an inventor has already publicly disclosed an invention prior to filing a patent application, for what is the public bargaining?

## C. The European Patent Office

The EPC establishes a number of divisions at the European Patent Office, which are the Receiving Section, Search Divisions, Examining Divisions, Opposition Divisions, Legal Division, Boards of Appeal, and Enlarged Board of Appeals (art. 15 EPC). The Boards of Appeal, as their name suggests, review the decisions of the various divisions. The Boards of Appeal and the President of the EPO may refer questions of law to the Enlarged Board of Appeals. In deciding a case, a Board of Appeal may exercise any of the powers conferred by the EPC on the department from which an appeal is taken, or it may remit a case back to that department for further action consistent with its decision (art. 111 EPC).

The Boards of Appeal and Enlarged Board of Appeals have developed a substantial case law regarding the interpretation and application of the EPC. In the *Procter & Gamble* decision of a Technical Board of Appeal that follows, the relationship among the various examining and opposition divisions, and the Boards, is considered. The decision includes a very useful discussion of the doctrine of *res judicata*, which plays an important role in IPRs law generally. Under what circumstances have two parties exhausted their IPRs claims against each other in the courts? Under what circumstances, if any, does the decision in a case involving two parties bind a third party not represented in that case? For example, does a finding that a patent is valid in one proceeding preclude a challenge to the patent in another proceeding? The principles elucidated in the following decision may be helpful to answering these questions.

### *Procter & Gamble v. Unilever*

Decision of Technical Board of Appeal 3.3.1 Dated 3 May 1996 T 167/93 - 3.3.1

Composition of the board:
Chairman: A. J. Nuss
Members: J. M. Jonk, S. C. Perryman
Patent proprietor/Appellant: The Procter & Gamble Company

52. 450 U.S. 175 (1981).

Opponent/Respondent: Unilever PLC/Unilever N.V. . . .
Article: 54, 56, 111(2), 113(1), 125 EPC . . .

## Headnote

A decision of a Board of Appeal on appeal from an Examining Division has no binding effect in subsequent opposition proceedings or on appeal therefrom, having regard both to the EPC and "res judicata" principle(s).

## Reasons for the Decision

1. The appeal is admissible.

2. The first issue to be dealt with is the Appellant's submission on res judicata. The Appellant was arguing that the Opposition Division was bound by the ratio decidendi of the remitting decision T 298/87 of the Board of Appeal, setting aside the decision of the Examining Division refusing the present patent application on the ground of lack of inventive step in view of document (3). In the Appellant's view, this also meant that all findings of facts from document (3) on which the binding part of the decision rested were not open to reconsideration and thus equally binding.

2.1 This issue requires a preliminary investigation of whether there is any legal basis under the European Patent Convention for such a binding effect.

The only explicit reference to any binding effect of a decision of a Board of Appeal (other than the Enlarged Board) is in Article 111(2) EPC stating:

> "If the Board of Appeal remits the case for further prosecution to the department whose decision was appealed, that department shall be bound by the ratio decidendi of the Board of Appeal, in so far as the facts are the same. If the decision which was appealed emanated from the Receiving Section, the Examining Division shall similarly be bound by the ratio decidendi of the Board of Appeal." (Emphasis by the Board)

2.2 There is no reference here to an Opposition Division being bound by a decision of a Board of Appeal on appeal from an Examining Division. The basis, if any, for such binding effect could thus only be under Article 125 EPC stating

> In the absence of procedural provisions in this Convention, the European Patent Office shall take into account the principles of procedural law generally recognized in the Contracting States, or some principle developed by interpretation of the European Patent Convention.

2.3 To discover principles of procedural law generally recognized in the Contracting States it is useful first to turn to maxims of Roman Law, as these have proved themselves in practice over many centuries, have fundamentally influenced the laws of all Contracting States, and survive, though possibly in slightly modified form, in these laws today. In this case, where the Appellant has referred to a principle of res judicata to support his argument, relevant maxims are:

> (1) Res inter alios judicata alii non praejudicat.
> (Dig, 2, 7, §2 in Corpus iuris civilis, editio stereotypa, Bd. 1, Berlin 1908)
>
> A matter adjudged between others does not prejudice third parties.
>
> (2) Res judicata pro veritate accipitur.
> (Digest 1, 5, 25 in Op. cit.)
>
> The adjudged matter is to be accepted as truth.
>
> (3) Res judicatas restaurari exemplo grave est.
> (Codex Just. 7, 52, 4 in Corpus iuris civilis, editio stereotypa, Bd. 2, Berlin 1877)

> To reopen adjudged matters is undesirable because of the [bad] example set.
>
> (4) Expedit rei publicae, ut finis sit litium.
> (Cod. Just. 7, 52, 2 (Caracalla); 2, 4, 10 (Philipp); 3, 1, 16 (Justinian) in Corpus iuris civilis, editio stereotypa, Bd. 1, Berlin 1908)

It is in the public interest that there be an end to litigation.

The principle of res judicata is thus a compromise between the right of all parties to a fair hearing (maxim (1)), and a desire to bring litigation to a speedy end (maxims (2) to (4)).

2.4 This is also accepted under the national laws of at least certain Contracting States as set out below:

2.4.1 For the purpose of English law it is useful to quote the following definitions taken from Halsbury's Laws of England, Fourth Edition Reissue 1992, Volume 16:

> "There is said to be an estoppel where a party is not allowed to say that a certain statement of fact is untrue, whether in reality it is true or not. Estoppel may therefore be defined as a disability whereby a party is precluded from alleging or proving in legal proceedings that a fact is otherwise than it has been made to appear by the matter giving rise to that disability." (§951)
>
> "Estoppel per rem judicatam arises:
>
> (1) where an issue of fact has been judicially determined in a final manner between the parties by a tribunal having jurisdiction, concurrent or exclusive in the matter, and the same issue comes directly in question in subsequent proceedings between the same parties (this is sometimes known as cause of action estoppel);
> (2) where the first determination was by a court having exclusive jurisdiction, and the same issue comes incidentally in question in subsequent proceedings between the same parties (this is sometimes known as issue estoppel)" (§953)

2.4.2 For French law, the Code Civil Art. 1351 states:

> L'autorité de la chose jugée n'a lieu qu'à l'égard de ce qui a fait l'objet du jugement. Il faut que la chose demandée soit fondée sur la même cause; que la demande soit entre les mêmes parties, et formée par elles et contre elles en la même qualité.
>
> The binding effect of the adjudged matter only exists for what was the object of the judgment. It is necessary that the relief sought is based on the same cause of action; that the suit is between the same parties, and for and against them in the same legal capacity.

2.4.3 In respect of German law §325 Zivilprozeßordnung (Rechtskraft und Rechtsnachfolge) states that:

> Das rechtskräftige Urteil wirkt für und gegen die Parteien und die Personen, die nach dem Eintritt der Rechtshängigkeit Rechtsnachfolger der Parteien geworden sind oder den Besitz der in Streit befangenen Sache in solcher Weise erlangt haben, daß eine der Parteien oder ihr Rechtsnachfolger mittelbarer Besitzer geworden ist.
>
> A legally binding judgment has force for and against the parties and persons, who after the start of litigation became successors of the parties or obtained possession of the thing in dispute in such a manner, that one of the parties or its successors has become the mediate owner.

2.5 Without needing to consider the laws of the Contracting States in more detail, in the Board's judgment, it can be seen from the above that any generally recognized principle of estoppel by rem judicatam for the Contracting States is of extremely narrow scope as it will involve something that has been:

(a) judicially determined
(b) in a final manner
(c) by a tribunal of competent jurisdiction,
(d) where the issues of fact are the same,

(e) the parties (or their successors in title) are the same, and
(f) the legal capacities of the parties are the same.

2.6 In cases T 843/91 (OJ EPO 1994, 832) and T 934/91 (OJ EPO 1994, 184) relied on by the Appellant, all criteria (a) to (f) were met, as the proceedings in both cases involved a second appeal in the same opposition proceedings. Here, however at least criterion (e) is not met, as the Respondent was not a party to the application proceedings in which decision T 298/87 issued.

2.7 As stated above, the principle of res judicata is based on public policy that there should be an end to litigation. But the European Patent Convention specifically provides that the grant of a patent should be considered both at a first examination stage (Articles 96 and 97) and at an opposition stage (Articles 99 to 102), and Article 113(1) EPC provides that "The decisions of the European Patent Office may only be based on grounds or evidence on which the parties concerned have had an opportunity to present their comments." In the Board's view these explicit provisions of the Convention preclude any implicit public policy preventing a matter being considered a second time in judicial proceedings, that is estoppel per rem judicatam, from being applicable. Further, to consider in opposition proceedings whether certain lines of argument are precluded on some principle of res judicata, would itself be an undue complication. As a party in opposition proceedings is free to adopt as its own argument the reasons given in a decision of a Board of Appeal in ex parte proceedings, it is this Board's view that the aim of speedy proceedings is best served, if all the issues in opposition proceedings are decided by the relevant tribunal on its own view of the facts, free from res judicata considerations relating to decisions made during the examination proceedings.

. . .

2.10 Thus, this Board can see no basis for res judicata in the present case, either under the wording of Article 111 or 125 EPC, or on the basis of any interpretation of the European Patent Convention.

2.11 This is a situation where in accordance with the Enlarged Board Decision G 5/83 (OJ EPO 1985, 64, point 5), it is legitimate to take into account the preparatory documents and the circumstances of the conclusion of the treaty in order to confirm the meaning that the Board believes correct.

2.11.1 The penultimate version of what is now Article 111(2) EPC read:

> "All further decisions on the same application or patent involving the same facts shall be based on the ratio decidendi of the Board of Appeal" (see document BR/184 e/72 of the Historical documentation relating to the European Patent Convention).

2.11.2 The reason for the change from that version to the present one appears from document BR/209 e/72 zat/QU/K of the Historical documentation relating to the European Patent Convention. This shows that it resulted from a joint proposal of the German, British, French and Dutch delegations, in which the committee agreed basically with their suggestion to avoid having a decision of a Board of Appeal from being binding on the Opposition Division or the courts of the individual states or the revocation divisions of the second convention. The committee however approved a change to make clear that the department to which the matter is remitted is bound by the ratio decidendi in so far as the facts are the same.

2.11.3 The Board thus concludes that a decision of a Board of Appeal on appeal from an Examining Division has no binding effect in subsequent Opposition proceedings or on appeal therefrom, having regard both to the European Patent Convention and "res judicata" principle(s).

## NOTES AND QUESTIONS

**1.** The Board of Appeal invokes maxims of Roman law since, according to the Board, these maxims "have fundamentally influenced the law of all Contracting States, and survive, though possibly in slightly modified form, in these laws today." Do you think this was an appropriate way for the Board to determine the procedural rules common to the contracting states of the EPC? What other method(s) might you have suggested?

**2.** It is interesting to note that the drafters of the EPC finally undertook to narrow the effect of decisions of the Boards of Appeal. In *Biogen, supra* section I.C.2, the UK Supreme Court held that the decision of the EPO Board of Appeal regarding the same patent was not binding on the U.K. courts. If the penultimate version of Article 111(2) EPC referred to by the Board of Appeal (in *Procter & Gamble*) had been adopted, do you think the result in *Biogen* would have been different? Would it be preferable that national courts in EPC states be required to follow the decisions of Boards of Appeal?

## D. Regional Trade Agreements and Patent Norms

### WHO-WIPO-WTO (2020)

### Review of Relevant Provisions in Free Trade Agreements Promoting Access to Medical Technologies and Innovation

#### (a) Review of selected IP provisions

When the TRIPS Agreement entered into force in 1995, there were 44 FTAs in force that had been notified to the WTO. At the time of writing, December 2019, the number of notified FTAs had surpassed 300. Some merely reaffirm the principles of the TRIPS Agreement. Many contain obligations to accede to a range of WIPO conventions and treaties, for example, the Paris Convention, the Patent Cooperation Treaty, the Patent Law Treaty or the Trademark Law Treaty. They reaffirm the principles of non-discrimination (i.e. national treatment and most-favoured-nation treatment) enshrined in the TRIPS Agreement. . . . Additionally, certain standards found in FTAs that relate to patent protection and regulatory exclusivities, as well as IPR enforcement, are particularly relevant to pharmaceutical and biotherapeutic products, as well as other health technologies.

Eighty-two per cent of the FTAs that entered into force after 2005 contain IP provisions. Among these, 20 per cent contain provisions that require the parties to implement more extensive protection and enforcement of IPRs than the standards provided for in the TRIPS Agreement. Such provisions are often referred to as "TRIPS plus". The non-discrimination principles under the TRIPS Agreement require parties to those FTAs to extend the application of any higher standards to all other WTO members. . . .

While there is no unique approach to IP standards in FTAs, certain commonalities in terms of specifying and increasing IP standards can nevertheless be observed. Provisions with a bearing on the health technologies typically cover one or more of the following subjects:

#### (i) Patent law

Several FTAs contain detailed provisions on various aspects of patent law. For example, some FTAs specify how patentability criteria and the requirement of sufficient disclosure are to be applied. . . . Some FTAs provide that patents must be available for inventions claimed as being at least one of the following: new uses of a known product; new methods of using a known product; or new processes of using a known product.

FTAs may include provisions foregoing the application of otherwise permissible exclusions from patentability and exceptions and limitations to patent rights in domestic law, or, on the contrary, making their application mandatory. . . . FTA provisions may thus expressly require the patentability of plants and animals (see Article 15.9.2 of the FTA between Morocco and the United States). But they may also require the parties to provide for regulatory review exception in domestic law. . . . Article 18.49 of the CPTPP, for example, states that "each Party shall adopt or maintain a regulatory review exception for pharmaceutical products."

#### (ii) Patent term extension

A number of FTAs require the possibility of extending the 20-year term of protection, which has to be available under the TRIPS Agreement, for, among other things, pharmaceutical products. The purpose of such an extension is to compensate the patent owner for the time it takes to obtain marketing approval, or for processing delays in the patent office. Some WTO members provide such extensions in the form of patent term extensions or adjustments, while others make supplementary protection certificates available.

#### (iii) Grounds for granting compulsory licences

The TRIPS Agreement does not establish an exhaustive list of grounds for granting compulsory licences. Provisions in certain FTAs, such as Article 16.7(6) in the United States-Singapore FTA, Article 17.9(7) in the United States–Australia FTA and Article 4(20) in the United States–Jordan FTA, limit grounds to remedies under competition law, situations of extreme urgency and public non-commercial use.

#### (iv) Exhaustion regime

Under the TRIPS Agreement, WTO members are free to choose the exhaustion regime that best meets their domestic policy objectives (see section C.3(f)). This freedom is confirmed in a number of FTAs. However, some FTAs specifically provide for the right of a patent owner to limit parallel imports through contracts.

#### (v) Regulatory exclusivities

. . . The WTO TRIPS Agreement does not require WTO members to provide for regulatory exclusivities in domestic legislation.

Some FTAs specify that a period of regulatory exclusivity is required and some FTAs provide for regulatory exclusivities in the context of implementing Article 39.3 of the WTO TRIPS Agreement (see Chapter II, sections A.6(f) and B.1(c)). In some cases, regulatory exclusivities are prescribed for a number of years (see Table 4.3). Certain FTAs provide for the possibility of extending exclusivity periods. Some FTAs require the parties to apply exclusivity periods when new clinical information is submitted in support of a previously approved product covering a new indication, formulation or method of administration.

In certain FTAs, data exclusivity also covers cases in which an FTA party permits the granting of a marketing approval of regulated products on the basis of an earlier marketing approval of the same or similar product in a third country. This has the effect of preventing generic companies from relying on the test data supplied by the originator company to another country's government, even if no test data have been supplied to the government of the country in which the generic company seeks to market its product. Parties to FTAs have implemented such obligations in different ways.

A number of FTAs provide for additional data and/or market exclusivity for biotherapeutic products, beyond the exclusivity periods for small-molecule medicines . . . In many jurisdictions,

no distinction was made between biotherapeutics and small-molecule medicines in terms of data and/or market exclusivity prior to signing an FTA. For example, Article 20.49 of the

USMCA as initially agreed in 2018 provided for a period of at least ten years of test data protection for new biotherapeutic products. In December 2019, the Parties agreed, among others, to make changes to the intellectual property chapter and to remove this obligation. Following ratification by all Parties, the Agreement entered into force in July 2020. During the negotiations for the TPP, the length of regulatory exclusivity for biotherapeutic products was also debated. One concern was that a lengthening of the exclusivity period for biotherapeutic products to 12 years would lead to substantially increased health expenditures. These provisions, among others, were suspended in the final text of the CPTPP.

#### (vi) Patent linkage

While the TRIPS Agreement does not include any requirement regarding patent linkage, a number of FTAs include provisions to that effect . . . In practice, it has been observed that countries that have agreed to patent linkage provisions in FTAs still retain some flexibility and discretion in implementing certain features of the system domestically (Son et. al, 2018).

## NOTES AND QUESTIONS

**1.** For a related description and analysis of the continuing evolution of provisions in trade and investment agreements that may impact access to medicines and other public health matters, *see* Frederick M. Abbott, *The Evolution of Public Health Provisions in Preferential Trade and Investment Agreements of the United States*, in CURRENT ALLIANCES IN INTERNATIONAL INTELLECTUAL PROPERTY LAWMAKING: THE EMERGENCE AND IMPACT OF MEGA-REGIONALS, GLOBAL PERSPECTIVES FOR THE IP SYSTEM 45-63 (P. Roffe & X. Seuba eds., 4 CEIPI-ICSTD 2017), available at SSRN: https://ssrn.com/abstract=3032085.

**3.** Patent provisions in recently negotiated bilateral trade agreements of the United States are largely consistent with U.S. law and practice. But U.S. patent law continuously changes through acts of the executive, legislative, and judicial branches. How will entering into binding international agreements affect U.S. domestic evolution of patent norms?

**4.** As noted in the WHO-WIPO-WTO report, twelve countries of the Asia-Pacific region, including the United States, negotiated the Trans-Pacific Partnership (TPP) Agreement, which was signed on February 4, 2016. Among the most contentious provisions in the negotiations, if not the most contentious, was a proposal by the United States to provide exclusive marketing rights for newly-approved biologic medicines for a period of 12 years. Ultimately, the TPP negotiators agreed on an 8-year (or 5+3) period of market exclusivity for biologics despite the misgivings of a number of negotiating governments. However, following withdrawal of the signature of the United States from the TPP, the remaining 11 countries eliminated the provisions on biologics exclusivity, along with several other provisions favorable to the U.S. pharmaceutical industry. The revised agreement, the Comprehensive and Progressive Agreement for Trans-Pacific Partnership (CPTPP), signed on March 8, 2018, does not extend market exclusivity for biologic drugs.

**5.** As noted in Chapter 1, section IV.A.5, the USMCA among Canada, Mexico, and the U.S. that entered into force on July 1, 2020, contains several provisions specifically directed towards strengthening patent protection, particularly as related to the pharmaceutical sector, in Chapter 20, Intellectual Property Rights. These include: (1) Article 20. F.9 that defines as "more than five years" an "unreasonable delay" in the issuance of a patent after filing, and for which a patent term adjustment should be made; (2) Article 20.F.11 providing that for a new pharmaceutical product a patent term adjustment should be made to compensate the patent owner for "unreasonable curtailment of the effect of patent term as a result of the marketing approval process"; (3) Article 20.F.16 according to which a patent owner with respect to a pharmaceutical product must be notified of a third-party submission for marketing approval of the product and given the opportunity to seek a preliminary injunction or equivalent measures (so-called "linkage"). Other provisions providing greater protection for pharmaceutical originator companies involve regulatory data-based marketing exclusivity, discussed in Chapter 5; trademark-related rules and penalties, discussed in Chapter 3; and additional investment protections, discussed in Chapter 4.

# IV. SELECTED NATIONAL PATENT SYSTEMS

## A. China

Since it began to liberalize its domestic market in the late 1980s, China has undergone one of the most rapid and profound economic transformations in world history. This has certainly *not* been because China introduced strong intellectual property protection. While China introduced a wide range of IP legislation and joined the major international IP agreements, at least until recently, China's record on IP enforcement has been weak.

**Wei Zhuang***

### *Evolution of the Patent System in China*

#### 1 Introduction

China's stunning economic performance over the past three decades has largely relied on its manufacturing competitive advantage which is to a great extent based on cheap labour, low-cost resources and extensive environment pollution. In order to achieve sustainable economic growth, the Chinese government seeks to transform itself from a global manufacturing hub to an innovation engine by 2020. The issuance of the landmark document titled 'The National Outline for Medium and Long Term Science and Technology Development Planning (2006–2020)' (hereafter 'the MLP') has mapped out such a transition. The MLP aims to enhance indigenous innovation capabilities through a variety of policies and measures, including financial and taxation policies encouraging technological innovation at the enterprise level and safeguarding the interests of intellectual property rights (IPR) owners. Despite the recent patent explosion in China, it remains to be seen precisely what effects these policies will have on China's technological progress.

#### 1.1 A Patent Boom in China

China has experienced a boom in both patent filings and patents in recent years. Published patent applications from China's patent office have risen by an average of 16.7 per cent annually from 171,000 in 2006 to nearly 314,000 in 2010. Out of all patents filed in China, the percentage of domestic applications rose to nearly 73 per cent in 2010 from less than 52 per cent in 2006, suggesting that Chinese entities have outpaced foreign companies in the patent surge. A closer look at the patent data seems to confirm this view. According to the Annual Report of China Valid Patent 2011 (Excerpt), China had a total of 2,739,906 valid patents by the end of 2011. Valid invention patents totalled 696,939, an increase of 23.4 per cent

* In Emerging Markets and the World Patent Order 155 (F.M. Abbott, C.M. Correa & P. Drahos eds., 2013).

compared with the year 2010. Invention patents developed by domestic companies accounted for 52 per cent of the total in 2011, while the ratio was just 1 percent in 2001.

The growth in patent applications and patents in China has been strongly encouraged by the strengthening of patent protection and innovation policies. It is highly likely that this trend will continue. As part of its 12th Five-Year Plan (2011-15) for National Economic and Social Development, China has set itself very ambitious goals in terms of R&D expenditure and invention patents. China is attempting to raise its R&D expenditure to 2.2 per cent as a proportion of GDP and is aiming for 3.3 invention patents for every 10,000 head of population by 2015.

### 1.2 The Patent Quality Challenge Facing China

Yet, quantity is one thing, quality is quite another. Through analysis of a variety of patent statistics, the European Union Chamber of Commerce in China (EUCCC) finds that 'China's progress in patent quality lags behind its rates of patent filings.' Under Chinese patent law, patent protection is available in three forms: invention patent, utility model patent and design patent. The utility model and design patents generally contain small and incremental innovations and are not subject to substantive examination. By the end of 2011, utility models and designs accounted for 40.9 per cent and 33.7 per cent of the total valid patents in China, while the percentage of invention patents was relatively low at 25.4 per cent. The composition of valid patents held by domestic patentees was even less balanced. Invention patents accounted for only 15.3 per cent, whereas utility models constituted 48.2 per cent and designs comprised 36.6 per cent.

Furthermore, most of the invention patents in China have been accused of 'embodying little technological progress' and being 'driven mainly by incentives put in place by the Chinese government to encourage patenting directly'. The average life span of invention patents awarded to domestic entities (around 6.9 years) is significantly lower than for foreign-owned invention patents in China (around 10.3 years). Of invention patents owned by Chinese entities 54.3 per cent maintain validity for less than five years and only 4.8 per cent are in force for over ten years. In contrast, 84.8 per cent of foreign invention patents remain in force for over five years and 24.7 per cent remain valid for more than ten years. The patents with longer life span generally embody higher levels of innovation and economic value. Few patent inventions owned by Chinese entities are at the frontier of world innovation. In 2010, only 0.6 per cent of US utility patents granted were owned by Chinese entities. Worse still, foreign firms generally do not file patents on their breakthrough inventions in China, further suggesting that China's patent ecosystem may be composed of few highest-quality patents.

Moreover, China's patent portfolio in high-tech fields is particularly inadequate. The sectoral composition of patents held by Chinese entities favours traditional sectors, including food, chemicals, civil engineering and medicine, whereas 'foreign investors still hold the advantage in high-tech industries, especially in optics, transportation, audio-visual technology, medical technology, semiconductors and engines.'

On the whole, China has a patent quality problem. What policies and laws has China enacted to tackle the low patent quality issue? Making the patent system work does not necessarily lead to welfare efficiency. What are the rules designed to address social welfare concerns specific to China? Before answering these questions, the chapter first studies the historical development of the Chinese patent system.

. . .

## 3 The Third Revision of the Chinese Patent Law

With the explosion of patenting activity in China in the past few years, the protection of intellectual property rights (IPRs) has increased in significance on the political agenda. The

State Council issued the Outline of the National Intellectual Property Strategy (NIPS) in June 2008 which aims to improve 'China's capacity to create, utilize, protect and administer intellectual property, making China an innovative country.' In response to this national strategy, China revised its patent law on 27 December 2008 for the third time. Major changes in the third revision can be summarized as follows: first, encouraging indigenous innovation through strengthening patent protection, promoting patent disclosure and improving patent quality; second, facilitating the wide use of technology through, for example, codifying the prior art defence and redefining co-owners' rights; finally, in order to balance patent rights and public interest, the revision improved the compulsory licensing system, introduced disclosure rules for inventions relying on genetic resources, explicitly allowed parallel imports and introduced the Bolar exception.

### 3.1 enhancing innovation capability

Echoing the Outline of NIPS to build an innovative nation, for the first time China has included the enhancement of innovation capabilities as one of the legislative objectives of its patent law. China's latest five-year plan (2011-15) emphasizes that China 'will strive to speed up the construction of an innovative country.' Ensuring patent quality, strengthening patent protection and making full use of patent information are considered essential for building up indigenous innovation capacity.

#### 3.1.1 Patentability standard raised

Under the previous Chinese patent law, the mere use or knowledge of an invention or a utility model outside China did not destroy novelty. To improve patent quality, the 2008 Patent Law has adopted the more common 'absolute novelty' principle under which 'prior art' refers to any technology known to the public in China or abroad before the filing date. This change may shut the door to 'patent hijacking,' and address the concern of 'junk patents.'

Meanwhile, in order to raise the quality of design patents, the amendment extends the 'absolute novelty' requirements to patentable designs. A design patent has to be significantly different from a prior design or combinations of the features of prior designs. Additionally, patent protection is no longer available for two-dimensional designs of images, colours, or the combination of the two, which mainly serve as indicators. After 1 October 2009 when the new patent law took effect, the threshold for design patents became higher and the number of 'junk design' patents was expected to be reduced.

#### 3.1.2 Strengthening patent protection

***Exclusive rights to offer for sale granted to design patentees***

Under the previous Chinese patent law, an offer for sale did not constitute infringement with respect to a design patent. In order to enhance the level of design patent protection, Article 67 of the 2008 amendment has granted design patentees the right to exclude others from offering to sell. This change enables design patent holders to pursue claims of infringement by advertisements, displaying in exhibitions or through other methods without permission.

***Codification of pre-litigation evidence preservation***

Pre-litigation evidence preservation has been provided in the 2001 Judicial Interpretation, yet a party can only file an application for evidence preservation when enforcing a pre-litigation injunction to cease a patent infringement. In order to prevent the accused infringer from destroying evidence before litigation, Article 67 of the 2008 Chinese Patent Law allows the patentee or interested party to file an independent application of evidence preservation.

Due to this change, prosecuting patent infringements becomes much easier and the legitimate interests of patent holders can be protected more effectively.

***Increased infringement damages***

In order to more effectively deter patent infringement, the 2008 amendment increased monetary damages. For the first time, the law explicitly stipulates that the damages shall include the patentee's reasonable expenses for taking actions against infringement. The administrative penalty that may be imposed is increased from three times to four times the illegal earnings, whereas the fine that may be imposed for the case in which there is no illegal gain has been increased from RMB 50,000 to RMB 200,000. The 2008 Patent Law has codified statutory damages and doubled both the upper and lower limits of the amount. These enhanced penalties for the act of patent infringement will better serve the interest of patent holders.

### 3.1.3 Facilitating dissemination of patent information

Dissemination of patent information is very important for stimulating innovation, reducing duplicative R&D activities, preventing the public from incautious infringement of patent rights, and ultimately promoting technological progress and economic and social development. For the purpose of meeting the growing public demands for patent information, China decided to improve its patent information service. The 2008 amendment explicitly obliges the patent administration department under the State Council to 'release patent-related information in a complete, accurate and timely manner, and publish patent gazettes on a regular basis'. The importance of patent information is further stressed by the National Patent Development Strategy (2011–20). According to the Strategy, China will establish a user-oriented, coordinated and cooperative patent information management and operational mechanism. By 2015, a national patent data centre, five regional patent information service centres and 47 local patent information service centres are expected to be established.

In addition to the amendments to the patent law, China has outlined in its 12th five-year plan priorities for the development of strategic emerging industries (SEIs) so as to achieve its innovation goals and transform its development pattern. The SEIs mainly cover seven areas: (1) energy-efficient, green technologies: (2) next-generation information technology; (3) pharmaceuticals and biotechnology; (4) high-end equipment manufacturing; (5) new energy; (6) new materials; and (7) new-energy vehicles. The share of SEI's total added-value in its GDP is expected to increase from 3 per cent in 2010 to 8 per cent by 2015.

## 3.2 Promoting the Utilization of Patents

Utilization of IP has been identified by the Outline of NIPS as one of China's primary IP goals for the near future. The 2008 amendment attempted to facilitate the commercialization of patents through incorporating prior art as a defence to infringement, promoting the exploitation of co-owned patents and removing the approval requirement for transfer of patent rights from Chinese nationals to foreigners.

### 3.2.1 Adding Provisions on Prior Art Defence

In previous patent infringement cases, the defendant would have to try and invalidate the patent before the Patent Re-examination Board (PRB) and the Court had to wait until the PRB's declaration of the invalidity of the patent before deciding no infringement was found. The whole process would take several years. Even if the accused infringer finally won the case, he would still suffer great losses in terms of time, money, market and reputation, which was unfair to those that utilized prior art or prior design. The 2008 amendment adds a new provision stipulating that if the alleged infringer can prove the technology or design he exploits is prior art or prior design, the infringement claim shall be dismissed. Notably, the absolute novelty principle, as discussed above, has expanded the scope of 'prior art' and 'prior design' and thus more prior art defence will be applied. This new provision will help stop accusations in bad faith and accordingly promote technology utilization.

#### 3.2.2 Encouraging the exploitation of co-owned patents

The previous Chinese Patent Law was silent on co-owners' rights. The 2008 amendment provided a new provision regarding the exploitation of jointly owned patents clarifying that when the patent co-owners have not reached agreement, any of the co-owners is entitled to exploit the patent independently or grant non-exclusive licences to others to exploit the patent. Such provisions prevent one of the co-owners from blocking the utilization of the patents rights arising from joint research efforts and ultimately promotes the exploitation and dissemination of the patented technologies.

#### 3.2.3 Removal of the approval requirement for technology transfer to foreigners

Under the 2000 Chinese Patent Law, any assignment of a patent or patent application from a Chinese entity to a foreigner needed to be approved by the competent authorities. This requirement was inconsistent with the Technology Export Regulations under which only transfers relating to technology that is restricted for export requires approval from provincial branches of the Ministry of Commerce of the People's Republic of China (MOFCOM). The approval requirement under the 2000 Patent Law makes transfer of Chinese patents to foreigners virtually impractical, in particular for non-restricted technologies which may comprise around 95 per cent of patentable inventions. The 2008 amendment makes it clear that transfer of Chinese patents or patent applications to a foreign entity shall be subject to the provisions of relevant laws and administrative regulations. Transfer of non-restricted patented technologies will no longer require prior approval.

### 3.3 Safeguarding Legitimate Rights and Interests of the Public and Preventing the Abuse of Patent Rights

Balancing the rights of patent holders and the public interest is another objective of the third Revision of the Chinese Patent Law. To address social welfare concerns, China incorporated the TRIPS flexibilities into its own law. In line with the relevant international treaties, China has improved the compulsory licensing system, incorporated mandatory disclosure of genetic resources, and broadened the scope of exception to patent infringements.

#### 3.3.1 Improving the Compulsory Licensing System

The latest amendments to the Chinese patent law introduce more detailed compulsory licence provisions which are largely in line with the Paris Convention and the TRIPS Agreement. These amendments aim to balance the interests of patent holders and users and address social welfare concerns, in particular regarding public health priorities.

Echoing Article 31 (k) of the TRIPS Agreement, the 2008 amendment has included illegal monopolistic actions as a new ground for compulsory licensing. The latest Measures for Compulsory Licensing of Patent Implementation (hereafter, 'the 2012 Measures') further clarify that such behaviour has to be determined to be anti-competitive under the law in an in-force judgment or determination by a judicial authority or an anti-monopoly law enforcement agency. This new provision signals China's desire to promote fair competition among enterprises and shows its determination to combat the monopolistic behaviours of certain patentees. Additionally, in response to Article 31 (c) of the TRIPS Agreement, the 2008 Patent Law provides that in the case of semi-conductor technologies, a compulsory licence can only be granted on the basis of illegal monopoly or for the purpose of the public interest.

The 2000 Patent Law permitted compulsory licences where an entity was unable to obtain a licence on reasonable terms and conditions within a reasonable period of time. Under the current Patent Law, however, the failure of prior negotiation efforts is only a pre-condition for granting compulsory licences where the patentee has not (fully) exploited within the stipulated time or where there are blocking patents.

The requirement to first make efforts to obtain authorization from the right holder is waived in an emergency or irregular event of the State, or for the purposes of the public interest. The competent department under the State Council is entitled to recommend SIPO to grant a compulsory licence to exploit the patent. However, application of the compulsory licensing system was unnecessarily limited to infectious diseases under the 2005 Measures for Implementing Compulsory Licensing of Patents Relating to Public Health Issues (the 2005 Measures). The 2012 Measures have removed such restrictions and allow compulsory licensing of patented pharmaceuticals for any public health purposes. The competent authority is now entitled to permit compulsory licensing for a much wider range of pharmaceuticals.

In response to paragraph 6 of the Doha Declaration on the TRIPS Agreement and Public Health, the 2008 Amendment provides a new definitive statutory basis to compel compulsory licences for the benefit of public health. Under Article 50, the competent authority may grant a compulsory licence to manufacture the patented drugs and export them to the following countries and regions: least developed countries or regions; and developed or developing Members that express their wish to import such medicine through informing the WTO in accordance with relevant international treaties.

Despite the fact that compulsory licensing has been available under the Chinese Patent Law since 1985, China has never granted a compulsory licence, even during the severe acute respiratory syndrome (SARS) outbreak in 2003. Recently, the Chinese public has been demanding compulsory licensing of drugs for hepatitis B, tuberculosis and AIDS. The latest amendments have paved the way for local manufacturing of generic drugs, making the system more compatible with the need to deal with public health crises. As one SIPO government official stated, if China were to begin granting compulsory licences, it would likely start with pharmaceutical patents.

### 3.3.2 Compulsory Disclosure Rules for Inventions Relying on Genetic Resources

The Convention on Biodiversity (CBD) requires that access to genetic resources shall follow the principles of state sovereignty, prior informed consent and benefits sharing, and further prescribes that the patent system shall facilitate, rather than hinder, the protection of genetic resources. Countries rich in genetic resources like India and Brazil, as well as industrialized countries such as Switzerland, Norway and Denmark, have introduced disclosure requirements in patent law to ensure that information on the provenance of claimed genetic resources is provided. As a country with abundant genetic resources, China has long been a victim of biopiracy. Genetic materials from wild soybeans, for instance, have been misappropriated by industrialized country companies to develop hybrids which are patented and exported to China again. To address the issue of biopiracy, for the first time, China incorporated tough disclosure rules for inventions relying on genetic resources into its current patent law in line with the CBD.

Under the 2008 China Patent Law, for an invention based on genetic resources, the applicant is obliged to disclose the direct and original source of the genetic resources. If the applicant is not able to state the original source, it or he shall state the reasons. Similar to the Andean Community and Costa Rica, China includes mandatory disclosure as one of the conditions for patentability. No patent rights shall be granted for inventions that are accomplished by relying on genetic resources which are illegally obtained or utilized. As SIPO explained, it is 'in the interest of China to follow the same practice of developing countries in an area where international treaties have always focused on the interest of developed countries.'

The 2010 Implementation Rules define 'genetic resources' as the materials of actual or potential value which are obtained from human bodies, animals, plants and microorganisms and contain functional units of heredity. 'Relying on genetic resources' refers to the use of the genetic function of the genetic resources. Yet, the impact of these provisions depends on what will constitute illegal acquisition and utilization. Biotechnology companies must comply with this new genetic disclosure requirement; otherwise, a Chinese patent will be rejected or invalidated. This is especially the case for applications originating from the US, Japan, Australia and some European countries where there is no equivalent mandatory disclosure requirement in their patent laws.

#### 3.3.3 Two newly added exceptions to patent infringement: parallel importation and Bolar Exemption

Article 69 of the 2008 Patent Law provides a series of exemptions for acts that shall not be deemed to be patent infringement. Parallel imports and Bolar exemption are two newly added causes for non-infringements.

***Parallel imports are explicitly permitted***

Under the TRIPS Agreement, WTO Member States are free to decide their positions in terms of the issue of exhaustion of IPRs. The previous Chinese patent law was silent on the issues of parallel imports. The 2008 China Patent Law clearly provides that when a patented product or a product directly obtained by using the patented method is sold with the permission of the patentee, any other person using, offering to sell, selling or importing that product shall not be deemed infringing a patent. This provision has confirmed the legality of parallel imports and thus introduced a regime of international exhaustion. No doubt, such international exhaustion will restrict the ability of the patent holders to charge higher prices in China than in other jurisdictions, as they will be vulnerable to being undercut by parallel importers.

***Bolar exception is introduced***

Bolar exception, first created in the US, deals with the use of an invention relating to a pharmaceutical product to conduct tests and obtain approval from a relevant authority, before the expiration of the patent, for commercialization of a generic version after the expiration of the patent. This exception aims to balance the interests of the patent holders and those of generic drug manufacturers by solving the problem of the lengthy regulatory approval time. The Bolar exemption has been adopted by many countries including the US, Canada, Japan and EU Members.

Following the international trend, the 2008 China Patent Law explicitly provides that manufacture, import or use of patented drugs or medical devices in order to provide necessary information for regulatory approval shall not be deemed as patent infringement. This provision enables the generic manufacturers to start producing patented drugs or medical devices before patents expire for the referred to purposes only, but ultimately facilitating faster access to drugs or medical devices at a lower price.

It is noted, however, that in contradiction to the practice of some countries, China does not provide any balancing provisions, e.g., patent term extension or a supplementary protection certificate, to compensate the patent holders for the restriction of their patent rights. This system has been criticized as 'unbalanced' mainly by the originator pharmaceutical industry for being in favour of the generic industry and acting as a disincentive for investments in pharmaceutical research in China, but it is fully consistent with the TRIPS Agreement and with the practice in many countries, where no particular impact on such investment has been observed. It is also to be noted that the WTO panel in the Canada–Pharmaceutical Patents case specially allowed a 'Bolar type' exception without patent term extension.

## 4 Conclusion

Compared to the earlier amendments, which were mainly driven by pressure from foreign investors and some WTO Members, the third revision of Chinese patent law was strongly driven by domestic demand for 'developing a strategy that balances IPRs, public interest and international obligations.' Accordingly, instead of largely relying on legal transplants, this revision is mainly based on China's own development needs and its domestic experience in the past 20 years against the background of strengthening self-innovation capacity.

Some changes, for instance, those dealing with genetic resources and the Bolar exception, have caused concern among industrial countries. Regarding the sanctions for failure to disclose the source of relevant genetic resources, the EUCCC argued that not granting the patent right might be unfair to the inventor who would usually not be the one breaching any regulation; with respect to the Bolar exception, the relevant government authorities and some pharmaceutical companies from the EU, Japan and the US considered that the 'Bolar exception' would create an imbalance between public and private interests and thus suggested that the relevant drug patent term should be extended. These views could be expected in light of the mercantile trade and investment perspectives of these countries.

However, changes have been carefully drawn up to establish a balance between private rights and public interest through, for example, providing greater legal certainty regarding patent rights and exceptions to patent infringement. Efforts have also been made to balance international obligations and specific domestic needs by including changes to safeguard Chinese national interests. Overall, the third revision to Chinese patent law has reflected the government's effort to promote domestic innovation and protect IP in accordance with international IP law. The effectiveness of such changes remains to be seen.

## NOTES AND COMMENTS

**1.** On October 17, 2020, the Standing Committee of the National People's Congress adopted the Fourth Amendment to the Chinese Patent Law, which came into force on June 1, 2021.

This amendment introduces several notable changes. Specifically, (i) it enhances the protection of design patents by allowing for patent protection of partial design, extending the patent term for design to 15 years, and establishing a domestic priority system; (ii) it increases compensation for patent infringement and shifts burden of proof in relation to damages towards infringer; (iii) with respect to pharmaceutical patents, it allows patent owners to request patent term extension to compensate for the time spent on obtaining marketing approval in China and establishes a patent linkage system; (iv) to encourage technology transfer and commercialization, it creates an "open licence" system; (v) it introduces a novelty grace period for disclosure in public interest in light of a national emergency or other extraordinary circumstance; and (iv) it requires the application of patent and the exercise of patent right to abide by the principle of good faith and prohibits the abuse of patent rights.

On the one hand, this amendment seeks to achieve sustainable development goal by strengthening patent protection, and facilitating innovation, transfer, and commercialization of technologies. On the other hand, it aims to keep pace with China's international commitments.

**2.** In Chapter 6, we will examine claims by the United States against China regarding its patent and transfer of technology laws and practices. The most serious claims of the United

States involve alleged Chinese demands that U.S.-based companies transfer technology as a condition of Chinese approval of joint venture foreign direct investment. The United States filed a Request for Consultations (RFC) at the WTO—a prelude to establishment of a dispute settlement panel—arguing that China discriminated against foreign (including U.S.) patent owners by imposing certain requirements that are not imposed on Chinese patent owners. This would be a form of national treatment discrimination. Specifically, the United States alleged that foreign licensors of patents must provide mandatory indemnification to Chinese licensees for third-party patent infringement claims against those licensees; prohibits grant backs of technology improvements by licensees to licensors; and mandates permission to licensees to continue using patented technologies after expiration of licenses. Each of these practices was said to apply to foreign licensors, but not to local Chinese companies. *See China—Certain Measures Concerning the Protection of Intellectual Property Rights*, Request for Consultations by the United States, WT/DS542/1, IP/D/38, March 26, 2018. The United States did not formally request establishment of a panel in this matter and it was reported that China had agreed to amend its legislation to apply it also to domestic licensors, thereby removing the basis for a discrimination claim.

**3.** *See* Note, *Patent Law for New Medical Uses of Known Compounds and Pfizer's Viagra Patent*, 46 IDEA 283 (2006), for some additional details regarding application of China's patent legislation.

## B. India

The adoption by India of a more market-oriented economic approach includes amendments to its Patents Act, which were mandated by the TRIPS Agreement. Like China, the acceleration of economic growth in India in the late 1990s and early twenty-first century can hardly be attributed to the introduction of strong intellectual property protection. In fact, India developed its highly successful generic pharmaceutical sector largely because it had elected not to provide pharmaceutical product patent protection until 2005. Now India also seeks to be among the countries that house "originators" of new pharmaceutical products.

**Frederick M. Abbott***

### *TRIPS II, Asia and the Mercantile Pharmaceutical War: Implications for Innovation and Access*

The internal Indian regulatory structure is undergoing a transformation, largely based on implementation of TRIPS I requirements as the ten-year pharmaceutical transition period ended on December 31, 2004.[24] Amendments to the Patents Act included implementation of pharmaceutical product patent protection.[25] Nine thousand "mailbox" applications

* Stanford Center for International Development Conference, Working Paper No. 308, Dec. 2006.

24. *See* Frederick M. Abbott, *The WTO Medicines Decision: World Pharmaceutical Trade and the Protection of Public Health*, 99 AJIL 317, at 320-23.

25. On April 5, 2005, the Patents (Amendment) Act was published as law. Gaz. India Extraordinary pt. II, sec. 1 (2005), Patents (Amendment) Act, 2005, No. 15, New Delhi, 5 Apr. 2005 (An Act further to amend the Patents Act, 1970). In addition to introducing pharmaceutical product patent protection, the 2005 amendments (1) defined "inventive step" to require technical advance as compared to existing knowledge, or having economic significance; (2) expressly limited patentability of different forms of the same substance absent a showing of a significant difference in efficacy; (3) maintained a reasonably strong form of pre-grant opposition; (4) eliminated an unnecessary hurdle to the grant of compulsory licenses under the WTO August 30, 2003 Decision; (5) clarified exports permitted under

are under review. The Act retained the institution of pre-grant opposition proceedings. The WTO August 30, 2003 waiver for exports under compulsory license was implemented.[26] A *sui generis* form of prior user right was adopted to permit continued production of generic versions of mailbox-patented products, with payment of reasonable royalty. India is taking steps to rapidly expand the capacity of its patent office and to increase regulatory oversight of pharmaceutical producers. The government seeks to ameliorate the public welfare impact of introducing product patents by extending price controls for a prescribed list of drugs.[27]

When India amended its Patent Act effective January 1, 2005 to extend to pharmaceutical product patents to comply with its TRIPS Agreement obligations, it included in Section 3(d) a limitation as to the circumstances in which new forms of known substances might be considered inventive, requiring an enhancement of known efficacy by the new form, and adding an explanation regarding the types of changes to pharmaceutical substances that would be considered new forms subject to the enhanced efficacy requirement. The Swiss pharmaceutical firm Novartis challenged the legislation principally on the grounds that it was inconsistent with Article 27.1 of the TRIPS Agreement, and also contravened the Indian Constitution. In the first part of its opinion on an appeal from the court of first instance, the High Court at Madras ruled that the TRIPS Agreement is not directly effective in Indian law based on the traditional treatment of treaties by the Indian Constitution. In the following excerpt, the High Court considers Novartis' claim that the legislative standard suffered from excessive vagueness and constituted an improper delegation of authority from the Indian Parliament. In doing so, it refers to the standards of the TRIPS Agreement in the context of discussing the object and purpose of the legislation.

## *Novartis v. Union of India*

In the High Court of Judicature at Madras Dated: 06.08.2007
The Hon'ble Mr. Justice R. Balasubramanian and
The Hon'ble Mrs. Justice Prabha Sridevan
W.P. Nos. 24759 and 24760 of 2006

. . .

13. Let us now test the argument advanced before this court by learned Senior Counsels on the validity of the amended section on the touchstone of Article 14 of the Constitution of India. As we understand the amended section, it only declares that the very discovery of a new form of a known substance which does not result in the enhancement of the known

---

the general compulsory licensing provision (e.g., expressly authorizing export of the nonpredominant part of production), as well as establishing certain presumptive time frames used in that provision; (6) improved a provision intended to permit parallel importation of patented products; and (7) allowed continued production in India of generic versions of medicines already on the market (if now patented by third parties under the mailbox system), with payment of a reasonable royalty—a form of "prior user right"—adapted to India's unique situation. Text available at http://www.ipindia.nic.in/writereaddata/Portal/IPOAct/1_69_1_patent_2005.pdf. *See also* D. G. Shah, Secretary General, Indian Pharmaceutical Alliance, *The New Indian Patent Law and August 30 Decision: The Response of the Generic Industry*, presentation to WHO-CIPIH Commission on Intellectual Property Rights, Innovation and Public Health, Geneva, Mar. 1, 2005 (PowerPoint), and Frederick M. Abbott, *India at the Crossroads: The Patents (Amendment) Bill 2003 and the Future of Public Health*, Proceedings of the India Federation of Chambers of Commerce and Industry (2004) and *Beginning of a New Policy Chapter*, Financial Express (India), June 4, 2005.

26. Regarding the WTO waiver, *see generally* Abbott, *WTO Medicines Decision*, *supra* note 24. The waiver provisions are only relevant when compulsory licenses are granted to export the predominant part of local production.

27. Deepali Gupta, *At What Price?*, Expresspharma, April 16-30, 2006.

efficacy of that substance, will not be treated as an invention. The position therefore is, if the discovery of a new form of a known substance must be treated as an invention, then the Patent applicant should show that the substance so discovered has a better therapeutic effect. Darland's Medical Dictionary defines the expression "efficacy" in the field of Pharmacology as "the ability of a drug to produce the desired therapeutic effect" and "efficacy" is independent of potency of the drug. Dictionary meaning of "Therapeutic," is "healing of disease—having a good effect on the body." Going by the meaning for the word "efficacy" and "therapeutic" extracted above, what the patent applicant is expected to show is, how effective the new discovery made would be in healing a disease/having a good effect on the body? In other words, the patent applicant is definitely aware as to what is the "therapeutic effect" of the drug for which he had already got a patent and what is the difference between the therapeutic effect of the patented drug and the drug in respect of which patent is asked for. Therefore it is a simple exercise of, though preceded by research,—we state—for any Patent applicant to place on record what is the therapeutic effect/efficacy of a known substance and what is the enhancement in that known efficacy. The amended section not only covers the field of pharmacology but also the other fields. As we could see from the amended section, it is made applicable to even machine, apparatus or known process with a rider that mere use of a known process is not an invention unless such a known process results in a new product or employs at least one new reactant. Therefore the amended Section is a comprehensive provision covering all fields of technology, including the field of pharmacology. In our opinion, the explanation would come in aid only to understand what is meant by the expression "resulting in the enhancement of a known efficacy" in the amended section and therefore we have no doubt at all that the Explanation would operate only when discovery is made in the pharmacology field. In 1989 (4) SCC Pg. 378 (*Aphali Pharma. Ltd. Vs. State of Maharashtra*), in laying down the law on "Explanation," the Supreme Court held as hereunder:

> "33. An Explanation, as was found in *Bihta Marketing Union vs. Bank of Bihar*, may only explain and may not expand or add to the scope of the original section. . . ."

. . .

In this case we find that the Explanation creates a deeming fiction of derivatives of a known substance are deemed to be the same substance unless they differ significantly in properties with regard to efficacy. Therefore it is clear from the amended section and the Explanation that in the pharmacology field, if a discovery is made from a known substance, a duty is cast upon the patent applicant to show that the discovery had resulted in the enhancement of a known efficacy of that substance and in deciding whether to grant a Patent or not on such new discovery, the Explanation creates a deeming fiction that all derivatives of a known substance would be deemed to be the same substance unless it differ[s] significantly in properties with regard to efficacy. In our opinion, the amended section and Explanation give importance to efficacy. We have already referred to the meaning of "efficacy" as given in Dorland's Medical Dictionary. Scientifically it is possible to show with certainty what are the properties of a "substance." Therefore when the Explanation to the amended section says that any derivatives must differ significantly in properties with regard to efficacy, it only means that the derivatives should contain such properties which are significantly different with regard to efficacy to the substance from which the derivative is made. Therefore in sum and substance what the amended section with the Explanation prescribes is the test to decide whether the discovery is an invention or not is that the Patent applicant should show the discovery has resulted in the enhancement of the known efficacy of that substance and if the discovery is nothing other than the derivative of a known substance, then, it must be shown that the properties in the derivatives differ significantly with regard to efficacy. As we stated earlier, due to the advanced technology in all fields of science, it is possible to show by giving necessary comparative details based on such science that the discovery of a new form a of known substance had resulted in the enhancement of the known efficacy of the original substance and the derivative so derived will not be the same substance, since the properties of the derivatives differ significantly with regard to efficacy. As rightly contended by learned Additional Solicitor General India and the lea[r]ned Senior Counsels and learned counsels for the Pharmaceutical Company opposing the Writ that the writ petitioner is not a novice to the pharmacology field but it, being [a] pharmaceutical giant in the whole of the world, cannot plead that they do not know what is meant by enhancement of a known efficacy and they cannot [k]now that the derivatives differ significantly in properties with regard to efficacy. Mr. P.S. Raman learned senior counsel argued that the Legislature, while enacting a Law, is entitled to create a deeming fiction and for that purpose, brought to our notice a judgment of the Supreme Court reported in AIR 1988 SC 191 (*M/s. J.K. Cotton Spinning and Weaving Mills Ltd. vs. Union of India*) where, in paragraph 40, the Supreme Court had said that "the Legislature is quite competent to enact a deeming provision for the purpose of assuming the existence of a fact which does not really exist." It is also stated in the very same paragraph that "it is well settled that a deeming provision is an admission of the non-existence of the fact deemed."

14. It is argued by learned Senior Counsels for the writ petitioners that it is possible for the Parliament to define in the Act itself what is meant by enhancement of a known efficacy and what is meant by differing significantly in properties with regard to efficacy. The above expressions are vague and ambiguous by themselves and therefore the meaning of such expressions ought to have been given in the Act or the amended section. Therefore when the meaning is not so given, then the vagueness and ambiguity in the provision would result in arbitrary exercise of power by the statutory authority. Opposing this argument, learned Additional Solicitor General of India would contend that Parliament is not an expert; it cannot foresee the future contingencies which may arise, when they enact an Act; therefore the Parliament always thinks it wise to use only general expressions in the Statute leaving it to the Court to interpret it depending upon the context in which it is used and the facts that are made available in each case. For this purpose, learned Additional Solicitor General brought to our notice the judgment of the Supreme Court reported in 1995 Supp. (1) SCC 235 (*Benilal vs. State of Maharashtra*) and 1980 (1) SCC 340 (*Registrar of Co-op. Societies vs. K. Kunjabmu*). Mr. P.S. Raman, learned senior counsel in supporting the argument of learned Additional Solicitor General that the Parliament cannot foresee things that may arise in the future, brought to our notice the judgment of the English Court reported in (1949) 2 All England Law Reports 155 (*Seaford Court Estates vs. Asher*), to understand and realise whether it would be possible at all to foresee things that may arise in the future when a Statute comes up for consideration before the Houses and what would be the duty of the Judge before whom interpretation of such a Statute arise for consideration. . . .

In 1980 (1) SCC 340 referred to *supra* the Supreme Court had held as hereunder:

"(1) Parliament and the State Legislatures function best when they concern themselves with general principles, broad objectives and fundamental issues, instead of technical or situational intricacies which are better left to better equipped full time expert executive bodies and specialist public servants. Parliament and the State Legislatures have neither the time or expertise to be involved in detail or circumstance, nor can visualise and provide for new strange unforeseen or unpredictable situations. That is the raison d'etre for delegated legislation. The power to legislate carries with it the power to delegate. But excessive delegation may amount to abdication. Delegation unlimited may invite despotism uninhibited. So the theory has been evolved that the legislature cannot delegate its essential legislative function. Legislate it must, by laying down policy and principle and delegate it may to fill in detail and carry out policy. The legislature may guide the delegate by speaking through the express provision empowering delegation or the other provisions of the statute such as the preamble, the scheme or even the very subject-matter of the statute. If guidance there is, wherever it may be found, the delegation is valid. A good deal of latitude has been held to be permissible in the case of taxing statutes and on the same principle generous degree of latitude must be permissible in the case of welfare legislation, particularly those statutes which are designed to further the Directive Principles of State Policy."

. . .

Therefore it is clear from the case laws referred to above that Parliament[] expresses its object and purpose in general terms when enacting a Statute and does not foresee the minute details that are likely to arise in the future and provide a solution for the same at the time when the Act itself is enacted. On the other hand, they would be acting wiser if they make only general expressions, leaving it to the experts/Statutory Authorities and then courts, to understand the general expressions used in the Statute in the context in which they are used in a case to case basis depending upon the facts available in each case. Using general expressions in a Statute, leaving the court to understand its meaning, would not be a ground to declare a section or an Act ultra vires, is the law laid down by the Supreme Court in Benilal's case referred to supra. Interpretation of a Statute must be to advance the object which the Act wants to achieve.

15. Now, we went through the statements of objects and reasons of Amending Act 15/2005. As rightly emphasized by Mr. Soli Sorabji learned senior counsel for the petitioners, the statement of objects and reasons for Amending Act 15/2005 emphasises in more than one place that the amendment is in the discharge of India's obligation to "TRIPS," which forms part of the "WTO" agreement. Therefore a need has arisen for us to look into the relevant Articles of "TRIPS" for the limited purpose of what obligations are created under "TRIPS," which, India was attempting to discharge by bringing in Amending Act 15/2005. Article 7 of "TRIPS" provides enough elbow room to a member country in complying with "TRIPS" obligations by bringing a law in a manner conducive to social and economic welfare and to a balance of rights and obligations. Article 1 of "TRIPS" enables a member country free to determine the appropriate method of implementing the provisions of this agreement within their own legal system and practice. But however, any protection which a member country provides, which is more extensive in nature than is required under "TRIPS," shall not contravene "TRIPS." Article 27 speaks about patentability. Lengthy arguments have been advanced by learned Additional Solicitor General appearing for the Government of India, learned senior counsels and learned counsels appearing for the pharmaceutical companies that India, being a welfare and a developing country, which is predominantly occupied by people below poverty line, it has a constitutional duty to provide good health care to its citizens by giving them easy access to life saving drugs. In so doing, the Union of India would be right, it is argued, to take into account the various factual aspects prevailing in this big country and prevent evergreening by allowing generic medicine to be available in the market. As rightly contended by the learned Additional Solicitor General of India, the Parliamentary debates show that welfare of the people of the country was in the mind of the Parliamentarians when Ordinance 7/2004 was in the House. They also had in mind the International obligations of India arising under "TRIPS" and under "WTO" agreement. Therefore the validity of the amended section on the touchstone of Article 14 of the Constitution of India must be decided having regard to the object which Amending Act 15/2005 wanted to achieve.

16. It is argued by the learned senior counsels for the petitioners that since the amended section uses only general expressions, leaving it to the Statutory Authority to understand what it means, the Statutory Authority is likely to act arbitrarily in exercising its discretion, since it has no guidelines. We have already held that the amended section cannot be said to be vague or ambiguous. We reiterate here at this stage that the amended section with its Explanation is capable of being understood and worked out in a normal manner not only by the Patent

applicant but also by the Patent controller. In other words, the patent controller would be guided by various relevant details which every patent applicant is expected to produce before him showing that the new discovery had resulted in the enhancement of the known efficacy; the derivatives differ significantly in properties with regard to efficacy and therefore it cannot be said that the patent controller had an uncanalised power to exercise, leading to arbitrariness. The argument that the amended section must be held to be bad in Law since for want of guidelines it gives scope to the Statutory Authority to exercise its power arbitrarily, has to be necessarily rejected since, we find that there are in-built materials in the amended section and the Explanation itself, which would control/guide the discretion to be exercised by the Statutory Authority. In other words, the Statutory Authority would be definitely guided by the materials to be placed before it for arriving at a decision. . . .

## NOTES AND QUESTIONS

**1.** The U.S. Patent and Trademark Office based decisions regarding the utility of pharmaceutical compounds on assessment of efficacy until it was precluded from doing so by the Court of Appeals for the Federal Circuit. In *In re Brana*, 51 F.3d 1560 (Fed. Cir. 1995), the U.S. PTO had rejected a patent application for an anticancer treatment on grounds that the applicant failed to demonstrate utility of the claimed compound through clinical testing on human beings intended to show efficacy. The Federal Circuit rejected efficacy in humans as the benchmark of utility of pharmaceutical substances in the following passages:

> "The Commissioner counters that such in vivo tests in animals are only preclinical tests to determine whether a compound is suitable for processing in the second stage of testing, by which he apparently means in vivo testing in humans, and therefore are not reasonably predictive of the success of the claimed compounds for treating cancer in humans. The Commissioner, as did the Board, confuses the requirements under the law for obtaining a patent with the requirements for obtaining government approval to market a particular drug for human consumption. See *Scott v. Finney*, 34 F.3d 1058, 1063, 32 U.S.P.Q.2D (BNA) 1115, 1120 (Fed. Cir. 1994) ('Testing for the full safety and effectiveness of a prosthetic device is more properly left to the Food and Drug Administration (FDA). Title 35 does not demand that such human testing occur within the confines of Patent and Trademark Office (PTO) proceedings.').
>
> . . .
>
> Our court's predecessor has determined that proof of an alleged pharmaceutical property for a compound by statistically significant tests with standard experimental animals is sufficient to establish utility. *In re Krimmel*, 48 C.C.P.A. 1116, 292 F.2d 948, 953, 130 U.S.P.Q. (BNA) 215, 219 (CCPA 1961); see also *In re Bergel*, 48 C.C.P.A. 1101, 292 F.2d 958, 130 U.S.P.Q. (BNA) 205 (CCPA 1961). In concluding that similar in vivo tests were adequate proof of utility the court in *In re Krimmel* stated:
>
>> We hold as we do because it is our firm conviction that one who has taught the public that a compound exhibits some desirable pharmaceutical property in a standard experimental animal has made a significant and useful contribution to the art, even though it may eventually appear that the compound is without value in the treatment in humans.
>
> Krimmel, 292 F.2d at 953, 130 U.S.P.Q. (BNA) at 219. . . .
>
> On the basis of animal studies, and controlled testing in a limited number of humans (referred to as Phase I testing), the Food and Drug Administration may authorize Phase II clinical studies. See 21 U.S.C. §355(i)(1); 5 C.F.R. §312.23(a)(5), (a)(8) (1994). Authorization for a Phase II study means that the drug may be administered to a larger number of humans, but still under strictly supervised conditions. The purpose of the Phase II study is to determine primarily the safety of the drug when administered to a larger human population, as well as its potential efficacy under different dosage regimes. See 21 C.F.R. §312.21(b).

> FDA approval, however, is not a prerequisite for finding a compound useful within the meaning of the patent laws. *Scott*, 34 F.3d 1058, 1063, 32 U.S.P.Q.2D (BNA) 1115, 1120. Usefulness in patent law, and in particular in the context of pharmaceutical inventions, necessarily includes the expectation of further research and development. The stage at which an invention in this field becomes useful is well before it is ready to be administered to humans. Were we to require Phase II testing in order to prove utility, the associated costs would prevent many companies from obtaining patent protection on promising new inventions, thereby eliminating an incentive to pursue, through research and development, potential cures in many crucial areas such as the treatment of cancer."

*Id.*, at 1567-68 (footnotes omitted). The reasoning of the Federal Circuit may certainly be questioned. The question of whether a claimed invention is "useful" can be assessed across the spectrum of endpoints. Is a drug compound useful because it can be tested on mice, or is it useful because it can be used to treat humans? Do you find the answer self-evident? The judgment by the High Court in Madras addressed the constitutional challenge that Novartis brought against Section 3(d) of India's Patents Act. It did not address the patentability of a specific claimed invention under the statute. The Indian Patent Office denied Novartis a patent on its anti-leukemia drug sold under the name Gleevec and Glivec on the basis that Novartis had failed to demonstrate that the beta-crystalline form of the compound for which Novartis sought a patent in India showed enhanced efficacy over the known form. Novartis challenged the determination of the Patent Office and the matter was decided by the Supreme Court of India in 2013.

## *Novartis v. India*

Civil Appeal Nos. 2706-2716 of 2013 (April 1, 2013)

### JUDGMENT

AFTAB ALAM, J.

. . .

3. What is the true import of section 3(d) of the Patents Act, 1970? How does it interplay with clauses (j) and (ja) of section 2(1)? Does the product for which the appellant claims patent qualify as a "new product" which comes by through an invention that has a feature that involves technical advance over the existing knowledge and that makes the invention "not obvious" to a person skilled in the art? In case the appellant's product satisfies the tests and thus qualifies as "invention" within the meaning of clauses (j) and (ja) of section 2(1), can its patentability still be questioned and denied on the ground that section 3(d) puts it out of the category of "invention"? On the answer to these questions depends whether the appellant is entitled to get the patent for the beta crystalline form of a chemical compound called Imatinib Mesylate which is a therapeutic drug for chronic myeloid leukemia and certain kinds of tumours and is marketed under the names "Glivec" or "Gleevec".

5. Jürg Zimmermann invented a number of derivatives of N-phenyl-2-pyrimidine-amine, one of which is CGP 571481 in free base form (later given the International Nonproprietary Name 'Imatinib' by the World Health Organisation). These derivatives, including Imatinib, are capable of inhibiting certain protein kinases. . . .The N-phenyl-2-pyrimidine-amine derivatives, including Imatinib, were submitted for patent in the US. The application was made on April 28, 1994 and patent was granted on May 28, 1996 under US Patent No. 5,521,184 (hereinafter referred to as 'the Zimmermann Patent'). The Zimmermann compounds (i.e., derivatives of N-phenyl-2-pyrimidine-amine) were also granted a European patent under Patent No. EP-A-0 564 409.

The appellant claims that beginning with Imatinib in free base form (as the 'educt'), in a two-stage invention they first produced its methanesulfonic acid addition salt, Imatinib Mesylate, and then proceeded to develop the beta crystalline form of the salt of Imatinib. . . .

8. The appellant filed the application (Application No.1602/MAS/1998) for grant of patent for Imatinib Mesylate in beta crystalline form at the Chennai Patent Office on July 17, 1998. In the application it claimed that the invented product, the beta crystal form of Imatinib Mesylate, has (i) more beneficial flow properties: (ii) better thermodynamic stability; and (iii) lower hygroscopicity than the alpha crystal form of Imatinib Mesylate. It further claimed that the aforesaid properties makes the invented product "new" (and superior!) as it "stores better and is easier to process"; has "better processability of the methanesulfonic acid addition salt of a compound of formula I", and has a "further advantage for processing and storing".

9. It is significant to note that the comparison of the aforesaid properties of the beta crystal form of Imatinib Mesylate was made with its alpha crystal form. In the patent application, there is no claim of superiority of the beta crystal form of Imatinib Mesylate in regard to the aforesaid three properties, or any other property, over the starting material Imatinib, or even over Imatinib Mesylate in amorphous form or any form other than the alpha crystal form. On the contrary, insofar as Imatinib in free base form is concerned . . .

10. . . . After the application was made and before it was taken up for consideration, a number of amendments were introduced in the Indian Patents Act, 1970, which brought about fundamental changes in the patent law of the country. The appellant was, however, fully aware of these changes in the law and, in order to reinforce its claim for patent for the subject product and to bring its claim within the four corners of the changed law, it filed four (4) affidavits of certain experts, two of which stated that the beta crystal form of Imatinib Mesylate has much higher bioavailability as compared to Imatinib in free base form. In due course, we shall examine how far the properties attributed to the subject product in the patent application and the affidavits make it "new" and entitled to grant of patent, but for the moment we may note how the case has come to the present stage.

13. The appellant's application for patent was taken out of the "mailbox" for consideration only after amendments were made in the Patents Act, with effect from January 1, 2005. But before it was taken up for consideration, the patent application had attracted five (5) pre-grant oppositions in terms of section 25(1) of the Act. And it was in response to the pre-grant oppositions that the appellant had filed the affidavits on the issue of bioavailability of Imatinib Mesylate in beta crystalline form.

14. The Assistant Controller of Patents and Designs heard all the parties on December 15, 2005, as provided under rule 55 of the Patent Rules, 2003, and rejected the appellant's application for grant of patent to the subject product by 5 (five) separate, though similar, orders passed on January 25, 2006 on the 5 (five) opposition petitions. The Assistant Controller held that the invention claimed by the appellant was anticipated by prior publication, i.e., the Zimmermann patent; that the invention claimed by the appellant was obvious to a person skilled in the art in view of the disclosure provided in the Zimmermann patent specifications; and further that the patentability of the alleged invention was disallowed by section 3(d) of the Act. . . .

17. The IPAB reversed the findings of the Assistant Controller on the issues of anticipation and obviousness. It held that the appellant's invention satisfied the tests of novelty and non-obviousness, and further that in view of the amended section 133, the appellant was fully entitled to get July 18, 1997, the date on which the patent application was made in Switzerland, as the priority date for his application in India. The IPAB, however, held that the patentability of the subject product was hit by section 3(d) of the Act. . . .

21. Against the order of the IPAB the appellant came directly to this Court in a petition under Article 136 of the Constitution. . . . In connection with the case of the appellant, the first and foremost thing that needs to be kept in mind is that it falls in the transitional period between two fundamentally different patent regimes. . . . Between January 1, 1995 and

January 1, 2005, the Patents Act, 1970, underwent wide ranging changes, but if we are asked to identify the single most important change brought about in the law of patent in India as a result of the country's obligations under the international agreement, we would unhesitatingly say the deletion of section 5 from the Patents Act, which opened the doors to product patents in the country. It is, however, important to note that the removal of section 5 from the statute book was accompanied by amendments in clauses (j) and (ja) of section 2(1), apart from some other ancillary clauses of section 2(1), as well as amendments in section 3, which redefined the concepts of invention and patentability. . . .

94. We have seen earlier that, in course of the debate in Parliament, an amendment (by way of addition) in clause (d) of section 3 was proposed by the Government in order to allay the fears of the members from the Opposition concerning the introduction of product patents for pharmaceuticals and agricultural chemicals, and it was on the Government's assurance that the proposed amendment in section 3(d) (besides some other changes in the Act) would take care of the apprehensions about the abuse of product patent in medicines and agricultural chemical substances that the Bill was passed by Parliament. We once again examine here what was the amendment introduced in section 3(d) by the amending Act of 2005. Immediately before its amendment in 2005, section 3(d) was, in the Patents (Amendment) Ordinance, 2004 (Ordinance No. 7 of 2004), as under:—

> "Section 3. What are not inventions.—The following are not inventions within the meaning of this Act,—
>
> (d) the mere discovery of any new property or mere new use for a known substance or of the mere use of a known process, machine or apparatus unless such known process results in a new product or employs at least one new reactant."

95. After the amendment with effect from Jan 1, 2005, section 3(d) stands as under:—

> "**Section 3. What are not inventions.**—The following are not inventions within the meaning of this Act,—
>
> (d) **the mere discovery of a new form of a known substance which does not result in the enhancement of the known efficacy of that substance or** the mere discovery of any new property or new use for a known substance or of the mere use of a known process, machine or apparatus unless such known process results in a new product or employs at least one new reactant.
>
> **Explanation.—For the purposes of this clause, salts, esters, ethers, polymorphs, metabolites, pure form, particle size, isomers, mixtures of isomers, complexes, combinations and other derivatives of known substance shall be considered to be the same substance, unless they differ significantly in properties with regard to efficacy."**

97. A perusal of the Parliamentary debate would further reveal that the whole debate centered on medicines and drugs. It would not be an exaggeration to say that eighty per cent of the debate was focused on medicines and drugs and the remaining twenty per cent on agricultural chemicals. In the entire debate, no substance of any other kind came under discussion.

98. The aforementioned amendment in section 3(d) is one of the most crucial amendments that saw the Bill through Parliament and, as noted, the amendment is primarily in respect of medicines and drugs. . . .

105. Admittedly, the genesis of this patent application lies in one of the derivatives of N-phenyl-2-pyrimidine-amine in free base called Imatinib, vide example 21 of the Zimmermann patent. According to the appellant, beginning with Imatinib, the subject product, i.e., Imatinib Mesylate in beta crystalline form, was brought to being by not one but two inventions. . . .

108. The subject product admittedly emerges from the Zimmermann patent. Hence, in order to test the correctness of the claim made on behalf of the appellant, that the subject product is brought into being through inventive research, we need to examine in some detail the Zimmermann patent and certain developments that took place on that basis.

109. An application for grant of patent for the Zimmermann invention (Pyrimidine Derivatives and Processes for the Preparation thereof) was filed in the United States of America on April 2, 1993, by Ciba Geigy1 (US Patent Application No. 08/042,322). This application was abandoned and another continuation-in-part application was then filed on April 28, 1994 (US Patent Application No. 5,521,184). The Zimmermann invention related to N-phenyl-2-pyrimidine-amine derivatives (called, "formula I" in the patent application), and the compounds thereof, the process for their preparation, and to their therapeutic uses. In the patent application, it was expressly stated that the compounds of formula I included their respective salts:

> "Salt-forming groups in a compound of formula I are groups or radicals having basic or acidic properties. Compounds having at least one basic group or at least one basic radical, for example a free amino group, a pyrazinyl radical or a pyridyl radical, **may form acid addition salts, for example with inorganic acids, such as hydrochloric acid, sulfuric acid or a phosphoric acid, or with suitable organic carboxylic or sulfonic acids**. . . ."
>
> Further:
>
> "Owing to the close relationship between the novel compounds in free form and in the form of their salts, including those salts that can be used as intermediates, for example in the purification of the novel compounds or for the identification thereof, hereinbefore and hereinafter **any reference to the free compounds should be understood as including the corresponding salts, where appropriate and expedient.**"

114. The US Patent No. 5,521,184 (the Zimmermann patent) was granted on May 28, 1996.

115. Later, the appellant made the application for patent for beta crystalline form of Imatinib Mesylate (the subject of the present appeals) in the US on January 18, 2000. The US patent for beta crystalline form of Imatinib Mesylate was granted to the appellant about five and a half years later on May 17, 2005 following the order of the US Appellate Court dated November 23, 2003. It is, however, interesting to note that Gleevec, the drug was launched much earlier in the market, on the basis of the Zimmermann patent itself.

116. On April 9, 1998, the appellant filed the Investigational New Drug Application (IND# 55,666) for Gleevec and on February 27, 2001, the original New Drug Application (NDA # 21-335) before the Food and Drug Administration (FDA), USA, for Imatinib Mesylate, formerly STI571, CGP57148B (capsules) for the treatment of patients with Chronic Myeloid Leukemia. The application contained results of extensive preclinical, technical and clinical research. . . .

117. In the patent information furnished in connection with the NDA as required under (US Code) 21 C.F.R. §314.53, the active ingredient of the drug was stated as Imatinib Mesylate. The Drug Substance (active ingredient), Drug Product (composition/formulation) and method of use were declared to be covered by US Patent No. 5,521,184 (i.e. the Zimmermann patent). It was further declared that the United States Patent No. 5,521,184 covered the composition, formulation, and/or method of use of Imatinib Mesylate (STI571).

119. The FDA approval for the drug Gleevec (Imatinib Mesylate) 50 mg and 100 mg capsules was granted vide Letter dated May 10, 2001. Following this, the drug was commercially launched in the market long before the grant of patent for beta crystalline form of Imatinib Mesylate.

120. In the package insert of Gleevec™ (Imatinib Mesylate capsules) the description of the drug was stated as follows:

> "GLEEVEC™ capsules contain imatinib mesylate equivalent to 100 mg of imatinib free base. Imatinib mesylate is designed chemically as 4-[(4-Methyl-1-piperazinyl)

methyl]-N-[4-methyl-3-[[4-(3-pyridinyl)-2-pyrimidinyl]amino]-phenyl] benzamide methanesulfonate. . . ."

121. After the grant of drug approval for Gleevec, on July 3, 2001, the appellant made a Patent Term Extension Application for the Zimmermann patent (US Patent No. 5,521,184) under 35 USC §156(g)(1)(B), for extending the term of the patent for the time taken in the regulatory review for Gleevec. This application leaves no room for doubt that Imatinib Mesylate, marketed under the name Gleevec, was submitted for drug approval as covered by the Zimmermann patent. . . .

123. It is noted above that the appellant had made an application no. 09/463,097 in the USA for grant of patent for beta crystalline form of Imatinib Mesylate. The application was rejected by the examiner and, against the examiner's decision, the appellant preferred an appeal (that is, appeal no. 2003-0919) before the Board of Patent Appeals and Interferences. The Board of Patent Appeals, by its judgment and order dated November 23, 2003, allowed the appellant's appeal and reversed the examiner's decision. . . .

124. From the above passage from the judgment, it is evident that, according to the Board of Patent Appeals, the Zimmermann patent teaches any person skilled in the art how to use Imatinib, a compound of formula I, or a pharmaceutically acceptable salt thereof, in a pharmaceutical composition for treating tumours or in a method of treating warm-blooded animals suffering from a tumoral disease. However, the Board of Patent Appeals held that the teaching in the Zimmermann patent did not go beyond Imatinib Mesylate and did not extend to beta crystalline form of Imatinib Mesylate, which represented a *manipulative step*[36] in a method of treating tumor disease in a patient.

126. From the above discussion it would be clear that the drug Gleevec directly emanates from the Zimmermann patent and comes to the market for commercial sale. Since the grant of the Zimmermann patent, the appellant has maintained that Gleevec (that is, Imatinib Mesylate) is part of the Zimmermann patent. It obtained drug approval for Gleevec on that basis. . . . Not only the appellant but the US Board of Patent Appeals, in its judgment granting patent for beta crystalline form of Imatinib Mesylate, proceeded on the basis that though the beta crystal form might not have been covered by the Zimmermann patent, the Zimmermann patent had the teaching for the making of Imatinib Mesylate from Imatinib, and for its use in a pharmacological compositions for treating tumours or in a method of treating warmblooded animals suffering from a tumoral disease. . . .

133. We thus find no force in the submission that the development of Imatinib Mesylate from Imatinib is outside the Zimmermann patent and constitutes an invention as understood in the law of patent in India. . . .

157. In light of the discussions made above, we firmly reject the appellant's case that Imatinib Mesylate is a new product and the outcome of an invention beyond the Zimmermann patent. We hold and find that Imatinib Mesylate is a known substance from the Zimmermann patent itself. Not only is Imatinib Mesylate known as a substance in the Zimmermann patent, but its pharmacological properties are also known in the Zimmermann patent and in the article published in the Cancer Research journal referred to above. The consequential finding, therefore, is that Imatinib Mesylate does not qualify the test of "invention" as laid down in section 2(1)(j) and section 2(1)(ja) of the Patents Act, 1970.

158. This leaves us with the beta crystal form of Imatinib Mesylate, which, for the sake of argument, may be accepted to be new, in the sense that it is not known from the Zimmermann

36. Not an "inventive step"! A "manipulative step" may or may not be an "inventive step", which is the requirement under Indian law.

patent. (Whether or not it involves an "inventive step" is another matter, and there is no need to go into that aspect of the matter now.) Now, the beta crystalline form of Imatinib Mesylate being a pharmaceutical substance and moreover a polymorph of Imatinib Mesylate, it directly runs into section 3(d) of the Act with the explanation appended to the provision. . . .

160. On facts also we are unable to accept that Imatinib Mesylate or even Imatinib was not a known substance with known efficacy. . . .

161. The subject product, that is, beta crystalline form of Imatinib Mesylate, is thus clearly a new form of a known substance, i.e., Imatinib Mesylate, of which the efficacy was well known. It, therefore, fully attracts section 3(d) and must be shown to satisfy the substantive provision and the explanation appended to it.

162. We now proceed to examine how far the beta crystalline form of Imatinib Mesylate stands up to the test of section 3(d) of the Act. It is noted, in the earlier part of judgment, that the patent application submitted by the appellant contains a clear and unambiguous averment that all the therapeutic qualities of beta crystalline form of Imatinib Mesylate are also possessed by Imatinib in free base. . . .

163. Now, when all the pharmacological properties of beta crystalline form of Imatinib Mesylate are equally possessed by Imatinib in free base form or its salt, where is the question of the subject product having any enhanced efficacy over the known substance of which it is a new form?

165. It further needs to be noted that, on the issue of section 3(d), there appears to be a major weakness in the case of the appellant. There is no clarity at all as to what is the substance immediately preceding the subject product, the beta crystalline form of Imatinib Mesylate.

170. It is to be noted that the higher solubility of the beta crystalline form of Imatinib Mesylate is being compared not to Imatinib Mesylate but, once again, to Imatinib in free base form. The whole case of the appellant, as made out in the subject application and the affidavits, is that the subject product, the beta crystalline form of Imatinib Mesylate, is derived from Imatinib, and that the substance immediately preceding the beta crystalline form is not Imatinib Mesylate but Imatinib in free base form. This position is sought to be canvassed in the subject application and the affidavits on the premise that the Zimmermann patent ended at Imatinib in free base and did not go beyond to Imatinib Mesylate. Not only is this premise unfounded as shown earlier, but the appellant itself appears to take a somewhat different stand, as before this Court it was contended that the subject product, in terms of invention, is two stages removed from Imatinib in free base, and the substance immediately preceding the subject product is Imatinib Mesylate (non-crystalline).

171. That being the position, the appellant was obliged to show the enhanced efficacy of the beta crystalline form of Imatinib Mesylate over Imatinib Mesylate (non-crystalline). There is, however, no material in the subject application or in the supporting affidavits to make any comparison of efficacy, or even solubility, between the beta crystalline form of Imatinib Mesylate and Imatinib Mesylate (non-crystalline).

172. As regards the averments made in the two affidavits, for all one knows the higher solubility that is attributed to the beta crystalline form of Imatinib Mesylate may actually be a property of Imatinib Mesylate itself. One does not have to be an expert in chemistry to know that salts normally have much better solubility than compounds in free base form. If that be so, the additional properties that may be attributed to the beta crystalline form of Imatinib Mesylate would be limited to the following:

i. More beneficial flow properties,
ii. Better thermodynamic stability, and
iii. Lower hygroscopicity

173. The aforesaid properties, ("physical attributes" according to Manley), would give the subject product improved processability and better and longer storability but, as we shall see presently, on the basis of those properties alone, the beta crystalline form of Imatinib Mesylate certainly cannot be said to possess enhanced efficacy over Imatinib Mesylate, the known substance immediately preceding it, within the meaning of section 3(d) of the Act.

180. What is "efficacy"? Efficacy means "the ability to produce a desired or intended result". Hence, the test of efficacy in the context of section 3(d) would be different, depending upon the result the product under consideration is desired or intended to produce. In other words, the test of efficacy would depend upon the function, utility or the purpose of the product under consideration. Therefore, in the case of a medicine that claims to cure a disease, the test of efficacy can only be "therapeutic efficacy". The question then arises, what would be the parameter of therapeutic efficacy and what are the advantages and benefits that may be taken into account for determining the enhancement of therapeutic efficacy? With regard to the genesis of section 3(d), and more particularly the circumstances in which section 3(d) was amended to make it even more constrictive than before, we have no doubt that the "therapeutic efficacy" of a medicine must be judged strictly and narrowly. Our inference that the test of enhanced efficacy in case of chemical substances, especially medicine, should receive a narrow and strict interpretation is based not only on external factors but there are sufficient internal evidence that leads to the same view. It may be noted that the text added to section 3(d) by the 2005 amendment lays down the condition of "enhancement of the known efficacy". Further, the explanation requires the derivative to "differ significantly in properties **with regard to efficacy**". What is evident, therefore, is that not all advantageous or beneficial properties are relevant, but only such properties that directly relate to efficacy, which in case of medicine, as seen above, is its therapeutic efficacy.

187. In whatever way therapeutic efficacy may be interpreted, this much is absolutely clear: that the physico-chemical properties of beta crystalline form of Imatinib Mesylate, namely (i) more beneficial flow properties, (ii) better thermodynamic stability, and (iii) lower hygroscopicity, may be otherwise beneficial but these properties cannot even be taken into account for the purpose of the test of section 3(d) of the Act, since these properties have nothing to do with therapeutic efficacy. . . .

189. . . .No material has been offered to indicate that the beta crystalline form of Imatinib Mesylate will produce an enhanced or superior efficacy (therapeutic) on molecular basis than what could be achieved with Imatinib free base in vivo animal model.

190. Thus, in whichever way section 3(d) may be viewed, whether as setting up the standards of "patentability" or as an extension of the definition of "invention", it must be held that on the basis of the materials brought before this Court, the subject product, that is, the beta crystalline form of Imatinib Mesylate, fails the test of section 3(d), too, of the Act.

191. We have held that the subject product, the beta crystalline form of Imatinib Mesylate, does not qualify the test of section 3(d) of the Act but that is not to say that section 3(d) bars patent protection for all incremental inventions of chemical and pharmaceutical substances. It will be a grave mistake to read this judgment to mean that section 3(d) was amended with the intent to undo the fundamental change brought in the patent regime by deletion of section 5 from the Parent Act. That is not said in this judgment.

192. Section 2(1)(j) defines "invention" to mean, "a new product or . . .", but the new product in chemicals and especially pharmaceuticals may not necessarily mean something altogether new or completely unfamiliar or strange or not existing before. It may mean something "different from a recent previous" or "one regarded as better than what went before" or "in addition to another or others of the same kind". However, in case of chemicals and especially pharmaceuticals if the product for which patent protection is claimed is a new form

of a known substance with known efficacy, then the subject product must pass, in addition to clauses (j) and (ja) of section 2(1), the test of enhanced efficacy as provided in section 3(d) read with its explanation.

195. In view of the findings that the patent product, the beta crystalline form of Imatinib Mesylate, fails in both the tests of invention and patentability as provided under clauses (j), (ja) of section 2(1) and section 3(d) respectively, the appeals filed by Novartis AG fail and are dismissed with cost.

## NOTES AND QUESTIONS

**1.** Novartis, Pfizer, and the U.S. Chamber of Commerce reacted to the decision of the Indian Supreme Court with charges that the decision threatened to undermine future innovation in the area of pharmaceuticals. Does anything about the Indian Supreme Court decision strike you as "anti-innovation"? *See also* Frederick M. Abbott, *The Judgment in Novartis v. India: What the Supreme Court of India Said*, Inside Views, IP-WATCH, April 4, 2013.

**2.** In March 2012, the Controller of Patents of India granted a compulsory license to the Indian generic manufacturer, NATCO, for the drug "Sorafenib tosylate" patented in India by Bayer and sold under the name Nexavar. (*In the matter of Natco and Bayer*, Compulsory License Application No. 1 of 2011 (Mumbai), granted March 9, 2012.) Nexavar is used in the treatment of kidney and liver cancer. Relying on the terms of the Indian Patents Act, the Controller granted the compulsory license on three grounds: (1) lack of accessibility, (2) lack of reasonable affordability, and (3) failure to work the patented locally. Bayer had argued that another Indian generic manufacturer, Cipla, was already supplying low-priced sorafenib to the Indian market (contending that the Bayer patent is invalid), and that Bayer had made some low-priced Nexavar available under an affordable access program. The Controller found that Bayer's prices far exceeded what the public could afford, including with governmental assistance, and that since Bayer contended that Cipla was acting illegally, it could not justify its own failure to provide access on the basis of Cipla's conduct. The Controller found that Bayer was obligated to manufacture the drug locally unless it provided some grounds making that impracticable. The Indian Intellectual Property Appellate Board affirmed the decision of the Controller on the grounds of lack of accessibility and lack of reasonable affordability, but it modified the holding regarding local working, essentially finding that the question whether local working is required must be determined on a case-by-case basis. (*Bayer v. India*, Intellectual Property Appellate Board, Chennai, decided March 4, 2013.) Bayer appealed to the Indian Supreme Court, which in December 2014 rejected the appeal.

# V. PATENTS AND THE CONVENTION ON BIOLOGICAL DIVERSITY (CBD)

## A. The CBD and the WTO TRIPS Agreement

See Chapter 1, section IX, including the Note summary of recent developments adapted from the 2006 Report of the Committee on International Trade Law to the International Law Association.

## B. The CBD at WIPO

The relationship between the CBD and international patent system has been the subject of extensive dialogue and study within WIPO as well as the WTO. The following is part of a WIPO study of disclosure requirements and how they might further the objectives of the CBD.

### WIPO Intergovernmental Committee on Intellectual Property and Genetic Resources, Traditional Knowledge and Folklore*

## *Technical Study on Disclosure Requirements in Patent Systems Related to Genetic Resources and Traditional Knowledge*

. . . The underlying, key issue is how to characterize the necessary relationship between the genetic resource and traditional knowledge on the one hand, and the claimed invention on the other. Discussion of possible disclosure requirements has already covered many ways of expressing this linkage. Better characterizing this linkage should also clarify the range and duration of obligations that may attach to such resources and knowledge, within the source country and in foreign jurisdictions, and how far these obligations "reach through" subsequent inventive activities and ensuing patent applications. General patent law principles provide certain more specific ways of expressing this relationship, even if the objective of the requirement is not conceived in traditional patent terms. Patent law may also be drawn on to clarify or implement more generally stated disclosure requirements: for example, a general requirement to disclose genetic resources used in the invention may be difficult to define in practice, and may [be] implemented through a more precise test that requires disclosure only when access to the resources would be necessary to reproduce the invention.

Another key issue is the legal basis of the disclosure requirement in question, and its relationship with the processing of patent applications, the grant of patents and the exercise of patent rights. This raises also the legal and practical interaction of the disclosure requirement with other areas of law beyond the patent system, including the law of other jurisdictions. Some of the legal and policy questions that arise are:

- the potential role of the patent system in one country in monitoring and giving effect to contracts, licenses, and regulations in other areas of law and in other jurisdictions, and the resolution of private international law or "choice of law" issues that arise in interpreting and applying across jurisdictions contract obligations and laws determining legitimacy of access and downstream use of GR/TK;
- the nature of the disclosure obligation, in particular whether it is essentially a transparency mechanism to assist with the monitoring of compliance with non-patent laws and regulations, or whether it incorporates compliance;
- the ways in which patent law and procedure can take account of the circumstances and context of inventive activity that are unrelated to the assessment of the invention itself and the eligibility of the applicant to be granted a patent;
- the situations in which national authorities can impose additional administrative, procedural or substantive legal requirements on patent applicants, within existing international legal standards applying to patent procedures, and the role of non-IP international law and legal principles in this regard;
- the legal and operational distinction (to the extent one can be drawn) between patent formalities or procedural requirements, and substantive criteria for patentability, and ways of characterizing the legal implications of such distinctions;
- clarification of the implications of issues such as the concept of "country of origin" in relation to genetic resources covered by multilateral access and benefit-sharing systems, differing

* Study No. 3, Feb. 2004, available at www.wipo.int.

> approaches to setting and enforcing conditions for access and benefit sharing in the context of patent disclosure requirements, and coherence between mechanisms for recording or certifying conditions of access and the patent system.

A further area for clarification is what actions of the inventor or patent applicant are to be monitored or regulated through a disclosure requirement—the actual use of the GR/TK (including its use in the inventive process), or the act of filing a patent application as such. The policy concern may relate to the legitimacy of the research or commercial behavior that makes use of the GR/TK (including prior informed consent of TK or GR holders). In this case, the patent application has a secondary role in providing evidence of such behavior. The concern may relate to the very filing [of] a patent application or holding a patent (for instance, where prior informed consent is given to research but not seeking IP, or prior informed consent includes agreement on assignment, coownership or similar disposition of ensuing IP).

The study concludes by noting that the core issues raised are the subjects of ongoing international policy debate. They may involve specific policy choices, such as the distinction between formal requirements or "form or contents" and substantive patent law and how to certify the basis of prior informed consent or legitimacy of access to GR/TK. It observes that some key legal concepts and approaches raised in the debate are so far untested, are the subject of policy development, or are in the early stages of implementation and practical experience, and thus cannot be definitively analyzed. Accordingly, the study is offered as a resource to facilitate the continuing debate, not to prescribe any particular approach.

## C. The CBD at WHO

When outbreaks of contagious pathogens occur, they create risks to public health not only for the people of the country in which the outbreak initially takes place, but they may also spill over and affect populations in a particular region, or throughout the world. The COVID-19 pandemic exemplified such a dangerous spillover effect, with devastating consequences not only for public health, but for the global economy as well. In order to develop vaccines, therapeutics, and diagnostics to combat dangerous pathogens, scientists require access to the pathogens themselves, and, in more recent years, access to the genetic code within those pathogens. Again, as illustrated in the case of COVID-19, the sequenced genetic code of the SARS-CoV-2 virus was sufficient to allow work to begin promptly on the development of "countermeasures."

The relationship between access to genetic resources and the sharing of the benefits of that access was the subject of significant international tension at the outset of the avian flu epidemic in the mid-2000s (see Note 5 below). The tensions arose when Indonesia indicated that it would refuse to supply samples of the virus until an agreement was worked out regarding its subsequent access to any health products developed to counter the virus. This immediately generated a dialogue revolving around whether viruses are "global public goods," materials in the "public domain," or subject to control by national sovereigns. There is a difference between global public goods, which in principle should be open to all but subject to an agreement about sharing (as in the deep seabed by way of illustration), and materials in the public domain, which in principle are freely available to all. Generally those favoring open access simply referred to viruses as global public goods. The WHO initially took the position that viruses are global public goods. However, various experts reminded WHO that pursuant to the Convention on Biological Diversity (CBD) and customary international law, national governments exercise sovereign control over resources located within their territories. In principle, there is no difference between oil reserves, forests, and pathogenic viruses. Indonesia might therefore be well within its rights to refuse to supply virus samples until its concerns were satisfied.

Negotiation of the PIP Framework took about two years, and ultimately produced a compromise on key issues. The WHO research centers that initially received vaccine samples would not seek to patent the genetic sequences of those samples. Private sector pharmaceutical companies that wanted access to samples would be required to enter into material transfer agreements. They would be allowed to patent new health products, but in return they would commit either to providing vaccines or other products as developed to a WHO stockpile, or they would engage in technology transfer to developing WHO members. This does not fulfill the early demands of Indonesia and its developing country supporters who had been looking for a firm commitment for assistance in building their domestic R&D and manufacturing capacity to address future outbreaks. It was a compromise. And this compromise shadows the current negotiations at WHO regarding a potential Pandemic Accord or amendments to the IHR.

Issues surrounding "inequitable" access to vaccines and other health products loomed large during the COVID-19 pandemic as people living in high and upper-middle income countries were vaccinated significantly earlier and in greater numbers than those in low and lower-middle income countries. As a consequence, there is attention being paid among developing countries to develop their own capacity to create and manufacture vaccines, therapeutics, and treatments so as to avoid dependence on high income countries in future public health emergencies. While some high income countries' governments express support for this initiative, as a practical matter not much changes. Some of the major vaccine producers have decided to address the problem by announcing that they will build their own facilities in lower income countries. High income governments continue to advocate for reliance on voluntary contributions during emergencies. Once again, the terms of access to genetic resources and information are one of the few bargaining chips in the hands of the developing countries who are demanding commitments to technology transfer and financing for their own efforts. The negotiations in late 2023 are contentious and slow-moving. It is not clear that the result will be an improvement from a developing country standpoint of the result achieved in the PIP Framework negotiations.

## NOTES AND QUESTIONS

**1.** Negotiations on an international legal instrument on IP issues related to GRs take place in the WIPO Intergovernmental Committee on Intellectual Property and Genetic Resources, Traditional Knowledge and Folklore. In July 2022, the WIPO General Assembly decided to convene a Diplomatic Conference to conclude an International Legal Instrument Relating to Intellectual Property, Genetic Resources and Traditional Knowledge Associated with Genetic Resources no later than 2024.

**2.** *See* ABS Capacity Development Initiative-WIPO, *A Guide to Intellectual Property Issues in Access and Benefit-sharing Agreements* (2018), http://www.wipo.int/edocs/pubdocs/en/wipo_pub_1052.pdf/.

**3.** An important U.S. federal decision concerning bio-prospecting in Yellowstone National Park is *Edmonds Institute v. Babbitt*, 93 F. Supp. 2d 63 (D.D.C. 2000). There has been increasing attention to the subject of access to biological resources and benefit sharing in the United States since that decision.

**4.** You represent a nongovernmental organization in India that is concerned with preventing foreign enterprises from patenting indigenous Indian plant varieties that exhibit commercially useful properties. Will requiring patent applicants in Europe, Japan, the United States, and elsewhere to disclose to the patent office the geographic location from where biological specimens were obtained adequately serve your client's interests? What other mechanisms might you suggest? How do potential enforcement costs affect your analysis?

**5.** Whether and to what extent patents should be granted on pathogenic biological materials as found in nature and/or as modified by human intervention was a significant issue in WHO negotiations regarding "pathogen sharing," as well as under the CBD and its recently negotiated Nagoya Protocol. *See* Frederick M. Abbott, *An International Legal Framework for the Sharing of Pathogens: Issues and Challenges*, ICTSD Programme on IPRs and Sustainable Development, Issue Paper No. 30, October 2010.

## VI. PATENT LICENSING, TRANSFER OF TECHNOLOGY, AND COMPETITION

The patent right is exploited in a number of different ways. Licensing plays a significant role in many of the ways a patent is used. The role of patent licensing, as well as possibilities for misuse, are considered in the following presentation made to the WIPO Open Forum on the draft Substantive Patent Law Treaty in March 2006.

**Frederick M. Abbott***

### *Patent Licensing, Competition Law and the Draft Substantive Patent Law Treaty*

1. Patent licensing may enhance the development of new technologies and making them available to the public.
   a. Patent licensing may facilitate access by researchers to third-party technologies and facilitate experimentation with a view toward commercialization or public use;[1]
   b. Patent licensing may facilitate movement of new technologies from the research phase to the commercialization phase as small and medium enterprises out-license inventions to more highly capitalized enterprises;
   c. Patent licensing may provide a means for enterprises to negotiate the "patent thicket" so as to overcome obstacles to incremental innovation
      i. In areas such as standards-setting, sharing of patented technologies may be necessary to maintenance of competitive markets. . . .
   d. Patent licensing may facilitate joint research and development, accelerating technology development and spreading risk;
   e. Patent licensing may facilitate partitioning of R & D and production functions, allowing production at most efficient locations without corollary investments in R & D.
2. Patent licensing is a tool for the transfer of technology between developed and developing countries.
   a. Positive welfare effects dependent on validity of underlying patent. Licensing and payment of royalties on technology otherwise in the public domain is unjustified social expense, [although services payment for training of personnel using public domain information may be justifiable—EDS.];

* March 2, 2006, Open Forum on the Draft Substantive Patent Law Treaty, World Intellectual Property Organization, Geneva, available at http://www.wipo.int.

1. Note that U.S. Supreme Court in *Merck v. Integra Lifesciences*, [545 U.S. 193 (2005)] dramatically expanded scope of permissible noninfringing uses of patented pharmaceutical technologies during drug research and development phase, reducing need for licensing prior to market entry.

b. "Securitization" of invention encourages sharing of information based on rent or royalty stream expectation;
c. Forms of enterprise combination and licensing arrangements highly variable—parent-subsidiary, joint venture, independent entities, etc.;
d. Extent to which patent licensing generates improvement to local technology capacity is context specific
    i. Patent licensing may take place in closely-guarded intracorporate setting which may limit local diffusion, or may take place in open setting (e.g., to university research institution) which may encourage diffusion
    ii. Associated "know-how" licensing affects level of technology transfer
    iii. Restrictive licensing terms may substantially affect economic and social value of patent license to transferee country.

3. Patent licensing is subject to anticompetitive abuse.
    a. "Patent pools" into which enterprises combine their technologies may be used to create prohibitive market entry barriers, facilitating cartelization of markets;
    b. Restrictive third-party licensing terms (e.g., exclusive grantbacks) may be used to foreclose emergence of competitors;
    c. Patent licensing terms can be used to leverage market power, such as through product tying arrangements and block licensing;
    d. Patent licensing agreements may include terms generally disfavored in competition law, such as fixing of resale prices, restricting output and dividing territories among horizontal competitors;
    e. No-challenge clauses in patent licenses encourage unearned surplus payments to holders of invalid patents;
    f. Patent licensing agreements merit particular scrutiny in the context of licensors holding dominant position on the relevant market.
4. Control of anticompetitive patent licensing is a generally accepted practice among states.
    a. The WTO TRIPS Agreement includes provisions which recognize that intellectual property rights may be abused, that authorize Members to regulate anticompetitive licensing practices and that encourage cooperation in enforcement (e.g., Articles 8.2, 31(k)-(l), 40).[2] Concern with anticompetitive patent licensing is reflected in the original International Trade Organization Charter;
    b. Paris Convention recognizes abuse of patents as grounds for compulsory licensing (Article 5A(2));
    c. Developed country regulation specifically addresses anticompetitive patent licensing arrangements
        i. *See, e.g.*, U.S. Department of Justice/Federal Trade Commission, Antitrust Guidelines for the Licensing of Intellectual Property (1995) [revised edition issued January 12, 2017—Eds.]. Also, the Supreme Court has ruled that patent misuse is an equitable defense to the enforcement of patents (e.g., in the case of certain product tying arrangements). *See also* U.S. Federal Trade Commission, To Promote Innovation: The Proper Balance of Competition and Patent Law and Policy (2003)
        ii. *See, e.g.*, European Commission Regulation No 772/2004 of 27 April 2004 on the application of Article 81(3) of the Treaty to categories of technology transfer agreements and Guidelines on the application of Article 81 of the EC Treaty to technology transfer agreements (2004/C/101/02) [Replaced by European Commission

2. *See* Frederick M. Abbott, *Are the Competition Rules in the WTO TRIPS Agreement Adequate?*, 7 J. Int'l Econ. L. 685 (2005 Oxford).

Guidelines on the application of Article 101 of the Treaty on the Functioning of the European Union to technology transfer agreements, 2014/C 89/03—Eds.]

iii. *See, e.g.*, Fair Trade Commission of Japan (FTCJ), Antimonopoly Act Guidelines Concerning Joint Research and Development, 20 April 1993 [*See also* Guidelines for the Use of Intellectual Property under the Antimonopoly Act (2007, revised 2016)—Eds.]

d. Developing countries address anticompetitive patent licensing through regulation and court decision
   i. *See, e.g.*, Andean Community, Decision 291, Article 14
   ii. Abuse of patent is common grounds in developing country patent legislation for grant of compulsory license
   iii. As a general proposition, developing countries have a lower level of competition law enforcement capacity than the OECD countries. Competition law enforcement tends to be fact intensive, complex and expensive.
e. Proposals from leading experts on competition law for international antitrust regulation routinely address anticompetitive patent licensing practices, *see* International Antitrust Working Group (W. Fikentscher, et al.), Draft International Antitrust Code, at Article 6: Restraints in Connection with Intellectual Property Rights[3];
f. Trend of regulation in OECD is to evaluate patent licensing restrictions under "rule of reason" approach and to limit inquiry where market share of parties is below defined threshold. Nonetheless, certain *per se* (or hardcore) prohibitions remain (e.g., in EU, against exclusive grantbacks)
   i. Specific doctrinal issues are continuously re-examined. For example, U.S. Supreme Court currently considering presumption of patent-based market power in context of tying arrangements (*Illinois Tool Works v. Independent Ink*, No. 04-1329). . . .
g. Current regulatory approach of OECD competition law authorities is not necessarily the best approach for developing countries which tend to have lower levels of enforcement capacity;
h. Developing countries may benefit from greater use of *per se* rules and other positive prohibitions such as characterized EU competition and technology law until 2004.[4]
   i. Developing countries are more likely to be patented-technology importers than exporters
   ii. Developing country markets are generally more susceptible to market power concentration among dominant enterprises than developed country markets
a. Competition law risk assessment should account for these factors. . . .

5. Rules regarding anticompetitive aspects of patent licensing are within the reasonable potential subject matter scope of a Substantive Patent Law Treaty. Such rules might take a positive form, prescribing certain types of conduct or establishing presumptions regarding certain types of conduct. Such rules might take a negative form, making clear that governments are permitted to regulate anticompetitive licensing practices notwithstanding positive obligations regarding the grant of patents. Such rules might include illustrative list of potentially anticompetitive licensing practices.

---

3. *Reprinted in* Public Policy and Global Technological Integration (F. Abbott & D. Gerber eds., 1997) (Kluwer), at Appendix 2. *See also* Wolfgang Fikentscher, *The Draft International Antitrust Code (DIAC) in the Context of International Technological Integration*, *id.* at 211.

4. *See* elaboration in F. Abbott, *supra* note 2.

a. The negotiating history of the GATT Uruguay Round and subsequent efforts within the WTO to establish mandatory positive competition rules suggest obstacles to that approach in the context of SPLT negotiations
   i. In TRIPS Agreement Art. 40, listing of anticompetitive licensing conditions is illustrative of subject matter that may be addressed, not prohibited as mandatory positive obligation
   ii. WTO Trade and Competition Working Group manifested disagreement on limited set of positive rules, with differences between governments at all levels of development.
b. Approaches to regulation of competition tend to vary over time within the same jurisdiction as industrial policy considerations shift. This may argue in favor of preserving regulatory flexibility;
c. Industrial policy considerations of developed and developing countries with respect to application of competition law to patent licensing may differ. Developing countries at different stages of development may also maintain differing industrial policy interests;
d. A negative approach would permit maintenance of regulatory flexibility. For example:

   > Nothing in this [SPLT] shall prevent or hinder a member state from prescribing or enforcing measures to address patent licensing conditions or practices determined to be anticompetitive. Such measures, which may be preventive and remedial, may be enforceable by private and government action, and may include civil damages and criminal penalties.

   Note that the foregoing does not address patent misuse in general because the subject matter of this presentation concerns patent licensing. However, it is reasonable to assume that additional negative provision should be included in SPLT to permit maintenance of regulatory flexibility regarding patent abuse in other contexts, such as abuse of patents by dominant enterprises;
e. A combination approach might negatively preserve regulatory flexibility and positively list potentially anticompetitive practices, along the lines of the WTO TRIPS Agreement
   i. An SPLT provision might also address enhanced enforcement cooperation and capacity-building. . . .

**John Barton***

## *New Trends in Technology Transfer: Implications for National and International Policy*

### Licensing

Very often, a developing-world firm will need to license in some or all of the technology it needs for a particular product. This is especially likely with globalization, for a firm that hopes to export to the developed world may need a license of developed-world patent rights covering the technology. Even [if] it is marketing locally, it may face local competition from developed nation firms who hold local patents; the firm needs to obtain a license to use the relevant

* ICTSD Intellectual Property and Sustainable Development Series, Issue Paper No. 18, Feb. 2007.

technology, unless it can find a way to design around those patents. And, the licensing of existing technology will often be cheaper and faster than re-engineering that technology.

In negotiating to obtain such a license, the bargaining position of the local firm depends on the economics of the specific situation. For the licensor (and to a certain extent for the developing nation's economy as well), licensed production is an alternative to FDI—a foreign firm can supply a global or a local market through its own facility in a developing nation or alternatively through license to a firm in a developing nation. Economics favors FDI over the license when technologies are changing very rapidly. This is because the relationship between the foreign supplier and the local manufacturer can be updated more easily through managerial negotiations within one entity than through formal revisions of a contract between two entities. The license is favored when the licensee brings special knowledge of the local environment, or when the technologies are changing in such a way that new licensors or licensees with new core expertise are needed from time to time. Thus, if the local firm holds important comparative advantages, such as the semiconductor production skills held by Taiwanese firms, then it is in a position to negotiate effectively for a cooperative agreement under which it obtains the necessary licenses. And, TRIPS probably favors FDI over licensing.[65]

If the agreement is to produce a product for a global market, the licensor will be interested in providing the best possible and most up-to-date technology. The globalization paradigm overrides the traditional product cycle model. In some cases, however, the purpose of the license will be for production for a local market. This is likely for service industries; it is also likely for very large markets such as China. In such a situation, the traditional 1970s concerns still apply: a foreign firm may be motivated to supply a less advanced technology for production for the local market, while holding its more advanced technologies for use for global markets and seeking to protect itself from local production with more advanced technologies. Such reticence to supply technology is also likely when the local license is compelled by regulations that, for example, require local partners and restrict FDI. These are contexts in which especially careful negotiation of specific licenses is essential, for the economic incentives of the two parties are less closely aligned than for production for export.

For many of today's technologies, particularly in the computer and communications sectors, new products require a variety of skills, more than available in any single firm. Hence, there is a need for strategic alliances and innovative licensing arrangements in order to produce a product—and a new developing-world firm may be able to develop and contribute one of the relevant areas of expertise. To make these efforts work, it is important to facilitate cooperative research efforts between firms and research entities of different nations. In many industries, strategic research alliances are a measure of the success of firms; they demonstrate that the science and technology are moving faster than can industrial organizations alone. In the biotechnology sector, these are both national and international and lead to what amounts to an integrated North Atlantic industry. In the semiconductor sector, the same kind of integration occurs across the Pacific. Such arrangements will be even more important for developing nations, who will often need access to foreign centers of excellence.

. . .

Insight from recently adopted National IP Strategies (i.e., policy measures taken up by government to improve its IP and innovation ecosystem) show that countries are increasingly considering the broader innovation ecosystem when it comes to policymaking on patent licensing and technology transfer issues. For instance, countries are aligning the goals of their National IP Strategy with the targets of other national plans. The Philippines' National IP

---

65. *See* J. Barton, Patents and the Transfer of Technology to Developing Countries, presented at OECD, Conference on IPR, Innovation and Economic Performance, Paris (Oct. 2003).

Strategy (adopted in 2020), as an example, purports to support the goals of the Philippines Development Plan, a national roadmap on inclusive innovation and entrepreneurship, the national R&D agenda, and a 10-point national socioeconomic agenda.[15] Some National IP Strategies articulate a national position on cross-cutting areas of IP and other public policy; Egypt's National IP Strategy 2022 calls for "implementing rational and balanced IP policies in the field of public health and access to medicine".[16]

Generally, with an overall goal to promote innovation and the generation and commercialization of IPRs, some National IP Strategies establish measures to better equip universities and research institutes with IP policies and training, as well as promote the use of policy levers outside of the IP system to promote R&D, technology transfer, and IP commercialization. These can include tax incentives, R&D-related government procurement, fostering academia-industry collaboration, or establishing R&D funding mechanisms.[17] Some countries acknowledge a need to update or improve the legal framework in the area of IP, technology transfer, and competition. The National IP Strategy of Brazil, for example, calls for

> ". . . continued efforts to identify important areas of study and research for the development of future improvements such as: i) interaction between IP laws and other laws to remove ambiguities and inconsistencies, if any; ii) IP interface with the free competition policy and laws provided for in the Constitution; iii) guidelines for authorities whose jurisdictions impact the administration or enforcement of IPR; iv) protection of business secrets; and v) identify, examine and propose measures to solve possible obstacles involving transfer of technology, know-how and licensing."

## NOTES AND QUESTIONS

**1.** Technology licensing certainly plays an important role in technology transfer but, as the foregoing discussion notes, the extent of technology diffusion is dependent on the terms of licenses and business contexts in which licensing is used. In the 1970s and 1980s, a substantial number of developing countries attempted to compel licensors to employ licensing terms that would encourage diffusion of technology into the local economy. The trend in the 1990s and 2000s has been away from such efforts and reliance on the "free market" to determine the terms of technology licensing. Why do you think developing countries were largely unsuccessful during the 1970s and 1980s in directing the terms of technology transfer? Is it because developed country enterprises own the vast preponderance of patents and thereby are in a stronger position to direct the terms of transfer? Or is it because governments are not well equipped to intervene in business decision making? What other factors may determine the success or failure of attempts by governments to control the terms of technology transfer?

Questions surrounding the terms of technology transfer and patent licensing surrounded the COVID-19 pandemic response. One of the authors of this book prepared a study of the

---

15. National Intellectual Property Strategy, Philippines 2020-2025, https://www.ipophil.gov.ph/national-intellectual-property-strategy-nips/#:~:text=The%20National%20Intellectual%20Property%20Strategy,agricultural%20self%2Dsufficiency%2C%20and%20inclusive/.

16. Egypt National Intellectual Property Strategy, Executive Summary, September 2022, https://www.sis.gov.eg/UP/Culture/Strategic%20Book%20(E).pdf.

17. *See, e.g.*, Albania National Intellectual Property Strategy, 2022-2025, http://dppi.gov.al/en/publikime/strategjia-kombetare/; Brazil National Intellectual Property Strategy, 2021, https://www.in.gov.br/web/dou/-/decreto-n-10.886-de-7-de-dezembro-de-2021-365433440; Colombia National Intellectual Property Policy, 2021, https://colaboracion.dnp.gov.co/CDT/Conpes/Econ%C3%B3micos/4062.pdf; National Intellectual Property Strategy, Philippines 2020-2025, https://www.ipophil.gov.ph/national-intellectual-property-strategy-nips/#:~:text=The%20National%20Intellectual%20Property%20Strategy,agricultural%20self%2Dsufficiency%2C%20and%20inclusive.

role of technology licensing during the pandemic for the WIPO Global Challenges Division. The technological response to the COVID-19 pandemic included a great deal of technology licensing and transfer, both in terms of licensing of basic technologies and downstream technologies used in manufacturing. The COVID-19 response was inequitable on a global basis, but there are a substantial number of reasons for this, including difficulties encountered in the creation of new vaccine candidates (including many failures), the delays inherent in clinical trials and regulatory approvals, difficulties encountered in establishing manufacturing processes and networks, and so forth. There is not much evidence that patents or other IP rights played a significant role in the problems associated with the pandemic response. That does not mean that the developers and owners of IP could not have done more to assist third parties in building manufacturing capacity, such as by transferring trade secret information and assisting with setting up production. But that is not an "IP" problem. It reflects the way the international system for the development, production, and distribution of health products is organized. Perhaps some governments could have "forced" vaccine developers based in their territories to transfer trade secret technology to additional manufacturers, but such action was not seriously contemplated by any government.

**2.** Might "neutral" consultants working on behalf of international or national development agencies seek to identify targets of opportunity for developing country industries to cooperate with developed country industries and help negotiate the terms of patent licensing arrangements?

**3.** Under the auspices of UNITAID, an independent Medicines Patent Pool (MPP) has been established with the objective of improving access to medicines in developing countries. MPP has described its operation and objectives as follows:

> MPP operates as a non-profit voluntary licensing mechanism through partnerships with originator pharmaceutical companies and generic manufacturers that facilitate access and promote innovation.
>
> MPP negotiates licences with patent holders and licenses those patents to multiple manufacturers, who develop the licensed medicine, including new formulations and combinations. The treatments are made available in a defined set of developing countries, sometimes in exchange for royalties.

As of June 2023, 18 patent holders have signed agreements with MPP, 60 generic manufacturers and product developers have sublicenses from MPP, and 148 countries have benefited from access to MPP-licensed products. MPP Strategy 2023-2025 identifies five strategic goals:

> 1 Expand access to innovation medicines for infectious diseases
>
> 2 Establish voluntary licensing as an impactful access mechanism for other diseases and conditions
>
> 3 Facilitate development and access to novel medical technologies
>
> 4 Accelerate equitable access to countermeasures for pandemics and other international health emergencies
>
> 5 Support diversified and sustainable manufacturing capacity

## NOTES

**1.** MPP's mandate includes treatments for people living with HIV, hepatitis C, and tuberculosis, as well as HIV-associated comorbidities. Since 2018, MPP has expanded its mandate to other patented essential medicines on the World Health Organization (WHO)'s Model List of Essential Medicines (EML) as well as medicines with strong potential for future inclusion on the EML. MPP temporarily expanded MPP's mandate to include COVID-19 treatments in 2018 and expanded its mandate into the licensing of technology with an initial focus on COVID-19 vaccines and pandemic preparedness in 2021.

**2.** The important relationship between competition law and IP is discussed more generally in Chapter 5.

## CHAPTER 3

# THE INTERNATIONAL TRADEMARK AND IDENTIFIER SYSTEM

## I. BASIC CHARACTERISTICS OF THE TRADEMARK, SERVICE MARK, TRADE NAME, DOMAIN NAME, AND GEOGRAPHICAL INDICATION

### A. Trademark Subject Matter

A trademark is a sign or symbol used to distinguish the goods or services of one enterprise from those of other enterprises in commerce. The function is fundamentally different from patents. While the latter protect innovation, the former essentially serves the purpose of allowing consumers to distinguish different products on the market. As a corollary, it forms the basis for investment in advertising and marketing of goods and services. Human beings are capable of identifying many different kinds of signs or symbols, including words, other alphanumeric combinations, designs, colors, sounds, scents, shapes, and even textures.

Trademarks and related forms of protection essentially serve three functions. While the first (i.e., distinguishing) is central in legally defining these instruments, investment protection and consumer protection are of equal importance.

*Distinguishing Products (Goods and Services)*

Conceptually, all types of signs or symbols are capable of allowing consumers to distinguish the goods or services of one enterprise from another. The term "trademark" may be used in a narrow sense in connection only with goods, and it may also be used in a broader sense to encompass services. The term "service mark" is specifically used with respect to services, such as accounting, banking, travel, and tourism services. However, even within the broad definition of trademark established by the WTO TRIPS Agreement, some limitations may be placed on the types of signs or symbols constituting trademarks.

*Investment Protection*

From an economic point of view, trademark protection, domain names, trade names, and geographical indications (i.e., identifiers) are employed to protect investment in branding. The resources spent on advertising depend upon trademark protection for success. Building the reputation of a product takes time and resources that intellectual property seeks to protect against "free-riding." Legally, the function of investment protection of trademarks has not yet been well developed within trademark law. Economic and social considerations may influence the legal assessment of trademarks implicitly, and play a role in defining the scope and boundaries of trademark law and of other identifiers.

*Consumer Information and Prevention of Deception*

Inherent to the function of distinguishing products for the purposes of branding, advertising, and markets is the interest of consumers to be able to distinguish products from each other in making choices on the market. Trademarks are an important ingredient of consumer information and a mainstay in realizing freedom of information. Moreover, the different forms of trademarks, including geographical indications, are part of the foundations of labeling of products, which has strongly increased in recent decades and accompanies the life cycle of products. Legally, labeling does not pertain to intellectual property protection but emanates mainly from health, environmental protection, sustainable development, and human rights concerns.

*Acquisition and Distinctiveness of Trademarks and Identifiers*

We are witnessing a gradual convergence of the basis on which trademark rights are recognized. In many national jurisdictions, principally those of civil law countries, trademark rights were traditionally granted solely on the basis of registration at a national (or regional) trademark office, except in the case of so-called well-known and famous trademarks, and without prejudice to protection under the laws of unfair competition. That traditional practice in civil law countries has been giving way to the recognition of rights also based on use (as in common law countries), largely grounded in an unfair competition approach. In other national jurisdictions, principally those of common law countries, trademark rights can be acquired by use in commerce, without the need for registration. However, in the common law countries trademark registration was and remains available and provides significant litigation advantages. Trademarks are ordinarily registered in these countries for reasons of legal security.

The trademark provides its holder with the right to prevent others from using the protected sign on identical or similar goods where such use is likely to cause consumer confusion. There are typically two key questions in a trademark infringement proceeding: first, whether the complainant holds a valid trademark; and second, whether the complained-against party is using it in a way likely to confuse consumers. There are a substantial number of elements that go into answering these questions.

### *1. Distinctiveness*

In order for a sign or symbol to serve as a trademark, it must be capable of distinguishing goods or services; that is, it must be "distinctive." A term that is commonly used in a language to identify a genus or class of thing (i.e., a "generic" term) may not serve as a trademark to identify that genus or class of thing. In English, the word "apple" may not be used as a trademark to identify a type of fruit because that is the generic term for a type of fruit. (On the other hand, "Apple" may be used to identify a computer because the term has no inherent connection to electronic goods.)

Some trademarks are "inherently distinctive." These are "arbitrary," "fanciful," or "suggestive" terms that do not have an established connection with a good or service. If a mark is inherently distinctive, the trademark holder does not need to prove that consumers identify it with its product. Trademarks may also be "descriptive," meaning consumers would ordinarily draw connections between the marks and the goods or services on which they are used (i.e., the marks, at least in part, describe the goods or services). In order for a descriptive term to be recognized as a trademark, its holder must demonstrate that it has become associated in the mind of consumers with the holder's good or service; that is, it has become "distinctive." This is often referred to as acquiring "secondary meaning." A trademark holder may demonstrate acquired distinctiveness or secondary meaning in a number of ways, including by conducting a consumer survey.

Trademarks normally inform markets and consumers in distinguishing products by using letters, symbols, pictures, and colors in combination. Some trademarks operate using sound or even smell. One of the most important issues in litigation related to the question of whether trademarks may consist of color as such, thus borrowing a public good and rendering it exclusive in certain circumstances. In the following decision, the U.S. Supreme Court considers whether a single color may serve as a trademark and, in doing so, provides a very useful introduction to the subject matter of the trademark.

## *Qualitex Co. v. Jacobson Products Co., Inc.*
514 U.S. 159 (1995)

Breyer, J., delivered the opinion for a unanimous Court.

The question in this case is whether the Lanham Trademark Act of 1946 (Lanham Act), 15 U.S.C. §§1051-1127 (1988 ed. and Supp. V), permits the registration of a trademark that consists, purely and simply, of a color. We conclude that, sometimes, a color will meet ordinary legal trademark requirements. And, when it does so, no special legal rule prevents color alone from serving as a trademark. . . .

The Lanham Act gives a seller or producer the exclusive right to "register" a trademark, 15 U.S.C. §1052 (1988 ed. and Supp. V), and to prevent his or her competitors from using that trademark, §1114(1). Both the language of the Act and the basic underlying principles of trademark law would seem to include color within the universe of things that can qualify as a trademark. The language of the Lanham Act describes that universe in the broadest of terms. It says that trademarks "include any word, name, symbol, or device, or any combination thereof," §1127. Since human beings might use as a "symbol" or "device" almost anything at all that is capable of carrying meaning, this language, read literally, is not restrictive. The courts and the Patent and Trademark Office have authorized for use as a mark a particular shape (of a Coca-Cola bottle), a particular sound (of NBC's three chimes), and even a particular scent (of plumeria blossoms on sewing thread). . . . If a shape, a sound, and a fragrance can act as symbols why, one might ask, can a color not do the same?

A color is also capable of satisfying the more important part of the statutory definition of a trademark, which requires that a person "use" or "intend to use" the mark

> "to identify and distinguish his or her goods, including a unique product, from those manufactured or sold by others and to indicate the source of the goods, even if that source is unknown." 15 U.S.C. §1127.

True, a product's color is unlike "fanciful," "arbitrary," or "suggestive" words or designs, which almost automatically tell a customer that they refer to a brand. *Abercrombie & Fitch Co. v. Hunting World, Inc.*, 537 F.2d 4, 9-10 (CA2 1976) (Friendly, J.); *see Two Pesos, Inc. v. Taco Cabana, Inc.*, 505 U.S. 763 (1992) (slip op., at 6-7). The imaginary word "Suntost," or the words "Suntost Marmalade," on a jar of orange jam immediately would signal a brand or a product "source"; the jam's orange color does not do so. But, over time, customers may come to treat a particular color on a product or its packaging (say, a color that in context seems unusual, such as pink on a firm's insulating material or red on the head of a large industrial bolt) as signifying a brand. And, if so, that color would have come to identify and distinguish the goods—i.e. to "indicate" their "source"—much in the way that descriptive words on a product (say, "Trim" on nail clippers or "Car-Freshner" on deodorizer) can come to indicate a product's origin. *See, e.g., J. Wiss & Sons Co. v. W. E. Bassett Co.*, 462 F.2d 567, 59 C.C.P.A. 1269, 1271 (Pat.), 462 F.2d 567, 569 (1972); *Car-Freshner Corp. v. Turtle Wax, Inc.*, 268 F. Supp. 162, 164 (SDNY 1967). In this circumstance, trademark law says that the word (e.g., "Trim"), although not inherently distinctive, has developed "secondary meaning." *See Inwood Laboratories, Inc. v. Ives Laboratories, Inc.*, 456 U.S. 844, 851, n. 11, 72 L. Ed. 2d 606, 102 S. Ct. 2182 (1982) ("secondary meaning" is acquired when "in the minds of the public, the primary significance of a product feature . . . is to identify the source of the product rather than the product itself"). Again, one might ask, if trademark law permits a descriptive word with secondary meaning to act as a mark, why would it not permit a color, under similar circumstances, to do the same?

We cannot find in the basic objectives of trademark law any obvious theoretical objection to the use of color alone as a trademark, where that color has attained "secondary meaning" and therefore identifies and distinguishes a particular brand (and thus indicates its "source"). In principle, trademark law, by preventing others from copying a source-identifying mark, "reduces the customer's costs of shopping and making purchasing decisions," 1 J. McCarthy, McCarthy on Trademarks and Unfair Competition §2.01[2], p. 2-3 (3d ed. 1994) (hereinafter McCarthy), for it quickly and easily assures a potential customer that this item—the item with this mark—is made by the same producer as other similarly marked items that he or she liked (or disliked) in the past. At the same time, the law helps assure a producer that it (and not an imitating competitor) will reap the financial, reputation-related rewards associated with a desirable product. The law thereby "encourages the production of quality products," *ibid.*, and simultaneously discourages those who hope to sell inferior products by capitalizing on a consumer's inability quickly to evaluate the quality of an item offered for sale. *See, e.g.*, 3 L. Altman, Callmann on Unfair Competition, Trademarks and Monopolies §17.03 (4th ed. 1983); Landes & Posner, The Economics of Trademark Law, 78 T. M. Rep. 267, 271-272 (1988); *Park 'N Fly, Inc. v. Dollar Park and Fly, Inc.*, 469 U.S. 189, 198, 83 L. Ed. 2d 582, 105 S. Ct. 658 (1985); S. Rep. No. 100-515, p. 4 (1988). It is the source-distinguishing ability of a mark—not its ontological status as color, shape, fragrance, word, or sign—that permits it to serve these basic purposes. *See* Landes & Posner, Trademark Law: An Economic Perspective, 30 J. Law & Econ. 265, 290 (1987). And, for that reason, it is difficult to find, in basic trademark objectives, a reason to disqualify absolutely the use of a color as a mark.

Neither can we find a principled objection to the use of color as a mark in the important "functionality" doctrine of trademark law. The functionality doctrine prevents trademark law, which seeks to promote competition by protecting a firm's reputation, from instead inhibiting legitimate competition by allowing a producer to control a useful product feature. It is the province of patent law, not trademark law, to encourage invention by granting inventors a monopoly over new product designs or functions for a limited time, 35 U.S.C. §§154, 173, after which competitors are free to use the innovation. If a product's functional features could be used as trademarks, however, a monopoly over such features could be obtained without regard to whether they qualify as patents and could be extended forever (because trademarks may be renewed in perpetuity). *See Kellogg Co. v. National Biscuit Co.*, 305 U.S. 111, 119-120, 83 L. Ed. 73, 59 S. Ct. 109 (1938) (Brandeis, J.); *Inwood Laboratories, Inc., supra*, at 863 (White, J., concurring in result) ("A functional characteristic is 'an important ingredient in the commercial success of the product,' and, after expiration of a patent, it is no more the property of the originator than the product itself") (citation omitted). Functionality doctrine therefore would require, to take an imaginary example, that even if customers have come to identify the special illumination-enhancing shape of a new patented light bulb with a particular manufacturer, the manufacturer may not use that shape as a trademark, for doing so, after the patent had expired, would impede competition—not by protecting the reputation of the original bulb maker, but by frustrating competitors' legitimate efforts to produce an equivalent illumination-enhancing bulb. *See, e.g., Kellogg Co., supra,* at 119-120 (trademark law cannot be used to extend monopoly over "pillow" shape of shredded wheat biscuit after the patent for that shape had expired). This Court consequently has explained that, "in general terms, a product feature is functional," and cannot serve as a trademark, "if it is essential to the use or purpose of the article or if it affects the cost or quality of the article," that is, if exclusive use of the feature would put competitors at a significant non-reputation-related disadvantage. *Inwood Laboratories, Inc.*, 456 U.S. at 850, n. 10.

Although sometimes color plays an important role (unrelated to source identification) in making a product more desirable, sometimes it does not. And, this latter fact—the fact that sometimes color is not essential to a product's use or purpose and does not affect cost or quality—indicates that the doctrine of "functionality" does not create an absolute bar to the use of color alone as a mark. *See Owens-Corning,* 774 F.2d at 1123 (pink color of insulation in wall "performs no non-trademark function"). It would seem, then, that color alone, at least sometimes, can meet the basic legal requirements for use as a trademark. It can act as a symbol that distinguishes a firm's goods and identifies their source, without serving any other significant function. *See* U.S. Dept. of Commerce, Patent and Trademark Office, Trademark Manual of Examining Procedure §1202.04(e), p. 1202-13 (2d ed. May, 1993) (hereinafter PTO Manual) (approving trademark registration of color alone where it "has become distinctive of the applicant's goods in commerce," provided that "there is [no] competitive need for colors to remain available in the industry" and the color is not "functional"); *see also* 1 McCarthy §§3.01[1], 7.26 ("requirements for qualification of a word or symbol as a trademark" are that it be (1) a "symbol" (2) "used . . . as a mark," (3) "to identify and distinguish the seller's goods from goods made or sold by others" but that it not be "functional"). Indeed, the District Court, in this case, entered findings (accepted by the Ninth Circuit) that show Qualitex's green-gold press pad color has met these requirements. The green-gold color acts as a symbol. Having developed secondary meaning (for customers identified the green-gold color as Qualitex's), it identifies the press pads' source. And, the green-gold color serves no other function. (Although it is important to use some color on press pads to avoid noticeable stains, the court found "no competitive need in the press pad industry for the green-gold color, since other colors are equally usable.") 21 U.S.P.Q.2D (BNA) at 1460. Accordingly, unless there is some special reason that convincingly militates against the use of color alone as a trademark, trademark law would protect Qualitex's use of the green-gold color on its press pads. . . .

The functionality doctrine, as we have said, forbids the use of a product's feature as a trademark where doing so will put a competitor at a significant disadvantage because the feature is "essential to the use or purpose of the article" or "affects [its] cost or quality." *Inwood Laboratories, Inc.*, 456 U.S. at 850, n. 10. The functionality doctrine thus protects competitors against a disadvantage (unrelated to recognition or reputation) that trademark protection might otherwise impose, namely their inability reasonably to replicate important non-reputation-related product features. For example, this Court has written that competitors might be free to copy the color of a medical pill where that color serves to identify the kind of medication (e.g., a type of blood medicine) in addition to its source. *See id.*, at 853, 858, n. 20 ("Some patients commingle medications in a container and rely on color to differentiate one from another"); *see also* J. Ginsburg, D. Goldberg & A. Greenbaum, Trademark and Unfair

Competition Law 194-195 (1991) (noting that drug color cases "have more to do with public health policy" regarding generic drug substitution "than with trademark law"). And, the federal courts have demonstrated that they can apply this doctrine in a careful and reasoned manner, with sensitivity to the effect on competition. Although we need not comment on the merits of specific cases, we note that lower courts have permitted competitors to copy the green color of farm machinery (because customers wanted their farm equipment to match) and have barred the use of black as a trademark on outboard boat motors (because black has the special functional attributes of decreasing the apparent size of the motor and ensuring compatibility with many different boat colors). *See Deere & Co. v. Farmhand, Inc.*, 560 F. Supp. 85, 98 (SD Iowa 1982), *aff'd*, 721 F.2d 253 (CA8 1983); *Brunswick Corp. v. British Seagull Ltd.*, 35 F.3d 1527, 1532 (CA Fed. 1994), *cert. pending*, No. 94-1075; *see also Nor-Am Chemical v. O. M. Scott & Sons Co.*, 4 U.S.P.Q.2D (BNA) 1316, 1320 (ED Pa. 1987) (blue color of fertilizer held functional because it indicated the presence of nitrogen). The Restatement (Third) of Unfair Competition adds that, if a design's "aesthetic value" lies in its ability to "confer a significant benefit that cannot practically be duplicated by the use of alternative designs," then the design is "functional." Restatement (Third) of Unfair Competition §17, Comment c, pp. 175-176 (1995). The "ultimate test of aesthetic functionality," it explains, "is whether the recognition of trademark rights would significantly hinder competition." *Id.*, at 176.

The upshot is that, where a color serves a significant nontrademark function—whether to distinguish a heart pill from a digestive medicine or to satisfy the "noble instinct for giving the right touch of beauty to common and necessary things." G. K. Chesterton, Simplicity and Tolstoy 61 (1912)—courts will examine whether its use as a mark would permit one competitor (or a group) to interfere with legitimate (nontrademark-related) competition through actual or potential exclusive use of an important product ingredient. That examination should not discourage firms from creating aesthetically pleasing mark designs, for it is open to their competitors to do the same. *See, e.g., W. T. Rogers Co. v. Keene*, 778 F.2d 334, 343 (CA7 1985) (Posner, J.). But, ordinarily, it should prevent the anticompetitive consequences of Jacobson's hypothetical "color depletion" argument, when, and if, the circumstances of a particular case threaten "color depletion."

## NOTES AND QUESTIONS

**1.** In *Qualitex*, the Supreme Court refers to the potential functionality of color, and specifically addresses the use of color to identify types of medicines. After the patent on a medicine has expired, generic producers may enter the market with the same product, bringing competition to the market for the medicine. Generic producers may prefer to use the same color used by the former patent holder because doctors and patients will identify the medicine with its original coloring. Has the Supreme Court endorsed this practice in *Qualitex*?

**2.** The term "generic" in the context of medicines has more than one meaning. The term is often used to distinguish between patented and off-patent versions of the same medicine, with "generic" referring to the off-patent version. The term is also used to distinguish between "branded" and "unbranded" versions of off-patent medicines. For example, "Bayer" is a brand name for "aspirin," which is unpatented. "Bayer Aspirin" is a branded medicine. Many chain stores also sell aspirin under a house label, typically at a lower price than branded aspirin. The medicine sold under the house label is often referred to as a "generic."

**3.** The use of colors—clearly in the public domain—often creates problems in trademark registration and protection. In *Christian Louboutin SAS v. Van Haren Schoenen BV*,

C-163/16, 12 June 2018,* the CJEU ruled that a color (red) applied to a part of a product (the sole of a high-heeled shoe) does not as such constitute a "shape" that would be excluded from trademark registration by virtue of a Trademark Directive (art. 3(1)(e)) exclusion from registrability for functional shapes.

> "25 [T]he mark at issue does not relate to a specific shape of sole for high-heeled shoes since the description of that mark explicitly states that the contour of the shoe does not form part of the mark and is intended purely to show the positioning of the red colour covered by the registration.
>
> 26 In any event, a sign, such as that at issue in the main proceedings, cannot be regarded as consisting 'exclusively' of a shape, where, as in the present instance, the main element of that sign is a specific colour designated by an internationally recognised identification code."

In the following 2002 decision, the Court of Justice of the European Union (CJEU) considers a question similar to that addressed by the U.S. Supreme Court in *Qualitex v. Jacobsen*, but with reference to the TRIPS Agreement and European legislation. The CJEU places particular emphasis on the role trademark registration plays in providing information to competitors in the economic marketplace. As you read the CJEU decision, consider whether it was approving the use of a single color as a trademark, as the U.S. Supreme Court has in *Qualitex*.

## *Heidelberger Bauchemie GmbH*

Judgment of the Court (Second Chamber), 24 June 2004

**In Case C-49/02**

REFERENCE to the Court under Article 234 EC by the Bundespatentgericht (Germany) for a preliminary ruling in the proceedings brought before that court by

Heidelberger Bauchemie GmbH

on the interpretation of Article 2 of the First Council Directive (89/104/EEC) of 21 December 1988 to approximate the laws of the Member States relating to trade marks (OJ 1989 L 40, p. 1),
THE COURT (Second Chamber),
composed of: C.W.A. Timmermans, President of the Chamber, J.-P. Puissochet, J.N. Cunha Rodrigues (Rapporteur), R. Schintgen and N. Colneric, Judges, gives the following:

**Judgment**

1. By order of 22 January 2002, received at the Court on 20 February 2002, the Bundespatentgericht (Federal Patents Court) referred to the Court for a preliminary ruling under Article 234 EC two questions on the interpretation of Article 2 of the First Council Directive (89/104/EEC) of 21 December 1988 to approximate the laws of the Member States relating to trade marks (OJ 1989 L 40, p. 1) (hereinafter "the Directive").

2. Those questions were raised in proceedings brought by Heidelberger Bauchemie GmbH (hereinafter "Heidelberger Bauchemie") against the refusal by the Deutsches Patentamt

* https://eur-lex.europa.eu/legal-content/EN/TXT/PDF/?uri=CELEX:62016CJ0163.

(German Patent Office) (hereinafter "the Patent Office") to register the colours blue and yellow as a trade mark for certain products used in the building trade.

### Legal Framework . . .

### Community Legislation

5. Article 2 of the Directive, headed "Signs of which a trade mark may consist," is worded as follows:

> A trade mark may consist of any sign capable of being represented graphically, particularly words, including personal names, designs, letters, numerals, the shape of goods or of their packaging, provided that such signs are capable of distinguishing the goods or services of one undertaking from those of other undertakings.

6. Article 3 of the Directive, headed "Grounds for refusal or invalidity" provides:

> . . . 3. A trade mark shall not be refused registration or be declared invalid in accordance with paragraph 1(b), (c) or (d) if, before the date of application for registration and following the use which has been made of it, it has acquired a distinctive character. Any Member State may in addition provide that this provision shall also apply where the distinctive character was acquired after the date of application for registration or after the date of registration. . . .

### The Main Proceedings and the Questions Referred

10. On 22 March 1995, Heidelberger Bauchemie applied to the Patent Office for the registration of the colours blue and yellow as a trade mark. The section headed "reproduction of the mark" comprised a rectangular piece of paper, the upper part of which was blue and the lower half yellow. The following description of the mark accompanied the application:

> The trade mark applied for consists of the applicant's corporate colours which are used in every conceivable form, in particular on packaging and labels.
> The specification of the colours is:
> RAL 5015/HKS 47—blue
> RAL 1016/HKS 3—yellow.

11. Registration of the mark was applied for in relation to a list of various products used in the building trade, including adhesives, solvents, varnishes, paints, lubricants and insulating materials.

12. By decision of 18 September 1996, the Patent Office rejected that application on the grounds, first, that the sign which it was sought to register was not capable of constituting a trade mark and was not capable of being represented graphically and, secondly, that the mark was devoid of any distinctive character. However, following the "black/yellow colour mark" decision of the Bundesgerichtshof (Federal Court of Justice) (Germany) of 10 December 1998, the Patent Office reviewed its position. By decision of 2 May 2000, it accepted that colours are in principle able to constitute a trade mark, but rejected the application on the ground of lack of any distinctive character. Heidelberger Bauchemie brought an appeal against that decision before the Bundespatentgericht.

13. The Bundespatentgericht considered that it was uncertain whether abstract, undelineated marks could be treated as "signs" capable of being represented graphically within the meaning of Article 2 of the Directive. . . .

14. In those circumstances, the Bundespatentgericht decided to stay the proceedings and to refer the following questions to the Court for a preliminary ruling. . . .

## The Questions Referred

15. By its questions, which should be dealt with together, the national court is essentially asking whether, and if so under what conditions, colours or combinations of colours designated in the abstract and without contours are capable of constituting a trade mark for the purposes of Article 2 of the Directive. . . .

19. Article 15(1) of the TRIPS Agreement provides that "combinations of colours . . . shall be eligible for registration as trade marks." However, that Agreement does not define a "combination of colours."

20. Since the Community is a party to the TRIPS Agreement, it is required to interpret its legislation on trade marks so far as possible in the light of the wording and purpose of that Agreement (*see*, to that effect, Case C-53/96 *Hermès* [1998] ECR I-3603, paragraph 28).

21. It should therefore be established whether Article 2 of the Directive can be interpreted as meaning that "combinations of colours" are capable of constituting a trade mark.

22. To constitute a trade mark under Article 2 of the Directive, colours or combinations of colours must satisfy three conditions. First, they must be a sign. Secondly, that sign must be capable of being represented graphically. Thirdly, the sign must be capable of distinguishing the goods or services of one undertaking from those of other undertakings (*see*, to that effect, [Case C-104/01] *Libertel* [2003] ECR I-3793, paragraph 23).

23. As the Court has already held, colours are normally a simple property of things (*Libertel*, paragraph 27). Even in the particular field of trade, colours and combinations of colours are generally used for their attractive or decorative powers, and do not convey any meaning. However, it is possible that colours or combinations of colours may be capable, when used in relation to a product or a service, of being a sign.

24. For the purposes of the application of Article 2 of the Directive, it is necessary to establish that in the context in which they are used colours or combinations of colours which it is sought to register in fact represent a sign. The purpose of that requirement is in particular to prevent the abuse of trademark law in order to obtain an unfair competitive advantage.

25. Moreover, it is clear from the Court's case-law (Case C-273/00 *Sieckmann* [2002] ECR I-11737, paragraphs 46 to 55, and *Libertel*, paragraphs 28 and 29) that a graphic representation in terms of Article 2 of the Directive must enable the sign to be represented visually, particularly by means of images, lines or characters, so that it can be precisely identified.

26. Such an interpretation is necessary for the proper working of the trade mark registration system.

27. The function of the requirement of graphic representation is in particular to define the mark itself in order to determine the precise subject of the protection afforded by the registered mark to its proprietor.

28. The entry of the mark in a public register has the aim of making it accessible to the competent authorities and to the public, particularly to economic operators.

29. On the one hand, the competent authorities must know with clarity and precision the nature of the signs of which a mark consists in order to be able to fulfill their obligations in relation to the prior examination of applications for registration and the publication and maintenance of an appropriate and precise register of trade marks.

30. On the other hand, economic operators must be able to acquaint themselves, with clarity and precision, with registrations or applications for registration made by their actual or potential competitors, and thus to obtain relevant information about the rights of third parties.

31. In those circumstances, in order to fulfil its role as a registered trade mark, a sign must always be perceived unambiguously and uniformly, so that the function of mark as an

indication of origin is guaranteed. In the light of the duration of a mark's registration and the fact that, as the Directive provides, it can be renewed for varying periods, the representation must also be durable.

32. It follows from the above that a graphic representation for the purpose of Article 2 of the Directive must be, in particular, precise and durable.

33. Accordingly, a graphic representation consisting of two or more colours, designated in the abstract and without contours, must be systematically arranged by associating the colours concerned in a predetermined and uniform way.

34. The mere juxtaposition of two or more colours, without shape or contours, or a reference to two or more colours "in every conceivable form," as is the case with the trade mark which is the subject of the main proceedings, does not exhibit the qualities of precision and uniformity required by Article 2 of the Directive, as construed in paragraphs 25 to 32 of this judgment.

35. Such representations would allow numerous different combinations, which would not permit the consumer to perceive and recall a particular combination, thereby enabling him to repeat with certainty the experience of a purchase, any more than they would allow the competent authorities and economic operators to know the scope of the protection afforded to the proprietor of the trade mark.

36. As regards the manner in which each of the colours concerned is represented, it is clear from paragraphs 33, 34, 37, 38 and 68 of *Libertel* that a sample of the colour concerned, accompanied by a designation using an internationally recognised identification code, may constitute a graphic representation for the purposes of Article 2 of the Directive.

37. As regards the question whether, for the purposes of this provision, colours or combinations of colours are capable of distinguishing the goods or services of one undertaking from those of other undertakings, it must be determined whether or not those colours or combinations of colours are capable of conveying precise information, particularly as regards the origin of a product or service.

38. It follows from paragraphs 40, 41 and 65 to 67 of *Libertel* that, whilst colours are capable of conveying certain associations of ideas, and of arousing feelings, they possess little inherent capacity for communicating specific information, especially since they are commonly and widely used, because of their appeal, in order to advertise and market goods or services, without any specific message.

39. Save in exceptional cases, colours do not initially have a distinctive character, but may be capable of acquiring such character as the result of the use made of them in relation to the goods or services claimed.

40. Subject to the above, it must be accepted that for the purposes of Article 2 of the Directive colours and combinations of colours, designated in the abstract and without contours, may be capable of distinguishing the goods or services of one undertaking from those of other undertakings.

41. It should be added that, even if a combination of colours which it is sought to register as a trade mark satisfies the requirements for constituting a trade mark for the purposes of Article 2 of the Directive, it is still necessary for the competent authority for registering trade marks to decide whether the combination claimed satisfies the other requirements laid down, particularly in Article 3 of the Directive, for registration as a trade mark in relation to the goods or services of the undertaking which has applied for its registration. That examination must take account of all the relevant circumstances of the case, including any use which has been made of the sign in respect of which trade mark registration is sought (*Libertel*, paragraph 76, and Case 363/99 *Koninklijke KPN Nederland* [2004] ECR I-0000, paragraph 37). That examination must also take account of the public interest in not unduly restricting the availability of colours for other traders who market goods or services of the same type as those in respect of which registration is sought (*Libertel*, paragraphs 52 to 56).

42. In light of the above, the answer to the questions must be that colours or combinations of colours which are the subject of an application for registration as a trade mark, claimed in the abstract, without contours, and in shades which are named in words by reference to a colour sample and specified according to an internationally recognised colour classification system may constitute a trade mark for the purposes of Article 2 of the Directive where:

— it has been established that, in the context in which they are used, those colours or combinations of colours in fact represent a sign, and
— the application for registration includes a systematic arrangement associating the colours concerned in a predetermined and uniform way.

Even if a combination of colours satisfies the requirements for constituting a trade mark for the purposes of Article 2 of the Directive, it is still necessary for the competent authority for registering trade marks to decide whether the combination claimed fulfils the other requirements laid down, particularly in Article 3 of the Directive, for registration as a trade mark in relation to the goods or services of the undertaking which has applied for its registration. Such an examination must take account of all the relevant circumstances of the case, including any use which has been made of the sign in respect of which trade mark registration is sought. That examination must also take account of the public interest in not unduly restricting the availability of colours for other traders who market goods or services of the same type as those in respect of which registration is sought. . . .

## NOTES AND QUESTIONS

**1.** The *Heidelberger Bauchemie* decision introduces some of the complexities of the EU trademark regime further discussed below in section V.A. Each of the EU member states has its own trademark law, which law must be compatible with the First Trade Marks Directive, which in 1988 acted to approximate the EU trademark law but left in place the national regulatory and judicial systems. In 1993 the European Union adopted the Community Trade Mark Regulation, which created a unitary mark (the "Community Trade Mark" or CTM) for the European Union and a new institution, the Office for Harmonization in the Internal Market (OHIM). More recently, the European Union "rebranded" its unitary trademark as the European Union Trade Mark or EUTM, and changed the name of the administrative office responsible for registration and related matters to the European Union Intellectual Property Office (EUIPO). Regulatory details of this transition are outlined in section V.A. At the judicial "top" of both the member state and EUTM systems is the CJEU, which has ultimate authority to interpret the law governing each of them. Though technically the two systems are separate, a decision by the CJEU regarding a question such as whether colors are appropriate trademark subject matter may apply with equal force to both trademark systems since each similarly defines trademark subject matter. Answers to some other trademark questions will be relevant to only one of the two systems.

**2.** Has the CJEU, like the U.S. Supreme Court in *Qualitex*, approved the use of a single color as a trademark?

**3.** A common form of media advertising involves combining the visual and aural image of an exciting or interesting event with a trademark—without conveying any direct information about a product. The objective is to associate a particular trademark with a positive (or even a negative) feeling such that when the consumer is faced with a choice among products, he or she will be drawn to the one that was advertised. In these circumstances, what function is the trademark performing?

**4.** In *Lego Juris A/S v. Office for Harmonisation in the Internal Market (Trade Marks and Designs) (OHIM)*, CJEU Case C-48/09 P, 14 Sept. 2010, the CJEU addressed the relationship between shape and function in the context of a product (the Lego building block), subject of an expired patent, saying:

> 38. According to settled case-law, trade mark law constitutes an essential element in the system of competition in the European Union. In that system, each undertaking must, in order to attract and retain customers by the quality of its goods or services, be able to have registered as trade marks signs enabling the consumer, without any possibility of confusion, to distinguish those goods or services from others which have another origin (see, to that effect, Case C-517/99 *Merz & Krell* [2001] ECR I-6959, paragraphs 21 and 22; Case C-206/01 *Arsenal Football Club* [2002] ECR I-10273, paragraphs 47 and 48; and Case C-412/05 P *Alcon* v *OHIM* [2007] ECR I-3569, paragraphs 53 and 54).
>
> 39. A product's shape is a sign which may constitute a trade mark. . . .
>
> 40. In the present case, it has not been disputed that the shape of the Lego brick has become distinctive in consequence of the use which has been made of it and is therefore a sign capable of distinguishing the appellant's goods from others which have another origin. . . .
>
> 45. First, the inclusion in Article 7(1) of Regulation No 40/94 of the prohibition on registration as a trade mark of any sign consisting of the shape of goods which is necessary to obtain a technical result ensures that undertakings may not use trade mark law in order to perpetuate, indefinitely, exclusive rights relating to technical solutions.
>
> 46. When the shape of a product merely incorporates the technical solution developed by the manufacturer of that product and patented by it, protection of that shape as a trade mark once the patent has expired would considerably and permanently reduce the opportunity for other undertakings to use that technical solution. In the system of intellectual property rights developed in the European Union, technical solutions are capable of protection only for a limited period, so that subsequently they may be freely used by all economic operators. . . .
>
> 47. Furthermore, the legislature has laid down with particular strictness that shapes necessary to obtain a technical result are unsuitable for registration as trade marks, since it has excluded the grounds for refusal listed in Article 7(1)(e) of Regulation No 40/94 from the scope of the exception under Article 7(3). If follows, therefore, from Article 7(3) of the regulation that, even if a shape of goods which is necessary to obtain a technical result has become distinctive in consequence of the use which has been made of it, it is prohibited from being registered as a trade mark (see by analogy, in relation to Article 3(3) of Directive 89/104, which is essentially identical to Article 7(3) of Regulation No 40/94, *Philips*, paragraph 57, and Case C-371/06 *Benetton Group* [2007] ECR I-7709, paragraphs 25 to 27).
>
> 48. Second, by restricting the ground for refusal set out in Article 7(1)(e)(ii) of Regulation No 40/94 to signs which consist "exclusively" of the shape of goods which is "necessary" to obtain a technical result, the legislature duly took into account that any shape of goods is, to a certain extent, functional and that it would therefore be inappropriate to refuse to register a shape of goods as a trade mark solely on the ground that it has functional characteristics. By the terms "exclusively" and "necessary," that provision ensures that solely shapes of goods which only incorporate a technical solution, and whose registration as a trade mark would therefore actually impede the use of that technical solution by other undertakings, are not to be registered.

**5.** In *Audi AG v. Office for Harmonisation in the Internal Market (Trade Marks and Designs) (OHIM)*, CJEU Case C-398/08 P, 21 Jan. 2010, the CJEU addressed trademark protection for advertising slogans, holding that such identifiers are subject to the same standards of assessment as other trademarks, stating:

> 39. The Court has therefore held, in particular, that an advertising slogan cannot be required to display "imaginativeness" or even "conceptual tension which would create surprise and so make a striking impression" in order to have the minimal level of distinctiveness required under Article 7(1)(b) of Regulation No 40/94 (*OHIM* v *Erpo Möbelwerk*, paragraphs 31 and 32; see also Case C-392/02 P *SAT.1* v *OHIM* [2004] ECR I-8317, paragraph 41).
>
> 40. In the present case, the reasoning followed by the General Court derives from an erroneous interpretation of the principles set out in paragraphs 36 to 39 of the present judgment.

41. It must be held that, even though the General Court stated in paragraph 36 of the judgment under appeal that it is clear from the case-law that registration of a mark cannot be excluded because of that mark's laudatory or advertising use, it went on to explain that the reason for its finding that the mark applied for lacks distinctive character was, in essence, the fact that that mark is perceived as a promotional formula: that is to say, its finding was made precisely on the basis of the mark's laudatory or advertising use. . . .

53. As the Board of Appeal stated in the contested decision, the expression "Vorsprung durch Technik" [meaning, *inter alia*, advance or advantage through technology] is a widely known slogan which Audi has been using for years to promote the sale of its motor vehicles. It was registered in 2001 as a Community trade mark for goods in Class 12 on the basis of proof that that slogan was widely known in German-speaking regions.

54. As regards the goods and services in question, other than those in Class 12, the Board of Appeal based its refusal of registration on the fact that the slogan "Vorsprung durch Technik" conveys an objective message to the effect that technological superiority enables the manufacture and supply of better goods and services. According to the Board of Appeal, a combination of words which limits itself to that banal objective message is, in principle, devoid of any inherently distinctive character and cannot therefore be registered unless it is shown that the public has come to perceive it as a trade mark.

55. That analysis shows that Article 7(1)(b) of Regulation No 40/94 was misapplied.

56. In that regard, it must be stated that all marks made up of signs or indications that are also used as advertising slogans, indications of quality or incitements to purchase the goods or services covered by those marks convey by definition, to a greater or lesser extent, an objective message. It is clear, however, from the case-law set out in paragraphs 35 and 36 of the present judgment that those marks are not, by virtue of that fact alone, devoid of distinctive character.

The issue of adequate specification with respect to the goods or services covered by a trademark registration was raised again before the CJEU in the following case involving use of the Nice Classification system, addressing whether it is acceptable for a trademark registrant to rely on a broad Nice class when it is providing a more limited range of goods or services. Note the references to the *Heidelberger Bauchemie* decision.

**6.** In *Chartered Institute of Patent Attorneys v. Registrars of Trade Marks*, CJEU Case C-307/20, Case C-307/20, on referral from the U.K. High Court of Justice, the CJEU addressed whether a trademark applicant could rely on the broad classifications of goods and services of the Nice Agreement for registration with respect to a narrow class of goods or services, or alternatively whether it is necessary to indicate the specific goods or services covered by the application. The CJEU said:

42. As regards the requirement of clarity and precision for the identification of the goods and services covered by an application to register a sign as a trade mark, it must be held that the application of certain provisions of Directive 2008/95 depends to a great extent on whether the goods or services covered by a registered trade mark are indicated with sufficient clarity and precision.

43. In particular, the question of whether or not any of the grounds for refusal or invalidity set out in Article 3 of the Directive apply to the mark must be assessed specifically by reference to the goods or services in respect of which registration is sought (see *Koninklijke KPN Nederland*, paragraph 33, and Case C239/05 *BVBA Management, Training en Consultancy* [2007] ECR I1455, paragraph 31).

. . .

45. Moreover, the Court has held that, although it is not necessary to specify in detail the service(s) for which registration is sought, since, to identify those services, it is sufficient to use general wording, the applicant must conversely be required to specify the goods or types of goods to which those services relate by means, for example, of other more specific details. Such details will make it easier to apply the articles of Directive 2008/95 referred to in the previous paragraphs, without appreciably limiting the protection afforded to the trade mark (see, by analogy, *Praktiker Bau- und Heimwerkermärkte*, paragraphs 49 to 51).

> 46. In that connection, it must be recalled that the entry of the mark in a public register has the aim of making it accessible to the competent authorities and to the public, particularly to economic operators (*Sieckmann*, paragraph 49, and Case C49/02 *Heidelberger Bauchemie* [2004] ECR I6129, paragraph 28).
>
> 47. On the one hand, the competent authorities must know with clarity and precision the nature of the signs of which a mark consists in order to be able to fulfil their obligations in relation to the prior examination of applications for registration and the publication and maintenance of an appropriate and precise register of trade marks (see, by analogy, *Sieckmann*, paragraph 50, and *Heidelberger Bauchemie*, paragraph 29).
>
> . . .
>
> 49. Accordingly, Directive 2008/95 requires the goods and services for which the protection of the trade mark is sought to be identified by the applicant with sufficient clarity and precision to enable the competent authorities and economic operators, on that basis alone, to determine the extent of the protection sought.
>
> . . .
>
> 54. In that connection, it must be observed that some of the general indications in the class headings of the Nice Classification are, in themselves, sufficiently clear and precise to allow the competent authorities to determine the scope of the protection conferred by the trade mark, while others are not such as to meet that requirement where they are too general and cover goods or services which are too variable to be compatible with the trade mark's function as an indication of origin.
>
> 55. It is therefore for the competent authorities to make an assessment on a case-by-case basis, according to the goods or services for which the applicant seeks the protection conferred by a trade mark, in order to determine whether those indications meet the requirements of clarity and precision.
>
> . . .
>
> 61. Accordingly, in order to respect the requirements of clarity and precision mentioned above, an applicant for a national trade mark who uses all the general indications of a particular class heading of the Nice Classification to identify the goods or services for which the protection of the trade mark is sought must specify whether its application for registration is intended to cover all the goods or services included in the alphabetical list of the particular class concerned or only some of those goods or services. If the application concerns only some of those goods or services, the applicant is required to specify which of the goods or services in that class are intended to be covered.

The standards of precision relating to goods and services to be addressed by a trademark, incorporating the Nice Agreement, developed in Case C-307/10 by the Court of Justice, continues to apply under revised Directive 2015/2436 and also applies to the registration of European trademarks under Regulation 2017/1001 on the EU Trade Mark. Note the importance of taking into account standards and disciplines entailed in instruments of international law to which Members and the European Union adhere.

### 2. *The Exclusion of Generic Names, Collective and Certified Marks*

The names of foodstuffs, in particular of cheeses and their geographical origins, gave rise to issues of distinctiveness in the recent cheese war over the terms EMMENTAL and GRUYERE, both depicting specific Cantons of Berne and of Fribourg, Switzerland, and of Savoy, France, respectively. Swiss cheese producers are keen to re-establish the exclusivity of these famous names as an asset for marketing and distinguishing the origin and qualities of their products abroad. These efforts have been successfully resisted by producers of hard cheeses abroad. Efforts to register these names as collective marks failed in litigation in the EU for EMMENTAL in 2022, and in the United States as a collective mark for GRUYERE in 2023.

Collective trademarks are owned by the association of producers. It responds to the criteria of distinctiveness, but can also be granted on the basis of geographical origin of the product (Article 74(1) EU Regulation 2017/100). Certified trademarks, on the other hand, are marks which are able to distinguish goods and services certified and monitored by the association of producers as the proprietor of the mark in terms of quality, accuracy, or other characteristics, modes of manufacturing of a good, or performance of a service. In the EU, the geographical origin of the product is excluded for certified marks (Article 83(1) EU Regulation 2017/100), but not so in the United States, 15 U.S.C. §1054 (Section 4 of the Lanham Act), 15 U.S.C §1127 (2021). However, other than geographical indications, discussed below, the quality of the product in collective and certified marks is not necessarily linked to the territory and region where the product typically is made.

While Emmental and Gruyère cheeses clearly and centuries ago originate in these two Swiss regions, the names have been widely used abroad to depict hard cheeses without distinguishing the origins and qualities of the respective products. According to the two following rulings, the names rather depict types of products that are deemed generic. They were held to fall short of trademark protection.

## *Judgment of the General Court (Tenth Chamber)*

24 May 2023 (*)

(EU trade mark – International registration designating the European Union – Word mark EMMENTALER – Absolute ground for refusal – Descriptive character – Article 7(1)(c) of Regulation (EU) 2017/1001 – Collective mark – Article 74(2) of Regulation 2017/1001 – Obligation to state reasons – Article 94 of Regulation 2017/1001)

In Case T2/21,

**Emmentaler Switzerland,** established in Berne (Switzerland), . . .

applicant,

v

**European Union Intellectual Property Office (EUIPO),** . . .

supported by **Federal Republic of Germany,** and by **French Republic,** and by **Centre national interprofessionnel de l'économie laitière (CNIEL),** established in Paris (France),

THE GENERAL COURT (Tenth Chamber),

composed, at the time of the deliberations, of A. Kornezov, President, K. Kowalik-Bańczyk and D. Petrlík (Rapporteur), Judges,

. . . gives the following

### Judgment

1 By its action under Article 263 TFEU, the applicant, Emmentaler Switzerland, seeks annulment of the decision of the Second Board of Appeal of the European Union Intellectual Property Office (EUIPO) of 28 October 2020 (Case R 2402/2019-2) ('the contested decision').

### Background to the dispute

2 On 4 October 2017, the applicant obtained international registration No 1378524 of the word sign EMMENTALER from the International Bureau of the World Intellectual

Property Organisation. On 7 December 2017, that international registration was notified to EUIPO, pursuant to Regulation (EU) 2017/1001 of the European Parliament and of the Council of 14 June 2017 on the European Union trade mark (OJ 2017 L 154, p. 1).

3 The goods in respect of which registration was sought are in Class 29 of the Nice Agreement Concerning the International Classification of Goods and Services for the Purposes of the Registration of Marks of 15 June 1957, as revised and amended, and correspond to the following description: 'Cheeses with the protected designation of origin "emmentaler"'.

4 By decision of 9 September 2019, the examiner rejected the application for registration on the basis of Article 7(1)(b) and (c) of Regulation 2017/1001, read in conjunction with Article 7(2) of that regulation.

5 On 25 October 2019, the applicant lodged an appeal with EUIPO against the examiner's decision.

6 By the contested decision, the Board of Appeal dismissed the appeal on the basis of Article 7(1)(c) of Regulation 2017/1001, on the ground that the mark applied for was descriptive.

. . .

## Law

9 In support of its action, the applicant relies on two pleas in law, alleging, first, infringement of Article 74(2) of Regulation 2017/1001 and, secondly, infringement of Article 7(1)(b) and (c) of that regulation.

10 Article 74(2) of Regulation 2017/1001 provides that, by way of derogation from Article 7(1)(c) of that regulation, signs or indications which may serve, in trade, to designate the geographical origin of the goods or services in question may constitute EU collective marks.

11 However, that provision, which provides for a derogation from the absolute ground for refusal laid down in Article 7(1)(c) of Regulation 2017/1001, must be interpreted strictly, such that its scope cannot cover signs which will be regarded as an indication of the kind, quality, quantity, intended purpose, value, time of production or other characteristic of the goods in question, but only those signs which will be regarded as an indication of the geographical origin of those goods (see, to that effect, judgment of 17 May 2011, *Consejo Regulador de la Denominación de Origen Txakoli de Álava and Others* v *OHIM (TXAKOLI)*, T341/09, EU:T:2011:220, paragraphs 33 and 35 and the case-law cited).

12 In the light of those principles, it is necessary first to examine the second plea in law, by which the applicant submits, inter alia, that the sign at issue does not designate a characteristic of the goods at issue, namely a type of cheese.

### The Second Plea in Law, Alleging Infringement of Article 7(1)(b) and (c) of Regulation 2017/1001

13 By its second plea, the applicant submits that the Board of Appeal infringed Article 7(1)(b) and (c) of Regulation 2017/1001. This plea is divided into two parts. The first part alleges that the contested decision infringes Article 7(1)(b) of Regulation 2017/1001, since that decision is based exclusively on Article 7(1)(c) of that regulation. The second part alleges, first, that the Board of Appeal incorrectly assessed the evidence and thus wrongly concluded that the mark applied for was descriptive of the goods at issue and, secondly, that it infringed its obligation to state reasons.

### The First Part of the Second Plea In Law, Alleging Infringement of Article 7(1)(b) of Regulation 2017/1001

. . .

18 . . . according to settled caselaw, a trade mark which is descriptive of the characteristics of goods or services for the purposes of Article 7(1)(c) of Regulation 2017/1001 is, on that account, necessarily devoid of any distinctive character in relation to those goods or services within the meaning of Article 7(1)(b) of that regulation (see judgment of 17 April 2013, *CONTINENTAL*, T383/10, EU:T:2013:193, paragraph 72 and the caselaw cited).

19 It follows that the Board of Appeal was entitled to confine itself to examining whether the mark applied for was descriptive within the meaning of Article 7(1)(c) of Regulation 2017/1001, without ruling on the application of other absolute grounds for refusal, such as that provided for in Article 7(1)(b) of that regulation.

20 Consequently, without it being necessary to rule on its admissibility, the first part of the second plea in law must be rejected as unfounded.

### The Second Part of the Second Plea in Law, Alleging Infringement of Article 7(1)(c) of Regulation 2017/1001 and of the obligation to state reasons

21 Article 7(1)(c) of Regulation 2017/1001 provides that 'trade marks which consist exclusively of signs or indications which may serve, in trade, to designate the kind, quality, quantity, intended purpose, value, geographical origin or the time of production of the goods or of rendering of the service, or other characteristics of the goods or service' are not to be registered.

22 Those signs or indications are regarded as incapable of performing the essential function of a trade mark, namely, that of identifying the commercial origin of the goods or services (judgments of 23 October 2003, *OHIM* v *Wrigley*, C191/01 P, EU:C:2003:579, paragraph 30; of 27 February 2002, *Eurocool Logistik* v *OHIM (EUROCOOL)*, T34/00, EU:T:2002:41, paragraph 37; and of 24 February 2021, *Liga Nacional de Fútbol Profesional* v *EUIPO (El Clasico)*, T809/19, not published, EU:T:2021:100, paragraph 29).

23 Under Article 7(2) of Regulation 2017/1001, Article 7(1)(c) of that regulation is to apply notwithstanding that the grounds of non-registrability obtain in only part of the European Union. Such a part may be comprised of a single Member State (see, to that effect, judgment of 22 June 2006, *Storck* v *OHIM*, C25/05 P, EU:C:2006:422, paragraphs 81 and 83).

24 For a sign to fall within the scope of the prohibition set out in Article 7(1)(c) of Regulation 2017/1001, it must suggest a sufficiently direct and concrete link to the goods or services in question to enable the public concerned immediately, and without further thought, to perceive a description of the category of goods and services in question or one of their characteristics (see judgments of 12 January 2005, *Deutsche Post EURO EXPRESS* v *OHIM (EUROPREMIUM)*, T334/03, EU:T:2005:4, paragraph 25 and the case-law cited, and of 22 June 2005, *Metso Paper Automation* v *OHIM (PAPERLAB)*, T19/04, EU:T:2005:247, paragraph 25 and the case-law cited).

25 The descriptive character of a sign can be assessed only by reference to the goods or services concerned and to the way in which it is understood by the relevant public (see judgments of 25 October 2005, *Peek & Cloppenburg* v *OHIM (Cloppenburg)*, T379/03, EU:T:2005:373, paragraph 37 and the case-law cited, and of 7 October 2015, *Cyprus* v *OHIM (ΧΑΛΛΟΥΜΙ and HALLOUMI)*, T292/14 and T293/14, EU:T:2015:752, paragraph 16 and the case-law cited.)

26 In the present case, the goods covered by the mark applied for, as set out in paragraph 3 above, are goods intended for all consumers. Consequently, the relevant public consists of the general public, as the Board of Appeal correctly found in paragraph 23 of the contested decision, without being challenged by the applicant.

27 In paragraph 24 of the contested decision, the Board of Appeal then found, essentially, that the sign EMMENTALER would be immediately understood by the part of the relevant public who speak Bulgarian, Danish, German, Estonian, Irish, French, Croatian, Hungarian, Dutch, Polish, Romanian, Slovak, Finnish, Swedish or English as designating a type of hard cheese containing holes.

28 The Board of Appeal justified that conclusion by relying on a series of factors which concerned, inter alia, the German- and French-speaking part of the relevant public.

29 The applicant submits that, by basing the contested decision on those factors, the Board of Appeal infringed Article 7(1)(c) of Regulation 2017/1001.

30 In paragraph 24 of the contested decision, the Board of Appeal relied, as regards the relevant German public, on several factors in support of its conclusion that the public understood the sign EMMENTALER as designating a type of cheese, the relevance of which is disputed by the applicant. These factors must now be examined.

### The Definition of the Term 'Emmentaler' in the Duden Dictionary

. . .

35 In those circumstances, the applicant's complaint that the Board of Appeal could not use the definition of the term 'emmentaler' in the *Duden* dictionary as one indication, among others, of the descriptive character of the sign, must be rejected.

### The Production of Emmentaler

36 In finding that the sign EMMENTALER designates a type of cheese, the Board of Appeal took into account the fact that, at the time when the application for the trade mark was filed, emmentaler was a cheese produced in several Member States, including Germany.

37 The applicant claims that the Board of Appeal's factual finding that emmentaler is a cheese produced in several Member States, including Germany, has not been proven. By basing its conclusion as to the descriptive character of the name Emmentaler on that assertion, the Board of Appeal thus infringed its obligation to state reasons.

38 Furthermore, according to the applicant, even if it is true that emmentaler was a cheese produced in those Member States at the time of the application for registration of the mark applied for, it could not have been lawfully placed on their market under the name Emmentaler on its own, that is to say, without that name being accompanied by the indication of the place of production. As regards, more particularly, Germany, that circumstance arises from the fact that that Member State is bound by the Treaty of 7 March 1967 concluded with Switzerland on the protection of indications of source and other geographical names ('the Switzerland-Germany Agreement'). That agreement reserves the use of that name for cheese produced in Switzerland and allows the use of the name Emmentaler to designate cheeses produced in Germany provided that that designation is accompanied by an indication of the country of production in characters identical in type, size and colour to those used for the name.

. . .

41 In the present case, the Board of Appeal did not expressly identify, in the contested decision, the evidence on which it had based its finding relating to the production of emmentaler in the Member States concerned.

42 However, the Board of Appeal referred in paragraph 25 of the contested decision 'to the observations of third-parties referred to in [paragraph 4 of that decision]'.

. . .

45 As regards, secondly, the production of emmentaler in Germany, it is apparent, first, from the observations of the Bundesministerium für Ernährung und Landwirtschaft (Federal Ministry of Food and Agriculture, Germany), the Milchwirtschaftlicher Verein Bayern eV (Dairy Association of Bavaria, Germany) and the MIV Milchindustrie-Verband eV (Dairy Industry Association, Germany), to which the Board of Appeal referred in paragraph 25 of the contested decision, that Germany produced 135 000 tonnes of emmentaler in 2016.

46 Next, it is not disputed that a substantial part of that production was placed on the German market. In that regard, it is apparent from the observations of the Dairy Association of Bavaria that, of the 135 000 tonnes of emmentaler produced in Germany in 2016, only 80 000 were exported. It follows that a substantial part of the quantity of emmentaler produced in Germany was placed on the market directly in Germany.

47 Finally, it follows from the aforementioned observations that the cheese production and marketing referred to in paragraphs 45 and 46 above concerned the name Emmentaler on its own. That finding is supported by a number of examples, reproduced in the observations referred to in paragraph 25 of the contested decision. Those cheeses, which come from a number of economic operators and were produced and placed on the market in Germany, bear that name without any indication of the country or place of production.

. . .

49 As regards the impact of that production of emmentaler in Germany on the relevant public's perception of the descriptive character of the sign EMMENTALER, it is apparent from the case-law that the production and marketing of a product under a certain name, without that name being used in a way which refers to the origin of that product, may constitute a relevant indication of whether that name has become generic (see, to that effect, judgments of 25 October 2005, *Germany and Denmark* v *Commission*, C465/02 and C466/02, EU:C:2005:636, paragraphs 75 to 100, and of 26 February 2008, *Commission* v *Germany*, C132/05, EU:C:2008:117, paragraphs 53 to 57).

50 The considerations set out in that case-law, although they concern the generic nature of a name, are also relevant to the examination of the descriptive character of signs. The characterisation of a sign as generic or descriptive is closely linked, as such a sign lacks distinctive character in both situations (see, to that effect, judgment of 24 May 2012, *Formula One Licensing* v *OHIM*, C196/11 P, EU:C:2012:314, paragraph 41).

51 Thus, in particular, the fact that several economic operators produce and market goods in a Member State bearing a certain sign, without that sign referring to a commercial or geographical origin of those goods, is likely to suggest that the relevant public perceives that sign as designating a characteristic of those goods and, therefore, as being descriptive.

52 It follows from the foregoing, first, that the applicant has not succeeded in disputing the fact that, as is apparent from the information set out in paragraphs 45 to 47 above, a significant quantity of cheese produced in Germany was marketed in that Member State under the name Emmentaler on its own. Secondly, as pointed out in paragraphs 49 to 51 above, that fact constitutes a valid indication that the relevant public perceives that designation as designating a characteristic of those goods and, therefore, as being descriptive.

53 In those circumstances, the question whether the placing on the German market of cheeses produced in Germany under the name Emmentaler on its own is compatible with the Switzerland-Germany Agreement is irrelevant, since the perception of the relevant public, in relation to which the descriptive character of the sign at issue must be assessed, in accordance

with the case-law cited in paragraph 25 above, is formed, inter alia, by its exposure to that sign as placed on the market. The relevant public will generally assume that the goods marketed in a Member State have been lawfully placed on the market of that Member State, without necessarily questioning whether there are alleged conflicts between legal norms.

54 Consequently, the applicant's complaint that the Board of Appeal could not rely on the production in Germany of the cheese described as Emmentaler as one indication among others of the descriptive character of that sign must be rejected.

**The German Cheese Regulation**

55 In order to demonstrate that the sign EMMENTALER designates a type of cheese, the Board of Appeal also relied on the German cheese regulation, according to which emmentaler is classified as a standard type of cheese

. . . .

60 . . . the applicant's complaint that the Board of Appeal could not rely on the German cheese regulation as an indication among others of the descriptive character of the sign must be rejected.

**The European Union's Position During the Negotiation of the Agreement Between Switzerland and the European Union**

. . .

63 According to the applicant, it is true that the European Union did not agree to include that designation in the list of geographical indications protected by the Agreement between Switzerland and the European Union. However, that fact alone does not lead to the conclusion that no protection by means of an EU collective mark is possible for the name Emmentaler on its own.

64 In that regard, it should be noted that, first, the Agreement between Switzerland and the European Union contains, in Appendix 1 thereto, a list of names of cheeses which are subject to mutual protection by the contracting parties as designations of origin and geographical indications.

65 However, the name Emmentaler was not included in that list.

66 Secondly, the reasons for that non-inclusion were described in a press release of the Swiss Federal Office for Agriculture of 17 December 2009, to which the Board of Appeal referred in paragraph 24 of the contested decision.

67 In that press release, the Federal Office for Agriculture noted that the negotiations on the Agreement between Switzerland and the European Union had been hampered for a long time by their divergent positions concerning the inclusion of the name Emmentaler in the list of designations of origin and geographical indications in the context of that agreement, since '[the European Union had considered] the name "[E]mmentaler" to be a generic name' and that '[it had] required that that name [could] be used in all Member States'. According to that press release, it was because of those differences that Switzerland and the European Union decided not to include the name Emmentaler in that list.

68 It is plausible that that position of the European Union has its origin in the fact that, as is apparent from paragraph 48 above, products bearing the designation Emmentaler on its own were placed on the market in at least some Member States, such as Germany, with the result that that position is likely to reflect the perception of the relevant public in the Member States, including the German public.

69 In those circumstances, the applicant's complaint that the Board of Appeal could not rely on that position as one indication among others that the term 'emmentaler' would be perceived by the German public as descriptive of a type of cheese must be rejected.

### The General Standard for Emmental Drawn Up by the Codex Alimentarius Commission

71 . . . it is clear, first of all, from the case-law that the fact that a name is defined as generic in the Codex Alimentarius is a relevant aspect for assessing whether the mark applied for may be descriptive of a type of cheese (see, to that effect and by analogy, judgments of 12 September 2007, *Consorzio per la tutela del formaggio Grana Padano* v *OHIM – Biraghi (GRANA BIRAGHI)*, T291/03, EU:T:2007:255, paragraph 67, and of 14 December 2017, *Consejo Regulador 'Torta del Casar'* v *EUIPO – Consejo Regulador 'Queso de La Serena' (QUESO Y TORTA DE LA SERENA)*, T828/16, not published, EU:T:2017:918, paragraph 34 and the case-law cited).

72 Next, according to the general standard for emmental (CXS 269-1967) drawn up by the Codex Alimentarius Commission, the term 'emmental' designates a ripened hard cheese which complies with the requirements listed in that standard. Under Article 7.1 of that standard, the sign EMMENTALER may be used in accordance with the general standard for the labelling of pre-packaged foodstuffs, provided that the product complies with the emmental standard.

73 It follows that the sign EMMENTALER is, in the context of the Codex Alimentarius, perceived as a name of a type of cheese with the characteristics set out in that standard.

. . .

76 In those circumstances, the Board of Appeal was entitled to rely on the general standard for emmental drawn up by the Codex Alimentarius Commission as one indication among others in order to conclude that the term 'emmentaler' was descriptive of the goods at issue.

. . .

### Conclusion on Descriptiveness

81 In the light of the evidence examined in paragraphs 31 to 80 above, the Board of Appeal was entitled to find, in paragraph 24 of the contested decision, without making an error of assessment, that the relevant German public immediately understood the sign EMMENTALER as designating a type of cheese.

82 In the light of the case-law referred to in paragraph 23 above, the Board of Appeal was therefore right to conclude that that sign was descriptive for the purposes of Article 7(1)(c) and Article 7(2) of Regulation 2017/1001, bearing in mind that it is sufficient that that ground for refusal exists in part of the European Union, which may consist, as the case may be, of a single Member State.

. . .

### The first plea, alleging infringement of Article 74(2) of Regulation 2017/1001

85 The applicant submits that the name Emmentaler on its own should enjoy protection as a collective mark under Article 74(2) of Regulation 2017/1001, since it refers to the geographical origin of the goods in question.

. . .

88 In the present case, it is apparent from paragraphs 31 to 82 above that the Board of Appeal was fully entitled to conclude that the term 'emmentaler' was descriptive of a type of cheese for the relevant German public and was not perceived as an indication of the geographical origin of that cheese.

89 Similarly, the applicant has not submitted to the Court any other specific evidence intended to show that that public understands that sign in that sense.

90 In those circumstances, the applicant cannot claim that the mark applied for must be protected under Article 74(2) of Regulation 2017/1001.

91 Consequently, the first plea in law must be rejected and, accordingly, the action must be dismissed in its entirety.

THE GENERAL COURT (Tenth Chamber)

hereby:

. . .

1. **Dismisses the action;**
2. **Orders the Emmentaler Switzerland to pay the costs.**

## *Interprofession Du Gruyere v. U.S.*

61 F.4th 407 (4th Cir. 2023)

Gregory, Chief Judge:

This case is about gruyere cheese—"widely considered among the greatest of all cheeses," according to the Oxford Companion to Cheese, J.A. 1771—and under what circumstances cheese can be labeled as such. Appellants are a Swiss consortium, Interprofession du Gruyère ("IDG"), and a French consortium, Syndicat Interprofessionel du Gruyère ("SIG") (together, "the Consortiums"), who believe that gruyere[1] should only be used to label cheese that is produced in the Gruyère region of Switzerland and France. Seeking to enforce this limitation in the United States, the Consortiums filed an application with the United States Patent and Trademark Office ("USPTO") to register the word "GRUYERE" as a certification mark. Appellees, the U.S. Dairy Export Council, Atalanta Corporation, and Intercibus, Inc. (together, "the Opposers"), opposed this certification mark because they believe the term is generic and therefore ineligible for such protection.

The USPTO's Trademark Trial and Appeal Board ("TTAB") agreed with the Opposers and held that "GRUYERE" could not be registered as a certification mark because it is generic. The Consortiums filed a complaint challenging the TTAB's decision in United States district court. The district court granted summary judgment for the Opposers on the same grounds as articulated in the TTAB's decision. This appeal followed.

Like a fine cheese, this case has matured and is ripe for our review. For the reasons to follow, we conclude that the term "GRUYERE" is generic as a matter of law and affirm the decision of the district court.

### I.

### A.

Gruyere cheese originated in the district of La Gruyère in the Canton of Fribourg, Switzerland in 1115 AD. The original area of production has since expanded to include other areas in Switzerland and neighboring areas of France. In the Gruyère region of Switzerland and France, "producers make cheese from the unpasteurized milk of cows that graze on alpine grasses. The resulting cheese goes through a rigorous aging and production process." J.A. 1878. Switzerland and France have approved "Gruyère" as a protected designation of origin ("PDO") and a protected geographical indication ("PGI"), respectively. As a general matter, PDO and PGI designations "guarantee that [a] food product originates in the specified region or follows a traditional production process." J.A. 1743. The PDO and PGI designations for "Gruyère" each set forth detailed requirements that dictate the process of gruyere production, including that the cheese be produced in specified areas of Switzerland (pursuant to the Swiss PDO) and France (pursuant to the French PGI).

Parallel protections do not exist in the United States. While the Food and Drug Administration ("FDA") has issued a standard of identity for "Gruyere cheese," 21 C.F.R. § 133.149(a), which sets forth requirements that must be met for cheese to be labeled as such, *see* 21 U.S.C. § 343(g), those requirements are far less stringent than those governing gruyere production in Switzerland and France. For example, and as specifically relevant to this appeal, the FDA standard of identity does not impose any geographic restrictions as to where gruyere-labeled cheese can be produced.

As a result, cheese — regardless of its location of production — has been labeled and sold as gruyere in America for decades. For example, starting in 1991, Roth Käse, an American cheesemaker, began producing cheese in Wisconsin that it labeled and sold as gruyere in the United States. Roth Käse was subsequently acquired by a Swiss company, Emmi International Limited ("Emmi"), and became Emmi Roth USA ("Emmi Roth"). Emmi Roth sells cheese through its own house brand, as well as through private label sales to third-party retailers that sell Emmi Roth cheese under their own brands and labels. Pursuant to an agreement between Emmi and IDG, Emmi Roth stopped labeling its house brand cheese as gruyere in May 2013. But this agreement only applies to Emmi Roth's house brand cheese; it does not preclude Emmi Roth's private label customers from labeling Emmi Roth cheese as gruyere. Such private label sales are substantial; between 2014 and 2020, Emmi Roth sold approximately [Redacted] pounds of its Wisconsin-produced cheese to its private label customers, and at least some of those private label customers resold Emmi Roth cheese as gruyere. Indeed, the record demonstrates that in 2020, Boar's Head and Wegmans resold [Redacted] pounds of Emmi Roth cheese as gruyere. And except for 2020, Wegmans sold more pounds of Emmi Roth cheese labeled as gruyere than it did Swiss-produced gruyere-labeled cheese each year between 2016 and 2021.

The record evidence demonstrates that numerous other retailers, including Kroger Company and Publix, have sold gruyere-labeled cheese that was produced in Wisconsin. Additionally, a company called Glanbia Nutritionals ("Glanbia") produces gruyere cheese in Blackfoot, Idaho. Glanbia sold over [Redacted] pounds of gruyere-labeled cheese in 2018 and 2019 and over [Redacted] pounds in 2020.

In addition to American-produced gruyere-labeled cheese, there is evidence that cheese has been imported from numerous countries and sold in the United States as gruyere. Approximately seven million pounds of gruyere cheese were imported from Switzerland in 2020, and in 2016, almost 40,000 pounds of French gruyere cheese were sold in the United States. But in addition to importation from Switzerland and France, United States Department of Agriculture ("USDA") data show that, at least since 1995, cheese has been imported to the United States under the category "Gruyere-Process Cheese, Processed, Not Grated or Powdered" from the Netherlands, Germany, Austria, Belgium, Luxembourg, and Denmark. J.A. 127. USDA data also reflect that between 2010 to 2020, cheese in that category was imported into the United States from Switzerland, France, the Netherlands, Germany, Egypt, Denmark, Austria, Belgium, Ireland, the Czech Republic, Italy, and Tunisia. While the record does not demonstrate how much of this cheese has been sold and labeled as gruyere in the United States, sales records show that, at a minimum, certain companies sold approximately [Redacted] pounds of German-produced cheese as gruyere in the United States in 2020 alone.

### B.

Seeking to curtail the indiscriminate labeling of cheese as gruyere in the United States, IDG applied to the USPTO in 2010 to register "LE GRUYERE" as a certification mark that would certify that the cheese originates in the Gruyère region of Switzerland. The USPTO refused registration of the applied-for mark because it found that "the relevant consuming public views gruyere as a firm, nutty flavored cheese that can be made anywhere. Therefore, gruyere is a generic designation for cheese." J.A. 647. IDG also applied for another certification mark in 2010. This mark would similarly certify that the cheese originates in the Gruyère region of Switzerland, but unlike the previously applied-for mark, this application did not only attempt to certify the words "LE GRUYERE." Rather, IDG applied to register a mark that "consists of the term 'LE GRUYÈRE SWITZERLAND' in a stylized font. The term 'Switzerland' appears within a solid bar directly under 'LE GRUYÈRE.' To the right appears a stylized square containing the letters 'AOC' and a stylized Swiss cross." J.A. 928. The USPTO granted registration of this requested certification mark in 2013. As a result, only cheese that originates in the Gruyère region of Switzerland can bear the following certification mark:

LE GRUYÈRE®
SWITZERLAND AOP

J.A. 928.

In addition to its efforts with the USPTO, IDG engaged in a letter-writing campaign asking retailers and manufacturers in the United States to stop labeling their non-Swiss cheeses as gruyere. While some retailers and manufacturers crumbled under IDG's pressure, numerous others declined IDG's request and continued labeling their cheese as gruyere.

### C.

On September 17, 2015, the Consortiums filed another application with the USPTO. In this application, the Consortiums sought to register the word "GRUYERE" as a certification mark. The certification mark would "certif[y] that the cheese originates in the Gruyère region of Switzerland and France," J.A. 383, and would preclude any cheese produced outside that region from using the "GRUYERE" label. The USPTO published the mark for opposition, and the Opposers filed Notices of Opposition.[3] The Opposers alleged that (1) the Consortiums failed to exercise legitimate control over the proposed certification mark, which prevents it from functioning as a certification mark; and (2) because gruyere is a generic name for cheese, it is unregistrable under the Trademark Act. As to the latter argument, a generic term is one that members of the relevant public understand as identifying the type, rather than the source, of a product. *In re Steelbuilding.com*, 415 F.3d 1293, 1296 (Fed. Cir. 2005). According to the Opposers, cheese consumers in the United States understand "GRUYERE" as identifying a type of cheese, rather than as a signifier that the cheese was produced in the Gruyère region of Switzerland and France.

The parties each submitted evidence to the TTAB. Following a trial, the TTAB issued a decision in favor of the Opposers. Based on its review of the evidence, the TTAB determined that the term "GRUYERE" is generic because "purchasers and consumers of cheese understand the term 'gruyere' as a designation that primarily refers to a category within the genus of cheese that can come from anywhere." J.A. 77. The TTAB declined to reach the Opposers' control argument.

### D.

The district court granted . . . [found] that "the factual record in this case points indisputably to the conclusion that cheese purchasers in the United States understand the term GRUYERE to refer to a generic type of cheese without reference to the geographic location where the cheese is produced." *Interprofession Du Gruyère v. U.S. Dairy Exp. Council*, 575 F. Supp. 3d 627, 638, 649 (E.D. Va. 2021). In so doing, the district court considered three categories of record evidence. First, the court found that the FDA standard of identity for "Gruyere cheese" indicates the mark is generic. *Id.* at 640–41. Second, the district court held that the USDA import data and related evidence, as well as evidence of domestically produced gruyere-labeled cheese, also favor a finding that the term is generic. *Id.* at 641–47. Third, the district court determined that evidence of common usage of the term gruyere supports the same conclusion. *Id.* at 647–49. . . .

The Consortiums timely appealed the district court's decision to this Court.

. . .

## III.

### A.

We begin with an overview of the legal framework governing this appeal. The central dispute in this case is whether the district court properly granted summary judgment for the Opposers on the ground that the Consortiums' proposed certification mark is generic. A certification mark is "any word, name, symbol, or device, or any combination thereof" that is used "to certify regional or other origin, material, mode of manufacture, quality, accuracy, or other characteristics of such person's goods or services or that the work or labor on the goods or services was performed by members of a union or other organization." 15 U.S.C. § 1127. Unlike a typical trademark, "[a] geographic certification mark is not used by the owner of the mark; rather, the owner of the certification mark controls how others use the mark." *Luxco, Inc. v. Consejo Regulador Del Tequila, A.C.*, 121 U.S.P.Q.2d 1477 (T.T.A.B. 2017). Certification mark "users apply the mark to the goods to indicate to consumers that the goods have been certified as meeting the standards set forth by the certifier (*i.e.*, the owner of the mark)." *Id.*

"[C]ertification marks, including indications of regional origin" are registrable "in the same manner and with the same effect as are trademarks." 15 U.S.C. § 1054. Therefore, as is the case with trademark registration, "[a] generic name—the name of a class of products or services—is ineligible" for registration as a certification mark. *USPTO v. Booking.com B. V.*, —— U.S. ——, 140 S. Ct. 2298, 2301, 207 L. Ed. 2d 738 (2020). "A generic term, by definition, identifies a type of product, not the source of the product." *Steelbuilding.com*, 415 F.3d at 1296. And even if a term was once non-generic, the term can become generic when it "ceases to identify in the public's mind the particular source of a product or service but rather identifies a class of product or service, regardless of source." *Glover v. Ampak, Inc.*, 74 F.3d 57, 59 (4th Cir. 1996). Pursuant to the Lanham Act, "[t]he primary significance of the registered mark to the relevant public . . . shall be the test for determining whether the registered mark has become the generic name of goods or services on or in connection with which it has been used." 15 U.S.C. § 1064(3). In other words, "[t]he critical issue in genericness cases is whether members of the relevant public primarily use or understand the term sought to be protected to refer to the genus of goods or services in question." *H. Marvin Ginn Corp. v. Int'l Assn. of Fire Chiefs, Inc.*, 782 F.2d 987, 989–90 (Fed. Cir. 1986). Moreover, "a term is generic if the relevant public understands the term to refer to part of the claimed genus of goods or services, even if the public does not understand the term to refer to the broad genus as a whole." *In re Cordua Rests., Inc.*, 823 F.3d 594, 605 (Fed. Cir. 2016).

The TTAB determined, and the parties do not dispute, that the genus of goods is "cheese" and "the relevant public consists of members of the general public who purchase or consume cheese." J.A. 41. Therefore, this appeal hinges on whether members of the general public who purchase or consume cheese primarily understand the term "GRUYERE" as referring to a type of cheese, rather than as indicating that the cheese was produced in the Gruyère region of Switzerland and France. "Evidence of what the relevant public understands the term to mean may come from direct consumer testimony, surveys, dictionary listings, newspapers, and other publications." *Loglan Inst., Inc. v. Logical Language Grp., Inc.*, 962 F.2d 1038, 1041 (Fed. Cir. 1992).

The opposer of the mark "bears the burden of proving generic-ness by a preponderance of the evidence." *Princeton Vanguard, LLC v. Frito-Lay N. Am., Inc.*, 786 F.3d 960, 965 (Fed. Cir. 2015). And, while whether a term is generic is a factual issue, this Court has recognized that summary judgment is appropriate in genericness cases when the evidence "is so one-sided that one party must prevail as a matter of law." *Retail Servs., Inc. v. Freebies Publ'g*, 364 F.3d 535, 542 (4th Cir. 2004) (quoting *Liberty Lobby*, 477 U.S. at 251–52, 106 S. Ct. 2505).

**B.**

[W]e . . . conclude that the term "GRUYERE" is generic as a matter of law.

**1.**

. . .

***a.***

As to their first argument, the Consortiums posit that the USPTO Guide applies only to trademarks—not certification marks—and, therefore, the district court erred in giving *Skidmore* deference to guidance they contend is irrelevant. The USPTO Guide explains that "[b]ecause standards of identity relate solely to production methods and ingredients, there is no requirement that the product come from a specific place, even though many of these terms identify a cheese or processed meat that once came only from the place referred to in the name. . . . *Therefore, such geo-significant terms differ from certification and collective marks of regional origin*, which are registrable under . . . 15 U.S.C. § 1054." J.A. 1500–01 (emphasis added). According to the Consortiums, this language indicates that the USPTO Guide does not apply to certification marks.

. . . to the extent that guidance informs the genericness inquiry for trademarks, so too, does it inform the genericness inquiry for certification marks.

Regardless of the relevance of the USPTO Guide, we believe the FDA standard of identity for "Gruyere cheese" is evidence that the term "GRUYERE" is generic. . . .

. . . because the FDA standard of identity for "Gruyere cheese" has set constraints for labeling products as gruyere since 1977, it follows that its requirements—which do not prescribe any limitations on where the cheese must be produced—accord with consumer expectations about the gruyere label.

In addition, the Federal Circuit, with its " 'extensive expertise' in the area of trademark law," *Snyder's-Lance, Inc. v. Frito-Lay North Am., Inc.*, 991 F.3d 512, 528 (4th Cir. 2021), has similarly relied on an agency regulation to determine that a term is generic.

. . . We . . . conclude that the FDA standard of identity for "Gruyere cheese," which does not link the production of the cheese to any geographic region, is evidence that the term "GRUYERE" is generic.

***b.***

In support of their second argument—that the FDA cannot "permit" labeling of cheese as gruyere—the Consortiums rely on *POM Wonderful LLC v. Coca-Cola Co.*, wherein the Supreme Court held that compliance with Federal FDCA and FDA labeling regulations did not preclude a private cause of action under the Lanham Act. 573 U.S. 102, 120–21, 134 S.Ct. 2228, 189 L.Ed.2d 141 (2014).

. . .

[T]hese arguments serve to demonstrate that the FDA standard of identity for "Gruyere cheese" cannot, on its own, preclude registration of the "GRUYERE" certification mark, we agree. But the district court did not hold that the FDA standard of identity for the term "Gruyere cheese" prevents its registration as a certification mark. Rather, the court found that "the FDA's standard of identity for GRUYERE *presents strong evidence* that GRUYERE is a generic term," *Interprofession Du Gruyère*, 575 F. Supp. 3d at 641 (emphasis added), which the Consortiums' contentions do not undermine. That is, *POM Wonderful* holds only that the FDCA does not preclude Lanham Act claims challenging food and beverage labels. 573 U.S. at 120–21, 134 S. Ct. 2228. The decision does not bear on whether the USPTO or courts can look to FDCA or FDA regulations as evidence in trademark or certification mark disputes.

Similarly, that certain cheeses are subject to both an FDA standard of identity and a certification mark demonstrates only that FDA standards of identity should not be used as conclusive evidence of genericness, not that standards of identity are irrelevant to the genericness inquiry. . . . [E]ven though Roquefort and Reggiano cheese may not be generic, their respective FDA standards of identity prescribe production and ingredient requirements for alternative (and, ostensibly, generic) names for those cheeses. It thus makes sense why an FDA standard of identity—which does not require cheese to be produced in any location—exists for those types of cheese which have both generic and non-generic labels. By contrast, the FDA standard of identity for "Gruyere cheese" does not recognize alternative names for the cheese, suggesting that consumers understand the "Gruyere cheese" label as indicating a type of cheese, rather than as indicating that the cheese comes from a particular source.

We therefore agree with the district court's conclusion that the FDA standard of identity for "Gruyere cheese" supports a finding that the term "GRUYERE" is generic.

## 2.

Next, the Consortiums contend that the district court drew erroneous inferences regarding gruyere-labeled cheese in the United States market that is imported from countries other than Switzerland and France and produced domestically. We conclude that while the district court made an improper inference in the Opposers' favor regarding the USDA import data, the evidence of imported and domestic gruyere cheese, too, favors a finding that "GRUYERE" is generic.

### *a.*

First, the district court concluded, based on the USDA import data, that "from 2010-2020, the majority of GRUYERE-labeled cheese imported into the United States was imported from the Netherlands and Germany, not from Switzerland or France." *Interprofession Du Gruyère*, 575 F. Supp. 3d at 641. . . .

We agree with the Consortiums that, to the extent the district court relied on the USDA table to conclude that the majority of gruyere-labeled cheese imported into the United States was from countries other than Switzerland and France, it erred. While evidence in the record shows significant sales of non-Swiss and non-French imported cheese labeled as gruyere in the United States, that evidence does not demonstrate that *all* of the cheese reflected in the USDA table was sold as gruyere in the United States. . . .

Given the lack of concrete evidence demonstrating that the cheese reflected in the USDA table was sold to consumers in the United States as gruyere and the conflicts between the USDA data and other evidence in the record, the district court's conclusion that the majority of imported gruyere-labeled cheese did not come from Switzerland and France constitutes an inference in favor of the Opposers, the party moving for summary judgment. Such an inference is plainly impermissible at this stage. *See Lone Star Steakhouse & Saloon, Inc. v. Alpha of Virginia, Inc.*, 43 F.3d 922, 928 (4th Cir. 1995).

However, the district court correctly concluded from the record evidence that the Opposers had "clearly demonstrated that hundreds of thousands of pounds of cheese produced outside the Gruyère region of Switzerland and France is imported into the United States and sold in the United States labeled as GRUYERE." . . . The undisputed evidence . . . establishes that a substantial quantity of cheese has been imported to the United States from countries other than Switzerland and France and sold to consumers as gruyere.

***b.***

. . .

As to the Consortiums' first argument, they are correct that the evidence does not establish that all of Emmi Roth's private label customers label and sell the cheese as gruyere. But the record does show that in 2020, Emmi Roth sold over [Redacted] pounds of private label cheese, of which private label customers resold, at the very least, [Redacted] pounds as gruyere. Moreover, an Emmi Roth corporate representative provided deposition testimony that "the majority of private label that's being done are calling it Gruyère," J.A. 1833, indicating that the quantity of Emmi Roth cheese resold as gruyere in 2020 exceeded [Redacted] pounds. . . .

The Consortiums' challenge to the district court's assessment of the Glanbia data is similarly unavailing. It is true that the label for Glanbia cheese in the record is for a forty-pound quantity of cheese and is, therefore, likely a wholesale label. But, in determining whether a term is generic, the Lanham Act directs us to determine "[t]he primary significance of the registered mark to the *relevant public*." 15 U.S.C. § 1064(3) (emphasis added). As the Sixth Circuit has recognized, "'[t]he relevant public' is a broad term that implies that in an appropriate case it could include professional buyers." *Nartron Corp. v. STMicroelectronics, Inc.*, 305 F.3d 397, 406 (6th Cir. 2002) (citation omitted). This is such an appropriate case. The relevant public "consists of members of the general public who purchase or consume cheese," J.A. 41, which undoubtedly includes purchasers of wholesale cheese. The district court thus properly relied on the evidence of Glanbia sales in concluding that millions of pounds of domestic-produced cheese are sold as gruyere in the United States.

. . . there is also undisputed evidence in the record that numerous other cheese companies and retailers have labeled their domestically produced cheese as gruyere. Indeed, IDG wrote letters to Red Apple Cheese, Burnett Dairy, Trader Joes, and Dairy Food USA, among others, demanding that they cease labeling their United States-produced cheese as gruyere. This evidence suggests that the quantity of domestically produced cheese labeled as gruyere exceeded [Redacted] pounds in 2020.

. . .

All told, the record reflects sales in 2020 of at least [Redacted] pounds of gruyere-labeled cheese that was produced outside of the Gruyère region of Switzerland and France. In *In Re Cooperativa Produttori Latte E Fontina Valle D'acosta*, the TTAB concluded that the term fontina "merely describes or is the generic name for a type of cheese," in part because "the record reveal[ed] that there is a *domestic* fontina cheese." 230 U.S.P.Q. 131 (T.T.A.B. Mar. 19, 1986). Here too, the evidence demonstrates the existence of a domestic gruyere cheese. And even more persuasively, the record establishes that, at least in 2020, non-Swiss and non-French cheese made up a substantial portion of the cheese sold as gruyere in the United States market. "This evidence is probative of generic use because the more members of the public see a term used by competitors in the field, the less likely they will be to identify the term with one particular producer" (or, in this case, one geographic region). . .

**3.**

Finally, the Consortiums challenge the district court's consideration of evidence of common usage of the term gruyere. Specifically, they contend that the district court erroneously concluded that two groups of evidence—(1) dictionary definitions of the term gruyere; and (2) references to gruyere in the media—support a finding that the term "GRUYERE" is generic.[7] For the following reasons, we agree with the Consortiums that the dictionary definition evidence here is not probative of genericness but conclude that the media references support a finding that "GRUYERE" is generic.

*a.*

First, the district court considered various definitions of "Gruyère" and "Gruyère cheese" . . .

The district court considered most, but not all, of the definitions in the record and concluded that "[v]iewed as a whole, the dictionary evidence points to the conclusion that the term GRUYERE is not restricted to cheese produced in the [Gruyère] region of Switzerland and France." . . . Recognizing the numerous dictionary definitions which define "Gruyère" or "Gruyère cheese" without reference to any geographic region, we cannot conclude that the dictionary evidence indicates that cheese consumers primarily understand the term "GRUYERE" to refer to cheese that is produced in the Gruyère region of Switzerland and France. However, given the conflicting 26 dictionary definitions, the district court erred insofar as it concluded that the definitions support a finding that the term is generic.

*b.*

Next, the district court considered references to gruyere in publications, articles, and other online media. For example, the record contains downloads from websites that include "Gruyere" on a list of "Wisconsin Cheese Traits," J.A. 1046–48; that sell gruyere that is domestic and imported from Austria; and that rank "Wisconsin Gruyere Cheese," "Austrian Alps Gruyere," and an "Italian Gruyere" cheese on a list of the "10 Best Gruyere Cheese Options," J.A. 1076–79. . . . Additionally, the district court noted that the Opposers had introduced numerous press articles that referred to gruyere without referencing production in Switzerland or France. The district court concluded that because of this substantial evidence, together with the fact that the Consortiums only offered "two online-dictionary definitions (discussed previously), one printout from Wikipedia, and one European cheese guide," the weight of the common usage evidence favors a finding of genericness. *Interprofession Du Gruyère*, 575 F. Supp. 3d at 648.

. . .

Second, the Consortiums posit that references to gruyere in recipes and menus that lack any mention of geographic origin do not show genericness. In support, the Consortiums cite *Luxco Inc.*, wherein the TTAB held that recipes referencing "Tequila" without indicating its geographic origin did "not show that consumers are unaware of the geographic origin of Tequila." 121 U.S.P.Q.2d 1477. We note that other courts have found that references to a term, without mention of who sells or manufactures it, indicate that the term is generic. . . . [E]ven accepting the Consortiums' argument, the Opposers offered evidence of numerous websites specifically describing gruyere as originating in places *other than* Switzerland and France, including Wisconsin and Austria, which supports a finding that the primary significance of the term to the relevant public is a type of cheese that can be produced anywhere.

Therefore, notwithstanding the neutral nature of the dictionary evidence, we conclude that the evidence of the common usage of gruyere favors a finding that the term is generic.

. . .

Having addressed the Consortiums' challenges to the district court's opinion, we conclude that, while the district court made certain improper inferences in its analysis, the record nevertheless contains evidence that is "so one-sided" that there is no genuine issue as to any material fact and Opposers must prevail as a matter of law. *Retail Servs., Inc.*, 364 F.3d at 542. The FDA standard of identity, the pervasive sales of non-Swiss and non-French cheese labeled as gruyere in the United States, and the common usage of gruyere "establish[ ] that when purchasers walk into retail stores and ask for [gruyere], they regularly mean" a type of cheese, and not a cheese that was produced in the Gruyère region of Switzerland and France. *Glover*, 74 F.3d at 59.

C.

The Consortiums attempt to overcome this overwhelming evidence by arguing that the district court could not have properly granted summary judgment where, as here, the Opposers failed to provide consumer survey evidence. This argument slices the cheese too thinly. It is true that survey evidence has become "almost de rigueur in litigation over genericness," *Convenient Food Mart, Inc. v. 6-Twelve Convenient Mart, Inc.*, 690 F. Supp. 1457, 1461 (D. Md. 1988) (cleaned up), but parties are "not required to provide direct evidence of consumer perception to support [their] genericness challenge[s] to [trademarks or certification marks]," *Royal Crown Co., Inc. v. The Coca-Cola Co.*, 892 F.3d 1358, 1370 (Fed. Cir. 2018). Indeed, "[e]vidence of the public's understanding of the mark may be obtained from *any competent source*, such as consumer surveys, dictionaries, newspapers and other publications." *Cordua Rests.*, 823 F.3d at 599 (emphasis added) (internal quotation marks and citation omitted); *see also Glover*, 74 F.3d at 59 (noting that evidence that a mark has become generic "may come from purchaser testimony, consumer surveys, listings and dictionaries, trade journals, newspapers, and other publications.").

Along similar lines, the Consortiums contend that summary judgment is improper in all cases where a term that was not "commonly used prior to its association with the products at issue" allegedly becomes generic over time. Reply Br. 26 (quotation omitted). As a threshold matter, the Consortiums have not brought evidence bearing on whether, at an earlier point in history, the term "GRUYERE" was in common use in the United States. But even assuming that was the case, this argument still fails. While "difficult questions may be presented when a term has . . . a meaning that has changed over time," *Booking.com B.V.*, 140 S. Ct. at 2307, the Consortiums point to no case where we have categorically held that those difficult questions cannot be resolved at summary judgment. . . .

In sum, the Consortiums cannot overcome what the record makes clear: cheese consumers in the United States understand "GRUYERE" to refer to a type of cheese, which renders the term generic.

IV.

For the foregoing reasons, we affirm the district court's summary judgment in favor of the Opposers.

*AFFIRMED*

## NOTES AND QUESTIONS

**1.** Note the predominant impact of factual evidence in assessing the genericness and the eligibility for collective and certified trademark protection. The more geographical names are widely used by producers and the public at large beyond the region, the less it is possible to roll back existing pattern of use. Note also that the prospects of exclusivity wanes when traditional brands are used in emigration and foreign direct investment beyond international trade.

**2.** The General Court strongly relies upon the use of Emmental in German cheese production, despite the fact that a Swiss-German Agreement reserves exclusivity. Should the Agreement be taken into account under Article 31(3)(c) of the Vienna Convention on the Law of Treaties in assessing the law in the European Union? Note that neither of the Courts have taken international law into account other than the Codex Alimenatrius, and no references to the TRIPS Agreement in particular can be found in the rulings.

**3.** The Court of Appeals for the Fourth Circuit relies for evidence upon the definition of Gruyere by the U.S. Food and Drug Administration which does not relate to geographical origin while conceding that FDA standards do not rule out an independent assessment under trademark law. Is it appropriate to rely upon Food Standards, the purpose of which essentially is the protection of public health, rather to food diversity?

**4.** The two rulings go counter to efforts in law to develop specialities, encourage food diversity, and foster high quality. But that protection is controversial both within the European Union and the United States due to competing producer interests. It is odd to note that the European Union denied protection to Emmental in negotiations while otherwise strongly fostering the idea of geographical indications.

**5.** Would it be possible to obtain a collective or certified trademark using the mark "Emmental Swiss Made", and "Gruyère Swiss Made" in the EU and the U.S.?

**6.** Which tools other than trademarks could be used? Are the rulings consistent with the obligations to protect geographical indications under Article 22 TRIPS Agreement? (*See infra* E.)

**7.** What strategy would you recommend producers in order to effectively protect geographical names and the capital and good will linked to it?

### *3. Consumer Information and Preventing Consumer Deception*

Once a complainant in a trademark infringement proceeding shows that it is the holder of a valid trademark, it must still demonstrate that the complained-against party is using the mark in a way that is likely to confuse consumers. When an identical mark is used on identical goods or services, a likelihood of confusion is typically presumed. However, more difficult cases arise when the sign used by the complained-against party is different than the trademark holder's mark—for example, when the spelling of a word is changed—or when the sign is used in connection with different goods or services—for example, when a trademark ordinarily used to identify automobiles is used to identify refrigerators. The following case illustrates the challenges of assessing consumer deception in a multilingual and culturally diverse environment.

---

## *Loutfi Management Propriété Intellectuelle SARL v. AMJ Meatproducts NV, Halalsupply NV*

Judgment of the Court (Tenth Chamber), 25 June 2015

Case C-147/14

(Reference for a preliminary ruling—Community trade mark—Regulation (EC) No 207/2009—Article 9(1)(b)—Effects—Rights conferred by a Community trade mark—Identical or similar signs—Prohibition of use—Likelihood of confusion—Assessment—Taking into consideration the use of a language other than an official language of the European Union)

Request for a preliminary ruling pursuant to Article 267 TFEU from the Hof van beroep te Brussel (Belgium), made by decision of 17 March 2014, received at the Court on 28 March 2014, in the proceedings

THE COURT (Tenth Chamber),
composed of C. Vajda, President of the Chamber, E. Juhász (Rapporteur) and D. Šváby, Judges . . .

## Judgment

1. The request for a preliminary ruling concerns the interpretation of Article 9(1)(b) of Council Regulation (EC) No 207/2009 of 26 February 2009 on the Community trade mark (OJ 2009 L 78, p. 1).

2. The request has been made in proceedings between Loutfi Management Propriété intellectuelle SARL ('Loufti'), on the one hand, and AMJ Meatproducts NV ('Meatproducts') and Halalsupply NV ('Halalsupply'), on the other hand, concerning an alleged infringement of two Community trade marks registered by Loutfi.

### Legal Context

3. Article 9(1) of Regulation No 207/2009 entitled 'Rights conferred by a Community trade mark', establishes the rights that are conferred on the proprietor of a Community trade mark. That provision states:

> "A Community trade mark shall confer on the proprietor exclusive rights therein. The proprietor shall be entitled to prevent all third parties not having his consent from using in the course of trade:
>
> a) any sign which is identical with the Community trade mark in relation to goods or services which are identical with those for which the Community trade mark is registered;
> b) any sign where, because of its identity with, or similarity to, the Community trade mark and the identity or similarity of the goods or services covered by the Community trade mark and the sign, there exists a likelihood of confusion on the part of the public; the likelihood of confusion includes the likelihood of association between the sign and the trade mark;
>
> . . ."

### The . . . Question Referred for a Preliminary Ruling

19. By its question the national court asks, in essence, if Article 9(1)(b) of Regulation No 207/2009 must be interpreted as meaning that, in order to assess the likelihood of confusion which may exist between a Community mark and a sign which cover the same or similar goods and which both contain a dominant Arabic word in Latin and Arabic script, those words being visually similar, in circumstances where the relevant public for the Community mark and for the sign at issue has a basic understanding of written Arabic, the meaning and the pronunciation of those words may or must be taken into account.

20. It should be noted at the outset that Regulation No 207/2009, and in particular Article 9(1)(b) thereof, do not make reference to the use of any particular language or alphabet which should or should not be taken into account in assessing the likelihood of confusion which might exist on the part of the public.

21. The likelihood of confusion must in particular be assessed by reference to the perception of the relevant public, which consists of average consumers of the products or services in question, who are reasonably well informed and reasonably observant and circumspect (see, to that effect, judgment in Henkel v OHIM, C456/01 P and C457/01 P, EU:C:2004:258, paragraph 35 and the case-law cited).

22. The determination of the relevant public and the finding of the identity or similarity of the goods and services covered by the Community trade marks and the sign considered, stem from the factual assessment that the national court must undertake. In the present case, the national court has found that the relevant public must be defined as being the public consisting of Muslim consumers of Arab origin who consume 'halal' food products in the European Union and who have at least a basic knowledge of written Arabic. In addition it has held . . . that the goods covered by the two Community marks and the sign considered are identical or at least similar.

23. As to the likelihood of confusion on the part of the public that may exist between the Community marks and the sign considered, according to the settled case-law of the Court the existence of such a likelihood must be appreciated globally, taking into account all factors relevant to the circumstances of the particular case. That assessment includes a visual, aural or conceptual comparison of the signs at issue, bearing in mind, in particular, their distinctive and dominant components (see, to that effect, judgments in *Aceites del Sur-Coosur v Koipe*, C498/07 P, EU:C:2009:503, paragraphs 59 and 60, and *XXXLutz Marken v OHIM*, C306/11 P, EU:C:2012:401, paragraph 39).

24. In this case the national court has held that the word elements 'EL BNINA', 'EL BENNA' and 'EL BAINA' were dominant both in the two Community trade marks and in the sign considered, as were, to a lesser extent, the words in Arabic script. It has also indicated that while visually those verbal elements presented a certain similarity, it followed from the documents lodged before it by Meatproducts and Halalsupply that the pronunciation and meaning of those word elements differed substantially.

25. It follows from the above that those phonetic and conceptual differences should be taken into account because, if they are not, the assessment of the likelihood of confusion could be made only partially and, as a result, without taking into account the overall impression made by the Community trade marks and the sign considered on the relevant public.

26. Therefore, the answer to the question referred for preliminary ruling is that Article 9(1)(b) of Regulation No 207/2009 must be interpreted as meaning that, in order to assess the likelihood of confusion that may exist between a Community trade mark and a sign which cover the same or similar goods and which both contain a dominant Arabic word in Latin and Arabic script, those words being visually similar, in circumstances where the relevant public for the Community mark and for the sign at issue has a basic knowledge of written Arabic, the meaning and pronunciation of those words must be taken into account.

27. Given that the reply to the question referred for a preliminary ruling can be inferred from the wording of Regulation No 207/2009 and the case-law of the Court relating to that regulation, it is not necessary to examine the possible effects of the provisions of the Charter of Fundamental Rights of the European Union on that reply.

## NOTES AND QUESTIONS

**1.** Under EU law, explained in section V.A, national courts may seek preliminary rulings by the Court of Justice of the European Union (CJEU). The ruling does not dispose of the case but expounds the interpretation of the pertinent provisions, in this case the notion of likelihood of confusion in comparing different trademarks.

**2.** In the present case, the trademarks look fairly similar, but differ in terms of pronunciation by Arabic speakers. In taking this into account, how do you deal with the fact that these products are also exposed to non-Arabic speakers in Belgium who are less able to distinguish the marks in reading the letters? Which group should be given priority in assessing the risk of confusion? How would you rule as a local judge?

The following recent decision by the trial court judge in India illustrates that an identical trademark may be used by independent parties with respect to different classes of goods, in this case beer and self-defense pepper spray. The plaintiff proceeded on grounds of trademark dilution or disparagement as compared with strict trademark infringement. In a dilution or disparagement cause of action, the trademark holder is not alleging that the complained-against party is competing for sales in the same market. The trademark holder is instead alleging that the complained-against party is causing injury to its brand.

## *Skol Breweries v. Unisafe Technologies*

In the High Court of Delhi at New Delhi CS(OS) 472/2006, I.A. No. 3194/2006
Pronounced on: 25.08.2010

Mr. Justice S. Ravindra Bhat, J.

1. The plaintiff, in this suit, seeks the relief of permanent injunction against the defendant alleging infringement, passing off and unfair competition in respect of its trade mark, "KNOCK OUT." Other consequential reliefs are also claimed.

2. The suit avers that the plaintiff is proprietor of the brand, KNOCK OUT for beer by virtue of an assignment deed dated 27.05. . . . It is stated that the said brand has been in existence for over two decades and enjoys large and established reputation both in the domestic, as well as international markets. The plaintiff, inter alia, is engaged in the business of brewing, distilling and marketing beer under various trademarks (Haywards 2000, Haywards 5000, Royal Challenge and Knockout). The brand KNOCK OUT has been in existence and continuous use since 1986 (by the plaintiff's predecessor in interest). . . .The registered trademarks of the plaintiff are:

Trade Mark Class Regn. No. Date Goods KNOCK OUT HIGH PUNCH WITH LOGO 32 450938 11.03.1986 Beer KNOCK OUT LABEL 32 450939 11.03.1986 Beer. The said trademark-registrations are subsisting and valid.

3. Further, it is stated that the KNOCK OUT beer is India's leading brand selling over 7 million cases. . . .

5. It is alleged that the defendant is manufacturing a self defence pepper spray under the trademark "KNOCK OUT," using the plaintiff's brand in entirety. The domain name of defendant's website, i.e. www.knockoutspray.com also amounts to violation of the plaintiff's rights. . . .

6. The plaintiff alleges that the actions of the defendant are with an intention to take unfair advantage of the goodwill and reputation enjoyed by its (the plaintiff's) trademark "KNOCK OUT.". . .

7. In its defence, the defendant states that it has been using the trade mark KNOCK OUT, since April, 2004 in respect of a self defence pepper spray. It has spent substantial amounts to popularize its product, but the plaintiff sought this injunctive relief only in March, 2006 almost two years after the defendant started its operations. Further, the goods of the plaintiff are entirely different from those of the defendant. The plaintiff's goods fall under class 32 and the defendant's goods fall under classes 5 and 9. The defendant asserts that the plaintiff's trademark cannot become a well-known trade mark within the meaning of Section 11 (Sic 2 (1)(zg)) of the Trade Marks Act, 1999. The defendant submits that "Knock out" being a common dictionary word, which means—punch to the forehead or a strike to the head to cause unconsciousness, cannot be monopolized by the plaintiff in the manner, as is sought. The adoption of the said mark by the defendant is stated to be bonafide, as the meaning of the said word is descriptive of the characteristic of the product, i.e. it is meant for self defence, and when used, it knocks-out (incapacitates) the attacker for some time, giving the victim opportunity to escape or get help.

. . .

9. What the plaintiff complains of here is trademark infringement, by dilution. Although, dilution is not expressly alluded to in the Act, the relevant provision is Section 29(4); it reads as follows:

Section 29. Infringement of registered trade marks

(1) A registered trade mark is infringed by a person who, not being registered proprietor or a person using by way of permitted use, uses in the course of trade, a mark which is identical with, or deceptively similar to, the trade mark in relation to goods or services in respect of

which the trade mark is registered and in such manner as to render the use of the mark likely to be taken as being used as a trade mark.

. . .

(4) A registered trade mark is infringed by a person who, not being a registered proprietor or a person using by way of permitted use, uses in the course of trade, a mark which—

(a) is identical with or similar to the registered trade mark; and (b) is used in relation to goods or services which are not similar to those for which the trade mark is registered; and (c) the registered trade mark has a reputation in India and the use of the mark without due cause takes unfair advantage of or is detrimental to, the distinctive character or repute of the registered trade mark.

10. In trademark dilution claims, the plaintiff has to establish the identity or similarity with the registered trademark; the goods, in question, of course, necessarily are dissimilar to the plaintiff's goods; the plaintiff has to also prove that his mark has "a reputation in India" and the use of that mark "without due cause" takes unfair advantage, or is "detrimental to" the distinctive character or repute of his (the plaintiff's) mark. At the heart of the claim is the duty to establish that the mark has "a reputation in India" which is not a requirement in the normal class of infringement. This duty is underscored by the circumstance that infringement (i.e. competing similar mark, in relation to similar goods) is presumed, by virtue of the mandate of Section 29(3); there is no such presumption in trademark dilution claims, and all the elements prescribed under Section 29(4) are to be made good, for a claim of infringement, through dilution, to succeed.

. . .

12. Dealing with whether, and to what extent a trader can claim exclusivity in relation to common words, this Court in *SBL Limited v. Himalaya Drug Company*, 67 (1997) DLT 803 (DB), through a division Bench said that:

> Nobody can claim exclusive right to use any generic word, abbreviation, or acronym which has become publici juris. In the trade of drugs it is common practice to name a drug by the name of the organ or ailment which it treats or the main ingredient of the drug. Such an organ ailment or ingredient being public jurisdiction or generic cannot be owned by anyone for use as a trademark.

. . .

Recently, in *Rhizome Distilleries P. Ltd. & Ors. v. Pernod Ricard S.A. France & Ors.*, 165 (2009) DLT 474 too, another Division Bench underlined that common words, generic or descriptive names, do not automatically evoke protection of the Court unless a plaintiff establishes that such marks have acquired secondary meaning: . . .

. . .

14. Another consideration which has to weigh with the Court is that the term Knock Out does not inherently describe the plaintiff's product. On the other hand, the defendant's pepper spray, it is claimed, has the attribute or ability to "knock out" the unwanted physical advances of a man, which may threaten the user. The defendant's mark, in the opinion of the Court, has greater degree of association or claim to descriptiveness of the product, than the plaintiff's. Here, the observations in *British Petroleum Company Ltd v. European Petroleum Distributors Ltd.*, [1968 RPC 54], are relevant:

> "In considering whether or not the mark is 'inherently adapted' to distinguish the goods it is relevant to ask oneself whether and to what extent if the proposed mark was not given a statutory protection, other producers of the goods would be likely in the normal course of events to wish to use the mark themselves. . . ."

. . .

17. There is no evidence on record, to establish that the plaintiff's KNOCK OUT has acquired distinctiveness and association with its product of such nature or fame that the

consumer or user only thinks of the plaintiff's brand of beer on any reference to the expression, Knock Out. The Court is evaluating the evidence, on the basis of material on record; it is essential that the plaintiff should rely on materials, which are not conjectural, but based on reality. The plaintiff has not led any evidence to show that there was likelihood of consumer confusion, or that the defendant, knowing the plaintiff's mark, deliberately chose to use it. The plaintiff was under an obligation to prove confusion, and not rely merely on the averments in the suit, and the documents filed, which it has failed to discharge.

18. Apart from the above considerations, there are some unusual elements to this case, which the Court cannot but help noticing. The lynchpin of the plaintiff's case is the strong message of "manliness" or machismo associated with the consumer of its KNOCK OUT beer. The plaintiff complains that this masculinity, as it were, is severely damaged by the defendant's use of the same KNOCK OUT term or mark, for the pepper spray it markets. The plaintiff is piqued, because of the manner by which the defendant is marketing, i.e. as an effective deterrent to aggressive or persistent unwanted male attention or physical advances, when it tends to threaten the (female) user. As mentioned earlier, the defendant's mark is closer in description of the product than the plaintiff's. If such is the case, the use of such an inherently descriptive mark is proper and legitimate. Furthermore, the speciousness of the plaintiff's argument is revealed if one examines it closely, for countenancing it would mean accepting that it is "masculine" or "manly" to indulge and persist in such unwarranted attentions towards women. If the argument implies that the plaintiff's product results in such "machismo" its utter untenability is laid bare, because it would amount to saying that consumption of the KNOCK OUT beer would result in such manliness that would need the use of pepper spray to stave of[f] uncalled[-for] physical advances. Surely that is not the result desired by the plaintiff, while advancing its contentions.

19. The Court is conscious that though the competing marks are similar, the consumer base is entirely different, as is the product. There is nothing to show that trade channels are common, or that the plaintiff's marks have acquired such degree of secondary distinctiveness that the term KNOCK OUT certainly, or almost invariably implies it or its product.

20. In view of the above conclusions, the Court is of opinion that the suit cannot succeed; it is accordingly dismissed. In the circumstances of the case, the parties are left to bear their costs.

## NOTES AND QUESTIONS

**1.** Why does the plaintiff beer producer proceed on a dilution or disparagement claim rather than strict trademark infringement?

**2.** The Delhi High Court's decision appears grounded in several factors: (1) the trademark at issue has a descriptive meaning; (2) the plaintiff has failed to establish that its mark has become well known in association with its product; (3) the defendant has plausible descriptive grounds for adopting the trademark in connection with its product; and (4) the plaintiff's theory of dilution or disparagement is contrary to good public policy.

**3.** India is part of the common law legal tradition. In this respect, the trial court may place greater reliance on precedent than statutory language as compared, for example, with the CJEU, whose decisions are more grounded in the civil law tradition.

## B. The Limits of the Trademark

The trademark is defined in terms of rights granted to the holder to prevent others from using without the right holder's consent identical or similar signs in the course of trade. This right is limited in a number of ways.

### 1. *Exhaustion of Trademark Rights and Fair Use*

The doctrine of exhaustion, introduced in Chapter 1 and considered in some detail with respect to patents in Chapter 2 and Chapter 4 in copyright, addresses the point at which the trademark holder's control over the good or service ceases. This termination of control is critical to the functioning of any market economy because it permits the free transfer of goods and services. Without an exhaustion doctrine, the original trademark holder would perpetually exercise control over the sale, transfer, or use of a good or service associated with the mark, and would control economic life.

A trademark is typically exhausted by the "first sale" (U.S. doctrine) or "placing on the market" (EU doctrine) of the good or service embodying it. The basic idea is that once the right holder has been able to obtain an economic return from the first sale or placing on the market, the purchaser or transferee of the good or service is entitled to use and dispose of it without further restriction.

The trademark gives its holder the exclusive right to place the good or service on the market, but it does not give the holder a right to control all uses of the trademark. Third parties are entitled to make "fair use" of the mark. There are a variety of contexts in which fair use may take place, some of which already were alluded to in the *Qualitex v. Jacobsen* decision. Resellers of trademarked products, or sellers of spare parts, typically must make some use of the trademark in order to make purchasers aware of the nature of the goods offered. Trademarks also may be used fairly in comparative advertisement and news reporting. Whether third-party use is "fair" will depend on the specific context of the use: A third party may be fairly using the mark to make consumers aware of the nature of the product, or a third party may be unfairly taking advantage by deliberately implying its own connection to the trademark holder. Trademarks are used in news reporting and in literary and academic references to refer to the "thing itself." A news reporter cannot very well be expected to refer to "the football club based in Manchester, England" every time he or she wishes to report on the exploits of Manchester United. Fair reference to the thing being described is sometimes referred to as "nominative fair use."

In the following decision, the Court of Justice of the European Union considers the extent to which a trademark holder, the maker of BMW automobiles, may prevent third parties from using its BMW mark in advertising second-hand BMWs and servicing them. In doing so, it sets limits on the rights of the trademark holder to control the secondary market in its products.

---

## *Judgment of the Court*

23 February 1999

(Trade-marks directive — Unauthorised use of the BMW trade mark in advertisements for a garage business)

In Case C-63/97,

REFERENCE to the Court under Article 177 of the EC Treaty by the Hoge Raad der Nederlanden (Netherlands) for a preliminary ruling in the proceedings pending before that court . . .

Bayerische Motorenwerke AG (BMW)
and
BMW Nederland BV and Ronald Karel Deenik

on the interpretation of Articles 5 to 7 of First Council Directive 89/104/EEC of 21 December 1988 to approximate the laws of the Member States relating to trade marks (OJ 1989 L 40, p. 1),

THE COURT,
composed of: G.C. Rodríguez Iglesias, President, P.J.G. Kapteyn, J.-P. Puissochet and P. Jann (Presidents of Chambers), C. Gulmann (Rapporteur), J.L. Murray, D.A.O. Edward, H. Ragnemalm, L. Sevón, M. Wathelet and R. Schintgen, Judges, gives the following :

## Judgment

1. By judgment of 7 February 1997, received at the Court on 13 February 1997, the Hoge Raad der Nederlanden (Supreme Court of the Netherlands) referred to the Court for a preliminary ruling under Article 177 of the EC Treaty five questions on the interpretation of Articles 5 to 7 of First Council Directive 89/104/EEC of 21 December 1988 to approximate the laws of the Member States relating to trade marks (OJ 1989 L 40, p. 1, "the directive").

2. Those questions were raised in proceedings between the German company Bayerische Motorenwerke AG (BMW) and the Netherlands company BMW Nederland BV (referred to separately as "BMW AG" and "BMW BV" and jointly as "BMW") and Mr Deenik, the owner of a garage, residing in Almere (Netherlands), concerning his advertisements for the sale of second-hand BMW cars and repairs and maintenance of BMW cars. . . .

6. In many countries, including, since 1930, the Benelux States, BMW AG markets vehicles which it has manufactured and in respect of which it has registered with the Benelux Trade Marks Office the trade name BMW and two figurative trade marks for, *inter alia*, engines and motor vehicles as well as for spare parts and accessories ("the BMW mark").

7. BMW AG markets its vehicles through a network of dealers. In the Netherlands it supervises the network with the help of BMW BV. Dealers are entitled to use the BMW mark for the purposes of their business, but are required to meet the high standards of technical quality deemed necessary by BMW in the provision of service and warranties and in sales promotion.

8. Mr Deenik runs a garage and has specialised in the sale of second-hand BMW cars and in repairing and maintaining BMW cars. He is not part of the BMW dealer network.

9. In the main proceedings BMW claimed that, in carrying on his business, Mr Deenik made unlawful use, in advertisements, of the BMW mark or, at the very least, of similar signs. By writ of 21 February 1994 it accordingly sought an order from the Rechtbank (District Court), Zwolle, restraining Mr Deenik from, in particular, using the BMW mark or any similar sign in advertisements, publicity statements or other announcements emanating from him, or in any other way in connection with his business, and claimed damages from him. BMW relied on its rights under Article 13A of the Uniform Benelux Law on Trade Marks in the version then in force.

10. The Rechtbank took the view that a number of statements made by Mr Deenik in his advertisements constituted unlawful use of the BMW mark, on the ground that they could give rise to the impression that they were put out by an undertaking entitled to use that mark, that is to say, an undertaking affiliated to the BMW dealer network. It therefore made an order prohibiting him from making such use of the BMW mark. However, the Rechtbank considered that Mr Deenik was entitled to use expressions such as "Repairs and maintenance of BMWs" in his advertisements, since it was sufficiently clear that these referred only to products bearing the BMW mark. Furthermore, the Rechtbank deemed permissible statements such as "BMW specialist" or "Specialised in BMWs," on the ground that BMW had not disputed the fact that Mr Deenik had specialist experience of BMW vehicles and it was

not for BMW to decide who were entitled to describe themselves as BMW specialists. The Rechtbank dismissed BMW's claim for damages.

11. BMW appealed against that judgment, requesting the Gerechtshof (Regional Court of Appeal), Arnhem, to rule that, by referring in advertisements to "Repairs and maintenance of BMWs" and by describing himself as a "BMW specialist" or as "Specialised in BMWs," Mr Deenik was infringing the trade-mark rights belonging to BMW. Upon the Gerechtshof's confirmation of the Rechtbank's judgment, BMW lodged an appeal in cassation against that decision on 10 November 1995 with the Hoge Raad.

12. In the circumstances the Hoge Raad decided to stay proceedings and refer the . . . questions to the Court for a preliminary ruling: . . .

29. It should in addition be borne in mind that Articles 6 and 7 of the directive contain rules limiting the right of the proprietor of a trade mark, under Article 5, to prohibit a third party from using his mark. In this connection, Article 6 provides *inter alia* that the proprietor of a trade mark may not prohibit a third party from using the mark where it is necessary to indicate the intended purpose of a product, provided that he uses it in accordance with honest practices in industrial or commercial matters. Article 7 provides that the proprietor is not entitled to prohibit the use of a trade mark in relation to goods which have been put on the market in the Community under that trade mark by the proprietor or with his consent, unless there exist legitimate reasons for him to oppose further commercialisation of the goods. . . .

## QUESTIONS 2 AND 3

31. By its second and third questions, which should be considered together, the national court is in substance asking whether the use of a trade mark, without the proprietor's authorisation, in order to inform the public that another undertaking carries out repairs and maintenance of goods covered by that trade mark or that it has specialised, or is a specialist, in such goods constitutes a use of that mark for the purposes of one of the provisions of Article 5 of the directive. . . .

42. Accordingly, the answer to be given to the second and third questions must be that the use of a trade mark, without the proprietor's authorisation, for the purpose of informing the public that another undertaking carries out the repair and maintenance of goods covered by that mark or that it has specialised or is a specialist in such goods constitutes, in circumstances such as those described in the judgment making the reference, use of the mark within the meaning of Article 5(1)(a) of the directive.

## QUESTIONS 4 AND 5

43. By its fourth and fifth questions, which should be considered together, the national court is in substance asking whether Articles 5 to 7 of the directive entitle the proprietor of a trade mark to prevent another person from using that mark for the purpose of informing the public that he carries out the repair and maintenance of goods covered by a trade mark and put on the market under that mark by the proprietor or with his consent, or that he has specialised or is a specialist in the sale or the repair and maintenance of such goods.

44. The Court is asked to rule, in particular, on the question whether the trade mark proprietor may prevent such use only where the advertiser creates the impression that his undertaking is affiliated to the trade mark proprietor's distribution network, or whether he may also prevent such use where, because of the manner in which the trade mark is used in the advertisements, there is a good chance that the public might be given the impression that the advertiser is using the trade mark in that regard to an appreciable extent for the purpose of advertising his own business as such, by creating a specific suggestion of quality.

45. In order to reply to that question, it must be pointed out that, in view of the answer given to the second and third questions that the use of the trade mark in the advertisements concerned in the main proceedings falls within the scope of Article 5(1)(a) of the directive, the use in issue may be prohibited by the trade mark proprietor unless Article 6, concerning the limitation of the effects of a trade mark, or Article 7, concerning exhaustion of the rights conferred by a trade mark, are applicable.

46. That question must be considered, first, in relation to the advertisements for the sale of second-hand cars and, second, in relation to the advertisements for the repair and maintenance of cars.

### The Advertisements for the Sale of Second-Hand Bmw Cars

47. As regards the advertisements for the sale of second-hand BMW cars put on the market under that trade mark by the trade mark proprietor or with his consent, the case-law of the Court should be borne in mind concerning the use of a trade mark to inform the public of the resale of goods covered by a trade mark.

48. In Case C-337/95 *Parfums Christian Dior v Evora* [1997] ECR I-6013, the Court first held, at paragraph 38, that on a proper interpretation of Articles 5 and 7 of the directive, when trade-marked goods have been put on the Community market by the proprietor of the trade mark or with his consent, a reseller, besides being free to resell those goods, is also free to make use of the trade mark in order to bring to the public's attention the further commercialisation of those goods.

49. In the same judgment, the Court then found, at paragraph 43, that damage done to the reputation of a trade mark may, in principle, be a legitimate reason, within the meaning of Article 7(2) of the directive, allowing the proprietor to oppose the use of his trade mark for further commercialisation of goods put on the Community market by him or with his consent. As regards prestige goods, the Court stated, at paragraph 45, that the reseller must not act unfairly in relation to the legitimate interests of the trade mark owner, but must endeavour to prevent his advertising from affecting the value of the trade mark by detracting from the prestigious image of the goods in question. At paragraph 48, the Court concluded that the proprietor of a trade mark may not rely on Article 7(2) to oppose the use of the trade mark, in ways customary in the reseller's sector of trade, for the purpose of bringing to the public's attention the further commercialisation of the trade-marked goods, unless it is established that such use seriously damages the reputation of the trade mark.

50. In the context of the present case, the consequence of that decision is that it is contrary to Article 7 of the directive for the proprietor of the BMW mark to prohibit the use of its mark by another person for the purpose of informing the public that he has specialised or is a specialist in the sale of second-hand BMW cars, provided that the advertising concerns cars which have been put on the Community market under that mark by the proprietor or with its consent and that the way in which the mark is used in that advertising does not constitute a legitimate reason, within the meaning of Article 7(2), for the proprietor's opposition.

51. The fact that the trade mark is used in a reseller's advertising in such a way that it may give rise to the impression that there is a commercial connection between the reseller and the trade mark proprietor, and in particular that the reseller's business is affiliated to the trade mark proprietor's distribution network or that there is a special relationship between the two undertakings, may constitute a legitimate reason within the meaning of Article 7(2) of the directive.

52. Such advertising is not essential to the further commercialisation of goods put on the Community market under the trade mark by its proprietor or with his consent or, therefore, to the purpose of the exhaustion rule laid down in Article 7 of the directive. Moreover, it is

contrary to the obligation to act fairly in relation to the legitimate interests of the trade mark owner and it affects the value of the trade mark by taking unfair advantage of its distinctive character or repute. It is also incompatible with the specific object of a trade mark which is, according to the case-law of the Court, to protect the proprietor against competitors wishing to take advantage of the status and reputation of the trade mark (*see, inter alia,* Case C-10/89 *HAG GF* [1990] ECR I-3711, "*HAG II*," paragraph 14).

53. If, on the other hand, there is no risk that the public will be led to believe that there is a commercial connection between the reseller and the trade mark proprietor, the mere fact that the reseller derives an advantage from using the trade mark in that advertisements for the sale of goods covered by the mark, which are in other respects honest and fair, lend an aura of quality to his own business does not constitute a legitimate reason within the meaning of Article 7(2) of the directive.

54. In that connection, it is sufficient to state that a reseller who sells second-hand BMW cars and who genuinely has specialised or is a specialist in the sale of those vehicles cannot in practice communicate such information to his customers without using the BMW mark. In consequence, such an informative use of the BMW mark is necessary to guarantee the right of resale under Article 7 of the directive and does not take unfair advantage of the distinctive character or repute of that trade mark.

55. Whether advertising may create the impression that there is a commercial connection between the reseller and the trade mark proprietor is a question of fact for the national court to decide in the light of the circumstances of each case.

### The Advertisements Relating to Repair and Maintenance of Bmw Cars

56. First, the Court finds that the rule concerning exhaustion of the rights conferred by a trade mark laid down in Article 7 of the directive is not applicable to the advertisements relating to repair and maintenance of BMW cars.

57. Article 7 is intended to reconcile the interests of trade-mark protection and those of free movement of goods within the Community by making the further commercialisation of a product bearing a trade mark possible and preventing opposition by the proprietor of the mark (*see*, to that effect, *Parfums Christian Dior*, paragraphs 37 and 38). Advertisements relating to car repair and maintenance do not affect further commercialisation of the goods in question.

58. None the less, so far as those advertisements are concerned, it is still necessary to consider whether use of the trade mark may be legitimate in the light of the rule laid down in Article 6(1)(c) of the directive, that the proprietor may not prohibit a third party from using the trade mark to indicate the intended purpose of a product or service, in particular as accessories or spare parts, provided that the use is necessary to indicate that purpose and is in accordance with honest practices in industrial or commercial matters.

59. In that regard, as the United Kingdom Government has observed, the use of the trade mark to inform the public that the advertiser repairs and maintains trade-marked goods must be held to constitute use indicating the intended purpose of the service within the meaning of Article 6(1)(c). Like the use of a trade mark intended to identify the vehicles which a non-original spare part will fit, the use in question is intended to identify the goods in respect of which the service is provided.

60. Furthermore, the use concerned must be held to be necessary to indicate the intended purpose of the service. It is sufficient to note, as the Advocate General did at point 54 of his Opinion, that if an independent trader carries out the maintenance and repair of BMW cars or is in fact a specialist in that field, that fact cannot in practice be communicated to his customers without using the BMW mark.

61. Lastly, the condition requiring use of the trade mark to be made in accordance with honest practices in industrial or commercial matters must be regarded as constituting in substance the expression of a duty to act fairly in relation to the legitimate interests of the trade mark owner, similar to that imposed on the reseller where he uses another's trade mark to advertise the resale of products covered by that mark.

62. Just like Article 7, Article 6 seeks to reconcile the fundamental interests of trade-mark protection with those of free movement of goods and freedom to provide services in the common market in such a way that trade mark rights are able to fulfil their essential role in the system of undistorted competition which the Treaty seeks to establish and maintain (*see*, in particular, *HAG II*, paragraph 13).

63. Consequently, for the reasons set out in paragraphs 51 to 54 of this judgment, which apply *mutatis mutandis*, the use of another's trade mark for the purpose of informing the public of the repair and maintenance of goods covered by that mark is authorised on the same conditions as those applying where the mark is used for the purpose of informing the public of the resale of goods covered by that mark.

64. In the light of the foregoing, the answer to be given to the fourth and fifth questions must be that Articles 5 to 7 of the directive do not entitle the proprietor of a trade mark to prohibit a third party from using the mark for the purpose of informing the public that he carries out the repair and maintenance of goods covered by that trade mark and put on the market under that mark by the proprietor or with his consent, or that he has specialised or is a specialist in the sale or the repair and maintenance of such goods, unless the mark is used in a way that may create the impression that there is a commercial connection between the other undertaking and the trade mark proprietor, and in particular that the reseller's business is affiliated to the trade mark proprietor's distribution network or that there is a special relationship between the two undertakings. . . .

## NOTES AND QUESTIONS

**1.** The Court of Justice of the European Union (CJEU) serves as guardian and ultimate interpreter of the Treaty on the Functioning of the European Union (TFEU) and subsidiary EU legislation. The courts of the EU member states ordinarily interpret and apply community legislation in litigation, but if the national courts are uncertain with respect to a proper interpretation, they may refer the matter to the CJEU. In the text case, the Supreme Court of the Netherlands (the "Hoge Raad") has referred the question of interpretation of the First Trade Marks Directive to the CJEU. When it renders its decision, the CJEU does not "direct" the national court, but rather provides an answer to the question that has been asked and relies on the national court to properly apply it in the case. This reflects the separation of EU and member state powers at the judicial level.

**2.** The CJEU has referred both to Article 7 of the Trade Marks Directive that provides for exhaustion of rights and Article 6 that addresses fair use. The two doctrines are closely related in that each places a limit on the scope of the rights of the trademark holder. Would BMW gain by exercising more control over downstream uses of its trademark? Who would lose?

**3.** Consider individuals who have purchased automobiles and wish to sell them by posting advertisements in newspapers or on the Internet. Is it feasible to sell a used car without referring to the manufacturer's trademark?

**4.** In *Ford Motor Company v Wheeltrims*, C-500/14, 6 Oct. 2015, the CJEU held that the owner of the trademark "Ford" cannot prevent its use by replacement part producers when necessary to restore the proper appearance of the vehicle ("The affixing by Wheeltrims of the Ford trade mark to the wheel covers it markets performs the function not of indicating the origin of such parts, but of identifying the manufacturer with reference to the product as a whole, namely the motor vehicle on which the wheel covers are mounted. That use of the Ford trade mark serves to reproduce, on the replacement part, an aesthetic and descriptive characteristic of the original part concerned, namely the wheel cover, a characteristic that must be regarded as essential for the purposes of restoring the original appearance of the complex product constituted by the motor vehicle as a whole. If producers of replacement parts for motor vehicles were not able to use trade marks for that purpose free competition would be impeded on the market concerned." *Id.*, para. 24.).

---

## *Junek Europ-Vertrieb v. Lohmann & Rauscher*

Judgment of the Court (Fifth Chamber), 17 May 2018

(Reference for a preliminary ruling—Intellectual property—Trade-mark law—Regulation (EC) No 207/2009—Article 13—Exhaustion of the rights conferred by a trade mark—Parallel imports—Repackaging of the product bearing the mark—New labelling—Conditions applicable to medical devices)

In Case C642/16,

REQUEST for a preliminary ruling under Article 267 TFEU from the Bundesgerichtshof (Federal Court of Justice, Germany), made by decision of 6 October 2015, and received at the Court on 14 December 2016, in the proceedings

Junek Europ-Vertrieb GmbH v Lohmann & Rauscher International GmbH & Co. KG

THE COURT (Fifth Chamber),
composed of J.L. da Cruz Vilaça, President of the Chamber, E. Levits, A. Borg Barthet (Rapporteur), M. Berger and F. Biltgen, Judges,
Advocate General: M. Bobek,
gives the following

### Judgment

1. This request for a preliminary ruling concerns the interpretation of Article 13(2) of Council Regulation (EC) No 207/2009 of 26 February 2009 on the European Union trade mark (OJ 2009 L 78, p. 1).

2. The request has been made in proceedings between Junek Europ-Vertrieb GmbH, parallel importer of sanitary preparations for medical purposes and dressings, and Lohmann & Rauscher International GmbH & Co. KG, manufacturer of such products, concerning dressings manufactured by the latter which were imported as parallel imports and marketed in Germany by Junek Europ-Vertrieb, after having been relabelled.

. . .

### Consideration of the Question Referred

21. By its question, the referring court asks, in essence, whether Article 13(2) of Regulation No 207/2009 must be interpreted as meaning that the proprietor of a mark may oppose the further commercialisation, by a parallel importer, of a medical device in its original

internal and external packaging when an additional label, such as that at issue in the main proceedings, has been added by the importer. More specifically, it wishes to know whether the principles developed by the Court in its judgments of 11 July 1996, *Bristol-Myers Squibb and Others* (C427/93, C429/93 and C436/93, EU:C:1996:282) and of 26 April 2007, *Boehringer Ingelheim and Others* (C348/04, EU:C:2007:249) apply without restriction to the parallel import of medical devices.

22. As a preliminary matter, it is necessary to recall the case-law of the Court and the principles developed by it as regards the parallel import of pharmaceutical products.

23. In that regard, it is clear from the settled case-law that the specific purpose of a mark is to guarantee the origin of the product bearing that mark and that a repackaging of that product carried out by a third party without the authorisation of the proprietor is likely to create real risks for that guarantee of origin (see, to that effect, judgment of 10 November 2016, *Ferring Lægemidler*, C297/15, EU:C:2016:857, paragraph 14 and the case-law cited).

24. According to the case-law of the Court, it is the repackaging of the trade-marked pharmaceutical products in itself which is prejudicial to the specific subject matter of the mark, and it is not necessary in that context to assess the actual effects of the repackaging by the parallel importer (see, to that effect, judgment of 26 April 2007, *Boehringer Ingelheim and Others*, C348/04, EU:C:2007:249, paragraph 15).

25. In addition, it must be observed that the Court has held, as regards Article 7(2) of the First Council Directive 89/104/EEC of 21 December 1988 to approximate the laws of the Member States relating to trade marks (OJ 1989 L 40, p. 1) the wording of which is equivalent to that of Article 13(2) of Regulation No 207/2009, that, under that provision, the trade mark proprietor's opposition to repackaging, in that it constitutes a derogation from free movement of goods, cannot be accepted if the proprietor's exercise of that right constitutes a disguised restriction on trade between Member States within the meaning of the second sentence of Article 36 TFEU (judgments of 23 April 2002, *Boehringer Ingelheim and Others*, C143/00, EU:C:2002:246, paragraph 18 and of 26 April 2007, *Boehringer Ingelheim and Others*, C348/04, EU:C:2007:249, paragraph 16 and the case-law cited).

26. A disguised restriction within the meaning of that provision will exist where the exercise by a trade mark proprietor of its right to oppose repackaging contributes to artificial partitioning of the markets between Member States and where, in addition, the repackaging is done in such a way that the legitimate interests of the proprietor are respected. This means, in particular, that the repackaging must not adversely affect the original condition of the product and must not be such as to harm the reputation of the mark (judgment of 26 April 2007, *Boehringer Ingelheim and Others*, C348/04, EU:C:2007:249, paragraph 17 and the case-law cited).

27. The Court thus laid down the principles on the restrictions on the exhaustion of the rights conferred by a trade mark in the context of the parallel importation of pharmaceutical products (judgments of 11 July 1996, *Bristol-Myers Squibb and Others*, C427/93, C429/93 and C436/93, EU:C:1996:282, paragraph 79, and of 26 April 2007, *Boehringer Ingelheim and Others*, C348/04, EU:C:2007:249, paragraph 32).

28. According to that case-law, pursuant to Article 7(2) of the First Directive 89/104, the proprietor of a mark may legitimately oppose the further commercialisation of a pharmaceutical product imported from another Member State in its original internal and external packaging with an additional external label applied by the importer, unless:

— it is established that the use of the trade mark rights by the proprietor thereof to oppose the marketing of the relabelled products under that trade mark would contribute to the artificial partitioning of the markets between Member States;
— it is shown that the repackaging cannot affect the original condition of the product inside the packaging;

— the new packaging states clearly who repackaged the product and the name of the manufacturer;
— the presentation of the repackaged product is not such as to be liable to damage the reputation of the trade mark and of its owner; thus, the packaging must not be defective, of poor quality, or untidy; and
— the importer gives notice to the trade mark proprietor before the repackaged product is put on sale, and, on demand, supplies him with a specimen of the repackaged product.

29. Thus, the five conditions referred to in the previous paragraph, which, when they are satisfied, preclude the proprietor of the mark from legitimately opposing the further commercialisation of the product concerned, only apply where the importer has repackaged that product.

30. As regards the concept of 'repackaging', the Court has clarified that it includes the relabelling of the pharmaceutical products bearing the mark (judgment of 26 April 2007, *Boehringer Ingelheim and Others*, C348/04, EU:C:2007:249, paragraph 28).

31. Nevertheless, it is necessary to note that the facts that gave rise to the judgments of 23 April 2002, *Boehringer Ingelheim and Others* (C143/00, EU:C:2002:246), and of 26 April 2007, *Boehringer Ingelheim and Others* (C348/04, EU:C:2007:249), which concerned additional labels being affixed to the packaging of the pharmaceutical products concerned, are different from the facts at issue in the main proceedings.

32. It is clear from paragraph 7 of the judgment of 23 April 2002, *Boehringer Ingelheim and Others* (C143/00, EU:C:2002:246), and paragraph 24 of the judgment of 26 April 2007, *Boehringer Ingelheim and Others* (C348/04, EU:C:2007:249) that, in the cases that gave rise to those judgments, in certain cases, a label including certain important information, such as the name of the parallel importer and its parallel import licence number, had been attached, in other cases, the product concerned had been repackaged in boxes which had been designed by the parallel importer and on which the mark had been reproduced and, in yet further cases, that product had been repackaged in boxes which had been designed by the parallel importer and which did not bear the mark, but only the generic name of the product. The Court added that, in all those cases of repackaging, the boxes contained a patient information leaflet in the language of the country of importation, namely English, which bore the mark at issue.

33. It follows that, in the cases that gave rise to those judgments, at issue was an intervention by the parallel importer that involved, not only affixing an additional external label to the packaging of the pharmaceutical products concerned or its repackaging, but also, in every case, the opening of the original packaging in order to insert an information leaflet in a language different from that of the country of origin of the product which bore the mark in question.

34. By contrast, in the case in the main proceedings, it must be observed, first, that the parallel importer has merely affixed an additional label to the unprinted part of the original packaging of the medical device in question, which, moreover, had not been opened. Second, the label is small in size and included, as the only information provided, the name, address and telephone number of the parallel importer, a barcode and a central pharmacological number which serves to organise the movement of the products with pharmacies.

35. Given that the packaging of the medical device concerned has not been modified and the original presentation of the packaging has not been affected other than by the attachment of a small label, which does not conceal the mark and which designates the parallel importer as responsible for placing it on the market by setting out his details, a barcode and a central pharmacological number, it cannot be held that the attachment of such a label constitutes repackaging within the meaning of the judgments of 23 April 2002, *Boehringer Ingelheim and Others* (C143/00, EU:C:2002:246), and of 26 April 2007, *Boehringer Ingelheim and Others* (C348/04, EU:C:2007:249).

36. Consequently, it cannot, in any event, be held that the attachment of such a label affects the specific purpose of the mark, which is to guarantee the origin of the product that it identifies.

37. In those circumstances, the attachment of an additional label, such as that at issue in the case in the main proceedings, by the parallel importer, namely by Junek Europ-Vertrieb, to the original packaging of the medical device, which has not been opened, is not a legitimate reason that justifies the proprietor of the mark, in this case Lohmann & Rauscher International, opposing the further commercialisation of the medical device concerned.

38. Therefore, the situation which gave rise to the case in the main proceedings constitutes a case of exhaustion of the rights conferred by a trade mark pursuant to Article 13(1) of Regulation No 207/2009.

39. Having regard to the foregoing considerations, the answer to the question referred is that Article 13(2) of Regulation No 207/2009 must be interpreted as meaning that the proprietor of a mark cannot oppose the further commercialisation, by a parallel importer, of a medical device in its original internal and external packaging where an additional label, such as that at issue in the case in the main proceedings, has been added by the importer, which, by its content, function, size, presentation and placement, does not give rise to a risk to the guarantee of origin of the medical device bearing the mark.

## NOTES AND QUESTIONS

**1.** The CJEU developed precise standards as to parallel imports of repacked pharmaceutical products using the original trademark (as opposed to generic drugs). It modified these standards for medical equipment. Do you think that these standards also apply to other consumer goods unrelated to health? What can be drawn from the overall purpose of preventing consumer deception while allowing for free flow of goods within the European Union and European Economic Area?

**2.** We examine the fair use of trademark in the context of an Internet domain name dispute, *infra* section VI.C, *Pfizer Inc. v. Van Robichaux.*

**3.** In *Jack Daniel's v. VIP Products*, 599 U.S. ___ (2023), the U.S. Supreme Court overturned a decision of the Ninth Circuit Court of Appeals that had exempted from infringement and dilution claims the use of a dog toy label similar to that of a well-known liquor brand, Jack Daniel's, based on the expressive content (i.e. parody) of the liquor brand. The Supreme Court held that when the "expressive" imitation mark (e.g., "Bad Spaniels") is being used to identify the source of the imitator's product (here a dog toy) there is no automatic trademark infringement exception for expression, but rather an ordinary likelihood of confusion infringement analysis applies. Likewise, the statutory non-commercial use exception from dilution actions does not apply when the imitator's mark is being used as a source identifier.

### *2. National, Regional, and International Exhaustion*

Trademark rights are typically granted by national (or regional) authorities. With the registration or acquisition of a trademark, the holder obtains a "bundle of rights" that it may exercise within the territory of the granting authority. When a good or service is first sold or marketed within the country, this exhausts the trademark right embodied in it. Yet, the same trademark holder may hold equivalent or "parallel" rights in many countries. The Coca-Cola Company, again for illustrative purposes, may hold trademark registrations for the Coca-Cola mark in virtually every country of the world. In Chapter 1, section VII.E, we introduced the distinction between national, regional, and international exhaustion of IP rights, and which doctrines are relevant to trademarks, just as patents (see Chapter 2, section II.A.4), and other forms of IP.

Trademark holder groups have long sought to shift the terminology of parallel trade so as to label parallel imports "gray market" goods. The implication is that such goods, while not "black market" or "illicit" goods, are somehow tainted. This campaign has enjoyed some success, and courts in the United States not infrequently refer to parallel imports as the "gray market." But there is nothing illegal or illicit in parallel trade. It provides significant benefits to consumers in the form of enhanced price competition, and parallel imports are commonly purchased by the largest retail stores. We do not adopt the "gray market" terminology here.

Countries need not, and often do not, adopt the same exhaustion rule across the spectrum of IPRs.[1] The United States, for example, follows a rule of international exhaustion among commonly controlled enterprises in trademarks (*see K mart v. Cartier, infra*), and a rule of international exhaustion with respect to patents (*see Impression Products, supra* Chapter 2) and copyright (*see Kirtsaeng v. John Wiley & Sons, infra* Chapter 4). Switzerland follows a rule of international exhaustion for copyright[2] and trademark,[3] but national exhaustion with respect to patent.[4] The European Union appears to follow a rule of regional exhaustion for copyright, patent, and trademark.[5] Consider that the preponderance of goods traded in world commerce is identified by a trademark. Far fewer goods are patented. All other things being equal, a rule that permits the segregation of national markets (i.e., national exhaustion) *may* have a broader impact on world trade if it applies to trademarked goods than if it is limited to patented goods.[6]

We examine the question of national, regional, and international exhaustion of trademark rights in some detail later in this chapter.

### 3. *Term of Protection*

There is no inherent limit on the term of protection for a trademark or service mark. A mark will remain valid for so long as it is used to identify goods or services in commerce, and provided that the mark does not lose its distinctive character. Trademark registration authorities typically require that registrations be renewed on a periodic basis, and the TRIPS Agreement (Art. 18) has set a minimum term of seven years for such renewals (as well as for the initial term of registration). Complex legal issues may arise in terminating and revoking existing trademarks; *see Peek & Cloppenburg KG, Hamburg v Peek & Cloppenburg KG*, Case C148/17, Düsseldorf, 18 Apr. 2018.

---

1. See generally Frederick M. Abbott, First Report (Final) to the International Trade Law Committee of the International Law Association on the Subject of Parallel Importation (June 1997), 1 J. Int'l Econ. L. 607 (1998); Frederick M. Abbott, Second Report (Final) to the Committee on International Trade Law of the International Law Association on the Subject of the Exhaustion of Intellectual Property Rights and Parallel Importation, presented in London, July 2000, at the 69th Conference of the International Law Association, rev. 1.1, available at SSRN: http://ssrn.com/abstract=1921856.

2. Chanel SA, Geneva and Chanel SA, Glarus v. EPA SA, BGE 122 II 469, Oct. 23, 1996.

3. *Imprafot AG v. Nintendo Co. et al.*, Swiss Federal Supreme Court, No. 4C.45/1998/zus, July 20, 1998.

4. *Kodak SA v. Jumbo-Markt AG*, 4C.24/1999/rnd, Dec. 7, 1999.

5. *See Silhouette,* supra Chapter 1, section VII.E, p. 102, regarding trademarks, and First and Second Reports, *supra*, regarding copyright and patent.

6. Patented goods may, on average, be more expensive than trademarked goods, so the extrapolation regarding overall impact on world trade would be complicated. Data collection by government authorities with respect to parallel trade is inadequate to permit an empirical assessment of this issue.

## C. Trade Names

A trade name is also an identifier. While a trademark identifies a good or service of an enterprise, the trade name identifies the enterprise itself. It is not uncommon for an enterprise to use the same trade name and trademark. As a well-known example, IBM is the trade name of a multinational enterprise, and it is also the trademark that this enterprise uses to identify its products and services. There is, however, no necessary link between a trade name and trademark. The name "Emily's Flower Shop" may serve as the identifier of a business, without also serving as the identifier of products or services of that business.

Article 8 of the Paris Convention for the Protection of Industrial Property establishes a general obligation for the protection of trade names, and specifies that such protection should be granted "without the obligation of filing or registration, whether or not it forms part of a trademark." The WTO Appellate Body has interpreted the subject matter "intellectual property" as used in the TRIPS Agreement to include trade names because Article 8 of the Paris Convention is incorporated by reference in the TRIPS Agreement. See discussion in *U.S.-Havana Club, infra* pages 419-425.

Holders of registered trademarks typically enjoy exclusive rights within a national or regional territory. The proprietors of trade names may enjoy more limited protection, confined even to a single town or part of a town. The owner of a local restaurant or cafe, for example, may be able to prevent a newcomer from using the same trade name in the same town. That restaurant or cafe owner may not be able to prevent a competitor from using the same trade name in a nearby town. This depends on principles of unfair competition law generally used to protect trade names.

## D. Domain Names

In recent years the "domain name" has taken its place alongside the trademark, service mark, and trade name as an important identifier for enterprises and their products and services.[7] A domain name is a human-friendly identifier of a location on the Internet,[8] and is composed of a registrant-specific term, followed by period or "dot" and a "generic Top Level Domain" (gTLD) (e.g., amazon.com) or its equivalent (e.g., country code).

Domain names are used to identify all manner of web sites on the Internet. Some of those web sites are commercially oriented. Many are not. From a business standpoint, the ability to establish an easily recognizable location on the Internet may have a very high commercial value. If a well-known trademark or service mark is incorporated in a domain name, this virtually assures a high volume of Internet traffic at the associated web site. A web site such as cnn.com may receive millions of visits every day. Yet, this propensity of trademarks and service marks to attract Internet users also offers an opportunity for third parties to take advantage of the commercial draw for their own benefit. If a person other than the trademark holder is successful in registering the same or a confusingly similar domain name, that third party may divert Internet traffic to its own web site, which may offer competing products, pornographic material, or other information not sponsored by or affiliated with the mark holder. Sometimes the successful third-party registrant of a mark in a domain name will attempt to sell it to

---

7. *See generally* Frederick M. Abbott, *On the Duality of Internet Domain Names: Propertization and Its Discontents*, 3 N.Y.U. J. Int. Prop. & Enter. L. 1 (2013), available at SSRN: http://ssrn.com/abstract=2257562.

8. The domain name is associated with an Internet Protocol (IP) number that identifies the location of a particular address typically including a host computer (or server) and a sub-location on that host.

the trademark holder. Unauthorized use of trademarks in domain names is more recently evidenced in a variety of schemes to defraud, including cloning of websites and use of near identical email addresses.

Yet, determining who is entitled to use a particular term in a domain name may be a complex matter. There are legitimate ways marks may be used without the consent of their holders in domain names, such as under "fair use" doctrine. A trademark may be identical to an individual's name, and individuals are generally allowed to use their own names in domain names, though this right is not unqualified.[9]

A domain name may identify a business enterprise without identifying a product or service in a trademark sense. In such cases, the domain name may perform a function much like that of a trade name.

The domain name may share characteristics of the trademark, service mark, and trade name, but it is a different form of identifier used in its own unique environment. The law surrounding the use and protection of domain names is explored in section VI of this chapter. The subject matter of domain names is becoming increasingly complex from a legal standpoint as the range of top-level domains has been widely opened up, and a number of new procedural mechanisms have been added for resolving potential conflicts between trademarks, other types of protected terms, and domain names.

## E. Geographical Indications

A geographical indication is the name of a territory that conveys an attribute of a product or the goodwill of producers of that place. The right to use a geographical indication is typically shared by a community of producers. An example of a geographical indication is "Champagne." That term refers to a region of France where quality sparkling wines are produced, and is used by wine makers of that region to identify their product. By virtue of long usage of the term "Champagne" by regional producers exercising control over production, consumers have come to associate the geographical name "Champagne" with certain qualities, and the term embodies the "goodwill" of its producers.

The right to use a geographical indication does not depend on objectively demonstrating a particular level of quality or characteristics of a product. Although consumers or experts might (or might not) be able to objectively distinguish between "Champagne" made by wine producers in France and "Sekt" made by wine producers in Germany (using the same bottle-fermenting process), legal reliance on such objective differentiation may not be feasible. Although Champagne might (or might not) have different characteristics than Sekt, it is not necessarily those characteristics that are protected by the geographical indication. Also protected is the goodwill or reputation of wine producers in the Champagne region built up over a long period of time.

In *Wineworths Group Ltd. v. Comite Interprofessionel du Vin de Champagne*, 2 NZLR 327 [1991] (*Wineworths v. CIVC*),[10] decided by the New Zealand Court of Appeal, an importer of Australian sparkling wines was sued by a French semi-official protective body for misuse of the term "Champagne" in connection with its marketing and sales activities. In finding for the French complainant, the court held that the name "Champagne" had acquired distinctiveness

9. Individuals with names that are identical to trademarks may be prevented from taking unfair commercial advantage of that fact.

10. This discussion and reference is taken from *Her Majesty the Queen, in right of her Government in New Zealand v. iSMER*, WIPO Case No. DBIZ2002-00270, decided Oct. 2, 2002.

among New Zealand consumers as associating a particular product with certain qualities, and that the producers of the "Champagne" region of France had acquired legally protectable goodwill in that name. Judge J. Gault stated:

> "Champagne is a geographical name. When used in relation to wine the primary significance it would convey to persons who know that would be as the geographical origin of the product. If the name conveys something of the characteristics of the wine it is because those familiar with wine sold by reference to the name associate those characteristics with it. . . . For suppliers the attracting force in the name constitutes a part of the goodwill of their business. That will be so whether the name is associated solely with one supplier or with a class of suppliers who stand in the same position to the name. The goodwill may be enjoyed among the whole population or among a particular market segment.
>
> That goodwill will be damaged if someone else uses the name in relation to a product in such a manner as to deceive purchasers into believing the product has the characteristics of products normally associated with the name when it does not. The damage may give rise to a claim for 'passing off' although deceptive trading would be a more accurate designation." (2 NZLR 327, 336)

Geographical indications are protected in different ways. Many countries protect them under unfair competition law, essentially prohibiting their use by persons not appropriately connected with the subject region. Other countries provide for the registration and protection of geographical indications as such, and may include administrative systems for their regulation. Still, other countries treat geographical indications as trademarks, including collective and certification marks.

Because the geographical indication is associated with a territory and may be used only by those with sufficient connection to the territory, it may not be licensed, assigned, or transferred in the sense of most other IPRs. The extent to which elements of the production process relating to the GI-protected good may be carried on outside the territory identified by the GI is not well settled.

The TRIPS Agreement established the first multilateral set of rules specifically directed to geographical indications, though this set of rules largely relied on the unfair competition provisions of the Paris Convention, and added a few enumerated requirements in respect to wines and spirits. The TRIPS Agreement mandated future negotiations on geographical indications. These negotiations are discussed later in this section.

The geographical indication is an identifier and, like the trademark and trade name, is capable of conferring exclusive rights for so long as the conditions that give rise to its protection endure.

The geographical indication as a form of intellectual property is distinguished from a "mark of origin" (sometimes referred to as an "indication of source") that is typically required to be placed on goods in international trade to allow customs and other regulatory authorities to identify the place where a product is made. The marking "made in China" allows customs authorities in the United States to determine the appropriate tariff applicable to goods that originate in China. This marking might be used to determine whether goods are subject to antidumping duties. As a matter of international trade law, it is unlawful to misdescribe the country of origin of goods because this practice may impede the application of various regulatory controls. The Paris Convention (Article 10) requires that governments provide for the seizure of goods bearing false indications of source, including country of origin markings, upon importation, and provides that producers from the falsely attributed territory should have the right to initiate actions for seizure.

**Frederick M. Abbott***

## *Geographical Indications at the Hong Kong Ministerial*
(Dec. 13-18, 2005)

1. Negotiations on geographical indications in the TRIPS Council illustrate the basic fact that intellectual property rights are instruments of industrial policy and that states express preferences not based on moral philosophy, but rather on whether they believe their national interests are maximized by granting or denying rights. Their expressed interests tend to be defined by larger producers who have the financial resources to make demands on the political process. . . .

4. WTO members each have offensive and defensive interests with respect to GIs and these interests vary along a spectrum. The fault line between offensive and defensive interests is sometimes characterized as "Old World" versus "New World," although it might also be characterized along efficiencies of agricultural production, marketing and franchising.

. . .

7. In a relatively simple economic calculation we can say that the EU interests in GIs are primarily offense, and the US interest primarily defensive, but there are US agricultural businesses which would welcome more protection such as the producers of Idaho potatoes and Washington apples.

8. For developing countries the picture is similar. Some developing countries have what they perceive as relatively strong offensive interests. Some in wine, some in teas and spices, some in rice varieties, some in spirit drinks. For most countries, the calculation is not easily made: but like the US, the large efficient agricultural producers like Argentina and Brazil oppose extension. The producers with major export markets in specific products, including smaller producing countries, occupy a movable middle ground.

9. For developing countries there is a factor that is less significant for the EU and the United States; and that is what the regulatory costs will be both on the offense and defensive sides. The creation of legal rights or interests—even if filing fees are reduced by a multilateral registration system—still require enforcement, which is predominantly under TRIPS a private matter. Considerable care must be taken not to conflate a system which theoretically allows protection in foreign markets and the costs of litigation in these foreign markets. There may be a tendency to overvalue the offensive interests and minimize the defensive costs. . . .

10. Because the picture is mixed, there is at present a stalemate. The United States will only move if the food—agriculture and food services—industries are willing to move, and this is not yet prepared. But over some period of time an accommodation a system meeting the EU part way could be worked out. If the EU makes GIs the sine qua non of agricultural reform, developing countries are put in a very serious posture of attempting to calculate the gains from expanded access to the EU market and reduction of damaging EU subsidies, versus the cost of giving EU agricultural products special protection in the market. This is a very difficult equation to solve. The US presumably will protect against a truly terrible deal.

* Presented at WTO Hong Kong Ministerial, ICSTD Session on Recovering Multilateralism in IP Policy Making: Can the WTO Deliver?, Dec. 15, 2005.

## NOTES AND QUESTIONS

**1.** The TRIPS Agreement includes, as part of its built-in agenda, negotiations toward the establishment of a multilateral register for geographical indications for wines and spirits for members participating in the system.[11] These negotiations have been going on for some time. At the Hong Kong Ministerial, WTO Members "agree[d] to intensify these negotiations in order to complete them within the overall time-frame for the conclusion of the negotiations that were foreseen in the Doha Ministerial Declaration."[12] There is also reference in Article 24.1 of the TRIPS Agreement to the possibility of further negotiation on specific indications following the Uruguay Round, but whether this refers to extension to products beyond wines and spirits is the subject of debate in the TRIPS Council. As with the relationship between the TRIPS Agreement and CBD, in Hong Kong, Members agreed that the Director-General should intensify negotiations on the subject and report to the General Council "no later than 31 July 2006." As of January 2011, while a substantial number of developing countries had moved to generally support the EU position on the extension of GIs protection, there had been no significant movement toward agreement at the WTO on the subject of geographical indications. The Director-General at the Geneva March 2010 stock-taking of the Doha Round reported only that "while my consultations have not created convergence they have certainly shed clearer light on the divergences."[13] The July 30, 2020 formal meeting of the TRIPS Special Session continued to reflect little progress toward consensus among negotiating members.[14]

**2.** While the geographical connection of some products is fairly well defined, this does not hold true in many cases. Thus, the introduction of additional layers of protection for geographical indications would almost certainly lead to controversies among important producing regions. Some of those conflicts would involve different developing countries with strong interests in geographic names.

**3.** There is also a question regarding the extent to which "country names" are protectable as intellectual property. New Zealand, for example, unsuccessfully claimed common law trademark rights in its country name "as such" in two domain name disputes (*see Her Majesty the Queen, in right of her Government in New Zealand v. iSMER*, WIPO Case No. DBIZ2002-00270, decided Oct. 2, 2002[15] and *Her Majesty the Queen, in right of her Government in New Zealand, as Trustee for the Citizens, Organizations and State of New Zealand, acting by and through the Honourable Jim Sutton, the Associate Minister of Foreign Affairs and Trade v. Virtual Countries, Inc*, Case No. D2002-0754, decided Nov. 27, 2002). Yet, while country names may not be trademarks "as such," there is interest among many governments in establishing some form of recognition of rights in country names beyond a right to protect against false attribution. The country name "Switzerland" (and the adjective "Swiss"), for example, conveys attributes of products and services to consumers. The country name is not infrequently used by

11. Article 23.4, TRIPS Agreement.

12. Hong Kong Ministerial Declaration, at para. 29.

13. *Lamy Opens Stocktaking Week with Hope for Strong Signal on Concluding the Round*, WTO: 2010 News Items: Trade Negotiations Committee, 22 March 2010, available at http://www.wto.org/english/news_e/news10_e/tnc_dg_stat_22mar10_e.htm.

14. Council for Trade-Related Aspects of Intellectual Property Rights — Special Session — Multilateral System of Notification and Registration of Geographical Indications for Wines and Spirits, Report by the Chairman, TN/IP/31, 22 Nov. 2022.

15. This decision was rendered under the .biz sunrise procedure (a process under which domain name applications within a new gTLD are subject to pre-registration challenge), and while New Zealand did not succeed on the trademark issue, it was awarded the domain name because it had some legitimate interest in it, which the respondent lacked (and conceded).

persons outside the country to identify products and services, notwithstanding the lack of any connection to the country. If these "non-Swiss" products and services do not meet the standards of quality or demonstrate the other characteristics expected by consumers, the goodwill enjoyed by manufacturers and service providers within Switzerland is affected. This may have an effect on the economy of the country. Yet efforts by some governments to negotiate toward increased protection of country names is resisted by others, particularly as such a move may raise questions regarding who controls use of the country name, and how it is controlled. By way of illustration, in the United States use of the designations "U.S.," "American," and similar terms by private parties is ubiquitous. Initiating a system to regulate such use would be difficult. In this regard, establishing the regime for additional protection for country names may be a rather complex legal and political undertaking. For a discussion of these issues within WIPO, *see, e.g.*, Standing Committee on the Law of Trademarks, Industrial Designs and Geographical Indications, Thirty-First Session, Geneva, March 17-21, 2014, Draft Report prepared by the Secretariat, paras. 135 et seq. (April 7, 2014).

**4.** One controversial issue under the TRIPS Agreement is whether there is a hierarchy or priority between trademarks and geographical indications. In other words, what happens when a trademark and geographical indication appear to be in conflict? This issue was addressed in a WTO panel decision involving a dispute between United States and the European Union, *European Communities—Protection of Trademarks and Geographical Indications for Agricultural Products and Foodstuffs*, Report of the Panel, WT/DS174/R, 15 Mar. 2005, presented *infra* p. 479-489.

**5.** Following a highly contentious negotiating process at WIPO, state parties to the Lisbon Agreement for the Protection of Appellations of Origin and their International Registration on May 20, 2015, adopted a new "Geneva Act" intended to expand the subject matter scope of the agreement to encompass all geographical indications. The Geneva Act entered into force on February 26, 2020. The process was made difficult because state parties to the Lisbon Agreement insisted that only parties to that agreement (the Lisbon Union) could participate as voting members of the diplomatic conference, which left out the United States and other countries where geographical indications are generally protected under trademark law. While the negotiations may have been at least a partial success from the standpoint of the Lisbon Union countries, because the Geneva Act is unlikely to attract countries not previously party to the Agreement, it will not act as a worldwide registration system for geographical indications. The Geneva Act effort was an attempt by the European Union to bypass the stalemate on a GI register and expanded scope of GI subject matter at the WTO. *See, e.g.*, *New Act of the Lisbon Agreement Encompasses All Geographical Indications, Allows Accession by Regional Organizations*, INTABulletin, June 15, 2015. For a somewhat more positive view of the outcome, *see, e.g.*, Catherine Saez, *An Interview with WIPO Director General Francis Gurry on the New Lisbon Act for GIs*, IP-Watch, May 25, 2015.

**6.** Given the difficulties to advance protection of GIs on the multilateral level, efforts shifted to bilateral and plurilateral fora. Canada recognized GI protection in the Comprehensive Economic and Trade Agreement with the European Union, and the Comprehensive and Progressive Transpacific Partnership Agreement, including GI protection among the 11 member states in the Pacific area. References can be found *infra* section I.G.

One of the most contested aspects of GI is the scope of protection. It explains much of the controversy on GIs. The European Union accords extensive subject matter protection, including to traditional agricultural products. In the following case, the CJEU decides on the extent of protection accorded to producers of ham in the Parma region of Italy.

## *Consorzio del Prosciutto Di Parma*

Judgment of the Court 20 May 2003

(Protected designations of origin — Regulation (EEC) No 2081/92 — Regulation (EC) No 1107/96 — Prosciutto di Parma — Specification — Requirement for ham to be sliced and packaged in the region of production — Articles 29 EC and 30 EC — Justification — Whether requirement may be relied on against third parties — Legal certainty — Publicity)

In Case C-108/01,

REFERENCE to the Court under Article 234 EC by the House of Lords (United Kingdom) for a preliminary ruling in the proceedings pending before that court between
Consorzio del Prosciutto di Parma,
Salumificio S. Rita SpA
And
Asda Stores Ltd, Hygrade Foods Ltd,

on the interpretation of Council Regulation (EEC) No 2081/92 of 14 July 1992 on the protection of geographical indications and designations of origin for agricultural products and foodstuffs (OJ 1992 L 208, p. 1), as amended . . . , and of Commission Regulation (EC) No 1107/96 of 12 June 1996 on the registration of geographical indications and designations of origin under the procedure laid down in Article 17 of Regulation No 2081/92 (OJ 1996 L 148, p. 1),

THE COURT,
composed of: G.C. Rodríguez Iglesias, President, J.-P. Puissochet, M. Wathelet, R. Schintgen and C.W.A. Timmermans (Presidents of Chambers), C. Gulmann (Rapporteur), D.A.O. Edward, P. Jann, V. Skouris, F. Macken, N. Colneric, S. von Bahr and J.N. Cunha Rodrigues, Judges, gives the following:

### Judgment . . .

### The Main Proceedings

22. Asda operates a chain of supermarkets in the United Kingdom. It sells among other things ham bearing the description Parma ham, purchased pre-sliced from Hygrade, which itself purchases the ham boned but not sliced from an Italian producer who is a member of the Consorzio. The ham is sliced and hermetically sealed by Hygrade in packets each containing five slices.

23. The packets bear the wording ASDA A taste of Italy PARMA HAM Genuine Italian Parma Ham.

24. The back of the packets states PARMA HAM All authentic Asda continental meats are made by traditional methods to guarantee their authentic flavour and quality and Produced in Italy, packed in the UK for Asda Stores Limited.

25. On 14 November 1997 the Consorzio brought proceedings by writ in the United Kingdom against Asda and Hygrade seeking various injunctions against them, essentially requiring them to cease their activities, on the ground that they were contrary to the rules applicable to Parma ham.

26. On 17 November 1997 it issued a notice of motion seeking the injunctions claimed in its writ and statement of claim.

27. Asda and Hygrade opposed the applications, arguing in particular that Regulation No 2081/92 and/or Regulation No 1107/96 did not confer on the Consorzio the rights it alleged.

28. The applications were dismissed.

29. The Consorzio appealed to the Court of Appeal (England and Wales). Salumificio was granted leave to intervene in the proceedings. The appeal was dismissed on 1 December 1998.

30. The Consorzio and Salumificio thereupon appealed to the House of Lords.

31. Since the House of Lords considered that the outcome of the case depended on the interpretation of Regulation No 2081/92 and Regulation No 1107/96, it decided to stay the proceedings and refer the following question to the Court for a preliminary ruling:

As a matter of Community law, does Council Regulation (EEC) No 2081/92 read with Commission Regulation (EC) No 1107/96 and the specification for the PDO [protected designation of origin] Prosciutto di Parma create a valid Community right, directly enforceable in the court of a Member State, to restrain the retail sale as Parma ham of sliced and packaged ham derived from hams duly exported from Parma in compliance with the conditions of the PDO but which have not been thereafter sliced, packaged and labelled in accordance with the specification? . . .

*Whether the use of a PDO may be subjected to a condition that operations such as the slicing and packaging of the product be carried out in the region of production*

50. It must [first] be concluded that Regulation No 2081/92 must be interpreted as not precluding the use of a PDO from being subject to the condition that operations such as the slicing and packaging of the product take place in the region of production, where such a condition is laid down in the specification.

*Whether the condition for the PDO Prosciutto di Parma that the product must be sliced and packaged in the region of production constitutes a measure having equivalent effect to a quantitative restriction on exports . . .*

59. . . . [W]here the use of the PDO Prosciutto di Parma for ham marketed in slices is made subject to the condition that slicing and packaging operations be carried out in the region of production, this constitutes a measure having equivalent effect to a quantitative restriction on exports within the meaning of Article 29 EC.

*Whether the condition that the product is sliced and packaged in the region of production is justified . . .*

62. It should be noted that, in accordance with Article 30 EC, Article 29 EC does not preclude prohibitions or restrictions on exports which are justified *inter alia* on grounds of the protection of industrial and commercial property.

63. Community legislation displays a general tendency to enhance the quality of products within the framework of the common agricultural policy, in order to promote the reputation of those products through *inter alia* the use of designations of origin which enjoy special protection (*see Belgium* v *Spain*, paragraph 53). That tendency took the form in the quality wines sector of the adoption of Council Regulation (EEC) No 823/87 of 16 March 1987 laying down special provisions relating to quality wines produced in specified regions (OJ 1987 L 84, p. 59), repealed and replaced by Council Regulation (EC) No 1493/1999 of 17 May

1999 on the common organisation of the market in wine (OJ 1999 L 179, p. 1). It was also manifested, in relation to other agricultural products, in the adoption of Regulation No 2081/92, which, according to its preamble, is intended *inter alia* to meet consumers' expectations as regards products of quality and an identifiable geographical origin and to enable producers, in conditions of fair competition, to secure higher incomes in return for a genuine effort to improve quality.

64. Designations of origin fall within the scope of industrial and commercial property rights. The applicable rules protect those entitled to use them against improper use of those designations by third parties seeking to profit from the reputation which they have acquired. They are intended to guarantee that the product bearing them comes from a specified geographical area and displays certain particular characteristics. They may enjoy a high reputation amongst consumers and constitute for producers who fulfil the conditions for using them an essential means of attracting customers. The reputation of designations of origin depends on their image in the minds of consumers. That image in turn depends essentially on particular characteristics and more generally on the quality of the product. It is on the latter, ultimately, that the product's reputation is based (*see Belgium* v *Spain*, paragraphs 54 to 56). For consumers, the link between the reputation of the producers and the quality of the products also depends on his being assured that products sold under the designation of origin are authentic.

65. The specification of the PDO Prosciutto di Parma, by requiring the slicing and packaging to be carried out in the region of production, is intended to allow the persons entitled to use the PDO to keep under their control one of the ways in which the product appears on the market. The condition it lays down aims better to safeguard the quality and authenticity of the product, and consequently the reputation of the PDO, for which those who are entitled to use it assume full and collective responsibility.

66. Against that background, a condition such as at issue must be regarded as compatible with Community law despite its restrictive effects on trade if it is shown that it is necessary and proportionate and capable of upholding the reputation of the PDO Prosciutto di Parma (*see*, to that effect, *Belgium* v *Spain*, paragraphs 58 and 59).

67. Parma ham is consumed mainly in slices and the operations leading to that presentation are all designed to obtain in particular a specific flavour, colour and texture which will be appreciated by consumers.

68. The slicing and packaging of the ham thus constitute important operations which may harm the quality and hence the reputation of the PDO if they are carried out in conditions that result in a product not possessing the organoleptic qualities expected. Those operations may also compromise the guarantee of the product's authenticity, because they necessarily involve removal of the mark of origin of the whole hams used.

69. By the rules it lays down and the requirements of the national provisions to which it refers, the specification of the PDO Prosciutto di Parma establishes a set of detailed and strict rules regulating the three stages which lead to the placing on the market of prepackaged sliced ham. The first stage consists of boning the ham, making bricks, and refrigerating and freezing them for slicing. The second stage corresponds to the slicing operations. The third stage is the packaging of the sliced ham, under vacuum or protected atmosphere. . . .

75. In this context, it must be accepted that checks performed outside the region of production would provide fewer guarantees of the quality and authenticity of the product than checks carried out in the region of production in accordance with the procedure laid down in the specification (*see*, to that effect, *Belgium* v *Spain*, paragraph 67). First, checks performed in accordance with that procedure are thorough and systematic in nature and are done by experts who have specialised knowledge of the characteristics of Parma ham. Second, it is

hardly conceivable that representatives of the persons entitled to use the PDO could effectively introduce such checks in other Member States.

76. The risk to the quality and authenticity of the product finally offered to consumers is consequently greater where it has been sliced and packaged outside the region of production than when that has been done within the region (*see*, to that effect, *Belgium* v *Spain*, paragraph 74).

77. That conclusion is not affected by the fact, pointed out in the present case, that the ham may be sliced, at least under certain conditions, by retailers and restaurateurs outside the region of production. That operation must in principle be performed in front of the consumer, or at least the consumer can require that it is, in order to verify in particular that the ham used bears the mark of origin. Above all, slicing and packaging operations carried out upstream of the retail sale or restaurant stage constitute, because of the quantities of products concerned, a much more real risk to the reputation of a PDO, where there is inadequate control of the authenticity and quality of the product, than operations carried out by retailers and restaurateurs.

78. Consequently, the condition of slicing and packaging in the region of production, whose aim is to preserve the reputation of Parma ham by strengthening control over its particular characteristics and its quality, may be regarded as justified as a measure protecting the PDO which may be used by all the operators concerned and is of decisive importance to them (*see*, to that effect, *Belgium* v *Spain*, paragraph 75).

79. The resulting restriction may be regarded as necessary for attaining the objective pursued, in that there are no alternative less restrictive measures capable of attaining it.

80. The PDO Prosciutto di Parma would not receive comparable protection from an obligation imposed on operators established outside the region of production to inform consumers, by means of appropriate labelling, that the slicing and packaging has taken place outside that region. Any deterioration in the quality or authenticity of ham sliced and packaged outside the region of production, resulting from materialisation of the risks associated with slicing and packaging, might harm the reputation of all ham marketed under the PDO Prosciutto di Parma, including that sliced and packaged in the region of production under the control of the group of producers entitled to use the PDO (*see*, to that effect, *Belgium* v *Spain*, paragraphs 76 and 77).

81. Accordingly, the fact that the use of the PDO Prosciutto di Parma for ham marketed in slices is conditional on the slicing and packaging operations being carried out in the region of production may be regarded as justified, and hence compatible with Article 29 EC. . . .

## NOTES AND QUESTIONS

**1.** The CJEU decision permits meatpackers in Italy to exercise "downstream" control over the way their product is distributed. Do you think this control is justified to protect the "integrity" of Parma ham? As an EU consumer, are you willing to pay a higher price for this type of ham because Italian meatpackers have sliced it?

**2.** The Parma ham decision may help illuminate why U.S. farmers and the food services industry are reluctant to extend the scope of protection for geographical indications. It may affect not only primary producers, but also food processors and marketers. *See also Federal Republic of Germany and Kingdom of Denmark v. Commission*, joined cases, C-465/02 and C-466/02, Oct. 2005, regarding protection of "feta" for a type of cheese.

## *Scotch Whisky Association v. Klotz*

Judgment of the Court (Fifth Chamber), 7 June 2018

(Reference for a preliminary ruling — Protection of geographical indications of spirit drinks — Regulation (EC) No 110/2008 — Article 16(a) to (c) — Annex III — Registered geographical indication 'Scotch Whisky' — Whisky produced in Germany and marketed under the designation 'Glen Buchenbach')

In Case C44/17,

REQUEST for a preliminary ruling under Article 267 TFEU from the Landgericht Hamburg (Regional Court, Hamburg, Germany), made by decision of 19 January 2017, received at the Court on 27 January 2017, in the proceedings

Scotch Whisky Association
v.
Michael Klotz,

THE COURT (Fifth Chamber), composed of J.L. da Cruz Vilaça, President of the Chamber, E. Levits, A. Borg Barthet, M. Berger (Rapporteur) and F. Biltgen, Judges, Advocate General: H. Saugmandsgaard Øe, gives the following:

### Judgment

1. This request for a preliminary ruling concerns the interpretation of Article 16(a) to (c) of Regulation (EC) No 110/2008 of the European Parliament and of the Council of 15 January 2008 on the definition, description, presentation, labelling and the protection of geographical indications of spirit drinks and repealing Council Regulation (EEC) No 1576/89 (OJ 2008 L 39, p. 16).

2. The request has been made in proceedings between the Scotch Whisky Association and Mr Michael Klotz, an online distributor of whisky, concerning an action seeking an order that Mr Klotz cease to market a whisky produced in Germany under the designation 'Glen Buchenbach'.

. . .

### The Dispute in the Main Proceedings and the Questions Referred for a Preliminary Ruling

8. The Scotch Whisky Association is an organisation constituted under Scottish law. Its objectives include protecting the trade in Scottish whisky both in Scotland and abroad.

9. Mr Klotz markets, via a website, a whisky under the designation 'Glen Buchenbach', which is produced by the Waldhorn distillery in Berglen, located in the Buchenbach valley in Swabia (Germany).

10. The label on the whisky bottles in question includes, in addition to a stylised depiction of a hunting horn (Waldhorn in German), the following information: 'Waldhornbrennerei' (Waldhorn distillery), 'Glen Buchenbach', 'Swabian Single Malt Whisky', '500 ml', '40% vol', 'Deutsches Erzeugnis' (German product), 'Hergestellt in den Berglen' (produced in the Berglen).

11. The Scotch Whisky Association brought an action before the Landgericht Hamburg (Regional Court, Hamburg, Germany) seeking an order that Mr Klotz, inter alia, cease to market that whisky, which is not Scotch whisky, under the designation 'Glen Buchenbach',

on the ground that use of that designation infringes, in particular, Article 16(a) to (c) of Regulation No 110/2008, which protects the geographical indications registered in Annex III to that regulation, which include 'Scotch Whisky'.

12. According to the Scotch Whisky Association, those provisions ensure that a geographical indication registered for a spirit drink is protected not only against the use of such an indication but also against any reference that suggests the geographical origin of that indication. It argues that because the designation 'Glen' is very widely used in Scotland instead of the word 'valley' and, in particular, as an element of the trade mark in the names of Scottish whiskies, it evokes in the relevant public an association with Scotland and Scotch Whisky despite the fact that other information is included on the label, which specifies that the product at issue is of German origin. Mr Klotz contends that the action should be dismissed.

. . .

### Consideration of the Questions Referred

* * *

### The Second Question

. . .

43. In order to provide the referring court with a useful answer, it should be borne in mind that Article 16(b) of Regulation No 110/2008 protects geographical indications from any 'evocation', 'even if the true origin of the product is indicated or the geographical indication is used in translation or accompanied by an expression such as "like", "type", "style", "made", "flavour" or any other similar term'.

44. According to the Court's case-law, the notion of 'evocation' covers a situation in which the term used to designate a product incorporates part of a protected geographical indication, so that when the consumer is confronted with the name of the product in question, the image triggered in his mind is that of the product whose indication is protected (judgment of 21 January 2016, Viiniverla, C75/15, EU:C:2016:35, paragraph 21 and the case-law cited).

45. Thus, for the purpose of finding there to be an 'evocation' within the meaning of Article 16(b) of Regulation No 110/2008, the Court has held that the national court must determine not only whether the term used to designate the product at issue incorporates a part of a protected geographical indication but also whether, when the consumer is confronted with the name of the product, the image triggered in his mind is that of the product whose indication is protected. Therefore, the national court must essentially rely on the presumed reaction of consumers in the light of the term used to designate the product at issue, it being essential that those consumers establish a link between that term and the protected geographical indication (judgment of 21 January 2016, Viiniverla, C75/15, EU:C:2016:35, paragraph 22).

46. It follows from the foregoing, as the Advocate General has stated . . . , that the partial incorporation of a protected geographical indication in the sign at issue is not an essential condition for Article 16(b) of Regulation No 110/2008 to apply. In assessing whether there is an 'evocation' within the meaning of that provision, it is therefore for the national court to determine whether, when the consumer is confronted with the name of the product, the image triggered in his mind is that of the product whose geographical indication is protected.

47. In that regard, the national court must, in making that assessment, refer to the perception of an average European consumer who is reasonably well informed and reasonably observant and circumspect (judgment of 21 January 2016, Viiniverla, C75/15, EU:C:2016:35, paragraphs 25 and 28).

48. In addition, the Court has held that it is legitimate to consider there to be an evocation of a protected geographical indication where, concerning products which are similar

in appearance, the sales names are phonetically and visually similar (judgment of 21 January 2016, Viiniverla, C75/15, EU:C:2016:35, paragraph 33 and the case-law cited).

49. However, as the Advocate General has stated . . . , identifying phonetic and visual similarity between the disputed designation and the protected geographical indication is likewise not an essential condition for establishing that there is an 'evocation' within the meaning of Article 16(b) of Regulation No 110/2008. It is only one of the factors to be taken into account by the national court when it assesses whether, when the consumer is confronted with the name of the product concerned, the image triggered in his mind is that of the product whose geographical indication is protected. Accordingly, it is possible that an 'evocation' may be found to exist even in the absence of such similarity.

50. In addition to the criteria relating to the incorporation of a part of a protected geographical indication in the disputed designation and to the phonetic and visual similarity between the designation and the indication, the Court has ruled that it is necessary, where appropriate, to take account of the criterion of 'conceptual proximity' between terms emanating from different languages, since such proximity, like the other criteria mentioned above, may also trigger an image in the consumer's mind which is that of the product whose geographical indication is protected, when he is confronted with a similar product bearing the disputed name (judgment of 21 January 2016, Viiniverla, C75/15, EU:C:2016:35, paragraph 35 and the case-law cited).

51. It follows from the foregoing that, for determining whether there is an 'evocation' within the meaning of Article 16(b) of Regulation No 110/2008, the decisive criterion is whether, when the consumer is confronted with a disputed designation, the image triggered directly in his mind is that of the product whose geographical indication is protected, a matter which it falls to the national court to assess, taking into account, as the case may be, the partial incorporation of a protected geographical indication in the disputed designation, any phonetic and/or visual similarity, or any conceptual proximity, between the designation and the indication.

52. In the case in the main proceedings, the referring court will therefore have to determine whether an average European consumer who is reasonably well informed and reasonably observant and circumspect thinks directly of the protected geographical indication, namely 'Scotch Whisky', when he is confronted with a comparable product bearing the disputed designation, in this case 'Glen', that court taking account, in the absence of (i) any phonetic and/or visual similarity between the disputed designation and the protected geographical indication and (ii) any partial incorporation of that indication in that designation, of conceptual proximity between the protected geographical indication and the disputed designation.

53. However, the criterion set out by the referring court in its second question for the purpose of establishing 'evocation' within the meaning of Article 16(b) of Regulation No 110/2008—namely that the disputed element of the sign at issue should evoke in the relevant public some kind of association with the protected geographical indication or the geographical area relating thereto—cannot be used, as it does not establish a sufficiently clear and direct link between that element and the indication concerned.

54. Furthermore, as the Advocate General has observed . . . , if it were sufficient, for the purpose of establishing such 'evocation', that the consumer make an association of any kind whatsoever with a protected geographical indication, that would result, first, in point (b) of Article 16 of Regulation No 110/2008 encroaching on the scope of the following provisions of that article, namely points (c) and (d), which cover situations in which the reference to a protected geographical indication is even more subtle than an 'evocation' of that indication.

55. Secondly, the use of such a criterion would extend the scope of Regulation No 110/2008 in an unforeseeable way and would give rise to significant risks, particularly for the legal certainty of the economic actors concerned. Indeed, as stated in recital 4 of that regulation, the EU legislature has sought to 'ensure a more systematic approach in the legislation governing spirit drinks', by setting out 'clearly defined criteria' for, inter alia, 'the protection of geographical indications'. Allowing a criterion as vague and far-reaching as that put forward by the referring court in its second question would not be consistent with that objective.

56. In view of all the foregoing considerations, the answer to the first part of the second question is that Article 16(b) of Regulation No 110/2008 must be interpreted as meaning that, for the purpose of establishing that there is an 'evocation' of a registered geographical indication, the referring court is required to determine whether, when the average European consumer who is reasonably well informed and reasonably observant and circumspect is confronted with the disputed designation, the image triggered directly in his mind is that of the product whose geographical indication is protected. In making that determination, the referring court, in the absence of (i) any phonetic and/or visual similarity between the disputed designation and the protected geographical indication and (ii) any partial incorporation of that indication in that designation, must take account of the conceptual proximity, if any, between the designation and the indication.

57. As regards the second part of the second question, which relates to the role that the context in which the disputed designation is embedded plays in the national court's assessment of whether there is an 'evocation' within the meaning of Article 16(b) of Regulation No 110/2008, the Court notes that it is apparent from the wording of that provision that there may be an 'evocation' even if the true origin of the product is indicated (judgment of 21 January 2016, Viiniverla, C75/15, EU:C:2016:35, paragraph 43 and the case-law cited).

58. The order for reference indicates that Mr Klotz, the defendant in the main proceedings, maintains that the designation 'Glen Buchenbach' is a play on words consisting of the name of the place of origin of the drink at issue in the main proceedings (Berglen) and the name of a local river ('Buchenbach'). However, the Court has already held that it is immaterial, so far as Article 16(b) of Regulation No 110/2008 is concerned, that the disputed designation corresponds to the name of the undertaking and/or the place where the product is manufactured (see, to that effect, judgment of 21 January 2016, Viiniverla, C75/15, EU:C:2016:35, paragraphs 42 to 45).

59. Moreover, as the Advocate General has observed in point 81 of his Opinion, the Court has also made clear that the fact that the disputed designation refers to a place of manufacture that is known to consumers in the Member State where the product is manufactured is not relevant for the purpose of assessing the concept of 'evocation' within the meaning of Article 16(b) of Regulation No 110/2008, since that provision protects registered geographical indications against any evocation throughout the territory of the European Union and, in view of the need to guarantee effective and uniform protection of those geographic indications in that territory, it covers all European consumers (judgment of 21 January 2016, Viiniverla, C75/15, EU:C:2016:35, paragraph 27).

60. In view of the foregoing considerations, the answer to the second part of the second question is that Article 16(b) of Regulation No 110/2008 must be interpreted as meaning that, for the purpose of establishing that there is an 'evocation' of a registered geographical indication, account is not to be taken either of the context surrounding the disputed element, or, in particular, of the fact that that element is accompanied by an indication of the true origin of the product concerned.

## NOTES AND QUESTIONS

**1.** How would you assess the case? Does "Glen" inherently evoke the image of Scotch Whiskey in relation to a German whiskey named Glen Buchenbach? How would you assess the perception of the average, reasonable consumer? To what extent can "Glen" be considered a generic geographical term?

**2.** Another key problem relates to defining the relationship of trademarks and geographical indications. Moreover, difficult issues arise in the context of multilevel European governance relating to the allocation of powers to regulate geographical indications and denominations. The following case illustrate the procedural complexity of litigation within the European context and issues and the tension between EU and national tools of protecting geographical indications. The European system of trademark protection is introduced and explained *infra* in section V.A of this chapter.

### *European Union Intellectual Property Office (EUIPO) and Commission v. Instituto dos Vinhos do Douro e do PortoIP and Portuguese Republic*

Judgment of the Court (Second Chamber), 14 September 2017

In Case C-56/16 P

(Appeal—EU trade mark—Regulation (EC) No 207/2009—Article 8(4) and Article 53(1)(c) and (2)(d)—EU word mark PORT CHARLOTTE—Application for a declaration of invalidity of that mark—Protection conferred on the earlier designations of origin 'Porto' and 'Port' under Regulation (EC) No 1234/2007 and under national law—Exhaustive nature of the protection conferred on those designations of origin—Article 118m of Regulation (EC) No 1234/2007—Concepts of 'use' and 'evocation' of a protected designation of origin)

APPEAL under Article 56 of the Statute of the Court of Justice of the European Union, brought on 29 January 2016,

European Union Intellectual Property Office (EUIPO), . . . appellant, supported by: European Commission, . . . intervener in the appeal,

the other parties to the proceedings being:

Instituto dos Vinhos do Douro e do PortoIP, established in Peso da Régua (Portugal), . . . applicant at first instance, supported by: Portuguese Republic, . . . intervener in the appeal,

Bruichladdich Distillery Co.Ltd, established in Argyll (United Kingdom), . . . intervener at first instance,

THE COURT (Second Chamber),
composed of M. Ilešič, President of the Chamber, A. Prechal (Rapporteur), A. Rosas, C. Toader and E. Jarašiūnas, Judges,

Advocate General: M. Campos Sánchez-Bordona,
gives the following:

## Judgment

. . .

## Findings of the Court

### The Second Ground of Appeal in the Cross-Appeal

110. By the second ground of appeal in its cross-appeal, alleging infringement of Article 118m(2)(a)(ii) of Regulation No 1234/2007, which provides that the designations of origin concerned are to be protected against any direct or indirect commercial use, even for products that are not comparable, in so far as that use exploits their reputation, IVDP [Instituto dos Vinhos do Douro e do PortoIP] criticises the General Court for holding, in . . . the judgment under appeal, that the [European Union Intellectual Property Office] Board of Appeal had been right in finding that the contested mark, namely the sign 'PORT CHARLOTTE', 'neither used nor evoked' the designation of origin 'Porto' or 'Port'.

111. That ground of appeal relates to the grounds set out in paragraphs 70 and 71 of the judgment under appeal, which are worded as follows:

> 70. In this connection, first, it must be observed that the protected appellation of origin of which the applicant is the proprietor, and which is entered in the E-Bacchus database, covers the names "[O]porto", "[P]ortvin", "[P]ortwein", "[P]ortwijn", "[V]in de [P]orto", "[P]ort [W]ine", [P]ort", "[V]inho do [P]orto" and "[P]orto". Consequently, it includes names, in different languages, composed either of two elements, namely "port" or "porto" and "wine" or of a single element, namely "oporto" or "porto". Secondly, as [EUIPO] submits, account should be taken of the fact that the contested mark also consists of an expression composed of two elements, namely "port" and "charlotte", which, like the expression "port wine", must be understood as forming a logical and conceptual unit. . . .
>
> 71. However, unlike the protected appellation of origin in question, the contested mark does not refer expressly to a wine, but to the female first name Charlotte, which is directly associated with the element "port", the primary meaning of which, in a number of European languages, including English and Portuguese, is harbour, namely a place situated on the coast or on a river. Therefore, as the Board of Appeal correctly found in paragraph 24 of the contested decision, the sign PORT CHARLOTTE, read as a whole as a logical and conceptual unit, will be understood by the relevant public as designating a harbour named after a person called Charlotte, with no direct link being made with the designation of origin "[P]orto" or "[P]ort" or a port wine. . . .

112. As IVDP has submitted, the word 'port' does not exist in Portuguese. What is more, the word used to designate a harbour, that is to say a place situated on the coast or on a river, is 'porto'. It follows that, regarding that specific issue, the General Court manifestly erred in regard to the facts.

113. The fact remains that, more generally, the General Court's assessment that the relevant public, namely the average consumer in the European Union with at least a basic knowledge of English or a Romance language, will understand the sign 'PORT CHARLOTTE' as designating a harbour named after a person called Charlotte, without making a direct link with the designation of origin 'Porto' or 'Port' or a port wine, is a factual assessment and cannot, as such and since IVDP has not established that there was a manifest distortion of evidence which is capable of affecting that assessment, be reviewed on appeal.

114. In addition, that assessment is not the result of an incorrect interpretation of the words 'any direct or indirect commercial use' in Article 118m(2)(a) of Regulation No 1234/2007.

115. The incorporation in a trade mark of a name which is protected under Regulation No 1234/2007, such as the designation of origin 'port', cannot be held to be capable of

exploiting the reputation of that designation of origin, for the purposes of Article 118m(2)(a)(ii) of that regulation, if that incorporation does not lead the relevant public to associate that mark or the goods in respect of which it is registered with the designation of origin concerned or the wine product in respect of which it is protected.

116. In the present case, the General Court, following an assessment of facts that is not open to challenge, found . . . that the sign 'PORT CHARLOTTE', since it consists of the term 'port' and the first name Charlotte, will be perceived by the relevant public as a logical and conceptual unit referring to a harbour, that is to say a place situated on the coast or on a river, with which a first name, which constitutes the most important and most distinctive element in the contested mark, is associated. According to the General Court, the relevant public will not perceive, in that sign, any geographical reference to the port wine covered by the designation of origin in question.

117. On the basis of that factual assessment, the General Court was entitled to hold, without erring in law, that the Board of Appeal had been right in finding that the contested mark could not, for the purposes of Article 118m(2)(a)(ii) of Regulation No 1234/2007, be regarded as using the designation of origin 'Porto' or 'Port'.

. . .

119. Consequently, the second ground of appeal in the cross-appeal must be rejected.

### The Third Ground of Appeal in the Cross-Appeal

120. By its third ground of appeal in the cross-appeal, IVDP submits that the General Court infringed Article 118m(2)(b) of Regulation No 1234/2007 by holding . . . that the use of the contested mark PORT CHARLOTTE, which is registered in respect of a whisky, did not involve 'misuse, imitation or evocation', within the meaning of that provision, of the protected designation of origin 'Porto' or 'Port'.

. . .

124. The General Court, without erring in law, applied the fundamental criterion deriving from that case-law, by holding . . . that, having regard to the findings set out in paragraph 71 of that same judgment, even though the term 'port' forms an integral part of the contested mark, the average consumer, even if he is of Portuguese origin or speaks Portuguese, in reaction to a whisky bearing that mark, will not associate it with a port wine covered by the designation of origin in question.

125. The General Court added . . . that that assessment is confirmed by the not insignificant differences between the respective features of a port wine and a whisky in terms of, inter alia, ingredients, alcohol content and taste, of which the average consumer is well aware and to which the Board of Appeal had rightly drawn attention. . . .

126. Since the assessments thus carried out by the General Court . . . of the judgment under appeal are factual assessments and IVDP has not established that there was any distortion of the evidence on the part of the General Court, those assessments cannot be criticised on appeal since they are, in addition, based on a correct interpretation of the concept of 'evocation' within the meaning of Article 118m(2)(b) of Regulation No 1234/2007.

127. The third ground of appeal in the cross-appeal must therefore be rejected.

## NOTES AND QUESTIONS

**1.** The case illustrates the legal avenues available within the European Union to challenge and examine the grant of trademarks which may conflict with geographical indications protected by member states. The system by now is firmly centralized. How much scope of protection do you think member states still enjoy to protect names and products outside of EU law?

**2.** Similar cases may arise in defining the relationship of existing trademarks and geographical indications both within the TRIPS Agreement and within domestic law. The complex relationship of trademarks and geographical indications under the TRIPS Agreement is addressed in section I.E *infra*. Article 22(3) requires WTO Members to refuse or invalidate the registration of a trademark "which contains or consists of geographical indications with respect to goods not originating in the territory indicated, if use of the indication in the trademark for such goods in that Member is of such a nature as to mislead the public as to the true place of origin." Article 24(5) of the Agreement, on the other hand, establishes a rule of priority for trademark protection where the trademark has been applied or registered in good faith prior in time to the protection of the geographical indication.

## F. Artificial Intelligence and Trademarks

AI and trademark law has not quite captured the public imagination in the same way that AI and copyright and AI and patent law has. Still, there a number of ways in which AI may significantly impact trademark law.

---

### *WIPO Revised Issues Paper on Intellectual Property Policy and Artificial Intelligence (2020)*

#### Issue 13: Trademarks

1. As trademarks do not have the equivalent of an author or inventor, AI does not affect the trademark system in the same way as the patents, designs and copyright systems. However, there may be areas of trademark law that may be impacted by AI.

2. Trademarks are intended to distinguish the origin of goods and services and to prevent consumer confusion. Current trademark law is therefore based on concepts of human perceptions and recollection both for determining whether a trademark is registrable and whether it is infringed. For example, applications for trademark registration may be rejected if the applicant's trademark is substantially identical with or deceptively similar to a trademark registered or applied for by another person in respect of similar goods or closely related services. In order to establish infringement a trademark owner generally needs to show that there is confusion as to the origin of the goods of services. Concepts of human perception and recollection also play a role in the laws passing off, prohibition against commercial misrepresentation of source or origins of goods (US Lanham Act, § 1125) or equivalent.

3. The emergence of AI and e-commerce platforms is changing the nature of the process of buying goods and services. There are ongoing discussions about the way that AI interacts with trademarks in the online environment. For example, AI assistants, search engines, customer service bots and online marketplaces play an important role in shaping the consumer decision-making process. The way that a consumer interacts with the online marketplace through AI may result in the presentation of only a limited number of brands to a consumer, or other alterations in the way that consumers make product selections.

4. In the case of trademarks, questions arise with respect to registrability, infringement and also unfair competition. Questions relating to the use of AI in trademark examination and prosecution are discussed [elsewhere in this Issue Paper].

(i) How, if at all, does AI impact trademark law?
(ii) Are there any concerns raised by ownership of trademarks with respect to AI?

(iii) Do the functions, law and practice of trademarks need to be reconsidered with the increasing use of AI in marketing and the proliferation of AI used by consumers in the context of Internet of Things applications?
(iv) Will the use of AI, knowingly or unknowingly, by the consumer for product selection affect brand recognition? Will principles of trademark law, such as distinctiveness, recollection, likelihood of confusion or the average consumer need to evolve due to the increasing use of AI? Are these issues for policymakers to consider?
(v) Who is ultimately responsible for AI's actions, in particular when recommendations include infringing products?
(vi) Does the use of AI raise unfair competition issues? Is this an issue that the IP system needs to address?

## NOTES AND QUESTIONS

**1.** How does AI impact how consumers engage with brands? Do you think the use of AI increases or decreases the likelihood of consumer confusion?

**2.** As AI is used to sell products on platforms such as Amazon, how would liability work if an AI ends up creating a listing that uses protected marks without authorization?

**3.** How might AI facilitate adjudication of trademark disputes?

## II. TRADEMARKS AT THE INTERNATIONAL LEVEL

### A. Introduction

The evolution of the multilateral system for the protection of trademarks has been substantially less controversial than the evolution of the system with respect to patents. Virtually all countries have recognized the basic economic and social value of allowing producers and suppliers of services to identify their output with distinctive markings. Trademarks enable consumers to make efficient and informed decisions about what they are buying. They encourage producers to invest in quality as repeat purchasing is facilitated. This is not to suggest the absence of economic and social issues as trademark holders seek to extend the scope of exclusive rights embodied in marks. It is only to suggest that there are good reasons why trademarks are not the subject of the same level of policy concern as patents, and why the evolution of multilateral protection has run more smoothly.

Two recent trends in the evolution of multilateral trademark rules include: (1) increased attention to protection for "well known" trademarks; and (2) more permissive rules concerning the licensing and transfer of marks (as the trademark itself has turned into a marketable commodity). Of course, the proliferation of the Internet and e-commerce has raised a host of new questions regarding the role of distinctive marks in this fluid environment. On the bilateral and plurilateral levels, the main emphasis has been on geographical indications.

### B. The Paris Convention and Trademarks

Multilateral rules for the protection of trademarks were adopted in the Paris Convention of 1883 along with rules for the protection of patents and industrial designs. As newspapers, magazines, and the word of mouth of travelers made consumers aware of the reputation of foreign products, it became increasingly important to consumers and producers that trademarks associated with products be genuine. This objective could be achieved by granting producers the opportunity to locally register and protect their trademarks. The Paris Convention incorporated provisions on national treatment, right of priority, and independence of trademarks similar to the provisions with regard to patents. We begin with a WIPO introduction to the provisions of the Paris Convention regarding trademarks.

## *The Paris Convention for the Protection of Industrial Property*

WIPO Intellectual Property Handbook, Chapter 5

### Principal provisions

[See the Paris Convention introduction in Chapter 2 for a description of general provisions, including national treatment.—Eds.]

### The Right of Priority . . .

5.30 The length of the priority period is different according to the various kinds of industrial property rights. For . . . trademarks it is six months. . . .

### Provisions Concerning Trademarks

### Use of Trademarks

5.67 The Convention touches on the issue of the use of marks in Article 5C(1), (2) and (3).

5.68 Article 5C(1) relates to the compulsory use of registered trademarks. Some of the countries which provide for the registration of trademarks also require that the trademark, once registered, be used within a certain period. If this use is not complied with, the trademark may be expunged from the register. For this purpose, "use" is generally understood as meaning the sale of goods bearing the trademark, although national legislation may regulate more broadly the manner in which use of the trademark is to be complied with. The Article states that where compulsory use is required, the trademark's registration may be cancelled for failure to use the trademark only after a reasonable period has elapsed, and then only if the owner does not justify such failure.

5.69 The definition of what is meant by "reasonable period" is left to the national legislation of the countries concerned, or otherwise to the authorities competent for resolving such cases. This reasonable period is intended to give the owner of the mark enough time and opportunity to arrange for its proper use, considering that in many cases the owner has to use his mark in several countries.

5.70 The trademark owner's justification of non-use would be acceptable if it were based on legal or economic circumstances beyond the owner's control, for example if importation of the marked goods had been prohibited or delayed by governmental regulations.

5.71 The Convention also establishes in Article 5C(2) that the use of a trademark by its proprietor, in a form differing in elements which do not alter the distinctive character of the mark as it was when formerly registered in one of the countries of the Union, shall not entail invalidation of the registration nor diminish the protection granted to the mark. The purpose of this provision is to allow for unessential differences between the form of the mark as it is registered and the form in which it is used, for example in cases of adaptation or translation of certain elements for such use. This rule applies also to differences in the form of the mark as used in the country of its original registration.

5.72 Whether in a given case the differences between the mark as registered and the mark as actually used alter the distinctive character is a matter to be decided by the competent national authorities.

### Concurrent Use of the Same Trademark by Different Enterprises

5.73 Article 5C(3) of the Convention deals with the case where the same mark is used for identical or similar goods by two or more establishments considered as co-proprietors of the trademark. It is provided that such concurrent use will not impede the registration of the trademark nor diminish the protection in any country of the Union, except where the said use results in misleading the public or is contrary to the public interest. Such cases could occur if the concurrent use misleads the public as to the origin or source of the goods sold under the same trademark, or if the quality of such goods differs to the point where it may be contrary to the public interest to allow the continuation of such use.

5.74 This provision does not, however, cover the case of concurrent use of the mark by enterprises which are not co-proprietors of the mark, for instance when use is made concurrently by the owner and a licensee or a franchisee. These cases are left for the national legislation of the various countries to regulate.

### Grace Period for the Payment of Renewal Fees

5.75 Article 5*bis* requires that a period of grace be allowed for the payment of fees due for the maintenance of industrial property rights. . . .

5.76 The countries of the Paris Union are obliged to accord a period of grace of at least six months for the payment of the renewal fees, but are free to provide for the payment of a surcharge when such renewal fees are paid within the period of grace. Moreover, the countries are free to provide for a period of grace longer than the minimum six months prescribed by the Convention.

5.77 During the period of grace, the registration remains provisionally in force. If the payment of the renewal fees (and surcharge where appropriate) is not made during the period of grace, the registration will lapse with retroactive effect to the original date of expiration.

### Independence of Trademarks

5.78 Article 6 of the Convention establishes the important principle of the independence of trademarks in the different countries of the Union, and in particular the independence of trademarks filed or registered in the country of origin from those filed or registered in other countries of the Union.

5.79 The first part of Article 6 states the application of the basic principle of national treatment to the filing and registration of marks in the countries of the Union. Regardless of the origin of the mark whose registration is sought, a country of the Union may apply only its domestic legislation when determining the conditions for the filing and registration of the mark. The application of the principle of national treatment asserts the rule of independence of marks, since their registration and maintenance will depend only on each domestic law.

5.80 This Article also provides that an application for the registration of a mark, filed in any country of the Union by a person who is entitled to the benefits of the Convention, may not be refused, nor may a registration be canceled, on the ground that filing, registration or renewal of the mark has not been effected in the country of origin. This provision lays down the express rule that obtaining and maintaining a trademark registration in any country of the Union may not be made dependent on the application, registration or renewal of the same mark in the country of origin of the mark. Therefore no action with respect to the mark in the country of origin may be required as a prerequisite for obtaining a registration of the mark in that country.

5.81 Finally, Article 6 states that a mark duly registered in a country of the Union shall be regarded as independent of marks registered in the other countries of the Union, including the country of origin. This means that a mark once registered will not be automatically affected by any decision taken with respect to similar registrations for the same marks in other countries. In this respect, the fact that one or more such similar registrations are, for example, renounced, cancelled or abandoned will not, *eo ipso*, affect the registrations of the mark in other countries. The validity of these registrations will depend only on the provisions applicable in accordance with the legislation of each of the countries concerned.

### Well-Known Trademarks

5.82 The Convention deals with well-known trademarks in Article 6*bis*. This Article obliges a member country to refuse or cancel the registration and to prohibit the use of a trademark that is liable to create confusion with another trademark already well known in that member country. The effect of this Article is to extend protection to a trademark that is well-known in a member country even though it is not registered or used in that country. The protection of the well-known trademark results not from its registration, which prevents the registration or use of a conflicting trademark, but from the mere fact of its reputation.

5.83 The protection of well-known trademarks is deemed justified on the grounds that a trademark that has acquired goodwill and a reputation in a member country ought to give rise to a right for its owner. The registration or use of a confusingly similar trademark would, in most cases, amount to an act of unfair competition and be prejudicial to the interests of the public, who would be misled by the use of a conflicting trademark for the same or identical goods than those in connection with which the well-known trademark is registered.

5.84 The trademark that is protected by Article 6*bis* must be a "well-known" trademark, as determined in a member country by its competent administrative or judicial authorities. A trademark may not have been used in a country, in the sense that goods bearing that trademark have not been sold there; yet that trademark may be well-known in the country because of publicity there or the repercussions in that country of advertising in other countries.

5.85 The protection of a well-known trademark under Article 6*bis* exists only where the conflicting trademark has been filed, registered or used for identical or similar goods, as determined by the administrative or judicial authorities of the country in which protection is claimed.

5.86 The protection of a well-known trademark under Article 6*bis* results from the obligation of a member country to take *ex officio*, where its legislation so permits, or at the request of an interested party, the following type of action:

- — first, refusal of the application for registration of the conflicting trademark;
- — second, cancellation of the registration of a conflicting trademark, allowing at least a period of five years from the date of registration within which a request for cancellation of the conflicting trademark may be made, unless that trademark was registered in bad faith, in which event no time limit may be fixed;
- — third, prohibition of the use of the conflicting trademark, the request for which may be within a period of time prescribed by a member country; however, no time limit may be fixed for such a request in the case of a conflicting trademark used in bad faith.

### State Emblems, Official Hallmarks and Emblems of International Organizations

5.87 The Convention deals with distinctive signs of States and international intergovernmental organizations in Article 6*ter*. . . .

### Assignment of Trademarks

5.93 Article 6*quater* of the Convention deals with the assignment of trademarks. The rule of Article 6*quater* arises because of the situation where a trademark is used by an enterprise in various countries and it is desired to make a transfer of the right to the trademark in one or more of those countries.

5.94 Some national legislations allow an assignment without a simultaneous or corresponding transfer of the enterprise to which the trademark belongs. Others make the validity of the assignment depend on the simultaneous or corresponding transfer of the enterprise.

5.95 Article 6*quater* states that it shall suffice for the recognition of the validity of the assignment of a trademark in a member country, that the portion of the business or goodwill located in that country be transferred to the assignee, together with the exclusive right to manufacture in the said country, or to sell therein, the goods bearing the trademark assigned. Thus, a member country is free to require, for the validity of the assignment of the trademark, the simultaneous transfer of the enterprise to which the trademark belongs, but such a requirement must not extend to parts of the enterprise that are located in other countries.

5.96 It should be noted that Article 6*quater* leaves a member country free not to regard as valid the assignment of a trademark with the relevant part of the enterprise, if the use of that trademark by the assignee would be of such a nature as to mislead the public, particularly as regards important features of the goods to which the trademark is applied. This freedom may be exercised, for example, if a trademark is assigned for part only of the goods to which it is applied, and if those goods are similar to other goods for which the trademark is not assigned. In such cases, the public may be misled as to the origin or essential qualities of similar goods to which the assignor and assignee will apply the same trademark independently.

**Protection of Trademarks Registered in One Country of the Union in Other Countries of the Union**

5.97 Parallel to the principle of independence of marks which is embodied in the provisions of Article 6, the Convention establishes a special rule for the benefit of owners of trademarks registered in their country of origin. This exceptional rule is governed by Article 6*quinquies* of the Convention.

5.98 The provisions of Article 6*quinquies* come into operation in the case where a registration in the country of origin is invoked in the country where protection is sought. Whereas the principle of national treatment of applications calls for the normal rule of complete independence of trademarks (as recognized in Article 6), in the exceptional situation regulated by Article 6*quinquies* the opposite rule prevails, providing for extraterritorial effects of the registration in the country of origin.

5.99 There are two main reasons for this special rule. On the one hand, it is in the interest of both owners of trademarks and the public to have the *same* trademark apply to the *same* goods in various countries. On the other hand, there are some important differences in the domestic legislation of the member countries regarding the registration of trademarks. As a consequence, the differences in domestic legislation could prevent this uniform use of the same trademark.

5.100 In order to diminish the impact of those differences on the registration of trademarks in respect of goods in international trade, Article 6*quinquies* of the Paris Convention establishes certain effects where registration in the country of origin has taken place and is invoked in another member country where registration and protection is sought. This provision has the effect of bringing about a certain uniformity of the law of the various countries as to the concept of trademarks.

5.101 For Article 6*quinquies* to apply it is necessary that the trademark concerned should be duly registered in the country of origin. A mere filing or use of the trademark in that country is not sufficient. Moreover, the country of origin must be a country of the Union in which the applicant has a real and effective industrial or commercial establishment or, alternatively, in which he has his domicile, or otherwise, the country of the Union of which he is a national.

5.102 The rule established by Article 6*quinquies* provides that a trademark which fulfils the required conditions must be accepted for filing and protected—*as is* (to use the expression found in the English version) or *telle quelle* (to use the expression adopted in the original French text)—in the other member countries, subject to certain exceptions. This rule is often called the "telle quelle" principle.

5.103 It is to be noted that the rule only concerns the form of the trademark. In this respect, the rule in this Article does not affect the questions relating to the nature or the function of the trademarks as conceived in the countries where protection is sought. Thus a member country is not obliged to register and extend protection to subject matter that does not fall within the meaning of a trademark as defined in the law of that country. If, for example, under the law of a member country, a three-dimensional object or musical notes indicating tunes is not considered a trademark in that country, it is not obliged to accept that subject matter for registration and protection.

5.104 Article 6*quinquies*, Section B, contains certain exceptions to the obligation of accepting a registered trademark "as is" for registration in the other countries of the Union. That list of exceptions is exhaustive so that no other grounds may be invoked to refuse or invalidate the registration of the trademark. However, the list does not exclude any ground for refusal of protection for which there is a need in national legislation.

5.105 The first permitted ground for refusal or invalidation of a trademark exists where the trademark infringes rights of third parties acquired in the country where protection is claimed. These rights can be either rights in trademarks already protected in the country concerned or other rights, such as the right to a trade name or a copyright.

5.106 The second permitted ground for refusal or invalidation is when the trademark is devoid of distinctive character, or is purely descriptive, or consists of a generic name.

5.107 The third permissible ground for refusal or invalidation exists where the trademark is contrary to morality or public order, as considered in the country where protection is claimed. This ground includes, as a special category, trademarks which are of such a nature as to deceive the public.

5.108 A fourth permissible ground for refusal or invalidation exists if the registration of the trademark would constitute an act of unfair competition.

5.109 A fifth and last permissible ground for refusal or invalidation exists where the trademark is used by the owner in a form which is essentially different from that in which it has been registered in the country of origin. Unessential differences may not be used as grounds for refusal or invalidation.

### Service Marks

5.110 A service mark is a sign used by enterprises offering services, for example, hotels, restaurants, airlines, tourist agencies, car-rental agencies, employment agencies, laundries and cleaners, etc., in order to distinguish their services from those of other enterprises. Thus service marks have the same function as trademarks, the only difference being that they apply to services instead of products or goods.

5.111 Article 6*sexies* was introduced into the Paris Convention in 1958 to deal specifically with service marks, but the revision Conference did not accept a more ambitious proposal to assimilate service marks to trademarks entirely. However, a member country is free to apply the same rules it applies for trademarks also to service marks in analogous situations or circumstances.

5.112 By virtue of Article 6*sexies*, member countries undertake to protect service marks, but are not required to provide for the registration of such marks. This provision does not oblige a member country to legislate expressly on the subject of service marks. A member country may comply with the provision not only by introducing special legislation for the protection of service marks, but also by granting such protection by other means, for example, in its laws against unfair competition.

### Registration in the Name of the Agent Without the Proprietor's Authorization

5.113 Article 6*septies* of the Convention deals with the relationship between the owner of a trademark and his agent or representative regarding registration or use of the trademark by the latter. . . .

### Nature of the Goods to Which a Trademark Is Applied

5.115 Article 7 of the Convention stipulates that the nature of the goods to which a trademark is to be applied shall in no case be an obstacle to the registration of the mark.

5.116 The purpose of this rule, and also the comparable rule in Article 4*quater* regarding patents for invention, is to make the protection of industrial property independent of the question whether goods in respect of which such protection would apply may or may not be sold in the country concerned.

5.117 It sometimes occurs that a trademark concerns goods which, for example, do not conform to the safety requirements of the law of a particular country. For instance, the food and drug laws of a country may prescribe requirements concerning the ingredients of a food product or the effects of a pharmaceutical product and allow its sale only after approval of the competent authorities, on the basis of an examination of the food product or of clinical trials as to the effect of the use of the pharmaceutical product on human beings or animals.

5.118 In all such cases, it would be unjust to refuse registration of a trademark concerning such goods. The safety or quality regulations may change and the product may be permitted for sale later on. In those cases where no such change is contemplated but the approval of the competent authorities of the country concerned is still pending, such approval, if imposed as a condition of filing or registration in that country, may be prejudicial to an applicant who wishes to make a timely filing for protection in another member country.

### Collective Marks

5.119 A collective mark may be defined as a sign which serves to distinguish the geographical origin, material, mode of manufacture, quality or other common characteristics of goods or services of different enterprises that simultaneously use the collective mark under the control of its owner. The owner may be either an association of which those enterprises are members or any other entity, including a public body.

5.120 Article 7*bis* of the Convention deals with collective marks. It obliges a member country to accept for filing and to protect, in accordance with the particular conditions set by that country, collective marks belonging to "associations." These will generally be associations of producers, manufacturers, distributors, sellers or other merchants, of goods that are produced or manufactured in a certain country, region or locality or that have other common characteristics. Collective marks of States or other public bodies are not covered by the provision.

5.121 In order that Article 7*bis* be applicable, the existence of the association to which the collective mark belongs must not be contrary to the law of the country of origin. The association does not have to prove that it conforms to the legislation of its country of origin, but registration and protection of its collective mark may be refused if the existence of the association is found to be contrary to that legislation.

5.122 Refusal of registration and protection of the collective mark is not possible on the ground that the association is not established in the country where protection is sought, or is not constituted according to the law of that country. Article 7*bis* adds a further stipulation that the association may not even be required to possess an industrial or commercial establishment anywhere. In other words, an association, without possessing any industrial or commercial establishment itself, may be one that simply controls the use of a collective mark by others.

### Trademarks Shown at International Exhibitions

5.123 The provision concerning marks shown at international exhibitions is contained in Article 11 of the Convention, which also applies to other titles of industrial property. . . .

### Provisions Concerning Industrial Designs, Trade Names, Appellations of Origin and Indications of Source And Unfair Competition . . .

### Trade Names

5.131 Trade names are dealt with by the Convention in Article 8. This Article states that trade names shall be protected in all the countries of the Union without the obligation of filing or of registration, whether or not they form part of a trademark.

5.132 The definition of a trade name for the purposes of protection, and the manner in which such protection is to be afforded, are both matters left to the national legislation of the countries concerned. Therefore, protection may result from special legislation on trade names or from more general legislation on unfair competition or the rights of personality.

5.133 In no case can protection be made conditional upon filing or registration of the trade name. However, if in a member country protection of trade names were dependent on the use of the name and to the extent that another trade name may cause confusion or prejudice with respect to the first trade name, such a requirement and criterion could be applied by that member country.

### Appellations of Origin and Indications of Source

5.134 Appellations of origin and indications of source are included among the various objects of protection of industrial property under the Paris Convention (Article 1(2)).

5.135 Both these objects can be referred to under the broader concept of geographical indications, although traditionally, and for the purposes of certain special treaties (e.g., the Madrid Agreement for the Repression of False or Deceptive Indications of Source on Goods and the Lisbon Agreement for the Protection of Appellations of Origin and their International Registration), both concepts have been distinguished.

5.136 Indications of source include any name, designation, sign or other indication which refers to a given country or to a place located therein, which has the effect of conveying the notion that the goods bearing the indication originate in that country or place. Examples of indications of source are the names of countries (e.g., Germany, Japan, etc.) or of cities (e.g., Hong Kong, Paris, etc.) when used on or in connection with goods in order to indicate their place of manufacture or their provenance.

5.137 Appellations of origin have a more limited meaning, and may be considered a special type of indication of source. An appellation of origin is the geographical name of a country, region or locality which serves to designate a product originating therein, the quality and characteristics of which are due exclusively or essentially to the geographical environment, including natural and human factors.

5.138 The Paris Convention contains in Articles 10 and 10*bis* provisions on the protection of indications of source. These provisions cover in general any direct or indirect use of a false indication of the source (including, where applicable, the appellation of origin) of the goods or the identity of the producer, manufacturer or merchant, as well as any act of unfair competition by the use of indications or allegations which are liable to mislead the public as to the nature or the characteristics of the goods for which they are applied.

5.139 The Convention requires the countries to seize the goods bearing false indications or to prohibit their importation, or otherwise to apply any other measures that may be available in order to prevent or stop the use of such indications. However, the obligation to seize goods on importation only applies to the extent that such a sanction is provided for under the national law.

5.140 The Convention provides that action may be taken not only by the public prosecutor but also by any interested party. In this connection, Article 10(2) states that any producer, manufacturer or merchant, whether a natural person or a legal entity, engaged in the production, manufacture or trade in such goods established in the locality, region or country falsely indicated as the source or in the country where such false indications are used, is in any case deemed to be an interested party. Moreover, Article 10*ter*, requires the countries to enable federations and associations representing interested industrialists, producers and merchants to take action before the competent authorities with a view to the repression of the acts referred to above.

**Unfair Competition**

5.141 The Convention provides in Article 10*bis* that the countries of the Union are bound to assure to persons entitled to benefit from the Convention effective protection against unfair competition. The Convention does not specify the manner in which such protection should be granted, leaving this to the laws existing in each of the member countries.

5.142 Article 10*bis* defines acts of unfair competition as those acts of competition which are contrary to honest practices in industrial or commercial matters. Further, the Article gives some typical examples of acts of unfair competition which should be prohibited in particular.

5.143 The first example refers to all acts of such a nature as to create confusion by any means whatever with the establishment, the goods or the industrial or commercial activities of a competitor. These acts cover not only the use of identical or similar marks or names, which could be attacked as an infringement of proprietary rights, but also the use of other means which can create confusion. Such could be the form of packages, the presentation or style used on products and on their corresponding outlets or points of distribution, titles of publicity, etc.

5.144 The second example relates to false allegations in the course of trade of such a nature as to discredit the establishment, the goods, or the industrial or commercial activities of a competitor. It has been left to the domestic legislation or case law of each country to decide whether, and in what circumstances, discrediting allegations which are not strictly untrue may also be considered acts of unfair competition.

5.145 The third example of acts of unfair competition concerns indications and allegations which are liable to mislead the public as to the nature, the manufacturing process, the characteristics, the suitability for their purpose or the quality of their goods. This provision may be distinguished from the previous cases to the extent that it is concerned with the interests and well-being of the public and is one of the provisions in the Convention that is more directly related to the consumer protection role of industrial property.

## NOTES AND QUESTIONS

**1.** Just as the Paris Convention does not define the patent, so it does not define the trademark. Just as for patents, several gaps regarding trademarks are addressed in the TRIPS Agreement.

**2.** The Paris Convention (art. 6) provides for the independence of trademarks. Note, however, that the Madrid Agreement Concerning the Registration of Marks (which is discussed later in this chapter) requires that a trademark be granted registration in one Madrid Agreement member country prior to the extension of that registration to other member countries via the Madrid registration system. (This rule is modified for the Madrid Protocol system, discussed *infra.*) For a five-year period following the Madrid Agreement international registration, cancellation of the initial national registration leads to invalidation of the mark in all Madrid Agreement countries. The independence of trademarks is therefore subject to certain limitations for trademark holders that make use of the Madrid Agreement registration system.

**3.** As noted earlier, Article 8 of the Paris Convention requires that all members provide protection for "trade names" (without imposing a registration requirement). The nature and scope of such protection is not defined.

## C. The Paris Convention and Well-Known Marks

### *1. Joint Recommendation Concerning Provisions on the Protection of Well-Known Marks*

Article 6*bis* of the Paris Convention provides limited guidance regarding how state parties are to determine whether marks are well known. In September 1999, the Assembly of the Paris Union and the WIPO General Assembly adopted a Joint Recommendation Concerning Provisions on the Protection of Well-Known Marks.[16] The preface to the Recommendation observed, "The Recommendation is the first implementation of WIPO's policy to adapt to the pace of change in the field of industrial property by considering new options for accelerating the development of international harmonized common principles." Article 2 of the Joint Recommendation provides, in part:

> Article 2
>
> Determination of Whether a Mark Is a Well-Known Mark in a Member State
>
> (1) *Factors for Consideration* (a) In determining whether a mark is a well-known mark, the competent authority shall take into account any circumstances from which it may be inferred that the mark is well known.
>
> (b) In particular, the competent authority shall consider information submitted to it with respect to factors from which it may be inferred that the mark is, or is not, well known, including, but not limited to, information concerning the following:
>
> 1. the degree of knowledge or recognition of the mark in the relevant sector of the public;
>
> 2. the duration, extent and geographical area of any use of the mark;
>
> 3. the duration, extent and geographical area of any promotion of the mark, including advertising or publicity and the presentation, at fairs or exhibitions, of the goods and/or services to which the mark applies;
>
> 4. the duration and geographical area of any registrations, and/or any applications for registration, of the mark, to the extent that they reflect use or recognition of the mark;
>
> 5. the record of successful enforcement of rights in the mark, in particular, the extent to which the mark was recognized as well known by competent authorities;
>
> 6. the value associated with the mark.
>
> (c) The above factors, which are guidelines to assist the competent authority to determine whether the mark is a well-known mark, are not pre-conditions for reaching that determination. Rather, the determination in each case will depend upon the particular circumstances of that case. In some cases all of the factors may be relevant. In other cases some of the factors may be relevant. In still other cases none of the

16. Joint Recommendation Concerning Provisions on the Protection of Well-Known Marks, *adopted by* the Assembly of the Paris Union for the Protection of Industrial Property and the General Assembly of the World Intellectual Property Organization (WIPO) at the Thirty-Fourth Series of Meetings of the Assemblies of the Member States of WIPO, September 20-29, 1999 (WIPO 2000), available at http://www.wipo.int.

factors may be relevant, and the decision may be based on additional factors that are not listed in subparagraph (b), above. Such additional factors may be relevant, alone, or in combination with one or more of the factors listed in subparagraph (b), above.

## NOTES AND QUESTIONS

**1.** A WIPO Joint Recommendation is not a new international agreement, and it is not a revision to, or amendment of, the Paris Convention. Its legal status is unclear. Nonetheless, it is likely to have influence on court decisions that consider the factors for establishing the well-known character of marks. Is there reason to be concerned that Joint Recommendations could be used as a means to circumvent the more cumbersome treaty-making and amendment processes at WIPO? What might you want to know about the process by which such Joint Recommendations are approved?

### *2. The Doctrine of Well-Known Marks in National Law*

In the following decision, the U.S. Court of Appeals for the Second Circuit examines the extent to which the well-known marks doctrine of the Paris Convention may control national law. The United States has maintained a longstanding embargo against Cuban enterprises doing business with or holding assets in the United States. A U.S.-based cigar company (General Cigar) registered in the United States a trademark ("Cohiba") widely known throughout the world in connection with cigar products of a Cuban enterprise (Cubatabaco). The Cuban enterprise sought to cancel the registration held by the U.S. company on the basis of its rights in the well-known mark, as well as to prevent the U.S. cigar company from advertising and selling cigars under the mark. As indicated in note 3 following the text case, this was not the last word in this affair.

This is not the first time a Cuban claim of rights in a well-known trademark has been tested against the U.S. legislative and regulatory embargo scheme. The first major case, involving the "Havana Club" mark for rum, eventually was the subject of a WTO Appellate Body decision, although the well-known marks doctrine played a limited role on that occasion. The Paris Convention rule at the center of the *U.S.-Havana Club* case was the "telle quelle" or "as is" rule of Article 6*quinquies*. We examine the decision of the Appellate Body in section II.D.2, *infra*.

## *Empresa Cubana del Tabaco v. Culbro*

399 F.3d 462 (2d Cir. 2005)

Straub, Circuit Judge:

Defendants-Counterclaimants-Appellants-Cross-Appellees, General Cigar Co., Inc., and General Cigar Holdings, Inc. ("General Cigar"), appeal from a judgment and permanent injunction of the United States District Court for the Southern District of New York (Robert W. Sweet, Judge), entered on May 6, 2004, finding in favor of Plaintiff-Counter-Defendant-Appellee-Cross-Appellant, Empresa Cubana del Tabaco, doing business as Cubatabaco ("Cubatabaco"), on its claim of trademark infringement under Section 43(a) of the Lanham Act, ordering cancellation of General Cigar's United States trademark registration for COHIBA cigars, permanently enjoining General Cigar from further use of the COHIBA mark, and ordering General Cigar to deliver to Cubatabaco all merchandise, packaging and other materials bearing the COHIBA name, to recall from retail customers and distributors products bearing the mark, and to inform customers and distributors that they could not sell General Cigar's COHIBA-labeled products in the United States. Cubatabaco has cross-appealed from the District Court's dismissal of its treaty-based and state law claims.

This appeal arises from a dispute between Cubatabaco, a Cuban company, and General Cigar, an American company, over who has the right to use the COHIBA mark on cigars. After filing an application to register the COHIBA mark in Cuba in 1969, Cubatabaco began selling COHIBA cigars in Cuba. Cubatabaco has sold COHIBA cigars outside of Cuba since 1982, but, because of the United States embargo against Cuban goods, imposed in 1963, Cubatabaco has never sold COHIBA cigars in the United States. General Cigar obtained a registration for the COHIBA mark in the United States in 1981 and sold COHIBA cigars in the United States from 1978 until late 1987. In 1992, General Cigar relaunched a COHIBA cigar in the United States and has sold cigars under that mark in the United States since that time.

Cubatabaco claims that it owns the U.S. COHIBA trademark because General Cigar abandoned its 1981 registration in 1987 and that, by the time General Cigar resumed use of the mark in 1992, the Cuban COHIBA mark was sufficiently well known in the United States that it deserved protection under the so-called "famous marks doctrine." The District Court agreed and found that, although Cubatabaco had never used the mark in the United States and was prohibited from doing so under the embargo, it nonetheless owned the U.S. COHIBA mark. The District Court concluded that by failing to use the COHIBA mark from late 1987 to 1992, General Cigar abandoned its 1981 registration. It found further that because the Cuban COHIBA mark was sufficiently well known in the United States by November 1992, the date General Cigar resumed its use of the mark, Cubatabaco was entitled to priority in asserting ownership of the mark. After finding that there was a likelihood of confusion between the Cuban COHIBA mark and the General Cigar COHIBA mark, the court granted judgment to Cubatabaco on its claim for trademark infringement under Section 43(a) of the Lanham Act, 15 U.S.C. §1125(a), cancelled General Cigar's registration of the mark, and enjoined General Cigar from using the mark. The court dismissed all other claims brought by Cubatabaco, including claims under international trademark treaties and New York law.

We do not reach the question of whether an entity that has not used a mark on products sold in the United States can nonetheless acquire a U.S. trademark through operation of the famous marks doctrine. We need not reach that question in this case because even were we to recognize and apply the famous marks doctrine, the Cuban embargo bars Cubatabaco's acquisition of the COHIBA mark via the famous marks doctrine. Therefore, we reverse the District Court's grant of judgment to Cubatabaco on its claim of trademark infringement under Section 43(a) of the Lanham Act. We affirm the District Court's dismissal of all other claims brought by Cubatabaco. . . .

### A. The Trademark Infringement Claim Fails Because Acquisition of the Mark Via the Famous Marks Doctrine Is Prohibited by the Embargo Regulations . . .

A transaction involving property in which a Cuban entity has an interest includes a transfer of property to a Cuban entity. "Property" includes trademarks, *id.* §515.311, and "transfers outside the United States" of United States trademark rights to Cuban entities are prohibited by §515.201(b)(2). "Transfer" is broadly defined to include "any . . . act . . . the . . . effect of which is to create . . . any right, remedy, power, privilege, or interest with respect to property." *Id.* §515.310. Cubatabaco's acquisition of the mark is a "transfer[] outside the United States with regard to any property or property interest subject to the jurisdiction of the

United States," *id.* §515.201(b)(2), because Cubatabaco's acquisition of the mark is a transfer of U.S. property rights from inside the United States to Cuba—a location "outside of the United States." Therefore, Cubatabaco's acquisition of the U.S. COHIBA mark through the famous marks doctrine is barred by §515.201(b)(2). . . .

### B. Cubatabaco's Claims for Injunctive Relief Based on Section 43(A) and the Paris Convention Fail Because They Entail A Transfer of Property Rights to Cubatabaco in Violation Of The Embargo. . .

#### 1. Section 43(a) Claim for Unfair Competition. . .

Cubatabaco's theory is that General Cigar's sale of COHIBA cigars in the United States violates Section 43(a) because it is likely to cause consumer confusion as to the source or attribution of those cigars. The confusion alleged by Cubatabaco in support of its Section 43(a) claim is derived solely from General Cigar's use of the COHIBA mark: Cubatabaco cannot obtain relief on a theory that General Cigar's use of the mark causes confusion, because, pursuant to our holding today, General Cigar's legal right to the COHIBA mark has been established as against Cubatabaco. General Cigar has a right to use the mark in the United States because it owns the mark in the United States.

In Part IA of this opinion we held that General Cigar has priority rights to the COHIBA mark in the United States as against Cubatabaco. . . . To allow Cubatabaco to prevail on a claim of unfair competition against General Cigar and to obtain an injunction prohibiting General Cigar from using the mark would turn the law of trademark on its head. None of United States law, the facts in this case, or international treaties warrants such acrobatics in this case. We therefore find that, on the facts of this case, Cubatabaco's Section 43(a) claim seeking an injunction against General Cigar's use of its duly registered COHIBA mark cannot succeed as a matter of law.

We do not find the analysis offered by the government and by Cubatabaco in defense of the recast Section 43(a) claim persuasive. It may be true that, as the government argues, "Cubatabaco's foreign registrations give it the right to register its COHIBA mark [in the United States], absent General Cigar's registration." Amicus Curiae Br. at 12. That is, however, a hypothetical circumstance upon which we need not speculate. As we hold today, General Cigar does have a valid registration on the COHIBA mark in the United States. Further, while it may be true, as the government points out, that Cubatabaco's COHIBA mark "was 'famous' and had secondary meaning in the United States before General Cigar's first use [of its COHIBA mark]," *id.*, we have already held that this fact cannot justify a transfer of property rights in the COHIBA mark to Cubatabaco via the "famous marks doctrine." We see no reason to alter that holding to allow Cubatabaco to achieve the same transfer via a route that is one step more circuitous than the path rejected above.

#### 2. Article 6bis Paris Convention

Cubatabaco maintains that even if the Regulations bar its acquisition of the mark, and even if it cannot obtain relief for an unfair competition claim under Section 43(a), it has a right under Article *6bis* of the Paris Convention, in conjunction with Sections 44(b) and (h) of the Lanham Act, to obtain cancellation of General Cigar's mark and an injunction against its use.

Article *6bis* of the Paris Convention provides that:

> (1) The countries of the Union undertake, ex officio if their legislation so permits, or at the request of an interested party, to refuse or to cancel the registration, and to prohibit the use, of a trademark which constitutes a reproduction, an imitation, or a translation, liable to create confusion, of a mark considered by the competent authority of the country of registration or use to be well known in that country as being already the mark of a person entitled to the benefits of

> this Convention and used for identical or similar goods. These provisions shall also apply when the essential part of the mark constitutes a reproduction of any such well-known mark or an imitation liable to create confusion therewith.
>
> (2) A period of at least five years from the date of registration shall be allowed for requesting the cancellation of such a mark. The countries of the Union may provide for a period within which the prohibition of use must be requested.
>
> (3) No time limit shall be fixed for requesting the cancellation or the prohibition of the use of marks registered or used in bad faith.

Paris Convention, Art. 6*bis*, 21 U.S.T. at 1640.

Both the United States and Cuba are parties to the Paris Convention. *Id.* at 1669, 1676.

According to Cubatabaco, Sections 44(b) and (h) incorporate treaty provisions relating to the "repression of unfair competition," and rights under Article 6*bis* fall into that category. Section 44(b) provides that:

> Any person whose country of origin is a party to any convention or treaty relating to trademarks, trade or commercial names, or the repression of unfair competition, to which the United States is also a party, or extends reciprocal rights to nationals of the United States by law, shall be entitled to the benefits of this section under the conditions expressed herein to the extent necessary to give effect to any provision of such convention, treaty or reciprocal law, in addition to the rights to which any owner of a mark is otherwise entitled by this chapter. . . .

Cubatabaco may be correct that Sections 44(b) and (h) incorporate Article 6*bis* and allow foreign entities to acquire U.S. trademark rights in the United States if their marks are sufficiently famous in the United States before they are used in this country. That is the view expressed by some commentators. *See* 4 McCarthy on Trademarks and Unfair Competition §29:4 (4th ed. 2004) ("In the author's view, the well-known or famous marks doctrine of Paris Convention Article 6*bis* is incorporated into United States domestic law though the operation of Lanham Act §43(a), §44(b) and §44(h)." (footnote omitted)).[10] However, we need not decide that broad question here because even assuming that the famous marks doctrine is otherwise viable and applicable, the embargo bars Cubatabaco from acquiring property rights in the U.S. COHIBA mark through the doctrine. The Embargo Regulations do not permit Cubatabaco to acquire the power to exclude General Cigar from using the mark in the United States. We do not read Article 6*bis* and Section 44(b) and (h) of the Lanham Act to require cancellation of General Cigar's properly registered trademark or an injunction against its use of the mark in the United States under these circumstances.

In any event, to the extent that the Paris Convention, standing alone, might pose an irreconcilable conflict to the Regulations, the latter will prevail. "An act of congress ought never to be construed to violate the law of nations, if any other possible construction remains." *Weinberger v. Rossi*, 456 U.S. 25, 32, 71 L. Ed. 2d 715, 102 S. Ct. 1510 (1982) (quotations and citations omitted). However, as we have recently recalled, "legislative acts trump treaty-made international law" when those acts are passed subsequent to ratification of the treaty and clearly contradict treaty obligations. *United States v. Yousef*, 327 F.3d 56, 110 (2d Cir. 2003) (citing *Breard v. Greene*, 523 U.S. 371, 376, 140 L. Ed. 2d 529, 118 S. Ct. 1352 (1998); *see also Whitney v. Robertson*, 124 U.S. 190, 194, 31 L. Ed. 386, 8 S. Ct. 456 (1888)

10. McCarthy asserts that claims for protection of "famous" marks should be brought under Section 43(a). *See* 4 McCarthy on Trademarks and Unfair Competition §29:4 ("Lanham Act §43(a) gives a foreign national without a federal registration of its mark standing to sue in a federal court, invoke the well-known marks doctrine of the Paris Convention Article 6*bis*, and prevail if its mark is so well-known in the U.S. that confusion is likely."). To the extent that a foreign entity attempts to utilize the famous marks doctrine as basis for its right to a U.S. trademark and seeks to prevent another entity from using the mark in the United States, the claim should be brought under Section 43(a). Under Section 43(a), both foreign and domestic entities can seek relief for infringement of unregistered marks.

(if a treaty and a federal statute conflict, "the one last in date will control the other"). The most recent iteration of the Paris Convention was ratified by the United States in 1970, *see* 21 U.S.T. 1583; whereas the Regulations were reaffirmed and codified in 1996 with the passage of the LIBERTAD Act, 110 Stat. 792 (1996), 22 U.S.C. §6032(h). In these circumstances, any claim grounded in the Paris Convention that presented an irreconcilable conflict with the Regulations would be rendered "null" by the Regulations. *Breard*, 523 U.S. at 376.

## II. Other Treaty Claims Brought Under Sections 44(B) and (H) of the Lanham Act . . .

### B. Treaty-Based Unfair Competition Claims. . .

In addition, Cubatabaco cannot maintain a claim for unfair competition under Article 10*bis* of the Paris Convention pursuant to Sections 44(b) and (h) of the Lanham Act. The Paris Convention requires that "foreign nationals . . . be given the same treatment in each of the member countries as that country makes available to its own citizens." *Vanity Fair Mills v. T. Eaton Co.*, 234 F.2d 633, 640 (2d Cir.), *cert. denied*, 352 U.S. 871, 1 L. Ed. 2d 76, 77 S. Ct. 96 (1956). "The Paris Convention provides for national treatment, and does not define the substantive law of unfair competition." *Mattel, Inc. v. MCA Records, Inc.*, 296 F.3d 894, 908 (9th Cir. 2002). As the Eleventh Circuit has explained:

> We agree that section 44 of the Lanham Act incorporated, to some degree, the Paris Convention. But we disagree that the Paris Convention creates substantive rights beyond those independently provided in the Lanham Act. As other courts of appeals have noted, the rights articulated in the Paris Convention do not exceed the rights conferred by the Lanham Act. Instead, we conclude that the Paris Convention, as incorporated by the Lanham Act, only requires "national treatment."

National treatment means that "foreign nationals should be given the same treatment in each of the member countries as that country makes available to its own citizens." So, Section 44 of the Lanham Act gives foreign nationals the same rights and protections provided to United States citizens by the Lanham Act. As such, foreign nationals like Plaintiff may seek protection in United States courts for violations of the Lanham Act. But the Paris Convention, as incorporated by Section 44 of the Lanham Act, creates no new cause of action for unfair competition. Any cause of action based on unfair competition must be grounded in the substantive provisions of the Lanham Act. *Int'l Cafe, S.A.L. v. Hard Rock Cafe Int'l (U.S.A.), Inc.*, 252 F.3d 1274, 1277-78 (11th Cir. 2001) (citations omitted). Therefore, we conclude that Cubatabaco cannot maintain a separate claim for unfair competition under Article 10*bis* and Sections 44(b) and (h). Rather, a claim for unfair competition must be brought under Section 43(a) or state law. *See Mattel*, 296 F.3d at 908.[14]

## NOTES AND QUESTIONS

**1.** The U.S. Supreme Court denied certiorari in *Empresa Cubana del Tabaco v. General Cigar Co.*, 547 U.S. 1205 (2006).

**2.** The rule that the later in time of a treaty or statute controls as a matter of internal law is longstanding U.S. constitutional doctrine. In this sense, it is unsurprising that the Court of Appeals decided that the embargo regulations take precedence over an inconsistent rule of the

14. In any event, as noted above, any irreconcilable conflict between the Paris Convention and the Regulations would be resolved in favor of the Regulations.

Paris Convention. But, without going further and transferring the mark to Cubatabaco, why did the Court of Appeals refuse to cancel General Cigar's "Cohiba" trademark registration?

**3.** The question asked in note 2 (already in the second edition of this book) was in fact pursued by Cubatabaco at the USPTO, with the Trademark Trial and Appeal Board (TTAB) initially ruling that the decision by the Second Circuit in the text case precluded it from seeking cancellation of General Cigar's trademark registrations. The Court of Appeals for the Federal Circuit reversed the TTAB (*Empresa Cubana Del Tabaco v. Gen. Cigar Co.*, 111 U.S.P.Q.2d 1058 (Fed. Cir. 2014)), authorizing Cubatabaco to proceed with its petitions for cancellation, and indicating that the text decision by the Second Circuit would not preclude it from registering the trademarks based on its Cuba registrations since this would not involve a prohibited transfer of property. The U.S. Supreme Court denied General Cigar's petition for certiorari in *General Cigar Co. v. Empresa Cubana del Tabaco*, 135 S. Ct. 1401 (2015).

**4.** It is central to the Court of Appeals decision to classify the trademark holder's right to exclude others as a "property" right, and thus subject to the embargo. Are "negative" rights to exclude "property"? Under any particular set of conditions?

**5.** U.S. business groups were almost uniformly opposed to the Court of Appeals decision because they fear that other governments will similarly refuse to acknowledge rights in well-known marks. *See, e.g.*, Amicus Brief of the National Foreign Trade Council to Supreme Court, filed Dec. 2, 2005.

## D. The WTO TRIPS Agreement and Trademarks

Negotiations during the GATT Uruguay Round with respect to trademarks were far less controversial than negotiations with respect to patents. In fact, many developing countries viewed an agreement protecting against trademark counterfeiting and copyright piracy as a preferable alternative to the more comprehensive TRIPS Agreement that was concluded. All (or virtually all) countries involved in the negotiations maintained trademark registration systems. There was little opposition to the premise that trademarks serve a useful economic function.

### *1. The TRIPS Agreement Text Analyzed*

The WTO TRIPS Agreement includes a section (Part II, sec. 2) with respect to trademarks. The following is from the UNCTAD/ICTSD TRIPS and Development Resource Book (2005), which explains the negotiating history of each provision of the TRIPS Agreement and provides interpretative guidance. Only the interpretative part of the chapter on trademarks is presented here, and then only in an excerpted format. The full text of the Resource Book is available online at http://www.iprsonline.org.

---

## *UNCTAD/ICTSD Resource Book on TRIPS and Development*

http://www.iprsonline.org*

### 3.1. Article 15

#### 3.1.3. Article 15.1: Definition

*Article 15 Protectable Subject Matter*

1. Any sign, or any combination of signs, capable of distinguishing the goods or services of one undertaking from those of other undertakings, shall be capable of constituting a

* In hardcover from Cambridge University Press (2005), at 228. The text has been adapted from the original by its author (who is also an author of this book).

trademark. Such signs, in particular words including personal names, letters, numerals, figurative elements and combinations of colours as well as any combination of such signs, shall be eligible for registration as trademarks.* Where signs are not inherently capable of distinguishing the relevant goods or services, Members may make registrability depend on distinctiveness acquired through use. Members may require, as a condition of registration, that signs be visually perceptible. . . .

### 3.1.3. Article 15.2

> 3. Paragraph 1 shall not be understood to prevent a Member from denying registration of a trademark on other grounds, provided that they do not derogate from the provisions of the Paris Convention (1967).

A Member might elect to refuse registration of a trademark on grounds other than that it does not distinguish the goods or services of an undertaking. For example, in the *U.S.-Havana Club* case decided by the WTO Appellate Body (AB), the United States had refused to register a mark on grounds that the party claiming ownership of the mark was not its rightful owner. The U.S. refusal was upheld by the AB as being within U.S. discretion to make determinations regarding the lawful holders of marks.

Article 6*quinquies* of the Paris Convention, which was at issue in the *U.S.-Havana Club* case, obligates Members to accept marks for registration in the same form ("as is," or "*telle quelle*") as registered in the country of origin. This rule was designed to prevent trademark registration authorities from requiring translations or other adaptations of marks to meet local preferences or rules. Under Article 15.2, a Member must comply with the "as is" obligation, and in that way it may not derogate from the Paris Convention. There are exceptions even to the "as is" obligation. That is, Article 6*quinquies*, Paris Convention, recognizes certain bases even for refusing to accept the same form of the mark.

The Paris Convention enumerates other bases on which the registration of trademarks may be denied (Article 6*bis* and 6*ter*). Article 6*bis* establishes an obligation to refuse third party registration of well-known marks. Treatment of well-known marks is addressed in sub-Section 3.2.2 below. Article 6*ter* creates obligations to refuse trademark registration for state flags and symbols.

### 3.1.3. Article 15.3: Use of Trademarks

> (1) Members may make registrability depend on use. However, actual use of a trademark shall not be a condition for filing an application for registration. An application shall not be refused solely on the ground that intended use has not taken place before the expiry of a period of three years from the date of application.

Trademark protection originated as a form of unfair competition law. The tort of "passing off" in Commonwealth jurisdictions evolved to address claims of taking unfair advantage of another person's trademark or business name. This cause of action did not depend on the registration of a mark. The concept is broader than trademark infringement, and could encompass misuse of trade names as well as other distinctive characteristics of a business. It was and remains the subject matter of common law. [On the common law doctrine of "passing off," *see* W.R. Cornish, Intellectual Property: Patents, Copyright, Trade Marks and Allied Rights (4th ed. 1999), at Chapter 16.] Protection of trademarks developed in the United States as a part of the law of unfair competition. Although trademarks long ago came to benefit from registration in the Commonwealth and U.S. legal systems, there remains the possibility to establish and enforce "common law" trademarks from use in commerce.

Before the TRIPS Agreement was negotiated, the United States required use of a trademark in commerce as a precondition to federal registration. This precondition was intended to assure that trademarks were associated only with real goods or services. Among other objectives, this would avoid a proliferation of unused marks on the records of the Patent and Trademark Office (USPTO). The use precondition also served as a reward to business enterprises that acted swiftly to put their goods and services on the market.

However, even without the complications that this use-based registration system created at the international level (since there was a basic incompatibility with most other countries that allowed registration without use), the precondition came to be seen as an impediment to more modern marketing strategies that involved the advertisement to the public of new goods and services before they were actually placed on the market. If use were a precondition for registration, business enterprises would face risks by advertising in advance of product and service introduction. Other businesses might actually use a mark on a good or service before the enterprise advertising it placed its own good or service on the market.

The U.S. moved to a modified use-based registration during the Uruguay Round as the advantages of a more globally-integrated trademark registration system became apparent to U.S. businesses. A Madrid Protocol-based registration system (administered by WIPO) could be employed to reduce registration inefficiencies, and some of the domestic difficulties that the use-based system presented for marketing strategies could be overcome. The U.S. system remains grounded in "use" as a condition of registration, but it is now acceptable to file for registration declaring "intent to use" a mark, and subsequently filing within a prescribed period a verification that the mark has actually been used in commerce. Formal registration of the mark does not occur until the applicant submits verification of actual use to the USPTO. In the meantime, the applicant benefits from priority "constructive use" of the mark that in effect precludes a third party from acquiring competing federal trademark rights during the intent-to-use period, and also allows infringement claims based on that constructive use.

Article 15.3, third sentence, provides that registration may not be denied during a three-year application period solely on the grounds of non-use. This in effect requires that a form of priority be established for unused marks included in filed applications since for a period of three years the mark should be treated (for application purposes) as if it is being used. However, this does not appear to require that an applicant be given rights as against an alleged infringer of an unused mark during the "priority" period since it refers only to the ultimate grant of registration, not to the interim period. It is for each Member to determine the effect of an application under national law. Article 4 of the Paris Convention provides a six-month right of priority in respect to the filing of trademark applications outside the country of first application. This prevents the intervening use of a mark or filing of an application from interfering with the rights of the priority holder.

Article 15.3, TRIPS Agreement, accommodates the U.S.-style registration system that continues to require use as a precondition to completion of registration, but permits an application to be filed prior to actual use. It is of interest that non-use cannot be the sole grounds for refusing registration during a three-year period, but otherwise the effects of an application are not stated.

### 3.1.3 Article 15.4

> 1. The nature of the goods or services to which a trademark is to be applied shall in no case form an obstacle to registration of the trademark.

Article 15.4 of the TRIPS Agreement essentially restates Article 7 of the Paris Convention, adding express reference to service marks.

. . . IPRs are not "market access" rights. The fact that Article 15.4 states that trademark registration must be granted in connection with all kinds of goods and services does not require that a Member allow such goods and services to be sold.

Article 6*quinquies* of the Paris Convention ("as is" or "*telle quelle*") permits trademark registration to be refused on grounds that the mark is "contrary to morality or public order and, in particular, of such a nature as to deceive the public." Note that reference is to the mark itself, and not to associated goods or services.

The question of morality or public order might arise in connection with goods such as cigarettes that are known to be harmful to health, the advertising or sale of which Members might choose to heavily regulate or even ban. Article 15.4 suggests that a mark used in connection with cigarettes may not be refused registration because of the product with which it is associated. This appears to create a tension with Article 6*quinquies* that permits refusal of registration of a mark on morality and public order grounds. This apparent tension might be resolved by interpreting Article 6*quinquies* to be limited to refusals for signs or symbols that are offensive "as such." Yet this is a difficult line to draw since a sign or symbol inherently acts to draw (or stimulate) a connection in the public mind to some good, service, activity or belief. A Member might argue that it is entitled to block the registration of a mark used on cigarettes not because of the product, but because promotion of the mark itself has adverse consequences for the public; that is, the mark "as such" is injurious to public order because it encourages a type of behaviour known to cause serious injury (and the behaviour is not linked or limited to the products of a particular enterprise). Whether or not this argument is persuasive, the critical point from a public policy perspective is that allowing registration of a trademark or service mark does not impair the government's authority to regulate the product associated with the mark. Even if a Member must allow registration of trademarks for cigarettes, it may ban (or limit) the sale of the cigarettes on public health grounds.

#### 3.1.3. Article 15.5

> 1. Members shall publish each trademark either before it is registered or promptly after it is registered and shall afford a reasonable opportunity for petitions to cancel the registration. In addition, Members may afford an opportunity for the registration of a trademark to be opposed.

Article 15.5 addresses the procedural issues of publication, cancellation and opposition. It is fairly straightforward. . . .

### 3.2. Article 16

#### 3.2.3. Article 16.1: Exclusive Rights

> 3. The owner of a registered trademark shall have the exclusive right to prevent all third parties not having the owner's consent from using in the course of trade identical or similar signs for goods or services which are identical or similar to those in respect of which the trademark is registered where such use would result in a likelihood of confusion. In case of the use of an identical sign for identical goods or services, a likelihood of confusion shall be presumed. The rights described above shall not prejudice any existing prior rights, nor shall they affect the possibility of Members making rights available on the basis of use. . . .

The rights are attributable to owners of "registered" trademarks. Members may, but need not, protect "common law" trademarks. In the *U.S.-Havana Club* case the United States was defending its right to determine who the "owner" of the subject trademark was, as a condition predicate to determining what the rights of that owner might be. . . .

The second sentence of Article 16.1 provides that, "In case of the use of an identical sign for identical goods or services, a likelihood of confusion shall be presumed." This provision should facilitate the successful prosecution of infringement claims where the intent to directly take advantage of the trademark owner is evident (*e.g.*, straightforward trademark counterfeiting). By establishing a presumption of likelihood of confusion where the signs and goods/services are identical, the burden is shifted to the alleged infringer to prove the absence of likelihood. This removes a significant evidentiary task from the trademark owner. It is, however, possible to rebut the presumption. Professor T. Cottier has noted that in cases of parallel importation (in countries following a rule of international exhaustion of trademarks), the presumption may be rebutted by showing that the goods were put on the market with the trademark owner's consent in another country. . . .

### 3.2.3. ARTICLE 16.2: WELL-KNOWN TRADEMARKS

> 3. Article *6bis* of the Paris Convention (1967) shall apply, *mutatis mutandis*, to services. In determining whether a trademark is well-known, Members shall take account of the knowledge of the trademark in the relevant sector of the public, including knowledge in the Member concerned which has been obtained as a result of the promotion of the trademark.

Article *6bis* of the Paris Convention addresses the subject of so-called "well-known" trademarks.

A special regime for such marks has the objective of providing protection for trademarks that are well known in a country as already belonging to a certain person, even though they are not, or not yet, protected in that country through a registration. In the absence of registration of the well-known mark, the conflicting mark could theoretically be registered and enforced to the detriment of the well-known mark, which would in most cases result in consumer confusion. Such practice is widely regarded as constituting an act of unfair competition, thus requiring the protection of the well-known trademark.

The necessity of protection of well-known marks usually arises in new markets, i.e. in countries previously closed to foreign traders or which, through an increase in economic development become attractive for the suppliers of branded products. In those cases, the owner of the well-known, but unregistered trademark is considered as worth of protection as if she/he had actually registered the mark. This shows that registration is not considered the ultimate criterion of protection. It is considered more important that the registration of the same or a similar mark by a third person could lead to *confusion of the public*, who would automatically associate the registered mark with the non-registered, but well-known owner or his products.

To make clear that well-known service marks are subject to protection on the same basis as trademarks (for goods), Article 16.2, TRIPS Agreement, first sentence, explicitly extends the protection of Article *6bis*, Paris Convention, to service marks.

Article *6bis*, Paris Convention, has been understood to leave substantial uncertainty regarding the standards states should apply in determining whether a mark is well known. Article 16.2, TRIPS Agreement, second sentence, addresses one aspect of that uncertainty. It establishes that the question whether a mark is well known should be determined in respect to the "relevant sector of the public." Assume, for example, that an enterprise is the leading manufacturer of sophisticated equipment used by scientific laboratories to determine the chemical composition of materials. The trademark of that enterprise might be very well known among all technical specialists in the field of chemical composition, but would likely be more or less completely unknown to the general public. Article 16.2 indicates that a mark should be considered well known based on the "relevant" sector of the public, which in such circumstances would be the technical specialists. There is a risk that defining "well known" in terms of the relevant sector of the public will lead to a proliferation of well known marks. This risk can be addressed by imposing a relatively high standard regarding the degree of knowledge of the mark among the relevant sector, which possibility is within the scope of the provision.

Article 16.2, second sentence, adds to its relevant sector clarification the phrase, "including knowledge in the Member concerned which has been obtained as a result of the promotion of the trademark." . . . The TRIPS text clarifies that a mark may be well known even if it has not been used on goods and services within the Member concerned, but has become known there through advertisement. . . .

### 3.2.3. Article 16.3: Well-Known Trademarks

> (2) Article 6*bis* of the Paris Convention (1967) shall apply, *mutatis mutandis*, to goods or services which are not similar to those in respect of which a trademark is registered, provided that use of that trademark in relation to those goods or services would indicate a connection between those goods or services and the owner of the registered trademark and provided that the interests of the owner of the registered trademark are likely to be damaged by such use.

Article 16.3, TRIPS Agreement, addresses the situation in which a third party uses a well-known mark in connection with goods or services for which the mark holder is not well known. This provision differs from Article 16.2. in three respects. First, the well-known mark in question is *registered*, as follows from the language of the provision (see quotation above). Second, the goods or services for which the confusingly similar trademark is used are different from those goods or services that are covered by the well-known mark. Third, this provision emphasizes protection of the *reputation* of the well-known mark. This is indicated by the last part of the paragraph, requiring that the "interests of the owner of the registered trademark are likely to be damaged" by the use of the third party's trademark (see below for details). Articles 16.2 TRIPS and 6*bis* of the Paris Convention do not contain such reference to the interests of the right holder, but focus on the likelihood of confusion of the public. Nevertheless, it has been observed that Article 16.3 TRIPS, by referring to Article 6*bis* of the Paris Convention, also takes account of the concern about confusion of the public.

To illustrate the operation of Article 16.3, consider the situation in which the well-known automobile trademark "AUDI" was used by a third party in connection with the marketing of television sets. To begin with, there would be a difficult question whether television sets might be part of the natural product line expansion of an automobile manufacturer in an ordinary trademark confusion sense (i.e., under Article 16.1). If so, there would be similarity between the television sets potentially covered by the registered trademark and the third party's television sets. Thus, the question of well-known marks might not arise since there may already be a likelihood of confusion between similar goods. However, if there is no likelihood of confusion in the *ordinary* trademark sense, Article 16.3 indicates that the finder of fact should proceed to ask whether a consumer would consider there to be a connection between the goods, even if not part of a natural product line expansion (i.e. the case of non-similarity of the goods). Would a consumer seeing the term "AUDI" on a television set think that there was a connection with the automobile company? In recent years there has been an increasing tendency for producers well known in one area of commerce to market into unrelated lines of commerce. Would it have been anticipated that the "Marlboro" and "Camel" cigarette marks would be used on clothing and shoes? In this context, Article 16.3, TRIPS Agreement, addresses a significant question regarding well-known marks.

Article 16.3 contains an important qualifier. The interests of the owner of the well known trademark must be "likely to be damaged by such use." There are two ways such damage might be foreseen. First, the well known trademark holder might itself have been planning to enter the same market as the third party using the mark. It would therefore be injured by the loss of a revenue opportunity. Second, the third party using the mark might be doing so in a way that would tarnish or injure the reputation of the trademark holder. The burden should presumably be on the trademark holder to establish the likelihood of damage since third party use of a mark in connection with a dissimilar product would not ordinarily be assumed to cause damage.

Subjective questions such as those involving the likelihood of damage from use of a mark on dissimilar goods may be answered differently in various Members. This is to be expected. In the application of TRIPS Agreement provisions such as Articles 16.2 and 16.3, the issue from a WTO legal standpoint is whether the rules are applied reasonably and in good faith, not whether an exact methodology is used to reach a definitive result.

### 3.3. Article 17: exceptions

*Exceptions*

> Members may provide limited exceptions to the rights conferred by a trademark, such as fair use of descriptive terms, provided that such exceptions take account of the legitimate interests of the owner of the trademark and of third parties.

Trademark rights involve exclusivity in signs or symbols. In effect a sign or symbol may be taken out of public usage and reserved to private control. When trademarks involve arbitrary combinations of letters and/or designs the effects on the public may be relatively inconsequential. However, there are a variety of contexts in which the effect on the public may be substantial.

When a descriptive word becomes the subject of trademark protection the capacity for expression is restricted. Even though the rights of the trademark holder are nominally limited to use with respect to certain goods or services in the course of trade, there is a chilling effect around the use of the word that discourages others from using it. The impact, both direct and indirect, of granting private rights in words is what motivates the prohibition on the grant of trademark rights in "generic" terms.

It is difficult for one enterprise to compare its goods with those of another without referring to the latter's goods by their trademark name. For this reason, the use of a competitor's mark in comparative advertising is typically allowed as an exception to the rights of the holder.

There are a number of other contexts in which trademarks are referred to without the consent of the owner. A common type of reference is in news reporting and commentary. It is often difficult to make reference to the goods or services of an enterprise without referring to the trademark name. Again consider the "AUDI" trademark. It would be difficult for the publishers of a magazine directed to auto enthusiasts to review the performance of AUDI automobiles without using the term "AUDI." The publisher could, of course, refer to an automobile manufacturer based in Germany with product lines known by certain characteristics, but this would strain writers and the reading public alike. The use by the publisher of the term AUDI in this context is a form of fair use of a trademark, sometimes referred to as "nominative fair use."

Like copyright, trademark protects only the identification of the product and not its function. Pharmaceutical manufacturers market drugs in colored capsules or tablets. Doctors, pharmacists and consumer-patients come to identify those drugs by their distinctive coloring. The users of the drugs come to rely on the color as a principal means for determining what to ingest. The color serves a critical function from a public health standpoint. When generic versions of a drug are produced by second-comers, significant problems for consumer-patients may arise if they are unable to identify the same medication by the same color. Color has taken on an important functional characteristic. The use by third parties of the same color on equivalent drugs may be justified on either of two bases. First, it might be said that the color is not serving a trademark function because it is functional, and thus not protected. Second, it might be said that use of the color is a limited exception to the rights of the trademark owner as a fair use in the public interest.

The Paris Convention does not expressly address the subject of exceptions to trademark rights, and from that standpoint Article 17, TRIPS Agreement, does not have a textual precedent at the multilateral level. This is similar to the circumstances of Article 30, TRIPS Agreement, with respect to patents. . . . While there may be a temptation to analogize because of the similar language of the three exception provisions, it is important to be aware that the forms of IPRs perform very different roles and that the public and private interests in each may be rather different.

The term "limited exception" is capable of different reasonable interpretations. In the *Canada-Generic Pharmaceuticals* case, the panel construed the language to refer to a narrow derogation. Canada had argued that a "limited exception" is an exception with defined boundaries. The text is susceptible to both interpretations.

Article 17 gives "fair use of descriptive terms" as illustration of a limited exception, but clearly not in an exclusive way, as is made clear by the use of the terms "such as." As noted above, there are a number of other types of limited exception that have been recognized in different legal systems.

Article 17 further provides that a limited exception should "take account of the legitimate interests of the owner of the trademark and of third parties." Application of this language will of necessity involve subjective judgments regarding the balance of public and private interests in trademarks. The panel in *Canada-Generic Pharmaceuticals* found that "legitimate interests" was to be understood more broadly than "legal interests" and to take into account broader social interests. Each of the trademark exceptions discussed above should be permissible within the scope of subjective balancing implicit in taking account of the legitimate interests of owners and third parties. [See *EC-Geographical Indications, infra* p. 479.]

### 3.4. Article 18: Term of Protection

*Term of Protection*

> Initial registration, and each renewal of registration, of a trademark shall be for a term of no less than seven years. The registration of a trademark shall be renewable indefinitely.

Prior to the TRIPS Agreement, WTO Members maintained significantly disparate renewal periods. Many trademark offices were (and remain) dependent on renewal fees to maintain their operations, and not surprisingly are anxious to collect fees. The seven-year minimum initial and renewal registration period was a compromise between the United States proposal for a minimum ten-year period and a developing country proposal to leave the question of duration to each Member.

Trademarks are capable of indefinite duration. This does not mean that trademark rights last indefinitely based on the mere payment of renewal fees. Trademarks are subject to cancellation on grounds such as non-use (*see* Article 19 below). Article 18, however, makes clear that there is no temporal limit to how long a trademark may remain valid if requirements for maintaining rights are satisfied.

### 3.5. Article 19: Requirement of Use

*Requirement of Use*

> 1. If use is required to maintain a registration, the registration may be cancelled only after an uninterrupted period of at least three years of non-use, unless valid reasons based on the existence of obstacles to such use are shown by the trademark owner. Circumstances arising independently of the will of the owner of the trademark which constitute an obstacle to the use of the trademark, such as import restrictions on or other government requirements for goods or services protected by the trademark, shall be recognized as valid reasons for non-use.
>
> 2. When subject to the control of its owner, use of a trademark by another person shall be recognized as use of the trademark for the purpose of maintaining the registration.

Article 19.1, TRIPS Agreement, first sentence, sets a three-year (uninterrupted) minimum term prior to which a registered mark may not be cancelled for non-use. The Paris Convention, at Article 5.C(1), provides that "the registration may be cancelled only after a reasonable period."

The TRIPS Agreement thus effectively defines the "reasonable period" of the Paris Convention.

Article 5.C(1), Paris Convention, and Article 19.1, TRIPS Agreement, first sentence, each provide a basis upon which the trademark owner can prevent cancellation. The Paris Convention permits the trademark owner to "justify his inaction." The TRIPS Agreement refers to the "existence of obstacles to such use." Neither formulation is clear as to what types of facts or circumstances might justify non-use, leaving substantial discretion to Members to delimit the scope of the grounds. They might be quite broad, for example, allowing the registered holder to justify non-use on grounds that it was unable to put a good into production for technical reasons. On the other hand, they might be narrow, for example, referring only to obstacles arising outside the trademark holder's control, such as a government ban on sales of the subject good.

The Paris Convention rule allowing owners to "justify" non-use might be construed not to provide an excuse when the government acted. The government's action might be construed to de-legitimize the trademark owner's excuse. Article 19.2, TRIPS Agreement, second sentence, makes clear that indeed the obstacle may arise from outside the trademark owner's control, including government-imposed restrictions on the subject goods or services. Thus, an excuse based on a legitimately-imposed government restriction should still constitute a legitimate excuse.

Article 19.2, TRIPS Agreement, provides for the situation in which the trademark is licensed by its owner to a third party. Use by the licensee is equivalent to use by the owner for purposes of preventing cancellation for non-use. However, the licensee's use of the mark is only covered "when subject to the control of its owner." It would appear that a "naked license," that is, a license under which the trademark holder merely collects royalties but does not supervise the licensee, may not constitute use under this provision. This is the logical import of the language and supported by the negotiating history which shows the language concerning control replacing an earlier text according to which only the owner's consent to use of the mark was required.

It might alternatively be argued that so long as the trademark owner holds a contractual interest in the mark the licensee is under its control (however loose) and that this may suffice for "control" within the meaning of Article 19.2. This does not seem very persuasive in light of the express language and negotiating history.

### 3.6. Article 20: Other Requirements

***Other Requirements***

> The use of a trademark in the course of trade shall not be unjustifiably encumbered by special requirements, such as use with another trademark, use in a special form or use in a manner detrimental to its capability to distinguish the goods or services of one undertaking from those of other undertakings. This will not preclude a requirement prescribing the use of the trademark identifying the undertaking producing the goods or services along with, but without linking it to, the trademark distinguishing the specific goods or services in question of that undertaking.

Prior to negotiation of the TRIPS Agreement, it was not unusual for national trademark legislation, particularly in developing countries, to include requirements concerning the manner in which trademarks could be used. The domestic licensee of a foreign-origin trademark might be required to use its own trademark alongside that of the licensor. Additional rules might prescribe the relative placement of local and foreign-origin marks on goods. Despite the "telle quelle" or "as is" rule regarding registration in the same form, a foreign-origin trademark owner might be required to transform its mark into a more locally-friendly form, such as by providing a translated version of descriptive terms. The development-oriented objective of such requirements, *inter alia*, was to assure that some name or trademark recognition was established in favour of a local enterprise, assuming that the foreign licensor's presence in the market might be transitory. By requiring the foreign licensor to link its mark with that of a local enterprise, developing country authorities encouraged continuity in business relationships since the licensor might be more reluctant to discontinue its association with a business with whose name or products it had been linked in the public mind. From the perspective of the foreign-origin licensor, this type of requirement presented obstacles to business planning. If the mark or name of a licensee (such as a distributor) was to be linked with the licensor's mark, the licensor risked injury to its own reputation based on actions of the licensee. Also, as the special requirements might discourage foreign-origin licensors from changing or discontinuing business relationships, this was not viewed positively by the licensors.

Article 20 precludes the imposition of "special requirements, such as use with another trademark, use in a special form or use in a manner detrimental to its capability to distinguish the goods or services of one undertaking from those of other undertakings." The first reference is clear, that is "with another trademark." The meaning of "special form" might refer either to a standard format prescribed for all trademark owners (such as "in translation," or in a particular size or colour scheme), or to a case-by-case determination by a trademark authority. It is less clear what is intended by "use in a manner detrimental to its capability to distinguish." Such a result might come about if a mark-owner is required to reduce the size or placement of its mark to a point that consumers would have difficulty recognizing it, or to place it alongside information or materials that likewise would reduce its impact on consumers. Thus, for example, a requirement to include the generic name of a product alongside a trademark might be argued to have such an effect. However, the legal formulation leaves substantial flexibility to the interpreter.

However, Article 20 specifically authorizes rules that require the mark or name of the producing enterprise to be included with that of the trademark owner. Such requirements are intended to serve a development objective by indicating to the public that a local producer is the *de facto* supplier of the goods or services, with the expectation that the local public will gain assurance regarding the capacity of local suppliers. At the same time, Article 20 provides that the local enterprise will use its mark "without linking it to, the trademark" of the subject owner. This is presumably intended to prevent the local enterprise from taking "unfair advantage" of the foreign-origin mark. There should be some form of differentiation, though Article 20 does not provide or suggest a specific means. Although this provision was negotiated in response to developing country insistence that they should be allowed to facilitate awareness of local production capacity, the text does not distinguish between local undertaking-producers and foreign undertaking-producers. If a Chinese producer is making a product on which a U.S. trademark is placed, and the product is being sold in Indonesia, the mark of the Chinese producer should just as well be required to appear (based on the principle of national treatment) as that of an Indonesian producer putting the U.S. mark on the product for sale in Indonesia.

## 3.7. Article 21: Licensing and Assignment

***Licensing and Assignment***

> Members may determine conditions on the licensing and assignment of trademarks, it being understood that the compulsory licensing of trademarks shall not be permitted and that the owner of a registered trademark shall have the right to assign the trademark with or without the transfer of the business to which the trademark belongs.

Trademarks were traditionally understood to serve as identifiers of the source of goods. The consumer expected that goods placed on the market by a particular producer would conform to the quality standards that the trademark, and thus the producer or source, represented. Consequently, in many legal systems it was not permitted to license a trademark to a third party or, if licensing was permitted (and this was largely a development of mid-20th century trademark law), the licensor was required to exercise control over the licensee so as to assure the consumer that the trademark continued to represent an equivalent product.

If a trademark was owned by a business, and the business was sold, there was generally not a legal obstacle to transfer of the mark along with the business. As businesses became more multinational, as well as subdivided into separate operating units, it became commonplace to sell and transfer part of the business, or business operations in a particular country, as opposed to selling and transferring an entire combined enterprise. National trademark laws, as well as Article 6*quater*(1) of the Paris Convention, acknowledged that assignment and transfer of a mark should be permitted to take place if at least "the portion of the business or goodwill located in that country be transferred to the assignee, together with the exclusive right to manufacture in the said country, or to sell therein, the goods bearing the mark assigned."

Article 21, TRIPS Agreement, acknowledges the right of Members to continue to impose restrictions on the licensing and assignment of trademarks. Members may, for example, continue to require that trademark licensors exercise adequate control over the activities of licensees so as to protect the source indication function of the mark (that is, the integrity of the mark from the standpoint of the consumer). The terms of the first clause are not restricted, "Members may determine conditions" on licensing and transfer. The limitations are set out in the second clause.

First, compulsory licensing of trademarks is not permitted. While Article 5.A of the Paris Convention authorizes the compulsory licensing of patents, Article 5.C does not specifically address compulsory licensing of trademarks. It provides that cancellation for non-use should only take place after a "reasonable period" (see sub-Section 2.1.1, *supra*). If a mark is cancelled, it becomes available for use by third parties. In an indirect way cancellation might be viewed as a form of compulsory licensing, but the two concepts are different.

Since trademarks are intended to indicate the source of products, it might seem contradictory to that basic function to permit compulsory licensing to third parties. The source of products would by definition change, and consumers might be misled. Yet there is perhaps more to this question than first meets the eye. Consider the situation in which a compulsory patent license is issued for a medicine. Prior to the introduction of the third-party version of medicine under compulsory license, it is marketed to doctor-pharmacist-consumers under the trademark of the patent holder company. The patent holder asserts that its trademark rights extend to the colour of the medicine tablet. If the colour of the tablet is not licensed along with the patent, this might lead to a situation of confusion in the consuming community (i.e. among doctors, patients and pharmacists). As a practical matter, under the TRIPS Agreement a compulsory license for the claimed mark—which is prohibited by Article 21—is not necessary for two reasons. Trademarks do not cover "function," and if the colour of a medicine tablet is performing a function for doctors, patients and pharmacists, the colour cannot be exclusively reserved to a trademark holder. In addition, Article 17 of the TRIPS Agreement permits limited exceptions to trademark rights, and a Member may recognize a "fair use" right in the mark in these circumstances.

Second, "the owner of a registered trademark shall have the right to assign the trademark with or without the transfer of the business to which the trademark belongs." This formula represents a break with the traditional view of the trademark as an indication of source. There is now permitted the "naked assignment" of marks. The trademark has in essence become a stand-alone commodity that can be traded just as lumber. This acknowledges a major change in the general principles underlying trademark law.

However, the fact that trademarks may be sold and transferred as commodities does not dispense with the basic requirements for the maintenance of marks. In countries where use is required to maintain marks, the new owner must assure that some use in connection with the covered goods or services is made so as to avoid cancellation after the minimum prescribed period has elapsed. Likewise, the mark cannot be allowed to become "generic" and thereby lose its trademark function. (Even a fanciful mark may become generic if it is widely used in reference to a product and the trademark owner does not take steps to assert its rights and control over the term.)

## 2. *WTO Appellate Body Interpretation of the TRIPS Agreement and Paris Convention*

In the *U.S.-Havana Club* case, excerpted below, the WTO Appellate Body for the first time addresses the trademark provisions of the TRIPS Agreement. In doing so, it answers a number of key questions concerning interpretation of the Paris Convention, as well as of the TRIPS Agreement.

The factual setting of the underlying dispute between private operators leading to the WTO case is complex, but may be briefly summarized.[17] Prior to the coming to power of the revolutionary government in Cuba, a family-owned Cuban enterprise made and sold rum under the trademark "Havana Club." That enterprise registered the Havana Club mark in Cuba and the United States. The revolutionary government confiscated the assets of the family-owned business, including the trademarks, and did not compensate the former owners. The former owners did not attempt to renew their trademark registration in the United States, and it lapsed. Subsequently, the Cuban state enterprise that succeeded to the mark in Cuba registered the mark in the United States.

In the 1990s, a France-based multinational liquor manufacturer and distributor (Pernod Ricard) entered into a joint venture with the Cuban state enterprise to sell Havana Club rum worldwide. The joint venture took assignment of the U.S.-registered trademark. In the same period, a U.S.-based (Bermuda incorporated) liquor manufacturer and distributor (Bacardi) purchased the residual interests of the former Cuban-family owners of the Havana Club mark, and began to sell rum under the Havana Club mark in the United States. The Cuban-French joint venture was precluded from selling into the U.S. market because of U.S. legislation and regulations that prevented Cuba and its nationals from doing business in and with the United States. Nonetheless, the Cuban-French joint venture sued the U.S. distributor in federal court in the United States for infringement of its trademark and trade name (and related unfair competition claims) to preserve its rights in the U.S. market.

While the infringement litigation was proceeding, the U.S. Congress passed legislation directed at trademarks and trade names that had been confiscated from Cuban nationals. This legislation retroactively invalidated the assignment of the Havana Club trademark registration to the Cuban-French joint venture, and denied Cuba the right to renew its registration of the Havana Club mark in the United States. In addition, the legislation instructed U.S. courts not to enforce rights in trademarks and trade names asserted by Cuban nationals or their successors-in-interest based on earlier confiscations. The federal court in which the Cuban-French joint venture brought its infringement and unfair competition action rejected the claims based on the newly adopted legislation. This decision was upheld by a federal appeals court, and the U.S. Supreme Court refused to grant a further right of appeal.

17. Summary taken from Frederick M. Abbott, *WTO Dispute Settlement Practice Relating to the TRIPS Agreement* in The WTO Dispute Settlement System 1995-2003 (F. Ortino & E.-U. Petersmann eds., 2005).

The European Union challenged the U.S. legislation, regulations, and court decision on a number of grounds. Its main argument was based on the "*telle quelle*" rule of the Paris Convention, which requires that state parties register marks previously registered in other parties "as is." The European Union further argued that the TRIPS Agreement requires WTO Members to recognize trademark ownership determinations made by the state in which a mark is initially registered. The European Union also said that the U.S. scheme deprived Cuba and third countries of national and most favored nation treatment. While the Appellate Body rejected the EU claims regarding the *telle quelle* rule and TRIPS Agreement rules on ownership, it accepted (contrary to the panel) that there were problems on the national treatment and MFN fronts. The portions of the AB decision dealing with national treatment and MFN are not reproduced here because the specific issues respecting the U.S. legislation are highly technical and rather unique to the circumstances. The AB's general pronouncements regarding the importance of the national treatment and MFN rules were excerpted in Chapter 1.

## *United States—Section 211 Omnibus Appropriations Act of 1998*
## *AB-2001-7*

Report of the Appellate Body*

### . . . v. Article 6 *Quinquies* of the Paris Convention (1967)

122. We turn now to the claims of the European Communities as they relate to Article 6*quinquies* of the Paris Convention (1967). Article 6*quinquies* A(1) reads:

> Every trademark duly registered in the country of origin shall be accepted for filing and protected *as is* in the other countries of the Union, subject to the reservations indicated in this Article. Such countries may, before proceeding to final registration, require the production of a certificate of registration in the country of origin, issued by the competent authority. No authentication shall be required for this certificate. (emphasis added)

123. Article 6*quinquies* forms part of the Stockholm Act of the Paris Convention, dated 14 July 1967. The Stockholm Act is a revision of the original *Paris Convention for the Protection of Industrial Property*, which entered into force on 7 July 1884. The parties to the Paris Convention, who are commonly described as the "countries of the Paris Union," are obliged to implement the provisions of that Convention.

124. Article 2.1 of the *TRIPS Agreement* provides that: "[i]n respect of Parts II, III and IV of this Agreement, Members shall comply with Articles 1 through 12, and Article 19, of the Paris Convention (1967)." Thus, Article 6*quinquies* of the Paris Convention (1967), as well as certain other specified provisions of the Paris Convention (1967), have been incorporated by reference into the *TRIPS Agreement* and, thus, the *WTO Agreement.*

125. Consequently, WTO Members, whether they are countries of the Paris Union or not, are obliged, under the *WTO Agreement*, to implement those provisions of the Paris Convention (1967) that are incorporated into the *TRIPS Agreement*. As we have already stated, Article 6*quinquies* of the Paris Convention (1967) is one such provision. . . .

130. Before examining the text of Article 6*quinquies*, we note that the Paris Convention (1967) provides two ways in which a national of a country of the Paris Union may obtain registration of a trademark in a country of that Union other than the country of the applicant's origin: one way is by registration under Article 6 of the Paris Convention (1967); the other is by registration under Article 6*quinquies* of that same Convention.

---

* WT/DS176/AB/R, 2 Jan. 2002.

131. Article 6(1) of the Paris Convention (1967) provides:

> The conditions for the filing and registration of trademarks shall be determined in each country of the Union by its domestic legislation.

132. Article 6(1) states the general rule, namely, that each country of the Paris Union has the right to determine the *conditions* for filing and registration of trademarks in its domestic legislation. This is a reservation of considerable discretion to the countries of the Paris Union—and now, by incorporation, the Members of the WTO—to continue, in principle, to determine for themselves the conditions for filing and registration of trademarks. Thus, in our view, the general rule under the Paris Convention (1967) is that national laws apply with respect to trademark registrations within the *territory* of each country of the Paris Union, subject to the requirements of other provisions of that Convention.[72] And, likewise, through incorporation, this is also now the general rule for all WTO Members under the *TRIPS Agreement.*

133. Therefore, an applicant who chooses to seek registration of a trademark in a particular foreign country under Article 6 must comply with the conditions for filing and registration specified in that country's legislation. Such an applicant is *not* obliged to register a trademark first in its country of origin in order to register that trademark in another country of the Paris Union. However, that applicant must comply with the conditions of that other country where registration is sought.

134. As we have stated, Article 6 is not the only way to register a trademark in another country. If an applicant *has* duly registered a trademark in its country of origin, Article 6*quinquies* A(1) provides an alternative way of obtaining protection of that trademark in other countries of the Paris Union. . . .

137. The participants to this dispute disagree on the scope of the requirement imposed by Article 6*quinquies* A(1) to accept for filing and protect trademarks duly registered in the country of origin "as is." Looking first to the text of Article 6*quinquies* A(1), we see that the words "as is" (or, in French, "telle quelle"[77]) relate to the trademark to be "accepted for filing and protected" in another country based on registration in the applicant's country of origin. The ordinary meaning of the words "as is" is "in the existing state."[78] The French term "telle quelle" can be defined as "sans arrangement, sans modification."[79] This suggests to us that the requirement of Article 6*quinquies* A(1) to accept for filing and protect a trademark duly registered in the applicant's country of origin relates at least to the *form* of the trademark as registered in the applicant's country of origin.[80] The question before us is whether the scope of this requirement also encompasses other features and aspects of that trademark as registered in the country of origin.

---

72. The discretion of countries of the Paris Union to legislate conditions for filing and registration is not unlimited. It is subject to the international minimum standard of trademark disciplines provided for in other Articles of the Paris Convention (1967). These include, for example, national treatment, as well as internationally agreed reasons for denying trademark registration, such as those provided for in Article 6*ter.* The Paris Convention (1967) limits also the legislative discretion of countries of the Union under Article 6(1) by setting out reasons that countries cannot invoke to deny trademark registration, for example in Article 6(2).

77. Article 29(1)(c) of the Paris Convention (1967) provides: "In case of differences of opinion on the interpretation of the various texts, the French text shall prevail."

78. *The New Shorter Oxford English Dictionary*, L. Brown (ed.), (Clarendon Press, 1993), Vol. I, p. 123.

79. *Le Petit Robert Dictionnaire de la Langue Française* (1995), p. 2220. Or in English, as it stands; without adjustments; without modification.

80. The participants agree that the requirement of Article 6*quinquies* A(1) *at the very least* relates to the form of the trademark, but they disagree on what else beyond form, if anything at all, that requirement includes.

138. According to one expert:

> . . . whenever a trademark is duly registered in the country of origin, the other countries of the Union are obliged to accept and protect it, even if, as regards its form, that is, with regard to the signs of which it is composed, such trademark does not comply with the requirements of the domestic legislation, subject to the additional rules, particularly the grounds for refusal or invalidation of any mark, considered on its individual merits, established in the Article. This rule will therefore apply to trademarks consisting of numbers, letters, surnames, geographical names, words written or not written in a certain language or script, and other signs of which the trademark is composed.[81] (italics and footnotes omitted).

139. However, this view is not determinative of the question before us. To resolve this question, we look to the context of Article 6*quinquies* A(1). We find that there is considerable contextual support for the view that the requirement to register a trademark "as is" under Article 6*quinquies* A(1) does *not* encompass all the features and aspects of that trademark. As we have stressed, Article 6(1) of the Paris Convention (1967) reserves to the countries of the Paris Union the right to determine the *conditions* for filing and registration of trademarks by their domestic legislation.[82] Article 6(1) confirms that the countries of the Paris Union did not relinquish their right to determine the conditions for filing and registration of trademarks by entering into the Paris Convention (1967)—subject, of course, to the other obligations of Paris Union countries under the Paris Convention (1967).[83] Clearly, if Article 6*quinquies* A(1) were interpreted too broadly, the legislative discretion reserved for Members under Article 6(1) would be significantly undermined.

140. To illustrate this point, we will assume for the moment, and solely for the sake of argument, that, as the European Communities argues, Article 6*quinquies* A(1) does require other countries to accept for filing and to protect duly registered trademarks in respect of *all their aspects*, including those other than the form of a trademark. If this were so, an applicant who is a national of a country of the Paris Union would have two choices: that applicant could request trademark registration under Article 6 in another country of the Paris Union—in which case, that registration would be subject to the trademark law of that other country. Or, that applicant could register the trademark in its country of origin and then invoke the right, pursuant to Article 6*quinquies* A(1), to request acceptance of that trademark for filing and protection in another country. In the latter case, that registration would be governed by the trademark law, not of the country in which the applicant sought registration under Article 6*quinquies* A(1), but of the applicant's country of origin. The "conditions" for registration imposed in the law of the other country of the Paris Union where registration was sought under Article 6*quinquies* A(1) would be irrelevant. If this were so, any such applicant would be able to choose between trademark registration under Article 6 and trademark registration under Article 6*quinquies*, depending on which *conditions* for filing and registration were viewed by the applicant as more favourable to the applicant's interests.[84] Consequently, within the territory of any country of the Paris Union other than the applicant's country of origin, a

81. See Bodenhausen, G.H.C, Guide to the Application of the Paris Convention for the Protection of Industrial Property as revised at Stockholm in 1967 (hereinafter "Guide to the Paris Convention"), United International Bureaux for the Protection of Intellectual Property, (1968, reprinted 1991), pp. 110-111.

82. We note that prior to the Revision Conference of Lisbon (1958), the requirements now found in Articles 6 and 6*quinquies* were contained in a single (original) Article 6. At the Revision Conference, it was decided to split the original Article in order to make clear the difference between the two alternative ways to obtain trademark registration explained above.

83. See *supra*, footnote 72.

84. As far as trademark protection within the territory of the Paris Union national's country of origin is concerned, such national could not avoid being subject to national trademark law.

national of a country of that Union could ensure that it would be subject to *either* the domestic trademark registration requirements of the country of origin (through recourse to Article 6*quinquies*) *or* the domestic trademark registration requirements of the other country where trademark registration is sought (through recourse to Article 6) — *whichever it preferred.* In other words, a national of a Paris Union country could circumvent the "use" requirements of a particular regime by registering in the jurisdiction that does not impose "use" requirements.

141. We are persuaded that the drafters of the Paris Convention did not intend such a result. If, even today, WTO Members have — as the European Communities concedes — reserved the right under the *TRIPS Agreement* to maintain domestic regimes of trademark ownership based on use, then it does not seem credible to us to contend — as the European Communities does — that many of those very same countries intended more than a century ago, in concluding the Paris Convention, or on the occasion of one of the subsequent Revision Conferences of the Paris Convention, to establish a global system for determining trademark ownership that could circumvent, and thereby undermine, a domestic regime of trademark ownership based on use.

142. We note that Article 6*quinquies* B provides that registration of a trademark covered by this Article may be neither denied nor invalidated, except for the reasons listed in subparagraphs B(1) through (3).[85]

These exceptions refer, *inter alia*, to acquired rights of third parties; to distinctiveness of character; and to morality, public order ("*ordre public*") and deceptiveness. . . .

145. Finally, we look to an agreed interpretation adopted at the conclusion of the original Paris Convention in 1883. The Final Protocol of the Paris Convention (1883) was considered to form an integral part of that Convention.[88] Paragraph 4 of that Final Protocol in 1883 explained that the provision, which later became Article 6*quinquies* A(1):[89]

> . . . should be understood in the sense that no trademark may be excluded from protection in one of the States of the Union for the sole reason that it does not comply, with regard to the signs of which it is composed, with the conditions of the laws of that State, provided it complies on this point with the laws of the country of origin and that it has been properly filed there. Subject to this exception, *which only concerns the form of the mark*, and subject to the provision of the other Articles of the Convention, *each State shall apply its domestic law.*[90](emphasis added)

146. As the European Communities has observed, this agreed interpretation was omitted at the Washington Revision Conference of 1911. Yet, like the Panel, we note that no

---

85. Article 6*quinquies* B provides:

Trademarks covered by this Article may be neither denied registration nor invalidated except in the following cases:

when they are of such a nature as to infringe rights acquired by third parties in the country where protection is claimed;

when they are devoid of any distinctive character, or consist exclusively of signs or indications which may serve, in trade, to designate the kind, quality, quantity, intended purpose, value, place of origin, of the goods, or the time of production, or have become customary in the current language or in the bona fide and established practices of the trade of the country where protection is claimed;

when they are contrary to morality or public order and, in particular, of such a nature as to deceive the public. It is understood that a mark may not be considered contrary to public order for the sole reason that it does not conform to a provision of the legislation on marks, except if such provision itself relates to public order.

This provision is subject, however, to the application of Article 10*bis*.

88. Final Protocol of the Paris Convention (1883), para. 7.

89. See *supra*, footnote 82.

90. Final Protocol of the Paris Convention (1883), para. 4.

delegation to that conference expressed the view at that time that this omission should change the meaning of the provision.[91] Indeed, as one WIPO publication states, "it is generally believed that such omission did not alter the intended sense of 'telle quelle' as it was made explicit in 1883."[92]On this, we simply observe that our interpretation of Article 6*quinquies* A(1) is not inconsistent with this interpretation.

147. We have already stated that we agree with the Panel that Section 211(a)(1) is a measure dealing, in the particular circumstances in which it applies, with the ownership of a defined category of trademarks. We also agree that the obligation of countries of the Paris Union under Article 6*quinquies* A(1) to accept for filing and protect a trademark duly registered in the country of origin "as is" does not encompass matters related to ownership.

148. For these reasons, we uphold the finding of the Panel in paragraph 8.89 of the Panel Report that Section 211(a)(1) is not inconsistent with Article 2.1 of the *TRIPS Agreement* in conjunction with Article 6*quinquies* A(1) of the Paris Convention (1967). . . .

### VII. ARTICLE 16 OF THE TRIPS AGREEMENT . . .

185. Article 16 of the *TRIPS Agreement* is entitled "Rights Conferred." Article 16.1 provides:

> The owner of a registered trademark shall have the exclusive right to prevent all third parties not having the owner's consent from using in the course of trade identical or similar signs for goods or services which are identical or similar to those in respect of which the trademark is registered where such use would result in a likelihood of confusion. In case of the use of an identical sign for identical goods or services, a likelihood of confusion shall be presumed. The rights described above shall not prejudice any existing prior rights, nor shall they affect the possibility of Members making rights available on the basis of use.

186. As we read it, Article 16 confers on the *owner* of a registered trademark an internationally agreed minimum level of "exclusive rights" that all WTO Members must guarantee in their domestic legislation. These exclusive rights protect the owner against infringement of the registered trademark by unauthorized third parties.[122]

187. We underscore that Article 16.1 confers these exclusive rights on the "owner" of a registered trademark. As used in this treaty provision, the ordinary meaning of "owner" can be defined as the proprietor or the person who holds the title or dominion of the property constituted by the trademark.[123] We agree with the Panel that this ordinary meaning does not clarify how the ownership of a trademark is to be determined. Also, we agree with the Panel that Article 16.1 does not, in express terms, define how ownership of a registered trademark is to be determined. Article 16.1 confers exclusive rights on the "owner," but Article 16.1 does not tell us who the "owner" *is.*

188. As the United States reminds us, and as the European Communities concedes, the last sentence of Article 16.1 acknowledges that WTO Members may make the rights available

91. "[I]t is not possible to conclude from this decision [at the Washington Conference of 1911] that agreement was reached regarding a different scope of application of the provision." Bodenhausen, *Guide to the Paris Convention, supra,* footnote 81, p. 110. Panel Report, para. 8.82.

92. Paris Centenary, 1983, WIPO Publication No. 875. Panel Report, footnote 124 to para. 8.82.

122. We note that, prior to the entry into force of the *TRIPS Agreement,* only Article 10*bis*(3) of the Paris Convention (1967) provided for a prohibition of "all acts of such a nature as to create confusion by any means whatever with the establishment, the goods, or the industrial or commercial activities of a competitor." *See,* Gervais, D., *The TRIPS Agreement—Drafting History and Analysis,* Sweet & Maxwell, London (1998), pp. 109-110.

123. *The New Shorter Oxford English Dictionary, supra,* footnote 78, Vol. II, p. 2059; *Black's Law Dictionary,* 7th ed., B.A. Garner (ed.), (West Group, 1999), p. 1130.

"on the basis of use" of the trademark. We read this to permit WTO Members to make the "exclusive rights" contemplated by Article 16.1 available within their respective jurisdictions on the basis of registration or use. The Panel concluded that Article 16.1 contemplates that different forms of entitlement may exist under the laws of different Members, and we agree. However, the *TRIPS Agreement* does not establish or prescribe a regime of ownership of trademarks.

189. In the absence of any *explicit* provisions defining ownership in the *TRIPS Agreement*, it is useful to look also at whether the *TRIPS Agreement*—including the Articles of the Paris Convention (1967) incorporated into it—contains an *implicit* definition of ownership. Turning first to the Paris Convention (1967), we see that, in response to a request for information by the Panel,[126] the Director-General of the International Bureau of the World Intellectual Property Organization ("WIPO") stated that "no provision [of the Paris Convention (1967)] addresses the question how the owner of a trademark has to be determined under the domestic law of States party to the Paris Convention." [127]

The Panel did not discuss this. However, the Panel seems to have taken the view that the definition of the conditions of ownership has been left to the legislative discretion of individual countries of the Paris Union by Article 6(1) of the Paris Convention (1967). We agree. . . .

### XI. ARTICLE 8 OF THE PARIS CONVENTION (1967)—TRADE NAMES . . .

333. We disagree with the Panel's reasoning and with the Panel's conclusion on the scope of the *TRIPS Agreement* as it relates to trade names.

334. To explain, we turn first to the Panel's interpretation of Article 1.2 of the *TRIPS Agreement*, which, we recall, provides:

> For the purposes of this Agreement, the term "intellectual property" refers to all categories of intellectual property that are the subject of Sections 1 through 7 of Part II.

335. The Panel interpreted the phrase "'intellectual property' refers to all categories of intellectual property that are the *subject* of Sections 1 through 7 of Part II" (emphasis added) as if that phrase read "intellectual property means those categories of intellectual property appearing in the *titles* of Sections 1 through 7 of Part II." To our mind, the Panel's interpretation ignores the plain words of Article 1.2, for it fails to take into account that the phrase "the subject of Sections 1 through 7 of Part II" deals not only with the categories of intellectual property indicated in each section *title*, but with other *subjects* as well. For example, in Section 5 of Part II, entitled "Patents," Article 27(3)(b) provides that Members have the option of protecting inventions of plant varieties by *sui generis* rights (such as breeder's rights) instead of through patents.[243]

---

126. Pursuant to Article 13 of the DSU.

127. The letter from the Director-General of the International Bureau of WIPO, dated 2 March 2001, states:

> Even though some provisions of the Paris Convention refer to the concept of trademark ownership (Article 5C(2) and (3), and Article 6*septies:* "proprietor," Article 6*ter*(1)(c): "owner," Article 6*bis*(1) "being already the mark of a person entitled to the benefits of this Convention"), ***no provision addresses the question how the owner of a trademark has to be determined under the domestic law of States party to the Paris Convention.*** (emphasis added)

Reproduced in relevant part in para. 6.41 of the Panel Report.

243. Article 27.3(b) of the *TRIPS Agreement* provides:

> Members may also exclude from patentability: . . .
>
> (b) plants and animals other than micro-organisms, and essentially biological processes for the production of plants or animals other than non-biological and microbiological processes. However, Members shall provide for the protection of plant varieties either by patents or by an effective *sui generis* system or by any combination thereof. The provisions of this subparagraph shall be reviewed four years after the date of entry into force of the WTO Agreement.

Under the Panel's theory, such *sui generis* rights would not be covered by the *TRIPS Agreement*. The option provided by Article 27(3)(b) would be read out of the *TRIPS Agreement*.

336. Moreover, we do not believe that the Panel's interpretation of Article 1.2 can be reconciled with the plain words of Article 2.1. Article 2.1 explicitly incorporates Article 8 of the Paris Convention (1967) into the *TRIPS Agreement*.

337. The Panel was of the view that the words "in respect of" in Article 2.1 have the effect of "conditioning" Members' obligations under the Articles of the Paris Convention (1967) incorporated into the *TRIPS Agreement*, with the result that trade names are not covered. We disagree.

338. Article 8 of the Paris Convention (1967) covers only the protection of trade names; Article 8 has no other subject. If the intention of the negotiators had been to exclude trade names from protection, there would have been no purpose whatsoever in including Article 8 in the list of Paris Convention (1967) provisions that were specifically incorporated into the *TRIPS Agreement*. To adopt the Panel's approach would be to deprive Article 8 of the Paris Convention (1967), as incorporated into the *TRIPS Agreement* by virtue of Article 2.1 of that Agreement, of any and all meaning and effect. As we have stated previously:

> One of the corollaries of the "general rule of interpretation" in the *Vienna Convention* is that interpretation must give meaning and effect to all the terms of a treaty. An interpreter is not free to adopt a reading that would result in reducing whole clauses or paragraphs of a treaty to redundancy or inutility.[244]

339. As for the import of the negotiating history, we do not see it as in any way decisive to the issue before us. The documents on which the Panel relied are not conclusive of whether the *TRIPS Agreement* covers trade names. The passages quoted by the Panel from the negotiating history of Article 1.2 do not even refer to trade names. There is nothing at all in those passages to suggest that Members were either for or against their inclusion. Indeed, the only reference to a debate about the categories for coverage in the *TRIPS Agreement* relates, not to trade names, but to trade secrets. The Panel itself acknowledged that "[t]he records do not contain information on the purpose of the addition" of the words "in respect of" at the beginning of Article 2.1. Therefore, we do not consider that any conclusions may be drawn from these records about the interpretation of the words "in respect of" in Article 2.1 as regards trade names.

340. Thus, in our view, the Panel's interpretation of Articles 1.2 and 2.1 of the *TRIPS Agreement* is contrary to the ordinary meaning of the terms of those provisions and is, therefore, not in accordance with the customary rules of interpretation prescribed in Article 31 of the *Vienna Convention*.[247] Moreover, we do not believe that the negotiating history confirms, within the meaning of Article 32 of the *Vienna Convention*, the Panel's interpretation of Articles 1.2 and 2.1.

341. For all these reasons, we reverse the Panel's finding in paragraph 8.41 of the Panel Report that trade names are not covered under the *TRIPS Agreement* and find that WTO Members do have an obligation under the *TRIPS Agreement* to provide protection to trade names.

---

244. Appellate Body Report, *US-Gasoline*, . . . , at 21. *See also* Appellate Body Report, *Japan-Alcoholic Beverages II*, . . . , at 106.

247. *See* Article 3.2 of the DSU.

## NOTES AND QUESTIONS

**1.** The Appellate Body has decisively rejected the European Union's argument that the "*telle quelle*" or "as is" rule of the Paris Convention addresses more than the form in which the foreign mark must be accepted for registration. There was very little support among international IP experts for that EU position from the outset of this case. A more interesting and debated question in this case was whether, as a matter of public international law, the United States had good grounds for refusing to recognize Cuba's taking of the former Cuban owners' assets, including trademark rights. Recall that the former owners were not U.S. (or other foreign) citizens, but rather nationals and residents of Cuba at the time of the confiscation. Thomas Cottier has argued that the U.S. refusal to recognize the acts of the Cuban government with respect to its own citizens may not be valid under international law, and therefore trademark ownership in the United States should properly reside with the Cuban-French joint venture. In the present case, this raises the question of whether the WTO Appellate Body could have invoked general principles of public international law to find U.S. legislation as to trademark ownership inconsistent with WTO norms. It did not. *See* discussion in F.M. Abbott & T. Cottier, *Dispute Prevention and Dispute Settlement in the Field of Intellectual Property Rights and Electronic Commerce: US-Section 211 Omnibus Appropriations Act 1998* ("Havana Club"), in TRANSATLANTIC ECONOMIC DISPUTES: THE EU, THE US, AND THE WTO (E.-U. Petersmann & M. Pollack eds., 2005).

**2.** Throughout the long history of the Paris Convention, the International Court of Justice has never been called upon to interpret its provisions. The WTO Appellate Body has now stepped in to perform this task. Why have states been reluctant to approach the ICJ? Why is the WTO Appellate Body a more attractive forum? Might the experience of litigating the Paris Convention before the WTO encourage some state party to bring a case at the ICJ? Is there a risk from potentially conflicting interpretations?

**3.** The Appellate Body relies on a former WIPO official's book for interpretive guidance with respect to the meaning of the *telle quelle* rule. This suggests a reasonably strong role for the WIPO Secretariat in the interpretation of the TRIPS Agreement.

**4.** The United States is a strong advocate of high standards of intellectual property protection. Yet, in the *Havana Club* case, it champions the right of each government to determine who the owner of a trademark is. Does this create risks for U.S. trademark owners?

## E. The Tobacco Cases

In early 2012, the Ukraine initiated a dispute settlement action against Australia at the WTO challenging Australia's adoption of tobacco plain packaging (TPP) legislation. The legislation establishes mandatory rules limiting the size, color, design, and placement of trademarks on tobacco (including cigarette) packaging. The TPP measures adopted by Australia were part of a broad regimen of rules intended to reduce tobacco smoking, which contributed substantially to the mortality rates in Australia and burdened the health care system. The tobacco industry strongly opposed the legislation arguing that it diminishes the value of trademarks and reduced the potential for cigarette companies to distinguish their brands among consumers. Australia's legislation reflected obligations and guidelines established by the WHO Framework Convention on Tobacco Control (FCTC), an international agreement adhered to by almost all countries.

A substantial portion of the first part of the Appellate Body decision addresses issues raised by the Dominican Republic and Honduras Technical Barriers to Trade (TBT Agreement). The TBT Agreement is intended to limit the adoption of regulatory standards or technical regulations by national governments that establish discriminatory barriers to trade. But the TBT Agreement makes clear that governments are permitted to adopt regulatory standards and technical regulations to address legitimate public purposes, including to protect public health. The TBT Agreement establishes a strong presumption that measures which conform to internationally accepted standards are compatible with the agreement. However, governments are permitted to adopt standards that are not reflecting international standards, but these standards or regulations do not enjoy the presumption of compatibility. The AB affirms that Australia's TPP technical regulations are compatible with the TBT Agreement as they are public health measures intended to achieve Australia's legitimate objective of reducing tobacco use, adopted with a reasonable scientific basis, and that the complaining countries did not establish that Australia could equally well meet its objectives through less trade restrictive means. The second part of the AB decision dealing with TRIPS issues largely refers back and relies on the discussion and analysis of science and policy in the first part addressing the Technical Barriers to Trade Agreement (TBT) in terms of the justification for Australia's trademark restrictions.

The predominant view among objective TRIPS experts was that Australia's TPP trademark restrictions were compatible with the TRIPS Agreement, including Article 20. In that regard, the decision by the AB in favor of Australia was no surprise. An adverse decision against Australia by would effectively have meant rejecting the well-considered view of the WHO and its member states regarding a very important public health agreement and would have opened up a major breach between the two organizations. With that said, the tobacco industry, by creating uncertainty, managed to delay the adoption of TPP legislation in a number of countries where it had been under consideration, and in that regard the lengthy dispute settlement process might be looked at from an industry standpoint as a tactical success—knowing in advance that success on the substantive merits was highly unlikely.

## *Australia – Certain Measures Concerning Trademarks, Geographical Indications and Other Plain Packaging Requirements Applicable to Tobacco Products and Packaging*

Reports of the Appellate Body*

AB-2018-4

AB-2018-6

5.7. Pursuant to the T[obacco] P[lain] P[ackaging] measures, all outer and inner surfaces of certain retail packaging of tobacco products must have a matt finish. The TPP measures further stipulate that the outer surfaces of these packages must be the colour Pantone 448C (drab dark brown), and that the inner surfaces of a cigarette pack or cigarette carton must be white. The inner surface of these packages (other than a cigarette pack or cigarette carton) must be either white or the colour of the packaging material in its natural state. The lining of a cigarette pack must be silver-coloured foil with a white paper backing. However, as the Panel noted, the colour requirements in the TPP measures do not apply to health warnings; the text of the brand, business or company name, or variant name; or the text of relevant legislative requirements.

5.8. In addition, the TPP measures prohibit the appearance of trademarks and marks anywhere on the retail packaging of tobacco products, with the exception of the brand name, business or company name, variant name, the relevant legislative requirements, and other trademarks and marks permitted by the TPP measures. The TPP measures make provision for

* WT/DS435/AB/R, WT/DS441/AB/R, 9 June 2020.

the appearance of origin marks, calibration marks, a measurement mark and trade description, a barcode, a fire-risk statement, a locally made product statement, the name and address of the person who packed the product or on whose behalf it was packed, and a consumer contact number. These markings must not obscure any relevant legislative requirement, or constitute or provide access to tobacco advertising and promotion.

5.9. Section 21 of the TPP Act, operating together with the TPP Regulations, prescribes the requirements for the manner in which the brand, business or company, or variant names for tobacco products may appear on the retail packaging of a tobacco product. With respect to cigarette packaging, any of these names must be printed in the Lucida Sans typeface in fonts no larger than 14-point size (for a brand, business, or company name) or 10-point size (for a variant name). The font must be normal weighted and in the colour Pantone Cool Gray 2C. In addition, the first letter in each word must be capitalised. No other upper case letters may be used. With respect to retail packaging other than retail packaging of cigarettes, names must meet the same specifications, but can be printed on the packaging or on an adhesive label fixed to the packaging. Such adhesive label must be in the colour Pantone 448C (drab dark brown), be no larger than reasonably necessary to print the permitted names, be fastened firmly to the retail packaging so as not to be easily removable, and not obscure any relevant legislative requirement.

5.10. Importantly, the requirements set out in the TPP Act and the TPP Regulations operate in conjunction with other legislative requirements that are not challenged in these disputes, including graphic health warnings (GHWs).

. . .

6.577. The starting point of our analysis is the text of the TRIPS Agreement. Given the unique structure of the TRIPS Agreement as compared to the other covered agreements1, in order to establish properly the right that is protected under Article 16.1 and the corresponding obligation on WTO Members, we consider it useful to place Article 16.1 in its proper context in the TRIPS Agreement.

6.578. Article 1.1 imposes an obligation on Members to "give effect to the provisions of" the TRIPS Agreement. Specifically, as regards trademarks, Members have an obligation to give effect to the provisions of Articles 15-21 of the TRIPS Agreement.

6.579. Article 15.1 defines the subject matter that is protectable as a trademark.1504 According to Article 15.1, any sign, or any combination of signs, capable of distinguishing the goods or services of one undertaking from those of other undertakings, shall be capable of constituting a trademark. Thus, a trademark serves to distinguish the goods or services of one undertaking from those of other undertakings. Article 15.1 also states that "[w]here signs are not inherently capable of distinguishing the relevant goods or services, Members may make registrability depend on distinctiveness acquired through use." Hence, Article 15.1 suggests that, in terms of eligibility for registration, the norm is the presentation of signs that are "inherently" distinctive. It is only in situations when a sign is not inherently distinctive that the "distinctiveness acquired through use" becomes relevant. We observe that the "distinctiveness" of a sign, discussed in Article 15.1, relates to the eligibility for registration of a sign as a trademark, and not to the rights conferred to the trademark owner once its trademark is registered. We recall that the question whether a sign is eligible for registration as a trademark is not at issue in these proceedings.

6.580. While Article 15 defines the subject matter that may be protected as a trademark and the rules governing the eligibility for registration of a sign as a trademark, Article 16 addresses the rights conferred on a trademark owner following such registration.1505 Article 16.1 states

> The owner of a registered trademark shall have the exclusive right to prevent all third parties not having the owner's consent from using in the course of trade identical or similar signs for goods

> or services which are identical or similar to those in respect of which the trademark is registered where such use would result in a likelihood of confusion. In case of the use of an identical sign for identical goods or services, a likelihood of confusion shall be presumed. The rights described above shall not prejudice any existing prior rights, nor shall they affect the possibility of Members making rights available on the basis of use.

. . .

6.582. Pursuant to Article 16.1, the owner of a registered trademark has the exclusive right to "prevent" all unauthorized third parties from behaving in a certain manner in the course of trade. Hence, the exclusive right conferred under Article 16.1 is one that grants a trademark owner the authority to "prevent" certain behaviour, which may be understood as the authority to "preclude, stop, or hinder"1508 such behaviour. As the panel in *EC – Trademarks and Geographical Indications (Australia)* said, the TRIPS Agreement "does not generally provide for the grant of positive rights to exploit or use certain subject matter, but rather provides for the grant of negative rights to prevent certain acts". Specifically, Article 16.1 grants a trademark owner the exclusive right to preclude unauthorized third parties from using, in the course of trade, identical or similar signs for goods or services that are identical or similar to those with respect to which the trademark is registered.

. . .

6.586. . . .We too have not come across any language in the TRIPS Agreement that endorses the position that the purpose of the exclusive right articulated in Article 16.1 is to allow a trademark owner to protect the distinctiveness of the trademark through the trademark owner's continued use of that trademark. . . . neither the TRIPS Agreement nor the provisions of the Paris Convention (1967) that are incorporated by reference into the TRIPS Agreement confer upon a trademark owner a positive right to use its trademark or a right to protect the distinctiveness of that trademark through use.

. . .

6.601. We recall that the "likelihood of confusion", which may result from the conduct of unauthorized third parties identified in Article 16.1, relates to the distinguishing function of the trademark in question, described in Article 15.1. However, as the Panel observed, "Members have not taken on a general responsibility for safeguarding the distinctiveness of signs, either before or after such signs have been registered as trademarks."1543 Moreover, except for the situation described in its second sentence, Article 16.1 does not delineate the criteria for the examination of whether an unauthorized third party's use of similar signs "would result in a likelihood of confusion". Thus, contrary to what Honduras suggests, Article 16.1 does not: (i) require Members to provide a "minimum opportunity" for a trademark owner to use its trademark in order to preserve or strengthen the distinctiveness of the trademark; (ii) provide the criteria for assessing whether the unauthorized use by third parties of similar signs has "result[ed] in a likelihood of confusion" with the registered trademark; or (iii) require Members to ensure that the factual scenario contemplated by the cumulative conditions in Article 16.1 occurs.

. . .

6.610. Furthermore, it is significant that unlike Article 17, Article 20 is not identified as an "exception" to the "rights conferred" on a trademark owner. Rather, Article 20 imposes a positive obligation limiting the regulatory autonomy that Members otherwise enjoy. As noted above, Article 20 imposes an obligation on Members to refrain from unjustifiably encumbering, by special requirements, "the use of a trademark in the course of trade". Significantly, Article 20 does not state that "the use of a trademark in the course of trade" is a right conferred on a trademark owner. Instead, this provision regulates the imposition of special requirements when a trademark owner is using its trademark in the course of trade. In the factual scenario where a trademark is being used in the course of trade, Article 20 protects such use from being unjustifiably encumbered by special requirements. Moreover, the words "unjustifiably encumbered" in Article 20 suggest that justifiable encumbrance by special requirements is compatible with that provision. Leaving aside the question of the standard against which an adjudicator should test whether an encumbrance is justifiable – which is at issue in these appellate proceedings1564 – the fact that Members should refrain from unjustifiable encumbrances does not suggest that Article 20 confers a right to use a trademark when special requirements are not involved. On the contrary, the provision allows, inversely, Members to justifiably encumber, by special requirements, the use of a trademark in the course of trade. Moreover, the second sentence of Article 20 "expressly provide[s] for conditions under which use can be encumbered" by indicating that the obligation outlined in the first sentence of Article 20 does "not preclude a requirement prescribing the use of the trademark" alongside another trademark. These reasons undermine Honduras' argument that "the 'exclusive rights' conferred by Article 16.1 are conferred against the background of a presumption of unencumbered use."

. . .

6.620. Honduras challenges the Panel's analysis under Article 20 of the TRIPS Agreement on two grounds. First, Honduras claims that the Panel erred in its interpretation of the term "unjustifiably" in Article 20.Second, assuming that the Panel's interpretation of Article 20 was correct, Honduras submits an alternative claim that the Panel erred in applying the legal standard that it had developed to the facts of the present dispute.1583 In this respect, Honduras argues that the Panel erred by: (i) focusing on the economic value of trademarks and in its assessment of the allegedly mitigating factors1584; (ii) finding that the TPP measures contribute to the reduction in the use of tobacco; (iii) rejecting the alternative less trademark-encumbering measures proposed by the complainants; and (iv) attributing undue legal weight to the F[ramework] C[onvention] on T[obacco] C[ontrol] guidelines.

. . .

6.641. Article 20 does not prohibit all measures that impose encumbrances on the use of a trademark in the course of trade. Rather, it proscribes only those special requirements that "unjustifiably encumber" the use of a trademark in the course of trade. This implies that there may be circumstances in which an "encumbrance" on the use of a trademark will be "justifiable". Accordingly, we do not share Honduras' view that Article 20 imposes a "general prohibition . . . on governmental encumbrances on use".1652 In this connection, we note that Article 19.1 of the TRIPS Agreement, which concerns the requirement of use, provides that "[c]ircumstances arising independently of the will of the owner of the trademark which constitute an obstacle to the use of the trademark, such as import restrictions on or other government requirements for goods or services protected by the trademark, shall be recognized as valid reasons for non-use." Article 19.1 thus contemplates that a Member may impose obstacles such as restrictions on goods or services protected by a trademark, which would result in the non-use of the trademark by its owner.

. . .

6.647 In our view, the term "unjustifiably" in Article 20 of the TRIPS Agreement reflects the degree of regulatory autonomy that Members enjoy in imposing encumbrances on the use of trademarks through special requirements. The reference to the notion of justifiability rather than necessity in Article 20 suggests that the degree of connection between the encumbrance on the use of a trademark imposed and the objective pursued reflected through the term "unjustifiably" is lower than it would have been had a term conveying the notion of "necessity" been used in this provision. Accordingly, a consideration of whether the use of a trademark has not been "unjustifiably" encumbered should not be equated with the necessity test within the meaning of Article XX of the GATT 1994 or Article 2.2 of the TBT Agreement.

. . .

6.649. . . In this connection, we note that Article 8 of the TRIPS Agreement, titled "Principles", provides, in paragraph 1, that Members may "adopt measures necessary to protect public health and nutrition, and to promote the public interest in sectors of vital importance to their socio-economic and technological development, provided that such measures are consistent with the provisions of this Agreement".1676 Measures seeking to protect public health and nutrition encompass a range of measures specifically contemplated by the TRIPS Agreement, including through exceptions to exclusive patent rights (Article 30), compulsory licences (Article 31), and the disclosure to the public of test data (Article 39.3). In this vein, we agree with the Panel that encumbrances on the use of trademarks by special requirements under Article 20 may also be imposed in pursuit of public health objectives.

. . .

6.658. Furthermore, we note that the Panel referred to paragraph 5(a) of the Doha Declaration to confirm that "Articles 7 and 8 of the TRIPS Agreement provide important context for the interpretation of Article 20."1696 It appears that the Panel had reached the conclusion about the contextual relevance of Articles 7 and 8 of the TRIPS Agreement before it turned to paragraph 5(a) the Doha Declaration and used the latter to simply reconfirm its view.1697 In particular, before turning to the Doha Declaration, the Panel observed that "Article 8 offers . . . useful contextual guidance for the interpretation of the term 'unjustifiably' in Article 20."1698 The Panel also remarked that the societal interests referred to in Article 8 may provide a basis of the justification of measures under Article 20.1699 Thus, we agree with Australia that, in any event, the reliance on the Doha Declaration was not of decisive importance for the Panel's reasoning since the Panel had reached its conclusions about the contextual relevance of Articles 7 and 8 of the TRIPS Agreement to the interpretation of Article 20 before it turned to the Doha Declaration. The Panel relied on the Doha Declaration simply to reconfirm its previous conclusions regarding the contextual relevance of Articles 7 and 8 of the TRIPS Agreement.

. . .

6.679. Thereafter, the Panel turned to its examination of whether the reasons for the application of the trademark requirements under the TPP measures sufficiently support the resulting encumbrances. In doing so, the Panel stated that it would have to assess the public health concerns that underlie the TPP measures' trademark requirements against the resulting encumbrances. Thereafter, the Panel stated that:

> The fact that these special requirements, as part of the overall TPP measures and in combination with other tobacco-control measures maintained by Australia, are capable of contributing, and do in fact contribute, to Australia's objective of improving public health by reducing the use of, and exposure to, tobacco products, suggests that the reasons for which these special requirements are applied provide sufficient support for the application of the resulting encumbrances on the use of trademarks.

6.680 The fact that the Panel made this statement upfront may have prompted Honduras' allegation that the Panel did not conduct any weighing and balancing. We note, however, that, after making that statement, the Panel elaborated on the reasons that led it to this conclusion. In particular, the Panel recalled its finding, made in the context of analysis under Article 2.2 of the TBT Agreement, that the rationale for the imposition of the TPP measures was that the removal of design features on retail packaging and cigarettes had been determined to be apt to reduce the appeal of tobacco products and increase the effectiveness of GHWs. The Panel then underscored that the standardization of packaging was an integral part of the TPP measures and recalled its previous rejection of a pre-vetting mechanism as an alternative measure due to administrative discretion embodied in such a mechanism. We consider that, by doing so, the Panel connected the requirements of the TPP measures to the public health concern that they sought to address, which demonstrated that Australia's public health objectives could be achieved only by uniform and standardized requirements that did not leave any space for possible administrative discretion or non-uniform application. Thereafter, the Panel addressed the complainants' arguments about the possible alternative less trademark-encumbering measures.

6.681. In light of the above, we do not agree with Honduras that the Panel did not undertake any weighing and balancing in its analysis. . . .

. . .

6.697. . . . Members enjoy a certain degree of regulatory autonomy in encumbering the use of trademarks by special requirements under Article 20 and an analysis of alternative measures is not required under this provision. In light of the contribution to Australia's objective that the trademark requirements of the TPP measures make, we consider that Australia's public health reasons for the adoption of the TPP measures sufficiently supported the far-reaching encumbrances on the use of trademarks resulting from the trademark requirements of the TPP measures.

## NOTES AND QUESTIONS

**1.** Up to the issuance of the Panel Report, the Australia TPP legislation had been subject to the WTO dispute settlement process for more than six years—far beyond the timelines of the DSU—plus another two years for the AB decision. Despite Australia's substantive success, has the tobacco industry successfully accomplished its objective of delaying the introduction of TPP measures in other countries? Leaving aside a few "outliers," experts considered the tobacco interest challenges at the WTO "unwinnable," but there is no penalty for pursuing.

**2.** The *Tobacco* case raised issues that are of substantial interest to other industry sectors, such as the food and food service industries, where regulation on health grounds is common, and is commonly challenged. What are the potential areas of interest in the decision for such other industries? What are the potential areas of interest for the regulators?

**3.** Is it appropriate from a global and/or national public policy standpoint that the WTO was made responsible for assessing the legitimacy of legislation adopted under the framework of a WHO Convention addressing public health? Does the "residence" of trade-economic power within the WTO distort global rulemaking and enforcement in favor of mercantile interests? If the WTO were to rule against Australia's TPP legislation, could the WHO (or Australia and/or others) bring an action at the International Court of Justice to seek an injunction against enforcement? What other recourse might there be? Would the Australian government comply with a WTO ruling against its public health legislation?

**4.** A private enterprise, Philip Morris, challenged plain packaging of cigarettes introduced in Uruguay under the Swiss-Uruguay bilateral investment treaty. The tribunal dismissed the claim essentially on grounds that trademark law in Uruguay does not entail a right to use the trademark and that Uruguay has properly used its policing powers in addressing the health-related issue (*see Philip Morris Brads Sarl, Philip Morris Products SA and Abal Hermonas v. Oriental Republic of Uruguay*, ICTSD Case No ARB/10/7, July 8, 2016, paras. 235-307, in particular 256, 260, 277 (expropriation and regulatory taking), paras 388-409 (fair and equitable treatment), 436-45 (Impairment of Use and Enjoyment of Investment) and 447-458 (use of trademark). Does the finding of the WTO panel under the TRIPS Agreement (see section E following) confirm or alter these findings subsequently under investment protection law?

**5.** Philip Morris (through its Asian subsidiary, Philip Morris Asia Limited), equally initiated an investor-to-state dispute settlement arbitration under an agreement between the Government of Australia and the Government of Hong Kong for the Promotion and Protection of Investments (1993), under UNCITRAL rules. According to Philip Morris, "Intellectual property is the core of Philip Morris' entire business because it underpins Philip Morris' branded products. . . . Australia's plain packaging legislation virtually eliminates Philip Morris' branded business by expropriating its valuable intellectual property" (Notice of Arbitration, 21 November 2011, at paras. 1.4-1.5).

On December 17, 2015, the Permanent Court of Arbitration tribunal found Philip Morris' claim inadmissible on abuse of rights grounds. The tribunal determined that PM Asia, in anticipation of the Australian Tobacco plain packaging (TPP) legislation, restructured their investments so that PM Asia would own both Philip Morris Australia (PM Australia) and PM Australia's subsidiary, Philip Morris Limited (PML). PM Asia's acquisitions allowed Philip Morris to possess entities in both Hong Kong and Australia and thus fall under the protection of the Hong Kong/Australia bilateral investment treaty (BIT). The tribunal concluded that Philip Morris altered their corporate structure with the intention of bringing a claim against Australia and the TPP measures under the BIT. Because the TPP measures were foreseen by PM Asia and motivated their corporate restructuring, the tribunal held the claim constituted an abuse of rights and precluded the tribunal from having jurisdiction to hear the case. Practical Law Arbitration, *PCA Publishes Jurisdiction and Admissibility Award Against Philip Morris*, Practical Law UK, May 25, 2016.

## F. The Interface Between Trademarks and Geographical Indications

The TRIPS Agreement includes a section addressing trademarks (Part II, sec. 2) and a section addressing geographical indications (Part II, sec. 3). The TRIPS Agreement does not, except in a few limited circumstances, address the relationship between the forms of IP protection.

The subject matter of GIs was introduced in section I.E, *supra*. Generally speaking, GIs may be protected by unfair competition law, as trademarks (including as collective and certification marks), by *sui generis* registration systems, and by administrative forms of protection. The TRIPS Agreement requires that wines and spirits receive specified minimum protection, and provides for the establishment of a common register with respect to wines for countries that choose to participate in it (TRIPS Agreement, art. 23).

In the United States, protection of geographical indications is principally provided through collective and certification marks. The United States does provide another form of GIs protection through its system for approving labels on wines and spirits (the Certificate of Labelling Approval or "COLA" system). This system is administered by the Alcohol and Tobacco Tax and Trade Bureau of the Department of the Treasury (TTB). The registration system is established pursuant to the Federal Alcohol Administration Act (27 U.S.C. §§201 et seq.), which is supplemented by Chapter 27 of the Code of Federal Regulations (27 C.F.R. §§1.1 et seq.).

In the European Union, protection of geographical indications is subject to a complex regulatory system that includes substantial conditions that producers must meet in order to obtain and maintain registration of GIs, and includes substantial oversight by national and EU regulatory authorities.

What happens when the rights of the trademark holder come into conflict with the rights of a holder of a GI? The following is an excerpt from the case brought by the United States against the European Union that addresses the relationship between trademarks and GIs (recall that part of this decision addressing national treatment appeared in Chapter 1).

This WTO panel decision includes the first application in a dispute settlement proceeding of Article 17 of the TRIPS Agreement regarding exceptions to the rights conferred by trademark, and for that reason is the special interest. Neither the European Union nor the United States appealed the panel decision to the Appellate Body.

## *European Communities—Protection of Trademarks and Geographical Indications for Agricultural Products and Foodstuffs Complaint by the United States*

Report of the Panel*

### . . . C. TRADEMARK CLAIM

#### 1. The Relationship Between Gis and Prior Trademarks . . .

7.512 The *United States* claims that the Regulation is inconsistent with Article 16.1 of the TRIPS Agreement because it does not ensure that a trademark owner may prevent uses of GIs which would result in a likelihood of confusion with a prior trademark. Its claim only concerns valid prior trademarks, not trademarks liable to invalidation because they lack distinctiveness or mislead consumers as to the origin of goods. It does not dispute that GIs that are identical or similar to trademarks may be used, but only to the extent that they do not result in a likelihood of confusion with respect to prior trademarks.

7.513 The *European Communities* responds that this claim is unfounded for several reasons: (1) Article 14(3) of the Regulation, in fact, prevents the registration of GIs, use of which would result in a likelihood of confusion with a prior trademark; (2) Article 24.5 of the TRIPS Agreement provides for the "coexistence" of GIs and prior trademarks; (3) Article 24.3 of the TRIPS Agreement requires the European Communities to maintain "coexistence"; and (4) in any event, Article 14(2) of the Regulation would be justified as a limited exception under Article 17 of the TRIPS Agreement.

7.514 For the sake of brevity, the Panel uses the term "coexistence" in this report to refer to a legal regime under which a GI and a trademark can both be used concurrently to some extent even though the use of one or both of them would otherwise infringe the rights conferred by the other. The use of this term does not imply any view on whether such a regime is justified. . . .

7.562 [T]he Panel considers that the United States has made a prima facie case that Article 14(3) of the Regulation cannot prevent all situations from occurring in which Article 14(2) would, in fact, limit the rights of a trademark owner.

7.563 Consistent with this view, it can be noted that the European Communities specifically rejected a proposal by a Committee of the European Parliament to amend Article 14(2) so as to subject it to the trademark owners' rights when Article 14 was amended in April 2003. This at least suggests that Article 14(3) was considered different from a blanket protection of trademark rights. . . .

7.567 . . . [T]he Panel considers that there is no evidence to show that it is possible to seek invalidation of a GI registration under Article 14(3) in *all* cases in which use of a GI would otherwise be found to infringe a prior trademark. In those cases where it is not possible, it would be necessary for the owner of a prior trademark to be able to anticipate, at the time of the proposed GI registration, all subsequent uses of the proposed GI that would result in a likelihood of confusion. There is no reason to believe that this is possible. The evidence submitted to the Panel shows that GI registrations under the Regulation simply refer to names without limiting the way in which they are used. Indeed, it became apparent in the course of the proceedings that what the United States regards as "trademark-like use" is, in the European Communities, considered perfectly legitimate use as a GI.[500] . . .

* WT/DS174/R, 15 Mar. 2005.

500. The United States submitted copies of the packaging of cheeses bearing the GIs "Esrom," "Bitto," "Bra" and "Tomme de Savoie" in Exhibit US-52. The European Communities submitted the approved specifications for these GIs in Exhibits EC-99 through EC-102. *See* the European Communities' response to Panel question No. 140 and the United States' comment on that response.

7.570 The United States also refers to specific cases in which the Regulation has been applied in support of its claim, as set out in the following paragraphs.

7.571 Article 14(3) of the Regulation has only been applied once. This was the case of "Bayerisches Bier," which was registered as a protected geographical indication in 2001 subject to the proviso that the use of certain prior trademarks, for example, BAVARIA and HØKER BAJER, was permitted to continue under Article 14(2). The GI refers to a beer and the trademarks are registered in respect of beer. The GI and the trademarks are, respectively, the words "Bavaria" or "Bavarian Beer" rendered in the German, English and Danish languages. Upon its registration, the EC Council concluded that the GI would not mislead the public as to the identity of the product, which is the standard embodied in Article 14(3) of the Regulation.

7.572 The United States alleges that the GI "Bayerisches Bier" could be used in a manner that would result in a likelihood of confusion with these prior trademarks. In response to a direct question from the Panel, the European Communities did not deny this specific allegation. It only responded that "in principle" a name registered following the assessment required by Article 14(3) "should not give rise to confusion when used subsequently" and submitted that "in practice" this may happen only when the registered name is used together with other signs or as part of a combination of signs. This was a conspicuous choice of words because in the same response it commented in detail on two other specific cases which it considered irrelevant to the dispute.[506]

7.573 The United States also alleges that three Czech beer GIs, "Budejovické pivo," "Českobudějovické pivo" and "Budějovický měšťanský var" could be used in a manner that would result in a likelihood of confusion with the prior trademarks BUDWEISER and BUD, registered in respect of beer.[507] The evidence shows that a court in a non-EC WTO Member found a reasonable probability that a substantial number of persons would be confused if the marks BUDEJOVICKY BUDVAR depicted in a special script, and BUDWEISER and BUD, were used together in relation to beer in a normal and fair manner and in the ordinary course of business, particularly the mark BUD.[508] However, courts in two other non-EC WTO Members found that the use of "Budìjovický Budvar" on specific beer labels did not give rise to a likelihood of confusion with the trademarks BUDWEISER and BUD, registered in respect of beer.[509] In response to a direct question from the Panel, the European Communities did not deny that these GIs could be used in a manner that would result in a likelihood of confusion with these prior trademarks. Instead, it pointed to an endorsement on the three GI

506. The European Communities submitted twice that the EC Council had concluded that the registration of this GI would not lead to a likelihood of confusion with these prior trademarks but this is different from the EC Council's conclusion as stated in the decision on registration. The European Communities later indicated in response to a question from the Panel that the EC Council's conclusion was that the signs were not sufficiently similar to mislead the public, which is closer to the wording of the conclusion as stated in the decision, but not necessarily a likelihood of confusion: see European Communities' first written submission, para. 288, fn. 140; rebuttal submission, para. 287; and responses to Panel questions Nos. 137 and 143 and compare Council Regulation (EC) No. 1347/2001 reproduced in Exhibits US-41 and EC-9 and the Commission Guide to the Regulation (August 2004 edition, p. 12) in Exhibit EC-64.

507. The evidence indicates that these trademarks are registered in at least two EC member States and rights to them appear to have been acquired through use in another EC member State: *see* Exhibits US-53, Section 3.6; US-51, para. 26; and US-82.

508. Judgement of the High Court of South Africa in *Budweiser Budvar National Corporation v. Anheuser-Busch Corporation*, dated 3 December 2003, reproduced in Exhibit US-82.

509. Judgement of the Federal Court of Australia in *Anheuser-Busch, Inc. v Budìjovický Budvar, Národní Podnik*, [2002] FCA 390 (dated 5 April 2002); judgement of the Court of Appeal of New Zealand in *Anheuser Busch Incorporated v Budweiser Budwar National Corporation & Ors* [2002] NZCA 264 (dated 19 September 2002) reproduced in Exhibits EC-117 and EC-118, respectively.

registrations that they apply "without prejudice to any beer trademark or other rights existing in the European Union on the date of accession." This might imply that it accepts a likelihood of confusion, but considers that there are other means besides Article 14(3) to deal with that. It also argued that these GIs were outside the terms of reference but the United States expressly clarified that it referred to them only as evidence in support of its claim and did not challenge these individual registrations in this panel proceeding.

7.574 There appears to be an inconsistency between the European Communities' position that Article 14(3) of the Regulation, in practice, prevents the registration of GIs, use of which would result in a likelihood of confusion with a prior trademark, and its decision to avoid contesting that there may be circumstances in which the four specific GIs referred to above could be used which would not result in a likelihood of confusion with these specific prior trademarks.

7.575 For the above reasons, the Panel considers that the European Communities has not rebutted the United States' prima facie case that Article 14(3) of the Regulation cannot prevent all situations from occurring in which a trademark would be subject to Article 14(2) and, hence, in which the Regulation would limit the rights of the owner of such a trademark.

7.576 The Panel will now proceed to examine whether the TRIPS Agreement requires Members to make available to trademark owners rights against the use of GIs.

### (D) Relationship Between Protection of Gis and Prior Trademarks Under the TRIPS Agreement

#### Article 16.1 of the Trips Agreement . . .

7.599 Although each of the Sections in Part II provides for a different category of intellectual property, at times they refer to one another,[547] as certain subject matter may be eligible for protection by more than one category of intellectual property. This is particularly apparent in the case of trademarks and GIs, both of which are, in general terms, forms of distinctive signs. The potential for overlap is expressly confirmed by Articles 22.3 and 23.2, which provide for the refusal or invalidation of the registration of a trademark which contains or consists of a GI.[548] . . .

7.601 The right which must be conferred on the owner of a registered trademark is set out in the first sentence of the text. There are certain limitations on that right which relate to use in the course of trade, the signs, the goods or services for which the signs are used and those with respect to which they are registered and the likelihood of confusion. The ordinary meaning of the text indicates that, basically, this right applies to use in the course of trade of identical or similar signs, on identical or similar goods, where such use would result in a likelihood of confusion. It does not specifically exclude use of signs protected as GIs.

7.602 The text of Article 16.1 stipulates that the right for which it provides is an "exclusive" right. This must signify more than the fact that it is a right to "exclude" others, since that notion is already captured in the use of the word "prevent." Rather, it indicates that this right belongs to the owner of the registered trademark alone, who may exercise it to prevent certain uses by "all third parties" not having the owner's consent. The last sentence provides for an exception to that right, which is that it shall not prejudice any existing prior rights. Otherwise, the text of Article 16.1 is unqualified.

547. For instance, Article 25.2 of the TRIPS Agreement refers to more than one category of intellectual property, as does Article 4 of the IPIC Treaty, as incorporated by Article 35 of the TRIPS Agreement.

548. Articles 22.3 and 23.2, respectively.

7.603 Other exceptions to the right under Article 16.1 are provided for in Article 17 and possibly elsewhere in the TRIPS Agreement. However, there is no implied limitation vis-à-vis GIs in the text of Article 16.1 on the exclusive right which Members must make available to the owner of a registered trademark. That right may be exercised against a third party not having the owner's consent on the same terms, whether or not the third party uses the sign in accordance with GI protection, subject to any applicable exception. . . .

**(f) Article 17 of the TRIPS Agreement . . .**

7.646 Article 17 provides as follows:

> EXCEPTIONS
>
> Members may provide limited exceptions to the rights conferred by a trademark, such as fair use of descriptive terms, provided that such exceptions take account of the legitimate interests of the owner of the trademark and of third parties.

7.647 Article 17 expressly permits Members to provide limited exceptions to the rights conferred by a trademark, which include the right provided for in Article 16.1 of the TRIPS Agreement. The Panel has already found that the Regulation limits the availability of the right provided for in Article 16.1. Therefore, to the extent that it satisfies the conditions in Article 17, this limitation will be permitted under the TRIPS Agreement.

7.648 Article 17 permits "limited exceptions." It provides an example of a limited exception, and is subject to a proviso that "such exceptions take account of the legitimate interests of the owner of the trademark and of third parties." The ordinary meaning of the terms indicates that an exception must not only be "limited" but must also comply with the proviso in order to satisfy Article 17. The example of "fair use of descriptive terms" is illustrative only, but it can provide interpretative guidance because, *a priori*, it falls within the meaning of a "limited" exception and must be capable of satisfying the proviso in some circumstances. Any interpretation of the term "limited" or of the proviso which excluded the example would be manifestly incorrect.

7.649 The structure of Article 17 differs from that of other exceptions provisions to which the parties refer. . . .

**Limited Exceptions**

7.650 The first issue to decide is the meaning of the term "limited exceptions" as used in Article 17. The United States interprets this in terms of a small diminution of rights. The European Communities does not disagree with this approach. The Panel agrees with the views of the Panel in *Canada-Pharmaceutical Patents*, which interpreted the identical term in Article 30, that "[t]he word 'exception' by itself connotes a limited derogation, one that does not undercut the body of rules from which it is made." The addition of the word "limited" emphasizes that the exception must be narrow and permit only a small diminution of rights. The limited exceptions apply "to the rights conferred by a trademark." They do not apply to the set of all trademarks or all trademark owners. Accordingly, the fact that it may affect only few trademarks or few trademark owners is irrelevant to the question whether an exception is limited. The issue is whether the exception to the *rights conferred by a trademark* is narrow.

7.651 There is only one right conferred by a trademark at issue in this dispute, namely the exclusive right to prevent certain uses of a sign, provided for in Article 16.1. Therefore, it is necessary to examine the exception on an individual "per right" basis. This is a legal assessment of the extent to which the exception curtails that right. There is no indication in the text of Article 17 that this involves an economic assessment, although economic impact can be taken into account in the proviso. In this regard, we note the absence of any reference to a "normal exploitation" of the trademark in Article 17, and the absence of any reference in

Section 2, to which Article 17 permits exceptions, to rights to exclude legitimate competition. Rather, they confer, *inter alia*, the right to prevent uses that would result in a likelihood of confusion, which can lead to the removal of products from sale where they are marketed using particular signs, but without otherwise restraining the manufacture, sale or importation of competing goods or services.

7.652 The right provided for in Article 16.1 contains several elements and an exception could, in principle, curtail the right in respect of any of them. We recall these elements in the text of that provision as follows:

> "The owner of a registered trademark shall have the exclusive right to prevent *all third parties* not having the owner's consent from using in the course of trade *identical or similar signs* for *goods or services which are identical or similar* to those in respect of which the trademark is registered where such use would result in *a likelihood of confusion.*" [emphasis added]

7.653 In principle, an exception could curtail the right of the owner in respect of the third parties concerned, or with respect to the identity or the similarity of the signs or the goods or services concerned or with respect to the degree of likelihood of confusion, or some combination of these. There may be other possibilities as well. The overriding requirement is that the exception must be "limited" and it must also satisfy the proviso, considered below. These elements provide a useful framework for an assessment of the extent to which an exception curtails the right provided for in Article 16.1.

7.654 The example in the text, "fair use of descriptive terms," provides guidance as to what is considered a "limited exception," although it is illustrative only. Fair use of descriptive terms is inherently limited in terms of the sign which may be used and the degree of likelihood of confusion which may result from its use, as a purely descriptive term on its own is not distinctive and is not protectable as a trademark. Fair use of descriptive terms is *not* limited in terms of the number of third parties who may benefit, nor in terms of the quantity of goods or services with respect to which they use the descriptive terms, although implicitly it only applies to those third parties who would use those terms in the course of trade and to those goods or services which those terms describe. The number of trademarks or trademark owners affected is irrelevant, although implicitly it would only affect those marks which can consist of, or include, signs that can be used in a descriptive manner. According to the text, this is a "limited" exception for the purposes of Article 17.

7.655 Turning to the Regulation, it curtails the trademark owner's right in respect of certain goods but not all goods identical or similar to those in respect of which the trademark is registered. It prevents the trademark owner from exercising the right to prevent confusing uses of a sign for the agricultural product or foodstuff produced in accordance with the product specification in the GI registration. We recall that, according to Article 2(2) of the Regulation . . . those goods must all be produced, processed and/or prepared in the region, specific place or, in exceptional cases, country, the name of which is used to describe them. Goods that are not from that geographical area may not use the GI. Further, according to Article 4 of the Regulation, all products using a GI must comply with a product specification. Products that do not so comply may not use the GI even if they are from the geographical area. The trademark owner's right against all other goods is not curtailed. We note that there is no limit in terms of the quantity of goods which may benefit from the exception, as long as they conform to the product specification. However, this cannot prevent the limitation on rights of owners of trademarks subject to Article 14(2) from constituting a limited exception for the purposes of Article 17, as fair use of descriptive terms implies no limit in terms of quantity either, and the text indicates that it is a limited exception for the purposes of Article 17. The quantity of goods which benefits from an exception may be related to the curtailment of the rights to prevent the acts of making, selling or importing a product, but these are not rights conferred by a trademark.

7.656 The Regulation curtails the trademark owner's right against certain third parties, but not "all third parties." It prevents the trademark owner from exercising the right to prevent confusing uses against persons using a registered GI on a good in accordance with its registration. This is a limitation on the third parties who may benefit from the exception. The trademark owner's right is not curtailed with respect to any other third parties.[580]

7.657 The Regulation curtails the trademark owner's right in respect of certain signs but not all signs identical or similar to the one protected as a trademark. It prevents the trademark owner from exercising its right to prevent use of an indication registered as a GI in accordance with its registration. We recall our finding . . . that the GI registration does not confer a positive right to use any other signs or combination of signs nor to use the name in any linguistic versions not entered in the register. The trademark owner's right is not curtailed against any such uses. If the GI registration prevented the trademark owner from exercising its rights against these signs, combinations of signs or linguistic versions, which do not appear expressly in the GI registration, it would seriously expand the exception and undermine the limitations on its scope.

7.658 Under the Regulation, once a GI has been registered and a trademark is subject to the coexistence regime under Article 14(2) . . . the GI may, in principle, be used without regard to the likelihood of confusion that it may cause. However, the Regulation refers to the likelihood or risk of confusion, with a given mark, which would result from use as a GI of an identical or similar sign, in Articles 7(5)(b), 12b(3) and 12d(3), in relation to the decision on whether to register a GI where an objection is admissible. Article 7(4) and, hence, Article 12b(3), provide a ground for objection where registration would jeopardize the existence of a mark, and Article 14(3) provides a ground for refusal of registration which refers to the trademark's reputation and renown and the length of time it has been used. . . .

7.659 The United States submitted that Article 14(2) eliminates the trademark owner's right, granting the owner only the right to continue to use the trademark. However, the European Communities has emphasized that the trademark owner retains the right to prevent the use of a name registered as a GI by any person in relation to any goods which originate in a different geographical area or which do not comply with the specifications, and that the positive right to use the GI extends only to the linguistic versions that have been entered in the register and not to other names or signs which have not been registered. Accordingly, on the basis of the terms of the GI Regulation and of the Community Trademark Regulation, and the explanation of them provided by the European Communities, the Panel finds that not only may the trademark continue to be used, but that the trademark owner's right to prevent confusing uses, is unaffected except with respect to the use of a GI as entered in the GI register in accordance with its registration. In view of these limitations, the scope of the exception in Article 14(2) falls far short of that which the United States initially claimed.[583]

7.660 Furthermore, the European Communities has explained that the use of a name registered as a GI is subject to the applicable provisions of the food labelling and misleading advertising directives so that the ways in which it may be used are not unlimited.

---

580. The United States refers to a case of trademark infringement in which the German Federal Supreme Court held that the concurrent use by Fiat of the SL trademark owned by Mercedes-Benz could put at risk the very existence of that trademark. Note that, in coming to its decision, the Court observed that "it could be expected that other vehicle manufacturers might soon follow the defendant's example." See United States' rebuttal submission, para. 173, fn. 167 and Exhibit US-67. The opportunity for all other potential competitors to use a trademark does not arise under the GI Regulation as it only permits use of a GI in accordance with its registration, including the product specifications.

583. See United States' first oral statement, para. 75. The United States appears to acknowledge that the GI registration does not extinguish the trademark owner's rights against other third parties, although it alleges that use of the GI will affect the distinctiveness of the trademark: see United States' second oral statement, para. 101. The Panel considers that issue in relation to the proviso to Article 17.

7.661 For the above reasons, the Panel finds that the Regulation creates a "limited exception" within the meaning of Article 17 of the TRIPS Agreement.

### The Proviso to Article 17

7.662 Limited exceptions must satisfy the proviso that "such exceptions take account of the legitimate interests of the owner of the trademark and of third parties" in order to benefit from Article 17. We must first establish what are "legitimate interests." Read in context, the "legitimate interests" of the trademark owner are contrasted with the "rights conferred by a trademark," which also belong to the trademark owner. Given that Article 17 creates an exception to the rights conferred by a trademark, the "legitimate interests" of the trademark owner must be something different from full enjoyment of those legal rights. The "legitimate interests" of the trademark owner are also compared with those of "third parties," who have no rights conferred by the trademark. Therefore, the "legitimate interests" at least of third parties, are something different from simply the enjoyment of their legal rights. This is confirmed by the use of the verb "take account of," which is less than "protect."

7.663 We agree with the following view of the Panel in *Canada-Pharmaceutical Patents*, which interpreted the term "legitimate interests" of a patent owner and third parties in the context of Article 30 as follows:

> To make sense of the term "legitimate interests" in this context, that term must be defined in the way that it is often used in legal discourse—as a normative claim calling for protection of interests that are "justifiable" in the sense that they are supported by relevant public policies or other social norms. In our view, this is also true of the term "legitimate interests" of a trademark owner and third parties in the context of Article 17.

7.664 The legitimacy of some interest of the trademark owner is assumed because the owner of the trademark is specifically identified in Article 17. . . .

7.665 Turning to the Regulation, the evidence shows that the owner's legitimate interest in preserving the distinctiveness, or capacity to distinguish, of its trademark can be taken into account in various ways. Article 7(4) of the Regulation provides that a statement of objection shall be admissible *inter alia* if it shows that the registration of the proposed GI would "jeopardize the existence . . . of a mark." This requires GI registration to be refused.

7.666 Article 14(3) also requires the refusal of GI registration in light of a trademark's reputation and renown and the length of time it has been used, if a particular condition is fulfilled. This addresses the distinctiveness, or capacity to distinguish, of prior trademarks and can ensure that, in cases where trademark owners' legitimate interests would be most likely to be affected, the exception in Article 14(2) simply does not apply. . . .

7.670 Where Articles 7(4) and 14(3) of the Regulation are unavailable, and a trademark is subject to Article 14(2), there remains the possibility that its distinctiveness will be affected by the use of the GI. We do not consider this fatal to the applicability of Article 17 given that, as a provision permitting an exception to the exclusive right to prevent uses that would result in a likelihood of confusion, it presupposes that a certain degree of likelihood of confusion can be permitted. In the light of the provisions of Articles 7(4) and 14(3), we are satisfied that where the likelihood of confusion is relatively high, the exception in Article 14(2) will not apply. In any event, even where the exception does apply, Article 14(2) expressly provides that the trademark may continue to be used, on certain conditions.

7.671 We also note that the proviso to Article 17 requires only that exceptions "take account" of the legitimate interests of the owner of the trademark, and does not refer to "unreasonabl[e] prejudice" to those interests, unlike the provisos in Articles 13, 26.2 and 30 of the TRIPS Agreement and Article 9(2) of the Berne Convention (1971) as incorporated by Article 9.1 of the TRIPS Agreement. This suggests that a lesser standard of regard for the legitimate interests of the owner of the trademark is required.

7.672 The United States submits that Article 17 of the TRIPS Agreement requires a case-by-case analysis and that a blanket exception *a priori* does not take into account the legitimate interests of trademark owners. The Panel observes that Articles 7(4) and 14(3) of the Regulation do require a case-by-case analysis at the time of a decision on GI registration and, even though they do not require a case-by-case analysis at the time of subsequent use, nothing in the text of Article 17 indicates that a case-by-case analysis is a requirement under the TRIPS Agreement. Whilst it may be true that in the United States the doctrine of "fair use" is applied by courts on a case-by-case basis, we do not consider that this is necessarily implied in the use of those words in the TRIPS Agreement.[588]

7.673 The Panel notes that there may be situations where, in order to take account of the legitimate interests of the owner of a trademark and third parties, practical conditions may be required to distinguish the goods with the trademark from those using the GI and to distinguish the respective undertakings.

7.674 For these reasons, the Panel considers that the exception created by the Regulation takes account of the legitimate interests of the owner of the trademark within the meaning of Article 17. This finding is confirmed by responses to a question from the Panel which revealed that, of over 600 GIs registered under the Regulation over a period of eight years, the complainants and third parties are unable to identify any that, in their view, could be used in a way that would result in a likelihood of confusion with a prior trademark, with four exceptions. Three of these are the Czech beer GIs, the registration of which is subject to the endorsement set out above. The only remaining example is "Bayerisches Bier," in respect of which the complainants have not shown an example of actual likelihood of confusion with a prior trademark.

7.675 We will now consider whether the exception created by the Regulation takes account of the legitimate interests of third parties.

7.676 The parties to this dispute agree that "third parties" for the purposes of Article 17 include consumers. The function of a trademark is to distinguish goods and services of undertakings in the course of trade. That function is served not only for the owner, but also for consumers. Accordingly, the relevant third parties include consumers.[589] Consumers have a legitimate interest in being able to distinguish the goods and services of one undertaking from those of another, and to avoid confusion.

7.677 Turning to the Regulation, Article 14(3) expressly addresses consumers, by providing for the refusal of GI registration where "registration is liable to mislead the consumer as to the true identity of the product." In the one instance in which Article 14(3) has been applied, the European Communities informs the Panel that:

> In essence, it was concluded that, although the products were similar, the signs were not sufficiently similar to mislead the public, having regard to the degree of recognition of the trademark in the different Member States.

588. If there were any doubt on this point, [one] can observe that this language in Article 17 was proposed in the TRIPS negotiations by the European Communities and Austria, and was not apparently intended to reflect the United States' practice: *see* "Synoptic tables setting out existing international standards and proposed standards and principles," prepared by the GATT Secretariat at the request of the Negotiating Group on Trade-related Aspects of Intellectual Property Rights, including trade in counterfeit goods (document MTN.GNG/NG11/W/32/Rev.2 dated 2 February 1990, p. 51).

589. This is confirmed by the reference in Article 16.2 to "the relevant sector of the public," in relation to well-known trademarks.

7.678 This indicates to the Panel that Article 14(3) of the Regulation was, in fact, applied to take account *inter alia* of the legitimate interests of consumers. . . .

7.686 For these reasons, the Panel considers that the exception created by the Regulation takes account of the legitimate interests of third parties within the meaning of Article 17.

7.687 On the basis of the evidence presented to the Panel, which is necessarily limited given that Article 14(3) of the Regulation has only been applied once, and for all of the above reasons, the Panel concludes that the European Communities has succeeded in raising a presumption that the exception created by the Regulation to the trademark owner's right provided for in Article 16.1 of the TRIPS Agreement is justified by Article 17 of the TRIPS Agreement. The United States has not succeeded in rebutting that presumption.

7.688 Therefore, the Panel concludes that, with respect to the coexistence of GIs with prior trademarks, the Regulation is inconsistent with Article 16.1 of the TRIPS Agreement but, on the basis of the evidence presented to the Panel, this is justified by Article 17 of the TRIPS Agreement.

## NOTES AND QUESTIONS

**1.** The panel accepts that some consumer confusion between existing trademarks and GIs will occur. Otherwise, there would be no need to invoke an exception. In what type of situation might this occur? If a German beer-producing region was successful in registering the GI "Bürger King," might that conflict with the registered trademark of the U.S.-based fast food chain "Burger King"? Would EU consumers be likely to think that the fast food outlet famous for hamburgers had decided to enter the beer business?

**2.** What limitations does the panel impose on the use of GIs that are permitted by application of Article 17 of the TRIPS Agreement? *Inter alia*, the European Union explained that "the positive right to use the GI extends only to the linguistic versions that have been entered in the register and not to other names or signs which have not been registered," and the panel noted that limitation. What is the basis for the limitations?

**3.** Recall from Chapter 1 that the EU GIs Regulation was found to be inconsistent with the TRIPS Agreement and GATT national treatment rules because it imposed burdensome conditions on foreign holders of GIs. These inconsistencies had effectively precluded foreign nationals from registering their GIs in the European Union. The possibility for conflict between prior trademarks and GIs was a relatively minor problem for the United States, which had some difficulty in providing examples where conflicts had arisen or might arise. Though there was one "big-ticket" case involving the "Budweiser" trademark for beer, even that conflict appeared to be at the margin of economic interest for the U.S. "Budweiser" owner, Anheuser-Busch.

**4.** The continuing saga of Anheuser-Busch and the Budweiser trademark in the European Union can be studied at *Anheuser-Busch v. OHIM*, ECJ Case C-214/09 P, 29 July 2010, where the ECJ refused to overrule the OHIM's decision to refuse Anheuser-Busch's application for registration of a CTM based on opposition by the Czech brewer Budějovický Budvar. Now that Anheuser-Busch is owned by a Belgium-based enterprise, InBev, do you think that the attitude of EU institutions toward full protection of the Budweiser trademark in the European Union may change?

**5.** In the *Canada-Generic Pharmaceuticals* case, *supra* Chapter 2, section II.B.1, the panel found that a provision of Canadian law that allowed stockpiling of generic drugs prior to expiration of the patent was inconsistent with Article 30, mainly because it did not restrict the quantity of drugs that could be stockpiled. Does the panel in the *EC-Geographical Indications* decision address the issue of quantity? Does it impose a limit? Is this consistent with the decision in the *Canada-Generic Pharmaceuticals* case?

**6.** The panel urges caution in using precedents under the exception provisions from the copyright and patent sections of the TRIPS Agreement in connection with Article 17. Why is this?

## G. TRIPS-plus Obligations in Bilateral and Plurilateral Agreements

Recent bilateral and multilateral agreements, in particular in CAFTA, CETA, and CPTPP, further developed standards. Importantly the latter agreements in particular extend the protection of geographical indications.

**Thomas Cottier, Dannie Jost & Michelle Schupp***

### *Setting the Scene: The Prospects of TRIPS-plus Protection in Future Mega-Regionals*

Geographical Indications and Trademarks

While trademarks chapters do not stray far from the basic framework in TRIPS, GIs show considerable development, especially in CETA which has three annexes listing the EU and Canada's GIs and product classes. Trademarks are dealt with in Articles 15 to 21 TRIPS and GIs in Articles 22 to 24. In CAFTA, Article 15.2 and 15.4 deal with trademarks and Article 15.3 with GIs. In CETA, Article 6.1 to 6.3 relate to trademarks and 7.1 to 7.8 deal with GIs. In the TPP, Section C, Articles 18.18 through 18.28 treat trademarks and Section E, Articles 18.30 to 18.36 TPP address GIs.

Starting with trademarks, perhaps not surprisingly, CAFTA and the TPP contain numerous verbatim or similar provisions, while CETA, as seen with copyrights, has a different orientation and addresses slightly different concerns.

What is new is the inclusion in CAFTA of "collective, certification and sound marks, which may include geographical indications and scent marks" thus significantly extending the minimal standard of protectable subject matter beyond Article 15 TRIPS.[2] CAFTA reproduces the GI definition verbatim from Article 22 TRIPS. The TPP leans on CAFTA's provision, entailing a provision on "Collective and Certification Marks",[3] and stating that "no party may require, as a condition of registration, that a sign be visually perceptible, nor may a Party deny registration of a trademark solely on the ground that the sign of which it is composed is a sound."[4] Recalling the last sentence of Article 15.1 TRIPS according to which "[m]embers may require, as a condition of registration, that signs be visually perceptible", TPP states exactly the opposite, while in most other Articles it leans on CAFTA's definitions, sustaining once more the parallel between the two agreements.

CAFTA also specifies that "the use of the term customary in common language [. . .] should not impair the use or effectiveness of trademarks used in relation to such goods."[5] In the TPP guidelines for determining whether a term is the term customary in the common language are provided.[6] "Rights conferred" as in Article 16 TRIPS is copied with the same

*. In Mega-Regional Trade Agreements 191-216 (Thilo Rensmann ed., 2017).

2. Article 15.2.1 CAFTA.

3. Article 18.19 TPP.

4. Article 18.18 TPP.

5. Article 15.2.2 CAFTA.

6. Article 18.33 TPP.

wording in CAFTA although "geographical indications" has been added to the use in the course of trade of identical or similar signs; giving the owner of a registered trademark the right to prevent third parties from using such signs. The TPP's provision reflects a mixture of TRIPS and CAFTA.[7]

Well-known trademarks in TRIPS are applied to goods or services "not similar to those in respect of which a trademark is registered", CAFTA changes the same sentence to "not identical or similar to those identified by a well-known trademark." CAFTA's provision goes further in referring to Article 6bis of the Paris Convention[8] in determining well-known trademarks and its scope of application extends to goods and not only to services.[9] The TPP partly copies the wording of CAFTA, providing more details, and stating that "no party may require as a condition for determining that a trademark is well-known that the trademark has been registered [. . .]."[10]

CAFTA expects parties to provide a system for registration of trademarks while also making available to the applicant the possibility to respond to communications, initial refusal and judicial appeal.[11] CETA uses different wording but expresses the same idea, while the TPP once again borrows from CAFTA.[12]

The Electronic Trademark System is a novelty. In all three agreements the main use would be for "application, registration and maintenance of trademarks" including an on-line public database.[13] CAFTA and the TPP use a classification of goods and services:[14] indicating trademarks by common names and following the grouping into classes that was established by the Nice Agreement.[15]

Terms of protection for trademarks are prolonged, both in CAFTA and in the TPP, three years more than the seven years of Article 18 TRIPS for initial registration and renewals of registrations, i.e. a total of ten years.[16] Regarding licensing, CAFTA and TPP state that parties may not require "recordal of trademark licenses to establish the validity of the license [. . .]."[17]

Domain names are addressed both in CAFTA and the TPP, the latter suggesting in addition to the provisions in CAFTA appropriate remedies for persons registering or holding domain names identical to or confusingly similar to trademarks. CAFTA requires management of the Contracting Parties' country-code top-level domain (ccLTD).[18]

CETA has a strong focus on GIs. CAFTA's definition of GIs corresponds to that of TRIPS, that is as indications "which identify a good as originating in the territory of a Member [. . .]" adding to this any form of signs or combination of signs.[19] CETA's definition also uses the one from TRIPS, but "goods" become "agricultural product or foodstuff," thus narrowing the scope.[20]

---

7. Article 15.2.3 CAFTA; Article 18.20 TPP.
8. Paris Convention for the Protection of Industrial Property (1883, 1967).
9. Article 15.2.5 CAFTA.
10. Article 18.22(1) TPP; TRIPS takes into account the knowledge in the relevant sector of the public, for a trademark to be well-known.
11. Article 15.2.6 CAFTA; TRIPS' registration depends on use.
12. Article 6.2 CETA, Article 18.23 TPP.
13. Article 15.2.7 CAFTA, Article 6.2 CETA, Article 18.24 TPP.
14. Article 15.2.8 CAFTA, Article 18.25 TPP.
15. Nice Agreement Concerning the International Classification of Goods and Services for the Purposes of the Registration of Marks, 1979.
16. Article 15.2.9 CAFTA, Article 18.26 TPP.
17. Article 15.2.10 CAFTA; Article 18.27 TPP.
18. Article 15.4 CAFTA; Article 18.28 TPP.
19. Article 15.3.1 CAFTA.
20. Article 7.1(a) CETA.

Legal means and procedures with respect to GIs are to be provided in respect of the identification and protection of GIs. Parties shall accept applications from persons from another Party without intercession by other parties on behalf of the applicant (no intermediary); there shall be minimum formalities; regulations shall be readily available to the public and applications shall be published.[21] CAFTA clarifies the relationship between trademarks and GIs expecting a request for protection or recognition of a GI to be refused if the latter "is likely to be confusingly similar" to a trademark subject to a pending application or registration, or existing trademarks, the rights of which have been acquired.[22]

CETA provides three Annexes where the scope is identified and a list of GIs is provided. The TPP defers to previous international agreements for protection or recognition of GIs and does not consider lists.[23] CETA specifies that protection of goods in the relevant annex "shall be provided even where the true origin of the product is indicated or the GI is used in translation or accompanied by [. . .] 'kind', 'type', 'style', 'imitation' or the like", providing also for enforcement by administrative action and notification if listed GIs are not or cease to be protected in the place of origin.[24] The topic of homonymous GIs is addressed by CETA; practical conditions are needed to differentiate homonymous GIs for products of the same product class.[25] A similar provision was not included in TPP.

Exceptions in CETA are relevant, since after giving a great deal of space to European GIs, the provision is providing for some advantages to the Canadian habits. Canada has no requirement to provide legal means to prevent the use of the GIs listed, "when the use of such terms is accompanied by expressions such as 'kind' [. . .] and is in combination with a legible and visible indication of the GI."[26] The protection of certain GIs could continue to be used in Canada by persons who had made commercial use of the GIs in the preceding five to ten years, until 18 October 2013. This provision pertains to specific product classes listed in the relevant annex.[27]

The starting date for the protection of CETA's listed GIs is the date of the signing of CETA or, if added after that date, the date of addition. The TPP works with the filing date.[28] The topic of translations is to be found in another provision of CETA that gives Canada more space in its own recognition of GIs. Thus if a translation of a GI is identical to or contains a customary term in common language, such "as the common name for a product in the territory of a Party", using that term in association with that product in that party's territory is allowed.[29] Regarding the use of customary names of varieties of plants or animal breeds, which exist in the territory of the party using them, are allowed.[30] TPP give discretion to the Party's authorities in determining whether a term is customary based on "how consumers understand the term in that party's territory."[31]

CETA states that the provisions on GIs shall not prejudice the right to use or register in Canada a trademark containing GIs of European origin if the terms are not used in such a way as to mislead the public in relation to the geographical origin of such goods.[32] The CETA

21. Article15.3.2-6 CAFTA; Article 18.31 and 18.32 TPP.
22. Article 15.3.7 CAFTA.
23. Article 7.2 and 7.3 CETA; Article 18.36 TPP.
24. Article 7.4 CETA.
25. Article 7.5 CETA.
26. Article 7.6.1 CETA.
27. Transitional periods of up to 5 years can be granted. Article 7.6.2-4 CETA.
28. Article 7.6.6 CETA; Article 18.35 TPP.
29. Article 7.6.7 CETA.
30. Article 7.6.8 CETA
31. Article 18.33 TPP.
32. Article 7.6.11 CETA.

Committee on GIs is entitled to add or remove GIs from the relevant list if "they have ceased to be protected or have fallen into disuse in their place of origin"; no addition is possible if, from the date of signing of CETA, those GIs are "registered" in the Register of the EU.[33]

The TPP contains a couple more provisions that are totally new and in neither CAFTA nor CETA. For example, the recognition of GIs that can be protected "through a trademark or *sui generis* system or other legal means."[34]

Also, if the GI has ceased to meet the conditions for original protection, the latter may be cancelled.[35] On multi-component terms, the TPP prescribes that individual components of multi-component terms that are protected as GIs in a party, shall not be protected in that party where the individual component is a customary language term in the common language "as the common name for associated goods."[36] Finally, a novelty in TPP is the provision that provides legal means against the use of a country name commercially in a way that would mislead consumers.[37]

## NOTES AND QUESTIONS

**1.** The Intellectual Property Rights chapter of the USMCA incorporates rules regarding the relationship between trademarks and geographical indications, allowing owners of pre-existing trademarks to object to the protection or recognition of GIs on grounds that they are likely to cause confusion with a pre-existing good faith trademark registration or pending application, or a pre-existing trademark, in a Party, or on grounds that the geographical indication is a term customary in the common language as the common name for the relevant good in the territory of a Party (Article 20.E.3). The IP chapter also requires that Parties implement means to challenge the recognition or protection of GIs that have been recognized or protected through an international agreement, though allowing exclusions for international agreements pre-dating NAFTA 2.0 (Article 20.E.7).

## III. TRADEMARK EXHAUSTION AND INTERNATIONAL TRADE

### A. U.S. Law on Trademarks and Parallel Imports

#### *1. K Mart v. Cartier*

U.S. law regarding international exhaustion of trademark rights is grounded in Section 526 of the Tariff Act of 1930, as interpreted by the U.S. Supreme Court in *K mart v. Cartier.* In *K mart,* a coalition of U.S. trademark industry groups challenged the Treasury Department's longstanding interpretation of the Tariff Act. Treasury Department regulations generally did not provide for blocking the importation of trademarked goods that had been placed on foreign markets by entities under common control with holders of U.S. registered trademarks, and these regulations did not provide for blocking the importation of trademarked goods that had been placed on foreign markets by authorized licensees of U.S. registered trademarks.

The Supreme Court responded to the challenge from the trademark industry coalition with a complex array of opinions. The practical result in *K mart* is not so complicated. The

33. Article 7.7 CETA.
34. Article 18.30 TPP.
35. Article 18.32.3 TPP.
36. Article 18.34 TPP.
37. Article 18.29 TPP.

Court affirms the Treasury Department's interpretation of the Tariff Act insofar as it prevented U.S. trademark holders from blocking parallel imports produced by commonly controlled enterprises (i.e., the "common control exception"). However, the Court rejects that portion of the Treasury regulation that prevented U.S. trademark holders from blocking parallel imports produced by foreign licensees.

It was largely in response to *K mart* that U.S. trademark holders began to assert rights to restrict imports of goods on the basis of copyrights in labels and package design.

## *K Mart v. Cartier*

486 U.S. 281 (1988)

Justice KENNEDY delivered the opinion of the Court with respect to Parts I, II-A, and II-C, and an opinion with respect to Part II-B, in which WHITE, J., joined.

A gray-market good is a foreign-manufactured good, bearing a valid United States trademark, that is imported without the consent of the United States trademark holder. These cases present the issue whether the Secretary of the Treasury's regulation permitting the importation of certain gray-market goods, 19 CFR §133.21 (1987), is a reasonable agency interpretation of §526 of the Tariff Act of 1930 (1930 Tariff Act), 46 Stat. 741, as amended, 19 U.S.C. §1526.

### I

### A

The gray market arises in any of three general contexts. The prototypical gray-market victim (case 1) is a domestic firm that purchases from an independent foreign firm the rights to register and use the latter's trademark as a United States trademark and to sell its foreign-manufactured products here. Especially where the foreign firm has already registered the trademark in the United States or where the product has already earned a reputation for quality, the right to use that trademark can be very valuable. If the foreign manufacturer could import the trademarked goods and distribute them here, despite having sold the trademark to a domestic firm, the domestic firm would be forced into sharp intrabrand competition involving the very trademark it purchased. Similar intrabrand competition could arise if the foreign manufacturer markets its wares outside the United States, as is often the case, and a third party who purchases them abroad could legally import them. In either event, the parallel importation, if permitted to proceed, would create a gray market that could jeopardize the trademark holder's investment.

The second context (case 2) is a situation in which a domestic firm registers the United States trademark for goods that are manufactured abroad by an affiliated manufacturer. In its most common variation (case 2a), a foreign firm wishes to control distribution of its wares in this country by incorporating a subsidiary here. The subsidiary then registers under its own name (or the manufacturer assigns to the subsidiary's name) a United States trademark that is identical to its parent's foreign trademark. The parallel importation by a third party who buys the goods abroad (or conceivably even by the affiliated foreign manufacturer itself) creates a gray market. Two other variations on this theme occur when an American-based firm establishes abroad a manufacturing subsidiary corporation (case 2b) or its own unincorporated manufacturing division (case 2c) to produce its United States trademarked goods, and then imports them for domestic distribution. If the trademark holder or its foreign subsidiary sells the trademarked goods abroad, the parallel importation of the goods competes on the gray market with the holder's domestic sales.

In the third context (case 3), the domestic holder of a United States trademark authorizes an independent foreign manufacturer to use it. Usually the holder sells to the foreign manufacturer an exclusive right to use the trademark in a particular foreign location, but conditions the right on the foreign manufacturer's promise not to import its trademarked goods into the United States. Once again, if the foreign manufacturer or a third party imports into the United States, the foreign-manufactured goods will compete on the gray market with the holder's domestic goods.

**B**

Until 1922, the Federal Government did not regulate the importation of gray-market goods, not even to protect the investment of an independent purchaser of a foreign trademark, and not even in the extreme case where the independent foreign manufacturer breached its agreement to refrain from direct competition with the purchaser. That year, however, Congress was spurred to action by a Court of Appeals decision declining to enjoin the parallel importation of goods bearing a trademark that (as in case 1) a domestic company had purchased from an independent foreign manufacturer at a premium. *See A. Bourjois & Co. v. Katzel*, 275 F. 539 (CA2 1921), *rev'd*, 260 U.S. 689, 43 S. Ct. 244, 67 L. Ed. 464 (1923).

In an immediate response to *Katzel*, Congress enacted §526 of the Tariff Act of 1922, 42 Stat. 975. That provision, later reenacted in identical form as §526 of the 1930 Tariff Act, 19 U.S.C. §1526, prohibits importing

> "into the United States any merchandise of foreign manufacture if such merchandise . . . bears a trademark owned by a citizen of, or by a corporation or association created or organized within, the United States, and registered in the Patent and Trademark Office by a person domiciled in the United States . . . , unless written consent of the owner of such trademark is produced at the time of making entry." 19 U.S.C. §1526(a).

The regulations implementing §526 for the past 50 years have not applied the prohibition to all gray-market goods. The Customs Service regulation now in force provides generally that "foreign-made articles bearing a trademark identical with one owned and recorded by a citizen of the United States or a corporation or association created or organized within the United States are subject to seizure and forfeiture as prohibited importations." 19 CFR §133.21(b) (1987). But the regulation furnishes a "common-control" exception from the ban, permitting the entry of gray-market goods manufactured abroad by the trademark owner or its affiliate:

> (c) Restrictions not applicable. The restrictions. . .do not apply to imported articles when:
>
> 1. Both the foreign and the U.S. trademark or trade name are owned by the same person or business entity; [or]
> 2. The foreign and domestic trademark or trade name owners are parent and subsidiary companies or are otherwise subject to common ownership or control.

The Customs Service regulation further provides an "authorized-use" exception, which permits importation of gray-market goods where

> "(3) the articles of foreign manufacture bear a recorded trademark or trade name applied under authorization of the U.S. owner. . . ."

19 CFR §133.21(c) (1987). Respondents, an association of United States trademark holders and two of its members, brought suit in Federal District Court in February 1984, seeking both a declaration that the Customs Service regulation, 19 CFR §§133.21(c)(1)-(3) (1987), is invalid and an injunction against its enforcement. . . .

. . . A majority of this Court now holds that the common-control exception of the Customs Service regulation, 19 CFR §§133.21(c)(1)-(2) (1987), is consistent with §526. *See* post (opinion of Brennan, J.). A different majority, however, holds that the authorized-use exception, 19 CFR §133.21(c)(3) (1987), is inconsistent with §526. *See* post (opinion of Scalia, J.). We therefore affirm the Court of Appeals in part and reverse in part.

## II

. . .

### B

. . . I conclude that subsections (c)(1) and (c)(2) of the Customs Service regulation, 19 CFR §§133.21(c)(1) and (c)(2) (1987), are permissible constructions designed to resolve statutory ambiguities. All Members of the Court are in agreement that the agency may interpret the statute to bar importation of gray-market goods in what we have denoted case 1 and to permit the imports under case 2a. *See* post (opinion of Brennan, J.); post (opinion of Scalia, J.). As these writings state, "owned by" is sufficiently ambiguous, in the context of the statute, that it applies to situations involving a foreign parent, which is case 2a. This ambiguity arises from the inability to discern, from the statutory language, which of the two entities involved in case 2a can be said to "own" the United States trademark if, as in some instances, the domestic subsidiary is wholly owned by its foreign parent.

A further statutory ambiguity contained in the phrase "merchandise of foreign manufacture," suffices to sustain the regulations as they apply to cases 2b and 2c. This ambiguity parallels that of "owned by," which sustained case 2a, because it is possible to interpret "merchandise of foreign manufacture" to mean (1) goods manufactured in a foreign country, (2) goods manufactured by a foreign company, or (3) goods manufactured in a foreign country by a foreign company. Given the imprecision in the statute, the agency is entitled to choose any reasonable definition and to interpret the statute to say that goods manufactured by a foreign subsidiary or division of a domestic company are not goods "of foreign manufacture." [4]

(1) Subsection (c)(3), 19 CFR §133.21(c)(3) (1987), of the regulation, however, cannot stand. The ambiguous statutory phrases that we have already discussed, "owned by" and "merchandise of foreign manufacture," are irrelevant to the proscription contained in subsection (3) of the regulation. This subsection of the regulation denies a domestic trademark holder the power to prohibit the importation of goods made by an independent foreign manufacturer where the domestic trademark holder has authorized the foreign manufacturer to use the trademark. Under no reasonable construction of the statutory language can goods made in a foreign country by an independent foreign manufacturer be removed from the purview of the statute.

(2) The design of the regulation is such that the subsection of the regulation dealing with case 3, §133.21(c)(3), is severable. . . . The severance and invalidation of this subsection will not impair the function of the statute as a whole, and there is no indication that the regulation would not have been passed but for its inclusion. Accordingly, subsection (c)(3) of §133.21 must be invalidated for its conflict with the unequivocal language of the statute.

---

4. I disagree with Justice Scalia's reasons for declining to recognize this ambiguity. *See* post. First, the threshold question in ascertaining the correct interpretation of a statute is whether the language of the statute is clear or arguably ambiguous. The purported gloss any party gives to the statute, or any reference to legislative history, is in the first instance irrelevant. Further, I decline to assign any binding or authoritative effect to the particular verbiage Justice Scalia highlights. . . .

## III

We hold that the Customs Service regulation is consistent with §526 insofar as it exempts from the importation ban goods that are manufactured abroad by the "same person" who holds the United States trademark, 19 CFR §133.21(c)(1) (1987), or by a person who is "subject to common . . . control" with the United States trademark holder, §133.21(c)(2). Because the authorized-use exception of the regulation, §133.21(c)(3), is in conflict with the plain language of the statute, that provision cannot stand. The judgment of the Court of Appeals is therefore reversed insofar as it invalidated §§133.21(c)(1) and (c)(2), but affirmed with respect to §133.21(c)(3).

It is so ordered.

Justice BRENNAN, with whom Justice MARSHALL and Justice STEVENS join, and with whom Justice WHITE joins as to Part IV, concurring in part and dissenting in part. . . .

I turn now to my small area of disagreement with the Court's judgment—the Court's conclusion that the authorized-use exception embodied in 19 CFR §133.21(c)(3) (1987) is inconsistent with the plain language of §526. In my view, §526 does not unambiguously protect from gray-market competition a United States trademark owner who authorizes the use of its trademark abroad by an independent manufacturer (case 3).

Unlike the variations of corporate affiliation in case 2, *see supra* . . . , the ambiguity in §526, admittedly, is not immediately apparent in case 3. In that situation, the casual reader of the statute might suppose that the domestic firm still "own[s]" its trademark. Any such supposition as to the meaning of "owned by," however, bespeaks stolid anachronism not solid analysis. It follows only from an understanding of trademark law that established itself long after the 1922 enactment and 1930 reenactment of §526. . . .

When §526 was before Congress, the prevailing law held that a trademark's sole purpose was to identify for consumers the product's physical source or origin. *See, e.g., Macmahan Pharmacal Co. v. Denver Chemical Mfg. Co.*, 113 F. 468, 475 (CA8 1901). "Under this early 'source theory' of protection, trademark licensing was viewed as philosophically impossible, since licensing meant that the mark was being used by persons not associated with the real manufacturing 'source' in a strict, physical sense of the word." 1 McCarthy, Trademarks and Unfair Competition, at 826; *see Macmahan Pharmacal Co., supra*, at 475 ("An assignment or license without [a] transfer [of the business] is totally inconsistent with the theory upon which the value of a trademark depends"); H. Nims, The Law of Unfair Competition and Trade-Marks 46 (1917) (identifying *Macmahan* as "the usual rule"). Thus, any attempt by a trademark holder to authorize a third party to use its trademark worked an abandonment of the trademark, resulting in a relinquishment of ownership. *See, e.g., Everett O. Fisk & Co. v. Fisk Teachers' Agency, Inc.*, 3 F.2d 7, 9 (CA8 1924).

Nor was it at all obvious then that a trademark owner could authorize the use of its trademark in one geographic area by selling it along with business and goodwill, while retaining ownership of the trademark in another geographic area. There were, as Justice Scalia points out, isolated suggestions that a foreign firm could validly assign to another the exclusive right to distribute the assignor's goods here under the foreign trademark. *See* post, at 326. The cases, however, were rife with suggestions to the contrary.[7] And we have found no contemporaneous

7. *See, e.g., Independent Baking Powder Co. v. Boorman*, 175 F. 448, 454 (CC NJ 1910) ("The assignor cannot, after the assignment, continue the same identical business and at the same places as before, under unassigned trademarks, and at the same time authorize his assignee to conduct the same business elsewhere under an assigned trademark"); *Eiseman v. Schiffer*, 157 F. 473 (CC SDNY 1907) (trademark owner may not assign trademark and then continue to engage in same business under different trademark).

case even suggesting that a domestic firm could retain ownership of a trademark after attempting to assign to another the right to use the trademark on goods that the other manufactured abroad. *Cf. Scandinavia Belting Co. v. Asbestos & Rubber Works of America, Inc.*, 257 F. 937, 956 (CA2 1919) (raising similar issue whether assignee of right to use trademark in the United States might use trademark on products not produced by the foreign manufacturer, but concluding "that question is not here and is not decided"). As one commentator writing as late as 1932 observed: "There is much confusion in the books in regard to the transferability of trade marks and trade names. The law on the matter is neither clearly stated nor always uniformly applied." Grismore, The Assignment of Trade Marks and Trade Names, 30 Mich. L. Rev. 490, 491.[8]

Not until the 1930's did a trend develop approving of trademark licensing—so long as the licensor controlled the quality of the licensee's products—on the theory that a trademark might also serve the function of identifying product quality for consumers. 1 McCarthy, Trademarks and Unfair Competition, at 827-829; *see* Grismore, 30 Mich. L. Rev., at 499. And not until the passage of the Lanham Trade-Mark Act in 1946 did that trend become the rule. *See, e.g., Dawn Donut Co. v. Hart's Food Stores, Inc.*, 267 F.2d 358, 366-367 (CA2 1959). Similarly, it was not until well after §526's enactment that it became clear that a trademark owner could assign rights in a particular territory along with goodwill, while retaining ownership in another distinct territory. *See, e.g., California Wine & Liquor Corp. v. William Zakon & Sons, Inc.*, 297 Mass. 373, 378, 8 N.E.2d 812, 814 (1937).

Manifestly, the legislators who chose the term "owned by" viewed trademark ownership differently than we view it today. Any prescient legislator who could have contemplated that a trademark owner might license the use of its trademark would almost certainly have concluded that such a transaction would divest the licensor not only of the benefit of §526's importation prohibition, but of all trademark protection; and anyone who gave thought to the possibility that a trademark holder might assign rights to use its trademark, along with business and goodwill, to an unrelated manufacturer in another territory had good reason to expect the same result. At the very least, it seems to me plain that Congress did not address case 3 any more clearly than it addressed case 2a, 2b, or 2c. To hold otherwise is to wrench statutory words out of their legislative and historical context and treat legislation as no more than a "collection of English words" rather than "a working instrument of government. . . ." *United States v. Dotterweich*, 320 U.S. 277, 280, 88 L. Ed. 48, 64 S. Ct. 134 (1943). . . .

Since I believe that the application of §526 to case 3 is ambiguous, the sole remaining question is whether Treasury's decision to exclude case 3 from §526's prohibition is entitled to deference. . . .

The legislative history that I have already discussed at length confirms Congress' intent to do exactly that, and merely to overrule *Katzel.* There is no more indication that Congress intended to permit a United States trademark holder to prohibit importation of trademarked goods manufactured abroad under its authorization than that Congress intended to permit a United States trademark holder to exclude goods produced by its affiliates or divisions abroad.

Finally, Treasury has, at least since 1951, declined to protect trademark holders who authorize the use of their trademarks abroad. Almost as soon as the Lanham Trade-Mark Act

---

8. Justice Scalia cites *United Drug Co. v. Theodore Rectanus Co.*, 248 U.S. 90, 100-101, 63 L. Ed. 141, 39 S. Ct. 48 (1918), and *Hanover Star Milling Co. v. Metcalf*, 240 U.S. 403, 415, 60 L. Ed. 713, 36 S. Ct. 357 (1916), in support of his contention that the law by 1920 clearly permitted a trademark owner to retain ownership and use a trademark in one territory after assigning the identical trademark along with goodwill in another. . . . Those cases held only that a firm can develop a trademark that is identical to a trademark already in use in a geographically distinct and remote area if the firm is unaware of the identity. Thus, those cases bore on the territorial extent of trademark protection, not on the transferability of a trademark by territory once developed.

codified the quality theory, enabling trademark holders to license the use of their trademarks without thereby relinquishing ownership, *see supra*, at 311, the Customs Service took the position that §526's protection would be unavailable to domestic firms that authorized independent foreign firms to use their trademarks. *See* Letter from Customs Commissioner Dow to Sen. Douglas (Mar. 23, 1951), App. 52, 53 ("[A] foreign subsidiary or licensee of the United States trademark is considered to stand in the same shoes as such trademark owner"). *See also* T. D. 69-12(2), 3 Cust. Bull., at 17. Particularly in light of that longstanding agency interpretation, I would uphold the authorized-use exception as reasonable.

Justice Scalia, with whom The Chief Justice, Justice Blackmun, and Justice O'connor join, concurring in part and dissenting in part.

I agree with the Court's analytic approach to this matter, and with its conclusion that subsection (c)(3) of the regulation, 19 CFR §133.21(c)(3) (1987), is not a permissible construction of §526(a) of the Tariff Act of 1930, 19 U.S.C. §1526(a). I therefore join Parts I, II-A, and II-C of the Court's opinion. In my view, however, subsections (c)(1) and (c)(2) of the regulation are also in conflict with the clear language of §526(a). I therefore decline to join Parts II-B and III of Justice Kennedy's opinion and dissent from that part of the judgment upholding subsections (c)(1) and (c)(2).

### I. . . .

Five Members of the Court (hereinafter referred to as "the majority") assert, however, that the regulation's treatment of situations 2b and 2c is attributable to the resolution of yet another ambiguity in §526(a). *See* ante, . . . (opinion of Kennedy, J.); ante, . . . (opinion of Brennan, J.). The statute excludes only merchandise "of foreign manufacture," which the majority says might mean "manufactured by a foreigner" rather than "manufactured in a foreign country." I think not. . . .

I find it extraordinary for this Court, on the theory of deferring to an agency's judgment, to burden that agency with an interpretation that it not only has never suggested, but that is contrary to ordinary usage, to the purposes of the statute, and to the interpretation the agency appears to have applied consistently for half a century.

## NOTES AND QUESTIONS

**1.** The U.S. Treasury Department has consistently opposed limitations on parallel imports of trademarked goods because of its conclusion that parallel imports promote price competition, and that the alleged (but generally unsubstantiated) assertions of injury to consumers can be addressed by means that are less likely to restrict competition.

**2.** Justice Brennan and Justice Scalia (in text not reproduced above) provide a historical perspective on the rights of trademark holders to license or transfer their marks. How does the TRIPS Agreement address these rights to license and transfer? What factors account for the changes?

**3.** In *Silhouette, supra* page [102], the CJEU ruled that holders of trademarks in the European Union may block the importation of goods first placed on the market outside the territory of the European Union. The United States provides less extensive rights to U.S. trademark holders. Does this "gap" adversely affect the United States?

**4.** As discussed in Chapter 4, the U.S. Supreme Court in 2013 decided in favor of international exhaustion with respect to copyright (*Kirtsaeng v. Wiley*, 568 U.S. 519, 133 S. Ct.

1351 (2013)). In 2017, the Court extended the principle of international exhaustion to include patents (*Impression Products, Inc. v. Lexmark Intern., Inc.*, 137 S. Ct. 1523 (2017); discussed in more detail in Chapter 2).

### a. The Post-*K mart* Material Differences Movement

In *K mart v. Cartier*, the U.S. Supreme Court interpreted Section 526 of the Tariff Act of 1930. Section 526 provides a basis for recording registered trademarks with the U.S. Customs Service, and for Customs Service blocking of infringing imports. There is another U.S. statute, Section 42 of the Lanham Act, which performs a function similar to that of Section 526 of the Tariff Act. It likewise provides a basis for recording registered trademarks with the Customs Service, and it is administered under the same rules of Title 19 of the Code of Federal Regulations as Section 526. The Customs Service has treated parallel imports of trademarked goods in the same manner under both statutes.

---

## *Lever Brothers v. United States*

981 F.2d 1330 (D.C. Cir. 1993)

Opinion for the Court filed by Circuit Judge SENTELLE.

The District Court entered a judgment invalidating the "affiliate exception" of 19 C.F.R. §133.21(c)(2) (1988) as inconsistent with the statutory mandate of the Lanham Act of 1946, 15 U.S.C. §1124 (1988), prohibiting importation of goods which copy or simulate the mark of a domestic manufacturer, and issued a nationwide injunction barring enforcement of the regulation with respect to any foreign goods bearing a valid United States trademark but materially and physically differing from the United States version of the goods. The United States appeals. We conclude that the District Court, obedient to our limited remand in a prior decision in this same cause, properly determined that the regulation is inconsistent with the statute. However, because we conclude that the remedy the District Court provided is overbroad, we vacate the judgment and remand for entry of an injunction against allowing the importation of the foreign-produced Lever Brothers brand products at issue in this case.

### I. BACKGROUND

Lever Brothers Company ("Lever US" or "Lever"), an American company, and its British affiliate, Lever Brothers Limited ("Lever UK"), both manufacture deodorant soap under the "Shield" trademark and hand dishwashing liquid under the "Sunlight" trademark. The trademarks are registered in each country. The products have evidently been formulated differently to suit local tastes and circumstances. The U.S. version lathers more, the soaps smell different, the colorants used in American "Shield" have been certified by the FDA whereas the colorants in British "Shield" have not, and the U.S. version contains a bacteriostat that enhances the deodorant properties of the soap. The British version of "Sunlight" dishwashing soap produces less suds, and the American version is formulated to work best in the "soft water" available in most American cities, whereas the British version is designed for "hard water" common in Britain.

The packaging of the U.S. and U.K. products is also somewhat different. The British "Shield" logo is written in script form and is packaged in foil wrapping and contains a wave motif, whereas the American "Shield" logo is written in block form, does not come in foil wrapping and contains a grid pattern. There is small print on the packages indicating where they were manufactured. The British "Sunlight" comes in a cylindrical bottle labeled "Sunlight

Washing Up Liquid." The American "Sunlight" comes in a yellow, hourglass-shaped bottle labeled "Sunlight Dishwashing Liquid."

Lever asserts that the unauthorized influx of these foreign products has created substantial consumer confusion and deception in the United States about the nature and origin of this merchandise, and that it has received numerous consumer complaints from American consumers who unknowingly bought the British products and were disappointed.

Lever argues that the importation of the British products was in violation of section 42 of the Lanham Act, 15 U.S.C. §1124 which provides that with the exception of goods imported for personal use:

> No article of imported merchandise which shall copy or simulate the name of the [sic] any domestic manufacture, or manufacturer . . . or which shall copy or simulate a trademark registered in accordance with the provisions of this chapter . . . shall be admitted to entry at any customhouse of the United States.

*Id.* The United States Customs Service ("Customs"), however, was allowing importation of the British goods under the "affiliate exception" created by 19 C.F.R. §133.21(c)(2), which provides that foreign goods bearing United States trademarks are not forbidden when "the foreign and domestic trademark or tradename owners are parent and subsidiary companies or are otherwise subject to common ownership or control."

In *Lever I*, we concluded that "the natural, virtually inevitable reading of section 42 is that it bars foreign goods bearing a trademark identical to the valid U.S. trademark but physically different," without regard to affiliation between the producing firms or the genuine character of the trademark abroad. . . .[4]

## II. Analysis . . .

Here the specific question at Step Two of *Chevron* is whether the intended prohibition of section 42 admits of an exception for materially different goods manufactured by foreign affiliates. . . . When we remanded this case, we indicated that the Government could not prevail unless it produced "persuasive evidence" rebutting our tentative reading of the statute, *Lever I*, 877 F.2d at 111, because the affiliate exception appears to contradict the clear implication of the language of section 42. The legislative history and administrative practice before us, as before the District Court, will not perform that onerous task.

### A. Legislative History And Administrative Practice Prior to Enactment Of Lanham Act . . .

The Supreme Court interpreted section 27 more broadly. In *A. Bourjois & Co. v. Katzel*, 260 U.S. 689, 67 L. Ed. 464, 43 S. Ct. 244 (1923), the Court held that a third party could not import a face powder manufactured in France when the plaintiff owned the United States trademarks for the product, even though the product sold was "the genuine product of the French concern. . . ." *Id.* at 691. The Supreme Court concluded that even an authentic foreign trademark on "genuine" merchandise may infringe a registered United States trademark. In another case that year involving the same Bourjois company, the Supreme Court held in a per curiam memorandum that third-party importation of goods bearing an authentic identical foreign trademark infringed the United States trademark owner's rights under section 27 and must be excluded from entry by Customs. *A. Bourjois & Co. v. Aldridge*, 263 U.S. 675,

4. In *Lever I*, we expressly recognized that our decision was not in conflict with the Supreme Court's decision in *K mart Corp. v. Cartier Inc.*, 486 U.S. 281, 100 L. Ed. 2d 313, 108 S. Ct. 1811 (1988), which upheld the affiliate exception against a challenge based on section 526 of the Tariff Act of 1930, 19 U.S.C. §1526 (1988), but "did not reach the question of the exception's validity under section 42 of the Lanham Act." *Lever I*, 877 F.2d at 108 & n.8.

68 L. Ed. 501, 44 S. Ct. 4 (1923) (answering questions certified to it by the Second Circuit at 292 F. 1013 (2d Cir. 1922)).

Until 1936, the regulations implementing section 27 quoted the statute, then provided for an absolute ban on imports bearing trademarks that copied or simulated United States marks. . . .

Section 518(b) of the 1936 regulations also included a "same person" exception, the first precursor of the affiliate exception:

> However, merchandise manufactured or sold in a foreign country under a trade-mark or trade name, which trade-mark is registered and recorded, shall not be deemed for the purpose of these regulations to copy or simulate such United States trade-mark or trade name if such foreign trade-mark or trade name and such United States trade-mark or trade name are owned by the same person, partnership, association, or corporation.

*Id.* The regulation did not explain the source of this exception, and there is no evidence that Customs considered the issue of physically different imports.

Several conclusions can be drawn from the pre-Lanham Act legislative history and administrative practice. First, at least until 1936, protection from unauthorized importation was consistently based upon ownership of a United States trademark, not upon the nature of the relationship between the trademark owner and the foreign producer. Second, as trademark law became more international, the trend was toward greater protection from foreign importation. Third, although the 1936 regulations implemented the first version of the affiliate exception, the specific question of materially different goods is nowhere addressed. . . .

### C. Legislative History and Developments Since Passage of Lanham Act

The Treasury Department's administrative practice after passage of the Lanham Act has been inconsistent. . . .

After Congress repeatedly considered and failed to enact the affiliate exception, the Treasury Department revived the exception. In 1972 the affiliate exception was adopted in the form at issue here. *See* 37 FR 20677 (1972). Under the 1972 regulations, section 42's protections were rendered inapplicable where:

> (1) Both the foreign and the U.S. trademark or trade name are owned by the same person or business entity;
>
> (2) The foreign and domestic trademark or trade name owners are parent and subsidiary companies or are otherwise subject to common ownership or control;
>
> (3) The articles of foreign manufacture bear a recorded trademark or trade name applied under authorization of the U.S. owner.

19 C.F.R. §133.21(c) (citations omitted).[5]

Neither the notice proposing the regulations, 35 FR 19269 (1970), nor the final notice adopting them, Treas. Dec. Int. Rev. 72-266, 6 Cust. B. & Dec. 538 (1972), explained their rationale. The statement accompanying the final rule contained no response to objections raised by several companies and associations. . . .

---

5. In *K mart Corp. v. Cartier, Inc.*, 486 U.S. 281, 100 L. Ed. 2d 313, 108 S. Ct. 1811 (1988), the Supreme Court struck down 19 C.F.R. §133.21(c)(3), which allowed the importation of foreign-made goods where the United States trademark owner has authorized the use of the mark, as in conflict with the unequivocal language of section 526 of the Tariff Act. Section 526 prohibits the importation of "any merchandise of foreign manufacture" bearing a trademark "owned by" a citizen of, or by a "corporation . . . organized within, the United States" unless written consent of the trademark owner is produced at the time of entry. 19 U.S.C. §1526. By a different majority, the Supreme Court upheld 19 C.F.R. §133.21(c)(2), the regulation at issue here, as consistent with section 526. As we noted above, the *K mart* case did not address the validity of these regulations under the Lanham Act. *See supra* note 4.

Customs' main argument from the legislative history is that section 42 of the Lanham Act applies only to imports of goods bearing trademarks that "copy or simulate" a registered mark. Customs thus draws a distinction between "genuine" marks and marks that "copy or simulate." A mark applied by a foreign firm subject to ownership and control common to that of the domestic trademark owner is by definition "genuine." Customs urges, regardless of whether or not the goods are identical. Thus, any importation of goods manufactured by an affiliate of a U.S. trademark owner cannot "copy or simulate" a registered mark because those goods are ipso facto "genuine."

This argument is fatally flawed. It rests on the false premise that foreign trademarks applied to foreign goods are "genuine" in the United States. Trademarks applied to physically different foreign goods are not genuine from the viewpoint of the American consumer. As we stated in *Lever I*:

> On its face . . . section [42] appears to aim at deceit and consumer confusion; when identical trademarks have acquired different meanings in different countries, one who imports the foreign version to sell it under that trademark will (in the absence of some specially differentiating feature) cause the confusion Congress sought to avoid. The fact of affiliation between the producers in no way reduces the probability of that confusion; it is certainly not a constructive consent to importation.

877 F.2d at 111.

There is a larger, more fundamental and ultimately fatal weakness in Customs' position in this case. Section 42 on its face appears to forbid importation of goods that "copy or simulate" a United States trademark. Customs has the burden of adducing evidence from the legislative history of section 42 and its administrative practice of an exception for materially different goods whose similar foreign and domestic trademarks are owned by affiliated companies. At a minimum, this requires that the specific question be addressed in the legislative history and administrative practice. The bottom line, however, is that the issue of materially different goods was not addressed either in the legislative history or the administrative record. It is not enough to posit that silence implies authorization, when the authorization sought runs counter to the evident meaning of the governing statute. Therefore, we conclude that section 42 of the Lanham Act precludes the application of Customs' affiliate exception with respect to physically, materially different goods. . . .

### IV. Conclusion

For the foregoing reasons, we affirm the District Court's ruling that section 42 of the Lanham Act, 15 U.S.C. §1124, bars the importation of physically different foreign goods bearing a trademark identical to a valid U.S. trademark, regardless of the trademark's genuine character abroad or affiliation between the producing firms. Injunctive relief, however, is limited to the two products which were the subject of this action. We therefore vacate the District Court's prior order to the extent that it renders global relief and remand for the entry of an injunction consistent with this opinion. . . .

## NOTES AND QUESTIONS

**1.** In *Lever Brothers*, the Court of Appeals holds that the common control doctrine adopted by the Supreme Court in *K mart* does not apply when there is a material physical difference between goods imported from an affiliated entity abroad and goods marketed domestically. The court says that *K mart* does not control the outcome of this case because the

Supreme Court expressly refrained from addressing the Lanham Act in *K mart* (*see* footnote 4 of opinion, *supra*).

**2.** In *Lever Brothers*, the U.S. trademark holder has sued the U.S. government, and not the importer. Why?

**3.** In reaction to the decision in *Lever Brothers*, the Treasury Department (and now Customs and Border Protection) adopted a rule permitting parallel importers to avoid application of the "Lever Rule" by labeling the goods as "materially different". Here is the relevant provision from the Code of Federal Regulations (CFR):

> "(b) Labeling of physically and materially different goods. Goods determined by the Customs Service to be physically and materially different under the procedures of this part, bearing a genuine mark applied under the authority of the U.S. owner, a parent or subsidiary of the U.S. owner, or a party otherwise subject to common ownership or control with the U.S. owner (see §§ 133.2(d) and 133.12(d) of this part), shall not be detained under the provisions of paragraph (c) of this section where the merchandise or its packaging bears a conspicuous and legible label designed to remain on the product until the first point of sale to a retail consumer in the United States stating that: "This product is not a product authorized by the United States trademark owner for importation and is physically and materially different from the authorized product." The label must be in close proximity to the trademark as it appears in its most prominent location on the article itself or the retail package or container. Other information designed to dispel consumer confusion may also be added." 19 CFR §133.23

Following the District of Colombia Circuit's decision in *Lever II*, the Court of Appeals for the Federal Circuit has permitted the blocking of parallel imports of trademark goods based on "material differences." The CAFC's leading decision on this subject is *Gamut Trading v. ITC*, an excerpt from which follows. Note that more effective labelling may "cure" the problems faced by the parallel importer.

## *Gamut Trading v. U.S. International Trade Commission*

200 F.3d 775 (Fed. Cir. 1999)

NEWMAN, CIRCUIT JUDGE.

This action for violation of §337 of the Tariff Act of 1930, 19 U.S.C. §1337, was initiated at the United States International Trade Commission ("ITC") on the complaint of the Kubota Corporation, a Japanese company ("Kubota-Japan"), owner of the registered United States trademark "Kubota," and its United States affiliated companies Kubota Tractor Corporation ("Kubota-US") and Kubota Manufacturing of America ("KMA"). Kubota-US is the exclusive licensee of the "Kubota" trademark in the United States, by agreement with Kubota-Japan which provides that the United States trademark and associated goodwill remain the exclusive property of Kubota-Japan.

The respondents are Gamut Trading Company and other entities (collectively "Gamut") that import from Japan and resell in the United States various models of used tractors of under 50 horsepower, all manufactured in Japan by the Kubota Corporation, used in Japan, and bearing the mark "Kubota" that had been properly affixed in Japan. Gamut was charged with violation of §337 of the Tariff Act of 1930, 19 U.S.C. §1337, which provides for exclusion of product bearing infringing marks and other remedies, based on asserted infringement of the United States trademark "Kubota":

> 19 U.S.C. §1337 UNFAIR PRACTICES IN IMPORT TRADE
>
> (a)(1)(C) The importation into the United States, the sale for importation, or the sale within the United States after importation by the owner, importer, or consignee, of articles that

infringe a valid and enforceable United States trademark registered under the Trademark Act of 1946.

Describing this case as one of "gray-market goods," the ITC issued a General Exclusion Order against importation of used Japanese tractors bearing the "Kubota" trademark, and Cease and Desist Orders against sale of such tractors that had already been imported into the United States. The principle of gray market law is that the importation of a product that was produced by the owner of the United States trademark or with its consent, but not authorized for sale in the United States, may, in appropriate cases, infringe the United States trademark.

On Gamut's appeal, we now affirm the decision of the ITC.

### Background

Kubota-Japan manufactures in Japan a large number of models of agricultural tractors, for use in Japan and other countries. Various tractor models are custom-designed for a particular use in a particular country. For example, tractor models that are designed for rice paddy farming are constructed for traction and maneuverability under wet, muddy conditions; these tractors have smaller tire separation in order to make tight turns in rice paddies, and are designed to function with rice paddy tillers, which contain narrow, light-weight blades. No corresponding model is designed for export to the United States.

In contrast, some tractor models that are intended to be used in the United States are specially constructed for lifting and transporting earth and rocks, and to function with rear cutters that contain heavy blades capable of cutting rough undergrowth; these models do not have a direct Japanese counterpart. The tractor models intended for sale and use in the United States bear English-language controls and warnings, and have English-language dealers and users manuals. They are imported by Kubota-US and sold through a nationwide dealership network which provides full maintenance and repair service and maintains an inventory of parts for these specific tractor models. Kubota-US conducts training classes for its dealership employees, instructing them on service and maintenance procedures.

Gamut purchases used Kubota tractors in Japan and imports them into the United States. The majority of the imported tractors are described as between 13 and 25 years old. All bear the mark "Kubota." The Kubota companies state that the importation and its extent came to their attention when United States purchasers sought service and repair or maintenance from Kubota-US dealerships.

#### The Gray Market

The term "gray market goods" refers to genuine goods that in this case are of foreign manufacture, bearing a legally affixed foreign trademark that is the same mark as is registered in the United States; gray goods are legally acquired abroad and then imported without the consent of the United States trademark holder. *See K Mart Corp. v. Cartier, Inc.*, 486 U.S. 281, 286-87, 6 U.S.P.Q.2D (BNA) 1897, 1899-1900, 100 L. Ed. 2d 313, 108 S. Ct. 1811 (1987) (discussing various gray-market conditions); 4 McCarthy on Trademark and Unfair Competition §29.46 (4th ed. 1997). The conditions under which gray-market goods have been excluded implement the territorial nature of trademark registration, and reflect a legal recognition of the role of domestic business in establishing and maintaining the reputation and goodwill of a domestic trademark.

Until the Supreme Court's decision in *A. Bourjois & Co. v. Katzel*, 260 U.S. 689, 67 L. Ed. 464, 43 S. Ct. 244 (1923), the prevailing rule in the United States was that the authorized sale of a validly trademarked product, anywhere in the world, exhausted the trademark's exclusionary right; thus the holder of the corresponding registered United States trademark was believed to have no right to bar the importation and sale of authentically marked foreign goods. However, in the *Bourjois* case the Court recognized the territorial boundaries of trademarks, stressing that the reputation and goodwill of the holder of the corresponding United States mark warrants protection against unauthorized importation of goods bearing the same mark, although the mark was validly affixed in the foreign country. In *Bourjois* the foreign-origin goods were produced by an unrelated commercial entity and imported by a third person, although the goods themselves were related in that the United States trademark owner bought its materials from the foreign producer. *See Id.* at 692.

Since the *Bourjois* decision, the regional circuits and the Federal Circuit have drawn a variety of distinctions in applying gray market jurisprudence, primarily in consideration of whether the foreign source of the trademarked goods and the United States trademark holder are related commercial entities and whether the imported goods bearing the foreign mark are the same as (or not materially different from) the goods that are sold under the United States trademark, applying a standard of materiality suitable to considerations of consumer protection and support for the integrity of the trademarks of domestic purveyors, all with due consideration to the territorial nature of registered trademarks in the context of international trade. . . .

### The "Kubota" Importations

The ALJ found that twenty-four models of the "Kubota" Japanese tractors imported by Gamut were materially different from any corresponding tractor imported by Kubota-US, and that one model was substantially the same. . . .

The Commission adopted the ALJ's Initial Decision as to the twenty-four models found to be infringing, and reversed the determination of no infringement by the Kubota L200. The Commission also found infringement by twenty additional tractor models not reviewed by the ALJ. For the Kubota L200 and the twenty additional models, the Commission found that the absence of English-language warning and instructional labels constituted a material difference from the "Kubota" brand tractors sold in the United States by Kubota-US, giving rise to trademark infringement by these unauthorized imports and violation of Section 337.

### The Question of Material Differences

Gamut argues that the ITC erred in finding that there are material differences between their imported tractors and those imported by Kubota-US. Gamut points out that materiality of product differences is determined by the likelihood of confusion of those whose purchasing choice would be affected by knowledge of the differences, *see Nestle*, 982 F.2d at 643, 25 U.S.P.Q.2D (BNA) at 1264, and that its purchasers know that they are purchasing a used Japanese tractor. Gamut states that a purchaser of a used tractor bearing Japanese labels would not be deceived into thinking that he/she is buying a new tractor designed for the United States market. Gamut states that any differences between the imported models and the United States models are readily apparent, and thus can not be a material difference.

The ITC rejected this argument, finding that it is not reasonable to expect that purchasers of used Kubota tractors will be aware of structural differences from the United States models and of the consequences of these differences for purposes of maintenance, service, and parts. This finding was supported by substantial evidence. Indeed, the marking of these tractors with the "Kubota" mark weighs against an inference that purchasers would be expected to be aware of or expect structural differences.

As precedent illustrates, differences that may be readily apparent to consumers may nevertheless be material. In *Nestle* the court found differences in quality, composition, and packaging to be material. In *Martin's Herend* the court found differences in the color, pattern or shape of porcelain figures to be material, although they would be apparent to an observer of the products side-by-side. Differences in labeling and other written materials have been deemed material, on the criteria of likelihood of consumer confusion and concerns for the effect of failed consumer expectations on the trademark holder's reputation and goodwill. *See Original Appalachian Artworks* (Spanish-origin "Cabbage Patch Kids" dolls were materially different because they had Spanish-language instructions and "adoption papers"); *PepsiCo v. Nostalgia Products Corp.*, 1990 U.S. Dist. LEXIS 18990, 18 U.S.P.Q.2D (BNA) 1404, 1405 (N.D. Ill. 1990) (materiality based on Mexican "Pepsi" labels that were in Spanish and did not contain a list of ingredients, along with quality control and marketing differences); *Fender Musical Instruments Corp. v. Unlimited Music Center Inc.*, 1995 U.S. Dist. LEXIS 15746, 35 U.S.P.Q.2D (BNA) 1053, 1056 (D. Conn. 1995) (material difference for guitars with Japanese language owner's manuals); *Osawa & Co. v. B&H Photo*, 589 F. Supp. 1163, 1169, 223 U.S.P.Q. (BNA) 124, 127 (S.D.N.Y. 1984) (material difference for camera equipment with foreign language instruction manuals); *Ferrero U.S.A, Inc. v. Ozak Trading Inc.*, 753 F. Supp. 1240, 1243-44, 18 U.S.P.Q.2D (BNA) 1052, 1055 (D.N.J. 1991) (material differences in the print and content of labels on "Tic-Tac" mints).

The Commission found that the imported used "Kubota" tractors lacked English instructional and warning labels, operator manuals, and service manuals. Labels are attached at various places on the tractor to instruct the user on the proper operation of the tractor and to warn of potential hazards, and include instructions on the direction of the engine speed hand throttle, the function of the transmission, the four-wheel drive, the power take-off speed, hydraulic power lift, and other controls on the tractor. The Commission found that such labels are necessary to safe and effective operation. The authorized "Kubota" tractors bear these labels in English; the permanent labels on the used imported tractors are in Japanese.

While it would be obvious to the purchaser that the warning and instructional labels are in Japanese, there was evidence before the ITC of consumer belief that the used tractors were sponsored by or otherwise associated with the Kubota-US distributorship/service system. . . .

The Kubota companies are not required to arrange to provide service to Gamut's imports in order to ratify these importations by mitigating their injury to the goodwill associated with the "Kubota" trademark. Whether or not the Kubota companies could arrange to service these tractors does not convert an otherwise infringing activity into an authorized importation. *See Osawa*, 589 F. Supp. at 1167-68, 223 U.S.P.Q. (BNA) at 126-27 (trademark holder incurred damage from the unauthorized importation of gray market cameras because it voluntarily bore the warranty expenses for servicing them).

In addition to the differences in labeling, service, and parts, the ALJ found that many of the tractors designed by Kubota for use in the United States are stronger structurally than the corresponding tractors made for use in Japan. For example, the ALJ found that some of the intended United States tractors were made with stronger front and rear axles, front axle brackets, chassis, power trail, and parts contained in the transmission, such as gears. The ALJ found that the stronger gears increase load-bearing capacity and bending strength, thereby reducing wear and tear. The ALJ found that some of the tractor models designed for the United States market have a stronger power take-off shaft, installed to accommodate the heavy load placed on the shaft by implements often used in the United States such as a rear cutter. The ALJ heard evidence that these structural differences significantly increase the likelihood of breakdowns of the less strong Japanese models. Although Gamut points to the absence of evidence of actual breakdown, the conceded or established differences in structural strength are relevant to the finding of material differences, and were properly considered by the Commission, along with the evidence concerning labelling, warnings, service, and parts.

Gamut raises the additional argument that in all events the Commission erred in law by applying the material differences test with the low threshold of precedent, because the imported tractors are not new but used. . . .

Substantial evidence supports the Commission's finding that consumers would consider the differences between the used imported tractors and the authorized Kubota-US tractors to be important to their purchasing decision, and thus material.

### Effect of the Fact that the Goods are Used

Gamut argues that this is not a "gray market" case because the imported tractors are simply durable used goods, rendering it irrelevant whether the trademark owner authorized their sale in the United States. Gamut also argues that imported goods must be sold in competition with the goods of the owner of the United States trademark in order for authentic foreign-marked goods to infringe any trademark rights, citing *K Mart v. Cartier*, 486 U.S. at 286, 6 U.S.P.Q.2D (BNA) at 1899-00. Gamut asserts that because Kubota-US sells new tractors in the United States and the respondents sell only used tractors, the goods are not in direct competition and the imported used tractors can not be held to be infringing gray market goods.

Direct competition between substantially identical goods is a factor to be considered, but it is not a prerequisite to trademark infringement. In *Safety-Kleen Corp. v. Dresser Indus.*, 518 F.2d 1399, 1404, 186 U.S.P.Q. (BNA) 476, 480 (CCPA 1975) the court explained that "While the similarity or dissimilarity of the goods or service should, in appropriate cases, be considered in determining likelihood of confusion . . . the law has long protected the legitimate interests of trademark owners from confusion among noncompetitive, but related, products bearing confusingly similar marks." Similar reasoning applies to products of the gray market.

As we have discussed, trademark law as applied to gray market goods embodies a composite of likelihood of consumer confusion as to the source of the goods, likelihood of consumer confusion arising from differences between the foreign and the domestic goods, impositions on the goodwill and burdens on the integrity of the United States trademark owner due to consumer response to any differences, and recognition of the territorial scope of national trademarks. Various of these factors acquire more or less weight depending on the particular situation. Although it is relevant to consider whether the imported product is new or used, other factors that may affect the reputation and the goodwill enuring to the holder of a trademark are not overridden by the fact that the product is known to be second-hand.

Courts that have considered the question and concluded that used goods can be gray market goods include [citations omitted]. . . .

The ALJ found that Kubota-US has established a reputation for safety, reliability, and service that consumers associate with the "Kubota" mark, and that the used tractors bearing the "Kubota" mark undermine the investment that Kubota-US made in consumer goodwill for "Kubota" products. These findings are supported by substantial evidence. The fact that the imported tractors are used does not prevent a finding of infringement of the United States "Kubota" trademark.

### Goodwill of the United States Trademark

Gamut points out that according to the trademark license agreement, Kubota-Japan owns the "Kubota" trademark in the United States and associated goodwill. Gamut argues that there can be no infringement of the United States trademark unless Kubota-Japan, as the trademark owner, demonstrates that it "has developed domestic goodwill, that is, independent of the goodwill associated with the mark world wide." The goodwill of a trademark is developed by use of the mark. The ALJ found that Kubota-US, through its large network of authorized dealers in "Kubota"-brand products, had established a reputation for product quality and service throughout the United States, establishing use of the mark accompanied by goodwill. This goodwill enures to the benefit of the trademark owner. Gamut's challenge to the standing of the complainants is not well founded.

**Remedy**

The ALJ recommended imposition of a general exclusion order as to the infringing tractor models, barring their importation and sale unless the tractors bore a permanent, non-removable label alerting the consumer to the origin of the used tractors and containing other information deemed necessary to mitigate consumer confusion. The ALJ also recommended that cease and desist orders be issued to bar the respondents from selling infringing used tractors already imported unless the tractors were appropriately labeled. The Commission, on giving full review to the ALJ's Initial Decision, including various modifications thereof, affirmed the ALJ's ruling that the vinyl decal label that was proposed by Gamut would not eliminate the likelihood of consumer confusion because of the high likelihood that the labels would be removed after importation and prior to sale. . . .

The Commission has broad discretion in selecting the form, scope and extent of the remedy in a Section 337 proceeding. . . .

An exclusion order is the Commission's statutory remedy for trademark infringement. 19 U.S.C. §1337(d). In addition, the Commission may issue cease and desist orders when it has personal jurisdiction over the party against whom the order is directed. 19 U.S.C. §1337(f). . . .

Accordingly, the Commission's decision is
AFFIRMED.

## NOTES AND QUESTIONS

**1.** In *SKF USA v. International Trade Commission*, 423 F.3d 1307 (Fed. Cir. 2005), the CAFC extended its holding in the *Gamut Trading* decision to differences in after-sales service and support accompanying a product, finding that such differences may be "material" and justify the blocking of parallel imports. However, in that case, the CAFC also said that "all or substantially all" of the trademark goods as to which protection against imports is sought must be accompanied by the relevant service and support. If the trademark owner sold goods both with and without service and support, it would be introducing confusion in the marketplace, and it could not then assert a claim based on consumer confusion against the parallel importer.

**2.** Both the *Gamut Trading* and *SKF USA* decisions arise under Section 337 of the Tariff Act of 1930, a provision that permits actions to prevent importation of goods that infringe U.S.-registered intellectual property. We will examine Section 337 in Chapter 6 on enforcement.

**3.** How are trademark holders likely to react to decisions such as *Gamut Trading* and *SKF USA*? Might they introduce low-cost product differences—such as instruction manuals or warning labels in different languages—to meet the CAFC's low material differences threshold? Is the CAFC attempting to provide a bypass around the *K mart* decision?

**4.** Some courts have held that unauthorized actions which modify the parallel imported goods or their containers in a way that deprives the trademark owner of the means to control quality can constitute trademark infringement. *See, e.g., Davidoff & Cie SA v. PLD International Corp.*, 56 U.S.P.Q.2d 1753, 2000 WL 1901542 (S.D. Fla. 2000), *aff'd*, 263 F.3d 1297, 60 U.S.P.Q.2d 1046 (11th Cir. 2001).

Circuit courts have been expanding application of the "material differences" rule to non-gray goods cases. *See, e.g., Dan-Foam A/S v. Brand Named Beds, LLC*, 500 F. Supp. 2d 296, 308-09 (S.D.N.Y. 2007) ("Much of the body of trademark law that has developed around 'gray goods' cases can be applied by analogy to sales by unauthorized United States retailers of goods bearing genuine trademarks that have been created by a trademark owner for the United States market.").

**5.** The USMCA incorporates criminal penalties for trademark infringement that raise potential concerns regarding legitimate parallel trade. In particular, Article 20.J.7(3) provides:

> "3. Each Party shall provide for criminal procedures and penalties to be applied in cases of willful importation102 and domestic use, in the course of trade and on a commercial scale, of a label or packaging:
>
> (a) to which a trademark has been applied without authorization that is identical to, or cannot be distinguished from a trademark registered in its territory; and
>
> (b) that is intended to be used in the course of trade on goods or in relation to services that are identical to goods or services for which that trademark is registered."

Consider the activities of a parallel trader that lawfully purchases a trademarked pharmaceutical product and repackages the product for any one of a number of legitimate reasons, for example to offer a reduced number of tablets or capsules for the consumer, or to add a language on the packaging. Such repackaging is typical for parallel traders in the European Union. Could such packaging and labeling activity be considered criminal under rules required by the USMCA? Given the jurisprudence of the U.S. Court of Appeals for the District of Columbia in *Lever Brothers v. United States, supra,* might the mere act of purchasing abroad and importing a pharmaceutical product including the "original" brand name on the package be considered a criminal offense? While this would seem fundamentally inconsistent with the Supreme Court's holding in *K mart v. Cartier,* recall that the DC Circuit sought to distinguish the various federal statutes under which imports may be blocked, and to limit the reach of the *K mart* holding.

## B. Trademark Exhaustion and the European Union

In its *Ideal Standard* decision, the European Court of Justice describes its "intra-Union" exhaustion doctrine in the field of trademarks.

### *IHT Internationale Heiztechnik GmbH and Another v. Ideal-Standard GmbH and Another*

(Case C-9/93) The Court of Justice of the European Communities [1994] 3 CMLR 857 22 June 1994

Panel: Presiding, Due CJ; Mancini, Moitino De Almeida, Diez De Velasco Ppc; Kakouris, Joliet

Headnote:

Reference from Germany by the Oberlandesgericht (Regional Court of Appeal), Dusseldorf, under Article 177 EC.

Decision: . . .

*The case law on Articles 30* [now renumbered as 34—Eds.] *and 36 trade mark law and parallel imports.*

On the basis of the second sentence of Article 36 of the Treaty the Court has consistently held:

> Inasmuch as it provides an exception to one of the fundamental principles of the Common Market, Article 36 in fact only admits of derogations from the free movement of goods where

such derogations are justified for the purpose of safeguarding rights which constitute the specific subject-matter of this property.

In relation to trade marks, the specific subject-matter of the industrial property is the guarantee that the owner of the trade mark has the exclusive right to use that trade mark, for the purpose of putting products protected by the trade mark into circulation for the first time, and is therefore intended to protect him against competitors wishing to take advantage of the status and reputation of the trade mark by selling products illegally bearing that trade mark.

An obstacle to the free movement of goods may arise out of the existence, within a national legislation concerning industrial and commercial property, of provisions laying down that a trade mark owner's right is not exhausted when the product protected by the trade mark is marketed in another Member State, with the result that the trade mark owner can [oppose] importation of the product into his own Member State when it has been marketed in another Member State.

Such an obstacle is not justified when the product has been put onto the market in a legal manner in the Member State from which it has been imported, by the trade mark owner himself or with his consent, so that there can be no question of abuse or infringement of the trade mark.

In fact, if a trade mark owner could prevent the import of protected products marketed by him or with his consent in another Member State, he would be able to partition off national markets and thereby restrict trade between Member States, in a situation where no such restriction was necessary to guarantee the essence of the exclusive right flowing from the trade mark (*see* Case 16/74, *CENTRAFARM v WINTHROP*).

So, application of a national law which would give the trade mark owner in the importing State the right to oppose the marketing of products which have been put into circulation in the exporting State by him or with his consent is precluded as contrary to Articles 30 and 36. This principle, known as the exhaustion of rights, applies where the owner of the trade mark in the importing State and the owner of the trade mark in the exporting State are the same or where, even if they are separate persons, they are economically linked. A number of situations are covered: products put into circulation by the same undertaking, by a licensee, by a parent company, by a subsidiary of the same group, or by an exclusive distributor.

There are numerous instances in national case law and Community case law where the trade mark had been assigned to a subsidiary or to an exclusive distributor in order to enable those undertakings to protect their national markets against parallel imports by taking advantage of restrictive approaches to the exhaustion of rights in the national laws of some States.

Articles 30 and 36 defeat such manipulation of trade marks rights since they preclude national laws which enable the holder of the right to oppose imports.

## NOTES AND QUESTIONS

**1.** Article 34 of the TFEU (formerly Article 30) provides:[18]

> Quantitative restrictions on imports and all measures having equivalent effect shall be prohibited between Member States.

18. In connection with adopting of the Amsterdam Treaty on European Union in 1997, the European Union renumbered the EC Treaty. In an apparent effort to maximize confusion for judges and lawyers, the provision of the EC Treaty that formerly allowed certain restrictions on trade (Article 36), was renumbered as the Article that formerly prohibited restrictions on trade (Article 30). The renumbering, interestingly enough, was purportedly undertaken to make the EC legal system less confusing for the ordinary citizen of the Union.

Article 36 of the TFEU provides:

> The provisions of Articles 34 and 35 shall not preclude prohibitions or restrictions on imports, exports or goods in transit justified on grounds of public morality, public policy or public security; the protection of health and life of humans, animals or plants; the protection of national treasures possessing artistic, historic or archaeological value; or the protection of industrial and commercial property. Such prohibitions or restrictions shall not, however, constitute a means of arbitrary discrimination or a disguised restriction on trade between Member States.

One of the principal objectives of the European Economic Community (established in 1958) was to eliminate tariffs and quotas that inhibited trade between its member states. Shortly after the Community came into being, the CJEU perceived that the free movement of goods and services might be substantially impaired by forms of regulation more subtle than tariffs and quotas, such as through the adoption of national regulatory schemes that directly or indirectly discriminated against outsiders. The TFEU did not specifically address each more subtle form of discrimination, so the Court began to fashion a jurisprudence based on Article 34 that characterized these other forms of discriminatory regulation as measures with the "equivalent effect" of quotas. There is today an extensive body of CJEU case law interpreting and applying Article 34, and considering its relationship to Article 36.

**2.** The main issue in the *IHT v. Ideal Standard* case was whether the holder of the "Ideal Standard" trademark in Germany—which holder was entirely separate from the holder of the same mark in France (due to a series of corporate divestitures and assignments)—could block import from France of goods labeled with the trademark (applied by the separate holder in France). The CJEU said that the absence of an economic link between the trademark holders prevented the German enterprise from exercising control over the quality of the goods made in France. On these grounds, the German enterprise was entitled to block the imports.

**3.** Another interesting problem was that the products made by the French enterprise differed from those made by the German enterprise. The trademark holder in Germany was using the mark to block imports of different goods. French law would not have permitted the trademark holder in France to prevent the use of its mark on the different goods, but German law allowed such prevention as to different goods (assuming there would be some consumer confusion). The CJEU observed that the First Trade Marks Directive did not harmonize the rules concerning likelihood of confusion, and that the issue of confusion was a matter to be assessed under German law.

**4.** In *Revlon v. Cripps & Lee, Court of Appeal* (Civil Division), [1980] FSR 85 22, the U.K. Court of Appeals refused to allow a U.S.-based multinational producer to use a trademark registered in the United Kingdom (by one corporate affiliate) to block importation of goods first sold in the United States with the consent of the U.S. parent company. Lord Sydney Templeman, author of the decision in that case, was subsequently appointed to the British Supreme Court.[19] He said:

> The plaintiffs complain that their sales of Revlon Flex products in the United Kingdom will suffer if the defendants sell their Revlon Flex products cheaply in this country. The plaintiffs also complain that the reputation which they have acquired in the United Kingdom by selling expensive goods will be damaged if the defendants sell similar goods cheaply. It is apparently common ground that the difference between brands of shampoos and hair conditioners depends not so much on the ingredients as on advertising and price. Assuming for the purposes of this appeal that Revlon products are expensive in the United Kingdom and are bought

19. Lord Templeman is skeptical about the claims of intellectual property right holder groups to benefit society. *See* Lord Sydney Templeman, *Intellectual Property*, 1 J. INT'L ECON. L 603 (1998).

> because they are expensive, this attempt by the plaintiffs to enforce price fixing by the back door is not sustainable. Revlon Inc. chose to obtain financial advantages by disposing of anti-dandruff medicated Revlon Flex products in such manner that the defendants are now able to sell those products cheaply in the United Kingdom. That choice which benefitted Revlon Inc. in the United States may damage Revlon Inc. through its subsidiaries operating in the United Kingdom. But in my judgment the plaintiff companies form part of a multi-national group, and are not entitled by asserting the English law of passing-off to prevent their own goods, put into circulation by their own group, from being exported from the United States and sold in the United Kingdom at prices determined by the importers. . . .
>
> In my judgment where a parent company chooses to manufacture and sell wholly or partly through a group of subsidiary companies in different parts of the world, products which bear the same trade mark and attract an international reputation, neither the parent nor any subsidiary can complain in the United Kingdom if those products are used, sold and re-sold under that trade mark.

Since this decision was rendered before the European Union adopted common legislation in the field of trademarks and the CJEU deprived the individual member states of the right to establish their own policies on the subject of international exhaustion.[20] Although the CJEU recognizes a rule of regional or intra-Union exhaustion among the EU member states, it has rejected international exhaustion. Though the ruling in *Revlon* has thus been superseded by later developments, it remains a classic articulation of the policies underlying international exhaustion. We may further ask whether the UK's withdrawal from the EU might cause a rethink of British rules on parallel importation? Might international exhaustion facilitate imports from the EU? Otherwise, might Brexit "partition" the UK and the EU from an IP enforcement standpoint?

**5.** Later in this chapter, we examine the European Union Trade Mark Regulation (EUTMR), which establishes a unitary mark (EUTM) valid throughout the European Union. The provision in the EUTMR regarding exhaustion provides:

> ARTICLE 15
>
> Exhaustion of the rights conferred by an EU trade mark
>
> 1. An EU trade mark shall not entitle the proprietor to prohibit its use in relation to goods which have been put on the market in the European Economic Area under that trade mark by the proprietor or with his consent.
>
> 2. Paragraph 1 shall not apply where there exist legitimate reasons for the proprietor to oppose further commercialisation of the goods, especially where the condition of the goods is changed or impaired after they have been put on the market.

Does the express language of the EUTMR tell you whether (or not) putting a product on the market outside the European Union with the consent of the trademark holder exhausts the EUTM?

## IV. TRADEMARK REGISTRATION AT THE MULTILATERAL LEVEL

Although business enterprises may acquire certain legal rights in trademarks under common law rules regarding their use in commerce, the principal mechanism for securing

20. *See Silhouette v. Hartlauer*, Court of Justice of the European Communities, [1998] 2 CMLR 953, *supra* page 102.

legal rights in trademarks is through registration of those marks with national, regional, and international authorities. Historically, businesses have more actively sought international trademark protection than international patent protection. There are a number of reasons for this. First, trademarks are easier to create than patentable inventions. For the most part, trademarks must only be distinct from other marks used on comparable goods or services, whereas patentable inventions must be new, useful, and nonobvious (as well as enabled). There is no requirement that trademarks be associated with innovative products. Trademarks, in short, are easier to come by than patentable inventions. Second, the process of securing patent protection at the international level is time consuming and expensive. Translating documents and appointing local agents generates considerable expense for patent applicants. Although decisions to undertake international trademark registration are not taken lightly, such decisions do not involve financial commitments as significant as those to seek international patent protection. Finally, there is generally a greater risk that trademarks may be misappropriated and misused in foreign countries than patentable inventions. The misappropriation of a patentable invention often requires production of that invention. Such production may be beyond the means of most would-be misappropriators. The misappropriation of a trademark may involve little more than applying a decal or stamp to an existing product — misleading consumers by taking advantage of the reputation of the foreign trademark holder. Trademark registration within each country or region is generally necessary to protect against this simple act of misappropriation.

Trademark protection is less an instrument of national and regional industrial policy than patent protection, and the harmonization of rules on trademark registration has been less controversial than such harmonization regarding patents. Trademark and service mark registrations are generally undertaken in respect to specific classes of goods and services. In 1957, an international agreement was reached on a standard system for classifying goods and services with respect to the registration of marks. The 1957 Nice Agreement Concerning the International Classification for the Purposes of the Registration of Marks provides a common format for designating the classes of goods and services, and is in wide use around the world.

## A. The Trademark Law Treaty and the Singapore Treaty on the Law of Trademarks

In 1994, the Trademark Law Treaty (TLT) was adopted at WIPO. The TLT entered into force in 1996. As of July 2023, it had attracted 54 adherents, among which are Colombia, Japan, Germany, South Korea, Switzerland, and the United States. The TLT establishes a maximum level of information that national authorities may require from trademark applicants — seeking to reduce the burden on applicants from complying with differing requirements. The TLT also provides an exhaustive list of requirements that may be imposed in connection with certain formalities such as changing the names and addresses of trademark registrants. The TLT adopts certain trademark application forms, which, if used by the applicant, must be accepted by the trademark registration office.

In September 2006, a new Singapore Treaty on the Law of Trademarks was adopted by WIPO members. The Singapore Treaty was signed by over 60 countries when it was adopted. The treaty entered into force on March 16, 2009 and as of July 2023, has 54 Contracting Parties. The Singapore Treaty was intended to remedy certain perceived limitations in the TLT. An excerpt from a summary of the treaty prepared by WIPO follows.

## *Summary of the Singapore Treaty on the Law of Trademarks* (2006)*

The objective of the Singapore Treaty is to create a modern and dynamic international framework for the harmonization of administrative trademark registration procedures. Building on the Trademark Law Treaty of 1994 (TLT), the Singapore Treaty has a wider scope of application and addresses more recent developments in the field of communication technologies. The Singapore Treaty is applicable to all types of marks registrable under the law of a given Contracting Party. Contracting Parties are free to choose the means of communication with their offices (including communications in electronic form or by electronic means of transmittal). Relief measures in respect of time limits as well as provisions on the recording of trademark licenses were introduced, and an Assembly of the Contracting Parties established. However, other provisions of the Singapore Treaty (such as the requirements to provide for multiclass applications and registrations and the use of the International ("Nice") Classification) closely follow the TLT. The two treaties are separate, and may be ratified or adhered to independently.

Unlike the TLT, the Singapore Treaty applies generally to all marks that can be registered under the law of a Contracting Party. Most significantly, it is the first international instrument dealing with trademark law to explicitly recognize non-traditional marks. The Treaty is applicable to all types of marks, including non-traditional visible marks, such as holograms, three-dimensional marks, color, position and movement marks, as well as non-visible marks such as sound, olfactory or taste and feel marks. The Regulations Under the Singapore Treaty on the Law of Trademarks provide for the mode of representation of these marks in applications, which may include non-graphic or photographic reproductions.

The Singapore Treaty leaves Contracting Parties the freedom to choose the form and means of transmittal of communications and whether to accept communications on paper, in electronic form or in another form. This has consequences on formal requirements for applications and requests, such as the signature on communications with the office. The Treaty maintains a very important provision of the TLT, namely that the authentication, certification or attestation of any signature on paper communications cannot be required. However, Contracting Parties are free to determine whether and how they wish to implement a system of authentication of electronic communications.

The Treaty provides for relief measures when an applicant or holder has missed a time limit in an action for a procedure before an office. Contracting Parties must make available, at their choice, at least one of the following relief measures: extension of the time limit; continued processing; and reinstatement of rights in so far as the failure to meet the time limit was unintentional or occurred in spite of due care required by the circumstances.

The Singapore Treaty includes provisions on the recording of trademark licenses, and establishes maximum requirements for requests for recordal, amendment or cancellation of the recordal of a license.

The creation of an Assembly of the Contracting Parties introduced a degree of flexibility in defining the details of administrative procedures to be implemented by national trademark offices, where it is anticipated that future developments in trademark registration procedures and practices will warrant amendments to those details. The Assembly is endowed with powers to modify the Regulations and the Model International Forms, where necessary, and can

* International Bureau of WIPO.

also address – at a preliminary level – questions relating to the future development of the Treaty.

Furthermore, the Diplomatic Conference adopted a Resolution Supplementary to the Singapore Treaty on the Law of Trademarks and the Regulations Thereunder, with a view to declaring an understanding by the Contracting Parties on several areas covered by the Treaty, namely: that the Treaty does not impose any obligations on Contracting Parties to (i) register new types of marks, or (ii) implement electronic filing systems or other automation systems. The Resolution also contains special provisions to provide developing and least developed countries with additional technical assistance and technological support to enable them to take full advantage of the provisions of the Treaty. It was recognized that LDCs shall be the primary and main beneficiaries of technical assistance by Contracting Parties. The Assembly monitors and evaluates, at every ordinary session, the progress of the assistance granted. Any dispute arising in relation to the interpretation or application of the Treaty is to be settled amicably through consultation and mediation under the auspices of the Director General of WIPO.

The Singapore Treaty was concluded in 2006 and entered into force in 2009.

The Treaty is open to States members of WIPO and to certain intergovernmental organizations. Instruments of ratification or accession must be deposited with the Director General of WIPO.

## B. The Madrid Agreement and Protocol

The Madrid Agreement Concerning the International Registration of Marks was adopted in 1891—shortly following the Paris and Berne Conventions. This Agreement enables a person who has secured a trademark registration in one contracting state to file an international application for registration with the International Bureau of WIPO. The international application is transmitted to trademark offices of other member countries designated by the applicant, and if there is no objection within an established time period, the international registration becomes effective for the countries designated by such application. Although 55 countries, including many European countries, are party to the Madrid Agreement as of July 2023 and it has been widely used by European trademark holders, the usefulness of the Madrid Agreement was limited because neither the United States nor Japan nor countries of Latin America (with the exception of Cuba) were parties.

In 1989, a Protocol Relating to the Madrid Agreement (Madrid Protocol) was adopted. The Protocol, which entered into force in 1996, is designed to address a number of the perceived defects in the Madrid Agreement. Under the Madrid Protocol, an international application for registration may be filed on the basis of an application in a Madrid Protocol country, dispensing with the requirement that a trademark be registered prior to filing the international application. There is the possibility of a longer time period during which a designated Protocol country may object to protection of the mark in that country. Under the Madrid Agreement, cancellation of the trademark in the initial country of registration within the first five years following international registration results in invalidation of the mark in all Madrid countries. Under the Madrid Protocol, upon a cancellation by the initial country of application, the international trademark holder may transform the mark into national applications based on the original filing date of the international application. Finally, the Protocol allows for the participation of the EU Office for Harmonisation in the Internal Market (OHIM) and use of the Community Trademark as the basis for an international application.

The relationship between the Madrid Agreement and the Madrid Protocol is defined by Article 9*sexies* of the Protocol.

The United States ratified and became party to the Madrid Protocol on November 3, 2003. The European Union and Japan have also joined. As of July 2023, there are 114 parties to the Madrid Protocol.

## *The Madrid Agreement Concerning the International Registration of Marks and the Protocol Relating to that Agreement: Objectives, Main Features, Advantages*[*]

### Introduction

1. The system of international registration of marks is governed by two treaties: the Madrid Agreement Concerning the International Registration of Marks, which dates from 1891, and the Protocol Relating to the Madrid Agreement, which was adopted in 1989, entered into force on December 1, 1995, and came into operation on April 1, 1996. Common Regulations under the Agreement and Protocol also came into force on that date. The system is administered by the International Bureau of WIPO, which maintains the International Register and publishes the WIPO Gazette of International Marks.

2. . . .

3. States party to the Agreement and/or the Protocol and organizations party to the Protocol are referred to collectively as Contracting Parties. A list of the Contracting Parties can be found at http://www.wipo.int. Together, they constitute the Madrid Union, which is a Special Union under Article 19 of the Paris Convention.

4. Every member of the Madrid Union is a member of its Assembly. Among the most important tasks of the Assembly are the adoption of the program and budget of the Union and the adoption and modification of the implementing regulations, including the fixing of fees connected with the use of the Madrid system.

### Objectives

5. The objectives of the system are two-fold. Firstly, it facilitates the obtaining of protection for marks (trademarks and service marks). The registration of a mark in the International Register produces, in the Contracting Parties designated by the applicant, the effects described in paragraph 31, below. Further Contracting Parties may be designated subsequently. Secondly, since an international registration is equivalent to a bundle of national registrations, the subsequent management of that protection is made much easier. There is only one registration to renew, and changes such as a change in ownership or in the name or address of the holder, or a limitation of the list of goods and services, can be recorded in the International Register through a single simple procedural step. On the other hand, if it is desired to transfer the registration for only some of the designated Contracting Parties, or for only some of the goods or services, or to limit the list of goods and services with respect to only some of the designated Contracting Parties, the system is flexible enough to accommodate this.

### Who May Use the Madrid System?

6. An application for international registration (an "international application") may be filed only by a natural person or a legal entity which has a real and effective industrial or commercial establishment in, or is domiciled in, or is a national of, a country which is party to the

[*] WIPO Publication No. 418(E) (2012).

Madrid Agreement or the Madrid Protocol, or who has such an establishment in, or is domiciled in, the territory of an intergovernmental organization which is a party to the Protocol, or is a national of a Member State of such an organization.

7. The Madrid system of international registration cannot be used by a person or legal entity which does not have the necessary connection, through establishment, domicile or nationality, with a member of the Madrid Union. Nor can it be used to protect a mark outside the Madrid Union.

### The International Application

8. A mark may be the subject of an international application only if it has already been registered (or, where the international application is governed exclusively by the Protocol, if registration has been applied for) in the Trademark Office of the Contracting Party with which the applicant has the necessary connection, as described in paragraph 6, above, to be able to file an international application. This Office is referred to as the Office of origin.

9. An international application must be presented to the International Bureau through the Office of origin. An international application which is presented direct to the International Bureau by the applicant will not be considered as such and will be returned to the sender.

10. The international application must contain, inter alia, a reproduction of the mark (which must be identical with that in the basic registration or basic application) and a list of the goods and services for which protection is sought, classified in accordance with the International Classification of Goods and Services (Nice Classification).

11. An international application may claim priority under Article 4 of the Paris Convention, whether from the application with the Office of origin or from a prior application filed with the Office of another country party to the Paris Convention or with the Office of a Member of the World Trade Organization.

12. An international application must designate the Contracting Parties in which the mark is to be protected. Where the Contracting Party whose Office is the Office of origin is a party to the Agreement but not the Protocol, only other States which are also party to the Agreement may be designated. Where the Contracting Party whose Office is the Office of origin is a party to the Protocol but not the Agreement, only other Contracting Parties which are also party to the Protocol may be designated. Where the Contracting Party whose Office is the Office of origin is a party to both the Agreement and the Protocol, any other Contracting Party may be designated.

13. The Contracting Party whose Office is the Office of origin cannot be designated in an international application; nor can it be designated subsequently.

14. The designation of a given Contracting Party is made under that treaty (Agreement or Protocol) which is common to the designated Contracting Party and the Contracting Party whose Office is the Office of origin. Where both Contracting Parties are party to both the Agreement and the Protocol, it is the Protocol which governs the designation.

15. There are therefore three kinds of international application:

> an international application governed exclusively by the Agreement; this means that all the designations are made under the Agreement; an international application governed exclusively by the Protocol; this means that all the designations are made under the Protocol; an international application governed by both the Agreement and the Protocol; this means that some of the designations are made under the Agreement and some under the Protocol.

16. An international application can be filed in any one of the three languages of the Madrid system, namely, English, French or Spanish. The Office of origin may, however, restrict the applicant's choice to only one language, or to two languages, or may permit the applicant to choose between any of the three languages.

17. The international application is subject to the payment of the following fees:

> a basic fee; a complementary fee in respect of each designated Contracting Party for which no individual fee is payable; a supplementary fee in respect of each class of goods and services beyond the third; no supplementary fee is payable however where all the designations are ones in respect of which an individual fee has to be paid.

18. . . .

19. For international applications filed by applicants whose country of origin is a Least Developed Country, in accordance with the list established by the United Nations, the basic fee is reduced to 10% of the prescribed amount.

20. These fees may be paid direct to the International Bureau or, where the Office of origin accepts to collect and forward such fees, through that Office.

21. The Office of origin must certify that the mark is the same as that in the basic registration or basic application, that any indications such as a description of the mark or a claim to color as a distinctive feature of the mark are the same as those contained in the basic registration or basic application, and that the goods and services indicated in the international application are covered by the list of goods and services in the basic registration or basic application.

22. The Office of origin must also certify the date on which it received the request to present the international application. This date is important; provided the application is received by the International Bureau within two months of that date (and provided that certain crucial elements are not missing), it is that date that will be the date of the international registration.

23. The International Bureau checks that the international application complies with the requirements of the Agreement or Protocol and the Common Regulations, including requirements relating to the indication of goods and services and their classification, and that the required fees have been paid. The Office of origin and the applicant are informed of any irregularities; these must be remedied within three months, otherwise the application will be considered abandoned.

24. Where the international application complies with the applicable requirements, the mark is recorded in the International Register and published in the Gazette. The International Bureau then notifies each Contracting Party in which protection has been requested.

### Examination by the Office of a Designated Contracting Party; Refusal of Protection

25. The Office of a designated Contracting Party examines the international registration in exactly the same way as an application filed directly. If grounds for objection are found during the ex officio examination, or if an opposition is filed, the Office has the right to declare that protection cannot be granted to the mark in that Contracting Party.

26. Any provisional refusal must be notified to the International Bureau by the Office of the Contracting Party concerned within the time limit specified in the Agreement or Protocol. This standard time limit is 12 months. A Contracting Party may however declare that, when it is designated under the Protocol, this time limit shall be replaced by 18 months. A Contracting Party that has made this declaration may further declare that a provisional refusal based on an opposition may be notified even after the expiry of this 18-month period.

27. . . .

28. The provisional refusal is recorded in the international Register and published in the Gazette and a copy is transmitted to the holder of the international registration.

29. Any procedure subsequent to the refusal, such as review, appeal or response to an opposition, is carried out directly between the holder and the Office concerned, without any involvement on the part of the International Bureau. However, once all the procedures

before that Office have been completed, the Office must send to the International Bureau a final statement. Depending upon the outcome of the case, such statement will confirm either that protection for the mark has been totally refused (Confirmation of Total Provisional Refusal), or that protection has been partially or totally granted to the mark, as the case may be (Statement of Grant of Protection Following a Provisional Refusal). This statement is recorded in the International Register, published in the Gazette and a copy is transmitted to the holder of the International Registration.

30. Where, before the expiry of the refusal period, all the procedures before an Office have been completed and the Office has found no grounds to refuse protection, the Office shall, as soon as possible, (and before the expiry of the refusal period), send to the International Bureau a statement to the effect that protection is granted to the mark (Statement of Grant of Protection where no Notification of Provisional Refusal has been Communicated). Such statement is recorded in the International Register and published in the Gazette and a copy is transmitted to the holder of the international registration.

### Effects of the International Registration

31. From the date of the international registration (or, in the case of a Contracting Party designated subsequently, from the date of that designation), the protection of the mark in each of the designated Contracting Parties is the same as if the mark had been the subject of an application for registration filed direct with the Office of that Contracting Party. If no provisional refusal is notified to the International Bureau within the relevant time limit, or if any such refusal is subsequently withdrawn, the protection of the mark in each designated Contracting Party is the same as if it had been registered by the Office of that Contracting Party.

32. An international registration is therefore equivalent to a bundle of national registrations. Although it is a single registration, protection may be refused by some of the designated Contracting Parties, or the protection may be limited or renounced with respect to only some of the designated Contracting Parties. Likewise an international registration may be transferred to a new owner with respect to only some of the designated Contracting Parties. An international registration may also be invalidated (for example, for non-use) with respect to one or more of the designated Contracting Parties. Moreover, any action for infringement of an international registration must be brought separately in each of the Contracting Parties concerned.

33. This is in contrast to a unitary regional right such as the Community trademark, which cannot be refused, limited or transferred with effect for only a part of the territory covered by the right, and which may be enforced by a single legal action covering infringement occurring anywhere in that territory.

### Dependence on the Basic Mark

34. For a period of five years from the date of its registration, an international registration remains dependent on the mark registered or applied for in the Office of origin. If, and to the extent that, the basic registration ceases to have effect, whether through cancellation following a decision of the Office of origin or a court, through voluntary cancellation or through non-renewal, within this five-year period, the international registration will no longer be protected. Similarly, where the international registration was based on an application in the Office of origin, it will be canceled if, and to the extent that, that application is refused or withdrawn within the five-year period, or if, and to the extent that, the registration resulting from that application ceases to have effect within that period.

35. The Office of origin is required to notify the International Bureau of facts and decisions concerning such ceasing of effect or refusal and, where appropriate, to request the cancellation (to the extent applicable) of the international registration. The cancellation is published in the Gazette and notified to the designated Contracting Parties.

36. If, within three months of such cancellation, the holder files an application for registration with the Office of a Contracting Party that had been designated under the Protocol, that application will be treated as if it had been filed on the date of the international registration or (as the case may be) the subsequent designation of the Contracting Party concerned. This option is not available in the case of a Contracting Party designated under the Agreement.

37. After the expiry of the period of five years mentioned in paragraph 34, the international registration becomes independent of the basic registration or basic application.

### Replacement of a National or Regional Registration by an International Registration

38. An international registration is deemed to replace a national or regional registration for the same mark and the same goods and services recorded in the name of the same person in a designated Contracting Party. . . .

### Subsequent Designation

39. The effects of an international registration can be extended to a Contracting Party not covered by the international application by filing a subsequent designation. Thus the holder of an international registration can expand the geographical scope of the protection of his mark in line with his business needs. Moreover a subsequent designation may be made in order to extend the protection of the mark to a Contracting Party which was not a party to the Agreement or Protocol at the time of the international application. The principles that determine whether such a designation can be made, and whether it is governed by the Agreement or by the Protocol, are as described in paragraphs 12 and 13, above.

### Changes in the International Register; Cancellation; Licenses

. . .

43. Information concerning such changes, cancellation and licenses is published in the Gazette and notified to the designated Contracting Parties.

44. No change may be made in the mark that is the subject of an international registration, either on renewal or at any other time. Nor may the list of goods and services be changed in a way that would extend the scope of protection.

### Duration of Registration; Renewal

45. An international registration is effective for 10 years. It may be renewed for further periods of 10 years on payment of the prescribed fees. The International Bureau sends a reminder to the holder and to his representative (if any) six months before renewal is due.

46. The international registration may be renewed in respect of all the designated Contracting Parties or in respect of only some of them. It may not however be renewed in respect of only some of the goods and services recorded in the International Register; if therefore the holder wishes, at the time of renewal, to remove some of the goods and services from the international registration, he must separately request cancellation in respect of those goods and services.

## NOTES AND QUESTIONS

**1.** The USPTO Trademark Manual of Examining Procedure (TMEP) includes Chapter 1900 with respect to the Madrid Protocol. It begins by observing:

> The Protocol Relating to the Madrid Agreement Concerning the International Registration of Marks ("Madrid Protocol") is an international treaty that allows a trademark owner to seek registration in any of the countries or intergovernmental organizations that have joined the Madrid Protocol by submitting a single application, called an international application. The international registration system is administered by the International Bureau ("IB") of the World Intellectual Property Organization ("WIPO"), in Geneva, Switzerland.
>
> The Madrid Protocol became effective in the United States on November 2, 2003. The Madrid Protocol Implementation Act of 2002, Pub. L. 107-273, 116 Stat. 1758, 1913-1921 ("MPIA") amended the Trademark Act to provide that:
>
> (1) the owner of a United States application and/or registration may seek protection of its mark in any of the countries or intergovernmental organizations party to the Madrid Protocol by submitting a single international application to the IB through the United States Patent and Trademark Office ("USPTO"); and (2) the holder of an international registration may request an extension of protection of the international registration to the United States. A notice of final rulemaking amending the Trademark Rules of Practice to incorporate the MPIA was published at 68 Fed. Reg. 55748 (Sept. 26, 2003).
>
> The Madrid Protocol, *Regulations Under the Protocol Relating to the Madrid Agreement Concerning the International Registration of Marks* (Regulations Rule(s) or Regs. Rule(s)), *Guide to the International Registration of Marks under the Madrid Agreement and the Madrid Protocol (Guide to International Registration)*, Administrative Instructions for the Application of the Protocol Relating to the MadridAgreement Concerning the International Registration of Marks (Administrative Instructions or Admin.Instrs.) are available on the IB's website, at https://www.wipo.int/madrid/en/. The Regulations are the procedures regarding the administration of the Madrid Protocol, pursuant to Madrid Protocol Article (Article)10(2)(iii).
>
> (TMEP July 2023.)

**2.** Note that the holder of a U.S. trademark seeking protection in the European Union has the option of filing an application under the Madrid Protocol designating the European Union and its EUTM. If the U.S. applicant has a real and effective commercial presence in an EU member state, it may also apply under the Madrid Agreement (assuming it had registered a trademark in a member state). Recall that application under the Madrid Agreement is predicated on an already-registered trademark.

## V. REGIONAL TRADEMARK SYSTEMS

### A. The EU Trademark System

The EU program to create a single market in the field of IPRs perhaps finds its furthest development in the field of trademarks. The two central pieces of Union legislation in this regard are the First Trade Marks Directive and the European Union [formerly Community] Trade Mark Regulation, as amended. These two legislative measures take different, but coordinated, approaches to the subject matter of trademarks. The First Trade Marks Directive was approved by the Council in 1988 and was intended only as a measure of "partial" approximation (or harmonization). The First Council Directive (89/104 EEC) was subsequently amended by the European Parliament and the Council in 2008 (Directive 2008/95 of 22 October 2008 to approximate the law of the member states relating to trademarks) and in 2015 (Directive 2015/2436 of 16 December 2008 to approximate the law of the member states relating to trademarks). In essence, the First Directive prescribed a set of basic trademark norms for the

EU member states, but left discretion to these states regarding the precise way in which these norms would be implemented in national law. Each member state would remain responsible for granting trademark registrations, and the courts of each member state would interpret national law in light of the Directive (subject to referral to the Court of Justice of the European Union (CJEU)). It would be possible for a trademark to be declared valid in the courts of one Union member state and invalid in the courts of another. Subsequent revisions increasingly limited the autonomy of member states as it became necessary in building a competitive internal market to seek stronger coherence not only in substance, but also in procedural requirements relating to national registration of trademarks and to combat counterfeiting in line with international obligations incurred under WTO law. Importantly, it became necessary to bring about better coordination with the Europe-wide system fully operating under EU law.

The initial Trade Mark Regulation, adopted by the Council in 1993, established, in parallel to national trademark systems, a Europe-wide protection based upon trademarks uniformly recognized throughout the Union and in all member states alike. The system gradually evolved and was subject to a major policy review of the overall trademark system initiated by the Council in 2010. The initial Council Regulation 40/94 of 20 December 1993 on the Community trademark was subsequently amended. Council Regulation (EC) 207/2009 of 26 February 2009 was replaced by Regulation 2015/2425 of the European Parliament and Council of 16 December 2015 and further codified and incorporated in Regulation 2017/2001 of 14 June 2017. The regulations amount to a full-fledged trademark code, addressing all pertaining aspects in terms of substance, including rules of conflict, procedures, and judicial protection within a total of 212 provisions. The system is further regulated and refined by regulations of the Commission under delegated powers, Commission Delegated Regulation 2018/625 of 5 March 2018 and Commission Implementing Regulation 2018/625 of 5 March 2018.

It is expected that the reformed EU-wide system of trademark protection will bring about significantly lower costs for trademark renewal (up to 37 percent), eliminate the requirement for graphic representation of a trademark, facilitate international registration, improve the rights of trademark owners to combat counterfeiting and to seize such goods, and further harmonize European and national rules on trademark protection (Michael Hawkins, *EU Trademark Reform: Where We Are, How We Got Here and What it Means for Users*, INTA BULLETIN, Nov. 15, 2015, available at http://www.inta.org/INTABulletin/Pages/EU_TM_Reform_Update_7020.aspx).

Formally framed as an EU regulation, the EUTMR is directly applicable in the law of the member states, and to the extent that matters are dealt with by the regulation, they pertain to the exclusive domain of the Union, and national legislatures (other than court of law) do not have discretion as to how the rules will be implemented. As a corollary, the regulation provides for the grant of a unitary European Union Trade Mark (EUTM) valid throughout the European Union. The EUTM is granted by a central office—the European Union Intellectual Property Office or EUIPO (prior to 2017, the Office for Harmonisation in the Internal Market (OHIM))—located in Alicante, Spain, and is subject to judicial review by the General Court and upon appeal by the Court of Justice of the European Union.

The system for resolving disputes concerning EUTMs is complex. Generally speaking, actions for invalidation or revocation of trademark registration are brought at the EUIPO, while trademark infringement actions and related matters are brought in the national courts of the EU member states that have been designated as "European Union Trade Mark Courts" of first and second instance (Art. 123). The shift of regulatory powers to the European Union is being compensated by decentralized adjudication. Matters pertaining to registration and opposition and thus the review of EUIPO decisions pertain to the General Court and the Court of Justice of the European Union. There is no appeal of national court decisions to Courts of the Union, but procedures are subject to preliminary rulings by the Court of Justice in matters pertaining to the interpretation of the provisions of the regulations (*see, e.g.*, *Ornua Co-operative Limited v. Tindale & Stanton Ltd España SL*, C-93/16, 20 July 2017, discussed below).

The national trademark systems operating under domestic law as partially harmonized by the Trade Mark Directive and the EUTM function side by side. Operators are able to choose among the two systems (and in addition the joint BOIP BENELUX system for protection in the Netherlands, Belgium, and Luxembourg), depending on market penetration, in addition to recourse to the international registration under the Madrid system discussed above.

The reader may take into account that much of the case law relates to the law of the First Directive of 1988 and the initial Trade Marks Regulation of 1993, under which the European Court of Justice produced a number of leading cases. Opinions and Judgment of that time remain of founding importance.

### *1. The Trade Marks Directive, the EU Treaty, and the European Trade Mark*

The following decision by the Court of Justice of the European Union reflects the complex institutional arrangement governing trademarks in the European Union. Here a German enterprise, Hukla, had registered a trademark in Spain. That registration was undertaken further to the rules established by the First Trade Marks Directive. Another European company, Matratzen Concord, subsequently applied for a Community Trade Mark (now European Trade Mark). That application was rejected following Hukla's opposition based on Hukla's preexisting Spanish trademark registration (the judicial proceedings concerning which proceeded all the way to a judgment by the CJEU). Subsequently, Matratzen Concord sought to invalidate Hukla's Spanish trademark before the courts of Spain on grounds that "Matratzen" is a generic term in German for mattress. The term, however, has no meaning in the Spanish language. A Spanish appeals court was uncertain whether the Treaty on the Functioning of the EU (TFEU) — which promotes the free movement of goods between EU member states — precludes granting trademark rights in a term that may be distinctive in Spain, but generic in Germany.

## *Matratzen Concord AG v. Hukla Germany SA*

Judgment of the Court (First Chamber) 9 March 2006

In Case C-421/04,

REFERENCE for a preliminary ruling under Article 234 EC from the Audiencia Provincial de Barcelona (Spain), made by decision of 28 June 2004, received at the Court on 1 October 2004, in the proceedings

Matratzen Concord AG v. Hukla Germany SA

THE COURT (First Chamber), composed of P. Jann, President of the Chamber, N. Colneric, J.N. Cunha Rodrigues, M. Ilešic (Rapporteur) and E. Levits, Judges. . . .

### Judgment

1. The reference for a preliminary ruling concerns the interpretation of Articles 28 EC and 30 EC.

2. This reference was made in the context of proceedings between Matratzen Concord AG (hereinafter "Matratzen Concord") and Hukla Germany SA (hereinafter "Hukla") concerning the validity of a national trade mark.

### Legal Context

3. Pursuant to Article 28 EC [now 34 TFEU—Eds.] "[q]uantitative restrictions on imports and all measures having equivalent effect shall be prohibited between Member States."

4. Article 30 [now 36 TFEU] EC provides:

> The provisions of Articles 28 and 29 [now 34 and 35 TFEU] shall not preclude prohibitions or restrictions on imports, exports or goods in transit justified on grounds of . . . the protection of industrial and commercial property. Such prohibitions or restrictions shall not, however, constitute a means of arbitrary discrimination or a disguised restriction on trade between Member States.

5. First Council Directive 89/104/EEC of 21 December 1988 to approximate the laws of the Member States relating to trade marks (OJ 1989 L 40, p. 1; hereinafter the "Directive") states, in the seventh recital in the preamble, that "attainment of the objectives at which this approximation of laws is aiming requires that the conditions for obtaining and continuing to hold a registered trade mark are, in general, identical in all Member States" and that "the grounds for refusal or invalidity concerning the trade mark itself. . .are to be listed in an exhaustive manner."

6. Article 3 of the Directive lays down the grounds for refusal to register a trade mark or of invalidity of a registered trade mark. In particular, Article 3(1)(b) and (c) provides:

> The following shall not be registered or if registered shall be liable to be declared invalid: . . .
> 4. trade marks which are devoid of any distinctive character;
> (c) trade marks which consist exclusively of signs or indications which may serve, in trade, to designate the kind, quality, quantity, intended purpose, value, geographical origin or the time of production of the goods or of rendering of the service, or other characteristics of the goods or service.

### The Main Action and the Question Referred to the Court

7. Hukla is the owner of the national word mark MATRATZEN, registered in Spain on 1 May 1994 to designate, inter alia, "rest furniture such as beds, sofa-beds, camp beds, cradles, divans, hammocks, bunk beds and carrycots, foldaway furniture, casters for beds and furniture, bedside tables, chairs, armchairs and stools, bed frames, straw mattresses, mattresses and pillows," which come within Class 20 of the Nice Agreement concerning the International Classification of Goods and Services for the Purposes of the Registration of Marks of 15 June 1957, as revised and amended.

8. On 10 October 1996 Matratzen Concord filed with the Office for Harmonisation in the Internal Market (Trade Marks and Designs) (OHIM) an application for registration of a composite word and figurative mark including the term "Matratzen," for various products coming within Classes 10, 20 and 24 of the Nice Agreement.

9. Hukla having filed a notice of opposition based on the earlier Spanish mark MATRATZEN, the said application was rejected by a decision of the Second Board of Appeal of OHIM of 31 October 2000. The action brought by Matratzen Concord against this

decision was rejected by the judgment of the Court of First Instance of 23 October 2002 in Case T-6/01 *Matratzen Concord* v *OHIM—Hukla Germany (Matratzen)* [2002] ECR II-4335), confirmed on appeal by the order of the Court of Justice of 28 April 2004 in Case C-3/03 P *Matratzen Concord* v *OHIM* [2004] ECR I-3657.

10. In parallel with the opposition procedure before the OHIM bodies and then the Community Courts, Matratzen Concord brought an action for cancellation of the national trade mark MATRATZEN before the Juzgado de Primera Instancia No 22 (Court of First Instance), Barcelona (Spain), on the basis of Article 11(1)(a), (e) and (f) of Ley 32/1988 de 10 de noviembre Marcas, BOE No 272 of 12 November 1988 (Law No 32/1988 of 10 November 1988 on trade marks). It submitted, in substance, that, given that the word "Matratzen" means "mattress" in German, the word of which the trade mark in question consists was generic and could mislead consumers regarding the nature, quality, characteristics or geographical origin of the products bearing the said mark.

11. Its action having been rejected by judgment of 5 February 2002, Matratzen Concord appealed to the Audiencia Provincial de Barcelona (Provincial Court of Barcelona).

12. That court states that the essential function of a trade mark is to enable the commercial origin of the goods and services bearing it to be identified and that, to that effect, Spanish case-law considers names borrowed from foreign languages to be arbitrary, capricious and fanciful, unless they resemble a Spanish word, making it reasonable to assume that the average consumer will be familiar with their meaning, or they have acquired a genuine meaning on the national market.

13. The Audiencia Provincial de Barcelona is nevertheless uncertain as to whether that interpretation is compatible with the concept of the "single market." It considers that generic words from the languages of the Member States must remain available to be used by any undertaking established in these States. Their registration as a trade mark in a Member State would facilitate monopolistic situations, which should be avoided in order to allow normal market forces to prevail, and could be considered an infringement of the prohibition on quantitative restrictions on imports as between the Member States, laid down in Article 28 EC.

14. The referring court considers that, in the pending case before it, the Spanish trade mark MATRATZEN puts its holder in a position to limit or restrict the import of mattresses from German-speaking Member States and, therefore, to prevent the free movement of goods.

15. That court is, uncertain however, as to whether such limitations or restrictions are capable of justification on the basis of Article 30 EC. In this respect, it points out that, in Case 192/73 *Van Zuylen* [1974] ECR 731, the Court affirmed the pre-eminence of the principle of the free movement of goods over the national protection of industrial property rights and stated that the reverse would lead to an undesirable partitioning of the markets, prejudicial to the free movement of goods and giving rise to disguised restrictions on trade between Member States.

16. Taking the view that the outcome of the dispute pending before it required an interpretation of Article 30 EC, the Audiencia Provincial de Barcelona decided to stay the proceedings and to refer the following question to the Court of Justice for a preliminary ruling:

> Can the validity of the registration of a trade mark in a Member State, when that trade mark is devoid of any distinctive character or serves, in trade, to designate the product which it covers or its kind, quality, quantity, intended purpose, value, geographical origin or other characteristics of goods, in the language of another Member State when that language is not spoken in the first Member State, as may be the case so far as concerns use of the Spanish trade mark "MATRATZEN," to designate mattresses and related products, constitute a disguised restriction on trade between Member States.

## The Question Referred

17. By its question, the referring court asks, in substance, whether Articles 28 EC and 30 EC must be interpreted as meaning that they preclude the registration in a Member State, as a national trade mark, of a term borrowed from the language of another Member State in which it is devoid of distinctive character or descriptive of the goods or services in respect of which registration is sought.

18. As a preliminary point, it should be noted that, in the context of the procedure established by Article 234 EC providing for cooperation between national courts and the Court of Justice, it is for the latter to provide the national court with an answer which will be of use to it and enable it to determine the case before it. To that end, the Court may find it necessary to consider provisions of Community law to which the national court has not referred in its question (*see*, in particular, Case C-230/98 *Schiavon* [2000] ECR I-3547, paragraph 37, and Case C-469/00 *Ravil* [2003] ECR I-5053, paragraph 27).

19. As is clear from the seventh recital in the preamble, the Directive lists in an exhaustive manner the grounds for refusal or invalidity of registration concerning the trade mark itself.

20. According to settled case-law, in a field which has been exhaustively harmonised at Community level, a national measure must be assessed in the light of the provisions of that harmonising measure and not of those of primary law (*see*, in particular, Case C-352/95 *Phytheron International* [1997] ECR I-1729, paragraph 17; Case C-324/99 *DaimlerChrysler* [2001] ECR I-9897, paragraph 32; and Case C-210/03 *Swedish Match* [2004] ECR I-11893, paragraph 81).

21. Consequently, it is the Directive, and in particular Article 3 thereof, on the absolute grounds for refusal or invalidity of registration, and not Articles 28 EC and 30 EC, which must be assessed to determine whether Community law precludes the registration of a national trade mark such as that at issue in the main proceedings.

22. Article 3 of the Directive does not include any ground for refusal to register specifically aimed at trade marks constituted by a term borrowed from the language of a Member State other than the State of registration in which it is devoid of distinctive character or descriptive of the goods or services in respect of which registration is sought.

23. Moreover, such a trade mark does not necessarily fall within the grounds for refusal to register relating to the lack of distinctive character or the descriptive character of the trade mark, referred to in points (b) and (c) respectively of Article 3(1) of the Directive.

24. In fact, to assess whether a national trade mark is devoid of distinctive character or is descriptive of the goods or services in respect of which its registration is sought, it is necessary to take into account the perception of the relevant parties, that is to say in trade and or amongst average consumers of the said goods or services, reasonably well-informed and reasonably observant and circumspect, in the territory in respect of which registration is applied for (*see* Joined Cases C-108/97 and C-109/97 *Windsurfing Chiemsee* [1999] ECR I-2779, paragraph 29; Case C-363/99 *Koninklijke KPNNederland* [2004] ECR I-1619, paragraph 77; and Case C-218/01 *Henkel* [2004] ECR I-1725, paragraph 50).

25. It is possible that, because of linguistic, cultural, social and economic differences between the Member States, a trade mark which is devoid of distinctive character or descriptive of the goods or services concerned in one Member State is not so in another Member State (*see*, by way of analogy, concerning the misleading nature of a trade mark, Case C-313/94 *Graffione* [1996] ECR I-6039, paragraph 22).

26. Consequently, Article 3(1)(b) and (c) of the Directive does not preclude the registration in a Member State, as a national trade mark, of a term borrowed from the language of another Member State in which it is devoid of distinctive character or descriptive

of the goods or services in respect of which registration is sought, unless the relevant parties in the Member State in which registration is sought are capable of identifying the meaning of the term.

27. This interpretation of the Directive is in accordance with the Treaty requirements, and in particular those of Articles 28 EC and 30 EC.

28. According to settled case-law, in the context of the application of the principle of the free movement of goods, the Treaty does not affect the existence of rights recognised by the legislation of a Member State in matters of intellectual property, but only restricts, depending on the circumstances, the exercise of those rights (Case 119/75 *Terrapin* [1976] ECR 1039, paragraph 5; Case 58/80 *Dansk Supermarked* [1981] ECR 181, paragraph 11; and order in *Matratzen Concord* v *OHIM*, paragraph 40).

29. Applying that case-law, the Court ruled, at paragraph 42 of the order in *Matratzen Concord* v *OHIM*—in which the Spanish trade mark MATRATZEN was already at issue, being the subject of the main proceedings—that the principle of the free movement of goods does not prohibit a Member State from registering as a national trade mark a sign which, in the language of another Member State, is descriptive of the goods or services concerned.

30. That also applies if the sign in question is, in the language of a Member State other than that of registration, devoid of distinctive character with regard to the goods or services covered by the application for registration.

31. It should be added that, as the Advocate General observed in points 59 to 64 of his Opinion, registration in a Member State of a trade mark such as that at issue in the main proceedings does not prohibit all use of the term constituting the trade mark by other traders in the said Member State.

32. In conclusion, the answer to the question referred is that Article 3(1)(b) and (c) of the Directive does not preclude the registration in a Member State, as a national trade mark, of a term borrowed from the language of another Member State in which it is devoid of distinctive character or descriptive of the goods or services in respect of which registration is sought, unless the relevant parties in the Member State in which registration is sought are capable of identifying the meaning of the term. . . .

## NOTES AND QUESTIONS

**1.** In paragraph 20, the CJEU says, "in a field which has been exhaustively harmonised at Community level, a national measure must be assessed in the light of the provisions of that harmonising measure and not of those of primary law." Yet, in paragraphs 28-30, the Court assesses its interpretation of the Directive under Articles 28 [34] and 30 [36] of the TFEU. Is the analytic approach consistent with its rhetoric?

**2.** The Advocate General pointed out that, even if trademark rights are granted for a German-language term in Spain, this would not necessarily preclude German exporters from using the relevant term in the Spanish market. Under what doctrine of trademark law might such use be allowed?

**3.** The case shows the remaining importance of national trademark systems operating under Directive 2015/2436 of 15 December 2015 and the WIPO Madrid system as it allows taking into account cultural and linguistic differences in trademark registration, which under the uniform European trademark system would lead to rejecting the application or validity of the mark, as the next case shows.

## *Ornua Co-Operative Ltd v. Tindale & Stanton Ltd España SL*

Judgement of the Court (Second Chamber), 20 July 2017

In Case C-93/16

REQUEST for a preliminary ruling under Article 267 TFEU from the Audiencia Provincial de Alicante (Provincial Court, Alicante, Spain), made by decision of 8 February 2016, received at the Court on 15 February 2016, in the proceedings

Ornua Co-operative Ltd, formerly The Irish Dairy Board Co-operative Ltd v Tindale & Stanton Ltd España SL,

THE COURT (Second Chamber), composed of M. Ilešič (Rapporteur), President of the Chamber, A. Prechal, A. Rosas, C. Toader and E. Jarašiūnas, Judges, Advocate General: M. Szpunar, gives the following:

### Judgment

1. This request for a preliminary ruling concerns the interpretation of Article 9 of Council Regulation (EC) No 207/2009 of 26 February 2009 on the [European Union] trade mark (OJ 2009 L 78, p. 1).

2. The request has been made in proceedings between Ornua Co-operative Ltd, formerly The Irish Dairy Board Co-operative Ltd ('Ornua'), and Tindale & Stanton Ltd España SL ('T & S') concerning the use by the latter of a sign which, according to Ornua, gives rise to a likelihood of confusion with the EU trade marks of which it is the proprietor and affects the reputation of those marks.

. . .

### The Dispute in the Main Proceedings and the Questions Referred for a Preliminary Ruling

9. Ornua is a company incorporated under Irish law whose economic activities are in the food sector. It markets, inter alia, butter and other dairy products.

10. It is the proprietor of several EU trademarks, including the word mark KERRYGOLD, registered in 1998 for goods in Class 29 of the Nice Agreement Concerning the International Classification of Goods and Services for the Purposes of the Registration of Marks of 15 June 1957, as revised and amended, namely, in particular butter and other dairy products, and the following two figurative marks registered respectively in 1998 and 2011 for the same class of goods (together, 'the KERRYGOLD EU trade marks'): [pictures omitted].

11. The goods on which those marks are affixed are exported to several countries. In the European Union, those goods are mainly sold in Spain, Belgium, Denmark, Germany, Ireland, Greece, France, Cyprus, Luxembourg, Malta, the Netherlands and the United Kingdom.

12. T & S is a company incorporated under Spanish law which imports and distributes, in Spain, margarines under the sign KERRYMAID. Those goods are manufactured in Ireland by Kerry Group plc.

13. Kerry Group has registered, in Ireland and the United Kingdom, the national mark KERRYMAID.

. . .

### The First Question

25. By its first question, the referring court asks, in essence, whether Article 9(1)(b) of Regulation No 207/2009 is to be interpreted as meaning that the fact that, in part of the European Union, an EU trade mark and a national mark peacefully coexist, allows, in view of the unitary nature of the EU trade mark, the conclusion that in another part of the European Union, where peaceful coexistence between that EU trade mark and the sign identical to that national mark is absent, there is an absence of the likelihood of confusion between that EU trade mark and that sign.

. . .

28. [T]he Court has already held that the exclusive right conferred by an EU trade mark on its proprietor, under Article 9(1) of Regulation No 207/2009, extends, as a rule, to the entire area of the European Union (see, to that effect, judgment of 12 April 2011, *DHL Express France*, C-235/09, EU:C:2011:238, paragraph 39).

29. As regards Article 9(1)(b) of that regulation, it is clear from the settled case-law of the Court that that article protects the proprietor of an EU trade mark against any use which adversely affects that trade mark's function of indicating origin or is liable to do so (judgment of 22 September 2016, *combit Software*, C223/15, EU:C:2016:719, paragraph 27 and the case-law cited).

30. The uniform protection thus conferred on the proprietor of the EU trade mark by that article is to entitle that proprietor, throughout the European Union, to prohibit a third party from using, in the course of trade and without the consent of that proprietor, an identical or similar sign for identical or similar goods or services which adversely affects that trade mark's function of indicating origin or is liable to do so and thus gives rise to a likelihood of confusion.

31. In order for the proprietor of the EU trade mark to avail himself of that right, there is no need for the use of the identical or similar sign creating a likelihood of confusion to take place throughout the entire territory of the European Union.

32. If the proprietor of the EU trade mark was only protected against infringements committed throughout the entire territory of the European Union, he would not be able to contest the use of identical or similar signs which give rise to a likelihood of confusion in only part of that territory, even though Article 9(1)(b) of Regulation No 207/2009 is intended to protect that proprietor, throughout the European Union, against any use which adversely affects his trade mark's function of indicating origin.

33. Consequently, when the use of a sign gives rise, in one part of the European Union, to a likelihood of confusion with an EU trade mark, whilst, in another part of the European Union, that same use does not give rise to such a likelihood of confusion, there is an infringement of the exclusive right conferred by that trade mark. In that case, the European Union trade marks court hearing the case must prevent the marketing of the goods concerned under the sign at issue throughout the entire territory of the European Union, with the exception of the part in respect of which there has been found to be no likelihood of confusion (judgment of 22 September 2016, *combit Software*, C223/15, EU:C:2016:719, paragraphs 25 and 36).

34. In the present case, it is clear from the documents before the Court that it is common ground between the parties to the main proceedings that there is peaceful coexistence between the KERRYGOLD EU trade marks and the national mark KERRYMAID in Ireland and the United Kingdom, since Ornua does not therefore oppose the use of that national mark in those Member States.

35. It is also common ground that such peaceful coexistence is absent in the part of the territory of the European Union which is the subject of the infringement action, namely

Spain, and that T & S's use of the sign KERRYMAID takes place there without Ornua's consent.

36. It is clear, moreover, from the case-law of the Court that the examination of the likelihood of confusion in part of the European Union must be based on a global assessment of all the relevant factors in the case concerned and that that assessment must include a visual, phonetic or conceptual comparison of the mark and the sign used by the third party, which may lead, in particular for linguistic reasons, to different conclusions for one part of the European Union and for another (see, to that effect, judgment of 22 September 2016, *combit Software*, C223/15, EU:C:2016:719, paragraphs 31 and 33 and the case-law cited).

37. It follows, as the Advocate General stated in . . . his Opinion, that in a situation such as that in the case in the main proceedings, in which peaceful coexistence between EU trade marks and a sign has been found in Ireland and the United Kingdom, the European Union trade marks court hearing infringement proceedings on the use of that sign in another Member State, here the Kingdom of Spain, cannot merely base its assessment on the peaceful coexistence prevailing in Ireland and the United Kingdom. That court must, on the contrary, make a global assessment of all the relevant factors.

38. Having regard to those considerations, the answer to the first question is that Article 9(1)(b) of Regulation No 207/2009 must be interpreted as meaning that the fact that, in part of the European Union, an EU trade mark and a national mark peacefully coexist, does not allow the conclusion that in another part of the European Union, where peaceful coexistence between that EU trade mark and the sign identical to that national mark is absent, there is no likelihood of confusion between that EU trade mark and that sign.

### The Second Question

39. By its second question, the referring court asks, in essence, whether Article 9(1)(b) of Regulation No 207/2009 must be interpreted as meaning that the elements which, according to the European Union trade marks court hearing an infringement action, are relevant to assess whether the proprietor of an EU trade mark is entitled to prohibit the use of a sign in part of the European Union not covered by that action, may be taken into account by that court to assess whether that proprietor is entitled to prohibit the use of that sign in the part of the European Union which is the subject of that infringement action.

40. As has been stated in paragraph 36 of the present judgment, the examination to be carried out by the competent European Union trade marks court must be based on a global assessment of all of the relevant factors of the case before it.

41. That global assessment must, as regards the visual, auditory or conceptual comparison between the EU trade mark at issue and the sign used by the third party, be based on the overall impression produced by that mark and that sign on the relevant public, which comprises the average consumer of the goods or services concerned, who is reasonably well informed and reasonably observant and circumspect (see, to that effect, judgment of 25 June 2015, *Loutfi Management Propriété Intellectuelle*, C147/14, EU:C:2015:420, paragraphs 21 and 25 and the case-law cited).

. . .

45. In that regard, account should be taken, in particular, of the overall presentation of the product marketed by the third party, the circumstances in which a distinction is made between that mark and the sign used by that the third party, and the effort made by that third party to ensure that consumers distinguish its products from those of which it is not the trade mark owner (see, to that effect, judgment of 17 March 2005, *Gillette Company and Gillette Group Finland*, C228/03, EU:C:2005:177, paragraph 46).

46. Although, for the purpose of assessing whether Ornua is entitled to prohibit the use of the sign KERRYMAID in Spain, the referring court should consider taking into account elements present in Ireland and the United Kingdom, it should first of all ensure that there is no significant difference between the market conditions or the sociocultural circumstances which may be observed, respectively, in the part of the European Union covered by the infringement action and in that in which the geographical area corresponding to the geographical word contained in the sign at issue. It cannot be excluded that the conduct which can be expected of the third party so that its use of the sign follows honest practices in industrial or commercial matters must be analysed differently in a part of the European Union where consumers have a particular affinity with the geographical word contained in the mark and the sign at issue than in a part of the European Union where that affinity is weaker.

47. In the light of the foregoing, the answer to the second question is that Article 9(1)(b) of Regulation No 207/2009 must be interpreted as meaning that the elements which, according to the European Union trade marks court hearing an infringement action, are relevant for assessing whether the proprietor of an EU trade mark is entitled to prohibit the use of a sign in part of the European Union not covered by that action, may be taken into account by that court to assess whether that proprietor is entitled to prohibit the use of that sign in the part of the European Union which is the subject of the infringement action, provided that the market conditions and the sociocultural circumstances are not significantly different in one of those parts of the European Union and in the other.

### The Third Question

48. By its third question, the referring court seeks, in essence, to ascertain whether Article 9(1)(c) of Regulation No 207/2009 must be interpreted as meaning that the fact that, in part of the European Union, an EU trade mark with a reputation and a sign peacefully coexist, having regard to the unitary character of the EU trade mark, allows the conclusion that in another part of the European Union, where that peaceful coexistence is absent, there is due cause legitimising the use of that sign.

. . .

52. That case-law ensures that the proprietor of an EU trade mark can either be entitled to the extended protection conferred by Article 9(1)(c) of Regulation No 207/2009 throughout the European Union, or cannot rely on it at all. Accordingly, the scope of the protection conferred by any EU trade mark has a uniform character on the entire territory of the European Union.

53. In contrast, in order for the proprietor of an EU trade mark having that extended protection to be able to rely on his right conferred by Article 9(1)(c), it is not at all necessary that the use of the sign infringing that right takes place on the entire territory of the European Union.

54. If that proprietor were only protected against infringements committed on the entire territory of the European Union, it would be impossible to contest infringements committed in only part of that territory, even though the purpose of Article 9(1)(c) of Regulation No 207/2009 is to protect that proprietor, throughout the European Union, from any use without due cause of an identical or similar sign which takes unfair advantage of the distinctive character or the repute of those marks or is detrimental to that distinctive character or repute.

55. In the present case, subject to verification by the referring court, it does not appear to be disputed that the KERRYGOLD EU trade marks have a reputation within the meaning of Article 9(1)(c) of Regulation No 207/2009.

56. Moreover, it is clear from the documents submitted to the Court that it is common ground between the parties to the main proceedings that there is, because of the peaceful coexistence in Ireland and the United Kingdom between those marks and the national mark KERRYMAID, due reason for the use of that sign in that part of the European Union.

57. As has already been pointed out in paragraph 35 of the present judgment, it is also common ground that such peaceful coexistence is absent in the part of the territory of the European Union which is the subject of the infringement action, namely Spain, and that T & S's use of the sign KERRYMAID takes place there without Ornua's consent.

58. Moreover, it is clear from the settled case-law of the Court that the examination of the existence of an infringement referred to in Article 9(1)(c) of Regulation No 207/2009 must be based on a global assessment which takes into account all the factors relevant to the case (judgments of 18 June 2009, *L'Oréal and Others*, C487/07, EU:C:2009:378, paragraph 44, and of 18 July 2013, *Specsavers International Healthcare and Others*, C252/12, EU:C:2013:497, paragraph 39).

59. It follows that, in the present case, where there is due cause legitimising the use of the sign KERRYMAID in Ireland and the United Kingdom because of the peaceful coexistence between the KERRYGOLD EU trade marks and the national mark at issue in those two Member States, the European Union trade marks court hearing an infringement action in respect of the use of that sign in another Member State cannot merely base its assessment on that peaceful coexistence in Ireland and the United Kingdom, but must, on the contrary, make a global assessment of all the relevant factors.

60. Therefore, the answer to the third question is that Article 9(1)(c) of Regulation No 207/2009 must be interpreted as meaning that the fact that, in part of the European Union, an EU trade mark with a reputation and a sign peacefully coexist, does not allow the conclusion that in another part of the European Union, where that peaceful coexistence is absent, there is due cause legitimising the use of that sign.

## NOTES AND QUESTIONS

**1.** This decision is important in two respects. First, it illustrates, similar to the *Matratzen Concord* case (section V.A.1 above), that while the European Union grants trademark registration for unitary marks that encompass the entire territory of the Union, there may yet be infringement cases where different national perceptions regarding similar trademarks will result in a finding of noninfringement in one member state, while infringement may be found as between the same competing marks in another member state. Second, ancillary to the first point, a party that has successfully defended against infringement in one member state may not simply invoke that defense in another member state, particularly if the circumstances are different.

## B. The Andean Community Trademark System

The intellectual property system of the Andean Community was introduced in Chapter 1. Decisions 486 and 689 of the Andean Community include common rules with respect to trademarks.[21] These common rules are applied by national trademark offices in each of the

21. Title IV, Decision 486, Common Intellectual Property Regime, Andean Community; Decision 689 Adaptation of certain articles of Decision 486 – Common Regime on Industrial Property, to allow the development and deepening of Industrial Property Rights through the internal regulations of the Member countries, available at http://www.sice.oas.org/trade/JUNAC/junaind.asp.

member countries,[22] and litigation to enforce rights is pursued in the national courts of each member country. The Court of Justice of the Andean Community has jurisdiction, *inter alia*, to consider actions by member countries and affected individuals with respect to the compatibility of national legislation and decisions with Andean law.[23]

Decision 486 provides for the international exhaustion of trademark rights at Article 158:

> **Article 158.**—Trademark registration shall not confer on the owner the rights to prevent third parties from engaging in trade in a product protected by registration once the owner of the registered trademark or another party with the consent of or economic ties to that owner has introduced that product into the trade of any country, in particular where any such products, packaging or packing as may have been in direct contact with the product concerned have not undergone any change, alteration, or deterioration.
>
> For the purposes of the preceding paragraph, two persons shall be considered to have economic ties when one of the persons is able to exercise a decisive influence over the other, either directly or indirectly, with respect to use of the trademark right or when a third party is able to exert that influence over both persons.

## NOTES AND QUESTIONS

**1.** The USMCA, as noted earlier, includes provisions regarding the relationship between trademarks and geographical indications, as well as provisions relating to enforcement of trademark rights in the import context. We discuss additional USMCA trademark enforcement provisions in Chapter 6.

# VI. INTERNET DOMAIN NAMES AT THE MULTILATERAL LEVEL

## A. The Nature of the Domain Name

**Frederick M. Abbott***

### *On the Duality of Internet Domain Names: Propertization and its Discontents*

#### II. Domain Names as Intellectual Property

#### A. The Technical Domain Name Function

A domain name shares characteristics with various forms of intellectual property as traditionally understood, but it does not fall neatly within "traditional" categories. To begin with, a domain name is similar in function to an old-fashioned telephone number. It tells a caller (in this case, the person through a device submitting an Internet query) where to route the call (in this case, to a particular server and/or sub-location). A random character string associated with an IP address could perform that function, and simply entering the appropriate IP address in

22. *Id.*, e.g., art. 138.

23. Treaty Creating the Court of Justice of the Cartagena Agreement (Amended by the Cochabamba Protocol), at, e.g., arts. 17-22.

* 3 N.Y.U. J. Intell. Prop. & Ent. L. 1 (Fall 2013), available at SSRN: http://ssrn.com/abstract=2257562.

a browser can perform it. But, it would be very difficult for Internet users to remember and enter strings of numbers to find who or what they are looking for, and the domain name is the "human friendly" way of solving the memory and data entry problem.[41]

### B. The Domain Name as Identifier

Broadly speaking, domain names fall into a number of different categories as identifiers. Some make use of generic or commonly descriptive terms, e.g., "health," "drugs," "travel," as a means to attract Internet users to sources of information for goods and services that may or may not be associated with a particular supplier/provider. Despite lacking trademark status, these domain names may have a substantial financial value because of the likelihood that Internet users will use these terms, perhaps along with a generic top-level domain (gTLD) such as ".com," when broadly searching for information and resources. . . . Many domain names incorporate the trademark or service mark of a business. Internet users seeking a business or its products (or services) commonly enter the trademark or service mark along with a gTLD to find the relevant resources, or enter the trademark or service mark in a browser and select the search result incorporating the trademark or service mark of the business.[43] The trademark or service mark of a business may appear in a domain name for reasons other than providing the location for goods and services. Commentators or critics of the business may use it in a legitimate way.[44] Typically with respect to legitimate noncommercial or fair use, the trademark or service mark will be combined with additional terms.[45] A subtype of the trademark-incorporating domain name is the "trade name" incorporating domain name.[46] From a technical IP standpoint, a trademark identifies a good or service that distinguishes one enterprise from another in commerce. A trade name is the name of a business that may or may not have trademark status. A third type of domain name is effectively a random or quasi-random alphanumeric string that does not signal the nature of the web location to which it will route the Internet user. There are a range of reasons why such random or quasi-random alphanumeric strings may be used.

"Identifiers" have constituted intellectual property rights (IPRs) subject matter since the inception of commerce.[47] Artisans' "marks" are as old as the crafting of pottery, whereby the artisan would identify his or her creation on the object. From the standpoint of the modern era, trademarks are subject matter of the Paris Convention on the Protection of Industrial Property of 1883 (and trade names are covered by that agreement).[48] There are other forms of IP that are identifiers, including geographical indications, appellations of origin, and other ways by which agricultural products have been designated.

41. It is a wonder, perhaps, that in the "old days" individuals were expected to remember 20 or so seven-digit telephone numbers to contact their family, friends, and business relations.

43. See 1 J. Thomas McCarthy, McCarthy on Trademarks and Unfair Competition §7:17.50 (4th ed. 2013) ("In the same way that businesses sometimes desire to have a prestige business address, businesses want a prestige address in cyberspace that corresponds to the trade name of the company or to a company trademark.").

44. See, e.g., *Pfizer Inc v. Van Robichaux*, WIPO Case No. D2003-0399, lipitor-info.com; *Sutherland Inst. v. Continuative L.L.C.*, WIPO Case No. D2009-0693, sutherlandinstitute.com.

45. See discussion of relationship between domain names incorporating trademark alone, and domain names using trademark in combination with other terms, in *Toyota Motor Sales, U.S.A. v. Tabari*, 610 F.3d 1171 (9th Cir. 2010).

46. See Abbott, Cottier & Gurry, . . . , at 378. For discussion of trade names under the TRIPS Agreement, see Appellate Body Report, United States—Section 211 Omnibus Appropriations Act of 1998, ¶¶333–41, WT/DS176/AB/R (Jan. 2, 2002).

47. McCarthy, supra note 43, §5:1 (describing the early origins of trade symbols).

48. Paris Convention for the Protection of Industrial Property, Mar. 20, 1883, 21 U.S.T. 1583, 828 U.N.T.S. 305.

While some forms of intellectual property require a creative element (e.g., patent and copyright), the trademark does not.[49] A trademark must be distinct from other trademarks for identical or similar goods, but it does not need to meet a standard of novelty or originality (although it may not be generic or commonly descriptive).[50]

## C. Domain Names as Intellectual Property

The domain name as an identifier may share characteristics with the trademark and trade name, but is it a distinct form of "intellectual property"?[51] To illustrate the question, suppose a person starting a new financial services consulting business registers as a domain name a previously unused alphanumeric string, "1q2r3s.com" and creates a commercial website. The name of the business on the website is "Financial Planning Associates", and the unique alphanumeric string in the domain name is not identifying the services business on the website. As a unique alphanumeric identifier, is the domain name "1q2r3s.com" a form of intellectual property distinct from a service mark or trade name because its sole function is to direct users to a location on the Internet? Is it intellectual property as such?

The U.S. Lanham Act defines "domain name"[52] and provides remedies against its misuse (see discussion of the ACPA supra), but the domain name as such is not accorded specific rights typical of IP. For example, the domain name is not associated with a specific statutory right to exclude third parties from infringing use. Moreover, U.S. statutory law does not include general provisions according protection to "intellectual property" as such, as distinct from the enumerated forms (e.g., patent, copyright, and trademark). A domain name may be a trademark, no doubt (e.g., Amazon.com).[53] To be clear concerning the illustration above, "1q2r3s.com" may well be registered as a trademark (or service mark) to the extent that it is used to identify the services of Financial Planning Associates.

But the domain name is not accorded its own unique statutory protection, though it may be protected on application of general unfair competition law. It may (or may not) be that domain names (and other "non-traditional" forms of identifier) should be accorded their own unique forms of protection. But, as a matter of current law, they are not.

## D. Trademarks as Property

### 1. Assignment and transfer

Legislatures and courts have long treated trademarks as a form of property capable of ownership. But, the transferability of trademark ownership has a complex history, and even today includes ambiguous elements and a divergence between U.S. law and international trademark law. In the United States, it has long been thought that a trademark should not be assigned and transferred without the business with which it is associated.[54] Since the function

49. See Abbott, Cottier & Gurry, . . . , at 354.

50. As discussed below, there are forms of intangible property that protect compilations of commercial information—database protection (e.g., in the European Union) and protection of undisclosed information in the form of regulatory data on pharmaceutical and agricultural chemical products (per Article 39.3 of the TRIPS Agreement)—that fall outside traditional notions of intellectual property.

51. See McCarthy, supra note 43, §7.17.50 ("Out of the millions of domain names, probably only a small percentage also play the role of a trademark or service mark.").

52. 15 U.S.C. §1127 states: "[t]he term "domain name" means any alphanumeric designation which is registered with or assigned by any domain name registrar, domain name registry, or other domain name registration authority as part of an electronic address on the Internet."

53. See, e.g., AMAZON.COM, Registration No. 2078496.

54. See generally, McCarthy, *supra* note 43, §§18:1–:11. A related discussion concerning licensing of trademarks is discussed in *K Mart Corp. v. Cartier, Inc.*, 486 U.S. 281, 313-15 (1988).

of a trademark is presumed to be providing consumers with information concerning relevant goods, or protecting trademark owners against misappropriation of their valuable corporate reputation, it is thought a logical corollary that the trademark should not be disassociated from the product purchased by the consumer or the reputation of the business owner. This concept or principle has been embodied in the U.S. both at common law and in Section 10 of the Lanham Act as a rule against "assignments in gross."[55] A trademark is assignable only with the goodwill of the business with which the mark is used.[56]

That being said, the U.S. appears to be acting inconsistently with Article 21 of the WTO TRIPS Agreement by maintaining Section 10 of the Lanham Act. Article 21 provides in relevant part, "the owner of a registered trademark shall have the right to assign the trademark with or without the transfer of the business to which the trademark belongs." This provision reflects the rule that apparently is most common outside the U.S.,[57] and it is difficult to stretch an interpretative argument that somehow the U.S. requirement to include the goodwill of a business in an assignment does not involve a requirement to transfer the business.

There are arguments on each side of the "assignments in gross" discussion. The U.S. position reflects the "world as it should be." If the trademark sends a signal to the consumer, why should the consumer bear the risk and consequences of new trademark ownership by an unrelated business? The TRIPS international position may better reflect the "world as it is." Trademarks have largely become commoditized. "Brands" include sports teams emblems more or less randomly placed on consumer goods. Should the law reflect preferred expectations or reality?

Fundamentally, trademarks are treated as a form of property that may be sold, assigned and transferred, both in the U.S. and elsewhere. In the U.S., there is a "rider" or condition attached to the property for purposes of assignment and transfer. It must be accompanied by the goodwill of the business.

### 2. Antidilution

A second element in the propertization or commodification of trademarks is the adoption of "antidilution" legislation and international rules. Article 6b of the Paris Convention provides special protection for "well-known" trademarks, which protection has been supplemented by TRIPS Agreement rules.[58] Domestic U.S. legislation extends rights to owners of famous trademarks to prevent third parties from using the mark on dissimilar goods or services (i.e., blurring) or from disparaging the trademark (i.e., tarnishment).[59] These rules in effect establish a property boundary around the trademark, protecting its owner against a third-party diminishing the value of its trademark asset. This goes beyond protecting the traditional trademark function of informing consumers as to the quality or characteristics of products, and towards protecting the trademark as property of its owner.

---

55. 15 U.S.C. §1060(a)(1)–(5) (2006) provides, inter alia, "[a] registered mark or a mark for which an application to register has been filed shall be assignable with the good will of the business in which the mark is used, or with that part of the good will of the business connected with the use of and symbolized by the mark." See McCarthy, supra note 43, at §18:2.

56. Although there may be some hints at a move away from strict application of this rule in the U.S., it appears still to represent good law. McCarthy, supra note 43, §18:10. McCarthy does not condone this as a mechanism for circumventing the anti-assignments-in-gross rule, but notes that goodwill "denotes only an intangible and ineffable concept: A concept which lies in the eye of the beholder." Because "goodwill" is a fairly flexible concept, the rule may not have great practical effect on transactions that realistically are assignments in gross. A recital of "associated goodwill" as part of transferring a trademark asset may be sufficient to satisfy most purposes.

57. Id.

58. See generally Abbott, Cottier & Gurry, supra note 7, at 363-70, 375-78.

59. See 15 U.S.C. §1125(c) (2006); see also *Nabisco, Inc. v. PF Brands, Inc.*, 191 F.3d 208 (2d Cir. 1999).

### 3. Intangible Asset Value

The typical business accounting treatment of the trademark is as an intangible asset.[60] That treatment varies depending on the jurisdiction. In the United States, the accounting and tax treatment may depend on whether the trademark was internally developed or purchased.[61] Regardless of the precise accounting treatment, the intangible asset value of trademarks is routinely calculated and reported by business information services, and the value of a brand may reach into the billions of U.S. dollars.[62]

## NOTE

**1.** The U.S. Supreme Court in *USPTO v. Booking.com*, 591 U.S. __ (2020), rejected determination by the USPTO that a generic term, i.e. "booking", appending a .com "suffix", may not be registered because addition of the generic top level domain (gTLD) .com may not confer trademark status. The Court said that Booking.com should be treated as other descriptive terms that may acquire secondary meaning among the consuming public, and it accepted determinations of the district and appeal courts which decided that the public had come to associate Booking.com with a source of services. The Court dismissed concern that allowing registration of Booking.com might discourage other service providers from using the term "booking" in conducting business, observing that such concerns may be raised with respect to many descriptive terms, and that trademark law doctrine permits third party use of common terms that are not serving as an identifier of a particular source.

## B. The Uniform Domain Name Dispute Resolution Policy (UDRP)

Following is an excerpt from WIPO's Second Report on the Domain Name Process that describes legal rules and a dispute settlement mechanism adopted to address domain names.

---

### *The Recognition of Rights and the Use of Names in the Internet Domain Name System*

Report of the Second WIPO Internet Domain Name Process September 3, 2001*

#### . . . WIPO's Prior Work

1. In June 1998, the National Telecommunications and Information Administration (NTIA), an agency of the United States Department of Commerce, issued a *Statement of Policy on the Management of Internet Names and Addresses* (the "White Paper"). The White Paper called for the creation of a new, private, not-for-profit corporation which would be responsible for coordinating certain DNS functions for the benefit of the Internet as a whole. Following the publication of the White Paper, a process occurred which resulted in the formation of the Internet Corporation for Assigned Names and Numbers (ICANN), a not-for-profit corporation

60. See McCarthy, supra note 43, at §2:19 ("In this sense, good will can be defined as the intangible value of a business beyond the value of its physical assets.").

61. See, e.g., Donald E. Kieso, Jerry J. Weygandt & Terry D. Warfield, Intermediate Accounting, 664-719 (14th ed. 2012).

62. Manish Modi, Coca-Cola Retains Title as World's Most Valuable Brand, Bloomberg (Oct. 2, 2012, 11:57 PM), http://www.bloomberg.com/news/2012-10-03/coca-cola-retains-title-as-world-s-most-valuable-brand-table-.html (based on Interbrand's Best Global Brands 2012 report).

* https://www.wipo.int/amc/en/processes/process2/report/html/report.html.

established under the laws of the State of California of the United States of America. The by-laws of ICANN and documentation on the various meetings that it has organized and activities that it has carried out are available on ICANN's web site, www.icann.org.

2. In response to growing publicity and concern over the interface between domain names and trademarks, and the lack of definition of the relation between these two species of identifiers, the White Paper also addressed certain intellectual property questions. In particular, the White Paper stated that the United States Government would "seek international support to call upon the World Intellectual Property Organization (WIPO) to initiate a balanced and transparent process, which includes the participation of trademark holders and members of the Internet community who are not trademark holders," to develop recommendations on certain aspects of the interface between domain names and trademarks, including "a uniform approach to resolving trademark/domain name disputes involving cyberpiracy."

3. Following the publication of the White Paper, and with the subsequent approval of its Member States, WIPO carried out between July 1998 and April 1999 an extensive and intensive process of consultations directed at developing recommendations on the issues which it was requested to address.

4. The WIPO Process, known as the WIPO Internet Domain Name Process, was conducted using a combination of Internet-based consultations, paper-based consultations and 17 physical meetings held in 14 countries. Participation was solicited from governments, intergovernmental organizations, professional and industry associations, corporations and individuals through three Requests for Comments. Responses were received to those Requests for Comments from 40 States, 6 intergovernmental organizations, 72 non-governmental organizations representing professional, industry and other special interests, 181 corporations and law firms and 182 individuals.

5. The Report of the WIPO Internet Domain Name Process, *The Management of Internet Names and Addresses: Intellectual Property Issues*, was published on April 30, 1999. The Report contained a series of recommendations. Chief amongst those recommendations was the establishment of a uniform dispute-resolution policy and procedure for resolving disputes over the alleged bad faith and deliberate misuse of trademarks through the registration of domain names in the generic top-level domains (gTLDs).com,.net and.org.

### The Uniform Domain Name Dispute Resolution Policy for gTLDs

6. Following the publication of the Report of the WIPO Internet Domain Name Process and certain consultation procedures in conformity with the by-laws of ICANN, ICANN adopted, in August 1999, a Uniform Domain Name Dispute Resolution Policy (UDRP), which entered into force for the gTLDs. .com, .net and .org on December 1, 1999, and January 1, 2000 (the policy was phased-in for registrars over the two dates).

7. The UDRP establishes a dispute-resolution procedure under which a complainant can seek the transfer or cancellation of a domain name registration in.com,.net or.org on the basis that (i) the domain name is identical or confusingly similar to a trademark in which the complainant has rights; (ii) the domain name holder has no rights or legitimate interests in respect of the domain name; and (iii) the domain name has been registered and is being used in bad faith. The UDRP is a mandatory procedure to which each applicant for a domain name registration in .com, .net or .org is required to submit, in the event that a complaint is lodged in respect of the applicant's registration.

8. ICANN has accredited four dispute-resolution service providers to administer disputes brought under the UDRP: the WIPO Arbitration and Mediation Center, the National Arbitration Forum, e-Resolution and the CPR Institute for Dispute Resolution.[24] Registrars

24. [e-Resolution is no longer an active dispute resolution service provider. — Eds.]

accredited by ICANN to accept registrations in.com,.net or.org are obligated to implement the results of panel decisions under the dispute resolution procedure.

## *New Generic Top-Level Domains: Intellectual Property Considerations*

WIPO Arbitration and Mediation Center*

### . . . 2.1. Domain Names and Trademarks

9. So far, IP protection in the DNS has focused on trademarks, a specific category of identifiers which serve to distinguish the goods or services of one company from those of another. As stated in the First WIPO Report:

> 11. [. . .] A trademark enables consumers to identify the source of a product, to link the product with its manufacturer in widely distributed markets. The exclusive right to the use of the mark, which may be of indefinite duration, enables the owner to prevent others from misleading consumers into wrongly associating products with an enterprise from which they do not originate.

10. Trademarks serve as a focus for the goodwill associated with a product as a result of investments in quality and marketing. Brand recognition through trademarks enables start-up companies to establish a successful business presence and more established brands to preserve their reputation and value. For a growing number of companies in developed and developing countries, trademarks have become the single most important business asset, their value often exceeding that of such companies' physical assets.

### 2.2. Domain Names and Other Identifiers

11. Other protected identifiers include trade names, personal names, geographical indications, International Nonproprietary Names (INNs) for pharmaceutical substances and the names and acronyms of international organizations (IGOs). Such identifiers have also become the subject of abusive practices in the DNS. To develop recommendations on means of dealing with such abuse, WIPO conducted the Second WIPO Internet Domain Name Process. The Second WIPO Report was published in September 2001 and discussed by the Member States of WIPO, who in September 2002 recommended to provide protection for country names and for the names and acronyms of IGOs in the UDRP. These recommendations (the "WIPO-2 Recommendations") were transmitted to ICANN in February 2003 and continue to be under ICANN's consideration.

### 2.3. Intellectual Property Concerns

12. Given the value of trademarks and other identifiers and the importance of the Internet as a commercial communication and marketing channel, rights owners are understandably worried that their identifiers fall victim to deceptive and abusive practices on the Internet. Undermining the status of such identifiers also compromises the credibility of the DNS and consumers' trust in the Internet as a medium for commercial exchange. The First WIPO Report found that:

> 315. [. . .] the priority concern of the trademark community does not relate to conflicts between parties who claim to have competing legitimate rights in the name (for example, different companies with the same trademark in different product lines or operating in different areas of the world), but focuses on cases of clear abuse, often directed at famous and well-known marks.

* Available at http://www.wipo.int, visited July 11, 2006.

13. Such concerns are based on previous experience with abusive practices in the existing open gTLDs where domain name registrations are granted purely on a "first come first served" basis. Such abuses have forced trademark owners to invest substantial human and financial resources in defending their interests. The damage that a trademark owner suffers as a result of the abusive registration and use of a domain name may well be extensive by virtue of the global accessibility of domain names. The First WIPO Report notes in this regard:

> 132. [. . .] A considerable disjunction exists between, on the one hand, the cost of obtaining a domain name registration, which is relatively cheap, and, on the other hand, the economic value of the damage that can be done as a result of such a registration and the cost to the intellectual property owner of remedying the situation through litigation, which may be slow and very expensive in some countries.

14. IP owners therefore often adopt a preventive approach by registering their most valuable identifiers (sometimes including misleading variations) in all relevant gTLDs in order to preempt abuse. Such defensive registrations cause substantial cost both for the registration of domain names as well as for the maintenance of large domain name portfolios. . . .

---

## *Update on Trademark-Related Aspects of the Domain Name System*

Document prepared by the Secretariat*

### I. Domain Name Case Administration

#### A. Uniform Domain Name Dispute Resolution Policy

2. The DNS raises a number of challenges for the protection of Intellectual Property (IP), which, due to the global nature of the Internet, call for an international approach. WIPO has addressed these challenges since 1998 by developing specific solutions, most notably in the First and Second WIPO Internet Domain Name Processes. Through the Arbitration and Mediation Center (Center), WIPO provides trademark owners with efficient international mechanisms to deal with the bad-faith registration and use of domain names corresponding to their trademark rights. The principal mechanism administered by the Center, the Uniform Domain Name Dispute Resolution Policy (UDRP) was adopted by the Internet Cooperation for Assigned Names and Numbers (ICANN) on the basis of recommendations made by WIPO in the First WIPO Internet Domain Name Process.

3. The UDRP is limited to clear cases of bad-faith, abusive registration and use of domain names and remains in high demand for trademark owners. Since December 1999, the Center has administered some 60,000 UDRP-based cases. Trademark holders in 2021 filed 5,128 UDRP-based complaints with the Center, a 22 per cent increase over 2020 filing (already a record at the time), and the sixth consecutive year that WIPO domain name case filings have surpassed 3,000. In 2021, the total number of domain names in WIPO UDRP-based cases brought by brand owners surpassed 100,000.

4. A diverse mixture of enterprises, institutions, and individuals used the Center's domain name dispute resolution procedures in 2021. The top sectors for complainant business activity were Banking and Finance; Internet and Information Technology (IT); Biotechnology and Pharmaceuticals; Retail; Food, Beverages, and Restaurants; and, Fashion. Nowadays, filings from rights owners include alleged fraudulent email or phishing schemes, impersonation, and other illicit uses of consumer-facing websites (e.g., counterfeits) associated with the disputed

* Standing Committee on the Law of Trademarks, Industrial Designs and Geographical Indications, SCT/46/3, Oct. 6, 2022.

domain names. More recently, cases have involved so-called homographic variations of trademarks with cybersquatters registering internationalized domain names (IDNs) which appear to be in "standard" Latin ASCII Script but employ IDN variations to trick users (i.e., profiting from visual similarity between different characters). Reflecting the global scope of this dispute mechanism, named parties to WIPO cases from UDRP inception through 2021 represented over 180 countries. In function of the language of the applicable registration agreement of the domain name at issue, WIPO UDRP proceedings have so far been conducted in nearly 30 languages.

5. All WIPO UDRP panel decisions are posted on the Center's website. Published in 2017, the Center's Third Edition of the WIPO Overview of WIPO Panel Views on Selected UDRP Questions (WIPO Overview 3.0) has been widely embraced by parties to proceedings and is applied by panelists across most cases nowadays. This globally-consulted online overview of decision trends on important case issues covers over 100 topics, including citations to almost 1,000 representative decisions from over 265 WIPO Panelists. To facilitate access to these decisions according to party business sector and dispute subject matter, the Center also offers an online searchable Legal Index of WIPO UDRP Decisions. These WIPO resources are accessible free of charge.

6. Mindful of WIPO's foundational role in the UDRP, the Center monitors developments in the DNS with a view to adjusting its resources and practices. With the exceptions of 2020 and 2021 given the global COVID-19 pandemic, the Center regularly organizes, including most recently in October 2022, Domain Name Dispute Resolution Workshops to update interested parties, as well as meetings of its Domain Name Panelists. In 2019, the UDRP passed 20 years of successful operation and the Center hosted a conference in Geneva to commemorate this milestone. The event both took stock and looked ahead in terms of UDRP jurisprudence, relevant Internet developments, and a range of other topical items such as platform ADR models.

## B. Country Code Top-Level Domains (ccTLDs)

7. The application of the UDRP is mandated for domain names registered in generic Top Level Domains (gTLDs) (such as .com) and more recently introduced New gTLDs. The Center however also assists ccTLD registries in their establishment of registration conditions and dispute resolution procedures that conform with international best practices in registry management and IP protection. Some ccTLD registries adopt the UDRP directly, while others have adopted UDRP-based procedures which take account of relevant national considerations. The Center provides domain name dispute resolution services to some 80 ccTLD registries, having commenced such services on a tailored basis for .BH and .البحرين (Bahrain) and for .SA and .السعودية (Saudi Arabia) in 2021, and .SN (Senegal) already in 2022, with yet further additions expected in 2022.

8. With further reference to WIPO's ccTLD assistance, in 2021 the Center provided policy support to a number of ccTLD registries. This included collaborating with relevant authorities to promote efficiency and harmonization of domain name dispute resolution mechanisms inter alia by updating as relevant the registration conditions, administrative processes, Policies, Rules, and/or WIPO Supplemental Rules for .AU (Australia), .BR (Brazil), .CH (Switzerland), .CN (China), .EU (European Union), .FR (France), .JP (Japan), .LV (Latvia), .MY (Malaysia), .SE (Sweden), .SN (Senegal), .TZ (Tanzania), and .UA (Ukraine).

9. In 2021, the Center hosted numerous virtual events including webinars to inform prospective and interested parties of the dispute resolution services for .AU (Australia) and .CH (Switzerland), ccTLDs with further webinars planned. The Center also organized and participated in an online ceremony to extend the Center's accreditation to manage .CN and .中国 (China) disputes as the first (and only) non-Chinese provider.

## II. Policy Developments in the Domain Name System

10. A number of policy developments in relation to ICANN present both opportunities and challenges for owners and users of IP rights. One is ICANN's introduction of hundreds of New gTLDs. Such New gTLDs may be of an "open" nature (similar to .com), or may take on more specific or restrictive characteristics, for example taking the form of .[brand], .[city], .[community], .[culture], .[industry], or .[language]. A noteworthy related development concerns the introduction of Internationalized Domain Names (IDNs) at the top level, such as .网店 (webshop/e-shop) and شبكة. (web/network). ICANN's expansion of the DNS also raises rights protection questions in connection with the Second WIPO Process.

### A. New Generic Top Level Domains (Gtlds)

11. ICANN implementation of its New gTLD Program, formally approved in June 2011, was detailed in its iterative "Applicant Guidebook". Delegation of the first New gTLDs into the Internet's Root Zone took place in October 2013; with over 1,200 gTLDs delegated by 2021 only a few (e.g., ".music") remain to launch. Together, these New gTLDs appear to have so far attracted some 29 million second-level registrations (owing e.g., to non-renewals, this figure is down from a prior 32 million). ICANN concluded its "New gTLD Subsequent Procedures Policy Development Process" (PDP) in 2020. While topics such as "Mitigating DNS Abuse" and "Closed Generics" remain under consideration, further ICANN processes including Generic Name Support Organization (GNSO) Council and ICANN Board consideration have seen this Subsequent Procedures process move towards an "Operational Design Phase" to prepare for future new gTLD rounds.

12. The Center remains committed to working with stakeholders to attempt to safeguard the observance of general principles of IP protection in New gTLDs. A number of RPMs specifically created for New gTLDs had emerged from a series of ICANN processes. Set out below is a broad description of these ICANN RPMs, for the top level and the second level respectively.

#### *(a) Top Level RPMs*

**(i) Pre-(TLD) Delegation Dispute Resolution Procedure**

13. This mechanism allowed trademark owners to lodge Legal Rights Objections (LRO) to New gTLD applications at the top level where certain substantive criteria were met. The Center assisted ICANN in the establishment of these criteria on the basis of the "WIPO Joint Recommendation Concerning Provisions on the Protection of Marks, and Other Industrial Property Rights in Signs, on the Internet".

14. Appointed by ICANN as the exclusive provider of LRO dispute resolution services, the Center received 69 compliant LRO filings, which it completed processing by September 2013. All WIPO LRO expert panel determinations are available on the Center's website as is a Center report on the LRO process. It is expected that a similar procedure would be available for subsequent New gTLD rounds.

**(ii) Post-(TLD) Delegation Dispute Resolution Procedure (PDDRP)**

15. In early 2009, the Center communicated to ICANN a specific substantive proposal for a permanent administrative option that would allow for the filing of a complaint with respect to an approved New gTLD registry operator whose manner of operation or use of its registry is alleged to cause or materially contribute to trademark abuse. The proposal's intent was to offer standardized assistance to ICANN's own compliance oversight responsibilities, by providing an administrative alternative to court litigation, encouraging responsible conduct by relevant actors and including appropriate safe-harbors.

16. Following various ICANN processes, including consultations with registry operators, the effectiveness of this PDDRP in the form adopted by ICANN remains uncertain,

in particular given the addition of overlapping procedural layers, and issues concerning the intended substantive scope of this mechanism (notably by ICANN having excluded the legal concept of "wilfull blindness"). In light of broader policy interests however, the Center in 2013 agreed with ICANN to become a provider for the trademark PDDRP.

#### *(b) Second Level RPMs*

**(i) Trademark Clearinghouse (TMCH)**

17. ICANN's New gTLD Program includes a Trademark Clearinghouse (TMCH) as a centralized repository of authenticated trademark data which may be invoked as the basis for using New gTLD RPMs. The Center commented that the TMCH should not unfairly burden rights holders in the treatment of trademark registrations legitimately obtained through varied examination and registration systems as applied in many global jurisdictions, and that, if and where relevant, practical measures may be envisaged to identify any allegedly inappropriate invocation of rights in specific contexts. According to the latest available information, it appears that the TMCH has received some 47,000 entries.

**(ii) Uniform Rapid Suspension (URS) System**

18. While importantly the UDRP remains available as a curative tool for New gTLD disputes involving the considered transfer of a disputed domain name to the trademark owner, ICANN has introduced what is intended to be a lighter second-level RPM for appropriate cases.

19. Having evolved from a sequence of ICANN processes and committees, the Uniform Rapid Suspension (URS) System continues to raise a number of questions, including its relationship to the UDRP. ICANN invited tenders from prospective URS providers, to which after careful consideration of the ICANN URS model, the Center has not been in a position to apply. The Center continues to closely monitor developments, including as to any evolution of the remedy offered by the URS procedure and, whether by contractual amendment or policy process, its potential applicability to incumbent TLDs such as ".com". In December 2019, ICANN upheld a request for reconsideration regarding its determination to include the URS procedure in the renegotiated .org Registry Agreement. There has been speculation as to whether the URS might in the future apply to the .net and .com registries – whether owing to an ICANN policy process or direct contract negotiations with the registry operator (as was the case e.g., with .cat, .jobs, .mobi, .org, .pro, .travel, and .xxx Top Level Domains). . .

## C. Panel Decisions Under the UDRP

Following are two panel decisions under the UDRP by one of the authors of this book. They each involve the same complainant, a major multinational pharmaceutical company. The first is a more typical type of complaint against a domain name registrant seeking to take unfair advantage of the trademark holder's rights—this is the prototypical "cybersquatting" case. The second involves a complex issue of fair use with potentially significant public policy implications.

### *Pfizer, Inc. v. Martin Marketing*

Case No. D2002-0793, WIPO Arbitration and Mediation Center
Administrative Panel Decision

#### 1. The Parties

The Complainant is Pfizer, Inc., a corporation organized in the State of Delaware, United States of America ("USA"), with place of business in New York, New York, USA.

The Respondent is Martin Marketing, with address in New York, New York, USA.

## 2. The Domain Name and Registrar

The disputed domain name is <viagra-nascar.com>.

The registrar of the disputed domain name is Intercosmos Media Group, Inc. dba directNIC.com ("Intercosmos"), with business address in New Orleans, Louisiana, USA.

## 3. Procedural History . . .

## 4. Factual Background

Complainant has registered the term "VIAGRA" as a trademark on the Principal Register at the United States Patent and Trademark Office (USPTO), Reg. No. 2,162,548, dated June 2, 1998, in International Class 5, covering " Compound for treating erectile dysfunction," asserting date of first use and first use in commerce of April 6, 1998 (Complaint, para. 12 & Annex 3). "VIAGRA" is a coined term with no denotative meaning (*id.* para. 12).

Complainant holds registrations for the "VIAGRA" trademark in many countries other than the United States (*id.*, para. 12 & Annex 4).

Complainant has registered the domain name <viagra.com> and maintains an active commercial website at Internet address (URL) <www.viagra.com> (*id.*, para. 12 & Annex 5).

Complainant has advertised its "VIAGRA" brand "sildenafil citrate" widely in the United States and in other countries (*id.*, para. 12). As a consequence of such advertising and news reports, Complainant's "VIAGRA" mark is well known in connection with a drug for the treatment of erectile dysfunction.

The National Association for Stock Car Racing ("NASCAR"), which claims ownership in the "NASCAR" trademark and service mark has consented to the transfer of the disputed domain name to Complainant (*id.*, para. 12 & Annex 6 (Affidavit of Karen B. Leetzow, Intellectual Property Counsel to NASCAR)). NASCAR has not authorized Respondent to use its trademark and service mark in a domain name or otherwise (*id.*).

Complainant is the sponsor of a car that has participated in the NASCAR Winston Cup Series. Such car has prominently displayed the "VIAGRA" mark, enjoyed success in the racing series and been featured in Complainant's television advertisements (*id.*, para. 12).

According to the Registrar's Verification to WIPO, "Martin Marketing" is the registrant of the disputed domain name <viagra-nascar.com>. The administrative contact is "Martin, Jim firstpharmacy@yahoo.com." The record of the disputed domain name was created on September 6, 2001, and was last updated on July 17, 2002.

Respondent has maintained an active commercial website at URL <www.viagra-nascar.com>. The home page of this website is headed with the terms "VIAGRA NASCAR" in large type, with the subheadings "MAIN/VIAGRA INFO/VIAGRA CAR/ORDER VIAGRA." The web pages include detailed information concerning VIAGRA, as well as detailed information concerning the NASCAR race car sponsored by Complainant. At the bottom of the web pages, the following appears in small type: "Copyright © 2001. Viagra Nascar. ALL RIGHTS RESERVED. All trademarks and registered trademarks are of their respective companies. Viagra® is a registered trade [unreadable from printout] site is in now [sic] way affiliated with Phizer [sic]. Only a physician should decide if Viagra® is appropriate for you. These pages are only a summary. If you have further questi [unreadable] information about Viagra®, visit viagra.com [hyperlink] or feel free to fill out our contact form or simply e-mail." (Complaint, Annex 11)

As of August 20, 2002, Respondent's website contained a hyperlink to <www.secure-medical.com/viagra-nascar.com/order.html>, which offered to sell VIAGRA product, as well as hyperlinks to websites selling jewelry and sporting tickets. A "pop-up" window also provided click-through links to an on-line gambling website <joebet.com> (*id.*, para. 12 & Annex 12), as well as other websites offering VIAGRA information, herbal virility solutions and tooth whitener (*id.*, para. 12 & Annexes 13-15).

The physical address provided by Respondent in its domain name registration apparently does not exist. The telephone number, as of August 14, 2002, was not working. (*Id.*, Affidavit of Toth, counsel for Complainant, at Annex 10.)

The Registration Agreement in effect between Respondent and Intercosmos subjects Respondent to Intercosmos' dispute settlement policy, the Uniform Domain Name Dispute Resolution Policy, as adopted by ICANN on August 26, 1999, and with implementing documents approved by ICANN on October 24, 1999. The Uniform Domain Name Dispute Resolution Policy (the "Policy") requires that domain name Registrants submit to a mandatory Administrative Proceeding conducted by an approved dispute resolution service provider, of which WIPO is one, regarding allegations of abusive domain name registration and use (Policy, paragraph 4(a)).

## 5. Parties' Contentions . . .

## 6. Discussion and Findings

The Policy is addressed to resolving disputes concerning allegations of abusive domain name registration and use. The Panel will confine itself to making determinations necessary to resolve this Administrative Proceeding.

It is essential to dispute resolution proceedings that fundamental due process requirements be met. Such requirements include that a respondent have notice of proceedings that may substantially affect its rights. The Policy, and the Rules for Uniform Domain Name Dispute Resolution Policy (the "Rules"), establish procedures intended to ensure that respondents are given adequate notice of proceedings commenced against them, and a reasonable opportunity to respond (*see, e.g.*, para. 2(a), Rules).

In this case, the Panel is satisfied that the Center took all steps reasonably necessary to notify the Respondent of the filing of the Complaint and initiation of these proceedings. Respondent transmitted an e-mail to the Center indicating that it was aware of the proceedings.

Paragraph 4(a) of the Policy sets forth three elements that must be established by a complainant to merit a finding that a respondent has engaged in abusive domain name registration and use, and to obtain relief. These elements are that:

i. Respondent's domain name is identical or confusingly similar to a trademark or service mark in which the Complainant has rights; and
ii. respondent has no rights or legitimate interests in respect of the domain name; and
iii. respondent's domain name has been registered and is being used in bad faith.

Each of the aforesaid three elements must be proved by a complainant to warrant relief.

Complainant is the holder of a trademark registration for the term "VIAGRA" on the Principal Register of the USPTO. It has registered the mark with other trademark authorities throughout the world. The term "VIAGRA" is arbitrary and distinctive. The "VIAGRA" mark is well known in respect to a drug addressing erectile dysfunction. The Panel determines that Complainant has rights in the trademark "VIAGRA." Those rights arose before Respondent's registration of the disputed domain name.

The disputed domain name <viagra-nascar.com> directly incorporates Complainant's mark as its lead term, and adds a hyphen and the trademark and service mark of a third party (as well as the gTLD ".com"). The addition of the third party mark does not eliminate the visual impression that the disputed domain name is associated with Complainant's trademark. Moreover, in light of Complainant's use of its mark in connection with the third party mark for its own advertising purposes, the combination of the two marks would convey to Internet users familiar with Complainant's advertising an expected association. In the circumstances of this proceeding, the addition of a hyphen and ".com" do not serve to alleviate potential Internet user confusion between the disputed domain name and Complainant's mark. Based on the overall visual impression and expected Internet user association, the Panel determines that the disputed domain name is confusingly similar to Complainant's "VIAGRA" mark.

Complainant has established the first element necessary for a finding of abusive domain name registration and use.

The second element of a claim of abusive domain name registration and use is that the Respondent has no rights or legitimate interests in respect of the domain name (Policy, paragraph 4(a)(ii)). The Policy enumerates several ways in which a Respondent may demonstrate rights or legitimate interests:

> "Any of the following circumstances, in particular but without limitation, if found by the Panel to be proved based on its evaluation of all evidence presented, shall demonstrate your rights or legitimate interests to the domain name for purposes of Paragraph 4(a)(ii)
>
> i. before any notice to you of the dispute, your use of, or demonstrable preparations to use, the domain name or a name corresponding to the domain name in connection with a bona fide offering of goods or services; or
> ii. you (as an individual, business, or other organization) have been commonly known by the domain name, even if you have acquired no trademark or service mark rights; or
> iii. you are making a legitimate noncommercial or fair use of the domain name, without intent for commercial gain to misleadingly divert consumers or to tarnish the trademark or service mark at issue." (Policy, paragraph 4(c).)

Respondent has offered no evidence that it has been commonly known by the disputed domain name. Respondent has no prior business association with Complainant and has used Complainant's mark in the disputed name to attract Internet users to a website where it offers to sell various products and services unconnected with Complainant or its trademarked product. Such use of the disputed domain name is not a fair use of Complainant's mark.

Complainant's mark is arbitrary and well known. Respondent was without doubt aware of Complainant's mark when it registered the disputed domain name, and would likewise be on constructive notice that Complainant would dispute its use of the mark in connection with its website. In the circumstances of this proceeding, in which Respondent has used the marks of two third parties without their consent to attract Internet users to a website where it offers for sale goods and services unconnected with those third parties, Respondent did not make a bona fide offering of goods prior to notice of a dispute.

Complainant has demonstrated that Respondent has no rights or legitimate interests in the disputed domain name, and has established the second element necessary for a finding of abusive domain name registration and use.

Respondent registered and used the disputed domain name to direct Internet users to a commercial website where it directly and indirectly offered for sale a variety of goods and services unconnected with Complainant, as well as offering for sale Complainant's product. Respondent included a small typeface disclaimer of association with Complainant at the bottom of certain web pages. However, that disclaimer is not adequate to overcome the overall impression created by Respondent's use of Complainant's mark in the domain name and again prominently on its home page (and elsewhere on its website) of an association with or sponsorship by Complainant. The Panel finds that Respondent has used the disputed domain name for commercial gain by creating confusion among Internet users as to Complainant's sponsorship of or affiliation with Respondent's website. Such use is in bad faith within the meaning of paragraph 4(b)(iv) of the Policy.

Complainant has satisfied the third element necessary for a finding of abusive domain name registration and use by Respondent.

Complainant has submitted authorization from the holder of the NASCAR trademark and service mark sufficient to relieve potential concern that transfer of the disputed domain name to Complainant would interfere with the rights of the third party trademark holder.

The Panel will therefore direct the registrar to transfer the disputed domain name to Complainant.

### 7. Decision

Based on its finding that the Respondent, Martin Marketing, has engaged in abusive registration and use of the domain name <viagra-nascar.com> within the meaning of paragraph 4(a) of the Policy, the Panel orders that the domain name <viagra-nascar.com> be transferred to the Complainant, Pfizer, Inc.

Frederick M. Abbott, Sole Panelist
November 15, 2002

---

## *Pfizer, Inc. v. Van Robichaux*

Case No. D2003-0399, WIPO Arbitration and Mediation Center
Administrative Panel Decision

### 1. The Parties

The Complainant is Pfizer Inc, New York, New York, United States of America, represented by Hale and Dorr, LLP of United States of America.

The Respondent is Van Robichaux, of New Orleans, Louisiana, United States of America, represented by Daniel W. Nodurft of New Orleans, Louisiana, United States of America.

### 2. The domain Name and Registrar

The disputed domain name <lipitorinfo.com> is registered with TierraNet d/b/a DomainDiscover.

### 3. Procedural History . . .

### 4. Factual Background

The Complainant has registered the word trademark "LIPITOR" on the Principal Register of the U.S. Patent and Trademark Office (USPTO), Reg. No. 2,074,561, dated June 24, 1997, in International Class 5, covering "Pharmaceutical preparations for use in the treatment of cardiovascular disorders and cholesterol reduction," claiming date of first use and use in commerce as January 28, 1997.[1] The Complainant has registered the word trademark "LIPITOR" and related word and/or design marks in numerous countries throughout the world, and applications are pending in various countries. "LIPITOR" is an arbitrary term coined by the Complainant (Complaint, para. 12 & Annexes 3-5).

---

1. The Complainant holds the mark by way of assignment to a wholly-owned subsidiary, Pfizer Ireland Pharmaceuticals. Complaint, para. 12 & Annex 3.

"LIPITOR" is marketed as a cholesterol-lowering medicine and is "the most prescribed cholesterol-lowering medicine in the United States and is the second largest selling pharmaceutical product of any kind in the world. Last year, worldwide sales of the LIPITOR product were $7.972 billion." The Complainant has spent substantial sums of money advertising and promoting its "LIPITOR" product in the United States and other countries (*Id.*, para. 12).

According to the Registrar's verification, the Respondent "Van Robichaux" is the registrant of the disputed domain name. According to a Better-Whois.com WHOIS database report submitted by the Complainant, the record of registration for the disputed domain name was created on August 14, 2002, and was last updated on February 12, 2003 (Complaint, Annex 1).

The Respondent, J. Van Robichaux, Jr., is an attorney with offices in New Orleans, Louisiana, USA. He provides information concerning his law practice at a website with Internet address at "www.robichauxlaw.com." This practice includes providing information to prospective clients concerning injuries that may have been caused to them by various medicines, including, for example "Baycol" and "Rezulin." An internal web page at "www.robic hauxlaw.com/rezulin.asp" includes information such as a description of the medicine, the problems that have been associated with it, a recommendation to seek medical attention as may be appropriate, and a part that states:

> "How can Robichaux Law firm help?
>
> We will investigate the relevant facts of your case, gather and evaluate your medical records, and take necessary legal steps to protect your legal rights once you become one of our clients.
>
> For a free consultation to see how we can help you Click Here" (dated June 24, 2003, Response, Annex 3).

The Respondent indicates that he rejected an offer from the Complainant to purchase the disputed domain name, although no details regarding the nature of that offer were provided by him (Response, para. III).

The disputed domain name has not been used by the Respondent to direct Internet users to an active website. However, the Respondent indicates that he would intend to use it to provide individuals with information about their legal rights and treatment options "should it ultimately be learned that 'lipitor' causes injuries to the consumer" (Response, para. III).

The Registration Agreement in effect between the Respondent and TierraNet d/b/a DomainDiscover, subjects the Respondent to dispute settlement under the Policy. The Policy requires that domain name Registrants submit to a mandatory Administrative Proceeding conducted by an approved dispute resolution service provider, of which the Center is one, regarding allegations of abusive domain name registration and use (Policy, paragraph 4(a)).

## 5. Parties' Contentions . . .

## 6. Discussion and Findings . . .

### A. Identical or confusingly similar

The Respondent has conceded that the Complainant has rights in the trademark "LIPITOR" and that the disputed domain name <lipitorinfo.com> is confusingly similar to that mark. The Panel finds that the Complainant has rights in the "LIPITOR" trademark, and that the disputed domain name is confusingly similar to it.

The Respondent has further acknowledged that it included the Complainant's mark in the disputed domain name precisely because it identifies the Complainant's widely sold medicine. This acknowledgement serves for present purposes to address the issue whether the "LIPITOR" mark is well known.[2]

### B. Rights or Legitimate Interests

The second element of a claim of abusive domain name registration is that the respondent has no rights or legitimate interests in respect of the domain name (Policy, para. 4(a)(ii)). The Policy enumerates several ways in which a respondent may demonstrate rights or legitimate interests:

> "Any of the following circumstances, in particular but without limitation, if found by the Panel to be proved based on its evaluation of all evidence presented, shall demonstrate your rights or legitimate interests to the domain name for purposes of Paragraph 4(a)(ii):
>
> i. before any notice to you of the dispute, your use of, or demonstrable preparations to use, the domain name or a name corresponding to the domain name in connection with a *bona fide* offering of goods or services; or
> ii. you (as an individual, business, or other organization) have been commonly known by the domain name, even if you have acquired no trademark or service mark rights; or
> iii. you are making a legitimate noncommercial or fair use of the domain name, without intent for commercial gain to misleadingly divert consumers or to tarnish the trademark or service mark at issue." (Policy, para. 4(c).)

The Respondent does not contend that it has been commonly known by the disputed domain name.

The Respondent had knowledge of the Complainant's mark when it registered the disputed domain name, and should reasonably have foreseen that the Complainant would object to its use. Whether an offering of legal services using reference to a mark in circumstances such as those present here might be a *bona fide* offering of services need not be decided, as the Panel considers that the Respondent had effective notice of a dispute prior to any such offering.

The Respondent principally claims "fair use" as a defense for using the Complainant's mark in its domain name. The Respondent essentially argues that in order to provide the public with information concerning the Complainant's product, including advice concerning treatment or legal advice, it is necessary or appropriate to use the Complainant's mark in its domain name.

The Respondent is seeking to establish a fair use defense without having actively used the Complainant's mark to identify a website. Paragraph 4(c)(iii) of the Policy refers to a respondent "making . . . fair use of the domain name." This sole panelist has in prior decisions under the Policy noted that the express requirement of "making" does not foreclose the establishment of a fair use defense in circumstances in which the disputed domain name has not been actively used. For example, in *Helen Fielding v. Anthony Corbert aka Anthony Corbett*, WIPO Case No. D2000-1000, (September 25, 2000), this panelist said:

> . . . the Panel notes that while paragraph 4(c)(i) of the Policy refers to "preparations to use" a domain name in the context of offering goods or services, paragraph 4(c)(iii) refers only to the

2. The Complainant has argued that the "LIPITOR" mark is well known, especially in the United States. The main evidence it has put forward to support this is the frequency with which the medicine is prescribed and its high level of sales. Because prescription medicines are prescribed by doctors to patient-consumers, generally by handwriting on a form, and are dispensed by pharmacists with often limited patient-consumer intervention, there is some difficulty in drawing a conclusion concerning consumer identification of a mark based on the volume of prescriptions and sales of a medicine. It will suffice for present purposes for the Panel to conclude that for persons with knowledge of the pharmaceutical sector, such as the Respondent, the mark "LIPITOR" is well known in the United States.

> active "making" of a "legitimate noncommercial or fair use." The express language of the Policy indicates that its drafters intended to limit the circumstances in which legitimate noncommercial or fair use could successfully be claimed. Applying the express language of the Policy to the Respondent's claim of legitimate noncommercial or fair use, the Panel finds that the Respondent is not "making" such legitimate non-commercial or fair use of the Complainant's mark in the disputed domain name.
>
> The Panel recognizes that there are contexts in which the registrant of a domain name should not be expected to make immediate use of that name, including for legitimate noncommercial or fair use purposes. For example, this sole panelist on a previous occasion has observed that a requirement of immediate use in hosting websites critical of trademark holders might stifle free expression by allowing such trademark holders to initiate abusive domain name proceedings before such domain names could effectively be put to active use.[3] Also, this sole panelist has recognized that a delay in using a domain name for a legitimate noncommercial or fair use purpose in response to a cease and desist demand might be justified.[4] [footnotes numbered 6 and 7, respectively, in quoted decision]

In *Fielding v. Corbert* the respondent had presented no evidence of a plan to make a legitimate noncommercial or fair use of the disputed domain name other than speculative statements in a response filed in the Administrative Proceeding, and had made an offer to sell the name for a substantial sum to the complainant.

The circumstances of the present case are clearly distinguished from those in *Fielding v. Corbert.* Here the Respondent presently maintains a website on which he offers information and representation in connection with potential legal claims associated with pharmaceutical products. He indicates that he does not yet have information concerning the Complainant's trademarked product that he considers would justify adding it to those he presently identifies as the potential subject of legal claims. There is very little reason to doubt that the Respondent will do exactly what he says he intends to do: that is, should he become aware of facts indicating this would be appropriate, he will use the disputed domain name to direct Internet users to a website where he will offer information about the Complainant's trademarked product and recommend that potential clients be in contact with him.

In these circumstances, the absence of active "making" use in connection with a website by the Respondent does not preclude a finding of rights or legitimate interests in the disputed domain name based on fair use. The Respondent is making use of the disputed domain name, but in a passive way. He has reserved it for future use in circumstances in which this is justified.

This does not answer the more fundamental question whether the proposed active use of the name would constitute fair use. If the Complainant has proven that the Respondent's proposed use of the disputed domain name would not be a fair one, the mere fact that the Respondent's present use is of a passive nature cannot establish a defense. In the proceeding, the Complainant bears the burden of proof in establishing the absence of rights or legitimate interests. Paragraph 4(a) of the Policy states "the complainant must prove that each of the[se] three elements are present." One element is that "you [the respondent] have no rights or legitimate interests in respect of the domain name" (Policy, Paragraph 4(a)(ii)).

The Complainant asserts that the Respondent will create initial interest confusion concerning its sponsorship or endorsement of the Respondent's website, and that creating such confusion for purposes of commercial gain precludes the establishment of a fair use defense. It further argues that even if the Respondent intends only noncommercial use of the disputed

3. *Wal-Mart Stores, Inc. v. Walsucks and Walmarket Puerto Rico*, WIPO Case No. D2000-0477, (July 20, 2000).

4. *Apple Computer, Inc. v. DomainHouse.com, Inc.*, WIPO Case No. D2000-0341, (July 5, 2000).

domain name, attracting Internet users by creating initial interest confusion is not permitted. It refers to the decision in *Banque Cantonale de Genève v. Primatex Group S.A.*, WIPO Case No. D2001-0477, (June 21, 2001), in support of the latter proposition. It suggests that the public interest will be harmed by the Respondent's activities because persons seeking information from the Complainant about the Complainant's product will find a website on which information is provided by the Respondent.

Before turning to the Respondent's defense, the Panel addresses the *Banque Cantonale de Genève v. Primatex Group S.A.* decision. In that proceeding, a respondent had used the trademark of a well known Swiss bank along with a common term ("-connection") in a domain name to direct Internet users to a noncommercial expression site that was sharply critical of the Bank. The panel in that proceeding suggested that a non-commercial expression site should in some manner identify itself as such in a domain name so that Internet users would not be misled by being transported to a site they had not elected to visit. The panel in that decision said:

> "Transparency starts with choosing a domain name which reflects the protest as opposed to a domain name which implies an affiliation to the trademark holder. If the protest is reflected in the domain name (for instance by adding the component '. . . sucks' or a similar element), Internet users have a choice to follow or not to follow the link. Otherwise, they may be misled.
>
> In this connection, it may be fair to state, however, that no *numerus clausus* of site names indicating protest or parody exists. It may even be legitimate, in some cases, to use a domain name denominating a corporation or public figure without qualifying additions. All depends from the circumstances of the individual case." *Id.*

The panel in *Banque Cantonale de Genève v. Primatex Group S.A.* wisely pointed out that disputes involving questions of fair use are context specific. There is a difference between an aggressive protest site directed at a Bank and a site maintained by a lawyer who is providing information and representation concerning potentially harmful pharmaceutical products. The interests of the public in information are different, and the motivations of the provider of information on the website are different. The complainant in *Banque Cantonale de Genève v. Primatex Group S.A* was Swiss and the respondent Panamanian. In the present proceeding, both parties are based in the United States, and the principal nexus of the Respondent's activities is likely to be in the United States. This decision should take into account the perspective of the U.S. judiciary on questions of fair use. In sum, the facts and circumstances of this proceeding are different than those in *Banque Cantonale de Genève v. Primatex Group S.A.*, and the determination in this proceeding is specific to its context.

The Respondent is essentially claiming "nominative fair use" of the Complainant's mark. In the Respondent's view, he should be able to refer to the Complainant's product by its trademark as a means of identification, rather than being required indirectly to describe the product, and he should be allowed do so in the domain name itself.[5]

This sole panelist, alone or as part of a three-person panel, has on a substantial number of occasions addressed the issue of fair use of marks in domain names. Each case is different, and the analysis in each is contextual, taking into account a number of factors. Two recent decisions of the U.S. Court of Appeals for the Ninth Circuit, *Playboy Enters. v. Welles*, 279 F.3d

---

5. In *Cairns v. Franklin Mint Co.*, 292 F.3d 1139 (9th Cir. 2002), the Court explained the distinction between a "nominative" fair use and "classic" fair use defense as follows:

> "The nominative fair use analysis is appropriate where a defendant has used the plaintiff's mark to describe the plaintiff's product, even if the defendant's ultimate goal is to describe his own product. Conversely, the classic fair use analysis is appropriate where a defendant has used the plaintiff's mark only to describe his own product, and not at all to describe the plaintiff's product." 292 F.3d, at 1152.

796 (9th Cir. 2002) and *Horphag Research v. Mario Pellegrini*, 328 F.3d 1108 (9th Cir. 2003), reaffirm a useful three-prong approach for determining whether third party use of a mark is "nominative fair use."

> This court looks to three factors in determining whether a defendant is entitled to the nominative fair use defense: (1) the product must not be readily identifiable without use of the mark; (2) only so much of the mark may be used as is reasonably necessary to identify the product; and (3) the user must do nothing that would, in conjunction with the mark, suggest sponsorship or endorsement by the trademark holder. *New Kids*, 971 F.2d at 308.[6]

The Respondent here is an attorney seeking to advise potential clients concerning treatment options and legal rights with respect to a particular medicine. The medicine is known to the public by its trademark name "LIPITOR." Few members of the public would be expected to understand a reference to "Pfizer's atorvastatin calcium product." "LIPITOR" is not readily identifiable without reference to the mark.

The Respondent has not used more of the mark in the domain name than is reasonably necessary to identify the product.[7]

Has the Respondent done anything that would, in conjunction with the mark, suggest sponsorship or endorsement by the trademark holder?

The use of the domain name <lipitorinfo.com> may initially suggest to Internet users who view it that it will direct them to a website sponsored by or affiliated with the Complainant. There may be, as the Complainant suggests, "initial interest confusion."

Some initial interest confusion will be associated with any domain name that incorporates a trademark, whether or not it is conjoined with "sucks" or another signal of impending disaffection. The domain name "LIPITOR-sucks" would initially attract Internet users by virtue of the trademark "LIPITOR" because some users would naturally be curious to find out why.[8] Indeed "LIPITOR-sucks" would provide notice that the referenced site was not sponsored by the Complainant before it was viewed, but there nonetheless would be Internet users who set out to seek information regarding the product from its producer who would visit it because of the mark incorporated in the name. This is a question of degree, and the point at which the Internet user becomes fully aware of the provider of content.[9]

---

6. As quoted in *Horphag Research v. Mario Pellegrini*, 328 F.3d 1108, at 1112 (9th Cir. 2003).

7. In *Playboy Enters. v. Welles*, 279 F.3d at 802, affirming *New Kids on the Block v. New America Publ'g, Inc.*, 971 F.2d 302, the Court referred to using the word mark of a competitor, but not its distinctive lettering or color scheme, as example of using only necessary parts of the mark.

8. This point was previously made by this sole panelist in *Wal-Mart Stores, Inc. v. Walsucks and Walmarket Puerto Rico*, WIPO Case No. D2000-0477, (July 20, 2000).

9. This sole panelist previously has pointed out the difference between using a trademark on a website and in a domain name from the standpoint of fair use. *See, e.g., Six Continents Hotels, Inc. v. Georgetown Inc.*, WIPO Case No. D2003-0214, (May 18, 2003), and *Six Contents Hotels, Inc. v. eGO*, WIPO Case No. D2003-0341, (July 3, 2003). A domain name that directly incorporates a trademark implicitly suggests an affiliation with the trademark holder. This distinction is recognized by federal courts in the United States. In *Playboy Enters. v. Welles*, the Court noted that its view of the nominative fair use defense might be influenced by whether the use would cause the alleged infringer's website to appear over the trademark holder's in web search results (noting that the uses by the alleged infringer were only in metatags). 279 F.3d, at 804. In *PACCAR Inc. v. Telescan Technologies*, 319 F.3d 242 (6th Cir. 2003), the Court of Appeals for the Sixth Circuit noted that domain names very often serve a source identification function, though rejecting a *per se* approach to trademark infringement, adopting instead use of an eight-factor test for determining likelihood of confusion. 319 F.3d, at 249-50. It went on to apply, without adopting, the Ninth Circuit's three-prong test of a nominative fair use defense, rejecting such a claim because of the combined factors of domain name usage and deliberate adoption by the alleged infringer of the trademark holder's distinctive styling on its website. 319 F.3d, at 256.

If any nominative fair use of domain names is to be permitted, initial interest confusion cannot standing alone act as a *per se* preclusion. In the context of the third prong of the Ninth Circuit's analytic approach, use of a mark in a domain name does not *standing alone* constitute doing something in conjunction with a mark that suggests sponsorship or endorsement by the trademark holder such as to bar a finding of nominative fair use.

The Respondent suggests that he would use the format of his existing informational web pages, plus a disclaimer, to make clear to any Internet user that the Complainant does not sponsor his website. The Respondent acknowledges by reference to another law firm's website that appropriate nominative fair use may require an express disclaimer of affiliation with the Complainant. Since the Respondent has not established a website addressed by the disputed domain name, the Panel is not in a position to evaluate his actual conduct. Nonetheless, since the Respondent has indicated his awareness of what an appropriate fair use might require, this would be consistent with allowing a passive nominative fair use defense that might later be adversely rebutted by the Respondent's conduct.

As the Complainant observes, the public has an interest in receiving information about medicines directly from their producers. The Complainant can and does maintain an active commercial website on which information concerning its medicine products is available.

The public also has an interest in learning of potential risks posed by medicines, and in securing the assistance of counsel as appropriate. This may be facilitated by the Respondent's proposed use of the disputed domain name.

The Respondent by his proposed use of the disputed domain name would not prevent the public from accessing information directly from the Complainant at the latter's website. The Respondent could provide information concerning "LIPITOR" to the public without using the mark in a domain name, although his communication to the public will be less effective that way. It would be exceedingly difficult for the Respondent to provide information about "LIPITOR" to the public on the Internet, or for the public to receive such information from the Respondent, without some use by the Respondent of the trademark (for example, on web pages addressed by other terms).

The Complainant has a commercial interest that conflicts with that of the Respondent. It is obviously in Complainant's best commercial interests that Internet users seeking information about "LIPITOR" not be directed to a site warning them of risks, and recommending adversary legal counsel.

As the Court of Appeals for the Ninth Circuit noted in *Playboy Enters. v. Welles*, a successful nominative fair use defense is not dependent on whether the party relying on it will make a profit from doing so.[10] The fact that Respondent may profit from use of the disputed domain name does not prevent him from establishing a nominative fair use defense.

As noted earlier, the Complainant bears the burden of proving that the Respondent does not have rights or legitimate interests in the disputed domain name (including by establishing a nominative fair use right to use the Complainant's mark in the name).

The Panel is not persuaded that the Complainant has carried its burden. The Complainant has established that it has rights in the mark in the disputed domain name and that the Respondent's proposed use of the name would conflict with its interests. The Respondent has presented a number of reasons why his use of the disputed domain name would be fair under the circumstances. The Respondent's showing has sufficiently rebutted the Complainant's showing so as to preclude the Panel from finding that the Respondent has no rights or legitimate interests in the disputed domain name.

10. 279 F.3d, at 801.

Proceedings under the Policy are intended to address "abusive" domain name registration and use. The Complainant is not suffering immediate harm. The Respondent is not actively using the disputed domain name. The Complainant may further pursue its interests in the courts. In light of the important public interests at stake and the reasonable nature of the Respondent's defense, the Panel does not consider it appropriate to deprive the Respondent of the disputed domain name in this Administrative Proceeding.

Having determined that the Complainant has not proven that the Respondent lacks rights or legitimate interests in the disputed domain name, the Panel will not address the issue of bad faith.

### 7. Decision

For all the foregoing reasons, the Complaint is denied.

Frederick M. Abbott, Sole Panelist
July 16, 2003

## NOTES AND QUESTIONS

**1.** The *Pfizer v. Van Robichaux* decision makes use of the doctrine of nominative fair use that largely evolved in the U.S. Court of Appeals for the Ninth Circuit. A notable decision that elaborates on that doctrine in the context of domain names is *Toyota v. Tabari*, 610 F.3d 1171 (9th Cir. 2010), involving <buy-a-lexus.com> and <buyorleaselexus.com>. This decision describes the typical Internet user as sophisticated, with significant searching skills and ability to rapidly distinguish trademark owner-sponsored and third-party-sponsored web sites (although a concurring opinion says this fact is not established). The Court of Appeals states that a domain name comprised solely of a trademark is presumed likely to cause consumer confusion and identification with the trademark owner, though additional terms may effectively eliminate that presumption. The Court holds that a defendant asserting nominative fair use in the context of an allegedly infringing domain name is subject to the three-prong test of *New Kids* (see text case above). A defendant need only demonstrate that it has used the trademark at issue to refer to the trademark good, and this shifts the burden of proof to the trademark owner to demonstrate likelihood of confusion (i.e., the trademark owner must prove defendant has suggested sponsorship or affiliation).

**2.** A respondent that loses a dispute decided by a panel under the Policy has the right to initiate litigation within ten days of notification of the decision, automatically preventing the registrar from transferring or canceling the disputed domain name. This option is used from time to time, though not often. Only in a few cases has a court effectively overturned the decision of a panel. *See Barcelona.Com v. Excelentisimo Ayuntamiento De Barcelona*, 330 F.3d 617 (4th Cir. 2002).

**3.** There has been modest academic criticism of decision making by panels under the Policy. Some conclude from an imbalance in decisions in favor of complainants that the process must somehow be biased in favor of trademark holders. *See, e.g.*, Michael Geist, *Fair.com?: An Examination of the Allegations of Systemic Unfairness in the ICANN UDRP* (2001), and *Fundamentally Fair.Com? An Update on Bias Allegations and the ICANN UDRP* (2002).[25] But

25. For a critique of Geist's almost wholly statistical approach, *see* International Trademark Association (INTA Internet Committee), *The UDRP by All Accounts Works Effectively, Rebuttal to Analysis and Conclusions of Professor Michael Geist in Fair.com and Fundamentally Fair.com* (2002).

this criticism may overlook or discount factors that help explain the imbalance. Compared to the large number of domain names that have been registered, the number of disputes is small. Hundreds of thousands of domain names are registered and maintained without incident. While registering a domain name is very inexpensive (today often less than $10), initiating a dispute under the Policy—while significantly less costly than court litigation—is nevertheless expensive, particularly as many complainants are represented by major law firms. Rational business enterprises do not set out to waste money on frivolous domain name challenges. The vast majority of complaints involve businesses that are able to demonstrate ownership of a trademark, and that have a reasonably good basis for believing they are the subject of abuse by a third-party domain name registrant. A substantial percentage of parties whose domain name registrations are challenged do not file a response, even though this is facilitated by tools provided on the WIPO web site. This context may help explain why the preponderance of UDRP decisions favor trademark holders.[26] The frequency of domain name disputes, and the percentage of trademark holder success, would be cut down by requiring *ex ante* review of domain name registration applications for conflict with existing trademark registrations (which, in fact, is required in some countries). Such a change would make the domain name registration process less efficient, increase its cost, and almost certainly reduce the number of registrations. Trademark holders would need to initiate fewer *ex post* complaints because there would be fewer cases of third-party abuse. The *ex post* percentage of UDRP decisions in favor of trademark holders would almost certainly decline because there would be fewer "obvious" cases of abuse, but at a significant cost to the public, which appears to appreciate the ease and low cost with which domain names may presently be registered.

**4.** What do you see as the costs and benefits of the UDRP process? Would it be preferable for all domain name disputes to be settled by national courts? Does the right to initiate litigation that automatically blocks transfer of a domain name based on a UDRP decision adequately protect the registrant?

**5.** The potential misuse of trademarks in domain names is not the only area where evolution of the Internet has challenged pre-existing paradigms of international trademark law. Trademark owners are concerned about auction web sites where there is the potential for sale of counterfeit goods, with the use of their marks in metatags and in other web content that may be made available to competitors for generating advertising links, and generally with the potential for trademark misuse absent traditional territorial limitations. The WIPO Secretariat has reviewed recent case law and proposals for new rules regarding protection of trademarks on the Internet in a report, "Trademarks and the Internet," prepared for the WIPO Standing Committee on the Law of Trademarks, Industrial Designs and Geographical Indications, SCT/244, August 31, 2010 (Twenty-Fourth Session of the SCT, Nov. 1-4, 2010, available at http://www.wipo.int).

## D. Implications of the New TLDs

As alluded to in the report by the WIPO Secretariat to member states, ICANN approved opening up the top-level domain name space (i.e., following the dot) to any party that could meet the established criteria for operating a registry, and provided that the proposed top-level domain (TLD) did not give rise to specific concerns, such as appropriating a term used by an established community. Putting aside the technical details and objection procedures, this means that instead

26. Statistically, three-person panels have supported Respondents at a somewhat more favorable rate than single-person panels. There may, again, be a fairly straightforward explanation for this. Respondents that are prepared to pay the higher fees associated with appointment of a three-person panel may be more likely to believe—and be able to support—that their claims to domain names are justified, and (unsurprisingly) their belief may be correct.

of the "traditionally" used generic top-level domains (gTLDs) such as .com, .net, .org, and .info, there are now over 1,000 TLDs. Some of these TLDs will be common dictionary terms and open to the public for registering domain names that associate a "second-level domain" with the TLD. Others are trademark terms, such as corporate brands, operating in a closed registration environment (e.g., second-level domains identifying various products offered under the brand controlled by the mark holder).

The idea of opening up the TLD environment raised a certain amount of alarm among corporate brand owners. In terms of cybersquatting or abuse most have long pursued defensive strategies involving registering virtually every conceivable word combination with (and variation of) their trademark with a relatively small number of gTLDs. When they have not been able to secure a particular domain name, they have initiated UDRP proceedings to challenge perceived abuses. But, a broad defensive registration strategy will be highly problematic when limitless second-level terms can be coupled with a large number of TLDs. Policing this new environment will be a challenge for the corporate brand owner.

Dispute settlement panels under the UDRP have tended to address the question whether a domain name is confusingly similar to a trademark in a relatively "simplified" manner focusing on visual impression. More in-depth jurisprudential analysis has focused on whether respondents accused of abusing trademarks have rights or legitimate interests in the disputed domain names, or have acted in bad faith. It is, however, possible that confusing similarity analysis will take on greater "depth" in the world of the new TLDs because it will be possible for registrants to make more refined distinctions in relation to brand owners. If a domain name registrant uses a second-level term that has not customarily been associated with the trademark owner's term used as a TLD, might that be sufficient to avoid a finding of confusing similarity? (To take an example, "Hilton" is the well-known mark of a hotel chain. The second-level domain "reservations" used in connection with ".hilton" (i.e., <reservations.hilton>) would presumably be considered confusingly similar to the trademark. But what about <bicycles.hilton>? Not so similar? What about <bedding.hilton>, <closets.hilton>, or <beaches.hilton>—more nuanced?[27] It is not that combination term domain names are a new phenomenon. UDRP panels have frequently been confronted with adjectives or common terms associated with trademarks. It can be argued that nothing is really changing. But, the new TLDs are being promoted to the public as distinct "properties" or regions, and this may affect how domain names are perceived. This may add a new element to the analysis. It is possible that dispute settlement panelists will become more inclined to look into the substance on web pages in the process of assessing confusing similarity to ascertain whether the use of a differentiated second-level domain is nonetheless being associated with products ordinarily connected with the trademark owner.

## E. A New Era of Cybercrime and Domain Names

When the UDRP was first adopted, the principal problems that trademark owners faced included use of well-known brand names to direct Internet users to pornographic content, and efforts by registrants to sell domain names incorporating well-known brands to the

27. This illustration assumes that the owner of the Hilton hotel trademark did not secure and control "Hilton" as a TLD, and that a third party did. The illustration might be more nuanced if it referred to a fairly well-known trademark that has other accepted meanings. In the process of rendering LRO decisions a number of such trademarks were assessed (such as "coach," "express," and "limited"). In each case a third party was permitted to proceed with establishing a TLD despite the objection of the trademark owner. So, for example, "handbag" combined with ".coach" would presumably be confusingly similar, but there are other terms where the similarity would not be so apparent.

trademark owner or a third party. More recently, bad-faith activities by domain name registrants extend to creating sophisticated replicas of corporate websites in efforts to lure unsuspecting Internet users to provide information and/or transfer funds, with the users believing that they are dealing with an established and reputable trademark owner. Domain names also form part of email addresses (i.e., the part of the address following the "@" sign), and various fraudulent phishing schemes use variations of trademark owner domain names to deceive recipients. These schemes can be very sophisticated, for example involving the use of an email format that includes otherwise legitimate information from the purported sender (e.g., a logo copied from the corporate website and the actual address of the legitimate business), but with an email address that differs only by a single letter in the top-level domain (e.g., using ".co" in place of ".com"). There are many variations on attempts to deceive Internet users using domain names. Substantial sums of money have been transferred by Internet users who thought they were dealing with a reputable supplier of goods or services when, in fact, the recipient of the transfer was a bad-faith actor. This new era of cybercrime calls for heightened attention by everyone involved in the system of domain name regulation.

# CHAPTER 4

# THE INTERNATIONAL COPYRIGHT SYSTEM

## I. COPYRIGHT AS AN INTELLECTUAL PROPERTY FORM

### A. Introduction

#### *1. A Wide Range of Activities*

Copyright, or in the European continental tradition, authors' rights and neighboring rights, is one of the most complex areas of intellectual property. It applies to a wide range of creative activities, from authors to artists, from music to visual arts, from composers to performers. It encompasses the worlds of broadcasting and media and architecture. It applies to individuals, collecting societies, as much as to globally operating corporations. The extension of copyright protection to computer software in the 1970s, replacing at that early stage the prospects of formal patent protection in the field, further enlarged the scope of application to the increasingly dominant information technology. Copyright is bound to play an important role in artificial intelligence and processes of automation.

Copyright, in other words, is at the heart of the information society. It is constantly confronted with changing and evolving technology. Among the different forms of intellectual property, copyright perhaps is the most difficult to understand. Principles and rules are framed at a high level of abstraction. Terms used do not necessarily convey what they mean. For example, broadcasting, distribution, and rental rights do not mean the right to undertake these activities, but rather the right to prevent and prohibit competitors from taking up such activities. The rights can only be understood in relation to the structure and operation of particular industries and creative activity. They vary depending upon the economic and societal structure at hand. The law cannot be fully understood outside its specific context. Problems and solutions vary among different industries. Given the broad scope of application it is not astonishing that the traditional distinctions between industrial property and copyright, expressed in the Paris and Berne Conventions, are increasingly blurred.

#### *2. Changing Technologies*

The Internet has exponentially expanded access to information and is changing the way people live and work around the world. Whether copyright laws are adequate to control distribution of expressive works on the Internet is an open question. Courts have been receptive to applying traditional copyright doctrine in the Internet arena (*see* discussion of evolving technologies in *Universal Studios v. Corley* (regarding DeCSS), *MGM v. Grokster*, and *American Broadcasting v. Aereo*, *infra*). Treaties and national legislation have been, or are being, adapted.

The EU Commission launched a major initiative with no less than 29 legislative proposals in 2016, including a new directive on copyright in the digital single market.

The rise of the Internet may suggest a decline in the relevance of national boundaries in the development and application of copyright and other intellectual property law. Certainly, the Internet gives its users the power to transmit data across national borders with relative ease. Yet, national governments may not be so willing to surrender local regulatory authority. The Internet may be a vector of "globalization," but there remains strong counterpressure to globalization reflecting values inherent in national sovereignty and the maintenance of local regulatory control. In sum, copyright is constantly challenged by technological advances, seeking to catch up in terms of effectiveness of protection and enforcement.

### *3. Diverging Cultural Backgrounds*

In addition to all these challenges, copyright in international law and relations struggles due to different philosophical and legal backgrounds in continental European authors' rights and Anglo-Saxon copyright. The following excerpt reflects on these historical differences that despite some convergence in the process of globalization still present difficulties in finding a common ground in international negotiations and treaty-making.

**Peter Baldwin***

## *The Battle Between Anglo-American Copyright and European Authors*

Works are created by their authors, reproduced and distributed by their disseminators, and enjoyed by the audience. These three actors, each with their own concerns, negotiate a delicate dance. Most generally, all must be kept content: the author productive, the disseminator profitable, and the audience enlightened. Get the balance wrong and things fall out of kilter. If authors become too exacting, the audience suffers. If the disseminators are greedy or the audience miserly, culture and eventually the public domain dissipate. . . .

The laws governing how artists, writers, musicians, choreographers, directors, and other authors relate to their works are usually called "copyright" in English. But this one word covers two different approaches. The very terms used to designate the European "authors' rights" alternative — *Urheberrecht* in German and *droit d'auteur* in French — voice a more encompassing approach. To capture it as we examine how these two approaches arose and evolved . . . [I] will attempt consistently to call the Anglo-American approach "copyright" and the continental European view "authors' rights." Copyright and authors' rights take very different approaches to authors and their social role. Seen historically over its long development, copyright has focused on the audience and its hopes for an expansive public domain. Authors' rights, in contrast, have targeted creators and their claims to ensure the authenticity of their works. Copyright's defenders see it as imbued with the spirit of the common good. Copyright promotes authors' creativity to benefit the public domain, allowing rights owners to exploit works efficiently. For its detractors copyright is philistine and commercial, treating noble creation as a mere commodity. It regards the creator as an entrepreneur and the work as a product.

* The Copyright Wars, Princeton Univ. Press, 2014.

The authors' rights tradition, in turn, valiantly protects the creator's vision from commercialization and exploitation. It claims to rest on the eternal verities of natural rights and regards copyright as a utilitarian, man-made creature of statute. For its detractors the authors' rights approach indulges seemingly whimsical artistes at the expense of the public. Its culturally conservative insistence that the creator retain the final say on a work's form hinders collective and collaborative efforts, let alone acknowledgment of the audience's role in determining a work's meaning. From this vantage the authors' rights approach embodies in statute an outmoded Romantic notion of the individual artiste, alone in a garret, dictating how his genius should be venerated. Copyright encourages innovation and promotes dissemination. Authors' rights restrain distribution, inhibiting experimentation and public exposure. Authors' rights speak for creators, while copyright favors disseminators and interpreters and ultimately the audience.

Copyright sees culture as a commodity. Its products can be sold and changed, largely like other property. But the authors' rights, especially their "moral rights," run counter to the market. Inalienable claims, they remain with the creators or their representatives even if they conflict with the commercial ambitions of the rights owners. The authors' rights ideology sees itself speaking for high culture. It is elitist and exclusive, while copyright is democratic and egalitarian. Copyright gives authors a limited economic monopoly over their work to stimulate their creativity, eventually enrich the public domain, and thereby serve the public interest. Private interests are thus subordinated to the public good. Authors' rights, in contrast, make no attempt to serve the public good as such, except tangentially insofar as happy authors better society.

The Continental ideology assumes that the author's and the audience's interests do not contradict each other directly. The public eventually benefits when authors are treated well. But copyright's adherents see a tense negotiation between author and audience. In their utilitarian calculation the public domain is served by protecting authors only as necessary to keep them contented and productive. Rewarding authors is not the goal but only the means to further their productivity. Social goals are preeminent, and the author's and the audience's claims do not always reconcile. "It is somehow typical of the American reasoning regarding copyright," says a French observer, "to oppose the interests of consumers to those of authors and performers." Authors' rights, in contrast, derive from natural rights. The Continental approach defends creators and their work. In a sense it seeks no other interest—public or otherwise. Authors' rights, says a distinguished French jurist, seek to protect the author, not society. Because it sets the author before all, writes a French law professor, balancing interests, on the model of the copyright systems, is foreign to the French tradition.

. . .

### Parsing the Differences Between Copyright and Authors' Rights

Differences between copyright and authors' rights are clear at a general and philosophical level. But in the hurly-burly of implementation and administration, they are frequently obscured by everyday practical considerations. Outcomes are often dictated by functional necessity, not philosophical disagreement. Courts on both sides of the Atlantic have sometimes reached similar conclusions, but for different reasons.

Let us therefore clarify the specific distinctions between these two systems. How have the ideological differences been expressed in law and jurisprudence? Among the concrete ways in which copyright and authors' rights have differed are these:

1. *Duration of term.* The Continental systems have historically had longer terms of protection for authors. . . . Recent standard French legal textbooks advocate perpetual rights in ways that are inconceivable in their Anglophone equivalents. In contrast, the American

Constitution prohibits perpetuity, specifically restricting copyright protection to limited times. . . . [T]he Anglophones have more often worried that the public domain would thus be curbed. Eldred v. Ashcroft (2003) challenged the constitutionality of extending terms for existing works after the United States had stretched them from fifty years postmortem to the EU norm of seventy. The Supreme Court, however, ruled that yet another retrospective extension of term did not render it unlimited and thus unconstitutional. Despite the plaintiffs' failure, Eldred highlighted a basic trans-Atlantic difference. Their lawyer, Lawrence Lessig, questioned whether there was a constitutional limit on America's ability to imitate the Europeans "as they continually expand the term in light of their own vision of what copyright is about." Europe had nothing like the American outpouring of legal opinion criticizing the relentless lengthening of copyright's duration. The globalization of intellectual property regulation has erased many of the actual differences between copyright and authors' rights. Most nations now have largely the same lengthy term durations. But their national preferences have been revealed by whether they have actively espoused long terms or have reformed only under pressure, with dispute and foot dragging. Seen historically, authors' right countries have favored longer terms, while copyright nations resisted them.

2. *Formalities of protection.* Based on authors' inherent claims to their work, the Continental approach has discounted the formalities traditionally required to protect works—registering, affixing notice to and depositing the work, renewing rights, and the like. Protection is triggered by the sheer fact of creation. . . . A 1975 US Senate report's first reason to support formalities was that they placed in the public domain the large body of published material that no one bothered to copyright. The opposition between the two systems can be summed up thus: in authors' rights works were born as private property. But in copyright they belonged automatically to the public domain unless the author took pains to register them. "No registration, no right." Formalities thus underlined the copyright thesis that intellectual property was not based on natural rights but was an artificial creation of statute. On this point, too, the two approaches have come to approximate each other. And yet the antagonism has not wholly vanished. The UK followed Berne's dictate to eliminate formalities in 1911, but it now also requires that authors formally assert their moral rights—a true muddle. Though the US eliminated formalities starting in 1976 as it edged toward joining Berne, American critics to this day still lament the sacrifice and have attempted to challenge its constitutionality, arguing that automatically protecting most works impedes the progress of science and the useful arts.

3. *Alienability.* Eighteenth-century reforms aimed to give authors property rights in their works to sell on the market. Unless the works were entirely theirs to alienate, they would receive less than full value. In this respect, copyright regarded the work as akin to other forms of property. After alienation the creator and creation had parted. In authors' rights systems, in contrast, works can never be wholly divorced from their creators. They retain significant control, even after having assigned economic rights. As a free man cannot sell himself into slavery, so the author cannot alienate his work. In German law authors quite simply cannot assign or transfer the work as such but only limited use rights. In France today moral rights (to which we come shortly) are inherently inalienable. [E]ven if alienated by contract, moral rights remain with the author. By contrast, in the Anglophone world rights (including those moral rights recognized in statute) are largely assignable. Indeed, as we will see with the work-for-hire doctrine, in legal terms owners are regarded as authors.

4. *Contracts.* Since copyright allows fuller alienability of works, contracts in the Anglosphere have usually been freer than in authors' rights countries. Continental nations often regulate how authors can transfer rights to future works. The French law of 1957, for example, forbade all blanket transfers of future works and then specified allowable transfers in numbing detail. Only five future works in any given genre within five years were legal. The publisher had to decide to accept each work within three months after submission. The

author was able to revoke the agreement if the publisher rejected two successive works in one genre, and so forth. The author was assumed to be the weaker party, in need of protection against rapacious disseminators. We want to defend the author against himself, explained Jean Zay, minister of education in the French Popular Front government of the late 1930s. Authors were helpless, unworldly *Luftmenschen,* unable to defend themselves—or so the French argued during their campaign to insert strong authorial rights into the U.N. Declaration of Human Rights in 1948. Copyright nations, on the other hand, have generally considered authors able to manage their own affairs. Authors are seen as free agents in the marketplace, knowing the value of their works and selling them only for a fair price. But even market-driven systems have sometimes cosseted them. The 1976 US Copyright Act allowed authors a second bite of the apple. After thirty-five years they could renegotiate terms (termination of transfer) since the "unequal bargaining position of authors" meant they could not know the value of their work until it had been exploited. But only rarely did US law allow copyright law to trump contract.

*5. Identity of the author and work-for-hire.* Work for an employer (work-for-hire) or by corporate or collective entities has been closely connected to alienability. The Continental systems have recognized mainly flesh-and-blood creators, not legal entities nor anyone other than the actual author. There are exceptions to this generalization. For collective works with many individual contributors, authorship is sometimes vested in corporate entities. In 1985 France vested rights for software in the corporate employer of the programmers. But, as a rule, even work done for hire in the French and German systems entitles employee authors to similar rights in their creations as their self-employed peers. In contrast, copyright systems have routinely vested authorship in corporate entities, attributed work-for-hire to the sponsoring entity, and resolved issues surrounding collective, collaborative, and corporate works by contract. Not only is the corporate entity behind the work the first owner of copyright, it is often regarded as the author too. Who was the author of Citizen Kane, Milos Forman asked rhetorically in 1994? And who is it today? RKO Pictures in 1941 and now Turner Broadcasting were—in his eyes—ludicrous answers. The 1909 US Copyright Act founded corporate authorship by including employers as authors of work for-hire. The 1911 UK Copyright Act introduced work-for-hire too and vested authorship of photographs and musical recordings in the corporate owner. The 1976 US Copyright Act deemed the employer of the creator not only the owner of "all of the rights comprised in the copyright" but also the author of the work. Work-for-hire demonstrated how copyright resisted Romantic ideas of individual authorship even as the Continent remained indebted to them. It remains perhaps the most important divergence between the two systems, especially considering the large fraction of all content that is produced as work-for-hire in the Anglo-Saxon nations.

*6. Exceptions to the author's exclusive rights.* As we would expect, the Anglophone nations have generally accepted broader exceptions to authorial rights, allowing other authors, interpreters, and the audience to make use of works without the permission of rights holders. The US "fair use" doctrine has allowed use of protected works without permission or compensation for broad, socially beneficial purposes. American practices have been more expansive than the "fair dealing" of other Anglophone nations. That in turn has tended to be more inclusive than the Continental counterparts, with their specific excepted uses enumerated in statute. Here too, international standardization has scrubbed away stark differences. But, as we will see, the issue has reappeared in recent years as France and Germany were pushed to expand their otherwise miserly exceptions to authorial rights.

*7. Compulsory licensing.* Compulsory licensing (sometimes known as equitable remuneration) allows works to be reproduced without the author's permission so long as certain criteria—usually royalty payment—are met. It has been used to bring works efficiently to the public without much regard for the author's rights, other than that of being paid.

It has meshed more naturally with copyright practices than the Continental approach and was adopted earlier and with less fuss in the Anglophone world. Licensing violated the core Continental principle of the author's exclusive rights since, in effect, it legalized infringement in return for automatically paid fines. Licensing destroyed his power of bargaining, George Bernard Shaw complained to a parliamentary committee in 1909. If competitors could issue their own editions at rates determined by law, the first publisher would offer less than for exclusive rights. Compulsory licensing thus spoke to the interests of the public and disseminators. Some advocates have seen it as a way to overcome the perennial conflict between authors' property rights and society's insistence on access. Squaring the circle, compulsory licensing granted authors their (pecuniary) due, perhaps even perpetually, while throwing open the doors to any royalty-paying disseminator. Both Mark Twain and Ezra Pound proposed systems of perpetual authorial rights, tempered by compulsory licensing to reprint. Compulsory licensing has also been used to override authors' attempts to suppress works altogether. Most nations allow new editions, even against the rights holder's will. The British 1842 Copyright Act permitted the Privy Council to grant compulsory licenses. Early in the twentieth century American and British composers were forced to accept compulsory licensing in return for being granted rights to sound recordings of their works. More recently, developing nations have favored compulsory licensing to gain better terms than those allowed by a classic regime of exclusive rights. And some open access advocates support licensing to break the "cyberlords' information monopolies."

*8. Originality*. We might have expected that the Continental nations, with their emphasis on the personal connection between author and work, would demand a higher standard of originality than the copyright countries. In fact, the contrast has not been dramatic. The Anglophone nations imposed a doctrine of "sweat of the brow," demanding effort but not necessarily creativity. The United States, however, also required a minimum level of originality. This was reaffirmed in 1991, when the Supreme Court refused protection to a telephone directory that had merely been copied from another. In the meantime the Continental originality bar has never been high, though it is defined more stringently in Germany than in France. In 1991, for example, the EU Software Directive broadly harmonized the standard of originality for computer programs at the Anglo-Saxon level. Such works had to be the author's own intellectual creation, but nothing more.

*9. Moral rights*. The fundamental premise of the European authors' rights ideology is to consider works as a form of property, sanctified by natural rights. During the nineteenth century this was expanded to include also a personal connection that—equally based on nature—reinforced the tie between authors and their works. Moral rights seek to protect in law that investment of authorial personality. By granting authors powers to control works even after they have sold their exploitation rights, moral rights privilege creators at the expense of disseminators, interpreters, and the audience. In Anglo-American copyright, in contrast, moral rights have played a much smaller role, protected—if at all—only incidentally or outside the copyright statutes.

## NOTES AND QUESTIONS

**1.** On the history of copyright, *see also* Sam Ricketson, *The Birth of the Berne Union, infra* section II.A.1, depicting the advent of international law in the field of copyright.

**2.** As you study subsequent sections, consider whether the cultural differences still play out or whether they have been overcome in international negotiations and approximation. To what extent do they continue to influence the interpretation of international agreements on copyright?

**3.** When considering this, reflect to what extent human rights could afford a bridge between the two traditional copyright cultures.

Before taking up copyright in international law, we discuss the basic features and problems of copyright protection using case law.

## B. Scope and Subject Matter of Copyright: Basic Features and Problems

Since the advent of the Berne Convention in 1886, copyright subject matter has been defined very broadly. That subject matter is the creative expression of artists and authors. Unlike patents, it does not extend to content and ideas, which remain freely usable. There is no limit on the form copyrightable expression may take, although national law may condition protection on its "fixation" in a tangible medium. While commonly thought of in connection with books, paintings, sculptures, music, and films, copyright may encompass product labels, computer software, clothing, and jewelry design. The "format" in which copyrightable expression appears is constantly changing, from film to videotape to DVD to MPEG file to video stream, and from vinyl record to CD to MP3 file to audio stream.

### *1. The Basic Idea/Expression Dichotomy*

Copyright protection extends to authors' and artists' creative expression. Legislatures and courts have consistently interpreted the term "expression" to exclude the protection of ideas or methods of operation that might be embodied in an expressive work. This was succinctly put by the U.S. Court of Appeals for the Second Circuit in *Computer Associates v. Altai.*

### *Computer Associates International v. Altai*

982 F.2d 693 (2d Cir. 1992)

Walker, Circuit Judge: . . .

It is a fundamental principle of copyright law that a copyright does not protect an idea, but only the expression of the idea. *See Baker v. Selden*, 101 U.S. 99, 25 L. Ed. 841 (1879); *Mazer v. Stein*, 347 U.S. 201, 217, 98 L. Ed. 630, 74 S. Ct. 460 (1954). This axiom of common law has been incorporated into the governing statute. Section 102(b) of the [U.S. Copyright] Act provides:

> In no case does copyright protection for an original work of authorship extend to any idea, procedure, process, system, method of operation, concept, principle, or discovery, regardless of the form in which it is described, explained, illustrated, or embodied in such work.

17 U.S.C. §102(b). *See also* House Report, at 5670 ("Copyright does not preclude others from using ideas or information revealed by the author's work.").

### *2. Research and Expression*

In the following case, the Swiss Supreme Court considers the distinction between expression and idea in the realm of science.[1] Frau X filed suit against Frau Y and Z publishing house for

1. The judicial system in Switzerland, typical for continental Europe, generally consists of three levels: First is the Bezirksgericht (Circuit Court), which has first instance jurisdiction within a small geographic region. The Obergericht or Kantonsgericht (Court of Appeals) is the second level, which decides all appeals in one state (a "Canton") of Switzerland. The highest Swiss Court is the Federal Court, located in Lausanne. In addition to performing the usual tasks of judicial review, this court, in the area of private law, acts as a court of second appeal with a view to bringing about the uniform interpretation of federal law in the Swiss federalist structure. Unlike the U.S. Supreme Court, the Swiss Federal Court does not have discretion to decide whether or not an appeal should be considered.

infringement of copyright, alleging that Frau Y used written results of Frau X's research in a public presentation before that research was published.[2]

## *Frau X v. Frau Y & Z Publishing House*

Bundesgericht (Swiss Federal Court) BGE 113 II 306, ([1989] ECC 232, 17 June 1987) (translation, as adjusted)*

### FACTS . . .

Frau X was a student of psychology at University of Zurich. Both her work for a licentiate and her dissertation were concerned with the life and work of the first child psychoanalyst, Hermine von Hug-Hellmuth. At the end of 1983, intending to have the results of her work published, she approached the Z publishing house. The publisher's reader informed her by telephone in March 1984 that publication of the two works in the form in which they then were was not possible but the publisher would be interested in the manuscripts if they were to be reworked. The reader added that she had passed the manuscripts on for an opinion to Frau Y, who, as Frau X knew, had announced a forthcoming lecture at the Zurich Psychoanalytic Seminar on "H Hug-Hellmuth and W Schmidt." Frau Y subsequently also got in touch with Frau X.

The lecture took place on 10 May 1984; it was recorded on a tape which is stored in the library of the Psychoanalytic Seminar. It is not clear whether the lecture has been published in an appropriate form.

In May 1985 Frau X started legal proceedings against Frau Y and the Z publishing house seeking in particular an injunction under threat of penalty on the first defendant against using any quotations or results of scientific research from either of her two unpublished manuscripts unless they were acknowledged as being such. She also asked that the first defendant be ordered to pay her 2,000 Sfr plus interest by way of moral redress and that both defendants be jointly held liable to pay 500 Sfr plus interest by way of damages.

The Zurich Obergericht (Court of Appeal) dismissed the action on 20 November 1986 on the grounds that the first defendant had not infringed any copyright or droit moral of the plaintiff and had not been guilty of unfair competition, that the second defendant was not responsible for the action of its reader, and that the plaintiff had suffered no harm as a result of the passing on of the manuscript.

The plaintiff appealed against that judgment and maintained her claims.

### DECISION: . . .

3. The plaintiff objects that the Obergericht was wrong in finding that there was no infringement by the first defendant of her copyright under section 1(2) of the Copyright Act. She argues in particular that a comparison of her work with the lecture in issue shows that various passages in her manuscripts are quoted and their substantive content is adopted in part. She says that the lower court did not go into the matter at all. Her theses were of an independent character, were the result of a personal intellectual performance and therefore should not have been quoted before publication even in extracts. The content of scientific works was not generally free for copyright purposes, so that, contrary to the view of the lower court, it

2. In section II.A.3.b, *infra*, we examine another part of this decision relating to "moral rights."

* In Swiss legal practice, names are deleted from published opinions with a view to protect the plaintiff's and defendant's privacy and integrity.

was not admissible to consider individual empirical facts in isolation or to refuse protection in advance in the case of scientific data and theses. Since the individual content of such works had to be sought in the selection and scientific processing of material which they undertook, the aspects relevant for copyright purposes had to be considered as a connected whole before it was possible to make a judgment on whether protection was available to the work.

(a) Literary works fall within the concept of a protected work within the meaning of section 1 of the Copyright Act if the specific presentation does not merely contain what is common property but, when taken as a whole, is to be regarded as a result of intellectual creative activity of an individual character or as the expression of a new original idea; for originality and individuality also count as essential characteristics of a protected work. (*See* 110 IV BGE 105 E 2; 106 II BGE 73-74; 100 II BGE 172, with further references in each case.) A scientific work is also covered by the statutory definition if it shows a minimum standard of creative performance. But for these purposes a scientific idea as such does not come into consideration. What a scientist states about external circumstances, operations or other matters of fact becomes free once it is published so far as the content is concerned, and is not in itself protected for copyright purposes even if it conveys new discoveries or has been worked out with effort (88 IV BGE 127). The content of a scientific idea is not the intellectual work involved therein but consists in the fact that it reveals previously unknown or little known facts. The result of the work, therefore, is freely usable as regards content, as befits the purpose of scientific investigation, which is oriented towards free access. Reservations remain only in the case of scientific discoveries in the technical field, which in appropriate cases can be subject to patent rights or protection by reference to secrecy or confidentiality. (Troller, Immaterialguterrecht I (3rd ed), p 355; Kummer, Das urheberrechtlich schutzbare Werk, pp 106 et seq.)

On the other hand, the specific presentation of a scientific work can be entitled to protection. This includes in the first instance the external form in which the work is communicated if it is clearly distinct from other persons' written work with the same content. For these purposes it evidently cannot be overlooked that for the author of such a work narrow boundaries tend to be set as regards its written formulation because he must adhere to specific sets of facts and in particular to technical language if he wishes to be taken seriously and to be understood (88 IV BGE 129). Where the form of communication is so tightly constricted by the scientific content that there is no longer any room for an individual or original formulation copyright protection disappears for that reason. (Kummer, op cit p 108.) In addition to the form given to it, a scientific work can also exhibit individual characteristics in the way in which it plans, selects and treats, and arranges and articulates the material, and it can thus establish copyright protection. (88 IV BGE 127; Troller, op cit I p 356, n 26; Ulmer, Urheber- und Verlsagsrecht (3rd ed), p 123.) Section 70 of the German Copyright Act is interpreted in the same way. (Judgments of the Federal Supreme Court at [1975] GRUR 667 et seq and [1982] UFITA 143 et seq.) Contrary to the plaintiff's view, however, it is not admissible to extend the copyright protection still further to the content of scientific works, as is advocated by some writers on the basis of the German conception. (Haberstumpf zur Individualitat wissenschaftlicher Sprachwerke, p 77 et seq, and at [1983] UFITA 41 et seq.)

Where, as in the present case, scientific works are concerned, an infringement of copyright may accordingly arise as a result of a third person adopting the specific form in which the work is presented or imitating it in its essential aspects. It is necessary to bear in mind in this connection that not only the work's scientific propositions as such but also forms of expression predetermined by them are freely available to the public, and furthermore that the selection, recording and articulation of the subject-matter only qualify for protection as a whole or in relation to connected parts of the work, but not so far as it simply concerns details of the work, such as data, evidence, examples or similar statements. The taking over of such details, even if they are many, is not an infringement of copyright because scientific statements which are common property do not become protected parts of a work as a result of the treatment or presentation of the subject-matter, which can confer copyright protection. Nor is this position altered by the principle that not only the work as a whole but also its individual parts can be entitled to protection if they satisfy the necessary conditions for protection (85 II BGE 123 E 3).

(b) When those criteria are applied there can be no objections under Federal law to the view of the lower court that the first defendant did not infringe any copyright owned by the plaintiff. At any rate, in so far as the first defendant adopted quotations and biographic details, one is dealing with pre-existing statements which are therefore in the public domain, nor do they enjoy copyright protection in respect of their content or of the predetermined form in which they are communicated. Accordingly the scientific thesis that the role of Hermine von Hug-Hellmuth must be seen in the light of the dispute between Freud and Jung about the origin of neuroses is not protected as a scientific proposition by reason of its content but at the most by reason of the characteristic written form in which it is expressed. The judgment in question found that in the proceedings at cantonal level the plaintiff did not argue that this thesis was adopted by the first defendant in the external form in which it was communicated in the plaintiff's two works. Accordingly the first defendant was able to consider the scientific propositions of the thesis in her lecture without infringing the plaintiff's copyright.

The position is not altered by the fact the plaintiff's two works were not published at the date when it is alleged that they were taken over. The publication of a protected work is decisive for the ability to quote passages from it or make it known publicly. (Ss 12(1)4 and 42 1(d) of The Copyright Act; Troller op cit II p 704; Ulmer op cit p 313; Lutz Die Schranken des Urheberrechts nach Schweizerischem Recht, Diss Zurich 1964, p 47; E Sciaroni, Das Zitatrecht, Diss Freiburg 1970 p 28.) But publication does not affect the distinction between the free and the restricted use of a work. There is therefore no need to decide whether the plaintiff's two works already counted as published for the purposes of the Act when approved by the faculty. It must still be borne in mind that the prohibition on quoting from unpublished works does not protect the author's publishing right, but his or her claim to prevent a distorting representation of the work and to reserve to himself or herself the right to determine the final version; and that condition is sufficiently satisfied if the work is fixed as regard its essential parts, which is generally the case where the competent body of an institute of further education has passed the work. (*Cf* Lutz, op cit p 47.)

## NOTES AND QUESTIONS

**1.** How did the Swiss Federal Court define the boundary between protectable expression and unprotectable content or idea?

**2.** The Court suggests that the means for expressing scientific ideas may be sufficiently constrained such that this expression cannot be an independently creative act for copyright purposes. In what cases are scientific propositions so clearly "true" in an objective sense that the personality of the researcher is not part of the scientific proposition? If a scientific proposition turns out to be false, does this falsity turn the proposition into creative expression within the scope of copyright protection?

**3.** In 1985, the German Federal Supreme Court imposed a minimum requirement of creative spark or innovation on the authors of computer programs as a condition of granting copyright protection. In the *Protection of Computer Programs*,[3] it said:

3. (I ZR 52/83), Bundesgerichtshof (German Federal Supreme Court), [1986] ECC 498, 9 May 1985.

> While it must be allowed that copyright protection is in principle possible for computer programs, it remains to be considered in individual cases whether the program and its preliminary stages do achieve a sufficiently creative level of originality within the meaning of section 2(2) of the Copyright Act. The question has to be answered in accordance with the principles developed hitherto in judicial decisions. On that basis the question of the level of originality is to be assessed according to the total impression of intellectual creativity of the specific composition, and that must be done moreover through an overall comparison with pre-existing compositions. (*See* 27 BGH 351, 356, et seq ("Candida" Script).) Such a comparison does not contain any test of novelty (which is not relevant to the question of copyright protection (*see* 18 BGHZ 319, 322 (Building Plan)), but answers the question whether the specific composition has individual characteristics compared with compositions already known. The starting point is known programs and the work produced in the individual stages of development with such known and usual arrangements, systems and principles of construction and treatment as they may have. Any forms of composition which remain in proximity to them do not possess a sufficiently creative level of originality; merely mechanical or technical advances on and developments of existing knowledge remain in this category. (*Cf* von Gamm: [1969] WRP 96, 99.) If creative characteristics are established by the test of an overall comparison with what is already known, they must then be set against the products of an average programmer. What the average composer can do, the merely workmanlike mechanical or technical combination and connection of the material, cannot be subject to any protection. Only after a substantial advance does the lower level of protectability begin, and it presupposes a clear superiority of the compositional activity in the matter of the selection, collection, arrangement and treatment of the information and instructions over the current average of achievement. (Thus the decided cases, most recently BGH: [1984] GRUR 659, 661, [1985] ECC 562 (Documents in Support of Tender)) Especial originality can also be achieved by the processing, reworking, and working-in of known elements and forms.
>
> The question of the creative level of composition does not in principle depend on the quantitative scope of the program, nor on the expenditure and costs with which it was created or on whether the problem posed was new. Furthermore, it is not decisive for the question of the quality of the work that a number of programmers given the same commission would develop differing programs. (*See* Frankfurt OLG: [1983] GRUR 753, 755.)

The approach of the German court was rejected by the European Union in adoption of the Software Directive, discussed *infra*, which forbade the application of any condition of originality other than that the program "is the author's own intellectual creation" (Software Directive, art. 1(3)). The Software Directive was largely a reaction to this German Supreme Court decision. Yet, the German Federal Supreme Court may merely have been ahead of its time. Courts in the United States have increasingly separated out (as unprotectable) elements of programs that are adopted for reasons having to do with the underlying technology of computers, such as the need for software to address and interact with hardware components, or to take advantage of drafting efficiencies.[4]

**4.** Compilations of factual material are protected by copyright if their arrangement embodies a creative act by the compiler.

### 3. *Fact and Expression*

It is generally accepted that "facts" are not protected by copyright. Facts identify persons, places, and events. A person who reports a fact does not create the subject matter he or she is reporting. Distinctive contribution by the author is lacking in the sense of copyright law.

4. *See, e.g., Computer Associates v. Altai, infra* section VI.A.

It follows from the lack of protection for facts that mechanically assembled facts are not subject to copyright protection. However, an author may well assemble facts in a creative way and earn copyright protection for the unique characteristics of the arrangement. The U.S. Supreme Court explains this in *Feist v. Rural Telephone.*

## *Feist Publications v. Rural Telephone Service*

499 U.S. 340 (1991)

Justice O'Connor delivered the opinion of the Court.

This case concerns the interaction of two well-established propositions. The first is that facts are not copyrightable; the other, that compilations of facts generally are. Each of these propositions possesses an impeccable pedigree. That there can be no valid copyright in facts is universally understood. The most fundamental axiom of copyright law is that "no author may copyright his ideas or the facts he narrates." *Harper & Row, Publishers, Inc. v. Nation Enterprises*, 471 U.S. 539, 556 (1985). Rural wisely concedes this point, noting in its brief that "facts and discoveries, of course, are not themselves subject to copyright protection.". . . At the same time, however, it is beyond dispute that compilations of facts are within the subject matter of copyright. Compilations were expressly mentioned in the Copyright Act of 1909, and again in the Copyright Act of 1976.

There is an undeniable tension between these two propositions. Many compilations consist of nothing but raw data—i.e., wholly factual information not accompanied by any original written expression. On what basis may one claim a copyright in such a work? Common sense tells us that 100 uncopyrightable facts do not magically change their status when gathered together in one place. Yet copyright law seems to contemplate that compilations that consist exclusively of facts are potentially within its scope.

The key to resolving the tension lies in understanding why facts are not copyrightable. The sine qua non of copyright is originality. To qualify for copyright protection, a work must be original to the author. *See Harper & Row, supra*, at 547-549. Original, as the term is used in copyright, means only that the work was independently created by the author (as opposed to copied from other works), and that it possesses at least some minimal degree of creativity. 1 M. Nimmer & D. Nimmer, Copyright §§2.01[A], [B] (1990) (hereinafter Nimmer). To be sure, the requisite level of creativity is extremely low; even a slight amount will suffice. The vast majority of works make the grade quite easily, as they possess some creative spark, "no matter how crude, humble or obvious" it might be. *Id.*, §1.08[C][1]. Originality does not signify novelty; a work may be original even though it closely resembles other works so long as the similarity is fortuitous, not the result of copying. To illustrate, assume that two poets, each ignorant of the other, compose identical poems. Neither work is novel, yet both are original and, hence, copyrightable. *See Sheldon v. Metro-Goldwyn Pictures Corp.*, 81 F.2d 49, 54 (CA2 1936). . . .

This Court has long recognized that the fact/expression dichotomy limits severely the scope of protection in fact-based works. More than a century ago, the Court observed: "The very object of publishing a book on science or the useful arts is to communicate to the world the useful knowledge which it contains. But this object would be frustrated if the knowledge could not be used without incurring the guilt of piracy of the book." *Baker v. Selden*, 101 U.S. 99, 103 (1880). We reiterated this point in *Harper & Row*:

> "No author may copyright facts or ideas. The copyright is limited to those aspects of the work—termed 'expression'—that display the stamp of the author's originality."
>
> "Copyright does not prevent subsequent users from copying from a prior author's work those constituent elements that are not original—for example . . . facts, or materials in the

public domain—as long as such use does not unfairly appropriate the author's original contributions." 471 U.S., at 547-548 (citation omitted).

This, then, resolves the doctrinal tension: Copyright treats facts and factual compilations in a wholly consistent manner. Facts, whether alone or as part of a compilation, are not original and therefore may not be copyrighted. A factual compilation is eligible for copyright if it features an original selection or arrangement of facts, but the copyright is limited to the particular selection or arrangement. In no event may copyright extend to the facts themselves.

## NOTES AND QUESTIONS

**1.** Later in the *Feist* decision, the U.S. Supreme Court held that the assembly by a telephone company of an alphabetical listing of names and telephone numbers (to form a directory) lacked the minimal creativity necessary to justify protection under copyright law. The decision prompted efforts by "database" compilers to secure additional protection for their work. These efforts succeeded in the European Union with adoption of the Database Directive, referenced *infra* section IV.A.2, which establishes a *sui generis* form of database protection.

**2.** Librarians and researchers are concerned about the prospects for enhanced database protection. If intellectual property protection for databases becomes commonplace, institutions that currently make information freely available may decide to impose "extraction" fees. This could have a chilling effect on research and access to knowledge.

**3.** Although the mechanical assembly of facts is not protectable by copyright, a database producer may be able to pursue a claim under unfair competition law, depending on the circumstances of the case. In other words, a database compiler may be able to demonstrate that a competitor has taken unfair commercial advantage of its efforts.

## C. Copying and Substantial Similarity

Copyright allows its holder to prevent unauthorized copying and distribution. It does not prevent a third party from independently creating the same (or a substantially similar) work. In this sense, copyright is fundamentally different from the patent. The holder of a patent has the right to prevent any third party from making or using the invention, even if the third party developed the invention without knowledge of what the patent holder had done. For this reason, the patent is sometimes referred to as a "hard" form of intellectual property. Because the copyright does not preclude independent creation, it is sometimes referred to as a "soft" form of intellectual property.

In addition to protecting the author's specific form of expression, copyright also protects against the unauthorized reproduction and distribution of derivative works such as translations and adaptations. There are many issues that arise in assessing whether a secondary work is merely an adaptation of an existing work, or is sufficiently transformed so as to constitute a "new" work.

Most copyright infringement lawsuits begin with the question whether the alleged infringer actually copied the relevant subject matter. It is often difficult for the copyright holder to directly prove copying. The act of copying may be "inferred" from the alleged infringer's access to the work and the degree of similarity.

The unauthorized reproduction of an author's work may take the form of direct or literal copying, in which case infringement of the author's rights may be relatively easy to determine (bearing in mind that there are defenses to literal copying, for example, under fair use doctrine). Unauthorized reproduction may also take the form of indirect or nonliteral copying, in which case the copying party is modifying the protected work in order to avoid the appearance of reproducing it. In the case of nonliteral copying, courts apply various tests to determine whether an allegedly infringing work is sufficiently similar to a protected work to violate the author's copyright. In the United States, for example, the traditional legal test is whether an allegedly infringing work is "substantially similar" to the protected work. Application of this test generally requires the use of subjective judgment.

Comparison of copyrighted works for substantial similarity involves determining an appropriate level of "abstraction." At the highest level of abstraction all movies are the same, that is, they are expressive cinematic works. At a lower level of abstraction, movies fall within broad categories (fictional and documentary). At progressively lower levels, movies have broad themes, plot outlines, titles, developed plot lines and characters, sets, and dialogue. At a relatively high level of abstraction — two people fall in love, get married, and endure hardship — hundreds if not thousands of films would be copies of each other. At this high level of abstraction, the movie is a common "idea." A "merger" between idea and expression takes place at this level. Only when an adequate level of detail is achieved may the author's expression become sufficiently distinctive to be protected against misappropriation.

It is not practical to define the appropriate level of abstraction at which comparison between allegedly infringing works should take place. The context in which such comparison takes place is always changing. Some courts have sought to distinguish between "objective" and "subjective" comparison of works. Objective comparison involves analytic dissection of the work — describing the characters, what they are doing, where they are living, and so forth — and seeking to evaluate similarity on the basis of the distilled factors. "Subjective" comparison looks instead to the impression the works make on the finder of fact. Viewing two movies side by side, do they seem to be similar?

Though one might expect courts to have evolved a straightforward body of rules for deciding such important questions, the creativity of authors and artists frustrates the judge. How does one formulate a rule for comparing two similar, but not identical, paintings or films? In recent years, there have a great number of cases regarding claims of misappropriating musical content. One such case was *Williams v. Gaye*, No. 15-56880 (9th Cir. 2018), where the U.S. Court of Appeals for the Ninth Circuit confirmed that Robin Thicke, Pharrell Williams, and Clifford Harris, Jr. have with their 2013 song "Blurred Lines" infringed the copyright of members of Marvin Gaye's family by copying his 1977 hit "Got to Give It Up". The musicians were ordered to pay about $5 million to Gaye's estate, plus half of future royalties for the song. The Court held that "Got to Give It Up" was entitled to broad copyright protection because musical compositions were not confined to a narrow range of expression and provided some helpful, although not uncontested, clarifications as to the tests of substantial similarity, in particular for musical compositions.

The Court held (footnotes omitted):

> We use a two-part test for substantial similarity: an extrinsic test and an intrinsic test. *Swirsky*, 376 F.3d at 845. For a jury to find substantial similarity, there must be evidence on both the extrinsic and intrinsic tests. *Id.* (citing *Rice v. Fox Broad. Co.*, 330 F.3d 1170, 1174 (9th Cir. 2003)). A district court applies only the extrinsic test on a motion for summary judgment, as the intrinsic test is reserved exclusively for the trier of fact. *Benay v. Warner Bros. Entm't, Inc.*, 607 F.3d 620, 624 (9th Cir. 2010).
>
> The extrinsic test is objective. *Swirsky*, 376 F.3d at 845. It "considers whether two works share a similarity of ideas and expression as measured by external, objective criteria." *Id.* Application of "[t]he extrinsic test requires 'analytical dissection of a work and expert testimony.'" *Id.* (quoting *Three Boys Music*, 212 F.3d at 485). An analytical dissection, in turn, "requires breaking the works 'down into their constituent elements, and comparing those

elements for proof of copying as measured by "substantial similarity."'" *Id.* (quoting *Rice v. Fox Broad. Co.*, 148 F. Supp. 2d 1029, 1051 (C.D. Cal. 2001)).

The intrinsic test, on the other hand, is subjective. *Three Boys Music*, 212 F.3d at 485. It "asks 'whether the ordinary, reasonable person would find the total concept and feel of the works to be substantially similar.'" *Id.* (quoting *Pasillas v. McDonald's Corp.*, 927 F.2d 440, 442 (9th Cir. 1991)).

"Because the requirement is one of substantial similarity to protected elements of the copyrighted work, it is essential to distinguish between the protected and unprotected material in a plaintiff's work." *Swirsky*, 376 F.3d at 845. Still, "substantial similarity can be found in a combination of elements, even if those elements are individually unprotected." *Id.* at 848; *see also Metcalf*, 294 F.3d at 1074 ("Each note in a scale, for example, is not protectable, but a pattern of notes in a tune may earn copyright protection."); *Three Boys Music*, 212 F.3d at 485-86 (upholding jury's finding of substantial similarity based on "a combination of unprotectible elements"). This principle finds particular relevance in application of the intrinsic test, as a trier of fact may "find that the over-all impact and effect indicate substantial appropriation," even if "any one similarity taken by itself seems trivial." *Sid & Marty Krofft Television Prods., Inc. v. McDonald's Corp.*, 562 F.2d 1157, 1169 (9th Cir. 1977) (quoting *Malkin v. Dubinsky*, 146 F. Supp. 111, 114 (S.D.N.Y. 1956)), superseded in part on other grounds, 17 U.S.C. §504(b); *see also Three Boys Music*, 212 F.3d at 485.

In *Computer Associates v. Altai, infra* section VI.A, the court assesses substantial similarity between computer programs.

## D. Term of Protection and the Public Domain

The protection afforded by copyright is of substantially longer duration than that afforded by patent. The Berne Convention and TRIPS Agreement minimum term of copyright is the author's life plus 50 years. This long duration is partially justified by the fact that copyright is weaker than the patent right, since it does not preclude independent creation. The term of copyright was extended to the author's life plus 70 years by the EU Copyright Directive, and this extension was followed by the United States. The U.S. term extension legislation was challenged by a number of groups on grounds, *inter alia*, that it was inconsistent with the Copyright and Patent Clause of the Constitution, which refers to the grant of exclusive rights for "limited Times." These groups worry that term extension has the effect of restricting the "public domain," that is, works free for all to use.

The following excerpts from the U.S. Supreme Court's decision in *Eldred v. Ashcroft* highlight the argument put forward on behalf of the U.S. copyright industries that failure to extend the copyright term would lead to a "protection gap" with the European Union, encouraging authors to publish outside the United States.

### *Eldred v. Ashcroft*

537 U.S. 186 (2003)

Justice GINSBURG delivered the opinion of the Court.

This case concerns the authority the Constitution assigns to Congress to prescribe the duration of copyrights. The Copyright and Patent Clause of the Constitution, Art. I, §8, cl. 8, provides as to copyrights: "Congress shall have Power . . . to promote the Progress of Science . . . by securing [to Authors] for limited Times . . . the exclusive Right to their . . . Writings." In 1998, in the measure here under inspection, Congress enlarged the duration of copyrights by 20 years. Copyright Term Extension Act (CTEA), Pub. L. 105-298, §102(b) and (d), 112 Stat. 2827-28 (amending 17 U.S.C. §§302, 304). As in the case of prior extensions, principally in 1831, 1909, and 1976, Congress provided for application of the enlarged terms to existing and future copyrights alike. . . .

The CTEA reflects judgments of a kind Congress typically makes, judgments we cannot dismiss as outside the Legislature's domain. As respondent describes, . . . a key factor in the CTEA's passage was a 1993 European Union (EU) directive instructing EU members to establish a copyright term of life plus 70 years. EU Council Directive 93/98, p. 4; *see* 144 Cong. Rec. S12377-S12378 (daily ed. Oct. 12, 1998) (statement of Sen. Hatch). Consistent with the Berne Convention, the EU directed its members to deny this longer term to the works of any non-EU country whose laws did not secure the same extended term. *See* Berne Conv. Art. 7(8); P. Goldstein, International Copyright §5.3, p. 239 (2001). By extending the baseline United States copyright term to life plus 70 years, Congress sought to ensure that American authors would receive the same copyright protection in Europe as their European counterparts.[11] The CTEA may also provide greater incentive for American and other authors to create and disseminate their work in the United States. *See* Perlmutter, Participation in the International Copyright System as a Means to Promote the Progress of Science and Useful Arts, 36 Loyola (LA) L. Rev. 323, 330 (2002) ("Matching the level of [copyright] protection in the United States [to that in the European Union] can ensure stronger protection for U.S. works abroad and avoid competitive disadvantages vis-à-vis foreign rightholders."); *see also id.*, at 332 (the United States could not "play a leadership role" in the give-and-take evolution of the international copyright system, indeed it would "lose all flexibility," "if the only way to promote the progress of science were to provide incentives to create new works"). . . .

Petitioners contend that even if the CTEA's 20-year term extension is literally a "limited Time," permitting Congress to extend existing copyrights allows it to evade the "limited Times" constraint by creating effectively perpetual copyrights through repeated extensions. We disagree.

As the Court of Appeals observed, a regime of perpetual copyrights "clearly is not the situation before us." 239 F.3d at 379. . . .

More forcibly, petitioners contend that the CTEA's extension of existing copyrights does not "promote the Progress of Science" as contemplated by the preambular language of the Copyright Clause. Art. I, §8, cl. 8. To sustain this objection, petitioners do not argue that the Clause's preamble is an independently enforceable limit on *Congress' power. See* 239 F.3d at 378. (Petitioners acknowledge that "the preamble of the Copyright Clause is not a substantive limit on Congress' legislative power." (internal quotation marks omitted)). Rather, they maintain that the preambular language identifies the sole end to which Congress may legislate; accordingly, they conclude, the meaning of "limited Times" must be "determined in light of that specified end.". . . The CTEA's extension of existing copyrights categorically fails to "promote the Progress of Science," petitioners argue, because it does not stimulate the creation of new works but merely adds value to works already created. . . .

We have also stressed, however, that it is generally for Congress, not the courts, to decide how best to pursue the Copyright Clause's objectives. . . .

Petitioners separately argue that the CTEA is a content-neutral regulation of speech that fails heightened judicial review under the First Amendment. We reject petitioners' plea for

11. Responding to an inquiry whether copyrights could be extended "forever," Register of Copyrights Marybeth Peters emphasized the dominant reason for the CTEA: "There certainly are proponents of perpetual copyright: We heard that in our proceeding on term extension. The Songwriters Guild suggested a perpetual term. However, our Constitution says limited times, but there really isn't a very good indication on what limited times is. The reason why you're going to life-plus-70 today is because Europe has gone that way. . . ." Copyright Term, Film Labeling, and Film Preservation Legislation: Hearings on H. R. 989 et al. before the Subcommittee on Courts and Intellectual Property of the House Committee on the Judiciary, 104th Cong., 1st Sess., 230 (1995) (hereinafter House Hearings).

imposition of uncommonly strict scrutiny on a copyright scheme that incorporates its own speech-protective purposes and safeguards. The Copyright Clause and First Amendment were adopted close in time. This proximity indicates that, in the Framers' view, copyright's limited monopolies are compatible with free speech principles. Indeed, copyright's purpose is to promote the creation and publication of free expression. As *Harper & Row* observed: "The Framers intended copyright itself to be the engine of free expression. By establishing a marketable right to the use of one's expression, copyright supplies the economic incentive to create and disseminate ideas." 471 U.S., at 558.

In addition to spurring the creation and publication of new expression, copyright law contains built-in First Amendment accommodations. *See id.*, at 560. First, it distinguishes between ideas and expression and makes only the latter eligible for copyright protection. . . . Due to this distinction, every idea, theory, and fact in a copyrighted work becomes instantly available for public exploitation at the moment of publication. *See Feist*, 499 U.S., at 349-350.

Second, the "fair use" defense allows the public to use not only facts and ideas contained in a copyrighted work, but also expression itself in certain circumstances. Codified at 17 U.S.C. §107, the defense provides: "The fair use of a copyrighted work, including such use by reproduction in copies . . ., for purposes such as criticism, comment, news reporting, teaching (including multiple copies for classroom use), scholarship, or research, is not an infringement of copyright." The fair use defense affords considerable "latitude for scholarship and comment," *Harper & Row*, 471 U.S., at 560, and even for parody, *see Campbell v. Acuff-Rose Music, Inc.*, 510 U.S. 569, 127 L. Ed. 2d 500, 114 S. Ct. 1164 (1994) (rap group's musical parody of Roy Orbison's "Oh, Pretty Woman" may be fair use). . . .

JUSTICE BREYER, dissenting.

The Constitution's Copyright Clause grants Congress the power to "*promote* the *Progress* of Science . . . by securing for *limited* Times to *Authors* . . . the exclusive Right to their respective Writings." Art. I, §8, cl. 8 (emphasis added). The statute before us, the 1998 Sonny Bono Copyright Term Extension Act, extends the term of most existing copyrights to 95 years and that of many new copyrights to 70 years after the author's death. The economic effect of this 20-year extension—the longest blanket extension since the Nation's founding—is to make the copyright term not limited, but virtually perpetual. Its primary legal effect is to grant the extended term not to authors, but to their heirs, estates, or corporate successors. And most importantly, its practical effect is not to promote, but to inhibit, the progress of "Science"—by which word the Framers meant learning or knowledge, E. Walterscheid, The Nature of the Intellectual Property Clause: A Study in Historical Perspective 125-126 (2002).

The majority believes these conclusions rest upon practical judgments that at most suggest the statute is unwise, not that it is unconstitutional. Legal distinctions, however, are often matters of degree. . . . And in this case the failings of degree are so serious that they amount to failings of constitutional kind. Although the Copyright Clause grants broad legislative power to Congress, that grant has limits. And in my view this statute falls outside them. . . .

Second, the Court relies heavily for justification upon international uniformity of terms. Ante, at 4, 14-15. Although it can be helpful to look to international norms and legal experience in understanding American law, cf. *Printz v. U.S.*, 521 U.S. 898, 977, 138 L. Ed. 2d 914, 117 S. Ct. 2365 (1997) (Breyer, J., dissenting), in this case the justification based upon foreign rules is surprisingly weak. Those who claim that significant copyright-related benefits flow from greater international uniformity of terms point to the fact that the nations of the European Union have adopted a system of copyright terms uniform among themselves. And the extension before this Court implements a term of life plus 70 years that appears to conform with the European standard. But how does "uniformity" help to justify this statute?

Despite appearances, the statute does not create a uniform American-European term with respect to the lion's share of the economically significant works that it affects—all works made "for hire" and all existing works created prior to 1978. . . . With respect to those works the American statute produces an extended term of 95 years while comparable European rights in "for hire" works last for periods that vary from 50 years to 70 years to life plus 70 years. Compare 17 U.S.C. §§302(c), 304(a)-(b) with Council Directive 93/98/EEC of 29 October 1993 Harmonizing the Term of Protection of Copyright and Certain Related Rights, Arts. 1-3, 1993 Official J. Eur. Cmty. 290 (hereinafter EU Council Directive 93/98). Neither does the statute create uniformity with respect to anonymous or pseudonymous works. Compare 17 U.S.C. §§302(c), 304(a)-(b) with EU Council Directive 93/98, Art. 1.

The statute does produce uniformity with respect to copyrights in new, post-1977 works attributed to natural persons. Compare 17 U.S.C. §302(a) with EU Council Directive 93/98, Art. 1(1). But these works constitute only a subset (likely a minority) of works that retain commercial value after 75 years. . . . And the fact that uniformity comes so late, if at all, means that bringing American law into conformity with this particular aspect of European law will neither encourage creation nor benefit the long-dead author in any other important way.

What benefit, then, might this partial future uniformity achieve? The majority refers to "greater incentive for American and other authors to create and disseminate their work in the United States," and cites a law review article suggesting a need to "avoid competitive disadvantages.". . . The Solicitor General elaborates on this theme, postulating that because uncorrected disuniformity would permit Europe, not the United States, to hold out the prospect of protection lasting for "life plus 70 years" (instead of "life plus 50 years"), a potential author might decide to publish initially in Europe, delaying American publication. . . . And the statute, by creating a uniformly longer term, corrects for the disincentive that this disuniformity might otherwise produce.

That disincentive, however, could not possibly bring about serious harm of the sort that the Court, the Solicitor General, or the law review author fears. For one thing, it is unclear just who will be hurt and how, should American publication come second—for the Berne Convention still offers full protection as long as a second publication is delayed by 30 days. *See* Berne Conv. Arts. 3(4), 5(4). For another, few, if any, potential authors would turn a "where to publish" decision upon this particular difference in the length of the copyright term. As we have seen, the present commercial value of any such difference amounts at most to comparative pennies. . . . And a commercial decision that turned upon such a difference would have had to have rested previously upon a knife edge so fine as to be invisible. A rational legislature could not give major weight to an invisible, likely nonexistent incentive-related effect.

But if there is no incentive-related benefit, what is the benefit of the future uniformity that the statute only partially achieves? Unlike the Copyright Act of 1976, this statute does not constitute part of an American effort to conform to an important international treaty like the Berne Convention. *See* H. R. Rep. No. 94-1476, pp. 135-136 (1976) (The 1976 Act's life-plus-50 term was "required for adherence to the Berne Convention"); S. Rep. No. 94-473, p. 118 (1975) (same). Nor does European acceptance of the longer term seem to reflect more than special European institutional considerations, i.e., the needs of, and the international politics surrounding, the development of the European Union. House Hearings 230 (statement of the Register of Copyrights); *id.*, at 396-398 (statement of J. Reichman). European and American copyright law have long coexisted despite important differences, including Europe's traditional respect for authors' "moral rights" and the absence in Europe of constitutional restraints that restrict copyrights to "limited Times." *See, e.g.*, Kwall, Copyright and the Moral Right: Is an American Marriage Possible? 38 Vand. L. Rev. 1, 1-3 (1985) (moral rights); House Hearings 187 (testimony of the Register of Copyrights) ("limited Times").

In sum, the partial, future uniformity that the 1998 Act promises cannot reasonably be said to justify extension of the copyright term for new works. And concerns with uniformity cannot possibly justify the extension of the new term to older works, for the statute there creates no uniformity at all. . . .

## NOTES AND QUESTIONS

**1.** In thinking about the "protection gap" argument, it may be helpful to note that the major copyright industry actors are multinational and lobby both in the United States and the European Union. Representatives of the same company will appear at EU Commission-sponsored meetings arguing for stronger protection to improve EU competitiveness vis-à-vis the United States, and fly across the Atlantic to appear at congressional hearings in the United States arguing that it is necessary to close the gap with the European Union.

**2.** Justice Breyer contends that additional royalty income to U.S. authors and artists creating new works will be very small. Who benefits from the term extension? Large entertainment companies with film and music libraries, as well as holders of copyrights in cartoon characters, lobbied heavily in favor of the extension.

**3.** The *Eldred v. Ashcroft* decision includes a discussion of the impact of copyright term extension on freedom of speech (or expression). Freedom of expression and copyright protection are inherently in tension. Although copyright law makes exception for the fair use of protected works in matters such as critical commentary, the application of the fair use exception is nonetheless subject to limitations. When expression is protected by copyright, it may no longer be used freely in an absolute sense. As with other fields of intellectual property protection, society makes a bargain. As encouragement for the creation of works that contribute to public well-being, the author or artist is granted an exclusive right to control his or her expression work for a limited time. A boundary is drawn around the work, and it becomes off limits from the standpoint of free expression (subject to fair use). There is always a risk that the public commons may become so cluttered with boundaries that free expression and the public good will suffer. *See* discussion in *Universal Studios v. Corley, infra.* The Berne Convention and TRIPS Agreement make provision for fair use, but they do not expressly address freedom of expression or speech. In fact, the Berne Convention provides that it does not interfere with the right of governments to control the distribution of expressive works (art. 17, Berne Convention).[5]

The right of free speech or expression will usually be guaranteed by the national constitution. Of course, not all governments or constitutions accord the same scope to this right. Nonetheless, the matter does not end at the national level. Regional and international human rights agreements and principles also recognize rights of speech and expression. (*See, e.g.*, the decision of the European Court of Human Rights in *Hertel v. Switzerland*, 25181/94 [1998] ECHR 77 (25 August 1998). Although this case principally involved conflict between freedom of expression and unfair competition law, the basic principles are similar.)

---

5. The Berne Convention provides:

Article 17 Possibility of Control of Circulation, Presentation and Exhibition of Works

The provisions of this Convention cannot in any way affect the right of the Government of each country of the Union to permit, to control, or to prohibit, by legislation or regulation, the circulation, presentation, or exhibition of any work or production in regard to which the competent authority may find it necessary to exercise that right.

**4.** Traditionally, U.S. and British copyright law required registration to obtain a copyright. With adherence to the Berne Convention, both countries abandoned this condition, because the Berne Convention states that copyright may not be bound by any formalities. But, whereas Great Britain fully eliminated the registration requirement, the United States still permits registration and encourages right holders to register by giving them an initial advantage in litigation. Are there reasonable grounds not to require registration of copyrights? Conversely, what justifies registration requirements with respect to patents, plant varieties, industrial designs, integrated circuit layout designs, and trademarks? The transition from registration to protection continues to raise issues of duration of copyright protection under the Berne Convention and the TRIPS Agreement. *See, e.g.*, *Montis Design v. Goossens Meubelen*, C-169/15, 20 Oct. 2016, addressing the non-retroactive character of copyright legislation in relation to works as to which copyright is already extinguished.

## E. The Dichotomy Between Private Use and Communication to the Public

In the field of information technology and streaming, the question of private use has been a major issue of debate on freedom of information versus copyright protection. Other than fair use, communication to the public is an essential prerequisite of copyright protection that does not extend to private use. The delineation has become most difficult in the digital age. The following case expounds the limitations of private use without authorization of the right holder in EU law.

### *Reha v. GEMA*

Judgment of the Court (Grand Chamber), 31 May 2016

(Reference for a preliminary ruling — Intellectual property — Copyright and related rights — Directive 2001/29/EC — Article 3(1) — Directive 2006/115/EC — Article 8(2) — Concept of 'communication to the public' — Installation of television sets by the operator of a rehabilitation centre making it possible for patients to watch television programmes)

In Case C117/15,

REQUEST for a preliminary ruling under Article 267 TFEU from the Landgericht Köln (Regional Court, Cologne, Germany), made by decision of 20 February 2015, received at the Court on 9 March 2015, in the proceedings

Reha Training Gesellschaft für Sport- und Unfallrehabilitation mbH v Gesellschaft für musikalische Aufführungs- und mechanische Vervielfältigungsrechte eV (GEMA), intervening parties: Gesellschaft zur Verwertung von Leistungsschutzrechten mbH (GVL),

THE COURT (Grand Chamber),
gives the following:

#### Judgment

1. This request for a preliminary ruling concerns the interpretation of Article 3(1) of Directive 2001/29/EC of the European Parliament and of the Council of 22 May 2001 on the harmonisation of certain aspects of copyright and related rights in the information society (OJ 2001 L 167, p. 10), and Article 8(2) of Directive 2006/115/EC of the European

Parliament and of the Council of 12 December 2006 on rental right and lending right and on certain rights related to copyright in the field of intellectual property (OJ 2006 L 376, p. 28).

2. This request has been made in proceedings between Reha Training Gesellschaft für Sport- und Unfallrehabilitation mbH ('Reha Training'), which operates a rehabilitation centre, and Gesellschaft für musikalische Aufführungs- und mechanische Vervielfältigungsrechte eV (GEMA), the company entrusted with the collective management of copyright in the musical sector in Germany, concerning the refusal of Reha Training to pay royalties on copyright and related rights in connection with making available protected works at that company's premises.

. . .

## The Dispute in the Main Proceedings and the Questions Referred for a Preliminary Ruling

11. The rehabilitation centre operated by Reha Training provides for accident victims to receive post-operative treatment on its premises with a view to permitting their rehabilitation.

12. Those premises include two waiting rooms and a training room in which, from June 2012 to June 2013, Reha Training allowed its patients to watch television programmes on television sets installed there. Those programmes could therefore be viewed by those who were at the rehabilitation centre for treatment.

. . .

15. The referring court takes the view, in accordance with the criteria set out in the Court's case-law relating to the interpretation of Directive 2001/29, that the making available of television programmes by Reha Training constitutes a communication to the public. That court also considers that the same criteria should apply to determine whether there is 'communication to the public' within the meaning of Article 8(2) of Directive 2006/115, but that the judgment of 15 March 2012 in *SCF* (C-135/10, EU:C:2012:140), prevents it giving a decision.

16. In that judgment the Court of Justice held that patients of a dental practice are not 'persons in general'. In the present case, since, as a rule, only the patients of Reha Training have access to the treatment provided by it, those patients cannot be categorised as 'persons in general', but constitute a 'private group'.

17. In its judgment of 15 March 2012 in *SCF* (C-135/10, EU:C:2012:140) the Court also held that the number of patients of a dental practice is not large, indeed it is insignificant, given that the group of persons present in that practice at the same time is, in general, very small. The category of persons formed by the patients of Reha Training would also seem to be limited.

18. Moreover, in that judgment, the Court ruled that the usual patients of a dental practice do not willingly listen to music there, since they enjoy it by chance, but do not choose to do so. In the present case, the patients of Reha Training in the waiting rooms and the training room also view and hear the television programmes without any active wish or choice on their part.

. . .

47. [This] Court has already held that the operators of a café-restaurant, a hotel or a spa establishment are such users and make a communication to the public if they intentionally broadcast protected works to their clientele, by intentionally distributing a signal by means of television or radio sets that they have installed in their establishment (see, to that effect, judgments of 7 December 2006 in *SGAE*, C306/05, EU:C:2006:764, paragraphs 42 and 47; 4 October 2011 in *Football Association Premier League and Others*, C403/08 and C429/08, EU:C:2011:631, paragraph 196; and 27 February 2014 in *OSA*, C351/12, EU:C:2014:110, paragraph 26).

53. In the light of various criteria laid down by the case-law of the Court, it must be determined whether the broadcast of television programmes, such as that at issue in the main proceedings, may be categorised as a 'communication to the public' within the meaning of Article 3(1) of Directive 2001/29 and Article 8(2) of Directive 2006/115.

54. In that connection, in the first place, as stated in paragraph 47 of the present judgment, the Court has already held that the operators of a café-restaurant, a hotel or a spa establishment carry out an act of communication where they intentionally broadcast protected works to their clientele by intentionally distributing a signal by means of television or radio sets which they have installed in their establishment.

55. Those situations are fully comparable with that at issue in the main proceedings in which, as is apparent from the order for reference, the operator of a rehabilitation centre intentionally broadcasts protected works to its patients by means of television sets installed in several places in that establishment.

56. Therefore, it must be held that such an operator carries out an act of communication.

57. In the second place, as regards the body of patients of a rehabilitation centre, such as that at issue in the main proceedings, it must be observed, first of all, that it is apparent from the documents submitted to the Court that they are persons in general.

58. Next, the circle of persons constituted by those patients is not 'too small or insignificant', it being understood, in particular, that those patients may enjoy works broadcast at the same time in several places in the establishment.

59. In those circumstances, it must be held that the body of patients of a rehabilitation centre, such as that at issue in the main proceedings, constitute a 'public', within the meaning of Article 3(1) of Directive 2001/29 and Article 8(2) of Directive 2006/115.

60. Finally, the patients of such a rehabilitation centre cannot, in principle, enjoy works broadcast without the targeted intervention of the operator of that centre. Furthermore, since the origin of the dispute in the main proceedings concerns the payment of royalties for copyright and related rights for the making available of protected works in that centre, it must be observed that those patients were clearly not taken into account when the original authorisation for the work to be made available was given.

61. It follows that the patients of a rehabilitation centre, such as that at issue in the main proceedings, constitutes a 'new public' within the meaning of the case-law referred to . . .

62. Having regard to the foregoing considerations, it must be held that the operator of a rehabilitation centre, such as that at issue in the main proceedings, carries out a communication to the public.

63. In the third place, as regards the profit-making nature of such a communication, it must be stated, as the Advocate General observed . . . , that, in the present case, the broadcasting of television programmes on television sets, in so far as it is intended to create a diversion for the patients of a rehabilitation centre, such as that at issue in the main proceedings, during their treatment or in the waiting time, constitutes the supply of additional services which, while not having any medical benefit, does have an impact on the establishment's standing and attractiveness, thereby giving it a competitive advantage.

64. It follows that, in a situation such as that at issue in the main proceedings, the broadcasting of television programmes by the operator of a rehabilitation centre, such as Reha Training, has a profit-making nature, capable of being taken into account in order to determine the amount of remuneration due, where appropriate, for such a broadcast.

65. Having regard to all of the foregoing considerations, the answer to the first three questions is that, in a case such as that in the main proceedings, in which it is alleged that the broadcast of television programmes by means of television sets that the operator of a rehabilitation centre has installed in its premises affects the copyright and related rights of a large

number of interested parties, in particular, composers, songwriters and music publishers, but also performers, phonogram producers and authors of literary works and their publishers, it must be determined whether such a situation constitutes a 'communication to the public', with regards to both Article 3(1) of Directive 2001/29 and Article 8(2) of Directive 2006/115 and in accordance with the same interpretation criteria. Furthermore, those two provisions must be interpreted as meaning that such a broadcast constitutes an act of 'communication to the public'.

## NOTES AND QUESTIONS

**1.** How does the Court justify different treatment of broadcast in a dental practice and a rehabilitation center? How is the threshold defined, and what does it mean for other institutions, such as small shops, hotels, or bars?

**2.** Would the European Union be entitled to exclude restaurants and shops from copyright levies? *See* the standards developed by WTO jurisprudence in *United States—Section 110(5) of the U.S. Copyright Act*, discussed *infra.*

**3.** Practical difficulties to distinguish between commercial and private copying led to the introduction of general fees levied upon copying works for whatever purpose, subject to a levy fee which is levied as tax upon owners of equipment. The CJEU confirmed that such taxes must not be levied on companies for activities clearly unrelated to private copying, and that exceptions must be framed in a nondiscriminatory manner and cannot be left to free contractual arrangements; *see Copydan Bandkopi*, C-463/12, EU:C:2015:44, 5 March 2015, and *Microsoft Mobile Sales International Oy et al.*, C-110/15, EU: C:2016:717, 22 September 2016.

## *Svenson v. Sverige Retriever AB*

Judgment of the Court (Fourth Chamber), 13 February 2014

(Reference for a preliminary ruling – Approximation of laws – Copyright and related rights – Directive 2001/29/EC – Information society – Harmonisation of certain aspects of copyright and related rights – Article 3(1) – Communication to the public – Meaning – Internet links ('clickable links') giving access to protected works)

In Case C-466/12,

REQUEST for a preliminary ruling under Article 267 TFEU from the Svea hovrätt (Sweden), made by decision of 18 September 2012, received at the Court on 18 October 2012, in the proceedings

Nils Svensson, Sten Sjögren, Madelaine Sahlman, Pia Gadd v Retriever Sverige AB,

THE COURT (Fourth Chamber),

composed of L. Bay Larsen, President of the Chamber, M. Safjan, J. Malenovský (Rapporteur), A. Prechal and S. Rodin, Judges,

Advocate General: E. Sharpston,

gives the following:

## Judgment

1. This request for a preliminary ruling concerns the interpretation of Article 3(1) of Directive 2001/29/EC of the European Parliament and of the Council of 22 May 2001 on the harmonisation of certain aspects of copyright and related rights in the information society (OJ 2001 L 167, p. 10).

2. The request has been made in proceedings between Mr Svensson, Mr Sjögren, Ms Sahlman and Ms Gadd, the applicants in the main proceedings, and Retriever Sverige AB ('Retriever Sverige') concerning compensation allegedly payable to them for the harm they consider they have suffered as a result of the inclusion on that company's website of clickable Internet links (hyperlinks) redirecting users to press articles in which the applicants hold the copyright.

. . .

### Consideration of the Questions Referred

#### The First Three Questions

. . .

22. An act of communication such as that made by the manager of a website by means of clickable links is aimed at all potential users of the site managed by that person, that is to say, an indeterminate and fairly large number of recipients.

23. In those circumstances, it must be held that the manager is making a communication to a public.

24. None the less, according to settled case-law, in order to be covered by the concept of 'communication to the public', within the meaning of Article 3(1) of Directive 2001/29, a communication, such as that at issue in the main proceedings, concerning the same works as those covered by the initial communication and made, as in the case of the initial communication, on the Internet, and therefore by the same technical means, must also be directed at a new public, that is to say, at a public that was not taken into account by the copyright holders when they authorised the initial communication to the public (see, by analogy, *SGAE*, paragraphs 40 and 42; order of 18 March 2010 in Case C136/09 *Organismos Sillogikis Diacheirisis Dimiourgon Theatrikon kai Optikoakoustikon Ergon*, paragraph 38; and *ITV Broadcasting and Others*, paragraph 39).

25. In the circumstances of this case, it must be observed that making available the works concerned by means of a clickable link, such as that in the main proceedings, does not lead to the works in question being communicated to a new public.

26. The public targeted by the initial communication consisted of all potential visitors to the site concerned, since, given that access to the works on that site was not subject to any restrictive measures, all Internet users could therefore have free access to them.

27. In those circumstances, it must be held that, where all the users of another site to whom the works at issue have been communicated by means of a clickable link could access those works directly on the site on which they were initially communicated, without the involvement of the manager of that other site, the users of the site managed by the latter must be deemed to be potential recipients of the initial communication and, therefore, as being part of the public taken into account by the copyright holders when they authorised the initial communication.

28. Therefore, since there is no new public, the authorisation of the copyright holders is not required for a communication to the public such as that in the main proceedings.

29. Such a finding cannot be called in question were the referring court to find, although this is not clear from the documents before the Court, that when Internet users click on the link at issue, the work appears in such a way as to give the impression that it is appearing on the site on which that link is found, whereas in fact that work comes from another site.

30. That additional circumstance in no way alters the conclusion that the provision on a site of a clickable link to a protected work published and freely accessible on another site has the effect of making that work available to users of the first site and that it therefore constitutes a communication to the public. However, since there is no new public, the authorisation of the copyright holders is in any event not required for such a communication to the public.

31. On the other hand, where a clickable link makes it possible for users of the site on which that link appears to circumvent restrictions put in place by the site on which the protected work appears in order to restrict public access to that work to the latter site's subscribers only, and the link accordingly constitutes an intervention without which those users would not be able to access the works transmitted, all those users must be deemed to be a new public, which was not taken into account by the copyright holders when they authorised the initial communication, and accordingly the holders' authorisation is required for such a communication to the public. This is the case, in particular, where the work is no longer available to the public on the site on which it was initially communicated or where it is henceforth available on that site only to a restricted public, while being accessible on another Internet site without the copyright holders' authorisation.

32. In those circumstances, the answer to the first three questions referred is that Article 3(1) of Directive 2001/29 must be interpreted as meaning that the provision on a website of clickable links to works freely available on another website does not constitute an act of communication to the public, as referred to in that provision.

### The Fourth Question

33. By its fourth question, the referring court asks, in essence, whether Article 3(1) of Directive 2001/29 must be interpreted as precluding a Member State from giving wider protection to copyright holders by laying down that the concept of communication to the public includes a wider range of activities than those referred to in that provision.

. . .

37. It follows that Article 3(1) of Directive 2001/29 cannot be construed as allowing Member States to give wider protection to copyright holders by laying down that the concept of communication to the public includes a wider range of activities than those referred to in that provision.

38. Such a conclusion is not affected by the fact, highlighted by the applicants in the main proceedings in their written observations, that Article 20 of the Berne Convention stipulates that the signatory countries may enter into 'special agreements' among themselves with a view to granting copyright holders more extensive rights than those laid down in that Convention.

39. In this connection, suffice it to recall that, when an agreement allows, but does not require, a Member State to adopt a measure which appears to be contrary to Union law, the Member State must refrain from adopting such a measure (Case C277/10 *Luksan* [2012] ECR, paragraph 62).

40. Since the objective of Directive 2001/29 would inevitably be undermined if the concept of communication to the public were construed as including a wider range of activities than those referred to in Article 3(1) of that directive, a Member State must refrain from exercising the right granted to it by Article 20 of the Berne Convention.

41. Therefore, the answer to the fourth question is that Article 3(1) of Directive 2001/29 must be interpreted as precluding a Member State from giving wider protection to copyright holders by laying down that the concept of communication to the public includes a wider range of activities than those referred to in that provision.

## NOTES AND QUESTIONS

**1.** Unless hyperlinking circumvents existing restrictions, it is not perceived to be a communication to a new public. What notion of public underlies the decision of the Court?

**2.** Look at the ruling in light of fragmentation of public spheres that we can increasingly observe with the advent of social media, information by hyperlinking is brought to audiences which would otherwise not have access to it as a practical matter. Would it be necessary to review the ruling in light of recent developments, or should it be maintained from the point of view of freedom of information and expression?

**3.** In 2021, the Court of Justice of the European Union decided in the case of *VG Bild-Kunst* (C-392/19, *VG Bild-Kunst v. Stiftung Preußischer Kulturbesitz*, Judgment of March 9, 2021, ECLI:EU:C:2021:181) that "where the copyright holder has adopted or imposed measures to restrict framing, the embedding of a work in a website page of a third party, by means of that technique, constitutes making available that work to a new public" and thus such a communication must be authorized by the copyright holder. This made a differentiation between clickable links (hyperlinking) and the embedding of content on third-party websites with the use of automatic/inline links (framing). The judgment is an extension of the ruling in *Svensson* and strengthens the position of copyright holders also with reference to works that are freely accessible to the public with the authorization of the copyright holder, where the copyright holder has adopted or imposed technological measures to restrict access to these works.

## *Stichting Brein v. Ziggo BV, XS4ALL Internet BV*

Judgment of the Court (Second Chamber), 14 June 2017

(Reference for a preliminary ruling—Intellectual and industrial property—Directive 2001/29/EC—Harmonisation of certain aspects of copyright and related rights—Article 3(1)—Communication to the public—Definition—Online sharing platform—Sharing of protected files, without the consent of the rightholder)

In Case C 610/15,

REQUEST for a preliminary ruling under Article 267 TFEU from the Hoge Raad der Nederlanden (Supreme Court of the Netherlands), made by decision of 13 November 2015, received at the Court on 18 November 2015, in the proceedings

Stichting Brein v Ziggo BV, XS4ALL Internet BV,

THE COURT (Second Chamber),

composed of M. Ilešič (Rapporteur), President of the Chamber, A. Prechal, A. Rosas, C. Toader and E. Jarašiūnas, Judges,

Advocate General: M. Szpunar,

gives the following:

### Judgment

1. This request for a preliminary ruling concerns the interpretation of Articles 3(1) and 8(3) of Directive 2001/29/EC of the European Parliament and of the Council of 22 May 2001 on the harmonisation of certain aspects of copyright and related rights in the information society (OJ 2001 L 167, p. 10), and of Article 11 of Directive 2004/48/EC of the

European Parliament and of the Council of 29 April 2004 on the enforcement of intellectual property rights (OJ 2004 L 157, p. 45, and corrigendum in OJ 2004 L 195, p. 16).

2. The request has been made in proceedings between, on the one hand, Stichting Brein, a foundation which safeguards the interests of copyright holders, and, on the other hand, Ziggo BV and XS4ALL Internet BV ('XS4ALL'), internet access providers, concerning requests made by Stichting Brein for an order requiring Ziggo BV and XS4ALL to block the domain names and IP addresses of the online sharing platform 'The Pirate Bay' ('online sharing platform TPB').

* * *

### The Dispute in the Main Proceedings and the Questions Referred for a Preliminary Ruling

8. Stichting Brein is a Netherlands foundation which safeguards the interests of copyright holders.

9. Ziggo and XS4ALL are internet access providers. A significant number of their subscribers use the online sharing platform TPB, an indexer of BitTorrent files. BitTorrent is a protocol through which users (known as 'peers') can share files. The essential characteristic of BitTorrent is that it divides files for sharing into segments, thus removing the need to rely on a central server to store those files, which lessens the burden on individual servers during the sharing process. In order to be able to share files, users must first download specific software called 'BitTorrent Client', which is not provided by the online sharing platform TPB. 'BitTorrent Client' is software which allows the creation of torrent files.

10. Users (called 'seeders') who wish to make a file on their computer available to other users (called 'leechers') have to create a torrent file through their BitTorrent Client. Torrent files refer to a central server (called a 'tracker') which identifies the users available to share a particular torrent file as well as the underlying media file. These torrent files are uploaded by the seeders to an online sharing platform, such as TPB, which then proceeds to index them so that they can be found by the users of the online sharing platform and the works to which those torrent files refer can be downloaded onto the users' computers in several segments through their BitTorrent Client.

11. 'Magnet links' are often used in place of torrent files. These links identify the content of a torrent file and refer to it through a digital fingerprint.

12. The torrent files offered on the online sharing platform TPB relate mainly to copyright-protected works, without the rightholders having given their consent to the operators or users of that platform to carry out the sharing acts in question.

13. In the context of the main proceedings, Stichting Brein's principal request is that Ziggo and XS4ALL be ordered to block the domain names and IP addresses of the online sharing platform TPB in order to prevent the services of those internet access providers from being used to infringe the copyright and related rights of the rightholders, whose interests Stichting Brein protects.

* * *

30. As regards, in the first place, the question of whether making available and managing an online sharing platform, such as that at issue in the main proceedings, is an 'act of communication' for the purposes of Article 3(1) of Directive 2001/29, it must be noted, as recital 23 of Directive 2001/29 states, that the author's right of communication to the public, provided for in Article 3(1), covers any transmission or retransmission of a work to the public by wire or wireless means, including broadcasting.

31. Furthermore, as is apparent from Article 3(1) of Directive 2001/29, in order for there to be an 'act of communication', it is sufficient, in particular, that a work is made available

to a public in such a way that the persons comprising that public may access it, from wherever and whenever they individually choose, irrespective of whether they avail themselves of that opportunity (see, to that effect, judgment of 26 April 2017, Stichting Brein, C527/15, EU:C:2017:300, paragraph 36 and the case-law cited).

* * *

35. In the present case it must be found, first, as the Advocate General has noted, . . . that it is not disputed that copyright-protected works are, by means of the online sharing platform TPB, made available to the users of that platform in such a way that they may access those works from wherever and whenever they individually choose.

36. Second, it is true, as noted by the referring court, that the works thus made available to the users of the online sharing platform TPB have been placed online on that platform not by the platform operators but by its users. However, the fact remains that those operators, by making available and managing an online sharing platform such as that at issue in the main proceedings, intervene, with full knowledge of the consequences of their conduct, to provide access to protected works, by indexing on that platform torrent files which allow users of the platform to locate those works and to share them within the context of a peer-to-peer network. . . .

37. The view must therefore be taken that the operators of the online sharing platform TPB, by making that platform available and managing it, provide their users with access to the works concerned. They can therefore be regarded as playing an essential role in making the works in question available.

38. Finally, the operators of the online sharing platform TPB cannot be considered to be making a 'mere provision' of physical facilities for enabling or making a communication, within the meaning of recital 27 of Directive 2001/29. It is clear from the order for reference that that platform indexes torrent files in such a way that the works to which the torrent files refer may be easily located and downloaded by the users of that sharing platform. Moreover, it is clear from the observations submitted to the Court that, in addition to a search engine, the online sharing platform TPB offers an index classifying the works under different categories, based on the type of the works, their genre or their popularity, within which the works made available are divided, with the platform's operators checking to ensure that a work has been placed in the appropriate category. In addition, those operators delete obsolete or faulty torrent files and actively filter some content.

39. In the light of the foregoing, the making available and management of an online sharing platform, such as that at issue in the main proceedings, must be considered to be an act of communication for the purposes of Article 3(1) of Directive 2001/29.

40. In the second place, in order to be categorised as a 'communication to the public', within the meaning of Article 3(1) of Directive 2001/29, the protected works must also in fact be communicated to a 'public' (judgment of 26 April 2017, Stichting Brein, C527/15, EU:C:2017:300, paragraph 43 and the case-law cited).

* * *

42. In the present case, it is apparent from the order for reference that a large number of subscribers to Ziggo and XS4ALL have downloaded media files using the online sharing platform TPB. It is also clear from the observations submitted to the Court that this platform is used by a considerable number of persons, the operators of TPB claiming, on their online sharing platform, to have several dozens of millions of 'peers'. In this respect, the communication at issue in the main proceedings covers, at the very least, all of the platform's users. These users can access, at any time and simultaneously, the protected works which are shared by means of the platform. Thus, that communication is aimed at an indeterminate number of

potential recipients and involves a large number of persons (see, to this effect, judgment of 26 April 2017, *Stichting Brein*, C527/15, EU:C:2017:300, paragraph 45 and the case-law cited).

43. It follows that, by a communication such as that at issue in the main proceedings, protected works are indeed communicated to a 'public' within the meaning of Article 3(1) of Directive 2001/29.

44. Furthermore, with regard to the question whether those works have been communicated to a 'new' public within the meaning of the case-law cited in paragraph 28 of the present judgment, the Court, in its judgment of 13 February 2014, Svensson and Others (C466/12, EU:C:2014:76, paragraphs 24 and 31) as well as in its order of 21 October 2014, BestWater International (C348/13, not published, EU:C:2014:2315, paragraph 14), has held that such a public is a public that was not taken into account by the copyright holders when they authorised the initial communication.

45. In the present case, it is apparent from the observations submitted to the Court, first, that the operators of the online sharing platform TPB were informed that this platform, which they make available to users and manage, provides access to works published without authorisation of the rightholders and, second, that the same operators expressly display, on blogs and forums available on that platform, their purpose to make protected works available to the users, and encourage the latter to make copies of those works. In any event, it is clear from the order for reference that the operators of the online sharing platform TPB could not be unaware that this platform provides access to works published without the consent of the rightholders, given that, as expressly highlighted by the referring court, a very large number of torrent files on the online sharing platform TPB relate to works published without the consent of the rightholders. In those circumstances, it must be held that there is communication to a 'new public' (see, to that effect, judgment of 26 April 2017, *Stichting Brein*, C527/15, EU:C:2017:300, paragraph 50).

46. Furthermore, there can be no dispute that the making available and management of an online sharing platform, such as that at issue in the main proceedings, is carried out with the purpose of obtaining profit therefrom, it being clear from the observations submitted to the Court that that platform generates considerable advertising revenues.

47. Therefore, it must be held that the making available and management of an online sharing platform, such as that at issue in the main proceedings, constitutes a 'communication to the public', within the meaning of Article 3(1) of Directive 2001/29.

48. In the light of all the foregoing considerations, the answer to the first question is that the concept of 'communication to the public', within the meaning of Article 3(1) of Directive 2001/29, must be interpreted as covering, in circumstances such as those at issue in the main proceedings, the making available and management, on the internet, of a sharing platform which, by means of indexation of metadata referring to protected works and the provision of a search engine, allows users of that platform to locate those works and to share them in the context of a peer-to-peer network.

## *GS Media BV v. Sanoma Media Netherlands BV, Playboy and Dekker*

Judgment of the Court (Second Chamber), 8 September 2016

(Reference for a preliminary ruling—Copyright and related rights—Directive 2001/29/EC—Information society—Harmonisation of certain aspects of copyright and related rights—Article 3(1)—Communication to the public—Definition—Internet—Hyperlinks giving access to protected works, made accessible on another website without the rightholder's consent—Works not yet published by the rightholder—Posting of such links for a profit)

In Case C160/15,

REQUEST for a preliminary ruling under Article 267 TFEU from the Hoge Raad der Nederlanden (Supreme Court of the Netherlands), made by decision of 3 April 2015, received at the Court on 7 April 2015, in the proceedings

GS Media BV v Sanoma Media Netherlands BV, Playboy Enterprises International Inc., Britt Geertruida Dekker,

THE COURT (Second Chamber),

composed of M. Ilešič (Rapporteur), President of the Chamber, C. Toader, A. Rosas, A. Prechal, and E. Jarašiūnas, Judges,

Advocate General: M. Wathelet,

gives the following

## Judgment

1. This request for a preliminary ruling concerns the interpretation of Article 3(1) of Directive 2001/29/EC of the European Parliament and of the Council of 22 May 2001 on the harmonisation of certain aspects of copyright and related rights in the information society (OJ 2001 L 167, p. 10).

2. The request has been made in proceedings between GS Media BV and Sanoma Media Netherlands BV ('Sanoma'), Playboy Enterprises International Inc. and Ms Britt Geertruida Dekker (together, 'Sanoma and Others'), concerning, inter alia, the posting on the GeenStijl.nl website ('the GeenStijl website'), operated by GS Media, of hyperlinks to other websites enabling photographs of Ms Dekker, taken for Playboy magazine ('the photos at issue'), to be viewed.

* * *

### The Dispute in the Main Proceedings and the Questions Referred for a Preliminary Ruling

6. At the request of Sanoma, which is the publisher of *Playboy* magazine, on 13 and 14 October 2011 the photographer, Mr C. Hermès, took the photos at issue, which were to be published in the December 2011 edition of that magazine. In that context, Mr Hermès granted Sanoma authorisation, on an exclusive basis, to publish those photos. He also granted Sanoma authorisation to exercise the rights and powers arising from his copyright.

7. GS Media operates the website GeenStijl, which includes, according to information provided by that website, 'news, scandalous revelations and investigative journalism with lighthearted items and wacky nonsense' and which is viewed daily by more than 230 000 visitors, making it one of the 10 most visited websites in the area of news in the Netherlands.

8. On 26 October 2011, the editors of the GeenStijl website received a message from a person using a pseudonym, which included a hyperlink to an electronic file hosted on the website Filefactory.com ('the Filefactory website'), located in Australia and dedicated to data storage. That electronic file contained the photos at issue.

9. On the same day, Sanoma asked GS Media's parent company to prevent the photos at issue being published on the GeenStijl website.

10. On 27 October 2011, an article relating to those photos of Ms Dekker, entitled '. . . ! Nude photos of . . . [Ms] Dekker', was published on the GeenStijl website, which included part of one of the photos at issue, and which ended with the following words: 'And now the

link with the pics you've been waiting for.' By clicking on a hyperlink accompanying that text, users were directed to the Filefactory website, on which another hyperlink allowed them to download 11 electronic files each containing one of those photos.

* * *

16. In December 2011, the photos at issue were published in *Playboy* magazine.

* * *

39. It is in the light, in particular, of those criteria that it is to be assessed whether, in a situation such as that at issue in the main proceedings, the fact of posting, on a website, a hyperlink to protected works, which are freely available on another website without the consent of the copyright holder, constitutes a 'communication to the public' within the meaning of Article 3(1) of Directive 2001/29.

40. In that regard, it should be recalled that, in the judgment of 13 February 2014, *Svensson and Others*, (C466/12, EU:C:2014:76), the Court interpreted Article 3(1) of Directive 2001/29 as meaning that posting hyperlinks on a website to works freely available on another website does not constitute a 'communication to the public' as covered by that provision. That interpretation was also adopted in the order of 21 October 2014, *BestWater International*, (C348/13, not published, EU:C:2014:2315) about such links using the technique known as 'transclusion' ('framing').

* * *

43. [I]t cannot be inferred either from the judgment of 13 February 2014, *Svensson and Others*, (C466/12, EU:C:2014:76) or from the order of 21 October 2014, *BestWater International*, (C348/13, not published, EU:C:2014:2315) that posting, on a website, hyperlinks to protected works which have been made freely available on another website, but without the consent of the copyright holders of those works, would be excluded, as a matter of principle, from the concept of 'communication to the public' within the meaning of Article 3(1) of Directive 2001/29. Rather, those decisions confirm the importance of such consent under that provision, as the latter specifically provides that every act of communication of a work to the public is to be authorised by the copyright holder.

* * *

47. For the purposes of the individualised assessment of the existence of a 'communication to the public' within the meaning of Article 3(1) of Directive 2001/29, it is accordingly necessary, when the posting of a hyperlink to a work freely available on another website is carried out by a person who, in so doing, does not pursue a profit, to take account of the fact that that person does not know and cannot reasonably know, that that work had been published on the internet without the consent of the copyright holder.

48. Indeed, such a person, by making that work available to the public by providing other internet users with direct access to it (see, to that effect, judgment of 13 February 2014, *Svensson and Others*, C466/12, EU:C:2014:76, paragraphs 18 to 23) does not, as a general rule, intervene in full knowledge of the consequences of his conduct in order to give customers access to a work illegally posted on the internet. In addition, where the work in question was already available with unrestricted access on the website to which the hyperlink provides access, all internet users could, in principle, already have access to it even the absence of that intervention.

49. In contrast, where it is established that such a person knew or ought to have known that the hyperlink he posted provides access to a work illegally placed on the internet, for example owing to the fact that he was notified thereof by the copyright holders, it is necessary

to consider that the provision of that link constitutes a 'communication to the public' within the meaning of Article 3(1) of Directive 2001/29.

50. The same applies in the event that that link allows users of the website on which it is posted to circumvent the restrictions taken by the site where the protected work is posted in order to restrict the public's access to its own subscribers, the posting of such a link then constituting a deliberate intervention without which those users could not benefit from the works broadcast (see, by analogy, judgment of 13 February 2014, *Svensson and Others*, C466/12, EU:C:2014:76, paragraphs 27 and 31).

51. Furthermore, when the posting of hyperlinks is carried out for profit, it can be expected that the person who posted such a link carries out the necessary checks to ensure that the work concerned is not illegally published on the website to which those hyperlinks lead, so that it must be presumed that that posting has occurred with the full knowledge of the protected nature of that work and the possible lack of consent to publication on the internet by the copyright holder. In such circumstances, and in so far as that rebuttable presumption is not rebutted, the act of posting a hyperlink to a work which was illegally placed on the internet constitutes a 'communication to the public' within the meaning of Article 3(1) of Directive 2001/29.

52. However, if there is no new public, there will be no communication to the 'public' within the meaning of that provision in the event that, referred to in paragraphs 40 to 42 of the present judgment, the works to which those hyperlinks allow access have been made freely available on another website with the consent of the rightholder.

* * *

54. As regards the case in the main proceedings, it is undisputed that GS Media operates the GeenStijl website and that it provided the hyperlinks to the files containing the photos at issue, hosted on the Filefactory website, for profit. It is also undisputed that Sanoma had not authorised the publication of those photos on the internet. Moreover, it appears to follow from the presentation of the facts, as they result from the order for reference, that GS Media was aware of that latter fact and that it cannot therefore rebut the presumption that the posting of those links occurred in full knowledge of the illegal nature of that publication. In those circumstances, it appears that, subject to the checks to be made by the referring court, by posting those links, GS Media effected a 'communication to the public', within the meaning of Article 3(1) of Directive 2001/29, and it is unnecessary to assess in that context the other circumstances referred to by that court, referred to in paragraph 26 of the present judgment.

55. Having regard to the foregoing considerations, the answer to the questions raised is that Article 3(1) of Directive 2001/29 must be interpreted as meaning that, in order to establish whether the fact of posting, on a website, hyperlinks to protected works, which are freely available on another website without the consent of the copyright holder, constitutes a 'communication to the public' within the meaning of that provision, it is to be determined whether those links are provided without the pursuit of financial gain by a person who did not know or could not reasonably have known the illegal nature of the publication of those works on that other website or whether, on the contrary, those links are provided for such a purpose, a situation in which that knowledge must be presumed.

## NOTES AND QUESTIONS

**1.** In balancing the interests between copyright protection and freedom of expression, the CJEU essentially relies, in assessing communication to the public, on the distinction of commercial and noncommercial use. How do you assess this categorical distinction in sensitive areas affecting personality protection?

**2.** What is the potential of human rights in assessing these difficult questions? See also *UPC Telekabel Wien GmbH v. Constantin Film Verleih GmbH*, C-314/12, *infra* section II.A.3.a, where the Court, in assessing internet retransmission, seeks to balance fundamental rights interests at stake in shaping the contours of injunctive relief.

**3.** Thomas Cottier argues in the excerpt in section I.G *infra* that copyright law should more strongly refer to the framework of human rights protection in assessing the interests at stake. Human rights both should provide the foundation upon which legislation is based and for adjudication of specific cases. Other than the categorical approach in the European legislative tradition, both for fair use and communication to the public, a fact intensive assessment should take place case by case commensurate with the Anglo-American tradition of fair use.

## F. Fair Use and Exceptions

The protection afforded by copyright is subject to important exceptions, among the most notable of which are rights of "fair use" accorded to certain copying and distribution. Fair use doctrines permit portions of copyrighted works to be used, for example, for news reference and instructional purposes. The right of fair use is related to freedom of expression.

### *Harper & Row, Publishers, Inc. v. Nation Enterprises*

471 U.S. 539 (1985)

Justice O'Connor delivered the opinion of the Court. . . .

Fair use was traditionally defined as "a privilege in others than the owner of the copyright to use the copyrighted material in a reasonable manner without his consent." H. Ball, Law of Copyright and Literary Property 260 (1944) (hereinafter Ball). The statutory formulation of the defense of fair use in the Copyright Act reflects the intent of Congress to codify the common-law doctrine. 3 Nimmer §13.05. Section 107 requires a case-by-case determination whether a particular use is fair, and the statute notes four nonexclusive factors to be considered. This approach was "intended to restate the [preexisting] judicial doctrine of fair use, not to change, narrow, or enlarge it in any way." H. R. Rep. No. 94-1476, p. 66 (1976) (hereinafter House Report).

"[The] author's consent to a reasonable use of his copyrighted works [had] always been implied by the courts as a necessary incident of the constitutional policy of promoting the progress of science and the useful arts, since a prohibition of such use would inhibit subsequent writers from attempting to improve upon prior works and thus . . . frustrate the very ends sought to be attained." Ball 260. Professor Latman, in a study of the doctrine of fair use commissioned by Congress for the revision effort, *see Sony Corp. of America v. Universal City Studios, Inc.*, 464 U.S., at 462-463, n. 9 (dissenting opinion), summarized prior law as turning on the "importance of the material copied or performed from the point of view of the reasonable copyright owner. In other words, would the reasonable copyright owner have consented to the use?" Latman 15.[3]

3. Professor Nimmer notes: "[Perhaps] no more precise guide can be stated than Joseph McDonald's clever paraphrase of the Golden Rule: 'Take not from others to such an extent and in such a manner that you would be resentful if they so took from you.'" 3 Nimmer §13.05[A], at 13-66, quoting McDonald, Non-infringing Uses, 9 Bull. Copyright Soc. 466, 467 (1962). This "equitable rule of reason," *Sony Corp. of America v. Universal City Studios, Inc.*, 464 U.S., at 448, "permits courts to avoid rigid application of the copyright statute when, on occasion, it would stifle the very creativity which that law is designed to foster." *Iowa State University Research Foundation, Inc. v. American Broadcasting Cos.*, 621 F.2d 57, 60 (CA2 1980). *See generally* L. Seltzer, Exemptions and Fair Use in Copyright 18-48 (1978).

As early as 1841, Justice Story gave judicial recognition to the doctrine in a case that concerned the letters of another former President, George Washington.

> "[A] reviewer may fairly cite largely from the original work, if his design be really and truly to use the passages for the purposes of fair and reasonable criticism. On the other hand, it is as clear, that if he thus cites the most important parts of the work, with a view, not to criticise, but to supersede the use of the original work, and substitute the review for it, such a use will be deemed in law a piracy." *Folsom v. Marsh*, 9 F. Cas. 342, 344-345 (No. 4,901) (CC Mass.)

As Justice Story's hypothetical illustrates, the fair use doctrine has always precluded a use that "[supersedes] the use of the original." *Ibid. Accord*, S. Rep. No. 94-473, p. 65 (1975) (hereinafter Senate Report).

The application of the fair use doctrine has been clarified in a number of subsequent cases. In the following, the seminal case of *Campbell v. Acuff-Rose* is included, as well as a discussion of the more recent decisions of the U.S. Supreme Court in *Google LLC v. Oracle America, Inc.* and *Andy Warhol Foundation for the Visual Arts, Inc. v. Goldsmith.*

## *Campbell v. Acuff-Rose Music, Inc.*

510 U.S. 569 (1994) (footnotes omitted)

Respondent Acuff-Rose Music, Inc., filed suit against petitioners, the members of the rap music group 2 Live Crew and their record company, claiming that 2 Live Crew's song, "Pretty Woman," infringed Acuff-Rose's copyright in Roy Orbison's rock ballad, "Oh, Pretty Woman." The District Court granted summary judgment for 2 Live Crew, holding that its song was a parody that made fair use of the original song. See Copyright Act of 1976, 17 U.S.C. §107. The Court of Appeals reversed and remanded, holding that the commercial nature of the parody rendered it presumptively unfair under the first of four factors relevant under §107; that, by taking the "heart" of the original and making it the "heart" of a new work, 2 Live Crew had, qualitatively, taken too much under the third §107 factor; and that market harm for purposes of the fourth §107 factor had been established by a presumption attaching to commercial uses.

. . .

> §107. Limitations on exclusive rights: Fair use
>
> "Notwithstanding the provisions of sections 106 and 106A, the fair use of a copyrighted work, including such use by reproduction in copies or phonorecords or by any other means specified by that section, for purposes such as criticism, comment, news reporting, teaching (including multiple copies for classroom use), scholarship, or research, is not an infringement of copyright. In determining whether the use made of a work in any particular case is a fair use the factors to be considered shall include—
>
> "(1) the purpose and character of the use, including whether such use is of a commercial nature or is for non-profit educational purposes;
>
> "(2) the nature of the copyrighted work;
>
> "(3) the amount and substantiality of the portion used in relation to the copyrighted work as a whole; and
>
> "(4) the effect of the use upon the potential market for or value of the copyrighted work.
>
> "The fact that a work is unpublished shall not itself bar a finding of fair use if such finding is made upon consideration of all the above factors." 17 U.S.C. §107 (1988 ed. and Supp. IV).

Congress meant §107 "to restate the present judicial doctrine of fair use, not to change, narrow, or enlarge it in any way" and intended that courts continue the common-law tradition of fair use adjudication. H.R. Rep. No. 94–1476, p. 66 (1976) (hereinafter House

Report); S.Rep. No. 94–473, p. 62 (1975) (hereinafter Senate Report). The fair use doctrine thus "permits [and requires] courts to avoid rigid application of the copyright statute when, on occasion, it would stifle the very creativity which that law is designed to foster." *Stewart v. Abend,* 495 U.S. 207, 236 (1990) (internal quotation marks and citation omitted).

The task is not to be simplified with bright-line rules, for the statute, like the doctrine it recognizes, calls for case-by-case analysis. *Harper & Row,* 471 U.S., at 560; *Sony,* 464 U.S., at 448, and n. 31; House Report, pp. 65–66; Senate Report, p. 62. The text employs the terms "including" and "such as" in the preamble paragraph to indicate the "illustrative and not limitative" function of the examples given, § 101; see *Harper & Row,* supra, at 561, which thus provide only general guidance about the sorts of copying that courts and Congress most commonly had found to be fair uses. Nor may the four statutory factors be treated in isolation, one from another. All are to be explored, and the results weighed together, in light of the purposes of copyright. *See Leval* 1110–1111; Patry & Perlmutter, *Fair Use Misconstrued: Profit, Presumptions, and Parody,* 11 Cardozo Arts & Ent. L. J. 667, 685–687 (1993) (hereinafter Patry & Perlmutter).

### A

The first factor in a fair use enquiry is "the purpose and character of the use, including whether such use is of a commercial nature or is for nonprofit educational purposes." §107(1). This factor draws on Justice Story's formulation, "the nature and objects of the selections made." *Folsom v. Marsh, supra,* at 348. The enquiry here may be guided by the examples given in the preamble to §107, looking to whether the use is for criticism, or comment, or news reporting, and the like, see §107. The central purpose of this investigation is to see, in Justice Story's words, whether the new work merely "supersede[s] the objects" of the original creation, *Folsom v. Marsh, supra,* at 348; accord, *Harper & Row, supra,* at 562 ("supplanting" the original), or instead adds something new, with a further purpose or different character, altering the first with new expression, meaning, or message; it asks, in other words, whether and to what extent the new work is "transformative." Leval 1111. Although such transformative use is not absolutely necessary for a finding of fair use, *Sony, supra,* at 455, n. 40, the goal of copyright, to promote science and the arts, is generally furthered by the creation of transformative works. Such works thus lie at the heart of the fair use doctrine's guarantee of breathing space within the confines of copyright, see, e.g., *Sony, supra,* at 478–480 (Blackmun, J., dissenting), and the more transformative the new work, the less will be the significance of other factors, like commercialism, that may weigh against a finding of fair use.

. . .

The germ of parody lies in the definition of the Greek parodeia, quoted in Judge Nelson's Court of Appeals dissent, as "a song sung alongside another." 972 F.2d, at 1440, quoting 7 Encyclopedia Britannica 768 (15th ed. 1975). Modern dictionaries accordingly describe a parody as a "literary or artistic work that imitates the characteristic style of an author or a work for comic effect or ridicule," or as a "composition in prose or verse in which the characteristic turns of thought and phrase in an author or class of authors are imitated in such a way as to make them appear ridiculous." For the purposes of copyright law, the nub of the definitions, and the heart of any parodist's claim to quote from existing material, is the use of some elements of a prior author's composition to create a new one that, at least in part, comments on that author's works. *See, e.g., Fisher v. Dees, supra,* at 437; *MCA, Inc. v. Wilson,* 677 F.2d 180, 185 (CA2 1981). If, on the contrary, the commentary has no critical bearing on the substance or style of the original composition, which the alleged infringer merely uses to get attention or to avoid the drudgery in working up something fresh, the claim to fairness in borrowing from another's work diminishes accordingly (if it does not vanish), and other factors, like the extent of its commerciality, loom larger. Parody needs to mimic an original to make its point, and so has some claim to use the creation of its victim's (or collective victims') imagination, whereas satire can stand on its own two feet and so requires justification for the very act of borrowing. *See ibid.*; Bisceglia, *Parody and Copyright Protection: Turning the Balancing Act Into a Juggling Act*, in ASCAP, Copyright Law Symposium, No. 34, p. 25 (1987).

The fact that parody can claim legitimacy for some appropriation does not, of course, tell either parodist or judge much about where to draw the line. Like a book review quoting the copyrighted material criticized, parody may or may not be fair use, and petitioners' suggestion that any parodic use is presumptively fair has no more justification in law or fact than the equally hopeful claim that any use for news reporting should be presumed fair, *see Harper & Row*, 471 U.S., at 561. The Act has no hint of an evidentiary preference for parodists over their victims, and no workable presumption for parody could take account of the fact that parody often shades into satire when society is lampooned through its creative artifacts, or that a work may contain both parodic and nonparodic elements. Accordingly, parody, like any other use, has to work its way through the relevant factors, and be judged case by case, in light of the ends of the copyright law.

Here, the District Court held, and the Court of Appeals assumed, that 2 Live Crew's "Pretty Woman" contains parody, commenting on and criticizing the original work, whatever it may have to say about society at large. As the District Court remarked, the words of 2 Live Crew's song copy the original's first line, but then "quickly degenerat[e] into a play on words, substituting predictable lyrics with shocking ones . . . [that] derisively demonstrat[e] how bland and banal the Orbison song seems to them." 754 F. Supp., at 1155 (footnote omitted). Judge Nelson, dissenting below, came to the same conclusion, that the 2 Live Crew song "was clearly intended to ridicule the white-bread original" and "reminds us that sexual congress with nameless streetwalkers is not necessarily the stuff of romance and is not necessarily without its consequences. The singers (there are several) have the same thing on their minds as did the lonely man with the nasal voice, but here there is no hint of wine and roses." 972 F.2d, at 1442. Although the majority below had difficulty discerning any criticism of the original in 2 Live Crew's song, it assumed for purposes of its opinion that there was some. *Id.*, at 1435–1436, and n. 8.

We have less difficulty in finding that critical element in 2 Live Crew's song than the Court of Appeals did, although having found it we will not take the further step of evaluating its quality. The threshold question when fair use is raised in defense of parody is whether a parodic character may reasonably be perceived. Whether, going beyond that, parody is in good taste or bad does not and should not matter to fair use. As Justice Holmes explained, "[i]t would be a dangerous undertaking for persons trained only to the law to constitute themselves final judges of the worth of [a work], outside of the narrowest and most obvious limits. At the one extreme some works of genius would be sure to miss appreciation. Their very novelty would make them repulsive until the public had learned the new language in which their author spoke." *Bleistein v. Donaldson Lithographing Co.*, 188 U.S. 239, 251 (1903) (circus posters have copyright protection); *cf. Yankee Publishing Inc. v. News America Publishing, Inc.*, 809 F. Supp. 267, 280 (SDNY 1992) (Leval, J.) ("First Amendment protections do not apply only to those who speak clearly, whose jokes are funny, and whose parodies succeed") (trademark case).

While we might not assign a high rank to the parodic element here, we think it fair to say that 2 Live Crew's song reasonably could be perceived as commenting on the original or criticizing it, to some degree. 2 Live Crew juxtaposes the romantic musings of a man whose fantasy comes true, with degrading taunts, a bawdy demand for sex, and a sigh of relief from paternal responsibility. The later words can be taken as a comment on the naivete of the original of an earlier day, as a rejection of its sentiment that ignores the ugliness of street life and the debasement that it signifies. It is this joinder of reference and ridicule that marks off the author's choice of parody from the other types of comment and criticism that traditionally have had a claim to fair use protection as transformative works.

The Court of Appeals, however, immediately cut short the enquiry into 2 Live Crew's fair use claim by confining its treatment of the first factor essentially to one relevant fact, the commercial nature of the use. The court then inflated the significance of this fact by applying a presumption ostensibly culled from Sony, that "every commercial use of copyrighted material is presumptively . . . unfair . . . ." *Sony*, 464 U.S., at 451. In giving virtually dispositive weight to the commercial nature of the parody, the Court of Appeals erred.

The language of the statute makes clear that the commercial or nonprofit educational purpose of a work is only one element of the first factor enquiry into its purpose and character. Section 107(1) uses the term "including" to begin the dependent clause referring to commercial use, and the main clause speaks of a broader investigation into "purpose and character." As we explained in *Harper & Row*, Congress resisted attempts to narrow the ambit of this traditional enquiry by adopting categories of presumptively fair use, and it urged courts to preserve the breadth of their traditionally ample view of the universe of relevant evidence. 471 U.S., at 561; House Report, p. 66. Accordingly, the mere fact that a use is educational and not for profit does not insulate it from a finding of infringement, any more than the commercial character of a use bars a finding of fairness. If, indeed, commerciality carried presumptive force against a finding of fairness, the presumption would swallow nearly all of the illustrative uses listed in the preamble paragraph of §107, including news reporting, comment, criticism, teaching, scholarship, and research, since these activities "are generally conducted for profit in this country." *Harper & Row, supra*, at 592 (Brennan, J., dissenting). Congress could not have intended such a rule, which certainly is not inferable from the common-law cases, arising as they did from the world of letters in which Samuel Johnson could pronounce that "[n]o man but a blockhead ever wrote, except for money." 3 *Boswell's Life of Johnson* 19 (G. Hill ed. 1934).

Sony itself called for no hard evidentiary presumption. There, we emphasized the need for a "sensitive balancing of interests," 464 U.S., at 455, n. 40, noted that Congress had "eschewed a rigid, bright-line approach to fair use," *id.*, at 449, n. 31, and stated that the commercial or nonprofit educational character of a work is "not conclusive," *id.*, at 448–449, but rather a fact to be "weighed along with other[s] in fair use decisions," *id.*, at 449, n. 32 (quoting House Report, p. 66). The Court of Appeals's elevation of one sentence from Sony to a per se rule thus runs as much counter to *Sony* itself as to the long common-law tradition of fair use adjudication. Rather, as we explained in *Harper & Row, Sony* stands for the proposition that the "fact that a publication was commercial as opposed to nonprofit is a separate factor that tends to weigh against a finding of fair use." 471 U.S., at 562. But that is all, and the fact that even the force of that tendency will vary with the context is a further reason against elevating commerciality to hard presumptive significance. The use, for example, of a copyrighted work to advertise a product, even in a parody, will be entitled to less indulgence under the first factor of the fair use enquiry than the sale of a parody for its own sake, let alone one performed a single time by students in school. See generally Patry & Perlmutter 679–680; *Fisher v. Dees*, 794 F.2d, at 437; *Maxtone-Graham v. Burtchaell*, 803 F.2d 1253, 1262 (CA2 1986); *Sega Enterprises Ltd. v. Accolade, Inc.*, 977 F.2d 1510, 1522 (CA9 1992).

### B

The second statutory factor, "the nature of the copyrighted work," §107(2), draws on Justice Story's expression, the "value of the materials used." *Folsom v. Marsh*, 9 F. Cas., at 348. This factor calls for recognition that some works are closer to the core of intended copyright protection than others, with the consequence that fair use is more difficult to establish when the former works are copied. *See, e.g., Stewart v. Abend*, 495 U.S., at 237–238 (contrasting fictional short story with factual works); *Harper & Row*, 471 U.S., at 563–564 (contrasting soon-to-be-published memoir with published speech); *Sony*, 464 U.S., at 455, n. 40 (contrasting motion pictures with news broadcasts); Feist, 499 U.S., at 348–351 (contrasting creative works with bare factual compilations); 3 M. Nimmer & D. Nimmer, Nimmer on Copyright §13.05[A][2] (1993) (hereinafter Nimmer); Leval 1116. We agree with both the District Court and the Court of Appeals that the Orbison original's creative expression for public dissemination falls within the core of the copyright's protective purposes. 754 F. Supp., at 1155–1156; 972 F.2d, at 1437. This fact, however, is not much help in this case, or ever likely to help much in separating the fair use sheep from the infringing goats in a parody case, since parodies almost invariably copy publicly known, expressive works.

## C

The third factor asks whether "the amount and substantiality of the portion used in relation to the copyrighted work as a whole," §107(3) (or, in Justice Story's words, "the quantity and value of the materials used," *Folsom v. Marsh, supra*, at 348) are reasonable in relation to the purpose of the copying. Here, attention turns to the persuasiveness of a parodist's justification for the particular copying done, and the enquiry will harken back to the first of the statutory factors, for, as in prior cases, we recognize that the extent of permissible copying varies with the purpose and character of the use. *See Sony, supra*, at 449–450 (reproduction of entire work "does not have its ordinary effect of militating against a finding of fair use" as to home videotaping of television programs); *Harper & Row, supra*, at 564 ("[E]ven substantial quotations might qualify as fair use in a review of a published work or a news account of a speech" but not in a scoop of a soon-to-be-published memoir). The facts bearing on this factor will also tend to address the fourth, by revealing the degree to which the parody may serve as a market substitute for the original or potentially licensed derivatives. *See* Leval 1123.

The District Court considered the song's parodic purpose in finding that 2 Live Crew had not helped themselves over-much. 754 F. Supp., at 1156–1157. The Court of Appeals disagreed, stating that "[w]hile it may not be inappropriate to find that no more was taken than necessary, the copying was qualitatively substantial. . . . We conclude that taking the heart of the original and making it the heart of a new work was to purloin a substantial portion of the essence of the original." 972 F.2d, at 1438.

The Court of Appeals is of course correct that this factor calls for thought not only about the quantity of the materials used, but about their quality and importance, too. In *Harper & Row*, for example, the Nation had taken only some 300 words out of President Ford's memoirs, but we signaled the significance of the quotations in finding them to amount to "the heart of the book," the part most likely to be news-worthy and important in licensing serialization. 471 U.S., at 564–566, 568 (internal quotation marks omitted). We also agree with the Court of Appeals that whether "a substantial portion of the infringing work was copied verbatim" from the copyrighted work is a relevant question, see *id.*, at 565, for it may reveal a dearth of transformative character or purpose under the first factor, or a greater likelihood of market harm under the fourth; a work composed primarily of an original, particularly its heart, with little added or changed, is more likely to be a merely superseding use, fulfilling demand for the original.

Where we part company with the court below is in applying these guides to parody, and in particular to parody in the song before us. Parody presents a difficult case. Parody's humor, or in any event its comment, necessarily springs from recognizable allusion to its object through distorted imitation. Its art lies in the tension between a known original and its parodic twin. When parody takes aim at a particular original work, the parody must be able to "conjure up" at least enough of that original to make the object of its critical wit recognizable. *See, e.g.*, *Elsmere Music*, 623 F.2d, at 253, n. 1; *Fisher v. Dees*, 794 F.2d, at 438–439. What makes for this recognition is quotation of the original's most distinctive or memorable features, which the parodist can be sure the audience will know. Once enough has been taken to assure identification, how much more is reasonable will depend, say, on the extent to which the song's overriding purpose and character is to parody the original or, in contrast, the likelihood that the parody may serve as a market substitute for the original. But using some characteristic features cannot be avoided.

We think the Court of Appeals was insufficiently appreciative of parody's need for the recognizable sight or sound when it ruled 2 Live Crew's use unreasonable as a matter of law. It is true, of course, that 2 Live Crew copied the characteristic opening bass riff (or musical phrase) of the original, and true that the words of the first line copy the Orbison lyrics. But if quotation of the opening riff and the first line may be said to go to the "heart" of the original, the heart is also what most readily conjures up the song for parody, and it is the heart at which parody takes aim. Copying does not become excessive in relation to parodic purpose merely because the portion taken was the original's heart. If 2 Live Crew had copied a significantly less memorable part of the original, it is difficult to see how its parodic character would have come through. *See Fisher v. Dees, supra*, at 439.

This is not, of course, to say that anyone who calls himself a parodist can skim the cream and get away scot free. In parody, as in news reporting, *see Harper & Row, supra*, context is everything, and the question of fairness asks what else the parodist did besides go to the heart of the original. It is significant that 2 Live Crew not only copied the first line of the original, but thereafter departed markedly from the Orbison lyrics for its own ends. 2 Live Crew not only copied the bass riff and repeated it,19 but also produced otherwise distinctive sounds, interposing "scraper" noise, over-laying the music with solos in different keys, and altering the drum beat. See 754 F. Supp., at 1155. This is not a case, then, where "a substantial portion" of the parody itself is composed of a "verbatim" copying of the original. It is not, that is, a case where the parody is so insubstantial, as compared to the copying, that the third factor must be resolved as a matter of law against the parodists.

Suffice it to say here that, as to the lyrics, we think the Court of Appeals correctly suggested that "no more was taken than necessary," 972 F.2d, at 1438, but just for that reason, we fail to see how the copying can be excessive in relation to its parodic purpose, even if the portion taken is the original's "heart." As to the music, we express no opinion whether repetition of the bass riff is excessive copying, and we remand to permit evaluation of the amount taken, in light of the song's parodic purpose and character, its transformative elements, and considerations of the potential for market substitution sketched more fully below.

### D

The fourth fair use factor is "the effect of the use upon the potential market for or value of the copyrighted work." §107(4). It requires courts to consider not only the extent of market harm caused by the particular actions of the alleged infringer, but also "whether unrestricted and widespread conduct of the sort engaged in by the defendant . . . would result in a substantially adverse impact on the potential market" for the original. Nimmer §13.05[A][4], p. 13–102.61 (footnote omitted); *accord, Harper & Row*, 471 U. S., at 569; Senate Report, p. 65; *Folsom v. Marsh*, 9 F. Cas., at 349. The enquiry "must take account not only of harm to the original but also of harm to the market for derivative works." *Harper & Row, supra*, at 568.

Since fair use is an affirmative defense, its proponent would have difficulty carrying the burden of demonstrating fair use without favorable evidence about relevant markets. In moving for summary judgment, 2 Live Crew left themselves at just such a disadvantage when they failed to address the effect on the market for rap derivatives, and confined themselves to uncontroverted submissions that there was no likely effect on the market for the original. They did not, however, thereby subject themselves to the evidentiary presumption applied by the Court of Appeals. In assessing the likelihood of significant market harm, the Court of Ap peals quoted from language in Sony that "'[i]f the intended use is for commercial gain, that likelihood may be presumed. But if it is for a noncommercial purpose, the likelihood must be demonstrated.'" 972 F.2d, at 1438, quoting *Sony*, 464 U.S., at 451. The court reasoned that because "the use of the copyrighted work is wholly commercial, . . . we presume that a likelihood of future harm to Acuff-Rose exists." 972 F.2d, at 1438. In so doing, the court resolved the fourth factor against 2 Live Crew, just as it had the first, by applying a presumption about the effect of commercial use, a presumption which as applied here we hold to be error.

No "presumption" or inference of market harm that might find support in Sony is applicable to a case involving something beyond mere duplication for commercial purposes. Sony's discussion of a presumption contrasts a context of verbatim copying of the original in its entirety for commercial purposes, with the noncommercial context of Sony itself (home copying of television programming). In the former circumstances, what Sony said simply makes common sense: when a commercial use amounts to mere duplication of the entirety of an original, it clearly "supersede[s] the objects," *Folsom v. Marsh, supra*, at 348, of the original and serves as a market replacement for it, making it likely that cognizable market harm to the original will occur. *Sony, supra*, at 451. But when, on the contrary, the second use is transformative, market substitution is at least less certain, and market harm may not be so readily inferred. Indeed, as to parody pure and simple, it is more likely that the new work will not affect the market for the original in a way cognizable under this factor, that is, by acting as a substitute for it ("supersed[ing] [its] objects"). *See* Leval 1125; Patry & Perlmutter 692, 697–698. This is so because the parody and the original usually serve different market functions. Bisceglia, ASCAP, Copyright Law Symposium, No. 34, at 23.

We do not, of course, suggest that a parody may not harm the market at all, but when a lethal parody, like a scathing theater review, kills demand for the original, it does not produce a harm cognizable under the Copyright Act. Because "parody may quite legitimately aim at garroting the original, destroying it commercially as well as artistically," B. Kaplan, *An Unhurried View of Copyright* 69 (1967), the role of the courts is to distinguish between "[b]iting criticism [that merely] suppresses demand [and] copyright infringement[, which] usurps it." *Fisher v. Dees*, 794 F.2d, at 438.

This distinction between potentially remediable displacement and unremediable disparagement is reflected in the rule that there is no protectible derivative market for criticism. The market for potential derivative uses includes only those that creators of original works would in general develop or license others to develop. Yet the unlikelihood that creators of imaginative works will license critical reviews or lampoons of their own productions removes such uses from the very notion of a potential licensing market. "People ask . . . for criticism, but they only want praise." S. Maugham, Of Human Bondage 241 (Penguin ed. 1992). Thus, to the extent that the opinion below may be read to have considered harm to the market for parodies of "Oh, Pretty Woman," see 972 F.2d, at 1439, the court erred. Accord, *Fisher v. Dees, supra*, at 437; Leval 1125; Patry & Perlmutter 688–691.

In explaining why the law recognizes no derivative market for critical works, including parody, we have, of course, been speaking of the later work as if it had nothing but a critical aspect (i.e., "parody pure and simple," *supra*, at 591). But the later work may have a more complex character, with effects not only in the arena of criticism but also in protectible markets for derivative works, too. In that sort of case, the law looks beyond the criticism to the other elements of the work, as it does here. 2 Live Crew's song comprises not only parody but also rap music, and the derivative market for rap music is a proper focus of enquiry, *see Harper & Row, supra*, at 568; Nimmer §13.05[B]. Evidence of substantial harm to it would weigh against a finding of fair use, because the licensing of derivatives is an important economic incentive to the creation of originals. *See* 17 U.S.C. §106(2) (copyright owner has rights to derivative works). Of course, the only harm to derivatives that need concern us, as discussed above, is the harm of market substitution. The fact that a parody may impair the market for derivative uses by the very effectiveness of its critical commentary is no more relevant under copyright than the like threat to the original market.

Although 2 Live Crew submitted uncontroverted affidavits on the question of market harm to the original, neither they, nor Acuff-Rose, introduced evidence or affidavits addressing the likely effect of 2 Live Crew's parodic rap song on the market for a nonparody, rap version of "Oh, Pretty Woman." And while Acuff-Rose would have us find evidence of a rap market in the very facts that 2 Live Crew recorded a rap parody of "Oh, Pretty Woman" and another rap group sought a license to record a rap derivative, there was no evidence that a potential rap market was harmed in any way by 2 Live Crew's parody, rap version. The fact that 2 Live Crew's parody sold as part of a collection of rap songs says very little about the parody's effect on a market for a rap version of the original, either of the music alone or of the music with its lyrics. The District Court essentially passed on this issue, observing that Acuff-Rose is free to record "whatever version of the original it desires," 754 F. Supp., at 1158; the Court of Appeals went the other way by erroneous presumption. Contrary to each treatment, it is impossible to deal with the fourth factor except by recognizing that a silent record on an important factor bearing on fair use disentitled the proponent of the defense, 2 Live Crew, to summary judgment. The evidentiary hole will doubtless be plugged on remand.

### III

It was error for the Court of Appeals to conclude that the commercial nature of 2 Live Crew's parody of "Oh, Pretty Woman" rendered it presumptively unfair. No such evidentiary presumption is available to address either the first factor, the character and purpose of the use, or the fourth, market harm, in determining whether a transformative use, such as parody, is a fair one. The court also erred in holding that 2 Live Crew had necessarily copied excessively from the Orbison original, considering the parodic purpose of the use. We therefore reverse the judgment of the Court of Appeals and remand the case for further proceedings consistent with this opinion.

---

As it is evident from the *Campbell* case, it is very often hard to draw the line between fair use and copyright infringement and this always demands a careful examination of the four factors based on the particular facts of the case. Often the outcome of the case may be important not only for the parties involved but also determine the path of a particular technology with spillovers on other companies and on the overall innovation environment. This was well-exemplified by the dispute between Oracle and Google with regard to the copyrightability of computer code and in particular Application Programming Interfaces (APIs) and their fair use by Google in the development of its Android operating system for mobile phones.

## Commentary on *Google LLC v. Oracle America, Inc.*, 141 S. Ct. 1183 (2021)*

In an era of rapid technological progress, copyright law risks becoming outdated. With no guidance from the Supreme Court in over twenty-five years, the application of fair use under

* Leading Case: Comment on 141 S. Ct. 1183 (2021), 135 Harv. L. Rev. 431 (2021) (footnotes omitted).

the Copyright Act of 1976—a four-factor statutory defense to copyright infringement claims—has been left largely to the speculation of scholars. This has been particularly troublesome in software, where developers have long been forced to rely on a confusing thicket of interpretations and assumptions lacking concrete legal assurances. A prolonged, multi-trial legal battle between two technology titans recently gave the Court cause to revisit fair use in software. Last Term, in *Google LLC v. Oracle America, Inc.*, the Supreme Court held that Google's copying of parts of the Java application programming interface (API) in its creation of the Android programming platform was fair use as a matter of law. In reaching this conclusion, the Court took a newly expansive view of transformativeness in the fair use analysis, recognizing the significance of Google's "reimplementation" of the Java API in a new context and the value of the third-party creativity the Android platform enabled. Although this development may feed concerns that fair use impinges on the transformation central to the derivative works right held exclusively by copyright owners, the Court's expansion of transformativeness in fair use accords with the constitutional goals of the Copyright Act.

In 2005, Google acquired Android, Inc., signaling the search company's intent to move into software development for the nascent mobile-device market. To attract "a sizeable number of skilled programmers" to develop applications for Google's Android-based smartphones, Google wanted its platform to take advantage of programmers' familiarity with the popular Java programming language. It negotiated with Java's developer Sun Microsystems to license Java technologies, but talks broke down over Sun's insistence that "all programs written on the Android platform be interoperable." Google then elected to create its Android platform independently.

However, to ensure that programmers' familiarity with Java would aid in developing Android applications, Google copied about 11,500 lines of code from the Java API. The Court identified this portion of the API as "declaring code," which matches a programmer's typed command to the code that actually performs it. Declaring code also reflects how Java's creators "arranged and grouped" different tasks, an organizational scheme known as "structure, sequence, and organization" (SSO). The code that actually performs the command, which the Court identified as "implementing code," accounted for the vast majority of the API that Google created for Android and was independently written by Google. In 2010, Oracle acquired Sun and the copyright to the Java computing platform, which includes the Java API. Oracle filed a suit against Google for copyright and patent infringement soon after.

Following trial, a jury rejected Oracle's patent claims and found copyright infringement only with respect to "nine lines of code," but could not agree on "whether Google could successfully assert a fair use defense." The district court held for Google that the API portion it had copied was an unprotected method of operation under the Copyright Act. Both parties appealed.

The Federal Circuit affirmed in part and reversed in part. It found that the declaring code and the SSO were copyrightable because Google was not bound to the naming conventions and structure of the Java API. Thus, Google could have written its own declaring code. Finding an insufficient record for a de novo review of Google's fair use defense, the court remanded for another trial on that question. The Supreme Court denied Google's petition for a writ of certiorari.

A second jury then found that Google's use of the Java API had been fair. The district court denied Oracle's motion for judgment as a matter of law, finding that the jury could "reasonably have found for either side on . . . fair use." Oracle renewed its motion, adding a motion for a new trial, which the district court also denied. Oracle appealed.

The Federal Circuit reversed and remanded again. The court concluded that the question of "whether the use at issue is ultimately a fair one is . . . review[ed] de novo." The court proceeded to reject the jury's findings in favor of Google on three of the four fair use factors. The balance tipped back in Oracle's favor, and the court found that Google's use of the Java API was "not fair as a matter of law." This time, the Supreme Court granted certiorari.

The Supreme Court reversed and remanded, with Justice Breyer writing for the majority. It began by affirming that the constitutional objective of copyright is "to promote the Progress of Science and useful Arts." After reviewing the statutory background, the Court, to "answer [no] more than [was] necessary to resolve the . . . dispute," assumed for the sake of argument that the Java API may be copyrightable. The Court also agreed with the Federal Circuit that " 'fair use' [was] a legal question for judges to decide de novo." It then dismissed Google's Seventh Amendment arguments, proceeding to the fair use analysis.

The Court found that all four factors favored Google and held that Google's copying was fair use as a matter of law. For "expository purposes," the majority opinion began by examining the second factor: the nature of the copyrighted work. It noted at the outset that although software is copyrightable, all code is not created equal. The declaring code—which was designed to be intuitive and easy to use—was primarily functional and lacked the same creative "magic" of an implementing program. And unlike standalone software, the declaring code was embedded in a larger interface comprised mostly of uncopyrightable ideas and the creative expression of users. Indeed, much of its value was generated not by the copyright holder, but by the community of programmers taking the time to learn the API. For these reasons, the declaring code was "further than are most computer programs . . . from the core of copyright," if it was "copyrightable at all." The Court thus viewed this factor as weighing in favor of fair use.

Turning to the first factor, the Court next addressed the purpose and character of the use. Drawing on the rule articulated nearly three decades earlier in *Campbell v. Acuff-Rose Music, Inc.*, the majority considered whether Google's use imbued the copied code "with new expression, meaning or message," or, more simply, whether it was "transformative." Justice Breyer noted that the purpose of "virtually any unauthorized use of a copyrighted computer program" will necessarily be functional in service of "accomplish[ing] particular tasks," just as Google's was. Ending the inquiry there would thus "severely limit the scope of fair use" for software. As such, he asserted: "[W]e must go further." To that end, the Court looked to Google's creation of the entire Android platform, in which it "reimplemented" the API, and all the new products and programming opportunities that Android created in turn. Even allowing that Google's use was "commercial in nature," the majority found in favor of fair use on this factor.

In addressing the third factor—the amount and substantiality of the use—the majority noted that when the amount copied is "tethered to a [copier's] valid, transformative purpose," the factor will "generally weigh in favor of fair use." Here, the Court characterized Google's "basic objective" as allowing programmers to use their pre-existing knowledge of the Java API to create new programs for Android. As declaring code was the "key" to "unlock[ing] the programmers' creative energies," this factor weighed in favor of fair use.

Finally, the Court reached the fourth factor, assessing the potential market harm from Google's copying. The Court noted that the "potential loss of revenue [was] not the whole story," and that it also had to consider "the source of the loss" in addition to any "public benefits the copying [would] likely produce." While the Court conceded that Google made a "vast amount of money" from Android it returned to the idea that the value Google derived from using the API was generated by "programmers'[] investment in Sun Java programs." These two considerations, in combination with "creativity-related harms to the public" that might result from copyright enforcement, convinced the majority that the fourth factor weighed in favor of fair use as well. As such, the Court declared Google's copying fair use as a matter of law.

Justice Thomas dissented. He asserted that the majority skipped over the copyrightability analysis, thereby ignoring "half the relevant statutory text and distort[ing] its fair-use analysis."

He argued that by failing to analyze the Copyright Act's definition of a copyrightable "computer program," the Court created a distinction between implementing and declaring code that Congress had previously "rejected." The dissent went on to critique the majority's analysis of the fair use factors and concluded that three of the four "weigh[ed] decidedly against Google."

*Google v. Oracle* has been hailed as a "huge win for developers and consumers," not to mention a "win for innovation" more broadly. Despite the majority's reluctance to rule directly on the question of API copyrightability, this case's holding will "provide[] breathing room" to software developers employing similar strategies to create their products. However, because transformativeness was likely determinative of fair use here, the Court's analysis may appear to some to impinge on the derivative works right belonging exclusively to the copyright holder under the Copyright Act. The Act defines derivative works as those "based upon one or more preexisting works," such that the original has been "recast, transformed, or adapted." Since findings of both an infringement of the derivative works right and a valid fair use defense to copyright infringement entail a transformativeness analysis, the debate over which serves to limit the other is ongoing. The Court's expansive view of transformativeness in the fair use inquiry rightly placed a further limit on the derivative works right, allowing for broader applications of fair use in service of copyright's goal of promoting innovation.

Transformativeness has become virtually dispositive of fair use findings since the Court introduced it. In *Campbell*, the Court used the word "transformative" to describe the purpose and character of a fair use, and it explicitly stated that "the more transformative" a work, the less "other factors, like commercialism," will weigh against a fair use finding. Truly transformative works, the Court wrote, would "lie at the heart of the fair use doctrine's guarantee of breathing space within the confines of copyright" while "generally further[ing]" copyright's constitutional goals.86 Courts employ "transformative use" to conceptualize the level of creative input required for a fair use defense to succeed. The concept's growing centrality to the fair use analysis has, predictably, made it critical to copyright stakeholders and litigators.

Given this increasing reliance on transformativeness, courts have attempted to draw an administrable line dividing the contexts of derivative works and fair use. Lower courts have largely come to treat transformation in derivative works as "changes of form" and transformation in fair use as changes in purpose. For example, translating a book into a new language or recording a text into an audiobook might constitute changes in form, falling within the derivative works right of the original copyright owner. This is because the overall message of the work remains unchanged, despite the additional effort or creativity required to make the derivative work. However, taking several pages of the same written text and crossing out certain words to convert the prose into a work of erasure poetry would likely constitute a change in purpose, thereby supporting a finding of fair use, especially if the message of the new poem consisted of commentary on or critique of the underlying work.

Some courts have nonetheless objected to the predominance of the transformative use analysis, fearing that it will supersede the derivative works right entirely. *Kienitz v. Sconnie Nation LLC*, which concerned a photographer's infringement action against a company that sold apparel incorporating one of his photos, contained a rare, explicit judicial recognition of the tension between fair use and the derivative works right. The *Kienitz* court expressed skepticism of the Second Circuit's treatment of transformativeness as dispositive of the fair use inquiry, fearing that excessive focus thereon "not only replaces the [other fair use factors] but also could override [statutory protections for] derivative works." The Seventh Circuit asserted that "[t]o say that a new use transforms the work is precisely to say that it is derivative." Justice Thomas expressed similar worries in his *Google* dissent.

However, the *Kienitz* court's definition of derivative use—as any "new use [that] transforms the work"—is itself an example of courts' tendency to enlarge an already overbroad derivative works right. In the late nineteenth century, copyright expanded to include certain derivative uses that previously belonged to the public domain. Since then, copyright protections have broadened through statutory expansions, leading many to characterize copyright legislation as a "one-way ratchet" in the direction of increased protections. Courts have exacerbated this trend by untethering the final clause of derivative works' statutory definition—consisting of "any other form in which the work is recast, transformed, or adapted"—from the nine specific examples of derivative use provided by the rest of the definition. The result, as exemplified by *Kienitz*, has been the equation of transformation as generically understood with derivative use as a copyright term of art.

Given the overbreadth of the derivative works right, the Court's expansion of transformativeness for the purposes of the fair use inquiry in Google brings an overly restrictive copyright doctrine back into the proper equilibrium. Contrary to much of the handwringing about the harms to authors from fair use impingements on the derivative works right, fair use's expansion in the 1990s is a relatively recent development, and it has been to the clear benefit of innovation, especially for software. Just as an overexpansive conception of transformative use can threaten the derivative works right, an overexpansive view of what constitutes a derivative work can threaten fair use. Thus, to the extent its conception of transformativeness expanded into territory previously occupied by derivative works, the Court only reasserted the proper "breathing space" in the face of previous overbroad constructions.

Against this backdrop, the *Google* Court correctly adopted an expansive view of transformative use in two important ways. First, it treated Google's end goal of enabling future creative works by third-party developers as a transformative purpose independent from the particular function for which Google reimplemented the Java API. In seeking "to expand the use and usefulness of Android-based smartphones" by offering "programmers a highly creative and innovative [new] tool for a smartphone environment," Google engaged in precisely the kind of innovation contemplated by the Copyright Clause. Second, the Court held that even exact copies serving the same purpose as the original may constitute fair uses where they occur in sufficiently different contexts—in this case a "distinct and different computing environment." This emphasis on the shift from computers to smartphones is tied to the "change in form" that courts have identified with derivative works in other contexts. However, the Court's disaggregation of "form" into copied content and altered context was correct in recognizing the importance of this distinction in the software realm, where similar reimplementations have long been a key ingredient of innovation.

While *Google* signals an expansion in the scope of fair use, it also takes a necessary step to realign modern copyright law with its constitutional goals. The scope of the fair use doctrine has undoubtedly expanded since the Court's last fair use decision in Campbell, but this shift occurred in response to a copyright status quo that was overly restrictive in the first place, and could well become so again. The majority's reasoning will give lower courts the freedom to consider clearly transformative uses that would otherwise be masked by the functional nature of software. It will allow them to do the same in less cutting-edge circumstances, but with similarly positive results for innovation. While restricting the rights of copyright holders, the Court's approach took an important step to further the constitutional goal of copyright law: to "promote the Progress of Science and useful Arts."

---

This expansive view of transformativeness may have been however curtailed in the 2023 decision of the U.S. Supreme Court in *Andy Warhol Foundation for the Visual Arts, Inc. v. Goldsmith,* 598 U.S. ___ 2023. The facts of the case were relatively straightforward: In 1981 Lynn Goldsmith, a photographer, took a series of photographs of Prince on assignment for Newsweek and retained copyright over the images. Following the release of Prince's Purple

Rain in 1984, the magazine *Vanity Fair* licensed one of those photos, a single black and white full length portrait photograph that previously unpublished. It was agreed the photograph would be used as an "artistic reference for an illustration" that would be used only once. The magazine commissioned Andy Warhol to create a highly colorized silkscreen using just Prince's head from the photograph, illustrating the feature "Purple Fame". Goldsmith was credited for the "source photograph" and received $400. Warhol created subsequently 16 variants of the Prince portrait and these remained in his private collection and were after Warhol's death managed by the Andy Warhol Foundation for the Visual Arts (AWF). After Prince died in 2016, Vanity Fair's parent company (Condé Nast) asked AWF about reusing the 1984 Vanity Fair image for a special edition magazine that would commemorate Prince. When Condé Nast learned about the other Prince Series images, it opted instead to purchase a license from AWF to publish Orange Prince. Goldsmith alleged that she had been unaware of the existence of the illustration and the Prince series until she came across the magazine. Goldsmith notified AWF of her belief that it had infringed her copyright. AWF then sued Goldsmith for a declaratory judgment of noninfringement or, in the alternative, fair use. Goldsmith counterclaimed for infringement. The District Court considered the four fair use factors in 17 U.S.C. §107 and granted AWF summary judgment on its defense of fair use. The Court of Appeals reversed, finding that all four fair use factors favored Goldsmith. Before the Supreme Court, the sole question asked was whether the first fair use factor, "the purpose and character of the use, including whether such use is of a commercial nature or is for nonprofit educational purposes," §107(1), weighs in favor of AWF's recent commercial licensing to Condé Nast.

In a 7-2 decision written by Justice Sotomayor the Court decided that the fair use requirements were not satisfied.

## *Andy Warhol Foundation for the Visual Arts, Inc. v. Goldsmith*

598 U.S. ___ 2023*

The "purpose and character" of AWF's use of Goldsmith's photograph in commercially licensing Orange Prince to Condé Nast does not favor AWF's fair use defense to copyright infringement. Pp. 12–38.

(a) AWF contends that the Prince Series works are "transformative," and that the first fair use factor thus weighs in AWF's favor, because the works convey a different meaning or message than the photograph. But the first fair use factor instead focuses on whether an allegedly infringing use has a further purpose or different character, which is a matter of degree, and the degree of difference must be weighed against other considerations, like commercialism. Although new expression, meaning, or message may be relevant to whether a copying use has a sufficiently distinct purpose or character, it is not, without more, dispositive of the first factor. Here, the specific use of Goldsmith's photograph alleged to infringe her copyright is AWF's licensing of Orange Prince to Condé Nast. As portraits of Prince used to depict Prince in magazine stories about Prince, the original photograph and AWF's copying use of it share substantially the same purpose. Moreover, AWF's use is of a commercial nature. Even though Orange Prince adds new expression to Goldsmith's photograph, in the context of the challenged use, the first fair use factor still favors Goldsmith. Pp. 12–27.

(1) The Copyright Act encourages creativity by granting to the creator of an original work a bundle of rights that includes the rights to reproduce the copyrighted work and to

* For a quick overview of the issues, provided here is the Court Report's headnote and not the actual Court's language.

prepare derivative works. 17 U.S.C. §106. Copyright, however, balances the benefits of incentives to create against the costs of restrictions on copying. This balancing act is reflected in the common-law doctrine of fair use, codified in §107, which provides: "[T]he fair use of a copyrighted work, . . . for purposes such as criticism, comment, news reporting, teaching . . . , scholarship, or research, is not an infringement of copyright." To determine whether a particular use is "fair," the statute enumerates four factors to be considered. The factors "set forth general principles, the application of which requires judicial balancing, depending upon relevant circumstances." *Google LLC v. Oracle America, Inc.*, 593 U. S. ___, ___.

The first fair use factor, "the purpose and character of the use, including whether such use is of a commercial nature or is for nonprofit educational purposes," §107(1), considers the reasons for, and nature of, the copier's use of an original work. The central question it asks is whether the use "merely supersedes the objects of the original creation . . . (supplanting the original), or instead adds something new, with a further purpose or different character." *Campbell v. Acuff-Rose Music, Inc.*, 510 U.S. 569, 579 (internal quotation marks and citations omitted). As most copying has some further purpose and many secondary works add something new, the first factor asks "whether and to what extent" the use at issue has a purpose or character different from the original. *Ibid.* (emphasis added). The larger the difference, the more likely the first factor weighs in favor of fair use. A use that has a further purpose or different character is said to be "transformative," but that too is a matter of degree. *Ibid.* To preserve the copyright owner's right to prepare derivative works, defined in §101 of the Copyright Act to include "any other form in which a work may be recast, transformed, or adapted," the degree of transformation required to make "transformative" use of an original work must go beyond that required to qualify as a derivative.

The Court's decision in Campbell is instructive. In holding that parody may be fair use, the Court explained that "parody has an obvious claim to transformative value" because "it can provide social benefit, by shedding light on an earlier work, and, in the process, creating a new one." 510 U.S., at 579. The use at issue was 2 Live Crew's copying of Roy Orbison's song, "Oh, Pretty Woman," to create a rap derivative, "Pretty Woman." 2 Live Crew transformed Orbison's song by adding new lyrics and musical elements, such that "Pretty Woman" had a different message and aesthetic than "Oh, Pretty Woman." But that did not end the Court's analysis of the first fair use factor. The Court found it necessary to determine whether 2 Live Crew's transformation rose to the level of parody, a distinct purpose of commenting on the original or criticizing it. Further distinguishing between parody and satire, the Court explained that "[p]arody needs to mimic an original to make its point, and so has some claim to use the creation of its victim's (or collective victims') imagination, whereas satire can stand on its own two feet and so requires justification for the very act of borrowing." *Id.*, at 580–581. More generally, when "commentary has no critical bearing on the substance or style of the original composition, . . . the claim to fairness in borrowing from another's work diminishes accordingly (if it does not vanish), and other factors, like the extent of its commerciality, loom larger." *Id.*, at 580.

*Campbell* illustrates two important points. First, the fact that a use is commercial as opposed to nonprofit is an additional element of the first fair use factor. The commercial nature of a use is relevant, but not dispositive. It is to be weighed against the degree to which the use has a further purpose or different character. Second, the first factor relates to the justification for the use. In a broad sense, a use that has a distinct purpose is justified because it furthers the goal of copyright, namely, to promote the progress of science and the arts, without diminishing the incentive to create. In a narrower sense, a use may be justified because copying is reasonably necessary to achieve the user's new purpose. Parody, for example, "needs to mimic an original to make its point." *Id.*, at 580–581. Similarly, other commentary or criticism that targets an original work may have compelling reason to "conjure up" the original by borrowing from it. *Id.*, at 588. An independent justification like this is particularly relevant to assessing fair use where an original work and copying use share the same or highly similar purposes, or where wide dissemination of a secondary work would otherwise run the risk of substitution for the original or licensed derivatives of it. *See, e.g., Google*, 593 U. S., at ___ (slip op., at 26).

In sum, if an original work and secondary use share the same or highly similar purposes, and the secondary use is commercial, the first fair use factor is likely to weigh against fair use, absent some other justification for copying. Pp. 13–20.

(2) The fair use provision, and the first factor in particular, requires an analysis of the specific "use" of a copyrighted work that is alleged to be "an infringement." §107. The same copying may be fair when used for one purpose but not another. *See Campbell*, 510 U.S., at 585. Here, Goldsmith's copyrighted photograph has been used in multiple ways. The Court limits its analysis to the specific use alleged to be infringing in this case—AWF's commercial licensing of Orange Prince to Condé Nast—and expresses no opinion as to the creation, display, or sale of the original Prince Series works. In the context of Condé Nast's special edition magazine commemorating Prince, the purpose of the Orange Prince image is substantially the same as that of Goldsmith's original photograph. Both are portraits of Prince used in magazines to illustrate stories about Prince. The use also is of a commercial nature. Taken together, these two elements counsel against fair use here. Although a use's transformativeness may outweigh its commercial character, in this case both point in the same direction. That does not mean that all of Warhol's derivative works, nor all uses of them, give rise to the same fair use analysis. Pp. 20–27.

(b) AWF contends that the purpose and character of its use of Goldsmith's photograph weighs in favor of fair use because Warhol's silk-screen image of the photograph has a different meaning or message. By adding new expression to the photograph, AWF says, Warhol made transformative use of it. Campbell did describe a transformative use as one that "alter[s] the first [work] with new expression, meaning, or message." 510 U.S., at 579. But *Campbell* cannot be read to mean that §107(1) weighs in favor of any use that adds new expression, meaning, or message. Otherwise, "transformative use" would swallow the copyright owner's exclusive right to prepare derivative works, as many derivative works that "recast, transfor[m] or adap[t]" the original, §101, add new expression of some kind. The meaning of a secondary work, as reasonably can be perceived, should be considered to the extent necessary to determine whether the purpose of the use is distinct from the original. For example, the Court in *Campbell* considered the messages of 2 Live Crew's song to determine whether the song had a parodic purpose. But fair use is an objective inquiry into what a user does with an original work, not an inquiry into the subjective intent of the user, or into the meaning or impression that an art critic or judge draws from a work.

Even granting the District Court's conclusion that Orange Prince reasonably can be perceived to portray Prince as iconic, whereas Goldsmith's portrayal is photorealistic, that difference must be evaluated in the context of the specific use at issue. The purpose of AWF's recent commercial licensing of Orange Prince was to illustrate a magazine about Prince with a portrait of Prince. Although the purpose could be more specifically described as illustrating a magazine about Prince with a portrait of Prince, one that portrays Prince somewhat differently from Goldsmith's photograph (yet has no critical bearing on her photograph), that degree of difference is not enough for the first factor to favor AWF, given the specific context and commercial nature of the use. To hold otherwise might authorize a range of commercial copying of photographs to be used for purposes that are substantially the same as those of the originals.

AWF asserts another related purpose of Orange Prince, which is to comment on the "dehumanizing nature" and "effects" of celebrity. No doubt, many of Warhol's works, and particularly his uses of repeated images, can be perceived as depicting celebrities as commodities. But even if such commentary is perceptible on the cover of Condé Nast's tribute to "Prince Rogers Nelson, 1958–2016," on the occasion of the man's death, the asserted commentary is at *Campbell*'s lowest ebb: It "has no critical bearing on" Goldsmith's photograph, thus the commentary's "claim to fairness in borrowing from" her work "diminishes accordingly (if it does not vanish)." *Campbell*, 510 U.S., at 580. The commercial nature of the use, on the other hand, "loom[s] larger." *Ibid.* Like satire that does not target an original work, AWF's asserted commentary "can stand on its own two feet and so requires justification for the very act of borrowing." *Id.*, at 581. Moreover, because AWF's copying of Goldsmith's photograph was for a commercial use so similar to the photograph's typical use, a particularly compelling justification is needed. Copying the photograph because doing so was merely helpful to convey a new meaning or message is not justification enough. Pp. 28–37.

(c) Goldsmith's original works, like those of other photographers, are entitled to copyright protection, even against famous artists. Such protection includes the right to prepare derivative works that transform the original. The use of a copyrighted work may nevertheless be fair if, among other things, the use has a purpose and character that is sufficiently distinct from the original. In this case, however, Goldsmith's photograph of Prince, and AWF's copying use of the photograph in an image licensed to a special edition magazine devoted to Prince, share substantially the same commercial purpose. AWF has offered no other persuasive justification for its unauthorized use of the photograph. While the Court has cautioned that the four statutory fair use factors may not "be treated in isolation, one from another," but instead all must be "weighed together, in light of the purposes of copyright," *Campbell*, 510 U.S., at 578, here AWF challenges only the Court of Appeals' determinations on the first fair use factor, and the Court agrees the first factor favors Goldsmith. P. 38.

## NOTES AND QUESTIONS

**1.** Justice Elena Kagan wrote a dissent in the *Warhol* case and was joined by the chief justice, John Roberts, arguing for the artistic value of appropriation and illustrating this with examples from Shakespeare to Nick Cave. Kagan concluded her dissenting opinion by stating: " 'Inhibit[ing] subsequent writers' and artists from 'improv[ing] upon prior works'—as the majority does today—will 'frustrate the very ends sought to be attained' by copyright law. *Harper & Row*, 471 U.S., at 549. It will stifle creativity of every sort. It will impede new art and music and literature. It will thwart the expression of new ideas and the attainment of new knowledge. It will make our world poorer." Do you agree with Justice Kagan's position or do you rather think that the *Warhol* judgment would not have such far-reaching effects and the balance of rights between original and follow-up creators is still given?

**2.** Recent litigation involving generative AI platforms suggests that the scope of fair use will undoubtedly be a point of contention. Before *Warhol*, it seemed likely that a court could find the use of unlicensed training data to be insulated by fair use, as the use of content to "train" a platform that generates content could be found to be transformative, as the Courts have established with regard to Google's searchable databases (*Authors Guild v. Google, Inc.*, 804 F.3d 202, 217 (2d Cir. 2015). Do you think that *Warhol*'s decision may have created an obstacle in this regard?

## G. The Prospects of Human Rights in Copyright

Both communication to the public and fair use exceptions pose difficult questions in particular in the field of Internet regulation. Other than property rights, freedom of expression and information, and the right to do business, courts have not taken recourse to human rights standards, in particular to protection of personality and privacy, or human dignity. Following the general discussion on intellectual property and human rights, the following excerpt discusses the potential impact of human rights in assessing and balancing different interests at stake, both in domestic and international law. The approach also contributes to enhancing transparency and to overcoming historical divides between legislative and rigid exceptions in European law and a case-to-case-based approach to fair use in the Anglo-American tradition.

**Thomas Cottier***

## *Copyright and the Human Right to Property: A European and International Case Law Approach*

. . .

[T]he relationship of copyright and human rights is a complex one and cannot be readily addressed without taking into account the particular structure of the legal instrument and court system at hand. What generally can be said it that assessments are fact intensive and depend on the particular configuration of the case. Yet, it clearly is not a matter of simply juxta-positioning IPRs and human rights. The United States Supreme Court famously stressed the importance of copyright protection as a precondition of freedom of expression. Moreover, human rights may particularly support and protect the dimension of moral rights, invoking Article 12 of the Universal Declaration on Human Rights and related rights: 'No one shall be subjected to arbitrary interference with his privacy, family, home or correspondence, nor to attacks upon his honour and reputation. Everyone has the right to the protection of the law against such interference or attacks.' Finally, procedural rights and due process are of utmost importance in support of right-holders seeking to obtain IPR protection, in particular in patent and trademark law and other forms dependent upon registration. It may, on the other, also restrict excessive standards of copyright protection. Importantly, however, for courts having comprehensive jurisdiction, it is not simply a matter of balancing all the interests at stake, but to develop a proper methodology which recognises the framework of human rights as a starting point in defining copyright protection in particular in the Post-Gutenberg Age.

### A. Constitutional Approach

It is submitted that a constitutional approach based upon fundamental and human rights guarantees should be used whenever possible in order to design and legally assess compatibilities of copyright law as a utilitarian concept. Human rights provide an overarching valuational framework. It offers the constitutional background for legislation, and the starting point of analysis. It shapes the legal methodology accordingly. Assessing compatibility with human right entails a different approach from generally and pragmatically balancing IPRs and human rights. The constitutional perspective may produce the same results as generally balancing interest taken on par. Methodologically, however, it is fundamentally different.

To start with, legislators and all courts can and should take into account the differences of the legal nature of property rights and human rights; while the first ones are conventional and agreed, the latter do not depend upon positive law and the essence of rights needs to be respected by legislation and cannot be completely restricted and suppressed. The special

* In Intellectual Property and the Judiciary (Christophe Geiger, Craig Nord and Xavier Leuba eds., forthcoming 2018); also in Thomas Cottier, *Copyright and Human Rights: The Impact of International and European Law*, 26 Annali Italiani di Diritto d'Autore Della Cultura e Dello Spectacolo 518-37 (2017) (footnotes omitted).

status of property rights as an institutional guarantee inherently assumes a serving function and can only exist to the extent that the property regime, as defined in statutory law and precedents, is compatible with the overarching spectrum of human rights and the essence of these rights. The utilitarian concept of copyright and related rights thus is to be mainstreamed along human rights. No longer should we operate distinctions of private and public law in the field of intellectual property and copyright in particular. They certainly do no longer exist in European and international economic law. Both being private rights and monopolies granted by government, they support and restrict human rights at the same time. To the extent that they support IPRs, this should translate into the formulation and interpretation of intellectual property standards. To the extent IPRs restrict human rights, the formulation and interpretation is subject to the three-step conditions of a clear legal basis in statutory law, overriding public interest and the test of proportionality. This perspective will allow coping better with ongoing and challenging technological change. Human rights make sure that we do not lose sight of what in the end of the day intellectual property protection is called upon to serve and to protect. This is particularly true for the law of the European Union to which human rights fully apply under the Charter of Fundamental Rights.

### The Impact of the Charter of Fundamental Rights

With the entry into force of the Charter of Fundamental Rights, including protection of IPRs in Article 17, experts and politicians are called upon to take human rights into account in designing and shaping copyright in positive law. Lawyers and the Court are today offered the option to plead in a constitutional law mode and argue that secondary EU law, or its application, is consistent or inconsistent with fundamental rights enshrined in the Charter. Beyond property rights, a host or rights are potentially affected. We recall in particular Article 1: human dignity, Article 3: right to integrity of the person, Article 7: respect for private and family life, Article 8: protection of personal data, Article 11: freedom of expression and information, Article 13: freedom of arts and sciences, Article 14: right to education, Article 16: freedom to conduct a business, Article 20: equality before the law, Article 26: integration of persons with disabilities, Article 38: consumer protection, Article 41: right to good administration, Article 42: access to documents, Article 47: the right to effective remedy and to a fair trial and additional procedural guarantees in Articles 48-50 of the Charter. All these rights and provisions are potentially relevant in shaping standards of copyright. They all may be relevant in reviewing such standards before a court of law.

In addressing a matter pertaining to copyright or related rights, it is a matter of landscaping the human rights environment in a first step. Which rights are affected and concerned? Which rights are supported and which rights are restricted by the copyright provision? These rights may be mutually supporting, or competing and conflicting. Legislators and courts need to accommodate them to the utmost extent possible. It goes without saying that this is a difficult task expounding diverging conflicting interests. But landscaping human rights offers the possibility to discuss all pertinent and legally relevant interests in a transparent manner. It offers the grounds for balancing and compromise in the process of legislation. When copyright limits fundamental rights, the Charter offers a methodology to assess resulting restrictions. Article 52(1) sets out the requirements to be met to the extent that human rights are restricted. They essentially relate to the rule of law, respect of the essence of the right, public interest or protection of other rights, and proportionality of the measure at stake:

> 1. Any limitation on the exercise of the rights and freedoms recognised by this Charter must be provided for by law and respect the essence of those rights and freedoms. Subject to the principle of proportionality, limitations may be made only if they are necessary and genuinely

> meet objectives of general interest recognised by the Union or the need to protect the rights and freedoms of others.

The configuration is comparable to the methodology developed by constitutional courts, the European Court on Human Rights and the Court of the European Union in assessing restrictions of the four freedoms. It was in particular applied in adjudicating intellectual property rules in domestic law of Member States and resulting quantitative restrictions. The Court assesses whether one of the fundamental freedoms or any other provision of the TFEU is affected. If yes, it is a matter of examining whether the provisions can be justified under existing restrictions, in particular within Article 34 or by Article 36 TFEU.

Balancing property rights and human rights at stake is particularly difficult in the digital economy. Directive 2001/29/EC of the European Parliament and of the Council of May 2001 on the harmonisation of certain aspects of copyright and related rights in the information society stipulates that '[t]he proposed harmonization will help to implement the four freedoms of the internal market and relates to compliance with the fundamental principles of law and especially of property, including intellectual property, and freedom of expression and the public interest.' It further recognizes that '[a] fair balance of rights and interests between the different categories of rightholders, as well as between the different categories of rightholders and users of protected subject-matter must be safeguarded. The existing exceptions and limitations to the rights as set out by the Member States have to be reassessed in the light of the new electronic environment.' The Directive offers strong intellectual property protection in Article 3 as reproduction rights and communications to the public by the rightholder or with its consent do not exhaust copyright and thus establishes control over digital content for no less than 70 years post mortem. The legal status of distribution rights is less clear. According to Article 4(2) they equally do not exhaust 'in respect of the original or copies of the work except where the first sale or other transfer of ownership in the Community of that object is made by the right holder or with his consent.' Since first sale or transfer depends upon consent it would seem that distribution rights are subject to regional exhaustion in result. The balance with human rights concerns and other interests is sought in Article 5 which entails a host of exceptions to reproduction and distribution rights, subject to the three-step-test (Para 5). From a human rights angle, legal licenses and fair use are important for the purposes of teaching and research (3a), uses for people with disabilities (3b), reproduction by the press (3c), quotations for criticism and review (3d), use of political speech (3f), use during religious celebrations (3g), advertising public exhibitions and sale of artistic works (3j), use for purpose of caricature (3k), use for research and private purposes (3n, 2b), and public libraries (2c). The list looks fairly random; it is the result of specific lobby efforts rather than a methodological approach. Important concerns are not reflected. Freedom of information, essential for the operation of a market economy and thus the common market, is not included.

Indeed, the question arises whether the classical rule-exception model, the model of strong copyright protection subject to listed exceptions is able to properly reflect a human rights-based approach. We recalled that property rights conceptually are subject to legislation, while human rights are a matter not at the disposition of legislation. It follows that a proper balance of property and human rights primarily requires reshaping property within the framework of Article 52 of the Charter of Fundamental Rights, rather than simply adding a random and even exhaustive list of fair use exemptions to strongly protected rights. The topic is widely debated, and it goes beyond the scope of this paper to summarize the debate. Except for Peukert, the methodology of restricting human rights has not been prominently featured so far. Discussions generally focus on the general relationship of copyright and human rights and the issue as to which of them should prevail.

Restrictions of human rights, in particular freedom of information and freedom of expression by means of intellectual property and copyright are duly possible up to the point that the essence of human rights is affected. Sufficiently precise legal foundations of intellectual property rights, the public interest in protecting them and encouraging innovation and investment can be readily met. The critical test, in my view, is necessity and proportionality. The latter is able to offer appropriate guidance in reshaping property rights. Proportionality essentially consists of three components: the measure is necessary, the measure is suitable and able to achieve the goal, and the means of the measure do not exceed of what is necessary to achieve the goal. The relationship of end and means perhaps is the most important factor in guiding shaping property rights. From this angle, the present scope of copyright protection in the Post Gutenberg era is asked into question. Assessing proportionality, the duration of rights goes beyond of what is necessary to recuperate investments and efforts made. Incentives to create do not depend any longer upon duration of 70 years *post mortem* protection but may return to dimensions of the Act of Anne in the digital era. Dissemination of information requires reviewing exhaustion of rights. Intangible goods and services are not excluded from this doctrine and restriction. It is difficult to see why digital reproduction rights do not exhaust, while distribution rights are subject to the first sale doctrine and transfer of ownership by consent in accordance with Article 4(2) of the 2001/29 EC directive. It would seem appropriate to develop an exhaustion doctrine able to preserve incentives to create and invest and limit free flow of information in the public domain only to the extent necessary to achieve these goals. The question arises whether control over the first release of copies and control of timing does not suffice. Moreover, downstream digital operations beyond contractual relations are almost impossible to control and monitor. Legal security and dissemination of information under freedom of information and expression speak in favour of a more open approach. Digital copyright should be redefined to international exhaustion upon first sale and release of the content. It could be made subject to a general legal requirement to indicate the source and the name of the author, but without the restrictions on certain contents currently listed in Article 5(2)(c) of the directive 2001/29 EC. From the point of view of freedom of information, expression and free speech, limitations of fair use on 'current economic, political or religious topics' at the exclusion of other content cannot be justified under copyright law which must be neutral on content. Importantly, it should also include commercial speech essential in the operation of a market economy.

### 6.3. Testing the Case of Hyperlinking

Returning to the case of *GS Media v. Sanova Media*, addressing the issue of copyright clearance for hyperlinking and discussed at the outset, it would be a matter of assessing firstly which human rights are affected in the case: Article 16 right to do business, Article 17 protection of property, Article 11 freedom of information and expression and Article 1 human dignity and Article 6 respect of private and family life. It is one thing to have explicit pictures printed in a magazine and another to have them circulated digitally with global access and distribution. Copyright clearance for hyperlinking is supported by the right to do business, the right to property, human dignity and respect of private and family life. It is countervailed by the freedom of information and expression, and the right to do business by users.

Applying the test of Article 52 of the Charter, Article 3(1) of Directive 2001/29 offers an adequate legal basis setting out copyright and the right to control any communication to the public of their work. There is a public interest in granting exclusive right in order to encourage investment, in line with the right to property and to do business, and human dignity and respect of privacy in this particular case. Freedom of information and expression, on the other hand, support hyperlinking and access to materials published. There is a general interest in wide and robust dissemination of information, albeit a question mark remains in the particular case.

These elements should inform the interpretation of the notion of communication to the public. Duties of care in checking whether communication to the public was authorized or not, should be defined in accordance with human rights affected in a particular case. Materials affecting human dignity and personality, also taking into account personality rights in article 12 of the Universal Declaration on Human Rights, evidently require a standard of stricter scrutiny than materials of general interest and importance for debate or commercial information. In this particular case, it would seem important to require an assessment of the lawfulness of release and publication by users before hyperlinking is allowed to take place. Whether or not this hyperlinking takes place for commercial or non-commercial purposes cannot be relevant. Human dignity and personality is affected either way, and users should assume appropriate responsibility and liability. Secondly, it is difficult to separate the economic impact along the lines of commercial or non-commercial activities. Publication for non-commercial purposes may equally affect economic and thus copyright interests.

Rather than relying upon categorical distinctions, it is submitted that users should be obliged to verify copyright clearance taking into account the content of the publication. Content of personal sensitivity should be cleared prior to hyperlinking, and users should be obliged to make the effort of verifying whether the material was released for publication or not. For other content—and what amounts to the mainstream of publications—a standard would be sufficient to assess whether the user knew, or was reasonably able to know, whether the material was not authorised to be communicated to the public in the first place. Freedom of information and access to information and dissemination are of overriding general interest and down-stream hyperlinking of originally unauthorised materials should be generally lawful, unless the user acts in bad faith and contrary to what he or she knew or could have reasonably known. This is the test the TRIPs Agreement applies to illegal incorporation of microchips into products legally traded. Remedies are limited to damages in such cases for stock at hand. This approach could also be suitable in the field of copyright. Good faith and reducing copyrights to liability rules, as suggested by Jerome Reichman and Keith Maskus, would seem suitable to address the problem of unlawful hyperlinking a fast moving reality as a general rule. It also shows that human rights approaches do not necessarily go against intellectual property rights, but may assist in finding more appropriate rules in the fast moving reality of the Post-Gutenberg era of digital trade than stretching existing and traditional concepts made for the printing age.

## NOTES AND QUESTIONS

**1.** Assess to what extent that the approach of liability rules not excluding the use of copyrighted materials could be suitable to address the problem of Internet transmission short of consent by copyright owners. *See UPC Telekabel Wien GmbH v. Constantin Film Verleih GmbH*, C-314/12, *infra* section II.A.3.a. In this case, the Court engages in extensive balancing of human rights setting out conditions for injunctive relief.

## H. Artificial Intelligence and Copyright

Copyright law is important for AI, and AI has disruptive potential for copyright law. With respect to the former, AI is generally software or computer code, and so generally eligible for copyright protection as a literary work including as source code (programming language) and object code (the machine language in 1s and 0s).

With respect to the later, many AI systems, particularly those based on machine learning, need to be "trained" on data to perform useful tasks. For example, an AI designed to perform facial recognition may need to be trained on images of faces. This training process may not involve a human being looking at the images, but will likely involve the images being digitally copied. If those images are copyright protected and if an AI developer uses them without the right holder's permission, does that constitute copyright infringement?

In 2022 and 2023, some high-profile lawsuits were filed against developers of generative AI systems for copyright infringement arising from AI training. For instance, Getty Images, Inc. ("Getty"), a large supplier of stock images such as photographs, sued Stability AI ("Stability") in both the United States and United Kingdom for, among other things, training its system "Stable Diffusion" on Getty's copyright protected content without permission. *See Getty Images (US), Inc. v. Stability AI, Inc.*, 1:23-cv-00135, (D. Del.). Getty alleges that Stability could have purchased a license to its content but did not. By contrast, some of the other parties suing generative AI developers like OpenAI for copyright infringement claim they do not want AI developers using their work at all, regardless of whether renumeration is paid.

Whether the use of copyright protected content for training AI constitutes copyright infringement likely depends on whether it is considered fair use in the United States, or, in jurisdictions with a closed list of exceptions to infringement, whether it fits within an exception. For example, Japan was the first country to pass a statutory amendment to its copyright law specifically to exempt this sort of activity from infringement. These laws are often referred to as "text and data mining" ("TDM") exceptions. TDM narrowly refers to the analysis of data set to derive insights, but more broadly can also refer to using data to train AI models. By contrast to Japan, the European Union, in its 2019 Directive on Copyright in the Digital Single Market, adopted a relatively narrow exception for TDM that only applied to certain non-commercial uses.

The United Kingdom Intellectual Property Office ("UKIPO") subsequently conducted two stakeholder consultations on AI and IP, one a broad survey of issues, and the second focused specifically on three issues: copyright protection for AI-generated (or computer-generated) works, TDM exceptions for copyright infringement, and patent protection for AI-generated inventions. The outcome was for the UKIPO to recommend the adoption of a broad TDM exception including for commercial activity, but this was ultimately not adopted after rights holders successfully lobbied against it.

## *UKIPO, Consultation outcome, Artificial Intelligence and Intellectual Property: copyright and patents: Government response to consultation*

Updated 28 June 2022

### Executive Summary[2]

1. Artificial intelligence (AI) is a transformative technology, which is already revolutionising many areas of our lives. The Taskforce on Innovation, Growth and Regulatory Reform (TIGRR) report urged UK leadership on AI. Unleashing the power of AI is a top priority in

2. UKIPO, Consultation outcome, Artificial Intelligence and Intellectual Property: copyright and patents: Government response to consultation, Updated 28 June 2022, https://www.gov.uk/government/consultations/artificial-intelligence-and-ip-copyright-and-patents/outcome/artificial-intelligence-and-intellectual-property-copyright-and-patents-government-response-to-consultation.

the plan to be the most pro-tech Government ever. The National AI Strategy sets out how the Government aims to secure the UK's position amongst the global AI superpowers.

2. AI can support innovation and creativity in a range of ways. It can be a tool for scientists, entrepreneurs, and artists, enabling new human inventions and creations. Some believe that AI will soon be inventing and creating things in ways that make it impossible to identify the human intellectual input in the final invention or work. Some feel this is happening now.

3. Intellectual property (IP) gives researchers, inventors, creators, and businesses the confidence to invest their time, energy and money in doing something new. UK business invests more than £130 billion a year in knowledge assets. IP rights protect around £63 billion of this. These assets are vital to the industries that bring us the innovation and products that add value to our lives.

4. The Government sought evidence and views on a range of options on how AI should be dealt with in the patent and copyright systems. This response sets out the conclusions of that process.

5. We considered three specific areas:

- copyright protection for computer-generated works (CGWs) without a human author
- licensing or exceptions to copyright for text and data mining (TDM), which is often significant in AI use and development
- patent protection for AI-devised inventions

6. For computer-generated works, we plan no changes to the law. There is no evidence at present that protection for CGWs is harmful, and the use of AI is still in its early stages. As such, a proper evaluation of the options is not possible, and any changes could have unintended consequences. We will keep the law under review and could amend, replace or remove protection in future if the evidence supports it.

7. For text and data mining, we plan to introduce a new copyright and database exception which allows TDM for any purpose. Rights holders will still have safeguards to protect their content, including a requirement for lawful access.

8. For AI-devised inventions we plan no change to UK patent law now. Most respondents felt that AI is not yet advanced enough to invent without human intervention. But we will keep this area of law under review to ensure that the UK patent system supports AI innovation and the use of AI in the UK. We will seek to advance AI inventorship discussions internationally to support UK economic interests.

. . .

18. We held six roundtables in November and December 2021. Participants included individuals, large and small businesses, and a range of organisations. Contributors were from sectors including the creative industries, tech industry, pharmaceuticals, the third sector, academia, and legal and IP professions. More than 60 people participated in the roundtables and shared their experiences and thoughts. There were also 88 written submissions received. We also talked to AI service/equipment providers, artists, entrepreneurs, inventors, academics and other IP offices.

**Copyright in computer-generated works**
**Summary**

19. Computer-generated works (CGWs) are copyright works without a human author. They are currently protected in UK copyright law. As part of our consultation, we asked whether they should continue to be protected and, if so, how. We also asked about related issues: the impacts of similar provisions in designs law, and risks of false attribution.

20. 61 written responses expressed a view on one or more of these issues. The majority favoured no change to the law (Option 0). Fewer respondents supported either of the other two options. Many, on all sides, said that there is little evidence of protection for CGWs having significant impacts at present.

21. We have decided to adopt Option 0: make no changes to the law. There is no evidence at present that protection for CGWs is harmful, and the use of AI is still in its early stages. As such, a proper evaluation of the options is not possible, and any changes could have unintended consequences. But we will keep the law under review and could amend, replace or remove protection in future if the evidence supports it.

. . .

### Other CGW related issues

27. We also asked about the implications of AI and our policy on CGWs on protection for designs. Few responses addressed this question. No significant concerns were raised about the implications of protecting AI-generated material on the designs system.

28. Many respondents gave views on the risks of CGWs being falsely attributed to human authors. This might be for the extra term of protection available to human-authored works, or for reputational reasons. Several respondents raised concerns about this issue. But most considered that existing law would be adequate. In particular, respondents highlighted laws on passing off, fraud, privacy, and the need to establish authorship in cases of alleged copyright infringement. We agree with this assessment and do not see a need for intervention on this issue.

. . .

## Text and Data Mining

### Summary

31. Text and data mining (TDM) means using computational techniques to analyse large amounts of information to identify patterns, trends and other useful information. TDM is used for training AI systems, amongst other uses. It also has uses in research, journalism, marketing, business analytics and by cultural heritage organisations. The consultation outlined options in relation to text and data mining, which developers of AI and other copyright users had identified in the call for views.

32. Although factual data, trends and concepts are not protected by copyright, they are often embedded in copyright works. Data mining systems copy works to extract and analyse the data they contain. Unless permitted under licence or an exception, making such copies will constitute copyright infringement.

33. Some rights holders license their works to allow TDM, but others do not. This has financial costs for people using data mining software. To reduce these costs for researchers, an exception to copyright for TDM was introduced in 2014. This is set out in section 29A of the Copyright, Designs and Patents Act 1988. It is limited to non-commercial research, following EU rules which were in place at its creation.

34. Several other countries have introduced copyright exceptions for TDM. These encourage AI development and other services to locate there. Territories with exceptions include the EU, Japan and Singapore. TDM may also be fair use under US law, depending on the facts.

35. The consultation sought views on how to make it easier for people to data mine copyright materials. It did this with a view to supporting AI and wider innovation in the UK, in line with Government priorities on AI, data and innovation.

36. 65 respondents expressed a preference, with a spread of views across the responses. Almost no quantitative evidence was provided on the licensing environment or other questions.

37. Rights holders favoured no change or licensing solutions to help make more material available for TDM. Users of copyright and database material favoured a wider exception. They highlighted the costs of licensing and difficulties in obtaining licences, especially when many rights holders are involved.

38. The Government has decided to introduce a new copyright and database exception which allows TDM for any purpose, along the lines of Option 4. This option is the most supportive of AI and wider innovation.

. . .

### Other Data Mining Issues

54. Respondents to the consultation raised issues related with data mining, including data protection. The uses of data other than under the copyright framework are outside the scope of this consultation.

55. Data ethics and standards were other areas of interest for respondents. Ethical questions can relate to personal data and what data should be used for training AI and other TDM uses. Data ethics are often considered in relation to scientific research. Standards questions concerned formats and types of data, which can vary even in the same type of copyright work, for example. The regulation of data standards and data ethics are not a part of the copyright framework and are outside the scope of this consultation.

56. Some respondents suggested tax incentives for AI developers to reduce costs. This should help them buy licences from rights holders. Taxation policy is outside the scope of this consultation.

57. Some respondents felt that the introduction of an exception under options 3 and 4 would lead to unfair competition in some sectors. Competition issues are generally a matter for the Competition and Markets Authority. However, the economic impact of exceptions on both users and rights holders will be in the impact assessment accompanying any legislation.

### Conclusion

58. The Government has decided to introduce a new copyright and database right exception which allows TDM for any purpose. The Government will identify suitable legislation to make the required changes in due course.

59. Introducing an exception which applies to commercial TDM will bring benefits to a wide range of stakeholders in the UK. These include researchers, AI developers, small businesses, cultural heritage institutions, journalists, and engaged citizens. Targeted products and services will benefit businesses and customers. Research outcomes could also benefit the wider public. This could be, for example, by supporting research and innovation in public health. Some in the creative industries also use TDM and AI to understand their market or create new works – they will also see benefits. The benefits will be reducing the time needed to obtain permission from multiple rights holders and no licence fee to pay. This will speed up the TDM process and development of AI.

60. These changes make the most of the greater flexibilities following Brexit. They will help make the UK more competitive as a location for firms doing data mining.

61. Rights holders will no longer be able to charge for UK licences for TDM and will not be able to contract or opt-out of the exception. The new provision may also affect those who have built partial business models around data licensing. However, rights holders will still have safeguards to protect their content. The main safeguard will be the requirement for

lawful access. That is, rights holders can choose the platform where they make their works available, including charging for access via subscription or single charge. They will also be able to take measures to ensure the integrity and security of their systems.

62. The Government's ambition is to make the UK a global centre for AI innovation. The new exception will ensure the UK's copyright laws are among the most innovation-friendly in the world. All users of data mining technology will benefit, with rights holders having safeguards to protect their content.

## NOTES AND QUESTIONS

**1.** Should the use of copyright-protected content without authorization for training AI constitute copyright infringement? How might this impact the development of AI and markets for copyright protected content? How might this impact markets for training data? Should only TDM uses be allowed, such as a research-based or non-commercial activities? How will infringement be detected and enforced? Should AI developers have to disclose what training data they have used, and whether it has copyright protection?

**2.** Another hot topic in AI and copyright is the creation of AI-generated works, or works created without a traditional human author. How else might you define an AI-generated work, and why might it matter? Should the absence of a human author impact protectability? Do you think it matters whether the issue is approached from the Anglo-Saxon "copyright" perspective or the continental European "author's rights" perspective? If there is a right, who (or what) would own that right? Who (or what) would be the author? Should AI-generated works have a separate sui generis system of protection (e.g., with reduced term of protection or other limitations)? Is it possible to determine whether a work is AI-generated?

**3.** If an AI-generated work is substantially similar to an existing work, would this constitute copyright infringement? Who (or what) would be liable?

**4.** AI-generated works also raise issues with copying artists' style. Style is not generally protectable per se, but has traditionally been relatively difficult to copy. By contrast, AI may be able to copy an artist's style with ease and create additional works in their style. Should the artist be able to prevent this? Should the artist be paid for having their style copied? Should AI-generated works be allowed to copy the name, image, and likeness of individuals without their permission?

**5.** "Deep fakes", the simulated likeness of a person and their attributions such as appearance and voice, have become common place. These can be used for political manipulation or disinformation, or to create sexualized content of a person without their permission. Should these technologies be banned or limited? How could that work? Is copyright law an appropriate vehicle for regulation?

# II. MULTILATERAL COPYRIGHT NORMS

## A. The Berne Convention

International norms on copyright are rooted in the Berne Convention for the Protection of Literary and Artistic Works, dating back in its initial form to 1886.[6] The main substantive provisions of the Berne Convention were supplemented by the copyright provisions of

6. The texts of all WIPO Conventions discussed in this section may be found at http://www.wipo.int.

the TRIPS Agreement, which incorporates by reference substantial parts of the Berne text. In addition to the TRIPS Agreement, the so-called neighboring rights to copyright are the subject of several separate international agreements, including the Rome Convention for the Protection of Performers, Producers of Phonograms and Broadcasting Organisations (Rome Convention) and the Geneva Convention for the Protection of Producers of Phonograms against Unauthorized Duplication of Their Phonograms (Geneva Convention). Neighboring rights subject matter that is covered by the Rome and Geneva Conventions is also the subject of new rules of the TRIPS Agreement. Subsequent to the entry into force of the TRIPS Agreement, two new treaties—the WIPO Copyright Treaty and the WIPO Performances and Phonograms Treaty—were concluded. These treaties supplement the rules of the Berne and Rome Conventions. One objective of the negotiators of these new treaties, collectively known as the WIPO Internet Treaties, was to create consistency between WTO and WIPO rules. The WIPO Internet Treaties also create rules for the digital environment that are not found in the TRIPS Agreement. This is a complex system of agreements, adopted in different times and sometimes with overlapping subject matter. In 2012, the Beijing Treaty on Audiovisual Performances was signed by a substantial number of WIPO members. The principal objective of this treaty is to establish rights in favor of performers of audiovisual works. The Beijing Treaty entered into force on April 28, 2020. In 2013, the Marrakesh Treaty to Facilitate Access to Published Works for Persons Who Are Blind, Visually Impaired, or Otherwise Print Disabled (VIP Treaty) was signed by a substantial number of WIPO members. This agreement obligates member states to make exceptions in copyright law to facilitate availability of works and accessible format for the visually impaired. It entered into force on September 30, 2016.

As with other areas of international intellectual property rights (IPRs) regulation, the rules of the Berne Convention, TRIPS Agreement, and other multilateral treaties are incorporated and transformed in regional, national, and subnational law. Because the multilateral agreements allow flexibility in implementation, there are variations across national laws.

### *1. Historical Perspective*

The following excerpt provides a historical perspective on international copyright protection, including the background of the Berne Convention negotiations. It is of some interest that many of the countries that today are the main advocates of strong copyright protection went through long periods as copyright "pirates." These countries discovered the virtues of copyright protection only after developing a strong domestic creative community interested in securing copyright protection abroad. For instance, until the 1950s, the United States maintained a "manufacturing clause" in its copyright statute and effectively offered copyright protection only for materials printed in the United States.[7]

**Sam Ricketson***

## *The Birth of the Berne Union*

We are celebrating today the centenary of the first true multilateral convention on copyright, the Berne Convention for the Protection of Literary and Artistic Works. I use the adjective

7. *See* Hamish R. Sandison, *The Berne Convention and the Universal Copyright Convention: The American Experience*, in The Centenary of the Berne Convention, Conference, at 11-22 (Intellectual Property Law Unit, Queen Mary College, University of London and British Literary and Artistic Copyright Association, London, April 17-18, 1986).

* The Centenary of the Berne Convention, Conference (Intellectual Property Law Unit, Queen Mary College, University of London and British Literary and Artistic Copyright Association London, April 17-18, 1986).

"true" advisedly, as prior to the Berne Convention there had been other multilateral conventions on copyright. However, these had been of limited territorial effect and had been entered into in order to overcome particular political problems, such as those that existed in Germany and Italy prior to the unification of those countries. The Berne Convention, on the other hand, was open to all states without restriction, as long as they were prepared to comply with the obligations embodied therein. It is also important to see the Convention in a broader context as it was only one of series of impressive multilateral conventions that came into existence during this period. Of these, the International Telegraph Convention, the Universal Postal Convention, and, of course, the Paris Convention for the Protection of Industrial Property still remain in force today. The Berne Convention, then, can be seen as a manifestation of a period when human society was attempting, in a high-minded but practical spirit, to bring about change and development across a whole range of matters through international cooperation. . . .

In 1886, most national copyright laws were not much more than a few decades old. The United Kingdom was, of course, an exception as it had enacted the first modern copyright statute as far back as 1709 (the "Act of Anne"). The scope of this Act was quite limited, and it was restricted to books, but during the next hundred years protection was extended in piecemeal fashion to other kinds of works, including engravings, sculptures and dramatic works. In most other European countries, however, the situation as regarded the protection of authors was similar to that which had obtained in the United Kingdom prior to 1709: there was no express recognition of authors' rights, and the only protection available was that accorded through the grant of privileges or monopolies for the printing of particular books. These privileges were usually granted by governments to publishers and printers, rather than authors. It is ironic, perhaps, that we should today be meeting in the Hall of the Stationers' Company as this was the trade association whose members traditionally exercised the printing monopolies that were granted by the Crown in the sixteenth and seventeenth centuries in this country.

A similar situation prevailed for longer in most European countries, in particular France, the German and Italian states and Spain. Even in this country, the members of the Stationers' Company strove long and hard throughout the eighteenth century to retain their traditional privileges with respect to the printing of books. Thus, it was not until the end of that century that it was firmly established that the rights accorded under the Act of Anne were authors' rights, rather than publishers' or printers' rights. In France, on the other hand, completely new ground was broken when the ancient regime was swept away by the Revolution of 1789. The rights of man, now enshrined in the new revolutionary laws, were soon recognised to include the rights of authors in their works. A Law of 1791 therefore accorded an exclusive right of public performance to the authors of dramatic and musical works for a period lasting five years after their deaths. A second Law of 1793 granted, in respect of all works, what we would now call an "exclusive reproduction right," enduring for the life of the author. There was a conscious philosophical basis to these laws that was lacking in the Act of Anne, in that the former conceived of the rights of authors as being rooted in natural law, with the consequence that these laws were simply according formal recognition to rights that were already in existence. In the years following the French Revolution this new conception of authors' rights spread to other continental European countries, in particular Belgium, the Netherlands and the Italian states. . . . [B]y 1886 almost all the European states, including the newly unified states of Italy and Germany, had enacted their own copyright laws. Outside of Europe, the United States had had a copyright law since 1791, and laws on copyright were to be found in seven other states of Latin America. A number of other countries, such as Greece, Bulgaria and Turkey, protected authors' rights in a partial or incidental fashion through provisions in their general civil, criminal or press laws.

Many of these new laws drew on the models provided by the two French Laws of 1791 and 1793, although it should be noted that French copyright law continued to develop rapidly throughout the nineteenth century and to do so as much through the jurisprudence as through legislative enactments. Nevertheless, while the principal issues addressed by national laws were the same, the solutions adopted were often quite different. Most laws extended protection to a wide range of productions of a literary and artistic character, including works intended for public presentation, such as musical and dramatic works. But some categories of works, such as architectural, oral and choreographic works, were protected only in a few countries, and there were widely differing approaches to the protection of photographic works. Great diversity also existed in relation to the matter of duration of protection. In two Latin American countries, Guatemala and Mexico, this was perpetual, but in all other countries protection was limited in time. This was usually for a period comprising the life of the author together with a fixed period after his death. France had led the way here with a *post mortem autoris* term of 50 years, but 1879 Spain adopted a period of 80 years, and other nations had terms ranging between 5 and 50. A few other countries, such as the United States of America had terms that were not fixed to the life of the author, and some, including the United Kingdom, accorded different terms of protection to different categories of works. Finally, in Italy there was a system of paying public domain, under which works were protected absolutely for a given period (the author's life or 40 years after publication), and this was followed by a further period of 40 years during which the work might be used by third parties subject to a payment of a compulsory royalty to the author.

The rights protected under these early national laws also varied considerably although the principal ones recognised were those of reproduction and public performance. The right to make translations was recognised to differing degrees and was often of far shorter duration than the other rights, particularly in case of foreign authors. . . . [M]ost laws required that the author comply with some kind of formality before protection would be accorded. The nature and effect of these formalities differed widely from country to country, but the chief ones were registration, the deposit of copies and the making of declarations. In some cases, failure to comply with formalities was fatal, meaning that the work fell into the public domain; in other cases, it meant merely that the copyright owner was unable to enforce his rights until he rectified the omission. By 1886, only a few countries, including Belgium, Germany and Switzerland (but not France), had abolished formalities altogether. . . .

The above sketch has concentrated on the contents of national copyright laws in the pre-1886 period. However, it will be clear that there is an equally important international dimension to the protection of authors' works. Literary and artistic works and musical compositions recognise no national boundaries, even where translation into another language is required for a work to be fully appreciated in a particular country. Thus it was that after the need for protection of authors by national laws had been recognised, the works of these authors still remained vulnerable to copying and exploitation abroad. These activities, commonly referred to as "piracy," had been a long-established feature of European social and cultural life, and this continued to be the case for a considerable time after the enactment of national copyright laws. The attitudes of many countries to these practices were highly anomalous: whilst prepared to protect their own authors, they did not always regard the piracy of foreign authors' works as unfair or immoral. Some countries, in fact, openly countenanced piracy as contributing to their educational and social needs and as reducing the prices of books for their citizens. The particular victims of these practices were the United Kingdom and France. During the eighteenth century English authors suffered from the activities of Irish pirates who could flood both the English and other markets with cheap reprints; after the Act of Union with Ireland in 1800, the chief threat came from the publishing houses of the United States and this continued to be a major problem for the rest of the century. French authors, in turn, suffered from the activities of pirates located in Switzerland, Germany, Holland, and, in particular, Belgium. By the early nineteenth century, Brussels was a major centre for the piracy of French books, and this led to considerable strains in the relations between France and Belgium. Piracy was likewise rampant between the different German and Italian states.

This widespread piracy of foreign works was the principal reason for the development of international copyright relations in the mid-nineteenth century. The arguments that raged both for and against the protection of foreign authors at this time have a surprisingly modern ring to them. On the one hand, it could be said that the activities of the pirates resulted in cheaper copies and the greater availability of the work in question. In countries hungry for knowledge and enlightenment, this could only be to the advantage of the public interest and this, indeed, was the reason for the persistent refusal of the United States to protect foreign works throughout the nineteenth century. On the other hand the moral and practical arguments in the author's favour were obvious: not only was he being robbed of the fruits of his creativity, but this would discourage him from continuing to create, with resultant loss to his own, and other, countries.

It is hard to identify the point at which a country no longer sees advantage in the piracy of foreign works, and decides to extend protection to the authors of such works. It may be that the activities of its own authors have increased, and that the latter now desire protection for their own works abroad. It may also be that, after a while, a country wishes to obtain some kind of international respectability, and to avoid the opprobrium of being labelled as a nation of pirates. Another factor may be that countries with large literary and artistic outputs bring pressure to bear on their more recalcitrant neighbours, promising various forms of trade advantage in return for copyright protection for their authors. Finally, pirate nations may come to recognise that the rights of authors in their works are of a proprietary nature, and that they should therefore be protected internationally in the same way as other property of foreigners. All these factors were certainly applicable in the case of Belgium, which, in the mid-nineteenth century, switched suddenly from being the chief centre of piracy for French works to being one of the most zealous defenders of authors' rights. The same factors applied to many other countries as they began to enter into international copyright relations with each other. Indeed, agreements between states and the formal sanctions of copyright law were not always necessary to achieve protection for foreign authors, at least in a limited form, as systems of "courtesy" copyright operated with some effect during this time and sometimes predated formal international agreements. This was particularly so in the United States, where the major publishing houses observed an unwritten custom whereby each would refrain from publishing editions of foreign works in respect of which another had reached a publishing agreement with the author. This system of mutual self-restraint had several advantages for the parties concerned: it protected the first American publisher of a foreign work from the unfettered copying of his edition, and gave the author the opportunity of earning some remuneration, even if he were unable to prevent the American publication of his work in the first place. As a consequence, authors such as Dickens and Trollope received large sums in respect of the American sales of their works, although they did not enjoy protection under United States copyright law.

"Courtesy copyright," however, is only a partial substitute for full copyright protection, and, in any case, it was not really of great significance outside the American market. . . .

Bilateral copyright agreements . . . had, in fact, become quite common by the middle of the century. . . . The basis of the majority of these conventions was national treatment, but, as stated above, they also contained a number of common rules which each country undertook to apply in its protection of works from the other country. There was usually a statement of the categories of works covered by the agreement, and specific provision was generally made for the protection of translation and performing rights. Restrictions in respect of particular kinds of use were also often allowed relating, for example, to education or the reproduction of newspaper articles. The scope and detail of these provisions differed considerably from one convention to another, but the most "advanced," in terms of protection of authors' interests, were to be found in the conventions made by France, Germany and Italy in the early 1880s. With regard to duration of protection, most of the pre-1886 conventions required material reciprocity, providing that country A was not obliged to protect the works of country B for any longer period than that accorded by state B to its own works, and in any event for no longer than country A protected its own nationals.

There were wider discrepancies with respect to formalities. . . . Matters were further complicated by the fact that the duration of many conventions was uncertain, in that they were linked to some wider treaty of trade or commerce between the countries in question and might suddenly fall to the ground if the latter was revoked or renegotiated. Another source of uncertainty arose from the insertion of "most favoured nation" clauses in many copyright conventions. The effect of these was that the contracting parties agreed to admit each other to the benefits that might be accorded to a third state under another treaty that was made by one of them with that state. The effect of such clauses was that a copyright convention between countries A and B might be abrogated, in whole or in part, by the terms of another convention made by either country A or B with country C if this agreement contained additional measures for the protection of copyright. While these clauses did not mean any loss or protection for authors, they obviously made it difficult for an author from country A to know, at any one time, what level of protection he was entitled to in country B, and vice versa.

It will be clear that this network of bilateral agreements meant that there was little uniformity in the protection that an author might expect to receive in countries other than his own. As far as Europe was concerned, the threat posed by international piracy earlier in the century had largely disappeared by 1886, but quite a number of European states still remained reluctant to enter bilateral agreements on copyright. . . . The most important of these countries was the United States, which throughout the nineteenth century continued to be a major centre for pirated works and resisted efforts by other countries, in particular the United Kingdom, to draw it into bilateral agreements. Several such attempts were made, but the vested interests of publishers and printers, on the one hand, and the voracious appetite for cheap books from the rapidly growing American population, on the other, doomed them to failure. . . .

In the light of the above, it was not surprising that moves for a more widely based and uniform kind of international copyright protection began in the middle of the nineteenth century.

## NOTES AND QUESTIONS

**1.** The early forms of protection granted for books and other printed material were generally in favor of publishers, and not in favor of authors. Today, the largest streams of copyright revenue flow to the producers of films and television programs such as Disney, Comcast, and Netflix. The rights of authors are certainly the subject of copyright protection, yet have the basic economics of the copyright industries changed very much from the Middle Ages?

**2.** The Internet and related digital delivery systems allow authors to bypass large producer/publishers and benefit more directly from their creative acts. Are producers and publishers needed in the new digital environment? Are we in the midst of the next revolution in copyright? We will be looking at this digital dimension more closely.

**3.** Consider the copyright "pirates" of today's China and the copyright pirates of the Industrial Age in the United States. British publishers were unhappy with American pirates in 1870, and U.S. publishers are unhappy with Chinese pirates today. Did the American pirates have a better justification for their conduct than the Chinese pirates? Are these somehow different than Internet users that employ copyrighted works to create memes and mash-ups online?

## 2. *Berne Convention Norms*

Next is a description of the terms of the Berne Convention by the International Bureau of WIPO.

---

# *The Berne Convention for the Protection of Literary and Artistic Works**

### HISTORY

5.165 Copyright protection on the international level began by about the middle of the nineteenth century on the basis of bilateral treaties. A number of such treaties providing for mutual recognition of rights were concluded but they were neither comprehensive enough nor of a uniform pattern.

5.166 The need for a uniform system led to the formulation and adoption on September 9, 1886 of the Berne Convention for the Protection of Literary and Artistic Works. The Berne Convention is the oldest international treaty in the field of copyright. . . .

5.167 The Berne Convention has been revised several times in order to improve the international system of protection which the Convention provides. Changes have been effected in order to cope with the challenges of accelerating development of technologies in the field of utilization of authors' works, in order to recognize new rights as also to allow for appropriate revisions of established ones. . . .

5.169 The aim of the Berne Convention, as indicated in its preamble, is "to protect, in as effective and uniform a manner as possible, the rights of authors in their literary and artistic works."

Article 1 lays down that the countries to which the Convention applies constitute a Union for the protection of the rights of authors in their literary and artistic works.

### PRINCIPAL PROVISIONS

### Basic Principles

5.170 The Convention rests on three basic principles. Firstly, there is the principle of "national treatment," according to which works originating in one of the member States are to be given the same protection in each of the member States as these grant to works of their own nationals.

Secondly, there is automatic protection, according to which such national treatment is not dependent on any formality; in other words protection is granted automatically and is not subject to the formality of registration, deposit or the like. Thirdly, there is independence of protection, according to which enjoyment and exercise of the rights granted is independent of the existence of protection in the country of origin of the work.

### Works Protected

5.171 Article 2 contains a non-limitative (illustrative and not exhaustive) list of such works, which include any original production in the literary, scientific and artistic domain, whatever may be the mode or form of its expression. Derivative works, that is those based on other pre-existing works, such as translations, adaptations, arrangements of music and other

* WIPO Intellectual Property Handbook (as of April 2006).

alterations of a literary or artistic work, receive the same protection as original works (Article 2(3)). The protection of some categories of works is optional; thus every State party to the Berne Convention may decide to what extent it wishes to protect official texts of a legislative, administrative and legal nature (Article 2(4)), works of applied art (Article 2(7)), lectures, addresses and other oral works (Article 2*bis*(2)) and works of folklore (Article 15(4)). Furthermore, Article 2(2) provides for the possibility of making the protection of works or any specified categories thereof subject to their being fixed in some material form. For instance, protection of choreographic works may be dependent on their being fixed in some form. . . .

### Owners of Rights

5.173 Article 2(6) lays down that protection under the Convention is to operate for the benefit of the author and his successors in title. For some categories of works, however, such as cinematographic works (Article 14*bis*), ownership of copyright is a matter for legislation in the country where protection is claimed.

### Persons Protected

5.174 Authors of works are protected, in respect of both their unpublished or published works if, according to Article 3, they are nationals or residents of a member country; alternatively, if, not being nationals or residents of a member country, they first publish their works in a member country or simultaneously in a non-member and a member country.

### Minimum Standards Of Protection

5.175 Certain minimum standards of protection have been prescribed relating to the rights of authors and the duration of protection.

### Rights Protected

5.176 The exclusive rights granted to authors under the Convention include the right of translation (Article 8), the right of reproduction in any manner or form, which includes any sound or visual recording, (Article 9), the right to perform dramatic, dramatico-musical and musical works (Article 11), the right to broadcast and communicate to the public, by wire, rebroadcasting or loudspeaker or any other analogous instrument, the broadcast of the work (Article 11*bis*), the right of public recitation (Article 11*ter*), the right to make adaptations, arrangements or other alterations of a work (Article 12) and the right to make cinematographic adaptations and reproductions of a work (Article 14). The so-called "droit de suite" provided for in Article 14*ter* (concerning original works of art and original manuscripts) is optional and applicable only if legislation in the country to which the author belongs permits.

5.177 Independently of the author's economic rights, Article 6*bis* provides for "moral rights"—that is, the right of the author to claim authorship of his work and to object to any distortion, mutilation or other modification of, or other derogatory action in relation to, the work which would be prejudicial to his honor or reputation.

### Limitations

5.178 As a sort of counterbalance to the minimum standards of protection there are also other provisions in the Berne Convention limiting the strict application of the rules regarding exclusive right. It provides for the possibility of using protected works in particular cases without having to obtain the authorization of the owner of the copyright and without having to pay any remuneration for such use. Such exceptions, which are commonly referred to as free use of protected works, are included in Articles 9(2) (reproduction in certain special cases), 10 (quotations and use of works by way of illustration for teaching purposes), 10*bis* (reproduction of newspaper or similar articles and use of works for the purpose of reporting current events) and 11*bis*(3) (ephemeral recordings).

5.179 There are two cases where the Berne Convention provides the possibility of compulsory licenses—in Articles 11*bis*(2), for the right to broadcast and communicate to the public, by wire, rebroadcasting or loudspeaker or any other analogous instrument, the broadcast of the work, and 13(1) for the right of recording musical works.

5.180 As far as the exclusive right of translation is concerned, the Berne Convention offers a choice, in that a developing country may, when acceding to the Convention, make a reservation under the so-called "ten-year rule" (Article 30(2)(b)). This provides for the possibility of reducing the term of protection in respect of the exclusive right of translation; this right, according to the said rule, ceases to exist if the author has not availed himself of it within 10 years from the date of first publication of the original work, by publishing or causing to be published, in one of the member countries, a translation in the language for which protection is claimed.

### Duration of Protection

5.181 The minimum standards of protection provided for in the Berne Convention also relate to the duration of protection. Article 7 lays down a minimum term of protection, which is the life of the author plus 50 years after his death.

5.182 There are, however, exceptions to this basic rule for certain categories of works. For cinematographic works, the term is 50 years after the work has been made available to the public, or, if not made available, then 50 years after the making of such a work. For photographic works and works of applied art, the minimum term of protection is 25 years from the making of the work (Article 7(4)).

5.183 A majority of countries in the world have legislated for life plus a 50-year term of protection since it is felt fair and right that the lifetime of the author and the lifetime of his children should be covered; this could also provide the incentive necessary to stimulate creativity, and constitute a fair balance between the interests of the authors and the needs of society.

5.184 The term of protection, in so far as moral rights are concerned, extends at least until the expiry of the economic rights.

### Application in Time

5.185 The Protection under the Berne Convention is retrospective, since it applies to all works which, at the moment of its coming into force for a specific country, have not yet fallen into the public domain in the country of their origin through the expiry of the term of protection.

## The Latest (Paris) Act of the Convention . . .

5.191 The Revision Conference convened in Paris in 1971 was predominantly concerned with finding solutions in order to support the universal effect of the Convention and to establish an appropriate basis for its operation, particularly in relation to developing countries. The question was asked whether it was fair and workable to ask the developing countries to take on obligations under the Convention that were agreed upon by developed countries, without taking into consideration the special circumstances of the former. There was certainly a challenge then posed to international copyright itself and this was, in a manner, sorted out through the give-and-take that culminated in the special provisions concerning developing countries that were incorporated in an Appendix, which now forms an integral part of the Convention, open to developing countries concerning translation and reproduction of works of foreign origin.

The Appendix augments the Convention's existing exceptions to the author's exclusive rights, including those of reproduction and translation (Articles 2*bis*, 9(2), 10(2), 10*bis*) and the ten-year rule (Article 30(2)(b)).

5.193 According to this Appendix, countries which are regarded as developing countries in conformity with the established practice of the General Assembly of the United Nations may, under certain conditions, depart from the minimum standards of protection provided for in the Convention. This exceptional regime concerns two rights, the right of translation and the right of reproduction. . . .

## NOTES AND QUESTIONS

**1.** Leading up to negotiation of the WTO TRIPS Agreement, the Organisation for Economic Co-operation and Development (OECD) industry groups criticized the Paris Convention for its lack of adequate subject matter coverage with respect to patents. By contrast, Article 2 of the Berne Convention provides broad subject matter coverage for copyright. In light of Article 2, were the provisions of the TRIPS Agreement on computer programs and compilations necessary? Is there a risk associated with adding express subject matter coverage for new technologies? In other words, if some new subject matter is expressly covered, might it be implied that other new subject matter is not covered without an express reference?

**2.** Article 2(2) Berne Convention, permits members to require that a copyrighted work be fixed in some tangible form. By way of illustration, the U.S. Copyright Act, Section 102, refers to "original works of expression fixed in any tangible medium of expression, now known or later developed, from which they can be perceived, reproduced, or otherwise communicated, either directly or with the aid of a machine or device." What types of expressive works are not fixed in a tangible medium of expression?

**3.** Article 2(3) Berne Convention extends copyright protection to translations (as well as to adaptations, arrangements, and other alterations). In the highly integrated global economy, the economic value of translation rights should be apparent. Article 21 Berne Convention and the referenced Appendix authorize developing countries to grant compulsory licenses for the translation and reproduction of copyrighted works under specified terms and conditions. The Appendix generally requires that a work has not been translated and made available at a reasonable cost. Article 21 and the Appendix are incorporated by reference in the TRIPS Agreement (TRIPS, Article 9.1).

**4.** Note that pursuant to Article 3(1)(a) Berne Convention, unpublished works are protected. Article 3(1)(b) provides protection to works first published in a Berne member country even if the author is not a national of a Berne member. This article provides a mechanism that permits Berne protection to be secured "through the back door"; this provision was quite important for American authors so long as the United States had not adhered to the Berne Convention. Now that Berne Convention membership has become virtually universal, this provision is of lesser importance.

**5.** Article 6*bis* addresses the subject of "moral rights" of authors, a topic we consider in detail later in this chapter. The TRIPS Agreement expressly excludes Article 6*bis* Berne Convention from its incorporated provisions (TRIPS, Article 9.1).

**6.** The term of copyright protection generally required by Article 7(1) Berne Convention is the life of the author plus 50 years. However, members may grant a longer term of protection (Article 7(6)) and, as we saw in *Eldred v. Ashcroft*, the European Union and the United States have extended the term to the author's life plus 70 years. Article 7(8) is of particular importance in the context of nations and regions with differing durations of copyright protection. What is the effect of Article 7(8) Berne Convention?

**7.** The basic protection of the Berne Convention is set out in Article 9(1), that is, the "exclusive right of authorizing the reproduction of these works, in any manner or form." The most important exceptions to the author's exclusive rights are in Article 9(2), which generally establishes the rights referred to as "fair use" rights. Specific embodiments of fair use rights are set forth in Articles 10 and 10*bis* Berne Convention.

**8.** Article 11*bis* establishes the rights to broadcast "to the public" by wireless means, (Article 11*bis*(1)(i)), and by wire or by rebroadcasting when the communication is made by an organization other than the "original one" (Article 11*bis*(1)(ii)). The meaning of the various phrases in Article 11*bis* has been the subject of considerable litigation in national and regional courts. For example, Cable News Network (CNN) fought a long court battle in France against a Paris hotel that claimed that its guest rooms were not public areas, and that it was thus entitled to retransmit CNN satellite signals to its guests without payment. CNN eventually prevailed. *See, e.g., Cable News Network Inc. and another v. Novotel SA*, Tribunal de Grande Instance (District Court), Paris, [1991] ECC 492, 14 Feb. 1990, holding that a hotel room is a "private" as opposed to "public" place, subsequently overturned by the Cour de Cassation. *Cable News Network and CNN International Sales Limited v. Novotel Paris-Les Halles SA*, Cour de Cassation (Supreme Court) [1994 ECC 530], 6 Apr. 1994. The question of what constitutes transmission of a broadcast work to "the public" was a major element of the U.S. Supreme Court's 2014 decision in *American Broadcasting Cos. v. Aereo*, 573 U.S. 431 (2014), although this decision did not purport to interpret the Berne Convention:

> . . . we must consider whether Aereo performs petitioners' works "publicly," within the meaning of the Transmit Clause. Under the Clause, an entity performs a work publicly when it "transmit[s] . . . a performance . . . of the work . . . to the public." §101. Aereo denies that it satisfies this definition. It reasons as follows: First, the "performance" it "transmit[s]" is the performance created by its act of transmitting. And second, because each of these performances is capable of being received by one and only one subscriber, Aereo transmits privately, not publicly. Even assuming Aereo's first argument is correct, its second does not follow.
>
> . . .
>
> We assume arguendo that Aereo's first argument is correct. Thus, for present purposes, to transmit a performance of (at least) an audiovisual work means to communicate contemporaneously visible images and contemporaneously audible sounds of the work. . . .
>
> We do not see how the fact that Aereo transmits via personal copies of programs could make a difference. The Act applies to transmissions "by means of any device or process." Ibid. And retransmitting a television program using user-specific copies is a "process" of transmitting a performance. A "cop[y]" of a work is simply a "material objec[t] . . . in which a work is fixed . . . and from which the work can be perceived, reproduced, or otherwise communicated." Ibid. So whether Aereo transmits from the same or separate copies, it performs the same work; it shows the same images and makes audible the same sounds. Therefore, when Aereo streams the same television program to multiple subscribers, it "transmit[s] . . . a performance" to all of them.
>
> Moreover, the subscribers to whom Aereo transmits television programs constitute "the public." Aereo communicates the same contemporaneously perceptible images and sounds to a large number of people who are unrelated and unknown to each other. This matters because, although the Act does not define "the public," it specifies that an entity performs publicly when it performs at "any place where a substantial number of persons outside of a normal circle of a family and its social acquaintances is gathered." Ibid. The Act thereby suggests that "the public" consists of a large group of people outside of a family and friends.
>
> Neither the record nor Aereo suggests that Aereo's subscribers receive performances in their capacities as owners or possessors of the underlying works. This is relevant because when an entity performs to a set of people, whether they constitute "the public" often depends upon their relationship to the underlying work. When, for example, a valet parking attendant returns

cars to their drivers, we would not say that the parking service provides cars "to the public." We would say that it provides the cars to their owners. We would say that a car dealership, on the other hand, does provide cars to the public, for it sells cars to individuals who lack a pre-existing relationship to the cars. Similarly, an entity that transmits a performance to individuals in their capacities as owners or possessors does not perform to "the public," whereas an entity like Aereo that transmits to large numbers of paying subscribers who lack any prior relationship to the works does so perform.

Finally, we note that Aereo's subscribers may receive the same programs at different times and locations. This fact does not help Aereo, however, for the Transmit Clause expressly provides that an entity may perform publicly "whether the members of the public capable of receiving the performance . . . receive it in the same place or in separate places and at the same time or at different times." Ibid. In other words, "the public" need not be situated together, spatially or temporally. For these reasons, we conclude that Aereo transmits a performance of petitioners' copyrighted works to the public . . . [citations omitted] (Slip Opinion at 11-15)

**9.** In *VCAST Limited v. RTI SpA*, C-265/16, 29 Nov. 2017, the CJEU reached a conclusion similar to that of the U.S. Supreme Court on a similar (though different) set of facts:

14. VCAST is a company incorporated under UK law which makes available to its customers via the Internet a video recording system, in storage space within the cloud, for terrestrial programmes of Italian television organisations, among which are those of RTI.

15. It is apparent from the order for reference that, in practice, the user selects a programme on the VCAST website, which includes all the programming from the television channels covered by the service provided by that company. The user can specify either a certain programme or a time slot. The system operated by VCAST then picks up the television signal using its own antennas and records the time slot for the selected programme in the cloud data storage space indicated by the user. That storage space is purchased by the user from another provider.

. . .

40. It follows from Article 3 of Directive 2001/29 that any communication to the public, including the making available of a protected work or subject matter, requires the rightholder's consent, given that, as is apparent from recital 23 of that directive, the right of communication of works to the public should be understood in a broad sense covering any transmission or retransmission of a work to the public by wire or wireless means, including broadcasting.

41. In that respect, the Court has already held that the concept of 'communication to the public' includes two cumulative criteria, namely an 'act of communication' of a work and the communication of that work to a 'public' (judgment of 31 May 2016, *Reha Training*, C117/15, EU:C:2016:379, paragraph 37).

. . .

46. In the present case, the service provider at issue in the main proceedings records programmes broadcast and makes them available to its customers via the Internet.

47. In the first place, it is evident that the sum of the persons targeted by that provider constitutes a 'public' within the meaning of the case-law cited in . . . the present judgment.

48. In the second place, the original transmission made by the broadcasting organisation, on the one hand, and that made by the service provider at issue in the main proceedings, on the other, are made under specific technical conditions, using a different means of transmission for the protected works, and each is intended for its public (see, to that effect, judgment of 7 March 2013, *ITV Broadcasting and Others*, C607/11, EU:C:2013:147, paragraph 39).

49. The transmissions referred to thus constitute communications to different publics, and each of them must therefore receive the consent of the rightholders concerned.

50. In those circumstances, it is no longer necessary to examine whether the publics targeted by those communications are identical or whether the public targeted by the service provider at issue in the main proceedings constitutes a new public (see, to that effect, judgment of 7 March 2013, *ITV Broadcasting and Others*, C607/11, EU:C:2013:147, paragraph 39).

51. It follows that, without the rightholder's consent, the making of copies of works by means of a service such as that at issue in the main proceedings could undermine the rights of that rightholder.

52. Accordingly, such a remote recording service cannot fall within the scope of Article 5(2)(b) of Directive 2001/29.

53. In those circumstances, there is no longer any need to verify whether the conditions imposed by Article 5(5) of that directive have been complied with.

54. In view of all the foregoing considerations, the answer to the questions asked is that Directive 2001/29, in particular Article 5(2)(b) thereof, precludes national legislation which permits a commercial undertaking to provide private individuals with a cloud service for the remote recording of private copies of works protected by copyright, by means of a computer system, by actively involving itself in the recording, without the rightholder's consent.

**10.** The CJEU argues that exceptions must be narrowly construed. How can this doctrine be justified in the process of balancing different interests at stake?

**11.** Compare the U.S. and EU approaches to fair use. The latter operates with legislative exceptions narrowly defined, such as private use. Does the case law confirm the cultural differences expounded upon in the introductory section of this chapter?

**12.** As we will examine, the Berne Convention and TRIPS Agreement permit exceptions for fair use of copyrighted works. The availability and scope of the exceptions remains, for the most part, subject to national law within the bounds of international law. We also examine, *infra*, a WTO panel decision that gives extensive consideration to the permissible scope of the fair use exception under the TRIPS Agreement (and the incorporated Berne Convention provisions).

**13.** Article 14*ter*(1) Berne Convention refers to the *droit de suite*, which requires that an author (and his or her heirs) collect an interest in the sale of a work of art or original manuscript in any sale after its first transfer. However, this right only extends to Berne members that choose to prescribe it by legislation, and it only benefits foreign authors whose home country also prescribes such rights (Article 14*ter*(2) Berne Convention).

**14.** We have previously observed that copyright and other IPRs do not afford market access rights. Article 17 Berne Convention establishes a right in favor of governments to prohibit the distribution of any copyrighted work. Does the fact that governments exercise that right as they "may find it necessary" suggest any meaningful limitation on the right?

**15.** Might you have foreseen that Article 18 concerning the retroactive application of Berne protection would be the subject of a major trade dispute? It was. Article 70.2 TRIPS provides that questions relating to copyright in existing works will be governed solely by the terms of Article 18 Berne Convention. Article 14 TRIPS extended the term of protection for performers and producers of phonograms to 50 years from the calendar year of fixation, extending well beyond the 20-year term prescribed by the Rome Convention for such subject matter. When Japan implemented the TRIPS Agreement provisions with respect to performers and producers of phonograms, it presumed that works existing for more than 20 years had fallen into the public domain, and therefore were not subject to TRIPS protection (per Article 18(2) Berne Convention). The United States vehemently objected, arguing that the TRIPS Agreement specifically contemplated the extension of copyright to existing works. Japan eventually conceded and adopted legislation extending protection, though not because it was convinced of the soundness of any U.S. legal argument. What do you think?

**16.** Note again, as in the Paris Convention, the possibility of referral of a dispute to the International Court of Justice (Article 33 Berne Convention)[8] – a possibility that has however been not used in practice.

---

8. Berne Convention, Article 33:

[DISPUTES: 1. JURISDICTION OF THE INTERNATIONAL COURT OF JUSTICE; 2. RESERVATION AS TO SUCH JURISDICTION; 3. WITHDRAWAL OF RESERVATION]

(1) Any dispute between two or more countries of the Union concerning the interpretation or application of this Convention, not settled by negotiation, may, by any one of the countries concerned, be brought before the International Court of Justice by application in conformity with the Statute of the Court, unless

### *3. Berne Convention in National Law*

The Berne Convention may be applied directly by the courts of a contracting state when the constitution of that state permits the direct application of treaties. The Convention may also be transformed into national law by the legislature or parliament of a contracting state. Even when a national legislature has adopted copyright legislation specifically to implement the provisions of the Berne Convention, the Convention may be referred to by courts either to aid in the interpretation of that national legislation, or to fill a gap in the legislation. The extent to which a court may directly rely on the provisions of the Convention (e.g., to fill a gap) will depend on the way in which the national constitution regards treaty law.[9]

#### a. Internet Retransmission

The following case addressed the status of Internet providers being intermediaries in distributing and streaming copyright protected content. The case is noteworthy for its effort to find a balanced solution taking into account fundamental rights at stake.

## *UPC Telekabel Wien GmbH v. Constantin Film Verleih GmbH and Wega Filmproduktionsgesellschaft mbH*

Judgment of the Court (Fourth Chamber), 27 March 2014

(Request for a preliminary ruling—Approximation of laws—Copyright and related rights—Information society—Directive 2001/29/EC—Website making cinematographic works available to the public without the consent of the holders of a right related to copyright—Article 8(3)—Concept of 'intermediaries whose services are used by a third party to infringe a copyright or related right'—Internet service provider—Order addressed to an internet service provider prohibiting it from giving its customers access to a website—Balancing of fundamental rights)

In Case C-314/12,

REQUEST for a preliminary ruling under Article 267 TFEU from the Oberster Gerichtshof (Austria), made by decision of 11 May 2012, received at the Court on 29 June 2012, in the proceedings

UPC Telekabel Wien GmbH v Constantin Film Verleih GmbH, Wega Filmproduktionsgesellschaft mbH,

---

the countries concerned agree on some other method of settlement. The country bringing the dispute before the Court shall inform the International Bureau; the International Bureau shall bring the matter to the attention of the other countries of the Union.

(2) Each country may, at the time it signs this Act or deposits its instrument of ratification or accession, declare that it does not consider itself bound by the provisions of paragraph (1). With regard to any dispute between such country and any other country of the Union, the provisions of paragraph (1) shall not apply.

(3) Any country having made a declaration in accordance with the provisions of paragraph (2) may, at any time, withdraw its declaration by notification addressed to the Director General. . . .

9. In this context, *see also* the doctrines of consistent interpretation and direct effect, discussed *supra* Chapter 1, section VII.H.

THE COURT (Fourth Chamber),

composed of L. Bay Larsen, President of the Chamber, K. Lenaerts, Vice-President of the Court, acting as a judge of the Fourth Chamber, M. Safjan, J. Malenovský (Rapporteur) and A. Prechal, Judges,

Advocate General: P. Cruz Villalón,

gives the following:

## Judgment

1. This request for a preliminary ruling concerns the interpretation of Article 5(1) and (2)(b) and Article 8(3) of Directive 2001/29/EC of the European Parliament and of the Council of 22 May 2001 on the harmonisation of certain aspects of copyright and related rights in the information society (OJ 2001 L 167, p. 10), and of certain fundamental rights enshrined in EU law.

2. The request has been made in proceedings between (i) UPC Telekabel Wien GmbH ('UPC Telekabel') and (ii) Constantin Film Verleih GmbH ('Constantin Film') and Wega Filmproduktionsgesellschaft mbH ('Wega') concerning an application for UPC Telekabel to be ordered to block the access of its customers to a website making available to the public some of the films of Constantin Film and of Wega without their consent.

## Legal Context

### The Dispute in the Main Proceedings and the Questions Referred for a Preliminary Ruling

11. Having established that a website was offering, without their agreement, either a download or 'streaming' of some of the films which they had produced, Constantin Film and Wega, two film production companies, referred the matter to the court responsible for hearing applications for interim measures with a view to obtaining, on the basis of Article 81(1a) of the UrhG, an order enjoining UPC Telekabel, an internet service provider, to block the access of its customers to the website at issue, inasmuch as that site makes available to the public, without their consent, cinematographic works over which they hold a right related to copyright.

. . .

## Consideration of the Questions Referred

. . .

### The First Question

23. By its first question, the referring court asks, essentially, whether Article 8(3) of Directive 2001/29 must be interpreted as meaning that a person who makes protected subject-matter available to the public on a website without the agreement of the rightholder, for the purpose of Article 3(2) of that directive, is using the services of the internet service provider of the persons accessing that subject-matter, which is to be regarded as an intermediary within the meaning of Article 8(3) of Directive 2001/29.

. . .

32. Accordingly, given that the internet service provider is an inevitable actor in any transmission of an infringement over the internet between one of its customers and a third party, since, in granting access to the network, it makes that transmission possible (see, to that effect, the order in Case C557/07 *LSG-Gesellschaft zur Wahrnehmung von Leistungsschutzrechten* [2009] ECR I1227, paragraph 44), it must be held that an internet service provider, such as

that at issue in the main proceedings, which allows its customers to access protected subject-matter made available to the public on the internet by a third party is an intermediary whose services are used to infringe a copyright or related right within the meaning of Article 8(3) of Directive 2001/29.

. . .

### The Third Question

42. By its third question, the referring court asks, essentially, whether the fundamental rights recognised by EU law must be interpreted as precluding a court injunction prohibiting an internet service provider from allowing its customers access to a website placing protected subject-matter online without the agreement of the rightholders when that injunction does not specify the measures which that access provider must take and when that access provider can avoid incurring coercive penalties for breach of that injunction by showing that it has taken all reasonable measures.

43. In this respect, as is apparent from Recital 59 in the preamble to Directive 2001/29, the rules for the injunctions which the Member States must lay down pursuant to Article 8(3) of the directive, such as those relating to the conditions to be met and the procedure to be followed, are a matter for national law.

44. That said, those national rules, and likewise their application by the national courts, must observe the limitations arising from Directive 2001/29 and from the sources of law to which Recital 3 in its preamble refers (see, to that effect, *Scarlet Extended*, paragraph 33 and the case-law cited there).

45. In order to assess whether an injunction such as that at issue in the main proceedings, taken on the basis of Article 8(3) of Directive 2001/29, is consistent with EU law, it is therefore necessary to take account in particular of the requirements that stem from the protection of the applicable fundamental rights, and to do so in accordance with Article 51 of the Charter of Fundamental Rights of the European Union ('the Charter') (see, to that effect, *Scarlet Extended*, paragraph 41).

46. The Court has already ruled that, where several fundamental rights are at issue, the Member States must, when transposing a directive, ensure that they rely on an interpretation of the directive which allows a fair balance to be struck between the applicable fundamental rights protected by the European Union legal order. Then, when implementing the measures transposing that directive, the authorities and courts of the Member States must not only interpret their national law in a manner consistent with that directive but also ensure that they do not rely on an interpretation of it which would be in conflict with those fundamental rights or with the other general principles of EU law, such as the principle of proportionality (see, to that effect, Case C275/06 *Promusicae* [2008] ECR I271, paragraph 68).

47. In the present case, it must be observed that an injunction such as that at issue in the main proceedings, taken on the basis of Article 8(3) of Directive 2001/29, makes it necessary to strike a balance, primarily, between (i) copyrights and related rights, which are intellectual property and are therefore protected under Article 17(2) of the Charter, (ii) the freedom to conduct a business, which economic agents such as internet service providers enjoy under Article 16 of the Charter, and (iii) the freedom of information of internet users, whose protection is ensured by Article 11 of the Charter.

48. As regards the freedom to conduct a business, the adoption of an injunction such as that at issue in the main proceedings restricts that freedom.

49. The freedom to conduct a business includes, inter alia, the right for any business to be able to freely use, within the limits of its liability for its own acts, the economic, technical and financial resources available to it.

50. An injunction such as that at issue in the main proceedings constrains its addressee in a manner which restricts the free use of the resources at his disposal because it obliges him to take measures which may represent a significant cost for him, have a considerable impact on the organisation of his activities or require difficult and complex technical solutions.

51. However, such an injunction does not seem to infringe the very substance of the freedom of an internet service provider such as that at issue in the main proceedings to conduct a business.

52. First, an injunction such as that at issue in the main proceedings leaves its addressee to determine the specific measures to be taken in order to achieve the result sought, with the result that he can choose to put in place measures which are best adapted to the resources and abilities available to him and which are compatible with the other obligations and challenges which he will encounter in the exercise of his activity.

53. Secondly, such an injunction allows its addressee to avoid liability by proving that he has taken all reasonable measures. That possibility of exoneration clearly has the effect that the addressee of the injunction will not be required to make unbearable sacrifices, which seems justified in particular in the light of the fact that he is not the author of the infringement of the fundamental right of intellectual property which has led to the adoption of the injunction.

54. In that regard, in accordance with the principle of legal certainty, it must be possible for the addressee of an injunction such as that at issue in the main proceedings to maintain before the court, once the implementing measures which he has taken are known and before any decision imposing a penalty on him is adopted, that the measures taken were indeed those which could be expected of him in order to prevent the proscribed result.

55. None the less, when the addressee of an injunction such as that at issue in the main proceedings chooses the measures to be adopted in order to comply with that injunction, he must ensure compliance with the fundamental right of internet users to freedom of information.

56. In this respect, the measures adopted by the internet service provider must be strictly targeted, in the sense that they must serve to bring an end to a third party's infringement of copyright or of a related right but without thereby affecting internet users who are using the provider's services in order to lawfully access information. Failing that, the provider's interference in the freedom of information of those users would be unjustified in the light of the objective pursued.

57. It must be possible for national courts to check that that is the case. In the case of an injunction such as that at issue in the main proceedings, the Court notes that, if the internet service provider adopts measures which enable it to achieve the required prohibition, the national courts will not be able to carry out such a review at the stage of the enforcement proceedings if there is no challenge in that regard. Accordingly, in order to prevent the fundamental rights recognised by EU law from precluding the adoption of an injunction such as that at issue in the main proceedings, the national procedural rules must provide a possibility for internet users to assert their rights before the court once the implementing measures taken by the internet service provider are known.

58. As regards intellectual property, it should be pointed out at the outset that it is possible that the enforcement of an injunction such as that in the main proceedings will not lead to a complete cessation of the infringements of the intellectual property right of the persons concerned.

59. First, as has been stated, the addressee of such an injunction has the possibility of avoiding liability, and thus of not adopting some measures that may be achievable, if those measures are not capable of being considered reasonable.

60. Secondly, it is possible that a means of putting a complete end to the infringements of the intellectual property right does not exist or is not in practice achievable, as a result of which some measures taken might be capable of being circumvented in one way or another.

61. The Court notes that there is nothing whatsoever in the wording of Article 17(2) of the Charter to suggest that the right to intellectual property is inviolable and must for that reason be absolutely protected (see, to that effect, *Scarlet Extended*, paragraph 43).

62. None the less, the measures which are taken by the addressee of an injunction, such as that at issue in the main proceedings, when implementing that injunction must be sufficiently effective to ensure genuine protection of the fundamental right at issue, that is to say that they must have the effect of preventing unauthorised access to the protected subject-matter or, at least, of making it difficult to achieve and of seriously discouraging internet users who are using the services of the addressee of that injunction from accessing the subject-matter made available to them in breach of that fundamental right.

63. Consequently, even though the measures taken when implementing an injunction such as that at issue in the main proceedings are not capable of leading, in some circumstances, to a complete cessation of the infringements of the intellectual property right, they cannot however be considered to be incompatible with the requirement that a fair balance be found, in accordance with Article 52(1), in fine, of the Charter, between all applicable fundamental rights, provided that (i) they do not unnecessarily deprive internet users of the possibility of lawfully accessing the information available and (ii) that they have the effect of preventing unauthorised access to protected subject-matter or, at least, of making it difficult to achieve and of seriously discouraging internet users who are using the services of the addressee of that injunction from accessing the subject-matter that has been made available to them in breach of the intellectual property right.

64. In the light of the foregoing considerations, the answer to the third question is that the fundamental rights recognised by EU law must be interpreted as not precluding a court injunction prohibiting an internet service provider from allowing its customers access to a website placing protected subject-matter online without the agreement of the rightholders when that injunction does not specify the measures which that access provider must take and when that access provider can avoid incurring coercive penalties for breach of that injunction by showing that it has taken all reasonable measures, provided that (i) the measures taken do not unnecessarily deprive internet users of the possibility of lawfully accessing the information available and (ii) that those measures have the effect of preventing unauthorised access to the protected subject-matter or, at least, of making it difficult to achieve and of seriously discouraging internet users who are using the services of the addressee of that injunction from accessing the subject-matter that has been made available to them in breach of the intellectual property right, that being a matter for the national authorities and courts to establish.

## NOTES AND QUESTIONS

**1.** The case shows the complexity of legal issues in Internet transmissions and the difficulties to realize and enforce copyright in the digital age.

**2.** In balancing different interests and fundamental rights at stake, the Court recognizes that protection of copyright is not absolute and is subject to restrictions imposed due to freedom of information and the right to do business.

**3.** In assessing injunctive relief, what role could the principle of proportionality play, which the Court does not explicitly mention, but which is inherent to restrictions of fundamental rights, including property rights?

### b. Moral Rights

The Berne Convention requires the recognition of "*droit moral*" or "moral rights" at Article 6*bis*. These include the right of attribution and the right to prevent a mutilation or other abuse of the work that would disparage the reputation of the author. The concept of moral rights was developed in Italy in the 1930s and eventually introduced into the Berne Convention, prior to the advent of human rights protection in the field.

In some legal systems, an author's moral rights are considered inalienable—they cannot be waived or released—and they are not subject to sale or transfer in connection with the author's economic rights in a work. It is often said that one of the greatest differences between Continental European and Anglo-American copyright law is the treatment of moral rights of authors. These differences, discussed in section I above, are often attributed to fundamental disparities in the way in which the respective cultures view the role of the artist in society—the theory being that the Continental European countries place a higher value on artistic expression than the Anglo-American countries do. Moreover, the lack of attention to the moral rights of artists, at least in the United States, is often attributed to the free market capitalist philosophy, which emphasizes the right of individuals to dispose of their possessions as they please.

Whether or not differences arise from profound cultural disparities, it is true that U.S. businesses worry that allowing authors to retain residual rights in copyrighted works may lead to financial uncertainty. A business that contracts for the development of a computer program, and that by contract obtains the copyright to the resulting work, does not want to be faced with demands from the programmer that the work not be altered lest his or her reputation be injured. Likewise, the film producer who invests tens (or hundreds) of millions of dollars in a work does not want the screenwriter or the director objecting to the way the film is marketed on the basis of residual moral rights.

The tension between economics and art is not a new one. We might safely assume that since the very first commercial performances by singers, storytellers, and actors, there has been conflict between artists desiring to perform in their own style and producers of works (e.g., tavern or theater owners) seeking to please the general public and earn a greater return on investment. In a world in which a film studio may invest $200 million in a film and earn a gross return of $1 billion, the stakes in a conflict are heightened.

#### *i. Moral Rights in Continental Europe*

The first decision below is by the French Cour de Cassation, the highest civil court in France. The decision involves a widely reported dispute between the corporate owner of the copyright to the film *Asphalt Jungle*, co-directed by John Huston, and the heirs to Huston's estate.

## *Angelica Huston v. Turner Entertainment Co.*

French Cour de Cassation, [1992] ECC 334, 28 May 1991

Panel: Presiding, M Massip; MM Gregoire, Zennaro, Bernard de Sainte-Affrique, Thierry, Averseng, Lemontey and Gelineau-Larrivet, Judges; M Savatier, Associate Judge

### Headnote:

Appeal from the Cour d'Appel (Court of Appeal), Paris.

*Copyright. Literary or artistic works. Foreign works.* Copyright legislation provides that the integrity of a literary or artistic work must not be violated in France. These provisions are mandatory and apply no matter where in the world the work in question was published for the first time.

The Court allowed the appeal by the plaintiff and others, as heirs to John Huston, against the order of the court below, which refused to enjoin the television company La Cinq from transmitting a coloured version of the film, Asphalt Jungle, made by the defendant, which had succeeded to the producer's rights to the film.

### INTRODUCTION: . . .

No cases were cited.

### DECISION:

Second ground of appeal, first limb, by Mrs. Angelica Huston, Mr. Daniel Huston and Mr. Walter Huston, and third ground of appeal by SFAI and other legal persons.

The court referred to section 1(2) of Act 64-689 of 8 July 1964, together with section 6 of the Copyright Act of 11 March 1957.

According the former provision, the integrity of a literary or artistic work must not be violated, irrespective of the State in which the work is published for the first time. The person who is the author by the mere fact of creating it is invested with the droit moral granted to him by the latter provision. The application of these rules is mandatory.

Mrs Angelica Huston, Mr Daniel Huston and Mr Walter Huston are the heirs of John Huston, co-director of the film Asphalt Jungle (the French title being Quand la Ville Dort), which was made in black and white, but a colour version of which was made by Turner Entertainment Co, which has succeeded to the producer's rights. Relying on their right to compel respect for the integrity of John Huston's work, the appellant heirs, who have been joined in this appeal on a point of law by the various other appellants which are legal persons, asked the courts dealing with the main issue to prohibit the television company La Cinq from showing this new version. The appeal court dismissed the application on the ground that the factual matters and points of law raised by them "precluded the ouster of American law and setting aside of the contracts" between the producer and directors, which do not acknowledge that the latter are the authors of the film Asphalt Jungle.

In reaching its decision the appeal court infringed the abovementioned provisions by refusing to apply them.

Appeal allowed. Case remitted to the Cour d'Appel, Versailles for rehearing.

## NOTES AND QUESTIONS

**1.** The decision of the Cour de Cassation is to the point: French legislation on the question of moral rights is mandatory—it is not waived by the U.S. contract that transferred the copyright to the film producer. The French rule applies despite the fact that the film is of U.S. origin, and despite the fact that the French Cour d'Appel found that the contract should otherwise be governed by U.S. law. Do you think that this result is unusual from a general conflict of laws standpoint? In other words, do countries commonly mandate the application of their own rules to activities taking place within their territory, despite contractual provisions that might generally call for the application of another country's law? In fact, it is not so uncommon for states to mandate the application of their own rules in cases in which important public policy considerations are at stake. A court in one state may, for example, refuse to enforce a judgment rendered by a court in another state if the court in the second state failed to follow a due process rule that is considered essential under the law of the first state.

We earlier examined that part of the Swiss Supreme Court decision in *Frau X v. Frau Y & Z Publishing House* finding that Frau X did not have a copyright in her work because it constituted unprotectable scientific idea. In addition to claiming Frau Y's unlawful reproduction of her expressive work, Frau X claimed that Frau Y infringed her moral rights because she gave the impression to her audience that Frau Y was the author of Frau X's work. The Court also considers Frau X's unfair competition claim.

## *Frau X v. Frau Y & Z Publishing House*

Bundesgericht (Swiss Federal Court) BGE 113 II 306, [1989] ECC 232, 17 June 1987 (translation, as adjusted)

4. The plaintiff further accuses the first defendant of infringing her droit moral. According to the judgment under appeal that allegation had to be rejected because the quotations, data and propositions which were undoubtedly adopted were nevertheless not of such moment that one could talk of usurpation of the work, and because there was no other prejudice to the plaintiff's scientific reputation.

(a) Under Swiss legal theory and legislation an author is protected not only in his or her power to dispose of the work as the object of property rights, but also as regards his personal relationship to the work, that is as regards his droit moral as author, which are conceived as being a part or special aspect of general droit moral. The protection of that special droit moral arises in part from the provisions of the Copyright Act. . . .The protection arises further from Article 6 *bis* of the Berne Union Convention, and it first occurs in the revision made in Rome in 1928 (96 II BGE 420 E 6, with references).

Under section 28 of the Civil Code it is a condition precedent for claims arising out of droit moral that there is unlawful interference in personal relationships, which are understood as being the sphere of private life and the home, as well as a person's professional and private reputation. That is not to say that any relationship of the author to the work is sufficient to turn an alleged interference into an infringement of a personal right; for the general principle does not grant any claim to an exclusive right of disposal if the author's reputation is not affected; such an approach to the matter would have the end-result of creating a monopoly under section 28 of the Civil Code in something which is designated as freely available to the public under the statutory provisions on the specific subject-matter. The special statutory provision has precedence over the general provisions of the Civil Code and governs the area to which it applies to the exclusion of other rules. It is therefore not admissible to attempt to fill alleged gaps in copyright law by an indirect route through the general principle (110 II BGE 417 E 3a, with references). In the matter of copyright this principle only covers claims which are not subject to the rules of the legislation on the specific subject-matter, such as the author's claim to have his scientific achievement acknowledged, to have his work protected against distortion, or to have access to research documentation. (Engel in [1982] GRUR 709 et seq.) This corresponds to Article 6*bis*(1) of the Berne Union Convention, under which, independently of the author's copyright and even after transfer of such copyright, the author still has the right in particular to object to any distortion, mutilation or other alteration of the work which could be prejudicial to his honour or reputation; under the 1948 Revision the concept also includes anything else which would be prejudicial. For these purposes it is sufficient that the alteration or other prejudicial action is apt to injure his reputation or honour (96 II BGE 421).

(b) The plaintiff attacks the first defendant's manner of proceeding inasmuch as the latter took quotations, data and propositions from her works without stating the source. She supports her claim in this respect with section 26(2) of the Copyright Act, but overlooks the fact that, as shown by heading III, that provision belongs to "Exceptions from Copyright Protection," and therefore presupposes a protected work or a protected part of a work. (Troller, op cit II, p 704; Sciaroni, op cit, pp 28 et seq.) What is available for public use, however, enjoys no copyright protection, and therefore also establishes no duty to attach a statement of source to quotations. The plaintiff, therefore, is likewise unable to derive anything from the general right of personality which will protect her scientific statements, regardless of whether or not her works have to be treated as published.

The Obergericht must also be agreed with in its finding that there was no infringement of the plaintiff's right to acknowledgment of her scientific achievement. It is true that rights of personality give the author a claim in particular to the protection of any reputation and honour which the work may establish for him (84 II BGE 573); he can also oppose the usurpation of authorship by third parties. As the court below correctly held, however, that presupposes that the work is claimed as an individual achievement as regards its essential parts or characteristic features. That cannot be seriously maintained in the present case, especially as according to the findings on the factual aspects the quotations, data and propositions taken over word-for-word or merely in substance cannot qualify for copyright protection.

5. In the same way the accusation that the first defendant's actions are to be regarded as a breach of good faith for the purposes of section 1 of the Unfair Competition Act fails in the first instance by reason of the fact that conduct which is not to be objected to under the specific legislative provisions on intangible property rights also does not in principle contravene the provisions of the Unfair Competition Act (110 IV BGE 107 E 4 and 108 II BGE 331 E 5a, with citation). No doubt on the basis of the general stipulation contained in section 1(1) of the Act an exception would be made for the case of conduct which amounts to a systematic approximation or a deliberate covert approach to another person's work (108 II BGE 74-75 and 332; 104 II BGE 334 E 5b). But this is clearly not such a case. The passages listed by the defendant, consisting of three quotations, five items biographical data and a scientific proposition (thesis), which are allegedly extracted from her two works, make it impossible to conclude that the first defendant, in the exercise of an economic activity, usurped rights in specific parts of the work or even the authorship of the whole presentation, as the plaintiff seeks to argue.

Finally, the plaintiff claims damages for breach of contract and on the grounds of vicarious liability because the reader of the second defendant acting without authority and therefore unlawfully passed her manuscripts on to the first defendant. It is not necessary for present purposes to decide how the facts stand with regard to those claims, for the plaintiff acknowledges in the appeal that she authorised the first defendant to refer to both works under certain "restrictive" conditions. In so doing she herself removes the basis of her objection that the publishing company passed the manuscripts on without authority and thereby made it possible for the first defendant to adopt the passages in question.

Appeal dismissed. Judgment of the lower court reaffirmed.

## NOTES AND QUESTIONS

**1.** Does the author in this case have "personal rights" in her work that copyright has not adequately protected? Do you agree with the Court's view that if material used in the lecture is not protected as creative expression, its author cannot have a moral right in the work?

**2.** Toward the end of its opinion, the Swiss Federal Court considers the plaintiff's unfair competition claim. While accepting that the usurpation of another person's work might constitute unfair competition, the Court says that the offending conduct must be systematic or involve a deliberate approach to the other person. In this regard, the Court says that appropriation, *inter alia*, of the plaintiff's thesis makes it impossible to conclude that a sufficiently great usurpation occurred. Perhaps the Court was not terribly impressed by the plaintiff's thesis. But as a general proposition, might not a single scientific proposition or thesis be of enormous economic and social value such that its usurpation would constitute a great harm to its creator? What if a rival physicist had broken into Albert Einstein's apartment in Berne and shortly thereafter published Einstein's theory of relativity under a different name?

**3.** The Swiss Supreme Court emphasizes that general principles of civil law should not be used to address gaps in IP protection deliberately left open by the legislature. Intellectual property law is drafted with exceptions to further the public interest. Is it sensible that courts should not allow those gaps to be closed by general principles of unfair competition?

**4.** Law professors and other academics make their reputations—and thus help determine their living conditions—on the basis of their creative scholarship. Law professors routinely circulate their work to colleagues prior to publication for criticism, editorial suggestion, and so forth, with the aim of improving the final product. Though it is certainly not unheard of, it is in fact rather rare to hear a complaint that one professor has "misappropriated" another's unpublished thesis. What do you think might motivate law professors, or research scientists, to respect the interests of their colleagues in such work? Is it protection by copyright or unfair competition law? Is it high moral standards? Is some other potential "collegial sanctioning mechanism" at work? Does such a sanctioning mechanism operate in the business sector?

### *ii. Moral Rights in the United States*

In the 1976 *Monty Python* decision that follows, the U.S. Court of Appeals for the Second Circuit elaborated a basis under the copyright statute of the United States, as well as under a statute on unfair competition, for the attribution of certain moral rights to authors.

## *Gilliam v. American Broadcasting Companies, Inc.*

538 F.2d 14 (2d Cir. 1976)

### Prior History:

Appeal from a denial of a preliminary injunction to enjoin broadcast of edited television programs that allegedly infringed appellants' copyright and violated the Lanham Act §43(a), 15 U.S.C. §1125(a).

### Disposition: Reversed and Remanded . . .

Lumbard, Circuit Judge:

Plaintiffs, a group of British writers and performers known as Monty Python,[1] appeal from a denial by Judge Lasker in the Southern District of a preliminary injunction to restrain the American Broadcasting Company (ABC) from broadcasting edited versions of three separate programs originally written and performed by Monty Python for broadcast by the British Broadcasting Corporation (BBC). We agree with Judge Lasker that the appellants have demonstrated that the excising done for ABC impairs the integrity of the original work. We further find that the countervailing injuries that Judge Lasker found might have accrued to ABC as a result of an injunction at a prior date no longer exist. We therefore direct the issuance of a preliminary injunction by the district court. . . .

### I . . .

American copyright law, as presently written, does not recognize moral rights or provide a cause of action for their violation, since the law seeks to vindicate the economic, rather than the personal, rights of authors. Nevertheless, the economic incentive for artistic and intellectual creation that serves as the foundation for American copyright law, *Goldstein v. California*,

1. Appellant Gilliam is an American citizen residing in England.

412 U.S. 546, 37 L. Ed. 2d 163, 93 S. Ct. 2303 (1973); *Mazer v. Stein*, 347 U.S. 201, 98 L. Ed. 630, 74 S. Ct. 460 (1954), cannot be reconciled with the inability of artists to obtain relief for mutilation or misrepresentation of their work to the public on which the artists are financially dependent. Thus courts have long granted relief for misrepresentation of an artist's work by relying on theories outside the statutory law of copyright, such as contract law, *Granz v. Harris*, 198 F.2d 585 (2d Cir. 1952) (substantial cutting of original work constitutes misrepresentation), or the tort of unfair competition, *Prouty v. National Broadcasting Co.*, 26 F. Supp. 265 (Mass. 1939). *See* Strauss, The Moral Right of the Author 128-138, in Studies on Copyright (1963). Although such decisions are clothed in terms of proprietary right in one's creation, they also properly vindicate the author's personal right to prevent the presentation of his work to the public in a distorted form. *See Gardella v. Log Cabin Products Co.*, 89 F.2d 891, 895-96 (2d Cir. 1937); Roeder, The Doctrine of Moral Right, 53 Harv. L. Rev. 554, 568 (1940).

Here, the appellants claim that the editing done for ABC mutilated the original work and that consequently the broadcast of those programs as the creation of Monty Python violated the Lanham Act §43(a), 15 U.S.C. §1125(a).[10] This statute, the federal counterpart to state unfair competition laws, has been invoked to prevent misrepresentations that may injure plaintiff's business or personal reputation, even where no registered trademark is concerned. *See Mortellito v. Nina of California*, 335 F. Supp. 1288, 1294 (S.D.N.Y. 1972). It is sufficient to violate the Act that a representation of a product, although technically true, creates a false impression of the product's origin. *See Rich v. RCA Corp.*, 390 F. Supp. 530 (S.D.N.Y. 1975) (recent picture of plaintiff on cover of album containing songs recorded in distant past held to be a false representation that the songs were new); *Geisel v. Poynter Products, Inc.*, 283 F. Supp. 261, 267 (S.D.N.Y. 1968).

These cases cannot be distinguished from the situation in which a television network broadcasts a program properly designated as having been written and performed by a group, but which has been edited, without the writer's consent, into a form that departs substantially from the original work. "To deform his work is to present him to the public as the creator of a work not his own, and thus makes him subject to criticism for work he has not done." Roeder, *supra*, at 569. In such a case, it is the writer or performer, rather than the network, who suffers the consequences of the mutilation, for the public will have only the final product by which to evaluate the work. Thus, an allegation that a defendant has presented to the public a "garbled," *Granz v. Harris, supra* (Frank, J., concurring), distorted version of plaintiff's work seeks to redress the very rights sought to be protected by the Lanham Act, 15 U.S.C. §1125(a), and should be recognized as stating a cause of action under that statute. *See Autry v. Republic Productions, Inc.*, 213 F.2d 667 (9th Cir. 1954); *Jaeger v. American Intn'l Pictures, Inc.*, 330 F. Supp. 274 (S.D.N.Y. 1971), which suggest the violation of such a right if mutilation could be proven.

During the hearing on the preliminary injunction, Judge Lasker viewed the edited version of the Monty Python program broadcast on December 26 and the original, unedited version. After hearing argument of this appeal, this panel also viewed and compared the two versions. We find that the truncated version at times omitted the climax of the skits to which appellants' rare brand of humor was leading and at other times deleted essential elements in the schematic development of a story line.[12] We therefore agree with Judge Lasker's conclusion

---

10. That statute provides in part: Any person who shall affix, apply, or annex, or use in connection with any goods or services, . . . a false designation of origin, or any false description or representation . . . and shall cause such goods or services to enter into commerce . . . shall be liable to a civil action by any person . . . who believes that he is or is likely to be damaged by the use of any such false description or representation.

12. A single example will illustrate the extent of distortion engendered by the editing. In one skit, an upper class English family is engaged in a discussion of the tonal quality of certain words as "woody" or "tinny." The father soon begins to suggest certain words with sexual connotations as either "woody" or "tinny," whereupon the mother fetches a bucket of water and pours it over his head. The skit continues from this point. The ABC edit eliminates this middle sequence so that the father is comfortably dressed at one moment and, in the next moment, is shown in a soaked condition without any explanation for the change in his appearance.

that the edited version broadcast by ABC impaired the integrity of appellants' work and represented to the public as the product of appellants what was actually a mere caricature of their talents. We believe that a valid cause of action for such distortion exists and that therefore a preliminary injunction may issue to prevent repetition of the broadcast prior to final determination of the issues.[13] . . .

For these reasons we direct that the district court issue the preliminary injunction sought by the appellants.

Gurfein, Circuit Judge, concurring:

I concur in my brother Lumbard's scholarly opinion, but I wish to comment on the application of Section 43(a) of the Lanham Act, 15 U.S.C. §1125(a).

I believe that this is the first case in which a federal appellate court has held that there may be a violation of Section 43(a) of the Lanham Act with respect to a common-law copyright. . . .

In the present case, we are holding that the deletion of portions of the recorded tape constitutes a breach of contract, as well as an infringement of a common-law copyright of the original work. There is literally no need to discuss whether plaintiffs also have a claim for relief under the Lanham Act or for unfair competition under New York law. I agree with Judge Lumbard, however, that it may be an exercise of judicial economy to express our view on the Lanham Act claim, and I do not dissent therefrom. I simply wish to leave it open for the District Court to fashion the remedy.

The Copyright Act provides no recognition of the so-called *droit moral*, or moral rights of authors. Nor are such rights recognized in the field of copyright law in the United States. *See* 1 Nimmer on Copyright, §110.2 (1975 ed.). If a distortion or truncation in connection with a use constitutes an infringement of copyright, there is no need for an additional cause of action beyond copyright infringement. *Id.* at §110.3. An obligation to mention the name of the author carries the implied duty, however, as a matter of contract, not to make such changes in the work as would render the credit line a false attribution of authorship, *Granz v. Harris*, 198 F.2d 585 (2d Cir. 1952).

So far as the Lanham Act is concerned, it is not a substitute for droit moral which authors in Europe enjoy. If the licensee may, by contract, distort the recorded work, the Lanham Act does not come into play. If the licensee has no such right by contract, there will be a violation in breach of contract. The Lanham Act can hardly apply literally when the credit line correctly states the work to be that of the plaintiffs which, indeed it is, so far as it goes. The vice complained of is that the truncated version is not what the plaintiffs wrote. But the Lanham Act does not deal with artistic integrity. It only goes to misdescription of origin and the like. *See Societe Comptoir De L'Industrie Cotonniere Etablissements Boussac v. Alexander's Dept. Stores, Inc.*, 299 F.2d 33, 36 (2 Cir. 1962).

The misdescription of origin can be dealt with, as Judge Lasker did below, by devising an appropriate legend to indicate that the plaintiffs had not approved the editing of the ABC version. With such a legend, there is no conceivable violation of the Lanham Act. If plaintiffs

13. Judge Gurfein's concurring opinion suggests that since the gravamen of a complaint under the Lanham Act is that the origin of goods has been falsely described, a legend disclaiming Monty Python's approval of the edited version would preclude violation of that Act. We are doubtful that a few words could erase the indelible impression that is made by a television broadcast, especially since the viewer has no means of comparing the truncated version with the complete work in order to determine for himself the talents of plaintiffs. Furthermore, a disclaimer such as the one originally suggested by Judge Lasker in the exigencies of an impending broadcast last December would go unnoticed by viewers who tuned into the broadcast a few minutes after it began. We therefore conclude that Judge Gurfein's proposal that the district court could find some form of disclaimer would be sufficient might not provide appropriate relief.

complain that their artistic integrity is still compromised by the distorted version, their claim does not lie under the Lanham Act, which does not protect the copyrighted work itself but protects only against the misdescription or mislabeling.

So long as it is made clear that the ABC version is not approved by the Monty Python group, there is no misdescription of origin. So far as the content of the broadcast itself is concerned, that is not within the proscription of the Lanham Act when there is no misdescription of the authorship.

I add this brief explanation because I do not believe that the Lanham Act claim necessarily requires the drastic remedy of permanent injunction. That form of ultimate relief must be found in some other fountainhead of equity jurisprudence.

## NOTES AND QUESTIONS

**1.** In discussing the traditional U.S. reluctance to recognize moral rights, the Second Circuit observes that it is difficult to reconcile the economic incentive for creation that American copyright law is intended to provide, on the one hand, with a lack of attention to the reputation of authors and artists. A good reputation, the court suggests, is a predicate of economic success. Do you agree with the court's perspective?

**2.** In *Dastar v. Twentieth Century Fox*, 539 U.S. 23 (2003), the U.S. Supreme Court rejected the "origin" theory of Lanham Act application to misattribution, but allowed that "misrepresentation" of nature, characteristics or quality under 15 USC § 1125(a)(1)(B) may apply.

Some 20 years after *Monty Python*, the U.S. Court of Appeals for the Second Circuit again addressed the subject of moral rights in *Carter v. Helmsley-Spear.* In this case, the court is called upon to interpret and apply an amendment to the U.S. Copyright Act, the Visual Artists Rights Act of 1990, which expressly incorporates moral rights into federal law though, as we will see, in a limited way.

## *Carter v. Helmsley-Spear*

71 F.3d 77 (2d Cir. 1995)

Cardamone, Circuit Judge: . . .

### B. Visual Artists Rights Act of 1990

Although bills protecting artists' moral rights had first been introduced in Congress in 1979, they had drawn little support. *See* Copyright Law at 1018 n.1. The issue of federal protection of moral rights was a prominent hurdle in the debate over whether the United States should join the Berne Convention, the international agreement protecting literary and artistic works. Article 6*bis* of the Berne Convention protects attribution and integrity, stating in relevant part:

> Independently of the author's economic rights, and even after the transfer of the said rights, the author shall have the right to claim authorship of the work and to object to any distortion, mutilation or other modification of, or other derogatory action in relation to, the said work, which would be prejudicial to his honor or reputation.

Berne Convention for the Protection of Literary and Artistic Works, September 9, 1886, art. 6*bis*, S. Treaty Doc. No. 27, 99th Cong., 2d Sess. 41 (1986).

The Berne Convention's protection of moral rights posed a significant difficulty for U.S. adherence. *See* Copyright Law at 1022 ("The obligation of the United States to provide droit moral . . . was the single most contentious issue surrounding Berne adherence".); Nimmer at 8D-15 ("During the debate over [the Berne Convention Implementation Act], Congress faced an avalanche of opposition to moral rights, including denunciations of moral rights by some of the bill's most vociferous advocates".); H.R. Rep. No. 514, 101st Cong., 2d Sess. 7 (1990), *reprinted in* 1990 U.S.C.C.A.N. 6915, 6917 ("After almost 100 years of debate, the United States joined the Berne Convention. . . . Consensus over United States adherence was slow to develop in large part because of debate over the requirements of Article *6bis*.").

Congress passed the Berne Convention Implementation Act of 1988, Pub. L. No. 100-568, 102 Stat. 2853 (1988), and side-stepped the difficult question of protecting moral rights. It declared that the Berne Convention is not self-executing, existing law satisfied the United States' obligations in adhering to the Convention, its provisions are not enforceable through any action brought pursuant to the Convention itself, and neither adherence to the Convention nor the implementing legislation expands or reduces any rights under federal, state, or common law to claim authorship of a work or to object to any distortion, mutilation, or other modification of a work. *See id.* §§2, 3; *see also* S. Rep. No. 352, 100th Cong., 2d Sess. 9-10 (1988), *reprinted in* 1988 U.S.C.C.A.N. 3706, 3714-15.

Two years later Congress enacted the Visual Artists Rights Act of 1990 (VARA or Act), Pub. L. No. 101-650 (tit. VI), 104 Stat. 5089, 5128-33 (1990). Construing this Act constitutes the subject of the present appeal. The Act protects both the reputations of certain visual artists and the works of art they create. It provides these artists with the rights of "attribution" and "integrity." . . .

> These rights are analogous to those protected by Article *6bis* of the Berne Convention, which are commonly known as "moral rights." The theory of moral rights is that they result in a climate of artistic worth and honor that encourages the author in the arduous act of creation.

H.R. Rep. No. 514 at 5 (internal quote omitted). The Act brings to fruition Emerson's insightful observation ["[A] country is not truly civilized 'where the arts, such as they have, are all imported, having no indigenous life.'" From earlier in the decision.—Eds.].

Its principal provisions afford protection only to authors of works of visual art—a narrow class of art defined to include paintings, drawings, prints, sculptures, or photographs produced for exhibition purposes, existing in a single copy or limited edition of 200 copies or fewer. 17 U.S.C. §101 (Supp. III 1991). With numerous exceptions, VARA grants three rights: the right of attribution, the right of integrity and, in the case of works of visual art of "recognized stature," the right to prevent destruction. 17 U.S.C. §106A (Supp. III 1991). For works created on or after June 1, 1991—the effective date of the Act—the rights provided for endure for the life of the author or, in the case of a joint work, the life of the last surviving author. The rights cannot be transferred, but may be waived by a writing signed by the author. Copyright registration is not required to bring an action for infringement of the rights granted under VARA, or to secure statutory damages and attorney's fees. 17 U.S.C. §§411, 412 (1988 & Supp. III 1991). All remedies available under copyright law, other than criminal remedies, are available in an action for infringement of moral rights. 17 U.S.C. §506 (1988 & Supp. III 1991). With this historical background in hand, we pass to the merits of the present litigation. . . .

### III. Work Made For Hire

Also excluded from the definition of a work of visual art is any work made for hire. 17 U.S.C. §101(B). A "work made for hire" is defined in the Copyright Act, in relevant part, as "a work prepared by an employee within the scope of his or her employment." *Id.* §101(1). Appellants maintain the work was made for hire and therefore is not a work of visual art under VARA. The district court held otherwise, finding that the plaintiffs were hired as independent contractors. [The court goes on to determine that the work of art at issue in this case was a "work made for hire" and therefore did not benefit from the protection of the VARA.]

## NOTES AND QUESTIONS

**1.** The Court of Appeals recounts the tremendous opposition to incorporation of Article 6*bis* of the Berne Convention into U.S. law. The act approving adherence to the Berne Convention and implementing it into U.S. law expressly precludes direct reliance on the Convention as a source of rights.[10]

**2.** The "work made for hire" doctrine in U.S. law finds its counterpart in other countries and regions. The essence of the doctrine is that when a work is produced by an author or artist within the course and scope of employment for another person, that other person will hold the copyright to the work. As the court observes in the preceding case, there are a variety of factors that may go into determining whether an author or artist stands in an employee-employer relationship. The work made for hire doctrine is of paramount importance in the business context, and lawyers who represent businesses that contract for expressive works—including computer software—must pay very close attention to which party will hold the copyright at the end of the day.

**3.** The updated North American Free Trade Agreement (NAFTA), now known as the United States–Mexico–Canada Agreement (USMCA), addresses the relationship between economic (and contractual) rights and moral rights with the following provision:

> Article 20.H.10: Contractual Transfers
>
> Each Party shall provide that for copyright and related rights, any person acquiring or holding any economic right[61] in a work, performance or phonogram:
>
> (a) may freely and separately transfer that right by contract; and
>
> (b) by virtue of contract, including contracts of employment underlying the creation of works, performances or phonograms, shall be able to exercise that right in that person's own name and enjoy fully the benefits derived from that right.[62]

What moral rights do artists and authors retain under this USMCA provision? To what extent may the transferee of economic rights in a work modify the original without the consent of the artist or author?

**4.** In 2018, Judge Frederic Block of the United States District Court for the Eastern District of New York ruled that a Queens real estate developer violated the rights of graffiti artists when he whitewashed and painted over their works on 5Pointz, a sprawling building complex in Long Island City, Queens, without due warning in 2013. A jury made the decision upholding that the artists' VARA rights were violated by the destruction of their work, and Judge Block awarded the maximum amount of $150,000 for each of the 45 works that were destroyed, making for the total sum of $6.75 million. The decision was affirmed in 2019, in particular that temporary artwork may achieve recognized stature so as to be protected

10. 17 U.S.C. §104(c).

61. For greater certainty, this provision does not affect the exercise of moral rights.

62. Nothing in this Article affects a Party's ability to establish: (i) which specific contracts underlying the creation of works, performances or phonograms shall, in the absence of a written agreement, result in a transfer of economic rights by operation of law; and (ii) reasonable limits to protect the interests of the original right holders, taking into account the legitimate interests of the transferees.

from destruction by VARA and that the plaintiffs' work had achieved that stature. The U.S. Supreme Court declined a request to review the case and this has been seen as a win for street art. Do you think that such a finding is right and that damages should be paid in such cases?

## B. The TRIPS Agreement

Thomas Cottier introduces below the main features of the TRIPS Agreement relating to copyright.

**Thomas Cottier***

### *The Agreement on Trade Related Aspects of Intellectual Property Rights (TRIPS)*

#### D. Standards Concerning the Availability, Scope and Use of Intellectual Property Rights (Part II)

##### 1. Copyright and Related Rights

The provisions related to copyright are set out in Articles 9 to 14 of the TRIPs Agreement. Besides obligating all WTO Members (including prior non-signatories) to comply with the substantive provisions of the Berne Convention, the TRIPs Agreement adds new provisions and clarifies those guaranteed by the Berne Convention. The rights of authors of literary and artistic works are addressed in Articles 9 to 12, the rights of performers, phonogram producers, and broadcasting organizations mainly in Article 14. The protection of performers' rights, which was traditionally limited to European civil law countries, is for the first time dealt with in a multilateral treaty of wider geographical coverage. The TRIPs copyright provisions against counterfeiting and piracy are of particular significance to producers of computer programs and phonograms. . . .

Article 9:2 awards copyright protection only to expressions and not to ideas, procedures, methods of operation, or mathematical concepts as such. The excluded elements are not defined by TRIPs, thus leaving it, subject to treaty interpretation, to Member states and domestic courts to decide what exactly constitutes, for example, a non-protected "procedure" or "method of operation" in software as opposed to protected expression.

Article 10 expands the traditional subject matter of copyright to include computer programs and compilations of data by creating an obligation to protect them as literary works. Like Article 2:5 of the Berne Convention, Article 10:2 of the TRIPs Agreement requires originality in the selection and arrangement of the contents of a compilation. Merely creating a list of works or extracts without engaging in any creative activity is not sufficient to merit copyright protection. If the database is protectable, the copyright protection only extends to the creative elements (e.g., the selection and arrangement of the data) and does not "extend to the material or data itself."

Article 11 provides the exclusive right to authors and their successors to authorize or prohibit the commercial rental of their computer programs and, subject to a so-called impairment test, to their cinematographic works.

Following Article 7:1 of the Berne Convention, Article 12 of the TRIPs Agreement sets the term of protection of most works that are calculated on a basis other than the life of the author to a minimum duration of fifty years from the end of the calendar year of authorized

* The World Trade Organization: Legal, Economic and Political Analysis 1082-1085 (Patrick F.J. Macrory, Arthur E. Appleton & Michael G. Plummer eds., 2005).

publication, making, or phonogram fixation/performance. Under Article 14:5 a term of twenty years is to apply to the rights of broadcasters, respectively, supplementing the twenty-five year term of protection for photographic works which is provided for in Article 7:4 of the Berne Convention.

Article 13 requires Members to confine limitations or exceptions to exclusive rights to (i) "certain special cases" which (ii) do not conflict with normal exploitation of the work, and (iii) do not unreasonably prejudice the legitimate interests of the right holder. The Panel first applied this test in the case *United States-Section 110(5) of the U.S. Copyright Act.* Since the wording of Article 13 has its roots in Article 9:2 of the Berne Convention, the Panel emphasized that the "preparatory works of Article 9(2) . . . and its application in practice may be of contextual relevance in interpreting Article 13 of the TRIPs Agreement." By applying the above three-prong test to the provisions of the U.S. statute at issue, it held that the exemption in U.S. copyright law from copyright liability for business establishments not exceeding a specified size to transmit or retransmit television or radio broadcasts of non-dramatic musical works failed the first criterion, since too many retail establishments were covered by the exemption to constitute only "certain special cases." However, the Panel found that the home-style exemption, which provided a similar exemption for certain small restaurants and retail outlets using "a single receiving apparatus of a kind commonly used in private homes," satisfied all three conditions of Article 13. The Panel stressed that, in addition to the actual effect on the market, the potential effect of an exemption should be taken into consideration as well when assessing the permissibility of the exemptions. In doing so, the Panel referred to similar concepts and interpretation standards developed in past GATT/WTO dispute settlement practice. It deemed it appropriate to develop an interpretation of the legal protection of IP right holders that is compatible with the treatment of products under GATT and services/service suppliers under GATS.

In the field of neighboring rights, Article 14 grants improved protection of rights of performers, phonogram producers, and broadcasting organizations. With respect to performers, Article 14:1 sets out the protection to be granted (i.e., preventing unauthorized phonogram fixation, reproduction of such fixations, broadcasting by wireless means and communication to the public). Phonogram producers enjoy exclusive rights over the reproduction of their phonograms in Article 14:2 and exclusive rental rights under Article 14:4. Finally, Article 14:3 requires that broadcasting organizations be given the right to prohibit the fixation, reproduction of fixations, wireless re-broadcasting, and communication to the public of television broadcasts in Article 14:3. According to Article 14:6, Members may provide for conditions, limitation, exceptions and reservations to the extent permitted by the Rome Convention, principally those provided for by Articles 12, 15 and 16 of the Convention.

## NOTES AND QUESTIONS

**1.** By way of contrast with the patent provisions of the TRIPS Agreement, the copyright section devotes little attention to the subject matter of protection — addressing computer software and compilations. The main focus of the TRIPS provisions is granting an additional form of distribution right (i.e., the rental right), and enhancing the rights of performers, producers, and broadcast organizations — the traditional beneficiaries of neighboring rights. From the standpoint of the copyright industries, the TRIPS Agreement was needed not so much to enhance or clarify the scope of rights, but to provide the leverage by which enforcement of these rights could be secured, particularly in developing countries.

### *1. The TRIPS Agreement and Its Relationship to the Berne Convention*

Article 9.1 TRIPS establishes the relationship between the Agreement and the Berne Convention. It obliges the WTO members to comply with Articles 1 through 21 of the Berne Convention. As discussed above, moral rights, however, are explicitly exempted from protection in Article 9, referring to Article 6*bis* of the Berne Convention. In the following case, *United States—Section 110(5) of the U.S. Copyright Act*, the Panel addresses, *inter alia*, the relationship between the TRIPS Agreement and the Berne Convention. In the course of its opinion, the Panel clarifies the relationship between the TRIPS and Berne provisions. It not only states that the rules of the Berne Convention "have to be read as applying to WTO Members," but also that the Berne *acquis* has been incorporated into TRIPS. It held that "the Berne Convention and the TRIPS Agreement form part of the overall framework for multilateral protection." The Panel further points out that, "if the incorporation was not intended to cover the Berne *acquis*, the TRIPS Agreement would have explicitly so provided." Generally, "one should avoid interpreting the TRIPS Agreement to mean something different than the Berne Convention except where this is explicitly provided for."

## *United States—Section 110(5) of the U.S. Copyright Act*

Report of the Panel*

### II. Factual Aspects

2.1 The dispute concerns Section 110(5) of the U.S. Copyright Act of 1976, as amended by the Fairness in Music Licensing Act of 1998 ("the 1998 Amendment"), which entered into force on 26 January 1999. The provisions of Section 110(5) place limitations on the exclusive rights provided to owners of copyright in Section 106 of the Copyright Act in respect of certain performances and displays. . . .

2.4 Subparagraph (A) of Section 110(5) essentially reproduces the text of the original "homestyle" exemption contained in Section 110(5) of the Copyright Act of 1976. When Section 110(5) was amended in 1998, the homestyle exemption was moved to a new subparagraph (A) and the words "except as provided in subparagraph (B)" were added to the beginning of the text. . . .

2.9 The 1998 Amendment has added a new subparagraph (B) to Section 110(5), to which we, for the sake of brevity, hereinafter refer to as a "business" exemption. It exempts, under certain conditions, communication by an establishment of a transmission or retransmission embodying a performance or display of a nondramatic musical work intended to be received by the general public, originated by a radio or television broadcast station licensed as such by the Federal Communications Commission, or, if an audiovisual transmission, by a cable system or satellite carrier.

2.10 The beneficiaries of the business exemption are divided into two categories: establishments other than food service or drinking establishments ("retail establishments"), and food service and drinking establishments. In each category, establishments under a certain size limit are exempted, regardless of the type of equipment they use. The size limits are 2,000 gross square feet (186 $m^2$) for retail establishments and 3,750 gross square feet (348 $m^2$) for restaurants. . . .

* World Trade Organization, Report of the Panel, WT/DS160/R, 15 June 2000.

## VI FINDINGS . . .

## D. Substantive Aspects of the Dispute

### 1. General Considerations About the Exclusive Rights Concerned and Limitations Thereto . . .

#### *(b) Limitations and Exceptions*

**(i) Introduction**

6.30 A major issue in this dispute is the interpretation and application to the facts of this case of Article 13 of the TRIPS Agreement. The U.S. defense is firmly based upon it. . . .

**(iii) The minor exceptions doctrine . . .**

*The legal status of the minor exceptions doctrine under the TRIPS Agreement*

6.60 Having concluded that the minor exceptions doctrine forms part of the "context" of, at least, Articles 11*bis* and 11 of the Berne Convention (1971) by virtue of an agreement within the meaning of Article 31(2)(a) of the Vienna Convention, which was made between the Berne Union members in connection with the conclusion of the respective amendments to that Convention, we next address the second step of our analysis outlined above. This second step deals with the question whether or not the minor exceptions doctrine has been incorporated into the TRIPS Agreement, by virtue of its Article 9.1, together with Articles 1-21 of the Berne Convention (1971) as part of the Berne *acquis.*

6.61 We note that the express wording of Article 9.1 of the TRIPS Agreement neither establishes nor excludes such incorporation into the Agreement of the minor exceptions doctrine as it applies to Articles 11, 11*bis*, 11*ter*, 13 and 14 of the Berne Convention (1971).

6.62 We have shown above that the minor exceptions doctrine forms part of the context, within the meaning of Article 31(2)(a) of the Vienna Convention, of at least Articles 11 and 11*bis* of the Berne Convention (1971). There is no indication in the wording of the TRIPS Agreement that Articles 11 and 11*bis* have been incorporated into the TRIPS Agreement by its Article 9.1 without bringing with them the possibility of providing minor exceptions to the respective exclusive rights. If that incorporation should have covered only the text of Articles 1–21 of the Berne Convention (1971), but not the entire Berne *acquis* relating to these articles, Article 9.1 of the TRIPS Agreement would have explicitly so provided.

6.63 Thus we conclude that, in the absence of any express exclusion in Article 9.1 of the TRIPS Agreement, the incorporation of Articles 11 and 11*bis* of the Berne Convention (1971) into the Agreement includes the entire *acquis* of these provisions, including the possibility of providing minor exceptions to the respective exclusive rights.

6.64 We find confirmation of our interpretation in certain references to the minor exceptions doctrine in the documentation from the GATT Uruguay Round negotiations on the TRIPS Agreement. . . .

6.66 In the area of copyright, the Berne Convention and the TRIPS Agreement form the overall framework for multilateral protection. Most WTO Members are also parties to the Berne Convention. We recall that it is a general principle of interpretation to adopt the meaning that reconciles the texts of different treaties and avoids a conflict between them. Accordingly, one should avoid interpreting the TRIPS Agreement to mean something different than the Berne Convention except where this is explicitly provided for. This principle is in conformity with the public international law presumption against conflicts, which has been applied by WTO panels and the Appellate Body in a number of cases. We believe that our interpretation of the legal status of the minor exceptions doctrine under the TRIPS Agreement is consistent with these general principles. . . .

**(vi) Summary of limitations and exceptions**

6.92 In the light of the foregoing analysis, we conclude that the context of Articles 11 and 11*bis* of the Berne Convention (1971) comprises, within the meaning of Article 31(2)(a) of the Vienna Convention, the possibility of providing minor exceptions to the exclusive rights in question. This minor exceptions doctrine has been incorporated into the TRIPS Agreement, by virtue of its Article 9.1, together with these provisions of the Berne Convention (1971). Therefore, the doctrine is relevant as forming part of the context of Articles 11(1)(ii) and 11*bis*(1)(iii) of the Berne Convention (1971) as incorporated into the TRIPS Agreement.

6.93 As regards the scope of permissible limitations and exceptions under the minor exceptions doctrine, we conclude that the doctrine is primarily concerned with de minimis use, but that otherwise its application is not limited to the examples contained in the reports of the Berne Convention revision conferences held in Brussels and Stockholm, to exclusively non-commercial uses or to exceptions in national legislation that existed prior to 1967. However, we note that the reports of the Brussels and Stockholm Conferences are inconclusive about the precise scope of exceptions that can be provided in national legislation.

6.94 We conclude that Article 13 of the TRIPS Agreement applies to Articles 11*bis*(1)(iii) and 11(1)(ii) of the Berne Convention (1971) as incorporated into the TRIPS Agreement, given that neither the express wording nor the context of Article 13 or any other provision of the TRIPS Agreement supports the interpretation that the scope of application of Article 13 is limited to the exclusive rights newly introduced under the TRIPS Agreement. . . .

## 2. The Three Criteria Test under Article 13 of the TRIPS Agreement

### *(a) General introduction*

6.97 Article 13 of the TRIPS Agreement requires that limitations and exceptions to exclusive rights (1) be confined to certain special cases, (2) do not conflict with a normal exploitation of the work, and (3) do not unreasonably prejudice the legitimate interests of the right holder. The principle of effective treaty interpretation requires us to give a distinct meaning to each of the three conditions and to avoid a reading that could reduce any of the conditions to "redundancy or inutility." The three conditions apply on a cumulative basis, each being a separate and independent requirement that must be satisfied. Failure to comply with any one of the three conditions results in the Article 13 exception being disallowed. Both parties agree on the cumulative nature of the three conditions. The Panel shares their view. It may be noted at the outset that Article 13 cannot have more than a narrow or limited operation. Its tenor, consistent as it is with the provisions of Article 9(2) of the Berne Convention (1971), discloses that it was not intended to provide for exceptions or limitations except for those of a limited nature. The narrow sphere of its operation will emerge from our discussion and application of its provisions in the paragraphs which follow. . . .

### *(c) "Not conflict with a normal exploitation of the work"*

**(i) General interpretative analysis . . .**

6.173 We agree with the European Communities that whether a limitation or an exception conflicts with a normal exploitation of a work should be judged for each exclusive right individually. We recall that this dispute primarily concerns the exclusive right under Article 11*bis*(1)(iii) of the Berne Convention (1971) as incorporated into the TRIPS Agreement, but also the exclusive right under Article 11(1)(ii). In our view, normal exploitation would presuppose the possibility for right holders to exercise separately all three exclusive rights guaranteed under the three subparagraphs of Article 11*bis*(1), as well as the rights conferred by other provisions, such as Article 11, of the Berne Convention (1971). If it were permissible to limit by a statutory exemption the exploitation of the right conferred by the third subparagraph of Article 11*bis*(1) simply because, in practice, the exploitation of the rights conferred by the first and second subparagraphs of Article

11*bis*(1) would generate the lion's share of royalty revenue, the "normal exploitation" of each of the three rights conferred separately under Article 11*bis*(1) would be undermined.

6.174 An individual analysis of the second condition for each exclusive right conferred by copyright is in line with the GATT/WTO dispute settlement practice. One panel found that GATT non-discrimination clauses do not permit balancing more favourable treatment under some procedure against a less favourable treatment under others. As another panel put it, an element of more favourable treatment would only be relevant if it would always accompany and offset an element of differential treatment causing less favourable treatment. While these cases involved the GATT non-discrimination clauses, we believe that the general principle embodied therein is mutatis mutandis relevant to the issue at hand.

6.175 We also note that the amplification of broadcast music will occur in establishments such as bars, restaurants and retail stores for the commercial benefit of the owner of the establishment. Both parties agree on the commercial nature of playing music even when customers are not directly charged for it. It may be that the amount yielded from any royalty payable as a consequence of this exploitation of the work will not be very great if one looks at the matter in the context of single establishments. But it is the accumulation of establishments which counts. . .

6.176 That leaves us with the question of how to determine whether a particular use constitutes a normal exploitation of the exclusive rights provided under Articles 11*bis*(1)(iii) and 11(1)(ii) of the Berne Convention (1971). . .

6.183 We believe that an exception or limitation to an exclusive right in domestic legislation rises to the level of a conflict with a normal exploitation of the work (i.e., the copyright or rather the whole bundle of exclusive rights conferred by the ownership of the copyright), if uses, that in principle are covered by that right but exempted under the exception or limitation, enter into economic competition with the ways that right holders normally extract economic value from that right to the work (i.e., the copyright) and thereby deprive them of significant or tangible commercial gains.

6.184 In developing a benchmark for defining the normative connotation of normal exploitation, we recall the European Communities' emphasis on the potential impact of an exception rather than on its actual effect on the market at a given point in time, given that, in its view, it is the potential effect that determines the market conditions.

6.185 We note that a consideration of both actual and potential effects when assessing the permissibility of the exemptions would be consistent with similar concepts and interpretation standards as developed in the past GATT/WTO dispute settlement practice. . . . Given that the agreements covered by the WTO form a single, integrated legal system, we deem it appropriate to develop interpretations of the legal protection conferred on intellectual property right holders under the TRIPS Agreement which are not incompatible with the treatment conferred to products under the GATT, or in respect of services and service suppliers under the GATS, in the light of pertinent dispute settlement practice.

6.186 Therefore, in respect of the exclusive rights related to musical works, we consider that normal exploitation of such works is not only affected by those who actually use them without an authorization by the right holders due to an exception or limitation, but also by those who may be induced by it to do so at any time without having to obtain a licence from the right holders or the CMOs representing them. Thus we need to take into account those whose use of musical works is free as a result of the exemptions, and also those who may choose to start using broadcast music once its use becomes free of charge.

6.187 We base our appraisal of the actual and potential effects on the commercial and technological conditions that prevail in the market currently or in the near future. What is a normal exploitation in the market-place may evolve as a result of technological developments or changing consumer preferences. Thus, while we do not wish to speculate on future developments, we need to consider the actual and potential effects of the exemptions in question in the current market and technological environment.

6.188 We do acknowledge that the extent of exercise or non-exercise of exclusive rights by right holders at a given point in time is of great relevance for assessing what is the normal exploitation with respect to a particular exclusive right in a particular market. However, in certain circumstances, current licensing practices may not provide a sufficient guideline for assessing the potential impact of an exception or limitation on normal exploitation. For example, where a particular use of works is not covered by the exclusive rights conferred in the law of a jurisdiction, the fact that the right holders do not license such use in that jurisdiction cannot be considered indicative of what constitutes normal exploitation. The same would be true in a situation where, due to lack of effective or affordable means of enforcement, right holders may not find it worthwhile or practical to exercise their rights.

6.189 Both parties are of the view that the "normalcy" of a form of exploitation should be analysed primarily by reference to the market of the WTO Member whose measure is in dispute, i.e., the U.S. market in this dispute. The European Communities is also of the view that comparative references to other countries with a similar level of socio-economic development could be relevant to corroborate or contradict data from the country primarily concerned. We note that while the WTO Members are free to choose the method of implementation, the minimum standards of protection are the same for all of them. In the present case it is enough for our purposes to take account of the specific conditions applying in the U.S. market in assessing whether the measure in question conflicts with a normal exploitation in that market, or whether the measure meets the other conditions of Article 13. . . .

[Subsequently, the Panel applied the three conditions contained in Article 13 of the TRIPS Agreement to the exemptions as set forth in Section 110(5) of the U.S. Copyright Act. The Panel held that the homestyle exemption met these requirements, unlike the business exemption, which was therefore considered inconsistent with Articles 11*bis*(1)(iii) and 11(1)(ii) of the Berne Convention (1971) as incorporated into the TRIPS Agreement by Article 9.1 of that Agreement.]

### 2. *The China–Intellectual Property Rights Case*

The following case decided by a WTO Panel in 2009 essentially concerns enforcement of intellectual property rights and will be discussed in Chapter 6. However, the case also entails issues pertaining to the protection of copyright under the TRIPS Agreement and the Berne Convention. The Copyright Law of the People's Republic of China essentially exempted works not authorized for circulation by government authorities from copyright protection. The first sentence of Article 4 of the Chinese law provided that "[w]orks the publication or distribution of which is prohibited by law shall not be protected by this Law."

## *China—Measures Affecting the Protection and Enforcement of Intellectual Property Rights*

Report of the Panel WT/DS362/R (26 January 2009)*

### Claim Under Article 5(1) of the Berne Convention (1971), as Incorporated by Article 9.1 of the TRIPS Agreement

#### Main Arguments of the Parties

7.16 The United States claims that Article 4(1) of China's Copyright Law denies the protection of the Copyright Law to certain categories of works, and refers to the text of that sentence. The United States recalls that China, during a review of its legislation in the Council

* Footnotes omitted.

for TRIPS in 2002, explained that this sentence referred to works of which the publication or distribution was prohibited by such laws and regulations as the Criminal Law, the Regulation on the Administration of Publishing Industry, the Regulation on the Administration of Broadcasting, the Regulation on the Administration of Audiovisual Products, the Regulation on the Administration of Films and the Regulations on the Administration of Telecommunication. The United States gives examples of four regulations that prohibit the publication or distribution of works under various circumstances. The United States claims that Article 4(1) of China's Copyright Law denies to the authors of works "the publication or distribution of which is prohibited by law" the broad set of rights enumerated in Article 10 of the Copyright Law, which largely encompasses the rights contemplated by the provisions of the Berne Convention (1971). Nor do authors of works denied protection of the Copyright Law benefit from the remedies specified in Articles 46 and 47 of the Copyright Law. Consequently, the authors of such works do not enjoy the minimum rights that are "specially granted" by the Berne Convention, inconsistently with Article 5(1) of that Convention. The United States submitted more detailed arguments with respect to content review in relation to Article 5(2) of the Berne Convention (1971). . . .

7.17 China responds that copyright vests upon creation and is independent of publication. Article 2 of the Copyright Law grants full copyright protection by expressly incorporating into Chinese law the rights conferred under international agreements, including the Berne Convention and the TRIPS Agreement. In contrast, Article 4(1) of the Copyright Law is extremely limited in scope. China, like many other countries in the world, bans from publication and dissemination such works as those that consist entirely of unconstitutional or immoral content. Article 4(1) simply provides that such a work shall not be protected by the Copyright Law. China argued in its first written submission that the application of Article 4(1) was not dependent on content review or any other regulatory regime related to publication and that the only result of a finding of prohibited content in that process was a denial of authority to publish, not a denial of copyright. Specifically, China argued that works that fail content review were not denied copyright protection. Article 17 of the Berne Convention (1971) subjects to the sovereign power of governments all of the rights otherwise granted by that Convention.

. . .

### Consideration by the Panel

#### Construction of the Measure at Issue

7.28 The Panel notes that this claim challenges China's Copyright Law, in particular Article 4(1), not as it has been applied in any particular instance but "as such." The parties have disagreed on the proper interpretation of that measure since shortly after the first substantive meeting. Therefore, the Panel is obliged, in accordance with its mandate, to make an objective assessment of the meaning of the relevant provisions of that measure. In this context, the Panel is mindful that, objectively, a Member is normally well-placed to explain the meaning of its own law. However, in the context of a dispute, to the extent that either party advances a particular interpretation of a provision of the measure at issue, it bears the burden of proof that its interpretation is correct. The Panel emphasizes that it examines the measure solely for the purpose of determining its conformity with China's obligations under the TRIPS Agreement.

7.29 The United States claims that Article 4(1) of the Copyright Law on its face denies immediate, automatic protection to certain works of creative authorship.

7.30 China responds that this claim is based on the "mistaken view" that copyright protection in China is contingent upon successful completion of content review. In the course of addressing the issue of when copyright vests under Chinese law, China acknowledged that Article 4(1) of the Copyright Law denies protection to certain works due to their content.

7.31 The United States stated at the first substantive meeting that, in view of that acknowledgement, China appeared simply to concede that Article 4 of the Copyright Law was inconsistent with China's obligations under the TRIPS Agreement. Canada and the European Communities, as third parties, took the same view. Argentina considered that the text of Article 4 was straightforward.

7.32 After that meeting, China clarified the terms of its earlier acknowledgement. It clarified that Article 4(1) denies "copyright protection" in the sense of enforcement but does not disturb "copyright."

7.33 The United States dismissed China's clarification as an "artificial distinction."

. . .

[Following analysis of the provisions of the Copyright Law resolving arguments concerning interpretation of Chinese and English translations, the panel addresses pertinent provisions of the TRIPS Agreement and the Berne Convention:]

## Article 5(1) of the Berne Convention (1971), as Incorporated by Article 9.1 of the TRIPS Agreement

7.104 This claim is made under Article 9.1 of the TRIPS Agreement, insofar as it incorporates Article 5(1) of the Berne Convention (1971). Article 9.1 of the TRIPS Agreement provides as follows:

> "Members shall comply with Articles 1 through 21 of the Berne Convention (1971) and the Appendix thereto. However, Members shall not have rights or obligations under this Agreement in respect of the rights conferred under Article 6*bis* of that Convention or of the rights derived therefrom."

7.105 The United States and China are both WTO Members and, accordingly, both are bound by the TRIPS Agreement, including the incorporated provisions of the Berne Convention (1971). The provisions of the Berne Convention (1971) incorporated by Article 9.1 of the TRIPS Agreement include Article 5(1) of that Convention, which provides as follows:

> "(1) Authors shall enjoy, in respect of works for which they are protected under this Convention, in countries of the Union other than the country of origin, the rights which their respective laws do now or may hereafter grant to their nationals, as well as the rights specially granted by this Convention."

7.106 Article 5(1) of the Berne Convention (1971) provides for the enjoyment of two overlapping sets of rights that have been described as "the twin pillars on which protection under the Convention rests." First, there are "the rights which their respective laws do now or may hereafter grant to their nationals." This is a national treatment obligation. The request for establishment of a panel included a claim under this part of Article 5(1) with respect to the Copyright Law in conjunction with certain other measures . . . , but this claim was not pursued.

7.107 Second, there are "the rights specially granted by this Convention." This term is not defined. However, Article 5(1) refers to rights that authors shall enjoy in respect of works. Articles 6*bis*, 8, 9, 11, 11*bis*, 11*ter*, 12, 14, 14*bis* and 14*ter* all provide for such rights. Nevertheless, the incorporation of provisions of the Berne Convention (1971), including Article 5, is subject to the terms of Article 9.1 of the TRIPS Agreement (quoted at paragraph 7.104 above). Therefore, "the rights specially granted by this Convention" as used in Article 5(1) of that Convention, as incorporated by Article 9.1 of the TRIPS Agreement, do not include the rights referred to in Article 6*bis* of the Berne Convention (1971). This Report refers to these rights in that sense.

7.108 The United States' claim relates to these rights, as a group. It makes a separate claim with respect to Article 5(2) of the Berne Convention (1971), which the Panel does not consider in this sub-section of this Report.

7.109 China submits that it has implemented Article 5(1) of the Berne Convention (1971). It offers no defence based on the terms of that Article but rather refers to Article 17 of the Berne Convention (1971), which the Panel addresses at paragraphs 7.120 to 7.139 below.

7.110 The Panel notes that the "rights specially granted" by the Berne Convention (1971), as incorporated by the TRIPS Agreement, include the exclusive right of making and of authorizing translation of works (in Article 8) and the exclusive right of authorizing reproduction of works (in Article 9), to name but the first two substantive rights.

7.111 As regards China's implementation of the "rights specially granted" by the Berne Convention (1971), the United States refers to the rights enumerated in Article 10 of the Copyright Law, as well as Articles 46 and 47 of the same Law. It does not challenge any of these particular Articles of the Copyright Law.

7.112 China agrees that it grants to authors all the substantive protections of the Berne Convention, in addition to others, through Article 10 of the Copyright Law. It submits that Article 10 of the Copyright Law fully complies with all Berne Convention requirements.

7.113 The Panel notes that many of the rights listed in subparagraphs (5) to (17) of the first paragraph of Article 10 of the Copyright Law provide for rights specially granted by the Berne Convention (1971), that the second paragraph of Article 10 provides that copyright owners may authorize others' exercise of these economic rights, and that these rights appear to be exclusive. . . . Therefore, the Panel finds that it is Article 10 of the Copyright Law that implements rights specially granted by the Berne Convention (1971).

7.114 The Panel recalls its finding . . . that Article 4(1) of the Copyright Law denies the protection of Article 10 to certain works, including those of WTO Member nationals, as the United States claims. The Panel observes that no party alleges that the denial of protection under Article 4(1) of the Copyright Law is permitted by any of the exceptions available with respect to certain specific rights under Articles 9(2), 10 or 10*bis* of the Berne Convention (1971). Nor does any party allege that the denial of protection under Article 4(1) of the Copyright Law is permitted by the exceptions provision in Article 13 of the TRIPS Agreement.

7.115 The Panel notes that both sets of rights under Article 5(1) of the Berne Convention (1971) relate to "works" for which authors are protected under that Convention. The categories of "works" in respect of which authors shall enjoy the rights specially granted by the Convention vary according to the terms of each Article granting the relevant right. For example, the rights of reproduction (Article 9) and of broadcasting (Article 11*bis*) are granted to authors of "literary and artistic works." That expression is defined, in a non-exhaustive manner, in Article 2(1) of the Berne Convention (1971).

7.116 The Panel recalls its finding . . . that the class of works denied protection under Article 4(1) of the Copyright Law includes works that have failed content review and, to the extent that they constitute copyright works, the deleted portions of works edited to satisfy content review. The Panel also recalls its findings . . . regarding the meaning of the word "works" as used in the Copyright Law, in particular in Article 4(1). No party has disputed that the "works" to which the Copyright Law, in particular Article 4(1), applies include at least some, if not all, the categories of works falling within the definition of "literary and artistic works" in Article 2(1) of the Berne Convention (1971). It is not disputed that the "works" to which Article 4(1) of China's Copyright Law applies are more extensive than those for which protection may be refused or limited under other provisions of Article 2, and under Article 2*bis*, of the Berne Convention (1971).

7.117 For the above reasons, the Panel finds that the Copyright Law is sufficiently clear on its face for the United States to have established that the Copyright Law, specifically Article 4(1), is inconsistent with Article 5(1) of the Berne Convention (1971), as incorporated by Article 9.1 of the TRIPS Agreement. This finding is subject to the Panel's consideration of Article 17 of the Berne Convention (1971), set out below.

7.118 The Panel recalls its finding at . . . and confirms that this conclusion does not apply to works never submitted for content review in China, works awaiting the results of content review in China and the unedited versions of works for which an edited version has been approved for distribution in China. However, the Panel recognizes that the potential denial of copyright protection, in the absence of a determination by the content review authorities, implies uncertainty with respect to works that do not satisfy the content criteria prior to a determination under Article 4(1) of the Copyright Law, with the consequent impact on enjoyment of rights described above. Therefore, the Panel reiterates for the record the firm position of China taken in these proceedings that:

> "Copyright vests at the time that a work is created, and is not contingent on publication. Unpublished works are protected, foreign works not yet released in the Chinese market are protected, and works never released in the Chinese market are protected."; and
>
> "Works that are unreviewed are decidedly not 'prohibited by law.' "

7.719 China has an international obligation to protect copyright in such works in accordance with Article 5(1) of the Berne Convention (1971), as incorporated by Article 9.1 of the TRIPS Agreement.

### Article 17 of the Berne Convention (1971) as Incorporated by Article 9.1 of the TRIPS Agreement

7.120 China raises a defence under Article 17 of the Berne Convention (1971), as incorporated by Article 9.1 of the TRIPS Agreement. China submits that all rights granted to authors under the Berne Convention (1971) are limited by Article 17 of that Convention, that Article 17 is not an exhaustive codification of the sovereign right to censor and that Article 17 is drafted using very expansive language "that effectively denies WTO jurisdiction in this area."

7.121 The United States responds that Article 17 of the Berne Convention (1971) does not authorize a content review system that denies all enforceable copyright protection to all works that have not been approved for publication or distribution.

7.122 The Panel recalls that Article 9.1 of the TRIPS Agreement, quoted at paragraph 7.104 above, incorporates Article 17 of the Berne Convention (1971). Article 17 of the Berne Convention (1971) provides as follows:

> "The provisions of this Convention cannot in any way affect the right of the Government of each country of the Union to permit, to control, or to prohibit, by legislation or regulation, the circulation, presentation, or exhibition of any work or production in regard to which the competent authority may find it necessary to exercise that right."

7.123 "The provisions of this Convention" as referred to in Article 17 include Article 5(1) of the Berne Convention (1971).

7.124 The parties agree that Article 17 confirms that governments have certain rights to control the exploitation of works. They do not agree as to whether those rights include a denial of all copyright protection with respect to particular works.

7.125 The Panel observes that the terms of Article 17 include certain broad phrases, notably "cannot in any way affect" and "any work or production." The use of the words "any work" (although it is slightly different in the French text) confirms that the subject-matter dealt with by Article 17 is the same as that addressed by the other substantive provisions of the Convention. However, these phrases are not used in isolation but refer to the right of a government to "permit, to control, or to prohibit . . . the circulation, presentation, or exhibition" of any work or production.

7.126 The right of a government "to control, or to prohibit" the "circulation, presentation, or exhibition" of any work or production clearly includes censorship for reasons of public order. Both China and the United States referred to the records of the diplomatic conferences of the Berne Convention, opinions in the academic literature and (in the case of China) to the WIPO Guide to the Berne Convention, that explained that Article 17 relates mainly to censorship and public order.

7.127 The Panel accepts that the three terms "circulation, presentation, or exhibition" are not necessarily an exhaustive list of the forms of exploitation of works covered by Article 17. However, a noticeable feature of these three terms is that they do not correspond to the terms used to define the substantive rights granted by the Berne Convention (1971), although they may be included within some of those rights or they may refer to acts incidental to the exercise of some of those rights. The word "exhibition" is not even used in the provisions setting out the substantive rights granted by the Convention. Therefore, it cannot be inferred that Article 17 authorizes the denial of all copyright protection in any work.

7.128 The Panel appreciates that the position may be somewhat different under Article 10 of China's Copyright Law. Article 10 of the Copyright Law grants in subparagraph (6) "the right of distribution", in subparagraph (8) "the right of exhibition," and in subparagraph (10) "the right of presentation," which may correspond to the "circulation, presentation, or exhibition" of any work in Article 17 of the Berne Convention (1971). Article 10 of the Copyright Law also grants in subparagraph (1) "the right of publication," as well as the "right of distribution," both of which appear to be directly contrary to a prohibition of the publication and/or dissemination of a work due to illegal content, as referenced in Article 4(1) of the Copyright Law. To the extent that Article 10 of the Copyright Law might provide rights additional to, or broader than, those specially granted by the Berne Convention (1971), as incorporated in the TRIPS Agreement and, hence, that Article 4(1) of that Law might deny such rights, the Panel makes no finding.

7.129 The Panel does note that the *second* sentence of Article 4 of the Copyright Law (that is not the subject of the claim in this dispute) may already address China's public policy concerns with respect to some of these rights. The second sentence of Article 4 provides as follows:

> "Copyright owners, in exercising their copyright, shall not violate the Constitution or laws or prejudice the public interests."

7.130 This provision does not deny copyright protection but, as China acknowledges, obliges copyright owners and authorized parties to respect the law in the exercise of their rights. In contrast, the first sentence of Article 4 of the Copyright Law denies all copyright protection with respect to particular works.

7.131 China draws the Panel's attention to the WIPO Guide to the Berne Convention, which states as follows regarding Article 17 of the Berne Convention (1971):

> "It covers the right of governments to take the necessary steps to maintain public order. On this point, the sovereignty of member countries is not affected by the rights given by the Convention. Authors may exercise their rights only if that exercise does not conflict with public order. The former must give way to the latter. The Article therefore gives Union countries certain powers to control."

7.132 The Panel agrees with this interpretation. A government's right to permit, to control, or to prohibit the circulation, presentation, or exhibition of a work may interfere with the exercise of certain rights with respect to a protected work by the copyright owner or a third party authorized by the copyright owner. However, there is no reason to suppose that censorship will eliminate those rights entirely with respect to a particular work.

7.133 With respect to those rights that are granted by the Berne Convention (1971), China is unable to explain why Article 4(1) of its Copyright Law provides for the complete denial of their protection with respect to particular works. Without prejudice to the range of rights that are granted by the Berne Convention (1971), it suffices to note that they are mostly exclusive rights of authorizing certain acts with respect to protected works. An exclusive right of authorizing necessarily entails the right to prevent others from carrying out the relevant acts with respect to protected works. China is unable to explain why censorship interferes with copyright owners' rights to prevent third parties from exploiting prohibited works.

7.134 China argues that such copyright protection is a "legal and material nullity," as economic rights are pre-empted by public prohibition. It also argues that copyright enforcement is meaningless in this context. China asks the Panel to note that Article 4(1) of the Copyright Law is an exceedingly narrow provision of law with negligible implications in the marketplace and in terms of any nullification or impairment of benefits to Members.

7.135 The Panel notes that copyright and government censorship address different rights and interests. Copyright protects private rights, as reflected in the fourth recital of the preamble to the TRIPS Agreement, whilst government censorship addresses public interests.

7.136 In response to a question from the Panel, China indicated that it "will always enforce copyrights against infringing edited versions, even when there is no edited version authorized by the author." It did not explain how this was possible under its law. In response to another question from the Panel, China indicated that if an unprotected, prohibited work later becomes legal, it will protect copyright in the work going forward. This might require a new court or NCAC determination but, in China's view, such a requirement does not constitute a formality under Article 5(2) of the Berne Convention (1971). In any event, the Panel recalls that Article 4(1) of the Copyright Law produces commercial uncertainty prior to a determination that a work is prohibited.

7.137 China maintains that public censorship renders private enforcement unnecessary, that it enforces prohibitions on content seriously, and that this removes banned content from the public domain more securely than would be possible through copyright enforcement. The Panel notes that these assertions, even if they were relevant, are not substantiated.

7.138 The Panel also recalls that if a measure infringes China's obligations under a covered agreement, in accordance with Article 3.8 of the DSU, this is considered prima facie to constitute a case of nullification or impairment. Even if the measure at issue has had no actual impact on foreign works to date, it has a *potential* impact on works of WTO Member nationals.

7.139 For the above reasons, the Panel confirms its finding . . . and concludes that, notwithstanding China's rights recognized in Article 17 of the Berne Convention (1971), the Copyright Law, specifically Article 4(1), is inconsistent with Article 5(1) of the Berne Convention (1971), as incorporated by Article 9.1 of the TRIPS Agreement.

## NOTES AND QUESTIONS

**1.** We now have WTO dispute settlement panel decisions addressing the scope of exceptions in the fields of patent (*Canada—Generic Pharmaceuticals, supra* Chapter 2), trademark (*EC—Geographical Indications, supra* Chapter 3), and copyright (*U.S.—Copyright Act, China—Intellectual Property Rights, supra*). It is of some interest that none of these panel decisions were appealed to the Appellate Body, even though most WTO dispute settlement decisions are appealed, and the Appellate Body often disagrees with the panel on issues of legal doctrine (even if, less frequently, on the practical outcome). What do you think accounts for the absence of appeals on decisions relating to IP exceptions? Are governments reluctant to request the "last word" on the scope of exceptions from the Appellate Body? Is it just a coincidence that in these four cases both governments were satisfied with the outcome? Could it be that the inconsistencies of domestic law with international law are more obvious than in other cases?

**2.** The WTO dispute settlement system is effectively determining the international scope of permissible exceptions in copyright law. Does the WTO adequately replicate national constitutional systems and courts such that you are comfortable with allocating this decision making "upward" to the global level of judicial governance?

**3.** What can we learn from *China—Measures Affecting the Protection and Enforcement of Intellectual Property Rights* for the trade and human rights debate? While the authorization of content cannot exclude copyright protection, it nevertheless inhibits the circulation of copyright protected material. How does that relate to freedom of expression and freedom of information? The same problem arose in relation to authorization exclusively reserved to state-controlled enterprises of audiovisual services in *China—Measures Affecting Trading Rights and Distribution Services and Certain Publications and Audiovisual Entertainment Products*, Report by the Appellate Body, WT/DS 363/AR/R (21 Dec. 2009). In this case, the Appellate Body found that authorization regarding public morals exclusively granted to state-owned companies discriminates against foreign-controlled operators. It fails the necessity test under the general exception clauses and is inconsistent with WTO law.

## C. The WIPO Copyright Treaty

The TRIPS Agreement negotiations focused on "trade-related" aspects of IPRs. It was not until somewhat late in the TRIPS negotiations (which formally commenced in 1986) that it became apparent that development of the Internet and other digital media might play a significant role in international commerce. In this regard, the TRIPS Agreement was a step behind developments in the global economic arena even before the proverbial ink had dried. One step following the TRIPS Agreement would be the negotiation of new rules for the digital environment. The first set of these negotiations took place within WIPO.

### *1. Negotiation*

In the following brief excerpt, Pamela Samuelson describes and analyzes the final stage of negotiation of the WIPO Copyright Treaty (WCT) in 1996.

**Pamela Samuelson***

## *The U.S. Digital Agenda at WIPO*

### I. Introduction

In December 1996, the World Intellectual Property Organization (WIPO) hosted a diplomatic conference in Geneva to consider three proposals to update world intellectual property law. The conferees considered draft treaties to revise treatment of copyright issues, legal protection for sound recordings, and legal protection for the contents of databases. Each

* 37 Va. J. Int'l L. 369 (1997).

contained provisions intended to respond to challenges that global digital networks pose for intellectual property law. . . .

The digital agenda that Clinton administration officials pursued in Geneva was almost identical to the digital agenda they had put before the U.S. Congress during roughly the same time period. Notwithstanding the fact that this digital agenda had proven so controversial in the U.S. Congress that the bills to implement it were not even reported out of committee, Clinton administration officials persisted in promoting these proposals in Geneva and pressing for an early diplomatic conference to adopt them. For a time, it appeared that administration officials might be able to get in Geneva what they could not get from the U.S. Congress, for the draft treaties published by WIPO in late August 1996 contained language that, if adopted without amendment at the diplomatic conference in December, would have substantially implemented the U.S. digital agenda, albeit with some European gloss. Had this effort succeeded in Geneva, Clinton administration officials would almost certainly have then argued to Congress that ratification of the treaties was necessary to confirm U.S. leadership in the world intellectual property community and to promote the interests of U.S. copyright industries in the world market for information products and services. . . .

### III. Components of the U.S. Digital Agenda and How They Fared at WIPO

The U.S. White Paper's digital agenda aimed to:

> 1. give copyright owners control over every use of copyrighted works in digital form by interpreting existing law as being violated whenever users make even temporary reproductions of works in the random access memories of their computers;
>
> 2. give copyright owners control over every transmission of works in digital form by amending the copyright statute so that digital transmissions will be regarded as distributions of copies to the public;
>
> 3. eliminate fair-use rights whenever a use might be licensed . . .;
>
> 4. deprive the public of the "first sale" rights it has long enjoyed in the print world . . . because the White Paper treats electronic forwarding as a violation of both the reproduction and distribution rights of copyright law;
>
> 5. attach copyright management information to digital copies of a work, ensuring that publishers can track every use made of digital copies and trace where each copy resides on the network and what is being done with it at any time;
>
> 6. protect every work technologically (by encryption, for example) and make illegal any attempt to circumvent that protection; [and]
>
> 7. force online service providers to become copyright police. . . .

The only new element in the U.S. digital agenda at WIPO, as compared with the digital agenda reflected in the White Paper, was a late-added proposal by the U.S. delegation calling for a treaty to create a new form of legal protection for the contents of databases. U.S. officials submitted this in reaction to a European proposal that they apparently thought needed improvement.

. . .

### IV. Reflections on the Outcome in Geneva . . .

#### B. Measures of Success for the U.S. Digital Agenda at WIPO

Whether one judges U.S. efforts to promote a digital agenda at WIPO as a success or a failure depends on what one decides to measure. By comparison with the high-protectionist agenda reflected in the White Paper and the U.S. submissions to WIPO, one would have to say that the U.S. efforts were largely unsuccessful. The conference rejected the temporary copying proposals that had initially had U.S. support. It decided to treat digital transmissions as communications to the public, rather than as distributions of copies (which may bring with it a widened possibility for some private transmissions of works). The treaty not only preserved existing user right privileges in national laws; it recognized that new exceptions might appropriately be created. The Chairman's variant on the U.S. White Paper's anti-circumvention provision garnered almost no support. Even though the treaty contains a rights management information provision, it is watered down by comparison with what the U.S. delegation had sought. Moreover, the U.S. model for a database treaty was so objectionable that it was dropped virtually without discussion from the agenda in Geneva.

Seen from another perspective, however, the U.S. digital agenda had considerable success. It is now clear that copyright law applies in the digital environment, and that storage of protected works is a reproduction that can be controlled by copyright owners. The treaty also protects copyright owners from digital transmissions insofar as they constitute communications to the public. The treaty reaffirms the three-step test that limits national authority to adopt exceptions or limitations to certain special cases that do not conflict with a normal exploitation of the work or unreasonably prejudice the legitimate interests of the author. It also requires states to have adequate protection and effective remedies against circumvention technologies and services, and to protect rights management information from alteration and removal insofar as these conceal or facilitate infringement. Finally, WIPO is to sponsor further discussions concerning a database treaty.

The copyright treaty that emerged from the diplomatic conference was a real success for the United States in part because that treaty is actually more consistent with the letter and spirit of U.S. copyright law than the digital agenda that Commissioner Lehman initially sought to promote in Geneva.

## NOTES AND QUESTIONS

**1.** Pamela Samuelson called attention to a provision added to the WIPO Copyright Treaty's preamble at the diplomatic conference that recognizes the need to maintain a balance among interests. Why might a provision in the preamble of a treaty be important? The preamble does not create specific rights or obligations. How might it be used?

**2.** Negotiation of the WCT illustrated—as does Article 6 of the TRIPS Agreement—that governments do not agree on an approach to the exhaustion of rights in the international context. It was once again made clear in the WCT negotiations that the subject matter remains sufficiently controversial that an attempt to find common ground might have impeded the successful conclusion of the treaty. The Chairman's drafts of the Copyright Treaty and the Performances and Phonograms Treaties included alternatives that would either have precluded international exhaustion, or reserved discretion regarding the exhaustion approach to the contracting states. The Chairman's drafts did not propose an alternative mandating international exhaustion. *See* Chairman of the Committee of Experts, Basic Proposal for the Substantive Provisions of the Treaty on Certain Questions Concerning the Protection of Literary and Artistic Works to be Considered by the Diplomatic Conference, WIPO Doc. CRNR/DC/4, Aug. 30, 1996, at art. 8. Examine Article 6(2) of the WCT and Article 8(2) and 12(2) of the WIPO Performances and Phonograms Treaty. The exhaustion approach has been left again to the discretion of contracting states.

**3.** Telecommunications service providers played a major role in the WCT negotiations. These providers were greatly concerned over potential liability for content carried over the Internet and other digital transmission media to which they provide access. The concerns of the service providers are addressed *in extenso* in the U.S. Digital Millennium Copyright Act and the EU law on intermediaries' liability, see *infra*, as well as in the IP chapters of bilateral and regional trade agreements of the United States.

### 2. *Norms of the WCT*

The following excerpt from the WIPO Intellectual Property Handbook describes the resulting WCT norms.

## *The WIPO Copyright Treaty (WCT)**

#### Introduction . . .

5.211 After the adoption of the TRIPS Agreement under the auspices of GATT, the preparatory work of new copyright and related rights norms in the WIPO committees was intensified to deal with problems not addressed by the TRIPS Agreement. To this end, in 1996 the WIPO Diplomatic Conference on Certain Copyright and Related Rights Questions adopted two treaties, the WIPO Copyright Treaty (WCT) and the WIPO Performances and Phonograms Treaty (WPPT). . . .

#### Substantive Provisions of the WCT

#### Provisions Relating to the So-Called "Digital Agenda"

5.217 During the preparatory work, it became clear that the most important and most urgent task was to clarify existing norms and, where necessary, create new norms to respond to the problems raised by digital technology, and particularly by the Internet. The issues addressed in this context were referred to as the "digital agenda."

5.218 The provisions of the WCT relating to the "agenda" cover the following issues—the rights applicable to the storage and transmission of works in digital systems, the limitations on and exceptions to rights in a digital environment, technological measures of protection and rights management information. As discussed below, the right of distribution may also be relevant in respect of transmissions in digital networks; its scope, however, is much broader. Also due to its relationship with the right of rental, the right of distribution is discussed, together with the former right, below.

#### Storage of Works in Digital Form in an Electronic Medium

5.219 In June 1982, a WIPO/Unesco Committee of Governmental Experts clarified that storage of works in an electronic medium is reproduction. The Diplomatic Conference adopted an agreed statement which reads as follows: "The reproduction right, as set out in Article 9 of the Berne Convention, and the exceptions permitted thereunder, fully apply in the digital environment, in particular to the use of works in digital form. It is understood that the storage of a protected work in digital form in an electronic medium constitutes a reproduction within the meaning of Article 9 of the Berne Convention."

5.220 It follows from this first sentence that Article 9(1) of the Convention is fully applicable. This means that the concept of reproduction under Article 9(1) of the Convention, which extends to reproduction "in any manner or form" irrespective of the duration of the reproduction, must not be restricted merely because a reproduction is in digital form through

* WIPO Intellectual Property Handbook (as of April 2006).

storage in an electronic memory, and just because a reproduction is of a temporary nature. It also follows from the same first sentence that Article 9(2) of the Convention is also fully applicable, which offers an appropriate basis to introduce any justified exceptions such as the above-mentioned cases of transient and incidental reproductions in national legislation, in harmony with the "three-step test" provided for in that provision of the Convention (see below, in this section, under "Limitations and Exceptions").

5.221 The second sentence of the agreed statement confirms the definition of storage of works. It is another matter that the word "storage" may still be interpreted in somewhat differing ways.

### Transmission on Digital Networks

5.222 During the preparatory work, an agreement emerged that the transmission of works on the Internet and in similar networks should be the object of an exclusive right of authorization of the author or other copyright owner, with appropriate exceptions. . . .

5.225 A specific solution was therefore adopted, which provided that the act of digital transmission should be described in a neutral way, free from specific legal characterization; that such a description should not be excessively technical and, at the same time, should convey the interactive nature of digital transmissions; that, in respect of legal characterization of the exclusive right—that is, in respect of the actual choice of the right or rights to be applied—sufficient freedom should be left to national legislation; and, finally, that the gaps in the Berne Convention in the coverage of the relevant rights—the right of communication to the public and the right of distribution—should be covered. This solution was referred to as the "umbrella solution."

5.226 The WCT applies this "umbrella solution" by extending applicability of the right of communication to the public to all categories of works, and clarifies that that right also covers transmissions in interactive systems described in a manner free of legal characterization. Thus Article 8 of the Treaty reads as follows: "Without prejudice to the provisions of Articles 11(1)(ii), 11*bis*(1)(i) and (ii), 11*ter*(1)(ii), 14(1)(ii) and 14*bis*(1) of the Berne Convention, authors of literary and artistic works shall enjoy the exclusive right of authorizing any communication to the public of their works, by wire or wireless means, including the making available to the public of their works in such a way that members of the public may access these works from a place and at a time individually chosen by them." It was stated in the Diplomatic Conference that Contracting Parties are free to implement the obligation to grant an exclusive right to authorize such "making available to the public" also through the application of a right other than the right of communication to the public or through the combination of different rights. By the "other" right, first of all, the right of distribution was meant, but "other" right might also be a specific new right such as that of making available to the public as provided for in Articles 10 and 14 of the WPPT.

5.227 An agreed statement was adopted concerning this Article 8. It reads as follows: "It is understood that the mere provision of physical facilities for enabling or making a communication does not in itself amount to communication within the meaning of this Treaty or the Berne Convention. It is further understood that nothing in Article 8 precludes a Contracting Party from applying Article 11*bis*(2)." This statement is intended to clarify the issue of liability of service and access providers in digital networks like the Internet: it is evident that, if a person engages in an act not covered by a right provided in the Convention (and in corresponding national laws), such person has no direct liability for the act covered by such a right.

### Limitations and Exceptions in the Digital Environment

5.228 An agreed statement was adopted in this respect, which reads as follows: "It is understood that the provisions of Article 10 [of the Treaty] permit Contracting Parties to carry forward and appropriately extend into the digital environment limitations and exceptions in their national laws which have been considered acceptable under the Berne Convention. Similarly, these provisions should be understood to permit Contracting Parties to devise new exceptions and limitations that are appropriate in the digital network environment. It is also understood that Article 10(2) [of the Treaty] neither reduces nor extends the scope of applicability of the limitations and exceptions permitted by the Berne Convention." The provisions of Article 10 of the Treaty referred to in the agreed statement are discussed below. It is obvious that extending limitations and exceptions into the digital environment, or devising new exceptions and limitations for such environment, is subject to the three-step test included in that Article (see below, in this section, under "Limitations and Exceptions").

### Technological Measures of Protection and Rights Management Information

5.229 No rights in respect of digital uses of works, particularly uses on the Internet, may be applied efficiently without the support of technological measures of protection and rights management information necessary to license and monitor uses. The application of such measures and information are left to the interested right-owners, but appropriate legal provisions are included in Articles 11 and 12 of the Treaty.

5.230 Under Article 11 of the Treaty, Contracting Parties must provide "adequate legal protection and effective legal remedies against the circumvention of effective technological measures that are used by authors in connection with the exercise of their rights under this Treaty or the Berne Convention and that restrict acts, in respect of their works, which are not authorized by the authors concerned or permitted by law."

5.231 Article 12(1) of the Treaty obliges Contracting Parties to "provide adequate and effective legal remedies against any person knowingly performing any of the following acts knowing, or with respect to civil remedies having reasonable grounds to know, that it will induce, enable, facilitate or conceal an infringement of any right covered by this Treaty or the Berne Convention, (i) to remove or alter any electronic rights management information without authority; (ii) to distribute, import for distribution, broadcast or communicate to the public, without authority, works or copies of works knowing that electronic rights management information has been removed or altered without authority." Article 12(2) defines "rights management information" as meaning "information which identifies the work, the author of the work, the owner of any right in the work, or information about the terms and conditions of use of the work, and any numbers or codes that represent such information, when any of these items of information is attached to a copy of a work or appears in connection with the communication of a work to the public."

5.232 An agreed statement was adopted by the Diplomatic Conference concerning Article 12 of the Treaty, which is in two parts. The first part reads: "It is understood that the reference to infringement of any right covered by this Treaty or the Berne Convention includes both exclusive rights and rights of remuneration." The second part reads: "It is further understood that Contracting Parties will not rely on this Article to devise or implement rights management systems that would have the effect of imposing formalities which are not permitted under the Berne Convention or this Treaty, prohibiting the free movement of goods or impeding the enjoyment of rights under this Treaty."

### Other Substantive Provisions . . .

5.235 Article 3 of the Treaty, dealt with above, also prescribes the *mutatis mutandis* application of Articles 2 and 2*bis* of the Berne Convention. The scope of the subject matter covered by copyright, particularly in relation to computer programs and databases, was explored in the WCT. The Treaty shares the same concept of literary and artistic works as is found in the Berne Convention. The Treaty also includes, however, some clarifications on the matter in common with those in the TRIPS Agreement.

5.236 First, Article 2 of the Treaty clarifies that "Copyright protection extends to expressions and not to ideas, procedures, methods of operation or mathematical concepts as such." This is virtually the same as the clarification included in Article 9.2 of the TRIPS Agreement. Nor is the principle reflected in Article 2 new in the context of the Berne Convention, since countries party to the Convention have always understood the scope of protection under the Convention in that way.

5.237 Second, Articles 4 and 5 of the Treaty contain clarifications concerning the protection of computer programs as literary works and of compilations of data (databases), which are similar to those included in Article 10 of the TRIPS Agreement. Two agreed statements specify that the scope of protection for computer programs under Article 4 of the Treaty and for compilations of data (databases) under Article 5 of the Treaty "is consistent with Article 2 of the Berne Convention and on par with the relevant provisions of the TRIPS Agreement."

**Rights to Be Protected**

5.238 Article 6(1) of the WCT provides an exclusive right to authorize the making available to the public of originals and copies of works through sale or other transfer of ownership, that is, an exclusive right of distribution. Under the Berne Convention, it is only in respect of cinematographic works that such a right is granted explicitly. Such a right, surviving at least until the first sale of copies, may be deduced as an indispensable corollary to the right of reproduction, and, in some legal systems, the right of distribution is in fact recognized on this basis. Article 6(1) of the WCT should be considered at least a useful clarification of the obligations under the Berne Convention (and also under the TRIPS Agreement, which includes by reference the relevant provisions of the Convention), and at the most as adding to both.

5.239 Article 6(2) of the Treaty deals with the issue of the exhaustion of the right of distribution. It does not oblige Contracting States to choose national/regional exhaustion or international exhaustion—or to regulate at all the issue of exhaustion—of the right of distribution after the first sale or other first transfer of ownership of the original or a copy of the work, with the authorization of the author.

5.240 Article 7 of the Treaty provides an exclusive right of authorizing commercial rental to the public in respect of the same categories of works—computer programs, cinematographic works and works embodied in phonograms, as determined in the national laws of Contracting Parties—as those covered by Articles 11 and 14.4 of the TRIPS Agreement, and with the same exceptions.

The exceptions are in respect of computer programs which are not themselves the essential objects of the rental, in respect of cinematographic works unless commercial rental leads to widespread copying of such works, materially impairing the exclusive right of reproduction, and in respect of a Contracting Party which, on April 15, 1994, had and still has in force a system of equitable remuneration for rental of copies of works included in phonograms, instead of an exclusive right: in the latter case the Contracting Party may maintain that system provided that commercial rental does not give rise to the material impairment of the exclusive right of authorization.

5.241 An agreed statement was adopted by the Diplomatic Conference on Articles 6 and 7 of the Treaty. It reads: "As used in these Articles, the expressions 'copies' and 'original and copies,' being subject to the right of distribution and the right of rental under the said Articles, refer exclusively to fixed copies that can be put into circulation as tangible objects."

**Duration of Protection of Photographic Works**

5.242 Article 9 of the WCT removes the unjustified discrimination against photographic works as to the duration of protection. It obliges Contracting Parties not to apply Article 7(4) of the Berne Convention, which, as also for works of applied art, prescribes a shorter term—25 years—for photographic works than for the general 50-year term.

**Limitations and Exceptions**

5.243 Paragraph (1) of Article 10 determines the types of limitations on, or exceptions to, the rights granted under the Treaty which may be applied, while paragraph (2) of that Article provides criteria for the application of limitations of, or exceptions to, the rights under the Berne Convention.

5.244 Both paragraphs use the three-step test included in Article 9(2) of the Berne Convention to determine the limitations and exceptions allowed. That is to say, exceptions and limitations are only allowed in certain special cases:

—provided that they do not conflict with a normal exploitation of the work;
—provided that they do not unreasonably prejudice the legitimate interests of the authors.

5.245 Under Article 9(2) of the Berne Convention, this test is applicable only to the right of reproduction, while both paragraphs of Article 10 of the Treaty cover all rights provided for in the Treaty and the Berne Convention respectively. In this, the provisions of Article 10 are similar to Article 13 of the TRIPS Agreement, which applies the same test for all rights provided for in the TRIPS Agreement, either directly or through inclusion by reference to the substantive provisions of the Berne Convention.

**Application in Time**

5.246 Article 13 of the WCT refers simply to Article 18 of the Berne Convention to determine the works to which the Treaty applies at the moment of its entry into force for a given Contracting State, and stipulates that the provisions of that Article must also be applied to the Treaty.

**Enforcement of Rights**

5.247 Article 14, paragraph (1) is a *mutatis mutandis* version of Article 36(1) of the Berne Convention. It provides that "Contracting Parties undertake to adopt, in accordance with their legal systems, the measures necessary to ensure the application of this Treaty."

5.248 Paragraph (2) of Article 14 is a *mutatis mutandis* version of the first sentence of Article 41.1 of the TRIPS Agreement. It reads: "Contracting Parties shall ensure that enforcement procedures are available under their law so as to permit effective action against any act of infringement of rights covered by this Treaty, including expeditious remedies to prevent infringements and remedies which constitute a deterrent to further infringements.". . .

## NOTES AND QUESTIONS

**1.** In the *United States—Copyright Act* decision, *supra*, the panel also addressed the issue of the role of the WCT in the interpretation of the TRIPS Agreement. The panel said:

> 6.70 In paragraph 6.66 we discussed the need to interpret the Berne Convention and the TRIPS Agreement in a way that reconciles the texts of these two treaties and avoids a conflict between them, given that they form the overall framework for multilateral copyright protection. The same principle should also apply to the relationship between the TRIPS Agreement and the WCT. The WCT is designed to be compatible with this framework, incorporating or using much of the language of the Berne Convention and the TRIPS Agreement. The WCT was unanimously concluded at a diplomatic conference organized under the auspices of WIPO in December 1996, one year after the WTO Agreement entered into force, in which 127 countries participated. Most of these countries were also participants in the TRIPS negotiations and are Members of the WTO. For these reasons, it is relevant to seek contextual guidance also in the WCT when developing interpretations that avoid conflicts within this overall framework, except where these treaties explicitly

> contain different obligations. The subsequent WCT was designed to be compatible with the TRIPS and the Berne Convention framework and should [be] seen as a part of the overall framework of multilateral copyright.

**2.** As in the TRIPS Agreement, rental rights are expressly limited to computer programs, videos, and phonograms (which include CDs). Why is the rental right limited to these three subject matters? Why is the video rental right only applicable when such rental has led to widespread copying of videos to the detriment of the author?

### *3. Implementation of the WCT at National and Regional Levels*

In 1998, two years after conclusion of the WCT, the United States enacted the Digital Millennium Copyright Act (DMCA), which revised substantial parts of Title 17 of the U.S. Copyright Act to implement the WCT. In 2001, the European Union adopted Directive 2001/29/EC of the European Parliament and of the Council of 22 May 2001 on the harmonisation of certain aspects of copyright and related rights in the information society (OJ 2001 L 167, p. 10) and a number of follow-up instruments to clarify the responsibilities of intermediaries for third-party infringements. Implementation of the WCT is taking place around the globe.

The DMCA makes certain amendments to existing copyright rules. It also adds new sections to the U.S. Copyright Act. For instance, new Section 512 creates so-called "safe harbors". Online service providers are granted immunity from damage awards if they remove, upon notification by the copyright owner, allegedly infringing material – the "notice and take down" procedure.[12]

In addition, newly added Section 1201 of the Copyright Act makes it a copyright offense to circumvent a technological measure that effectively controls access to a copyrighted work, or to manufacture, sell, or traffic in products the only significant purpose for which is circumvention.[13] This section finds its basic premise in Article 11 of the WCT.

Article 11 of the WCT provides flexibility for implementing "adequate legal protection and effective legal remedies." Section 1201 of the U.S. Copyright Act[14] has become the subject of debate concerning the scope and limitations of the legal protection it affords.[15] Some claim the U.S. Congress went well beyond the requirements of the WCT, mainly due to the successful efforts of copyright-dependent industry interest groups seeking broad anticircumvention provisions.[16] Some legal scholars, civil liberties groups, and computer-technology interest groups have argued that DMCA's anticircumvention provisions will hinder legitimate justification for bypassing access controls, including for reverse engineering, fair use, and scientific research.

A typical technological measure is "CSS" (Content Scrambling System) copy protection encoded on DVDs. Independent programmers developed software called "DeCSS," which breaks the scrambling algorithm of the CSS system, permitting copying and access by non-authorized operating systems.

*Universal City Studios v. Corley*, decided on November 28, 2001 by the U.S. Court of Appeals for the Second Circuit, provides background on technical issues and was the first case to address the scope and constitutionality of the DMCA's Section 1201. It is followed by

---

12. *See* 17 U.S.C. §512. The procedures are detailed in subsections 512(c)(3), 512(f), and 512(g).

13. *See* 17 U.S.C. §1201.

14. For a detailed overview of the provisions, *see* https://www.copyright.gov/fedreg/2005/70fr57526.htmland *Universal City Studios v. Corley, infra.*

15. For background, *see* Pamela Samuelson, *Intellectual Property and the Digital Economy: Why the Anti-circumvention Regulations Need to Be Revised,* 14 Berkeley Tech. L. J. 1 (1999).

16. *Id.* at 2.

the CJEU's interpretation of EU copyright harmonizing legislation addressing technological protection measures.

## *Universal City Studios v. Corley*

273 F.3d 429 (2d Cir. 2001)

NEWMAN, CIRCUIT JUDGE.

When the Framers of the First Amendment prohibited Congress from making any law "abridging the freedom of speech," they were not thinking about computers, computer programs, or the Internet. But neither were they thinking about radio, television, or movies. Just as the inventions at the beginning and middle of the 20th century presented new First Amendment issues, so does the cyber revolution at the end of that century. This appeal raises significant First Amendment issues concerning one aspect of computer technology—encryption to protect materials in digital form from unauthorized access. The appeal challenges the constitutionality of the Digital Millennium Copyright Act ("DMCA"), 17 U.S.C. §1201 et seq. (Supp. V 1999) and the validity of an injunction entered to enforce the DMCA.

Defendant-Appellant Eric C. Corley and his company, 2600 Enterprises, Inc., (collectively "Corley," "the Defendants," or "the Appellants") appeal from the amended final judgment of the United States District Court for the Southern District of New York (Lewis A. Kaplan, District Judge), entered August 23, 2000, enjoining them from various actions concerning a decryption program known as "DeCSS." *Universal City Studios, Inc. v. Reimerdes*, 111 F. Supp. 2d 346 (S.D.N.Y. 2000) ("*Universal II*"). The injunction primarily bars the Appellants from posting DeCSS on their web site and from knowingly linking their web site to any other web site on which DeCSS is posted. *Id.* at 346-47. We affirm.

### INTRODUCTION

Understanding the pending appeal and the issues it raises requires some familiarity with technical aspects of computers and computer software, especially software called "digital versatile disks" or "DVDs," which are optical media storage devices currently designed to contain movies. Those lacking such familiarity will be greatly aided by reading Judge Kaplan's extremely lucid opinion, *Universal City Studios, Inc. v. Reimerdes*, 111 F. Supp. 2d 294 (S.D.N.Y. 2000) ("*Universal I*"), beginning with his helpful section "The Vocabulary of this Case" *id.* at 305-09. . . .

In November 1999, Corley posted a copy of the decryption computer program "DeCSS" on his web site, http://www.2600.com ("2600.com"). DeCSS is designed to circumvent "CSS," the encryption technology that motion picture studios place on DVDs to prevent the unauthorized viewing and copying of motion pictures. Corley also posted on his web site links to other web sites where DeCSS could be found.

Plaintiffs-Appellees are eight motion picture studios that brought an action in the Southern District of New York seeking injunctive relief against Corley under the DMCA. Following a full non-jury trial, the District Court entered a permanent injunction barring Corley from posting DeCSS on his web site or from knowingly linking via a hyperlink to any other web site containing DeCSS. *Universal II*, 111 F. Supp. 2d at 346-47. The District Court rejected Corley's constitutional attacks on the statute and the injunction. *Universal I*, 111 F. Supp. 2d at 325-45.

Corley renews his constitutional challenges on appeal. Specifically, he argues primarily that: (1) the DMCA oversteps limits in the Copyright Clause on the duration of copyright protection; (2) the DMCA as applied to his dissemination of DeCSS violates the First Amendment because computer code is "speech" entitled to full First Amendment protection and the DMCA fails to survive the exacting scrutiny accorded statutes that regulate "speech"; and (3) the DMCA violates the First Amendment and the Copyright Clause by unduly obstructing the "fair use" of copyrighted materials. Corley also argues that the statute is susceptible to, and should therefore be given, a narrow interpretation that avoids alleged constitutional objections.

**BACKGROUND . . .**

## I. CSS

The movie studios were reluctant to release movies in digital form until they were confident they had in place adequate safeguards against piracy of their copyrighted movies. The studios took several steps to minimize the piracy threat. First, they settled on the DVD as the standard digital medium for home distribution of movies. The studios then sought an encryption scheme to protect movies on DVDs. They enlisted the help of members of the consumer electronics and computer industries, who in mid-1996 developed the Content Scramble System ("CSS"). CSS is an encryption scheme that employs an algorithm configured by a set of "keys" to encrypt a DVD's contents. The algorithm is a type of mathematical formula for transforming the contents of the movie file into gibberish; the "keys" are in actuality strings of 0's and 1's that serve as values for the mathematical formula. Decryption in the case of CSS requires a set of "player keys" contained in compliant DVD players, as well as an understanding of the CSS encryption algorithm. Without the player keys and the algorithm, a DVD player cannot access the contents of a DVD. With the player keys and the algorithm, a DVD player can display the movie on a television or a computer screen, but does not give a viewer the ability to use the copy function of the computer to copy the movie or to manipulate the digital content of the DVD. . . .

## II. DeCSS

In September 1999, Jon Johansen, a Norwegian teenager, collaborating with two unidentified individuals he met on the Internet, reverse-engineered a licensed DVD player designed to operate on the Microsoft operating system, and culled from it the player keys and other information necessary to decrypt CSS. The record suggests that Johansen was trying to develop a DVD player operable on Linux, an alternative operating system that did not support any licensed DVD players at that time. In order to accomplish this task, Johansen wrote a decryption program executable on Microsoft's operating system. That program was called, appropriately enough, "DeCSS." . . .

In November 1999, Corley wrote and placed on his web site, 2600.com, an article about the DeCSS phenomenon. His web site is an auxiliary to the print magazine, 2600: The Hacker Quarterly, which Corley has been publishing since 1984. As the name suggests, the magazine is designed for "hackers," as is the web site. While the magazine and the web site cover some issues of general interest to computer users—such as threats to online privacy—the focus of the publications is on the vulnerability of computer security systems, and more specifically, how to exploit that vulnerability in order to circumvent the security systems. Representative articles explain how to steal an Internet domain name and how to break into the computer systems at Federal Express. *Universal I*, 111 F. Supp. 2d at 308-09.

Corley's article about DeCSS detailed how CSS was cracked, and described the movie industry's efforts to shut down web sites posting DeCSS. It also explained that DeCSS could be used to copy DVDs. At the end of the article, the Defendants posted copies of the object and source code of DeCSS. In Corley's words, he added the code to the story because "in a journalistic world, . . . you have to show your evidence . . . and particularly in the magazine that I work for, people want to see specifically what it is that we are referring to," including "what evidence . . . we have" that there is in fact technology that circumvents CSS. Trial Tr. at 823. Writing about DeCSS without including the DeCSS code would have been, to Corley, "analogous to printing a story about a picture and not printing the picture." *Id.* at 825. Corley also added to the article links that he explained would take the reader to other web sites where DeCSS could be found. *Id.* at 791, 826, 827, 848.

2600.com was only one of hundreds of web sites that began posting DeCSS near the end of 1999. The movie industry tried to stem the tide by sending cease-and-desist letters to many of these sites. These efforts met with only partial success; a number of sites refused to remove DeCSS. In January 2000, the studios filed this lawsuit.

## III. The DMCA

The DMCA was enacted in 1998 to implement the World Intellectual Property Organization Copyright Treaty ("WIPO Treaty"), which requires contracting parties to "provide adequate legal protection and effective legal remedies against the circumvention of effective technological measures that are used by authors in connection with the exercise of their rights under this Treaty or the Berne Convention and that restrict acts, in respect of their works, which are not authorized by the authors concerned or permitted by law." WIPO Treaty, Apr. 12, 1997, art. 11, S. Treaty Doc. No. 105-17 (1997), available at 1997 WL 447232. Even before the treaty, Congress had been devoting attention to the problems faced by copyright enforcement in the digital age. Hearings on the topic have spanned several years. . . .

The Act contains three provisions targeted at the circumvention of technological protections. . . .

The DMCA contains exceptions for schools and libraries that want to use circumvention technologies to determine whether to purchase a copyrighted product, 17 U.S.C. §1201(d); individuals using circumvention technology "for the sole purpose" of trying to achieve "interoperability" of computer programs through reverse-engineering, *id.* §1201(f); encryption research aimed at identifying flaws in encryption technology, if the research is conducted to advance the state of knowledge in the field, *id.* §1201(g); and several other exceptions not relevant here.

The DMCA creates civil remedies, *id.* §1203, and criminal sanctions, *id.* §1204. It specifically authorizes a court to "grant temporary and permanent injunctions on such terms as it deems reasonable to prevent or restrain a violation." *id.* §1203(b)(1). . . .

## Discussion . . .

## III. Constitutional Challenges Based on the First Amendment

### A. Applicable Principles . . .

#### 4. The Scope of First Amendment Protection for Decryption Code

In considering the scope of First Amendment protection for a decryption program like DeCSS, we must recognize that the essential purpose of encryption code is to prevent unauthorized access. Owners of all property rights are entitled to prohibit access to their property by unauthorized persons. Homeowners can install locks on the doors of their houses. Custodians of valuables can place them in safes. Stores can attach to products security devices that will activate alarms if the products are taken away without purchase. These and similar security devices can be circumvented. Burglars can use skeleton keys to open door locks. Thieves can obtain the combinations to safes. Product security devices can be neutralized.

Our case concerns a security device, CSS computer code, that prevents access by unauthorized persons to DVD movies. . . .

DeCSS is computer code that can decrypt CSS. In its basic function, it is like a skeleton key that can open a locked door, a combination that can open a safe, or a device that can neutralize the security device attached to a store's products. DeCSS enables anyone to gain access to a DVD movie without using a DVD player.

The initial use of DeCSS to gain access to a DVD movie creates no loss to movie producers because the initial user must purchase the DVD. However, once the DVD is purchased, DeCSS enables the initial user to copy the movie in digital form and transmit it instantly in virtually limitless quantity, thereby depriving the movie producer of sales. The advent of the Internet creates the potential for instantaneous worldwide distribution of the copied material.

At first glance, one might think that Congress has as much authority to regulate the distribution of computer code to decrypt DVD movies as it has to regulate distribution of skeleton keys, combinations to safes, or devices to neutralize store product security devices. However, despite the evident legitimacy of protection against unauthorized access to DVD movies, just like any other property, regulation of decryption code like DeCSS is challenged in this case because DeCSS differs from a skeleton key in one important respect: it not only is capable of performing the function of unlocking the encrypted DVD movie, it also is a form of communication, albeit written in a language not understood by the general public. As a communication, the DeCSS code has a claim to being "speech," and as "speech," it has a claim to being protected by the First Amendment. But just as the realities of what any computer code can accomplish must inform the scope of its constitutional protection, so the capacity of a decryption program like DeCSS to accomplish unauthorized—indeed, unlawful—access to materials in which the Plaintiffs have intellectual property rights must inform and limit the scope of its First Amendment protection. *Cf. Red Lion*, 395 U.S. at 386 ("Differences in the characteristics of new media justify differences in the First Amendment standards applied to them.").

With all of the foregoing considerations in mind, we next consider the Appellants' First Amendment challenge to the DMCA as applied in the specific prohibitions that have been imposed by the District Court's injunction.

### B. First Amendment Challenge

The District Court's injunction applies the DMCA to the Defendants by imposing two types of prohibition, both grounded on the anti-trafficking provisions of the DMCA. The first prohibits posting DeCSS or any other technology for circumventing CSS on any Internet web site. *Universal II*, 111 F. Supp. 2d at 346-47, P 1 (a), (b). The second prohibits knowingly linking any Internet web site to any other web site containing DeCSS. *Id.* At 347, P 1 (c). The validity of the posting and linking prohibitions must be considered separately.

#### 1. Posting

The initial issue is whether the posting prohibition is content-neutral, since, as we have explained, this classification determines the applicable constitutional standard. The Appellants contend that the anti-trafficking provisions of the DMCA and their application by means of the posting prohibition of the injunction are content-based. They argue that the provisions "specifically target . . . scientific expression based on the particular topic addressed by that expression—namely, techniques for circumventing CSS.". . . We disagree. The Appellants' argument fails to recognize that the target of the posting provisions of the injunction—DeCSS—has both a nonspeech and a speech component, and that the DMCA, as applied to the Appellants, and the posting prohibition of the injunction target only the nonspeech component. . . .

As a content-neutral regulation with an incidental effect on a speech component, the regulation must serve a substantial governmental interest, the interest must be unrelated to the suppression of free expression, and the incidental restriction on speech must not burden substantially more speech than is necessary to further that interest. *Turner Broadcasting*, 512 U.S. at 662. The Government's interest in preventing unauthorized access to encrypted copyrighted material is unquestionably substantial, and the regulation of DeCSS by the posting prohibition plainly serves that interest. Moreover, that interest is unrelated to the suppression of free expression. . . .

Posting DeCSS on the Appellants' web site makes it instantly available at the click of a mouse to any person in the world with access to the Internet, and such person can then instantly transmit DeCSS to anyone else with Internet access. Although the prohibition on posting prevents the Appellants from conveying to others the speech component of DeCSS, the Appellants have not suggested, much less shown, any technique for barring them from making this instantaneous worldwide distribution of a decryption code that makes a lesser restriction on the code's speech component. . . .

### 2. Linking

In considering linking, we need to clarify the sense in which the injunction prohibits such activity. Although the injunction defines several terms, it does not define "linking." Nevertheless, it is evident from the District Court's opinion that it is concerned with "hyperlinks," *Universal I*, 111 F. Supp. 2d at 307; *see id.* at 339 . . . . With a hyperlink on a web page, the linked web site is just one click away.

In applying the DMCA to linking (via hyperlinks), Judge Kaplan recognized, as he had with DeCSS code, that a hyperlink has both a speech and a nonspeech component. It conveys information, the Internet address of the linked web page, and has the functional capacity to bring the content of the linked web page to the user's computer screen (or, as Judge Kaplan put it, to "take one almost instantaneously to the desired destination," *id.*). . . .

Applying the *O'Brien/Ward/Turner Broadcasting* requirements for content-neutral regulation, Judge Kaplan then ruled that the DMCA, as applied to the Defendants' linking, served substantial governmental interests and was unrelated to the suppression of free expression, *id.* We agree. He then carefully considered the "closer call," *id.*, as to whether a linking prohibition would satisfy the narrow tailoring requirement. In an especially carefully considered portion of his opinion, he observed that strict liability for linking to web sites containing DeCSS would risk two impairments of free expression. Web site operators would be inhibited from displaying links to various web pages for fear that a linked page might contain DeCSS, and a prohibition on linking to a web site containing DeCSS would curtail access to whatever other information was contained at the accessed site. *Id.* at 340.

To avoid applying the DMCA in a manner that would "burden substantially more speech than is necessary to further the government's legitimate interests," *Turner Broadcasting*, 512 U.S. at 662 (internal quotation marks and citation omitted), Judge Kaplan adapted the standards of *New York Times Co. v. Sullivan*, 376 U.S. 254, 283, 11 L. Ed. 2d 686, 84 S. Ct. 710 (1964), to fashion a limited prohibition against linking to web sites containing DeCSS. He required clear and convincing evidence

> that those responsible for the link (a) know at the relevant time that the offending material is on the linked-to site, (b) know that it is circumvention technology that may not lawfully be offered, and (c) create or maintain the link for the purpose of disseminating that technology.

*Universal I*, 111 F. Supp. 2d at 341. He then found that the evidence satisfied his three-part test by his required standard of proof. *Id.* . . .

Mindful of the cautious approach to First Amendment claims involving computer technology expressed in *Name.Space*, 202 F.3d at 584 n.11, we see no need on this appeal to determine whether a test as rigorous as Judge Kaplan's is required to respond to First Amendment objections to the linking provision of the injunction that he issued. It suffices to reject the Appellants' contention that an intent to cause harm is required and that linking can be enjoined only under circumstances applicable to a print medium. As they have throughout their arguments, the Appellants ignore the reality of the functional capacity of decryption computer code and hyperlinks to facilitate instantaneous unauthorized access to copyrighted materials by anyone anywhere in the world. Under the circumstances amply shown by the record, the injunction's linking prohibition validly regulates the Appellants' opportunity instantly to enable anyone anywhere to gain unauthorized access to copyrighted movies on DVDs.

At oral argument, we asked the Government whether its undoubted power to punish the distribution of obscene materials would permit an injunction prohibiting a newspaper from printing addresses of bookstore locations carrying such materials. In a properly cautious response, the Government stated that the answer would depend on the circumstances of the publication. The Appellants' supplemental papers enthusiastically embraced the arguable analogy between printing bookstore addresses and displaying on a web page links to web sites at which DeCSS may be accessed. Supplemental Brief for Appellants at 14. They confidently asserted that publication of bookstore locations carrying obscene material cannot be enjoined consistent with the First Amendment, and that a prohibition against linking to web sites containing DeCSS is similarly invalid. *Id.*

Like many analogies posited to illuminate legal issues, the bookstore analogy is helpful primarily in identifying characteristics that distinguish it from the context of the pending dispute. If a bookstore proprietor is knowingly selling obscene materials, the evil of distributing such materials can be prevented by injunctive relief against the unlawful distribution (and similar distribution by others can be deterred by punishment of the distributor). And if others publish the location of the bookstore, preventive relief against a distributor can be effective before any significant distribution of the prohibited materials has occurred. The digital world, however, creates a very different problem. If obscene materials are posted on one web site and other sites post hyperlinks to the first site, the materials are available for instantaneous worldwide distribution before any preventive measures can be effectively taken.

This reality obliges courts considering First Amendment claims in the context of the pending case to choose between two unattractive alternatives: either tolerate some impairment of communication in order to permit Congress to prohibit decryption that may lawfully be prevented, or tolerate some decryption in order to avoid some impairment of communication. Although the parties dispute the extent of impairment of communication if the injunction is upheld and the extent of decryption if it is vacated, and differ on the availability and effectiveness of techniques for minimizing both consequences, the fundamental choice between impairing some communication and tolerating decryption cannot be entirely avoided.

In facing this choice, we are mindful that it is not for us to resolve the issues of public policy implicated by the choice we have identified. Those issues are for Congress. Our task is to determine whether the legislative solution adopted by Congress, as applied to the Appellants by the District Court's injunction, is consistent with the limitations of the First Amendment, and we are satisfied that it is.

## IV. Constitutional Challenge Based on Claimed Restriction of Fair Use

Asserting that fair use "is rooted in and required by both the Copyright Clause and the First Amendment," . . . the Appellants contend that the DMCA, as applied by the District Court, unconstitutionally "eliminates fair use" of copyrighted materials. . . . We reject this extravagant claim.

Preliminarily, we note that the Supreme Court has never held that fair use is constitutionally required, although some isolated statements in its opinions might arguably be enlisted for such a requirement. . . .

We need not explore the extent to which fair use might have constitutional protection, grounded on either the First Amendment or the Copyright Clause, because whatever validity a constitutional claim might have as to an application of the DMCA that impairs fair use of copyrighted materials, such matters are far beyond the scope of this lawsuit for several reasons. In the first place, the Appellants do not claim to be making fair use of any copyrighted materials, and nothing in the injunction prohibits them from making such fair use. They are barred from trafficking in a decryption code that enables unauthorized access to copyrighted materials.

Second, as the District Court properly noted, to whatever extent the anti-trafficking provisions of the DMCA might prevent others from copying portions of DVD movies in order to make fair use of them, "the evidence as to the impact of the anti-trafficking provisions of the DMCA on prospective fair users is scanty and fails adequately to address the issues." *Universal I*, 111 F. Supp. 2d at 338 n.246.

Third, the Appellants have provided no support for their premise that fair use of DVD movies is constitutionally required to be made by copying the original work in its original format. Their examples of the fair uses that they believe others will be prevented from making all involve copying in a digital format those portions of a DVD movie amenable to fair use, a copying that would enable the fair user to manipulate the digitally copied portions. One example is that of a school child who wishes to copy images from a DVD movie to insert into the student's documentary film. We know of no authority for the proposition that fair use, as protected by the Copyright Act, much less the Constitution, guarantees copying by the optimum method or in the identical format of the original. Although the Appellants insisted at oral argument that they should not be relegated to a "horse and buggy" technique in making fair use of DVD movies, the DMCA does not impose even an arguable limitation on the opportunity to make a variety of traditional fair uses of DVD movies, such as commenting on their content, quoting excerpts from their screenplays, and even recording portions of the video images and sounds on film or tape by pointing a camera, a camcorder, or a microphone at a monitor as it displays the DVD movie. The fact that the resulting copy will not be as perfect or as manipulable as a digital copy obtained by having direct access to the DVD movie in its digital form, provides no basis for a claim of unconstitutional limitation of fair use. A film critic making fair use of a movie by quoting selected lines of dialogue has no constitutionally valid claim that the review (in print or on television) would be technologically superior if the reviewer had not been prevented from using a movie camera in the theater, nor has an art student a valid constitutional claim to fair use of a painting by photographing it in a museum. Fair use has never been held to be a guarantee of access to copyrighted material in order to copy it by the fair user's preferred technique or in the format of the original.

## Conclusion

We have considered all the other arguments of the Appellants and conclude that they provide no basis for disturbing the District Court's judgment. Accordingly, the judgment is affirmed.

## *Nintendo Co. Ltd and Others v. PC Box Srl and 9Net Srl*

Judgment of the Court (Fourth Chamber), 23 January 2014

(Directive 2001/29/EC – Copyright and related rights in the information society – Concept of 'technological measures' – Protection device – Equipment and protected complementary products – Similar complementary devices, products or components from other undertakings – Exclusion of any interoperability between them – Scope of those technological measures – Relevance)

In Case C-355/12,

REQUEST for a preliminary ruling under Article 267 TFEU from the Tribunale di Milano (Italy), made by decision of 22 December 2011, received at the Court on 26 July 2012, in the proceedings

Nintendo Co. Ltd,
Nintendo of America Inc.,
Nintendo of Europe GmbH
v
PC Box Srl,
9Net Srl,

THE COURT (Fourth Chamber),

composed of L. Bay Larsen, President of the Chamber, K. Lenaerts, Vice-President of the Court, acting as Judge of the Fourth Chamber, M. Safjan (Rapporteur), J. Malenovský and A. Prechal, Judges,

Advocate General: E. Sharpston,

Registrar: A. Impellizzeri, Administrator, having regard to the written procedure and further to the hearing on 30 May 2013, after considering the observations submitted on behalf of: . . . gives the following:

### Judgment

1. The request for a preliminary ruling concerns the interpretation of Article 6 of Directive 2001/29/EC of the European Parliament and of the Council of 22 May 2001 on the harmonisation of certain aspects of copyright and related rights in the information society (OJ 2001 L 167, p. 10).

2. The request has been made in proceedings between, on the one hand, Nintendo Co. Ltd, Nintendo of America Inc. and Nintendo of Europe GmbH (collectively 'the Nintendo undertakings'), and, on the other, PC Box Srl ('PC Box') and 9Net Srl ('9Net'), concerning the sale, by PC Box, of 'mod chips' and of 'game copies' ('PC Box equipment') through the website managed by PC Box and hosted by 9Net.

### Legal Context

#### The Dispute in the Main Proceedings and the Questions Referred for a Preliminary Ruling

9. The Nintendo undertakings, members of a group which creates and produces videogames, market two types of products for those games, namely portable systems, 'DS' consoles and fixed console videogame systems, 'Wii' consoles.

10. The Nintendo undertakings have adopted technological measures, namely a recognition system installed in the consoles, and the encrypted code of the physical housing system onto which the videogames which are protected by copyright are registered. Those measures have the effect of preventing the use of illegal copies of videogames. Games lacking a code cannot be launched on either of the two types of equipment marketed by the Nintendo undertakings.

. . .

14. PC Box markets original Nintendo consoles together with additional software consisting of certain applications from independent manufacturers, 'homebrews' created specifically to be used in such consoles and the use of which requires the prior installation of PC Box equipment which deactivates the installed device which constitutes the technological protection measure.

15. In the opinion of PC Box, the actual purpose pursued by the Nintendo undertakings is to prevent use of independent software which does not constitute an illegal copy of videogames, but which is intended to enable MP3 files, movies and videos to be read on consoles, in order to fully use those consoles.

. . .

## Consideration of the Questions Referred

. . .

24. As regards Article 6 of Directive 2001/29, it is important to note that it requires the Member States to provide adequate legal protection against the circumvention of any effective 'technological measure' which is defined, in paragraph 3, as any technology, device or component that, in the normal course of its operation, is designed to prevent or restrict acts, in respect of works or other subject-matter, which are not authorised by the rightholder of any copyright or any right related to copyright as provided for by law or the *sui generis* right provided for in Chapter III of Directive 96/9.

25. Those acts constitute, as is apparent from Articles 2 to 4 of Directive 2001/29, the reproduction, the communication to the public of works and making them available to the public, and the distribution of the original or copies of works. The legal protection referred to in Article 6 of that directive applies only in the light of protecting that rightholder against acts which require his authorisation.

26. In that regard, it must be stated, in the first place, that there is nothing in that directive to suggest that Article 6(3) thereof does not refer to technological measures such as those at issue in the main proceedings, which are partly incorporated in the physical housing systems of games and partly in consoles which requires interaction between them.

27. Indeed, as the Advocate General noted . . ., it is apparent from that provision that the concept of 'effective technological measures' is defined broadly and includes application of an access control or protection process, such as encryption, scrambling or other transformation of the work or other subject-matter or a copy control mechanism. Such a definition, moreover, complies with the principal objective of Directive 2001/29 which, as is apparent from recital 9 thereof, is to establish a high level of protection in favour, in particular, of authors, which is crucial to intellectual creation.

28. In those circumstances, it must be considered that technological measures such as those at issue in the case in the main proceedings, which are partly incorporated in the physical housing of videogames and partly in consoles and which require interaction between them, fall within the concept of 'effective technological measures' within the meaning of Article 6(3) of Directive 2001/29 if their objective is to prevent or to limit acts adversely affecting the rights of the holder protected by them.

29. In the second place, it is necessary to examine according to which criteria the scope of legal protection against circumventing technological protection measures within the meaning of Article 6 of Directive 2001/29 should be assessed.

30. As the Advocate General noted . . ., the examination of that question requires that account be taken of the fact that legal protection against acts not authorised by the rightholder of any copyright must respect the principle of proportionality, in accordance with Article 6(2) of Directive 2001/29, interpreted in the light of recital 48 thereof, and should not prohibit devices or activities which have a commercially significant purpose or use other than to circumvent the technical protection.

31. Accordingly, that legal protection is granted only with regard to technological measures which pursue the objective of preventing or eliminating, as regards works, acts not authorised by the rightholder of copyright referred to in . . . the present judgment. Those measures must be suitable for achieving that objective and must not go beyond what is necessary for this purpose.

32. In those circumstances, it is necessary to examine whether other measures or measures which are not installed in consoles could have caused less interference with the activities of third parties not requiring authorisation by the rightholder of copyright or fewer limitations to those activities, while still providing comparable protection of that rightholder's rights.

33. Accordingly, it is relevant to take account, inter alia, of the relative costs of different types of technological measures, of technological and practical aspects of their implementation, and of a comparison of the effectiveness of those different types of technological measures as regards the protection of rightholder's rights, that effectiveness however not having to be absolute.

34. The assessment of the scope of the legal protection at issue would not have to be carried out, as the Advocate General noted . . ., by reference to the particular use of consoles, as envisaged by the copyright holder. It would, however, have to take account of the criteria laid down, as regards the devices, products or components capable of circumventing the protection of effective technological measures, in Article 6(2) of Directive 2001/29.

35. More specifically, that provision requires the Member States to provide adequate legal protection against those devices, products or components which have the purpose of circumventing that protection of effective technological measures which have only a limited commercially significant purpose or use other than to circumvent that protection, or are primarily designed, produced, adapted or performed for the purpose of enabling or facilitating that circumvention.

36. In that regard, with a view to examining the purpose of those devices, products or components, the evidence of actual use which is made of them by third parties will, in the light of the circumstances at issue, be particularly relevant. The referring court may, in particular, examine how often PC Box's devices are in fact used in order to allow unauthorised copies of Nintendo and Nintendo-licensed games to be used on Nintendo consoles and how often that equipment is used for purposes which do not infringe copyright in Nintendo and Nintendo-licensed games.

37. In the light of the foregoing, the answer to the questions referred is that Directive 2001/29 must be interpreted as meaning that the concept of an 'effective technological measure', for the purposes of Article 6(3) of that directive, is capable of covering technological measures comprising, principally, equipping not only the housing system containing the protected work, such as the videogame, with a recognition device in order to protect it against acts which are not authorised by the holder of any copyright, but also portable equipment or consoles intended to ensure access to those games and their use.

38. It is for the national court to determine whether other measures or measures which are not installed in consoles could cause less interference with the activities of third parties or limitations to those activities, while still providing comparable protection of the rightholder's rights. Accordingly, it is relevant to take account, inter alia, of the relative costs of different types of technological measures, of technological and practical aspects of their

implementation, and of a comparison of the effectiveness of those different types of technological measures as regards the protection of the rightholder's rights, that effectiveness however not having to be absolute. That court must also examine the purpose of devices, products or components, which are capable of circumventing those technological measures. In that regard, the evidence of use which third parties actually make of them will, in the light of the circumstances at issue, be particularly relevant. The national court may, in particular, examine how often those devices, products or components are in fact used in disregard of copyright and how often they are used for purposes which do not infringe copyright.

**Mira Burri and Zaira Zihlmann***

## *Intermediaries' Liability in Light of the Recent EU Copyright Reform*

. . .

### II. Intermediaries as Key Actors in Copyright Enforcement

#### 1. From Analogue to Digital

At the time when the international copyright regime was created back in the 19th century, the relevant technology that permitted multiplication and distribution of copyrighted works was the printing press. The Internet came only a century later, so neither the 1886 Berne Convention nor even the 1995 WTO Agreement on Trade-Related Aspects of Intellectual Property Rights (TRIPS) contain any specific rules for digital technologies or intermediaries' liability, except for the fact that TRIPS extended the scope of copyright to explicitly cover computer programs and databases. The international community was quick however to acknowledge the far-reaching effects of digitization, both as a powerful tool to create and distribute content and as a potential enhancer of copyright infringement. While the enforcement of copyright has always been demanding, in the online environment, characterized by its borderless nature, easy access by everyone, and perfect reproduction of original works that can be instantaneously distributed to millions, it almost seemed impossible. Policy-makers were confronted yet again with the fundamental questions underlying copyright of how to secure an effective protection of the copyright holders' package of rights, while at the same time allow the public to access and use works, and engage in creative activities. The stakes and the risks on both sides appear somewhat higher in the digital space, which on the one hand, permits massive copyright infringement and on the other hand, enables unprecedented user-driven creativity. With the adoption of the WIPO Copyright Treaty in 1996, the international community moved towards designing some solutions in the domain of digital copyright; these were however cautiously formulated and left room for different implementation approaches, as at the time the Internet was still quite young. Neither were many of the applications we use today known, nor could the pervasive societal embeddedness of the digital medium be fully anticipated. A critical development in the post-WIPO Copyright Treaty environment, that this article discusses, is the increased role of Internet intermediaries in the field of copyright enforcement and their effective emancipation into critical copyright management actors. As rightsholders were "faced with a major enforcement failure", it appeared appropriate that intermediaries carry some of the burden and costs associated with copyright enforcement,

---

* 11 Indian Journal of Intellectual Property 35 (2021).

especially as they are well positioned and technically capable to monitor, filter, block, and disable infringing materials. At the same time, this liability ought not to be too burdensome, since this would limit the companies' economic freedom and hamper growth and innovation. A model of limited and conditional liability, the so-called "safe harbour", was created as a solution but implemented differently at the national levels – in the European Union, through the 2000 E-Commerce Directive and in the United States, through the 1998 Digital Millennium Copyright Act (DMCA). We briefly discuss the existing different approaches to intermediaries' liability before looking at newer developments and the 2019 EU Copyright Directive in particular.

### 2. Different Approaches to Intermediaries' Liability

Systems for intermediary governance can largely be split into two groups. On the one hand, there are horizontal systems that install rules for all types of intermediaries' liability – be it with regard to hate speech, misleading information, trademark or copyright infringements, as the EU framework does. On the other hand, there are systems, such as Section 512 DMCA, that specifically target copyright violations. Both systems seek to strike a balance between the different interests involved by creating certain "safe harbours" as mechanisms to mitigate the risk of legal liability of Internet intermediaries while providing copyright holders with protection and ways that enable them to have their content removed online.

The DMCA and the E-Commerce Directive, albeit with some differences, enact to this effect a "notice and takedown" procedure, in the sense that once notified of an alleged infringement, intermediaries must expeditiously take down the said content. There are a number of variations of the safe harbour regime, known under the umbrella term "notice and action". Besides the notice and takedown procedure, the best-known other procedures are the so-called "notice and notice" and "notice and stay down". While similar in the triggering by a notification, they differ in the required intermediary's response and ultimately, in the resulting balance of interests. In case of the notice and notice procedures, as found in Canada, Chile and South Korea, the intermediary forwards the received notice to the content provider and she is given the opportunity to take action to restore compliance with all legal requirements or to defend her behaviour within a certain time limit. The "notice and stay down" regime is substantially more stringent and the provider must additionally to taking the notified content down, prevent the (re)upload of the same or similar content. Such a procedure has been applied in Germany and has recently been established in the Swiss copyright law.

Many intermediaries have in addition to the legally prescribed measures implemented proactive enforcement measures, such as filters or monitoring mechanisms, to detect infringing content, largely as a response to pressure from rightsholders. YouTube, for instance, introduced its automated content recognition and filtering mechanism, known as "Content ID", as a reaction to being exposed to a major copyright lawsuit in 2012. Such mechanisms have come to be known as "DMCA plus" systems, since they go beyond the DMCA requirements, shift responsibilities and move from reactive to proactive methods. Although these applications may offer efficient tools to deal with the allegedly vast amount of infringing content, they do come with some negative implications, in particular with regard to the fair use of copyrighted content or the use of works in the public domain, as the example at the outset of this article showed.

The safe harbour model has evolved over the years, especially as the role of intermediaries has increased due to the ongoing platformization of the digital space. There is a discrete trend towards heightened responsibilities that these intermediaries should assume, and the need for this shift, while pushed by rightsholders has become now largely acknowledged by policy-makers too. The new EU Copyright Directive is an expression of this recognition and marks a significant step towards making intermediaries active "gatekeepers" of content uploaded and shared by their users. It effectively changes the existing regime and has been fittingly labelled as "safe harbor's coup de grace". This rings true in particular if one looks at the new liabilities created under Article 17 of the Directive.

. . .

## IV. Article 17 of the EU Copyright Directive

### 1. Rationale behind Article 17

Article 17 has been prompted by the so-called "value gap". The term describes the (alleged) imbalance between the revenues Internet service providers generate from the use of copyright protected content uploaded by their users and the revenues copyright holders obtain. The problem was said to arise from the safe harbour regime established by the E-Commerce Directive, as this provides platforms with a liability privilege and does not incentivize them to enter into licensing agreements or otherwise provide for conditions more accommodating for rightsholders. From the EU perspective, the problem was only more acute, as most dominant platforms are US-based and the generated revenues rarely remain in the EU. Article 17 sought to address this "value gap" problem by effectively changing the intermediaries' liability regime existing under Article 14 of the E-Commerce Directive.

### 2. Scope and Obligations under Article 17

In contrast to the initial proposal, Article 17 no longer targets information society service providers as a generic category but defines a new sub-category of "online content-sharing service providers" (OCSSPs). OCSSP is "a provider of an information society service of which the main or one of the main purposes is to store and give the public access to a large amount of copyright-protected works or other protected subject matter uploaded by its users, which it organizes and promotes for profit-making purposes". Certain providers, such as non-profit online encyclopedias, open source software-developing and sharing platforms, as well as business-to-business cloud services, are excluded. These exclusions are based on the recognition that the notice and takedown system of the E-Commerce Directive works well enough for most ISPs and that Article 17 may harm entities which do not bear the risks of infringement that it is designed to address. The scope of application is further narrowed down by Recitals 62 and 63, which demand among other things a case-by-case evaluation taking into account the platforms' audience and amount of uploaded copyright works. Overall, although the scope of application has been reduced in comparison to the Commission's proposal, the vague language used leaves a number of questions open and induces uncertainty. For now, it appears clear that Article 17 captures user generated content hosting providers of a particular size, such as YouTube and Facebook.

Article 17(1) stipulates that when an OCSSP gives the public access to copyright-protected works or other subject matter uploaded by its users, the provider performs an act of communication to the public or an act of making available to the public. Thus, Article 17(1) renders OCSSPs primary liable for copyright infringements committed by its users. It is further clarified that the limitation of liability, as established in Article 14(1) E-Commerce Directive, does not apply to situations covered by Article 17, and this effectively creates a *lex specialis* rule for the said particular category of hosting providers.

The liability regime of Article 17 follows a two-level approach – on the one hand, it prescribes direct liability and specifies on the other hand distinct ways to "escape" this liability burden. OCSSPs can avoid liability in two ways: First, they must obtain an authorization from rightsholders, for example, by concluding a licensing agreement (Article 17(1), second sentence). Such authorization covers also non-commercial user actions as well as user activities that do not generate significant revenues. If no authorization is granted, pursuant to

Article 17(4), the provider is not liable if three cumulative conditions are met: OCSSPs must demonstrate that they have (1) made best efforts to obtain an authorization from the right holder; (2) made best efforts to ensure that specific content is as inaccessible as possible, and (3) disabled access or removed content expeditiously after becoming aware of it and made best efforts to prevent future uploads of the respective content. When determining whether the provider has complied with these obligations, Article 17(5) requires in light of the principle of proportionality certain aspects to be taken into account, such as (a) the type, the audience and the size of the service and the type of content uploaded by the users, as well as (b) the availability of suitable and effective means, including their cost for the provider. Additional "bright-line" limitations are given by Article 17(6). It specifies that new online content-sharing service providers whose services have been available to the public in the Union for less than three years and which have an annual turnover below EUR 10 million are exempted from the obligation set out paragraph 4 point (b) – that is, they just have to act expeditiously, upon receiving a sufficiently substantiated notice, to disable access to the notified works or to remove those works from their websites. This limitation does not however apply when the average number of monthly unique visitors exceeds 5 million.

Article 17(7) demands in addition that the cooperation between OCSSPs and rightsholders does not result in the prevention of justified use of copyright protected content. Consequently, EU Member States must ensure that users are able to rely on exceptions and limitations to copyright for the purposes of quotation, criticism, review, caricature, parody or pastiche. This is a new provision in comparison to the original Commission's proposal and it does recognize the fact that many websites contain significant amounts of user-generated works, such as remixes and mashups, which may be lawful under EU copyright law. Next to this explicit reference to fair use situations, Article 17(9) sets out complaint and redress mechanisms as procedural safeguards.

Article 17(8) states further that the application of Article 17 shall not lead to any general monitoring obligation. It however obliges OCSSPs to provide rightsholders, at their request, with certain information. Finally, Article 17(10) requires the European Commission to organize stakeholder dialogues in order to discuss best practices for cooperation between the platform providers and the rightsholders.

### 3. Critical Analysis of Article 17's Liability Regime

Against the backdrop of the complex liability regime under Article 17 and the so created "escape" routes, it is fair to ask how viable these really are, whether certain negative effects may be triggered in the course of their implementation, and how these potential harms can be mitigated. The following sections seek to address these questions.

#### 3.1. The Licensing Approach and its Pitfalls

Article 17(1) demands authorization from the rightsholders as the default way to avoid primary liability and mentions licensing as a way to receive such authorization. Other options include collective licensing mechanisms or statutory licensing. Whereas it is understandable that Article 17(1) tries to encourage rights clearance initiatives, it confronts the platform with an enormously cumbersome obligation which bears a resemblance to a "mission impossible", as it is hard to imagine that a platform can obtain all the necessary licenses for all the works uploaded by its users. The impossibility of this task is linked on the one hand to the existence of overlapping rights – so for instance, most videos involve next to copyright(s), rights of phonogram or film producers, and/or performers' rights, which can belong or be managed by different entities. On the other hand, while it may be feasible for platform providers to contact rightsholders known to them, as well as the collecting societies, in the case of unknown rightsholders, this is evidently not the case. Copyright does not demand formalities to be awarded and there is nothing like a global or even national register for all protected works that can be consulted. In the absence of such a register, platforms cannot identify rightsholders of works uploaded by users and must rely on the declarations of uploaders or those claiming to be rightsholders. This is problematic given that false copyright claims are common and many user uploads do not contain any copyright information at all. As Dusollier notes the situation is close to a paradox since: "how to contact copyright owners to get the proper authorization for a content that could be identified only when put online, which will be infringing if no licence precedes its making available?".

Even if the platform is able to identify and contact a rightsholder, it may encounter other difficulties. These include, among others, the fact that rightsholders are under no obligation to enter into licensing agreements offered under fair terms. Furthermore, it is doubtful that copyright holders and collecting societies will offer all-embracing umbrella licenses. Platforms will need to probably make use of algorithmic tools to ensure that the content being uploaded does not exceed the limits of the acquired licenses and in this sense even licensing can be a starting point for algorithmic enforcement measures. Such measures may affect the freedom of users to actively participate in the creation of online content, as a user-generated remix will not pass the content filter if it is not compliant with the repertoire and usage restrictions set out in the licensing agreements. Platforms that rely on licensing agreements are also likely to focus on mainstream works and face difficulties in providing access to the wide variety of content uploaded by users with different social, cultural, and ethnic backgrounds. Given the adversities in meeting the requirements set out in Article 17(1), it may be assumed that platforms will heavily rely on the second option of filtering to avoid liability.

### 3.2. The Promises and Perils of Filtering

#### *3.2.1. Filtering Obligations under Article 17*

As explained earlier, platforms must meet three cumulative conditions in order to avoid direct liability. OCSSPs must demonstrate that they have (a) made best efforts to obtain an authorization, and (b) made, in accordance with high industry standards of professional diligence, best efforts to ensure the unavailability of specific works for which the rightsholders have provided the relevant and necessary information; and in any event (c) acted expeditiously, upon receiving a sufficiently substantiated notice from the rightsholders, to disable access to, or to remove from their websites, the notified works, and made best efforts to prevent their future uploads. The qualification of "best efforts" appears particularly important for understanding the real implications of the provision; yet, the Directive offers little guidance to this effect. One can assume that the Directive's implementation in the Member States is likely to bring more clarity but the development of different standards is also possible.

With regard to the first condition of making "best efforts" to obtain authorization, one can think of several possibilities. One option may be that the OCSSP would have to proactively identify each piece of protected material and the respective rightsholder and then offer fair licensing conditions. Yet, this would amount to a general monitoring obligation for all uploaded content and would thus contradict Article 17(8), Article 15 of the E-Commerce Directive, as well as the fundamental freedom of the OCSSPs to conduct business in accordance with Article 16 of the Charter of Fundamental Rights. Another possibility would be to oblige rightsholders to always take the first step and notify the OCSSP that unlicensed protected material is available on the platform. This would result in the OCSSP only having to react when notified by the rightsholder. However, such an interpretation would likely contradict the very aim of the Directive to strengthen the negotiating position of rightsholders and reduce some of their burden. Finally, one can imagine a somewhat more pragmatic approach: If the content is obviously protected material and the rightsholders are publicly known, the OCSSP must actively contact these known rightsholders and offer serious negotiations on licensing terms. If the content is not obviously protected material or no rightsholder is known, the OCSSP may remain passive until the rightsholders, including collective management organizations, contact the provider. As soon as the OCSSP receives such notification, it must then react and start negotiations.

The second condition specified in Article 17(4) is the obligation of the provider to make best efforts to ensure the unavailability of specific works for which the rightsholders have provided relevant and necessary information. This sets out a proactive duty of care and necessitates the active involvement of the rightsholders. In case the OCSSP is provided with the relevant information, it must block the upload of the respective content in accordance with high industry standards of professional diligence. Although this formulation is technology-neutral and unlike the initially proposed Article 13 does not explicitly mention the use of content recognition technologies, there is wide agreement that this requirement can hardly be met by anything else than algorithmic driven tools (also referred to as "upload filters"). This marks a distinct "shift from a regime in which the law is enforced after a violation of law has taken place (*ex post*) to a system where technology ensures that violations do not even occur in the first place (*ex ante*)".

Another question that arises in this context is to what extent removing content demands monitoring. Some suggest that this will result in general monitoring, while others share the view that such review of content is only specific monitoring and would not conflict with the ban on general monitoring under Article 17(8). If the latter view is not supported, there may be a major conflict with EU primary law, as discussed above in the two *SABAM* cases, where the CJEU did not stop short of finding an infringement of the E-Commerce Directive but considered this also a serious infringement of fundamental rights – in particular the users' right to the protection of their personal data and the freedom to receive and impart information.

Similar problems exist also with regard to the third and last obligation that a provider must fulfil to avoid liability in that OCSSPs must act expeditiously and disable access to infringing content or remove it from their platform upon receiving a substantiated notice from the rightsholders, and make best efforts to prevent future uploading of the respective content. This effectively changes the "notice and takedown" mechanism and includes a new "stay down" obligation, which although already introduced through national jurisprudence and practiced by some countries, such as Germany, is novel for EU law. Under the notice and stay down regime, a submitted notification does not only address a one-time infringement but triggers an ongoing duty of the intermediary to prevent the same infringement in the future. The Directive does not mention a specific measure to prevent the re-upload of content but states that OCSSPs must have made "best efforts to prevent their future uploads in accordance with point (b)". Hence again, the provider is likely to make use of automatic content recognition technologies to fulfil the stay down obligation. The question of whether this involves general monitoring is pertinent again. Some authors are of the opinion that an obligation to detect future infringements which are not only the same but merely similar does not constitute a general but a specific monitoring obligation and is therefore permissible. Others argue that it is difficult to imagine how providers can ensure that copyright protected works are not re-uploaded unless they use a technological tool that systematically monitors all uploaded content.

Although no longer mentioned explicitly in Article 17, the preceding analysis shows that OCSSPs can *de facto* meet the statutory requirements only if they use automated content recognition technology and so the rhetoric question of to filter or not filter seems to be answered in the positive. While the use of technology for copyright enforcement is not entirely new, what is distinct in the case of the new EU copyright framework is the legislative incentive and legitimization of the introduction of such systems through Article 17. Senftleben qualifies this as "institutionalized algorithmic enforcement" and this development opens an array of questions with regard to users' rights, transparency and due process.

## NOTES AND QUESTIONS

**1.** Note that the Court does not include the WIPO Treaty in its analysis. Would this have made a difference?

**2.** What is the impact of freedom to do business and to serve other programs which may interfere with copyright-protected ones? Does it boil down to apply the principle of proportionality in assessing infringing activities deployed by extraneous equipment?

**3.** Do you find the new EU liability regime too onerous? What are the dangers of automated filtering systems? Can a proper balance between rightsholders' interests and users' rights be attained?

## D. Neighboring Rights and the WIPO Performances and Phonograms Treaty (WPPT)

### *1. The Problem of Performance*

*Schweizerische Interpreten-Gesellschaft and Others v. X and Z,* decided in 1984, illustrates why performers sought new standards of protection. This decision was rendered a decade before conclusion of the TRIPS Agreement and the WIPO Performances and Phonograms Treaty, and prior to Swiss amendments to its copyright law in 1992 (described following the decision). Though Switzerland had signed the Rome Convention in 1961, it did not ratify the Convention until September 1993.

---

### *Schweizerische Interpreten-Gesellschaft and Others v. X and Z*

Bundesgericht (Swiss Federal Court) BGE 110 II 411, [1986] ECC 384, October 2, 1984

#### HEADNOTE:

Appeal from the Obergericht (Cantonal Court of Appeal), Zurich. . . .

#### FACTS:

A

On the evening of 2 November 1980 the Zurich Opera gave a gala performance of the opera "Tosca" by Giacomo Puccini. At that time X was still a member of the Opera chorus. That evening he sat for almost the entire performance in the second row of a so-called relatives' box, where he made sound recordings with a cassette recorder. He was seen doing this, allegedly accompanied by Mrs Z. In January 1981 he was reported by the Schweizerische Interpreten-Gesellschaft for infringement of copyrights.

In the criminal investigation, which was extended to Mrs Z, X admitted that he had made sound recordings of approximately 15 musical stage works between the middle of 1979 and December 1980 in the Zurich Opera, and had sold approximately the same number of cassettes at cost price. Mrs Z stated, as an accused, that she had advertised in the October 1980 issue of the magazine Opernwelt for people who wanted to exchange opera recordings, but only a few prospective purchasers had replied and she had sold them recordings of the opera "Tristan und Isolde" at cost price. Both accused denied that they had commercial intentions. The District Prosecutor's Office, Zurich, and, following an appeal, on 8 October 1982 the State Prosecutor of the Canton of Zurich discontinued the criminal proceedings because performances by performing artists (performers) are not protected by copyright.

Thereupon the Interpreten-Gesellschaft applied to the Single Judge of the District Court, Zurich, who on 20 October 1982 prohibited the accused, as a precautionary measure, from re-selling sound recordings of the Zurich Opera, subject to a penalty, and provisionally impounded the recordings, which had been placed in the criminal files.

**B**

In October 1983 the Society, together with seven musicians who had sung at the gala performance of 2 November 1980, brought an action against X and Mrs Z in the Appeal Court of the Canton of Zurich. The plaintiffs sought an injunction prohibiting the defendants from selling and exploiting commercially sound recordings originating from the Opera House, subject to a penalty; an order requiring them to disclose the volume of their sales and to surrender all receipts; and an order for the destruction of the impounded tapes and cassettes.

The defendants opposed these applications.

By judgment of 26 January 1984 the Appeal Court dismissed the action and rescinded the precautionary measures ordered by the Single Judge.

**C**

The plaintiffs have appealed against that judgment, maintaining their original applications. The defendants ask the Court to dismiss the appeal and to uphold the judgment appealed against.

**JUDGMENT:**

The plaintiffs maintain that performers also create works within the meaning of the Copyright Act and can therefore invoke the protection of the Act if their performances are to be regarded as artistic. In particular, a musical stage work is achieved only by the activity of all the performers, including the musicians of an orchestra. To refuse them protection for their performance is clearly contrary to the words and meaning of section 4(1)(2) and 4(2) of the Copyright Act, which lays down mandatory protection providing that the other requirements of copyright law are met. The Appeal Court, on the other hand, agrees with the defendants that a new work is not created by the performance of an orchestra or chorus, so that its members cannot be regarded as creators within the meaning of the Act; this applies in cases where, as here, we are not concerned with an interpretative achievement of a work, but the performance of a famous opera. . . .

However, the plaintiffs' submissions in support of their argument fail owing to the definition of a copyright-protected work. . . . A work capable of copyright protection, within the meaning of section 1(2) of the Copyright Act, presupposes an original creation, i.e. an achievement of creative intellectual activity with a minimum degree of its own personal character. (*See* BGE 105 II 299 and 85 II 123 para 3, with references.) The plaintiffs appreciate that this also applies to the individual performance of a performer. Contrary to their objections, however, protection for a performance cannot be inferred from the wording of the Act, nor can it be acknowledged regardless of the latitude which an individual performer has within a group of musicians or singers who are attuned to each other. There can be no serious question of this at least in relation to a classical opera, as here, the performance of which is predetermined in every detail by the composer, the producer and the conductor. In such a case an exception is justified at the most in relation to the conductor and soloists, but not other participants who are members of an orchestra or choir. It is unnecessary to decide here what the position would be with regard to so-called aleatoric works by modern composers, which give the performer wide latitude, which is not the same thing, or in the case of improvisations and variations.

(b) This is also the prevailing view of legal theorists. . . . Troller (In Immaterialguterrecht 1, 3rd edition, pp 391-2) likewise now (differing from the second edition (At p 501 et seq) accepts that conductors and soloists are able to fashion musical works individually but that orchestras and choruses cannot take part in this process because they have to subordinate their view of the work to that of the conductor. He regrets that the legislature and certain theorists do not include protection for creative performers in the ambit of the Copyright Act, regardless of the power to fashion a work, and that neither the revised Berne Convention nor the Universal Copyright Convention mentions such protection, but leaves it to State Parties.

Attempts by these States to reach an objectively satisfactory solution show similar tendencies. In several European countries the rights of performing artists are protected by special legislation on the assumption that the performance does not give them a copyright in the work performed. (*See* Frank Gotzen, Das Recht des Interpreten in der Europäischen Wirtschaftsgemeinschaft, p 49 et seq.) In other countries, by contrast, such protection is not given in any legislation but is left to the courts in individual cases. This applies to Switzerland, where neither the current law nor the new Copyright Bill contains, provisions for the protection of performing artists; on the contrary, according to the explanatory memorandum to the Bill, such provisions are to remain separate from copyright and incorporated in another field of law or a separate Act if necessary. (*See* BB1 [1984] III p 198 et seq.)

In the present case, however, it is unnecessary to give a final answer to the question whether and, if so, to what extent qualified performers can invoke copyright protection. No doubt, there is much to be said for the proposition that conductors and soloists in particular fashion musical works individually in performance and may thereby create a work at second hand if they have enough latitude. However, this cannot be said in general of any performance of a work of classical music by elite participants, however high the qualitative level. The Court does not wish to diminish their contributions in any way, but the plaintiff members of the orchestra cannot claim copyright protection for their own contribution for this reason.

[The court subsequently rejected both the plaintiffs' allegation of unfair competition and the claim of infringement of its personality rights (*Persönlichkeitsrecht*). The court held that results of effort and labor that are not or are no longer protectable under copyright law may not be protected by means of competition law or right of personality indirectly. Exceptions to this rule should only apply if there are additional circumstances justifying the application of these provisions. Accordingly, the Federal Court dismissed the appeal and upheld the judgment of the Cantonal Appeal Court.]

## NOTES AND QUESTIONS

**1.** Title 3 of the 1992 Swiss Federal Law on Copyright and Neighboring Rights Protection (Bundesgesetz über das Urheberrecht und verwandte Schutzrechte), adopted well after the text decision, addressed neighboring rights, and Article 33 granted performance rights to artists, including the right to authorize sound recordings (Article 33(c)). Article 34 concerned the distribution of rights among performing groups, and provided that in the case of a choral, orchestral, or theatrical performance, the rights are shared among soloists, producers, conductors, and the representative of the artists' group. It would appear that all of the aforementioned parties must consent to authorize a sound recording. May we assume that the result in the text case would be different after the changes to Swiss law brought about by the 1992 law?

**2.** The Rolling Stones first recorded "(I Can't Get No) Satisfaction" in 1965. Since then, how many times do you think the group has performed that song live? When they performed it live during their world tour in 2022, was there a creative element in the performances? Under the rules applied by the Swiss Supreme Court in the text case, would the group have been able to prevent its audiences from making sound recordings of "Satisfaction"?

### 2. *The Rome, Geneva, and Brussels Conventions*

Until the TRIPS Agreement (and subsequent WPPT), the most widely adhered-to multilateral agreement concerning rights of performers, producers, and broadcasters was the Rome Convention (1961). The following excerpt from the WIPO Intellectual Property Handbook describes the main features of the Rome Convention. This is followed by a brief description of the Geneva Convention (1971) and the Brussels Satellite Convention (1974).

## *Special Conventions in the Field of Related Rights: The International Convention for the Protection of Performers, Producers of Phonograms and Broadcasting Organizations ("The Rome Convention")**

#### . . . The Minimum Protection Required by the Convention

5.500 The minimum protection guaranteed by the Convention to performers is provided by "the possibility of preventing certain acts" done without their consent. Instead of enumerating the minimum rights of performers, this expression was used in order to allow countries like the United Kingdom to continue to protect performers by virtue of penal statutes, determining offenses and penal sanctions under public law. It was agreed, however, that the enumerated acts which may be prevented by the performer, require his consent in advance. In fact, the possibility of preventing certain acts as defined in the Convention amounts to a distinct bundle of rights granted to performers.

5.501 The restricted acts comprise: broadcasting or communication to the public of a "live" performance; recording an unfixed performance; reproducing a fixation of the performance, provided that the original fixation was made without the consent of the performer or the reproduction is made for purposes not permitted by the Convention or the performer (Article 7).

5.502 Producers of phonograms have the right to authorize or prohibit the direct or indirect reproduction of their phonograms (Article 10). The Rome Convention does not provide for any right to authorize performances of the phonogram and does not explicitly prohibit distribution or importation of unauthorized duplicates of phonograms.

5.503 Broadcasting organizations have the right to authorize or prohibit: the simultaneous rebroadcasting of their broadcasts, the fixation of their broadcasts, the reproduction of unauthorized fixations of their broadcasts or reproduction of lawful fixations for illicit purposes and the communication to the public of their television broadcasts by means of receivers in places accessible to the public against payment. It should be noted, however, that this last-mentioned right does not extend to communication to the public of merely sound broadcasts, and that it is a matter for domestic legislation to determine the conditions under which such a right may be exercised. It should also be observed that the Rome Convention does not protect against distribution by cable of broadcasts.

#### Provisions for Discretionary Regulation of the Exercise of Rights

5.504 The Rome Convention, over and above the minimum requirements of protection, also contains provisions allowing national laws to regulate certain aspects of protection at their discretion. . . .

5.507 Concerning both the protection of performers and producers of phonograms, Article 12 (perhaps the most controversial part of the Convention) provides that if a

* WIPO Intellectual Property Handbook.

phonogram published for commercial purposes is used directly for broadcasting or any communication to the public, an equitable remuneration shall be paid by the user to the performers, or to the producers of the phonogram, or to both. This Article does not grant any right to either the performers or producers of phonograms to authorize or to prohibit the secondary use of a phonogram. By guaranteeing a single remuneration for the use of the phonogram it seems to establish a sort of non-voluntary license. It does not, however, obligatorily specify the beneficiary or beneficiaries of the remuneration for the secondary use of the performance and the phonogram embodying it.

Article 12 only says that at least one of the interested parties should be paid for the use; nevertheless it provides that in the absence of agreement between these parties, domestic law may optionally lay down the conditions for the sharing of this remuneration.

5.508 The implementation of these provisions, however, can be excluded or restricted by the Contracting States at any time by an appropriate notification (Article 16(1)(a)). A State may declare that it will not apply the provisions of Article 12. A Contracting State may declare that it will not apply this article in respect of certain uses. . . .

### Limitations

5.509 The Rome Convention allows for certain limitations of the rights granted and, as regards the performers, also imposes limitations on rights itself.

5.510 Any Contracting State may provide for exceptions as regards private use, use of short excerpts in connection with reporting current events, ephemeral fixation by a broadcasting organization by means of its own facilities and for its own broadcasts, and for all kinds of use solely for the purpose of teaching or scientific research (Article 15(1)). This latter possibility of introducing exceptions may be of special benefit to developing countries.

5.511 Besides the exceptions specified by the Convention, any Contracting State may also provide for the same kind of limitations with regard to the protection of performers, producers of phonograms and broadcasting organizations as it provides for in connection with copyright protection. There is, however, an important difference: compulsory licenses may be provided for only to the extent to which they are compatible with the Rome Convention (Article 15(2)).

5.512 In view of the cinematographic industry's interest in exclusively exploiting the contributions made to their productions, Article 19 of the Rome Convention provides that once a performer has consented to the incorporation of his performance in a visual or audiovisual fixation, he shall have no further rights under the Rome Convention as regards the performance concerned.

### Duration of Protection

5.513 The minimum term of protection under the Rome Convention is a period of twenty years, to be computed from the end of the year in which the fixation was made, as far as phonograms and performances incorporated therein are concerned, or the performance took place, as regards performances not incorporated in phonograms, or the broadcast took place, for broadcasts (Article 14).

### Restriction of Formalities

5.514 If a country requires compliance with formalities as a condition of protecting related rights in relation to phonograms, these should be considered as fulfilled if all copies in commerce of the published phonogram or their containers bear a notice consisting of the symbol P, accompanied by the year date of the first publication. If the copies of their containers do not identify the producer or his licensee, the notice shall also include the name of the owner of the rights of the producer, and if the copies or their containers do not identify the principal performers, the notice shall also include the name of the person who owns the rights of such performers (Article 11). It should be emphasized that this provision is *not* a formality requirement; it is a restriction of formalities, which may be required by some national laws. . . .

#### THE OTHER SPECIAL CONVENTIONS

5.524 Besides the Rome Convention of 1961, a basic legal instrument discussed in the previous section, two other international instruments have been drawn up with regard to certain related rights. These are the Convention for the Protection of Producers of Phonograms Against Unauthorized Duplication of Their Phonograms, concluded in Geneva in October 1971 and generally referred to as "the Phonograms Convention," and the Convention Relating to the Distribution of Programme-Carrying Signals Transmitted by Satellite, concluded in Brussels in May 1974 and known briefly as "the Satellites Convention." These two Conventions are also within the area of related rights, and their purpose is to protect producers of phonograms and broadcasting organizations, respectively, against certain prejudicial acts that have been widely recognized as infringements or acts of piracy.

5.525 With regard to the Rome Convention, the Phonograms Convention and the Satellites Convention may be regarded as special agreements, the conclusion of which is reserved for Contracting States insofar as the agreements grant to performers, producers of phonograms or broadcasting organizations more extensive rights than those granted by the Rome Convention, or contain other provisions not contrary to that Convention (Article 22 of the Rome Convention).

## NOTES AND QUESTIONS

**1.** The United States did not join the Rome Convention because, *inter alia*, the United States did not recognize performers' rights, but it is a party to the Geneva Convention. The Geneva Convention provides protection to producers against unauthorized duplication of phonograms. The United States amended its copyright legislation in connection with implementation of the TRIPS Agreement to recognize the rights of performers (U.S. Copyright Act, §1101), but it has not acceded to the Rome Convention.

**2.** The transmission of broadcast signals by satellite has become a commonplace mode of distributing copyrighted works. The signal transmitted from a satellite to the earth creates a "footprint" or "zone of illumination" that is often larger than a single country, and it may often exceed the geographical area for which rights to broadcast, retransmit, etc., have been secured from the copyright holder.

The Brussels Convention establishes a few basic principles regulating satellite transmissions, such as the principle obligating contracting states to take steps to prevent the misappropriation of signals within their territory. However, the rules of the Brussels Convention are limited. They do not seek to establish what country's rules should govern the interests of copyright holders. The Convention establishes obligations only with respect to satellite signals intended for retransmission to the public. It does not apply to signals that are intended for direct reception by the public. As of 2018, only 38 countries were party to the Brussels Convention.

### 3. *The WIPO Performances and Phonograms Treaty (WPPT)*

#### a. WPPT Norms

The WPPT was adopted alongside the WCT in 1996 in Geneva. Like the WCT, the WPPT was intended to make WIPO-administered rules consistent with those of the TRIPS

Agreement, and to go further by addressing issues presented by digital technologies. WIPO describes the elements of the WPPT.

## *The WIPO Performances and Phonograms Treaty (WPPT)**

### Introduction

5.553 The WIPO Diplomatic Conference on Certain Copyright and Neighboring Rights Questions, held in Geneva in December 1996, adopted two treaties: the WIPO Copyright Treaty (the third section dealt with in this chapter) and the WIPO Performances and Phonograms Treaty (WPPT).

5.554 In view of the technological developments of the 1980s, as also in the field of copyright, it was recognized that guidance in the form of recommendations, guiding principles and model provisions would no longer suffice, and that binding new norms were indispensable. The WCT and the WPPT were prepared in parallel at the same Diplomatic Conference.

### Legal Nature of the WPPT and Its Relationship with Other International Treaties

5.555 The WPPT has a certain relationship with the Rome Convention which has been regulated in a way similar to the relationship between the TRIPS Agreement and the Rome Convention. . . .

### Substantive Provisions of the WPPT

#### Provisions Relating to the So-Called "Digital Agenda"

5.559 The provisions of the WPPT relating to the "digital agenda" cover the following issues: certain definitions, rights applicable to storage and transmission of performances and phonograms in digital systems, limitations on and exceptions to rights in a digital environment, technological measures of protection and rights management information. As discussed below, the right of distribution may also be relevant in respect of transmissions in digital networks; its scope, however, is much broader. Also due to its relationship with the right of rental, the right of distribution is discussed, together with the former right, below.

#### Definitions

5.560 The WPPT follows the structure of the Rome Convention, in the sense that it contains, in Article 2, a series of definitions. The definitions cover more or less the same terms as those which are defined in Article 3 of the Rome Convention: "performers," "phonogram," "producer of phonograms," "publication," "broadcasting." They cover more, in the sense that the WPPT also defines "fixation" and "communication to the public," and less, in the sense that they do not define "reproduction" and "rebroadcasting."

5.561 The impact of digital technology is present in the definitions, on the basis of the recognition that phonograms do not necessarily mean the fixation of sounds of a performance or other sounds any more; now they may also include fixations of (digital) representations of sounds that have never existed, but that have been directly generated by electronic means.

* WIPO Intellectual Property Handbook.

The reference to such possible fixations appears in the definitions of "phonogram," "fixation," "producer of phonogram," "broadcasting" and "communication to the public." It should be stressed, however, that the reference to "representations of sounds" does not expand the relevant definitions as provided under existing treaties; it only reflects the desire to offer a clarification in the face of advancing technology.

### Storage of Works in Digital Form in an Electronic Medium

5.562 In June 1982, a WIPO/UNESCO Committee of Governmental Experts clarified that storage of works and objects of related rights in an electronic medium is reproduction. The Diplomatic Conference adopted an agreed statement which reads: "The reproduction right, as set out in Articles 7 and 11 [of the WPPT], and the exceptions permitted thereunder through Article 16 [of the WPPT], fully apply in the digital environment, in particular to the use of performances and phonograms in digital form. It is understood that the storage of a protected performance or phonogram in digital form in an electronic medium constitutes a reproduction within the meaning of these Articles."

5.563 The first sentence states the obvious, that the provisions of the Treaty on the rights of reproduction are fully applicable in a digital environment. The concept of reproduction must not be restricted merely because a reproduction is in digital form through storage in an electronic memory, or because a reproduction is of a temporary nature. It also follows from the same first sentence that Article 16 of the Treaty is also fully applicable, offering an appropriate basis to introduce any justified exceptions, such as in respect of certain transient and incidental reproductions, in national legislation, in harmony with the "three-step test" provided for in that provision of the Treaty (see below).

5.564 The second sentence of the agreed statement simply confirms the definition of storage of works. It is another matter that the word "storage" may still be interpreted in somewhat differing ways.

### Transmission in Digital Networks

5.565 The background to the provisions of the WPPT concerning transmission of works in digital networks, including the so-called "umbrella solution," can be found in the third section of this chapter.

5.566 In the WPPT, the relevant provisions regarding transmission in digital networks are Articles 10 and 14, under which performers and producers of phonograms, respectively, must enjoy "the exclusive right of authorizing the making available to the public" of their performances fixed in phonograms and of their phonograms, respectively, "by wire or wireless means, in such a way that members of the public may access them from a place and at a time individually chosen by them."

Taking into account the freedom of Contracting Parties to choose differing legal characterization of acts covered by certain rights provided for in the treaties, it is clear that, also in this case, Contracting Parties may implement the relevant provisions not only by applying such a specific right but also by applying some other rights such as the right of distribution or the right of communication to the public—providing their obligations to grant an exclusive right of authorization concerning the acts described are fully respected.

5.567 On the question of whether the mere provision of physical facilities for enabling or making a communication in itself amounts to communication within the meaning of the WCT or the Berne Convention, the agreed statement, which was adopted in relation to Article 8 of the WCT, intends to clarify the issue of the liability of service and access providers in digital networks like the Internet.

It is clear that, although this was not stated explicitly, the principle reflected in the agreed statement is also applicable, *mutatis mutandis*, to the above-mentioned provisions of Articles 10 and 14 of the WPPT concerning "making available to the public."

### Limitations and Exceptions in the Digital Environment

5.568 The Diplomatic Conference affirmed that the agreed statement concerning limitations and exceptions is applicable *mutatis mutandis* also to Article 16 of the WPPT on limitations and exceptions. That provision of the WPPT is discussed below. It is obvious that any limitations and exceptions — existing or new — in the digital environment are only applicable if they are acceptable under the "three-step test" indicated in Article 16(2) of the Treaty (see below).

### Technological Measures of Protection and Rights Management Information

5.569 The provisions in Articles 18 and 19 of the WPPT concerning technological measures and rights management information correspond to the similar provisions of the WCT (see the third section dealt with in this chapter).

5.570 An agreed statement was adopted by the Diplomatic Conference concerning Article 12 of the WCT, which contains provisions similar to those of Article 19 of WPPT. The first part of the agreed statement reads: "It is understood that the reference to 'infringement of any right covered by this Treaty or the Berne Convention' includes both exclusive rights and rights of remuneration."

The second part reads: "It is further understood that Contracting Parties will not rely on this Article to devise or implement rights management systems that would have the effect of imposing formalities which are not permitted under the Berne Convention or this Treaty, prohibiting the free movement of goods or impeding the enjoyment of rights under this Treaty." The Diplomatic to Article 19 of the WPPT.

### Other Substantive Provisions

#### Criteria for Eligibility

5.571 Article 3 provides for the application of the criteria under the Rome Convention (Articles 4, 5, 17 and 18).

#### National Treatment

5.572 Article 4 provides for the same kind of national treatment as that prescribed by Article 3.1 of the TRIPS Agreement in respect of related rights, that is, national treatment only extends to the rights granted under the Treaty.

#### Coverage of the Rights of Performers

5.573 The coverage of the rights of performers is similar to that under the TRIPS Agreement; it only extends to live aural performances and performances fixed in phonograms, except for the right of broadcasting and communication to the public of live performances, which under Article 6(i) extends to all kinds of live performances, not only to aural ones (as under the second sentence of Article 14.1 of the TRIPS Agreement).

5.574 It is a question for interpretation whether the right to authorize fixation of unfixed performances under Article 6(ii) extends to all fixations or only to fixations on phonograms. The text of the provision may suggest a broader coverage; if, however, the definition of "fixation" under Article 2(c) is also taken into account, it seems that a narrower interpretation is justified. According to the said definition, "fixation" only means "the embodiment of *sounds, or the representation thereof*, from which they can be perceived, reproduced or communicated through a device" (emphasis added). Thus, Article 6(ii) seems to only extend to fixation on phonograms.

### Moral Rights of Performers

5.575 Article 5(1) provides as follows: "Independently of a performer's economic rights, and even after the transfer of those rights, the performer shall, as regards his live aural performances or performances fixed in phonograms, have the right to claim to be identified as the performer of his performances, except where omission is dictated by the manner of the use of the performance, and to object to any distortion, mutilation or other modification of his performances that would be prejudicial to his reputation." This provision, in its main lines, follows Article 6*bis* of the Berne Convention (on the moral rights of authors) but it requires a somewhat lower level of protection: in respect of the right to be identified as the performer, the element of practicability is built in, and the scope of "the right to respect" is also narrower. Article 5(2) and (3), on the duration of protection of, and the means of redress for safeguarding, the rights, are *mutatis mutandis* versions of Article 6*bis*(2) and (3) of the Berne Convention.

### Economic Rights of Performers

5.576 In addition to the "right of making available," discussed above under the "digital agenda," and a right of distribution, discussed below, the WPPT provides for practically the same economic rights for performers—right of broadcasting and communication to the public of unfixed performances (but in Article 6(ii) it is added: "except where the performance is already a broadcast performance"), right of reproduction and right of rental (Articles 6, 7 and 9)—as the rights granted in the TRIPS Agreement (Articles 14.1 and 14.4).

5.577 As far as the distribution right is concerned, Article 8(1) provides that performers have an exclusive right of authorizing the making available to the public of the original and copies of their performances fixed in phonograms, through sale or other transfer of ownership. Article 8(2) deals with the issue of the exhaustion of this right. It does not oblige Contracting States to choose national/regional exhaustion or international exhaustion, or to regulate at all the issue of exhaustion.

### Rights of Producers of Phonograms

5.578 In addition to the right of "making available" discussed above under the "digital agenda" and a right of distribution, the WPPT provides the same rights for producers of phonograms—right of reproduction and right of rental (Articles 11 and 13)—as those granted under the TRIPS Agreement (Articles 14.2 and 14.4).

5.579 Article 12 contains, *mutatis mutandis*, the same provisions concerning a right of distribution for producers of phonograms in respect of their phonograms, as Article 8 does concerning such a right for performers in respect of their performances fixed in phonograms (see above).

### Right to Remuneration for Broadcasting and Communication to the Public

5.580 Article 15 provides practically the same kind of right of remuneration to performers and producers of phonograms as Article 12 of the Rome Convention (except that, while the latter leaves it to national legislation whether this right is granted to performers, to producers or to both, the former provides that this right must be granted to both, in the form of a single equitable remuneration) and with the same extent of possible reservations as under Article 16.1(a) of the Rome Convention.

5.581 A specific feature of Article 15 appears in paragraph (4) which provides as follows: "For the purposes of this Article, phonograms made available to the public by wire or wireless means in such a way that members of the public may access them from a place and at a time individually chosen by them shall be considered as if they had been published for commercial purposes."

### Limitations and Exceptions

5.582 Under Article 16(1) of the WPPT, Contracting Parties may "provide for the same kinds of limitations or exceptions with regard to the protection of performers and producers of phonograms as they provide for, in their national legislation, in connection with the protection of copyright in literary and artistic works." This provision corresponds in substance to Article 15.2 of the Rome Convention. It is, however, an important difference that the Rome Convention, in its Article 15.1, also provides for specific limitations independent of those provided for in a given domestic law concerning copyright protection. Two of those specific limitations (use of short excerpts for reporting current events and ephemeral fixations by broadcasting organizations) are in harmony with the corresponding provisions of the Berne Convention; the third specific limitation, however, is not, since it provides for the possibility of limitations in respect of private use without any further conditions, while, in the Berne Convention, limitations for private use are also covered by the general provisions of Article 9(2) and, consequently, are subject to the "three-step test" (see under the WCT, paragraph 5.244).

5.583 If a country adheres to both the WCT and the WPPT, which is desirable, on the basis of the above-quoted Article 16(1) of the WPPT, it is obliged to apply the "three-step test" also for any limitations and exceptions to the rights provided for in the WPPT. Article 16(2) of the WPPT, however, contains a provision which prescribes this directly also (and, thus, that test is applicable irrespective of whether or not a given country also adheres to the WCT); it reads: "Contracting Parties shall confine any limitations of or exceptions to rights provided for in this Treaty to certain special cases which do not conflict with a normal exploitation of the performance or phonogram and do not unreasonably prejudice the legitimate interests of the performer or of the producer of the phonogram."

### Transferability of Rights

5.584 The Treaty—similarly to the Berne Convention and the WCT—does not contain any limitation on the transferability of economic rights. The transferability of economic rights is confirmed also by the introductory phrase of Article 5(1) on moral rights of performers which reads: "Independently of a performer's economic rights and *even after the transfer of those rights. . . .*" (emphasis added).

### Duration of Protection

5.585 Under Article 17 of the WPPT, the "term of protection to be granted to performers shall last, at least, until the end of a period of 50 years computed from the end of the year in which the performance was fixed in a phonogram."

5.586 The term of protection of phonograms differs in substance from the term provided for in the TRIPS Agreement. Under Article 14.5 of the Agreement, the 50-year term is always computed from the end of the year in which the fixation was made, while under Article 17(2) of the WPPT, the term is calculated from the end of the year in which the phonogram was published, and it is only in case of absence of publication that it is calculated as under the

TRIPS Agreement. Since publication normally takes place after fixation, the term under the Treaty, in general, is somewhat longer.

**Formalities**

5.587 Under Article 20 of the WPPT, the enjoyment and exercise of rights provided for in the Treaty must not be subject to any formality. . . .

**Audiovisual Performances**

5.592 The definitions of the terms "phonogram" and "fixation" in Article 2(b) and (c) of the WPPT limit the application of the Treaty to recordings of sounds. As regards audiovisual use of performances (that is use through moving images, with or without sound) the WPPT only grants protection against live broadcasting (Article 6(i)). The 1996 Diplomatic Conference which adopted the WPPT also discussed a possible extension of the scope of protection to cover such audiovisual use, but agreement was not reached at the time. . . .

## NOTES AND QUESTIONS

**1.** The WPPT grants rights to performers and producers of phonograms that are more extensive than the rights afforded by the Rome Convention. It also addresses new technologies that enable the delivery of sound recordings over the Internet and other digital networks. The term of protection under the WPPT is 50 years as compared with the Rome term of 20 years. The 50-year term is consistent with the provisions of the TRIPS Agreement. The Rome Convention to some extent favors the interests of producers. The WPPT Treaty appears to carry forward territorial limitations with respect to the rights of performers by making their treatment subject to qualifications of the Rome Convention (*see* art. 3(2), WPPT in conjunction with art. 4, Rome). These qualifications are incorporated by reference in the TRIPS Agreement, which permits WTO Members to provide conditions and limitations on the rights of performers and producers consistent with the Rome Convention (art. 14.6, TRIPS).

**2.** In the United States, sound recordings (e.g., phonograms) are defined by the Copyright Act as copyright subject matter.[11] Recall that in 1998, the U.S. Congress enacted the Sonny Bono Copyright Term Extension Act (CTEA), extending the term of copyright to the life of author plus 70 years (see *Eldred v. Ashcroft, supra*).[12]

**3.** Art. 2(b) of the WPPT defines "phonogram" as the "fixation of the sounds of a performance or of other sounds, or of a representation of sounds, other than in the form of a fixation incorporated in a cinematographic or other audiovisual work." Therefore, audiovisual use is not protected under the WPPT (with the exception of protection against live broadcasting as set forth in Article 6). As the WPPT addressed the rights of performers in respect of audiovisual performances only to a limited extent, negotiations were initiated for a treaty to protect audiovisual performances. In 2012, a substantial number of WIPO members signed the Beijing Treaty on Audiovisual Performances that since its entry to force in 2020 substantially enhances the protection of performers of audiovisual works on an international basis. The Beijing Treaty grants performers four kinds of economic rights for their performances fixed in audiovisual fixations, such as motion pictures: (i) the right of reproduction; (ii) the right of distribution; (iii) the right of rental; and (iv) the right of making available. As to unfixed

11. 17 U.S.C. §102(7).
12. *See* Sonny Bono Copyright Term Extension (CTEA) Act, Pub. L. 105-298, Oct. 27, 1998, §102.

(live) performances, the Treaty grants performers three kinds of economic rights: (i) the right of broadcasting (except in the case of rebroadcasting); (ii) the right of communication to the public (except where the performance is a broadcast performance); and (iii) the right of fixation. The Treaty also grants performers moral rights, that is, the right to claim to be identified as the performer (except where such an omission would be dictated by the manner of the use of the performance); and the right to object to any distortion, mutilation, or other modification that would be prejudicial to the performer's reputation, taking into account the nature of the audiovisual fixations.

The Treaty provides that performers shall enjoy the right to authorize the broadcasting and communication to the public of their performances fixed in audiovisual fixations. However, Contracting Parties may notify that instead of the right of authorization, they will establish a right to equitable remuneration for the direct or indirect use of performances fixed in audiovisual fixations for broadcasting or communication to the public. Any Contracting Party may restrict or – provided that it makes a reservation to the Treaty – deny this right. In the case and to the extent of a reservation by a Contracting Party, the other Contracting Parties are permitted to deny, vis-à-vis the reserving Contracting Party, national treatment ("reciprocity").

As to limitations and exceptions, Article 13 of the Beijing Treaty incorporates the "three-step" test to determine limitations and exceptions, as provided for in Article 9(2) of the Berne Convention, extending its application to all rights. The accompanying Agreed Statement provides that the Agreed Statement of Article 10 WCT applies similarly to the Beijing Treaty, that is, that such limitations and exceptions as established in national law in compliance with the Berne Convention may be extended to the digital environment. Contracting States may devise new exceptions and limitations appropriate to the digital environment subject to the conditions of the "three-step" test. The term of protection must be at least 50 years. The enjoyment and exercise of the rights provided for in the Treaty cannot be subject to any formality.

The Treaty obliges further Contracting Parties to provide for legal remedies against the circumvention of technological measures (e.g., encryption) used by performers in connection with the exercise of their rights, and against the removal or altering of information—such as the indication of certain data that identify the performer, performance and the audiovisual fixation itself – necessary for the management (e.g., licensing, collecting and distribution of royalties) of the said rights ("rights management information").[13]

### b. WPPT Norms and the Internet

Business enterprises and individuals engaged in the commercial recording, distribution, and sale of copyrighted musical compositions and sound recordings were granted extensive legal protection in the WPPT. During the last several years, however, these interested groups were confronted with major challenges arising from continuously evolving technologies. New storage methods for digital data have been developed, coding audiovisual information, including movies and music, in a digital compressed format (e.g., MPEG, in the context of audio coding referred to as MP3).[14] The combination with broader Internet-connection bandwidth allows more efficient data exchange and storage of sound files. On the other hand, the emergence of so-called file sharing or "Peer-to-Peer" (P2P) systems provided a forum for large-scale data exchanges among Internet users.[15]

13. WIPO, https://www.wipo.int/treaties/en/ip/beijing/summary_beijing.html.
14. For more details, *see* https://mpeg.chiariglione.org/.
15. For a technical background, *see, e.g.*, http://en.wikipedia.org/wiki/Peer-to-peer.

The most prominent first-generation file-sharing system was "Napster." Napster, a software application created in 1999 by a 19-year-old student, facilitated the transmission of audio files between and among its users via free-download software. Napster did not store the individual user's audio files on its servers, but it stored the user's MP3 file names (i.e., personal library) and created a "collective directory" of files available for transfer during the time the user was logged onto the Napster system. The recording industry initiated legal proceedings against Napster. Eventually, the U.S. Court of Appeals for the Ninth Circuit held that Napster's service constituted both vicarious and contributory infringement of copyrighted works under the U.S. Copyright Act.[16] Yet, by the time the decision was rendered, Napster was already succeeded by myriad new P2P software. New software providers were more "copyright aware," having learned from the Napster experience. They developed more decentralized (sometimes anonymous) network systems and did not play an active role in connecting the users.

Next follows *MGM v. Grokster*, decided by the U.S. Supreme Court in 2005. The Court distinguishes Napster's and Grokster's roles in the file-sharing process. *MGM v. Grokster* does not directly apply the WPPT. There is no mention of the treaty in the opinion. Nonetheless, the decision addresses sounds that have been fixed in a digital medium for reproduction through a device, and that are accessible to individuals at a time and place of their own choosing. The Supreme Court's decision is likely to be looked at in other jurisdictions in both the copyright and neighboring rights contexts.

## *Metro-Goldwyn-Mayer Studios v. Grokster*

545 U.S. 913 (2005)

Justice Souter delivered the opinion of the Court.

The question is under what circumstances the distributor of a product capable of both lawful and unlawful use is liable for acts of copyright infringement by third parties using the product. We hold that one who distributes a device with the object of promoting its use to infringe copyright, as shown by clear expression or other affirmative steps taken to foster infringement, is liable for the resulting acts of infringement by third parties.

### I

### A

Respondents, Grokster, Ltd., and StreamCast Networks, Inc., defendants in the trial court, distribute free software products that allow computer users to share electronic files through peer-to-peer networks, so called because users' computers communicate directly with each other, not through central servers. The advantage of peer-to-peer networks over information networks of other types shows up in their substantial and growing popularity. Because they need no central computer server to mediate the exchange of information or files among users, the high-bandwidth communications capacity for a server may be dispensed with, and the need for costly server storage space is eliminated. Since copies of a file (particularly a popular one) are available on many users' computers, file requests and retrievals may be faster than on other types of networks, and since file exchanges do not travel through a server, communications can take place between any computers that remain connected to the network without risk that a glitch in the server will disable the network in its entirety. Given these benefits in

16. *A&M Records v. Napster*, 239 F.3d 1004 (9th Cir. 2001).

security, cost, and efficiency, peer-to-peer networks are employed to store and distribute electronic files by universities, government agencies, corporations, and libraries, among others.[1]

Other users of peer-to-peer networks include individual recipients of Grokster's and StreamCast's software, and although the networks that they enjoy through using the software can be used to share any type of digital file, they have prominently employed those networks in sharing copyrighted music and video files without authorization. A group of copyright holders (MGM for short, but including motion picture studios, recording companies, songwriters, and music publishers) sued Grokster and StreamCast for their users' copyright infringements, alleging that they knowingly and intentionally distributed their software to enable users to reproduce and distribute the copyrighted works in violation of the Copyright Act, 17 U.S.C. §101 et seq. (2000 ed. and Supp. II). MGM sought damages and an injunction.

Discovery during the litigation revealed the way the software worked, the business aims of each defendant company, and the predilections of the users. . . .

Although Grokster and StreamCast do not therefore know when particular files are copied, a few searches using their software would show what is available on the networks the software reaches. . . .

But MGM's evidence gives reason to think that the vast majority of users' downloads are acts of infringement, and because well over 100 million copies of the software in question are known to have been downloaded, and billions of files are shared across the FastTrack and Gnutella networks each month, the probable scope of copyright infringement is staggering.

Grokster and StreamCast concede the infringement in most downloads. . . .

Grokster and StreamCast are not, however, merely passive recipients of information about infringing use. The record is replete with evidence that from the moment Grokster and StreamCast began to distribute their free software, each one clearly voiced the objective that recipients use it to download copyrighted works, and each took active steps to encourage infringement. . . .

In addition to this evidence of express promotion, marketing, and intent to promote further, the business models employed by Grokster and StreamCast confirm that their principal object was use of their software to download copyrighted works. . . .

Finally, there is no evidence that either company made an effort to filter copyrighted material from users' downloads or otherwise impede the sharing of copyrighted files. Although Grokster appears to have sent e-mails warning users about infringing content when it received threatening notice from the copyright holders, it never blocked anyone from continuing to use its software to share copyrighted files. . . . StreamCast not only rejected another company's offer of help to monitor infringement . . . but blocked the Internet Protocol addresses of entities it believed were trying to engage in such monitoring on its networks. . . .

## B

. . . The District Court held that those who used the Grokster and Morpheus software to download copyrighted media files directly infringed MGM's copyrights, a conclusion not contested on appeal, but the court nonetheless granted summary judgment in favor of Grokster and StreamCast as to any liability arising from distribution of the then current versions of their software. Distributing that software gave rise to no liability in the court's view, because its use did not provide the distributors with actual knowledge of specific acts of infringement. . . .

1. Peer-to-peer networks have disadvantages as well. Searches on peer-to-peer networks may not reach and uncover all available files because search requests may not be transmitted to every computer on the network. There may be redundant copies of popular files. The creator of the software has no incentive to minimize storage or bandwidth consumption, the costs of which are borne by every user of the network. Most relevant here, it is more difficult to control the content of files available for retrieval and the behavior of users.

The Court of Appeals affirmed. 380 F.3d 1154 (CA9 2004). In the court's analysis, a defendant was liable as a contributory infringer when it had knowledge of direct infringement and materially contributed to the infringement. But the court read *Sony Corp. of America v. Universal City Studios, Inc.*, 464 U.S. 417 . . . (1984), as holding that distribution of a commercial product capable of substantial noninfringing uses could not give rise to contributory liability for infringement unless the distributor had actual knowledge of specific instances of infringement and failed to act on that knowledge. The fact that the software was capable of substantial noninfringing uses in the Ninth Circuit's view meant that Grokster and StreamCast were not liable, because they had no such actual knowledge, owing to the decentralized architecture of their software. The court also held that Grokster and StreamCast did not materially contribute to their users' infringement because it was the users themselves who searched for, retrieved, and stored the infringing files, with no involvement by the defendants beyond providing the software in the first place.

The Ninth Circuit also considered whether Grokster and StreamCast could be liable under a theory of vicarious infringement. The court held against liability because the defendants did not monitor or control the use of the software, had no agreed-upon right or current ability to supervise its use, and had no independent duty to police infringement. We granted certiorari.

## II

### A

MGM and many of the amici fault the Court of Appeals's holding for upsetting a sound balance between the respective values of supporting creative pursuits through copyright protection and promoting innovation in new communication technologies by limiting the incidence of liability for copyright infringement. The more artistic protection is favored, the more technological innovation may be discouraged; the administration of copyright law is an exercise in managing the trade-off. *See Sony Corp. v. Universal City Studios, supra*, at 442, 78 L. Ed. 2d 574, 104 S. Ct. 774; *see generally* Ginsburg, Copyright and Control over New Technologies of Dissemination, 101 Colum. L. Rev. 1613 (2001); Lichtman & Landes, Indirect Liability for Copyright Infringement: An Economic Perspective, 16 Harv. J. L. & Tech. 395 (2003).

The tension between the two values is the subject of this case, with its claim that digital distribution of copyrighted material threatens copyright holders as never before, because every copy is identical to the original, copying is easy, and many people (especially the young) use file-sharing software to download copyrighted works. This very breadth of the software's use may well draw the public directly into the debate over copyright policy. . . .

The argument for imposing indirect liability in this case is, however, a powerful one, given the number of infringing downloads that occur every day using StreamCast's and Grokster's software. When a widely shared service or product is used to commit infringement, it may be impossible to enforce rights in the protected work effectively against all direct infringers, the only practical alternative being to go against the distributor of the copying device for secondary liability on a theory of contributory or vicarious infringement. *See In re Aimster Copyright Litigation*, 334 F.3d 643, 645-646 (CA7 2003).

One infringes contributorily by intentionally inducing or encouraging direct infringement, *see Gershwin Pub. Corp. v. Columbia Artists Management, Inc.*, 443 F.2d 1159, 1162 (CA2 1971), and infringes vicariously by profiting from direct infringement while declining to exercise a right to stop or limit it, *Shapiro, Bernstein & Co. v. H. L. Green Co.*, 316 F.2d

304, 307 (CA2 1963).[9] Although "the Copyright Act does not expressly render anyone liable for infringement committed by another," *Sony Corp. v. Universal City Studios*, 464 U.S., at 434, 78 L. Ed. 2d 574, 104 S. Ct. 774 these doctrines of secondary liability emerged from common law principles and are well established in the law, *id.*, at 486, 78 L. Ed. 2d 574, 104 S. Ct. 774 (Blackmun, J., dissenting). . . .

### B

Despite the currency of these principles of secondary liability, this Court has dealt with secondary copyright infringement in only one recent case, and because MGM has tailored its principal claim to our opinion there, a look at our earlier holding is in order. In *Sony Corp. v. Universal City Studios, supra*, this Court addressed a claim that secondary liability for infringement can arise from the very distribution of a commercial product. There, the product, novel at the time, was what we know today as the videocassette recorder or VCR. Copyright holders sued Sony as the manufacturer, claiming it was contributorily liable for infringement that occurred when VCR owners taped copyrighted programs because it supplied the means used to infringe, and it had constructive knowledge that infringement would occur. At the trial on the merits, the evidence showed that the principal use of the VCR was for "time-shifting" or taping a program for later viewing at a more convenient time, which the Court found to be a fair, not an infringing, use. . . . There was no evidence that Sony had expressed an object of bringing about taping in violation of copyright or had taken active steps to increase its profits from unlawful taping. . . . Although Sony's advertisements urged consumers to buy the VCR to " 'record favorite shows' " or " 'build a library' " of recorded programs. . . . (Blackmun, J., dissenting), neither of these uses was necessarily infringing. . . .

On those facts, with no evidence of stated or indicated intent to promote infringing uses, the only conceivable basis for imposing liability was on a theory of contributory infringement arising from its sale of VCRs to consumers with knowledge that some would use them to infringe. . . . But because the VCR was "capable of commercially significant noninfringing uses," we held the manufacturer could not be faulted solely on the basis of its distribution. . . .

This analysis reflected patent law's traditional staple article of commerce doctrine, now codified, that distribution of a component of a patented device will not violate the patent if it is suitable for use in other ways. . . .

In sum, where an article is "good for nothing else" but infringement, *Canda v. Michigan Malleable Iron Co.*, [124 F. 486 (C.A. 6 1903)], at 489, there is no legitimate public interest in its unlicensed availability, and there is no injustice in presuming or imputing an intent to infringe. . . . Conversely, the doctrine absolves the equivocal conduct of selling an item with substantial lawful as well as unlawful uses, and limits liability to instances of more acute fault

9. We stated in *Sony Corp. of America v. Universal City Studios, Inc.*, 464 U.S. 417, 78 L. Ed. 2d 574, 104 S. Ct. 774 (1984), that " 'the lines between direct infringement, contributory infringement and vicarious liability are not clearly drawn.'. . . Reasoned analysis of [the *Sony* plaintiffs' contributory infringement claim] necessarily entails consideration of arguments and case law which may also be forwarded under the other labels, and indeed the parties . . . rely upon such arguments and authority in support of their respective positions on the issue of contributory infringement," *id.*, at 435, n. 17, 78 L. Ed. 2d 574, 104 S. Ct. 774 (quoting *Universal City Studios, Inc. v. Sony Corp.*, 480 F. Supp. 429, 457-458 (CD Cal. 1979)). In the present case MGM has argued a vicarious liability theory, which allows imposition of liability when the defendant profits directly from the infringement and has a right and ability to supervise the direct infringer, even if the defendant initially lacks knowledge of the infringement. *See, e.g., Shapiro, Bernstein & Co. v. H. L. Green Co.*, 316 F.2d 304, 308 (CA2 1963); *Dreamland Ball Room, Inc. v. Shapiro, Bernstein & Co.*, 36 F.2d 354, 355 (CA7 1929). Because we resolve the case based on an inducement theory, there is no need to analyze separately MGM's vicarious liability theory.

than the mere understanding that some of one's products will be misused. It leaves breathing room for innovation and a vigorous commerce. . . .

The parties and many of the amici in this case think the key to resolving it is the *Sony* rule and, in particular, what it means for a product to be "capable of commercially significant noninfringing uses." *Sony Corp. v. Universal City Studios, supra,* at 442, 78 L. Ed. 2d 574, 104 S. Ct. 774. MGM advances the argument that granting summary judgment to Grokster and StreamCast as to their current activities gave too much weight to the value of innovative technology, and too little to the copyrights infringed by users of their software, given that 90% of works available on one of the networks was shown to be copyrighted. Assuming the remaining 10% to be its noninfringing use, MGM says this should not qualify as "substantial," and the Court should quantify *Sony* to the extent of holding that a product used "principally" for infringement does not qualify. . . . As mentioned before, Grokster and StreamCast reply by citing evidence that their software can be used to reproduce public domain works, and they point to copyright holders who actually encourage copying. Even if infringement is the principal practice with their software today, they argue, the noninfringing uses are significant and will grow.

We agree with MGM that the Court of Appeals misapplied *Sony*, which it read as limiting secondary liability quite beyond the circumstances to which the case applied. *Sony* barred secondary liability based on presuming or imputing intent to cause infringement solely from the design or distribution of a product capable of substantial lawful use, which the distributor knows is in fact used for infringement. The Ninth Circuit has read *Sony*'s limitation to mean that whenever a product is capable of substantial lawful use, the producer can never be held contributorily liable for third parties' infringing use of it; it read the rule as being this broad, even when an actual purpose to cause infringing use is shown by evidence independent of design and distribution of the product, unless the distributors had "specific knowledge of infringement at a time at which they contributed to the infringement, and failed to act upon that information." 380 F.3d at 1162 (internal quotation marks and alterations omitted). Because the Circuit found the StreamCast and Grokster software capable of substantial lawful use, it concluded on the basis of its reading of *Sony* that neither company could be held liable, since there was no showing that their software, being without any central server, afforded them knowledge of specific unlawful uses.

This view of *Sony*, however, was error, converting the case from one about liability resting on imputed intent to one about liability on any theory. Because *Sony* did not displace other theories of secondary liability, and because we find below that it was error to grant summary judgment to the companies on MGM's inducement claim, we do not revisit *Sony* further, as MGM requests, to add a more quantified description of the point of balance between protection and commerce when liability rests solely on distribution with knowledge that unlawful use will occur. It is enough to note that the Ninth Circuit's judgment rested on an erroneous understanding of *Sony* and to leave further consideration of the *Sony* rule for a day when that may be required.

### C

*Sony*'s rule limits imputing culpable intent as a matter of law from the characteristics or uses of a distributed product. But nothing in *Sony* requires courts to ignore evidence of intent if there is such evidence, and the case was never meant to foreclose rules of fault-based liability derived from the common law.[10] *Sony Corp. v. Universal City Studios*, 464 U.S., at 439, 78

10. Nor does the Patent Act's exemption from liability for those who distribute a staple article of commerce, 35 U.S.C. §271(c), extend to those who induce patent infringement, §271(b).

L. Ed. 2d 574, 104 S. Ct. 774 ("If vicarious liability is to be imposed on Sony in this case, it must rest on the fact that it has sold equipment with constructive knowledge" of the potential for infringement). Thus, where evidence goes beyond a product's characteristics or the knowledge that it may be put to infringing uses, and shows statements or actions directed to promoting infringement, Sony's staple-article rule will not preclude liability.

The classic case of direct evidence of unlawful purpose occurs when one induces commission of infringement by another, or "entices or persuades another" to infringe, Black's Law Dictionary 790 (8th ed. 2004), as by advertising. . . .

The rule on inducement of infringement as developed in the early cases is no different today.[11] . . .

For the same reasons that Sony took the staple-article doctrine of patent law as a model for its copyright safe-harbor rule, the inducement rule, too, is a sensible one for copyright. We adopt it here, holding that one who distributes a device with the object of promoting its use to infringe copyright, as shown by clear expression or other affirmative steps taken to foster infringement, is liable for the resulting acts of infringement by third parties. We are, of course, mindful of the need to keep from trenching on regular commerce or discouraging the development of technologies with lawful and unlawful potential. Accordingly, just as Sony did not find intentional inducement despite the knowledge of the VCR manufacturer that its device could be used to infringe, 464 U.S., at 439, n. 19, 78 L. Ed. 2d 574, 104 S. Ct. 774, mere knowledge of infringing potential or of actual infringing uses would not be enough here to subject a distributor to liability. Nor would ordinary acts incident to product distribution, such as offering customers technical support or product updates, support liability in themselves. The inducement rule, instead, premises liability on purposeful, culpable expression and conduct, and thus does nothing to compromise legitimate commerce or discourage innovation having a lawful promise.

## III

### A

The only apparent question about treating MGM's evidence as sufficient to withstand summary judgment under the theory of inducement goes to the need on MGM's part to adduce evidence that StreamCast and Grokster communicated an inducing message to their software users. . . .

In StreamCast's case, of course, the evidence just described was supplemented by other unequivocal indications of unlawful purpose in the internal communications and advertising designs aimed at Napster users ("When the lights went off at Napster . . . where did the users go?". . .). . . .

Three features of th[e] evidence of intent are particularly notable. First, each company showed itself to be aiming to satisfy a known source of demand for copyright infringement, the market comprising former Napster users. StreamCast's internal documents made constant reference to Napster, it initially distributed its Morpheus software through an OpenNap program compatible with Napster, it advertised its OpenNap program to Napster users, and its Morpheus software functions as Napster did except that it could be used to distribute more kinds of files, including copyrighted movies and software programs. Grokster's name is apparently derived from Napster, it too initially offered an OpenNap program, its software's function is likewise comparable to Napster's, and it attempted to divert queries for Napster onto its own Web site. Grokster and StreamCast's efforts to supply services to former Napster

11. Inducement has been codified in patent law. *Ibid.*

users, deprived of a mechanism to copy and distribute what were overwhelmingly infringing files, indicate a principal, if not exclusive, intent on the part of each to bring about infringement.

Second, this evidence of unlawful objective is given added significance by MGM's showing that neither company attempted to develop filtering tools or other mechanisms to diminish the infringing activity using their software. While the Ninth Circuit treated the defendants' failure to develop such tools as irrelevant because they lacked an independent duty to monitor their users' activity, we think this evidence underscores Grokster's and StreamCast's intentional facilitation of their users' infringement.[12]

Third, there is a further complement to the direct evidence of unlawful objective. It is useful to recall that StreamCast and Grokster make money by selling advertising space, by directing ads to the screens of computers employing their software. As the record shows, the more the software is used, the more ads are sent out and the greater the advertising revenue becomes. Since the extent of the software's use determines the gain to the distributors, the commercial sense of their enterprise turns on high-volume use, which the record shows is infringing.[13] This evidence alone would not justify an inference of unlawful intent, but viewed in the context of the entire record its import is clear.

The unlawful objective is unmistakable.

### B

In addition to intent to bring about infringement and distribution of a device suitable for infringing use, the inducement theory of course requires evidence of actual infringement by recipients of the device, the software in this case. As the account of the facts indicates, there is evidence of infringement on a gigantic scale, and there is no serious issue of the adequacy of MGM's showing on this point in order to survive the companies' summary judgment requests. Although an exact calculation of infringing use, as a basis for a claim of damages, is subject to dispute, there is no question that the summary judgment evidence is at least adequate to entitle MGM to go forward with claims for damages and equitable relief. . . .

In sum, this case is significantly different from *Sony* and reliance on that case to rule in favor of StreamCast and Grokster was error. *Sony* dealt with a claim of liability based solely on distributing a product with alternative lawful and unlawful uses, with knowledge that some users would follow the unlawful course. The case struck a balance between the interests of protection and innovation by holding that the product's capability of substantial lawful employment should bar the imputation of fault and consequent secondary liability for the unlawful acts of others.

MGM's evidence in this case most obviously addresses a different basis of liability for distributing a product open to alternative uses. Here, evidence of the distributors' words and deeds going beyond distribution as such shows a purpose to cause and profit from third-party acts of copyright infringement. If liability for inducing infringement is ultimately found, it will not be on the basis of presuming or imputing fault, but from inferring a patently illegal objective from statements and actions showing what that objective was.

---

12. Of course, in the absence of other evidence of intent, a court would be unable to find contributory infringement liability merely based on a failure to take affirmative steps to prevent infringement, if the device otherwise was capable of substantial noninfringing uses. Such a holding would tread too close to the *Sony* safe harbor.

13. . . . [T]he distribution of a product can itself give rise to liability where evidence shows that the distributor intended and encouraged the product to be used to infringe. In such a case, the culpable act is not merely the encouragement of infringement but also the distribution of the tool intended for infringing use.

There is substantial evidence in MGM's favor on all elements of inducement, and summary judgment in favor of Grokster and StreamCast was error. On remand, reconsideration of MGM's motion for summary judgment will be in order.

The judgment of the Court of Appeals is vacated, and the case is remanded for further proceedings consistent with this opinion.

It is so ordered.

## NOTES AND QUESTIONS

**1.** The successful launch of Spotify, Apple Music, Pandora and similar streaming services has provided a substantial measure of relief to the recording industry and associated artists, but widespread unauthorized sharing of audio and video files continues. There appears to be at least some difference in attitude among generations, with older Internet users more willing to pay for content than younger. Of course, this could simply be explained by the fact that older users are more likely to be generating income and therefore have the capacity to pay.

**2.** It is often pointed out that many individuals who would not contemplate "shoplifting" a CD from a brick-and-mortar store are willing to "misappropriate" copyrighted works over the Internet. What may account for these different attitudes toward misappropriation? Do individuals inherently associate "tangible" goods such as CDs with labor for which they are willing to compensate, while not associating digital bits with labor? Do people avoid shoplifting only because they fear being caught?

**3.** Since the earliest days of personal computing, software developers have attempted to protect against the unauthorized copying of data with technical measures. While some of these technical measures have inhibited unauthorized copying, they certainly have not controlled the problem of software "piracy," nor in the case of audio and video files do technical protection measures seem likely to keep ahead of those attempting to defeat them. Legal solutions such as recording industry litigation threats against university administrators, and searches of student dormitories (with seizure of computers) are very unpleasant and seem unlikely to generate respect for copyright protection. Historically, problems of controlling large-scale "misappropriation" of copyrighted works—such as tape recording of over-the-air music broadcasts—have been addressed by imposing a tax or royalty on the sale of the hardware that enables the copying. The tax or royalty is then distributed to copyright holders based on formulas reflecting the popularity of their works. Is this a feasible solution to problems such as peer-to-peer file sharing of audio and video files? What are the foreseeable impediments to such a system? Have digital streaming services put the concerns of copyright owners to rest?

### *4. Broadcast, Cablecast, and Webcast*

The issue of an enhanced and updated protection for broadcasting organizations has been on the WIPO agenda since 1998, when the Standing Committee on Copyright and Related Rights (SCCR) was established. The adoption of a WIPO Broadcasting Organizations Treaty would harmonize the protection granted to broadcasting organizations by setting minimum standards internationally and seeks to be an effective anti-piracy instrument to protect program-carrying signals on a global scale. In 2023, a Second Revised Draft Text for the WIPO Broadcasting Organizations Treaty (SCCR/43/3) was distributed that seeks to attain a common ground of the scope of protection taking into account the various legal traditions. The Treaty would allow (but not require) the grant of exclusive intellectual property rights to the "signals" transmitted entirely over the Internet – a result not provided for under the

Rome Convention or Brussels Convention. The scope of limitations and exceptions has been improved but continues to permit exclusive rights over a broadcast signal that can curtail uses allowed under copyright law, such as quotation and access for people with disabilities.[17] While there has been a lot of support from broadcasting organizations, many, such as, for instance, the Electronic Frontier Foundation, fear that the new WIPO Treaty may have unintended consequences and harm innovation in the digital environment, as broadcasters would have unchecked control over other copyright holders, and even works in the public domain.

## E. The Marrakesh Treaty to Facilitate Access to Published Works for Persons Who Are Blind, Visually Impaired, or Otherwise Print Disabled

The Marrakesh Treaty was adopted on June 27, 2013 in Marrakesh and joined the body of copyright-related treaties administered by WIPO. The treaty seeks to facilitate access to copyright protected works by blind, visually impaired, and otherwise print-disabled persons. Conceptually, the treaty expounds a number of mandatory exceptions which signatories agree to introduce in domestic legislation. As of July 2023, the treaty had 93 contracting parties and entered into force on 30 September 2016.

The following facts sheet published by WIPO provides a survey of the treaty.

---

### *Main Provisions and Benefits of the Marrakesh Treaty (2013)**

#### Background

Each year, of the millions of books published worldwide, only between 1 and 7 percent (see World Blind Union (WBU) press release, June 2013) are made available to the 285 million persons in the world who are blind, visually impaired and print disabled, 90 per cent of whom live in low-income settings in developing countries (see World Health Organization online Factsheet on Visual Impairment and Blindness). The Marrakesh Treaty to Facilitate Access to Published Works for Persons Who Are Blind, Visually Impaired, or Otherwise Print Disabled ("the Marrakesh Treaty") was adopted by the Member States of the World Intellectual Property Organization (WIPO) on June 27, 2013, to address this problem, commonly referred to as the global book famine.

Conceived in line with the human rights principles outlined in the Universal Declaration of Human Rights and the United Nations Convention on the Rights of Persons with Disabilities (UNCRPD), the Marrakesh Treaty is the first copyright treaty to include a clear human rights perspective. The Marrakesh Treaty demonstrates that copyright systems are an important part of the solution to the challenge of improving access to books and other printed works for persons with print disabilities.

#### Main Elements of the Treaty

##### Definitions

The definitions provided in the Marrakesh Treaty are fundamental to understanding its scope and application. These definitions provide clarity on: who will be able to enjoy the limitations

---

17. For a discussion, *see, e.g.*, P. Bernt Hugenholtz, *The WIPO Broadcasting Treaty: Comments on the Second Revised Draft*, 84 Joint PIJIP/TLS Research Paper Series (2023), available at: https://digitalcommons.wcl.american.edu/research/84/.

* World Intellectual Property Organization, http://www.wipo.int/treaties/en/ip/marrakesh/ (visited July 28, 2018).

and exceptions outlined in the Treaty (the "beneficiaries"), what can be made accessible (the "works") and into which formats such works can be adapted ("accessible formats").

A "beneficiary" is defined as someone affected by one or more in a range of disabilities that interfere with the effective reading of printed material. This broad definition includes persons who are visually impaired as well those with a physical disability that prevents them from holding and manipulating a book.

The definitions of "works" and "accessible format copy" are closely related to the concept of beneficiaries in the sense that "works" refers to those materials that the "beneficiary" would not be able to read or access, except in an alternative or accessible format. The definition of "works" within the Treaty is limited to materials in the form of text, notation and/or related illustration, and an agreed statement by the Contracting Parties provides that this also includes audiobooks

The definition of "accessible format copy" is fairly broad and covers any format that permits a person with a visual impairment or other print disability to have access to the content as feasibly and comfortably as a person without such a disability, including digital formats.

The Marrakesh Treaty recognizes that governmental and non-governmental organizations play an important role in providing persons with print disabilities with access to alternative format materials. For that reason the Treaty allows these organizations to perform certain acts, otherwise prohibited under copyright law, in order to assist the "beneficiaries". In the definition, the Marrakesh Treaty states that "authorized entities" need to observe some conditions regarding the use of the work, for example ensuring that only those individuals considered as "beneficiaries" according to the Treaty will enjoy access to accessible format copies. The Marrakesh Treaty does not require an organization to fulfill any formalities or undertake specific procedures to obtain recognition as an "authorized entity". However, the Treaty does not forbid such measures and thus gives Member States the leeway to create such procedures at the national level.

### Obligations

The Marrakesh Treaty requires that Contracting Parties fulfill two main obligations when implementing the Treaty at the national level, although they may do so according to their own legal systems. The first is to provide for a limitation or an exception to copyright in order to allow "beneficiaries" and "authorized entities" to undertake any changes needed to make a copy of a work in an accessible format for persons with a print disability. The second is to allow the exchange across borders of those accessible copies produced according to the limitations and exceptions provided in the Marrakesh Treaty, or in accordance with the operation of law.

### Relationship with Other International Treaties

The Marrakesh Treaty has no formal relationship with other treaties and does not affect the obligations Member States have assumed under other international agreements. In fact, the Marrakesh Treaty reinforces the need for Contracting Parties to comply with their international obligations regarding the creation of limitations and exceptions at the national level. In international instruments, that obligation usually relates to the so-called three-step test that can be found in the Berne Convention, the WIPO Copyright Treaty and the TRIPS Agreement. In general, and depending on the exact wording of the instrument where it appears, the three-step test provides that limitations and exceptions in national legislation should be confined to:

i. certain special cases;
ii. that do not conflict with the normal exploitation of the work
iii. that do not unreasonably prejudice the legitimate interests of the rightholder.

### Benefits of Adherence

The Marrakesh Treaty has one shared goal and benefit: To increase access to books, magazines and other printed materials for the world's population of persons with print disabilities.

It is anticipated that the Treaty will have concrete positive effects in all countries where it is implemented, including developing and least developed countries, where the greatest numbers of persons with print disabilities live. Anticipated benefits include:

> a) Improved awareness of the challenges faced by the print-disabled community and persons with disabilities: The Marrakesh Treaty is an instrument that fosters discussion and raises awareness about the need for policies that benefit persons with disabilities. For example, the implementation of the Marrakesh Treaty could provide access to works for persons with other types of disabilities, or trigger actions to implement additional provisions of the UNCRPD, in favor of the wider community of persons with disabilities.
>
> b) Greater access to education: There is no doubt that education plays a crucial role in society and that it has an immeasurable impact on an individual's life. Access to educational materials in accessible formats is essential to enable persons with print disabilities to pursue educational opportunities. At the same time, educational institutions are only able to offer their services to individuals with print disabilities if they too have access to accessible format materials. The Marrakesh Treaty will improve the availability of accessible format educational materials so that persons with print disabilities can enjoy equal access to education.
>
> c) Enhanced social integration and cultural participation: Having equal access to common sources of knowledge and information is crucial not only for learning, but also for social inclusion and cultural participation. By improving access to both educational and leisure materials, the Marrakesh Treaty will facilitate greater inclusiveness and participation by persons with print disabilities in the cultural and social life of their communities.
>
> d) Leisure materials such as books, newspapers and magazines have a clear entertainment and information function in society, as well as an important role in the expression and dissemination of local culture. It is equally important that persons with print disabilities in the community have access to these materials, which afford them the opportunity to fully participate in cultural developments as consumers or as creators.
>
> e) Poverty alleviation and increased contributions to the national economy: Individual professional development is highly dependent on educational attainment. By providing access to learning materials in accessible formats, the implementation of the Marrakesh Treaty can be a powerful tool for poverty alleviation, providing persons with print disabilities with opportunities for professional growth, allowing them to contribute to their local economies and become economically self-sufficient.

In addition, by increasing the focus on accessible format works and improving the certainty about the system for their production and distribution under national copyright laws, the Marrakesh Treaty will strengthen local publishing industries and increase investment in copyright industries, which are key drivers for economic growth and development.

## III. EXHAUSTION AND THE MOVEMENT OF COPYRIGHTED WORKS IN INTERNATIONAL TRADE

### A. National and International Exhaustion

In Chapter 1, we introduced the subject of IPRs exhaustion and its relationship to the movement of goods in international trade. We have further examined exhaustion rules in respect of patents (Chapter 2) and trademarks (Chapter 3). It was earlier observed that countries do not necessarily follow the same rule of exhaustion with respect to all categories of intellectual property. Countries may, and do, adopt a different rule of exhaustion for copyright than they adopt with respect to patent.

Copyright affects a wide range of subject matter and its role in the international movement of goods may be broader than immediately apparent. For example, automobile producers attempt to protect the design of spare body parts with copyright, and to prevent the movement of such parts across national borders. A rule of national exhaustion of copyright may enable the producer to segregate markets. A rule of international exhaustion in copyright, on the other hand, may require the producer to make products available at roughly the same prices across world markets. Debate concerning copyright exhaustion has been quite intense in countries such as Australia and New Zealand, which have traditionally confronted higher prices based on their relative isolation from other major OECD markets.[18] Some of the best empirical studies of the impact of exhaustion rules on prices have been conducted in Australia and New Zealand.

In the United States, product labels may be protected by copyright.[19] Following the U.S. Supreme Court decision in *K mart v. Cartier, supra* Chapter 3, U.S. manufacturers increasingly turned to copyright as a means to block parallel importation of products that they (including their affiliates) had put on the market in foreign countries. This led to a division among the Courts of Appeals regarding whether the Copyright Act could be used for that purpose.

To resolve a split among the Circuits, in 1998, the Supreme Court decided *Quality King v. L'anza*. The holding of the *Quality King* decision directly applied to copyrighted subject matter produced within the United States, exported, and subsequently imported into the United States. Because of the complex construction of the U.S. Copyright Act and one passage of dicta included in the *Quality King* opinion, it could not be assumed that the rule of exhaustion announced by the Court in that case would govern the situation in which copyrighted goods are first sold outside the United States. The Supreme Court, in the following opinion by Justice Breyer, came down resoundingly in favor of international exhaustion for copyrighted works. Writing in dissent, Justice Ginsburg favored rejecting international exhaustion mainly because it is disfavored by the U.S. Trade Representative.

## *Kirtsaeng, dba Bluechristine99 v. John Wiley & Sons, Inc.*

568 U.S. 519 (2013)

JUSTICE BREYER delivered the opinion of the Court.

Section 106 of the Copyright Act grants "the owner of copyright under this title" certain "exclusive rights," including the right "to distribute copies . . . of the copyrighted work to the public by sale or other transfer of ownership." 17 U. S. C. §106(3). These rights are qualified, however, by the application of various limitations set forth in the next several sections of the Act, §§107 through 122. Those sections, typically entitled "Limitations on exclusive rights," include, for example, the principle of "fair use" (§107), permission for limited library archival reproduction, (§108), and the doctrine at issue here, the "first sale" doctrine (§109).

---

18. Australia and New Zealand each adopted legislation permitting parallel importation of works protected by copyright. The legislation adopted by Australia distinguishes among different types of copyrighted works. *See* Chris Creswell, *Recent Developments in Australia and New Zealand,* paper presented to ILA Trade Law Committee meeting of November 6-7, 1998, Geneva; and Abraham Van Melle, *Parallel Importing in New Zealand: Historical Origins, Recent Developments, and Future Directions,* [1999] EIPR 63. In the case of New Zealand, at least, this action led to a diplomatic protest by the U.S. government. *See* details in Frederick M. Abbott, *Second Report (Final) to the Committee on International Trade Law of the International Law Association on the Subject of the Exhaustion of Intellectual Property Rights and Parallel Importation,* presented in London, July 2000 at the 69th Conference of the International Law Association, rev. 1.1.

19. Recall that in *Feist v. Rural Telephone, supra,* the Supreme Court imposed a low threshold of originality.

Section 109(a) sets forth the "first sale" doctrine as follows:

> "Notwithstanding the provisions of section 106(3) [the section that grants the owner exclusive distribution rights], the owner of a particular copy or phonorecord *lawfully made under this title* . . . is entitled, without the authority of the copyright owner, to sell or otherwise dispose of the possession of that copy or phonorecord." (Emphasis added.)

Thus, even though §106(3) forbids distribution of a copy of, say, the copyrighted novel Herzog without the copyright owner's permission, §109(a) adds that, once a copy of Herzog has been lawfully sold (or its ownership otherwise lawfully transferred), the buyer of that copy and subsequent owners are free to dispose of it as they wish. In copyright jargon, the "first sale" has "exhausted" the copyright owner's §106(3) exclusive distribution right.

What, however, if the copy of Herzog was printed abroad and then initially sold with the copyright owner's permission? Does the "first sale" doctrine still apply? Is the buyer, like the buyer of a domestically manufactured copy, free to bring the copy into the United States and dispose of it as he or she wishes?

To put the matter technically, an "importation" provision, §602(a)(1), says that

> "[i]mportation into the United States, without the authority of the owner of copyright under this title, of copies . . . of a work that have been acquired outside the United States is an infringement of the exclusive right to distribute copies . . . *under section 106*. . . ." 17 U. S. C. §602(a)(1) (2006 ed., Supp. V) (emphasis added).

Thus §602(a)(1) makes clear that importing a copy without permission violates the owner's exclusive distribution right. But in doing so, §602(a)(1) refers explicitly to the §106(3) exclusive distribution right. As we have just said, §106 is by its terms "[s]ubject to" the various doctrines and principles contained in §§107 through 122, including §109(a)'s "first sale" limitation. Do those same modifications apply—in particular, does the "first sale" modification apply—when considering whether §602(a)(1) prohibits importing a copy?

In Quality King Distributors, Inc. v. L'anza Research Int'l, Inc., 523 U. S. 135, 145 (1998), we held that §602(a)(1)'s reference to §106(3)'s exclusive distribution right incorporates the later subsections' limitations, including, in particular, the "first sale" doctrine of §109. Thus, it might seem that, §602(a)(1) notwithstanding, one who buys a copy abroad can freely import that copy into the United States and dispose of it, just as he could had he bought the copy in the United States.

But *Quality King* considered an instance in which the copy, though purchased abroad, was initially manufactured in the United States (and then sent abroad and sold). This case is like *Quality King* but for one important fact. The copies at issue here were manufactured abroad. That fact is important because §109(a) says that the "first sale" doctrine applies to "a particular copy or phonorecord lawfully made under this title." And we must decide here whether the five words, "lawfully made under this title," make a critical legal difference.

Putting section numbers to the side, we ask whether the "first sale" doctrine applies to protect a buyer or other lawful owner of a copy (of a copyrighted work) lawfully manufactured abroad. Can that buyer bring that copy into the United States (and sell it or give it away) without obtaining permission to do so from the copyright owner? Can, for example, someone who purchases, say at a used bookstore, a book printed abroad subsequently resell it without the copyright owner's permission?

In our view, the answers to these questions are, yes. We hold that the "first sale" doctrine applies to copies of a copyrighted work lawfully made abroad.

## I

### A

Respondent, John Wiley & Sons, Inc., publishes academic textbooks. Wiley obtains from its authors various foreign and domestic copyright assignments, licenses and permissions—to the point that we can, for present purposes, refer to Wiley as the relevant American copyright owner.

. . . [T]here are two essentially equivalent versions of a Wiley textbook, 654 F. 3d, at 213, each version manufactured and sold with Wiley's permission: (1) an American version printed and sold in the United States, and (2) a foreign version manufactured and sold abroad. And Wiley makes certain that copies of the second version state that they are not to be taken (without permission) into the United States. Ibid.

Petitioner, Supap Kirtsaeng, a citizen of Thailand, moved to the United States in 1997 to study mathematics at Cornell University. Ibid. He paid for his education with the help of a Thai Government scholarship which required him to teach in Thailand for 10 years on his return. . . . Kirtsaeng successfully completed his undergraduate courses at Cornell, successfully completed a Ph.D. program in mathematics at the University of Southern California, and then, as promised, returned to Thailand to teach. Ibid. While he was studying in the United States, Kirtsaeng asked his friends and family in Thailand to buy copies of foreign edition Englishlanguage textbooks at Thai book shops, where they sold at low prices, and mail them to him in the United States. Id., at 7-8. Kirtsaeng would then sell them, reimburse his family and friends, and keep the profit. . . .

### B

In 2008 Wiley brought this federal lawsuit against Kirtsaeng for copyright infringement. 654 F.3d, at 213. Wiley claimed that Kirtsaeng's unauthorized importation of its books and his later resale of those books amounted to an infringement of Wiley's §106(3) exclusive right to distribute as well as §602's related import prohibition. 17 U. S. C. §§106(3) (2006 ed.), 602(a) (2006 ed., Supp. V).

See also §501 (2006 ed.) (authorizing infringement action). App. 204–211. Kirtsaeng replied that the books he had acquired were " 'lawfully made' " and that he had acquired them legitimately. . . .

Thus, in his view, §109(a)'s "first sale" doctrine permitted him to resell or otherwise dispose of the books without the copyright owner's further permission. Id., at 2-3.

. . .

We granted Kirtsaeng's petition for certiorari to consider this question in light of different views among the Circuits. Compare id., at 221 (case below) ("first sale" doctrine does not apply to copies manufactured outside the United States), with Omega S. A. v. Costco Wholesale Corp., 541 F. 3d 982, 986 (CA9 2008) ("first sale" doctrine applies to copies manufactured outside the United States only if an authorized first sale occurs within the United States), aff'd by an equally divided court, 562 U. S. (2010), and Sebastian Int'l, Inc. v. Consumer Contacts (PTY) Ltd., 847 F. 2d 1093, 1098, n. 1 (CA3 1988) (limitation of the first sale doctrine to copies made within the United States "does not fit comfortably within the scheme of the Copyright Act").

## II

We must decide whether the words "lawfully made under this title" restrict the scope of §109(a)'s "first sale" doctrine geographically. The Second Circuit, the Ninth Circuit, Wiley, and the Solicitor General (as amicus) all read those words as imposing a form of geographical limitation. . . . [T]he Solicitor General says that those five words limit the "first sale" doctrine's applicability to copies " 'made subject to and in compliance with [the Copyright Act],' " which (the Solicitor General says) are copies "made in the United States.". . .

Under any of these geographical interpretations, §109(a)'s "first sale" doctrine would not apply to the Wiley Asia books at issue here. And, despite an American copyright owner's permission to make copies abroad, one who buys a copy of any such book or other copyrighted work—whether at a retail store, over the Internet, or at a library sale—could not resell (or otherwise dispose of) that particular copy without further permission.

Kirtsaeng, however, reads the words "lawfully made under this title" as imposing a non-geographical limitation. He says that they mean made "in accordance with" or "in compliance with" the Copyright Act. . . . In that case, §109(a)'s "first sale" doctrine would apply to copyrighted works as long as their manufacture met the requirements of American copyright law. In particular, the doctrine would apply where, as here, copies are manufactured abroad with the permission of the copyright owner. See §106 (referring to the owner's right to authorize).

In our view, §109(a)'s language, its context, and the common-law history of the "first sale" doctrine, taken together, favor a non-geographical interpretation. We also doubt that Congress would have intended to create the practical copyright-related harms with which a geographical interpretation would threaten ordinary scholarly, artistic, commercial, and consumer activities. See Part II–D, infra. We consequently conclude that Kirtsaeng's nongeographical reading is the better reading of the Act.

### A

The language of §109(a) read literally favors Kirtsaeng's nongeographical interpretation, namely, that "lawfully made under this title" means made "in accordance with" or "in compliance with" the Copyright Act. The language of §109(a) says nothing about geography. The word "under" can mean "[i]n accordance with." 18 Oxford English Dictionary 950 (2d ed. 1989). See also Black's Law Dictionary 1525 (6th ed. 1990) ("according to"). And a nongeographical interpretation provides each word of the five-word phrase with a distinct purpose. The first two words of the phrase, "lawfully made," suggest an effort to distinguish those copies that were made lawfully from those that were not, and the last three words, "under this title," set forth the standard of "lawful[ness]." Thus, the nongeographical reading is simple, it promotes a traditional copyright objective (combatting piracy), and it makes word-by-word linguistic sense.

The geographical interpretation, however, bristles with linguistic difficulties. It gives the word "lawfully" little, if any, linguistic work to do. (How could a book be unlawfully "made under this title"?) It imports geography into a statutory provision that says nothing explicitly about it. And it is far more complex than may at first appear.

To read the clause geographically, Wiley, like the Second Circuit and the Solicitor General, must first emphasize the word "under." Indeed, Wiley reads "under this title" to mean "in conformance with the Copyright Act where the Copyright Act is applicable." Brief for Respondent 15. Wiley must then take a second step, arguing that the Act "is applicable" only in the United States. Ibid. And the Solicitor General must do the same. See Brief for United States 6 ("A copy is 'lawfully made under this title' if Title 17 governs the copy's creation and the copy is made in compliance with Title 17's requirements"). See also post, at 7 (Ginsburg, J., dissenting) ("under" describes something "governed or regulated by another").

One difficulty is that neither "under" nor any other word in the phrase means "where." See, e.g., 18 Oxford English Dictionary, supra, at 947–952 (definition of "under"). It might mean "subject to," see post, at 6, but as this Court has repeatedly acknowledged, the word evades a uniform, consistent meaning. See Kucana v. Holder, 558 U. S. 233, 245 (2010) ("'under' is chameleon"); Ardestani v. INS, 502 U. S. 129, 135 (1991) ("under" has "many dictionary definitions" and "must draw its meaning from its context").

A far more serious difficulty arises out of the uncertainty and complexity surrounding the second step's effort to read the necessary geographical limitation into the word "applicable" (or the equivalent). Where, precisely, is the Copyright Act "applicable"? The Act does not instantly protect an American copyright holder from unauthorized piracy taking place abroad. But that fact does not mean the Act is inapplicable to copies made abroad. . . .

The appropriateness of this linguistic usage is underscored by the fact that §104 of the Act itself says that works "*subject to protection under this title*" include unpublished works "without regard to the nationality or domicile of the author," and works "first published" in any one of the nearly 180 nations that have signed a copyright treaty with the United States. §§104(a), (b) (2006 ed.) (emphasis added); §101 (2006 ed., Supp. V) (defining "treaty party"); U. S. Copyright Office, Circular No. 38A, International Copyright Relations of the United States (2010). Thus, ordinary English permits us to say that the Act "applies" to an Irish manuscript lying in its author's Dublin desk drawer as well as to an original recording of a ballet performance first made in Japan and now on display in a Kyoto art gallery. Cf. 4 M. Nimmer & D. Nimmer, Copyright §17.02, pp. 17-18, 17-19 (2012) (hereinafter Nimmer on Copyright) (noting that the principle that "copyright laws do not have any extraterritorial operation" "requires some qualification").

. . . [W]e believe that geographical interpretations create more linguistic problems than they resolve. And considerations of simplicity and coherence tip the purely linguistic balance in Kirtsaeng's, nongeographical, favor.

### B

Both historical and contemporary statutory context indicate that Congress, when writing the present version of §109(a), did not have geography in mind.

. . .

### C

A relevant canon of statutory interpretation favors a nongeographical reading. "[W]hen a statute covers an issue previously governed by the common law," we must presume that "Congress intended to retain the substance of the common law." Samantar v. Yousuf, 560 U. S. 305 n. 13 (2010) (slip op., at 14, n. 13). See also Isbrandtsen Co. v. Johnson, 343 U. S. 779, 783 (1952) ("Statutes which invade the common law . . . are to be read with a presumption favoring the retention of long-established and familiar principles, except when a statutory purpose to the contrary is evident").

The "first sale" doctrine is a common-law doctrine with an impeccable historic pedigree. In the early 17th century Lord Coke explained the common law's refusal to permit restraints on the alienation of chattels. Referring to Littleton, who wrote in the 15th century, Gray, Two Contributions to Coke Studies, 72 U. Chi. L. Rev. 1127, 1135 (2005), Lord Coke wrote:

> "[If] a man be possessed of . . . a horse, or of any other chattell . . . and give or sell his whole interest . . . therein upon condition that the Donee or Vendee shall not alien[ate] the same, the [condition] is voi[d], because his whole interest . . . is out of him, so as he hath no possibilit[y] of a Reverter, and it is against Trade and Traffi[c], and bargaining and contracting betwee[n] man and man: and it is within the reason of our Author that it should ouster him of all power given to him." 1 E. Coke, Institutes of the Laws of England §360, p. 223 (1628).

A law that permits a copyright holder to control the resale or other disposition of a chattel once sold is similarly "against Trade and Traffi[c], and bargaining and contracting." Ibid.

With these last few words, Coke emphasizes the importance of leaving buyers of goods free to compete with each other when reselling or otherwise disposing of those goods. American law too has generally thought that competition, including freedom to resell, can work to the advantage of the consumer. See, e.g., Leegin Creative Leather Products, Inc. v. PSKS, Inc., 551 U. S. 877, 886 (2007) (restraints with "manifestly anticompetitive effects" are per se illegal; others are subject to the rule of reason (internal quotation marks omitted)); 1 P. Areeda & H. Hovenkamp, Antitrust Law ¶100, p. 4 (3d ed. 2006) ("[T]he principal objective of antitrust policy is to maximize consumer welfare by encouraging firms to behave competitively").

The "first sale" doctrine also frees courts from the administrative burden of trying to enforce restrictions upon difficult-to-trace, readily movable goods. And it avoids the selective enforcement inherent in any such effort. Thus, it is not surprising that for at least a century the "first sale" doctrine has played an important role in American copyright law. See Bobbs-Merrill Co. v. Straus, 210 U. S. 339 (1908); Copyright Act of 1909, §41, 35 Stat. 1084. See also Copyright Law Revision, Further Discussions and Comments on Preliminary Draft for Revised U. S. Copyright Law, 88th Cong., 2d Sess., pt. 4, p. 212 (Comm. Print 1964) (Irwin Karp of Authors' League of America expressing concern for "the very basic concept of copyright law that, once you've sold a copy legally, you can't restrict its resale").

The common-law doctrine makes no geographical distinctions; nor can we find any in Bobbs-Merrill (where this Court first applied the "first sale" doctrine) or in §109(a)'s predecessor provision, which Congress enacted a year later. See supra, at 12. Rather, as the Solicitor General acknowledges, "a straightforward application of Bobbs-Merrill" would not preclude the "first sale" defense from applying to authorized copies made overseas. Brief for United States 27. And we can find no language, context, purpose, or history that would rebut a "straightforward application" of that doctrine here.

. . .

### D

Associations of libraries, used-book dealers, technology companies, consumer-goods retailers, and museums point to various ways in which a geographical interpretation would fail to further basic constitutional copyright objectives, in particular "promot[ing] the Progress of Science and useful Arts." U. S. Const., Art. I, §8, cl. 8.

The American Library Association tells us that library collections contain at least 200 million books published abroad (presumably, many were first published in one of the nearly 180 copyright-treaty nations and enjoy American copyright protection under 17 U. S. C. §104, see supra, at 10); that many others were first published in the United States but printed abroad because of lower costs; and that a geographical interpretation will likely require the libraries to obtain permission (or at least create significant uncertainty) before circulating or otherwise distributing these books.

. . .

Technology companies tell us that "automobiles, microwaves, calculators, mobile phones, tablets, and personal computers" contain copyrightable software programs or packaging. . . . Many of these items are made abroad with the American copyright holder's permission and then sold and imported (with that permission) to the United States. . . . A geographical interpretation would prevent the resale of, say, a car, without the permission of the holder of each copyright on each piece of copyrighted automobile software. Yet there is no reason to believe that foreign auto manufacturers regularly obtain this kind of permission from their software component suppliers, and Wiley did not indicate to the contrary when asked. . . . Without that permission a foreign car owner could not sell his or her used car.

Retailers tell us that over $2.3 trillion worth of foreign goods were imported in 2011. . . . American retailers buy many of these goods after a first sale abroad. . . . And, many of these items bear, carry, or contain copyrighted "packaging, logos, labels, and product inserts and instructions for [the use of] everyday packaged goods from floor cleaners and health and beauty products to breakfast cereals.". . . The retailers add that American sales of more traditional copyrighted works, "such as books, recorded music, motion pictures, and magazines" likely amount to over $220 billion . . . (electronic game industry is $16 billion). A geographical interpretation would subject many, if not all, of them to the disruptive impact of the threat of infringement suits. . . .

. . .

These examples, and others previously mentioned, help explain why Lord Coke considered the "first sale" doctrine necessary to protect "Trade and Traffi[c], and bargaining and contracting," and they help explain why American copyright law has long applied that doctrine. Cf. supra, at 17–18.

Neither Wiley nor any of its many amici deny that a geographical interpretation could bring about these "horribles"—at least in principle. Rather, Wiley essentially says that the list is artificially invented.

. . . [W]e believe that the practical problems that petitioner and his amici have described are too serious, too extensive, and too likely to come about for us to dismiss them as insignificant—particularly in light of the ever-growing importance of foreign trade to America. See The World Bank, Imports of goods and services (% of GDP) (imports in 2011 18% of U. S. gross domestic product compared to 11% in 1980), online at http://data.worldbank.org/indicator/NE.IMP.GNFS.ZS? (as visited Mar. 15, 2013, and available in Clerk of Court's case file). The upshot is that copyright-related consequences along with language, context, and interpretive canons argue strongly against a geographical interpretation of §109(a).

## III

Wiley and the dissent make several additional important arguments in favor of the geographical interpretation. First, they say that our *Quality King* decision strongly supports its geographical interpretation. . . .

. . . The language "lawfully made under this title" was not at issue in *Quality King*; the point before us now was not then fully argued; we did not canvas the considerations we have here set forth; we there said nothing to suggest that the example assumes a "first sale"; and we there hedged our statement with the word "presumably." Most importantly, the statement is pure dictum. It is dictum contained in a rebuttal to a counterargument. And it is unnecessary dictum even in that respect. Is the Court having once written dicta calling a tomato a vegetable bound to deny that it is a fruit forever after?

To the contrary, we have written that we are not necessarily bound by dicta should more complete argument demonstrate that the dicta is not correct. Central Va. Community College v. Katz, 546 U. S. 356, 363 (2006) ("[W]e are not bound to follow our dicta in a prior case in which the point now at issue was not fully debated"); Humphrey's Executor v. United States, 295 U. S. 602, 627–628 (1935) (rejecting, under stare decisis, dicta, "which may be followed if sufficiently persuasive but which are not controlling"). And, given the bit part that our Quality King statement played in our *Quality King* decision, we believe the view of stare decisis set forth in these opinions applies to the matter now before us.

. . . Wiley and the dissent claim that a nongeographical interpretation will make it difficult, perhaps impossible, for publishers (and other copyright holders) to divide foreign and domestic markets. We concede that is so. A publisher may find it more difficult to charge different prices for the same book in different geographic markets. But we do not see how these facts help Wiley, for we can find no basic principle of copyright law that suggests that publishers are especially entitled to such rights.

The Constitution describes the nature of American copyright law by providing Congress with the power to "secur[e]" to "[a]uthors" "for limited [t]imes" the "exclusive [r]ight to their . . . [w]ritings." Art. I, §8, cl. 8. The Founders, too, discussed the need to grant an author a limited right to exclude competition. Compare Letter from Thomas Jefferson to James Madison (July 31, 1788), in 13 Papers of Thomas Jefferson 440, 442-443 (J. Boyd ed. 1956) (arguing against any monopoly) with Letter from James Madison to Thomas Jefferson (Oct. 17, 1788), in 14 id., at 16, 21 (J. Boyd ed. 1958) (arguing for a limited monopoly to secure production). But the Constitution's language nowhere suggests that its limited exclusive right should include a right to divide markets or a concomitant right to charge different purchasers different prices for the same book, say to increase or to maximize gain. Neither, to our knowledge, did any Founder make any such suggestion. We have found no precedent suggesting a legal preference for interpretations of copyright statutes that would provide for market divisions. Cf. Copyright Law Revision, pt. 2, at 194 (statement of Barbara Ringer, Copyright Office) (division of territorial markets was "primarily a matter of private contract").

To the contrary, Congress enacted a copyright law that (through the "first sale" doctrine) limits copyright holders' ability to divide domestic markets. And that limitation is consistent with antitrust laws that ordinarily forbid market divisions. Cf. *Palmer v. BRG of Ga., Inc.*, 498 U.S. 46, 49-50 (1990) (per curiam) ("[A]greements between competitors to allocate territories to minimize competition are illegal").Whether copyright owners should, or should not, have more than ordinary commercial power to divide international markets is a matter for Congress to decide. We do no more here than try to determine what decision Congress has taken.

Fourth, the dissent and Wiley contend that our decision launches United States copyright law into an unprecedented regime of "international exhaustion.". . . But they point to nothing indicative of congressional intent in 1976. The dissent also claims that it is clear that the United States now opposes adopting such a regime, but the Solicitor General as amicus has taken no such position in this case. In fact, when pressed at oral argument, the Solicitor General stated that the consequences of Wiley's reading of the statute (perpetual downstream control) were "worse" than those of Kirtsaeng's reading (restriction of market segmentation). . . .

Moreover, the exhaustion regime the dissent apparently favors would provide that "the sale in one country of a good" does not "exhaus[t] the intellectual-property owner's right to control the distribution of that good elsewhere." Post, at 18-19. But our holding in *Quality King* that §109(a) is a defense in U. S. courts even when "the first sale occurred abroad," 523 U. S., at 145, n. 14, has already significantly eroded such a principle.

## IV

For these reasons we conclude that the considerations supporting Kirtsaeng's nongeographical interpretation of the words "lawfully made under this title" are the more persuasive. The judgment of the Court of Appeals is reversed, and the case is remanded for further proceedings consistent with this opinion.

It is so ordered.

Justice Ginsburg, with whom Justice Kennedy joins, and with whom Justice Scalia joins except as to Parts III and V–B–1, dissenting.

"In the interpretation of statutes, the function of the courts is easily stated. It is to construe the language so as to give effect to the intent of Congress." *United States v. American Trucking Assns., Inc.*, 310 U. S. 534, 542 (1940). Instead of adhering to the Legislature's design, the Court today adopts an interpretation of the Copyright Act at odds with Congress' aim to protect copyright owners against the unauthorized importation of low-priced, foreign-made copies of their copyrighted works. The Court's bold departure from Congress' design is all the more stunning, for it places the United States at the vanguard of the movement for "international exhaustion" of copyrights—a movement the United States has steadfastly resisted on the world stage.

To justify a holding that shrinks to insignificance copyright protection against the unauthorized importation of foreign-made copies, the Court identifies several "practical problems." Ante, at 24. The Court's parade of horribles, however, is largely imaginary. Congress' objective in enacting 17 U. S. C. §602(a)(1)'s importation prohibition can be honored without generating the absurd consequences hypothesized in the Court's opinion. I dissent from the Court's embrace of "international exhaustion," and would affirm the sound judgment of the Court of Appeals.

## I

Because economic conditions and demand for particular goods vary across the globe, copyright owners have a financial incentive to charge different prices for copies of their works in different geographic regions. Their ability to engage in such price discrimination, however, is undermined if arbitrageurs are permitted to import copies from low-price regions and sell them in high-price regions. The question in this case is whether the unauthorized importation of foreign-made copies constitutes copyright infringement under U. S. law.

. . .

## IV

Unlike the Court's holding, my position is consistent with the stance the United States has taken in international trade negotiations. This case bears on the highly contentious trade issue of interterritorial exhaustion.

. . . [T]he United States has steadfastly "taken the position in international trade negotiations that domestic copyright owners should . . . have the right to prevent the unauthorized importation of copies of their work sold abroad." Id., at 22. . . .

. . . Even if the text and history of the Copyright Act were ambiguous on the answer to the question this case presents—which they are not, see Parts II–III, supra 16—I would resist a holding out of accord with the firm position the United States has taken on exhaustion in international negotiations. *Quality King*, I acknowledge, discounted the Government's concerns about potential inconsistency with United States obligations under certain bilateral trade agreements. See 523 U. S., at 153-154. See also *Quality King* Brief 22-24 (listing the agreements). That decision, however, dealt only with copyright-protected products made in the United States. See 523 U. S., at 154 (Ginsburg, J., concurring). *Quality King* left open the question whether owners of U. S. copyrights could retain control over the importation of copies manufactured and sold abroad—a point the Court obscures, see ante, at 33 (arguing that *Quality King* "significantly eroded" the national-exhaustion principle that, in my view, §602(a)(1) embraces). The Court today answers that question with a resounding "no," and in doing so, it risks undermining the United States' credibility on the world stage. While the Government has urged our trading partners to refrain from adopting international-exhaustion regimes that could benefit consumers within their borders but would impact adversely on intellectual-property producers in the United States, the Court embraces an international-exhaustion rule that could benefit U.S. consumers but would likely disadvantage foreign holders of U. S. copyrights. This dissonance scarcely enhances the United States' "role as a trusted partner in multilateral endeavors." Vimar Seguros y Reaseguros, S. A. v. M/V Sky Reefer, 515 U. S. 528, 539 (1995).

V

I turn now to the Court's justifications for a decision difficult to reconcile with the Copyright Act's text and history.

A

The Court asserts that its holding "is consistent with antitrust laws that ordinarily forbid market divisions." Ante, at 32. See also ante, at 18 (again referring to anti-trust principles). Section 602(a)(1), however, read as I do and as the Government does, simply facilitates copyright owners' efforts to impose "vertical restraints" on distributors of copies of their works. See Forsyth & Rothnie 435 ("Parallel importation restrictions enable manufacturers and distributors to erect 'vertical restraints' in the market through exclusive distribution agreements."). See generally Leegin Creative Leather Products, Inc. v. PSKS, Inc., 551 U. S. 877 (2007) (discussing vertical restraints). We have held that vertical restraints are not per se illegal under §1 of the Sherman Act, 15 U. S. C. §1, because such "restraints can have procompetitive effects." 551 U. S., at 881-882. . . .

Rather than adopting the very international-exhaustion rule the United States has consistently resisted in international-trade negotiations, I would adhere to the national-exhaustion framework set by the Copyright Act's text and history. Under that regime, codified in §602(a)(1), Kirtsaeng's unauthorized importation of the foreign-made textbooks involved in this case infringed Wiley's copyrights. I would therefore affirm the Second Circuit's judgment.

## NOTES AND QUESTIONS

**1.** In *Quality King*, a unanimous Supreme Court questioned whether the policies underlying *K mart's* limited right to block parallel imports should extend to the case in which a U.S. producer is deliberately engaging in international price discrimination. Should governments encourage their producers to sell more cheaply abroad than at home? Why?

**2.** In *Quality King*, the U.S. Justice Department argued to the Supreme Court that it should interpret the Copyright Act in a way that would not conflict with international trade agreements the United States signed with several countries. A conflicting interpretation, according to the Justice Department, would embarrass the United States in the conduct of foreign relations. A number of commentators suggested that the Justice Department was attempting to force a change in U.S. domestic law through the "back door" of international relations. In her dissent in *Wiley*, Justice Ginsburg acknowledged that the Supreme Court in *Quality King* had dismissed the significance of international trade negotiations in the context of interpreting the Copyright Act, but she sought to distinguish that on grounds that the Supreme Court had only been considering products initially exported from the United States. Yet in *Quality King* the Supreme Court had not even hinted at such a distinction when discussing external trade negotiations.

**3.** Subsequent to the *Quality King* case, but prior to *Wiley*, the question whether copyrighted works first produced and sold outside the United States are subject to international exhaustion, with parallel importation into the United States permitted, was tested before the Ninth Circuit Court of Appeals in *Omega v. Costco*, 541 F.3d 982 (9th Cir. 2008). The *Omega v. Costco* case involved luxury watches produced and first sold in Switzerland, and imported to the United States by a discount reseller. In a brief procedural decision, an evenly divided Supreme Court (one Justice not participating) declined to take a position, essentially leaving standing the Ninth Circuit decision, but without other precedential effect (*Costco v. Omega*, 562 U.S. 40 (2010).

**Robert H. Rotstein, Emily F. Evitt & Matthew Williams***

## *The First Sale Doctrine in the Digital Age*

An English professor purchases an original edition of Rabbit Run from a quaint used bookstore. A newlywed couple holds a yard sale where the wife sells the husband's collection of "National Lampoon" and "American Pie" DVDs. A photography enthusiast purchases new editing software, loads it onto his hard drive, and lends the disc containing the software to his neighbor. An enterprising college student rips her entire CD collection onto an iPod and is inspired to start a business selling ready loaded iPods. A bookworm purchases a Kindle and dozens of e-books, decides she prefers the touch and feel of paper, and sells her Kindle—e-books and all—to a friend. On their face, these scenarios have little in common. However, each scenario raises questions concerning the applicability of copyright law's first sale doctrine and its contemporary scope.

### The First Sale Doctrine: General Background

Under §106 of the U.S. Copyright Act, copyright owners have six exclusive rights: (1) reproduction; (2) preparation of derivative works; (3) distribution; (4) public performance; (5) public display; and (6) digital public performance of sound recordings. The third right gives copyright owners the exclusive right to distribute copies of their works to the public, including by offering copies for sale, lease, or auction. Under the first sale doctrine, however, in most circumstances the distribution right is extinguished when a copyright owner transfers ownership of a particular legal copy of a work to another person. Specifically, §109(a) of the Copyright Act provides:

> Notwithstanding the provisions of section 106(3), the owner of a particular copy or phonorecord lawfully made under this title, or any person authorized by such owner, is entitled, without the authority of the copyright owner, to sell or otherwise dispose of the possession of that copy or phonorecord.

The first sale doctrine provides a defense to copyright infringement. A defendant may rely on the first sale doctrine as a defense to an alleged violation of the distribution right if he overcomes the burden of proving that he lawfully owned the copy that he distributed. The first sale doctrine, however, is not universally applicable. Section 109(a) provides that the defense extends only to "the owner of a particular copy[.]" This language is clarified in §109(d), which states, "The privileges prescribed by subsection[] (a) . . . do not, unless authorized by the copyright owner, extend to any person who has acquired possession of the copy or phonorecord from the copyright owner, by rental, lease, loan, or otherwise, without acquiring ownership of it." Under this provision, it is clear that Congress intended to allow copyright owners to enter transactions that do not involve transfers of ownership and therefore do not constitute "first sales." Moreover, Congress expressly stated in §109(b) that there is no first sale right to rent, lease, or lend phonorecords embodying sound recordings or to rent, lease, or lend copies of a computer program for direct or indirect commercial gain. The overall first sale scheme "rest[s] on the principle that the copyright owner is entitled to realize the full value of each copy or phonorecord upon its disposition." The theory is that the price charged for the initial sale of a copyrighted book will account for the purchaser's ability to subsequently resell the book. Thus, if a book's resale value is $5, the book's initial price point can be set $5 higher, such that a book with an initial value of $7 can be sold for $12. The author captures the value

* 22 Intell Prop. & Tech. L.J. 23-28 (2010).

of both the initial sale and the resale in the initial value, and the purchaser is then free to dispose of his or her copy as the purchaser sees fit.

. . .

### Three Contemporary First Sale Paradigms

With the advent of modern technology, the use of many copyrighted works, such as software, has become intertwined with the reproduction of these works. This poses a challenge for the first sale doctrine, which applies to the distribution right but not to their production right. Thus, today the first sale doctrine is best understood in terms of three paradigms:

1. Traditional: cases in which transfer of possession of the physical copy of a copyrighted work does not implicate the reproduction right;
2. Transfer of tangible/intangible property: when reproduction is necessary to attendant use of technology; and
3. Transfer of intangible property only.

. . .

### Traditional

Even today, there are still traditional applications of the first sale doctrine in which the transfer of possession of the physical copy of a copyrighted work does not implicate the reproduction right. For example, whether a hard copy book was sold or lent would not ordinarily implicate the reproduction right because one does not have to reproduce a book to use it for its primary purpose. The same is true with more advanced technology, such as a DVD. In these situations, to determine whether the first sale doctrine applies, the inquiry should generally focus on the contractual relationship between the transferor and transferee.

More recently, in *UMG Recordings, Inc. v. Augusto*, [558 F. Supp. 2d 1055 (C.D. Cal. 2008),] Judge James Otero of the Central District of California analyzed first sale in the context of an individual who repeatedly acquired and sold on eBay "promotional" copies of music CDs without authorization. Judge Otero concluded that the individual's resale of these promotional copies was protected by the first sale doctrine; the case is currently on appeal to the Ninth Circuit.

. . .

### Transfer of Tangible/Intangible Property

The second modern first sale paradigm involves situations in which reproduction is necessary to attendant use of technology. The classic example is software, because the user not only needs the physical medium of copyrighted expression (e.g., a disc) but also must copy the intangible work of copyrighted software to another medium (e.g., a hard drive). Consequently, software transfers implicate at least two separate rights: (1) distribution, to which the first sale doctrine is relevant, and (2) reproduction, to which the first sale doctrine has no relevance. Sorting out the scope and applicability of these two rights can be difficult.

There is extensive case law from district and appellate courts across the country analyzing whether consumer transactions involving software resident on discs constitute sales or licenses for the purpose of the first sale doctrine. Two frequently cited district court cases within the Ninth Circuit, both involving Adobe software products, illustrate the issues involved.

First, in *Adobe Sys. Inc. v. One Stop Micro, Inc.*, [84 F. Supp. 2d 1086 (N.D. Cal. 2000)], a Northern District of California court concluded that the first sale doctrine did not apply.

Judge Ware considered whether defendant One Stop Micro infringed Adobe's distribution rights by acquiring educational copies of Adobe software that sell at a discounted price from authorized Adobe distributors, repackaging the software to remove the "educational" labels from the products, and reselling the software. One Stop Micro argued that it was protected by the first sale doctrine because Adobe's agreements with its authorized educational distributors included words such as "purchase," "own," and "resell." Judge Ware disagreed, however, and concluded, based on "undisputed evidence submitted by Adobe regarding the intent of the parties in entering into the agreement, trade usage, the unique nature of distributing software, as well as the express restrictive language of the contract," that Adobe's end user license agreement, which was incorporated into Adobe's agreements with its distributors, clearly provided purchasers with a mere license, rather than ownership, of the software.

By contrast, in *Softman Products Co. v. Adobe Sys. Inc.*, [171 F. Supp. 2d 1075 (C.D. Cal. 2001)], a Central District of California case very similar to *One Stop Micro*, Judge Pregerson concluded that the first sale doctrine applied. Softman Products Company bought "collections" of Adobe software products that were bundled together at a discount. Softman then sold the individual products from the collections separately and made a profit. As in *One Stop*, the Adobe agreements at issue stated that Adobe was only licensing the software involved. However, Judge Pregerson concluded that these licensing agreements were mere "labels" and that "the reality of the business environment[] suggests that Adobe sells its software to distributors." He also distinguished *One Stop* as a case that was more about removing the "educational" stickers from the software than anything else. Summarizing the core issue involved, Judge Pregerson stated: "Adobe frames the issue as a dispute about the ownership of intellectual property. In fact, it is a dispute about the ownership of individual pieces of Adobe software."

### Transfer of Intangible Property Only

The third contemporary first sale scenario arises when there are multiple copyrighted works on one device, but the physical copy of each copyrighted work need not be transferred each time. This paradigm is exemplified by the Kindle and the iPod. In theory, first sale should not apply to an individual work contained on one of these devices. Some advocates, however, argue that the first sale defense applies to all copies, no matter what form. Such arguments completely ignore the fact that the reproduction right, not simply the distribution right, is implicated by the transfer of intangible property.

An interesting question is whether the sale of the Kindle itself containing lawfully downloaded material would be subject to the first sale doctrine. In this scenario, a user's right to sell a lawfully loaded Kindle might be limited because of the copyright owner's ability to limit the reproduction right. This relates to the technology used to view books on a Kindle; presumably the Kindle user makes a digital copy each time a book is loaded for reading. These digital copies, in turn, are covered by the reproduction right, which is not governed by the first sale doctrine. Courts have held that copying software from a storage medium onto hardware causes a copy to be made, and "[i]n the absence of ownership of the copyright or express permission by license, such acts constitute copyright infringement." Thus, because viewing books on a Kindle requires making a digital copy, there is no legal reason why the copyright holder cannot limit that reproduction right to the original Kindle owner and effectively bar the sale of a legally loaded Kindle.

Finally, as discussed in the context of software, ripping CDs onto an iPod and then selling the CDs and/or the iPod poses a variation of the borrow/copy problem. . . .

## B. Unique Characteristics of Audiovisual Services

The *Quality King v. L'anza* decision deals with a copyright associated with a tangible product. Yet, copyrighted works may be disseminated to the public in ways disassociated from a tangible product. We have, for example, seen the problems that arise when music files are disassociated from CDs and are shared on the Internet. *Coditel v. Cine Vog*, decided by the CJEU, is one of the earliest cases to address the difference from an exhaustion standpoint between the sale of a tangible copyrighted work and the making available to a wide public of a copyrighted work (disassociated from a tangible product). The CJEU confronts certain special characteristics of the film distribution and television broadcast industries. A film differs from a book or newspaper in that the film depends on repeated showings to generate an adequate economic return. If the initial showing of a film is treated as a "first sale" for exhaustion purposes, artists and producers of films may not recover their investments.

### *Coditel v. Cine Vog Films*

(preliminary ruling requested by the Cour d'Appel, Brussels) (Case 62/79)
European Court of Justice [1980] ECR 881, [1981] 2 CMLR 362, 18 March 1980

PANEL: H. KUTSCHER, PRESIDENT, A. O'KEEFFE and A. TOUFFAIT, (Presidents of Chambers), J. MERTENS DE WILMARS, P. PESCATORE, Lord MACKENZIE STUART, G. BOSCO, T. KOOPMANS and O. DUE, JUDGES

Decision: . . .

The facts of the case bearing upon the outcome of the dispute were summarized by the Cour d'Appel as follows. By an agreement of 8 July 1969 Les Films la Boetie, acting as the owner of all the proprietary rights in the film "Le Boucher," gave Cine Vog the "exclusive right" to distribute the film in Belgium for seven years. The film was shown in cinemas in Belgium starting on 15 May 1970. However, on 5 January 1971 German television's first channel broadcast a German version of the film and this broadcast could be picked up in Belgium. Cine Vog considered that the broadcast had jeopardized the commercial future of the film in Belgium. It relied upon this ground of complaint both against Les Films la Boetie, for not having observed the exclusivity of the rights which it had transferred to it, and against the Coditel companies for having relayed the relevant broadcast over their cable diffusion networks. . . .

Believing that that submission bears upon the interpretation of the Treaty, the Cour d'Appel referred to the Court of Justice the following two questions:

> 1. Are the restrictions prohibited by Article 59 of the Treaty establishing the European Economic Community only those which prejudice the provision of services between nationals established in different Member States, or do they also comprise restrictions on the provision of services between nationals established in the same Member State which however concern services the substance of which originates in another Member State?
>
> 2. If the first limb of the preceding question is answered in the affirmative, is it in accordance with the provisions of the Treaty on freedom to provide services for the assignee of the performing right in a cinematographic film in one Member State to rely upon his right in order to prevent the defendant from showing that film in that State by means of cable television where the film thus shown is picked up by the defendant in the said Member State after having been broadcast by a third party in another Member State with the consent of the original owner of the right? . . .

The second question raises the problem of whether Articles 59 and 60 of the Treaty prohibit an assignment, limited to the territory of a Member State, of the copyright in a film, in view of the fact that a series of such assignments might result in the partitioning of the Common Market as regards the undertaking of economic activity in the film industry.

A cinematographic film belongs to the category of literary and artistic works made available to the public by performances which may be infinitely repeated. In this respect the problems involved in the observance of copyright in relation to the requirements of the Treaty are not the same as those which arise in connection with literary and artistic works the placing of which at the disposal of the public is inseparable from the circulation of the material form of the works, as in the case of books or records.

In these circumstances the owner of the copyright in a film and his assigns have a legitimate interest in calculating the fees due in respect of the authorization to exhibit the film on the basis of the actual or probable number of performances and in authorizing a television broadcast of the film only after it has been exhibited in cinemas for a certain period of time. It appears from the file on the present case that the contract made between Les Films la Boetie and Cine Vog stipulated that the exclusive right which was assigned included the right to exhibit the film "Le Boucher" publicly in Belgium by way of projection in cinemas and on television but that the right to have the film diffused by Belgian television could not be exercised until 40 months after the first showing of the film in Belgium.

These facts are important in two regards. On the one hand, they highlight the fact that the right of a copyright owner and his assigns to require fees for any showing of a film is part of the essential function of copyright in this type of literary and artistic work. On the other hand, they demonstrate that the exploitation of copyright in films and the fees attaching thereto cannot be regulated without regard being had to the possibility of television broadcasts of those films. The question whether an assignment of copyright limited to the territory of a Member State is capable of constituting a restriction on freedom to provide services must be examined in this context.

Whilst Article 59 of the Treaty prohibits restrictions upon freedom to provide services, it does not thereby encompass limits upon the exercise of certain economic activities which have their origin in the application of national legislation for the protection of intellectual property, save where such application constitutes a means of arbitrary discrimination or a disguised restriction on trade between Member States. Such would be the case if that application enabled parties to an assignment of copyright to create artificial barriers to trade between Member States.

The effect of this is that, whilst copyright entails the right to demand fees for any showing or performance, the rules of the Treaty cannot in principle constitute an obstacle to the geographical limits, which the parties to a contract of assignment have agreed upon in order to protect the author and his assigns in this regard. The mere fact that those geographical limits may coincide with national frontiers does not point to a different solution in a situation where television is organized in the Member States largely on the basis of legal broadcasting monopolies, which indicates that a limitation other than the geographical field of application of an assignment is often impracticable.

The exclusive assignee of the performing right in a film for the whole of a Member State may therefore rely upon his right against cable television diffusion companies which have transmitted that film on their diffusion network having received it from a television broadcasting station established in another Member State, without thereby infringing Community law.

Consequently the answer to the second question referred to the Court by the Cour d'Appel, Brussels, should be that the provisions of the Treaty relating to the freedom to provide services do not preclude an assignee of the performing right in a cinematographic film in a Member State from relying upon his right to prohibit the exhibition of that film in that State, without his authority, by means of cable diffusion if the film so exhibited is picked up and transmitted after being broadcast in another Member State by a third party with the consent of the original owner of the right.

It is clear from the answer given to the second question that Community law, on the assumption that it applies to the activities of the cable diffusion companies which are the subject-matter of the dispute brought before the national court, has no effect upon the application by that court of the provisions of copyright legislation in a case such as this. Therefore there is no need to answer the first question. . . .

On those grounds,

THE COURT, in answer to the questions referred to it by the Cour d'Appel, Brussels, by judgment of 30 March 1979, hereby rules:

The provisions of the Treaty relating to the freedom to provide services do not preclude an assignee of the performing right in a cinematographic film in a Member State from relying upon his right to prohibit the exhibition of that film in that State, without his authority, by means of cable diffusion if the film so exhibited is picked up and transmitted after being broadcast in another Member State by a third party with the consent of the original owner of the right.

## C. Alterations of Works

### *Art & Allposters International BV v. Stichting Pictoright*

Judgment of the Court (Fourth Chamber), 22 January 2015

(Reference for a preliminary ruling—Intellectual property—Copyright and related rights—Directive 2001/29/EC—Article 4—Distribution right—Exhaustion rule—Concept of 'object'—Transfer of the image of a protected work from a paper poster to a painter's canvas—Replacement of the medium—Impact on exhaustion)

In Case C419/13,

REQUEST for a preliminary ruling under Article 267 TFEU from the Hoge Raad der Nederlanden (Netherlands), made by decision of 12 July 2013, received at the Court on 24 July 2013, in the proceedings

Art & Allposters International BV

v

Stichting Pictoright,

THE COURT (Fourth Chamber),

composed of L. Bay Larsen, President of the Chamber, K. Lenaerts, Vice-President of the Court, acting as a Judge of the Fourth Chamber, K. Jürimäe (Rapporteur), M. Safjan and A. Prechal, Judges,

Advocate General: P. Cruz Villalón,

Registrar: C. Strömholm, Administrator,

having regard to the written procedure and further to the hearing on 22 May 2014, after considering the observations submitted on behalf of: . . . gives the following

## JUDGMENT

1. This request for a preliminary ruling concerns the interpretation of Article 4 of Directive 2001/29/EC of the European Parliament and of the Council of 22 May 2001 on the harmonisation of certain aspects of copyright and related rights in the information society (OJ 2001 L 167, p. 10).

2. The request has been made in proceedings between Art & Allposters International BV ('Allposters') and Stichting Pictoright ('Pictoright') regarding a possible infringement, by Allposters, of copyright exploited by Pictoright, resulting from the transfer of images of protected works from a paper poster to a painter's canvas and the sale of those images on that new medium.

. . .

### The Dispute in the Main Proceedings and the Questions Referred for a Preliminary Ruling

14. Pictoright is a Netherlands copyright collecting society which looks after the interests of copyright owners affiliated to it. It also safeguards, in the Netherlands, the interests of foreign artists and their heirs on the basis of agreements concluded with foreign entities with the same purpose. Pictoright is mandated to exploit copyright on behalf of the rightholders in particular by licensing and by taking action against infringements of that copyright.

15. Allposters, through its websites, markets posters and other reproductions depicting the works of famous painters, which are covered by the copyright exploited by Pictoright. Among other products, Allposters offers its clients reproductions in the form of posters, framed posters, posters on wood and images on canvases. In order to produce an image on canvas, a synthetic coating (laminate) is first applied to a paper poster depicting the chosen work. Next, the image on the poster is transferred from the paper to a canvas by means of a chemical process. Finally, that canvas is stretched over a wooden frame. The image of the work disappears from the paper backing during the process. Allposters refers to both it and its result as 'canvas transfer'.

16. Pictoright opposed the sale of canvas transfers reproducing works protected by copyright without the consent of its clients, the holders of that copyright, calling on Allposters to cease that activity and threatening legal proceedings.

. . .

### Consideration of the Questions Referred for a Preliminary Ruling

22. The jurisdiction of the Court, in the procedure laid down in Article 267 TFEU, is confined to considering provisions of EU law only and it has no jurisdiction to rule on the compatibility of national law, including the case-law of the Member States, with EU law (see, to that effect, *Triveneta Zuccheri and Others* v *Commission*, C347/87, EU:C:1990:129, paragraph 16, and *Schwarz*, C321/07, EU:C:2009:104, paragraph 48).

23. In those circumstances, the questions referred, which should be considered together, must be understood to mean that the referring court is asking, in essence, whether the rule of exhaustion of the distribution right set out in Article 4(2) of Directive 2001/29 applies in a situation where a reproduction of a protected work, after having been marketed in the European Union with the copyright holder's consent, has undergone an alteration of its medium, such as the transfer of that reproduction from a paper poster onto a canvas, and is placed on the market again in its new form.

24. As a preliminary matter, it should be noted that Pictoright is of the view that, owing to the significant alteration undergone by the posters in the process of transfer onto the canvases of reproductions of protected works, those canvases are adaptations of those works, which are

not covered by the distribution right. It submits that the adaptation right in the field of copyright is not harmonised in EU law but is governed by Article 12 of the Berne Convention.

25. It should therefore be assessed whether the facts at issue in the main proceedings fall within the scope of Directive 2001/29.

26. With regard to the adaptation right, it is true that Article 12 of the Berne Convention confers on authors of literary or artistic works an exclusive right of authorising adaptations, arrangements and other alterations of their works and that there is no equivalent provision in Directive 2001/29.

27. However, and without having to interpret the concept of 'adaptation' within the meaning of Article 12, it is sufficient to state that both the paper poster and the canvas transfer contain the image of a protected artistic work and thus fall within the scope of Article 4(1) of Directive 2001/29 as copies of a protected work marketed within the European Union. That provision recognises the exclusive right of authors, in respect of the original of their works or of copies thereof, to authorise or prohibit any form of distribution to the public by sale or otherwise.

28. It must therefore be held that the facts at issue in the main proceedings fall within the scope of Article 4 of Directive 2001/29.

29. With regard to the conditions of application of the exhaustion rule, it follows from Article 4(2) of Directive 2001/29 that the distribution right is not exhausted in respect of the original or copies of a work, except where the first sale or other transfer of ownership in the European Union of that object is made by the rightholder or with his consent.

. . .

37. It follows from the foregoing considerations that the EU legislature, by using the terms 'tangible article' and 'that object', wished to give authors control over the initial marketing in the European Union of each tangible object incorporating their intellectual creation.

38. That finding, as the European Commission correctly states, is supported by international law, and in particular by the WIPO Copyright Treaty, in the light of which Directive 2001/29 must be interpreted as far as possible (see, to that effect, judgments in *Laserdisken*, EU:C:2006:549, paragraphs 39 and 40; *Peek & Cloppenburg*, C456/06, EU:C:2008:232, paragraphs 30 and 31; *Football Association Premier League and Others*, C403/08 and C429/08, EU:C:2011:631, paragraph 189; and *Donner*, C5/11, EU:C:2012:370, paragraph 23).

39. Article 6(1) of that Treaty provides that authors of literary and artistic works are to enjoy the exclusive right of authorising the making available to the public of the original and copies of their works through sale or other transfer of ownership. In that regard, the significance of the term 'copy' was explained by the Contracting Parties by an agreed statement concerning Articles 6 and 7 of the Treaty adopted by the Diplomatic Conference of 20 December 1996, at which the Treaty itself was also adopted. According to that statement, 'the expressions "copies" and "original and copies" being subject to the right of distribution and the right of rental under the said Articles, refer exclusively to fixed copies that can be put into circulation as tangible objects'.

40. Accordingly, it should be found that exhaustion of the distribution right applies to the tangible object into which a protected work or its copy is incorporated if it has been placed onto the market with the copyright holder's consent.

41. In the second place, it must be assessed whether the fact that the object, which was marketed with the copyright holder's consent, has undergone subsequent alterations to its physical medium has an impact on exhaustion of the distribution right within the meaning of Article 4(2) of Directive 2001/29.

42. In the case in the main proceedings, the alteration carried out consists in a transfer of the image of an artistic work from a paper poster onto a painter's canvas, by means of the process described in . . . this judgment, resulting in the replacement of the paper

medium by a canvas. It follows from the observations of the parties in the main proceedings that that technique increases the durability of the reproduction, improves the quality of the image in comparison with the poster and provides a result closer to the original of the work.

43. In that regard, it must be held that, as the French Government correctly argues, a replacement of the medium, as was carried out in the case in the main proceedings, results in the creation of a new object incorporating the image of the protected work, whereas the poster itself ceases to exist. Such an alteration of the copy of the protected work, which provides a result closer to the original, is actually sufficient to constitute a new reproduction of that work, within the meaning of Article 2(a) of Directive 2001/29, which is covered by the exclusive right of the author and requires his authorisation.

44. Allposters nevertheless maintains that the transfer onto canvas cannot be categorised as reproduction on the ground that there is no multiplication of copies of the protected work since the image is transferred and no longer appears on the poster. It explains that the ink which reproduces the work is not altered and that the work itself is not affected in any way.

45. That argument cannot be accepted. The fact that the ink is saved during the transfer cannot affect the finding that the image's medium has been altered. What is important is whether the altered object itself, taken as a whole, is, physically, the object that was placed onto the market with the consent of the rightholder. That does not appear to be the case in the dispute in the main proceedings.

46. Consequently, the consent of the copyright holder does not cover the distribution of an object incorporating his work if that object has been altered after its initial marketing in such a way that it constitutes a new reproduction of that work. In such an event, the distribution right of such an object is exhausted only upon the first sale or transfer of ownership of that new object with the consent of the rightholder.

47. That interpretation is supported by the principal objective of Directive 2001/29 which, according to recitals 9 and 10 of that directive, is to establish a high level of protection of, inter alia, authors, allowing them to obtain an appropriate reward for the use of their works (see judgments in *SGAE*, C306/05, EU:C:2006:764, paragraph 36; *Peek & Cloppenburg*, EU:C:2008:232, paragraph 37; and *Football Association Premier League and Others*, EU:C:2011:631, paragraph 186).

48. However, it follows from the arguments advanced before the Court by the parties in the main proceedings that the copyright holders did not consent to the distribution of the canvas transfers, at least not expressly. Accordingly, applying the rule of exhaustion of the distribution right would deprive those rightholders of the possibility of prohibiting those objects from being distributed or, in the event of distribution, of requiring appropriate reward for the commercial exploitation of their works. In that regard, the Court has already held that, in order to be appropriate, such remuneration must be reasonable in relation to the economic value of the exploitation of the protected work (see, by analogy, judgment in *Football Association Premier League and Others*, EU:C:2011:631, paragraphs 107 to 109). As regards canvas transfers, the parties in the main proceedings acknowledge that their economic value significantly exceeds that of posters.

49. Having regard to all the foregoing considerations, the answer to the questions asked is that Article 4(2) of Directive 2001/29 must be interpreted as meaning that the rule of exhaustion of the distribution right set out in Article 4(2) of Directive 2001/29 does not apply in a situation where a reproduction of a protected work, after having been marketed in the European Union with the copyright holder's consent, has undergone an alteration of its medium, such as the transfer of that reproduction from a paper poster onto a canvas, and is placed on the market again in its new form.

## NOTES AND QUESTIONS

**1.** According to the CJEU, the special characteristics of the film and broadcast industries made it necessary to provide limitations on the exhaustion of copyright for these media. The same was found to be the case in alterations of artworks sold on the Internet. In what other copyright contexts do you think that limitations on the principle of exhaustion might be necessary?

**2.** In 2020 the CJEU issued the *Tom Kabinet* decision (C-263/18, ECLI:EU:C:2019:1111) concerning the digital exhaustion of e-books. In the case, two associations representing Dutch publishers, sought an injunction to stop the online platform Tom Kabinet from making available "second-hand" e-books to its members. The platform offered e-books that were either donated by other members or purchased by Tom Kabinet. The files were watermarked to certify their lawful origin and offered for download against payment of a fixed price. E-books could also be sold or donated to Tom Kabinet in exchange for credits for future purchases. In contrast to its *UsedSoft* ruling (C-128/11, ECLI:EU:C:2012:407), which permitted digital exhaustion of software, the CJEU denied the soundness of digital exhaustion if applied to more traditional works, such as books, in light of the different economic and functional characteristics of their exploitation compared to those of software. The CJEU stressed that, unlike material copies, digital files are not subject to deterioration by use, and the exchange of used copies does not entail additional effort or cost. Thus, the second-hand market for digital copies can have a significant impact on the original market of the work, and consequently, on the ability of rightholders to obtain an appropriate reward.[20] Do you think that there should different regimes of exhaustion of different types of content?

**3.** The *Coditel* and *Art & Allposters* and *Tom Kabinet* decisions are addressed only to the intra-Union context. Do you think that the same policy considerations that motivated the CJEU in these decisions should also apply in the international exhaustion of copyright context?

**4.** Issues associated with international exhaustion and intangible copyrighted works have yet to be explored in the same depth as issues of exhaustion associated with tangible products, including traditional copyrighted works such as books. The problems are similar to those associated with file-sharing networks. Copying and distribution of intangible works across national borders is conceptually similar to copying and distribution within a single country. Permission to make a single copy does not constitute permission to make an indefinite number of copies. If a single copy has been authorized and sold, there is no special reason to confine its resale or movement within a single geographic territory, even if that movement is across a computer network. On the other hand, authorization and sale of a single copy within one country does not specially constitute authorization for indefinite replication and distribution of the work among many countries, even across a computer network. Do you see other issues associated with international exhaustion and copyrighted works disassociated from tangible products?

20. For a case study, *see* Caterina Sganga, *Is the Digital Exhaustion Debate Really Exhausted? Some Afterthoughts on the Grand Chamber Decision in Tom Kabinet (C-263/18)*, Kluwer Copyright Blog, May 19, 2020, available at https://copyrightblog.kluweriplaw.com/2020/05/19/is-the-digital-exhaustion-debate-really-exhausted-some-afterthoughts-on-the-grand-chamber-decision-in-tom-kabinet-c-263-18/.

# IV. REGIONAL COPYRIGHT SYSTEMS

## A. EU Harmonization Measures

### *1. Consequences of Different Rules*

We have earlier examined EU approximation efforts in the fields of patent and trademark and frequently come across such measures on copyright in the case-law of the CJEU discussed above. Early on, *Warner Brothers v. Christiansen* heightened awareness that intra-EU trade distortions might arise from different member state approaches in copyright. This decision notes the emergence of a new form of right for the copyright holder—the right to control the renting out of the work—distinct from the right to sell or communicate to the public. The *Warner Brothers v. Christiansen* case helped form the background for the rental right embodied in the TRIPS Agreement.

---

### *Warner Brothers Inc. and Metronome Video ApS v. Erik Viuff Christiansen*

Court of Justice of the European Communities, 1988 ECJ CELEX LEXIS 2016,
Judgment of the Court of 17 May 1988

Reference for a preliminary ruling: OEstre Landsret—Denmark Copyright—Objection to the hiring-out of video-cassettes Case 158/86, 686J0158

Introduction:
In Case 158/86

REFERENCE to the Court under Article 177 of the EEC Treaty by the OEstre Landsret, Copenhagen, for a preliminary ruling in the action pending before that court between

Warner Brothers Inc.,
Metronome Video ApS
and Erik Viuff Christiansen

on the interpretation of Articles 30, 36 and 222 of the EEC Treaty with regard to the action taken by an owner of exclusive rights in Denmark to restrain hiring-out in Denmark of a video-recording marketed in another Member State by the same owner of the exclusive rights or with his consent.

The Court composed of: G. Bosco, President of Chamber, for the President, O. Due and J.C. Moitinho de Almeida (Presidents of Chambers), T. Koopmans, U. Everling, K. Bahlmann, Y. Galmot, R. Joliet and F. Schockweiler, Judges,

Advocate General: G. F. Mancini . . .

Judgment by: Galmot

#### Judgment:

1. By order dated 11 June 1986, which was received at the Court on 1 July 1986, the OEstre Landsret referred to the Court for a preliminary ruling under Article 177 of the EEC Treaty a question on the interpretation of Articles 30 and 36 [now 34 and 36—Eds.] of the EEC Treaty, with a view to establishing the extent to which national copyright legislation regarding the hiring-out of video-cassettes is compatible with the free movement of goods.

2. The question was raised in the context of proceedings brought by two companies, Warner Brothers Inc. (hereinafter referred to as "Warner") and Metronome Video ApS (hereinafter "Metronome"), against Mr Erik Viuff Christiansen.

3. Warner, the owner in the United Kingdom of the copyright of the film "Never Say Never Again," which it produced in that country, assigned the management of the video production rights in Denmark to Metronome.

4. The video-cassette of the film was on sale in the United Kingdom with Warner's consent. Mr Christiansen, who manages a video shop in Copenhagen, purchased a copy in London with a view to hiring it out in Denmark and imported it into that Member State for that purpose.

5. On the basis of Danish legislation, which enables the author or producer of a musical or cinematographic work to take action to restrain the hiring-out of videograms of that work until such time as he gives his consent, Warner and Metronome obtained an injunction from the Copenhagen City Court prohibiting the defendant from hiring out the video-cassette in Denmark. . . .

8. In submitting the question the national court seeks to ascertain, in essence, whether Articles 30 and 36 of the EEC Treaty preclude the application of national legislation which gives an author the right to make the hiring-out of video-cassettes conditional on his authorization, where those video-cassettes have already been put into circulation with his consent in another Member State whose legislation allows the author to control their initial sale without giving him the right to prohibit them from being hired out.

9. It should be noted that, unlike the national copyright legislation which gave rise to the judgment of 20 January 1981 in Joined Cases 55 and 57/80 *Musik Vertrieb Membran v GEMA* (1981) ECR 147, the legislation which gives rise to the present preliminary question does not enable the author to collect an additional fee on the actual importation of recordings of protected works which are marketed with his consent in another Member State, or to set up any further obstacle whatsoever to importation or resale. The rights and powers conferred on the author by the national legislation in question comes into operation only after importation has been carried out.

10. None the less, it must be observed that the commercial distribution of video-cassettes takes the form not only of sales but also, and increasingly, that of hiring-out to individuals who possess video-tape recorders. The right to prohibit such hiring-out in a Member State is therefore liable to influence trade in video-cassettes in that State and hence, indirectly, to affect intra-Community trade in those products. Legislation of the kind which gave rise to the main proceedings must therefore, in the light of established case-law, be regarded as a measure having an effect equivalent to a quantitative restriction on imports, which is prohibited by Article 30 of the Treaty.

11. Consideration should therefore be given to whether such legislation may be considered justified on grounds of the protection of industrial and commercial property within the meaning of Article 36—a term which was held by the Court, in its judgment of 6 October 1982 in Case 262/81 *Coditel v Cine-Vog* (1982) ECR 3381, to include literary and artistic property.

12. In that connection it should first be noted that the Danish legislation applies without distinction to video-cassettes produced in situ and video-cassettes imported from another Member State. The determining factor for the purposes of its application is the type of transaction in video-cassettes which is in question, not the origin of those video-cassettes. Such legislation does not therefore, in itself, operate any arbitrary discrimination in trade between Member States.

13. It should further be pointed out that literary and artistic works may be the subject of commercial exploitation, whether by way of public performance or of the reproduction and marketing of the recordings made of them, and this is true in particular of cinematographic works. The two essential rights of the author, namely the exclusive right of performance and the exclusive right of reproduction, are not called in question by the rules of the Treaty.

14. Lastly, consideration must be given to the emergence, demonstrated by the Commission, of a specific market for the hiring-out of such recordings, as distinct from their sale. The existence of that market was made possible by various factors such as the improvement of manufacturing methods for video-cassettes which increased their strength and life in use, the growing awareness amongst viewers that they watch only occasionally the video-cassettes which they have bought and, lastly, their relatively high purchase price. The market for the hiring-out of video-cassettes reaches a wider public than the market for their sale and, at present, offers great potential as a source of revenue for makers of films.

15. However, it is apparent that, by authorizing the collection of royalties only on sales to private individuals and to persons hiring out video-cassettes, it is impossible to guarantee to makers of films a remuneration which reflects the number of occasions on which the video-cassettes are actually hired out and which secures for them a satisfactory share of the rental market. That explains why, as the Commission points out in its observations, certain national laws have recently provided specific protection of the right to hire out video-cassettes.

16. Laws of that kind are therefore clearly justified on grounds of the protection of industrial and commercial property pursuant to Article 36 of the Treaty.

17. However, the defendant in the main proceedings, relying on the judgments of 22 January 1981 in Case 58/80 *Dansk Supermarked v Imerco* (1981) ECR 181 and of 20 January 1981 *Musik Vertrieb Membran v GEMA*, cited above, contends that the author is at liberty to choose the Member State in which he will market his work. The defendant in the main proceedings emphasizes that the author makes his choice according to his own interests and must, in particular, take into consideration the fact that the legislation of certain Member States, unlike that of certain others, confers on him an exclusive right enabling him to restrain the hiring-out of the recording of the work even when that work has been offered for sale with his consent. That being so, a maker of a film who has offered the video-cassette of that film for sale in a Member State whose legislation confers on him no exclusive right of hiring it out (as in the main proceedings) must accept the consequences of his choice and the exhaustion of his right to restrain the hiring-out of that video-cassette in any other Member State.

18. That objection cannot be upheld. It follows from the foregoing considerations that, where national legislation confers on authors a specific right to hire out video-cassettes, that right would be rendered worthless if its owner were not in a position to authorize the operations for doing so. It cannot therefore be accepted that the marketing by a film-maker of a video-cassette containing one of his works, in a Member State which does not provide specific protection for the right to hire it out, should have repercussions on the right conferred on that same film-maker by the legislation of another Member State to restrain, in that State, the hiring-out of that video-cassette.

19. In those circumstances, the answer to be given to the question submitted by the national court is that Articles 30 and 36 of the Treaty do not prohibit the application of national legislation which gives an author the right to make the hiring-out of video-cassettes subject to his permission, when the video-cassettes in question have already been put into circulation with his consent in another Member State whose legislation enables the author to control the initial sale, without giving him the right to prohibit hiring-out. . . .

## NOTES AND QUESTIONS

**1.** Christiansen points out that Warner Brothers elected to put its video cassette on the market in the United Kingdom where the law provided that a first sale exhausted the copyright holder's right to control further distribution of the cassette. Warner Brothers profited from the first sale in the United Kingdom. By enabling Warner Brothers to control the rental in Denmark, the Court is allowing Warner Brothers to obtain additional profits from the same video cassette. Has the Court persuaded you that Warner Brothers needed the additional right to control the rental of the cassette in Denmark?

**2.** Computer software vendors tend to characterize their transactions with consumers as "licenses." In essence, software vendors assert that their transactions with consumers are not sales, but rather rentals under restrictive conditions. As we review the EU Rental Rights Directive and Computer Software Directive, consider the potential impact of these directives on the typical vendor to end-user consumer software transaction.

### *2. Harmonization of EU Copyright Law*

In *Warner Brothers v. Christiansen*, the ECJ permitted differences in member state IPRs laws to act as a barrier to the free movement of goods. A primary objective of the European Union is to create a "single market" for goods and services, and it was a logical next step for EU authorities to seek removal of the barrier. To this effect, the European Union has adopted a great number of harmonization instruments in the domain of copyright law. While copyright and related rights continue to be addressed in national law, it is fair to say that key areas of modern copyright law have been thus comprehensively addressed on the regional level by European law, amounting to one of the most harmonized fields of law. The following information is provided by the Commission's website and regularly updated (https://ec.europa.eu/digital-single-market/en/eu-copyright-legislation):

> The EU's regulatory framework for copyright and neighbouring rights (*acquis*) consists of 13 directives and 2 regulations, harmonizing the essential rights of authors, performers, producers and broadcasters:
>
> - Directive on the harmonisation of certain aspects of copyright and related rights in the information society ("InfoSoc Directive"), 22 May 2001
> - Directive on rental right and lending right and on certain rights related to copyright in the field of intellectual property ("Rental and Lending Directive"), 12 December 2006
> - Directive on the resale right for the benefit of the author of an original work of art ("Resale Right Directive"), 27 September 2001
> - Directive on the coordination of certain rules concerning copyright and rights related to copyright applicable to satellite broadcasting and cable retransmission ("Satellite and Cable Directive"), 27 September 1993
> - Directive on the legal protection of computer programs ("Software Directive"), 23 April 2009
> - Directive on the enforcement of intellectual property right ("IPRED"), 29 April 2004
> - Directive on the legal protection of databases ("Database Directive"), 11 March 1996
> - Directive on the term of protection of copyright and certain related rights amending the previous 2006 Directive ("Term Directive"), 27 September 2011
> - Directive on certain permitted uses of orphan works ("Orphan Works Directive"), 25 October 2012
> - Directive on collective management of copyright and related rights and multi-territorial licensing of rights in musical works for online use in the internal market ("CRM Directive"), 26 February 2014
> - Directive on certain permitted uses of certain works and other subject matter protected by copyright and related rights for the benefit of persons who are blind, visually impaired

or otherwise print-disabled (Directive implementing the Marrakech Treaty in the EU), 13 September 2017

- Regulation on the cross-border exchange between the Union and third countries of accessible format copies of certain works and other subject matter protected by copyright and related rights for the benefit of persons who are blind, visually impaired or otherwise print-disabled (Regulation implementing the Marrakech Treaty in the EU), 13 September 2017
- Regulation on cross-border portability of online content services in the internal market ("Portability Regulation"), 14 June 2017
- Directive on copyright and related rights in the Digital Single Market ("DSM Directive"), 17 April 2019
- Directive on the exercise of copyright and related rights applicable to certain online transmissions of broadcasting organisations and retransmissions of television and radio programmes ("Satellite and Cable II"), 17 April 2019

Three additional instruments (Directive 87/54/EC, Council Decision 94/824/EC and Council Decision 96/644/EC) harmonise the legal protection of topographies of semiconductor products. Moreover, the E-Commerce Directive [now replaced by the Digital Services Act] and the Conditional Access Directive also contain provisions relevant to the exercise and the enforcement of copyright.

The overall goal in the EU harmonisation efforts is to enable copyright protected goods (e.g. books, music, films, software etc.) and services (e.g. services offering access to these goods) to move freely within the internal market.

. . .

In the context of the Digital Single Market Strategy for Europe (COM(2015) 192 final issued May 6, 2015, the Commission set out the challenges for copyright in a digital single market:

BETTER ACCESS TO DIGITAL CONTENT—A MODERN, MORE EUROPEAN COPYRIGHT FRAMEWORK

Copyright underpins creativity and the cultural industry in Europe. The EU strongly relies on creativity to compete globally and is a world leader in certain copyright-intensive sectors. Digital content is one of the main drivers of the growth of the digital economy. 56% of Europeans use the internet for cultural purposes and spending on digital entertainment and media is predicted to see double digit growth rates (around 12%) for the next five years. Behaviour is changing as consumers increasingly view content on mobile devices and expect to be able to access content from everywhere and wherever they are.

Barriers to cross-border access to copyright-protected content services and their portability are still common, particularly for audiovisual programmes. As regards portability, when consumers cross an internal EU border they are often prevented, on grounds of copyright, from using the content services (e.g. video services) which they have acquired in their home country. . . .

In addition, when trying to access or purchase online copyright-protected content from another Member State, consumers are sometimes told that it is unavailable or cannot be accessed from their own country. This situation is partly linked to the territoriality of copyright and difficulties associated with the clearing of rights. In other cases, the lack of availability and/or access may result from contractual restrictions between rights holders and distributors, or from business decisions taken by distributors. This may sometimes be due to the role territorial exclusivity plays in the financing of certain types of (audiovisual) works.

Innovation in research for both non-commercial and commercial purposes, based on the use of text and data mining (e.g. copying of text and datasets in search of significant correlations or occurrences) may be hampered because of an unclear legal framework and divergent approaches at national level. The need for greater legal certainty to enable researchers and educational institutions to make wider use of copyright-protected material, including across borders, so that they can benefit from the potential of these technologies and from cross-border collaboration will be assessed, as with all parts of the copyright proposals in the light of its impact on all interested parties.

> An effective and balanced civil enforcement system against commercial scale infringements of copyright is central to investment in innovation and job creation. In addition the rules applicable to activities of online intermediaries in relation to copyright protected works require clarification, given in particular the growing involvement of these intermediaries in content distribution. Measures to safeguard fair remuneration of creators also need to be considered in order to encourage the future generation of content.
>
> Europe needs a more harmonised copyright regime which provides incentives to create and invest while allowing transmission and consumption of content across borders, building on our rich cultural diversity. To this end, the Commission will propose solutions which maximise the offers available to users and open up new opportunities for content creators, while preserving the financing of EU media and innovative content. Furthermore, the Commission will review the satellite and cable directive 6 to assess the need to enlarge its scope to broadcasters' online transmissions and the need to tackle further measures to ensure enhanced cross-border access to broadcasters' services in Europe.
>
> The Commission will make legislative proposals before the end of 2015 to reduce the differences between national copyright regimes and allow for wider online access to works by users across the EU, including through further harmonization measures. The proposals will include: (i) portability of legally acquired content, (ii) ensuring cross-border access to legally purchased online services while respecting the value of rights in the audiovisual sector, (iii) greater legal certainty for the cross-border use of content for specific purposes (e.g. research, education, text and data mining, etc.) through harmonised exceptions,(iv) clarifying the rules on the activities of intermediaries in relation to copyright-protected content and, in 2016, (v) modernising enforcement of intellectual property rights, focusing on commercial-scale infringements (the 'follow the money' approach) as well as its cross-border applicability.

## NOTES AND QUESTIONS

**1.** Copyright is embedded in the overall framework of the European internal market rules on goods and services and competition. It is influenced by other instruments, in particular relating to the digital economy. In particular, the Regulation (EU) 2017/1128 of the European Parliament and of the Council of 14 June 2017 on cross-border portability of online content services in the internal market, OJ L168/1, 30 June 2017, which entered into force on 20 March 2018 profoundly affects and reduces territoriality of copyright protection in the European Union.

**2.** Directive (EU) 2019/789 of the European Parliament and of the Council of 17 April 2019 laying down rules on the exercise of copyright and related rights applicable to certain online transmissions of broadcasting organisations and retransmissions of television and radio programmes, and amending Council Directive 93/83/EEC seeks to improve Union and EEA-wide access to online television programs, complementing the Satellite and Cable Directive to digital technologies. It establishes the principle of the "country of origin" for the clearance of rights for certain online transmissions of broadcasters, helping broadcasters to make the vast majority of their content (news, cultural, political, documentary, or entertainment programs, for instance) available online also in other member states. It extends the system of compulsory collective management currently applicable to cable retransmission to other equivalent digital retransmissions. The Directive also lays down rules that regulate the use of protected works or other subject matter via "direct injection", i.e., the technique by which a broadcaster transmits its signal to distributors via a private line – in a way that those signals cannot be received by the general public during that transmission – and, subsequently, the distributor offers the relevant programs to the public. When direct injection is used, and there is no parallel transmission of the same programs by the broadcaster itself, the broadcasting organization and the signal distributor are deemed to be participating in a single act of communication to the public. This means that both parties need to obtain authorization for their respective participation in that activity. The Directive, which is in force since June 2021, thus strongly impacts the transnational operation of copyright within the European Economic Area.

**3.** Bear in mind the legal nature of EU directives. Unlike regulations, which are directly applicable in the national legal system and relied upon by individuals, directives "shall be binding, as to the result to be achieved, upon each Member State to which it is addressed, but shall leave to the national authorities the choice of form and methods."[21] As a general rule, directives do not automatically become part of the national legal system and are not directly applicable (self-executing). Only if specific requirements are met,[22] however, might they have "direct effect," that is, giving a right to individuals to "base a claim in, and be granted relief from, the domestic courts" on the basis of the provisions of the directive.[23] If a member state does not implement (or incorrectly implements) the obligations into national law, the domestic court is still obliged to construe its law in the light of the purpose of the directive, and individuals can sue the member state for damages if the directive is not implemented on time.[24]

## V. REGIONAL AND BILATERAL TRADE AGREEMENTS

In Chapters 1 and 2, we discussed the use by the United States, the European Union, and other countries of bilateral and regional trade agreements to negotiate higher standards of intellectual property rights protection than are presently achievable at the WTO or WIPO. As in the other fields of intellectual property, TRIPS-plus provisions are included also in relation to copyright, most of them pertaining to improving the enforcement which faces particular challenges in the digital age. Following is an excerpt from a World Bank Trade Note that discusses this phenomenon in the context of copyright.

**Carsten Fink & Patrick Reichenmiller***

### *Tightening TRIPS: The Intellectual Property Provisions of Recent US Free Trade Agreements*

#### Copyright Protection

TRIPS requires copyright to be protected for the life of the author plus 50 years. Except for the FTAs extend this term by an additional 20 years.

Most bilateral FTAs include obligations against circumventing so-called technological protection measures—devices and software developed to prevent unauthorized copying

21. Article 288 Treaty on the Functioning of the European Union (ex. Article 249(3) of the Consolidated Version of the Treaty Establishing the European Community).

22. *Id.* at 142.

23. *Id.* at 141. *See also* T. Cottier & K. Nadakavukaren Schefer, *The Relationship between World Trade Organization Law, National and Regional Law*, 1 J. Int'l Econ. L. 83 (1998), at 91 for a detailed analysis of "direct effect." However, an individual can only rely on a directive's direct effect vis-à-vis the government (vertical) and not vis-à-vis other individuals (horizontal). For detailed overviews, further references, and a listing of the requirements for direct effect of directives, *see* The Evolution of EU Law (P. Craig & G. Burca eds., 1999), at 340, and the decisions of the European Court of Justice in, *inter alia, Marshall v. Southampton and South West Hampshire Area Health Authority*, ECR (152/84), 1986, at 723 ff, and *Paola Faccini Dori v. Recreb Srl*, ECR (C-91/92), I-3325, 1994, at 3347 ff.

24. *Francovich and Bonifaci v. Italy*, ECR I-5357, 1991, at 5415 ff.

* World Bank Trade Note 20, Feb. 7, 2005.

of digital works. This issue is not covered under TRIPS. It only came to prominence with advances in information and communication technologies that greatly facilitated the copying of any literary or artistic work in digital form. The US Digital Millennium Copyright Act of 1998 strengthened standards on circumventing technologies designed to prevent unauthorized copying of digital content. These standards found their way to varying degrees into seven of the bilateral agreements. Related provisions in six of the FTAs define the liability of Internet Service Providers (ISPs) when copyright infringing content is distributed through their servers and networks. Again, these provisions are based on standards found in the US Digital Millennium Copyright Act.

In copyright infringement cases, all bilateral FTAs — except for the US-Vietnam Agreement — place the burden of proof on the defending party to show that works are in the public domain. TRIPS does not have any obligation on this question. The FTAs thus strengthen the position of copyright holders, as artistic and literary works should generally be considered as protected — unless they obviously belong to the public domain.

As in the case of pharmaceutical products, TRIPS does not mandate any rule on the permissibility of parallel imports of copyrighted works — such as books or musical CDs — that have been lawfully sold in foreign markets. Some countries, for example New Zealand, have permitted parallel importation of certain copyrighted products as a way to stimulate price competition. By contrast, the bilateral agreements with Jordan and Morocco give copyright holders the right to block parallel importation. . . .

### Economic and Social Implications . . .

Most countries have industries that rely on copyright protection and that may benefit from strengthened protection. And new technologies that greatly facilitate the copying of digital works pose challenges that policymakers need to address. At the same time, copyright laws have historically sought to strike a balance between the interests of copyright producers and the interests of the general public. So-called fair use exemptions allow the copying of protected works for educational or research purposes.

There are concerns that new rules on the term of protection, technological protection measures, the liability of Internet services providers, and the burden of proof in case of copyright infringement could diminish the rights of consumers and the general public (CIPR, 2002).

Such concerns have also been voiced in the United States itself, not only by consumer rights advocates and academic institutions, but also by computer manufacturers and communications service providers that distribute copyrighted works. For example, specific amendments to the Digital Millennium Copyright Act have been proposed that would permit the circumvention of technological protection measures if such action does not result in an infringement of a copyrighted work. Ensuring fair use of copyrighted material seems particularly important for accessing educational material. The opportunities and gains from the use of digital libraries, Internet-based distance learning programs, or online databases would be limited if access to such tools is unaffordable or otherwise restricted by copyright law.

Finally, strengthening the enforcement of intellectual property rights can be a costly exercise — both in terms of budgetary outlays and the employment of skilled personnel. For developing countries that face many institutional deficiencies, a critical question is whether stronger enforcement of IPRs would draw away financial and human resources from other development priorities.

The following excerpt offers an account of TRIPS-plus provisions in recent bilateral and regional negotiations, next to the frequent obligation to adhere to existing WIPO agreements:

**Thomas Cottier, Dannie Jost & Michelle Schupp***

## *Setting the Scene: The Prospects of TRIPS-plus Protection in Future Mega-Regionals*

### Copyright and Neighbouring Rights

The basic provisions of the TRIPS Agreement addressing the topic of "Copyright and Related Rights" are to be found in Articles 9 to 14 TRIPS Agreement. The CAFTA Agreement [the Central America-Dominican Republic Free Trade Agreement (CAFTA-DR) is composed of the United States and Costa Rica, the Dominican Republic, El Salvador, Guatemala, Honduras, and Nicaragua], here used as an analysis template, deals with these provisions in Article 15.5 through 15.7, CETA in Article 5.1 to 5.6 and TPP in Article 18.57 to 18.71 (Section H). CAFTA's right of reproduction partly uses the wording of TRIPS and of the Berne Convention,[1] adding firstly to the categories "authors" (present in the Berne Convention) while TRIPS only cites "performers" and "producers". Secondly, it adds that the term "reproductions" covers "all reproductions [. . .] in any manner or form, permanent or temporary (including temporary storage in electronic form)". This provision has been copied almost verbatim in TPP, but does not include the wording "permanent or temporary".[2]

The right of distribution of CAFTA (almost verbatim in TPP: "right to authorize or prohibit the making available"), gives authors, performers and producers of phonograms the right of distribution of their works, both for originals and copies.[3] The hierarchy provision is again the same in CAFTA as in TPP, abating hierarchy between the categories of author, performer and producer of phonograms: when authorization both from the author and a performer or producer owning rights therein: both authorizations are needed and neither has greater importance than the other.[4]

TRIPS terms of protection have been prolonged both in CAFTA and in TPP.[5] CAFTA's terms calculated on a basis other than the life of a natural person vary between 70 years in case of authorized publication and failing such authorized publication, within 50 years of creation. The terms calculated on the basis of the life of a natural person "shall be no less than the life of the author and 70 years from the author's death" in CAFTA and in TPP. The possibility of contractual transfer of economic rights on a work, performance or phonogram held by any person by virtue of a contract is foreseen in that person shall be able to exercise such rights enjoying the deriving benefits in that person's own name.[6]

A provision on technological protection measures (TPM) is to be found in all three "post-TRIPS agreements". CAFTA is once more copied almost verbatim in TPP and some parts are also to be found in CETA.[7] The provision requires legal protection and remedies against the circumvention of effective technological measures used by authors, performers or producers of phonograms in connection with the exercise of their rights. CETA provides a shorter

* In Mega-Regional Trade Agreements 191-216 (Thilo Rensmann ed., 2017).

1. Berne Convention for the Protection of Literary and Artistic Works, 1886, Article 9(1).
2. Article 14.1 and Article 14.2 TRIPS; Article 15.5.1 CAFTA; Article 18.58 TPP.
3. Article 15.5.2 CAFTA, Article 18.60 TPP.
4. Article 15.5.3 CAFTA, Article 18.61 TPP.
5. Article 12 TRIPS, Article 15.5.4 CAFTA, Article 18.63 TPP.
6. Article 15.5.6 CAFTA; Article 18.67 TPP.
7. Article 15.5.7 CAFTA; Article 5.3 CETA and Article 18.68 TPP.

article some parts of which are copied from CAFTA while CAFTA's wording is long and very detailed, as is that of the TPP (copied nearly verbatim).

The three interregionals exhibit a concern with the protection of rights management information.[8] The wording is nearly the same in CAFTA and the TPP. Some parts of CETA are also copied from CAFTA. The provisions address the protection and remedies against persons performing acts,[9] knowingly without authority, knowing that those acts will facilitate infringement of copyrights or related rights.

CAFTA and TPP contain a specific provision concerning government use of software only as authorized.[10] In TPP, once again the provision is essentially identical to that of CAFTA, with one major difference. While CAFTA recommends that each Party shall issue appropriate laws, orders, regulations, or decrees to actively regulate the acquisition and management of software for such use (e.g. inventories), TPP is more restrictive, saying that government agencies should only use non-infringing computer software protected by copyright and related rights, and further binds use to as authorised by the relevant licence.

Article 15.6 CAFTA, based on Article 14.1 TRIPS, deals only with obligations pertaining specifically to copyright. The TPP uses the same wording as CAFTA, and CETA uses different words for essentially the same provision. That is, authors should have the exclusive right to authorize or prohibit the communication to the public of their works by wire or wireless means whether directly or indirectly; including the making available so that members can access these works from places and at times chosen by them, thus giving more space to authors than under TRIPS.[11]

The TPP agreement further includes a provision on copyright collective management that recognizes the role of collective management societies in collecting and distributing royalties, based on fair practices.[12]

Unlike the TPP, CETA does not strictly follow the template of CAFTA and has its own structure; thus apart from the few Articles cited previously, it contains several additional Articles that may be listed as "TRIPS-plus provisions".

Protection granted[13] refers not only to TRIPS, but also to compliance with the WIPO Copyright Treaty,[14] the WIPO Performance and Phonograms Treaty,[15] and Articles 1 to 22 of the Rome Convention.[16] The Articles further emphasize that "nothing in the chapter shall be construed as restricting each Party's ability to limit intellectual property protection to performances that are fixed in phonograms."

Additionally, liability of intermediary service providers is addressed in that parties are expected to provide for limitations or exceptions in their domestic legislation when intermediary service providers are intermediaries for the infringements of copyright and related rights,

8. Article 15.5.8 CAFTA, Article 5.4 CETA, Article 18.69 TPP. "Rights management information" means information that identifies the work, the author of the work or the producer or the owner of any right in the work, see CETA Article 5.4(1) footnote 49.

9. E.g. "remove or alter any electronic rights management information [. . .], make available to the public copies of works [. . .] knowing that electronic rights management information has been removed or altered without authority.", Article 5.4(1)(a) and (b) CETA.

10. Article 15.5.9 CAFTA, Article 18.80 TPP.

11. Article 15.6 CAFTA, Article 5.2.1 CETA, Article 18.59 TPP.

12. Article 18.70 TPP.

13. Article 5.1 CETA.

14. WIPO Copyright Treaty (WCT), 1996.

15. WIPO Performances and Phonograms Treaty (WPPT), 1996.

16. Rome Convention for the Protection of Performers, Producers of Phonograms and Broadcasting Organizations, 1961.

and such is taking place on or through communication networks relating to the provision or use of their services.[17]

With regard to camcording, the last article of the CETA copyright chapter, addresses the providing of criminal procedures and penalties to be imposed on persons who make a copy a work being shown "in a motion picture exhibition, without authorization of the theatre manager or the holder of copyright in a cinematographic work".[18]

## NOTES AND QUESTIONS

**1.** As with other areas of IPRs protection, there are reasons to question whether standards adopted by and appropriate for the United States, the European Union, and other advanced industrialized countries are equally appropriate for developing countries. The U.S. Digital Millennium Copyright Act involves complex procedural mechanisms that give a decided advantage to better-financed parties. This is a problem for individuals and small-business owners in the United States who may find it difficult to participate in litigation. When comparably complex procedural mechanisms are mandated for developing countries, the imbalance between the capacity of well-financed foreign copyright industries and local individuals and business owners is even more pronounced.

**2.** The decision of the United States in 2017 to abstain from the TTP led to partial renegotiations and suspension of some of the intellectual property disciplines among the 11 parties that later agreed upon the Comprehensive and Progressive Agreement for Trans-Pacific Partnership (CPTTP). In copyright and neighboring rights, the CPTPP suspends the original TPP obligation on the term of protection for copyright of 70 years after the death of the author and a provision on national treatment on payments on copyright and related rights, as well as provisions on technological protection measures (TPMs, or "digital locks") and rights management information (RMI or "digital watermarks on copyrighted works), *see* Government of Canada, *What Does the CPTPP Mean for Intellectual Property?*, http://international.gc.ca/trade-commerce/trade-agreements-accords-commerciaux/agr-acc/cptpp-ptpgp/sectors-secteurs/ip-pi.aspx?lang=eng. *See also* Pratyush Nath Upreti, *From TPP to CPTPP: Why Intellectual Property Matters*, 13 Journal of Intellectual Property Law & Practice 100 (2018).

**3.** The USMCA in effect re-introduces the provisions relating to enhanced protection for copyright that were made inapplicable subsequent to the withdrawal of the United States signature from the TPP. USMCA, for example, imposes detailed obligations on the parties with respect to preventing circumvention of technological protection measures (TPMs), including with respect to devices, products, or components that may facilitate such circumvention (Article 20.H.11). USMCA also effectively requires ISPs to maintain notice and takedown processes in favor of copyright owners (Article 20.J.11). Other USMCA provisions relating to enforcement are discussed in Chapter 6.

## VI. COPYRIGHT IN SOFTWARE AND OPEN SOURCE

We have witnessed the all-encompassing importance of information technology in copyright throughout this chapter. We therefore conclude by addressing the role of copyright in computer programs, engineering, and reverse engineering, and we discuss exclusivity in its tension

17. Article 5.5 CETA.
18. Article 5.6 CETA.

to open access to programs and content. This problem also strongly relates to competition policy and cannot be dealt with in isolation in intellectual property law. We seek to explore the impact of international law in the field. Article 10 of the TRIPS Agreement extended copyright protection to computer programs and compilations of data. It multilateralized an approach which, at the time, was spearheaded by the United States. The Agreement does not offer detailed regulation, and no case law has evolved as of today in WTO dispute settlement. The field continues to strongly depend upon implementation by domestic law and case law. The latter was predominant, in a process of trial and error, in defining the boundaries of copyright protection for computer programming.

## A. Copyright in Software

The importance of computer software to modern economic life is self-evident. Yet, computer software entered the mainstream legal world only in the 1970s as its commercial exploitation began to be commonplace. There were many questions about computer software that lawyers confronted. It is generally quite easy to copy software. In making a program available to a purchaser, licensee, or beta-tester, how could the creator be assured that the software would not be copied, used, and/or redistributed? The commercialization of software appeared to depend upon some form of legal protection. Yet, what form?

Patents are fairly cumbersome. The application process is lengthy and technical. Both novelty and inventive step are elements that may be difficult to satisfy in the software patenting context. Moreover, commercial software is always changing. One version of a program is soon superseded by another as new features are added and bugs (or programming errors) are worked out. A single concept may be embodied in several different versions of the same program written in different programming languages. Would it be possible to draft individual patent applications in a way that would encompass the evolutionary and differentiated character of software? Would a new application need to be filed each time some substantial change to a program was made? Finally, and perhaps most important, it was unclear whether the basic algorithms underlying computer programs are patentable subject matter, because it has long been understood that mathematical formulas are not patentable as such (in that they are thought to represent laws of nature or discoveries).[25]

One potential alternative to the patent was *sui generis* protection that would take into account the unique characteristics of software. *Sui generis* protection might include several characteristics of the patent—such as a prohibition against independent creation and protection of the overall concept—while perhaps enjoying a moderate term of protection. The government of Japan advocated the development of a form of *sui generis* protection, and there was no shortage of proposals in Europe and the United States.

Ultimately, the practical needs of industry triumphed over the government policy makers. Lawyers used the tools at hand to fashion protection for their clients under the copyright laws. There were (and are) decided advantages to copyright. First, copyright laws were in place throughout most of the world, so there would be no time lost in the negotiation and implementation of new norms. Second, copyright protection is automatic. Under the

25. Just what is an *algorithm* has been the subject of debate. One of the authors of this book was some years ago jogging in the hills of Los Angeles with a pioneer of the personal computer industry when the author realized he needed to return to their hotel for a meeting. Not knowing how to get back to the hotel, he asked for directions from the computer scientist. "Well," queried the scientist, "Do you know what an algorithm is?" The author replied, "Perhaps, but in any event why don't you tell me?" "Allow me to explain by illustration," said the scientist. "To return to the hotel, you will always run straight, except that you will turn right at every third stoplight, and left at the only stop sign between here and the hotel. In other words," he continued, "an algorithm is a set of instructions expressed as a mathematical formula."

Berne Convention, the absence of formalities is prescribed. (Recall that in the early 1980s the United States was not party to the Berne Convention.) Thus, assuming that software would be considered copyrightable subject matter, protection would be easy to obtain. Third, copyright law is flexible. Each addition or change to a program would automatically be the subject of protection. Fourth, copyright is of long duration, and while this long duration may not always be of practical use, it was perceived as preferable to the shorter terms generally proposed for *sui generis* protection. Finally, there was the perspective of the practicing lawyers who represented clients in the computer industry. The patent bar of each country is highly specialized, and qualification for the patent bar generally requires technical training. Many lawyers representing the computer industry were not patent lawyers, and these lawyers stood to lose substantial business if representation of the software industry were channeled to the patent bar. There was an incentive for the non-patent lawyer to promote copyright protection or a form of *sui generis* protection outside the specialized patent field.

The adoption of the copyright as the accepted method for protecting computer software left myriad questions to be answered. Though some of the most basic questions have been the subject of fairly consistent legislative and judicial rule making, many questions remain unevenly answered (or not answered at all). Moreover, the computer software industry is dynamic—the "thing" that is covered by copyright protection continues to evolve. In addition, as the "open source movement" (introduced in the next section) illustrates, shifting "business models" alter the landscape on which questions are set.

Of course, the United States over the past decade has opened the field of computer software "as such" to patent protection. Numerous difficulties have resulted.

Though more than 30 years have passed since it was decided, the *Computer Associates v. Altai* decision substantially shapes the "state of the art" in U.S. case law concerning software as copyrightable subject matter.

## *Computer Associates International v. Altai*

982 F.2d 693 (2d Cir. 1992)

WALKER, CIRCUIT JUDGE: . . .

Among other things, this case deals with the challenging question of whether and to what extent the "non-literal" aspects of a computer program, that is, those aspects that are not reduced to written code, are protected by copyright. While a few other courts have already grappled with this issue, this case is one of first impression in this circuit. As we shall discuss, we find the results reached by other courts to be less than satisfactory. Drawing upon longstanding doctrines of copyright law, we take an approach that we think better addresses the practical difficulties embedded in these types of cases. In so doing, we have kept in mind the necessary balance between creative incentive and industrial competition. . . .

### BACKGROUND . . .

### II. FACTS . . .

The subject of this litigation originates with one of CA's marketed programs entitled CA-SCHEDULER. CA-SCHEDULER is a job scheduling program designed for IBM mainframe computers. . . .

. . . ADAPTER plays an extremely important role. It is an "operating system compatibility component," which means, roughly speaking, it serves as a translator. . . .

Starting in 1982, Altai began marketing its own job scheduling program entitled ZEKE. The original version of ZEKE was designed for use in conjunction with a VSE operating system. By late 1983, in response to customer demand, Altai decided to rewrite ZEKE so that it could be run in conjunction with an MVS operating system.

At that time, James P. Williams ("Williams"), then an employee of Altai and now its President, approached Claude F. Arney, III ("Arney"), a computer programmer who worked for CA. Williams and Arney were longstanding friends, and had in fact been co-workers at CA for some time before Williams left CA to work for Altai's predecessor. Williams wanted to recruit Arney to assist Altai in designing an MVS version of ZEKE. . . .

. . . They decided to name this new component-program OSCAR. . . .

The first generation of OSCAR programs was known as OSCAR 3.4. From 1985 to August 1988, Altai used OSCAR 3.4 in its ZEKE product, as well as in programs entitled ZACK and ZEBB. In late July 1988, CA first learned that Altai may have appropriated parts of ADAPTER. After confirming its suspicions, CA secured copyrights on its 2.1 and 7.0 versions of CA-SCHEDULER. CA then brought this copyright and trade secret misappropriation action against Altai.

Apparently, it was upon receipt of the summons and complaint that Altai first learned that Arney had copied much of the OSCAR code from ADAPTER. After Arney confirmed to Williams that CA's accusations of copying were true, Williams immediately set out to survey the damage. Without ever looking at the ADAPTER code himself, Williams learned from Arney exactly which sections of code Arney had taken from ADAPTER.

Upon advice of counsel, Williams initiated OSCAR's rewrite. The project's goal was to save as much of OSCAR 3.4 as legitimately could be used, and to excise those portions which had been copied from ADAPTER. Arney was entirely excluded from the process, and his copy of the ADAPTER code was locked away. Williams put eight other programmers on the project, none of whom had been involved in any way in the development of OSCAR 3.4. Williams provided the programmers with a description of the ZEKE operating system services so that they could rewrite the appropriate code. The rewrite project took about six months to complete and was finished in mid-November 1989. The resulting program was entitled OSCAR 3.5.

From that point on, Altai shipped only OSCAR 3.5 to its new customers. Altai also shipped OSCAR 3.5 as a "free upgrade" to all customers that had previously purchased OSCAR 3.4. While Altai and Williams acted responsibly to correct Arney's literal copying of the ADAPTER program, copyright infringement had occurred. . . .

## Discussion . . .

## I. Copyright Infringement . . .

For the purpose of analysis, the district court assumed that Altai had access to the ADAPTER code when creating OSCAR 3.5. . . . [O]ur analysis will proceed along the same assumption.

As a general matter, and to varying degrees, copyright protection extends beyond a literary work's strictly textual form to its non-literal components. As we have said, "it is of course essential to any protection of literary property . . . that the right cannot be limited literally to the text, else a plagiarist would escape by immaterial variations." *Nichols v. Universal Pictures Co.*, 45 F.2d 119, 121 (2d Cir. 1930) (L. Hand, J.), *cert. denied*, 282 U.S. 902, 75 L. Ed. 795, 51 S. Ct. 216 (1931). Thus, where "the fundamental essence or structure of one work is duplicated in another," 3 Nimmer, §13.03[A][1], at 13-24, courts have found copyright infringement. . . .

### A. Copyright Protection for the Non-Literal Elements Of Computer Programs

It is now well settled that the literal elements of computer programs, i.e., their source and object codes, are the subject of copyright protection. *See Whelan*, 797 F.2d at 1233 (source and object code). . . . Here, as noted earlier, Altai admits having copied approximately 30% of the OSCAR 3.4 program from CA's ADAPTER source code, and does not challenge the district court's related finding of infringement.

In this case, the hotly contested issues surround OSCAR 3.5. As recounted above, OSCAR 3.5 is the product of Altai's carefully orchestrated rewrite of OSCAR 3.4. After the purge, none of the ADAPTER source code remained in the 3.5 version; thus, Altai made sure that the literal elements of its revamped OSCAR program were no longer substantially similar to the literal elements of CA's ADAPTER. . . .

CA argues that, despite Altai's rewrite of the OSCAR code, the resulting program remained substantially similar to the structure of its ADAPTER program. As discussed above, a program's structure includes its nonliteral components such as general flow charts as well as the more specific organization of inter-modular relationships, parameter lists, and macros. In addition to these aspects, CA contends that OSCAR 3.5 is also substantially similar to ADAPTER with respect to the list of services that both ADAPTER and OSCAR obtain from their respective operating systems. We must decide whether and to what extent these elements of computer programs are protected by copyright law. . . .

#### 1. Idea vs. Expression Dichotomy

It is a fundamental principle of copyright law that a copyright does not protect an idea, but only the expression of the idea. *See Baker v. Selden*, 101 U.S. 99, 25 L. Ed. 841 (1879); *Mazer v. Stein*, 347 U.S. 201, 217, 98 L. Ed. 630, 74 S. Ct. 460 (1954). This axiom of common law has been incorporated into the governing statute. Section 102(b) of the Act provides:

> In no case does copyright protection for an original work of authorship extend to any idea, procedure, process, system, method of operation, concept, principle, or discovery, regardless of the form in which it is described, explained, illustrated, or embodied in such work.

17 U.S.C. §102(b). *See also* House Report, at 5670 ("Copyright does not preclude others from using ideas or information revealed by the author's work.").

Congress made no special exception for computer programs. To the contrary, the legislative history explicitly states that copyright protects computer programs only "to the extent that they incorporate authorship in programmer's expression of original ideas, as distinguished from the ideas themselves." *Id.* at 5667; *see also id.* at 5670 ("Section 102(b) is intended . . . to make clear that the expression adopted by the programmer is the copyrightable element in a computer program, and that the actual processes or methods embodied in the program are not within the scope of copyright law."). . . .

Drawing the line between idea and expression is a tricky business. Judge Learned Hand noted that "nobody has ever been able to fix that boundary, and nobody ever can." *Nichols*, 45 F.2d at 121. Thirty years later his convictions remained firm. "Obviously, no principle can be stated as to when an imitator has gone beyond copying the 'idea,' and has borrowed its 'expression,'" Judge Hand concluded. "Decisions must therefore inevitably be ad hoc." *Peter Pan Fabrics, Inc. v. Martin Weiner Corp.*, 274 F.2d 487, 489 (2d Cir. 1960).

The essentially utilitarian nature of a computer program further complicates the task of distilling its idea from its expression. *See SAS Inst.*, 605 F. Supp. at 829; *cf.* Englund, at 893. In order to describe both computational processes and abstract ideas, its content "combines creative and technical expression." *See Spivack*, at 755. The variations of expression found in purely creative compositions, as opposed to those contained in utilitarian works, are not directed towards practical application. For example, a narration of Humpty Dumpty's demise, which would clearly be a creative composition, does not serve the same ends as, say, a recipe for scrambled eggs—which is a more process oriented text. Thus, compared to aesthetic works, computer programs hover even more closely to the elusive boundary line described in §102(b).

The doctrinal starting point in analyses of utilitarian works, is the seminal case of *Baker v. Selden*, 101 U.S. 99, 25 L. Ed. 841 (1879). . . .

The Supreme Court found nothing copyrightable in Selden's bookkeeping system, and rejected his infringement claim regarding the ledger sheets. The Court held that:

> The fact that the art described in the book by illustrations of lines and figures which are reproduced in practice in the application of the art, makes no difference. Those illustrations are the mere language employed by the author to convey his ideas more clearly. Had he used words of description instead of diagrams (which merely stand in the place of words), there could not be the slightest doubt that others, applying the art to practical use, might lawfully draw the lines and diagrams which were in the author's mind, and which he thus described by words in his book.
>
> The copyright of a work on mathematical science cannot give to the author an exclusive right to the methods of operation which he propounds, or to the diagrams which he employs to explain them, so as to prevent an engineer from using them whenever occasion requires.

*Id.* at 103.

To the extent that an accounting text and a computer program are both "a set of statements or instructions . . . to bring about a certain result," 17 U.S.C. §101, they are roughly analogous. In the former case, the processes are ultimately conducted by human agency; in the latter, by electronic means. In either case, as already stated, the processes themselves are not protectable. But the holding in *Baker* goes farther. The Court concluded that those aspects of a work, which "must necessarily be used as incident to" the idea, system or process that the work describes, are also not copyrightable. 101 U.S. at 104. Selden's ledger sheets, therefore, enjoyed no copyright protection because they were "necessary incidents to" the system of accounting that he described. *Id.* at 103. From this reasoning, we conclude that those elements of a computer program that are necessarily incidental to its function are similarly unprotectable.

While *Baker v. Selden* provides a sound analytical foundation, it offers scant guidance on how to separate idea or process from expression, and moreover, on how to further distinguish protectable expression from that expression which "must necessarily be used as incident to" the work's underlying concept. . . .

### 2. Substantial Similarity Test for Computer Program Structure

#### *Abstraction-Filtration-Comparison . . .*

As discussed herein, we think that district courts would be well-advised to undertake a three-step procedure, based on the abstractions test utilized by the district court, in order to determine whether the non-literal elements of two or more computer programs are substantially similar. This approach breaks no new ground; rather, it draws on such familiar copyright doctrines as merger, scène à faire, and public domain. In taking this approach, however, we are cognizant that computer technology is a dynamic field which can quickly outpace judicial decisionmaking. Thus, in cases where the technology in question does not allow for a literal application of the procedure we outline below, our opinion should not be read to foreclose the district courts of our circuit from utilizing a modified version.

In ascertaining substantial similarity under this approach, a court would first break down the allegedly infringed program into its constituent structural parts. Then, by examining each of these parts for such things as incorporated ideas, expression that is necessarily incidental to those ideas, and elements that are taken from the public domain, a court would then be able to sift out all non-protectable material. Left with a kernel, or possibly kernels, of creative expression after following this process of elimination, the court's last step would be to compare this material with the structure of an allegedly infringing program. The result of this comparison will determine whether the protectable elements of the programs at issue are substantially similar so as to warrant a finding of infringement. It will be helpful to elaborate a bit further.

### *Step One: Abstraction*

As the district court appreciated, *see Computer Assocs.*, 775 F. Supp. at 560, the theoretic framework for analyzing substantial similarity expounded by Learned Hand in the *Nichols* case is helpful in the present context. In *Nichols*, we enunciated what has now become known as the "abstractions" test for separating idea from expression:

> Upon any work . . . a great number of patterns of increasing generality will fit equally well, as more and more of the incident is left out. The last may perhaps be no more than the most general statement of what the [work] is about, and at times might consist only of its title; but there is a point in this series of abstractions where they are no longer protected, since otherwise the [author] could prevent the use of his "ideas," to which, apart from their expression, his property is never extended.

*Nichols*, 45 F.2d at 121.

While the abstractions test was originally applied in relation to literary works such as novels and plays, it is adaptable to computer programs. In contrast to the *Whelan* approach, the abstractions test "implicitly recognizes that any given work may consist of a mixture of numerous ideas and expressions." 3 Nimmer §13.03[F] at 13-62.34-63.

As applied to computer programs, the abstractions test will comprise the first step in the examination for substantial similarity. Initially, in a manner that resembles reverse engineering on a theoretical plane, a court should dissect the allegedly copied program's structure and isolate each level of abstraction contained within it. This process begins with the code and ends with an articulation of the program's ultimate function. Along the way, it is necessary essentially to retrace and map each of the designer's steps — in the opposite order in which they were taken during the program's creation. See Background: Computer Program Design, *supra.*

As an anatomical guide to this procedure, the following description is helpful:

> At the lowest level of abstraction, a computer program may be thought of in its entirety as a set of individual instructions organized into a hierarchy of modules. At a higher level of abstraction, the instructions in the lowest-level modules may be replaced conceptually by the functions of those modules. At progressively higher levels of abstraction, the functions of higher-level modules conceptually replace the implementations of those modules in terms of lower-level modules and instructions, until finally, one is left with nothing but the ultimate function of the program. . . . A program has structure at every level of abstraction at which it is viewed. At low levels of abstraction, a program's structure may be quite complex; at the highest level it is trivial. . . .

### *Step Two: Filtration*

Once the program's abstraction levels have been discovered, the substantial similarity inquiry moves from the conceptual to the concrete. Professor Nimmer suggests, and we endorse, a "successive filtering method" for separating protectable expression from non-protectable material. *See generally* 3 Nimmer §13.03[F]. This process entails examining the structural components at each level of abstraction to determine whether their particular inclusion at that level was "idea" or was dictated by considerations of efficiency, so as to be necessarily incidental to that idea; required by factors external to the program itself; or taken from the public domain and hence is nonprotectable expression. *See also* Kretschmer, at 844-45 [Mark T. Kretschmer, *Copyright Protection for Software Architecture: Just Say No!*, 1988 Colum. Bus. L. Rev. 823

(1988)] (arguing that program features dictated by market externalities or efficiency concerns are unprotectable). The structure of any given program may reflect some, all, or none of these considerations. Each case requires its own fact specific investigation.

Strictly speaking, this filtration serves "the purpose of defining the scope of plaintiff's copyright." *Brown Bag Software v. Symantec Corp.*, 960 F.2d 1465, 1475 (9th Cir.) (endorsing "analytic dissection" of computer programs in order to isolate protectable expression), *cert. denied*, 113 S. Ct. 198, 121 L. Ed. 2d 141 (1992). By applying well developed doctrines of copyright law, it may ultimately leave behind a "core of protectable material." 3 Nimmer §13.03[F][5], at 13-72. Further explication of this second step may be helpful.

**(a) Elements Dictated by Efficiency.** The portion of *Baker v. Selden*, discussed earlier, which denies copyright protection to expression necessarily incidental to the idea being expressed, appears to be the cornerstone for what has developed into the doctrine of merger. . . .

CONTU recognized the applicability of the merger doctrine to computer programs. In its report to Congress it stated that:

> Copyrighted language may be copied without infringing when there is but a limited number of ways to express a given idea. . . . In the computer context, this means that when specific instructions, even though previously copyrighted, are the only and essential means of accomplishing a given task, their later use by another will not amount to infringement.

CONTU Report at 20. While this statement directly concerns only the application of merger to program code, that is, the textual aspect of the program, it reasonably suggests that the doctrine fits comfortably within the general context of computer programs.

Furthermore, when one considers the fact that programmers generally strive to create programs "that meet the user's needs in the most efficient manner," Menell, at 1052 [Peter S. Menell, *An Analysis of the Scope of Copyright Protection for Application Programs*, 41 Stan. L. Rev. 1045 (1989)], the applicability of the merger doctrine to computer programs becomes compelling. In the context of computer program design, the concept of efficiency is akin to deriving the most concise logical proof or formulating the most succinct mathematical computation. Thus, the more efficient a set of modules are, the more closely they approximate the idea or process embodied in that particular aspect of the program's structure.

While, hypothetically, there might be a myriad of ways in which a programmer may effectuate certain functions within a program—i.e., express the idea embodied in a given subroutine—efficiency concerns may so narrow the practical range of choice as to make only one or two forms of expression workable options. *See* 3 Nimmer §13.03[F][2], at 13-63; *see also Whelan*, 797 F.2d at 1243 n.43 ("It is true that for certain tasks there are only a very limited number of file structures available, and in such cases the structures might not be copyrightable . . ."). Of course, not all program structure is informed by efficiency concerns. *See* Menell, at 1052 (besides efficiency, simplicity related to user accommodation has become a programming priority). It follows that in order to determine whether the merger doctrine precludes copyright protection to an aspect of a program's structure that is so oriented, a court must inquire "whether the use of this particular set of modules is necessary efficiently to implement that part of the program's process" being implemented. Englund, at 902. If the answer is yes, then the expression represented by the programmer's choice of a specific module or group of modules has merged with their underlying idea and is unprotected. *Id.* at 902-03. . . .

**(b) Elements Dictated by External Factors.** We have stated that where "it is virtually impossible to write about a particular historical era or fictional theme without employing certain 'stock' or standard literary devices," such expression is not copyrightable. *Hoehling v. Universal City Studios, Inc.*, 618 F.2d 972, 979 (2d Cir.), *cert. denied*, 449 U.S. 841,

66 L. Ed. 2d 49, 101 S. Ct. 121 (1980). For example, the *Hoehling* case was an infringement suit stemming from several works on the Hindenberg disaster. There we concluded that similarities in representations of German beer halls, scenes depicting German greetings such as "Heil Hitler," or the singing of certain German songs would not lead to a finding of infringement because they were " 'indispensable, or at least standard, in the treatment of' " life in Nazi Germany. *Id.* (*quoting Alexander v. Haley*, 460 F. Supp. 40, 45 (S.D.N.Y. 1978)). This is known as the *scenes à faire* doctrine, and like "merger," it has its analogous application to computer programs. *Cf. Data East USA*, 862 F.2d at 208 (applying scène à faire to a home computer video game).

Professor Nimmer points out that "in many instances it is virtually impossible to write a program to perform particular functions in a specific computing environment without employing standard techniques." 3 Nimmer §13.03[F][3], at 13-65. This is a result of the fact that a programmer's freedom of design choice is often circumscribed by extrinsic considerations such as (1) the mechanical specifications of the computer on which a particular program is intended to run; (2) compatibility requirements of other programs with which a program is designed to operate in conjunction; (3) computer manufacturers' design standards; (4) demands of the industry being serviced; and (5) widely accepted programming practices within the computer industry. *Id.* at 13-66-71.

Courts have already considered some of these factors in denying copyright protection to various elements of computer programs. . . .

Building upon this existing case law, we conclude that a court must also examine the structural content of an allegedly infringed program for elements that might have been dictated by external factors.

**(c) Elements Taken from the Public Domain.** Closely related to the non-protectability of *scenes à faire*, is material found in the public domain. Such material is free for the taking and cannot be appropriated by a single author even though it is included in a copyrighted work. *See E.F. Johnson Co. v. Uniden Corp. of America*, 623 F. Supp. 1485, 1499 (D. Minn. 1985); *see also Sheldon*, 81 F.2d at 54. We see no reason to make an exception to this rule for elements of a computer program that have entered the public domain by virtue of freely accessible program exchanges and the like. *See* 3 Nimmer §13.03[F][4]; *see also Brown Bag Software*, 960 F.2d at 1473 (affirming the district court's finding that " 'plaintiffs may not claim copyright protection of an . . . expression that is, if not standard, then commonplace in the computer software industry.' "). Thus, a court must also filter out this material from the allegedly infringed program before it makes the final inquiry in its substantial similarity analysis.

*Step Three: Comparison*

The third and final step of the test for substantial similarity that we believe appropriate for non-literal program components entails a comparison. Once a court has sifted out all elements of the allegedly infringed program which are "ideas" or are dictated by efficiency or external factors, or taken from the public domain, there may remain a core of protectable expression. In terms of a work's copyright value, this is the golden nugget. *See Brown Bag Software*, 960 F.2d at 1475. At this point, the court's substantial similarity inquiry focuses on whether the defendant copied any aspect of this protected expression, as well as an assessment of the copied portion's relative importance with respect to the plaintiff's overall program. . . .

### 3. Policy Considerations

We are satisfied that the three step approach we have just outlined not only comports with, but advances the constitutional policies underlying the Copyright Act. Since any method that tries to distinguish idea from expression ultimately impacts on the scope of copyright protection afforded to a particular type of work, "the line [it draws] must be a pragmatic one, which also keeps in consideration 'the preservation of the balance between competition and protection. . . .'" *Apple Computer* [*v. Franklin Computer Corp.*], 714 F.2d [1240] at 1253 (citation omitted). . . .

[W]e are unpersuaded that the test we approve today will lead to the dire consequences for the computer program industry that plaintiff and some amici predict. To the contrary, serious students of the industry have been highly critical of the sweeping scope of copyright protection engendered by the *Whelan* rule, in that it "enables first comers to 'lock up' basic programming techniques as implemented in programs to perform particular tasks." Menell, at 1087; *see also Spivack*, at 765 (*Whelan* "results in an inhibition of creation by virtue of the copyright owner's quasi-monopoly power").

To be frank, the exact contours of copyright protection for non-literal program structure are not completely clear. We trust that as future cases are decided, those limits will become better defined. Indeed, it may well be that the Copyright Act serves as a relatively weak barrier against public access to the theoretical interstices behind a program's source and object codes. This results from the hybrid nature of a computer program, which, while it is literary expression, is also a highly functional, utilitarian component in the larger process of computing. . . .

### II. Trade Secret Preemption

[In the second part of its opinion, the Second Circuit considers the relationship between state trade secret law and federal copyright law. The court holds that state trade secret law is not preempted by federal copyright law to the extent that there is an additional substantive element to a state trade secret law cause of action. The court held: "[A] state law claim based solely upon Altai's" use, "by copying, of ADAPTER's non-literal elements could not satisfy the governing 'extra element' test, and would be preempted by section 301. However, where the use of copyrighted expression is simultaneously the violation of a duty of confidentiality established by state law, that extra element renders the state right qualitatively distinct from the federal right, thereby foreclosing preemption under section 301." Judge Altimari dissented from the court's preemption analysis.]

## NOTES AND QUESTIONS

**1.** The second step in the court's analytical process is "filtration." The court observes that the expression in computer programs is often dictated by functional concerns—for example, the microprocessor requests that data be transmitted from the disk drive—and that there are a limited number of relatively efficient ways to frame such requests. The court does not want expression that is dictated by such functional concerns to be protected by copyright. Moreover, the court notes that some types of program instruction are commonplace—analogizing to *scenes à faire* doctrine, which precludes the copyrighting of commonplace descriptions and events (*e.g.*, "under a clear blue sky").

**2.** Some courts may find it difficult to apply the tests articulated in *Computer Associates.* Is the *Computer Associates* analysis practical in the global context?

**3.** Recall the German Supreme Court's decision in the *Protection of Computer Programs* case, *supra*, that program elements dictated by functionality should be filtered out, and that originality should reflect more than the skill of the average programmer. Is that decision consistent with the decision in *Computer Associates*? Consider also the recent CJEU decision in *SAS v. World Programming* set forth below.

The United Kingdom ratified the WIPO Copyright Treaty in December 2009, nine years after it was approved by the EU Council. The Treaty entered into force for the European Union in 2010. The *SAS Institute v. World Programming Limited* case, initially argued before the UK High Court, is an example dealing with the interpretation of the WIPO Copyright Treaty, the TRIPS Agreement, and the EU Software Directive under UK legislation. UK law does not expressly limit the scope of copyright to the expression of ideas (not encompassing the ideas themselves). This case raised several important issues related to copyright in computer programs, including programming languages, interfaces, and program functionality. The case is important for the doctrine of consistent interpretation of domestic and international law; see *supra* Chapter 1, section VII. The judgment of the European Court of Justice rendered in response to referral from the UK High Court substantially defines the scope of copyright protection of computer programs, with critical elements regarding uses that are excluded from copyright protection.

## *SAS Institute Inc. v. World Programming Inc.*

Judgment of the Court (Grand Chamber), 2 May 2012

(Intellectual property — Directive 91/250/EEC — Legal protection of computer programs — Articles 1(2) and 5(3) — Scope of protection — Creation directly or via another process — Computer program protected by copyright — Reproduction of the functions by a second program without access to the source code of the first program — Decompilation of the object code of the first computer program — Directive 2001/29/EC — Copyright and related rights in the information society — Article 2(a) — User manual for a computer program — Reproduction in another computer program — Infringement of copyright — Condition — Expression of the intellectual creation of the author of the user manual)

In Case C-406/10,

REFERENCE for a preliminary ruling under Article 267 TFEU from the High Court of Justice of England and Wales, Chancery Division (United Kingdom), made by decision of 2 August 2010, received at the Court on 11 August 2010, in the proceedings

SAS Institute Inc. v World Programming Ltd,

THE COURT (Grand Chamber),

Advocate General: Y. Bot,

gives the following

### Judgment

23. SAS Institute is a developer of analytical software. It has developed an integrated set of computer programs over a period of 35 years which enables users to carry out a wide range of data processing and analysis tasks, in particular, statistical analysis ('the SAS System'). The core component of the SAS System, called 'Base SAS', enables users to write and run their own application programs in order to adapt the SAS System to work with their data (Scripts). Such Scripts are written in a language which is peculiar to the SAS System ('the SAS Language').

24. WPL perceived that there was a market demand for alternative software capable of executing application programs written in the SAS Language. WPL therefore produced the 'World Programming System', designed to emulate the SAS components as closely as possible in that, with a few minor exceptions, it attempted to ensure that the same inputs would

produce the same outputs. This would enable users of the SAS System to run the Scripts which they have developed for use with the SAS System on the 'World Programming System'.

. . .

### Consideration of the Questions Referred

#### Questions 1 to 5

29. By these questions, the national court asks, in essence, whether Article 1(2) of Directive 91/250 must be interpreted as meaning that the functionality of a computer program and the programming language and the format of data files used in a computer program in order to exploit certain of its functions constitute a form of expression of that program and may, as such, be protected by copyright in computer programs for the purposes of that directive.

. . .

39. On the basis of those considerations, it must be stated that, with regard to the elements of a computer program which are the subject of Questions 1 to 5, neither the functionality of a computer program nor the programming language and the format of data files used in a computer program in order to exploit certain of its functions constitute a form of expression of that program for the purposes of Article 1(2) of Directive 91/250.

40. As the Advocate General states . . ., to accept that the functionality of a computer program can be protected by copyright would amount to making it possible to monopolise ideas, to the detriment of technological progress and industrial development.

41. Moreover, point 3.7 of the explanatory memorandum to the Proposal for Directive 91/250 [COM(88) 816] states that the main advantage of protecting computer programs by copyright is that such protection covers only the individual expression of the work and thus leaves other authors the desired latitude to create similar or even identical programs provided that they refrain from copying.

42. With respect to the programming language and the format of data files used in a computer program to interpret and execute application programs written by users and to read and write data in a specific format of data files, these are elements of that program by means of which users exploit certain functions of that program.

43. In that context, it should be made clear that, if a third party were to procure the part of the source code or the object code relating to the programming language or to the format of data files used in a computer program, and if that party were to create, with the aid of that code, similar elements in its own computer program, that conduct would be liable to constitute partial reproduction within the meaning of Article 4(a) of Directive 91/250.

44. As is, however, apparent from the order for reference, WPL did not have access to the source code of SAS Institute's program and did not carry out any decompilation of the object code of that program. By means of observing, studying and testing the behaviour of SAS Institute's program, WPL reproduced the functionality of that program by using the same programming language and the same format of data files.

45. The Court also points out that the finding made in paragraph 39 of the present judgment cannot affect the possibility that the SAS language and the format of SAS Institute's data files might be protected, as works, by copyright under Directive 2001/29 if they are their author's own intellectual creation (see *Bezpečnostní softwarová asociace*, paragraphs 44 to 46).

46. Consequently, the answer to Questions 1 to 5 is that Article 1(2) of Directive 91/250 must be interpreted as meaning that neither the functionality of a computer program nor the programming language and the format of data files used in a computer program in order to exploit certain of its functions constitute a form of expression of that program and, as such, are not protected by copyright in computer programs for the purposes of that directive.

### Questions 6 and 7

47. By these questions, the national court asks, in essence, whether Article 5(3) of Directive 91/250 must be interpreted as meaning that a person who has obtained a copy of a computer program under a licence is entitled, without the authorisation of the owner of the copyright in that program, to observe, study or test the functioning of that program in order to determine the ideas and principles which underlie any element of the program, in the case where that person carries out acts covered by that licence with a purpose that goes beyond the framework established by the licence.

. . .

50. The Court observes that, from the wording of that provision, it is clear, first, that a licensee is entitled to observe, study or test the functioning of a computer program in order to determine the ideas and principles which underlie any element of the program.

51. In this respect, Article 5(3) of Directive 91/250 seeks to ensure that the ideas and principles which underlie any element of a computer program are not protected by the owner of the copyright by means of a licensing agreement.

52. That provision is therefore consistent with the basic principle laid down in Article 1(2) of Directive 91/250, pursuant to which protection in accordance with that directive applies to the expression in any form of a computer program and ideas and principles which underlie any element of a computer program are not protected by copyright under that directive.

53. Article 9(1) of Directive 91/250 adds, moreover, that any contractual provisions contrary to the exceptions provided for in Article 5(2) and (3) of that directive are null and void.

54. Second, under Article 5(3) of Directive 91/250, a licensee is entitled to determine the ideas and principles which underlie any element of the computer program if he does so while performing any of the acts of loading, displaying, running, transmitting or storing that program which he is entitled to do.

55. It follows that the determination of those ideas and principles may be carried out within the framework of the acts permitted by the licence.

56. In addition, the 18th recital in the preamble to Directive 91/250 states that a person having a right to use a computer program should not be prevented from performing acts necessary to observe, study or test the functioning of the program, provided that these acts do not infringe the copyright in that program.

57. As the Advocate General states . . ., the acts in question are those referred to in Article 4(a) and (b) of Directive 91/250, which sets out the exclusive rights of the rightholder to do or to authorise, and those referred to in Article 5(1) thereof, relating to the acts necessary for the use of the computer program by the lawful acquirer in accordance with its intended purpose, including for error correction.

58. In that latter regard, the 17th recital in the preamble to Directive 91/250 states that the acts of loading and running necessary for that use may not be prohibited by contract.

59. Consequently, the owner of the copyright in a computer program may not prevent, by relying on the licensing agreement, the person who has obtained that licence from determining the ideas and principles which underlie all the elements of that program in the case where that person carries out acts which that licence permits him to perform and the acts of loading and running necessary for the use of the computer program, and on condition that that person does not infringe the exclusive rights of the owner in that program.

60. As regards that latter condition, Article 6(2)(c) of Directive 91/250 relating to decompilation states that decompilation does not permit the information obtained through its application to be used for the development, production or marketing of a computer program substantially similar in its expression, or for any other act which infringes copyright.

61. It must therefore be held that the copyright in a computer program cannot be infringed where, as in the present case, the lawful acquirer of the licence did not have access to the source code of the computer program to which that licence relates, but merely studied, observed and tested that program in order to reproduce its functionality in a second program.

62. In those circumstances, the answer to Questions 6 and 7 is that Article 5(3) of Directive 91/250 must be interpreted as meaning that a person who has obtained a copy of a computer program under a licence is entitled, without the authorisation of the owner of the copyright, to observe, study or test the functioning of that program so as to determine the ideas and principles which underlie any element of the program, in the case where that person carries out acts covered by that licence and acts of loading and running necessary for the use of the computer program, and on condition that that person does not infringe the exclusive rights of the owner of the copyright in that program.

**Questions 8 and 9**

63. By these questions, the national court asks, in essence, whether Article 2(a) of Directive 2001/29 must be interpreted as meaning that the reproduction, in a computer program or a user manual for that program, of certain elements described in the user manual for another computer program protected by copyright constitutes an infringement of that right in the latter manual.

64. It is apparent from the order for reference that the user manual for SAS Institute's computer program is a protected literary work for the purposes of Directive 2001/29.

65. The Court has already held that the various parts of a work enjoy protection under Article 2(a) of Directive 2001/29, provided that they contain some of the elements which are the expression of the intellectual creation of the author of the work (Case C5/08 *Infopaq International* [2009] ECR I6569, paragraph 39).

66. In the present case, the keywords, syntax, commands and combinations of commands, options, defaults and iterations consist of words, figures or mathematical concepts which, considered in isolation, are not, as such, an intellectual creation of the author of the computer program.

67. It is only through the choice, sequence and combination of those words, figures or mathematical concepts that the author may express his creativity in an original manner and achieve a result, namely the user manual for the computer program, which is an intellectual creation (see, to that effect, *Infopaq International*, paragraph 45).

68. It is for the national court to ascertain whether the reproduction of those elements constitutes the reproduction of the expression of the intellectual creation of the author of the user manual for the computer program at issue in the main proceedings.

69. In this respect, the examination, in the light of Directive 2001/29, of the reproduction of those elements of the user manual for a computer program must be the same with respect to the creation of the user manual for a second program as it is with respect to the creation of that second program.

70. Consequently, in the light of the foregoing considerations, the answer to Questions 8 and 9 is that Article 2(a) of Directive 2001/29 must be interpreted as meaning that the reproduction, in a computer program or a user manual for that program, of certain elements described in the user manual for another computer program protected by copyright is capable of constituting an infringement of the copyright in the latter manual if—this being a matter for the national court to ascertain—that reproduction constitutes the expression of the intellectual creation of the author of the user manual for the computer program protected by copyright.

## NOTES AND QUESTIONS

**1.** In *DVD Copy Control Ass'n (DVD CCA) v. Bunner*,[26] an injunction had been issued to prevent Andrew Bunner from making available on his web page DeCSS software he had previously downloaded from the Internet. DVD CCA claimed that the publishing on or linking to web sites containing DeCSS software constituted trade secret misappropriation under California law. Bunner argued that republishing information widely available on the Internet (such as DeCSS) was protected by the First Amendment and the injunction thus violated his constitutional rights. The California Supreme Court agreed with the basic proposition that the distribution of computer code is protectable as free speech. However, in the case of publishing code protected by trade secret law, an injunction would be "content neutral" (i.e., not based on the particular content of the speech, but rather a legitimate tool to protect trade secrets), and constitutionally permissible. The California Supreme Court remanded the case to the California Court of Appeal, which found that DVD CCA failed to establish that the DeCSS code made widely available on the Internet was subject to trade secret protection (*DVD Copy Control Ass'n v. Bunner* (6th Dist. Cal. App.), 116 Cal. App. 4th 241 (2004) (*request for review by Cal. Sup. Ct. denied*, 2004 Cal. LEXIS 8697 (Cal., Sept. 15, 2004))). A portion of that decision is excerpted in the discussion of trade secrets, *infra* Chapter 5, section V.A.

**2.** At the outset of this Chapter, *supra* section I.B.2, we noted that the EU Software Directive was in good part a response to the decision of the German Supreme Court in the *Inkasso [re Protection of Computer Programs]* case that copyright protection for computer programs required creativity above the skill of the average computer programmer. We also noted that the trend in U.S. law was to narrow the scope of copyright protection for computer programs, removing protection from functional elements. Is it fair to say that the decision of the CJEU in *SAS v. World Programming* continues this trend toward limiting copyright protection for computer programs? Do you sense that U.S. and EU trade negotiators demanding strict protection for intellectual property, including copyright, may be out of sync with their national courts? Or not?

**3.** *Computer Associates v. Altai* and, more recently, *SAS Institute Inc. v. World Programming Ltd*, are landmark decisions with respect to the question of copyright protection of computer software. They define the "proprietary" elements of software. The latter decision may have been partly influenced by developments during the last few decades with the advent of a new concept altering the concept of property in the context of computer software. The "open source" movement is evolving and dynamic, creating a new software environment and innovation model.

## B. Open Source and the Public Domain

Throughout this chapter the issue of public domain was mentioned several times. The importance of public domain is widely recognized—promotion of education and follow-on innovation, as well as low-cost access to information, are examples. The following excerpt from a WIPO study on the public domain explains the recent private initiatives aimed at promotion of better access to information and development of the public domain.

26. Supreme Court of California, 2003 Cal. LEXIS 6295, 31 Cal. 4th 864, Aug. 25, 2003.

## *Scoping Study on Copyright and Related Rights and the Public Domain*

Prepared by Severine Dusollier WIPO, May 7, 2010

. . .

### Copyleft, Open Source or Open Access Licensing

#### 1. Notion

Unhappy with the extension of intellectual property, some creators have set up alternative regimes for exercising copyright. The first and best known is the open source software movement that was born in the 80's to counteract the proprietary exercise of copyright in software, considered by many as excessive and far-fetched and at odds with the needs of the community of software developers and users. Many licenses have been developed with common features that give some basic freedoms to the licensees, such as the right to reproduce, communicate or distribute the work to the public for free, and oblige the licensor to provide the source code of the program.

That first idea inspired and gave its name to a larger movement whose key purpose was to use the copyright to share one's works and grant large freedoms of use to the public. That movement has adopted many names. Open source is the germinal term that has embraced a myriad of licenses governing free software. It insists on the core obligation arising from such licenses—the obligation to provide the source code of the software. The movement or licenses promoting non-proprietary software are also generally dubbed as F/OSS, standing for Free/Open-Source Software (or even FLOSS, for Free, Libre, Open Source Software).

While the principles of open source have spread beyond software, these open-source initiatives have forsaken the "source" element to prefer instead "open access" or "open content." The openness of the resource, whether such openness lies in its access or use, is there emphasized. Following a body of literature applying the economic concept of the "commons" to intellectual property, many projects have also borrowed that word to signify the newly gained communality of the resources that the open access and sharing initiatives could yield. The term "commons-based initiatives" has sometimes served to designate sharing projects in copyright or patent fields.

Also taken from open-source software, the term "copyleft" gained momentum in the open-access schemes and in the literature describing them. It results from a play on words where copy *left* stands in stark contrast to copy *right*—"left" versus "right"—but also progressive versus conservative (applying to what was perceived, by the copyleft proponents, as the "right-wing" and conservative position of the proprietary copyright), "right" as legal entitlement versus "left" as relinquishment of the property. . . .

Software, works or inventions distributed to the public under an open source or copyleft licensing regime are often said to be in the public domain. This is not accurate as the decision to license the use of one's works under a copyleft license does not amount to a relinquishment of copyright, but rather as an exercise thereof, albeit different. Based on licenses granting the right to copy, distribute, communicate and sometimes modify the work to any user of the work, open access licensing can be seen as pursuing a similar objective to the public domain, i.e. promoting the free availability, use and exploitation of creative expressions.

#### 2. Presentation of Main Licensing Regimes

##### (i) Open Source Software

The history of open-source software is now well known and documented. Reacting to the early development of licensing practices aimed at restricting the "rights of use" of software and of the increasing closure of the source code, Richard Stallman imagined a new model of software distribution, that would fit more closely with the habits of the programmers' community. This alternate framework was named "free software" in order to convey the freedom to access and use the software.

The history of open-source software then took different paths. Richard Stallman founded the Free Software Foundation, which has developed and continues to manage the General Public License ("GPL"), the first license embedding free software principles. The development of the operating system Linux by a student quickly gave a market pedigree to the idea of free software, demonstrating the possible commercial success of this new model. A schism occurred in 1998 when less radical programmers launched the Open Source Initiative whose objective was to develop open-source principles that could be seen not only as a confrontation to the practices of the software industry but that could be part of a business strategy. They invented the term "open source" to emphasize not the freedom to use but the necessity to make the source code of the software available. This meeting also gave birth to the Open Source Definition, which lays down the key elements and provisions that a license should include to merit the open-source label. This definition contains ten "commandments" that form a sort of label certificate. They combine the four basic freedoms that a free or open-source license should grant: (1) the freedom to run the program, for any users or purpose (e.g., for commercial purpose or not); (2) the right to obtain access to source code; (3) the freedom to redistribute copies; and (4) the freedom to improve the program and release improvements if desired.

Eventually the open source software movement gave birth to more than one hundred open-source licenses that are in use worldwide. The GPL represents the biggest share of the licenses now employed on the market. Most of them originate from a US-based legal philosophy and writing. One European license, the EUPL (European Public License) has been recently developed by the European Commission to be applied to software in a way that would be compliant with the EU regulatory framework.

### (ii) Creative Commons

Lawrence Lessig, a well-known scholar in cyberspace law, has followed Richard Stallman and the overall open-source movement by imagining the transposition of the copyleft model at work in free software to other types of creation. He founded the Creative Commons ("CC") project and organization in 2001. The main objective of Creative Commons parallels that of the free software movement, i.e. to grant basic freedoms of copying and distributing a copyrighted work to users, but has devised licenses applicable to any type of literary and artistic work and not only software.

Besides developing licenses applicable outside of software, Creative Commons departs from the open-source model used in software by giving the author choices among different licenses. Each license grants diverse rights to the user. When deciding to license his/her work under Creative Commons, an author can choose whether he/she will allow the work to be modified by the user, whether he/she wants to limit uses of the work to non-commercial purposes, and whether he/she wants to oblige the user to grant the same freedom of use when the latter modifies the work and publicly communicates the derivative work. Regardless of which Creative Commons license the author chooses, a work should be attributed to its author when it is disseminated.

Creative Commons offers six different licenses for the author to choose from, divided into three basic characteristics: Commercial/Non-Commercial, Derivative Works/Non-Derivative Works, and Share Alike/Non-Share Alike. Each license grants a worldwide, royalty-free, non-exclusive, perpetual license to the user to reproduce, display, perform, communicate, and distribute copies of the work. Depending on the type of license selected, the right to create derivative works or to use the work for commercial purposes might also be granted. All rights not expressly granted by the licensor are reserved with the exception of limitations to copyright that are not prejudiced by the license. The so-called Share Alike licenses require that the further distribution of derivative works be made under the same license terms. . . .

. . . To some extent, Creative Commons can be said to provide a useful answer to the needs of some communities of creators who might consider sharing as the normal way of disseminating their creation, whether artistic, informational, scientific or functional.

Other free licenses have been developed for artistic creation such as the *Licence Art Libre*, in France in 1999, but they are less used now than Creative Commons.

#### (iii) Open Access to Scientific Publications

Open-access ideology has also spread to the field of scientific publications where it has been seen as a strategy for counteracting the increasing commodification of scientific publications and the reduced availability of scientific knowledge. In the realm of scientific publications, the open-access dogma has been applied by putting in place free electronic distribution of scholarly journals in almost all fields of science and by setting up central repositories of open-access journals such as the OpenDOAR (Open Directory of Open Access Repositories) that contains more than 14,000 sources of academic open access repositories or journals.

Open-access ideology in the realm of scientific publications has been aided by the fact that many research organizations, universities, libraries, research funding agencies, and publishers have signed the Berlin Declaration on Open Access to Knowledge in the Sciences and Humanities. This declaration requires authors associated with the signatories to grant to all users a free worldwide right to access their works and requires that the works be deposited in at least one online repository enabling open access, unrestricted distribution, interoperability, and long-term archiving. Publication of scientific results or articles in open access is increasingly the norm in scientific research. It does not follow any particular licensing framework for enabling open access, but rather relies on existing licensing platforms such as Creative Commons or lets the authors or the open-access repositories draft their own open-access policy.

The following excerpt by Lawrence Lessig points out that open source is not free intellectual property protection, but depends on copyright protection to remain "open."

**Lawrence Lessig***

## *Open Source Baselines: Compared to What?*

. . . [H]ere lies the puzzle: by distributing the source code with the object code, open source and free software developers give their competitors free access to any value that they might have added to the software they are distributing. A developer thus cannot capture that value for him- or herself, but rather gives at least a part of it away. How then can developers have sufficient incentive to innovate? What motivates them to develop in this way? How can developers sustain the costs of development if they must hand to their competitors all the value they have created?

My aim here is to disentangle this puzzle. Open source and free software have played an important part in the growth of the Internet. The puzzle about their existence comes from a mistaken baseline of comparison. Properly understood, these movements are completely

* GOVERNMENT POLICY TOWARD OPEN SOURCE SOFTWARE 50 (Robert W. Hahn ed., 2003).

consistent with a tradition of innovation and development outside the context of software. They may seem unique within the software industry, but they are not unique against the background of development or innovation generally. . . .

### THE NATURE OF OPEN SOURCE AND FREE SOFTWARE

Open source and free software give consumers and the public something more than proprietary software does: the ability to tinker and modify. Such software gives the public the benefit of the information contained within the code. Yet open source and free software don't provide these values by forfeiting public law protection. Open source and free software are not "in the public domain." Copyrights still attach to their creative content. Thus copyright law continues to control how this content can be used and distributed. Open source and free software producers use this control to impose conditions upon the use of their code. These conditions vary significantly depending upon whether the code is free or open source. But these conditions are not options. They are requirements imposed by the force of law.

Not all software-related content is protected in this way. There are important software related products that are within the public domain. The TCP/IP (Transmission Control Protocol/Internet Protocol), for example, which forms the basic protocols of the Internet, is in the public domain. Anyone is free to implement it without the permission of a copyright holder. This enabled many to build TCP/IP networks inexpensively and ensured that no one had the power to control how TCP/IP would develop.

But being in the public domain also means that TCP/IP could in principle be hijacked. A major producer of TCP/IP technology could extend the protocol in a way that benefits its own interests and weakens its competitors. It could do this because the nature of the public domain is that anyone is free to build as they wish. HTML (Hypertext Markup Language) is an example of a protocol that was in the public domain. Netscape and Microsoft each tried to extend the protocol in ways that benefited its own implementation. This competition may or may not have been beneficial to the spread of the World Wide Web. But whether or not it was, hijacking was possible because the underlying protocol was not protected.

By staying outside the public domain, open source and free software at least have the potential to protect themselves against the hijacker. Using copyright law, they have the power to require certain conditions before their code is used in ways that implicate the exclusive rights protected by copyright law. Thus, like proprietary software, open source and free software depend upon copyright; like proprietary software, open source and free software make themselves available only under certain conditions. The important difference among these three forms of software is simply the difference in conditions.

Proprietary software is made available upon the payment of a price (which sometimes is zero). In exchange for a price, the user ordinarily licenses the object code. Object code, because it is compiled into a form that is effectively opaque to humans, does not transmit the information it contains; it is simply a machine that induces another machine to function in a particular way. But attached to that machine is a license supported by copyright law. That license sets the terms according to which one may use the licensed machine. In the ordinary proprietary model, you are not permitted to sell the code you have licensed, nor are you permitted to modify and redistribute it. Proprietary code gives you the right to use the machine you've licensed, just like a rental from Hertz gives you the right to use the car you've leased.

Open source and free software impose different conditions upon users. And while the variety of open source and free software licenses is broad, we can identify essentially two sorts: copylefted software and noncopylefted software.

Copylefted software is software that is licensed under terms that require follow-on users to require others to adopt the same license terms for work derived from the copylefted code.

The principle is "share and share alike." Noncopylefted open source software imposes no such condition on subsequent use. With copylefted software, the price of admission is that if you redistribute modified versions of the copylefted code, you must redistribute it under similar license terms; with noncopylefted software, no such price is demanded.

The most famous example of copylefted code is the GNU/Linux operating system. GNU/Linux is licensed under the GNU General Public License (GPL). The GPL requires that anyone who modifies and redistributes GPL-covered code do so under a GPL license. For example, if an enterprising coder modified Linux to run seamlessly Windows and Macintosh programs, he would be free to redistribute that modified GNU/Linux only if he did so under a GPL license. And since a GPL license also requires that the source code of a GPL work be made available for free, this Linux innovator would likely face competition from copycat competitors. If the coder had in fact produced an operating system that could run programs from other operating systems directly, then many would likely take it and sell it in competition with him. The GPL guarantees that "freedom."

It is for this reason that some argue that the copyleft requirement is too steep a price for developers to pay. The freedom of a single developer to build a cross-platform-compatible version of Linux, for example, might well be defeated by the copyleft condition (assuming that the costs of such a project are extremely high and that the developer would need to recover those costs from the sale of copies of the resulting operating system). But this condition is not necessarily any more expensive than the conditions imposed by proprietary code. If our Linux developer wanted to create a modified, cross-platform-compatible version of Windows, he would be no more free to redistribute the resulting Microsoft code than he would be free to distribute the modified Linux code under the GPL. If he could get the permission of Microsoft at all, no doubt he would have to pay a high price. The difference then is not that one licensing system imposes burdens while the other does not; the difference is in the nature of the burdens.

Noncopylefted open source software does not impose this condition on subsequent licensing. Not only is a user free to build upon it, but it also does not require that such building be released under similar licensing terms. . . .

No doubt, from a private perspective, the differences among these types of software are important. . . .

From the perspective of the public, however, another difference is significant. To understand this difference, however, requires a bit more explanation about the economics of software.

### SOFTWARE AND PUBLIC GOODS . . .

Goods can be mixed — possessing both public and private attributes. Software is an example: it can be produced as a purely private good, but it can also be produced in a way that promotes certain public goods. These public goods might be divided between pure and "qualified" public goods. The information about how a program works — how it achieves its functionality — that is contained within its source code is a pure public good. If made available generally, then my consumption of that knowledge would leave as much for you as before. If made available generally, then it would be hard to exclude my knowledge of it to the extent that knowledge is known generally.

In contrast, the digital copy of a particular software product could be considered a qualified public good, meaning simply that it requires some resources in order to be obtained. My having a copy of your program doesn't interfere with your having a copy of your program. But it may take resources to produce that copy of your program. Likewise, an unprotected digital copy can be made available to all if it is made available to some, but it takes resources to move that content (the cost of electricity to run the network, for example). As modern digital technologies reduce these necessary resources to zero, this means in effect that software can be made available just as easily as a pure public good. . . .

Software developers, however, have tools beyond intellectual property law that they can deploy to balance the public goods nature of software. Proprietary software providers, for example, can add excludability to their software by never releasing its source code: by compiling the source code and distributing just its object code, they can make the information within the product effectively excludable. Compilation makes the source code secret, and secrecy adds to the providers' ability to recover value.

Software providers can also make software effectively rivalrous. Copy protection technologies, for example, can make particular copies of software exclusive to particular owners. Properly deployed, these technologies can make it effectively impossible for you to use my software when I am using it. This again makes it easier for the producer to recover the value of his production by eliminating another public goods aspect of the digital product.

Thus two sets of tools—one public, the other private—are available to the software provider for balancing (or defeating) the public goods character of code. These tools in turn overlap. An author doesn't have to choose between copy protection technologies and copyright or between compiled code and law—he gets both. And by combining both kinds, a producer will get more value and will, to some extent and in some contexts, increase the incentive to produce.

Yet at some point, the combination of this public and private protection may reduce, rather than increase, social welfare—at least if the protection is too strong. These protections raise the price of information above its marginal cost of production. This means less information is being distributed than is economically efficient. Economics resents a price above marginal cost. Any gap may be a necessary evil to induce production, but as with all necessary evils, it should be tolerated only so far as it is truly necessary. A gap may be justified by the need to solve the provision problem, but if the controls extend beyond the justification, they reduce social welfare. Some control is needed, but some control is far less than perfect control. And hence the problem of social policy is how best to balance a necessary evil against access to information at its marginal cost—that is, free.

These familiar ideas are presented here to remind us of a point that is too often forgotten in the debate about open source and free software: the strong bias of public policy should be to spread public goods at their marginal cost. Compromises are no doubt necessary if private actors are to contribute voluntarily to the production of public goods; but public entities, such as governments, should not indulge in these compromises unless they are necessary. Between two systems for producing a public good, one that releases the information produced by that good freely and one that does not, all things being equal, public policy should favor free access. This is not because of some egalitarian bias or because of ideals about social equality but for purely neoclassical economic reasons: free access brings the cost of information down to its marginal cost, and neoclassical economics favors price at marginal costs. If the problems of incentives have already been solved for a particular good or class of goods—no doubt a large assumption, but for some important software goods a true one—then there is no further reason to exclude access to the public goods produced. Or if the provision problem is sufficiently solved by other systems of incentive, then again there is no reason to exclude the public goods produced.

From a social perspective, this means that there is a difficult choice between these two forms of production. If social good is the sum of private and public goods, then we cannot pick between open and proprietary software in the abstract. On the one hand, open source and free software dominate proprietary software in spreading a public good. Yet on the other hand, if there is insufficient incentive to produce software under the open source and free software models, then the private good from software will also be underproduced.

When society faces a difficult social choice that is usually a good reason to let both forms of production compete in the market. And thus no one sensible is calling for a requirement that all software be free or that free software be banned. Yet some do argue against open source and free software, sometimes motivated by a belief that its business model is a failure and sometimes motivated by a view that at least some forms of free software are dangerous to "software ecology."

The economics of open source and free software is just beginning to be understood. A growing body of literature increasingly demonstrates how individuals could have sufficient private incentive to solve the provision problem, even though they cannot capture the full value of what they produce. . . .

### Conclusion

There is a reason for public policy to prefer a world where software is open and free. That reason cannot trump all other considerations, and it alone does not support a general rule that would banish proprietary code. But the reason does motivate an inquiry into whether free and open source code can be adequately produced. Economists have just begun a formal inquiry into that question. That inquiry could be helped with a bit of perspective: by seeing the parallel between open source and free software production and other more familiar modes of production, we are more likely to accept the conclusion of economists that open code is often possible and often very valuable.

I have argued in favor of government neutrality regarding open and proprietary software—as long as the interests the government reckons are sufficiently broad. If they are, then the government will often arrive at the conclusion that open code is preferable to proprietary code. At the very least, such an approach would lead to the conclusion that the government should not allow software patents to tilt the competitive horizon against open code projects.

## NOTES AND QUESTIONS

**1.** Economists have dealt extensively with the underlying question of why anyone would take time and effort to write software for free? They identify several "intrinsic" and "extrinsic" factors.[27] Motivation is extrinsic if personal needs are satisfied indirectly; for example, a certain activity is performed in order to earn money, which can then be used to address personal needs. In the case of intrinsic motivation, the activity itself satisfies personal needs (*e.g.*, pleasure, fun, reaching self-defined goals). Extrinsically motivated actors participate in the open source community for several reasons. For instance, they sell services using open source software (available at low cost) or sell complementary products (e.g., servers). Furthermore, publishing the source code offers the possibility that other programmers improve, maintain, and further develop the software at low cost. Finally, open software projects can be "signed" by the author, thereby "signaling" the author's abilities to potential employers. On the other hand, participation in open source may also be motivated intrinsically. Eric S. Raymond, one of the leading figures in the open source movement, considers the joy of programming an innovative and functioning piece of code, and the respect and reputation gained from it, as a major motivation for programmers to participate in the open source movement.[28] Might it be a combination of extrinsic and intrinsic motivation that makes the open source movement a successful alternative software development model?

---

27. *See, e.g.*, Lerner & Tirole, *Some Simple Economics of Open Source*, 50 J. Indus. Econ. 197 (2002).

28. *See* Eric S. Raymond, *Homesteading the Noosphere* (2000), http://www.catb.org/esr/writings/cathedral-bazaar/homesteading/ (last visited December 21, 2023).

**2.** Lessig points out that copyleft software is licensed under a General Public License (GPL). The most widely used GPL is called "GNU Public License." The GNU GPL gives the user the right to copy, re-transmit, and modify the software, and to have access to the source code. The GNU GPL must be included with each copy and alteration of the original program. Some authors refer to this effect as being "viral," since any software combined with software under GPL protection is from then on "infected" (i.e., subject to the GPL and thus open source). A number of alternative licensing systems have evolved,[29] and "open source" software licensing can be a complex endeavor, as exemplified by the *Google v. Oracle* case, *infra*.

**3.** Open source makes available the code of a computer program for others to view and manipulate, but this should not be conflated with "free software." There are large publicly traded companies such as Red Hat—which acquired by IBM for $34 billion—that work with open source platforms but license their software products, often for considerable fees. While conceptually every business can write its own code based on open source, there is a great deal of specialized expertise involved in developing and maintaining software that helps to run large-scale enterprises, and having the ability to see the underlying code and change it is not the same as having the ability (and interest) to write and maintain it. The Internet is replete with offers to license for a price software products, including website content management software that is built on an open source platform.

**4.** Considering the rigidity of applying copyright in the digital space and the uncertainties around the application of exceptions and limitations for follow-up works, Lawrence Lessig launched in 2001 the international nonprofit organization Creative Commons (https://creativecommons.org/). The Creative Commons licenses provide an easy way to manage the copyright terms that attach automatically to all creative material under copyright. The licenses allow that material to be shared and reused under terms that are flexible and legally sound, as they are tailored along the 80-plus national copyright systems. Creative Commons offers a core suite of six copyright licenses (combining attribution, non-commercial use, non-derivative works, and share-alike) that are non-exclusive and royalty-free. There is also the possibility to waive copyright under the CC0 license to the extent permitted under the applicable law. The Creative Commons licenses have become widely used by international organizations, governments, public institutions, and online creators. Do you find the Creative Commons licenses an appropriate solution to the challenges of online content distribution, use and re-use?

**5.** There are now many active proponents of open source. For an overview of the relationship between the public domain and copyright, *see, e.g.*, *The Public Domain: Enclosing the Commons of the Mind*, by David Boyle.[30]

## C. The Impact of Competition Law and Policy

In essence, intellectual property grants a producer an exclusive monopoly allowing to offset and prevent unfair competition and free-riding. It bears to potential of an abuse of such wide-reaching powers. Such abuses are addressed by means of competition law and policy. Intellectual property and thus copyright is embedded in these disciplines. Article 40(2) of the TRIPS Agreement allows Members to operate domestic standards of competition law and policy.

Competition law and policy is of major importance in defining the scope and exceptions to copyright in software. We discuss the underpinnings in Chapter 6, but note at this stage

29. For an illustrative overview, *see* http://www.gnu.org/philosophy/license-list.html or https://opensource.org/licenses/category.

30. Available at http://www.thepublicdomain.org/ (visited December 21, 2010).

the importance of the most extensive and complex case ever decided by the General Court (formerly the Court of First Instance) of the European Union, *Microsoft Corp. v. Commission of the European Union*, Case T-201/04, 1 September 2007, that addresses the relationship of software protection and competition law. The case is not limited to applying EU law but also discusses the status of the TRIPS Agreement and the TBT Agreement of the WTO, the latter in relation to the Microsoft trademark.

In *Microsoft v. Commission*, the focus was on whether Microsoft could be lawfully obliged to supply and authorize competitors to use interoperability information and refrain from tying obligations by means of compulsory licensing imposed by the Commission to offset an alleged abuse of dominant position. The Court assessed the circumstances by reference to which abusive conduct must be analyzed, expounding relevant case law, including *RTE v. Commission* ("*Magill*"), Joined Cases 241/91 P and C 242/91 P (para. 107, applying competition law to copyright) (paras. 291-336).

The Court recalled that the refusal by a company holding a dominant position to grant a license cannot in itself constitute an abuse, and that it is only in exceptional circumstances that the exercise of intellectual property rights may give rise to an abuse of law (para. 331). The Court sets out the relevant circumstances which in particular qualify for exceptional consideration: (i) the refusal relates to a product indispensable to the exercise of a particular activity on a neighboring market; (ii) the refusal effectively excludes competition; and (iii) the refusal prevents the appearance of a new product relating to IP (paras. 332-35).

One of the most important aspects of the case is the assessment of de facto industry standards which companies with dominant market power are able to deploy. By establishing narrow and privileged links between Windows client PCs and workgroup server operating systems, it was de facto imposing the Windows domain architecture as an industry standard (para. 392). Other than technical regulations adopted by governments, such standards are not generally available and thus depend upon voluntary or compulsory licensing.

In reply to the claim that the Commission did not properly take into account the impact of the TRIPS Agreement, in particular Article 13 and the three-step test, Article 31 on compulsory licenses and Article 39 on trade secrets, the Court referred to the denial of direct effect of WTO law in EU law (paras 777-805). A similar finding is made in relation to the TBT Agreement and the complaint of denigrating the Microsoft trademark (paras. 1168-93).

The bundling of Windows Media Player with the Windows client PC operating system, being two different programs, was analyzed and found to be unlawfully tying these programs and to violate Article 82 ECT (para 839-975).

## NOTES AND QUESTIONS

**1.** What would be the impact of giving direct effect to TRIPS provisions, or at least of seeking to apply the doctrine of consistent interpretation of EU law with TRIPS obligations in international law? Could WTO cases, discussed *supra*, provide appropriate guidance in assessing the complaint?

**2.** We consider these and other points in Chapter 5.

## CHAPTER 5

# COMPETITION LAW AND *SUI GENERIS* SYSTEMS OF INTELLECTUAL PROPERTY PROTECTION: TRADITIONAL KNOWLEDGE, PLANT VARIETY PROTECTION, UNDISCLOSED INFORMATION, INDUSTRIAL DESIGNS, AND INTEGRATED CIRCUITS

## I. INTRODUCTION

The intellectual property system essentially emerged from the philosophy of protecting competitors against appropriations of costly efforts and unfair competition. Eventually, the different forms of intellectual property protection discussed in previous chapters emerged. New technologies and developments have brought about new potential for unfair competition. These technologies and developments are partly addressed under existing forms of intellectual property protection, such as software under copyright or patent law, and partly addressed under laws against unfair competition; eventually, this may lead to new and specific forms of protection, often called *sui generis* forms and systems of protection. This chapter explains the foundations and the relevance of unfair competition laws and competition policy (antitrust) for the international system. It addresses emerging *sui generis* forms of protecting traditional knowledge in the context of genetic engineering, and then turns to well-established and existing forms of *sui generis* protection, in particular plant variety protection, undisclosed information, and finally, the protection of industrial designs and integrated circuits.

# II. PROTECTION AGAINST UNFAIR COMPETITION: THE RELATIONSHIP TO INTELLECTUAL PROPERTY AND ANTI-TRUST RULES

## A. UNFAIR COMPETITION RULES (Art. 10*bis* PARIS CONVENTION and TRIPS)

Different views exist on the relationship of unfair competition and intellectual property rights. On the one hand, they are perceived to be conceptually different in terms of foundation and application. On the other hand, unfair competition principles are considered the very foundation of intellectual property rights, grounded in notions of fairness. While different views influence the interpretation of intellectual property and unfair competition in domestic law, international law considers the two jointly, both forming part of the TRIPS Agreement and thus of WTO law. The panel in *Australia – Plain Packaging* recognized the rules on unfair competition in Article 10*bis* of the Paris Convention to form part of the TRIPS Agreement.

### *Australia – Certain Measures Concerning Trademarks, Geographical Indications and Other Plain Packaging Requirements Applicable to Tobacco Products and Packaging*

DS WT/DS435/R, WT/DS441/R WT/DS458/R, WT/DS467/R (28 June 2018)

Reports of the Panels*

. . .

**7.3.6 Article 10*bis* of the Paris Convention (1967), as incorporated by Article 2.1 of the TRIPS Agreement**

7.3.6.1 Introduction

7.2607. We will now address the complainants' claims under Article 2.1 of the TRIPS Agreement in conjunction with Article 10*bis* of the Paris Convention (1967), paragraphs 1, 3(1) and 3(3), which concerns repression of unfair competition.

7.2608. Paragraph 1 of Article 2 of the TRIPS Agreement, entitled "Intellectual Property Conventions", reads as follows:

> In respect of Parts II, III and IV of this Agreement, Members shall comply with Articles 1 through 12, and Article 19, of the Paris Convention (1967).

7.2609. Article 10*bis* of the Paris Convention (1967) reads as follows:

> (1) The countries of the Union are bound to assure to nationals of such countries effective protection against unfair competition.
>
> (2) Any act of competition contrary to honest practices in industrial or commercial matters constitutes an act of unfair competition.
>
> (3) The following in particular shall be prohibited:
>
> 1. all acts of such a nature as to create confusion by any means whatever with the establishment, the goods, or the industrial or commercial activities, of a competitor;
>
> 2. false allegations in the course of trade of such a nature as to discredit the establishment, the goods, or the industrial or commercial activities, of a competitor;

* Footnotes omitted.

> 3. indications or allegations the use of which in the course of trade is liable to mislead the public as to the nature, the manufacturing process, the characteristics, the suitability for their purpose, or the quantity, of the goods.

7.2610. The complainants claim that the TPP measures are inconsistent with Article 2.1 of the TRIPS Agreement in conjunction with Article 10*bis* of the Paris Convention (1967).

7.2611. Australia asks the Panel to reject these claims in their entirety.

7.2612. The parties disagree on whether Article 10*bis* of the Paris Convention (1967), as incorporated into the TRIPS Agreement by means of a reference in its Article 2.1, covers both the requirements within the TPP measures that affect the use of trademarks, GIs and other categories of IP rights on tobacco retail packaging and products ("trademark requirements") and the requirements that concern other physical features of tobacco retail packaging and products ("format requirements"). We will, therefore, first consider the scope of the incorporation of Article 10*bis* of the Paris Convention (1967) through Article 2.1 of the TRIPS Agreement.

7.2613. We will then consider the interpretation of Article 10*bis* of the Paris Convention (1967), before addressing the complainants' claims that the TPP measures are inconsistent with Australia's obligations under paragraphs 1, 3(1) and 3(3) of Article 10*bis* of the Paris Convention (1967) as incorporated into the TRIPS Agreement.

**7.3.6.2 Scope of incorporation of Article 10*bis* of the Paris Convention (1967) through Article 2.1. of the TRIPS Agreement.**

. . .

7.3.6.2.2 Analysis by the Panel

7.2619. We recall that paragraph 1 of Article 2 of the TRIPS Agreement provides that:

> *In respect of Parts II, III and IV of this Agreement,* Members shall comply with Articles 1 through 12, and Article 19, of the Paris Convention (1967). (emphasis added)

7.2620. It is undisputed, in these proceedings, that the incorporation resulting from Article 2.1 of the TRIPS Agreement includes Article 10*bis* of the Paris Convention (1967). However, the parties have different views on the scope of this incorporation, and how this affects the application of this provision to their claims in relation to the TPP measures.

. . .

7.2626. The question before us, therefore, is as to how the terms "[i]n respect of Parts II, III and IV of this Agreement" in Article 2.1 of the TRIPS Agreement affect the scope of the requirement, established through Article 2.1 of the TRIPS Agreement, for WTO Members to comply with Article 10*bis* of the Paris Convention (1967) and assure effective protection against unfair competition as provided for in that provision.

7.2627. The term "in respect of" is defined as "as regards, as relates to; with reference to". The ordinary meaning of this term, together with the grammatical structure of Article 2.1, therefore suggests that Members shall comply with the identified provisions of the Paris Convention (1967) as those Paris Convention provisions relate to Parts II, III and IV of the TRIPS Agreement. We understand this reference to relate to the subjects addressed in Parts II, III and IV, namely standards of protection, domestic enforcement, and acquisition and maintenance of IP rights. The phrase "[i]n respect of Parts II, III and IV of this Agreement" thus makes clear that the articles of the Paris Convention (1967) incorporated by reference may have a bearing not only on standards concerning the availability, scope and use of IP rights (Part II), but also on enforcement of IP rights (Part III), and the acquisition and maintenance of IP rights (Part IV). The articles of the Paris Convention (1967), in turn, concern the protection of industrial property.

. . .

7.2631. In light of the above, we find that, pursuant to the second sub-clause of Article 2.1 of the TRIPS Agreement, Members are required to comply with Article 10*bis* of the Paris

Convention (1967), and that the term "in respect of" in the first sub-clause of Article 2.1 does not have the effect of conditioning the scope of the incorporation of the obligation under Article 10*bis* to cover only those acts of unfair competition that relate to the types of subject-matter addressed in Parts II, III or IV of the TRIPS Agreement.

7.2632. We further observe that the challenged measures in this case, the TPP measures, include features that may be seen as relating to various categories of IP addressed in Part II of the TRIPS Agreement. Specifically, it is undisputed that they affect the use of trademarks and GIs, and they may also affect other categories of IP, such as industrial designs and patents. In light of this also, we find it appropriate not to limit our consideration of how the TPP measures relate to the protection against unfair competition to how they relate to any particular subject-matter addressed in Part II, III or IV of the TRIPS Agreement.

7.2633. With these initial determinations in mind, we first consider the interpretation of Article 10*bis*, to inform our assessment of the complainants' claims that the TPP measures are inconsistent with Australia's obligations under paragraphs 3(1), and 3(3) of Article 10*bis* of the Paris Convention (1967) as incorporated into the TRIPS Agreement.

**7.3.6.3 Interpretation of Article 10*bis* of the Paris Convention (1967), as incorporated through Article 2.1 of the TRIPS Agreement**

. . .

7.3.6.3.3 Analysis by the Panel

7.2662. We recall that, under Article 2.1 of the TRIPS Agreement, "[i]n respect of Parts II, III and IV of the Agreement, Members shall comply with Article 1 through 12, and Article 19, of the Paris Convention (1967)". We recall that Article 10*bis* of the Paris Convention (1967) reads as follows:

> (1) The countries of the Union are bound to assure to nationals of such countries effective protection against unfair competition.
>
> (2) Any act of competition contrary to honest practices in industrial or commercial matters constitutes an act of unfair competition.
>
> (3) The following in particular shall be prohibited:
>
> 1. all acts of such a nature as to create confusion by any means whatever with the establishment, the goods, or the industrial or commercial activities, of a competitor;
> 2. false allegations in the course of trade of such a nature as to discredit the establishment, the goods, or the industrial or commercial activities, of a competitor;
> 3. indications or allegations the use of which in the course of trade is liable to mislead the public as to the nature, the manufacturing process, the characteristics, the suitability for their purpose, or the quantity, of the goods.

7.2663. Paragraph 1 of Article 10*bis*, as incorporated into the TRIPS Agreement by means of a reference in its Article 2.1, [. . .] requires Members to assure to nationals of Members effective protection against unfair competition. While paragraph 1 requires that such protection is "effective", it does not determine the means by which Members are to assure such protection or elaborate on the meaning of unfair competition.

7.2664. "[A]n act of unfair competition" is defined in paragraph 2 of Article 10*bis* as being "[a]ny act of competition contrary to honest practices in industrial or commercial matters" (emphasis added). The term "competition" in the context of commerce is defined as "rivalry in the market, striving for custom between those who have the same commodities to dispose of". This is also how the panel in Mexico – Telecoms understood this term "in its relevant economic sense".

7.2665. The noun "act" means "something done or effected; a deed". The term "act of competition", in the context of "industrial or commercial matters", suggests something that is done by a market actor to compete against other actors in the market.

7.2666. The ordinary meaning of the adjective "honest" in conjunction with an action such as "practice" is "done with or expressive of truthfulness, fairness, or integrity of character or intention; free from deceit; genuine, sincere." As regards the term "practice", the Appellate Body considered as relevant the following definitions: " 'habitual doing or carrying out of something; usual or customary action or performance'; 'custom; a habit; a habitual action'; 'action of doing something; performance, operation; method of action or working'." How commercial matters are habitually carried out is likely to vary from market to market and change over time. Taken together, these definitions suggest that an "act of competition" is contrary to "honest practices" if it is done in a manner that is contrary to what would usually or customarily be regarded as truthful, fair and free from deceit within a certain market.

7.2667. Accordingly, we understand the definition of "an act of unfair competition" in paragraph 2 as referring to something that is done by a market actor to compete against other actors in the market in a manner that is contrary to what would usually or customarily be regarded as truthful, fair and free from deceit within a certain market.

7.2668. The chapeau of paragraph 3 provides that "[t]he following in particular shall be prohibited" (emphasis added). The relevant definition of "in particular" is "[a]s one distinguished from others of a number". We understand that paragraph 3 is linked to paragraph 2 of Article 10*bis* in that the acts from which the acts listed in paragraph 3 are distinguished are other acts of unfair competition, as defined in paragraph 2. Therefore, we understand that the types of acts listed in paragraph 3 are instances of "act[s] of competition contrary to honest practices in industrial or commercial matters", and that there may be other types of dishonest commercial practices that meet the definition in paragraph 2, which more broadly refers to "[a]ny act of competition contrary to honest practices in industrial or commercial matters" (emphasis added). Furthermore, the chapeau of paragraph 3 is worded as a binding obligation in respect of the types of acts listed under its subparagraphs, providing that "[t]he following in particular shall be prohibited" (emphasis added). In other words, paragraph 3 requires Members to prohibit the types of dishonest commercial practices mentioned in its subparagraphs.

7.2669. Overall, therefore, paragraph 1, read together with paragraphs 2 and 3, requires that a Member, in the process of assuring effective protection against acts of unfair competition, within the meaning of paragraph 2, has to prohibit the types of practices in industrial and commercial matters that fall under paragraph 3. Pursuant to paragraph 1, protection against such acts must be "effective". Paragraph 1, however, is silent as to the standard to be applied to determine which industrial and commercial practices – beyond those covered by paragraph 3 – should be considered dishonest in a particular Member, against which that Member consequently must assure effective protection.

7.2670. We note that the parties share the view that it would be possible for a measure to be inconsistent with paragraph 1 without being inconsistent with any of the sub-paragraphs of paragraph 3. Indonesia reads paragraph 1 as creating a broader obligation than paragraph 3, and characterizes the examples in paragraph 3 as establishing "minimum protection". Australia takes the view that a measure could be inconsistent with paragraph 1, even if the relevant conduct does not specifically fall under any of the sub-paragraphs of paragraph 3, provided that such conduct is "of the same nature and scope" as the acts listed in paragraph 3. We will now turn to these questions.

7.2671. As we determined above, we understand "an act of unfair competition" in paragraph 2 as referring to something that is done by a market actor to compete against other actors in the market, in a manner that is contrary to what would usually or customarily be regarded as truthful, fair and free from deceit within a certain market. How industrial and commercial matters are usually or customarily carried out differs from market to market, as do the perceptions of and the standards for determining what constitutes "honest" commercial practices. In this regard, we observe that there may be some diversity in how domestic legal systems approach the repression of unfair competition and what types of acts they cover. A WIPO commentary, provided to the Panel by the WIPO Secretariat in response to the Panel's request for information, notes that, while most countries with special laws on unfair competition have adopted definitions that are the same or similar to the one used in Article 10*bis*(2), using terms such as "honest trade practices", perceptions of notions such as "honest practices" vary:

> It is true that describing unfair competition as acts contrary to "honest trade practices", "good faith" and so on does not make for clear-cut, universally accepted standards of behavior, since the meaning of the terms used is rather fluid. The standard of "fairness" or "honesty" in competition is no more than a reflection of the sociological, economic, moral and ethical concepts of a society, and may therefore differ from country to country (and sometimes even within a country). That standard is also liable to change with time.

7.2672. We read this passage as illustrative also for the purposes of understanding the definition of an act of unfair competition contained in Article 10*bis*(2). In our view, the reference in that definition to "honest practices" does not suggest that a single "clear-cut, universally accepted standard of behaviour" applies in determining whether a commercial practice is "honest". Rather, it suggests that this assessment should be made in light of what constitutes "honest practices" in the relevant market.

7.2673. In this respect, the notion of "honest practices" resembles another notion referred to in the WTO agreements, namely "public morals". The panel in US – Gambling, in interpreting Article XIV(a) of the GATS, found that "the term 'public morals' denotes standards of right and wrong conduct maintained by or on behalf of a community or nation". It also noted that "the content of these concepts for Members can vary in time and space, depending upon a range of factors, including prevailing social, cultural, ethical and religious values". Similarly, the panel in China – Publications and Audiovisual Products, in interpreting Article XX(a) of the GATT 1994, noted that "the content and scope of the concept of 'public morals' can vary from Member to Member, as they are influenced by each Member's prevailing social, cultural, ethical and religious values".

7.2674. The context provided by other provisions of the TRIPS Agreement referring to morality point in a similar direction. Article 6quinquies of the Paris Convention (1967), as incorporated into the TRIPS Agreement, allows a Member to deny or invalidate, under certain circumstances, a trademark that is "contrary to morality or public order". As Bodenhausen notes, the grounds for refusal or invalidation of a trademark exist when such a trademark is contrary to morality or public order "as considered in the country where protection is claimed". Article 27.2 of the TRIPS Agreement allows Members to exclude from patentability inventions "the prevention within their territory of the commercial exploitation of which is necessary to protect ordre public or morality" (emphasis added), suggesting that the necessity of preventing commercial exploitation on the grounds of morality is to be considered in respect of a particular territory.

7.2675. Therefore, the notion of "honest practices" as used in the definition of an act of unfair competition in Article 10*bis*(2) should be interpreted with reference to standards of honest conduct habitually applied and maintained in the domestic market at issue. What is to be considered as the market concerned needs to be determined based on the circumstances of a particular case. We note in this respect that the fact that what is considered to constitute an "honest practice" may vary from Member to Member does not render the obligation discretionary. If certain acts objectively fall within what is considered, within the domestic market at issue, "contrary to honest practices in industrial or commercial matters", then they will constitute an act of unfair competition subject to the obligation in Article 10*bis*.

7.2676. This understanding is confirmed by the preparatory works of the Paris Convention (1967). The original 1883 Paris Convention did not address unfair competition. The first mention of it was included in Article 10*bis* of the 1900 Brussels Act5360, and the current wording was introduced at the 1925 Hague Revision Conference.5361 The Drafting Committee introduced the final text with, inter alia, the following comments:

> [O]n a jugé utile, en renforçant l'obligation prise par les pays contractants à Washington, d'établir le principe qu'il fallait atteindre la concurrence déloyale sous toutes ses formes et de donner seulement comme un exemple minimum les deux groupes de faits qu'on était unanimes à ranger parmi les actes de concurrence déloyale.

7.2677. The aforementioned WIPO commentary further confirms that the three practices listed in paragraph 3 that "in particular" have to be prohibited "must not be seen as exhaustive, but rather as the minimum protection that has to be granted by all member States".

7.2678. These elements confirm that the practices enumerated in paragraph 3 of Article 10*bis* are examples of dishonest practices and constitute an internationally agreed minimum as regards the types of dishonest practices that countries of the Paris Union are to prohibit. This does not detract from the fact that paragraph 2 sets the scope of the definition of "an act of unfair competition" as including "[a]ny" act of competition contrary to honest practices in commercial matters. The countries of the Union are, therefore, bound to provide effective protection against any acts of unfair competition falling within the definition in paragraph 2. This must comprise – at a minimum – the categories of practices mentioned in paragraph 3. The preparatory works cited above make it clear that, while the negotiators did not endeavour to specify other specific categories of practices against which all countries would be bound to assure effective protection, they had the intention of addressing unfair competition "sous toutes ses formes" ("in all of its forms"), and that the specific situations identified in paragraph 3 were provided "seulement comme un exemple minimum" ("only as a minimum example").

7.2679. Accordingly, WTO Members are required not only to prohibit the three specific types of acts identified in paragraph 3 of Article 10*bis*, but also to provide effective protection against all acts falling more generally within the scope of its paragraph 2. While a Member is required to prohibit the types of dishonest practices in industrial and commercial matters enumerated in its paragraph 3, the scope of other practices in industrial and commercial matters against which it is bound to assure effective protection needs to be considered in the context of the legal systems and conceptions of what constitutes an act contrary to what would usually or customarily be regarded as truthful, fair and free from deceit within the domestic market at issue.

7.2680. We further note that, as observed by the Dominican Republic and Indonesia, protection against unfair competition serves to protect competitors as well as consumers, together with the public interest. We agree with the analysis in the WIPO commentary, to which the Dominican Republic refers, that when determining "honesty" in business dealings, all these factors have to be taken into account. This approach is consistent with Article 7 of the TRIPS Agreement, entitled "Objectives", which reflects the intention of establishing and maintaining a balance between the societal objectives mentioned therein. Consequently, a determination of what amounts to an act that is contrary to honest practices in commercial matters may, depending on the circumstances, reflect a balancing of these interests.

7.2681. We further note that this interpretation is consistent with the relevant context in the TRIPS Agreement, into which Article 10*bis* is incorporated by means of the reference in its Article 2.1. In this regard, we note that the second and third sentences of Article 1.1 of the TRIPS Agreement provide that "Members may, but shall not be obliged to, implement in their law more extensive protection than is required by this Agreement, provided that such protection does not contravene the provisions of this Agreement", and "Members shall be free to determine the appropriate method of implementing the provisions of this Agreement within their own legal system and practice."

7.2682. The second sentence of Article 1.1 makes it clear that the TRIPS Agreement is a minimum standards agreement. As the panel in China – Intellectual Property Rights noted, it "clarifies that the provisions of the Agreement are minimum standards only, in that it gives Members the freedom to implement a higher standard, subject to a condition". Furthermore, the third sentence clarifies that the TRIPS Agreement is not intended to harmonize laws between Members. As the Appellate Body noted in India – Patents, "Members, therefore, are free to determine how best to meet their obligations under the TRIPS Agreement within the context of their own legal systems". We also note that the third sentence of Article 1.1 of the TRIPS Agreement leaves it to that Member to choose the appropriate methods within its own legal system and practice to repress any such dishonest practice.

7.2683. In response to a question from the Panel, Honduras, Cuba, and Indonesia argue that Article 10*bis* could cover more than "acts of unfair competition" as defined in its paragraph 2 because Article 10*bis*(1) requires effective protection against "unfair competition".

7.2684. Article 10*bis*(2) defines the term "act of unfair competition", whereas Article 10*bis*(1) requires effective protection against "unfair competition". We do not, however, read the omission of the word "act" from paragraph 1 as extending the scope of Article 10*bis* beyond acts of unfair competition as defined in paragraph 2. As described above, the term "competition" refers, in the relevant economic sense, to "[r]ivalry in the market, striving for custom between those who have the same commodities to dispose of." This definition entails that competition is a process between market actors. By referring to competition, Article 10*bis*(1) thus requires effective protection against unfair competition between market actors. This is underscored by the three subparagraphs of Article 10*bis*(3) which are each based on the assumption that unfair competition involves an action of market actors. Subparagraphs 1 and 2 of Article 10*bis*(3) both refer to something being done to a "competitor", which implies that a competing market operator is involved in what amounts to unfair competition. Likewise, subparagraph 3 of Article 10*bis*(3) regulates the use of certain types of "indications or allegations . . . in the course of trade", implying that unfair competition relates to actions undertaken by actors operating on the market. We also do not have any indication from the preparatory work of Article 10*bis* and its subsequent amendments that would suggest any intention by negotiators to address unfair competition in relation to anything other than business competition involving market actors.

## NOTES AND QUESTIONS

**1.** The panel subsequently found that the Australian regulation of plain packing of tobacco products is not contrary to unfair competition. The findings of the panel on Article 10*bis* as incorporated in the TRIPS Agreement were not appealed. The findings thus stand and are open for further applications.

**2.** The inclusion of Article 10*bis* of the Paris Convention in the TRIPS Agreement not only renders the principles of fairness in market conduct fully open do dispute settlement under the DSU of the WTO. It also opens the principles against unfair competition to other regulatory areas not or not sufficiently covered by the disciplines of intellectual property rights under its different forms.

**3.** How would you assess and describe the relationship of unfair competition and intellectual property rights upon integrating its principles into the TRIPS Agreement? Does it confirm the view that unfair competition amounts to the overall foundation of IPRs, are does it support the view that unfair competition is a separate concept? Some of these issues are considered in the following excerpts written prior to the panel's finding in *Australia – Plain Packaging*.

**Thomas Cottier & Christophe Germann***

## *Teaching Intellectual Property, Unfair Competition and Anti-Trust Law*

. . .

The main function of intellectual property laws is to provide incentives for innovation and creation in the form of exclusive rights that can be considered as private monopolies, either limited in time (patents, copyright, related rights etc.) or for potentially unlimited duration (indefinitely renewable trademark registrations, trade names etc.). Intellectual property works as an instrument to appropriate knowledge that is understood in a broad sense as encompassing, in particular, scientific and artistic content as well as market relevant information. The forms of protection provided by intellectual property laws range from patents for inventions over exclusive rights on industrial models, plant varieties, layout designs or integrated circuits, industrial design, to copyright and related rights. The protection of undisclosed information functions as a supplement to the patent system. Trademarks, geographical indications and, to some extent, protection of industrial designs, on the other hand, are intended to serve as identifiers and as incentives for investments in reputation (goodwill, quality). In this light, the individual user's primary interest lies in obtaining access to protected goods and services under affordable conditions, and to not be misled with respect to identifiers. The classical approach is based on a duality of paradigms where the patent paradigm typically protects functional or utilitarian achievements, whereas the copyright paradigm protects creative results that do not need to show practical applications such as artistic works. This duality has, however, been gradually eroded, for example in the area of information technology where copyright is used to protect software.

A further category of intellectual property rights to be labeled as "identifiers" protects distinctive signs such as trademarks, trade names or geographical indications. Eventually, intellectual property law traditionally also includes rules prohibiting unfair competition although these rules do not provide exclusive rights.

Unfair competition law commonly protects fair competition with a particular focus on good faith in business dealings and fair business practices. Like intellectual property rights, unfair competition law essentially aims at protecting physical and legal persons (individuals and companies) against "free riding" on investment in knowledge and the fruits of labors created by others.

Competition (anti-trust) legislation typically aims at protecting the market, and more precisely at preserving an effective competitive framework that shall promote the best quality of goods and services at the lowest cost for consumers, as well as ensure the suppliers' freedom of access to the market and the demands associated with freedom of choice. Competition rules, or anti-trust rules, essentially operate as legal restrictions on the freedom of contract between economic operators who are mutually placed in a competitive relationship. The law intervenes

* In Teaching of Intellectual Property: Principles and Methods 130-66 (Yo Takagi, Larry Allman & Mpazi A. Sinjela eds., 2008) (footnotes omitted).

to avoid collusion and concertation which diminishes workable competition to the detriment of consumers. Also, competition law disciplines the conduct of dominant operators who otherwise need not consider other market participants. Anti-trust thus operates as a limitation on freedom of conduct to the benefit of markets and consumers.

Often, intellectual property rights are considered anathema to competition as they offer exclusive rights and thus exclude competition. However, they form as essential basis for competition. Without proper protection, investment will not be encouraged and third parties cannot be prevented from free-riding and unfairly using the fruits of investment without compensation. In operational terms, intellectual property protection and protection against unfair competition are complementary, as they essentially pursue comparable goals. Anti-trust rules, on the other hand, provide a counterbalance to the granting of exclusive rights. They assist in combating abuses of such rights detrimental to competition on markets.

. . .

In mature legal orders, the disciplines of intellectual property, competition law (anti-trust) and unfair competition rules develop in tandem and provide an appropriate balance. In many quarters of the world, such a basis does not yet exist. While international law prescribes advanced standards of intellectual property and rudimentary rules on unfair competition by means of international treaty obligations, in particular the Agreement on Trade-Related Aspects of Intellectual Property Rights (TRIPS Agreement) of the World Trade Organization (WTO), anti-trust rules have largely remained a matter of domestic law, still lacking in many countries. Vice-versa, competition law may be developed while common standards of intellectual property protection remain deficient, as has been the case in European Community law. Overall, this results in constellations of imbalance which future efforts on the national, international and regional levels need to remedy.

. . .

## Protection Against Unfair Competition

. . .

### Relationship to Intellectual Property Protection

Since unfair competition law and the protection of intellectual property pursue partly overlapping goals and objectives, the two areas have developed a rather complex relationship, which may vary, again, from country to country. A few general observations can be made on the basis of selected case law.

#### Independent Application

In many instances, unfair competition rules serve to supplement what intellectual property laws do not or cannot provide in particular circumstances. For example, according to the Swiss Federal Court, trademark legislation constitutes no special law vis-à-vis unfair competition legislation that would allow the former to prevail as *lex specialis* over the latter. This case law concludes that trademark and unfair competition laws obey different rationales. Unfair competition law aims at promoting fair and undistorted competition. As a consequence, a trademark owner may not use her exclusive rights in a way that qualifies as unfair competition. Article 3 lit. d of the Swiss Unfair Competition Act prohibits an indication or make-up and presentation of a product *(Aufmachung)* that leads to confusion in respect of older goods or services. The Court recalled that any behavior that is misleading or that otherwise infringes the principle of good faith and that influences the relationship between competitors or between supply and demand is deemed to be unfair and illicit.

Unfair competition law may substitute for protection where such protection is not available under intellectual property laws. A good example is the protection equivalent to moral rights in US law. In *Gilliam v. American Broadcasting Companies, Inc. (ABC)* ["Monty Python Case," *supra* Chapter 4], the appellants invoked the theory that the editing cuts made by the broadcaster without their consent constituted an actionable mutilation of their work. This cause of action, which seeks redress for the deformation of an artist's work, finds its roots in the continental concept of *droit moral*, or moral rights, as set forth in Article 6*bis* of the Berne Convention. US copyright law does not recognize moral rights since this law seeks to vindicate the economic, rather than the personal, rights of authors. However, the economic incentives for artistic and intellectual creation that serves as the foundation of the American Copyright Act, cannot be reconciled with the inability of artists to obtain relief for mutilation or misrepresentation of their work to the public on which the artists are financially dependent. American courts have long granted relief for misrepresentation of an artist's work by relying on theories outside the statutory law of copyright, such as contract law, or the tort of unfair competition. In the case at stake, Monty Python's members claimed that the editing done for ABC on their television programs violated the Lanham Act §43(a), 15 U.S.C §1125(a), the federal unfair competition act. This statute provides in particular that any person affixing, applying, annexing, or using in connection with any goods or services a false designation of origin, or any false description or representation, and causing such goods or services to enter into commerce, shall be liable to a civil action by any person who believes that he is or is likely to be damaged by the use of any such false description or representation.

### Pre-Emption of Unfair Competition Rules

Protection under unfair competition law should generally not be considered as an alternative to intellectual property protection. Pursuant to the principle of pre-emption, protection under unfair competition law will be generally denied—except in certain cases of confusion—if protection under specific intellectual property rights were available, at least for a certain period of time, and expired thereafter. For example, in *Schweizerische Interpreten-Gesellschaft*, [*supra* Chapter 4,] the Swiss Federal Court stated that gaps in a particular law relating to intangible property rights cannot be closed by means of the general clause of the Swiss Unfair Competition Act. In principle, the results of efforts and labor which, according to the special law, are no longer protected or cannot be protected at all, may be used by anyone, even competitors. An interpretation to the contrary would amount to a monopolization of non-copyrighted content. The Court further recalled that the only exception allowed by case law related to special circumstances under which a particular conduct or measures are genuinely unfair and therefore justify the application of the general clause of the Unfair Competition Law.

The principle of pre-emption, emanating from the principles of *lex specialis derogat legi generali*, takes its substantive legitimacy from the assumption that intellectual property law is supposed to materialize a specific balance of the various stakeholders' interests (creators, innovators, users and society) by featuring built-in "competitive antibodies" that promotes innovation and creation within the paradigm of monopoly-like exclusive rights. Applying unfair competition rules would therefore in general, undermine the balance between appropriation and public domain.

### Basis for Codification of Intellectual Property

Unfair competition law often serves as a basis for intellectual property legislation. In various jurisdictions, legislators have the tendency to codify consolidated case law on unfair competition caused by confusion and misappropriation within their intellectual property legislation, in particular within laws on trademarks, trade names and geographical indications. In this way, intellectual property laws dealing with these issues are eroding the proper scope of application of unfair competition laws. This tendency is reinforced by international instruments such as the TRIPS Agreement harmonizing the approaches that deal with the prohibition of confusion and misappropriation, discussed below.

### Protection In International Law

#### Foundations

National legislation, divergent as it may be, has to be consistent with applicable international instruments, such as the TRIPS Agreement and the Paris Convention. We therefore focus on common rules available in international law and thus binding on many countries being part of global law. Protection was recognized as forming part of intellectual property for more than a century. In 1900, the Brussels Diplomatic Conference for the Revision of the Paris Convention for the Protection of Industrial Property introduced Article 10*bis* that specifically addresses unfair competition. It was eventually revised in the Stockholm Act of 1967 of the Paris Convention. . . . .

The provision on unfair competition in Article 10*bis* of the Paris Convention is broadly termed and refers to elusive concepts, requiring careful interpretation. The norm obliges WTO Members (and other Member States party to the Paris Convention) to provide appropriate protection in domestic jurisdictions, and to enact, if necessary, appropriate legislation. The terms primarily leave the determination of the notion of honesty in industrial and commercial matters to the national courts and administrative authorities. They are not strictly limited to producer and consumer relations. Member States of the Paris Union are free to grant protection against certain acts even if the parties involved are not competing against each other.

While leaving ample room to domestic jurisdiction, international law nevertheless provides guidance as to the scope and interpretation of these broad precepts and principles. Firstly, Members need to respect requirements emanating from other applicable regional and international treaties, in particular international instruments on human rights. Secondly, the notions of honest business practices, and the constellations addressed in the non-exhaustive list, are notions of international law. They are subject to specification in dispute settlement and fully operational in international disputes brought before the WTO. It is submitted that these specifications amount to minimal standards which Members will need to respect, irrespective of domestic definitions adopted in legislation and case law. Also, it is submitted that these minimal standards are suitable for direct effect before domestic courts and administrative authorities, where constitutional law so permits. The provision of Article 10*bis*, paragraph 1, does not imply a dualistic concept. At any rate, and once a substantial body of case law exists on the subject in WTO law, national courts should take it into account under the doctrine of consistent interpretation. Domestic terms of unfair competition should be construed in the light of minimal standards emanating from Article 10*bis* of the Paris Convention.

#### Protection Against Dishonest Practices, Confusion and False Allegations

Pursuant to Article 10*bis*, paragraph 2 of the Paris Convention, any act of competition contrary to honest practices in industrial or commercial matters constitutes an act of unfair competition. Unfair competition in the relationship between competitors may take various forms. Article 10*bis*, paragraph 3 of the Paris Convention mentions in particular all acts of such a nature as to create confusion by any means whatever with the establishment, the goods, or the industrial or commercial activities, of a competitor (sub-para. 1), as well as false allegations in the course of trade of such a nature as to discredit the establishment, the goods, or the industrial or commercial activities, of a competitor (sub-para. 2).

Article 10*bis*, paragraph 3 provides for a non-exhaustive list of dishonest practices that shall be prohibited including acts creating confusion by any means whatever with the establishment, the goods, or the industrial or commercial activities, of a competitor, false and discrediting or misleading indications and allegations. It aims at protecting competitors against a risk of confusion and false allegations having a discrediting effect, as well as the public against misleading information as to the nature, the manufacturing process, the characteristics, and the suitability for their purpose, or the quantity, of the goods.

Article 10*bis*, paragraph 3(1) of the Paris Convention does not make the prohibition of confusion conditional to intent or negligence in acting or omitting to act. Bad faith, however, may be taken into account in respect of the sanction for an infringement. Likelihood of confusion is sufficient. It is therefore not necessary that the confusion actually has taken place. Confusion mainly occurs in relation to indications of origin of goods and services (confusion as to affiliation or as to sponsorship and to their appearance (confusion as to product shape). Accordingly, for generic and commonplace goods and services the likelihood of confusion can normally be denied since they no longer have an original or distinctive character. Specific trademark and trade name legislation provides protection against confusion, and often makes recourse to unfair competition redundant. However, intellectual property protection may not always be appropriate and adequate, for example, in the case of protection of well-known trademarks as addressed by Article 6*bis* of the Paris Convention and Article 16 of the TRIPS Agreement. Member States may implement the prohibition to use a well-known trademark pursuant to Article 6*bis* of the Paris Convention on the national level via their unfair competition legislation, in the absence of corresponding restrictions in their trademark legislation.

**Protection Against Free Riding**

Undue advantage of efforts and achievement by others and recognized by consumers and other market participants may be taken by imitating products and services or their identifiers, including trade marks, trade names and other forms of commercially relevant indications. Article 10*bis* of the Paris Convention encapsulates this under the doctrine of competition contrary to honest practices in paragraph 2, while leaving it, astonishingly, without mention in the non-exclusive list of paragraph 3. Preventing and combating free riding on work and products of others is an essential and core function of unfair competition rules and of intellectual property protection alike. Whereas free riding is considered as a dishonest business practice under unfair competition law, it is deemed to hinder innovation, creativity and the supply of reliable market information under intellectual property law.

Protection against free riding amounts to one of the major functions of intellectual property and its different forms. Unfair competition rules take place where such protection is not sufficiently available or existent. They provide complementary protection. For example, a school may offer a particular curriculum or training program, composed in a particular manner. It is neither protected by trademark or copyright. Competitors nevertheless are not allowed to imitate the structure of the program without the consent of the school. As a prerequisite of the protection against free riding on a firm's identity and reputation, the indication, the good or service must have some distinctiveness. In other words, unfair competition does not protect against the imitation of mere banality. However, the degree of distinctiveness may be lower than what is required under intellectual property legislation.

The TRIPS Agreement further elaborates protection against free riding in relation to geographical indications, to undisclosed information and to test data. Today, and due to WTO law, these areas clearly pertain to the protection of intellectual property, but remain essentially informed in terms of foundations and scope to the protection of unfair competition. The respective provisions refer to Article 10*bis* of the Paris Convention.

Article 22, paragraph 2(a) of the TRIPS Agreement protects geographical indications to the extent that the designation or presentation of a product suggests that the product originates in a geographical area different from the true place of origin in a manner which misleads the public as to the geographical origin of the good. Except for wines and spirits in accordance with Articles 22 and 23 of the TRIPS Agreement, the indication of the true origin of the product protects from violating the obligation. For example, it is possible to label "Gruyere Cheese made in the US" since consumers are thus informed about the true origin of the product despite the fact that the product is based upon qualities relating to a Swiss region. Protection therefore is limited. This explains why enhanced protection applicable to wines and spirits is thought to be extended to all agricultural products in the Doha Round negotiations.

The question arises as to whether such use may otherwise constitute an act of unfair competition in accordance with paragraph 2(b) of the provision, which generally refers to Article 10*bis* of the Paris Convention. To the extent that—despite the absence of confusion as to the true origin—the product is essentially based upon free riding in terms of traditional know-how and experience and thus traditional knowledge, a case can be made under Article 10*bis* of the Paris Convention.

The same relationship is contemplated by the protection of undisclosed information (trade secrets) pursuant to Article 39 of the TRIPS Agreement. Provided that the conditions under Article 39.2 of the TRIPS Agreement regarding the secrecy and commercial value of the information are met, natural and legal persons shall have the possibility of preventing information lawfully within their control from being disclosed to, acquired by, or used by others without their consent in a manner contrary to honest commercial practices. Such practices have in common a business's attempt vis-à-vis other businesses to succeed in competition without relying on its own achievements in terms of quality and price of its products and services, but rather by taking undue advantage of the work of another (free riding) or by influencing consumer demand with false or misleading statements.

Article 39.3 of the TRIPS Agreement provides that WTO Members must protect undisclosed test or other data that took considerable effort to be generated, against unfair commercial use when they require that such data must be submitted to their agencies for the purpose of marketing approval for pharmaceutical or agricultural chemical products utilizing new chemical entities. Furthermore, WTO Members must protect such data against disclosure, except where necessary to protect the public or unless steps are taken to ensure that the data are protected against fair commercial use [further elaborated on *infra*].

Legally, the provision can be seen as an enlargement of the list of acts that are prohibited under Article 10*bis*, para. 3 of the Paris Convention. In other words, Article 39.3 of the TRIPS Agreement addresses the unfair use of undisclosed data submitted to authorities by private competitors. . . .

A recent example of linking new forms of protection to unfair competition and eventually intellectual property rights can be observed with the emerging protection of traditional knowledge. While currently left in the public domain, traditional knowledge can be freely used in the context of biotechnology as an important source of information and a basis for new products which are eligible for patent protection. . . .

Finally, a potential field of application of unfair competition rules in international law relates to the protection of Internet domain names involving more than one jurisdiction, which are dealt with by the Mediation and Arbitration Center of the WIPO. For the time being, the substantive rules only provide rules for the conflict between a domain name and a trademark, where the domain name registered by the domain name registrant is identical or confusingly similar to a trademark in which the complainant has rights (para. 4(a) UDRP).

In this case, the rights of the trademark owner prevail over the interests of the domain name registrant unless the latter is in good faith. However, there is no similar dispute settlement mechanism available with respect to conflicts between domain names and trade names. These cases are essentially dealt with under the unfair competition law of national or regional jurisdictions. Corresponding judgments may be substantially more difficult and costly to enforce in foreign jurisdictions as arbitration awards under the UDRP. It would therefore be suitable to extend protection to such signs by taking recourse to Article 10*bis* of the Paris Convention, or to create appropriate additional rules under the UDRP. Again, it is a matter of refining intellectual property protection on the basis of experiences made under the case law approach of unfair competition protection.

**Thomas Cottier & Gabriela Wermelinger***

## *Implementing and Enforcing Corporate Social Responsibility: The Potential of Unfair Competition Rules in International Law*

Codes of Conduct and principles of CSR contained in official documents issued by the United Nations, the International Labour Organization (ILO) and the Organization for Economic Co-operation and Development (OECD) essentially amount to commitments by governments to create appropriate framework conditions supporting MNCs in the pursuit of good governance entailed in these instruments, for example the United Nations Global Compact, the Universal Declaration on Human Rights, the OECD Guidelines for Multinational Enterprises (OECD Guidelines), the International Organization for Standardization (ISO) 26000 Guidance Standard of Social Responsibility (ISO 26000), the ILO Core Conventions and the Declaration on Fundamental Principles and Rights at Work (Instruments of the ILO), the ILO Tripartite Declaration of Principles concerning Multinational Enterprises and Social Policy (ILO MNE Declaration) and the Global Reporting Initiative (GRI). MNCs should be supported, and not impeded, in the pursuit of these goals by other binding rules. The main and binding frame for MNCs will be found in domestic law and binding international agreements, such as the law of the WTO or preferential trade and investment agreements. Instruments of CSR are issued not only by governments and international organizations but also by non-state actors. Moreover, the former two are also bound by such instruments in the sense that their own policies and rules should allow the principles to be taken into account within the body of binding law. Thus, unless rules on CSR form part of a binding agreement, governments essentially pledge to act on the basis of, and in accordance with, the rules and principles expounded for MNCs in these instruments. They are formally part of soft law, and thus not strictly binding per se. However, the pledge to act accordingly amounts to a unilateral promise, and failure to act frustrates legitimate expectations on the part of other States as well as the MNCs concerned. States, in other words, are bound by the *principle of good faith* and the *protection of legitimate expectations*. To the extent that a promise to create appropriate framework conditions was made but not followed up, it may trigger legal consequences under *good faith* protection. The *doctrine of estoppel* may be invoked by other States provided that they took action, made dispositions and suffered damages due to the lack of implementation by the promising party to the instrument. Likewise, the *doctrine of estoppel*, expressing a general principle of law, may also be invoked by MNCs vis-à-vis the host State.

* In CORPORATE SOCIAL RESPONSIBILITY: VERBINDLICHE STANDARDS DES WETTBEWERBSRECHTS? 81, 83-97 (Reto M. Hilty & Frauke Henning-Bodewig eds., 2014).

If dispositions were made which are eventually frustrated because domestic legislation is not adjusted accordingly, and which do not allow policies to be adopted in line with the international CSR instrument adopted, responsibility for unlawful act may be induced under state responsibility in international law. In conclusion, while formally soft law, these instruments are not void of normative effect for governments and oblige them to adopt the necessary measures facilitating implementation by MNCs.

MNCs, on the other hand, are not directly bound by these instruments, unless such effects are provided for in domestic law. Codes and principles require additional commitments which amount to unilateral declarations and promises on the part of the companies. These pledges and commitments are expressed by the policy statements and measures taken by companies on the basis of such soft law instruments. The unilateral promise of a company to act in certain ways and not in others equally creates legitimate expectations. Investors, partners and consumers rely upon such pledges in making business decisions. Trading shares of companies may be influenced in various ways. Investors will take these commitments into account. Consumers may make decisions to buy based upon the information provided and the promises made as to human rights standards, labour standards in production, and transparency. The pledge forms the reputation of a company. While these commitments again are often considered to amount to no less than soft law and thus to be non-binding in nature, and mainly a tool in promoting the company's reputation and marketing, the *principle of good faith* and the *protection of legitimate expectations* again and equally apply, this time in domestic law. To the extent that the company does not live up to the expectations created by its pledges and promises, it frustrates legitimate expectations; and the *doctrine of estoppel*, as a general principle of law, equally applies to such constellations. Frustrated shareholders, investors and consumers may invoke the doctrine to the extent that they had made dispositions in light of the pledge, and eventually incurred disadvantages and losses. Competitors complying with standards adopted may suffer losses in the market as they face difficulties in competing with lower prices that were made possible due to the lack of implementation by other competitors and yet higher shares due to disregarded pledges made by the latter. *Estoppel* requires the company to remedy the situation or pay compensation to investors and consumers who are negatively affected. Again, it is wrong to assume that CSR commitments by companies are without legal effects and implications. Companies need to carefully consider what they are pledging and to make sure that they live up to the expectations created by their commitment.

It would seem, however, that there is still little awareness about the potential implications of fairness, *good faith* and the *doctrine of protecting legitimate expectations* in the field of CSR. The discourse on realizing and enforcing CSR, it would seem, does not sufficiently take these principles into account. It can neither be found in the preambles of respective instruments, nor is it part of the operative principles, nor can it be found in respective chapters on enforcement strategies. Equally, we find no recourse in CSR documents to the principles of unfair competition which in return implement the principles of fairness and good faith in addressing the conduct of private operators.

...

Recourse to unfair competition law in the context of CSR responsibility is still in its infancy. The most prominent case to be found is *Kasky v. Nike Inc.*,[1] adjudicated in 2003. Kasky, a consumer activist complained that Nike was not living up to its CSR pledges, in terms of labour standards and conditions in factories operating in Vietnam, Indonesia and China. It was alleged that the company uses child labour, exposes children to long working

1. *Kasky v. Nike, Inc.*, California Supreme Court, 45 P 3d 243 (Cal. 2002) and *Kasky v. Nike, Inc.*, US Supreme Court, 539 U.S. 654 (2003).

hours and offers only a payment of less than the minimum wages. It was further alleged that workers in a factory in Vietnam were exposed to carcinogens at levels 177 times higher than the limits set out in local standards. The subcontractors of Nike were alleged to be violating domestic law, and Nike was alleged not to be living up to its own CSR standards. Nike had stated in its reports that subcontractors did adhere [to] Nike's own standards which exclude sweated labour. Moreover, Nike had commissioned an external report which had confirmed, upon inspection of production sites that the subcontractors were largely respecting Nike's CSR standards. Kasky alleged that Nike made false and misleading statements and had acted unfairly and deceptively in violation of the law of unfair competition of the State of California. The complaint was brought as a public action as admitted 'on behalf of the General Public of the State of California' under the Act.

The case was dismissed by the trial court and the California Court of Appeal on the grounds that Nike is protected by the first Amendment of the US Constitution, protecting free speech. Upon appeal, the judgment was reversed by the Supreme Court of California. The court essentially followed the claims made and found a violation of unfair competition rules based upon the discrepancy between CSR pledges and the business conduct of the company and its subcontractors. This divergence and discrepancy between pledges made, reporting and perceptions conveyed to the public at large, on the one hand, and the realities of business conduct on the other hand, amounts to an act of unfair competition. The United States Supreme Court denied *certiorari*; the fundamental issue of to what extent CSR pledges are protected by free speech, and thus also the right to lie, remain a constitutionally open issue under the strict standards of free speech protection in the United States. The case, however, is a landmark one as it shows the potential to enforce CSR pledges in court and to increase awareness that these commitments are legally relevant and go way beyond being a tool of marketing and for favourably influencing the perceptions of consumers and investors.

Similarly, the *Lidl Case*[2] dealt with the impact of unfair competition rules on statements by companies relating to their business conduct. In 2006, Lidl became a member of the 'Business Social Compliance Initiative' (BSCI) which is aimed at improving working conditions along entire global supply chains. The BSCI code of conduct is based on the ILO's regulatory framework on labour rights, including, among others, the limitation of working hours, regulating salaries and the elimination of discrimination. Even though, according to the principles of BSCI, its members are not per se bound by them and obliged to guarantee these social standards, Lidl has referred on its website to 'safeguarding social standards' and has stated that compliance with social standards by the BSCI is mandatory for its suppliers. It thus evoked the impression that its suppliers are already complying with such standards and in particular has emphasized that its decision to purchase from suppliers depends upon compliance, even though in reality, working conditions on the production site are nowhere near the level of the standards promoted. The European Center for Constitutional and Human Rights (ECCHR), the Clean Clothes Campaign (CCC) and the Hamburg Consumer Protection Agency argued that the advertising campaign by Lidl misleads socially conscious consumers into purchasing a product and thus violates the German law on unfair competition (UWG). Again, although companies are not required to guarantee the adherence of suppliers to social standards, explicit pledges made by Lidl in advertising campaigns created legitimate expectations for consumers and stakeholders. 10 days after the filing of the case, Lidl made a declaration that it would

2. *Consumer Protection Agency Hamburg v. Lidl*, filed at the Heilbronn District Court on 6 April 2010 and supported by an initiative of the European Center for Constitutional and Human Rights (ECCHR) and the Clean Clothes Campaign (CCC). The case was decided only 10 days later through a declaration by Lidl that it would refrain from allegedly misleading advertising. For the indictment see http://www.vzhh.de/recht/30332/Lidl_Kl age.pdf (in German).

cease to imply to consumers that membership to the BSCI would bind Lidl to comply with its social standards and that such compliance is a given.

The discrepancy and gap between information provided, public perceptions and the reality is also at the heart of comparable constellations around labelling. The so called *Blue Angel*[3] judgment of the German Supreme Court adjudicated in 1988, is a leading case in point. Blue Angel is a public label issued by the United Nations Environmental Programme (UNEP), initiated by the German Government. The complainant alleged that the defendant, while properly describing the products in accordance with the label requirements, used additional tools, so called 'wobblers,' to market the products concerned. These wobblers, which were attached to the shelves and attracted consumers in the store, failed to contain all the relevant consumer information required by the labelling programme, and allegedly misinformed consumers. The German Supreme Court followed the arguments of the plaintiff and ruled that the labels evoke erroneous perceptions of the quality of the product concerned. The Court noted that the Blue Angel label implies environmental soundness of the product while the reasons establishing such soundness were not communicated. Missing substantiation could mislead a substantial proportion of the consumers. It was held that the business practice amounts to a violation of Article 5 of the German Unfair Competition Act. The Court held that strict standards need to be applied to environmental advertising. In particular, the Court emphasized that environmental labels reflected in higher prices evoke an impression of environmental sustainability, i.e. addressing environmental concerns and worries of consumers. Again, the gap between perceptions evoked and the realities amounted to consumer deception and unfair competition.

. . .

The inclusion of Article 10*bis* of the Paris Convention in the TRIPS Agreement thus defines the mechanisms enforcing disciplines on CSR commitments. Firstly, WTO law obliges Members, equal to the Paris Convention, to implement principles and rules of unfair competition law in domestic legislation. A WTO Member that is not providing principles and rules suitable to enforce CSR commitments made by private companies may be challenged and called upon to defend its legislation before a panel and the Appellate body, both of which are mandated to assess compatibility of domestic legislation with obligations under WTO law. The host country of subsidiaries of an MNC or of competitors may complain that an industrialized or emerging member country does not sufficiently live up to CSR pledges made and thus engages in unfair competition. Such complaints may be triggered by the failure of domestic courts to remedy a discrepancy and gap between CSR commitments made by a domiciled company and business and labour relations practiced within the country or abroad. There may be a lack of legislation, or insufficient standing to bring a complaint by consumers, competitors and workers suffering from unfair trade practices.

Article 10*bis* of the Paris Convention as incorporated in the TRIPS Agreement offers the potential to explore, on a case-by-case basis, the scope of protection offered by unfair competition against failures of States to discipline companies which fail to honour the CSR commitments they have made. It will also allow an assessment of the extent to which recourse to free speech may allow dispensation from living up to such commitments under WTO law. For example, had the US Supreme Court found in the *Nike* case that conduct of Nike is protected by free speech rather than commercial speech, a WTO panel would need to assess to what extent free speech undermines the commitments made under Article 10*bis* of the Paris Convention, in particular para. 3(3). The relationship of trade and human rights is not

3. *Blauer Engel*, German Supreme Court, BGH—I ZR 219/87, decision from 20 October 1988, Citation BGHZ 105, 277.

limited to adjudicating exemptions under Article XX GATT. It also plays a role in interpreting the provisions of the Paris Convention and the TRIPS Agreement. A panel would thus be required to make findings on free speech and commercial speech in the context of unfair competition rules. The case law may eventually develop appropriate findings as to the relationship of the two competing areas and values. The point made is that Article 10*bis* Paris Convention offers a valuable starting point in developing the law applicable to voluntary commitments that will be made by companies under CSR in the coming years and decades, addressing the discrepancy and gap between promises made, perceptions shaped and conduct on the ground. Private operators do not have recourse to WTO dispute settlement. It is up to governments to decide whether a case should be taken up. WTO law does not offer compensation and is unable to undo injustices done in the past. The remedy is geared to improvement of the law for the future. Lack of implementation of rulings may trigger the withdrawal of tariff and non-tariff concessions and market access for the defendant concerned. Limiting market access rights to defendant parties and thus to companies operating from the defendant's soil, amounts to a major incentive to comply in the first place and to avoid trade restrictions in sectors of importance to the country concerned. . . .

## NOTES AND QUESTIONS

**1.** Unfair competition law can be considered a common underlying policy for the different forms of IPRs. However, as stated above, the relationship of the two systems has been controversial. In the case *Frau X v. Frau Y & Z Publishing House*, discussed in Chapter 4, the Swiss Federal Court denied the subsidiary invocation of competition law after ruling out an infringement of the plaintiff's copyright for her thesis. Recent jurisprudence, however, emphasizes the mutually supportive role of intellectual property rights and of unfair competition; BHG I ZR 188/11 (*Hard Rock Café*), German Supreme Court, 15 Aug. 2013. The Court held that trademark law and unfair competition law are not mutually exclusive, but apply in parallel and are mutually supportive. What are the implications of these diverging views? How would you define the relationship between unfair competition and IPRs? Should unfair competition apply to conduct and use of information which is in the public domain and not protected by IPRs?

**2.** Recourse to unfair competition rules for the purposes of enforcing obligations voluntarily incurred by companies on social conduct (corporate social responsibility) offers an interesting avenue for interest groups and NGOs to monitor and challenge corporate conduct. Should companies be entitled to invoke freedom of speech against allegations of unfairly violating a promised course of conduct?

**3.** Following the discussion on protection of traditional knowledge (TK) through competition law and the possible application of Article 10*bis* of the Paris Convention, we will have a look at the possibilities for a *sui generis* system for TK in Section III of this chapter. Try to identify which advantages and challenges are inherent to each of the solutions.

## B. COMPETITION LAW (ANTI-TRUST) AND INTELLECTUAL PROPERTY

Other than unfair competition, competition law or anti-trust rules are not part of international law. Efforts to bring about shared disciplines under the roof of the WTO, aspired under the so- called Singapore issues, were abandoned. The field was left to domestic law, and the jurisdictions of the United States and the European Union dominating under principles of extraterritorial application. Since the adoption of the WTO Agreements in 1995, many more countries have adopted anti-trust rules. They cooperate within the International Competition Network. The TRIPS Agreement recognizes the relevance of anti-trust rules. Article 8(2) reads: "Appropiate measures, provided that they are consistent with the provisions of this Agreement, may be needed to prevent the abuse of intellectual property rights by the right holders or the resort to practices which unreasonably restrain trade or adversely affect the international transfer of technology". Article 40 specifies: "Members agree that some licensing practices or conditions pertaining to intellectual property rights which restrain competition may have adverse effects on trade and may empede the transfer and dissemination of technology". The following paragraphs entail carve-outs to the effect that intellectual property rights under the TRIPS Agreement cannot be invoked to curb the effect of domestic anti-trust rules. The following excerpts broadly address the complex relationship of competition law and intellectual property.

**Thomas Cottier & Christophe Germann***

## *Teaching Intellectual Property, Unfair Competition and Anti-Trust Law*

. . .

### Relationship to Intellectual Property Protection

#### Coexistence, Tensions and Balance

Intellectual property and competition law are necessary, but not sufficient, conditions of a competitive environment. Operationally, they create a dialectical tension and require mutual balancing. On the one hand, exclusive rights granted under intellectual property by definition exclude competition in a particular setting and allow excluding third parties from directly competing with the right holder. On the other hand, competition law seeks to facilitate direct competition and tends to limit the use of exclusive rights.

. . . In the United States . . . the detrimental effects of per se prohibitions were removed under the influence of the Chicago School, and eventually gave way to a case-by-case analysis, based on the rule of reason. All pertinent factors are taken into account, and licensing agreements are examined under what is called the "post-Chicago" approach. A comparable, albeit not similar, development can be observed in European Community law. As a result, competition law and intellectual property interact in a most complex manner, strongly dependent upon the case law of the courts.

#### Anti-Trust Guidelines and Block Exemptions for Licensing of Intellectual Property

Defining the relationship of competition law and intellectual property on a case-by-case basis responds to the needs of reality, but offers little legal security for business transactions. Authorities have, therefore, made attempts to codify pertinent principles and rules applicable to licensing of intellectual property rights. In the United States, the Justice Department and the Federal Trade Commission enacted Anti-trust Guidelines for Licensing of Intellectual Property in 1995. [Eds. Note: Updated 2017] Building upon case law, these guidelines define allowable terms for intellectual property licensing agreements.

* In TEACHING OF INTELLECTUAL PROPERTY: PRINCIPLES AND METHODS 130-66 (Yo Takagi, Larry Allman & Mpazi A. Sinjela eds., 2008) (footnotes omitted).

Similarly, the European Commission enacted Technology Transfer Block Exemptions in 1996. They were subsequently revised in 2004. These regulations define transfer agreements which are automatically exempt from the application of Article 81 of the EC Treaty [Eds. Note: Now Art. 101 of TFEU] where market shares do not exceed 20 per cent.

**Intellectual Property Rights and the Essential Facilities Doctrine**

Dominant positions may be based upon intellectual property rights, such as patents. Competition law breaks them by imposing compulsory licensing, i.e. the obligation to allow third parties to use such rights against compensation. Prominently, the "essential facility doctrine" serves as a legal concept, initially developed by US case law, to address such constellations. This doctrine — which is not restricted to intellectual property — may impose restrictions on companies exclusively controlling an essential facility (such as a port, a railway station, a utility, a network). In the absence of voluntarily granting reasonable access to competitors on a contractual basis, competition authorities and courts may order such access. The US Supreme Court first articulated this doctrine in *United States v. Terminal Railroad Ass'n*, 224 U.S. 383 (1912). In this case, a group of railroads controlling all railway bridges and switching yards into and out of St. Louis prevented competing railroad services from offering transportation to and through that destination. This, the court held, constituted both an illegal restraint of trade and an attempt to monopolize. Because the essential facilities doctrine represents a divergence from the general rule that even a monopolist may choose with whom to deal, courts have established widely adopted tests that parties must meet before a court will require a monopolist to grant access to an essential asset to its competitors. Specifically, to establish anti-trust liability under the essential facilities doctrine, a party must prove four factors: (1) control of the essential facility by a monopolist; (2) competitor's inability practically or reasonably to duplicate the essential facility; (3) the denial of the use of the facility to a competitor; and (4) the feasibility of providing the facility to competitors.

This test for anti-trust liability has been adopted by virtually every United States court to consider an "essential facilities" claim. Rulings of these courts also suggest that anti-trust liability under the essential facilities doctrine is particularly appropriate when denial of access is motivated by an anti-competitive animus — usually demonstrated by a change in existing business practices with the apparent intent of harming rivals.

In view of the various contexts in which the essential facilities doctrine has been applied, courts have declined to impose any artificial limit on the kinds of products, services, or other assets to which the doctrine may appropriately be applied. . . . The European Court of Justice, albeit refraining from adopting the terminology of essential facilities, adopted an essentially similar approach. It is summarized in the Advocate General's opinion of May 28, 1998 in the *Oscar Bronner* case.

In the recent *IMS* case concerning a statistical device ("brick structure") aimed at presenting sales data of pharmaceutical product and protected by copyright, the European Court of Justice recalled that, according to settled case law, refusal to grant a license, even if it is the act of an undertaking holding a dominant position, does not per se constitute an abuse of such a position. It is a legitimate exercise of intellectual property rights. However, pursuant to this case law, the exercise of an exclusive right by the owner may, in exceptional circumstances, involve abusive conduct. The Court held that such exceptional circumstances were present in a previous case dealing with intellectual property rights, namely the *Magill* case. Several television channels in a dominant position relied on the copyright conferred by national legislation on the weekly listings of their programs in order to prevent another undertaking from publishing joint information on those programs together with commentaries, on a weekly basis. In this case, the exceptional circumstances resulted from three sets of considerations. Firstly, from the fact that the refusal in question concerned a product (information on the weekly schedules of certain television channels), the supply of which was indispensable for carrying on the business in question (the publishing of a general television guide). Secondly, from the consideration that, without that information, the person wishing to produce such a guide would find it impossible to publish it and offer it for sale. Thirdly, from the fact that such refusal prevented the emergence of a new product for which there was a potential consumer demand, the fact that it was not justified by objective considerations, and was likely to exclude all competition in the secondary market. This last condition relates to the consideration that, in the balancing of the interest in protection of the intellectual property right and the economic freedom of its owner against the interest in protection of free competition, the latter can prevail only where refusal to grant a license prevents the development of the secondary market to the detriment of consumers. Therefore, the denial by an undertaking in a dominant position to allow access to a product protected by an intellectual property right, where that product is indispensable for operating on a secondary market, may be regarded as abusive only where the undertaking which requested the license does not intend to limit itself essentially to duplicating the goods or services already offered on the secondary market by the owner of the intellectual property right, but intends to produce new goods or services not offered by the owner of the right and for which there is a potential consumer demand. In the *IMS* case, the Court eventually held that the refusal to grant a license constituted an abuse of a dominant position within the meaning of Article 82 EC [now Art. 102 TFEU] where the following conditions are fulfilled:

> (a) the undertaking which requested the license intends to offer, on the market at stake, new products or services not offered by the owner of the intellectual property right and for which there is a potential consumer demand;
>
> (b) the refusal is not justified by objective considerations;
>
> (c) the refusal is such as to reserve to the owner of the intellectual property right the market at stake by eliminating all competition on that market.

The Court confirmed that the application of the essential facilities doctrine to positions dominating the market based on their intellectual property rights requires the supply of a good or service that must be new. In comparison, this condition of novelty must not be fulfilled in those cases where intellectual property rights are not relevant for the essential facility. This additional requirement makes sense from the perspective of the rationale underlying the grant of intellectual property rights, i.e. the promotion of innovative and creative efforts.

## NOTES AND QUESTIONS

**1.** The relationship between intellectual property rights and anti-trust law may be assessed differently depending on the field and context of application. For example, patents and other forms of market exclusivity (e.g., based on regulatory data protection) may allow their owners to charge very high prices for pharmaceutical products. In high-income countries (HICs) such as Switzerland, consumers and the public health system may be able to cope with such prices. In low- and middle-income countries (LMICs), such prices may effectively constitute a denial of treatment. In assessing whether patent-based pricing is "excessive" from a competition law standpoint, it may be appropriate to place the burden of justifying prices on the patent owners in LMICs, even if that would not be the case in HICs. For an assessment of the relationship between competition law and IP rights in the context of LMICs, *see* Frederick M. Abbott, Sean M. Flynn, Carlos M. Correa, Jonathan Michael Berger & Natasha Nayak, UNDP, *Using Competition Law to Promote Access to Health Technologies: A Guidebook for Low- and Middle-Income Countries*, United Nations Development Program (F.M. Abbott ed., 2014), available at SSRN: http://ssrn.com/abstract=2439416.

**2.** The USMCA includes Chapter 21 on Competition Policy. The chapter does not prescribe substantive competition rules. It imposes detailed obligations on the Parties with respect to procedures that should be followed in conducting investigations and enforcement actions. Such rules are in a concrete sense TRIPS-plus. Their invocation by private sector companies—through their governments—is likely to make it more difficult for competition authorities to pursue investigations and enforcement actions. The United States, which long opposed negotiation of multilateral competition rules has now signed on to the idea of limiting their application in the interest of protecting its multinational private sector companies. Alleged breaches of Chapter 21 are not subject to state-to-state dispute settlement, but only may be the subject of consultations (Article 21.6-7).

## C. Pricing and Intellectual Property Rights

**Frederick M. Abbott**

### *Prosecuting Excessive Pricing of Pharmaceuticals under Competition Law: Evolutionary Development**

#### I. Introduction

#### A. Background

Access to healthcare is a concern for individuals around the world. Pharmaceutical products, including therapeutics, vaccines and diagnostics, play a major role in the global healthcare system. Concerns regarding affordability and access to pharmaceutical products are long-standing. They are relevant across the range of disease conditions and the manner of addressing them. They affect high-income, middle-income and low-income countries. The COVID-19 pandemic starkly illustrated the intensity of global and local discourse that may take place when pharmaceutical products are not made available in a timely and accessible manner.

There are various legislative and regulatory tools that can be used to address affordability and access to pharmaceutical products. Such tools, including price control systems, are widely employed. For example, in Europe, where most of the cases discussed in this article arose, price control systems are common. Yet despite the availability and use of these tools, the price of pharmaceutical products in Europe may be high and, as illustrated in this article, may also be "excessive." Excessive pricing often signals that the national or regional regulatory system for medicines is in some way broken in the sense that pharmaceutical industry actors are able to exploit defects to enable excessive pricing. There are, as will be described, business models consciously built around exploiting "niches" where single suppliers of pharmaceutical products can dominate the market and charge excessive prices. These niches are advertised to investors as attractive opportunities.

Competition or antitrust law is used to address pharmaceutical products and markets, just as it is used to address other subject matter, whether that be automobiles, banks, energy supplies or smartphones. For example, to address abuses involving agreements to fix prices and allocate markets, or to address problematic mergers and acquisitions.

* Columbia Science and Technology Law Review, Vol. 24, No. 2, pgs. 173-247 (2023), available at SSRN: https://ssrn.com/abstract=4320036 or http://dx.doi.org/10.2139/ssrn.4320036.

In Europe and some other jurisdictions (for example, South Africa) competition laws expressly make it unlawful to abuse a dominant market position to charge an unfair price. Yet, until a decade ago, competition authorities were reluctant to pursue excessive pricing cases, including with respect to pharmaceuticals. A substantial part of this article is devoted to describing a significant shift in attitude. In Europe prosecutions involving charges of excessive pricing of pharmaceuticals are now fairly common. The South African Competition Authority currently is pursuing a case addressing excessive pricing of a patented treatment for breast cancer.

In the United States, controversy over the terms of programs such as Medicare and Medicaid, and the pricing of widely used therapeutic treatments such as insulin, are a routine part of the daily news cycle. Yet competition authorities in the United States do not pursue excessive pricing causes of action, primarily because the federal courts have not been receptive. The courts have questioned whether such prosecutions are technically feasible and whether judges are the right arbiters. This article shows the feasibility of prosecuting cases of excessive pricing. It has been "proven" in Europe. The United States is lagging, and it should be catching up.

This article begins by describing how the landscape of excessive pricing has shifted over the past decade, particularly within Europe, from hesitancy to endorsement, mainly through the pursuit of a series of cases involving excessive pricing of off-patent pharmaceutical products. Before providing the details of these cases, this article briefly explains rules deriving from the seminal judgment of the Court of Justice of the European Union in the *United Brands* case on which these prosecutions rely. The article then provides details of seven prosecuted cases, and one settlement, in Europe. "How" it was done is an important part of the proof of feasibility.

The article then describes and analyzes an ongoing prosecution in South Africa involving pricing of the breast cancer treatment Herceptin. This case is distinguished from those in Europe as it concerns a patent-protected drug. Analysis of excessive pricing in cases involving originator drugs that include research and development ("R&D") expenses, risk and patents is inherently more complex than addressing generic drugs marketed without substantial investment in R&D.

Based on the cases so far prosecuted, the article synthesizes common elements or approaches that might be used by competition authorities in the future. There are "learning curves" as competition authorities sort through the various technical issues involved in pharmaceutical production and distribution, and associated pricing decisions. Prosecutors should reference and rely on approaches that have previously been developed so that the "wheel" need not be reinvented for each case.

Competition authorities are government offices and must deal with budgetary and staffing limitations. Attention should be focused on improving the efficiency of prosecutions to reduce costs and accelerate timelines.

The article suggests that the jurisprudence surrounding competition law prosecutions for excessive pricing could be improved in at least two ways. First, courts or legislative authorities could adopt "per se" rules such that when pricing for generic products exceeds a certain level (above cost-plus) it is automatically deemed to be excessive so that courts and prosecuting authorities do not need to engage in further in-depth investigation and analysis.

Cases that are not captured by the *per se* rules will remain. This article suggests preferred methodologies for establishing excessive pricing in such cases, including cases involving originator products where there is R&D risk adjustment involved.

The article then proposes reexamining the jurisprudence arising out of *United Brands*. It recommends moving from the "two step" test to a rule of reason type balancing test to assess whether a price is excessive under the circumstances.

The article finally turns to the United States and the judicial reluctance to accept excessive pricing causes of action noting that there is some change in the wind as evidenced, *inter alia*, by the Federal Trade Commission ("FTC")/States Attorney General prosecution in the case involving Martin Shkreli. The article finally suggests that the FTC pursue a Sector Study looking to determine whether abuses involving niche pharmaceutical products and excessive pricing are taking place in the United States.

### B. The Changing Landscape

As of 2011, an Organisation for Economic Co-operation and Development ("OECD") compilation of views of competition authorities regarding excessive pricing reported that there had been no prosecutions in the pharmaceutical sector outside one in South Africa in the early 2000's. At that time competition authorities on the whole expressed a cautious attitude about the prospects for moving forward in this area.

European competition authorities have moved forcefully ahead in prosecuting excessive pricing, having initiated eight such prosecutions since 2011. They have collectively imposed more than $600 million in fines. So far, the prosecutions in Europe have involved generic (off-patent/off-regulatory exclusivity) products, though two involve an orphan drug designation.

South Africa has prosecuted two cases based on excessive pricing of originator/patent protected drugs. The first, more than a decade ago, and the second now under submission to the Competition Tribunal with respect to excessive pricing of Herceptin. As we consider potential reforms of competition law globally it is important to examine the 2018 amendments to South Africa's Competition Act that work improvements on the approach originally derived from the Court of Justice of the European Union ("CJEU") (formerly European Court of Justice) jurisprudence in *United Brands*.

The United States traditionally has been the leader in policing the pharmaceutical sector against anticompetitive abuse, particularly through the work of the FTC. Yet in the arena of excessive pricing, Europe and South Africa have moved substantially ahead.

An important take-away from the European prosecutions involving the generics sector is that there is no practical reason why excessive pricing prosecutions cannot be successfully pursued in the United States, and elsewhere. The Europeans have shown that it can be done. It is time to lay out a roadmap for the United States and other countries drawing lessons from the European and South African experience.

## II. Europe

### A. The CJEU and the Two-Step Test

European competition authorities and courts have a certain advantage in that the text of Article 102 of the Treaty on the Functioning of the European Union (TFEU) expressly establishes the charging of unfair selling prices as a form of abuse of dominant position. A successful prosecution for excessive pricing under Article 102 of the TFEU requires that the party under investigation holds a dominant position on the relevant market for the product(s), as the cause of action

is grounded in abuse of dominant position.

. . .

## III. South Africa

. . .

### B. The Competition Act as Amended in 2018

The South African competition authority noted in its submission to the 2011 OECD excessive pricing report that the related provisions of its Competition Act (89 of 1998), Secs. 1(ix) & 8(a) were based on the two-step test of the CJEU in United Brands.300 In 2018, with effect in 2019, South Africa amended Section 8 to incorporate and modify the definitional element previously in Section 1, and to elaborate a more sophisticated approach to analyzing claims of excessive pricing. It is worthwhile to set out relevant terms of the revised Section 8:

> (1) It is prohibited for a dominant firm to—
> (a) *charge an excessive price* to the detriment of consumers or customers;
> (b) refuse to give a competitor access to an essential facility when it is economically feasible to do so;
> (c) . . .
> (d) . . .
> (2) *If there is a prima facie case of abuse of dominance because the dominant firm charged an excessive price, the dominant firm must show that the price was reasonable.*
> (3) Any person determining whether a price is an excessive price *must determine if that price is higher than a competitive price and whether such difference is unreasonable, determined by taking into account all relevant factors*, which may include—
> (a) *the respondent's price-cost margin, internal rate of return, return on capital invested or profit history*;
> (b) the respondent's prices for the goods or services—
> (i) in markets in which there are competing products;
> (ii) to customers in other geographic markets;
> (iii) for similar products in other markets; and
> (iv) historically;
> (c) relevant comparator firm's prices and level of profits for the goods or services in a competitive market for those goods or services;
> (d) the *length of time* the prices have been charged at that level;
> (e) the structural characteristics of the relevant market, including the extent of the respondent's market share, *the degree of contestability of the market, barriers to entry and past or current advantage that is not due to the respondent's own commercial efficiency or investment, such as direct or indirect state support for a firm or firms in the market*; and
> (f) any regulations made by the Minister, in terms of section 78 regarding the calculation and determination of an excessive price. (emphasis added).

There are a number of notable features to the 2018 amendments which align with this author's perspective regarding movement away from the CJEU's two-step test toward a more contextual approach along the lines of a rule of reason analysis.

In practical terms, one of the most significant innovations of the 2018 Amendments may prove to be the procedural shifting of the burden of proof in section 8(2). That is, once the competition authority has made out a *prima facie* case that the respondent party holds a dominant position and has charged an excessive price, the burden shifts to that respondent to "show that the price was reasonable."

. . .

## VII. The Way Forward for the U.S.

### A. Philosophical Persuasion

Focusing on the situation of the United States, it seems accepted that the Sherman Act itself does not preclude federal courts from adjudicating causes of action involving claims of excessive pricing as an abuse of monopoly under Section 2. It seems equally well established at least for the moment the courts have not yet allowed for that possibility. On one hand, the federal courts have resisted based on a philosophical view of the Sherman Act as directed toward removing supply side constraints so as to return the market to competitive equilibrium. There is here the matter of convincing the federal courts that there are parts of the pharmaceutical sector that do not "self-correct" based on intellectual property and/or regulatory features in one form or another. While the US Supreme Court helped to clear the path by holding in *FTC v. Actavis* [570 U.S. 136 (2013)] that validly granted patents do not provide a shield against antitrust liability, this view has yet to manifest itself as a willingness to address abusive patents or other regulatory exclusivities by charging excessive prices. Persuading the federal courts to address excessive pricing under the Sherman Act will require persuading them that protecting consumers should be on an equal footing with removing supply-side constraints. European and South African prosecutions might help persuade the federal courts on this account, but the work of US academics, including lawyers and economists, may be needed to help in the persuasion.

### C. Legislative Change

An alternative to persuasion regarding judicial philosophy would be an amendment to the Sherman Act to align it with Article 102 of the TFEU and similarly drafted competition statutes. That is, adding language to the effect that the charging of unfair purchase or selling prices constitutes an abuse of monopoly. While this might be the easier route in terms of producing the desired result, it may be the more difficult route from a political standpoint.

## NOTES AND QUESTIONS

**1.** In 2023, the pharmaceutical originator companies in the United States have initiated litigation against the federal government arguing that legislation authorizing negotiation of pharmaceutical prices with the industry is unconstitutional (Patrick Wingrove, Pharmaceutical trade group sues U.S. over Medicare drug price negotiation plans, Reuters, June 21, 2023) ("In response to the previous lawsuits, the White House said there is nothing in the U.S. Constitution that prevents Medicare from negotiating lower drug prices.")* Though the theory about price negotiation from the pharmaceutical industry may appear "far-fetched", there is some history of sympathy from the federal courts to industry push-back against government attempts to control pharmaceutical prices. At the very least, it may have the effect of delaying the implementation of the government's approach, giving the industry more time to lobby for change in Congress. The U.S. Congress has a history of backing away from addressing pharmaceutical pricing concerns. This is an often-repeated story.

## D. Essential Facilities and Intellectual Property Rights

The leading "Magill" case squares intellectual property as a monopoly right and disciplines of competition law in the European Union. On appeal, the ECJ (today CJEU) confirmed the findings of the Court of First Instance (today General Court) and of the Commission in issuing a compulsory license in response to an abuse of a dominant position. The 1995 case laid the foundations of the essential facilities doctrine in European law:

---

* https://www.reuters.com/world/us/us-sued-block-program-that-gives-medicare-power-negotiate-drug-prices-2023-06-21/.

## *Radio Telefis Eireann (RTE) and Independent Television Publications Ltd (ITP) v. Commission of the European Communities ("Magill TV Guide")*

Judgement of the Court, 6 April 1995

In Joined Cases C-241/91 P and C-242/91 P

1. Competition—Dominant position—Concept—Monopoly of broadcasting companies over information relating to weekly programme listings (EEC Treaty, Art. 86)
2. Competition—Dominant position—Copyright—Weekly listings of television programmes—Exercise of copyright—Abuse—Conditions (EEC Treaty, Art. 86)

In Joined Cases C-241/91 P and C-242/91 P,
Radio Telefis Eireann (RTE), . . .
and
Independent Television Publications Ltd (ITP),

. . .

THE COURT,
composed of: G.C. Rodríguez Iglesias (Rapporteur), President, F.A. Schockweiler and P.J.G. Kapteyn (Presidents of Chambers), G.F. Mancini, C.N. Kakouris, J.C. Moitinho de Almeida and J.L. Murray, Judges,
Advocate General: C. Gulmann,

. . .

### Grounds

1. By application lodged at the Court Registry on 19 September 1991, Radio Telefis Eireann ("RTE"), notified of the judgment of the Court of First Instance in Case T-69/89 *RTE v Commission* [1991] ECR II-485 ("the RTE judgment") on 10 July 1991, the date of judgment, appealed against that judgment on the ground of non-compliance with Community law.

2. By application lodged at the Court Registry on 19 September 1991, Independent Television Publications Ltd ("ITP"), notified of the judgment of the Court of First Instance of 10 July 1991 in Case T-76/89 *ITP v Commission* [1991] ECR II-575 ("the ITP judgment") on 12 July 1991, appealed against that judgment on the ground of non-compliance with Community law.

. . .

6. According to the judgments of the Court of First Instance, most households in Ireland and 30% to 40% of households in Northern Ireland can receive television programmes broadcast by RTE, ITV and BBC.

7. At the material time, no comprehensive weekly television guide was available on the market in Ireland or in Northern Ireland. Each television station published a television guide covering exclusively its own programmes and claimed, under Irish and United Kingdom legislation, copyright protection for its own weekly programme listings in order to prevent their reproduction by third parties.

8. RTE itself published its own weekly television guide, while ITV did so through ITP, a company established for that purpose.

9. ITP, RTE and BBC practiced the following policy with regard to the dissemination of programme listings. They provided their programme schedules free of charge, on request, to

daily and periodical newspapers, accompanied by a licence for which no charge was made, setting out the conditions under which that information could be reproduced. Daily listings and, if the following day was a public holiday, the listings for two days, could thus be published in the press, subject to certain conditions relating to the format of publication. Publication of "highlights" of the week was also authorized. ITP, RTE and the BBC ensured strict compliance with the licence conditions by instituting legal proceedings, where necessary, against publications which failed to comply with them.

10. Magill TV Guide Ltd ("Magill") attempted to publish a comprehensive weekly television guide but was prevented from doing so by the appellants and the BBC, which obtained injunctions prohibiting publication of weekly television listings.

11. Magill lodged a complaint with the Commission on 4 April 1986 under Article 3 of Regulation No 17 of the Council of 6 February 1962, the First Regulation implementing Articles 85 and 86 of the Treaty (OJ, English Special Edition 1959-1962, p. 87) ("Regulation No 17") seeking a declaration that the appellants and the BBC were abusing their dominant position by refusing to grant licences for the publication of their respective weekly listings. The Commission decided to initiate a proceeding, at the end of which it adopted Decision 89/205/EEC of 21 December 1988 relating to a proceeding under Article 86 of the EEC Treaty (IV/31.851—Magill TV Guide/ITP, BBC and RTE) (OJ 1989 L 78, p. 43) ("the decision"), which was the subject-matter of the proceedings before the Court of First Instance.

12. In that decision the Commission found that there had been a breach of Article 86 of the EEC Treaty and ordered the three organizations to put an end to that breach, in particular "by supplying . . . third parties on request and on a non-discriminatory basis with their individual advance weekly programme listings and by permitting reproduction of those listings by such parties". It was also provided that, if the three organizations chose to grant reproduction licences, any royalties requested should be reasonable.

13. By order of 11 May 1989 in Joined Cases 76, 77 and 91/89 R *RTE and Others v Commission* [1989] ECR 1141, the President of the Court of Justice, at the request of the applicants, ordered suspension "of the operation of Article 2 of the . . . decision in so far as it obliges the applicants to bring the infringement found by the Commission to an end forthwith by supplying each other and third parties on request and on a non-discriminatory basis with their individual advance weekly programme listings and by permitting reproduction of those listings by such parties".

14. At first instance the two appellants sought annulment of the Commission decision and an order requiring it to pay the costs of the proceedings.

15. The Court of First Instance dismissed the appellants' applications and ordered them to pay the costs.

. . .

### The Existence of an Abuse of a Dominant Position

. . .

31. In the light of the foregoing considerations, the Court of First Instance found that, although the programme listings were at the material time protected by copyright as laid down by national law, which still determined the rules governing that protection, the conduct at issue could not qualify for such protection within the framework of the necessary reconciliation between intellectual property rights and the fundamental principles of the Treaty concerning the free movement of goods and freedom of competition. The aim of that conduct was clearly incompatible with the objectives of Article 86 (ITP judgment, paragraph 60).

32. The Court of First Instance accordingly dismissed the plea in law based on breach of Article 86.

### Existence of a Dominant Position

. . .

46. So far as dominant position is concerned, it is to be remembered at the outset that mere ownership of an intellectual property right cannot confer such a position.

47. However, the basic information as to the channel, day, time and title of programmes is the necessary result of programming by television stations, which are thus the only source of such information for an undertaking, like Magill, which wishes to publish it together with commentaries or pictures. By force of circumstance, RTE and ITP, as the agent of ITV, enjoy, along with the BBC, a de facto monopoly over the information used to compile listings for the television programmes received in most households in Ireland and 30% to 40% of households in Northern Ireland. The appellants are thus in a position to prevent effective competition on the market in weekly television magazines. The Court of First Instance was therefore right in confirming the Commission's assessment that the appellants occupied a dominant position (see the judgment in Case 322/81 Michelin, cited above, paragraph 30).

### (b) Existence of Abuse

48. With regard to the issue of abuse, the arguments of the appellants and IPO wrongly presuppose that where the conduct of an undertaking in a dominant position consists of the exercise of a right classified by national law as "copyright", such conduct can never be reviewed in relation to Article 86 of the Treaty.

49. Admittedly, in the absence of Community standardization or harmonization of laws, determination of the conditions and procedures for granting protection of an intellectual property right is a matter for national rules. Further, the exclusive right of reproduction forms part of the author's rights, so that refusal to grant a licence, even if it is the act of an undertaking holding a dominant position, cannot in itself constitute abuse of a dominant position (judgment in Case 238/87 *Volvo*, cited above, paragraphs 7 and 8).

50. However, it is also clear from that judgment (paragraph 9) that the exercise of an exclusive right by the proprietor may, in exceptional circumstances, involve abusive conduct.

51. In the present case, the conduct objected to is the appellants' reliance on copyright conferred by national legislation so as to prevent Magill—or any other undertaking having the same intention—from publishing on a weekly basis information (channel, day, time and title of programmes) together with commentaries and pictures obtained independently of the appellants.

52. Among the circumstances taken into account by the Court of First Instance in concluding that such conduct was abusive was, first, the fact that there was, according to the findings of the Court of First Instance, no actual or potential substitute for a weekly television guide offering information on the programmes for the week ahead. On this point, the Court of First Instance confirmed the Commission's finding that the complete lists of programmes for a 24-hour period—and for a 48-hour period at weekends and before public holidays—published in certain daily and Sunday newspapers, and the television sections of certain magazines covering, in addition, "highlights" of the week's programmes, were only to a limited extent substitutable for advance information to viewers on all the week's programmes. Only weekly television guides containing comprehensive listings for the week ahead would enable users to decide in advance which programmes they wished to follow and arrange their leisure activities for the week accordingly. The Court of First Instance also established that there was a specific, constant and regular potential demand on the part of consumers (see the *RTE* judgment, paragraph 62, and the *ITP* judgment, paragraph 48).

53. Thus the appellants—who were, by force of circumstance, the only sources of the basic information on programme scheduling which is the indispensable raw material for compiling a weekly television guide—gave viewers wishing to obtain information on the choice

of programmes for the week ahead no choice but to buy the weekly guides for each station and draw from each of them the information they needed to make comparisons.

54. The appellants' refusal to provide basic information by relying on national copyright provisions thus prevented the appearance of a new product, a comprehensive weekly guide to television programmes, which the appellants did not offer and for which there was a potential consumer demand. Such refusal constitutes an abuse under heading (b) of the second paragraph of Article 86 of the Treaty.

55. Second, there was no justification for such refusal either in the activity of television broadcasting or in that of publishing television magazines (*RTE* judgment, paragraph 73, and *ITP* judgment, paragraph 58).

56. Third, and finally, as the Court of First Instance also held, the appellants, by their conduct, reserved to themselves the secondary market of weekly television guides by excluding all competition on that market (see the judgment in Joined Cases 6/73 and 7/73 *Commercial Solvents v Commission* [1974] ECR 223, paragraph 25) since they denied access to the basic information which is the raw material indispensable for the compilation of such a guide.

57. In the light of all those circumstances, the Court of First Instance did not err in law in holding that the appellants' conduct was an abuse of a dominant position within the meaning of Article 86 of the Treaty.

58. It follows that the plea in law alleging misapplication by the Court of First Instance of the concept of abuse of a dominant position must be dismissed as unfounded. It is therefore unnecessary to examine the reasoning of the contested judgments in so far as it is based on Article 36 of the Treaty.

**Effects on Trade Between Member States (Second Plea in the Appeal in Case C-241/91 P)**

. . .

70. In this case, the Court of First Instance found that the applicant had excluded all potential competitors on the geographical market consisting of one Member State (Ireland) and part of another Member State (Northern Ireland) and had thus modified the structure of competition on that market, thereby affecting potential commercial exchanges between Ireland and the United Kingdom. From this the Court of First Instance drew the proper conclusion that the condition that trade between Member States must be affected had been satisfied.

71. It follows that the plea in law alleging misapplication by the Court of First Instance of the concept of trade between Member States being affected must be dismissed.

**The Berne Convention (Third Plea in the Appeal In Case C-241/91 P)**

72. So far as the Berne Convention ("the Convention") is concerned, RTE had submitted before the Court of First Instance that Article 9(1) thereof conferred an exclusive right of reproduction and that Article 9(2) allowed a signatory State to permit reproduction only in certain special cases, provided that such reproduction did not conflict with normal exploitation of the work and did not unreasonably prejudice the legitimate interests of the author. From this RTE deduced that Article 2 of the contested decision was incompatible with the Convention inasmuch as it conflicted with the normal exploitation of RTE's copyright in the programme listings and seriously prejudiced its legitimate interests (*RTE* judgment, paragraph 100).

. . .

83. It is appropriate to observe at the outset, as the Court of First Instance did, that the Community is not a party to the Convention for the Protection of Literary and Artistic Works.

. . .

86. The Court of First Instance was therefore correct to hold that Article 9 of the Convention cannot be relied on to limit the powers of the Community, as provided for in

the EEC Treaty, since the Treaty can be amended only in accordance with the procedure laid down in Article 236.

87. It follows that the plea that the Court of First Instance failed to have proper regard to the Convention must be dismissed as unfounded.

. . .

104. It follows that the appeals must be dismissed in their entirety.

## NOTES AND QUESTIONS

**1.** While the Court does not mention the essential facilities doctrine, it implicitly recognized the public function of TV advertising and the need for a comprehensive guide being in the public interest and practices preventing the publication of such a guide to amount to an abuse of copyright law. The case at the time gave rise to much discussion as to the scope of the essential facilities doctrine in Europe; criticism of a potentially expansive application led to a more restrictive concept in *Oskar Bronner GmbH & Co v. Mediaprint Zeitung- und Zeitschriftenverlag GmbH*, C-7/97, 26 Nov. 1998.

**2.** The relationship of competition law and intellectual property was discussed earlier in *Volvo v. Veng*, Case C-238/87, 5 Oct. 1988 (design rights) and subsequently in *IMS Health GmbH v. NDC Health GmbH & Co*, Case-418/01, 29 Apr. 2004 (copyright).

**3.** In *Microsoft v. Commission*, C-T-201/04, 17 Sept. 2007, the Court of First Instance (today the General Court) extensively dealt with the interface of copyright in software and the abuse of a dominant position and the treatment of private de facto industry standards in competition law; see Chapter 4, section VI.C, pp. 713-714.

**4.** How do you assess the impact of these decisions for other forms of intellectual property rights, in particular the field of patents? Does it affect regulations of industry standards or access to essential medicines, or influence the framing of private public partnerships?

**5.** Do you see a need to take up competition law again at the WTO in light of strong intellectual property standards in the TRIPS Agreement and TRIPS-plus in Preferential and Regional Trade Agreements? What are the pros and cons of doing so, from the point of view of industrialized and developing countries?

**6.** Note that competition law is limited to ex post controls and subject to expensive procedures and litigation. It makes a significant contribution to embed intellectual property in economic law, but we cannot dispense with finding an appropriate balance with the IP system itself.

We reiterate the importance to distinguish competition law and policy (antitrust) in domestic or regional law from the protection of unfair competition under Article 10*bis* of the Paris Convention. These disciplines have barely been applied and discovered in the field of intellectual property. The following excerpts argue that unfair competition has considerable potential for the protection of traditional knowledge and for the enforcement of, and compliance with, standards of corporate social responsibility.

# III. TRADITIONAL KNOWLEDGE IN THE INTERNATIONAL INTELLECTUAL PROPERTY SYSTEM

## A. Claims and Efforts to Bringing About Protection

Globalization, scientific progress, and new concepts in research and development have widened the access to new fields of knowledge allotted in societies all over the world. Traditional knowledge, gathered, developed, and passed on over generations in indigenous communities, has gradually been discovered as a vast source of know-how for public and private investment. The understanding of nature, terrain, and species behavior in certain areas has proven essential for environmental planning and engineering. Knowledge about plants and their use in farming and health is of great interest to agricultural and pharmaceutical providers.[1]

However, the trade-off between public interest in accessibility of knowledge and the protection of investment in its creation is particularly apparent in the domain of TK. The philosophical foundation of IP protection—the adequate remuneration for intellectual effort and investment—is controversial in the context of the commercial use of TK. The nature of TK, often preserved and passed on in tribal, intergenerational, and sometimes secret processes, triggers several questions: How can TK be acquired without interfering with customs and self-determination of its holders, and how can a system of fair and equitable sharing of benefits derived from that knowledge be created? How can the issue of biopiracy be addressed, and when is TK considered to be in the public domain and hence hindering patentability of inventions?

Traditional knowledge, a good mainly available in developing countries, plays an important role in the assessment of the legitimacy of the international IP system. The interface of TK, IP, and other frameworks like the Convention on Biological Diversity (CBD) and International Convention for the Protection of New Varieties of Plants (UPOV) produced an intense debate in various fora including discussions about the integration of concepts like prior informed consent (PIC), equitable benefit sharing (EBS as framed by Article 8(j) CBD), and disclosure of sources into the international IP system. While some voice doubts about the need for specific legal treatment of TK,[2] others consider the creation of a *sui generis* system an adequate means for the equitable treatment of traditional knowledge.

---

## *Intellectual Property and Genetic Resources, Traditional Knowledge and Traditional Cultural Expressions*

World Intellectual Property Organization (2020)

### What are Traditional Knowledge, Traditional Cultural Expressions and Genetic Resources?

#### Traditional knowledge

The term "traditional knowledge" or its abbreviation "TK" is sometimes used as shorthand for the entire field of TK and TCEs. However, nowadays, WIPO most often distinguishes between TK and TCEs, because, from an IP standpoint, a different set of policy questions arises and distinct legal tools are likely to apply for their protection.

TK is a living body of knowledge that is developed, sustained and passed on from generation to generation within a community, often forming part of its cultural or spiritual identity. In a few words, TK is understood as:

- knowledge, know-how, skills, innovations or practices;
- that are passed between generations;
- in a traditional context; and

1. *See* WIPO, Intellectual Property and Traditional Knowledge (WIPO Publication 920(E)), p. 5.

2. *See* Stephen R. Munzer & Kal Raustiala, *The Uneasy Case for Intellectual Property Rights in Traditional Knowledge*, 27 Cardozo Arts & Ent. L.J. 37-97 (2009).

- that form part of the traditional lifestyle of indigenous and local communities who act as their guardian or custodian.

TK can be, for example, agricultural, environmental or medicinal knowledge, or knowledge associated with GRs. Examples include, among thousands of others:

- knowledge about traditional medicines;
- traditional hunting or fishing techniques;
- knowledge about animal migration patterns or water management. . .

### Who are the Holders of Traditional Knowledge and Traditional Cultural Expressions?

One central issue in the debate over the protection of TK and TCEs is the identity of their owners, bearers or custodians. It is generally agreed that protection should principally benefit TK/TCEs holders, in particular the indigenous peoples and local communities that develop, maintain and identify culturally with them and seek to pass them on between generations. TK/TCEs are generally regarded as collectively originated and held, so that any rights and interests in this material should vest in communities rather than in individuals, including in cases where TK/ TCEs are developed by an individual member of a community. In some instances though, beneficiaries may also include recognized individuals within the communities, such as certain traditional healers or individual farmers working within the community. Typically, this recognition arises through customary understandings, protocols, laws or practices. It could be that more than one community qualifies for protection of their TK/TCEs, including communities which share the same or similar TK/TCEs in different countries.

### What Does "Protection" Mean?

Protection of traditional knowledge and traditional cultural expressions

"Protection" can mean different things, depending on the context in which the term is used, but WIPO is concerned with a very specific understanding of the term: the use of IP tools and principles to prevent unauthorized or inappropriate uses of TK/TCEs by third parties. Put differently, the form of protection being developed at WIPO is the application of IP law, values and principles to prevent misuse, misappropriation, copying, adaptation or other kind of illicit exploitation. The objective, in short, is to make sure that the intellectual innovation and creativity embodied in TK or TCEs are not wrongly used. IP protection can entail recognizing and exercising exclusive rights, i.e., excluding others from carrying out certain acts. IP protection can also include non-proprietary forms of protection like moral rights, equitable compensation schemes and protection against unfair competition. . . .

### Two Approaches to Intellectual Property Protection

The IP system can be approached from two different angles to ensure protection of TK and TCEs. These two approaches—generally referred to as "positive" and "defensive" protection—can be undertaken together in a complementary way.

Under a first approach—"positive protection"—the IP system is designed to enable holders, if they so wish, to acquire and assert IP rights in their TK and TCEs. This can allow them to prevent unwanted, unauthorized or inappropriate uses by third parties (including culturally offensive or demeaning use) and/or to exploit TK/ TCEs commercially, for example through the granting of licenses, as a contribution to their economic development. In brief, positive protection is the granting of rights that empower communities to promote their TK/TCEs, control their uses by third parties and benefit from their commercial exploitation.

A second approach—"defensive protection"—is designed to prevent the illegitimate acquisition or maintaining of IP rights by third parties. Stated otherwise, defensive protection aims to stop people outside the community from acquiring IP rights over TK and TCEs. India, for example, has compiled a searchable database of traditional medical knowledge that can be used as evidence of prior art by patent examiners when assessing patent applications. Defensive strategies might also be used to protect sacred cultural manifestations, such as sacred symbols or words, from being registered as trademarks.

In short, a range of IP tools can be used to protect TK and TCEs. For their holders, positive protection means making use of these tools for their own purposes. Defensive protection, in contrast, means preventing anyone else from having access to these tools, when it would go against the interests of TK and TCE holders.

**Wend Wendland, Director, Traditional Knowledge Division, WIPO and Secretary of the WIPO Intergovernmental Committee (IGC)**

## *Is an International Agreement on IP, Genetic Resources and Associated Traditional Knowledge Finally in Sight?*

WIPO Magazine, February 2023

In a dramatic development July 2022, WIPO member states decided to fast-track negotiations on genetic resources and associated traditional knowledge by convening a Diplomatic Conference to conclude an international agreement on these matters no later than 2024. This step-change development, welcomed by many countries, is also revitalizing discussions on traditional knowledge more broadly and traditional cultural expressions/expressions of folklore. These exciting developments come after many years of intensive negotiations and mounting concerns about how they would evolve.

A Diplomatic Conference is a high-level meeting, where representatives of member countries come together to finalise and adopt an international treaty or convention. Countries and regional organizations that sign up to the treaty would then integrate its provisions into their national laws.

Successful conclusion of a diplomatic conference would bring to a close a long, complex, and often frustrating negotiation and would launch a new phase of work at WIPO on these issues. The ups and downs of these negotiations, spanning more than two decades, are outlined in a WIPO Magazine article published in February 2022. That article expands on the political, legal, regulatory and economic benefits of such an agreement and the broader work of the WIPO Intergovernmental Committee (IGC), in which the negotiations are taking place.

### How the Prospect of a Diplomatic Conference Came into Sight

At the 2022 session of WIPO's annual General Assembly (GA), member states took a decision to convene two diplomatic conferences; one on genetic resources and associated traditional knowledge and one on a design law treaty to harmonize the formalities associated with acquiring design rights. The decision resulted from discussions on a proposal by the African Group of countries. However, game-changing developments in relation to the handling of matters at the GA 2022, played a significant role in enabling the decision to be taken by consensus, as outlined below.

### Unpacking the GA's Decision

The IGC, which works on IP issues surrounding traditional knowledge, traditional cultural expressions and genetic resources, had met in June 2022, under its 2022-2023 mandate and work program. As required by the GA 2021, it submitted a factual report with recommendations to the GA 2022.

The report provided details of two IGC sessions held earlier in 2022 on genetic resources in which negotiations had stalled on the IGC's principal negotiating text, a draft Consolidated Document Relating to Intellectual Property and Genetic Resources. Many (although not all) members favoured the text of an international legal instrument prepared by a former chair of the IGC, Ian Goss, under his own responsibility, the so-called Chair's Text, as the basis of future work.

The expectation, at GA 2022, was that the IGC's report would simply be noted with support expressed for the Committee's continued work. Instead, the GA convened the diplomatic conference and stated that the Chair's Text would serve as the basis for that negotiation.

Two countries formally disassociated themselves from the decision. A few others expressed their misgivings, but decided not to block the consensus.

A game-changing development in GA 2022 played a significant role in enabling the decision to be taken "by consensus." While discussing another agenda item, member states had opted to vote, instead of relying on the traditional practice of consensual decision-making. Moving forward, exercising the option to vote may affect intergovernmental decision-making at WIPO on a range of issues. . . .

On the substance of the negotiation itself, the IGC will meet in a Special Session ahead of the preparatory committee, from September 4 to 8, 2023, to "further close any existing gaps to a sufficient level." These meetings will take place at WIPO's headquarters in Geneva, Switzerland, and will be open to accredited observers in line with established practice.

The GA 2022 decided that the Chair's Text referred to above will constitute the substantive articles of the "basic proposal". The basic proposal is the draft text to be considered by the Diplomatic Conference. However, the preparatory committee will also incorporate into that text "such further agreements of the IGC as are reached [. . .] with the understanding that any Member State and the Special Delegation of the European Union may make proposals at the Diplomatic Conference.". . .

## The High-Level Policy Conundrum

Modern life sciences research, including through the use of genetic resources and traditional knowledge, offers humanity great benefits. However, many countries have been concerned that patents are granted for inventions that are based on genetic resources and their associated traditional knowledge, but that do not fulfill patentability requirements, such as novelty, inventiveness or industrial applicability. The granting of such "erroneous patents", it is argued, facilitates the misappropriation of genetic resources and their associated traditional knowledge. This is referred to colloquially as "biopiracy."

How then can the patent system help scientists, businesses and public sector research institutions realize the immense benefits of scientific research while simultaneously protecting the interests of biodiversity-rich countries, Indigenous Peoples, local communities and the broader scientific community?

## What's up for Negotiation?

Many argue that a new disclosure requirement in patent law would help to achieve this balance. But what is the scope and, indeed, the rationale for such a new requirement? And what are the arguments against it?

Transparency through the disclosure of a description of inventions is a defining feature of the patent system. Under current patent law, in order to obtain patent protection for any invention, it is necessary, among other things, to disclose sufficiently detailed technical information about it. From society's viewpoint, such disclosure is critical to promote scientific and technological progress and further innovation. This is one of the primary justifications for the patent system.

The proposal at the heart of the upcoming diplomatic conference is that applicants seeking patents for inventions that are based on genetic resources and associated traditional knowledge should include certain additional information, as part of the patent application. This includes information about the source or origin of the genetic resources and associated traditional knowledge.

At present, such information does not normally need to be disclosed in a patent application, as it is generally not relevant to determining the patentability of an invention.

### Arguments in Favor of an Additional Disclosure Requirement

Proponents argue that an additional disclosure requirement would increase legal certainty, transparency and efficiency within the patent system. For example, it would, help patent examiners identify relevant prior art and thereby reduce the risk of granting patent rights for inventions that do not meet the requirements of novelty and inventive step.

They also argue that such a disclosure obligation will make it possible to monitor the contribution of genetic resources and associated traditional knowledge to patentable inventions. Since some countries have legislation which requires prior informed consent and benefit-sharing arrangements to be agreed before accessing a resource and related knowledge, it will help ensure that such knowledge and resources are used with the permission of the countries and/or communities from which they originate, enabling them to benefit in some way from the resulting inventions.

They argue that new disclosure obligations may prevent misappropriation and promote the fair and equitable sharing of benefits between users and providers of genetic resources and associated traditional knowledge. Holders include biodiversity-rich countries and Indigenous Peoples and local communities, while users are those with the modern technologies to exploit the scientific and commercial potential of these resources.

At present, more than 30 countries, including a mix of developing and developed countries, have adopted, or are in the process of adopting, some form of this kind of additional disclosure requirement in their national laws. The WIPO publication entitled Key Questions on Patent Disclosure Requirements for Genetic Resources and Traditional Knowledge examines and compares these national provisions.

### What the Opponents are Saying

Opposing views, however, claim that such a new disclosure obligation would impede innovation, with inventors turning increasingly to secrecy to protect their innovations. They claim it would create uncertainty for patent applicants, investors and the R&D sector and would be burdensome, expensive and time-consuming for patent applicants and patent offices to implement. They also argue that the patent system is not designed to implement objectives or goals external to the IP system (such as ABS objectives). Those opposing new disclosure requirements advocate for the greater use of databases – see below.

### What the Chair's Text Says

The Chair's Text proposes that such a disclosure requirement should form a mandatory part of patent law. Why? To enhance the efficacy, transparency and quality of the patent system, and prevent patents from being granted erroneously for inventions that are not novel or inventive with regard to genetic resources and associated traditional knowledge.

The Chair's Text sets out the proposed content of the requirement, as well as its subject matter scope, exceptions and limitations, temporal and geographic/spatial scope, sanctions for non-compliance, relationship with other instruments and other matters. An informal summary of the Chair's Text sums up the main provisions.

The Chair's Text also proposes that databases of information about genetic resources and traditional knowledge should be established and made accessible to patent examiners to reduce the risk of patents being granted erroneously. Databases are another tool that some argue can help to address the high-level policy conundrum identified earlier. . . .

### A Final Word

The decision by GA 2022 to accelerate negotiations on genetic resources and associated traditional knowledge is a step-change in the work of the IGC. The decision itself, while dramatic, is procedural throat-clearing – much substantive work lies ahead. Born of understandable frustration with the slow progress made in the IGC over the years, this unanticipated jolt has brought into sight the exciting possibility of bringing these long-standing negotiations to a successful conclusion.

## B. Traditional Knowledge and Unfair Competition

**Thomas Cottier & Ana Jevtic***

### *The Protection Against Unfair Competition in WTO Law: Status, Potential And Prospects*

### III Emerging Fields of Protection Against unfair Competition in Wto Law

Much of WTO law is dedicated to securing fair conditions of competition for foreign products, both goods and services. The basic principles of non-discrimination, most-favoured-nation (MFN) and national treatment, much as transparency, the disciplines on subsidies and on dumping, as well as the restraints imposed on trade remedies, protect legitimate expectations as to conditions of competition. The same is true for intellectual property protection. A wide variety of specialized norms assume such a function, and recourse to Article 10*bis* of the Paris Convention has been made so far. It is relevant, however, in areas still lacking specific rules or in which non-violation complaints cannot bring about relief from trade distortions induced by measures formally outside the scope of positive WTO law. . . .

#### The Protection of Traditional Knowledge

Motives for providing protection to traditional knowledge (TK) are diverse and imply both legal and moral aspects. [See further information on protection of TK and relevant case law below.] TK has been widely recognized as a valuable source of information essential to the achievement of sustainable development. . . .

The protection of traditional knowledge has been one of the major issues of intellectual property reform in the WTO. No explicit reference and recognition is given in the TRIPS Agreement, and the subject was established as a matter requiring further work and negotiations

* Technology and Competition: Contributions in Honour of Hanns Ullrich 669-95 (Josef Drexl ed., 2009).

in the Doha Development Agenda of 2001. The mandate was introduced in response to the demand of countries with high biodiversity seeking to obtain a better balance of returns on bio-prospecting and recourse to modern biotechnology. It was meant to supplement mechanisms of benefit sharing under the contractual and uneven system of the Convention on Biodiversity. Negotiations so far have focused on amending patent rules relating to disclosure of sources. No agreement has so far been reached. This is even more the case for protecting TK on the basis of a *sui generis* system of intellectual property protection. Negotiations are scheduled to continue, and it is evident that all further progress on protecting innovation in genetic engineering will depend upon a solution to the problem of protecting TK.

The issue of TK is very challenging, and the establishment of a proper system of *sui generis* protection based upon traditional intellectual property rights (TIP-Rights) will take some time. . . .

Given the difficulties and complexity of the matter, recourse to Article 10*bis* of the Paris Convention currently offers the most promising avenue to address inherent problems of misappropriation and free-riding in the use of genetic materials in combination with TK. The broad concept of unfair competition, the need to assess it on a case by case basis, taking into account the context, allows experience to be gained in this field on the basis of positive law. The process may eventually support negotiations and the emergence of a *sui generis* system.

Unfair competition protection as a basis for TK protection has been particularly supported with the acknowledgement of operational legal principles by the WIPO Secretariat, whereby prohibition of unfair competition and thus protection against misappropriation is particularly emphasized. The paper contains a comprehensive list of acts of misappropriation that any applicable system of protection should be able to suppress.

Indeed, core concerns of TK protection essentially boil down to the act of misappropriation of TK and free-riding on it. Misappropriation includes any act of acquisition or appropriation of TK by unfair or illicit means. One of the most widespread examples of misappropriation of TK is related to the wrongful granting of patents covering TK. They occur in relation to either the definition of prior art which is constructed in such a way as not to recognize information available to the public through use or oral traditions outside their domestic jurisdictions; or in connection with the absence or inadequacy of the information available to patent examiners. A patent applicant may thus be conferred a monopoly right to exploit a product based on a biological resource or related TK which actually is in the public domain. It is illustrative to cite the *Enola bean* case in which the patent owner was using its exclusive right to ban the sale of imported beans with similar characteristics to the one described in the patent. Four problems may be highlighted:

a) the lack of evidence that any of the similar beans actually had the same characteristics as the actual patented *invention*, as a consequence of the broadly established claims of the patent;
b) that in the basis of the patent was a traditional way of cultivation which cannot be described as novel;
c) that no benefit sharing was organized with the original holders of this knowledge, although they themselves were no longer allowed to use it without authorization of the new patent holder in countries where the new patent holder had obtained patent protection;
d) that producers of exporting countries were prevented from trading with traditionally produced beans.

In another example, the *Hoodia* case, the patent was obtained over the plant named hoodia, which possesses ingredients with appetite-suppressing characteristics. Such plants, before a patent was claimed, were used by indigenous people, known as Khomani or San, as an appetite suppressant to help them to survive while hunting in the desert. The patent was obtained by a South African governmental institution (the South African Council for Scientific and Industrial Research—CSIR) and was meant to be developed as Africa's first best-seller drug. However, no discussion with the Khomani people, as the custodians of the knowledge, on the use of the hoodia plant had taken place prior to the patent application. It was only after being criticized by NGOs and domestic organizations that the CSIR entered into the benefit sharing agreement on the exploitation of the drug with the holders of the knowledge.

This type of situation can best be assessed under the doctrine of misappropriation under Article 10*bis* of the Paris Convention. It can be looked at on a case-by-case basis, without requiring prior registration of rights. It is available as long as the particular circumstances that trigger the protection continue to exist. It offers a basis to challenge use and effectiveness of intellectual property titles which were obtained without taking into account the legitimate interests of the stewards and custodians of TK. The remedy offered will entail a ban on commercialization of the product concerned. In doing so, it offers a strong incentive to take these interests into account prior to commercialization and to seek negotiated settlements of permission to use TK and to bring about effective benefit sharing.

The approach based upon unfair competition and misappropriation is the more important as it has been recognized and adopted in domestic law, in particular that of developed countries mainly benefiting from intellectual property protection and modern technology. Although an explicit prohibition can be found only in the Swiss law (Article 5 of the Swiss Unfair Competition Act prohibiting the unfair imitation of articles reflecting certain distinguished qualities), other jurisdictions have also broadly developed this doctrine. Importantly, Swiss law considers a pure imitation as the act of unfair competition as such. Under US law, actionable misappropriation will occur under certain conditions:

a) the claimant offers a distinctive product which has a certain value;
b) the defendant is free riding by copying the product in that he engages in direct competition;
c) which as a consequence has the impact either to the detriment of the claimant's actual or potential market or to the confusion as to the origin of the product.

Although we find here the possibility of claiming misappropriation in case of detrimental impact even on a *potential* market, or—importantly to our subject—in case of confusion as to the origin of the product; a direct competitive relationship seems nonetheless to be required.

A similar approach to that of the US has been adopted in German jurisprudence, taking into account the damage the claimant may suffer. A designation of commercial originality can be given here if the article can be attributed individuality or uniqueness. According to UK regulations, in the situation in which the infringer engages in direct competition, copying is to be considered unfair.

WTO law and dispute settlement offers the foundations to assess whether domestic regulations as applied to issues of TK comply with the standards set out in Article 10*bis* of the Paris Convention. We recall that even though the provision clearly emphasizes three examples (confusion, discrediting and misleading the public), it does not limit the protection to the listed acts of unfair behaviour. Instead, Article 10*bis* provides fertile ground for condemning *any* act of competition that is contrary to honest practices in industrial and commercial matters. Although it does not especially address acts of misappropriation, a flexible definition of unfairness in this provision allows taking misappropriation acts into account in further shaping and framing the concept of "dishonest business practice" in the context of a particular case.

Considering that the WTO Agreements are unambiguous on the issue that the international legal system prevails over national legislations, WTO Members are obliged to ensure the conformity of their laws, regulations and administrative procedures with the obligations set out in WTO Agreements. WTO Members could therefore bring a case before the Dispute Settlement Body against any Member whose unfair competition legislature is not in line with Article 10*bis*, either because the Member has not provided any protection against unfair competition at all, or if its regulations on unfair competition do not give full effect to the principle established in Article 10*bis*. When Members do maintain regulations against unfair competition, the Panel or Appellate Body will indeed have to assess whether national legislations afford comparable protection against unfair competition to that set forth in Article 10*bis* of the Paris Convention. It should be kept in mind that WTO Members do not have the obligation to provide uniform protection against unfair competition. As a consequence of a broad definition of Article 10*bis* on the basis of which many Members developed their unfair competition law, it is reasonable to expect different regulations in this area as well as different treatment of unfairness. However, irrespective of this fact, Members are compelled to have at least an equivalent level of protection securing fairness for TK holders.

## C. Traditional Knowledge in the Patent System

In recent years, holders of TK have started to oppose patents containing their knowledge: The widely discussed cases of Turmeric (U.S. Patent No. 5401504) and Neem (European Patent No. 436257) involved patents that were challenged, reexamined, and annulled by the patent offices that had granted them. In both cases, evidence was put forward by the opponents that both Turmeric and Neem were used in traditional farming and agriculture for centuries, thus hindering the novelty and inventive step of the granted patents. In the Hoodia case, the EPO came to a different conclusion in the assessment of the impact of TK on patentability.

**Kari Moyer-Henry, Ph.D.***

### *Patenting Neem and Hoodia: Conflicting Decisions Issued by the Opposition Board of the European Patent Office*

#### The Hoodia Plant

#### Background

Hoodia gordonii (Hoodia) is a cactus that was used by the San People of South Africa for generations as an appetite suppressant during times of famine, low food supply, or long nomadic hunting trips. As the San remain a partially nomadic people today, Hoodia was likely used to allow them to make it on their long desert journeys with little to no supplies. South Africa's national laboratory began investigating the science behind the appetite-suppressing nature of Hoodia as part of a study of indigenous foods. In 1963, the Council for Scientific and Industrial Research (CSIR) isolated a chemical they called P57 as the active ingredient responsible for appetite suppression.

The CSIR in South Africa was established in 1945 by an act of Parliament and is the leading scientific and technology, research and development, and implementation organization in Africa. The purpose of CSIR is to engage in directed and multidisciplinary research and technological innovation, as well as industrial and scientific development to improve the quality of life of African people. But perhaps the primary goal of the organization is to improve the

* 27 Biotechnology Law Report 1-10 (2008), available at http://www.liebertonline.com/doi/abs/10.1089/blr.2008.9991.

national competitiveness of South Africa in the global economy. Approximately 40% of the CSIR's annual income is provided by a grant from Parliament, with additional income being provided by royalties, licenses and dividends from an intellectual property portfolio and commercial companies created by the CSIR.

### The Patent

The controversy involving Hoodia was largely twofold. The subject matter of the patent application was problematic for the EPO examiner. The Examining Division initially found that the subject matter lacked an inventive step because the traditional knowledge of the San people provided enough information to lead a person skilled in the art to use Hoodia extract as an appetite suppressant. The CSIR appealed the rejection of the patent. They argued, using prior art to demonstrate, that the traditional use of Hoodia plant parts by the San people did not disclose that "an extract from . . . Hoodia could be used [for] manufacture of a medicament" for use as an appetite suppressant.

Ultimately, the Appeal Board concluded "a skilled person, knowing that consumption of parts of a fibrous, water-storing plant of the genus Trichocaulon very efficiently 'removed the pangs of hunger,' could not obviously derive from this disclosure that an extract from the plant could be used for the manufacture of an appetite-suppressant, anti-obesity medicament." With that conclusion, the subject matter included an inventive step and was therefore patentable. But this conclusion by the Board does not seem logical because even a person not skilled in the art of the invention could make the obvious connection that extracts from a plant consumed by an ancient people to stave off hunger could be used to combat obesity by piggy-backing on the appetite suppressant effects of ingesting certain plant components. Obviously, a person eating less because he/she doesn't feel hungry can lose weight. Despite this obvious lack of a true inventive step, the CSIR overcame the obstacle at the EPO, but they were not out of the woods completely.

### The Real Controversy

The government-funded CSIR patented its discovery of P57 without communicating with the San or crediting them with the discovery of Hoodia. The CSIR then licensed use of P57 to Phytopharm, a British pharmaceutical research company. Subsequently, Phytopharm subleased the rights to P57 to Pfizer. In addition, poor public relations on the part of CSIR scientists contributed to the start of the San's opposition to the Hoodia patent. When asked how the traditional knowledge of the San aided their research of Hoodia, the scientists incorrectly stated that the San people were extinct. This errant statement, combined with the previous poor treatment of the San by CSIR, caused the South African San Council to file suit against the CSIR and its licensees.

The San first learned of the patent through a Phytopharm press release. The San felt exploited by CSIR because they had provided the national laboratory with the knowledge necessary to further their research. The San people expected the laboratory to act as advocates for them in furthering their rights and benefits in return for the information they provided to CSIR that ultimately advanced research.

### The Outcome

When accused of biopiracy by the San, CSIR and Phytopharm did the only thing they could do to protect their investments. The government offered a settlement to the San for use of their knowledge. Beginning in March 2003, San in four countries—South Africa, Botswana, Namibia and Angola—were guaranteed at least four payments of $30,000 during clinical testing of Hoodia. In addition, Pfizer agreed to profit sharing with the San at a rate of 6% of the royalties received on the market. Subsequently, when the Hoodia patent was granted in 2006, there was no opposition filed with the EPO. Once the Hoodia patent was granted, it provided the CSIR with protection in an array of member countries. . . . The family of patents totals 76 members derived from 58 applications to provide an expansive range of protection for the invention.

## Mixed Messages

### Can the Contradictory Decisions by the Epo be Reconciled?

The treatment of the Hoodia patent by the EPO was in response to the mistakes made during the handling of the neem patent. The Examining Division was proceeding cautiously in its handling of another patent application based on traditional knowledge. In regard to the neem patent, some opponents accused the EPO of merely skimming over the references to traditional knowledge in the Grace application. The opponents felt a closer examination of the Indian traditional knowledge in the application would have led the Examining Division to reject the application initially for lack of inventive step, thereby avoiding the subsequent 10-year battle to invalidate the patent. Thus, the Hoodia patent was originally denied by the Examining Division "for lack of inventive step (Art. 56 EPC) in view of the traditional knowledge of the San people."

Still, there remains a simpler explanation for the outcome of these two patent applications. The response of the Indian people and the San people to the use of their respective traditional knowledge played a tremendous role in the final outcome of each controversy. The Indian government in particular attacked the neem patent with vigor . . . . It is clear that the opposition to the Grace patent was not going to stop fighting until the neem patent was defeated. In contrast, the San have largely embraced their place in the history of biotechnology, and with the signing of the licensing agreement, the San have renewed faith. The San see the commercialization of Hoodia and their part in it as a way to guarantee that the modern world recognizes the wealth to be found in the San's ancient knowledge. For a society struggling against extinction, "at least one tradition in their dying culture might be saved.". . .

The San people never filed any opposition to the granted Hoodia patent because it would only do them greater harm to do so. Under the agreement, the San people have a financial interest in the promotion of their plant and their culture. The San people are an example of how many indigenous communities could benefit from the revenue generated by profit-sharing agreements. Although it may not be the most equal division of profits for the San, the agreement still provides a significant means for them to take control over their future and plan the health and well-being of their community. Alternatively, the Indian people saw the Grace patent as another attempt to exploit their resources and steal their culture from them. Even though they were promised that the neem patent was not being sought in India, they were not willing to compromise with big industry over something they felt belonged to them entirely. Therefore, the Hoodia patent could have easily ended up revoked, just as the neem patent was, if the San people had reacted to the situation as the Indian government did.

### Policy Implications

The EPO's decision to reject the neem patent was a strategic one. The Opposition Board had not agreed with the opponents and their argument that the patent constituted a "de facto monopoly on a single plant variety" or that it was a violation of "public order and morality." On the other hand, they accepted the opponents' argument that patents should not be granted for common traditional knowledge, but pointed out that this argument should be used for establishing "prior art" and is not a question of morality in the sense of the European

Patent Convention. This distinction was crucial for maintaining the proper role of the EPO. Rather than base their decision on standards not well defined, specifically morality, and certain to be insufficient depending on the time and societal values applied, the Board framed the decision around the long established requirement for an inventive step. In doing so, the Board set a precedent for recognizing traditional knowledge as prior art.

India has altered its policy on traditional knowledge in response to the argument that the traditional knowledge of Indian farmers does not qualify as prior art because it could not be found in printed publications prior to the filing date of the application. India has been translating ancient texts containing traditional remedies into electronic form. The sole purpose of making such records available to patent offices in English, German, French, Japanese, and Spanish is to prevent further exploitation of Indian tradition by foreign industry.

As early as 1999, Indian legislature began working to amend the Patent Act to expressly provide patent protection to indigenous peoples. Similarly, in 2000, the World Intellectual Property Organization (WIPO) General Assembly created the Intergovernmental Committee on Intellectual Property and Genetic Resources, Traditional Knowledge and Folklore (IGC) to "progress towards a shared international understanding of how best to protect TK and TCEs against misappropriation and misuse." Just last month, the member states of WIPO reaffirmed their commitment "to forging ahead with efforts to reach international consensus on the protection of traditional knowledge, genetic resources and folklore." The goal of these initiatives is to move close to stronger legal recognition of and protection for traditional knowledge in order to strengthen the rights of the member countries domestically while protecting the interest of each internationally.

The contradictory decisions by the EPO regarding the validity of the neem and Hoodia patents were based ultimately on the determination of whether the subject matter of each patent included an inventive step. However, the evidence presented by the EPO in support of their decisions does not actually fit the conclusions. Specifically, the Grace patent that was clearly based on an inventive step beyond the knowledge held by the Indian farmers was denied for lack of inventive step. The Appeals Board decided it would be easier to base their decision on the lack of inventive step rather than the more controversial, and perhaps more accurate, reason of morality that was so strongly advocated by the opponents to the patent. In regard to the Hoodia patent, the conclusion by the Appeals Board that there was an inventive step coincided with the decision by the San people to sign a licensing agreement for the use of their traditional knowledge. These seemingly unsupported decisions by the EPO result in the creation of an equally weak and unjust patent policy. The patent policy of the EPO should be fair to all applicants, not just those who can avoid opposition filings, as the CSIR and Phytopharm were able to. But until there are guidelines in place that clearly address the issue of traditional knowledge as prior art and the right of indigenous peoples to protect their traditional knowledge, the patent policy will remain unjust.

### Biotechnology Implications

There needs to be a consensus about what can and cannot be patented. Currently, no such agreement exists. As a result, pharmaceutical companies feel forced to go to extraordinary lengths to gain protection for their products. Companies are filing broader patent applications in greater numbers. The EPO is suffering from a backlog of applications waiting for examination. According to Sjoerd Hoestra, director of a biotechnology department at the EPO, "[more than] 60 percent of applications are [rejected]; they are not worth [patenting because of] a lack of balance between disclosure and invention."

The need for clear regulations on biotechnology goes well beyond the EPO. An international solution is required if there is ever going to be harmony between the biotechnology industry and the patent offices. The industry will suffer and decline if there is no guarantee that the high expenditures on research costs and decades of development will be recouped. In turn, the suffering will reach the public because companies will put less capital into research and development for fear that they will never be able to recover the cost.

## D. The Quest for Sui Generis Rights

**Thomas Cottier & Marion Panizzon***

### *Legal Perspectives on Traditional Knowledge: The Case for Intellectual Property Protection*

#### II A Proposal for Traditional IP Rights in Traditional Knowledge

#### A. Subject Matter and Beneficiaries of the Rights

#### 1. Subject Matter

This study suggests a . . . general term—Traditional Intellectual Property Rights ("TIP Rights")—that is left deliberately open to encompass new and changing forms of traditional knowledge. TIP rights express the concept of a *sui generis* private law entitlement vested in communities which covers data and information about plant genetic resources for food and agriculture (PGRFA) and medicinal plants. The concept encompasses methods of use and includes the seed that embodies a given community's traditional knowledge. . . .

#### 2. Rights Holders

We believe that a TIP right should be inclusive, rather than exclusive, with respect to prospective beneficiaries of protection. It should encompass the spectrum of all relevant persons touched by such a law, ranging from individuals to communities, from associations to cooperatives. Given the strong intergenerational component of TK, it will be difficult to identify a single holder. Because TK is often held by families and even lineages, TIP rights should partake of a communitarian nature. . . .

That the TIP right as such is reserved for a collective entity hardly presents a new phenomenon in IP law. Consider, for example, that even a modem patent law deals more with teams of inventors than single persons, and "most intellectual property assets are owned by collective entities, which in many cases represent large and diffuse groups of individuals."

. . . Given that different communities [in different regions of the world] might assert parallel rights to the same traditional knowledge, cooperative efforts in assigning or transferring such knowledge to firms for industrial application would be in their mutual interests. Also beneficial might be agreements setting prices for such purposes, short of collusion running afoul of antitrust laws. In this regard, states participating in the proposed IP regime would need to adopt appropriate exceptions for collective administration of TIP rights, so as to avoid pitting different communities against one another in ways that would drive down the prices paid for their traditional knowledge. It would undermine a primary goal of establishing such rights if antitrust laws would deny traditional communities an exceptional use of monopolistic market power.

* *Legal Perspective on Traditional Knowledge: The Case for Intellectual Property Protection*, 7 J. Int'l Economic Law 371 (2004).

### B. The Content and Scope of Rights

. . . The scope of protection may range from fully developed property rights to a limited entitlement focusing on compensation without entailing powers to prevent others from using materials for commercial purposes. However, it should be clear that TIP rights only extend to commercial activities undertaken by public or private entities. The very rationale for such rights is to introduce a new level of economic benefits that alters the balance of power between those who possess traditional knowledge and commercial actors who seek to exploit and build upon such knowledge with a view to marketing new products.

In keeping with general principles of intellectual property law, activities partaking of private use should not be covered. Nothing therefore would bar individuals from using TK generated by others for private purposes short of engaging in commercial activities.

A difficult question arises from the need to compensate holders of rights in TK adequately when a TK component is claimed as part of a "combination patent" in jurisdictions that recognize such patents. Here the object is to prevent would-be patentees from avoiding the need to license the traditional knowledge or otherwise to compensate its holders simply because they filed for a combination patent. Similarly, policy makers must decide whether to allow potential licensees to test their products and obtain market approval prior to obtaining the consent of the right holders.

Where the TK is associated with a biological resource, as when it pertains to the effects of medicinal plants or the specific quality of a crop, the TIP right must necessarily encompass certain uses one can elicit of that plant. An open question is whether the genetic information encapsulated within the plant (or seed) should be eligible for any form of IP protection. The communities have usually neither identified the genetic sequences making up the seed nor have they matched the function of any given seed to a certain strand of the genetic code, and for contemporary international treaty law, genetic information falls under the research exemption.

. . . Logically, the poorest developing countries would prefer a strong exclusive property right in TK, unencumbered by research exceptions that required all users to be licensed. Users, especially those in developed countries, may prefer to limit the right to compensation or to adopt the compensatory liability regime (CLR) proposed by Professor Reichman.

Between an exclusive right and a clear entitlement to compensatory liability lies the possibility of adopting a misappropriation regime. Such a regime, as suggested by Professor Correa among others, seems consistent with a broader unfair competition approach, which others have proposed. The African Group within the Council for TRIPS endorsed the misappropriation approach in 2003. An approach rooted in unfair competition can benefit from Article 10*bis* of the Paris Convention for the Protection of Industrial Property. Just as undisclosed information has been protected on this basis by Article 39 of the TRIPS Agreement, which established a new IPR category in international law, so it can be argued that to use information and knowledge generated by others and expressed in a specific product is unfair to the extent that it serves to facilitate copies or a derived product without the consent of the creator.

All of these proposals need to be carefully evaluated in light of their potential impact on the free flow of genetic material envisaged by the FAO's International Treaty and their human rights implications.

### C. The Duration of Rights

IPRs that stimulate innovation and creation are generally limited in time. After a period in which innovators reap their rewards, innovation enters the public domain of human knowledge and becomes freely available. With TIP rights, the process is reversed. Traditional knowledge that resides in the public domain without being privatized by law becomes, as of a particular date, subject to an intellectual property right owned by an individual or a community.

Active use of TK should constitute the required limit of protection. Rights to TK should only arise so long as the process or information exists within, and is being used by, a particular community. Once it fades into the past, it is no longer of commercial interest to the community and should no longer be granted protection.

When the use of active TK is protected, however, the period of liability for specific uses will have to be determined by law. Regardless of whether an exclusive rights regime or a compensatory liability regime is adopted, the question arises as to how long the licensee must remain liable to the licensor. The problem here is that a new product will often only be placed on the market after a number of years of research and testing, and the amount of equitable sharing of benefits cannot be properly defined during the first years of licensing.

One solution would be to differentiate the licensing fees according to a menu of options, with one charge for a period of R&D, and additional compensation to become due once the product reaches the market. Such compensation would then be limited for a certain period of time sufficient to generate adequate profit sharing. At some point, e.g. after 10 years, the duty to compensate would cease and the use of TK by that licensee would no longer trigger a duty to remunerate the right holder.

We stress that the TIP rights in traditional knowledge as such should not lapse and would again become operational if the TK were used by another economic operator or for different purposes. At this point, the process of licensing or compensatory liability would revive and additional revenues would be generated. In effect, one could envisage that TK protection could last indefinitely, so long as active use is made of the relevant information, and this solution would be consonant with the intergenerational and incremental nature of traditional knowledge.

## D. The Creation and Registration of Rights

### 1. Registration Requirements

Costly registration procedures can be avoided by linking the registration process to existing and updated inventories of knowledge. In addition to a registration requirement for TK holders, industries interested in using TK could be obliged to disclose the origin of the genetic resources in question.

This requirement, in turn, would help to foster the creation of TK inventories.

However, according to de Carvalho, a disclosure requirement seems incompatible with the TRIPS Agreement. . . .

Registration of the right itself can be either declaratory or constitutive. A declaratory registration might have the advantage that it could strengthen the claims of traditional communities against infringement prior to the vesting of a formal legal title. An examination would presuppose the creation of a core of examiners specialized in the IP rights of indigenous people.

The problem of finding the resources to apply for adequate protection and/or enforcement of a TIP right in TK is aggravated by the manner in which knowledge has often been unsystematically transmitted from one generation to another. Ideally, these rights should be registered at the international level by an international organization, in cooperation with national agencies and NGOs. Information technology facilitates linking different sources and building a coherent system. Registered information about TK and its uses should be made publicly available, as in patent law.

An optimal solution aimed at reducing registration costs must invest a TIP right with a built in "presumption of protection" in traditional knowledge. Any user of TK would labor under a burden to disclose the origin of biological or genetic resources and to establish that he had obtained prior informed consent to their use, unless these resources were otherwise demonstrably free of claims by indigenous people or in the public domain. Such disclosure and prior informed consent requirements have not yet been included in international patent treaties. Yet, conditioning the grant of a patent on such a requirement would successfully link the objectives of the CBD access and benefit-sharing system to that of IPRs protection.

. . .

### CONCLUSIONS

We contend that IP protection for traditional knowledge must be shaped by an international agreement specifically designed for this purpose. Neither the national sovereignty approach of the CBD nor the public goods approach of the FAO's International Treaty is alone sufficient effectively to empower communities whose TK has enabled them to identify, collect, develop, and conserve plant genetic resources for food and agriculture.

We, therefore, propose the creation of a traditional intellectual property right (TIP right), the scope of which will need to be more fully defined, but which at least should entail a right to compensatory liability. We support the requirements of prior informed consent and disclosure of origin as a precondition to patent applications. At the same time, we stress that existing IPRs and TIP rights are not mutually exclusive. Quite the opposite, they all need to be made part of an overall package of measures to support viable agricultural structures in developing countries. In particular, stronger protection of geographical indications of origin would further enhance the potential to develop local and international niche markets for products based on traditional knowledge.

If action is taken at the international level to implement IPRs for traditional knowledge along the lines we envision, the end results should become part of the global trading system and thus of WTO law. We maintain that it is only the WTO, which combines global trade rules with worldwide IP protection that can ensure better market access and conditions for commercially valuable assets resulting from a TK-related production process.

In an age of globalization, monetary value creates power, and trade transcends borders. Those whose traditional knowledge acquires value in identifiable plant genetic resources for food and agriculture and in the corresponding seed will not become "players" in the global market place unless these assets attract tradable IPRs. International disputes arising from the exercise of these rights should be resolved within the existing dispute settlement framework, and trade-related enforcement mechanisms should ensure that treaty rights are fully implemented. The Least Developed Countries would particularly benefit from such an arrangement, and it would thus help to rebalance the social costs of the TRIPS Agreement.

## NOTES AND QUESTIONS

**1.** The prevention of "erroneously granted patents" is one of the measures a *sui generis* system for TK has to provide for. Other major fields of work are the disclosure of origin and source of information used in patent claims and the provision of evidence of benefit sharing and prior informed consent in patent applications. What other measures, apart from intervention in the application process of patents, would you consider suitable to enforce the rights of TK holders?

**2.** Patents are one form of IP that is affected by the protection of TK. Considering other fields of economic activity, for example, the tourism and souvenir industry, what other interfaces of IP and TK can you think of?

**3.** As discussed above, some countries are encouraging the documentation of TK at least for the defensive purpose of preventing misappropriation by patent applicants unrelated to the TK community. Regarding documentation of traditional medical knowledge, *see generally* Ryan Abbott, *Documenting Traditional Medical Knowledge*, World Intellectual Property Organization (2014), available at SSRN: http://ssrn.com/abstract= 2406649.

**4.** As noted by WIPO, "The WIPO Intergovernmental Committee on Intellectual Property and Genetic Resources, Traditional Knowledge and Folklore (IGC) undertakes text-based negotiations to finalize an agreement on an international legal instrument(s) for the protection of traditional knowledge (TK), traditional cultural expressions (TCEs) and genetic resources (GRs)." (https://www.wipo.int/tk/en/igc/). On July 21, 2022, the WIPO General Assembly decided to convene a Diplomatic Conference to conclude an International Legal Instrument Relating to Intellectual Property, Genetic Resources and Traditional Knowledge Associated with Genetic Resources no later than 2024. The General Assembly 2022 decided that the text of an international legal instrument prepared by a former chair of the IGC, Ian Goss, under his own responsibility (the so-called "Chair's Text") will constitute the substantive articles of the "basic proposal." The basic proposal is the draft text to be considered by the Diplomatic Conference. The Chair's Text and further information regarding the Diplomatic Conference on Intellectual Property and Genetic Resources is available at https://www.wipo.int/diplomatic-conferences/en/genetic-resources /index.html (visited July 12, 2023).

**5.** The protection of traditional knowledge is also envisaged by international environmental law. Fair and equitable sharing of the benefits arising out of the utilization of genetic resources is one of the three objectives of the Convention on Biological Diversity. As an international agreement, it aims at sharing the benefits arising from the utilization of genetic resources in a fair and equitable manner, including by appropriate access to genetic resources and by appropriate transfer of relevant technologies, taking into account all rights over those resources and to technologies, and by appropriate funding, thereby contributing to the conservation of biological diversity and the sustainable use of its components.

**6.** The Nagoya Protocol on Access to Genetic Resources and the Fair and Equitable Sharing of Benefits Arising from their Utilization to the Convention on Biological Diversity was adopted by the Conference of the Parties to the Convention on Biological Diversity at its tenth meeting on October 29, 2010 in Nagoya, Japan. The Nagoya Protocol entered into force on October 12, 2014, which is 90 days after the date of deposit of the fiftieth instrument of ratification in accordance with Article 33.

**7.** The Nagoya Protocol addresses the "traditional knowledge associated with genetic resources" several times. In accordance with Article 3 this Protocol also applies to traditional knowledge associated with genetic resources within the scope of the Convention and to the benefits arising from the utilization of such knowledge.

**8.** Discuss to what extent the implementation of the Convention on Biological Diversity and the Nagoya Protocol essentially depend upon the formulation of *sui generis* TIP Rights, and to what extent implementation can be achieved without the support of unfair competition rules and new disciplines of intellectual property.

In the next section, we examine additional specific subject matter areas of intellectual property protection. For each of these areas, there is generally a combination of protective schemes available, and approaches to protection vary among countries. Nonetheless, there are multilateral rules addressing each of these subject matter areas and related forms of protection.

# IV. THE INTERNATIONAL SYSTEM FOR THE PROTECTION OF PLANT VARIETIES

## A. Introduction

Plant varieties play an enormously important role in human affairs.[3] Success or failure in producing foodstuffs is a life or death matter for large parts of the world's population. For many nations, agriculture is the dominant field of economic activity. Even in nations where agriculture is a less significant component of economic activity, there remains intense interest in maintaining farm communities and promoting food security. Disputes concerning agricultural subsidies remain at the heart of the World Trade Organization agenda. Although the protection afforded to plant varieties as a matter of intellectual property law does not receive the level of public attention accorded to pharmaceutical patents or copyrights in music, the direction of public interest should not obscure the fundamental importance of intellectual property rights in plant varieties.

Innovation in the field of agriculture has been important to human civilization since farmers first began to cultivate crops. Increasing crop yields has long been a goal of agricultural research and development (R&D). Two recent trends in agricultural R&D are rather important to understanding ongoing debates concerning the scope of plant variety protection. The first is the biotechnology revolution brought about by advances in genetic engineering. New technologies make possible comparatively rapid development of new plant varieties with yield and disease-resistance characteristics that might substantially relieve pressures on the world food supply. Of course, concerns about the effects of genetically modified organisms (GMOs) on human health and the environment are the subject of intense public discussion, and these concerns directly and indirectly influence the IP dialogue. This is one important illustration of the general point that IP is often closely interlinked with social questions, and that IP issues must be considered in their social context.

The second recent trend is a pronounced shift in agricultural R&D from public sector institutions to the private sector. The shift toward privately funded R&D has enhanced business interest in expanding the scope of plant variety protection. Yet, farmers throughout much of the world operate with limited capital resources. For them, the introduction of better though more expensive plant varieties may be a mixed blessing. Without access to new plant varieties, the marginal farmer may be replaced by large-scale agribusiness. The social consequences could be rather dramatic.[4] Plant variety protection therefore is often combined with so-called farmer's rights or privilege allowing use of genetic resources without IP-owner consent, though in some cases subject to financial compensation.

## B. Plant Variety Protection as an IP Form

Plant varieties are protected by patent and by *sui generis* registration systems. In each case, there are various approaches followed by different countries. Plant varieties may be protected by more than one form of IP.

---

3. *See, e.g.*, Geoff Tansey, *Trade, Intellectual Property, Food and Biodiversity[:] A Discussion Paper*, Quaker Peace and Service, London (1999).

4. The protection of plant varieties has long been controversial at the international level. A major part of agricultural research and development historically has been financed and/or undertaken by public authorities, and the results of this research have often been made freely available. There has been reluctance to apply IPRs-related limitations to the fruits of public research, and there has been some worry that private sector dominance of the agricultural research area would have adverse consequences, particularly in developing countries.

The United States today allows the protection of plant varieties by utility patent, plant patent, and *sui generis* plant variety protection. The availability of all three forms of protection for the same plant variety was recognized by the U.S. Supreme Court in *J.E.M. AG Supply v. Pioneer Hi-Bred*, decided in 2001. The decision provides a useful introduction to the different forms of protection.

## *J.E.M. AG Supply v. Pioneer Hi-Bred*
534 U.S. 124 (2001)

Justice Thomas delivered the opinion of the Court.

This case presents the question whether utility patents may be issued for plants under 35 U.S.C. §101 (1994 ed.), or whether the Plant Variety Protection Act, 84 Stat. 1542, as amended, 7 U.S.C. §2321 et seq., and the Plant Patent Act of 1930, 35 U.S.C. §§161-164 (1994 ed. and Supp. V), are the exclusive means of obtaining a federal statutory right to exclude others from reproducing, selling, or using plants or plant varieties. We hold that utility patents may be issued for plants. . . .

Several years after *Chakrabarty*, the PTO Board of Patent Appeals and Interferences held that plants were within the understood meaning of "manufacture" or "composition of matter" and therefore were within the subject matter of §101. *Ex parte Hibberd*, 227 U.S.P.Q. (BNA) 443, 444 (1985). It has been the unbroken practice of the PTO since that time to confer utility patents for plants. To obtain utility patent protection, a plant breeder must show that the plant he has developed is new, useful, and non-obvious. 35 U.S.C. §§101-103 (1994 ed. and Supp. V). In addition, the plant must meet the specifications of §112, which require a written description of the plant and a deposit of seed that is publicly accessible. *See* 37 CFR §§1.801-1.809 (2001).

Petitioners do not allege that Pioneer's patents are invalid for failure to meet the requirements for a utility patent. Nor do they dispute that plants otherwise fall within the terms of §101's broad language that includes "manufacture" or "composition of matter." Rather, petitioners argue that the PPA and the PVPA provide the exclusive means of protecting new varieties of plants, and so awarding utility patents for plants upsets the scheme contemplated by Congress. . . . We disagree. Considering the two plant specific statutes in turn, we find that neither forecloses utility patent coverage for plants.

### II

The 1930 PPA conferred patent protection to asexually reproduced plants. Significantly, nothing within either the original 1930 text of the statute or its recodified version in 1952 indicates that the PPA's protection for asexually reproduced plants was intended to be exclusive.

Plants were first explicitly brought within the scope of patent protection in 1930 when the PPA included "plants" among the useful things subject to patents. . . .

This provision limited protection to the asexual reproduction of the plant. Asexual reproduction occurs by grafting, budding, or the like, and produces an offspring with a genetic combination identical to that of the single parent — essentially a clone.[9] The PPA also amended Revised Statutes §4888 by adding, "No plant patent shall be declared invalid on the

9. By contrast, sexual reproduction occurs by seed and sometimes involves two different plants.

ground of noncompliance with this section if the description is made as complete as is reasonably possible." Id., §2, 46 Stat. 376.

In 1952, Congress revised the patent statute and placed the plant patents into a separate chapter 15 of Title 35 entitled, "Patents for plants." 35 U.S.C. §§161-164.[10] This was merely a housekeeping measure that did nothing to change the substantive rights or requirements for a plant patent. A "plant patent"[11] continued to provide only the exclusive right to asexually reproduce a protected plant, §163, and the description requirement remained relaxed, §162.[12] Plant patents under the PPA thus have very limited coverage and less stringent requirements than §101 utility patents.

Importantly, chapter 15 nowhere states that plant patents are the exclusive means of granting intellectual property protection to plants. . . .

. . . [I]n 1930 Congress believed that plants were not patentable under §101, both because they were living things and because in practice they could not meet the stringent description requirement. Yet these premises were disproved over time. As this Court held in *Chakrabarty*, "the relevant distinction" for purposes of §101 is not "between living and inanimate things, but between products of nature, whether living or not, and human-made inventions." 447 U.S. at 313. In addition, advances in biological knowledge and breeding expertise have allowed plant breeders to satisfy §101's demanding description requirement.

Whatever Congress may have believed about the state of patent law and the science of plant breeding in 1930, plants have always had the potential to fall within the general subject matter of §101, which is a dynamic provision designed to encompass new and unforeseen inventions. "A rule that unanticipated inventions are without protection would conflict with the core concept of the patent law that anticipation undermines patentability." *Id.*, at 316.

Petitioners essentially ask us to deny utility patent protection for sexually reproduced plants because it was unforeseen in 1930 that such plants could receive protection under §101. Denying patent protection under §101 simply because such coverage was thought technologically infeasible in 1930, however, would be inconsistent with the forward-looking perspective of the utility patent statute. As we noted in *Chakrabarty*, "Congress employed broad general language in drafting §101 precisely because [new types of] inventions are often unforeseeable." *Ibid.* . . .

### B

By passing the PVPA in 1970, Congress specifically authorized limited patent-like protection for certain sexually reproduced plants. Petitioners therefore argue that this legislation evidences Congress' intent to deny broader §101 utility patent protection for such plants. Petitioners' argument, however, is unavailing for two reasons. First, nowhere does the PVPA purport to provide the exclusive statutory means of protecting sexually reproduced plants. Second, the PVPA and §101 can easily be reconciled. Because it is harder to qualify for a

10. The PPA, as amended, provides: "Whoever invents or discovers and asexually reproduces any distinct and new variety of plant, including cultivated sports, mutants, hybrids, and newly found seedlings, other than a tuber propagated plant or a plant found in an uncultivated state, may obtain a patent therefor, subject to the conditions and requirements of this title." 35 U.S.C. §161.

11. Patents issued under §161 are referred to as "plant patents," which are distinguished from §101 utility patents and §171 design patents.

12. To obtain a plant patent under §161 a breeder must meet all of the requirements for §101, except for the description requirement. *See* §162 ("No plant patent shall be declared invalid for noncompliance with section 112 [providing for written description] of this title if the description is as complete as is reasonably possible").

utility patent than for a Plant Variety Protection (PVP) certificate, it only makes sense that utility patents would confer a greater scope of protection.

1

The PVPA provides plant variety protection for:

> "The breeder of any sexually reproduced or tuber propagated plant variety (other than fungi or bacteria) who has so reproduced the variety. . . ." 7 U.S.C. §2402(a).

Infringement of plant variety protection occurs, inter alia, if someone sells or markets the protected variety, sexually multiplies the variety as a step in marketing, uses the variety in producing a hybrid, or dispenses the variety without notice that the variety is protected.

Since the 1994 amendments, the PVPA also protects "any variety that is essentially derived from a protected variety," §2541(c)(1), and "any variety whose production requires the repeated use of a protected variety," §2541(c)(3). *See* Plant Variety Protection Act Amendments of 1994, §9, 108 Stat. 3142. Practically, this means that hybrids created from protected plant varieties are also protected; however, it is not infringement to use a protected variety for the development of a hybrid. *See* 7 U.S.C. §2541(a)(4).[11]

The PVPA also contains exemptions for saving seed and for research. A farmer who legally purchases and plants a protected variety can save the seed from these plants for replanting on his own farm. *See* §2543 ("It shall not infringe any right hereunder for a person to save seed produced by the person from seed obtained, or descended from seed obtained, by authority of the owner of the variety for seeding purposes and use such saved seed in the production of a crop for use on the farm of the person . . ."); *see also Asgrow Seed Co. v. Winterboer*, 513 U.S. 179, 130 L. Ed. 2d 682, 115 S. Ct. 788 (1995). In addition, a protected variety may be used for research. *See* 7 U.S.C. §2544 ("The use and reproduction of a protected variety for plant breeding or other bona fide research shall not constitute an infringement of the protection provided under this chapter"). The utility patent statute does not contain similar exemptions.[12]

Thus, while the PVPA creates a statutory scheme that is comprehensive with respect to its particular protections and subject matter, giving limited protection to plant varieties that are new, distinct, uniform, and stable, §2402(a), nowhere does it restrict the scope of patentable subject matter under §101. With nothing in the statute to bolster their view that the PVPA provides the exclusive means for protecting sexually reproducing plants, petitioners rely on the legislative history of the PVPA. They argue that this history shows the PVPA was enacted because sexually reproducing plant varieties and their seeds were not and had never been intended by Congress to be included within the classes of things patentable under Title 35.

The PVPA itself, however, contains no statement that plant variety certificates were to be the exclusive means of protecting sexually reproducing plants. The relevant statements in the legislative history reveal nothing more than the limited view of plant breeding taken by some Members of Congress who believed that patent protection was unavailable for sexually reproduced plants. This view stems from a lack of awareness concerning scientific possibilities.

11. It is, however, infringement of a utility patent to use a protected plant in the development of another variety. . . .

12. The dissent argues that our "reading would destroy" the PVPA's exemptions. . . . Yet such bold predictions are belied by the facts. According to the Government, over 5,000 PVP certificates have been issued, as compared to about 1,800 utility patents for plants. Since 1985 the PTO has interpreted §101 to include utility patents for plants and there is no evidence that the availability of such patents has rendered the PVPA and its specific exemptions obsolete.

Furthermore, at the time the PVPA was enacted, the PTO had already issued numerous utility patents for hybrid plant processes. Many of these patents, especially since the 1950's, included claims on the products of the patented process, i.e., the hybrid plant itself. *See* Kloppenburg 264. Such plants were protected as part of a hybrid process and not on their own. Nonetheless, these hybrids still enjoyed protection under §101, which reaffirms that such material was within the scope of §101.

2 . . .

To be sure, there are differences in the requirements for, and coverage of, utility patents and plant variety certificates issued pursuant to the PVPA. . . .

It is much more difficult to obtain a utility patent for a plant than to obtain a plant variety certificate because a utility patentable plant must be new, useful, and nonobvious, 35 U.S.C. §§101-103. In addition, to obtain a utility patent, a breeder must describe the plant with sufficient specificity to enable others to "make and use" the invention after the patent term expires. §112. The disclosure required by the Patent Act is "the quid pro quo of the right to exclude." *Kewanee Oil Co. v. Bicron Corp.*, 416 U.S. 470, 484, 40 L. Ed. 2d 315, 94 S. Ct. 1879 (1974). The description requirement for plants includes a deposit of biological material, for example seeds, and mandates that such material be accessible to the public. *See* 37 CFR §§1.801-1.809 (2001); *see also* App. 39 (seed deposits for U.S. Patent No. 5,491,295).

By contrast, a plant variety may receive a PVP certificate without a showing of usefulness or nonobviousness. *See* 7 U.S.C. §2402(a) (requiring that the variety be only new, distinct, uniform, and stable). Nor does the PVPA require a description and disclosure as extensive as those required under §101. The PVPA requires a "description of the variety setting forth its distinctiveness, uniformity and stability and a description of the genealogy and breeding procedure, when known." 7 U.S.C. §2422(2). It also requires a deposit of seed in a public depository, §2422(4), but neither the statute nor the applicable regulation mandates that such material be accessible to the general public during the term of the PVP certificate. *See* 7 CFR §97.6 (2001).

Because of the more stringent requirements, utility patent holders receive greater rights of exclusion than holders of a PVP certificate. Most notably, there are no exemptions for research or saving seed under a utility patent. Additionally, although Congress increased the level of protection under the PVPA in 1994, a plant variety certificate still does not grant the full range of protections afforded by a utility patent. . . .

## III

We also note that the PTO has assigned utility patents for plants for at least 16 years and there has been no indication from either Congress or agencies with expertise that such coverage is inconsistent with the PVPA or the PPA. The Board of Patent Appeals and Interferences, which has specific expertise in issues of patent law, relied heavily on this Court's decision in *Chakrabarty* when it interpreted the subject matter of §101 to include plants. *In re Hibberd*, 227 U.S.P.Q. (BNA) 443 (1985). This highly visible decision has led to the issuance of some 1,800 utility patents for plants. Moreover, the PTO, which administers §101 as well as the PPA, recognizes and regularly issues utility patents for plants. In addition, the Department of Agriculture's Plant Variety Protection Office acknowledges the existence of utility patents for plants.

In the face of these developments, Congress has not only failed to pass legislation indicating that it disagrees with the PTO's interpretation of §101, it has even recognized the availability of utility patents for plants. In a 1999 amendment to 35 U.S.C. §119, which concerns the right of priority for patent rights, Congress provided: "Applications for plant breeder's rights filed in a WTO [World Trade Organization] member country . . . shall have the same effect for the purpose of the right of priority . . . as applications for patents, subject to the same conditions and requirements of this section as apply to applications for patents." 35 U.S.C. §119(f) (1994 ed., Supp. V). Crucially, §119(f) is part of the general provisions of Title 35, not the specific chapter of the PPA, which suggests a recognition on the part of Congress that plants are patentable under §101.

### IV

For these reasons, we hold that newly developed plant breeds fall within the terms of §101, and that neither the PPA nor the PVPA limits the scope of §101's coverage. As in *Chakrabarty*, we decline to narrow the reach of §101 where Congress has given us no indication that it intends this result. 447 U.S. at 315-316. Accordingly, we affirm the judgment of the Court of Appeals.

Justice BREYER, with whom Justice STEVENS joins, dissenting.

The question before us is whether the words "manufacture" or "compositions of matter" contained in the utility patent statute, 35 U.S.C. §101 (1994 ed.) (Utility Patent Statute), cover plants that also fall within the scope of two more specific statutes, the Plant Patent Act of 1930 (PPA), 35 U.S.C. §161 et seq. (1994 ed. and Supp. V), and the Plant Variety Protection Act (PVPA), 7 U.S.C. §2321 et seq. I believe that the words "manufacture" or "composition of matter" do not cover these plants. That is because Congress intended the two more specific statutes to exclude patent protection under the Utility Patent Statute for the plants to which the more specific Acts directly refer. And, as the Court implicitly recognizes, this Court neither considered, nor decided, this question in *Diamond v. Chakrabarty*, 447 U.S. 303, 65 L. Ed. 2d 144, 100 S. Ct. 2204 (1980). Consequently, I dissent. . . .

## NOTES AND QUESTIONS

**1.** As the Supreme Court observes, a key difference between the exclusive rights accorded the utility or plant patent holder, and the holder of a plant breeder's certificate, is that the former allows the holder to prevent farmers from replanting seeds. From the standpoint of both seed vendors and farmers, there is clearly a material financial difference depending upon which form of protection is employed. Yet, patents are not a panacea for seed vendors because bringing enforcement actions against individual farmers is expensive and time-consuming, and requires monitoring of individual farmer practices. For this reason, biotechnology enterprises have sought to develop so-called terminator genes, which will physically prevent seeds generated by plants embodying the technology from reproducing. The development and employment of terminator gene technology has been highly controversial because of concerns that the genetic characteristics may inadvertently spread and result in a proliferation of non-reproducing plants.

## C. Farmer's Privilege

### *Saatgut Treuhandverwaltungs GmbH v. Gerhard Und Jürgen Vogel GbR*

Judgment of The Court (Second Chamber), 25 June 2015

(Reference for a preliminary ruling — Community plant variety rights –Regulation (EC) No 2100/94 — Derogation provided for in Article 14 –Use by farmers of the product of the harvest for propagating purposes without the holder's authorisation — Farmers under an obligation to pay equitable remuneration for such use — Period within which that remuneration must be paid in order to be able to benefit from the derogation — Whether it is possible for the holder to have recourse to Article 94 — Infringement)

In Case C242/14,

REQUEST for a preliminary ruling under Article 267 TFEU from the Landgericht Mannheim (Germany), made by decision of 9 May 2014, received at the Court on 19 May 2014, in the proceedings

SaatgutTreuhandverwaltungs GmbH

v.

Gerhard und Jürgen Vogel GbR,

Jürgen Vogel,
Gerhard Vogel,
THE COURT (Second Chamber),
composed of R. Silva de Lapuerta, President of the Chamber, J.-C. Bonichot, A. Arabadjiev, J.L. da Cruz Vilaça and C. Lycourgos (Rapporteur), Judges,
Advocate General: N. Jääskinen,

. . .

#### Judgment

1. This request for a preliminary ruling concerns the interpretation of certain provisions of Council Regulation (EC) No 2100/94 of 27 July 1994 on Community plant variety rights (OJ 1994 L 227, p. 1) and Commission Regulation (EC) No 1768/95 of 24 July 1995 implementing rules on the agricultural exemption provided for in Article 14(3) of Regulation No 2100/94 (OJ 1995 L 173, p. 14).

2. The request has been made in proceedings between Saatgut-Treuhandverwaltungs GmbH ('STV'), which represents the interests of the holder of Community plant variety rights in respect of the winter barley variety 'Finita', and Gerhard und Jürgen Vogel GbR, an agricultural company, Mr G. Vogel and Mr J. Vogel, the personally liable partners in that company (together, 'the Vogels') concerning the Vogels' planting of that variety.

#### Legal Context

##### Regulation No 2100/94

. . .

4. Article 14 of Regulation No 2100/94, entitled 'Derogation from Community plant variety right', is worded as follows:

1. Notwithstanding Article 13(2), and for the purposes of safeguarding agricultural production, farmers are authorised to use for propagating purposes in the field, on their own holding, the product of the harvest which they have obtained by planting, on their own holding, propagating material of a variety other than a hybrid or synthetic variety, which is covered by a Community plant variety right.

2. The provisions of paragraph 1 shall only apply to agricultural plant species of:

. . .

(b) Cereals:

. . .

Hordeum vulgare L.— Barley

. . .

3. Conditions to give effect to the derogation provided for in paragraph 1 and to safeguard the legitimate interests of the breeder and of the farmer shall be established, before the entry into force of this Regulation, in implementing rules pursuant to Article 114, on the basis of the following criteria:

. . .

— small farmers shall not be required to pay any remuneration to the holder;

. . .

— other farmers shall be required to pay an equitable remuneration to the holder, which shall be sensibly lower than the amount charged for the licensed production of propagating material of the same variety in the same area; the actual level of this equitable remuneration may be subject to variation over time, taking into account the extent to which use will be made of the derogation provided for in paragraph 1 in respect of the variety concerned; . . .

— monitoring compliance with the provisions of this Article or the provisions adopted pursuant to this Article shall be a matter of exclusive responsibility of holders; in organising that monitoring, they may not provide for assistance from official bodies;

— relevant information shall be provided to the holders on their request by farmers and by suppliers of processing services; relevant information may equally be provided by official bodies involved in the monitoring of agricultural production, if such information has been obtained through ordinary performance of their tasks, without additional burden or costs. . . .

. . .

11. STV is an association of plant variety right holders that manages, inter alia, the rights of the holder of the winter barley variety 'Finita', which is protected under Regulation No 2100/94. STV publishes on its website a list setting out all the protected plant varieties the rights to the administration of which it has been granted in the course of various marketing years, as well as the planting fees payable for those varieties. Moreover, each year STV asks farmers, without specifying a particular variety, to provide information on any planting of protected plant varieties for which STV administers the rights, sending to them planting declaration forms for that purpose, together with a guide listing all the protected varieties for which it administers the rights in the relevant marketing year and the corresponding right holders and persons enjoying rights of exploitation. The Vogels, which do not have any contractual relations with STV, did not respond to those requests for information.

12. On 16 December 2011, STV became aware, through a processor, that in the marketing year 2010/11 the Vogels had, among other things, arranged for 35 quintals [1 quintal = 100 kg] of seed of the winter barley variety 'Finita' to be processed.

13. By letter of 31 May 2012, STV asked the Vogels to verify the information concerning the planting of the winter barley variety 'Finita' disclosed by that processor and to send it information concerning that planting, directing them to reply by 20 June 2012 at the latest. The Vogels did not reply to that reply.

14. By letter of 27 July 2012, STV claimed from the Vogels payment of EUR 262.50, corresponding to the full fee that would be due for licensed use of seeds of the winter barley variety 'Finita', known as the 'C-Licence', as compensation for the damage suffered as a result of the undisclosed planting of that protected variety. As no such payment was forthcoming, STV brought an action on 18 March 2013 seeking such compensation on the basis of Article 94(1) and (2) of Regulation No 2100/94.

15. In support of its action, STV argues that the Vogels are required to pay to it reasonable compensation in an amount equivalent to the full C-Licence fee, pursuant to Article 94(1) of Regulation No 2100/94, because they carried out planting 'without being entitled to do so' within the meaning of that provision, and were not entitled to avail themselves of the derogation provided for in Article 14(1) of the regulation as they had failed to comply with the requirement to pay equitable remuneration laid down in the fourth indent of Article 14(3) of that regulation. STV also claims that that payment requirement is enforceable irrespective of whether a request for information has been made by the holder of the protected plant variety concerned and that the farmer must make the payment prior to sowing and, in any event, by the end of the marketing year in which the protected variety was planted. STV is also of the view that the information published on its website and the guide listing all the protected varieties the rights to the management of which it has been granted, which is sent each year to farmers, enables the Vogels to calculate themselves, and therefore pay, the amount due for planting those varieties.

16. The Vogels claim that they are not liable for payment of an amount equivalent to the full C-Licence fee by way of compensation. They submit that they owe, at the most, a reduced fee, on the ground that the planting was 'authorised' within the meaning of Article 14(1) of Regulation No 2100/94. They also contend that they were not under any obligation to reply to the request for information of 31 May 2012, as that request did not relate to the current marketing year. According to the Vogels, there would have to be an infringement of the obligation to provide information in order for the conditions governing entitlement to compensation to be satisfied.

17. The referring court has expressed doubts concerning STV's claim that the farmer is required to pay, of his own initiative, the remuneration referred to in the fourth indent of Article 14(3) of Regulation No 2100/94 before sowing, in particular in the light of Article 6(1) of Regulation No 1768/95. It observes that the latter provision would appear to preclude the inference that the farmer is required to pay that remuneration in advance, before sowing. Furthermore, that court states that if that remuneration could be paid after planting the protected variety, the question then arises as to the date by which the farmer is required to pay that remuneration in order to be able to benefit from the derogation provided for in Article 14 of Regulation No 2100/94 and thus fall outside the infringement provisions laid down in Article 94 of the regulation. According to the referring court, the provisions of Regulation Nos 2100/94 and 1768/95 do not provide a clear and unambiguous answer to that question, which the Court has not had occasion to address.

18. In those circumstances, the Landgericht Mannheim decided to stay the proceedings and to refer the following questions to the Court for a preliminary ruling:

> '(1) Is a farmer who has planted propagating material obtained from a protected plant variety without having concluded a contract for so doing with the plant variety right holder required to pay reasonable compensation, as provided for in Article 94(1) of Regulation No 2100/94, and—if he has acted intentionally or negligently—to compensate the holder for any further damage resulting from the infringement of the plant variety right in accordance with Article 94(2) of that regulation, where he has not yet fulfilled his obligation under the fourth indent of Article 14(3) of that regulation, in conjunction with Articles 5 and 6 of Regulation No 1768/95, to pay an equitable remuneration (planting fee) at the time when he actually made use of the product of the harvest for propagating purposes in the field?

(2) If the first question is to be answered to the effect that the farmer can still fulfil his obligation to pay an equitable planting fee even after he has actually made use of the product of the harvest for propagating purposes in the field, are the aforementioned provisions to be interpreted as fixing a period within which a farmer who has planted propagating material obtained from a protected plant variety must fulfil his obligation to pay an equitable planting fee in order for the planting to be capable of being regarded as "authorised" for the purposes of Article 94(1) of Regulation No 2100/94 in conjunction with Article 14 of that regulation?'

### Consideration of the Questions Referred

19. By its questions, which it is appropriate to consider together, the referring court seeks to ascertain, in essence, the period within which a farmer who has planted propagating material obtained from a protected plant variety (farm-saved seed) without having concluded a contract for so doing with the holder of the plant variety right concerned must comply with the requirement to pay the equitable remuneration due under the fourth indent of Article 14(3) of Regulation No 2100/94 ('the equitable remuneration by way of derogation') in order to be able to benefit from the derogation from the obligation to obtain the holder's authorisation provided for in Article 14.

20. It should be noted, first, that Article 13(2) of Regulation No 2100/94 provides that the authorisation of the holder of the plant variety right is required, in respect of variety constituents or harvested material of the protected variety, inter alia, for production or reproduction (multiplication). In that context, Article 14(1) of that regulation establishes a derogation from that rule, insofar as use of the product of the harvest obtained by farmers, on their own holding, for propagating purposes in the field is not conditional upon authorisation by the holder of the right where they fulfil certain conditions expressly set out in Article 14(3) of that regulation (see judgment in *Geistbeck*, C509/10, EU:C:2012:416, paragraphs 21 and 22).

21. One of those conditions, set out in the fourth indent of Article 14(3) of Regulation No 2100/94, requires payment to be made, by way of derogation from the authorisation requirement, to the holder of the plant variety right concerned of equitable remuneration in respect of such use.

22. A farmer who does not pay equitable remuneration to the holder when he uses the product of the harvest obtained by planting propagating material of a protected variety cannot rely on Article 14(1) of Regulation No 2100/94 and, therefore, must be regarded as having undertaken, without being entitled to do so, one of the acts set out in Article 13(2) of that regulation. Accordingly, it follows from Article 94 of that regulation that an action may be brought against such a farmer by the holder for an injunction in respect of the infringement or for payment of fair compensation, or both. If the infringement is intentional or negligent, the farmer is also obliged to pay damages to make good the loss suffered by the holder (judgment in *Schulin*, C305/00, EU:C:2003:218, paragraph 71).

23. The referring court is uncertain, first, whether the farmer concerned must pay the equitable remuneration by way of derogation before actually using the product of the harvest for propagating purposes in the field.

24. In that regard, Article 6 of Regulation No 1768/95, which establishes the implementing rules in respect of the obligation to pay equitable remuneration by way of derogation, provides in the second subparagraph of paragraph 1 thereof that while the holder of the protected plant variety concerned may determine the date and manner of payment, he may not determine a date for payment which is earlier than the date on which the obligation to pay such equitable remuneration arose. In accordance with the first subparagraph of Article 6(1) of that regulation, that obligation arises when the farmer actually makes use of the product of the harvest of the protected variety for propagating purposes in the field. It follows that such a farmer may still fulfil that obligation after he has sown the product of the harvest of the protected variety, as that date of actual use of the product for propagating purposes in the field is

not the deadline by which payment of equitable remuneration by way of derogation must be made but the date from which that remuneration becomes payable.

25. While that provision makes it possible to assert that a farmer may still fulfil his obligation to pay equitable remuneration by way of derogation after he has actually sown the product of the harvest of the protected variety, there is no indication whatsoever in that provision of the period within which the farmer is required to pay that remuneration when no date for payment has been set, under the second subparagraph of Article 6(1) of Regulation No 1768/95, by the holder of the right to the protected variety.

26. In that regard, the Vogels and the Spanish Government maintain, in essence, that that period may run indefinitely. They rely specifically on Article 6(1) of Regulation No 1768/95, stating in that regard that, while that provision governs the date on which the payment obligation arises, it does not lay down any deadline for payment.

27. That interpretation cannot be accepted, however.

28. In the first place only by defining a payment period is it possible to ensure that such proceedings are effective.

29. In the second place, it should be recalled that the holders of plant variety rights alone are responsible for the control and supervision of the use of the protected varieties in the context of authorised planting and they depend, therefore, on the good faith and cooperation of the farmers concerned (judgment in *Geistbeck*, C509/10, EU:C:2012:416, paragraph 42). Accordingly, the absence of a precisely defined period within which farmers are required to comply with the obligation to pay equitable remuneration by way of derogation is liable to encourage farmers to defer that payment indefinitely, in the hope of avoiding payment altogether. To allow farmers to avoid complying with their own obligations towards holders in such a way would be at odds with the objective set out in Article 2 of Regulation No 1768/95 of maintaining a reasonable balance between the legitimate interests of the farmers and the holders concerned.

31. Thus, . . . if he has failed to pay the equitable remuneration by way of derogation within the period that expires at the end of the marketing year during which he planted propagating material obtained from a protected plant variety, without having concluded a contract for so doing with the plant right holder, a farmer must be regarded as having effected, without being entitled to do so, one of the acts set out in Article 13(2) of Regulation No 2100/94, which entitles the holder to bring the forms of action provided for in Article 94 of that regulation.

32. In the light of the foregoing considerations, the answer to the questions referred is that, in order to be able to benefit from the derogation provided for in Article 14 of Regulation No 2100/94 from the obligation to obtain the authorisation of the holder of the plant variety right concerned, a farmer who has planted propagating material obtained from a protected plant variety (farm-saved seed) without having concluded a contract for so doing with the holder, is required to pay the equitable remuneration by way of derogation within the period that expires at the end of the marketing year during which that planting took place, that is, no later than 30 June following the date of reseeding.

## D. Plant Patents and Exhaustion of Rights

The question how the rights of owners of patents on plants and the rights of farmers are to be defined is of obvious importance. A farmer purchases patented seeds for the purpose of planting and harvesting a commercially valuable crop. That crop may include "new" seeds created by natural processes (perhaps aided or altered by genetic intervention of the patent owner). The farmer is typically the owner of the crop and may control its sale. But, may the farmer plant the newly generated seeds to create another crop? Can the farmer use newly generated seeds to continuously expand the area of planting and cultivation? Can the farmer sell the seeds to third parties? The major agricultural patent owners like Monsanto attempt to impose answers on farmers through contracts or licenses associated with the purchase of seeds. Companies like Monsanto use these contracts because the answer as to whether and how the purchaser of a patented product that "self-regenerates" may take advantage of that property's inherent characteristics is not self-evident, though the Supreme Court of the United States apparently thinks it is, as expressed in *Bowman v. Monsanto.*

## *Bowman v. Monsanto*

569 U.S. 278 (2013)

KAGAN, J., delivered the opinion for a unanimous Court.

. . .

Under the doctrine of patent exhaustion, the authorized sale of a patented article gives the purchaser, or any subsequent owner, a right to use or resell that article. Such a sale, however, does not allow the purchaser to make new copies of the patented invention. The question in this case is whether a farmer who buys patented seeds may reproduce them through planting and harvesting without the patent holder's permission. We hold that he may not.

### I

Respondent Monsanto invented a genetic modification that enables soybean plants to survive exposure to glyphosate, the active ingredient in many herbicides (including Monsanto's own Roundup). Monsanto markets soybean seed containing this altered genetic material as Roundup Ready seed. Farmers planting that seed can use a glyphosate-based herbicide to kill weeds without damaging their crops. Two patents issued to Monsanto cover various aspects of its Roundup Ready technology, including a seed incorporating the genetic alteration. See Supp. App. SA1-21 (U.S. Patent Nos. 5,352,605 and RE39, 247E); see also 657 F.3d 1341, 1343-1344 (C.A. Fed. 2011).

Monsanto sells, and allows other companies to sell, Roundup Ready soybean seeds to growers who assent to a special licensing agreement. . . . That agreement permits a grower to plant the purchased seeds in one (and only one) season. He can then consume the resulting crop or sell it as a commodity, usually to a grain elevator or agricultural processor. See 657 F.3d, at 1344-1345. But under the agreement, the farmer may not save any of the harvested soybeans for replanting, nor may he supply them to anyone else for that purpose. These restrictions reflect the ease of producing new generations of Roundup Ready seed. Because glyphosate resistance comes from the seed's genetic material, that trait is passed on from the planted seed to the harvested soybeans: Indeed, a single Roundup Ready seed can grow a plant containing dozens of genetically identical beans, each of which, if replanted, can grow another such plant—and so on and so on. . . . The agreement's terms prevent the farmer from co-opting that process to produce his own Roundup Ready seeds, forcing him instead to buy from Monsanto each season.

Petitioner Vernon Bowman is a farmer in Indiana who, it is fair to say, appreciates Roundup Ready soybean seed. He purchased Roundup Ready each year, from a company affiliated with Monsanto, for his first crop of the season. In accord with the agreement just described, he used all of that seed for planting, and sold his entire crop to a grain elevator (which typically would resell it to an agricultural processor for human or animal consumption).

Bowman, however, devised a less orthodox approach for his second crop of each season. Because he thought such late-season planting "risky," he did not want to pay the premium price that Monsanto charges for Roundup Ready seed. . . . He therefore went to a grain elevator; purchased "commodity soybeans" intended for human or animal consumption; and planted them in his fields. Those soybeans came from prior harvests of other local farmers. And because most of those farmers also used Roundup Ready seed, Bowman could anticipate that many of the purchased soybeans would contain Monsanto's patented technology. When he applied a glyphosate-based herbicide to his fields, he confirmed that this was so; a significant proportion of the new plants survived the treatment, and produced in their turn a new crop of soybeans with the Roundup Ready trait. Bowman saved seed from that crop to use in his late-season planting the next year—and then the next, and the next, until he had harvested eight crops in that way. Each year, that is, he planted saved seed from the year before (sometimes adding more soybeans bought from the grain elevator), sprayed his fields with glyphosate to kill weeds (and any non-resistant plants), and produced a new crop of glyphosate-resistant—i.e., Roundup Ready—soybeans.

After discovering this practice, Monsanto sued Bowman for infringing its patents on Roundup Ready seed. Bowman raised patent exhaustion as a defense, arguing that Monsanto could not control his use of the soybeans because they were the subject of a prior authorized sale (from local farmers to the grain elevator). The District Court rejected that argument, and awarded damages to Monsanto of $84,456. The Federal Circuit affirmed. It reasoned that patent exhaustion did not protect Bowman because he had "created a newly infringing article." 657 F.3d, at 1348. The "right to use" a patented article following an authorized sale, the court explained, "does not include the right to construct an essentially new article on the template of the original, for the right to make the article remains with the patentee." *Ibid.* (brackets and internal quotation marks omitted). Accordingly, Bowman could not " 'replicate' Monsanto's patented technology by planting it in the ground to create newly infringing genetic material, seeds, and plants." *Ibid.*

We granted certiorari to consider the important question of patent law raised in this case, 568 U.S.____, 133 S. Ct. 420, 184 L. Ed.2d 251 (2012), and now affirm.

## II

The doctrine of patent exhaustion limits a patentee's right to control what others can do with an article embodying or containing an invention. Under the doctrine, "the initial authorized sale of a patented item terminates all patent rights to that item." *Quanta Computer, Inc. v. LG Electronics*, Inc., 553 U.S. 617, 625, 128 S. Ct. 2109, 170 L. Ed. 2d 996 (2008). And by "exhaust[ing] the [patentee's] monopoly" in that item, the sale confers on the purchaser, or any subsequent owner, "the right to use [or] sell" the thing as he sees fit. *United States v. Univis Lens Co.*, 316 U.S. 241, 249-250, 62 S. Ct. 1088, 86 L. Ed. 1408 (1942). We have explained the basis for the doctrine as follows: "[T]he purpose of the patent law is fulfilled with respect to any particular article when the patentee has received his reward . . . by the sale of the article"; once that "purpose is realized the patent law affords no basis for restraining the use and enjoyment of the thing sold." Id., at 251, 62 S. Ct. 1088.

Consistent with that rationale, the doctrine restricts a patentee's rights only as to the "particular article" sold, ibid.; it leaves untouched the patentee's ability to prevent a buyer from making new copies of the patented item. "[T]he purchaser of the [patented] machine . . . does not acquire any right to construct another machine either for his own use or to be vended to another." *Mitchell v. Hawley*, 16 Wall. 544, 548, 21 L. Ed. 322 (1873); see *Wilbur-Ellis Co. v. Kuther*, 377 U.S. 422, 424, 84 S. Ct. 1561, 12 L. Ed. 2d 419 (1964) (holding that a purchaser's "reconstruction" of a patented machine "would impinge on the patentee's right 'to exclude others from making' . . . the article" (quoting 35 U.S.C. §154 (1964 ed.))). Rather, "a second creation" of the patented item "call[s] the monopoly, conferred by the patent grant, into play for a second time." *Aro Mfg. Co. v. Convertible Top Replacement Co.*, 365 U.S. 336, 346, 81 S. Ct. 599, 5 L. Ed. 2d 592 (1961). That is because the patent holder has "received his reward" only for the actual article sold, and not for subsequent recreations of it. *Univis*, 316 U.S., at 251, 62 S. Ct. 1088. If the purchaser of that article could make and sell endless copies, the patent would effectively protect the invention for just a single sale. Bowman himself disputes none of this analysis as a general matter: He forthrightly acknowledges the "well settled" principle "that the exhaustion doctrine does not extend to the right to 'make' a new product." Brief for Petitioner 37 (citing *Aro*, 365 U.S., at 346, 81 S. Ct. 599).

Unfortunately for Bowman, that principle decides this case against him. Under the patent exhaustion doctrine, Bowman could resell the patented soybeans he purchased from the grain elevator; so too he could consume the beans himself or feed them to his animals. Monsanto, although the patent holder, would have no business interfering in those uses of Roundup Ready beans. But the exhaustion doctrine does not enable Bowman to make additional patented soybeans without Monsanto's permission (either express or implied). And that is precisely what Bowman did. He took the soybeans he purchased home; planted them in his fields at the time he thought best; applied glyphosate to kill weeds (as well as any soy plants lacking the Roundup Ready trait); and finally harvested more (many more) beans than he started with. That is how "to 'make' a new product," to use Bowman's words, when the original product is a seed. . . . Because Bowman thus reproduced Monsanto's patented invention, the exhaustion doctrine does not protect him.

This conclusion applies however Bowman acquired Roundup Ready seed: The doctrine of patent exhaustion no more protected Bowman's reproduction of the seed he purchased for his first crop (from a Monsanto-affiliated seed company) than the beans he bought for his second (from a grain elevator). The difference between the two purchases was that the first—but not the second—came with a license from Monsanto to plant the seed and then harvest and market one crop of beans. We do not here confront a case in which Monsanto (or an affiliated seed company) sold Roundup Ready to a farmer without an express license agreement. For reasons we explain below, we think that case unlikely to arise. See *infra*, at 1768. And in the event it did, the farmer might reasonably claim that the sale came with an implied license to plant and harvest one soybean crop.

Were the matter otherwise, Monsanto's patent would provide scant benefit. After inventing the Roundup Ready trait, Monsanto would, to be sure, "receiv[e] [its] reward" for the first seeds it sells. *Univis*, 316 U.S., at 251, 62 S. Ct. 1088. But in short order, other seed companies could reproduce the product and market it to growers, thus depriving Monsanto of its monopoly. And farmers themselves need only buy the seed once, whether from Monsanto, a competitor, or (as here) a grain elevator. The grower could multiply his initial purchase, and then multiply that new creation, ad infinitum—each time profiting from the patented seed without compensating its inventor. Bowman's late-season plantings offer a prime illustration. After buying beans for a single harvest, Bowman saved enough seed each year to reduce or eliminate the need for additional purchases. Monsanto still held its patent, but received no gain from Bowman's annual production and sale of Roundup Ready soybeans. The exhaustion doctrine is limited to the "particular item" sold to avoid just such a mismatch between invention and reward.

. . .

Bowman principally argues that exhaustion should apply here because seeds are meant to be planted. The exhaustion doctrine, he reminds us, typically prevents a patentee from controlling the use of a patented product following an authorized sale. And in planting Roundup Ready seeds, Bowman continues, he is merely using them in the normal way farmers do.

Bowman thus concludes that allowing Monsanto to interfere with that use would "creat[e] an impermissible exception to the exhaustion doctrine" for patented seeds and other "self-replicating technologies."...

But it is really Bowman who is asking for an unprecedented exception—to what he concedes is the "well settled" rule that "the exhaustion doctrine does not extend to the right to 'make' a new product."

Still, Bowman has another seeds-are-special argument: that soybeans naturally "self-replicate or 'sprout' unless stored in a controlled manner," and thus "it was the planted soybean, not Bowman" himself, that made replicas of Monsanto's patented invention. . . . ("[F]armers, when they plant seeds, they don't exercise any control . . . over their crop" or "over the creative process"). But we think that blame-the-bean defense tough to credit. . . .

Our holding today is limited—addressing the situation before us, rather than every one involving a self-replicating product. We recognize that such inventions are becoming ever more prevalent, complex, and diverse. In another case, the article's self-replication might occur outside the purchaser's control. Or it might be a necessary but incidental step in using the item for another purpose. Cf. 17 U.S.C. §117(a)(1) ("[I]t is not [a copyright] infringement for the owner of a copy of a computer program to make . . . another copy or adaptation of that computer program provide[d] that such a new copy or adaptation is created as an essential step in the utilization of the computer program"). We need not address here whether or how the doctrine of patent exhaustion would apply in such circumstances. In the case at hand, Bowman planted Monsanto's patented soybeans solely to make and market replicas of them, thus depriving the company of the reward patent law provides for the sale of each article. Patent exhaustion provides no haven for that conduct. We accordingly affirm the judgment of the Court of Appeals for the Federal Circuit.

It is so ordered.

## NOTES AND QUESTIONS

**1.** Could one equally well argue that Monsanto knew what it was doing when it went into the seed business, and that an inherent property of seeds is that they regenerate into new plants, which may then generate new seeds, and so on? This is an inherent characteristic of the patented product that Monsanto is developing and selling. The farmer is not making a new product. The farmer is making use of the original product exactly the way "nature intended." Inherent logic does not really seem to favor the Supreme Court's approach. Instead, the Supreme Court is making a policy decision, which may well reflect the preferred policy of the U.S. Congress. That is, Monsanto's ability to generate profits through higher price sales of patented seeds should be protected on the theory that Monsanto will be encouraged to invest in new R&D for further improved agricultural products. Recall that historically most agriculture-related R&D was funded by governments and the objective was to increase crop output for the benefit of the public. Only in the past 30 years or so has there been a marked shift toward private market R&D solutions for agricultural products.

**2.** The Biotechnology Directive of the European Union expressly authorizes farmers to save and replant patented seeds, providing:

> Article 11
>
> 1. By way of derogation from Articles 8 and 9, the sale or other form of commercialisation of plant propagating material to a farmer by the holder of the patent or with his consent for agricultural use implies authorisation for the farmer to use the product of his harvest for propagation or multiplication by him on his own farm, the extent and conditions of this derogation corresponding to those under Article 14 of Regulation (EC) No 2100/94.

Article 14 of Regulation (EC) No 2100/94 was the subject of the *STV* case excerpted above. Note that case involved a protected plant variety under EU law (see discussion *infra* of the EU plant variety protection regime), and that this provision of the biotechnology directive is referring to patents.

Monsanto's contract with patented seed purchasers precludes replanting saved seed (without specific authorization), and the U.S. Supreme Court's decision "normalizes" Monsanto's practice.

**3.** Do you think that a European farmer working with "replanted" Monsanto seeds can lawfully export crops harvested from such seeds to the United States? Recall that patented products produced on the basis of processes that would have infringed if performed in the United States constitute infringing products. What facts might be important to completing your analysis?

## E. Multilateral Agreements

### *1. The WTO TRIPS Agreement*

As of 2023, there are 164 Members of the WTO, all of which are parties to the TRIPS Agreement. The TRIPS Agreement provisions regarding plant variety protection are therefore the most widely adopted rules in this area. Article 27.1, TRIPS Agreement, obligates Members to extend patent subject matter coverage to all fields of technology. Article 27.3 establishes certain exceptions, including the following:

> 3. Members may also exclude from patentability: . . .
>
> (b) plants and animals other than micro-organisms, and essentially biological processes for the production of plants or animals other than non-biological and microbiological processes. However, Members shall provide for the protection of plant varieties either by patents or by an effective *sui generis* system or by any combination thereof. The provisions of this subparagraph shall be reviewed four years after the date of entry into force of the WTO Agreement.

Without doubt, WTO Members may exclude plant varieties from the subject matter scope of patent protection. Many Members make this exclusion. In addition, by reference to "essentially biological processes for the production of plants," Members may exclude traditional cross-breeding and related techniques from the scope of process patent protection. However, if Members do not provide patent protection for plant varieties, they must provide some form of "effective *sui generis* system," alone or in combination with patent protection. We turn to this momentarily.

Members must also provide patent protection for the production of plants through "non-biological and microbiological processes." The language of Article 27.3(b) was adapted from Article 53(b) of the European Patent Convention.[5]

There has been substantial debate over the meaning of this requirement. One question is whether genes or gene sequences constitute "microbiological process[es]" that must be subject

5. Article 53(b) of the European Patent Convention, however, mandated certain exclusions from patentability, for example, plant and animal varieties, rather than merely allowing such exclusions. It provides:

> Article 53
>
> Exceptions to patentability European patents shall not be granted in respect of:
>
> (a) inventions the publication or exploitation of which would be contrary to "ordre public" or morality, provided that the exploitation shall not be deemed to be so contrary merely because it is prohibited by law or regulation in some or all of the Contracting States;
>
> (b) plant or animal varieties or essentially biological processes for the production of plants or animals; this provision does not apply to microbiological processes or the products thereof.

to patenting. The information contained in genetic structures does not fall within the generally accepted definition of a "micro-organism."[6]

Neither genes nor the information in genes is a "unicellular organism with dimensions beneath the limits of vision which can be propagated and manipulated in a laboratory." Certain WTO Members have allowed the patenting of elements of the human body isolated from it by technical means (including gene sequences). But this does not mean that such patenting is a requirement of the TRIPS Agreement. The meaning of the terminology adapted from the European Patent Convention was sufficiently ambiguous that the European Union adopted the Biotechnology Directive to address the many unanswered questions.[7]

We have previously considered issues of patenting of genetic information in Chapter 2 and do not pursue that further here.

Limiting the discussion to protection of plant varieties, as such, Members may provide effective *sui generis* protection. There is no "common understanding" concerning the appropriate rules for plant variety protection. Some developed countries have argued that compliance with the latest version of the International Convention for the Protection of New Varieties of Plants (the 1991 Act, discussed *infra*) is the only acceptable effective form of *sui generis* protection. However, based on the negotiating history and terms of the TRIPS Agreement, this view is rejected by many Members, including but not limited to a number of developing countries.[8]

Article 27.3(b) of the TRIPS Agreement was adopted subject to review by the TRIPS Council beginning in 1999. That review is ongoing, and includes consideration of the disclosure of source and origin of genetic resources, as discussed in Chapters 1 and 2.

---

6. The Technical Board of Appeal of the European Patent Office has defined "microorganism" as follows:

> According to the current practice of the EPO, the term "microorganism" includes not only bacteria and yeasts, but also fungi, algae, protozoa and human, animal and plant cells, i.e. all generally unicellular organisms with dimensions beneath the limits of vision which can be propagated and manipulated in a laboratory. Plasmids and viruses are also considered to fall under this definition (*cf.* Guidelines for Examination, C-IV, 3.5).

This practice is consistent with the objective teleological interpretation of Article 53(b) EPC, second half-sentence, in particular with the principle of equal treatment (*cf.* paragraph 32 *supra*), and is, therefore, fully acceptable. Furthermore, this practice takes clearly into account the developments of modern industrial microbiology (*cf., for example*, A. Kocková-Kratochvilová, "Characteristics of Industrial-40-T 0356/93 1171.D. . ./. . . Microorganisms," in "Biotechnology," 1981, Vol. 1, H.-J. Rehm & G. Reed eds., Verlag Chemie, Weinheim, Chapter 1, pages 5 to 71, in particular page 7), fulfilling thereby an objective purpose of Article 53(b) EPC, second half-sentence." (*Plant Genetic Systems/Patentee v. Greenpeace/Opponent*, T 0356/93–3.3.4, 21 Feb. 1995).

7. See EU Biotechnology Directive:

> Article 5
>
> 1. The human body, at the various stages of its formation and development, and the simple discovery of one of its elements, including the sequence or partial sequence of a gene, cannot constitute patentable inventions.
>
> 2. An element isolated from the human body or otherwise produced by means of a technical process, including the sequence or partial sequence of a gene, may constitute a patentable invention, even if the structure of that element is identical to that of a natural element.
>
> 3. The industrial application of a sequence or a partial sequence of a gene must be disclosed in the patent application.

8. For a more complete discussion, including negotiating texts, *see* UNCTAD/ICTSD Resource Book on TRIPS and Development, at 388-412.

## 2. *The UPOV Convention*

Multilateral efforts toward plant variety protection began with the 1961 Act of the International Convention for the Protection of New Varieties of Plants (UPOV).[9] This was followed by revisions, notably a 1978 Act, and, most recently, a 1991 Act of UPOV. Of 78 UPOV members,[10] 17 countries are party to the 1978 Act, and 59 countries and 2 organizations (African Intellectual Property Organization and European Union) to the 1991 Act.[11]

### a. 1991 Act

Under the 1991 Act, a system of plant variety protection should grant a plant "breeder's right" with respect to a "variety" that is "new," "distinct," "uniform," and "stable." These criteria differ from the criteria for the grant of a utility patent.

"Novelty" generally requires that a variety has not been sold or marketed in the country where the application is filed earlier than one year before the filing date. The variety may not have been sold or marketed in the territory of any other UPOV country earlier than four years before that same filing date (and earlier than six years for trees or vines).

"Distinctness" requires that a variety be clearly distinguishable from other commonly known varieties.

"Uniformity" that a variety must be sufficiently uniform in its relevant characteristics, subject to variation that may be expected from its propagation.

"Stability" requires that the relevant characteristics of the variety remain unchanged after repeated propagation.

"Denomination" requires that the variety be given a name that will not be misleading or confusing as to the value of the variety or the identity of the breeder.

Under the 1991 Act, the plant breeder's right extends to seven acts in respect to propagating material of a variety that requires the breeder's authorization: (1) production or reproduction (multiplication); (2) conditioning for the purpose of propagation; (3) offering for sale; (4) selling or other marketing; (5) exporting; (6) importing; and (7) stocking for any of the purposes mentioned in (1) through (6).

The breeder's right is subject to certain limited exceptions (e.g., acts done for experimental purposes). In addition, each party to the 1991 Act of UPOV *may* allow farmers certain privileges with respect to use of protected varieties for reproduction on their farm holdings. Article 15(2) ("Exceptions to the Breeder's Right") provides:

> (2) [Optional exception] Notwithstanding Article 14, each Contracting Party may, within reasonable limits and subject to the safeguarding of the legitimate interests of the breeder, restrict the breeder's right in relation to any variety in order to permit farmers to use for propagating purposes, on their own holdings, the product of the harvest which they have obtained by planting, on their own holdings, the protected variety or a variety covered by Article 14(5)(a)(i) or Article 14(5)(a)(ii).

The duration of the breeder's right must be a minimum of 20 years from the date of grant, and for trees and vines a minimum of 25 years.

The 1991 Act of UPOV provides for a one-year priority period from the date of filing the first application in a UPOV member. It also requires each country party to extend national treatment to persons of other UPOV members.

---

9. Information and texts with respect to UPOV may be found at http://www.upov.int/. The UPOV web site also includes a database of national legislation with respect to plant breeder rights.

10. As of April 25, 2023.

11. The European Union is a party to the 1991 Act in addition to its individual member states.

#### b. 1978 Act

The 1978 Act of UPOV uses a more general formula than the 1991 Act for the characteristics of plant varieties that are subject to protection. "[T]he variety must be clearly distinguishable by one or more important characteristics from any other variety whose existence is a matter of common knowledge at the time when protection is applied for. . . . The characteristics which permit a variety to be defined and distinguished must be capable of precise recognition and description." (art. 6(1)(a), UPOV 1978).

More important, the exclusive rights granted to the breeder are less extensive. The 1978 Act allows the breeder to prevent:

— the production for purposes of commercial marketing
— the offering for sale
— the marketing

of the reproductive or vegetative propagating material, as such, of the variety. (art. 5(1), UPOV 1978).

There is no prohibition against use of the reproductive material (e.g., seeds) for purposes of reproduction, planting, and harvesting of crops. Thus, parties to the 1978 Act are free to grant farmers' rights with respect to saved seed, without applying the "within reasonable limits and subject to the safeguarding of the legitimate interests of the breeder" constraint of the 1991 Act. Note that the breeders' rights under the 1978 Act are conditioned on commercial marketing or sale of seeds. Farming communities may share seed (i.e., without commercial sale). However, national law may still regulate or restrict such activity.

The breeder's right under the 1978 Act generally must be a minimum of 15 years from the date of the title of protection (art. 8, 1978 Act).

The reasons why some countries prefer the 1978 Act to the 1991 Act should be apparent. Countries that are net importers of plant varieties (including seed) prefer to allow their farmers wider use (e.g., replanting) of seeds that have already been purchased, and a shorter duration of protection. However, adherence to the 1978 Act is not open to new members.[12] Countries wishing to adhere to UPOV may now only opt for the 1991 Act.

## F. Regional Systems for Plant Variety Protection

### *1. The EU System*

The EU system for the protection of plant varieties is introduced in the following article by the President of the Community Plant Variety Office (CPVO).

**Bart Kiewiet***

---

## *Plant Variety Protection in the European Community*

### 1. Introduction

If breeders want to prevent the free use by others of the varieties they have developed, they can seek legal (IPR) protection for their varieties in the form of a plant variety right, also called "plant breeders' right." . . .

---

12. *See, e.g.*, UPOV Press Release No. 29, March 24, 1998, available at http://www.upov.int/en/news/pressroom/29.htm.

* World Patent Information 319-27 (2005). The author is president of the Community Plant Variety Office (CPVO).

In the European Community two options for plant variety protection exist: national protection (21 national schemes with national coverage) and protection on the Community level. . . .

## 2. The Community Plant Variety Office

The Community Plant Variety Office, the CPVO, has been created by Council Regulation (EC) no 2100/94 of 27 July 1994 ("the Basic Regulation") "for the purpose of the implementation of" that regulation. It has its seat in Angers, France.

The core business of the CPVO encompasses:

- The formal examination of applications (article 53).
- The substantive examination of applications (article 54).
- The technical examination of candidate varieties (articles 55-58).
- The refusal of applications (article 61).
- The granting of the Community PVR (article 62).
- The approval of variety denominations (article 63).
- The declaration of nullity of Community PVRs (article 20).
- The cancellation of Community PVRs.

### 2.1. Community Agency

The CPVO is a so-called Community agency, a body governed by European public law, distinct from the Community institutions such as Council and Commission, that has its own legal personality and, in the case of the CPVO, its own financial resources. . . .

### 2.4. The Board of Appeal

Within the CPVO organization there has been established a Board of Appeal (article 45). With two exceptions, where a direct appeal to the Court of Justice of the European Communities ("the European Court") is possible, decisions of the CPVO can be challenged before its Board of Appeal. . . .

Against decisions of the Board of Appeal further appeal can be lodged to the European Court (Article 73). This task has been delegated to the Court of first instance. Until now this possibility has not been used by parties that were affected by Board decisions. . . .

## 3. Substantive Matters

### 3.1. Subject Matter

The substantive part of the Basic Regulation is based on the 1991 version of the UPOV convention.

The subject matter of a Community plant variety right, is a plant variety. In order to be eligible for protection a variety has to be distinct, uniform and stable (the DUS requirements), new and have an adequate variety denomination. . . .

### 3.5. Relation to National Systems

As said the Community system exists in parallel with the national PVR systems of the EU Member States. All but four of these states have adopted PVR legislation. The national systems are not harmonised and based on different versions of the UPOV convention.

The Community system offers protection on a Community scale. On the basis of one application a Community plant variety right can be obtained that is valid in the territory of all the Member States of the European Community. National protection is limited of course to the territory of the state in question. It is up to the breeder seeking PVR protection in the

European Community to decide what type of protection he prefers. If he sees a market for a new variety in more than two Member States the Community option is the logical choice.

As follows from article 92 of the Basic Regulation any variety which is the subject of a Community plant variety right shall not be the subject of a national plant variety right or any patent for that variety. It is nevertheless not prohibited that part of a variety, for instance a gene coding for a disease resistance, is protected by a patent whereas the variety as such is protected with a Community plant variety right.

### 3.6. The Scope of the Right

The scope of Community plant variety rights is to a high degree similar to that of a utility patent even though there are some differences due to the specific nature of plant variety rights. The scope of rights is mentioned in Article 13(2) of the Basic Regulation and includes the exclusive right for the holder to produce and reproduce, condition for the purpose of propagation, sell, market, import and export to the Community and stocking material (variety constituents/harvested material) of the variety. In addition to acts effected in relation to the protected variety itself, acts effected in relation to essentially derived varieties, other indistinct varieties and hybrid varieties dependent on the protected variety for their production may also constitute infringements (Article 13(2) read in conjunction with Article 13(5)).

### 3.7. Derogations

There are important derogations of the scope of the right laid down in Articles 14-16. Article 14 sets out the terms for the so-called agricultural exemption (farmers' privilege). This exemption gives farmers the right to use farm saved seed without the consent of the owner (right holder) of the variety in question. However, the farmer, with the exception of small farmers, must pay the holder an equitable remuneration which shall be sensibly lower than the amount charged for the licensed product (Article 14(3)). If the parties can not agree upon the level of the remuneration, such remuneration should be 50% of the amounts charged for the licensed production of propagating material (Article 5 of Council Regulation No 1768/95).

Article 15 of the Basic Regulation excludes from the exclusive rights of the PBR holder "breeding for noncommercial purposes and breeding for the purpose of discovering and developing other varieties" (the breeders exemption). Such a breeders exemption, considered as one of the important characteristics of UPOV style PVP legislation, does not exist as such in respect of patents.

### 3.8. Compulsory Licensing

In line with the UPOV convention article 29(1) contains the provision that compulsory (exploitation) licences shall be granted only on grounds of public interest.

Recently a new paragraph has been added to this article introducing the possibility of granting a compulsory licence to the holder of a patent for a biotechnological invention incorporated in a protected variety. In order to qualify for such compulsory licence, the patent holder has to demonstrate that: (i) he/she has applied unsuccessfully to the holder of the plant variety right to obtain a contractual licence and (ii) the invention constitutes significant technical progress of considerable economic interest compared with the protected variety.

In the case a holder of a Community plant variety right has been granted—by a competent national patent authority—a compulsory licence for the non-exclusive use of a patented invention incorporated in the protected variety in question, a cross-licence shall be granted, on application, to the holder of the patent (article 29(5a)).

The competent authority for granting such compulsory licences or cross-licences is the CPVO. The new provisions laid down in article 29 as regards (cross) compulsory licences to be granted to patent holders should, as follows from article 12 of the so-called Biotech Directive find their complement in the provisions of national patent legislation in the EU member states containing provisions to grant compulsory licences in respect of patented inventions to holders of Community plant variety rights.

### 3.9. Enforcement

Under Community law, there is no legal system in place as regards infringement procedures for plant variety rights. The procedures in such proceedings are governed by national law. However, the Basic Regulation provides some basic conditions regarding civil claims, infringements and jurisdiction (Articles 94-107).

These rules together with the Lugano Convention ensure that there will always be a competent court to deal with infringements of Community plant variety rights (Article 101). Article 103 provides that, where jurisdiction lies with national courts, the rules of procedure of the relevant State governing the same type of action relating to corresponding national property rights shall apply.

Article 105 requires a national court or other body hearing an action relating to a community plant variety right to treat the right as valid. This provision underlines the fact that only the Office is competent with regard to the nullification or cancellation of a Community plant variety right.

Article 107 provides that Member States shall take all appropriate measures to ensure that the same provisions are made applicable to penalize infringements of Community plant rights as apply to the matter of infringements of corresponding national rights. Accordingly, even though the Basic Regulation is silent as regards the sanction of seizure and destruction of infringing material, a holder of a Community plant variety right may ask a national court for such a remedy if such remedy is provided for under national law.

The Basic Regulation states that the holder has a right to a reasonable compensation in case there is an infringement of his rights (Article 94(1)). This is the case even if the infringer was in good faith. However, if it is established that the infringement was carried out intentionally or negligently, the infringer shall be liable to compensate the holder of the CPVR for any further damage resulting from the act of infringement. In cases of slight negligence, such claims may be reduced according to the degree of such slight negligence, but not however to the extent that they are less than the advantage derived there from by the person who committed the infringement (Article 94(2)). Article 95 provides that the holder of a Community plant variety right may require reasonable compensation from any person who has, in the time between publication of the application for a Community plant variety right and grant thereof, affected an act that he would be prohibited from performing subsequent thereto. . . .

## 4. Procedures

The procedures to be followed and the conditions required in relation to a variety submitted for Community protection can be summarized as follows.

### 4.1. Where to Apply?

An application for plant variety protection can be made in any of the twenty official languages of the European Community direct to the CPVO or to one of the national agencies in a Member State, which in turn will take the necessary steps to send it on to the CPVO.

### 4.2. Who Can Apply?

Any individual or company whose domicile or headquarters is located in the European Union.

Individuals or companies from a state which is a member of the International Union for the protection of new varieties of plants (UPOV) but not a member of the European Union can also apply, provided that an agent domiciled in the Community has been nominated.

### 4.3. Checking the Application

When an application is received, the CPVO checks to see that it is complete and eligible and that the variety is novel (see below). If no impediment is found at this stage, the CPVO arranges for a technical examination of the variety submitted.

### 4.4. Technical Examination

The purpose of the technical examination is to ensure that in respect of a candidate variety the criteria of distinctness, uniformity and stability, are complied with. The CPVO does not itself carry out these examinations. They are entrusted to bodies deemed competent by the CPVO Administrative Council. At present more than 20 examination offices have obtained the qualification "competent." The major ones are: the Bundessortenamt in Germany, GEVES in France, NIAB in the UK and the Raad voor het Kwekersrecht in the Netherlands. All the offices performing examinations on behalf of the CPVO render similar services in the framework of national listing and plant variety protection systems.

Examinations have to be conducted in accordance with guidelines laid down by the CPVO. Varieties submitted for protection are compared during the examination with other varieties submitted for Community protection and with appropriate varieties of common knowledge at the time of application.

### 4.5. Grant of Title

If the CPVO is of the opinion that the findings of the examination are sufficient to base a decision upon, it decides whether or not to grant a Community plant variety right. In the case of a successful application, the CPVO issues the title holder with a certificate attesting to the grant of protection and a copy of the decision containing an official, detailed description of the variety in question.

In the case, that the examination does not lead to clear conclusions, for instance in respect of the assessment of distinctness, an extension of the examination period, with the same sample, can be ordered. It is the responsibility of the breeder to submit sample material, that meets the relevant conditions in respect of germination, flowering, etc. Only in very exceptional cases the breeder will be offered the possibility to submit a new sample, if the first sample does not perform adequately.

Community protection may be granted as a general rule for twenty-five (25) years, or for thirty (30) years in the case of vines, potatoes and trees. These periods are maxima. For each year of protection an annual fee has to be paid. When the commercial lifetime of a variety is shorter than the maximum protection period, the breeder could decide to give up protection.

### 4.6. Appeals

This subject is covered by Section 2.4 above.

### 4.7. Status Information and Publicity

Every two months the CPVO publishes an Official Gazette containing all the information appearing in its Registers, in particular applications for protection, proposals for variety denomination and grants of titles. Any other information the CPVO feels the public should be informed about may also be published in the Gazette.

Furthermore the CPVO has created a Website which contains comprehensive information about the Community system. The website contains all the information published in the Gazette. Due to legal restrictions the information published on the web has not yet an official status. Furthermore all relevant legislation, news, texts of presentations can be found on the non-confidential part of the web site.

The CPVO is in close co-operation with UPOV in the process of creating a data base for variety denominations to be fed by all the UPOV Member States. In first instance this data base will only be accessible to authorities within the European Community responsible for national PVR and listing systems. Once the data base is well established it could be made available for all the users of the Community system.

### 5. The State of the System . . .

The high number of applications for Community protection (the number of applications received by the CPVO — more than 20,000 — is higher than the sum of the national applications received by the national PVR authorities within the European Community over the same time period) shows that protection on a European scale is an attractive alternative for national protection for those varieties which have an international market. . . .

## NOTES AND QUESTIONS

**1.** The Plant Variety Regulation assures the farmer a right to use saved seed, and except with respect to small farmers, upon payment of the reasonable royalty. Do you think this compensatory model of IP protection might have utility in other fields? Note that systems of copyright protection often make use of compensatory models.

**2.** The Plant Variety Regulation assures biotechnology patent holders of a license to use a protected variety, and assures the owner of a protected variety a license to use a third-party patent. What are the conditions upon which such licenses are granted? Are these conditions consistent with the provisions of Article 31 of the TRIPS Agreement — which applies only to patents? Does Article 31(l), TRIPS Agreement, apply?

**3.** On the complex interplay between techniques of biotechnological modification, food safety and environmental protection, *see, e.g.*, Court of Justice of the European Union Press Release No. 111/18 Luxembourg, 25 July 2018, Judgment in Case C-528/16, *Confédération Paysanne and Others v. Premier Ministre and Ministre de l'Agriculture, de l'Agroalimentaire et de la Forêt*:

> "Organisms obtained by mutagenesis are GMOs and are, in principle, subject to the obligations laid down by the GMO Directive. However, organisms obtained by mutagenesis techniques which have conventionally been used in a number of applications and have a long safety record are exempt from those obligations, on the understanding that the Member States are free to subject them, in compliance with EU law, to the obligations laid down by the directive or to other obligations. Unlike transgenesis, mutagenesis is a set of techniques which make it possible to alter the genome of a living species without the insertion of foreign DNA. Mutagenesis techniques have made it possible to develop seed varieties which are resistant to selective herbicides." https://curia.europa.eu/jcms/upload/docs/application/pdf/2018-07/cp180111en.pdf.

# V. THE INTERNATIONAL SYSTEM FOR THE PROTECTION OF TRADE SECRET AND REGULATORY DATA

## A. Trade Secrets as Intellectual Property Form

"Trade secret" or confidential, or undisclosed, commercial information is traditionally protected in civil and common law countries against misappropriation through dishonest practices. Prior to the TRIPS Agreement, there was no specific multilateral obligation to offer protection for trade secrets. Article 10*bis* of the Paris Convention establishes an obligation to provide protection against unfair competition, but the terms of that article leave some doubt as to whether an obligation to protect trade secrets is created.

A trade secret is generally understood as information with commercial value that has not been publicly disclosed by its holder, and that the holder has taken reasonable steps to protect. Trade secrets may include information as diverse as customer lists, manufacturing processes, and food recipes.

With the TRIPS Agreement, trade secret protection has been recognized as a form of intellectual property, and it has been gaining enhanced importance in recent years. Businesses often exclusively rely upon trade secrets in defending their first mover advantage, while shunning the costs for patent protection and worse, in defending patents against appropriations before courts of law. Often, combinations are used. Patents alone would not allow copying a particular piece of equipment and product. While this strategy works well in the field of engineering, chemical and pharmaceutical industries, strongly depending upon chemical formula, continue to strongly depend upon patents as risk of disclosure remains high. Their focus on trade secrets is in the field of test data exclusivity and to make sure that data submitted for regulatory approval is not passed on by the authorities to competitors.

Legally, trade secret and patent protection may be available for the same subject matter, and the inventor of a new product or process usually must choose the more desirable form of protection. The trade secret has two principal advantages compared with the patent. First, there is no limitation on the term of trade secret protection. Its holder is protected against misappropriation for so long as the information remains secret. The term of the patent, by way of contrast, is (generally) 20 years from the date of application. Second, the holder of a trade secret is not required to disclose that information to the public, and is, in fact, precluded from doing so in order to preserve protection. The patenting process, on the other hand, typically mandates disclosure of the invention. Perhaps the most frequently cited example of successful trade secret protection is the holding of the Coca-Cola formula for more than 100 years.

The major disadvantage of trade secret protection, as compared to patent protection, is that trade secret protection does not preclude reverse engineering and use. Anyone may attempt to replicate the information comprising the trade secret, and make use of it. The patent, by way of contrast, precludes independent creators from commercial use of an invention, and effectively precludes reverse engineering. The patent grants its holder the right to exclude others from the market, while the trade secret does not.

For many innovators, the reason for seeking patent protection (even given the limited term) is that the product can be replicated by others once it is made public. Advances in technology continue to improve the opportunities for reverse engineering even in highly technical fields. Pharmaceutical innovators traditionally have opted for patent protection because the chemical formulas for new drugs are usually subject to fairly rapid reverse engineering.

Yet, many industrial companies successfully guard production processes and methods that are critical to their competitive position with trade secret, and its importance as a tool of IP protection should not be underestimated.

The experience of the COVID-19 pandemic, the rapid but uneven deployment of vaccines produced in complex value chains entailing patents and undisclosed information highlights the conceptual challenges related to undisclosed information, in particular the absence of rules relating to fair use or compulsory licensing.

## *Kewanee Oil v. Bicron Corp.*

416 U.S. 470 (1974)

Mr. Chief Justice Burger delivered the opinion of the Court. . . .

Ohio has adopted the widely relied-upon definition of a trade secret found at Restatement of Torts §757, comment b (1939). *B. F. Goodrich Co. v. Wohlgemuth*, 117 Ohio App. 493, 498, 192 N.E.2d 99, 104 (1963); *W. R. Grace & Co. v. Hargadine*, 392 F.2d 9, 14 (CA6 1968). According to the Restatement,

> "[a] trade secret may consist of any formula, pattern, device or compilation of information which is used in one's business, and which gives him an opportunity to obtain an advantage over competitors who do not know or use it. It may be a formula for a chemical compound, a process of manufacturing, treating or preserving materials, a pattern for a machine or other device, or a list of customers."

The subject of a trade secret must be secret, and must not be of public knowledge or of a general knowledge in the trade or business. *B. F. Goodrich Co. v. Wohlgemuth, supra*, at 499, 192 N.E.2d, at 104; *National Tube Co. v. Eastern Tube Co.*, 3 Ohio C.C.R. (n.s.) 459, 462 (1902), *aff'd*, 69 Ohio St. 560, 70 N.E. 1127 (1903). This necessary element of secrecy is not lost, however, if the holder of the trade secret reveals the trade secret to another "in confidence, and under an implied obligation not to use or disclose it." *Cincinnati Bell Foundry Co. v. Dodds*, 10 Ohio Dec. Reprint 154, 156, 19 Weekly L. Bull. 84 (Super. Ct. 1887). These others may include those of the holder's "employees to whom it is necessary to confide it, in order to apply it to the uses for which it is intended." *National Tube Co. v. Eastern Tube Co., supra*, at 462. Often the recipient of confidential knowledge of the subject of a trade secret is a licensee of its holder. *See Lear, Inc. v. Adkins*, 395 U.S. 653 (1969). The protection accorded the trade secret holder is against the disclosure or unauthorized use of the trade secret by those to whom the secret has been confided under the express or implied restriction of nondisclosure or nonuse. The law also protects the holder of a trade secret against disclosure or use when the knowledge is gained, not by the owner's volition, but by some "improper means," Restatement of Torts §757 (a), which may include theft, wiretapping, or even aerial reconnaissance. A trade secret law, however, does not offer protection against discovery by fair and honest means, such as by independent invention, accidental disclosure, or by so-called reverse engineering, that is by starting with the known product and working backward to divine the process which aided in its development or manufacture.

Novelty, in the patent law sense, is not required for a trade secret, *W. R. Grace & Co. v. Hargadine*, 392 F.2d, at 14. "Quite clearly discovery is something less than invention." *A. O. Smith Corp. v. Petroleum Iron Works Co.*, 73 F.2d 531, 538 (CA6 1934), *modified to increase scope of injunction*, 74 F.2d 934 (1935). However, some novelty will be required if merely because that which does not possess novelty is usually known; secrecy, in the context of trade secrets, thus implies at least minimal novelty. . . .

Trade secret law and patent law have co-existed in this country for over one hundred years. Each has its particular role to play, and the operation of one does not take away from the need for the other. Trade secret law encourages the development and exploitation of those items of lesser or different invention than might be accorded protection under the patent laws, but which items still have an important part to play in the technological and scientific advancement of the Nation. Trade secret law promotes the sharing of knowledge, and the efficient operation of industry; it permits the individual inventor to reap the rewards of his labor by contracting with a company large enough to develop and exploit it. . . .

## NOTES AND QUESTIONS

**1.** Until 1996, trade secret protection in the United States was largely a matter of state civil law. However, the Economic Espionage Act of 1996 made the theft of trade secrets a federal criminal offense, accompanied by potentially severe civil and criminal penalties (e.g., 18 U.S.C. §1832). While the criminal offenses may be prosecuted only by federal authorities (and not by private parties in civil litigation), they nonetheless raise the stakes for those who might engage in industrial espionage. In 2016, the U.S. Congress adopted the Defend Trade Secrets Act, 18 U.S.C. §1836 et seq., which provided trade secret owners with the option to bring claims for trade secret misappropriation in federal court under a federal cause of action. The new legislation was modeled on the Uniform Trade Secrets Act (UTSA) that had largely been the model for trade secret statutes throughout the United States. One of the objectives of the legislation was to establish a level of uniformity among trade secret laws among the states, as well as to give claimants more convenient forums for initiating litigation. However, the legislation expressly provides that it does not preempt state trade secret law, leaving some uncertainty regarding how the objective of making the treatment of trade secrets more uniform will be accomplished. Presumably the federal courts will create a body of federal common law on trade secrets rather than relying on state court doctrine. We discuss the protection of regulatory data *infra.*

**2.** Industrial espionage is practiced as businesses seek information about the new products, marketing campaigns, and service promotions of competitors. One of the most widely reported cases of misappropriation of trade secrets involved a senior executive of General Motors who, in accepting a senior position at Volkswagen, took with him extensive information concerning GM's arrangements with its suppliers. *See* Keith Bradsher, *Former G.M. Executive Indicted on Charges of Taking Secrets*, N.Y. Times, May 23, 2000.

**3.** One of the most difficult problems in trade secret law concerns the treatment of knowledge obtained by employees in the course of their employment. Even if an employee has signed a confidentiality agreement and does not intend to breach a confidence, when that employee goes to work for a rival company in the same field some "secret" information may be indirectly or directly used at the new job. Airtight protection of corporate information could not be maintained without making it difficult for employees to move between jobs. This would result in an inefficient labor market, and it would operate as a serious infringement on personal liberties. Courts have tended to address this problem by requiring the holder of trade secret information to demonstrate the misappropriation of documents or the misuse of specific product information.

**4.** In notes following the *Universal Studios v. Corley* excerpt, *supra* Chapter 4, section II.C.3, we referred to the decision of the California Court of Appeal in *DVD Copy Control Ass'n v. Bunner* (6th Dist. Cal. App.), 116 Cal. App. 4th 241 (2004) (*request for review by Cal. Sup. Ct. denied*, 2004 Cal. LEXIS 8697 (Cal., Sept. 15, 2004)), which held that Bunner's posting of the DeCSS program on his web site did not violate trade secret rights of the program developer. The Court of Appeal said, *inter alia:*

DVD CCA urges us, in effect, to ignore the fact that the allegedly proprietary information may have been distributed to a worldwide audience of millions prior to Bunner's first posting. According to DVD CCA, so long as Bunner knew or should have known that the information he was republishing was obtained by improper means, he cannot rely upon the general availability of the information to the rest of the world to avoid application of the injunction to him. In support of this position, DVD CCA contends that the denial of an injunction would offend the public policies underlying trade secret law, which are to enforce a standard of commercial ethics, to encourage research and invention, and to protect the owner's moral entitlement to the fruits of his or her labors. . . . DVD CCA points out that these policies are advanced by making sure that those who misappropriate trade secrets do not avoid "judicial sanction" by making the secret widely available.

The first problem with this argument is that by denying a preliminary injunction the court does not per se protect a wrongdoer from judicial sanction, which in most cases would come following trial on the merits.

(8) Second, the evidence in this case is very sparse with respect to whether the offending program was actually created by improper means. Reverse engineering alone is not improper means. . . . Here the creator is believed to be a Norwegian resident who probably had to breach a Xing license in order to access the information he needed. We have only very thin circumstantial evidence of when, where, or how this actually happened or whether an enforceable contract prohibiting reverse engineering was ever formed.

Finally, assuming the information was originally acquired by improper means, it does not necessarily follow that once the information became publicly available that everyone else would be liable under the trade secret laws for republishing it simply because they knew about its unethical origins. In a case that receives widespread publicity, just about anyone who becomes aware of the contested information would also know that it was allegedly created by improper means. Under DVD CCA's construction of the law, in such a case the general public could theoretically be liable for misappropriation simply by disclosing it to someone else. This is not what trade secret law is designed to do.

(9) It is important to point out that we do not assume that the alleged trade secrets contained in DeCSS became part of the public domain simply by having been published on the Internet. Rather, the evidence demonstrates that in this case, the initial publication was quickly and widely republished to an eager audience so that DeCSS and the trade secrets it contained rapidly became available to anyone interested in obtaining them. Further, the record contains no evidence as to when in the course of the initial distribution of the offending program Bunner posted it. Thus, DVD CCA has not shown a likelihood that it will prevail on the merits of its claim of misappropriation against Bunner. 116 Cal. App. 4th 241, 252-53.

What implications do you see for trade secret protection from the *Bunner* decision?

**5.** On May 19, 2014, the United States Department of Justice announced the filing of criminal charges against five Chinese government officials for computer hacking, economic espionage, and other offenses directed at six American victims in the U.S. nuclear power, metals, and solar products industry. The charges included theft of trade secrets intended to benefit, among others, Chinese state-owned enterprises. *See* U.S. Department of Justice, Office of Public Affairs, *U.S. Charges Five Chinese Military Hackers for Cyber Espionage Against U.S. Corporations and a Labor Organization for Commercial Advantage*, May 19, 2014, http://www.justice.gov/opa/pr/2014/May/14-ag-528.html.

## B. Trade Secret and the TRIPS Agreement

The principal multilateral agreement establishing trade secret norms is the TRIPS Agreement. The TRIPS Agreement accomplishes this by specifying that Article 10*bis* of the Paris Convention applies to "undisclosed information" (art. 39.1, TRIPS Agreement), and then by defining what shall constitute protection of undisclosed information (art. 39.2, *id.*). Article 39.2 provides:

> 2. Natural and legal persons shall have the possibility of preventing information lawfully within their control from being disclosed to, acquired by, or used by others without their consent in a manner contrary to honest commercial practices [Note 10] so long as such information:
>    (a) is secret in the sense that it is not, as a body or in the precise configuration and assembly of its components, generally known among or readily accessible to persons within the circles that normally deal with the kind of information in question;
>    (b) has commercial value because it is secret; and
>    (c) has been subject to reasonable steps under the circumstances, by the person lawfully in control of the information, to keep it secret.
>
> [Note 10] For the purpose of this provision, "a manner contrary to honest commercial practices" shall mean at least practices such as breach of contract, breach of confidence and inducement to breach, and includes the acquisition of undisclosed information by third parties who knew, or were grossly negligent in failing to know, that such practices were involved in the acquisition.

The terms of Article 39.2 are consistent with the traditional treatment of trade secrets in common and civil law countries. Interpretation of Article 39.2 has not been a source of controversy among WTO Members. Recall that the TRIPS Agreement provides flexibility for each Member to implement its requirements in light of their customary practices.

Article 39.2 TRIPS is explicitly based upon unfair competition, based upon Article 10*bis* of the Paris Convention, discussed above in Cottier & Germann, pages 723-729. Other than in copyright and patent law, the TRIPS Agreement does not explicitly address fair use or compulsory licensing for the purpose of technology dissemination called upon by Article 7 of the TRIPS Agreement. Given the fact technological knowledge often amounts to a combination of patents and undisclosed information, and a product cannot be successfully produced without access to the latter, the potential for express legal rules addressing the sharing and pooling of trade secrets beyond voluntary licensing is apparent. The recognition of trade secrets or undisclosed information as a proper intellectual property right in the TRIPS agreement entails that is subject to a proper balance of rights and obligations expressed in the objectives of Article 7 TRIPS Agreement. The following excerpts expound the problem and argue that international law does not restrict compelled sharing of undisclosed information.

**David S. Levine & Joshua D. Sarnoff***

## *Compelling Trade Secret Sharing*

### Introduction

The unprecedented COVID-19 virus has brought to the forefront many questions associated with exclusive rights, information sharing, and innovation. How do we get effective vaccines, therapeutics, diagnostics, medical devices, and personal protective equipment ("PPE") quickly, safely, and affordably to people around the world? More specifically, how do we ensure that effective products in sufficient quantities are researched and developed ("R&D"), approved by regulatory agencies, and produced for public distribution; that repairs of existing

* 74 Hastings L.J. 987 (2023) (footnotes omitted).

equipment can be performed as needed; that such health products are affordable; and that the needed products are equitably distributed globally and locally? Among the many challenges on the road to these outcomes is the difficult question of how to handle information that is valuable in part because others do not know it. In other words, what do we do about trade secrets? Addressing this issue will continue to be critical to COVID-19 responses, as well as to responses to future pandemics and similar worldwide problems.

Because trade secrecy can apply to wide swaths of information, it can shield a shockingly broad range of critical and lifesaving information from view. For this reason, assertions of trade secrets constitute much of the primary knowledge necessary for countries to combat and even potentially eradicate COVID-19. Indeed, trade secrets are everywhere in the battle to defeat COVID-19, including clinical trial data, pharmaceutical- and medical-equipment manufacturing processes, and regulatory compliance information.

Trade secrets raise three primary issues. First, if an entity is forced to share trade secrets to expedite development and to expand supply of needed products, must or should the government compensate the rights holder? Although we address this question, we think it is largely unnecessary to answer it. This is because compensation is not *required* under international law (at least to address public health emergencies); because national law may sometimes already provide for compensation when compelling licensing, as well as when mandating sharing that eliminates secrecy; and because we think *reasonable* compensation *should* normally be provided for compelled trade secret sharing. Second, does international law prohibit governments from compelling the sharing of trade secrets, including by compulsory licensing? The short answer is no. Third, what authorities currently exist or could be adopted for governments to compel the sharing of trade secrets? We present a general overview of a range of existing authorities, as well as a framework for addressing the latter two questions and understanding the complexity of the first question.

. . .

## I. Trade Secret and Related Protection

Trade secrets are comprised by a complicated and diverse body of law with significant variations in international and national law, including those that address limitations on and exceptions to trade secret rights. Trade secret applications are extremely fact- and sector-specific, and the existence of a trade secret must be assessed individually against its value in the industry sector in which it operates. Therefore, few blanket prohibitions or rules of conduct apply when discussing the role of trade secrets in innovation and production.

In the COVID-19 context, trade secret law raises a critical policy question: Is information sharing needed to rapidly combat the spread of disease and to enable vaccine production? In the case of COVID-19 vaccines, potential trade secrets included manufacturing processes, test data, medical formulas, and other biological resources. Vaccines, other biologic medicines, cell lines, genomic information, and other biological material can also be held as trade secrets. Similarly, data about the effectiveness of medicines and vaccines are trade secrets. Manufacturing processes can be a paradigmatic trade secret, or can fall into the amorphous quasi-trade secret categories of "know-how" or "show how." All of this information is essential to the rapid development of, and access to, safe and effective COVID-19 diagnostics, treatments, and vaccines worldwide.

Similarly, data for developing vaccines may be held as trade secrets. Typically, clinical data are not required to be made public as a condition of regulatory marketing approvals, even if the government can use such data when evaluating requests for generic product approvals. In many cases, such data and methods need not be disclosed to assure compliance with good manufacturing practices that permit product marketing. Methods of assuring that the public can "make and use" patent disclosures and legal authorizations in the patent context, such as compulsory patent licenses, cannot assure private access when needed to scale up research, development, regulatory approvals, and manufacturing supplies.

Methods for manufacturing may also be treated as trade secrets. Such methods often are colloquially labeled "know-how," a subset of trade secrecy doctrine involving information that is valuable and difficult to transfer, but that is not necessarily secret. Such information may not always be protectable under trade secret law. Nonetheless, because of its value and difficulty to acquire, know-how that does not achieve trade secret status operates similarly to trade secrecy as property that can be licensed.

In the case of COVID-19 research, product development, commercialization, and data and manufacturing processes are key trade secrets. After all, if a company knows what works and what does not, then it has a competitive advantage over others who lack that knowledge. When it possesses efficient means of production, the trade secret owner enjoys a significant competitive advantage. As has been evident regarding COVID-19 vaccine production from the beginning, such information sharing is critical to worldwide supply needs, but has occurred only to a limited extent through voluntary licensing among a mostly restricted set of global pharmaceutical companies and manufacturers. Global pharmaceutical companies have rejected requests from various generic pharmaceutical producers to license the trade secrets and know-how in order to scale up production.

. . .

## A. What are Trade Secrets?

Often labeled as "confidential information" or "proprietary information," trade secrets encompass vast quantities of information needed to discover, test, create, and manufacture diagnostics, treatments, medicines, and vaccines. Chemical formulas are classic trade secrets. So are processes for manufacturing. Even "negative information"—information about what does not work—can be a trade secret.

Trade secret legal protections stem back to at least the early 1800s in England. In the United States, the Supreme Court of Massachusetts appears to be the first court to describe a view on trade secret protections. The famous example of the "best-kept trade secret in the world" involves the recipe for Coca Cola. The exclusivity of the formula makes the soft drink an "extremely valuable asset" that competing innovators may want to uncover in order to enter competition and make the item less exclusive.

Trade secrets are often, but are not always, a prerequisite to product, process, and commercial service development and innovation, as well as to the advancement of knowledge and science. Federal laws, primarily the Federal Defend Trade Secrets Act ("DTSA"), and state laws modeled after the Uniform Trade Secret Act ("UTSA") enable trade secret owners like pharmaceutical companies to bring trade secret misappropriation actions against former employees and others, particularly competitors who gain unauthorized access to their claimed trade secrets. The Federal Economic Espionage Act ("EEA") allows federal prosecutors to bring criminal actions under certain circumstances, especially those involving what is colloquially called computer "hacking." Other federal and state laws can be used to prevent public disclosure of information that has been previously disclosed to public authorities. As a result, trade secrets are a powerful exemption from state and federal access-to-information laws, like the Freedom of Information Act ("FOIA"). At the international level, the European Union's Trade Secrets Directive and the WTO's TRIPS Agreement article 39 provide or require similar trade secrets protections.

Under the UTSA, a trade secret is defined as

> a formula, process, device, or other business information that is kept confidential to maintain an advantage over competitors; information – including a formula, pattern, compilation, program, device, method, technique, or process – that (1) derives independent economic value,

> actual or potential, from not being generally known or readily ascertainable by others who can obtain economic value from its disclosure or use, and (2) is the subject of reasonable efforts, under the circumstances, to maintain its secrecy.

The UTSA was enacted in 1979 and has been adopted by forty-nine states, the District of Columbia, Puerto Rico, and the U.S. Virgin Islands. Prior to the UTSA, "the improper use or disclosure of trade secrets was traditionally a common law tort."

On the federal level, trade secret theft is prohibited by the EEA and, more recently, the DTSA. Congress passed the EEA as the "first major federal statute to address trade ecret misappropriation"; it "criminalized trade secret misappropriation and authorized broad domestic and international enforcement measures against trade secret misappropriation." The EEA criminalized trade secret theft as a response to an "environment of digitalization and intense worldwide competition." Under the EEA, the federal government alone can prosecute such theft.

Ongoing concern about the EEA's (and state law in May 2016, and allows trade secret owners to bring a civil action in federal court for trade secret misappropriation. The DTSA is functionally similar to the UTSA and "is not intended to alter the balance of current trade secret law or . . . specific court decisions." The DTSA has been described as a "wake-up call" to companies that value and protect their intellectual property as trade secrets.

Unlike patents, regulatory entities do not grant or confirm trade secrets; rather, one has a trade secret by keeping valuable information secret. Thus, there is no specified term for trade secrets; instead, they exist for as long as they remain secret. Importantly, trade secrets can be lost due to no fault of the trade secret owner or any act of misappropriation. This can happen, for instance, if the trade secrets are reverse engineered or independently discovered by another and thereafter made generally known.

The best way to keep a trade secret is simply not to disclose it. However, while that works as a theoretical matter (and most jurisdictions also require affirmative measures to protect secrecy), in most instances, it renders the trade secret nearly useless. Thus, the paradigm trade secret suit is one alleging the trade secret's misappropriation by a former employee or competitor that hires the employee through alleged theft-typically in violation of contractual obligations of the employee, or enabled by sloppy trade secret management.

The use of trade secrets is either by the entity that owns it or, as is relevant here, by another person or entity under a license. Trade secrets are not meant to be shared unless the owner authorizes the sharing, and then (usually) under a requirement of secrecy imposed on the authorized party. As a result, trade secrets rely heavily on licensing. As the American Law Institute has explained:

Exploiting the value of trade secrets through licensing has long been a common practice. Arguably, no other form of intellectual property is more dependent on licensing mechanisms than trade secrets. The license instrument provides the mechanism for conveying the benefits embodied by the trade secret to the awaiting public while still protecting and creating incentives for the labor and effort expended on marshalling of the trade secret.

As discussed in Part II, licensing is at the center of the COVID-19 trade secrecy challenges. Vaccine manufacturers generally have been unwilling to share their trade secrets in ways that would sufficiently advance widespread worldwide access to affordable vaccines. Even as overall production of COVID- 19 vaccines has increased over time, the inequitable distribution of and access to vaccines has persisted, and may have increased. We can, and must, do better.

Additionally, there are three amorphous categories of informational concepts related to trade secrets that are also at play. The first (and easiest to understand) is "confidential information." Such information has been "roughly" defined as

> data, technology, or know-how that is known by a substantial number of persons in a particular industry (such that its status as a technical "trade secret" is in doubt) but that, nonetheless,

> retains some economic and /or competitive value by virtue of the fact that it is unknown to certain industry participants.

While this information is not technically a trade secret, its limited availability renders it valuable. Thus, we consider it here in light of its need for distribution to combat COVID-19 (albeit without having to overcome trade secret law challenges).

Arguably the most amorphous informational concept is the know-how associated with vaccine manufacturing. "Know-how" is a highly controversial term in trade secret law generally because "there are so many types of proprietary information that have value in an industrial environment." As Eckstrom explains:

> Know-how encompasses trade secrets and unpatented manufacturing processes as well as other industrial or commercial techniques outside the public domain. . . . Intangibles, such as laboratory practice, sampling techniques, marketing schemes, and the availability of consultations with skilled technicians or professional advisors, acting for the licensor, also fall within the definition of valuable, and therefore licensable, know-how.

For present purposes, we define "know-how" (sometimes referred to by others as "tacit knowledge") as valuable information that may not rise to the level of a trade secret, and therefore is not protected by trade secret law if it is used in a way unauthorized by its owner. Nonetheless, because it is valuable and not easily accessible, absent a voluntary license, its sharing requires some "nudging" or "compulsion."

Lastly, some information that might be a trade secret can be designated as "show-how." This distinction has little meaning in the world of trade secrecy generally (because information is either a trade secret or it is not), but is important to delineate for purposes of this Article because of its need for sharing in order to address COVID-19's (and similar future) challenges. Put simply, whereas "know-how can be committed fairly easily to paper or to some other recorded form, . . . show-how can only be transmitted effectively by demonstration, e.g., by in-house training." Like know-how, sharing "show how" requires a similar "nudge" or "compulsion."

Importantly, "know-how" and "show-how" should not be confused with the "general skill and knowledge" held by individuals that is never treated as proprietary relative to others. Such information, like what an employee learns about how to do their job, while valuable, is not the property of the entity that helped the employee acquire it. Instead, it is treated as information that may be used freely by the individual and competitors or others who may seek to employ the individual's knowledge.

In sum, trade secrets, confidential information, know-how, and show-how are all at play in the COVID-19 arena. Because the lines between these concepts are blurry, and to avoid confusion, we will often collectively refer to all of them as "trade secrets." Where necessary, we may draw lines between trade secrets and the other informational concepts due to their differing methodologies for sharing and degrees of legal protection.

. . .

## III. Compelling Trade Secret Sharing Complies with International Treaty Law

To assess whether international treaty law prohibits or supports compelling trade secret sharing requires an understanding of a few basic principles. First, it is important to understand exactly what international treaty law prohibits or authorizes generally, before analyzing the legality of government measures compelling trade secrets sharing from one private entity to another under specific international treaties. It is also important to distinguish the sharing of codified knowledge (including, for example, clinical trial data already in the government's possession) from compelling companies to share uncodified know-how and show-how (such as by providing employees to train others). Furthermore, any government-compelled actions may either make the trade secret public (and thus destroy its secrecy) or may only assure competitors' abilities to use the trade secret (as by compelled licensing that also requires secrecy relative to the general public). Either the loss of the trade secret through publicity or the government-authorized third-party use of the secret may be compensated. This should (in most cases) avoid concerns about uncompensated regulatory expropriation of the value of the trade secret. Finally, even if international law does not prohibit, or even if it explicitly authorizes, compelled trade secret sharing, national laws may need to be amended or, as discussed below in Part IV.A, existing national legal authorities may need to act by, for example, issuing orders compelling the sharing.

Determining the relevant treaty principles is a complex but not insurmountable endeavor. As discussed in Subpart A, the WTO's TRIPS Agreement is the principal international treaty governing intellectual property. The TRIPS Agreement incorporates relevant provisions of the Paris Convention for the Protection of Industrial Property. But the TRIPS Agreement does not expressly or impliedly prohibit governments from compelling trade secret sharing, unlike its provision expressly prohibiting compulsory licensing of trademarks. This is true even if trade secrets, unlike trademarks, are not viewed as property rights but only things warranting regulatory protection. Further, as a matter of interpretation, the obligations for trade secrets ("undisclosed information") apply only to protection against "unfair competition," defined as "disclos[ure] . . . or use[]" "contrary to honest commercial practices"; for "undisclosed test or other data," the provision applies only to protection against "unfair commercial use." Although the nature of the prohibited acts has not been officially interpreted in any dispute resolution proceeding in the WTO, it is unlikely that the TRIPS Agreement prohibits *government* decisions to compel sharing of such information for public need or public benefit, as the recited prohibitions are focused on *commercial* morality.

Even if the TRIPS Agreement did impliedly prohibit compelled licensing or other compelled sharing of trade secrets, the TRIPS Agreement's national security exception may authorize national governments to compel trade secret sharing in a pandemic. Specifically, article 73 provides that "nothing in this Agreement shall be construed: . . . to prevent a Member from taking any action which it considers necessary for the protection of its essential security interests . . . taken in time of war or other emergency in international relations." Similarly, potential residual authority to regulate-and thus to adopt limitations and exceptions to TRIPS obligations-also might authorize such actions. The WTO's international obligations and enforcement provisions, moreover, do not actually prevent countries from adopting measures that diverge from TRIPS treaty requirements. Rather, the WTO treaty structure only requires countries to come into prospective conformity with obligations, and, absent such conformity, authorizes compensation or trade retaliation ("suspension of concessions") to countries that bring successful claims of another country's failure to implement WTO treaty requirements. In short, the TRIPS Agreement cannot and does not prohibit member countries from compelling trade secret sharing to address public health needs.

As discussed in Subpart B, the TRIPS Waiver Proposal would have suspended national obligations regarding trade secret TRIPS requirements, which would then have precluded any claims in the WTO *even if* the TRIPS Agreement were somehow thought to preclude compelled trade secret sharing. The Ministerial Decision that was adopted, however, does not address trade secrets directly, so Subpart A's discussion remains highly relevant (as it would for any non-COVID-19 pandemic or other health emergency).

Finally, as discussed in Subpart C, countries that compel trade secret sharing might be subject to investor-state treaty claims for compensation if adequate compensation for the loss of trade secrecy or for the compelled third party uses were not already provided. But adoption of the Ministerial Decision might nevertheless inform any interpretation of investor-state obligations to preclude compensation. Regardless of compensation, however, any such investor-state claims would not preclude countries from adopting the discussed measures, nor authorize any injunctive relief to prevent the trade secret sharing from being compelled.

### A. The TRIPS Agreement Does not Prohibit Compelled Trade Secret Sharing

As shown below, the plain text of the TRIPS Agreement, traditional interpretive principles, legislative history, and the national security exception all support an interpretation of the TRIPS Agreement to retain within national discretion the authority to compel trade secret sharing. The contrary view is likely the result of misplaced (and particularly American) concerns that governments should not compel the actions of individuals or of corporations, and should not intrude on markets to establish "industrial policy." As the COVID-19 example has shown (and as discussed in regard to the Defense Production Act below), however, governments (including the U.S. government) engage in industrial policy all the time, and have done so particularly in the context of pandemic responses.

#### 1. Textual Interpretation of TRIPS Supports the View That It Does Not Prohibit Governments from Compelling Trade Secret Sharing.

The TRIPS Agreement imposes on countries obligations to adopt minimum requirements for protection of various forms of intellectual creations or intangible products, or associations with them. These include the obligations to protect trade secrets against "unfair competition," and undisclosed test or other data noted above against "unfair commercial use." Unlike with trademarks, however, the TRIPS Agreement does not prohibit compulsory licensing (much less compelled sharing) of trade secrets or undisclosed data. And unlike for patents, the TRIPS Agreement does not regulate compulsory licensing of trade secrets.

As a general rule, any interpretation of the TRIPS Agreement applies the interpretive principles of the Vienna Convention on the Law of Treaties, particularly articles 31 and 32. Article 31 provides the "[g]eneral rule of interpretation":

. . .

Thus, the Vienna Convention requires understanding the text of the TRIPS Agreement in good faith and in light of its language, structure, and context. If interpretation remains ambiguous, negotiating history may also be consulted.

That brings us to what the TRIPS Agreement actually prohibits as a textual matter, and in particular whether article 39 limits or prohibits *governments* from compelling the sharing or licensing of trade secrets without authorization by the trade secret owner. Significantly, for trade secrets in general ("undisclosed information"), the TRIPS Agreement requires *only* that they be protected against disclosure, acquisition, or use by third parties "in a manner contrary to honest commercial practices." The latter phrase is explained in a footnote to "mean at least practices such as breach of contract, breach of confidence and inducement to breach, and includes *the acquisition* of undisclosed information *by third parties* who knew, or were grossly negligent in failing to know, that such practices were involved in the acquisition." Therefore, the focus is not only on commercial actions (and thus commercial actors), but also third parties who know or should know that their actions are *improper.*

Importantly, nothing suggests *any* application to government action, much less any limitation on governments' ability to provide such disclosures for use by third parties. Nor does it imply that action by a government, when authorized by law to *provide or compel sharing of* such information would be either a "commercial" activity or one "contrary to honest commercial practices." In contrast, and particularly where significant investments were made to develop the trade secrets, some may view the receipt and use by third parties of government-compelled, shared information (particularly if uncompensated) as "unfair" and "contrary to honest commercial practices." We do not share that view, based on the text and structure of TRIPS.

This "plain" textual meaning of article 39's prohibition requirements is supported by inferences derived by the structure of the text and the context of usage within the TRIPS Agreement. Because they overlap with traditional "canons of construction" and background understandings of international law regarding the nature of sovereignty and treaty-based limits on such sovereignty, they are addressed collectively in the next Subpart.

### 2. Canons of Construction and General Principles Against Legislating Unexpressed Treaty Provisions by Interpretation Support the View That the TRIPS Agreement Does Not Preclude Compelled Trade Secret Sharing or Licensing.

Starting with the text of the TRIPS Agreement, two standard structural interpretive principles apply. The first is the *expressio unius est exclusio alterius* canon of construction, where a text having expressed something implies the exclusion of something not mentioned-and conversely where the failure to express something implies its exclusion where something similar is mentioned elsewhere. By expressly adopting a prohibition on compulsory licensing of trademarks, the TRIPS Agreement should be understood to impose *no* similar prohibition on compulsory licensing or compulsory sharing of trade secrets. Similarly, had the drafters intended to impose conditions on compulsory licensing of trade secrets, they would have imposed conditions such as those for patent compulsory licensing. By expressing prohibitions and conditions elsewhere, the Agreement should be understood to impose no similar prohibitions or conditions where they are not mentioned.

The second relevant structural canon of construction is the rule of interpreting language to avoid redundancy or surplusage. This canon establishes that the TRIPS drafters' failure to impose any prohibition on compulsory sharing or licensing of trade secrets cannot evidence an intent to make the obligation to protect trade secrets non-derogable in this regard. Otherwise, the prohibition against compulsory trademark licensing would be unnecessary surplusage.

Although there are alternative structural canons of construction that could be supplied to contradict the application of any particular canon there is no *compelling* reason to adopt alternative interpretations to those above. In contrast, Eric Solovy and Deepak Raju argue that the definition of such *commercial* practices is not exhaustive, without addressing the interpretive canons above or the additional interpretive canon *ejusdem generis* (that a general term is to be construed in light of the specific examples recited for its application). They further argue that the *absence* of any codified exceptions in article 39.3 (other than the public health exception) means that the TRIPS Agreement can *only* be interpreted under Vienna Convention principles as *prohibiting* compulsory licensing of trade secrets. Courts and arbitral bodies applying the Vienna Convention, however, are reluctant to impose terms or conditions that treaty language does not itself supply. This is because treaties by their very nature are limitations on the otherwise unfettered sovereignty of nations. Thus, such "derogations" from the natural state of international relations are to be construed narrowly.

### 3. The Drafting History Regarding Trade Secrets and Undisclosed Information Supports the View That the TRIPS Agreement Does Not Preclude Compelled Trade Secret Sharing.

The lack of a textual prohibition on compelled trade secret sharing or compulsory trade secret licensing (as supported by structural inferences in the text) is also evident from the drafting history. Still, it is important to remember that Vienna Convention article 32 provides for resort to such materials *only* when interpretation under article 31 "leaves the meaning ambiguous or obscure[] or . . . leads to a result which is manifestly absurd or unreasonable"; neither of which applies here. Thus, this Subpart is only offered to rebut possible counterarguments based on drafting intent, as the text, structure, and context of interpretation already provide a clear and unambiguous understanding.

During the drafting of TRIPS, the parties approached trade secret protection tentatively, incorporating the principles of the Paris Agreement, which were understood to retain significant flexibility for national approaches to protecting against what the parties viewed as improper "commercial" behaviors, and debating strenuously over the new and additional protections for pharmaceutical and agricultural data submitted to governments to obtain regulatory marketing approval. Thus, the failure to reach agreement on, or to even discuss, compulsory trade secret sharing or licensing invokes the principle of the Vienna Convention and the WTO's interpretive framework that matters not resolved by treaty text are left to country discretion. This issue also recurs below in Subpart B, when discussing retained regulatory powers and implied power to adopt exemptions to explicit TRIPS requirements.

The context of the Paris Agreement and its interpretation was clearly relevant to what was negotiated in the relevant provisions of TRIPS. As Bodenhausen has noted:

> What is to be understood by "competition" will be determined in each country according to its own concepts: countries may extend the notion of acts of unfair competition to acts which are not competitive in a narrow sense, that is, within the same branch of industry or trade, but which unduly profit from a reputation established in another branch of industry or trade and thereby weaken such reputation. Any act of competition will have to be considered unfair if it is contrary to honest practices in industrial or commercial matters.

Again, nothing here addresses actions by the government to regulate industrial and commercial matters, including mandated sharing of undisclosed information.

Rather, regulation of commercial activity by *government* action in protection of undisclosed information was specifically addressed *only* in TRIPS article 39.3, and then only for "pharmaceutical or . . . agricultural chemical products which utilize new chemical entities," and only in regard to "the submission of undisclosed test or other data." Again, what is required by the governments to which such data has been supplied is protection against "unfair commercial use" of that information. The subsequent sentence, moreover, expressly requires, "[i]n addition," the protection of such data against "disclosure," "except where necessary to protect the public, or unless steps are taken to ensure that the data are protected against unfair commercial use." The use of "[i]n addition" strongly suggests that the drafting parties understood that disclosure by a *government* was *not* included within the prohibition against "unfair commercial use" in the prior sentence. Thus, government *regulation* of information within a private company's possession that compels private trade secret *sharing* from one company to another is not addressed at all, and article 39.3 restricts *disclosure by the government* of only certain kinds of data already in its possession. Even then, the government *may* disclose that information to commercial parties where needed to protect the public or where doing so will not result in "unfair" commercial use. Again, what is "unfair" in this context is unlikely to include anything that the government requires for public health.

Further, as Gervais has noted, it is wholly unclear from the negotiating history and subsequent interpretation of TRIPS that it requires *data exclusivity* under article 39.3 as a necessary form of protection against "unfair commercial use" of pharmaceutical or agricultural chemical data submitted to government authorities as part of regulatory approvals. To the extent that article 39.3 only requires data compensation, again it would impose no barrier to compelled trade secret sharing or compulsory licensing.

Moreover, the Doha Declaration on the TRIPS Agreement and Public Health is a "subsequent agreement" for interpretation, which affirmed "that the Agreement can and should be interpreted and implemented in a manner supportive of WTO members' right to protect public health and, in particular, to promote access to medicines for all." A group of countries thus took the view that data exclusivity is not required by TRIPS. This view was explicitly recognized by commentators such as Gervais:

> In sum, one can safely conclude that the protection required goes beyond nondisclosure. Beyond that, whether it requires full "data exclusivity" is much less clear, especially in light of variegated state practice, positions articulated at the TRIPS Council, and the negotiating history. It seems safe to conclude that data exclusivity is one safe form of implementation of art. 39.3. There may, however, be other forms of protection meant to target unfair commercial use that would be considered to meet the obligations contained in art. 39.3. This assessment should be done on a case-by-case basis.

In sum, the TRIPS Agreement does not expressly or impliedly prohibit the government from compelling trade secret sharing among private companies or from compelling third-party trade secret licensing. Nor does it impose any requirements that would be inconsistent with a government undertaking such actions. In fact, subsequent negotiation of "TRIPS-plus" provisions that require data exclusivity suggests that the TRIPS Agreement by itself does *not* require data exclusivity, even without regard to the provision authorizing the disclosure of submitted regulatory data for marketing approval "where necessary to protect the public."

Although bilateral or multilateral "TRIPS-plus" treaties may potentially add to TRIPS article 39.3 requirements by imposing data-exclusivity requirements for pharmaceutical and agricultural data, such treaties typically do not prevent countries from taking regulatory actions to protect public health. And in any event, such TRIPS-plus agreements may lack any enforcement mechanisms other than the inherent risk of trade retaliation or war. Accordingly, the TRIPS Agreement simply does not prohibit countries from compelling trade secret sharing or trade secret licensing *to or among* private entities as a *regulatory* matter to protect public health, and it is unlikely that any TRIPS-plus data-exclusivity requirements do so as well.

#### 4. The National Security Exception and Implied Authority to Adopt Regulatory Exceptions

Even assuming that the TRIPS Agreement prohibits compelled trade secret sharing or licensing under article 39, article 73's national security exception provides adequate authority to adopt domestic measures as "exceptions or limitations" to article 39's requirement. Specifically, article 73 provides that "nothing in this Agreement shall be construed: . . . to prevent a Member from taking any action which it considers necessary for the protection of its essential security interests . . . taken in time of war or other emergency in international relations." Significantly, the article by its own terms focuses on a member's self-determined perception of "necessity," which may largely preclude contrary judgments by the WTO's Dispute Settlement Understanding. In contrast, one panel decision (that the complainant, Qatar, agreed not to seek adoption of by the Dispute Settlement Body) held such determinations justiciable, imposing an objective reasonableness test for invoking the security exception and requiring a plausible relationship to that emergency for the measures being challenged. Even if such a holding (which contradicts the position of the United States and other powerful nations that the national declaration of an emergency in international relations is not justiciable) were to extend in the future to the context of pandemic diseases, it is unlikely that a national declaration would be held objectively unreasonable, or that actions taken to address public health threats such as compulsory licensing of trade secrets would be found to be improper exercises of the exception. Particularly because of the express "protect the public" language of article

39.3, it is highly unlikely that the WHO would find members that compelled trade secret sharing to address public health needs to be in violation of their TRIPS obligations. But again, even if it did, this would not prohibit the members from legally imposing such measures; it would only authorize trade sanctions against the member or compensation for rights holders in response to the measures.

Further, the TRIPS Agreement is to be interpreted in light of its objectives and principles, and with regard to the regulatory authority of states to protect public health. As noted in an important WTO Appellate Body decision regarding a regulation that required tobacco trademark owners to use plain packaging, the exclusionary trademark rights in the TRIPS Agreement do not convey "positive" rights to use the trademark that are subject to regulatory control to protect public health. Rather, the TRIPS Agreement only conveys negative rights against third parties that make unfair commercial use of the same trademark. Similarly, nothing in the TRIPS Agreement treats as a "positive right" the required trade secret protection against unfair competition by third parties in article 39.2. Nor does TRIPS treat as a positive right the government's obligation to protect from disclosure regulatory submission data for new chemical entities for pharmaceutical and agricultural products in article 39.3. Rather, governments retain the power and duty to regulate commercial activity to protect the public.

This interpretation of article 39's obligations on member states as preserving states' right to regulate is consistent with the principles and objectives of the TRIPS Agreement. As article 8.1's "principles" explain: "Members may, in formulating or amending their laws and regulations, adopt measures *necessary to protect public health* and nutrition, and to promote the public interest in sectors of vital importance to their socio-economic and technological development, provided that such measures are consistent with the provisions of this Agreement." As noted, regulatory measures to compel trade secret sharing are consistent with article 39, and may be "necessary to protect public health."

Importantly, the TRIPS Agreement provides no express provision restricting trade secret exceptions and limitations to article 39 obligations. This stands in stark contrast to the article 13 and article 30 "three-step" tests for assessing exceptions or limitations to copyrights and patent rights. Thus, even if article 39's interpretation were ambiguous about governments' regulatory authority to compel trade secret sharing, article 8.1, the *expressio unius* canon, and the presumption that states retain authority except where expressly prohibited would suggest reading TRIPS to permit unrestricted (reasonable) limitations or exceptions to article 39 obligations.

Similarly, article 8.2 provides that "[a]ppropriate measures, provided that they are consistent with the provisions of this Agreement, may be needed to prevent the abuse of intellectual property rights by right holders or the resort to practices which unreasonably restrain trade *or adversely affect the international transfer of technology.*"[231] Government authority to compel the *international* sharing of trade secrets-including but not limited to trade secrets necessary for manufacturing, or submitted clinical trial and other data needed for foreign regulatory approvals-would similarly prevent such rights from adversely affecting international transfer of technology and would simultaneously address worldwide public health needs.

Article 66.2, moreover, *obligates* developed country members to provide incentives to private entities to foster technology transfer to least-developed country members: "Developed country Members *shall provide* incentives to enterprises and institutions in their territories for the purpose of promoting and encouraging technology transfer to least-developed country Members in order to enable them to create a sound and viable technological base." Although private actions are voluntary under article 66.2, government creation of incentives for such private actions are not. Accordingly, failure to implement this domestic-law incentives requirement may be taken into account when considering what measures have become "necessary to protect public health" in developing countries. Where the failure to provide such incentives results in a lack of technology transfer for local R&D and manufacture of needed medical products, developed country members may be understood to have violated their TRIPS obligations. Conversely, compelled trade secret sharing by developed country members may be viewed as one such "incentive" in the strong form of a legal requirement.

Finally, it is important to remember human rights obligations when interpreting treaty requirements, which may form *jus cogens* or create other obligations in addition to topical treaty rights and obligations. Article 15(1)(b) of the International Covenant on Economic, Social and Cultural Rights "recognize[s] the right of everyone . . . [t]o enjoy the benefits of scientific progress and its applications." Access to needed medical products to protect against or to treat pandemic disease and potential death should clearly fall within the scope of that right, as well as the article 12(1) "right of everyone to the enjoyment of the highest attainable standard of physical and mental health." As noted in the UN Economic and Social Council Committee on Economic, Social and Cultural Rights, General Comment 25:

> The term "benefits" refers first to the material results of the applications of scientific research, such as vaccinations, fertilizers, technological instruments and the like. Secondly, benefits refer to the scientific knowledge and information directly deriving from scientific activity, as science provides benefits through the development and dissemination of the knowledge itself. Lastly, benefits refer also to the role of science in forming critical and responsible citizens who are able to participate fully in a democratic society.

Obviously, intellectual property withholding-such as the failure to share trade secret know-how and clinical data-may be in substantial tension with access to these "material results." This is particularly likely if such withholding results in disease or death that prevents citizens from "participat[ing] fully" in society. Thus, General Comment 25 states that "States should take appropriate measures to foster the positive effects of intellectual property on the right to participate in and to enjoy the benefits of scientific progress and its applications, while at the same time avoiding its possible negative effects."

In summary, the TRIPS Agreement (and other agreements) do not prohibit compelled trade secret sharing or compulsory trade secret licensing. Arguments to the contrary are simply misguided. Such arguments, moreover, are harmful in that they discourage countries from exercising their authority to compel such sharing to address worldwide pandemic technology-development, manufacturing, and regulatory-approval needs. The relevant questions are thus what domestic authorities exist to take such action (as addressed in Part IV), and whether governments have the political will to exercise those authorities. But before turning to those authorities, it is worth discussing both the pending TRIPS Waiver proposals and the potential for governments to face monetary liability under ISDS (also referred to as "bilateral investment treaties" or "international investment agreements" ("IIAs")) regarding claims for compensation, in addition to any compensation that may be provided or required when governments compel such trade secret sharing or trade secret licenses.

## NOTES AND QUESTIONS

**1.** Note the difference between compelling rightholders to disclose undisclosed information to the benefit of a competitor (horizontal relation) and for government use (vertical relation). Which of the arguments made in favour of compelling disclosure relate to one or the other configuration?

2. As noted in Chapter 2, part of the negotiations at the World Health Organization on a Pandemic Accord and potential amendment of the International Health Regulations (2005) involves enhancing the capacity within low- and middle-income countries to develop and manufacture vaccines. Negotiators are by now aware that merely "waving patents" does not

provide a sufficient basis for building up sophisticated vaccine capacity, and that access to the know-how involved is imperative. No one seriously disputes that premise. The questions rather involve the extent to which private sector actors can or should be required to participate in technology transfer, including know-how covered by trade secret, to third parties. Companies such as Moderna have said that rather than transfer trade secrets they will build new factories in low- and middle-income countries.*

**3.** The paper does not discuss the implications of *Australia – Plain Packaging* (DS 435, D International Health Regulations S 441, DS 458, DS 467) dealing with governmental restrictions on the use of trademarks under Article 20 TRIPS. What lessons can be learned for government use from the case, in particular the recognition of a legitimate interest to use a trademark, while denying a right to use in relation to governmental powers? (Cf. Chapter 3, section II.E, pp. 426-432.)

**4.** What lessons can be drawn for the protection of trade secrets as an intellectual property right from the overall requirement to balance rights and obligations as a core concern of the underlying philosophy discussed in Chapter 1?

**5.** The USMCA incorporates a number of substantive and enforcement provisions with respect to trade secret protection, including a definition of "misappropriation" and "Manner contrary to honest commercial practices" (Article 20.I.3), as well as a provision foreclosing Parties from imposing "excessive or discriminatory conditions" on licenses "that dilute the value of the trade secrets" (Article 20.I.7). It requires the Parties to provide criminal procedures and penalties for "unauthorized and willful misappropriation of a trade secret" (Article 20.I.2).

## C. Regulatory Data Protection as an IP Form

Governments request or require the submission of data from business enterprises for a wide variety of reasons. Data may be requested (or demanded) for the purpose of:

- investigating allegations of misconduct, such as in the antitrust enforcement context
- the evaluation of merger and acquisition proposals
- in the context of monitoring economic activity
- to assess tax liability, or to assure compliance with securities regulation
- to evaluate whether products meet certain regulatory standards.

In all of these circumstances, the business enterprise may want to protect submitted data against disclosure to competitors.

It is common for national legislation to require government agencies to protect against disclosure data designated by its submitter as confidential business information, except as such disclosure is authorized by law. Disclosure may be authorized for a variety of reasons, including to protect public health or safety or to further a legitimate law enforcement objective.

Data submitted for regulatory purposes may not be "intellectual property" in the ordinary sense of that term, just as information contained in databases may not constitute intellectual property. However, that information may have commercial value because a substantial investment was required to assemble it, and because that information would have commercial value to a competitor who could use the information without repeating its assembly.

Prior to the TRIPS Agreement, there were no multilaterally agreed norms on the protection of data submitted to governments for regulatory purposes.

---

* See Frederick Abbott, Intellectual Property and Technology Transfer for COVID-19 Vaccines: Assessment of the Record, Study for the WIPO Global Challenges Division, https://www.wipo.int/publications/en/details.jsp?id=4684&plang=EN.

## D. Regulatory Data and the TRIPS Agreement

Negotiations during the GATT Uruguay Round regarding the protection of regulatory data were highly contentious, and the resulting rules of Article 39.3 have been equally contentious. The following excerpt from the UNCTAD/ICTSD Resource Book on TRIPS and Development introduces the TRIPS Agreement rules.

### *Article 39.3*

UNCTAD/ICTSD Resource Book on TRIPS and Development*

Members, when requiring, as a condition of approving the marketing of pharmaceutical or of agricultural chemical products which utilize new chemical entities, the submission of undisclosed test or other data, the origination of which involves a considerable effort, shall protect such data against unfair commercial use. In addition, Members shall protect such data against disclosure, except where necessary to protect the public, or unless steps are taken to ensure that the data are protected against unfair commercial use.

#### 3.3.1. Conditions for Protection of Data Submitted for Marketing Approval

A basic premise for the application of Article 39.3 is that a Member imposes an obligation to submit data as a condition to obtain the marketing approval of pharmaceutical or agrochemical products. This provision does not apply when it is not necessary to submit such data, for instance, when marketing approval is granted by the national authority relying on the existence of a prior registration elsewhere.[1034]

The subject matter of the protection under this Article is *undisclosed* information contained in written material which details the results of scientific health and safety testing of drugs and agrochemicals, in relation to human, animal and plant health, impact on the environment and efficacy of use. This information is not "invented" or "created" but developed according to standard protocols. The protected data may also include manufacturing, conservation and packaging methods and conditions, to the extent that their submission is needed to obtain marketing approval.

The data to be protected must relate to a "new chemical entity." The Agreement does not define what should be meant by "new." Members may apply a concept similar to the one applied under patent law, or consider that a chemical entity is "new" if there were no prior application for approval of the same drug. Article 39.3 does not clarify either whether newness should be absolute (universal) or relative (local).[1035]

Based on the ordinary meaning of the terms used, Article 39.3 would not apply to new uses of known products, nor to dosage forms, combinations, new forms of administration, crystalline forms, isomers, etc., of existing drugs, since there would be no novel chemical entity involved.

Article 39.3 does not define any substantive standard for granting protection (like inventive step or novelty), but simply mandates protection when obtaining the data involved "a

* Available at http://www.iprsonline.org.

1034. In this case the authority does not require test data, but takes its decision on the basis of the registration granted in a foreign country.

1035. *See* T. Cook (2000). *Special Report: The protection of regulatory data in the pharmaceutical and other sectors*, Sweet & Maxwell, London, p. 6.

considerable effort." The text is vague about the type of effort involved (technical, economic?) and also with respect to its magnitude. (When would it be deemed "considerable"?) The wording used here is broader than that employed in Article 70.4—where reference to "significant investment" is made. A reasonable understanding would be that the "effort" involved should not only be significant in economic terms but also from a technical and scientific point of view, including experimental activities.

### 3.3.2. Forms of Protection of Data Submitted for Marketing Approval

The protection to be granted under Article 39.3 is twofold: against "unfair commercial use" and against disclosure of the relevant protected information.

Considerable controversy exists about the interpretation of the extent of the obligation to protect against "unfair commercial use." According to one view, the sole or most effective method[1036] for complying with this obligation is by granting the originator of data a period of *exclusive* use thereof, as currently mandated in some developed countries. Under this interpretation, national authorities would not be permitted, during the exclusivity period, to rely on data they have received in order to assess subsequent applications for the registration of similar products.[1037]

According to another view, Article 39.3 does not require the recognition of exclusive rights, but protection in the framework of unfair competition rules. Thus, a third party should be prevented from using the results of the test undertaken by another company as background for an independent submission for marketing approval, if the respective data had been acquired through dishonest commercial practices. However, under that provision a governmental authority would not be prevented from relying on the data presented by one company to assess submissions by other companies relating to similar products. If the regulatory body were not free, when assessing a file, to use all the knowledge available to it, including data from other files, a great deal of repetitive toxicological and clinical investigation will be required, which will be wasteful and ethically questionable. This position is also grounded on the pro-competitive effects of low entry barriers for pharmaceutical product. The early entry of generic competition is likely to increase the affordability of medicines at the lowest possible price.[1038]

On the other hand, protection is to be ensured against disclosure of the confidential data by governmental authorities, subject to the two exceptions mentioned in Article 39.3: a) when disclosure is necessary to protect the public; and b) when steps are taken to ensure that the

---

1036. *See, e.g.*, the Communication from the European Union and its member states on *The relationship between the provisions of the TRIPS Agreement and access to medicines*, IP/C/W/280, 12 June 2001. A similar view is expressed by R. Kampf, *Patents versus Patients?, in* Archiv des Völkerrechts, vol. 40 (2002), pp. 90-234, on p. 120, 121.

1037. The rationale behind this position is that "equity demands that protection be provided for data, which can cost the original submitter several million dollars to produce. Disclosing this data to the public or allowing its use by another applicant unfairly denies the compiler of the data the value of its efforts and grants an economic advantage to later applicants for marketing approval, enabling them to avoid the cost of developing test data for their own products. Countries that allow such unfair advantages to later applicants discourage developers of new pharmaceuticals and agricultural chemicals from seeking to introduce their state-of-the-art products in the country's market. So, not only is such protection required by the TRIPS Agreement, it is both equitable and wise from a public and health policy standpoint." *See* C. Priapantja, (2000), *Trade Secret: How does this apply to drug registration data?* Paper presented at "ASEAN Workshop on the TRIPS Agreement and its Impact on Pharmaceuticals," Department of Health and World Health Organization, May 2-4, p. 4.

1038. *See* Carlos Correa, *Protection of Data Submitted for the Registration of Pharmaceuticals: Implementing the Standards of the TRIPS Agreement*, South Centre, Geneva 2002 (available at http://www.southcentre.org/publications/protection/toc.htm).

data will not be used in a commercially unfair manner. Under these exceptions, disclosure may be permissible, for example, to allow a compulsory licensee to obtain a marketing approval, particularly when the license is aimed at remedying anti-competitive practices or at satisfying public health needs.

## NOTES AND QUESTIONS

**1.** Rules regarding protection of data submitted for regulatory purposes may have a profound effect on the functioning of the pharmaceuticals market. Innovator companies invest substantial sums in conducting clinical trials of new medicines and pursuing approval of those medicines with regulatory agencies such as the U.S. Food and Drug Administration. These innovator companies seek to protect their investment in the clinical trial process. Generic pharmaceutical producers submit applications for approval of copies of innovator medicines based on demonstrating "bioequivalence." That is, the generic producer need only demonstrate that its product is essentially the same as the innovator drug. It would be unethical to require generic producers to conduct redundant clinical trials because some of the test subjects receive placebo rather than therapy. Moreover, redundant clinical testing would be a waste of financial resources. Establishing the proper scope of protection for regulatory data in the pharmaceutical sector involves striking a balance between the interests of the innovator companies in protecting investment and the interests of the general public in more rapid access to low-priced medicines. There are very large sums of money at stake in the debate over the appropriate level of protection for regulatory data in the pharmaceutical sector.

**2.** Similar issues arise in other regulatory sectors. For example, when the U.S. Environmental Protection Agency assesses the safety of industrial chemicals, the producer of those chemicals submits data regarding production processes. That data is of interest to competitors, but it is also of interest to nongovernmental organizations seeking to assess potential environmental impact. Should the government have a monopoly over assessment of environmental risk? How can data be made accessible to public interest groups but at the same time be protected against "unfair commercial use" by competitors?

**3.** Article 39.3 of the TRIPS Agreement expressly refers to pharmaceutical and agricultural chemical products using "new chemical entities". As a matter of common understanding, a biologic drug formed from biological substances such as cells or parts of cells would not be considered "chemical entities", which instead refer to combinations of small molecules, i.e. basic chemical components. This may help to explain why pharmaceutical companies have been so anxious to negotiate market exclusivity protection for new biologic drugs in bilateral and regional trade agreements. On its face, new biologic drugs are not subject to protection by Article 39.3 of the TRIPS Agreement. The industry might argue that biologic drugs were not prevalent at the time the TRIPS Agreement was negotiated and that Article 39.3 should be read broadly to incorporate changes in the industry sector. But, biologic drugs are regulated separately through national/regional legislation and by national regulatory authorities. Regulatory authorities do not simply read their former mandates on chemical drugs to apply to biologic drugs. Why should the TRIPS Agreement be interpreted that way?

## E. Regional Systems for the Protection of Regulatory Data

### *1. Protection of Regulatory Data in the European Union*

The *AKZO* case is the landmark decision in EU law concerning the obligation of the EC Commission to treat business secrets as confidential. In this case, the Commission asked for several sensitive documents in a competition law investigation. AKZO was obliged to produce these documents to the Commission by former Article 213 of the EC Treaty (now Article 284) as well as the corresponding provisions of Regulation No. 17 dealing with competition procedure. Later, the Commission communicated some of the documents to the intervener and only informed AKZO afterwards. In considering if this behavior of the Commission was correct, the Court of Justice of the European Union interpreted the secrecy obligation of the Commission in relation to the rights of third parties of access to the file, and it implemented a high-level duty to protect business secrets.

## *AKZO Chemie BV and AKZO Chemie UK Ltd v. Commission of the European Communities*

Judgment of the Court (Fifth Chamber) of 24 June 1986, Case 53/85 Court of Justice of the European Communities

Prior history: application requesting the Court to declare void the decision of the Commission of the European Communities of 14 December 1984 concerning the communication to a third party of documents stated to be confidential, disposition: on those grounds, the Court (fifth chamber) hereby:

(1) Declares void the decision which the Commission notified to the applicant by letter of 18 December 1984;
(2) Dismisses the remainder of the application;
(3) Orders the Commission to pay the costs.

Introduction: In case 53/85

AKZO Chemie BV . . .

vs.

Commission of the European Communities . . .

Application requesting the Court to declare void the decision of the Commission of the European Communities of 14 December 1984 concerning the communication to a third party of documents stated to be confidential. . . .

Judgment by: Joliet

### Judgment:

By an application lodged at the Court registry on 22 February 1985, AKZO Chemie BV and AKZO Chemie UK Ltd., whose registered offices are at Amersfoort (Netherlands) and Walton-on-Thames (United Kingdom) respectively, brought an action under the second paragraph of Article 173 of the EEC Treaty requesting the Court to declare void the Commission's decision of 18 December 1984 to communicate documents of a confidential nature to a third party who had submitted a complaint.

AKZO Chemie BV and AKZO Chemie UK Ltd. are part of the AKZO group which is the largest supplier in the Community of benzoyl peroxide, a chemical product which is used in the making of plastics and as a bleach for the treatment of flour. . . .

AKZO is alleged to have threatened to force ECS from the flour additives market through a policy of selective, abnormally low prices if ECS extended its activities to the market in organic peroxides for the plastics industry and to have actually carried out that threat. On 15 June 1982 ECS made a complaint to the Commission alleging an infringement of Article 86 of the EEC Treaty. As a result of that complaint, officials of the Commission carried out an investigation in December 1982 at the offices of AKZO Chemie BV and of AKZO Chemie

UK Ltd. under Article 14(3) of Regulation No. 17/62. On that occasion the officials obtained various documents belonging to AKZO. . . .

On 14 December 1984 the Commission communicated to ECS certain annexes to the statement of objections and only informed AKZO that it had done so in a letter of 18 December 1984. In its letter, the Commission emphasized that it was for it to decide whether or not documents were confidential. It stated that it had followed the list drawn up by AKZO with a few exceptions in regard to which it provided a brief explanation.

By an application lodged at the Court registry on 22 February 1985, AKZO brought an action for a declaration that the Commission's decision to transmit certain confidential documents to ECS was void. In its application AKZO also sought an order from the Court requiring the Commission to demand ECS to return the documents transmitted to it.

By order of 10 July 1985, the Court granted ECS leave to intervene in the proceedings in support of the Commission's conclusions.

### Admissibility of the Action . . .

It is certainly true that the documents were transmitted with a view to facilitating the examination of the case. However, the measure adversely affecting the applicant is, as is clear from the foregoing paragraphs, the decision in which the Commission considered that the documents in question did not qualify for the confidential treatment guaranteed by Community law and could therefore be communicated. That measure is definitive in nature and is independent of any decision on the question whether Article 86 [now Article 82] of the Treaty has been infringed. The opportunity which the applicant has to bring an action against a final decision establishing that the competition rules have been infringed is not of such a nature as to provide it with an adequate degree of protection of its rights in the matter. On the one hand, it is possible that the administrative procedure will not result in a decision finding that an infringement has been committed. On the other hand, if an action is brought against that decision, it will not in any event provide the applicant with the means of preventing the irreversible consequences which would result from improper disclosure of certain of its documents.

AKZO's interest in contesting the decision in question cannot be denied on the ground that in this case the decision had already been implemented at the time when the action was brought. The annulment of such a decision is of itself capable of having legal consequences, in particular by preventing a repetition by the Commission of the practice complained of and by rendering unlawful the use by ECS of any documents improperly communicated to it.

It follows that the applicant's claim for a declaration that the contested decision is void is admissible. . . .

### Substance of the Case

The applicant puts forward three submissions in support of its application. In the first place, it alleges that by communicating to ECS certain documents which were all in some way confidential, the Commission acted in breach of its obligation not to disclose information which is covered by the obligation of professional secrecy or which is subject to protection as a business secret. In the second place, by communicating to ECS certain documents which the latter could use in the legal proceedings pending in the [U]nited [K]ingdom, the Commission infringed Article 20(1) of Regulation No. 17/62 which provides that information acquired by the Commission in the exercise of its powers of investigation may be used only for the purpose for which it was obtained. Finally, the Commission has infringed Article 185 [now Article 242] of the Treaty inasmuch as, by implementing its decision before notifying it to the applicant, it deprived the latter of the possibility of applying for an order suspending the operation of that decision at the same time as it instituted proceedings for annulment.

The Commission, with whose arguments the intervener essentially agrees, considers first of all that documents constituting evidence of an infringement of Article 86 of the Treaty, such as those communicated to ECS, are not of a confidential nature. It goes on to emphasize that ECS was given access to the documents only on the express condition that it would not use them for any purpose other than the proceedings before the Commission. Finally, it denies that there was any infringement of Article 185 of the Treaty because it did not adopt any decision which could be the subject of an application for annulment.

In the first place, it must be borne in mind that Article 214 [now Article 287] of the Treaty requires the officials and other servants of the institutions of the Community not to disclose information in their possession of the kind covered by the obligation of professional secrecy. Article 20 of Regulation No. 17/62, which implements that provision in regard to the rules applicable to undertakings, contains in paragraph (2) a special provision worded as follows: "without prejudice to the provisions of Articles 19 and 21, the Commission and the competent authorities of the member states, their officials and other servants shall not disclose information acquired by them as a result of the application of this Regulation and of the kind covered by the obligation of professional secrecy."

The provisions of Articles 19 and 21, the application of which is thus reserved, deal with the Commission's obligations in regard to hearings and the publication of decisions. It follows that the obligation of professional secrecy laid down in Article 20(2) is mitigated in regard to third parties on whom Article 19(2) confers the right to be heard, that is to say in regard, in particular, to a third party who has made a complaint. The Commission may communicate to such a party certain information covered by the obligation of professional secrecy in so far as it is necessary to do so for the proper conduct of the investigation.

However, that power does not apply to all documents of the kind covered by the obligation of professional secrecy. Article 19(3) which provides for the publication of notices prior to the granting of negative clearance or exemptions, and Article 21 which provides for the publication of certain decisions, both require the Commission to have regard to the legitimate interest of undertakings in the protection of their business secrets. Business secrets are thus afforded very special protection. Although they deal with particular situations, those provisions must be regarded as the expression of a general principle which applies during the course of the administrative procedure. It follows that a third party who has submitted a complaint may not in any circumstances be given access to documents containing business secrets. Any other solution would lead to the unacceptable consequence that an undertaking might be inspired to lodge a complaint with the Commission solely in order to gain access to its competitors' business secrets.

It is undoubtedly for the Commission to assess whether or not a particular document contains business secrets. After giving an undertaking an opportunity to state its views, the Commission is required to adopt a decision in that connection which contains an adequate statement of the reasons on which it is based and which must be notified to the undertaking concerned. Having regard to the extremely serious damage which could result from improper communication of documents to a competitor, the Commission must, before implementing its decision, give the undertaking an opportunity to bring an action before the Court with a view to having the assessments made reviewed by it and to preventing disclosure of the documents in question.

In this case, the Commission gave the undertaking concerned an opportunity to make its position known and adopted a decision containing an adequate statement of the reasons on which it was based and concerning both the confidential nature of the documents at issue and the possibility of communicating them. At the same time, however, by an act which cannot be severed from that decision, the Commission decided to hand over the documents to the third party who had made the complaint even before it notified its findings to that undertaking. It thus made it impossible for the undertaking to avail itself of the means of redress provided by Article 173 [now Article 230] in conjunction with Article 185 of the Treaty with a view to preventing the implementation of a contested decision.

That being the case, the decision which the Commission notified to the applicant by letter of 18 December 1984 must be declared void without there being any need to determine whether the documents communicated to the intervener did in fact contain business secrets.

## NOTES AND QUESTIONS

**1.** Article 287 (formerly Article 214) of the EC Treaty provides: "The members of the institutions of the Community, the members of committees, and the officials and other servants of the Community shall be required, even after their duties have ceased, not to disclose information of the kind covered by the obligation of professional secrecy, in particular information about undertakings, their business relations or their cost components."

**2.** Following the adoption and entry into force of the TRIPS Agreement, trade secret protection in Member States remained diverse and incoherent. Directive (EU) 2016/943 of the European Parliament and the Council of 8 June 2016 on the protection of undisclosed know-how and business information (trade secrets) against their unlawful acquisition, use and disclosure, OJ 15.6.2016 L 151/1, brought about harmonization of trade secret protection within the European Union and EEA. The directive regulates scope of protection, acquisition, and exceptions (excerpts below), as well as measures, procedures, and remedies, in particular the preservation of confidentiality in legal proceedings. The directive regulates safeguards, provisional measures, and damages. It results in essentially codifying a new chapter of unfair competition in the context of the single market, taking into account free movement of goods and services as well as fundamental rights.

## *Directive (EU) 2016/943 of the European Parliament and of the Council*

of 8 June 2016 on the protection of undisclosed know-how and business information (trade secrets) against their unlawful acquisition, use and disclosure

Whereas:

(1) Businesses and non-commercial research institutions invest in acquiring, developing and applying know-how and information which is the currency of the knowledge economy and provides a competitive advantage. This investment in generating and applying intellectual capital is a determining factor as regards their competitiveness and innovation-related performance in the market and therefore their returns on investment, which is the underlying motivation for business research and development. Businesses have recourse to different means to appropriate the results of their innovation-related activities when openness does not allow for the full exploitation of their investment in research and innovation. Use of intellectual property rights, such as patents, design rights or copyright, is one such means. Another means of appropriating the results of innovation is to protect access to, and exploit, knowledge that is valuable to the entity and not widely known. Such valuable know-how and business information, that is undisclosed and intended to remain confidential, is referred to as a trade secret.

(2) Businesses, irrespective of their size, value trade secrets as much as patents and other forms of intellectual property right. They use confidentiality as a business competitiveness and research innovation management tool, and in relation to a diverse range of information that

extends beyond technological knowledge to commercial data such as information on customers and suppliers, business plans, and market research and strategies. Small and medium-sized enterprises (SMEs) value and rely on trade secrets even more. By protecting such a wide range of know-how and business information, whether as a complement or as an alternative to intellectual property rights, trade secrets allow creators and innovators to derive profit from their creation or innovation and, therefore, are particularly important for business competitiveness as well as for research and development, and innovation-related performance.

. . .

Member States shall ensure that an application for the measures, procedures and remedies provided for in this Directive is dismissed where the alleged acquisition, use or disclosure of the trade secret was carried out in any of the following cases:

(a) for exercising the right to freedom of expression and information as set out in the Charter, including respect for the freedom and pluralism of the media;
(b) for revealing misconduct, wrongdoing or illegal activity, provided that the respondent acted for the purpose of protecting the general public interest;
(c) disclosure by workers to their representatives as part of the legitimate exercise by those representatives of their functions in accordance with Union or national law, provided that such disclosure was necessary for that exercise;
(d) for the purpose of protecting a legitimate interest recognised by Union or national law. . . .

## 2. *Pharmaceutical Regulatory Data in the European Union*

The European Union has increasingly taken over regulation of the internal pharmaceuticals market from its member states. In 1992, the European Union adopted a regulation providing for the extension of the term of pharmaceutical patents to compensate for the period during which regulatory approval for a medicine covered by the patent was sought.[13] The patent holder is issued a "supplementary protection certificate" or "SPC," which extends the effective term of the patent. The period of supplementary protection may not be greater than five years.[14]

In 2004, in connection with the establishment of a European Medicines Agency responsible for approval of the marketing of medicines throughout the European Union,[15] the European Union adopted a common standard of data exclusivity.[16] This new system is referred

13. Council Regulation (EEC) No 1768/92 of 18 June 1992 concerning the creation of a supplementary protection certificate for medicinal products, OJ L 182, 02/07/1992.

14. *Id.* at Article 13, providing:

Duration of the certificate

1. The certificate shall take effect at the end of the lawful term of the basic patent for a period equal to the period which elapsed between the date on which the application for a basic patent was lodged and the date of the first authorization to place the product on the market in the Community reduced by a period of five years.

2. Notwithstanding paragraph 1, the duration of the certificate may not exceed five years from the date on which it takes effect.

15. Regulation (EC) No 726/2004 of the European Parliament and of the Council of 31 March 2004 laying down Community procedures for the authorization and supervision of medicinal products for human and veterinary use and establishing a European Medicines Agency, OJ L 136/1, 30/4/2004.

16. Directive 2004/27/EC of the European Parliament and of the Council of 31 March 2004 amending Directive 2001/83/EC on the Community code relating to medicinal products for human use, OJ L 136/34, 30/4/2004 (Community Code Amendments).

to as the 8 + 2 + 1 system. Amendments to the Community Code on Medicinal Products provide that a generic producer may seek approval of a bioequivalent product eight years following authorization of an innovator "reference" product, and in doing so may rely on the data submitted in connection with approval of the reference product.[17] However, even if approval is granted earlier, the generic product may not be placed on the market until ten years following initial authorization of the "reference" product.[18] There is thus a ten-year period of marketing exclusivity in favor of the innovator product. In addition, a one-year period may be added to the ten-year marketing exclusivity period if, during the first eight years of that period, "the marketing authorization holder obtains an authorisation for one or more new therapeutic indications which, during the scientific evaluation prior to their authorisation, are held to bring a significant clinical benefit in comparison with existing therapies."[19]

All countries newly acceding to the European Union must accept the foregoing rules regarding marketing exclusivity. This has proven difficult and controversial for countries such as Hungary, which housed a successful and dynamic generic pharmaceutical sector prior to joining the European Union.

## F. Bilateral and Regional Trade Agreements and the Protection of Regulatory Data

At the urging of U.S. and European research-based pharmaceutical companies, the United States Trade Representative and the European Commission have pursued a policy of demanding extensive commitments for the protection of pharmaceutical regulatory data in bilateral and regional trade agreement negotiations. The lacuna of regulating the duration of test data exclusivity in Article 39.3, TRIPS Agreement, led to the introduction of specific time periods in preferential trade agreements in terms of TRIPS-plus obligations.

Other aspects of the FTA program are described in another excerpt from the World Bank Trade Note by Fink and Reichenmiller (see also Chapter 1, section V.A; Chapter 4, section V; and Chapter 6, section III).

**Carsten Fink & Patrick Reichenmiller***

### *Tightening TRIPS: The Intellectual Property Provisions of Recent US Free Trade Agreements*

. . . [O]btaining marketing approval for drugs requires the submission of test data on a drug's safety and efficacy to regulatory authorities. Such data is protected by separate legal instruments that differ from country to country. The TRIPS Agreement only requires test data to be protected against "unfair commercial use." By contrast, most of the bilateral agreements explicitly mandate test data exclusivity, as provided for under US law. Once a company has submitted original test data, no competing manufacturer is allowed to rely on these data for a period of five years to request marketing approval for its own drug. The new compilation of comparable test data by competing manufacturers may take several years and may be prohibitively expensive. Thus, test data exclusivity may pose a second obstacle for governments to effectively use compulsory licensing.

17. Art. 10(1), Community Code, as amended.
18. *Id.*
19. *Id.*
* World Bank Trade Note No. 20, Feb. 7, 2005.

Several of the bilateral agreements go further on data exclusivity. When pharmaceutical companies seek marketing approval for previously unapproved uses of already registered drugs, regulatory authorities typically require the submission of "new" clinical information. The agreements with Morocco and Bahrain provide for an additional 3 year data exclusivity period triggered by such new clinical information. Drugs benefiting from this type of marketing exclusivity do not only include new patented products, but also older generic products for which the patents have expired (though generic competition for previously approved uses of such drugs would remain unaffected).

Sometimes drug regulatory authorities recognize the marketing approval decisions of foreign regulators in granting marketing approval for the same product at home. The intellectual property chapter of the US-Singapore Agreement mandates, in this case, that foreign data exclusivity also applies at home. In other words, no competing manufacturer is allowed to rely on the test data submitted to a *foreign* regulator for seeking own marketing approval at home.

The agreements with Australia, Bahrain, and the DR-CAFTA countries are still more far reaching on the cross-border application of data exclusivity. Even if regulatory authorities do not recognize foreign marketing approvals, competing manufacturers are prevented from using test data submitted to a drug regulatory agency in another territory. In other words, test data exclusivity applies automatically in all FTA jurisdictions, once a company submits test data to a drug regulator in one territory—even outside the FTA area. . . .

Are the provisions on marketing approval during the patent term, test data exclusivity, and parallel importation at odds with the Doha Declaration on TRIPS and Public Health? This Declaration—issued at the WTO Ministerial Meeting in Doha, Qatar in 2001—recognized the gravity of the public health problems afflicting many developing countries and least developing countries. Among other things, it reaffirmed the right of WTO members to use the flexibilities of TRIPS in the area of compulsory licensing and parallel importation to ". . . *promote access to medicines for all.*" Moreover, in August 2003, WTO members created a special mechanism under the TRIPS Agreement that allows countries with insufficient manufacturing capacity to effectively use compulsory licenses by importing generic drugs (*see* Fink, 2003). Technically, the Doha Declaration and the August 2003 Decision by WTO members do not address questions of marketing approval during the patent term and test data exclusivity. However, the provisions of the FTAs in these areas can still be seen as being at odds with the spirit of these multilateral accords, to the extent that they preclude the effective use of compulsory licenses.

In side letters to the US-DR-CAFTA, US-Morocco and US-Bahrain agreements, the respective governments shared understandings that the intellectual property chapters do not affect their ability to ". . . *take necessary measures to protect public health by promoting medicines for all* [. . .]." In a recent letter to a Member of the US Congress on the US-Morocco FTA, the General Counsel of the United States Trade Representative (USTR) further clarified:

> [. . .] if circumstances ever arise in which a drug is produced under a compulsory license, and it is necessary to approve that drug to protect public health or effectively utilize the TRIPS/health solution, the data protection provision in the FTA would not stand in the way.
>
> [. . .] As stated in the side letter, the letter constitutes a formal agreement between the Parties. It is, thus, a significant part of the interpretive context for this agreement and not merely rhetorical. According to Article 31 of the Vienna Convention on the Law of Treaties, which reflects customary rules of treaty interpretation in international law, the terms of a treaty must be interpreted "in their context," and that "context" includes "any agreement relating to the treaty which was made between all the parties in connection with the conclusion of the treaty."

At the same time, the US Government does not view the side letters as creating any kind of exemption that would allow parties to the FTAs to ignore obligations in the agreements' intellectual property chapters. The side letters merely signal the signing governments' belief that the intellectual property rules of the FTAs will not interfere with the protection of public health.

**Thomas Cottier, Dannie Jost & Michelle Schupp***

## *Setting the Scene: The Prospects of TRIPS-Plus Protection in Future Mega-Regionals*

### TEST DATA EXCLUSIVITY

Test data exclusivity for agricultural, chemical and pharmaceutical products prior to market approval is another central issue in the three interregionals. The period of data exclusivity ranges from five,[1] eight,[2] or ten years.[3]

CAFTA establishes a period of data exclusivity for new 'products' of either five years (pharmaceuticals) or ten years (agricultural chemicals), whereas TRIPS leaves the period for new chemical entities unspecified, thus also potentially zero years, if one was able to establish the absence of 'unfair commercial use' for said 'new chemical entity'. The shift in terminology from 'new chemical entity' in TRIPS to 'new product' in CAFTA can be interpreted as "casting the monopoly net wider."[4]

CETA deals in two separate provisions with data protection for pharmaceuticals[5] and for plant protection products.[6] In the market approval process, it provides data exclusivity (no use of the data by a third party) for 'new chemical entities' for a period of 'not less than six years' from the date on which market approval was granted for pharmaceuticals, and ten years for plant protection products. In addition, CETA provides a period of market exclusivity for a pharmaceutical product based on the test data submitted to the regulatory agency, of not less than eight years,[7] thus giving a manufacturer of a new generic product a window of two years to obtain marketing approval (using the data of the originator pharmaceutical rights owner).

In TPP minimum data exclusivity period for agricultural chemicals, biologics and pharmaceuticals in separate provisions, with the durations being ten, eight and five years, respectively.[8]

### BIOLOGICS

The TPP suggests that there is a new area of contention: the protection of pharmaceuticals based on biologics (aka biologicals). While certain biologics (vaccines) are more than a century old, new biologics and advanced therapeutic strategies present a challenge for the industry. Thus in TPP the offers on the table for exclusivity on (clinical, safety, effectiveness) data

* In MEGA-REGIONAL TRADE AGREEMENTS 191-216 (Thilo Rensmann ed., 2017).

1. Article 15.10.1(a) CAFTA for pharmaceuticals; Article 18.50.1(ii) TPP for a new pharmaceutical product.
2. Article 18.52.1(a) TPP for new biologics.
3. Article 15.10.1(a) CAFTA for agricultural products.
4. Godoy (n 21) 116.
5. Article 10 CETA.
6. Article 11 CETA.
7. Article 10.2(b) CETA.
8. Article 18.47 TPP for agricultural chemicals, Article 18.50 TPP for pharmaceuticals, and Article 18.52 for biologics.

submitted for the first marketing approval of a pharmaceutical that is a biologic[9] ranged from 0 to 12 years.[10] The arguments were and are many, and commentators express a range of opinions between this being a matter of life and death to the well-worn argument that exclusivity is "essential for incentivizing investments in the technologies and rewarding the innovators who are willing to take these risks."[11] This particular issue not only reflects the state of the art in therapeutics, but it also raises fundamental questions regarding the mechanisms used to grant monopoly rights to products of fundamental relevance to public policy. It will be interesting to see if this issue is raised in the TTIP negotiations and how it will be solved. The European Medicines Agency (EMA)[12] put in place a policy on 1 January 2015 establishing that "clinical data cannot be considered commercially confidential information." If this is to be interpreted as meaning that such clinical data is outside the scope of TRIPS 39(2) and (3) then the whole construct of data exclusivity could collapse.

## NOTES AND QUESTIONS

**1.** As the excerpt shows, stronger research data protection and exclusivity is not limited to developing countries but equally includes countries like Canada or Israel. Both were the subject of aggressive complaint from the U.S. Trade Representative for many years, and each has recently adopted an approach to protection of pharmaceutical regulatory data more consistent with U.S. preferences.

**2.** In addition to generally including the template of the United States for free trade agreements that obligate other countries to maintain a 5-year period of market exclusivity for new small chemical drugs, plus 3-year extensions for additional clinical studies and indications. As initially agreed, the USMCA would have obligated the Parties to provide 10-year terms of market exclusivity for new biologics (Article 20.F.14). This was 2 years longer than the 8-year biologic market exclusivity term included in the TPP (prior to the withdrawal of US signature), and represents another ratcheting up of protection standards imposed in favor of the originator (biologic) pharmaceutical industry. However, Democrats in the U.S. Congress objected to extending market exclusivity protection for new biologic products to the USMCA, and with agreement of Canada and Mexico (which had each opposed the provision in the first place), this new provision on market exclusivity was removed from the USMCA as it finally entered into force.

**3.** India is home to the developing world's most successful generic pharmaceutical sector. Having revised its patent legislation in 2005 to comply with its January 1, 2005 obligation to provide pharmaceutical product patent protection, India is under pressure from Europe and the United States to adopt a new approach to protection of regulatory data. In addition to seeking pharmaceutical regulatory data-based marketing exclusivity in bilateral and regional trade negotiations, the United States also bargains for such exclusivity when countries seek to join the WTO. China, for example, agreed to provide a six-year period of pharmaceutical

---

9. For the purpose of the TPP IP chapter a biologic is a vaccine, protein, plasma-derived product, or blood-derivative, but the definition is not settled. For an authoritative discussion on this topic see: Sarah K Branch and Israel Agranat, '"New Drug" Designations for New Therapeutic Entities: New Active Substance, New Chemical Entity, New Biological Entity, New Molecular Entity' (2014) 57 Journal of Medicinal Chemistry 8729.

10. Article QQ.E.20 TPP (leaked version 2014).

11. Kristina M Lybecker, 'When Patents Aren't Enough: Why Biologics Necessitate Data Exclusivity Protection' (2014) 40 1427, 1442.

12. Clinical Trial Regulation EU No. 536/2014 Recital 68; Article 81(4).

marketing exclusivity in connection with its accession in 2001. Paragraph 284 of the Report of the Working Party on the Accession of China, WT/ACC/CHN/49, 1 Oct. 2001, provides:

> The representative of China further confirmed that China would, in compliance with Article 39.3 of the TRIPS Agreement, provide effective protection against unfair commercial use of undisclosed test or other data submitted to authorities in China as required in support of applications for marketing approval of pharmaceutical or of agricultural chemical products which utilized new chemical entities, except where the disclosure of such data was necessary to protect the public, or where steps were taken to ensure that the data are protected against unfair commercial use. This protection would include introduction and enactment of laws and regulations to make sure that no person, other than the person who submitted such data, could, without the permission of the person who submitted the data, rely on such data in support of an application for product approval for a period of at least six years from the date on which China granted marketing approval to the person submitting the data. During this period, any second applicant for market authorization would only be granted market authorization if he submits his own data. This protection of data would be available to all pharmaceutical and agricultural products which utilize new chemical entities, irrespective of whether they were patent-protected or not. The Working Party took note of these commitments.

The commitment in paragraph 284 of the Working Party Report should be read in conjunction with paragraph 342 of the report, and Article 1(3) of the Protocol of Accession, WT/L/432, 23 Nov. 2001, which together establish the legally binding nature of the commitment.

**4.** Why are pharmaceutical companies not satisfied with the protection for inventions provided by patents? What are the advantages provided by regulatory marketing exclusivity? The straightforward answer is that the companies understand that patents are inherently vulnerable to challenge on the various grounds described in Chapter 2, and protection as insecure. As a general proposition, grants of market exclusivity based on approval of new drugs or biologic products are not subject to challenge and litigation. Or, at least, such challenges are relatively rare and the law on such challenges is not well developed. Regulatory market exclusivity, in short, is more secure than patent protection.

## VI. THE INTERNATIONAL SYSTEM FOR THE PROTECTION OF INDUSTRIAL DESIGN AND INTEGRATED CIRCUIT LAYOUT DESIGN

### A. Design Protection as an IP Form

The design of products, whether purely artistic or commercially useful, creates appeal for the consumer. Product design is particularly important in industries whose products are not readily differentiated on the basis of technical performance. A "designer" blouse may serve precisely the function as a plain cotton T-shirt, but consumers pay more for the designer blouse because they appreciate its aesthetic elements.

Design has an inherent relationship with function. On the one hand, design possibilities are limited by function. At a certain stage, extravagance or fantasy in design can impede function. There may be endless ways to conceive of the design of a shoe or airplane, but not all of them will result in a functional piece of footwear or a vehicle that flies. On the other hand, design can facilitate function. Certain designs of automobiles take advantage of aerodynamics and decrease air resistance to increase speed or reduce fuel consumption.

The protection of industrial designs has long been problematic. The traditional forms of IP protection—copyright, patent, and trademark—may be applicable in many cases, but their application poses problems.

Copyright protects the creative expression of artists and authors, and is not limited in respect to the media in which such expression may be embodied. Yet, copyright does not protect function or idea, and courts have faced seemingly intractable difficulties in devising methodologies for separating form from function. In addition, because designs in many fields (such as fashion) tend to be similar, it is difficult to act against "similar" works. Also, copyright does not protect against independent creation and, particularly in the international context, proving that a second-comer "copied" raises an evidentiary hurdle.

A "utility patent" may protect a functional design. However, the criteria of novelty, inventive step, and usefulness may be difficult to meet, particularly in the realm of incremental design changes. Moreover, obtaining a utility patent, particularly for a number of countries, is a costly and time-consuming enterprise. For industries where design changes are routinely introduced to stimulate consumer demand—such as textiles and automobiles—the cost and administrative obstacles to using the utility patent for protection may be insurmountable in all but rare cases.

Trademarks protect distinctive signs, and in some countries (such as the United States) trademark protection has been extended broadly to cover "trade dress," including product and packaging design. However, as with copyright, trademark (and trade dress) does not extend to function, and courts also have difficulty separating trademark-related design and function. Also, since countries follow substantially different approaches to trade dress, relying on this approach internationally presents problems.

To address the obstacles inherent in applying copyright, (utility) patent, and trademark to industrial designs, some countries have adopted approaches more uniquely suited to this subject matter. The United States has a system for the grant of "design patents" that are similar to utility patents, except that instead of demonstrating the "usefulness" of a novel design, the applicant must show that its design is "ornamental" or nonfunctional (and the term of protection is limited to 14 years). More commonly, however, countries have adopted systems of design "registration" that do not include substantive examination and that employ standards of novelty less stringent than those for patents. We will take a look at the EU registration system.

In *Best Lock v. Ilco*, the U.S. Court of Appeals for the Federal Circuit addresses the tension between form and function in relation to design patent protection. The differing views of the majority and dissent illustrate the difficulty regulators have encountered in drawing the boundaries of design protection.

## *Best Lock v. Ilco Unican*

94 F.3d 1563 (Fed. Cir. 1996)

LOURIE, CIRCUIT JUDGE.

Best Lock Corporation appeals from the final decision of the United States District Court for the Southern District of Indiana in which the court held that Best Lock's U.S. Design Patent 327,636 was invalid. *Best Lock Corp. v. Ilco Unican Corp.*, 896 F. Supp. 836, 36 U.S.P.Q.2D (BNA) 1527 (S.D. Ind. 1995). Because the court did not clearly err in finding that the claimed design was functional and hence not ornamental, we affirm.

### BACKGROUND

This case involves a design patent for a key "blade." A typical key consists of a bow, which allows the user to turn the key in a corresponding lock, and a blade, which is the portion of the key inserted into the lock's keyway. When a key is manufactured, the key blade is "blank," i.e., the blade has not been cut or "bitted" with the combination required to operate the corresponding lock. Although a blank key blade will not operate the lock, the profile of the key blade is manufactured to fit into the corresponding lock's keyway. Subsequently, the blank key blade is cut to match the corresponding lock's combination.

In the replacement key market, a locksmith or a retail store with a key duplicating facility stocks blank key blades with various key profiles. . . . [T]he locksmith or retailer cuts the blade of the key blank with the combination required to operate the lock.

Best Lock manufactures and sells locks and keys used to maintain security at industrial, commercial, and institutional facilities. At these facilities, it is often feared that the keys used in their locks may readily be duplicated. Consequently, key and lock manufacturers, including Best Lock, have attempted to restrict unauthorized access to duplicate key blanks by obtaining utility or design patent protection on the keys. By obtaining patent protection, a company hopes to control the market for duplicate key blanks during the life of the patent.

Best Lock is the assignee of the two patents that were at issue before the district court, U.S. Patent 5,136,869 and U.S. Design Patent 327,636. The '869 patent, entitled "High Security Key and Cylinder Lock Assembly," claims an improved key blade and cylinder lock assembly that provides a wider key profile than standard keys and includes other features to deter lock picking. The '636 patent, entitled "Portion of a Key Blade Blank," claims the ornamental design for the operative portion of a key blade blank. . . . The '636 patent is the only design patent at issue on appeal. . . .

Ilco manufactures duplicate and replacement key blanks for existing locks. It sells its replacement key blanks to locksmiths and replacement key retailers. In 1993, Ilco copied the design of a Best Lock key, which had a key blade shaped like the design shown in the '636 patent. It subsequently distributed key blanks with that key blade shape at the annual convention of the Associated Locksmiths of America. In response, Best sued Ilco, alleging, *inter alia*, infringement of the '636 design patent and the '869 utility patent. Ilco counterclaimed, seeking a declaratory judgment of invalidity and noninfringement of both patents.

After a ten-day bench trial, the district court held that the '869 patent claims were invalid under 35 U.S.C. §102 because the claims were anticipated by the prior art. *Best Lock Corp. v. Ilco Unican Corp.*, 896 F. Supp. 836, 837, 36 U.S.P.Q.2D (BNA) 1527, 1528 (S.D. Ind. 1995). Best Lock has not appealed that holding. The court also held that the '636 design patent was invalid. In particular, the court found that Best Lock's key blades were not "a matter of ornamental concern to the purchaser or the user." *Id.* at 843, 36 U.S.P.Q.2D (BNA) at 1534. The court further found that the design patent was invalid because the shape of the blank key blade was dictated by its function. *Id.* Best Lock appeals, challenging the district court's decision regarding the '636 patent.

## Discussion

Under 35 U.S.C. §171, a design patent may be granted for a "new, original and ornamental design for an article of manufacture." However, if the design claimed in a design patent is dictated solely by the function of the article of manufacture, the patent is invalid because the design is not ornamental. *See Bonito Boats, Inc. v. Thunder Craft Boats, Inc.*, 489 U.S. 141, 148, 9 U.S.P.Q.2D (BNA) 1847, 1851, 103 L. Ed. 2d 118, 109 S. Ct. 971 (1989) ("To qualify for protection, a design must present an aesthetically pleasing appearance that is not dictated by function alone, and must satisfy the other criteria of patentability."); *see also In re Carletti*, 51 C.C.P.A. 1094, 328 F.2d 1020, 1022, 140 U.S.P.Q. (BNA) 653, 654 (CCPA 1964) ("It has long been settled that when a configuration is the result of functional considerations only, the resulting design is not patentable as an ornamental design for the simple reason that it is not 'ornamental'—was not created for the purpose of ornamenting."). A design is not dictated solely by its function when alternative designs for the article of manufacture are available. *See L.A. Gear, Inc. v. Thom McAn Shoe Co.*, 988 F.2d 1117, 1123, 25 U.S.P.Q.2D (BNA) 1913, 1917 (Fed. Cir.), *cert. denied*, 510 U.S. 908, 114 S. Ct. 291, 126 L. Ed. 2d 240 (1993). We review for clear error the district court's determination that the design claimed in the '636 patent is functional. *See id.* at 1124, 25 U.S.P.Q.2D (BNA) at 1917.

On appeal, Best Lock argues that the court erred in holding the '636 design patent invalid as being directed solely to a functional design. As support, it asserts that although a particular key and its corresponding lock must mate to operate the lock, an unlimited number of key blade and corresponding keyway designs are available. Choice of any particular design is arbitrary. Thus, Best Lock maintains that the key blade blank may have any number of different shapes and is therefore not dictated solely by functional concerns.

We disagree. The design shown in the claim of the '636 patent is limited to a blank key blade as shown in Figures 1-5 of the patent. Best Lock did not claim a design for the entire key.[2] See 37 C.F.R. §1.153 (1995) (The claim of a design patent "shall be in formal terms to the ornamental design for the article . . . as shown, or as shown and described."). The parties do not dispute that the key blade must be designed as shown in order to perform its intended function—to fit into its corresponding lock's keyway. An attempt to create a key blade with a different design would necessarily fail because no alternative blank key blade would fit the corresponding lock. In fact, Best Lock admitted that no other shaped key blade would fit into the corresponding keyway, and it presented no evidence to the contrary. Therefore, we find no clear error in the court's finding that the claimed key blade design was dictated solely by the key blade's function. Any aesthetic appeal of the key blade design shown in the '636 patent is the inevitable result of having a shape that is dictated solely by functional concerns.

Further, Best Lock's assertion that a variety of possible shapes of interfaces between keys and locks exists does not compel a different result. Clearly, different interfaces between key blades and corresponding lock keyways can be designed to permit the combination to function as a lock and key set. However, Best Lock's patent does not claim the combination of a lock and corresponding key. Instead, the claim in the '636 design patent is limited to a key blade, which must be designed as shown in the '636 patent in order to perform its intended function.

Moreover, the fact that Best Lock also has a design patent on the keyway that mates with the key blade shown in the '636 patent does not alter our analysis. The existence of a separate patent on the keyway is irrelevant to the construction of the '636 patent claim and to the ultimate determination that the claimed design is dictated solely by function. *See Elmer v. ICC Fabricating, Inc.*, 67 F.3d 1571, 1577, 36 U.S.P.Q.2D (BNA) 1417, 1421 (Fed. Cir. 1995) (construing design patent as limited to the article of manufacture "as shown and described" in the patent). The validity of a patent must be evaluated based on what it claims rather than on the totality of the claims of multiple patents.

For the foregoing reasons, the district court's finding that the claimed design is solely governed by functional concerns is not clearly erroneous. Consequently, we affirm its resulting conclusion that the '636 patent is invalid under 35 U.S.C. §171 for failure to satisfy the statute's ornamentality requirement.

Affirmed.

---

2. As our predecessor court previously held, a design for an article of manufacture may be embodied in less than all of an article of manufacture . . . at *In re Zahn*, 617 F.2d 261, 267, 204 U.S.P.Q. (BNA) 988, 994 (CCPA 1980).

Newman, Circuit Judge, dissenting.

I respectfully dissent. The design of this key blade profile meets the statutory criteria of design patent subject matter. . . .

The legal principles governing design patents have their foundation in the important decision of *Gorham Co. v. White*, 81 U.S. (14 Wall.) 511, 20 L. Ed. 731 (1871), wherein the Supreme Court explained:

> The appearance may be the result of peculiarity of configuration, or of ornament alone, or of both conjointly, but, in whatever way produced, it is the new thing, or product, which the patent law regards.

81 U.S. at 525. Courts have measured the term "ornamental" by the non-functionality that distinguishes the subject of a design patent from a utility patent, while recognizing that the design of a useful article is not insulated from the utility of the article. A review of patentable designs in general illustrates the mixture of functional and non-functional features embraced in the patented design. . . .

An effective design patent law must recognize the distinction between functionality of the article and of the particular design of the article or features thereof. *See L.A. Gear, supra*, (the sneaker tongue, moustache, delta wing, and side mesh, were useful parts of the sneaker, but the overall design of these features and the shoe was not dictated by function alone). This interaction of form and function does not remove the design from the statutory scope of the design patent law, or defeat the statutory patentability of a primarily non-functional design, although it is not always easy to draw a bright line between the functionality of an article and its design, as discussed by J.H. Reichman, Design Protection and the New Technologies: The United States Experience in a Transnational Perspective, 19 Balt. L. Rev. 6 (1989), for design patents often appear on quite mundane articles of manufacture. . . .

The design of the key blade profile is primarily non-functional, as the Patent and Trademark Office recognized in granting the patent in suit. The Manual of Patent Examining Procedure defines "design" as follows for purposes of §171:

> The design of an object consists of the visual characteristics or aspects displayed by the object. It is the appearance presented by the object which creates a visual impact upon the mind of the observer.

Since a design is manifested in appearance, the subject matter of a design patent application may relate to the configuration or shape of an object, to the surface ornamentation on an object, or both.

Design is inseparable from the object to which it is applied and cannot exist alone merely as a scheme of surface ornamentation. It must be a definite, preconceived thing, capable of reproduction and not merely the chance result of a method. MPEP §1502 (6th ed. 1995). *See also* 1 D. Chisum, Patents §1.04[2][a] (1996) ("[A] design rests on appearance created by the configuration of the article, surface ornamentation, or a combination of configuration and ornamentation.") (footnote omitted).

The parties to this litigation agree that there are myriad possible designs of key profiles. All keys require, of course, mating keyways. In holding that because the key must fit a keyway, the abstract design of the key profile is converted to one solely of function, the court creates an exception to design patent subject matter. An arbitrary design of a useful article is not statutorily excluded from §171 simply because in use it interacts with an article of complementary design. Although precedent is sparse, it is contrary to this holding. In *Motorola Inc.*

*v. Alexander Mfg. Co.*, 786 F. Supp. 808, 21 U.S.P.Q.2D (BNA) 1573 (N.D. Iowa 1991), the only United States case on this point of which we are aware, the court considered a design patent for a battery housing intended for use in a portable phone. Since the battery housing had to fit into the phone and a battery charger, the accused infringer argued that this function dictated the design. The court disagreed:

> The design of the battery housing was not dictated by the design of the battery charger because the charger did not exist when the housing was designed. The design of the phone was done concurrently with the battery housing. Therefore, the design of the battery housing cannot fairly be said to have been "dictated" by the design of the phone.

*Id.* at 812, 21 U.S.P.Q.2D at 1557. This reasoning is equally apt in this case. The design of the key profile was not dictated by the design of the keyway, and indeed the two share the same arbitrary design.

In sum, the fact that the key blade is the mate of a keyway does not convert the arbitrary key profile into a primarily functional design. It is not the design of the key profile that is functional, but the key itself. Thus I must, respectfully, dissent from the ruling of the panel majority that the design of the key blade profile is not patentable because the key blade requires a mating keyway.

## NOTES AND QUESTIONS

**1.** As noted earlier, the "design patent" is one of several forms of IP used to protect designs in the United States. "Trade dress" generally refers to the distinctive appearance adopted by a business for its products or services and is a form of trademark and unfair competition protection. Trade dress may take the form of a registered trademark, but it may also be the subject of unregistered common law trademark protection. The U.S. Supreme Court has addressed the nature of trade dress protection on several occasions. *See, e.g., Traffix Devices v. Mktg. Displays*, 532 U.S. 23 (2001); *Wal-Mart Stores, Inc. v. Samara Bros.*, 529 U.S. 205 (2000); *Two Pesos v. Taco Cabana*, 505 U.S. 763 (1992). Copyright is often invoked to protect fashion and jewelry design. *See, e.g., Langman Fabrics v. Graff Californiawear*, 160 F.3d 106 (2d Cir. 1998).

**2.** In recent years, the stakes in design patent litigation have risen considerably. Smartphone makers Apple and Samsung have engaged in some notable design patent battles in courts around the world. *See, e.g., Apple v. Samsung*, 678 F.3d 1314 (Fed. Cir. 2012), and *Apple Inc. v. Samsung Electronics Co.*, Wikipedia, https://en.wikipedia.org/wiki/Apple_Inc._v._Samsung_Electronics_Co.#:~:text=On%20August%2024%2C%202012%2C%20the,damages%20in%20its%20counter%20suit; Juli Clover, *Samsung and Apple Settle Long-Running Design Patent Dispute*, MacRumors, June 27, 2018, https://www.macrumors.com/2018/06/27/apple-samsung-patent-dispute-settled/.

**3.** During the Uruguay Round TRIPS Agreement negotiations, some industries actively sought improvements in design protection while other industries opposed it. The automotive industry favored lower standards for protection of designs, while the insurance industry sought to increase the required level of originality. The high-fashion design industry complained about the inefficiency of industrial design protection and called for more efficient and rapid registration systems (or improved protection through copyright). Yet, major clothing retailers were not anxious to see standards of protection raised. Why did these industries take the positions that they did?

## B. The Multilateral System for Protection of Design

### *1. The Provisions of the TRIPS Agreement*

**Thomas Cottier***

### *The Agreement on Trade Related Aspects of Intellectual Property Rights (TRIPS)*

#### Industrial Designs

#### Negotiating History

Negotiations on industrial designs were difficult. There was controversy as to whether the standards of protection to be granted for industrial design should be based on the protection available in Europe or in the United States. The EC wanted the United States to expand coverage of its domestic design patent law. The initial U.S. proposal excluded "functional" designs from protection and was limited to designs that are "new, original, ornamental and non-obvious." One of the main practical interests at stake was trade in automobile spare parts. The automotive industry sought to obtain protection from cheaper parts produced by foreign competitors. Extension of protection was, therefore, opposed by developing countries and the car insurance industry. The interests of the textile industry, which sought enhanced protection for fashion designs, were another driving force in the negotiations and resulted in modest improvements. Overall, the minimum standard of protection that was agreed maintains a reasonable level of creativity, but allows Members to grant more extensive protection if they so wish.

#### The Agreement

Members are obliged by *Article 25* to provide for the protection of independently created industrial designs that are new or original. Protection can be withheld from "designs dictated essentially by technical or functional considerations." Members must ensure that the requirements for obtaining protection for textile designs do not unreasonably impair the opportunity to obtain such protection. Article 25:2 was included in recognition of the short lifecycle of such design creations due to changes in fashion and amounts to a novel instrument in design protection. Together with Article 62, discussed in Part III(F) below, Article 25:2 creates an obligation to, and pressures for, facilitating filing procedures in countries notoriously slow in registering designs which depend on fashion cycles. Moreover, in many countries copyright protection can also be used as a possible way for protecting designs without any registration requirements.

### *2. The Hague Agreement Concerning the International Registration of Industrial Designs*

The Hague Agreement Concerning the International Registration of Industrial Designs provides a mechanism for registering industrial designs.[20]

---

* In 1 The World Trade Organization: Legal, Economic and Political Analysis 1041 (Patrick F. J. Macrory, Arthur E. Appleton & Michael G. Plummer eds., 2005).

20. Information and the text of the Agreement can be found at http://www.wipo.int.

The Hague Agreement is a registration mechanism and does not include substantive rules. Designs are protected only as provided for under the law of the countries where protection has been sought. Substantive examination and litigation are entirely left to the domestic entities under the national law of the parties. The system merely offers the possibility to lodge one single application for design protection for a number of countries and intergovernmental organizations. The main objective of the Hague System is to facilitate and economize the international registration of industrial designs.

There are more than 50 country parties to at least one of the three Acts of the Hague Agreement, the most recent of which (the Geneva Act) was concluded in 1999. One objective of the Geneva Act was to make the system more attractive to countries such as the United States, which do not employ design registration systems, but offer alternatives such as a design patent. The United States became party to the Geneva Act on May 13, 2015. A number of EU member states are party to the Hague Agreement and in 2008, the European Union itself became party to the Geneva Act.

### *3. Proposed Design Law Treaty*

In July 2022, the WIPO General Assembly approved the convening of a diplomatic conference no later than 2024 for a proposed international agreement pertaining to the protection of designs to facilitate cross border trade. A Preparatory Committee of the Diplomatic Conference to Conclude and Adopt a Design Law Treaty (DLT) will be held in October 2023. WIPO documents SCT/35/2 and SCT/35/3, as well as the 2019 proposal considered by the WIPO General Assembly on draft Articles and Regulations on Industrial Design Law and Practice, will constitute the substantive articles of the Basic Proposal for the Diplomatic Conference.

As noted by WIPO, "The proposed Design Law Treaty (DLT) aims to help designers obtain easier, faster and cheaper protection for their designs – both in home markets and abroad.

The proposed Treaty would streamline the global system for protecting designs, which are an integral part of many brands, by eliminating red tape and accelerating protection procedures. If approved, these changes would benefit the community of designers, with particular impact for smaller-scale designers with less access to legal support for registering their designs. In particular, the DLT would make it significantly easier for SMEs in low and medium income countries to obtain design protection overseas. . . .

Work on the simplification of procedures for the protection of industrial designs was initially started in the WIPO Standing Committee on the Law of Trademarks, Industrial Designs and Geographical Indications (SCT) in 2006 and gradually matured into a set of draft Articles and draft Regulations for a Treaty. Similar treaties already exist in the area of Patents (Patent Law Treaty of 2000) and Trademarks (Trademark Law Treaty of 1994 and Singapore Treaty on the Law of Trademarks of 2006)."

## NOTES AND QUESTIONS

**1.** The following excerpt from the Federal Register sets out the U.S. position with respect to how applications under the Geneva Act of the Hague Agreement, now in force for the United States, would be treated in U.S. law:

> Given the benefits to the users of the Hague system, the United States has been actively involved in the negotiations with the goal of obtaining a suitable agreement that could engender interest and support by United States industry and designers. Although protection for industrial designs

> is available in the United States under various laws, including patent, trademark, copyright, and unfair competition laws, the United States has taken the position that, if adopted, implementation of the new Act of the Hague Agreement would be through United States design patent law.[21]

Because design patents are subject to prior examination in the United States, while many foreign design registration systems do not entail prior examination (*see, e.g.*, EU Design Regulation system, next section *infra*), U.S. participation would offer limited opportunity for registration as compared with other Geneva Act contracting states.

## C. Regional Design Protection Systems

### *1. The EU Design Directive and Regulation*

The European Union has adopted a directive (1998)[22] and regulation (2001)[23] on the protection of designs that effectively establish a comprehensive system for design regulation within the European Union. Similar to the situation with respect to trademarks, the European Union first adopted a directive intended to approximate the laws of the member states, but maintaining the national authority to grant design rights, and allowing some flexibility within national legal systems with respect to implementation. The subsequent regulation is directly applicable in the law of the member states and establishes a single unified design protection right throughout the European Union, embodied in a "Community Design." The unregistered Community Design (or CD) right arises when the design is first made available to the public in the European Union and has a term of three years.[24] Registered CDs have a renewal term of five years from the date of filing the application, up to a maximum of 25 years.[25] The Community Design system, like the Community Trademark System (see Chapter 3, *supra*), is administered by the Office of Harmonization in the Internal Market (OHIM), situated in Alicante, Spain.

The Design Regulation establishes "newness" and "individual character" as the criteria for design protection.[26] Registration confers significant advantages. A registered CD protects against third-party use notwithstanding independent creation.[27] An unregistered CD is only protected against "copying."[28] In addition, a registered CD enjoys a presumption of validity in an infringement action.[29] The rights of the holder are subject to limitations, such as "acts done for experimental purposes."[30] The CD right is subject to a "prior use" right in favor of a third party who can establish good-faith use or serious preparations to use within the European

---

21. Patent and Trademark Office, Docket No. 990408092-0992-01, RIN 0651-ZA01, *Notice of Public Hearing and Request for Comments on the Proposed New Act of the Hague Agreement Concerning the International Registration of Industrial Designs*, 64 Fed. Reg. 19,135-139 (Apr. 19, 1999).

22. Directive 98/71/EC of the European Parliament and of the Council of 13 October 1998 on the legal protection of designs, OJ L 289, 28.10.1998, p. 28, available at http://oami.europa.eu/en/design/legalaspects.htm.

23. Council Regulation (EC) No 6/2002 of 12 December 2001 on Community designs (consolidated version), available at http://oami.europa.eu/en/design/legalaspects.htm.

24. Design Regulation, art. 11(1).

25. *Id.*, art. 12.

26. *Id.*, art. 4(1).

27. *Id.*, art. 19(1).

28. *Id.*, art. 19(2).

29. *Id.*, art. 85.

30. *Id.*, art. 20(1)(b).

Union prior to the filing or priority date of the application.[31] The Design Regulation includes an express intra-Union exhaustion rule.[32]

Newness or novelty involves a modest threshold of differentiation from "identical" designs previously made available to the public (Article 5, Design Regulation). Regarding "individual character,"

> [a] design shall be considered to have individual character if the overall impression it produces on the informed user differs from the overall impression produced on such a user by any design which has been made available to the public.

(Article 6, *id.*) CDs "shall not subsist in features of appearance of a product which are solely dictated by its technical function," nor in features that are necessary to permit the product (or a connected product) to function.[33]

Applications to register CDs are submitted to the OHIM, which examines the applications for compliance with formalities. If the formal requirements are met, the design is registered and published.[34] Any natural or legal person may apply to the OHIM to invalidate the registered design.[35] An initial decision regarding invalidity is made by administrators, but may be appealed to the Board of Appeal.[36] Decisions of the Board of Appeal may be taken to the Court of Justice of the European Union.[37]

Actions for infringement of the CD are brought before national courts of the EU member states that have been designated by those states as "Community design courts," which shall include courts of both first and second instance.[38] The Community design courts also have jurisdiction over actions for declaration of noninfringement (if permitted by national law), for declarations of invalidity of unregistered CDs, and over counterclaims for invalidity regarding registered CDs.[39]

The rules established by the EU Design Regulation do not interfere with the grant by the member states of national design rights providing simultaneous protection (which remain subject to the Design Directive),[40] or with respect to unregistered designs, trademarks, patents, utility models, and unfair competition. Designs may also be protected under copyright law applicable in the member states.[41] Provision is made in the Design Regulation for treatment of parallel legal actions,[42] and for the enforcement of judgments.[43]

---

31. *Id.*, art. 22. Note that since an unregistered design is not protected against independent creation, a prior use right in favor of an independent third-party creator is not required in respect to unregistered designs.

32. *Id.*, art. 22.

33. *Id.*, art. 8.

34. *Id.*, arts. 47-49. Publication is subject to deferral for up to 30 months. However, legal proceedings may only be instituted if the design had been previously communicated to the person against whom the action is brought. *Id.*, art. 50.

35. *Id.*, art. 52.

36. *Id.*, arts. 55-61.

37. *Id.*, art. 61.

38. *Id.*, art. 80.

39. *Id.*, art. 81.

40. *Id.*, art. 95.

41. *Id.*, art. 96.

42. *Id.*, art. 95.

43. *Id.*, art. 79.

## *Office for Harmonization in the Internal Market (Trade Marks and Designs) Designs Department—Invalidity Division*

Decision of the Invalidity Division of 20/09/05 In the Proceedings for a Declaration of Invalidity of a Registered Community Design

File Number ICD 000000388
Community Design 000150206-0002

Applicant: LENG-D'OR, S.A. [Spain]
Holder: Crown Confectionery Co., LTD. [Republic of Korea]

The Invalidity Division,
composed of Martin SCHLÖTELBURG (rapporteur), Paul MAIER (member) and José IZQUIERDO PERIS (member) took the following decision on 20/09/05:

1. The registered Community design No. 000150206-0002 is declared invalid.
2. The Holder shall bear the costs of the Applicant.

### I. FACTS, EVIDENCE AND ARGUMENTS

(1) The Community design No. 000150206-0002 (in the following: "the CD") has been registered in the name of the Holder with the date of filing of 20/02/04 and the date of priority of 19/01/04. In the CD, the indication of products reads "biscuits" and the design is represented in the following views (published at http://oami.eu.int/bulletin/rcd/2004/2004_045/000150206_0002.htm):

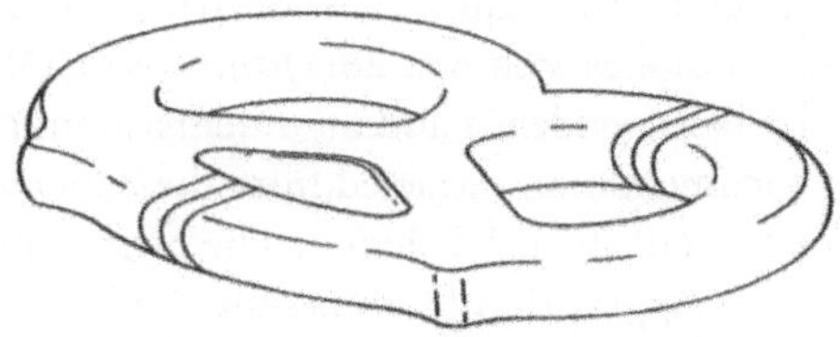

(2) On 01/07/04, the Applicant filed an application for a declaration of invalidity (in the following: "the Application") contesting the validity of the CD. . . .

(3) The Applicant, by referring to "the right recognised by article 25 point 1 section b, of the regulation in force in regard to Community Drawings and Models," claims "lack of novelty and singularity of the challenged Community design is lacking, prior and demanded requirements in articles 4, 5 and 6 of the Regulations for Community Drawings and Models." He argues that the CD "does not have any novelty and singularity necessary for its registration, given that the distinguished features presented by same are included in the number of biscuits and snacks located and contributed by my principal, which were made public in this specific industrial field prior to the Community Design application."

(4) As evidence, the Applicant provided "documentation extracted from the 'Google' public database," in particular "printout extracted from the 'Google' public database using the term referring to 'pretzels' and 'snacks' as the parameter" and "printout extracted from the 'Google' public database using the term referring to 'pretzels' " as well as "printout of images extracted from the 'Google' public database using the term referring to 'pretzels' as the parameter." In particular, the Applicant provided a printout of an article with the title "Field Reports: New twist on environmental compliance for snack maker" published in the

magazine "Food Engineering" (in the following: D1). The article bears the dating "Magazine issue date: 12/01/2002" and includes the following image (in the following: prior design):

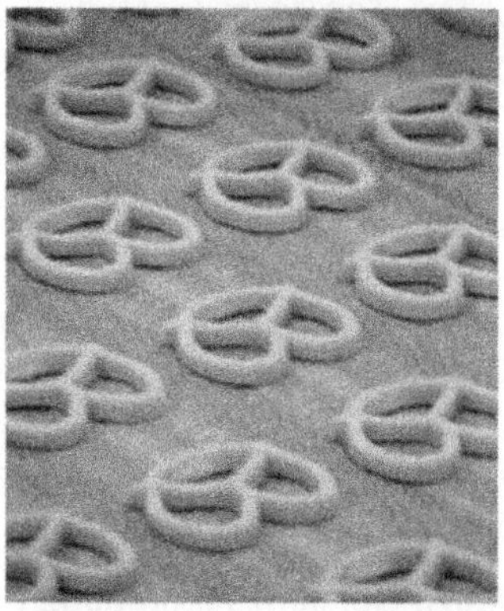

(5) The Holder did not submit observations.

(6) For further details to the facts, evidence and arguments submitted by the Applicant and the Holder reference is made to the documents on file.

## II. Grounds of the Decision

### A. Admissibility

(7) The request of the Applicant to declare the invalidity of the CD due to "lack of novelty and singularity of the challenged Community" is a statement of the grounds on which the Application is based. Therefore, the requirement of Art. 28(1)(b)(i) CDIR1 is fulfilled. Furthermore, the Application complies with Art. 28(1)(b)(v)(vi) CDIR, since the attachment contains an indication of the facts, evidence and arguments submitted in support of those grounds, in particular the "documentation extracted from the 'Google' public database" gives an indication and a reproduction of the prior design. The other requirements of Art. 28(1) CDIR are fulfilled as well. The Application is admissible. 1 Commission Regulation (EC) No 2245/2002 of 21 October 2002 implementing Council Regulation (EC) No 6/2002 on Community designs.

### B. Substantiation

#### B.1 Evidence

(8) D1 is a copy of an article from a magazine dated 12/01/02. Magazines are usually published and distributed. Furthermore, the Applicant submits elements that the earlier design could have been known in the normal course of business to the circles specialized in the sector concerned, operating within the Community. Therefore, D1 is considered as having been made available to the public prior to the date of filing of the CD in accordance with Article 7(1) CDR. The Holder did not put into question any of these elements which all together constitute prima facie evidence of a disclosure of D1 according to Article 7(1) CDR.

#### B.2 Novelty

(9) The CD consists essentially in the shape of a pretzel. The prior design shown in D1 and the CD do not show differences except for the lines across the pretzel. Such differences are considered immaterial details. The Holder does not indicate any further differences nor has made any submission. Therefore, the Invalidity Division must conclude that both designs are identical.

### C. Conclusion

(10) The CD lacks novelty. Therefore, it has to be declared invalid pursuant to Article 25(1)(b) CDR.

## III. Costs

(11) Pursuant to Article 70(1) CDR and Art. 79(1) CDIR, the Holder bears the costs incurred by him essential to the proceedings.

## IV. Right to Appeal

(12) An appeal shall lie from the present decision. Notice of appeal must be filed at the Office within two months after the date of notification of that decision. The notice is deemed to have been filed only when the fee for appeal has been paid. Within four months after the date of notification of the decision, a written statement setting out the grounds of appeal must be filed (Art. 57 CDR).

# NOTES AND QUESTIONS

**1.** The text decision illustrates the effect of absence of substantive examination of CD applications by OHIM. Presumably, prior examination would have resulted in rejection of the shape of a pretzel as a biscuit for lack of novelty. At the same time, a general requirement of prior examination would result in a much more complex registration system, and would present significant problems due, *inter alia*, to the necessity of compiling a database of prior art. On the other hand, registration of a CD does not by any means guarantee the holder the right to prevent others from using the design. It does provide a presumption in litigation in favor of the holder, but that is subject to challenge by an alleged infringer. An alleged infringer may counterclaim for invalidity. There is also a prior user right. Finally, in this proceeding, the losing party (registered CD holder) bears the costs of the action. Do you think the advantages of a low-cost rapid system of registration outweigh the disadvantages of imposing on the public the burden of challenging validity in litigation? Do the holders of CDs enjoy some additional "apparent power" to threaten third parties? Is there a better alternative to this registration system?

**2.** In November 2022, the European Commission adopted proposals to revise the Council Regulation (EC) No 6/2002 of 12 December 2001 on Community designs ("Community Design Regulation 2002") and Directive 98/71/EC of the European Parliament and of the Council of 13 October 1998 on the legal protection of designs ("Design Directive"). With the aim of modernizing design protection in the EU, the proposals call for broadening the "definition of products eligible for design protection to clearly cover those visualised in a graphic, embodied in a physical object or apparent from the spatial arrangement of items intended to form, in particular, an interior environment. In this context, it should also be recognised that the movement, transition or animation of features can contribute to the visual appearance of designs, in particular for designs that are not embodied in a physical object." (*See* Recital 9, Proposal for a Regulation of the European Parliament and of the Council amending Council Regulation (EC) No 6/2002 on Community designs and repealing Commission Regulation (EC) No 2246/2002.) The proposals also adjust the scope of design rights to enable right holders to more effectively address challenges brought by increased use of 3D printing technologies. (*See* Article 19 Proposal for a Regulation of the European Parliament and of the Council amending Council Regulation (EC) No 6/2002 on Community designs and repealing Commission Regulation (EC) No 2246/2002.)

## D. Fair Use and the Repair Clause

### *Acacia SRL v. Audi AG & Porsche AG*

Judgment of the Court (Second Chamber), 20 December 2017

(References for a preliminary ruling — Regulation (EC) No 6/2002 — Community designs — Article 110(1) — No protection — 'Repair' clause — Concept of 'component part of a complex product' — Repair of the complex product so as to restore its original appearance — Measures to be adopted by the user for the purposes of relying on the 'repair' clause — Replica car wheel rim identical to the original wheel rim design)

In Joined Cases C397/16 and C435/16,

REQUESTS for a preliminary ruling under Article 267 TFEU from the Corte d'appello di Milano (Court of Appeal, Milan, Italy) and from the Bundesgerichtshof (Federal Court of Justice, Germany), made by decisions of 15 and 2 June 2016, received at the Court, respectively, on 18 July and 4 August 2016, in the proceedings

Acacia Srl
v
Pneusgarda Srl, in insolvency,
Audi AG (C397/16),
and
Acacia Srl,
Rolando D'Amato
v
Dr. Ing. h.c. F.;Porsche AG (C435/16),

THE COURT (Second Chamber),
composed of M. Ilešič (Rapporteur), President of the Chamber, A. Rosas, C. Toader, A. Prechal and E. Jarašiūnas, Judges,
Advocate General: H. Saugmandsgaard Øe,
Registrar: R. Schiano, Administrator,
having regard to the written procedure and further to the hearing on 14 June 2017,
after considering the observations submitted on behalf of . . .
gives the following

#### Judgment

1. These requests for a preliminary ruling concern the interpretation of Article 110(1) of Council Regulation (EC) No 6/2002 of 12 December 2001 on Community designs (OJ 2002 L 3, p. 1).

2. The requests have been made in the context of two disputes between (i) Acacia Srl, on the one hand, and Pneusgarda Srl, in insolvency, and Audi AG, on the other, and (ii) Acacia and its managing director, Mr Rolando D'Amato, on the one hand, and Dr. Ing. h.c. F. Porsche AG ('Porsche'), on the other, concerning the alleged infringement, by Acacia, of Community designs of which Audi and Porsche are the holders.

. . .

10. Article 110 of Regulation No 6/2002, entitled 'Transitional provision' provides:

> '1. Until such time as amendments to this Regulation enter into force on a proposal from the Commission on this subject, protection as a Community design shall not exist for a design which constitutes a component part of a complex product used within the meaning of Article 19(1) for the purpose of the repair of that complex product so as to restore its original appearance.
>
> 2. The proposal from the Commission referred to in paragraph 1 shall be submitted together with, and take into consideration, any changes which the Commission shall propose on the same subject pursuant to Article 18 of Directive 98/71/EC.'

### The Disputes in the Main Proceedings and the Questions Referred for a Preliminary Ruling

#### Case C397/16

11. Audi is the holder of a number of Community designs of alloy car wheel rims.

12. Acacia manufactures, under the brand WSP Italy, alloy car wheel rims that are sold on its own website, which is available in several languages. According to the referring court, some of those wheel rims are identical to Audi's alloy wheel rims. The wheel rims manufactured by Acacia are stamped with the indication 'NOT OEM', which means not made by the original equipment manufacturer. The commercial and technical documents accompanying those products, the sales invoices and Acacia's internet site indicate that the wheel rims at issue are sold exclusively as replacement parts for the purpose of making repairs.

13. Audi brought an action before the Tribunale di Milano (District Court, Milan, Italy) seeking, in essence, a declaration that Acacia's manufacture and sale of the wheel rims at issue constitutes an infringement of its Community designs. That court upheld that action.

14. Acacia brought an appeal against that court's judgment before the Corte d'appello di Milano (Court of Appeal, Milan, Italy). That court, after noting inter alia the existence of conflicting rulings from Italian courts and courts of other Member States concerning the application of the 'repair' clause, held that there were serious doubts as to the interpretation of Article 110(1) of Regulation No 6/2002.

15. In those circumstances, the Corte d'appello di Milano (Court of Appeal, Milan) decided to stay the proceedings and to refer the following questions to the Court for a preliminary ruling:

#### Case C435/16

16. Porsche is the holder of a number of Community designs of alloy car wheel rims.

17. The wheel rims manufactured by Acacia, referred to in paragraph 12 of the present judgment, are sold, in Germany, on its internet site, which is directed at end consumers and is accessible in German. According to the referring court, some of those wheel rims are identical to Porsche's alloy wheel rims. That court observes that, according to Acacia, the rims it manufactures and which are intended for Porsche vehicles can be used only with Porsche vehicles. Porsche submits to that court that the rims in question are also offered in colours and sizes which do not correspond to the original products.

18. Porsche brought an action before the Landgericht Stuttgart (Regional Court, Stuttgart, Germany) seeking, in essence, a declaration that Acacia's manufacture and sale of the wheel rims at issue constitutes an infringement of its Community designs. That court upheld that action.

19. As the appeal brought by Acacia and Mr D'Amato was dismissed, they brought an appeal on a point of law (*Revision*) before the referring court. That court notes that the

outcome of the appeal on a point of law depends on whether Acacia may rely on the 'repair' clause in Article 110(1) of Regulation No 6/2002. However, the interpretation of that provision raises several difficulties.

20. In those circumstances, the Bundesgerichtshof (Federal Court of Justice, Germany) decided to stay the proceedings and to refer the following questions to the Court for a preliminary ruling:

. . .

### Consideration of the Questions Referred

#### The Second Question in Case C397/16 and the First Question in Case C435/16

29. By the second question in Case C397/16 and by the first question in Case C435/16, which it is appropriate to examine first and together, the referring courts ask, in essence, whether Article 110(1) of Regulation No 6/2002 must be interpreted as meaning that the 'repair' clause in it makes the exclusion of protection as a Community design for a design which constitutes a component part of a complex product which is used for the purpose of the repair of that complex product so as to restore its original appearance subject to the condition that the protected design is dependent upon the appearance of the complex product.

. . .

32. According to Article 110(1) of Regulation No 6/2002, 'protection as a Community design shall not exist for a design which constitutes a component part of a complex product used within the meaning of Article 19(1) for the purpose of the repair of that complex product so as to restore its original appearance'.

. . .

34. It . . . follows from the wording of Article 110(1) of Regulation No 6/2002 that the protected design's dependence upon the appearance of the complex product is not one of the conditions listed in that provision.

. . .

39. It is . . . apparent from the origin of Article 110(1) of Regulation No 6/2002 that the absence of a limitation on the scope of that provision to parts whose shape is fixed by the shape of the complex product stems from a choice made during the legislative process.

. . .

50. As is apparent from that explanatory memorandum, the protection granted by Community designs may cause adverse effects by removing or restricting competition on markets, as regards, inter alia, long lasting and expensive complex products such as cars, in respect of which the protection of designs that are applied to the particular component parts which make up the complex product may create a veritable captive market for those spare parts. In that context, the purpose of the 'repair' clause is to avoid the creation of captive markets in certain spare parts and, in particular, to prevent a consumer who has bought a long lasting and perhaps expensive product from being indefinitely tied, for the purchase of external parts, to the manufacturer of the complex product.

. . .

52. The aim of the 'repair' clause to liberalise, to a certain extent, the market in replacement parts is, moreover, corroborated by recital 19 and by Article 14 of Directive 98/71, according to which changes to national legal provisions relating to the use of the design of a component part used for the purpose of the repair of a complex product so as to restore its original appearance are permitted only if the purpose of those changes is to liberalise the market for the component parts at issue.

. . .

54. In the light of the foregoing considerations, the answer to the second question in Case C397/16 and the first question in Case C435/16 is that Article 110(1) of Regulation

No 6/2002 must be interpreted as meaning that the 'repair' clause in it does not make the exclusion of protection as a Community design for a design which constitutes a component part of a complex product which is used for the purpose of the repair of that complex product so as to restore its original appearance subject to the condition that the protected design is dependent upon the appearance of the complex product.

**The First Question in Case C397/16 and the Second Question in Case C435/16**

55. By the first question in Case C397/16 and by the second question in Case C435/16, which it is appropriate to examine secondly and together, the referring courts ask, in essence, to which conditions the 'repair' clause in Article 110(1) of Regulation No 6/2002 subjects the exclusion of protection as a Community design for a design which constitutes a component part of a complex product which is used for the purpose of the repair of a complex product so as to restore its original appearance.

. . .

61. In that regard, according to Article 4(2) of Regulation No 6/2002, a design applied to or incorporated in a product which constitutes a component part of a complex product is to be protected only to the extent that, first, the component part, once it has been incorporated into a complex product, remains visible during normal use of that product and, secondly, the visible features of the component part fulfil in themselves the requirements as to novelty and individual character set out in paragraph 1 of that article.

62. In the present case, it is common ground that this applies to the Community designs of car wheel rims of which Audi and Porsche are holders.

63. In the second place, Article 110(1) of Regulation No 6/2002 applies only to 'component parts of a complex product'.

64. It must be noted that Regulation No 6/2002 does not define the concept of 'component part of a complex product'. It is, however, apparent from Article 3(b) and (c) of that regulation that, first, 'product' means any industrial or handicraft item, including inter alia parts intended to be assembled into a complex product and, secondly, 'complex product' means a product which is composed of multiple components which can be replaced permitting disassembly and re-assembly of the product. Furthermore, in the absence of any definition of the term 'component part' in that regulation, it must be understood in accordance with its usual meaning in everyday language (see, to that effect, judgment of 4 May 2006, *Massachusetts Institute of Technology*, C431/04, EU:C:2006:291, paragraph 17 and the case-law cited).

65. In those circumstances, it must be held that, through the words 'component parts of a complex product', Article 110(1) of Regulation No 6/2002 covers multiple components, intended to be assembled into a complex industrial or handicraft item, which can be replaced permitting disassembly and re-assembly of such an item, without which the complex product could not be subject to normal use.

66. In the present case, a car wheel rim must be classified as a 'component part of a complex product' within the meaning of that provision, such a wheel rim being a component of a complex product which a car constitutes, without which that product could not be subject to normal use.

. . .

70. Any use of a component part for reasons of preference or purely of convenience, such as, inter alia, the replacement of a part for aesthetic purposes or customisation of the complex product is therefore excluded from the 'repair' clause.

. . .

74. It is further necessary that the repair be done so as to restore the complex product to its 'original' appearance. It follows that, in order for the 'repair' clause to be applied, the

component part must be used so as to restore the complex product to the appearance it had when it was placed on the market.

75. It must be concluded that the 'repair' clause applies only to component parts of a complex product that are visually identical to original parts.

76. Such an interpretation is, moreover, consistent with Article 26(2) of the Agreement on Trade-Related Aspects of Intellectual Property Rights, which provides that any exception to the protection of industrial designs must be limited and must not unreasonably conflict with the normal exploitation of such designs or unreasonably prejudice the legitimate interests of the owner, taking account of the legitimate interests of third parties. That is the situation in the present case, since the application of the 'repair' clause is limited to the use of a design that constitutes a component part of a complex product used for the sole purpose of permitting the actual repair of that complex product so as to restore its original appearance.

77. Any use of a component part which is not for the purpose of restoring a complex product to the appearance it had when it was placed on the market is, accordingly, excluded. That is the case if, inter alia, the replacement part does not correspond, in terms of its colour or its dimensions, to the original part, or if the appearance of a complex product was changed since it was placed on the market.

78. In the light of the foregoing considerations, the answer to the first question in Case C397/16 and the second question in Case C435/16 is that Article 110(1) of Regulation No 6/2002 must be interpreted as meaning that the 'repair' clause in it makes the exclusion of protection as a Community design for a design which constitutes a component part of a complex product which is used for the purpose of the repair of that complex product so as to restore its original appearance subject to the condition that the replacement part must have an identical visual appearance to that of the part which was originally incorporated into the complex product when it was placed on the market.

### The Third Question in Case C397/16 and the Third and Fourth Questions in Case C435/16

79. By the third question in Case C397/16 and by the third and fourth questions in Case C435/16, which it is appropriate to examine thirdly and together, the referring courts ask, in essence, whether Article 110(1) of Regulation No 6/2002 must be interpreted as meaning that, in order to rely on the 'repair' clause in that provision, the manufacturer or seller of a component part of a complex product must ensure and, in that case, how it must ensure, that the component part can be purchased exclusively for repair purposes.

. . .

82. Thus, it must be ascertained whether, when such use consists, as in the cases in the main proceedings, in the manufacture and sale of such a product, Article 110(1) of Regulation No 6/2002 imposes upon the manufacturer and the seller of that product who intend to make and sell it for the purposes of its actual use in accordance with the conditions laid down by that provision, certain obligations as regards compliance by downstream users with those conditions.

83. In that regard, it should be noted that the 'repair' clause exception to the principle of protection as a design requires the end user of the component part in question to use it in accordance with the conditions set out in Article 110(1) of Regulation No 6/2002, namely that he uses that component part in order to repair a complex product so as to restore its original appearance.

. . .

85. In that context, while the manufacturer or seller of a component part of a complex product cannot be expected to guarantee, objectively and in all circumstances, that the parts they make or sell for use in accordance with the conditions prescribed by Article 110(1) of Regulation No 6/2002 are, ultimately, actually used by end users in compliance with those

conditions, the fact remains that, in order to benefit from the derogatory regime thus put into place by that provision, such a manufacturer or seller is, as the Advocate General noted in points 131, 132 and 135 of his Opinion, under a duty of diligence as regards compliance by downstream users with those conditions.

86. In particular, they must, first of all, inform the downstream user, through a clear and visible indication on the product, on its packaging, in the catalogues or in the sales documents, on the one hand, that the component part concerned incorporates a design of which they are not the holder and, on the other, that the part is intended exclusively to be used for the purpose of the repair of the complex product so as to restore its original appearance.

87. Next, they must, through appropriate means, in particular contractual means, ensure that downstream users do not intend to use the component parts at issue in a way that does not comply with the conditions prescribed by Article 110(1) of Regulation No 6/2002.

88. Finally, the manufacturer or seller must refrain from selling such a component part where they know or, in the light of all the relevant circumstances, ought reasonably to know that the part in question will not be used in accordance with the conditions laid down in Article 110(1) of Regulation No 6/2002.

89. In the light of all the foregoing considerations, the answer to the third question in Case C397/16 and the third and fourth questions in Case C435/16 is that Article 110(1) of Regulation No 6/2002 must be interpreted as meaning that, in order to rely on the 'repair' clause contained in that provision, the manufacturer or seller of a component part of a complex product are under a duty of diligence as regards compliance by downstream users with the conditions laid down in that provision.

. . .

## NOTES AND QUESTIONS

**1.** The car industry, next to textiles, has been the most important sector relating to design protection. As car dealers and garages increasingly depend upon income from servicing car and repair, the scope of design protection has been most contentious; *see also Volvo v. Veng*, Case C-238/87, 5 Oct. 1988. Insurance companies lobbied for excluding spare parts from protection with a view to lower costs while producers argued in favor of extensive protection and thus tying consumers to the original producer of the car. The repair clause in terms of fair use seeks to strike a balance between these conflicting interests. How do you assess the balance struck from the point of view of the consumer?

**2.** The textile industry is strongly interested in design protection against copying and counterfeiting, but is often frustrated due to rapid fashion cycles. Enforcing design rights often takes time way beyond the fashion cycle and rapidly becomes obsolete.

## E. Layout Designs of Integrated Circuits

### *1. The Origin and Nature of the Sui Generis Integrated Circuit Layout Design Right*

The protection of intellectual property in integrated circuit (or semiconductor device) layout design is a *sui generis* form of IPR that developed largely in the 1980s.* Instead of protecting

* Section E is based on Frederick Abbott, Thomas Cottier & Francis Gurry, The International Intellectual Property System (1999), and Thomas Cottier, *The Agreement on Trade Related Aspects of Intellectual Property*, in 1 The World Trade Organization: Legal, Economic and Political Analysis 1041 (Patrick F. J. Macrory, Arthur E. Appleton & Michael G. Plummer eds., 2005).

these products by means of existing forms, such as patent, copyright, or industrial designs, the view prevailed that a separate instrument should be created. The initial impetus came from the U.S. semiconductor industry, which pursued and obtained domestic legislation on the subject. Similar legislation soon followed in Japan and the European Union.[44] In 1989, the Treaty on Intellectual Property in Respect of Integrated Circuits (IC or Washington Treaty) was concluded. This treaty has never entered into force because of industry concerns over certain terms. The TRIPS Agreement, however, incorporates the substantive provisions of the IC Treaty, with amendments designed to address those concerns.

An integrated circuit (IC) or semiconductor device is produced by depositing and etching a pattern of electricity-conducting materials, for example, aluminum, and insulating material onto a semiconducting base, usually silicon. The pattern forms a series of transistors designed to perform computational functions. By designing smaller transistors and placing them closer together, engineers can produce ICs that run faster. The pattern that is deposited and etched onto a semiconducting base is embodied in a three-dimensional map, referred to as a *mask work, layout design*, or *topography*, that is used to guide the complex equipment that creates the physical end-product IC. Once such a mask work is created, it can be used by any semiconductor foundry with the requisite technical expertise to produce the subject IC. The objective of the IC producer is to assure that its competitors are not able to use a mask work it has developed to create an identical or substantially similar product.

Engineers are able to reverse engineer a mask work starting with a finished IC product. This is a complex and costly process. Nevertheless, a reverse-engineered IC may be significantly less expensive to produce than a newly developed product.

IC layout design protection is generally secured by registration of the mask work with an appropriate national or regional authority. Examination of the application by such an authority to determine whether the mask work meets the substantive requirement of originality is not a precondition of registration demanded by the terms of the IC Treaty, and a substantive examination is not ordinarily undertaken by registering authorities. However, such a substantive examination does not appear to be precluded by the terms of the IC Treaty. Whether a registered mask work or layout design meets the relevant standards for protection is generally a matter for civil litigation following registration.[45]

## 2. *Integrated Circuit Protection in the TRIPS Agreement*

The provisions of Articles 35 to 38 of the TRIPS Agreement implement and reinforce the Washington Treaty. They are of particular importance not only to the protection of topographies as such, but also for all products that include topographies. The provisions significantly strengthen the legal position of the right holders as they are linked with the enforcement provisions. In order to avoid distortions caused by potential abuse of border enforcement procedures, it is necessary to equally protect the interest of importers and bring about an appropriate balance of interests.

Article 35 requires Member countries to protect the layout designs of integrated circuits in accordance with the provisions of the Washington Treaty. In addition, the TRIPS Agreement clarifies several points. In Article 38, the term of protection is extended from eight to ten years from the date of filing or from the first commercial exploitation wherever it occurs. Article

---

44. For these legislative references, *see* Frederick M. Abbott, *Introductory Note to WIPO: Treaty on Intellectual Property in Respect of Integrated Circuits*, 28 International Legal Materials 1477 (1989), at note 3.

45. Note, for example, that pursuant to the U.S. Semiconductor Chip Protection Act (1984), registration with the Copyright Office establishes a presumption that a mask work is protected, thereby placing the burden of proof on a party challenging the entitlement to protection. 17 U.S.C.A. §908(f).

36 defines the rights and their broad applicability to products containing infringing integrated circuits. The provision bans the import, sale, or distribution of unlawfully produced designs or circuits, and applies to the many products incorporating such designs or circuits. The breadth of product coverage made it imperative to limit the application to willful and negligent infringement. Article 37 excludes the *bona fide* buyer of counterfeited goods. Acts of incorporating a counterfeited layout design into an integrated circuit, or incorporating the latter into any product, are not deemed unlawful if the person performing the act did not know or had no reasonable ground to know when acquiring the product that it contained an unlawfully produced layout design. Given the number of integrated circuits contained in many products, this provision essentially limits the reach of the article to producers and traders, to the exclusion of consumers, since consumers are usually not in a position to know, and cannot be expected to know, the origin of layout designs incorporated in a product that they buy on the market.

## NOTES AND QUESTIONS

**1.** Integrated circuit layout design protection generally entitles the right holder to prohibit the unauthorized ***reproduction*** of its mask work in an IC. The use of the term "reproduction" in IC protection legislation, and in the IC Treaty, signifies that it is the copying of a protected design that is prohibited by the IC Treaty, since Article 9 of the Berne Convention uses the term "reproduction" to define the act that a copyright holder is entitled to authorize. In this regard, IC protection is more similar to copyright than patent protection. However, the term of IC layout design protection generally is ten years, which is a considerably shorter term than copyright protection, and about half that of patent protection.

**2.** Taiwan, which produces two-thirds of the world's semiconductors, has become a battleground in the war for semiconductor market preeminence. In several recent cases, Taiwanese prosecutors have accused Chinese companies of stealing trade secrets from businesses located in Taiwan such as Taiwan Semiconductor Manufacturing Co. and the United States' largest memory chip manufacturer, Micron Technology Inc. The upswing in Taiwanese technology theft cases may be a result of China's larger effort "both to pressure what it considers a breakaway province and to pursue its own strategic goal of reducing its reliance on foreign suppliers." Chuin-Wei Yap, *Taiwan's Technology Secrets Come Under Assault from China*, The Wall Street Journal, July 1, 2018, https://www.wsj.com/articles/taiwans-technology-secrets-come-under-assault-from-china-1530468440. Recent efforts in the United States and Europe to "reshore" semiconductor manufacturing is at least partially a consequence of concerns regarding Chinese use of foreign-developed (including Taiwanese) semiconductor designs as the basis for developing its internal semiconductor development and manufacturing capacity. This points to the limits of IP protection. Whether via legal rules or physical security measures, "intangible" assets are difficult to protect, particularly when a single thumb drive may contain the information needed to build and operate a semiconductor manufacturing facility.

## CHAPTER 6

# THE INTERNATIONAL SYSTEM FOR THE ENFORCEMENT OF INTELLECTUAL PROPERTY RIGHTS

## I. INTRODUCTION TO THE LEGAL AVENUES OF IPRS ENFORCEMENT

Judicial and administrative enforcement of intellectual property rights traditionally and exclusively pertained to the province of domestic law. States made available mechanisms of enforcement commensurate with domestic civil, administrative, and penal procedures, including customs administration, investment protection, and competition law and policy. These procedures were subject to MFN and national treatment obligations under GATT 1947, but otherwise left to domestic law. The enforcement of intellectual property rights in international relations was mainly dealt with by domestic rules on international private law, which eventually were partly harmonized by international rules on private law. Even in European integration, enforcement of rights was not a harmonized matter and essentially pertained to the member states, again subject to disciplines of non-discrimination.

Given this tradition, perhaps the most dramatic change in focus of international IPRs rulemaking from the Paris and Berne Conventions of the 1880s to the TRIPS Agreement concerns the enforcement of IPRs. In fact, the shift in institutional competence from WIPO to the WTO mainly reflected the perception by industry groups in the Organisation for Economic Cooperation and Development (OECD) that the system of treaties administered by WIPO did not sufficiently compel contracting states to implement and enforce IPRs protection. The TRIPS Agreement therefore introduced minimum standards to be respected in domestic law, not limited to substantive, but also extending to and including procedural standards and obligations.

Yet, despite the considerable attention paid to enforcement of IPRs in the TRIPS Agreement, and in bilateral and plurilateral agreements negotiated by the United States, the European Union, and other countries, the persistent lack of firm enforcement by certain countries is a priority trade and IPRs negotiation issue today. This priority manifested itself in the signing (and ultimate failure) of an Anti-Counterfeiting Trade Agreement (ACTA) in 2011 by a group largely comprised of developed countries that provoked a new round of controversy regarding the role of international IPRs rules. By mid-2018, dissatisfaction by the United States with China's IPRs-related practices — including claims regarding "forced" technology transfer — reached the threshold of a full-scale "trade war" encompassing the imposition of substantial tariff measures.

While governments agree to adopt and maintain standards for the protection of IPRs at international organizations in Geneva and elsewhere, enforcement generally takes place in national (and local) courts and administrative bodies. For many (or most) countries, enforcement of IPRs involves net royalty payments to companies based abroad (i.e., a financial outflow). In that context, whether one country can persuade another to enforce "in fact" IPRs rules depends, among other things, on their relative economic and political power. The United States, for example, may find it easier to persuade Costa Rica to enforce IPRs than to persuade China.

For the most part, enforcement of IPRs involves legal proceedings initiated by the right holder in a civil or administrative court in the country where the IPRs are held and infringement is alleged to be taking place. Depending on the circumstances, if the right holder is successful in its claim, an injunction against further acts of infringement may be obtained, a civil monetary judgment may be assessed and, in some cases, forfeiture of assets used in the infringing acts (and even beyond these) may be ordered. The execution of the judgment may require the aid of local law enforcement authorities and/or third parties, which may require further legal proceedings. If infringing goods are already in the local stream of commerce, it may be difficult to fully carry out a judgment.

Because of the difficulties inherent in pursuing remedies once infringing products have entered the local stream of commerce, IPRs holders concerned with cross-border trade have a strong preference for enforcement of "border measures." Customs authorities may be authorized or directed to prevent infringing or allegedly infringing goods from entering the stream of commerce within the national territory. In some cases, customs authorities may have standing instructions (based on IPRs "registers") to inspect and suspend (at least temporarily) the release of suspicious shipments. More generally, IPRs holders may initiate legal proceedings seeking orders directing customs authorities to prevent infringing goods from entering the country. One of the objectives of the countries negotiating the failed ACTA was to strengthen the role of customs authorities to police enforcement of IPRs at the border, including by acting on their own initiative (i.e., *ex officio*).

There is a marked trend in the enforcement of IPRs toward increased criminalization of acts of infringement. There are several reasons for this. The customary mechanism for IPRs enforcement is a civil complaint by the holder against an alleged infringer. Criminal infringement actions, on the other hand, are pursued by government authorities. This shifts the cost and responsibility (and risk) for enforcement from the private sector to the public sector, saving the expense for IPRs holders. Second, the threat of incarceration and criminal fines/forfeiture is presumably a more substantial deterrent to infringement than the threat of civil fine and injunction/forfeiture. The increased attention to criminalization raises important public policy questions. Excerpts of the following study elaborate on these questions from the point of view of economics. They show the tensions between enhanced protection and the impact on consumer welfare, and the dilemmas society and governments face in allocating resources to IPRs enforcement.

**Carsten Fink***

## *Enforcing Intellectual Property Rights: An Economic Perspective*

1. Upholding the protection of intellectual property rights (IPRs) has emerged as a prominent policy issue. The year 2007 alone saw a G-8 summit calling for stepped-up enforcement

* Advisory Committee on Enforcement, Fifth Session, Geneva, November 2-4, 2009, WIPO/ACE/5/6 (August 26, 2009) (footnotes omitted).

of IPRs, the initiation of a WTO dispute on China's IPRs enforcement regime, and the launch of inter-governmental negotiations towards an Anti-Counterfeiting Trade Agreement (ACTA). In addition, intellectual property chapters of free trade agreements (FTAs) negotiated over the past few years have introduced obligations on IPRs enforcement that go beyond multilateral standards inscribed in the WTO's Agreement on Trade Related Aspects of Intellectual Property Rights (TRIPS). Several developed countries, in turn, have called for renewed discussions on enforcement in the TRIPS Council.

2. Concerns about trademark counterfeiting, copyright piracy, and other forms of IPRs violations are not new. Already back in 1985, *Business Week* characterized counterfeiting as "*perhaps the world's fastest growing and most profitable business.*" Indeed, the desire to stem in trade in counterfeit goods was at the origin of the GATT negotiations which eventually led to the conclusion of the TRIPS Agreement. However, two developments have sharpened the policy discourse on IPRs violations in recent years.

3. First, rapid global economic integration and the fast growth of middle income countries—led by China and India—have raised the stakes for intellectual property-owning companies. They see counterfeiting and piracy as a constraint on their ability to expand sales in rapidly growing markets. More fundamentally, they also view IPRs infringements as a direct competitive threat, as firms in labor-abundant countries copy the latest technologies and undermine what is perceived to be their remaining competitive edge. In the United States, politicians have linked lax IPRs enforcement abroad to the country's persistent trade deficit, especially with China. While such a link has little economic basis—the trade balance primarily reflects the difference between domestic savings and investment—it carries political weight and is shaping US trade and foreign policy.

4. Second, counterfeiting and piracy are perceived to have reached unprecedented levels. In part, the growth of counterfeiting has been spurred by technological developments which have facilitated the copying of original products. For example, the emergence of easy-to-copy digital storage mediums has enabled the cheap reproduction of audiovisual and software products without any loss of quality. The spread of online patent databases has permitted easy access to new technologies.

5. Due to their illegal nature, there are no reliable figures on the sales of intellectual property infringing products. The OECD (2007) estimates that international trade in counterfeit and pirated goods in 2005 may have amounted to as much as 200 billion dollars, or slightly more than 2 percent of global merchandise trade. This figure understates global commerce in IPRs-infringing goods, as it excludes domestic sales and digital products distributed via the Internet. Even though there are no hard numbers on the growth of IPRs violations, anecdotal evidence suggests that their scale and scope is expanding. For example, newspaper articles and government surveys in recent years indicate that counterfeiting activity has expanded from luxury to common consumer goods, affecting products as diverse as automotive replacement parts, electrical appliances, and toys. In addition, intellectual property violations are increasingly linked to organized crime.

6. At one level, one might ask: why worry about IPRs enforcement as a matter of public policy? Governments set standards of intellectual property protection through national laws and ensuring that firms and individuals obey these laws seems only natural. To be sure, some observers have argued that the exclusive rights granted by intellectual property laws have become overly strong (Jaffee and Lerner, 2004 and Maskus and Reichman, 2004). However, no one would seriously argue for correcting this suspected overshooting of IPRs laws by promoting illegal behavior. If laws do not serve the public interest, they ought to be changed rather than disregarded.

7. Yet there is one important reason for regarding IPRs piracy as an issue of public policy: resources needed for enforcing IPRs are invariably scarce. Counterfeiting and product

piracy exist even in the richest countries which have the best staffed and best equipped law enforcement agencies. For example, the Business Software Alliance estimates that, in 2006, 45 percent of software was pirated in France, 28 percent in Germany, 25 percent in Japan, and 21 percent in the United States. Governments need to make choices about how many resources to spend on combating piracy, as opposed to enforcing other areas of law, building roads and bridges, protecting national security, and providing other public goods. Such choices are usually not stated in explicit terms, but they underlie every budgetary decision by federal and local governments. For example, greater spending on counter-terrorism in the United States after September 11, 2001 has left fewer resources for fighting crime, reportedly causing rates of crime to go up in many US cities. Deciding on appropriate spending for IPRs enforcement is especially difficult in developing countries, where many public goods are underprovided and enforcement challenges exist in many areas of law—fighting violence, guaranteeing real property rights, upholding contracts, stopping illegal logging of endangered forests, regulating traffic, and so on. This paper seeks to offer an economic perspective on policies towards IPRs enforcement. It draws on key insights from the economic literature to identify priorities for the allocation of scarce law enforcement resources. Two major themes emerge from this literature. First, different types of intellectual property infringements have different welfare effects, depending on underlying market failures and market characteristics. Past studies that have attempted to quantify the "losses" due to IPRs piracy have sometimes ignored these differences. Second, in designing an IPRs enforcement strategy, policymakers need to take into account the incentives of producers and consumers to break the law. Understanding these incentives offers important insights about the limits of government policy and the effectiveness of different types of enforcement activities.

. . .

## Trademark Counterfeiting

18. A crucial consideration for evaluating the welfare implications of trademark counterfeiting is whether consumers are misled by the falsified brand name attached to their purchases. For example, most buyers of a 10-dollar watch bearing the Rolex label know perfectly well that they acquire a fake product. Simple inspection can often reveal if a product is fake or genuine and, even if not, most consumers know that genuine Rolex watches do not sell for 10 dollars. By contrast, simple inspection may not easily reveal whether [a] pharmaceutical product is counterfeit and the purchase price alone is unlikely to offer additional information on the product's origin.

19. We will first analyze product counterfeiting assuming that buyers really do not know that they purchase a counterfeit product. We will then turn to the case where buyers know that they are purchasing a fake. As will become clear, the welfare consequences from counterfeiting in these two cases differ markedly.

### Case 1: Consumers are Misled

20. If consumers cannot by themselves distinguish fakes from originals, the presence of counterfeit goods undermines the signaling function of trademarks, as described in the previous section. Consumers will invariably be worse off. Purchasers of counterfeit products will, at best, derive a value from the product which is lower than the price they paid for it and, at worst, be exposed to physical harm if counterfeit products create health or safety risks. The consumption of misbranded products may also adversely affect other individuals—for example, when the intake of drugs with no or insufficient levels of active ingredients increases the risk of disease transmission or when defect[ive] vehicle replacement parts provoke traffic accidents. In the parlance of economists, the consumption of counterfeit goods may impose "negative externalities."

21. In the long-run, if consumers know that trademarks are imperfectly enforced, markets for certain high-quality goods may not exist to begin with. Consumers would not be willing to pay the full price of a high quality original, since they fear that their purchase may be a fake. At lower prices, in turn, producers of original products would not be willing to sell. In other words, the market failure of asymmetric information strikes exactly as George Akerlof predicted more than 30 years ago.

22. The only beneficiaries of counterfeiting are the producers of counterfeits. However, the benefits accruing to those producers are bound to be lower than the losses to consumers and original producers, such that economy-wide welfare is generally lower in the presence of counterfeiting.

23. This result holds for closed economies and for the world economy at large. What if counterfeit producers are located in certain countries and export the overwhelming share of production, with domestic sales constituting a negligible share of output? For example, 90 percent of IPRs-infringing activities seized at the European border in 2006 originated in only 8 countries, with China alone accounting for 79 percent of all seizures. Even though producers in these countries invariably profit from counterfeiting activities, it is not clear how far the economies hosting such producers gain as a whole. Welfare effects will depend on patterns of comparative advantage and, in particular, how production factors in those economies would be used if counterfeiting were not feasible. Nonetheless, stronger trademark enforcement may well lead to substantial short-run employment losses in the concerned countries—an issue to which we will return below.

### Case 2: Consumers are not Misled

24. If consumers are perfectly aware that their purchases are fakes, a natural question to ask is: why do they prefer a product bearing a falsified label to a "generic" product of identical quality? The only plausible explanation is that they derive prestige or status value from the display of a particular brand name. Prestige value may be partly imaginary, for example when a consumer derives pleasure from carrying the same handbag as a Hollywood actress. More often, consumers derive status value by belonging to an exclusive club of consumers who share the same preferences and are able to afford high-end products. Individual consumers' taste for status thus needs to be included in social welfare calculations. Such an exercise may at first seem tenuous. However, a taste for status is quite real. Why else would a consumer be ready to pay several thousand dollars for a brand-name watch, when a reliable generic timekeeper can be purchased for far less that amount? Indeed, the very presence of counterfeit status goods indicates that status matters.

25. What can we say about the welfare consequences of counterfeiting in these circumstances? To begin with, consumers who knowingly purchase fake products are likely to be better off from counterfeiting activity. They always have the option of buying either the original or a generic product of comparable quality. If they choose the fake product and are not mislead, their choice reflects a rational trade-off between price, status value, and quality.

26. For consumers of original products, a crucial question is whether and how their welfare is affected by the presence of fake goods. Suppose first that such consumers can perfectly observe whether other buyers acquire fake or original products. If so, their welfare is unaffected, as the composition of the exclusive club of original purchasers remains the same. Their welfare may even increase, as the presence of fakes may raise the status value derived from owning the "real thing."

27. However, in most cases, it is more likely that consumers of originals cannot tell whether other consumers own counterfeit or original products. For many fashion products and accessories, the difference between a fake and an original can only be ascertained by close inspection or by the fanciness of the store in which the product is bought. To the casual observer, fakes and originals are often indistinguishable. Indeed, consumers of fakes would

unlikely derive much status value from counterfeit products if they could not successfully pretend that they own the genuine product.

28. Grossman and Shapiro (1988b) develop a simple model in which the prestige value a consumer derives from a given brand is negatively related to the number of consumers who own products displaying the same brand name—regardless of whether those products are fake or genuine. The presence of fake goods thus undermines the prestige of owning the genuine product, leaving buyers of those genuine products worse-off from counterfeiting. However, Grossman and Shapiro show that the economy-wide welfare consequences from stronger trademark enforcement are ambiguous: depending on demand structures, the loss suffered by consumers of counterfeits may exceed the gain to consumers of originals.

29. Trademark owners will experience an increase in profits from stronger trademark enforcement, as some consumers switch from fakes to originals. In the long term, greater profitability in the market for genuine products will induce entry of additional firms. The arrival of additional brands brings about a dual benefit to consumers of originals: each brand is purchased by fewer consumers, thus raising the prestige value associated with each brand, and greater competition between brands leads to a fall in the price of those products. Notwithstanding these additional benefits from market entry, the welfare consequences of stronger trademark enforcement remain ambiguous, as the loss to consumers of counterfeits may still outweigh any gain to consumers of originals.

30. Two additional considerations further complicate an already complex assessment of the welfare effects from counterfeiting. First, the presence of status goods may lead those consumers who cannot afford originals to be envious of those who can. Since the presence of counterfeit products may reduce this form of jealousy, there may be additional welfare losses from stronger trademark enforcement. Second, since consumers able to afford original products are likely to have higher incomes than those unable to do so, stronger trademark enforcement may have distributional implications. A government seeking a more equal distribution of real incomes may assign a stronger weight to low income consumers in its social welfare calculations. On balance, the inclusion of distributional concerns along these lines makes it more likely that stepped-up trademark enforcement will lower economy-wide welfare—though, in the end, it remains an empirical question.

### Infringements of Copyright, Patents, and Related Iprs

31. In general, violations of copyright, patents, and related IPRs affect the policy trade-off outlined previously: they weaken incentives for investments in inventive and creative activities but benefit users of these rights by offering them access to IPRs-protected goods at competitive prices. If governments maintain socially optimal standards of protection, IPRs violations, by definition, will lead to a welfare loss. However, this is a big "if." Actual patent and copyright regimes are often the outcome of history, rules of thumb, and the influence of vested interests. Economic optimization hardly plays a role—not least because the social benefits of inventive and creative activities are unknown *ex-ante.* If the degree of protection as inscribed in laws is too strong, some levels of IPRs violations will increase welfare. If the degree of protection is too weak, any IPRs violation will invariably lower welfare.

32. An interesting question is how consumers of original products will fare upon stepped-up IPRs enforcement. Reduced competition from IPRs-infringing goods may increase the market power of the IPRs-holder, leading to higher prices for originals. However, the price effect will also depend on the price sensitivity of demand exhibited by the group of consumers that purchase originals. If their price sensitivity is lower than the average price sensitivity among all consumers in the economy, producers of originals may respond to stronger enforcement by lowering their prices. Such an outcome is consistent with consumers of originals being relatively well-off compared to consumers of illegitimate products. Indeed, original copyrighted works (e.g., audiovisual recordings) are sometimes more expensive in developing

countries with higher piracy rates, as copyright holders set prices mostly reflecting demand from high-income consumers. However, possible price effects upon stronger IPRs enforcement may well be small if the distribution of income is such that only few consumers will be able to switch from IPRs-infringing to legitimate goods.

33. As in the case of trademarks, stronger enforcement of copyright, patents, and related IPRs is likely to have distributional consequences, which governments may want to take into account in their social welfare calculations. How the distribution of real incomes will be affected will, in part, depend on the average incomes of consumers of illegitimate products relative to the average incomes of workers engaged in creative and inventive activities. In a developing country context, where most intellectual property is owned by foreign residents, governments seeking to promote a more equal distribution of real incomes may attach more weight to the welfare losses suffered by low income consumers of IPRs-infringing goods relative to the strengthened incentive for investments in creative and inventive activities. Yet again, the national and global welfare effects of stronger IPRs enforcement remain ultimately an empirical question.

## NOTES AND QUESTIONS

**1.** In assessing the options, who bears the costs and risks of private law enforcement, and who bears the costs and risks of penal prosecutions?

**2.** Lobbyists for right holders stress the importance of enhanced criminal penalties, in particular in the field of copyright piracy. Where would you agree to criminal measures from a developing country point of view, and where would you disagree, using the analysis by Fink?

**3.** Thomas Cottier suggested to introduce the idea of graduation to intellectual property protection and to shape obligations of countries in international law and in particular the TRIPS Agreement commensurate with their levels of social and economic development, using a number of thresholds and indicators which would trigger the operation of specific provisions. *From Progressive Liberalization to Progressive Regulation in WTO Law*, 9 J. Int'l Econ. L. 779-821 (2006). Do you think that such an approach could provide appropriate answers to the problems underlying the enforcement of intellectual property rights?

## II. MULTILATERAL IPRS ENFORCEMENT AGREEMENTS

### A. The TRIPS Agreement

#### *1. Enforcement Obligations*

**Thomas Cottier***

### *The Agreement on Trade Related Aspects of Intellectual Property Rights (TRIPS)*

#### Enforcement of Intellectual Property Rights (Part III)

Effective legal protection depends both on substantive norms and the efficient and fair administration of justice. This is equally true for intellectual property rights protection. In

* 1 The World Trade Organization: Legal, Economic and Political Analysis 1041 (Patrick F. J. Macrory, Arthur E. Appleton & Michael G. Plummer eds., 2005).

many countries, implementation of and respect for rights fails due to lack of adequate and effective legal protection before administrative and judicial authorities. This is particularly true for intellectual property since it is a complex area of law often unfamiliar to regular courts and often alien to the legal tradition of developing countries. Efforts in the GATT prior to the Uruguay Round focused on combating counterfeiting and piracy which essentially entailed efforts to improve domestic and border enforcement. It was clear from the outset that comprehensive negotiations on trade-related aspects of intellectual property protection in the GATT, and subsequently the WTO, could not be limited to the definition of minimum substantive standards, but would need to extend to standards on judicial, administrative and even penal protection of IPRs. These efforts amounted to one of the most interesting and challenging tasks of the negotiation. None of the conventions administrated by WIPO addresses the issue of effective enforcement. A common and new ground between different legal traditions and systems had to be found. Developing countries resisted these efforts for a long time on the ground that the issue of enforcement goes far beyond aspects of international trade. Moreover, improving enforcement would not come without additional financial burdens which were not considered a priority in the process of development. Negotiations were based upon comprehensive drafts submitted by the United States, the European Communities and Switzerland. They can be characterized as a process of mutual approximation or *approchement* between common law traditions which entail party-driven instruments such as pretrial discovery, and the European-based approach leaving procedures and investigation much more in the hand of the courts. The result amounts to a first and quite substantial harmonization of civil and administrative law procedures in international law, while leaving room for alternative solutions reflecting different legal traditions. Many of the provisions are expressed in non-mandatory terms, allowing Members, but not obliging them, to authorize judicial and administrative authorities to take certain measures. These formulations demonstrate, on the one hand, the remaining divergences between judicial systems. On the other hand, they also prescribe and confirm that such measures as authorized, but not mandated, by the Agreement do not amount to excessive procedural requirements and, consequently, cannot give rise to violation and non-violation complaints.

As the implementation of these rules in national legislation inherently reaches beyond the realm of intellectual property protection, the provisions of Part III of the TRIPs Agreement may be described as a body of common procedural standards in international law. The norms resulting from the negotiations reflect a considerable level of detail. They are particularly apt to be referred to in the process of interpretation and application of domestic law under the doctrine of consistent interpretation. They are equally suitable for direct effect where such effect is constitutionally permitted. These points are of particular importance for the European Community. By means of the provisions on enforcement, a common regional standard in EC law was achieved for which no internal jurisdiction or competence existed in internal, domestic EC law. It is no coincidence that the provisions on enforcement resulted in a considerable expansion of the jurisdiction of the European Court of Justice in matters relating to civil procedure, and the doctrines of consistent interpretation and direct effect were first probed by the court in the field of WTO law.

While compliance with Part III only required minor, but sometimes important changes in the legislation of industrialized countries, implementing legislation was often required in developing and transitional countries, assisting the process of reinforcing the rule of law and good governance. The Agreement, however, does not oblige Members to provide additional and special resources for the protection of intellectual property rights distinct from the resources provided for the enforcement of laws in general. Article 41:5 provides a significant limitation, stating that "[n]othing in this Part creates any obligation with respect to the distribution of resources as between enforcement of intellectual property rights and the enforcement of law in general." Developing country efforts to reinforce the judicial system for the purposes of intellectual property right protection, however, have to be supported by developed country Members through technical cooperation under Article 67 of the Agreement.

### General Obligations

Article 41 of the Agreement stipulates a number of fundamental principles which apply in general and to all the subsequent, more specialized provisions of Part III. It requires Members to ensure that enforcement procedures are available under their law that permit effective action against any act of infringement of intellectual property rights covered by the TRIPs Agreement, including expeditious remedies to prevent infringements and remedies which constitute a deterrent to further infringements. The relevant test in assessing enforcement procedures is trade-related, examining whether they create barriers to legitimate trade and whether they provide safeguards against their abuse. Article 41:2 requires the procedures to be fair and equitable. Standards of fairness and equity are incorporated in the provisions throughout this Part. In addition, they need to be defined by reference to general principles of law. Procedures must not be unnecessarily complicated or costly, and must not entail unreasonable time-limits or unwarranted delays. Article 41:3 entails the fundamental principle that a decision on the merits of a case is to be reasoned, preferably in writing. Oral decisions therefore are not prohibited, and may be applied primarily in the field of rapid, provisional measures. Decisions on the merits must be based solely upon evidence in respect of which the parties were offered an opportunity to be heard.

These important provisions apply to all judicial systems alike and embody the fundamental right to be heard and the right to reasoned decision-making. They also apply, in accordance with Article 62:4, to administrative revocation and *inter-partes* procedures, such as opposition, revocation and cancellation of rights. Article 41:4 builds upon the tradition of Article X:3(b) of the GATT and prescribes the obligation to provide for appeal mechanisms. Members are required to provide for review of final administrative decisions by independent judicial authorities. As to judicial decisions in civil matters, the agreement is limited to a minimal standard. Members are free to define the jurisdictional threshold for appeal commensurate with the importance of the case (e.g., in terms of monetary thresholds). Within this range, they need to provide at least for review of legal issues on the merits. There is no obligation to provide for a second level of appeal. As to penal cases, judicial review is required for convictions, but not for acquittals.

Implementation of Part III is supported by obligations of Members to cooperate in international law enforcement in accordance with Article 69 of the Agreement. Members are obliged to establish and notify contacts point in their administrations and be ready to exchange information on infringing goods. Particular emphasis is laid on cooperation and exchange of information between customs authorities "with regard to trade in counterfeit trademark goods and pirated copyright goods."

### Civil and Administrative Procedures and Remedies

The provisions of Section 2 of Part III of the TRIPs Agreement further specify the concept of fair and equitable procedural principles commensurate with well-established general rules of civil procedure. According to Article 49, they also apply to administrative procedures to the extent that "any civil remedy can be ordered as a result of administrative procedures on the merits of the case." The following requirements deserve particular emphasis:

Footnote 11 to Article 42 defines right holders entitled to civil procedures to include federations and associations having legal standing in accordance with domestic law. Parties shall be entitled to substantiate their claims. To this effect, the provision requires Members to allow representation by legal counsel. The requirement of personal appearance of right holders and defendants shall not be "overly burdensome"; an item of particular importance in transnational litigation. Defendants need to be served with sufficiently detailed and timely written notice. Subject to the constitutional law of Members, the confidential information of parties to the dispute needs to be protected, for example by making available a summary of factual evidence to the other party.

Article 43 contains important rules on evidence. Article 43:1 obliges Members to require parties to a dispute, based upon sufficiently substantiated claims, to produce evidence in administrative and judicial proceedings, subject to the protection of undisclosed information. If a party fails to produce such evidence, Article 43:2 empowers administrative and judicial authorities to make determinations based on the available evidence.

Article 44 addresses injunctions which are of particular importance in intellectual property litigation, especially in cases relating to counterfeiting or unlawful parallel trade. It requires domestic laws to grant power to local judicial authorities to prevent imminent infringements of intellectual property rights. This provision, applicable to proceedings on the merits and to be distinguished from independent provisional measures addressed in Article 50, sets forth minimum standards for injunctions requiring a party not to commit an infringement or to cease infringement. In particular, local judicial authorities should be empowered, immediately after customs clearance of such goods, to prevent the entry into the channels of commerce of imported goods that infringe an intellectual property right and to seize the respective goods. Members are not required to extend such mechanisms to situations where the importer did not know, or did not have reasonable grounds to know that dealing in such subject matter would entail the infringement of an intellectual property right. In such cases, the right holder would need to await the judgment on the merits.

Article 45 requires that the damages awarded must constitute adequate compensation for the injury, including payment of the expenses of the right holder which, depending on the judicial system, may also (but need not) include appropriate attorney's fees. This minimum obligation is limited to willful or careless infringement. In addition, authorities may have the power to recover profits and/or the payment of pre-established damages. This possibility is available also in cases where the infringers did not knowingly, or with reasonable grounds to know, engage in infringing activity.

In addition, local authorities shall have the mandatory authority under Article 46 to seize infringing goods and to prevent the further delivery of infringing services (e.g., film screenings). Instruments ("implements") that predominantly serve to create infringing goods ("*instrumenta sceleris*"), such as production facilities and machinery, computers, etc., are also to be subject to seizure. For many countries, this amounts to an important additional obligation, reinforcing the fight against counterfeiting at its source. Judicial authorities shall have the authority to remove infringing goods and implements from the channels of commerce without compensation. Subject to the constitutional requirements of Members and the principle of proportionality, this may also involve destruction. Counterfeit goods or unlawfully imported goods in parallel trade may be used and consumed outside the channel of commerce, for example by making them available to food and support programs. Authorities are obliged to engage in a process of balancing the interests involved with a view to preventing further violations. As a result, goods may stay in the channel of commerce, even though the treaty specifies that mere removal of trademarks is generally not sufficient to comply with the TRIPs Agreement.

Article 47 provides an arguably very effective tool for detecting the sources of infringements. Provided that the measure appears to be proportionate to the infringement, the judicial authorities shall have the authority to require the infringing person to disclose (i) the identity of third persons involved in the production and distribution of the infringing goods or services, and (ii) their channels of distribution. While these obligations strongly reinforce the position of right holders, Article 48 protects defendants against abusive claims and measures. The provision is designed to deal with cases of so-called procedural harassment where measures imposing unjustified restrictions were granted. Appropriate remedies to compensate for damage must be made available. Accordingly, the judicial authorities must have authority to order the applicants to pay the defendant's expenses, which may include appropriate attorneys' fees. Members may exempt both public authorities and officials from appropriate remedial measures where unjustified actions are taken in good faith in the course of enforcing intellectual property laws.

### Provisional Measures

Provisional measures applied for and granted beyond the ordinary civil or administrative remedies discussed above, amount to one of the most effective and important tools in enforcing intellectual property rights. Most cases against infringement or, as the case may be, unlawful importation and distribution by way of parallel trade, are settled by means of such procedures and do not reach the stage of ordinary and costly proceedings on the merits. The powers granted in Article 50 are of particular importance for trademark and copyright enforcement in the field of software protection as evidence of infringement can be easily destroyed upon notice of impending measures. A number of countries were obliged, following consultations under the DSU, to alter their legislation accordingly.

Article 50 is therefore a core provision of the TRIPs Agreement. Applying both to civil and administrative proceedings (Article 50:8), Article 50:1 obliges Members to make available prompt and effective provisional measures in order to (i) prevent an infringement from occurring, "in particular to prevent the entry into the channels of commerce in their jurisdiction or goods, including imported goods immediately after customs clearance," and (ii) "to preserve relevant evidence in regard of the alleged infringement." The Agreement sets detailed mandatory standards to this effect. In particular, according to Article 50:2 the judicial authorities shall have the authority to adopt such measures without having heard the defendant prior to taking action ("*inaudita altera parte*"). Such measures are subject to certain conditions set forth in Article 50:3 and 50:5: (i) the rights of the claimant must be reasonably established, (ii) any delay is likely to cause irreparable harm or where there is a risk of evidence being destroyed, and (iii) the goods concerned must be clearly identified and the applicant may therefore [be] required to supply additional information necessary for the identification of the goods. Upon taking measures *inaudita altera parte*, Article 50:4 requires that the defendant must be notified without delay of the measure and granted access to judicial review within a reasonable period to decide upon maintenance, revocation or modification of the measures. Article 50:6 of the Agreement requires that the provisional measures are revoked or otherwise cease to have effect upon request of the defendant, if the claimant does not initiate proceedings on the merit within a reasonable period of time. Such period is to be determined by the judicial authority ordering the provisional measure. Failing such determination, it shall not exceed 20 working days or 31 calendar days, whichever is shorter. This requirement and safeguard of linking provisional measures to proceedings on the merit amounts to a defining element of provisional measures compatible with WTO law. Article 50 gave rise to interpretation by the European Court of Justice and was applied in accordance with the doctrine of consistent interpretation with respect to both national law and the European trademark regulation. Furthermore, Article 50 is particularly suitable for direct effect when its safeguard provisions do not exist in domestic law. Under Article 50:7, courts may order the applicant to pay appropriate damages to the defendant, if the measure turns out to be unjustified.

### Special Requirements Related to Border Measures

Border measures operated by customs authorities provide the second central mainstay for enforcing intellectual property rights. Counterfeit goods are best intercepted at the point of importation. Once they have reached the channels of distribution, law enforcement is more difficult and burdensome as complaints may need to be filed in different jurisdictions.

The provisions of Section 4 of Part III of the TRIPs Agreement deal with measures ordered by custom administrations with respect to the importation of counterfeit trademarked or pirated copyrighted goods. "Counterfeit trademark goods" (not including geographical indications) and "pirated copyright goods" (including goods protected by neighboring rights) are defined in a footnote to Article 51. There is no obligation to apply this Section to patented products, industrial designs, layout-designs, or geographical indications. However, if border measures are extended to other forms, there must be compliance with the procedures set forth in the Agreement. Furthermore, Members can also provide the same measures against infringing goods destined for export from their territories.

Article 52 requires the applicant to provide *prima facie* evidence of an impending infringement, and conditions are defined to this effect. Upon acceptance of the application, the authority informs the applicant as to the duration of the measure taken and, in accordance with Article 54, both the applicant and the importer are promptly notified of the suspension of the release of the goods at stake.

Article 53 allows authorities to require a reasonable, non-deterrent security or an equivalent assurance sufficient to protect the interests of the defendant and the authority in case wrongful actions is taken and compensation is due in accordance with Article 56. In cases other than trademark counterfeiting and copyright piracy as defined above (industrial designs, patents, layout designs and undisclosed information) the importer or consignee of such goods is entitled to their release on the posting of a sufficient security. This reflects the fact that assessing violations of IPRs in these areas is more difficult than in the field of trademarks and copyright protection.

Article 55 defines the duration of suspension of release and the relationship to proceedings on the merits. Given the powerful impact of this instrument, customs authorities are obliged to release the goods if they are not informed within ten working days that proceedings on the merits have been initiated by the applicant or that the competent judicial authority has taken provisional measures prolonging the suspension of the goods in accordance with Article 50. If proceedings on the merits have been initiated, the defendant is entitled to initiate review of the measure and to be heard. Measures may be subsequently modified, revoked or confirmed within a reasonable period of time.

Article 56 addresses the indemnification of the importer and owner of the goods for injury due to wrongful detention of goods or through detention of goods released pursuant to Article 55. The provision obligates Members to grant authorities the authority to require the applicant to pay the owner of the goods or the consignee appropriate compensation for injury caused. The Agreement does not set forth any standards and criteria to this effect and Members may base such compensation on their tort law. Also, the provision is silent on the responsibility of customs authorities. Article 53 implies that the responsibility remains exclusively with the applicant vis-à-vis the defendant. Additional remedies for *ex officio* action are required by Article 58.

Under Article 57 Members are obliged to grant the local authorities power to allow the right holder to inspect the goods in order to substantiate its claim, and the importer must also be granted the right of inspection. The Members are to authorize their authorities to inform the right holder of the names and addresses of the consignor, the importer and the consignee, and of the quantity of the goods in question if a positive determination has been made on the merits of a case.

Customs authorities are not limited to acting upon motion by the applicant. According to Article 58, Members may, but are not obligated, to empower competent authorities to order *ex officio* enforcement measures relating to the protection of intellectual property on the basis of *prima facie* evidence. Where such powers exist, a number of safeguards must be respected: (i) authorities are entitled to request additional information from the right holder at any time, (ii) the importer and right holder need to be promptly informed about the suspension of customs clearance (Article 58(b) implies that appeal procedures shaped *mutatis mutandis* in accordance with Article 55 must be available to the importer); (iii) liability of public authorities and officials for unlawful suspension must be made available and can only be excluded for acts taken or intended in good faith. The standard provides minimum protection against willful or negligent infringement.

Article 59 renders the principles and rules of Article 46 on disposal or destruction of infringing goods applicable to *ex officio* measures. Other than in exceptional circumstances, counterfeit trademark goods may not be released into a third country in an unaltered state, thus somewhat limiting the flexibility available under Article 46. Under Article 60 Members may exclude *de minimis* imports from the application of the provisions in Section 4.

### Criminal Procedures

The TRIPs Agreement contains in Article 61 the first generation of penal provisions in the WTO system. It nevertheless leaves Members considerable flexibility in implementing the provision. Members are obligated to prosecute, at a minimum, willful trademark counterfeiting and copyright piracy (as defined in Article 51) on a commercial scale.[1] Penalties must include imprisonment and/or monetary fines. Members are obliged to set standards of punishment consistently with penalties provided for crimes of comparable gravity. In other words, they need to show consistency in their criminal policies. Penalties for other infringements, including negligent trademark or copyright violations, are permitted, but not required. Penal law must allow for the seizure, forfeiture and destruction of infringing goods and implements (defined in Article 46) in appropriate cases. The provision does allow Members to adopt extensive criminal sanctions without running the risk of facing challenges under violation or non-violation complaints, even though the threat of such sanctions may have considerable trade-restricting effects, for example in the field of internet communication.

## NOTES AND QUESTIONS

**1.** Prior to the TRIPS Agreement, protection of enforcement of intellectual property rights was limited to MFN and national treatment obligations under GATT 1947. In *US – Section 337 of the Tariff Act,* Report of the Panel, adopted 7 Nov. 1989, L/6439, 36S/345 (1990), it was found that the United States violated national treatment by treating imported products under patent protection before the United States International Trade Commission (USITC) less advantageously than domestic products in litigation in federal courts under the U.S. Patent Act. See *infra* section IV.B.1. With the incorporation of national treatment and MFN in the TRIPS Agreement, such cases today are also dealt with under the TRIPS Agreement, in parallel to GATT 1995.

**2.** National treatment remains an important ingredient for IP protection and enforcement. In 2018, the United States and the European Union requested consultation on

1. Even though Article 61 is framed as an alternative (by stating that criminal procedures and penalties be applied at least to trademark counterfeiting *or* copyright piracy), measures clearly need to be put in place for both trademarks *and* copyright.

discriminatory treatment in transfer of technology, including patent licensing: *China – Measures Affecting the Protection and Enforcement of Intellectual Property Rights*, DS 542, consultation requested by the United States, 23 Mar. 2018; *China – Certain Measures on the Transfer of Technology*, DS 549, consultation requested by the European Union, 1 June 2018. These claims relate to the substantive provisions of the TRIPS Agreement, but also have an indirect bearing on the realization and enforcement of IPRs; see also *infra* section II.A.2. The United States did not formally request establishment of a panel in this matter and it was reported that China had agreed to amend its legislation to apply it also to domestic licensors, thereby removing the basis for a discrimination claim.

### 2. *Enforcement in WTO Dispute Settlement*

The TRIPS Agreement entered new international legal ground when it imposed obligations on WTO Members to adequately and effectively enforce IPRs. The difficulties inherent in establishing a breach of obligations were to some extent foreseeable. Those difficulties are on display in connection with U.S. efforts to require China to better implement its enforcement commitments. The first excerpt below examines some of the complications involved in pursuing an enforcement action under TRIPS Agreement rules. This is followed by an excerpt from the decision of the WTO dispute settlement panel in the *China-Enforcement* case.

**Frederick M. Abbott***

## *China in the WTO 2006: "Law and its Limitations" in the Context of TRIPS*

### I. Introduction . . .

In February 2005, U.S. industry groups requested USTR to initiate a WTO dispute settlement action against China based on inadequate enforcement of intellectual property rights. USTR declined, largely on grounds that industry had not presented the kind of specific information that would be required to successfully pursue a WTO complaint. This was a significant decision reflecting a core problem the U.S. faces as it attempts to move forward at the WTO.

In April 2005, USTR announced the results of a so-called Special 301, "out of cycle review" of China's IPRs practices.[37] In addition to elevating China to "Priority Watch" country status (which is significantly less serious than designating China a priority foreign country), USTR indicated that it would invoke the provisions of Article 63 of the TRIPS Agreement which authorize a Member to formally request information from another Member regarding certain intellectual property-related matters. . . .

On October 25, 2005, in connection with a meeting of the TRIPS Council, the US Ambassador to the WTO, Peter Allgeir, transmitted a detailed request to the Chinese Ambassador to the WTO, Sun Zhenyu, regarding China's IPRs enforcement related activities. China was requested to respond on or before January 23, 2006. Japan and Switzerland made similar requests.

---

* In Developing Countries in the WTO: A Law and Economics Analysis (G. Bermann & P.C. Mavroidis eds., 2007).

37. Available at http://www.ustr.gov.

China's delegate questioned at the TRIPS Council meeting whether Article 63.3 of the TRIPS Agreement provides the basis for the broad request made by the United States. On December 22, 2006, the Chinese Ambassador sent a request for clarification of the legal basis of the request to the US Ambassador. As of February 2006, China had declined to formally respond to the U.S. request for information at the WTO. On February 15, 2006, USTR Robert Portman reiterated U.S. concerns with China's inadequate implementation of its IPRs-related commitments, and referred to action taken under Article 63 of the TRIPS Agreement at the WTO.

## II. WTO Dispute Settlement

. . .

The TRIPS Agreement broke new ground when it established a requirement for effective enforcement of intellectual property norms. There are no comparable requirements in the WIPO Conventions. Thus, a panel and the Appellate Body would need to establish new standards under which to assess a claim for failure to permit the effective enforcement of IPRs. What quantum of enforcement failures would constitute a systemic failure? How would individual claims of judicial or administrative failure be assessed? Would a panel assess the decisions of judges in particular cases to determine whether the law was correctly applied? What would be the standard of review?

There are other trade agreements which require countries to properly apply their own law. For example, the NAFTA requires its parties to properly administer their antidumping and countervailing duty laws, and there have been a significant number of Chapter 19 panel decisions making assessments under those standards. But, the NAFTA Chapter 19 rules do not ask a systemic question. Each case is evaluated on its individual merits. The NAFTA Supplemental Agreements on Environment and Labor each require the parties to effectively enforce their respective laws in these subject matter areas, and provide mechanisms for evaluating claims of noncompliance. The mechanisms for evaluation are different than traditional state to state dispute settlement mechanisms, as in the WTO. In the environmental sector, private parties are entitled to initiate claims before the Secretariat of the NAAEC Commission for Environmental Cooperation, which may ultimately result in the preparation and publication of a factual record. There is an alternative state to state dispute settlement mechanism for allegations of failure of effective enforcement of environmental law. This mechanism has never been used and raises questions similar to that which are raised under Article 41 of the TRIPS Agreement. It is doubtful that a panel or the Appellate Body will refer to agreements outside the WTO to establish standards on effective enforcement under the TRIPS Agreement because there is no comparable context. The WTO dispute settlement system would be in uncharted jurisprudential territory.

. . .

### C. Remedies

The Appellate Body characteristically recommends that a Member bring its measures into conformity with its WTO obligations. If it found that China was failing to implement its Article 61 obligations to provide adequate criminal sanctions against trademark counterfeiting and copyright piracy, it would presumably recommend that China remedy that failure. This could predictably lead to additional rounds of dispute settlement arbitration regarding whether China had in fact remedied the situation and, if not, what level of concessions the United States was entitled to withdraw. Such arbitrations would raise questions as difficult as those facing the panel and Appellate Body in the main dispute. How much criminal enforcement activity is required? How quickly can such a situation be remedied? Would the adequacy of the remedial measures be judged on the basis of the steps the government had taken or whether trademark counterfeiting and copyright piracy had actually been reduced? Are there reliable figures regarding the economic costs of counterfeiting and piracy?

None of this is to suggest that answers are beyond the capacity of the WTO dispute settlement system, but rather that almost any result is bound to be controversial. And this has the potential to create tensions within and for the WTO, regardless which of the main protagonists considers itself aggrieved.

## NOTES AND QUESTIONS

**1.** The article excerpted above goes on to observe that China is likely to strengthen enforcement of IPRs as local enterprises increase their attention to innovation and branding. In other words, China will enforce IPRs when it perceives it to be in its national interest. The TRIPS Agreement represents, in effect, an attempt to block this historic pattern. While the OECD countries may be successful in that effort with respect to less economically and politically powerful countries, the results are mixed with more economically and politically powerful countries like Brazil, China, and India.

**2.** U.S. foreign direct investors hold large stakes in China. U.S.-owned businesses produce in China for export to the United States and elsewhere. Does this restrict U.S. options for forcing China's hand with respect to IP enforcement?

**3.** Later in this chapter, we examine USTR's 2018 "Special 301" report with respect to China. This report sets out specific concerns with respect to IPRs practices.

As you read the following excerpt from *China—Measures Affecting the Protection and Enforcement of Intellectual Property Rights*, consider whether you accept a U.S. claim that it "won" the case, recognizing that this excerpt does not address all of the issues at stake.

## *China—Measures Affecting the Protection and Enforcement of Intellectual Property Rights*

Report of the Panel*

7.528 Part III of the TRIPS Agreement distinguishes between the treatment of wilful trademark counterfeiting and copyright piracy on a commercial scale, on the one hand, and all other infringements of intellectual property rights, on the other hand, in that only the former are subject to an obligation regarding criminal procedures and penalties. This indicates the shared view of the negotiators that the former are the most blatant and egregious acts of infringement. This view must inform the interpretation of Article 61.

7.529 The Panel recalls its findings at paragraph 7.241 above as to the circumstances of conclusion of the TRIPS Agreement with respect to enforcement procedures. Whilst some of the pre-existing international intellectual property agreements or conventions contain provisions on the characteristics of enforcement mechanisms, it is striking that none of them create any specific minimum standard for criminal enforcement procedures. Among the international intellectual property agreements with wide membership, Article 61 of the TRIPS Agreement is, in this sense, unique.

7.530 This reflects, in part, the fact that intellectual property rights are private rights, as recognized in the fourth recital of the Preamble to the TRIPS Agreement. In contrast,

* WT/DS362/R, 26 Jan. 2009.

criminal procedures are designed to punish acts that transgress societal values. This is reflected in the use of the word "penalties" in Article 61.

7.531 Bearing in mind these aspects of the context of the first sentence of Article 61, and the object and purpose of the TRIPS Agreement, the Panel now turns to the ordinary meaning of the words "on a commercial scale."

### (V) "ON A COMMERCIAL SCALE"

7.532 The parties adopt different approaches to the task of interpreting the phrase "on a commercial scale." The Panel will examine each of these approaches in turn, beginning with that of the complainant.

7.533 The ordinary meaning of the word "scale" is uncontroversial. It may be defined as "relative magnitude or extent; degree, proportion. Freq. in *on a grand, lavish, small,* etc. *scale.*" The ordinary meaning of the word includes both the concept of quantity, in terms of magnitude or extent, as well as the concept of relativity. Both concepts are combined in the notions of degree and proportion. Therefore, a particular "scale" compares certain things or actions in terms of their size. Some things or actions will be of the relevant size and others will not.

7.534 The relevant size is indicated by the word "commercial." The ordinary meaning of "commercial" may be defined in various ways. The following two definitions have been raised in the course of these proceedings:

> 1. Engaged in commerce; of, pertaining to, or bearing on commerce.
> 2. (. . .)
> 3. Interested in financial return rather than artistry; likely to make a profit; regarded as a mere matter of business."

7.535 The Panel considers the first definition to be apposite. It includes the term "commerce" which may, in turn, be defined as "buying and selling; the exchange of merchandise or services, esp. on a large scale." Reading this definition into the definition of "commercial" indicates that "commercial" means, basically, engaged in buying and selling, or pertaining to, or bearing on, buying and selling. A combination of that expanded definition of "commercial" and the definition of "scale" would render a meaning in terms of a relative magnitude or extent (of those) engaged in buying and selling, or a relative magnitude or extent pertaining to, or bearing on, buying and selling. This draws a link to the commercial marketplace.

7.536 The United States also submits that the word "commercial" scale draws a link to the commercial marketplace. However, it refers to elements of the first and third meanings in definition 3., but dismisses the relevance of the second meaning, "likely to make a profit," because it is different from the other two.

7.537 . . .

7.538 Therefore, the Panel considers that the first definition set out at paragraph 7.534 above is appropriate. However, the combination of that definition of "commercial" with the definition of "scale" presents a problem in that scale is a quantitative concept whilst commercial is qualitative, in the sense that it refers to the nature of certain acts. Some acts are in fact commercial, whilst others are not. Any act of selling can be described as commercial in this primary sense, irrespective of its size or value. If "commercial" is simply read as a qualitative term, referring to all acts pertaining to, or bearing on commerce, this would read the word "scale" out of the text. Acts on a commercial scale would simply be commercial acts. The phrase "on a commercial scale" would simply mean "commercial." Such an interpretation fails to give meaning to all the terms used in the treaty and is inconsistent with the rule of effective treaty interpretation.

. . .

7.543 . . . [T]he negotiators agreed in Article 61 to use the distinct phrase "on a commercial scale." This indicates that the word "scale" was a deliberate choice and must be given due interpretative weight. "Scale" denotes a relative size, and reflects the intention of the negotiators that the limitation on the obligation in the first sentence of the Article depended on the size of acts of counterfeiting and piracy. Therefore, whilst "commercial" is a qualitative term, it would be an error to read it solely in those terms. In context it must indicate a quantity.

7.544 A review of the uses of the word "commercial" throughout the TRIPS Agreement indicates that it links various activities, not simply selling, to the marketplace. It also shows that "commercial" activities cannot be presumed to be on a larger scale than others, such as "public non-commercial" activities, even though they would generally be larger than, say, "personal" or "domestic" use. The distinguishing characteristic of a commercial activity is that it is carried out for profit. The review of the uses of the word "commercial" also shows that, unlike all the others, Article 61 uses the word "commercial" to qualify a notion of size.

7.545 In the Panel's view, the combination of the primary definition of "commercial" and the definition of "scale" can be reconciled with the context of Article 61 if it is assessed not solely according to the nature of an activity but also in terms of relative size, as a market benchmark . . .

7.546 Turning to the arguments of the parties and various third parties on this point, they have attempted to give due meaning to both the terms "commerce" and "scale" in different ways. Initially, the United States submitted as follows:

> "those who engage in commercial activities in order to make a 'financial return' in the marketplace . . . are, by definition, therefore operating on a commercial scale" . . .

. . .

7.559 The Panel will follow the approach explained by the Appellate Body in EC—Chicken Cuts:

> "The Appellate Body has observed that dictionaries are a 'useful starting point' for the analysis of 'ordinary meaning' of a treaty term, but they are not necessarily dispositive. The ordinary meaning of a treaty term must be ascertained according to the particular circumstances of each case. Importantly, the ordinary meaning of a treaty term must be seen in the light of the intention of the parties 'as expressed in the words used by them against the light of the surrounding circumstances.'"

7.560 The Panel recalls that the dictionary definition of "scale" (quoted at paragraph 7.533 above) includes the entry "Freq. in on a grand, lavish, small, etc. scale." These examples show that the phrase "on a . . . scale" is frequently used. Therefore, the use of the words "on a commercial scale" as a phrase appears to be relevant to their ordinary meaning.

7.561 The circumstances surrounding the inclusion of the phrase "on a commercial scale" show that the phrase has been used and, in some cases, defined in the intellectual property legislation of various countries for periods stretching back almost a century. . . .

. . .

7.577 The Panel recalls its view at paragraph 7.545 above and, in light of the evidence considered above, finds that a "commercial scale" is the magnitude or extent of typical or usual commercial activity. Therefore, counterfeiting or piracy "on a commercial scale" refers to counterfeiting or piracy carried on at the magnitude or extent of typical or usual commercial activity with respect to a given product in a given market. The magnitude or extent of typical or usual commercial activity with respect to a given product in a given market forms a benchmark by which to assess the obligation in the first sentence of Article 61. It follows that what constitutes a commercial scale for counterfeiting or piracy of a particular product in a particular market will depend on the magnitude or extent that is typical or usual with respect to such a product in such a market, which may be small or large. The magnitude or extent of typical or usual commercial activity relates, in the longer term, to profitability.

7.578 The Panel observes that what is typical or usual in commerce is a flexible concept. The immediate context in the second sentence of Article 61, which is closely related to the first, refers to the similarly flexible concepts of "deterrent" and "corresponding gravity." Neither these terms nor "commercial scale" are precise but all depend on circumstances, which vary according to the differing forms of commerce and of counterfeiting and piracy to which these obligations apply.

. . .

### (IX) Conformity of the Measures at Issue with Respect to the Level of the Thresholds

7.600 The Panel recalls its finding at paragraph 7.545 above regarding the interpretation of the phrase "wilful trademark counterfeiting or copyright piracy 'on a commercial scale,'" as used in Article 61 of the TRIPS Agreement. The Panel recalls, in particular, that this is a relative standard, which will vary when applied to different fact situations.

7.601 The Panel notes that it is the standard in the treaty obligation that varies as applied to different fact situations, and not necessarily the means by which Members choose to implement that standard. The Panel recalls that the third sentence of Article 1.1 of the TRIPS Agreement, quoted and discussed at paragraphs 7.512 and 7.513 above, provides as follows:

> "Members shall be free to determine the appropriate method of implementing the provisions of this Agreement within their own legal system and practice."

7.602 This provision confirms that the TRIPS Agreement does not mandate specific forms of legislation. The Panel may not simply assume that a Member must give its authorities wide discretion to determine what is on a commercial scale in any given case, and may not simply assume that thresholds, including numerical tests, are inconsistent with the relative benchmark in the first sentence of Article 61 of the TRIPS Agreement. As long as a Member in fact provides for criminal procedures and penalties to be applied in cases of wilful trademark counterfeiting or copyright piracy on a commercial scale, it will comply with this obligation. If it is alleged that a Member's method of implementation does not so provide in such cases, that allegation must be proven with evidence. Therefore, the Panel will assess whether the evidence shows that China fails to provide for criminal procedures and penalties to be applied in any such cases.

7.603 The Panel begins with the first limb of the claim. In the first limb of the claim, the United States challenges the levels at which certain thresholds are set. Having chosen to challenge the level of a series of numerical thresholds as compared to a relative standard, it is necessary for the United States to demonstrate that the levels are higher than that standard as applied in certain factual situations. That calls for quantitative evidence. Later, the Panel will address the second limb of the claim, in which the United States challenges the factors taken into account by the criminal thresholds. That calls for qualitative evidence.

7.604 The parties agree that the standard of "a commercial scale" will vary by product and market and that the conformity of China's criminal thresholds with that standard must be assessed by reference to China's marketplace.

7.605 The Panel recalls that a previous Panel had occasion to apply certain relative standards in the TRIPS Agreement in quantitative terms.

7.606 . . . The Panel needs to consider the specific conditions applying in China's marketplace in assessing whether the measures in question, which exclude certain acts of infringement from particular liability, conform to the relative standard in Article 61. This applies a fortiori as the relative standard is set in terms of what is "on a commercial scale," which varies not only by market but also by product within the same market.

. . .

7.609 The Panel has reviewed the measures and agrees that, on their face, they do exclude certain commercial activity from criminal procedures and penalties. For example, some of the criminal thresholds are set in terms that refer expressly to commercial activity, such as "illegal business operation volume," which is defined in terms of "manufacture, storage, transportation, or sales" of infringing products, and "illegal gains" which is defined in terms of profit. However, based solely on the measures on their face, the Panel cannot distinguish between acts that, in China's marketplace, are on a commercial scale, and those that are not.

7.610 Certain thresholds are set in monetary terms, ranging from ¥20,000 profit to ¥50,000 turnover or sales. The measures, on their face, do not indicate what these amounts represent as compared to a relevant commercial benchmark in China. Each of these amounts represents a range of volumes of goods, which vary according to price. Another factor to take into account is the period of time over which infringements can be cumulated to satisfy these thresholds. One threshold is set not in monetary terms but rather at 500 ("copies" for the sake of simplicity). Whilst it is reasonably clear to the Panel how many goods that comprises with respect to certain traditional media, this is not, on its face, related to any relevant market benchmark in China either.

7.611 The Panel has noted the United States' repeated assertions that certain amounts constitute counterfeiting or piracy on a commercial scale. The most recurrent example concerns 499 copyright-infringing "copies," although it is not related to the same product in all examples or, sometimes, to any product. The only facts in these examples are amounts equal to, or slightly less than, those in the measures themselves. Those amounts, in combination with the monetary thresholds and the factors used in the thresholds, demonstrate the class of acts for which China does not provide criminal procedures and penalties to be applied. Those numbers and factors do not, in themselves, demonstrate what constitutes a commercial scale for any product or in any market in China.

. . .

7.615 In its rebuttal of China's assertion regarding the scale of commerce in China, the United States noted that the "commercial scale" standard was a relative one. It commented on the Economic Census statistics submitted by China but at the same time dismissed their relevance as they are aggregate statistics related to undefined average economic units. It also recalled an earlier assertion that the Chinese market, including the market for many copyright and trademark-bearing goods, is fragmented and characterized by a profusion of small manufacturers, middlemen, distributors, and small outlets at the retail level.

7.616 The Panel has reviewed the evidence in support of this assertion. The evidence comprises a quote from a short article from a US newspaper, the San Francisco Chronicle, titled "30,000-Store Wholesale Mall Keeps China Competitive" regarding the number of stores in a particular mall in Yiwu and the physical dimensions of some stalls; a statistic quoted from an extract from a management consultant report titled "The 2005 Global Retail Development Index" that the top ten retailers in China hold less than 2 per cent of the market, and another statistic that the top 100 retailers have less than 6.4 per cent; and a quote from an article in Time magazine titled "In China, There's Priceless, and for Everything Else, There's Cash" that a shopping mall in Luohu spans six floors of small stores.

7.617 The Panel finds that, even if these sources were suitable for the purpose of demonstration of contested facts in this proceeding, the information that was provided was too little and too random to demonstrate a level that constitutes a commercial scale for any product in China.

7.618 The United States referred to Canada's third party written submission, which had provided an estimate of China's gross domestic product per capita. It did not explain specifically how this figure was comparable to China's numerical thresholds.

7.619 The Panel considers GDP per capita a reliable indicator of average national income but not a sufficient indicator of a commercial scale, as it is calculated with a denominator of total population. The Panel also notes that GDP is a far more aggregated figure than those in the Economic Census statistics that the United States dismissed.

7.620 China submits that the United States must provide evidence that China's laws actually function to exclude a category of infringement that meets the "commercial scale" standard. Hypothetical examples do not qualify as sufficient evidence.

7.621 In response, the United States asserts that it, and a number of third parties, have provided "numerous, concrete illustrations" of commercial-scale piracy and counterfeiting that take place underneath China's thresholds. It refers to a "Report on Copyright Complaints, Raids and Resulting Criminal Actions in China" prepared by a coalition of trade associations in 2008 (the "CCA Report").

7.622 The Panel has reviewed the CCA Report to determine whether it bears out the United States' assertion. The CCA Report was originally submitted as a case example intended to show that the criminal thresholds create a "safe harbour" (an assertion not borne out by the data) and also to show that significant quantities of retail sales of infringing product take place in China at levels below China's thresholds.

7.623 The Panel notes that the question whether retail sales of infringing product take place below the thresholds is not dispositive of the claim, as the first sentence of Article 61 does not require Members to provide for criminal procedures and penalties to be applied to all such cases.

. . .

7.627 The United States also submitted other press articles to illustrate points in its first written submission, particularly regarding the calculation of certain thresholds. China objected at the outset arguing that "[t]he Panel can afford little or no weight to such anecdotal and potentially misinformed reports." The United States was puzzled by China's concern at its recourse to newspapers or other media. It recalled its prior attempts to obtain information from China pursuant to Article 63.3 of the TRIPS Agreement. China had declined to provide information and stated instead that its competent domestic IPR authorities had also made relevant information publicly available through their official websites, newspapers, magazines and other proper channels. The United States added that the information in newspapers and magazines is "drawn from a variety of well-established and well-regarded sources."

7.628 The Panel has reviewed the press articles and notes that none of them are corroborated, nor do they refer to events or statements that would not require corroboration. Whilst the publications are reputable, most of these particular articles are brief and are quoted either for general statements or random pieces of information. Most are anecdotal in tone, some repeating casual remarks about prices of fake goods, anonymous statements or speculation. They have titles including "Fake Pens Write Their Own Ticket," "Chasing copycats in a tiger economy," "Hollywood takes on fake Chinese DVDs," "Film not out yet on DVD? You can find it in China" and "Inside China's teeming world of fake goods." Most of the press articles are printed in US or other foreign English-language media that are not claimed to be authoritative sources of information on prices and markets in China. There are four press articles from Chinese sources, one from Xinhua News Agency and three from the English-language China Daily. Two are quoted simply to demonstrate the existence of certain goods in China; another quotes a vague statement from unnamed "market insiders" on how illegal publishers tend to work; and the other quotes an "insider" for the maximum and minimum prices of a range of pirated and genuine goods. One other alleged "recent news account" is not attributed to any source at all.

7.629 The Panel emphasizes that, in the absence of more reliable and relevant data, it has reviewed the evidence in the press articles with respect to a central point in this claim that is highly contested. The credibility and weight of that evidence are therefore critical to the Panel's task. For the reasons set out above, the Panel does not ascribe any weight to the evidence in the press articles and finds that, even if it did, the information that these press articles contain is inadequate to demonstrate what is typical or usual in China for the purposes of the relevant treaty obligation.

7.630 There is no indication that probative evidence on this point would be difficult to obtain.

. . .

7.632 For the above reasons, the Panel finds that the United States has not made a prima facie case with respect to the first limb of its claim under the first sentence of Article 61 of the TRIPS Agreement. The Panel will now turn to the second limb of the claim.

### (X) Other Indicia—Physical Evidence

. . .

7.652 . . ., the Panel does not consider that the United States has made a prima facie case with respect to other indicia of infringement, such as physical evidence including product components, packaging and materials or implements.

### (XI) Other Indicia—Impact on the Commercial Marketplace

7.653 With respect to the second limb of this claim, the United States also alleges that China's thresholds are tied to finished goods and therefore ignore other indicia of commercial scale operations, such as the impact that the piracy or counterfeiting has on the commercial marketplace and by extension, right holders.

. . .

7.661 For all the above reasons, the Panel does not consider that the United States has made a prima facie case with respect to impact on the commercial marketplace.

7.662 The Panel wishes to emphasize that its findings should not be taken to indicate any view as to whether the obligation in the first sentence of Article 61 of the TRIPS Agreement applies to acts of counterfeiting and piracy committed without any purpose of financial gain.

### (XII) Miscellaneous Factors

7.663 The United States asserted that the breadth of the term "on a commercial scale" presumes that a wide range of considerations should be probative of "commercial scale." However, it did not submit argument in support of any other considerations besides those discussed above.

. . .

7.667 Therefore, the United States did not relate these factors sufficiently to the measures at issue or to its claim to discharge its burden of proof.

7.668 The Panel recalls its findings at paragraphs 7.652, 7.661 and 7.667 above and finds that the United States has not made a prima facie case with respect to the second limb of its claim under the first sentence of Article 61 of the TRIPS Agreement.

### (XIII) Conclusion with Respect to the Claim Under the First Sentence of Article 61

7.669 In light of the Panel's findings at paragraphs 7.632 and 7.668 above, the Panel concludes that the United States has not established that the criminal thresholds are inconsistent with China's obligations under the first sentence of Article 61 of the TRIPS Agreement.

. . .

### 6. Conclusions With Respect to the Criminal Thresholds

7.681 The Panel recalls its conclusion at paragraph 7.669 above that the United States has not established that the criminal thresholds are inconsistent with China's obligations under the first sentence of Article 61 of the TRIPS Agreement.

7.682 The Panel exercises judicial economy with respect to the claims under Article 41.1 of the TRIPS Agreement and under the second sentence of Article 61 of the TRIPS Agreement (with respect to the criminal thresholds).

. . .

### 8. Concluding Remark

. . .

8.5 In this dispute, the Panel's task was not to ascertain the existence or the level of trademark counterfeiting and copyright piracy in China in general nor to review the desirability of strict IPR enforcement. The United States challenged three specific alleged deficiencies in China's IPR legal system in relation to certain specific provisions of the TRIPS Agreement. The Panel's mandate was limited to a review of whether those alleged deficiencies, based upon an objective assessment of the facts presented by the parties, are inconsistent with those specific provisions of the TRIPS Agreement.

## NOTES AND QUESTIONS

**1.** The United States has been pressing China for stronger enforcement of IP laws since at least the mid-1980s. Do you find it puzzling that after three-plus decades of voicing concern, the United States could not present "better evidence" of counterfeiting on a substantial scale in China? What do you think might account for the relative paucity of evidence? Is it possible that U.S.-based multinational companies doing business in China were not anxious to make public their specific complaints out of concern they might risk future business opportunities in China? If you find that plausible, how would you recommend pursuing stronger enforcement in China without presenting concrete evidence of TRIPS Agreement—inconsistent conduct?

**2.** With respect to note 1 above, the United States has, in fact, initiated a new and aggressive trade policy response to China's alleged failure to adequately protect IPRs as well as to "force" technology transfer from U.S. investors in China. We discuss the U.S. Section 301 action and measures taken against China later in this chapter.

**3.** In Chapter 1, the state-to-state WTO dispute settlement mechanism was introduced. In subsequent chapters, we examined a number of WTO dispute settlement decisions involving substantive compliance, including the *Canada-Generic Pharmaceuticals*, *U.S.-Havana Club*, *U.S.-Copyright Act* and *EC- Geographic Indications* decisions (as well as a decision involving implementation of procedural obligations, *India-Mailbox*, excerpted in Chapter 1). We refer back to the introduction and the referenced cases to illustrate operation of the state-to-state WTO dispute settlement mechanism.

Each of the cases previously examined involved a claim by one WTO Member against another alleging failure to comply with an obligation expressly imposed by the WTO TRIPS Agreement. In WTO terms, these cases involved "violation" complaints.

### 3. Violation and Non-Violation Complaints

There is another type of WTO complaint that one Member may bring against another. This type does not involve failure to comply with an express obligation. Instead, one Member alleges that another deprived it of benefits it legitimately expected to receive when it entered into the agreement, even though the other Member has not failed to comply with an express obligation. This is referred to as a "non-violation nullification or impairment complaint" or, more concisely, a "non-violation complaint."

The non-violation complaint has a sensible basis in traditional trade disputes. Assume that the United States and Australia negotiate over tariff rates. The United States agrees to reduce its tariffs on imports of Australian apples in exchange for Australia's agreement to reduce its tariffs on imports of American oranges. A reciprocal bargain is struck. From the U.S. side, the benefit is that the price of U.S.-grown oranges will be lower on the Australian market (and more price-competitive with oranges grown in Australia). Following conclusion of this deal, the Australian government grants a WTO-legal domestic farm subsidy to Australian orange growers, providing them with payments for oranges they produce and sell on the Australian market. As a result of the subsidy payments, Australian growers can sell their oranges at a lower price. From the standpoint of the United States, the value of the tariff reduction previously agreed to by Australia has been "nullified or impaired." That is, the competitive gain to U.S. orange growers from the tariff reduction has been reduced or eliminated even though, technically, Australia has not violated any express WTO obligation to the United States. An action by the United States against Australia in this context would be a "non-violation" action provided for by the WTO DSU (and also by the earlier GATT dispute settlement mechanism).

Is the same type of non-violation complaint sensible in the context of TRIPS? The following paper addressed this question from the standpoint of developing countries preparing for the 2003 WTO Cancún Ministerial Conference.

**Frederick M. Abbott***

## *Non-Violation Nullification or Impairment Causes of Action under the TRIPS Agreement and the Fifth Ministerial Conference: A Warning and Reminder*

At the Fourth Ministerial Conference in Doha, WTO Ministers directed the TRIPS Council to continue examining the scope and modalities for bringing non-violation nullification or impairment (hereinafter "non-violation") causes of action in dispute settlement under the TRIPS Agreement. The Decision on Implementation-Related Issues and Concerns stated:

* Quaker United Nations Office, Occasional Paper No. 11, July 2003, available at http://www.quno.org.

11. Agreement on Trade-Related Aspects of Intellectual Property Rights (TRIPS)

11.1 The TRIPS Council is directed to continue its examination of the scope and modalities for complaints of the types provided for under subparagraphs 1(b) and 1(c) of Article XXIII of GATT 1994 and make recommendations to the Fifth Session of the Ministerial Conference. It is agreed that, in the meantime, Members will not initiate such complaints under the TRIPS Agreement.

Article 64.2, TRIPS Agreement,[1] established a five-year moratorium on the initiation of non-violation and situation[2] complaints. During that period, Members were to examine the scope and modalities for such complaints and submit recommendations to the Ministerial Conference. A decision to approve such recommendations or to extend the five-year moratorium was to be made by consensus. The question of whether failure of the TRIPS Council to submit recommendations to the Ministerial Conference acts to continue the moratorium in force is debated. Regardless of one's views on this subject, there is a *substantial risk* that should Ministers *not act* to extend the moratorium at the Fifth Ministerial Conference (or adopt rules on scope and modalities), this will enable the initiation of non-violation complaints (as a consequence of the lapse of the period stated in Article 64.2).

From the standpoint of developing countries, the possibility of non-violation causes of action being brought under the TRIPS Agreement would give rise to serious risks. In the *India-Mailbox* decision,[3] in which the Appellate Body (AB) first interpreted the TRIPS Agreement, it stressed reliance on the express text of the agreement and discounted the significance of Member's expectations concerning its effects. Although the AB has given little indication that it would permit Members to significantly expand the agreement to encompass subject matter not expressly contemplated by the text, there remains the possibility of developing Members being forced to defend claims brought on non-violation grounds, even if for the most part such claims are ultimately rejected.

## Potential Claims

Intellectual property rights (IPRs) are "negative rights" in that they entitle their holders to prevent third parties from performing acts without their consent. IPRs are not "market access" rights. However, it might be argued that granting IPRs while limiting access to the market deprives the right holder of advantages expected to be gained when the TRIPS Agreement was negotiated. Concerns over a market access theory of TRIPS in relation to the audio-visual sector motivated the European Community (EC) to support the non-violation moratorium

1. Article 64

2. Subparagraphs 1(b) and 1(c) of Article XXIII of GATT 1994 shall not apply to the settlement of disputes under this Agreement for a period of five years from the date of entry into force of the WTO Agreement.

3. During the time period referred to in paragraph 2, the Council for TRIPS shall examine the scope and modalities for complaints of the type provided for under subparagraphs 1(b) and 1(c) of Article XXIII of GATT 1994 made pursuant to this Agreement, and submit its recommendations to the Ministerial Conference for approval. Any decision of the Ministerial Conference to approve such recommendations or to extend the period in paragraph 2 shall be made only by consensus, and approved recommendations shall be effective for all Members without further formal acceptance process.

2. "Situation" complaints may be brought under GATT Article XXIII:1(c), and by cross-reference under TRIPS Agreement Article 64.1, except as limited by the moratorium. Such complaints are addressed by the DSU in a manner that makes their successful pursuit unlikely. Article 26.2, DSU, requires the consensus adoption of panel reports on "situation" grounds. Situation complaints are not considered separately in this memorandum.

3. India-Patent Protection for Pharmaceutical and Agricultural Chemical Products, AB-1997-5, WT/DS50/AB/R, 19 Dec. 1997.

during the Uruguay Round. The EC was concerned that the United States of America (USA) would claim that granting copyrights to authors and artists, but restricting their capacity to show films, etc., in the EC, would deprive the USA of the benefit of its TRIPS bargain.

It is not difficult to foresee Members acting on behalf of pharmaceutical patent holders claiming that price controls operate to deprive them of the benefits of patent protection. While such a claim would be unlikely to succeed in light of Article 8.1, TRIPS Agreement, and the fact that price controls were present in many countries during the TRIPS negotiations, this may not preclude a Member from threatening such action, or bringing it.

There are many forms of government regulation that could be argued to be consistent with the TRIPS Agreement, yet to nullify or impair the expectations of IPRs holders. For example, tax policies with respect to IPRs may affect the profitability of IPRs-dependent industries and nullify or impair benefits. Regulatory measures such as packaging and labelling requirements, and consumer protection rules, might be applicable to trademark holders and affect their access to the market.

Many Members maintain rules on acceptable expression, that is, they censor certain materials as against public policy. Members on behalf of copyright holders may argue that rules restricting expression are inconsistent with copyright holders' interests.

As noted above, the EC and other Members regulate access to the market for expressive works based on cultural concerns. This inhibits market access by copyright holders and might form the subject of a non-violation complaint.

Non-violation causes of action could be used to threaten developing Members' use of flexibilities inherent in the TRIPS Agreement and intellectual property law more generally. Thus, for example, Members that adopt relatively generous fair use rules in the fields of copyright or trademark might find that they are claimed against for depriving another Member of the benefit of its bargain.

Actions taken by developing Members to implement exceptions to TRIPS patent rules under Articles 30, or to grant compulsory licenses under Article 31, could be alleged to deprive patent holders of their expectations. The application of copyright rules in the area of software protection involves substantial flexibility. The use of discretion to establish permissive uses of code (for example, on hardware or software interface efficiency grounds) might be subject to challenge.

Non-violation causes of action might also be foreseen in the area of enforcement. For example, while the TRIPS Agreement requires that adequate remedial measures be provided, in most cases it leaves to Members substantial discretion to determine the level of appropriate remedies. A Member could be claimed against for nullifying or impairing benefits by imposing insufficiently stringent remedies. Although the TRIPS Agreement does not require Members to provide or enforce forms of IP protection not specified in the agreement, it might be claimed that failure to extend protection to new forms nullified or impaired the TRIPS Agreement bargain.

Non-violation causes of action might be pleaded in addition (in the alternative) to violation causes of action. It might be that in many TRIPS cases developing countries would find themselves forced to defend an additional and ambiguous claim that would raise the level of uncertainty and increase legal costs.

This is not to discount the possibility that developing Members could affirmatively use the nonviolation cause of action, for example to claim that threats or penalties imposed by certain Members concerning measures permitted under the TRIPS Agreement are nullifying or impairing the benefits of the bargain. Yet imbalance in the financial capacity of Members to pursue legal claims suggests that the balance of benefits would favour developed Members with strong IPRs holder communities.

To be clear, this brief paper is not intended to suggest that the potential claims outlined above could be successfully pursued. To the contrary, the AB would likely seek to avoid expansion of the TRIPS Agreement text through the uncertain vehicle of non-violation claims. Developing Members might nonetheless face demands and pressures to modify measures or courses of conduct under the threat of such claims.

### An Issue Not to Overlook

The foregoing summary of non-violation actions that might arise suggests that the subject matter of non-violation nullification or impairment and Article 64.3, TRIPS Agreement, should not be overlooked among the myriad of issues that developing Members should address in the run-up to and at the Fifth Ministerial Conference. It is in the nature of a warning and reminder.

## NOTES AND QUESTIONS

**1.** From the WTO: At the 12th Ministerial Conference in Geneva in June 2022 ministers agreed to once again extend the moratorium until the 13th Ministerial Conference. In the interim, discussions on the applicability of these types of disputes to the TRIPS Agreement are to continue.

The Ministerial Decision on "TRIPS Non-Violation and Situation Complaints" of 17 June 2022 (WT/L/1137) says:

> "We take note of the work done by the Council for Trade-Related Aspects of Intellectual Property Rights pursuant to the General Council Decision of 10 December 2019 on "TRIPS Non-Violation and Situation Complaints" (WT/L/1080), and direct it to continue its examination of the scope and modalities for complaints of the types provided for under subparagraphs 1(b) and 1(c) of Article XXIII of GATT 1994 and make recommendations to the 13th Ministerial Conference. It is agreed that, in the meantime, Members will not initiate such complaints under the TRIPS Agreement."

In 2012 the WTO Secretariat prepared a note describing the views of various WTO Members on the issues involved in the non-violation debate with respect to TRIPS. *See Non-Violation and Situation Complaints*, Summary Note by the Secretariat, IP/C/W/349/Rev.2, 19 October 2012, Revision, https://www.wto.org/english/tratop_e/trips_e/ta_docs_e/6_ipcw349rev2_e.pdf.

**2.** The foregoing excerpt looks at non-violation complaints from the standpoint of developing countries, assuming that they are more likely to be on the "receiving end" of such complaints. Do you think the United States, the European Union, and other OECD countries may be vulnerable to such complaints? In what subject matter areas? Would it be possible to challenge, for example, price controls on pharmaceuticals by invoking non-violation in the realm of the TRIPS Agreement?

**3.** There is a difference in the WTO remedies available in a non-violation action as compared with a violation action. A Member against which a non-violation finding is made is not expected to modify or remove the measure against which the complaint was brought. Instead, it is expected to rebalance concessions with the complaining Member, such as by offering a compensating trade concession (art. 26, WTO DSU).

**4.** Non-violation complaints require that the measure at stake was not foreseeable, that is, that it was introduced only after a trade concession was made or an obligation to protect intellectual property was incurred. Practices and measures already existing at the time of negotiations do not qualify for non-violation. *See Japan—Photographic Film and Paper* (WT/DS44/R) para. 7.93 et seq.; THOMAS COTTIER & MATTHIAS OESCH, INTERNATIONAL TRADE REGULATION: LAW AND POLICY OF THE WTO, THE EUROPEAN UNION AND SWITZERLAND 127-36 (2005). It is therefore important to distinguish the political dimension of non-violation, which explains the moratorium, from strict legal requirements, which need to be met in dispute settlement.

**5.** Do you think that in light of the legal requirement of non-foreseeability, the TRIPS Agreement should follow ordinary rules and the moratorium should no longer be extended?

### 4. *Withdrawal of Concessions*

Under the terms of the WTO Dispute Settlement Understanding, a Member whose measures are found to be inconsistent with the terms of the TRIPS Agreement is expected to bring those measures into conformity within a reasonable period of time.[1] If this is not done, the prevailing Member is authorized to suspend concessions "equivalent to the level of the nullification or impairment."[2] The DSU establishes a nonbinding preference for withdrawal of concessions in the same "sector" as to which the finding of noncompliance is made. With respect to the TRIPS Agreement, "sector" is defined in terms of the categories of IP set out in Part II of the TRIPS Agreement (or Parts III or IV).[3] A finding of noncompliance in the field of patent protection preferably should lead to a withdrawal of concessions in the field of patent protection. However, the DSU also permits withdrawal of concessions more widely under the same "covered agreement" (e.g., under the TRIPS Agreement), and under other agreements (e.g., under the GATT 1994).[4]

Securing the possibility to withdraw concessions for a TRIPS violation in other areas of trade, including trade in goods and services ("cross-withdrawal" of concessions), was one reason why IP-dependent industry groups in the OECD sought to move IP subject matter protection from WIPO to the WTO. There is a practical basis for this. If a developing country tolerates the establishment of a large-scale counterfeiting industry within its borders, and the United States or the European Union seeks to penalize that country by refusing to provide patent or trademark protection to its nationals, this might result in a minor hardship. The developing country's domestic industry is not likely to be heavily IP-dependent. On the other hand, if the United States or the European Union bars importation of the main agricultural or textile products exported from that developing country, the resulting hardship might be quite serious.

The fact that WTO remedies are limited to the withdrawal of concessions establishes a significant imbalance in favor of large economy countries—both developed and developing. If the United States, the European Union, China, or Brazil suspends import concessions, this may have a material impact on any exporting country. If Nicaragua, on the other hand, suspends import concessions vis-à-vis the United States or China, the impact on the latter will be immaterial. As a practical matter, compliance with WTO obligations can be "compelled" only by the major economic powers.

1. *See* arts. 21-22, DSU.
2. *Id.*, art. 22.4.
3. *Id.*, art. 22.3(f)(iii).
4. *Id.*, art. 22.3.

## Frederick M. Abbott*

# *Cross-Retaliation in TRIPS: Options for Developing Countries*

## 2. WTO Jurisprudence and Experience in TRIPS Cross-Retaliation

Cross-retaliation under the TRIPS Agreement has twice been approved by WTO dispute settlement arbitrators. Ecuador followed-up on arbitrator approval by requesting and gaining DSB authorisation for TRIPS cross-retaliation against European Communities (EC). Cross-retaliation under TRIPS has not yet been implemented by any authorised country. There has been an additional cross-retaliation request by Brazil against the United States (US) but arbitration of that request is presently suspended by agreement of parties to the dispute.

### A. EC—Bananas III—Article 22.6 DSU Arbitration with Ecuador

The first proceeding under the DSU in which a WTO Member requested DSB authorisation to suspend concessions under the TRIPS Agreement, which was also the first proceeding in which TRIPS suspension was requested as a matter of "cross-retaliation," involved Ecuador's claim against the EC in respect to the latter's banana trading regime. Ecuador requested authorisation pursuant to Article 22.2 of the DSU to suspend concessions or other obligations under the TRIPS Agreement, GATT and GATS, with respect to findings of inconsistencies regarding the EC's banana regime under the GATT and GATS. The EC thereupon requested arbitration pursuant to Article 22.6 of the DSU.

In the *EC—Bananas III* arbitration, Ecuador's initial request for suspension indicated the amount of its proposed suspension, and the sectors and covered agreements under which it intended to suspend concessions. Despite EC objection, the arbitrators found that this met the minimum requirements for the information needed in a request for suspension. The arbitrators indicated that Ecuador might well be required to submit additional methodological information in response to a challenge by the EC.

The arbitrators found that the EC carried the burden of proof in establishing that Ecuador was *not* justified in its request for suspension authorisation. As in other DSU proceedings, once the EC had established a *prima facie* case of inconsistency, Ecuador would be required to present evidence to rebut that *prima facie* case.

The arbitrators determined that the TRIPS Agreement does not preclude the suspension of concessions, including in light of Articles 22.3(f)(iii) and 22.3(g)(iii) that define "sector" and "covered agreement" in relation to TRIPS.

The Panel determined that although Ecuador had a certain margin of appreciation in determining whether suspension of concessions in the same sector as where the injury occurred would be practicable or effective, its discretion was limited by the requirements of Article 22.3(b)-(d) with respect to the principles and procedures for making its determinations. The arbitrators are authorised to review compliance with the applicable principles and procedures. The arbitrators concluded that:

> In our view, the margin of review by the Arbitrators implies the authority to broadly judge whether the complaining party in question has considered the necessary facts objectively and whether, on the basis of these facts, it could plausibly arrive at the conclusion that it was not

* *Cross-Retaliation in TRIPS: Options for Developing Countries*, ICTSD Programme on Dispute Settlement and Legal Aspects of International Trade, Issue Paper No. 8, International Centre for Trade and Sustainable Development, Geneva, Switzerland (2009).

> practicable or effective to seek suspension within the same sector under the same agreements, or only under another agreement provided that the circumstances were serious enough.

The arbitrators observed that the objective of suspending concessions is to induce the complained-against party to fulfil its obligations, and that as a practical matter this may be extremely difficult in cases where there is a great imbalance in terms of trade volume and economic power between the country seeking to suspend concessions and the complained-against country. Particularly in respect to "primary goods" and "investment goods" (referring to inputs and capital equipment), it may well be counterproductive to suspend concessions (i.e. to increase tariffs) because this will increase costs for local manufacturers. Effects on consumer goods may be less important from the standpoint of establishing the practicability or effectiveness of suspension. Because Ecuador's banana sector formed a major part of its economic activity, and because the EC's failure to implement the decision adopted by the DSB plausibly contributed to a severe disruption of Ecuador's economy, Ecuador clearly demonstrated that circumstances were "serious enough" to seek suspension of concessions under a covered agreement (i.e. under the TRIPS Agreement) other than where the violation was found.

The arbitrators said that although Article 22 of the DSU does not expressly direct the arbitrators to make suggestions regarding how to implement their decision, in light of this being the first decision to address suspension under the TRIPS Agreement and Ecuador's expressed interest in hearing the arbitrators' views, there is nothing to prevent the arbitrators from making suggestions regarding implementation of the suspension.

The arbitrators noted that Ecuador should take care that suspension of IPRs affects only nationals of Members subject to the suspension. In some circumstances it may be difficult to determine the nationality of right holders.

The arbitrators favourably noted Ecuador's stated intention to implement the suspension by a government-sanctioned licensing system for the reproduction of certain copyrighted works (i.e. phonograms), as well as geographic indications (GIs) and industrial designs, suggesting this was perhaps a better approach than "simply abolish[ing]" IP rights and placing materials in the public domain. This licensing system would permit Ecuador to monitor the level of suspended concessions and terminate the suspension when appropriate. The panel also noted that economic operators in Ecuador should be cautious about reliance on a transitory suspension regime for investments "which might not prove viable in the longer term."

The arbitrators said that authorisation of the suspension of TRIPS obligations within Ecuador does not affect IPRs in other WTO Members. In considering exports of phonograms produced under a suspension regime, the arbitrators said that Ecuador should consider footnotes 13 and 14 to Article 51 of the TRIPS Agreement. While footnote 13 provides that a Member is not under obligation to block imports of goods put on the market in another Member by or with the consent of the copyright holder, phonogram copies authorised under a suspension regime would not be put on the market with consent. Members would remain obligated to apply Article 51 border measures with respect to goods produced without consent. The panel stated:

> Distortions in third-country markets could be avoided if Ecuador would suspend the [IPRs] in question only for the purposes of supply destined for the domestic market. An authorisation of a suspension requested by Ecuador does of course not entitle other WTO Members to derogate from any of their obligations under the TRIPS Agreement. Consequently, such DSB authorisation to Ecuador cannot be construed by other WTO Members to reduce their obligations under Part III of the TRIPS Agreement in regard to imports entering their customs territories.

The arbitrators took note that implementation of the suspension of TRIPS obligations "may give rise to legal difficulties or conflicts within the domestic legal system of the Member so authorised (and perhaps even of the Member(s) affected by such suspension)." They further noted that this is a matter entirely within the prerogative of the suspending Members, and that their domestic legal situation may be influenced by the specific measures used to implement the suspension.

In the *EC—Bananas III* arbitration, the arbitrators said it is not for WTO arbitrators to pass judgment on whether Ecuador, once authorised by the DSB to suspend TRIPS commitments, might act inconsistently with obligations under relevant WIPO Conventions. This is for Ecuador and the other parties to such treaties to consider.

The arbitrators authorised Ecuador to request suspension of concessions under the TRIPS Agreement from the DSB. The DSB authorised the suspension. However, following successful negotiation of a settlement with the EC, Ecuador did not implement the suspension.

One study of the Ecuadorian experience concludes that the threat of suspension of TRIPS concessions induced the EC to reach substantially more favourable settlement terms of market access for Ecuadorian-origin bananas than would have occurred in the absence of that threat.[2] The same study suggests that the threat of suspension of TRIPS concessions may have assisted in Ecuador's renegotiation of external debt. The study's author considers that Ecuador would have had very limited negotiating power had potential retaliation been available only with respect to goods or services for reasons similar to those identified by the arbitrators in *EC—Bananas III*; namely, that asymmetry in economic and trade weight and the potentially damaging domestic consequences of raising trade barriers leaves many developing countries without a realistic prospect of inducing compliance by major developed country actors.

## B. Other Multilateral Agreements on Enforcement

### *1. Paris and Berne Conventions*

We have previously noted that the Paris and Berne Conventions each permit recourse in the event of a dispute to the International Court of Justice, and that such possibility for state-to-state enforcement of IPRs obligations has not been used. We also noted that a proposal for a WIPO dispute settlement mechanism was briefly entertained following the TRIPS negotiations, but no such WIPO mechanism was adopted.

### *2. Activities of the WIPO Arbitration and Mediation Center*

In Chapter 3, the Uniform Domain Name Dispute Resolution Policy was addressed, including the availability of the WIPO Arbitration and Mediation Center and other dispute settlement service providers as a forum for claims regarding abusive domain name registration and use.

In addition to serving as a forum for domain name claims, the WIPO Arbitration and Mediation Center offers its services more generally in connection with mediation and arbitration of intellectual property-related disputes.[5] The WIPO Center has developed a set of Arbitration Rules (as well as Mediation Rules), and has prepared recommended clauses for insertion in contracts. The WIPO Center offers arbitration services in connection with licensing and other IP contract disputes, as well as for claims of infringement.

### *3. World Customs Organization*

A substantial part of IP enforcement activity involves the enforcement by customs authorities of border measures. The World Customs Organization (WCO) is an intergovernmental

2. McCall Smith, James, "Compliance Bargaining in the WTO: Ecuador and the Banana Dispute." In Negotiating Trade: Developing Countries in the WTO and NAFTA, ed. J. Odell, 257. Cambridge University Press, 2006.

5. Detailed information is available at http://www.wipo.int.

organization based in Brussels, Belgium, which facilitates cooperation among national and regional customs authorities. The WCO has increasingly turned attention to the problem of trade in counterfeit goods. For example, in 2004, it convened a Global Congress on Combating Counterfeiting, which resulted in the adoption of the Rome Declaration.[6] That Declaration recommended increased attention by Interpol, the WCO, and WIPO to the problem of counterfeiting, including by establishing capacity-building programs for national customs authorities. It also promoted private sector cooperation with the WCO. The Cancun Declaration, adopted at the Fifth Global Congress on Combating Counterfeiting in 2009, recommended expansion of the WCO's counterfeiting and piracy database. The WCO maintains an Enforcement Committee, and a Counterfeiting and Piracy Group, among other arrangements addressing enforcement matters.[7]

### *4. Organisation for Economic Cooperation and Development (OECD)*

The OECD has devoted attention to the problem of counterfeiting and has prepared analytic studies. In 2005, the OECD managed a project on counterfeiting and piracy, which appears to have been largely dormant since 2008-09. The OECD has, however, in recent years has published reports on trade in counterfeit and pirated goods – including trade in counterfeit pharmaceuticals and the misuse of small parcels for trade in counterfeit goods.[8]

It describes its work program as follows. This work appears to have been largely dormant since 2008-09.

---

## *OECD Project on Counterfeiting and Piracy**

### OECD Responds to Rising Concerns on the Impact of Counterfeiting and Piracy

Responding to concerns in governments and the business community, the OECD launched a project in 2005 to assess the magnitude and impact of counterfeiting and piracy. The objective of the project is to improve factual understanding and awareness of how large the problem is and the effects that infringements of intellectual property rights have on governments, business and consumers in member countries and non-member economies.

### What Does the Project Cover?

The project covers infringements of the intellectual property rights that are described and defined in the WTO Agreement on Trade Related Aspects of Intellectual Property Rights (TRIPS).

In addition to assessing economic effects, the current project analyses rising concerns over the health, safety and security threats that counterfeit and pirated products pose to consumers.

---

6. October 21-22, 2004, available at http://www.wcoomd.org.

7. *See* details at http://www.wcoomd.org/en/about-us/wco-working-bodies/enforcement_and_compliance.aspx.

8. *See, e.g.*, OECD, Trade in Counterfeit Pharmaceutical Products (2020), https://www.oecd.org/governance/illicit-trade/trade-in-counterfeit-pharmaceutical-products-a7c7e054-en.htm; OECD, Misuse of Small Parcels for Trade in Counterfeit Goods (2018), https://www.oecd.org/corruption-integrity/reports/misuse-of-small-parcels-for-trade-in-counterfeit-goods-9789264307858-en.html.

* OECD, Directorate for Science, Technology and Innovation, http://www.oecd.org/sti/ind/oecdprojectoncounterfeitingandpiracy.htm.

It also reviews trends and developments and assesses what is being done to combat the illicit practices.

### How is the Project Structured?

The project is being carried out in three separate phases.

Phase I focuses on tangible counterfeit and pirated products (*i.e.* physical products that infringe trademarks or copyrights), and to a lesser extent infringements of patents and design rights. This phase has been completed. The full report was published in June 2008. A November 2009 update on the magnitude of counterfeiting and piracy of tangible products is also available.

Phase II focused on piracy of digital content. The final report was published in July 2009.

Phase III will address infringements of other intellectual property rights.

### Who is the OECD Working With?

The project is being conducted in co-operation with international organisations that are active in the counterfeiting/piracy area, including the World Trade Organization, the World Customs Organization, the World Intellectual Property Organization, Interpol and relevant NGOs. Liaison with the business community and labour has been co-ordinated through the Business and Industry Advisory Committee to the OECD and the Trade Union Advisory Committee to the OECD.

### Earlier Work

This study expands considerably on a related project on the economic impact of counterfeiting that was carried out in 1998.

## NOTES AND QUESTIONS

**1.** As OECD governments are frustrated with their ability to negotiate stronger standards of IP protection at the WTO and WIPO, they turn their attention to alternative forums. The OECD is comprised of largely "like-minded" countries, and its agenda is often strongly supported by industry. However, as OECD governments discovered when attempting to conclude a Multilateral Agreement on Investment (MAI), failure to take into account the social consequences of a narrowly defined work program may result in considerable wasted effort. What are the potential social consequences of an aggressive anticounterfeiting program? What interests other than those of the IP-dependent industries should be taken into account?

**2.** Unauthorized downloading of MP3 files is considered copyright "piracy," a subcategory of counterfeiting. Should the interests of file-sharing communities be taken into account by the OECD?

**3.** Pharmaceutical companies typically argue that cross-border trade in medicines should be restricted because of counterfeiting concerns. Yet, the same companies have a strong economic interest in preventing cross-border trade in medicines from lower-priced markets (e.g., Canada) to higher-priced markets (e.g., the United States). How would you draw the line between legitimate public security concerns and private corporate interest?

## C. Plurilateral Agreement on Enforcement

### *1. The Anti-Counterfeiting Trade Agreement*

The Anti-Counterfeiting Agreement (ACTA) was an effort mainly of industrialized countries to introduce TRIPS-plus provisions in enforcement, partly in response to failed attempts in

WTO dispute settlement to remedy what the United States considered to be insufficient levels of enforcement. The Agreement, while still formally pending for entry into force, is not likely to formally materialize due to rejection of consent by the European Parliament.

## NOTES AND QUESTIONS

**1.** The final text of the ACTA can be found here: http://www.mofa.go.jp/policy/economy/i_property/pdfs/acta1105_en.pdf.

**2.** The ACTA was subject to approval of ratification and acceptance in its prospective country Parties. The European Parliament rejected approval of the agreement. *See, e.g.*, Eric Pfanner, *European Parliament Rejects Anti-Piracy Treaty*, July 4, 2012 ("The vote was not even close, with 478 members of Parliament opposing the treaty, only 39 supporting it and 146 abstaining. Under EU law, the treaty cannot go into effect without the Parliament's endorsement."). Following rejection by the EU Parliament, the U.S. Trade Representative appears to have lost interest in the matter, though USTR had suggested that the United States could ratify the agreement absent congressional approval (i.e., as an Executive Agreement). This was a fairly position was very difficult to reconcile with U.S. Constitutional requirements (*see, e.g.*, Gwen Hinze, *U.S. Law Professors Cast Further Doubt on ACTA's Constitutionality—State Department Confirms No ACTA Pre-Review*, EFF, May 16, 2012). It appears that for all intents and purposes the ACTA is "dead."

**3.** Is there a lesson to be drawn for government policymakers from the failure of the ACTA effort? Might it be that efforts to strengthen IP enforcement are better incorporated in broader trade and investment agreements in which a focused group of stakeholder advocates are less likely to be able to block approval because of countervailing stakeholder group interests? Is it easier to make "progress" by avoiding single-purpose agreements? At least until recently, that was the collective wisdom for approaching GATT/WTO negotiations in the "round" format that included so many different interest trade-offs that a single stakeholder group would be unlikely to block the collective group compromise.

## III. BILATERAL TRADE AGREEMENTS AND IPRS ENFORCEMENT

Throughout this book we have referred to in particular U.S. and EU efforts to strengthen IPRs protection through negotiation of bilateral commitments in free trade agreements. This effort extends to commitments regarding civil and criminal enforcement measures. Importantly, these standards are not limited to agreements of industrialized countries with developing and emerging countries, but equally among industrialized and among developing countries.

The EU-Canada Comprehensive Economic and Trade Agreement (CETA), provisionally applied as of September 21, 2017 (ratifications pending), comprises a comprehensive code of enforcement provisions, including border measures in Sec 3, chapter 20.32-20.49. These provisions essentially follow the structure of the TRIPS Agreement. They partly overlap and partly exceed levels of protection of TRIPS standards. The text is available at http://international.gc.ca/trade-commerce/trade-agreements-accords-commerciaux/agr-acc/ceta-aecg/text-texte/20.aspx?lang=eng.

Likewise, the Comprehensive and Progressive Agreement for Transpacific Partnership (CPTPP Agreement), signed March 8, 2018, entails a comprehensive code on IPR enforcement, incorporating Chapter 18, sections 18.71-18.77 on enforcement and border measures. It equally builds upon TRIPS standards. The text is available at http://international.gc.ca/trade-commerce/trade-agreements-accords-commerciaux/agr-acc/tpp-ptp/text-texte/18.aspx?lang=eng; the incorporation without modification into CPTPP is available at http://international.gc.ca/trade-commerce/trade-agreements-accords-commerciaux/agr-acc/cptpp-ptpgp/text-texte/cptpp-ptpgp.aspx?lang=eng.

In addition, these agreements include provisions on investment protection which explicitly include the protection of intellectual property rights (Chapter 8, CETA; Chapter 9, CPTPP). The relationship of intellectual property and investment in substance and enforcement and dispute settlement is discussed in Chapter 1, *supra* section V.

The following excerpt describes typical features of bilateral agreement to which the United States is a party.

**Carsten Fink & Patrick Reichenmiller***

## *Tightening TRIPS: The Intellectual Property Provisions of Recent US Free Trade Agreements*

### . . . Enforcement of Intellectual Property Rights

The TRIPS Agreement—for the first time in an international agreement on intellectual property—introduced detailed obligations on the enforcement of IPRs. Certainly, without judicial enforcement of intellectual property laws, rules on patents, copyright and other forms of protection could be seriously undermined. However, recognizing the institutional limitations existing in many developing countries, TRIPS does not create any obligation "*. . . with respect to the distribution of resources as between enforcement of intellectual property rights and the enforcement of law in general.*"

The agreements with Vietnam, Jordan, and Australia do not explicitly allow for the same institutional flexibility. In these cases, it may therefore be difficult to defend derogations from the specific enforcement provisions of the agreements' IPRs chapters with inherent institutional constraints, such as limited budgetary or human resources. The agreements with Singapore, Chile, Morocco, DR-CAFTA, and Bahrain go further in spelling out that resource constraints cannot be invoked as an excuse for not complying with the agreements' specific enforcement obligations. Indeed, some of the specific enforcement requirements of the FTAs seem to create additional institutional obligations. For example, as in the case of TRIPS, the FTAs require customs authorities to stop trade in counterfeit and pirated goods. But TRIPS only requires these measures for imported goods, whereas most FTAs mandate border measures for imported and exported goods and, in some cases, even transiting goods.

Finally, the enforcement rules of the bilateral agreements mandate a stronger deterrent against IPRs infringement. For example, TRIPS only requires the imposition of fines adequate to compensate IPRs holders for the monetary damages they suffered. In the case of copyright piracy and trademark counterfeiting, all of the FTAs require the imposition of fines irrespective of the injury suffered by IPRs holders. TRIPS only mandates criminal procedures in cases of willful trademark counterfeiting or copyright piracy on a commercial scale. Many FTAs go beyond this broad standard and define more explicitly the scope of infringement acts subject to criminal procedures—including, for example, copyright piracy with a significant aggregate monetary value, but not necessarily for financial gain. Thus, certain forms of end-user piracy may be considered a criminal offense. . . .

* World Bank Trade Note No. 20, Feb. 7, 2005.

### Intellectual Property Rights and Investment Rules

In addition to the rules contained in the intellectual property chapters of the FTAs, IPRs are subject to separate investment disciplines. . . . [S]ix of the bilateral agreements have separate chapters on investment. The US-Bahrain and US-Jordan FTAs do not have such chapters, but the respective governments have negotiated bilateral investment treaties (BITs) with similar provisions. As no multilateral agreement on investment exists at the WTO or elsewhere, these bilateral investment rules break new ground.

A common element of the recent US FTA investment chapters and BITs is that intellectual property rights are explicitly listed in the definition of what is considered an investment. Thus, the agreements' specific investment disciplines apply, in principle, to government measures affecting the intellectual property portfolios of foreign investors. This raises, for example, the question of whether granting a compulsory license is considered an act of expropriation. Five of the FTA investment chapters explicitly remove compulsory licenses from the scope of expropriation, as long as such licenses comply with the obligations of the TRIPS Agreement and the intellectual property chapter of the respective FTA. However, the US-Vietnam FTA and the two BITs with Bahrain and Jordan do not have a comparable safeguard. Thus, as an example, if Vietnam were to issue a compulsory license in case of a national emergency, could the patent holder challenge such a decision as an act of investment expropriation?

Questions like this may be important, as these investment agreements provide for direct investor-to-state dispute settlement—going beyond the more traditional state-to-state dispute settlement procedures included in trade agreements. An exception is the investment chapter of the US-Australia FTA, which only allows for the possibility that investor-to-state dispute settlement procedures be negotiated in future. Investor-to-state dispute settlement may be more attractive to foreign investors, who can seek arbitration awards for uncompensated expropriation. By contrast, state-to-state dispute settlement can typically authorize only the imposition of punitive trade sanctions.

Notwithstanding these considerations, the reach of investment agreements into the intellectual property domain is still untested and remains in many ways legally uncertain (Correa, 2004).

## NOTES AND QUESTIONS

**1.** The treatment of IPRs as an "investment" presupposes their characterization as a form of "property." Do IPRs have the same characteristics as real property and movable property? For example, is a trade secret a form of property? A trade secret holder may not prevent a third party from developing and using the same information. The right to exclude only arises in the event of dishonest commercial practices. How would an investment dispute arbitration panel decide on the value of an expropriated trade secret?

**2.** As Fink and Reichenmiller point out, provisions that exempt compulsory licensing from the rules protecting against expropriation (and requiring compensation) refer to such licensing when it complies with the TRIPS Agreement and the IPRs chapter of the relevant agreement. For example, Article 10.9 (Expropriation and Compensation) of Chapter 10 of the U.S.-Chile FTA provides:

> 5. This Article does not apply to the issuance of compulsory licenses granted in relation to intellectual property rights in accordance with the TRIPS Agreement, or to the revocation, limitation, or creation of intellectual property rights, to the extent that such revocation, limitation, or creation is consistent with Chapter Seventeen (Intellectual Property Rights).

Does this article preclude an IPRs holder from pursuing an investment dispute settlement claim based on a compulsory license? Might not an IPRs holder argue that the license was inconsistent with the TRIPS Agreement or the bilateral IPRs chapter?

**3.** Several IPRs-related proceedings initiated under investor-to-state dispute settlement (ISDS) chapters in trade and investment agreements have caused a number of governments to reconsider whether treating IPRs as a form of protected investment is a sound approach. The questionable proceedings include several unsuccessful actions based on alleged injury to tobacco company trademark interests, as well as the unsuccessful claim brought by the American pharmaceutical company, Eli Lilly, against the government of Canada based on alleged patent law inconsistencies with NAFTA (see Chapter 2, section I.C.3). The fact that the ISDS claims have so far been unsuccessful speaks positively about the capabilities of the arbitrators. But, unsuccessful claims still place significant burdens on governments required to defend against such claims, both in terms of human resources and financial outlays (though the latter may be recovered). Moreover, meritless claims may exert a "chilling" effect on adoption of legislation needed to protect the public interest, and this presumably helps explain why industry interests may pursue such claims without realistic prospects for success.

**4.** Note that these issues are addressed in CETA by excluding infringement of property under investment rules to the extent that measures are compatible and even incompatible with the TRIPS Agreement, see Chapter 1, *supra* pages 62-63.

**5.** The USMCA includes detailed provisions with respect to enforcement in its Intellectual Property Rights chapter (Chapter 20). These provisions incorporate elements from previously negotiated FTAs, elements from the ACTA and elements from the TPP. As discussed earlier, the USMCA requires the parties to maintain criminal penalties for unauthorized and willful misappropriation of trade secrets (Article 20.I.2), in addition to providing civil causes of action (Article 20.I.1).

**6.** The USMCA introduces authority in favor of customs authorities to take action against suspected counterfeit trademark goods or pirated copyright goods "in transit" (Article 20.J.6). Recall that a dispute arose within the WTO context over EU detention of patented goods (pharmaceutical products) in transit. Arguably there are grounds to distinguish the situation of patented and trademarked goods in terms of whether customs detention may be appropriate, and the USMCA does not apply the transit rule to patents. Nonetheless, extending the IP status of goods within a "transit country" to goods moving between the country of export and the country of import, each of which has its own IP system, raises serious issues regarding independence of IP rights and free movement of goods. While rules designed to protect the public from unscrupulous counterfeiters are important, such rules can also be misused to interfere with legitimate trade. As with most IP issues, the objective is to find the appropriate balance.

**7.** As noted in Chapter 3, the USMCA incorporates criminal penalties for willful importation and domestic use of labels or packaging to which a trademark has been applied without authorization (Article 20.J.7), and this provision may have significant implications for parallel traders.

**8.** The USMCA includes detailed rules regarding Internet Service Providers (ISPs), including the terms under which they enjoy protection from liability for the acts of users of their services (i.e., safe harbor)(Article 20.J.11). There is also a body of rules applicable to preventing circumvention of technological protection measures (TPMs)(Article 20.H.11), and protecting against removal, altering or misusing rights management information (RMI) (Article 20.H.12).

**9.** Consistent with prior practice, the United States-Mexico-Canada Agreement Implementation Act, [Public Law 116–113], sec. 102, bars the agreement from having direct (self-executing) effect in U.S. law.[9]

U.S.-based industry groups may be able to secure rules in bilateral trade agreements that are more favorable to them than comparable rules in domestic U.S. law. Congress routinely denies the bilateral agreements' "self-executing" effect in U.S. law. Technically, changes are made to domestic law only when Congress amends it. But there is a persistent question whether the negotiation of international commitments places pressure on Congress to amend U.S. law so as to bring it in line with those commitments. In the following excerpt, some differences between remedies as provided by U.S. law and the typical bilateral trade agreement are noted.

**Frederick M. Abbott***

## *Intellectual Property Provisions of Bilateral and Regional Trade Agreements in Light of U.S. Federal Law*

### Enforcement . . .

2. *Damages calculation.* The provisions of the FTAs regarding calculation of damages for infringement of IPRs set forth a methodology. For example, Article 15.11 of the U.S. Morocco FTA provides:

> (6)(b) in determining damages for infringement of intellectual property rights, its judicial authorities shall consider, *inter alia*, the value of the infringed-on good or service, measured by the suggested retail price or other legitimate measure of value submitted by the right holder.

The standard of "suggested retail price" is used in only one of the many U.S. statutes regulating intellectual property, that is, the prohibition in the Tariff Act of 1930 against the importation of goods bearing an infringing trademark.[22]

U.S. courts generally have substantial discretion in determining the basis for establishing the level of damages in cases of infringement. In a trademark infringement suit, the trademark holder is ordinarily required to prove its "actual damages" which would be based on the market price of its goods. The "suggested retail price" of a good or service will be the "market price" in only a limited number of cases. The Copyright Act also uses the measure of "actual damages," providing:

> (b) Actual damages and profits. The copyright owner is entitled to recover the actual damages suffered by him or her as a result of the infringement, and any profits of the infringer that are attributable to the infringement and are not taken into account in computing the actual damages. In establishing the infringer's profits, the copyright owner is required to present proof only of the infringer's gross revenue, and the infringer is required to prove his or her deductible expenses and the elements of profit attributable to factors other than the copyrighted work.

---

9. https://www.govinfo.gov/content/pkg/COMPS-15732/pdf/COMPS-15732.pdf.

* UNCTAD-ICTSD Project on IPRs and Sustainable Development, Issue Paper No. 12, Feb. 2006.

22. 19 USCS §1526 (f)(2)

For the first such seizure, the fine shall be not more than the value that the merchandise would have had if it were genuine, according to the manufacturer's suggested retail price, determined under regulations promulgated by the Secretary.

17 USC §504. A U.S. court might allow a trademark, copyright or patent holder to base its claim for remedies in an infringement action on the suggested retail price of its goods if there was no reasonable way to prove the actual selling price of the goods in the market. However, because the suggested retail price is a hypothetical price this would not be a first option.

The use of "suggested retail price" as the basis for calculating damages is also problematic because it suggests that the IPRs holder receives the "retail" price for its goods or services. In many cases, the IPRs holder will sell to intermediaries such as wholesalers and distributors and will receive a price substantially discounted from the suggested retail price, even assuming that the suggested retail price represents the price paid by the consuming public. The IPRs holder's "actual damages" should instead be based on the price it receives from the intermediaries.

The FTA provision does not limit courts solely to the consideration of "suggested retail price" in the calculation of damages. However, it requires the courts to take this measure into account when presented by the right holder. In doing so, it implies that using the basis of "suggested retail price" is a "safe harbor" under the FTA which can be used to avoid trade disputes.[73]

## NOTES AND QUESTIONS

**1.** From the perspective of U.S. IPRs holder interest groups doing business overseas, the level of penalties for infringement can rarely be "too high." Is the same perspective reasonable within the domestic U.S. context? What are the risks associated with an enforcement system that "over-penalizes" infringement?

# IV. THE ENFORCEMENT REGIMES OF THE EUROPEAN UNION AND OF THE UNITED STATES

## A. The EU Enforcement Regime

As the European Union has gradually taken over from its member states responsibility for establishing substantive IPRs standards (see, e.g., Chapter 4, section IV), so it has also increasingly set standards for the enforcement of IPRs.

### *1. IP Border Measures Regulation*

The European Union's first major effort in this area was a 1994 regulation that addressed border measures with respect to counterfeit trademarked and pirated copyrighted goods.[10] Because this measure concerned international trade, and because the European Union has exclusive competence in that area, there was a clear basis in the EC Treaty for this measure. (Recall from Chapter 1, section IV.A.1, the CJEU Advisory Opinion regarding EU membership in the WTO and the discussion of the respective competences of the European Union and its member states.) Border measures of the European Union are subject to the Union Customs Code, Regulation (EU) 952/2013, as amended by Regulation (EU) 2016/2339, which not only regulates customs

73. IPRs holders, similarly, are not obligated to present damage requests on the basis of "suggested retail price." They may present requests on the basis of other "legitimate measures" of value. The courts are required to consider those alternative valuations.

10. Council Regulation (EC) No 3295/94 of 22 December 1994, laying down measures to prohibit the release for free circulation, export, re-export or entry for a suspensive procedure of counterfeit and pirated goods, 1994 OJ L 341, Dec. 22, 1994.

but also partially implements the TRIPS Agreement in terms of border measures relating to counterfeit and pirated goods. In particular, Articles 197 and 198 of Regulation 952/2013 address the destruction and disposal of goods. These rules are not specific and are subject to special regulations.

In 2003, the original border measures regulation was replaced by a new regulation with a broader scope that extended to patents (including supplementary certificates of protection), plant variety rights, and geographical indications.[11] A right holder was entitled to file an application with the customs authorities requesting suspension of entry of infringing goods,[12] stating the period of time during which the customs authorities were expected to take action.[13] Customs authorities would suspend shipments suspected of infringing, and notify the right holder.[14] Customs authorities were also entitled to suspend shipments *ex officio* (i.e., on their own initiative) if they had reason to suspect an infringement. Generally, the right holder was expected to initiate proceedings under national law of the relevant member state seeking a determination of infringement.[15] This was supposed to occur within ten working days of notification of suspension, although the ten-working-day period might be extended for an additional ten working days.[16] Goods found to infringe an IPR would not be allowed to enter the European Union and could not be re-exported.[17] The member states made provision for the destruction of infringing goods, or other removal from the stream of commerce, as appropriately determined by the national authorities.[18] The 2003 IP Border Measures regulation provided the basis for the detention of generic drugs in transit based on allegations of patent infringement discussed in Chapters 1 and 2.

On June 12, 2013, the European Parliament and Council adopted a revised regulation No 608/2013 concerning customs enforcement of intellectual property rights (2013 IP Border Measures Regulation), that repealed the 2003 IP Border Measures Regulation.[19] One of the significant factors behind the Commission's proposal of the revised regulation was to address concerns raised in the context of the dispute with India and Brazil regarding seizures of medicines in transit. And, in the interim, as discussed in Chapter 1, the CJEU had decided the *Philips/Nokia* joined cases. As you will recall, the CJEU held that goods would not be subject to seizure merely on the basis of transiting an EU port or airport, although goods in transit could be detained based on suspicion of intended diversion to the EU market. It is notable that the Commission's initial proposal for a revised regulation (COM (2011) 285) was more attentive to addressing the issues raised in the dispute with India and Brazil than was the 2013 IP Border Regulation ultimately adopted by the Parliament and Council. Nonetheless, the revised 2013 Regulation eliminates the language on which the Dutch Supreme Court had relied in establishing its so-called "manufacturing fiction" that treated goods manufactured in India as if they had been manufactured in the Netherlands. The revised 2013 Regulation also, in recital 11, says that "in line with the Union's international commitments [under the

---

11. Council Regulation (EC) No 1383/2003 of 22 July 2003, concerning customs action against goods suspected of infringing certain intellectual property rights and the measures to be taken against goods found to have infringed such rights, OJ L 196/7, 2.8.2003.

12. *Id.*, art. 5. The 2003 border measures regulation allows customs authorities to suspend the release of goods suspected to infringe an intellectual property right even prior to a specific application from a right holder. *Id.*, art. 4.

13. *Id.*, arts. 5 and 8.

14. *Id.*, art. 9.

15. *Id.*, art. 13.

16. *Id.*, art. 13. This period may be extended for an additional ten working days.

17. *Id.*, art. 16.

18. *Id.*, art. 17.

19. Regulation (EU) No 608/2013 of the European Parliament and of the Council of 12 June 2013 concerning customs enforcement of intellectual property rights and repealing Council Regulation (EC) No 1383/2003.

Doha Declaration] and its development cooperation policy, with regard to medicines [in transit] . . . when assessing the risk of infringement of intellectual property rights, [customs authority should] take account of any substantial likelihood of diversion of such medicines onto the market of the Union." On the other hand, the 2013 IP Border Measures Regulation does not set out standards by which customs authorities are expected to assess risks of diversion, and leaves in the hands of the member states the determination as to whether a particular alleged act constitutes infringement.

It must be borne in mind, however, that the CJEU laid out standards in its *Philips/Nokia* decision in December 2011, and that customs authorities of the member states are bound to follow the jurisprudence of the CJEU. The Commission stresses this point in its adoption of Guidelines to customs authorities ("Guidelines of the European Commission concerning the enforcement by EU customs authorities of intellectual property rights with regard to goods, in particular medicines, in transit through the EU," February 1, 2012), stating:

> On 1 December 2011 the Court of Justice issued the judgment related to the joined cases C-446/09 (*Philips*) and C-495/09 (*Nokia*). In essence, the judgment addresses the question of whether goods coming from a nonmember State, which are imitations of goods protected in the European Union by a trade mark right or copies of goods protected in the European Union by copyright, a related right or a design, may be classified as 'counterfeit goods' or 'pirated goods' within the meaning of Regulation No 1383/2003 and, before the entry into force of that Regulation, within the meaning of Regulation No 3295/94 merely on the basis of the fact that they are brought into the customs territory of the European Union, without being released for free circulation there. Nevertheless, the findings of the Court go beyond this scope and are applicable to other intellectual property rights, such as patents.
>
> These Guidelines therefore aim, in addition, to clarify the scope for the customs control of any goods in transit through the territory of the EU in the light of the findings in the *Nokia-Philips* judgment.
>
> . . .
>
> Consequently, and in the light of certain cases of customs detentions on the grounds of patent infringement of shipments of medicines originating in a third country, it is understood that the mere fact that medicines are in transit through the EU territory, and there is a patent right applicable to such medicines in the EU territory, does not in itself constitute enough grounds for customs authorities in any Member State to suspect that the medicines at stake infringe patent rights. It is further understood that a situation in which medicines are in transit through EU territory, and there is adequate evidence that satisfies the customs authorities that there is a substantial likelihood of diversion of such medicines onto the EU market, may constitute enough grounds for customs authorities to suspect that the medicines at stake infringe patent rights.

## 2. *IP Enforcement Directive*

In 2004, the European Union adopted a directive on the enforcement of intellectual property rights.[20] This directive requires the member states to assure that IPRs holders have access to evidence regarding the activities of alleged infringers.[21] Member states must make available provisional measures, including preliminary injunctions to prevent "imminent infringement,"[22] and to make that available without the appearance of the alleged infringer, in particular when any delay would cause irreparable harm.[23] The directive specifies that member states judges

20. Directive 2004/48/EC of the European Parliament and of the Council of 29 April 2004 on the enforcement of intellectual property rights, OJ L 195/16, 2.6.2004.

21. *Id.*, arts. 6 and 8.

22. *Id.*, art. 9.

23. *Id.*, art. 9(4).

must be authorized to remove from commerce and/or destroy infringing goods,[24] issue permanent injunctions,[25] and assess damages taking into account "all appropriate aspects," including lost profits.[26] The unsuccessful party shall generally bear the legal costs of the proceeding.[27] Judicial authorities may order dissemination of information concerning the decision at the expense of the infringer.[28]

The directive on enforcement is without prejudice to the criminal law applicable in the member states with respect to intellectual property rights.[29] This directive represents a significant step in consolidation in the hands of EU legislators of authority to regulate IPRs.

Along with the IP Enforcement Directive, the European Union is also promoting closer cooperation between authorities for combating against counterfeiting and piracy. This was emphasized in several Resolutions, as a result of which a new platform for such collaboration was created—European Observatory on Counterfeiting and Piracy. This initiative is based on the existing Commission structures and its members represent both public and private sectors.

In December 2010, the EU Commission issued a report assessing the effectiveness of the IP Enforcement Directive that has been followed by a series of consultations.[30] As of Fall 2023, there is no Commission proposal for a revised IP Enforcement Directive. However, in November 2017, the Commission issued a Guidance document on certain aspects of the 2004 Directive that focused on ten issue areas. Relying principally on recent CJEU jurisprudence, the Commission made suggestions intended to harmonize or approximate the approaches being taken among national authorities with respect to enforcement issues, with considerable attention to achieving an appropriate balance of interests. In all events, the Guidance document provides a useful compilation of CJEU jurisprudence in areas such as liability of Internet service providers for allegedly protected content.[31]

### *3. Regulation on the Recognition and Enforcement of Judgments*

In 2000, the European Union adopted a regulation on jurisdiction and the recognition and enforcement of judgments in civil and commercial matters.[32] This regulation effectively supplanted the Brussels Convention on Jurisdiction and the Enforcement of Judgments in Civil and Commercial Matters of 1968 (as amended) for EU member states. The regulation adopted in 2000 was supplanted by Regulation (EU) No 1215/2012 of the European Parliament and of the Council of 12 December 2012 on jurisdiction and the recognition and enforcement of judgments in civil and commercial matters (recast).[33] Although this regulation is not specifically addressed to IPRs, it is important for the conduct of IP-related litigation in the European Union, including for the enforcement of judgments rendered by courts in

24. *Id.*, art. 10.
25. *Id.*, art. 11.
26. *Id.*, art. 13.
27. *Id.*, art. 14.
28. *Id.*, art. 15.
29. *Id.*, art. 2(3)(c).
30. Report from the Commission to the European Parliament, the Council, the European Economic and Social Committee, and the Committee of the Regions Application of Directive 2004/48/EC of the European Parliament and the Council of 29 April 2004 on the enforcement of intellectual property rights/COM/2010/0779 final. See consultations at: http://ec.europa.eu/internal_market/consultations/2011/intellectual_property_rights_en.htm.
31. COM(2017) 708—Guidance on certain aspects of Directive 2004/48/EC of the European Parliament and of the Council on the enforcement of intellectual property rights.
32. Council Regulation (EC) No 44/2001 of 22 December 2000 on jurisdiction and the recognition and enforcement of judgments in civil and commercial matters, OJ L 12/1, 16.1.2001.
33. https://eur-lex.europa.eu/legal-content/EN/TXT/HTML/?uri=CELEX:32012R1215&from=EN.

the European Union. The regulation establishes a general rule that a person domiciled in a member state should be sued in that member state.[34] However, suits involving contracts may be brought in the place of performance, and suits in tort where the harmful event occurred.[35] Article 24 expressly addresses IPRs and establishes "exclusive" jurisdiction, regardless of domicile:

> (4) in proceedings concerned with the registration or validity of patents, trade marks, designs, or other similar rights required to be deposited or registered, irrespective of whether the issue is raised by way of an action or as a defence, the courts of the Member State in which the deposit or registration has been applied for, has taken place or is under the terms of an instrument of the Union or an international convention deemed to have taken place.
>
> Without prejudice to the jurisdiction of the European Patent Office under the Convention on the Grant of European Patents, signed at Munich on 5 October 1973, the courts of each Member State shall have exclusive jurisdiction in proceedings concerned with the registration or validity of any European patent granted for that Member State;

This provision thus reflects a territorial perspective on registration and challenges to validity, and takes into account the special character of the European Patent Convention (see Chapters 1 and 2, *supra*) further to which rights established by European patents are governed by the law of the designated member states.

The regulation provides for recognition of judgments among the member states of the European Union, "without any special procedure being required."[36] Grounds for refusal to recognize are strictly limited, and include "if such recognition is manifestly contrary to public policy (ordre public) in the Member State addressed."[37] The regulation expressly precludes substantive review of a foreign member state judgment.[38] The regulation provides for enforcement by a member state of a judgment rendered in another member state when, on application of any interested party, it has been declared enforceable there.[39] The regulation includes an annex identifying the courts and competent authorities to which applications for enforcement are submitted, and provides that judgments will be declared enforceable immediately upon completion of formalities.[40] There is provision for appeal of the declaration of enforceability.

The regulation's facilities for the recognition and enforcement of judgments rendered by EU member state judicial authorities are *not* made available for judgments of judicial authorities outside the European Union.[41] The absence of a recognition and enforcement mechanism for non-EU judgments is one of the drivers behind an effort to draft a new Hague Convention on jurisdiction and foreign judgments in civil and commercial law matters. That effort has not, however, yielded results. One reason for the slow progress is lack of agreement concerning the treatment of IPRs-related disputes.

---

34. *Id.*, art. 2.
35. *Id.*, art. 5.
36. *Id.*, art. 36(1).
37. *Id.*, art. 45(1).
38. *Id.*, art. 52, "Under no circumstances may a judgment given in a Member State be reviewed as to its substance in the Member State addressed."
39. *Id.*, art. 42.
40. *Id.*, art. 61.
41. Except as may be provided to European Free Trade Area (EFTA) country judgments under the Lugano Convention (Lugano Convention of 1988 on jurisdiction and the enforcement of judgments in civil and commercial matters (*see* recital 7 of Regulation, *id.*)).

### 4. *Trade Barriers Regulation*

#### a. Main Regulation

In the next section we examine Section 301 of the U.S. Trade Act of 1974 (as amended). This controversial legislation, *inter alia*, allows interested persons to file complaints with the United States Trade Representative regarding foreign trade practices. In 1984, the European Union also adopted legislation that permitted interested persons to seek remedial action regarding certain foreign trade practices. This legislation was superseded by legislation adopted in December 1994, which took into account the establishment of the WTO.[42] It is commonly referred to as the "Trade Barriers Regulation" or "TBR." The TBR was less controversial than U.S. Section 301 because it was limited to actions that violate international trade rules, whereas Section 301 extended to a broad category of "unreasonable" trade practices. The EU legislation was revised in 2015 with adoption of Regulation (EU) 2015/1843.[43] Mainly based on the definition of "obstacles to trade" in the 2015 TBR,[44] the revised TBR appears to maintain the EU distinction from U.S. Section 301.

Under the 2015 TBR, a person acting on behalf of an EU industry, an EU enterprise, or an EU member state,[45] may request the EU Commission to investigate an "obstacle to trade" maintained by a foreign country that causes an "adverse trade effect." An obstacle to trade may be "any trade practice adopted or maintained by a third country in respect of which international trade rules establish a right of action; such a right of action exists when international trade rules either prohibit a practice outright, or give another party affected by the practice a right to seek elimination of the effect of the practice in question."[46] An "adverse trade effect" refers to a material negative impact on the economy of the European Union, a region, or a sector of economic activity.[47]

Following a threshold determination that there is sufficient evidence, the Commission will open an "examination procedure" regarding the alleged obstacle to trade, giving an affected foreign country notice and the opportunity to submit information.[48] If the Commission finds that the complaint is justified, it will initiate a procedure under the applicable legal mechanism, such as by filing a WTO dispute settlement complaint.[49]

As discussed in Chapter 1, as a general rule, WTO agreements are not directly effective in the law of the European Union or its member states. The TBR provides a mechanism to private citizens for enforcing (indirectly) WTO agreements as against foreign countries, although not against EU institutions or member states.

The TBR has been used once to address an alleged TRIPS Agreement violation.[50] It was used to initiate the WTO dispute settlement proceeding against the United States regarding the Copyright Act (see Chapter 4, section II.B.1, *supra*).

---

42. Council Regulation (EC) No 3286/94 of 22 Dec. 1994, laying down Community procedures in the field of the common commercial policy in order to ensure the exercise of the Community's rights under international trade rules, in particular those established under the auspices of the World Trade Organization, OJ L 349, 31. 12. 1994.

43. Regulation (EU) 2015/1843 of the European Parliament and of the Council of 6 Oct. 2015, laying down Union procedures in the field of the common commercial policy in order to ensure the exercise of the Union's rights under international trade rules, in particular those established under the auspices of the World Trade Organization (codification), https://eur-lex.europa.eu/legal-content/EN/TXT/HTML/?uri=CELEX:32015R1843&from=EN.

44. *Id.*, art 2.

45. *Id.*, arts. 3-4 & 6.

46. *Id.*, art. 2(1).

47. *Id.*, art. 2(4).

48. *Id.*, art 9.

49. *Id.*, arts. 13-14.

50. An important GATT dispute settlement case—the U.S.—Section 337 case (see Chapter 1, page 71 and section IV.B, *supra*)—was initiated under the 1984 predecessor to the TBR.

### b. Regulation Authorizing Suspension of Concessions

In 2014, the European Union adopted regulations that lay out the procedures to be followed when it takes measures to enforce its rights, such as by suspension or withdrawal of concessions following a favorable determination from the WTO dispute settlement body. In 2021, the EU amended those regulations to authorize suspension or withdrawal of concessions during the time frame when the WTO dispute settlement process remains "broken" based on the incapacity of the Appellate Body. The EU Commission describes the updated regulation:[51]

> The regulation sets out rules and procedures for the EU to suspend or withdraw its obligations under an international trade agreement in order to:
> respond to breaches of international trade rules by non-EU countries and enforce a judicial ruling in favour of the EU, to obtain a satisfactory solution that restores benefits for EU businesses;
> rebalance obligations under and in line with a trade agreement, when non-EU countries alter the treatment of goods from the EU, either temporarily through a safeguard measure or long-term through modifying tariff concessions.
> . . .
> Because a current lack of new appointments to the Appellate Body of the World Trade Organization (WTO) has meant that the second tier of its dispute settlement mechanism is not able to function, amending Regulation (EU) 2021/167 introduced some changes to Regulation (EU) No 654/2014.
> The amending Regulation (EU) 2021/167:
> allows enforcement action in situations where:
> the EU obtains a favourable ruling from a WTO dispute settlement panel,
> the process is then blocked because the non-EU country appeals to the non-functioning WTO Appellate Body, and does not agree to interim appeal arbitration under Article 25 of the WTO Dispute Settlement Understanding;
> allows enforcement action when:
> a trade partner under a bilateral or regional trade agreement imposes illegal trade measures, subsequently does not take the steps necessary for the dispute settlement process under that agreement to function;
> extends the scope of possible countermeasures to trade in services and some trade-related aspects of intellectual property rights. This extension is accompanied by safeguards to ensure that the most efficient and proportionate countermeasures are used and that EU Member States' authorities and stakeholders are consulted."

## B. The U.S. Enforcement Regime

### *1. Section 337 of the Tariff Act of 1930*

The United States maintains a specific legal procedure pursuant to which holders of IPRs may obtain orders directing the Customs Service to block importation of infringing goods. This is Section 337 of the Tariff Act of 1930. Under Section 337, the holder of a U.S. IPR initiates a complaint at the International Trade Commission (ITC) in Washington, D.C. The ITC is a "quasi-autonomous" agency of the federal government headed by six commissioners.[52]

---

51. EU rights to apply and enforce international trade rules, https://eur-lex.europa.eu/EN/legal-content/summary/eu-rights-to-apply-and-enforce-international-trade-rules.html.

52. Congress appoints the commissioners, with each major political party appointing three. The ITC also plays an important role in antidumping and countervailing duty cases, and in conducting studies regarding trade issues for Congress and the executive branch.

If threshold criteria are met, the Commission appoints an administrative law judge to make an initial determination regarding the complaint. The Section 337 procedure and available remedies are described in more detail below by the Commission. Decisions by the ITC under Section 337 are at least somewhat unique in that the President of the United States may decide on policy grounds that a decision should not be enforced, and such a decision was made in a dispute involving Samsung and Apple regarding a patent on a technical standard (see note 4 *infra*). Decisions by the ITC—although not presidential determinations—may be appealed to the Court of Appeals for the Federal Circuit.

In 1989, a GATT dispute settlement panel ruled that certain elements of Section 337, as then in force, were inconsistent with GATT national treatment rules. In effect, imported products alleged to infringe U.S. patents were treated less favorably than domestically produced products subject to patent litigation in federal court.[53] For example, a defendant in a Section 337 proceeding was not permitted to counterclaim on patent invalidity grounds, while such a counterclaim was a common defensive maneuver in federal district court patent infringement cases. Subsequent to the GATT panel decision, the United States amended Section 337 to make its procedures substantially more comparable to federal court proceedings under the Patent Act.

---

## *Section 337 Investigations at the U.S. International Trade Commission: Answers to Frequently Asked Questions*

U.S. International Trade Commission*

### Background on Section 337

Under Section 337 of the Tariff Act of 1930 (19 U.S.C. §1337), the Commission conducts investigations into allegations of certain unfair practices in import trade. Section 337 declares the infringement of certain statutory intellectual property rights and other forms of unfair competition in import trade to be unlawful practices. Most Section 337 investigations involve allegations of patent or registered trademark infringement.[1] Other forms of unfair competition, such as misappropriation of trade secrets, passing off, false advertising, and violations of the antitrust laws, may also be asserted.[2]

Section 337 investigations are initiated by the Commission following the receipt of a properly filed complaint that complies with the Commission's Rules.[3] A Commission notice

53. GATT Panel Report, *United States—Section 337 of the Tariff Act of 1930*, L/6439-36S/with 345, adopted Nov. 7, 1989.

* Publication No. 3708, July 2002, U.S. International Trade Commission, Washington, D.C., available at https://www.usitc.gov/publications/337/pub3708.pdf.

1. Section 337 specifically declares the infringement of the following statutory rights to be unlawful import practices: a U.S. patent or a U.S. copyright registered under Title 17, a registered trademark, a mask work registered under chapter 9 of Title 17, or a boat hull design protected under chapter 13 of Title 17. 19 U.S.C. §1337(a)(1)(B)-(E). In cases involving infringement of these intellectual property rights, there is no injury requirement.

2. In addition to unfair practices based upon infringement of certain specified statutory intellectual property rights, Section 337 also declares unlawful unfair methods of competition and unfair acts in the importation and sale of products in the United States, *the threat or effect of which* is to destroy or substantially injure a domestic industry, prevent the establishment of such an industry, or restrain or monopolize trade and commerce in the United States. Thus, in these types of investigations, threatened or actual injury must be shown.

3. Requirements for the contents of Section 337 complaints are set forth in 19 C.F.R. §§210.4, 210.12 and 68 Fed. Reg. 32971 (June 3, 2003).

announcing the institution of an investigation is published in the *Federal Register* whenever the Commission votes to institute a Section 337 investigation.

When an investigation is instituted, the Commission assigns an Administrative Law Judge to preside over the proceedings and to render an initial decision (referred to as an "Initial Determination") as to whether Section 337 has been violated. The Commission also assigns an investigative attorney from the Commission's Office of Unfair Import Investigations ("OUII"), who functions as an independent litigant representing the public interest in the investigation. The staff investigative attorney is a full party to the investigation. In the notice announcing initiation of an investigation, the Commission identifies the entities that may participate in the investigation as parties, namely, the complainant or complainants that allege a violation of Section 337, the respondent or respondents that are alleged to have violated Section 337, and the OUII staff attorney, who is formally known as the Commission Investigative Attorney.

Section 337 investigations are conducted in accordance with procedural rules that are similar in many respects to the Federal Rules of Civil Procedure. These Commission procedural rules (found in 19 C.F.R. Part 210) are typically supplemented by a set of Ground Rules issued by the presiding Administrative Law Judge. The procedural rules and Administrative Law Judge's Ground Rules provide important details regarding such matters as the taking of discovery and the handling of motions.

A formal evidentiary hearing on the merits of a Section 337 case is conducted by the presiding Administrative Law Judge in conformity with the adjudicative provisions of the Administrative Procedure Act (5 U.S.C. §§551 *et seq.*). Hence, parties have the right of adequate notice, cross-examination, presentation of evidence, objection, motion, argument, and other rights essential to a fair hearing.

Following a hearing on the merits of the case, the presiding Administrative Law Judge issues an Initial Determination (ID) that is certified to the Commission along with the evidentiary record. The Commission may review and adopt, modify, or reverse the Initial Determination or it may decide not to review the ID. If the Commission declines to review an ID, the ID becomes the final determination of the Commission.

In the event that the Commission determines that Section 337 has been violated, the Commission may issue an exclusion order barring the products at issue from entry into the United States, as well as a cease and desist order directing the violating parties to cease certain actions. The Commission's exclusion orders are enforced by the U.S. Customs Service.

Commission orders become effective within 60 days of issuance unless disapproved by the President for policy reasons. Appeals of Commission orders entered in Section 337 investigations are heard by the U.S. Court of Appeals for the Federal Circuit.

The ordinary remedy in a Section 337 proceeding is an exclusion order barring certain products from entering the United States, and directing identified parties to cease and desist from described acts, such as repeating attempts to unlawfully import. However, one of the distinguishing characteristics of Section 337 is that it also makes available to a complaining party the possibility for obtaining a "general exclusion order." Such an order literally prevents all products described by the order from entering the United States without permission of the IPRs holder, regardless of the identity of the importer. The following proceeding involving Pfizer's Viagra illustrates this remedial option.

The first document is an initial determination and recommendation by the administrative law judge. The second is an order by the Commission.

## *In the Matter of Certain Sildenafil or any Pharmaceutically Acceptable Salt Thereof, Such as Sildenafil Citrate, and Products Containing Same*

United States International Trade Commission Inv. No. 337-TA-489

Order No. 19: Initial Determination Granting in Part and Denying in Part Complainant's Motion for Summary Determination Respect to Domestic Industry and Violation of Section 337 Recommended Determination on Remedy and Bonding (October 27, 2003).

On October 6, 2003, complainant Pfizer, Inc. ("Pfizer") moved (489-008) pursuant to 19 C.F.R. §210.18 for *summary* determination on the issues of the existence of a domestic industry and violation of Section 337. On October 16, 2003, the Commission Investigative Staff ("Staff") filed a response in support of Pfizer's motion. No other responses to the motion were filed.

The instant motion is the culmination of this investigation, which began on January 29, 2003 with Pfizer's filing of a complaint with the Commission pursuant to Section 337 of the Tariff Act of 1930, as amended, 19 U.S.C. §1337. Pfizer's complaint alleged violations of Section 337 by all named respondents in connection with the importation, sale for importation, and sale within the United States after importation of certain sildenafil or any pharmaceutically acceptable salt thereof, such as sildenafil citrate, and products containing same. On February 27, 2003, the Commission issued a Notice of Investigation that was subsequently published in the Federal Register on March 6, 2003.

The Notice of Investigation listed 15 entities as respondents. . . . Of these, eleven were found to be in default, including domestic respondent #1 Aabaaca Viagra LLC of Reno, Nevada ("Aabaaca").[1] Two more were never found to have been served with the complaint and notice of investigation, and did not otherwise participate in the investigation.[2] One more respondent was terminated from this investigation on the basis of a settlement agreement.[3] One entered into a consent order stipulation with Pfizer that remains pending.[4] Thus, none of the named respondents have contested Pfizer's allegations that they have violated and continue to violate Section 337.

Pfizer's motion seeks, in addition to a summary determination of a Section 337 violation and the existence of a domestic industry, the entry of a general exclusion order against all infringing imports of accused sildenafil products. . . . Pfizer also seeks the entry of a cease and desist order against Respondent Aabaaca, the only domestic defaulting respondent in this case. . . .

### The Legal Framework of Pfizer's Motion

The standards for granting a motion for summary determination under 19 C.F.R. §210.18(a) are well-recognized and need no repetition here. . . . It is only useful to note for the purposes of the instant motion that the Commission's Rules require an appropriate, properly supported, unopposed motion for summary determination to be granted. . . .

---

1. The 11 defaulting respondents are as follows: Planet Pharmacy; LTMC, Ltd.; Aleppo Pharmaceutical Industries; #1 Aabaaca Viagra LLC; Zhejiang Medicines & Health Products Import & Export Co., Ltd.; Tianjin Shuaike Chemical Co., Ltd.; Sino Health Care Company of Sichuan; China Jiangsu International; Yiho Export & Import Co., Ltd.; and EBC Corporation.

2. The two respondents that were never found to have been formally served were Investment and Future Development Corp. SA, of Nicaragua; and Jiangxi Jilin Chemical Corp. Ltd., of China. . . .

3. The terminated respondent is Ezee Soulnature Healthcare Pvt. Ltd., of India ("Ezee"). . . .

4. The respondent that executed the pending consent order stipulation with Pfizer is Biovea. . . .

## THE ELEMENTS OF A SECTION 337 INVESTIGATION ARE SATISFIED BY PFIZER'S MOTION

Turning, then, to the matter at hand, Pfizer has amply established by "substantial, reliable, and probative evidence" that a violation has occurred and continues to occur, and that the *Spray Pumps* conditions [Certain Airless Paint Spray Pumps and Components Thereof, Inv. No. 337-TA-90, USITC Pub. No. 1199, Commission Opinion, 216 U.S.P.Q. 465 (U.S.I.T.C., November 1981)] for issuing a general exclusion order are present in this case.

### Infringement of the '534 Patent

Concerning violation of Section 337, Pfizer's motion establishes, and the Staff concurs, that there is a violation by reason of the Respondents' importation into the United States, sale for importation in the United States, or sale within the United States after importation, of certain sildenafil and pharmaceutically acceptable sales thereof, including sildenafil citrate, and products containing the same, that infringe one or more of claims 1-5 of Pfizer's U.S. Patent No. 5,250,534 (the "'534 patent"). . . . Pfizer's complaint includes a declaration of Rubie Ann Mages, Pfizer's Manager of Corporate Security, which details the instances of importation and sale of Respondents' accused products and identifies the chemical analysis of each product that was performed by Dr. John W. Thomas, Pfizer's Senior Research Scientist. The complaint also includes a declaration from Dr. Thomas demonstrating that the products imported into the United States by the Respondents contain sildenafil citrate and therefore infringe the '534 patent. Dr. Thomas" declaration includes detailed chemical analysis reports prepared by Pfizer that show the presence of sildenafil citrate in each defaulting respondent's product. Chemical analyses also demonstrate the presence of sildenafil citrate in the products of settling respondents Biovea and Ezee. Additionally, the Thomas declaration includes a claim chart demonstrating that the sildenafil citrate present in respondents' products is covered by claims 1-5 of the '534 patent.

## DOMESTIC INDUSTRY

Pfizer's motion, with Staff concurrence, also demonstrates that a domestic industry exists that practices the '534 patent in accordance with Section 337(a)(2) and (3). . . . Under Section 337(a)(3), a domestic industry exists: (1) if the domestic articles are "protected by the patent . . . concerned," i.e., practice one or more of the claims of the patent; and (2) if there exist in the United States with respect to those articles one or more of the following:

1. Significant investment in plant and equipment;
2. Significant employment of labor or capital; or
3. Substantial investment in the exploitation of the patent, including engineering, research and development, or licensing.

*See* 19 U.S.C. §1337(a)(3). Pfizer's motion satisfies both the first, so-called "technical prong" and the second, so-called "economic prong" of the domestic industry requirements.

Regarding the technical prong, the declaration of Dr. Thomas shows that each of claims 1-5 of the '534 patent embraces sildenafil, and pharmaceutically acceptable salts thereof, including sildenafil citrate. Sildenafil is the active ingredient in Viagra, Pfizer's domestic drug for the treatment of erectile dysfunction. Viagra contains sildenafil in the form of its citrate salt. . . . The Staff concurs with Pfizer's assertions. . . . With regard to the economic prong, Pfizer has submitted with its motion the declarations of Jose Torres and Sheldon Epstein, two Pfizer employees, stating that Viagra is manufactured at two Pfizer facilities in the United States. . . . One facility is located in Barceloneta, Puerto Rico, and the other in Brooklyn,

New York. In both plants, according to the declarations, bulk sildenafil citrate manufactured in Ireland is blended with various excipients to produce Viagra blend, which is then processed into Viagra tablets. The Staff concurs with these assertions as well. . . . Further in connection with the economic prong, the Torres and Epstein declarations state that Pfizer's total investment in plant and equipment used for the production of Viagra in the United States is approximately $5.756 million. . . . In addition, Pfizer employs approximately 2500 employees in the United States who are involved at least part-time in manufacturing and packaging activities relating to Viagra. Pfizer's annual labor costs relating to Viagra are approximately $11.066 million. The Staff also concurs with these statements.

In connection with Pfizer's research and development activities connected with exploitation of the '534 patent, Pfizer asserts in its motion, but does not support by any declaration or other evidence, that it has conducted extensive pre-market clinical testing of Viagra in the United States in order to ensure the safety and efficacy of Viagra, as well as to satisfy U.S. regulatory requirements. In 1995 and 1996, Pfizer asserts, it conducted eight major clinical trials of Viagra on human males in the United States, evaluating hundreds of subjects at numerous testing centers. Pfizer further states that since the approval of Viagra by the FDA in 1998, it has conducted, and continues to conduct, numerous additional clinical trials of Viagra throughout the United States. These tests, according to Pfizer, cost it several hundreds of millions of dollars.[15] . . .

### Validity of the '534 Patent

As for the validity of the '534 patent, its validity is presumed by law and has not been challenged in this proceeding by the Staff or by any Respondent. . . .

### Importation of Accused Products

Concerning importation of the accused products, the Mages declaration attached to the complaint demonstrates that each of the defaulting Respondents has imported accused sildenafil products into the United States. . . . The Staff concurs with these findings. . . .

### Conclusion on Violation of Section 337

In accordance with the foregoing reasons, Pfizer has demonstrated by "substantial, reliable, and probative evidence," with the concurrence of the Staff, that there is a violation of Section 337 by reason of the defaulting Respondents' importation into the United States, sale for importation, and sale within the United States after importation, of certain sildenafil or pharmaceutically acceptable salts thereof, such as sildenafil citrate, and products containing the same, that infringe claims 1-5 of the '534 patent.

### Recommended Determination on Remedy and Bonding

Finally, following the issuance of an initial determination on violation of Section 337, the administrative law judge must also issue a recommended termination concerning the appropriate remedy in the event that the Commission finds a violation of Section 337 and the amount of the bond to be posted by the respondents during the 60-day period of Presidential review of the Commission's action under Section 337(j). 19 C.F.R. §210.42(a)(l)(ii).

---

15. Although the Staff does not endorse Pfizer's research and development allegations solely because they have not been accompanied by a declaration under oath, it does not question their truthfulness.

## Propriety of a General Exclusion Order

In the case of a finding of violation of Section 337 by defaulting respondents under Section 337(g)(2), a general exclusion order may issue if the requirements of Section 337(d)(2) are met. 19 U.S.C. §1337(g)(2)(C). As mentioned earlier, these are the *Spray Pumps* factors, under which a general exclusion order is warranted if: "(A) a general exclusion from entry of articles is necessary to prevent circumvention of an exclusion order limited to products of named persons; or (B) there is a pattern of violation of this section and it is difficult to identify the source of infringing products." 19 U.S.C. §1337(d)(2).

Under *Spray Pumps*, a two-pronged test must be satisfied for issuance of a general exclusion order. There must be (1) "a widespread pattern of unauthorized use of [the] patented invention"; and (2) "certain business conditions from which one might reasonably infer that foreign manufacturers other than respondents to the investigation may attempt to enter the U.S. market with infringing articles." The following factors are considered relevant to demonstrating a widespread pattern of unauthorized use:

1. Commission determination of unauthorized importation into the United States of infringing articles by numerous foreign manufacturers; and
2. other evidence which demonstrates a history of unauthorized foreign use of the patented invention.

The Commission has also identified a number of factors relevant to showing "certain business conditions," including:

1. an established market for the patented product in the U.S. market and conditions of the world market; and
2. the availability of marketing and distribution networks in the United States for potential foreign manufacturers.

Both Pfizer and the Staff agree that there is a "widespread pattern of unauthorized use" in that numerous entities in India and China manufacture sildenafil citrate, and possibly Thailand as well. . . . They also agree that infringing sildenafil citrate is widely available on the Internet and through unsolicited bulk e-mail (also known colloquially as "spam"). Pfizer further asserts that "Customs and FDA have been overwhelmed by 'massive quantities' of pharmaceutical shipments that the [Customs Service Miami International Mail Branch] receives routinely from South and Central America, Canada, Europe, the Bahamas, and Mexico and many foreign prescription drugs have improperly entered the U.S. as a result.". . . As an example for this case, Pfizer cites a letter from a member of Congress to the Commissioner of the U.S. Food and Drug Administration stating that on May 6, 2003, the Miami Customs facility improperly released 1,233 packages labeled as "Sildenafil" or "generic Viagra" to consignees in the United States. *Id.*, citing Motion Exhibit 5 (Letter from W.J. "Billy" Tauzin et al. to The Honorable Mark B. McClellan, M.D., Ph.D. (June 5, 2003)).[19] [William Tauzin subsequently became President of PhRMA—Eds.]

Concerning the presence of "business conditions" influencing such unfair imports, Pfizer and the Staff agree that Viagra is a popular drug, sales of which were in excess of $1.5 billion in 2001. . . . Infringers offer their versions of Viagra over the Internet at significantly lower prices than Pfizer, often without requiring a prescription. *See id.* It is not difficult for foreign entities to gain access to the U.S. market, Pfizer notes, citing numerous foreign manufacturers of infringing sildenafil citrate products and ready access to the market through Internet sales.

19. The difficulties faced by Customs in stemming the tide of unauthorized drug imports raises a question of whether Customs is any more equipped to enforce a general exclusion order of this kind than it is to enforce FDA notices of detention for drugs that violate the Food, Drug and Cosmetic Act. Such "public interest" issues, however, cannot be addressed in this Initial Determination.

Concerning the possibility of circumvention, Pfizer and the Staff note the difficulty of identifying and shutting down individual suppliers. . . . Both note that infringers operating through Internet web sites typically offer very limited contact information, making it difficult to take effective action against individual suppliers.

Based on these considerations, it is readily apparent that the *Spray Pumps* factors have been satisfied by Pfizer in this case and that a general exclusion order is, therefore, warranted. . . .

### Respondents' Bond

In accordance with Section 337(j), the accused products are entitled to entry under bond during the 60-day period of Presidential review. 19 U.S.C. §1337(j). To the extent possible, the bond should be an amount that would be sufficient to protect the complainant from any injury. 19 C.F.R. §210.50(a)(3).

Although the Commission frequently sets the bond on the basis of a difference in sales prices between the patented domestic product and the infringing product, there is only limited evidence here of prices charged by the defaulting Respondents because they did not participate in the investigation. As Pfizer and the Staff both point out, the evidence that does exist is based on Pfizer's investigation and demonstrates a wide range of prices charged by the Respondents, generally well below the retail price charged for Pfizer's Viagra product. . . .

Where it has been difficult or impossible to calculate a bond based upon price differentials, and particularly where the respondents fail to provide discovery, the Commission has set the bond at 100 percent of the entered value of the infringing imported product. . . . Pfizer and Staff concur, and the undersigned recommends as appropriate, that the bond in this instance should be set at 100 percent of the entered value of Respondents' accused products during the Presidential review period.

Accordingly, Motion No. 489-008 is granted in part and denied in part to the extent set forth herein.

Pursuant to 19 C.F.R. §210.38(d), the Administrative Law Judge hereby CERTIFIES to the Commission the record in this investigation.

Pursuant to 19 C.F.R. §210.42(h), this Initial Determination shall become the determination of the Commission unless a party files a petition for review pursuant to 19 C.F.R. §210.43(a) or the Commission, pursuant to 19 C.F.R §210.44, orders on its own motion a review of the Initial Determination or certain issues therein.

So Ordered.

Charles E. Bullock

Administrative Law Judge

## *In the Matter of Certain Sildenafil or Any Pharmaceutically Acceptable Salt Thereof, Such as Sildenafil Citrate, and Products Containing Same*

United States International Trade Commission Inv. No. 337-TA-489, General Exclusion Order

The Commission has determined that there is a violation of section 337 of the Tariff Act of 1930 (19 U.S.C. §1337) in the unlawful importation and sale of certain sildenafil, or any pharmaceutically acceptable salt thereof, such as sildenafil citrate, and products containing same that infringe one or more of claims 1-5 of U.S. Patent No. 5,250,534 ("the '534 patent").

Having reviewed the record in this investigation, including the recommended determination of the presiding administrative law judge and the written submissions of the parties, the Commission has made its determination on the issues of remedy, the public interest, and bonding. The Commission has determined that the appropriate form of relief is a general exclusion order issued under section 337(d)(2) prohibiting the unlicensed importation of sildenafil, or any pharmaceutically acceptable salt thereof, such a sildenafil citrate, and products containing same covered by one or more of claims 1-5 of the '534 patent.

The Commission has also determined that the public interest factors enumerated in 19 U.S.C. §1337(d) do not preclude issuance of the general exclusion order, and that the bond during the Presidential review period shall be in the amount of 100 percent of the entered value of the products subject to this order.

Accordingly, the Commission hereby ORDERS THAT:

1. Sildenafil, or any pharmaceutically acceptable salt thereof, such as sildenafil citrate, and products containing same covered by one or more of claims 1-5 of U.S. Patent No. 5,250,534 are excluded from entry for consumption into the United States, entry for consumption from a foreign trade zone, or withdrawal from warehouse for consumption, for the remaining term of the patent, except under license of the patent owner or as provided by law.
2. Sildenafil, or any pharmaceutically acceptable salt thereof, such as sildenafil citrate, and products containing same that are excluded by paragraph 1 of this Order are entitled to entry for consumption into the United States, entry for consumption from a foreign trade zone, or withdrawal from warehouse for consumption, under bond in the amount of 100 percent of entered value pursuant to subsection (j) of section 337 of the Tariff Act of 1930, as amended, 19 U.S.C. §1337(j), from the day after this Order is received by the President until such time as the President notifies the Commission that he approves or disapproves this action but, in any event, not later than sixty (60) days after the date of receipt of this action.
3. In accordance with 19 U.S.C. §1337(l), the provisions of this Order shall not apply to products otherwise covered by this Order that are imported by and for the use of the United States, or imported for, and to be used for, the United States with the authorization or consent of the Government.
4. The Commission may modify this Order in accordance with the procedures described in section 210.76 of the Commission's Rules of Practice and Procedure, 19 C.F.R. §210.76.
5. The Secretary shall serve copies of this Order upon each party of record in this investigation and upon the Department of Health and Human Services, the Department of Justice, the Federal Trade Commission, and the Bureau of Customs and Border Protection.
6. Notice of this Order shall be published in the *Federal Register.*

By Order of the Commission.

## NOTES AND QUESTIONS

**1.** The issuance of the general exclusion order does not prevent a third party from challenging the validity of Pfizer's patent in a proceeding before the USPTO or in an ordinary federal court patent invalidity proceeding. If the patent were found to be invalid, the ITC could be petitioned to remove the general exclusion order.

**2.** Because it has obtained a general exclusion order, Pfizer does not need to bring individual claims for patent infringement—seeking injunction (and damages) against third parties attempting to import Viagra into the United States. Based on the general exclusion order, the Customs Service will routinely block imports by any third party. Note, however, that

Section 337 does not include a means for securing monetary damages such as are available in a patent infringement proceeding (although the ITC may assess civil fines in the event an order is violated). A patent holder may bring a suit for infringement and damages following a successful Section 337 action.

**3.** The ITC's general exclusion order does not apply to the federal government. This is consistent with 28 U.S.C. §1498, which generally exempts the federal government from patent infringement injunctions, permitting only claims for compensation before the Court of Claims.

**4.** As noted at the outset of this section, the President has the authority to disapprove enforcement of an ITC decision. The President has delegated this authority to the USTR. Following is an excerpt from the notification of disapproval from the USTR to the Chairperson of the ITC in regard to enforcement of a Samsung technical standards patent to block imports of certain Apple products. In disapproving enforcement of Samsung's patent, the USTR relies on a Department of Justice/USPTO Policy Statement regarding patents on technical standards. Such a Policy Statement is not a legislative measure, and USTR appears to be deciding that Samsung's behavior is anticompetitive, yet without Samsung having been the subject of an antitrust proceeding. Consider whether it is advisable from a legal standpoint to empower a single trade official to bar a legal remedy on the basis of his thoughts about antitrust policy. Might it have been more appropriate from a policy standpoint to require Apple to initiate its own antitrust proceeding against Samsung if it thought it had been subject to anticompetitive behavior?

EXECUTIVE OFFICE OF THE PRESIDENT
THE UNITED STATES TRADE REPRESENTATIVE
WASHINGTON, D.C. 20508
The Honorable Irving A. Williamson
Chairman
United States International Trade Commission
500 E Street, SW
Washington, DC 20436
August 3, 2013

RE: Disapproval of the U.S. International Trade Commission's Determination in the Matter of Certain Electronic Devices, Including Wireless Communication Devices, Portable Music and Data Processing Devices, and Tablet Computers, Investigation No. 337-TA-794.

Dear Chairman Williamson:

On June 4, 2013, the United States International Trade Commission ("Commission") determined that Apple Inc. ("Apple") had violated Section 337 of the Tariff Act of 1930, as amended, in the importation of certain devices, e.g., certain smartphones and tablet computers that infringe a U.S. patent owned by Samsung Electronics Co., Ltd. and Samsung Telecommunications America Inc. ("Samsung"). Following this determination, the Commission issued an exclusion order prohibiting the unlicensed importation of infringing devices, manufactured for or on behalf of Apple. The Commission also issued a cease and desist order that prevents Apple from engaging in certain activities, such as sale of these products in the United States.

Under section 337, the President is required to engage in a policy evaluation of the Commission's determinations to issue exclusion and cease and desist orders. The President may disapprove an order on policy grounds, approve an order, or take no action and allow the order to come into force upon the expiration of the 60-day review period. This authority has been assigned to the United States Trade Representative. The legislative history of section 337 lists the following considerations relevant to the policy review of the impact of the Commission's determination to issue an exclusion order: "(1) public health and welfare; (2) competitive conditions in the U.S. economy; (3) production of competitive articles in the United States; (4) U.S. consumers; and (5) U.S. foreign relations, economic and political."

In addition, on January 8, 2013, the Department of Justice and United States Patent and Trademark Office issued an important Policy Statement entitled "Policy Statement on Remedies for Standard-Essential Patents Subject to Voluntary FRAND Commitments" ("Policy Statement"). The Policy Statement makes clear that standards, and particularly voluntary consensus standards set by standards developing organizations ("SDO"), have incorporated important technical advances that are fundamental to the interoperability of many of the products on which consumers have come to rely, including the types of devices that are the subject of the Commission's determination. The Policy Statement expresses substantial concerns, which I strongly share, about the potential harms that can result from owners of standards-essential patents ("SEPs") who have made a voluntary commitment to offer to license SEPs on terms that are fair, reasonable, and non-discriminatory ("FRAND"), gaining undue leverage and engaging in "patent hold-up," i.e., asserting the patent to exclude an implementer of the standard from a market to obtain a higher price for use of the patent than would have been possible before the standard was set, when alternative technologies could have been chosen. At the same time, technology implementers also can cause potential harm by, for example, engaging in "reverse hold-up" ("hold-out"), e.g., by constructive refusal to negotiate a FRAND license with the SEP owner or refusal to pay what has been determined to be a FRAND royalty.

As the Policy Statement makes clear, whether public interest considerations counsel against a particular exclusion order depends on the specific circumstances at issue. The statement also explains that, to mitigate against patent hold-up, exclusionary relief from the Commission based on FRAND-encumbered SEPs should be available based only on the relevant factors described in the Policy Statement. The courts are also engaged on the issue of appropriate remedies for infringement of SEPs and we look forward to the development of appellate jurisprudence on this issue. The SEP Policy Statement is one part of the Administration's continuing efforts to consider the scope of appropriate remedies for owners of SEPs, and encourage the development of strong, innovative standards.

The Administration is committed to promoting innovation and economic progress, including through providing adequate and effective protection and enforcement of intellectual property rights. Relief available to the owners of intellectual property rights through section 337 is an important facet of achieving that objective. At the same time, standards, and particularly voluntary consensus-based standards set by SDOs, have come to play an increasingly important role in the U.S. economy. Important policy considerations arise in the enforcement of those patents incorporated into technical standards without which such standards cannot be implemented as designed, when the patent holder has made a voluntary commitment to offer to license these SEPs on FRAND terms. Licensing SEPs on FRAND terms is an important element of the Administration's policy of promoting innovation and economic progress and reflects the positive linkages between patent rights and standards setting.

I have reviewed the various policy considerations set out above based on the information provided in this case, including information developed in connection with the omission's determination. Although the parties dispute the facts vigorously, it is beyond the scope of this policy review to revisit the Commission's legal analysis or its findings based on its record. After extensive consultations with the agencies of the Trade Policy Staff Committee and the Trade Policy Review Group, as well as other interested agencies and persons, I have decided to disapprove the USITC's determination to issue an exclusion order and cease and desist order in this investigation. This decision is based on my review of the various policy considerations discussed above as they relate to the effect on competitive conditions in the U.S. economy and the effect on U.S. consumers.

. . .

This policy decision is not an endorsement or a criticism of the Commission's decision or analysis. My decision to disapprove this determination does not mean that the patent owner in this case is not entitled to a remedy. On the contrary, the patent owner may continue to pursue its rights through the courts.

Sincerely,
Ambassador Michael B. G. Froman

**5.** As a result of USTR's disapproval, reports indicated a drop in the number of standard-essential patent-related filings at the ITC. Concerns over the value of standard-essential patents, however, have been somewhat mitigated by a 2018 ITC decision to issue a limited exclusion order against Sony storage devices. *See* Ryan Davis, *ITC Becomes Ghost Town for Essential Patent Filings*, Law360, Aug. 8, 2014, https://www.law360.com/articles/565263/itc-becomes-ghost-town-for-essential-patent-filings; *see also* Tiffany Hu, *ITC Finds Sony Infringed Fujifilm Data Patent, Bans Imports*, Law360, Mar. 9, 2018, https://www.law360.com/articles/1020358?scroll=1, and Ryan Davis, *4 Ways the Apple-Samsung Case Shaped Patent Law*, Law360, June 29, 2018, https://www.law360.com/articles/1058254/4-ways-the-apple-samsung-case-shaped-patent-law.

## 2. *Other Statutory Authority Regarding Importation*

In Chapter 3, we examined *K mart v. Cartier* and *Lever Brothers v. United States*, each of which involved actions to block imports into the United States of products bearing trademarks alleged to infringe the rights of U.S. trademark holders. The *K mart* case was initiated under Section 526 of the Tariff Act of 1930 (19 U.S.C. §1526), while the *Lever Brothers* case was initiated under Section 42 of the Lanham Act (15 U.S.C. §1124). In Chapter 4, we examined *Kirtsaeng v. Wiley*, initiated pursuant to Section 602 of the Copyright Act. We refer to these cases for explanation of the statutory authority—in addition to Section 337—pursuant to which private litigants in the United States may seek to block importation of goods infringing U.S. copyright and trademark (as well as seek damages for unlawful importation).

These same statutes provide the basis for recording U.S. registered trademarks and copyrights, as well as unregistered trade names, with the U.S. Customs and Border Protection (CBP) (part of the Department of Homeland Security), and for detention by U.S. CBP authorities of goods infringing them. The relevant rules of U.S. CBP are codified at 19 C.F.R. Part 133. Upon detention of goods, the importer is notified and may provide evidence of authorization to import, pursuant to which evidence the goods will be released. If the importer does not, within 30 days of notice, obtain release of the goods, CBP commences proceedings for forfeiture. CBP has the authority to levy fines in respect of counterfeit trademark imports, and may refer trademark counterfeiting and copyright piracy cases to the Department of Justice for criminal prosecution. See for detailed explanation: What Every Member of the Trade Community Should Know About: CBP Enforcement of Intellectual Property Rights (https://www.cbp.gov/sites/default/files/assets/documents/2020-Feb/ICP-IPR-Enforcement-2012-Final.pdf)

CBP compiles data with respect to seizures of IPRs-infringing goods, broken down by commodity type and country of origin, and makes that data available online.

> Intellectual Property Rights Fiscal Year 2022 Seizure Statistics
>
> U.S. Customs and Border Protection (CBP) and U.S. Immigration and Customs Enforcement (ICE)-Homeland Security Investigation (HSI) seized 20,812 shipments containing goods that violated Intellectual Property Rights (IPR) in Fiscal Year (FY) 2022, which equates to nearly 25 million counterfeit goods. The total estimated manufacturer's suggested retail price (MSRP) of the seized goods, had they been genuine, was over $2.98 billion (USD). In FY 2022, ICE-HSI arrested 255 individuals, obtained 192 indictments, and received 95 convictions related to intellectual property crimes. . . .
>
> The People's Republic of China remained the primary source economy for counterfeit and pirated goods seized, accounting for a total estimated MSRP value of almost $1.8 billion (USD) or approximately 60% of the total estimated MSRP value of all IPR seizures.[4]

4. https://www.cbp.gov/trade/priority-issues/ipr#:~:text=U.S.%20Customs%20and%20Border%20Protection%20(CBP)%20and%20U.S.%20Immigration%20and,nearly%2025%20million%20counterfeit%20goods.

Of course, MSRP may not reflect the reality of the commercial marketplace, and is not representative of the ordinary "legitimate" import price of the products (which would typically be a wholesale price at the relevant distribution level).

### 3. *Section 301 and Special 301*

U.S. trade legislation provides a mechanism—Section 301 of the Trade Act of 1974 (as amended)—under which interested persons may initiate administrative proceedings at the Office of the United States Trade Representative (USTR) that may lead to a finding that a foreign country is engaging in unlawful or unreasonable trade practices.[54] Such administrative proceedings may also be self-initiated by USTR. Depending upon the nature of the finding, USTR may be obligated to negotiate a satisfactory resolution with the foreign country and, if unsuccessful, initiate a dispute settlement action at the WTO or under another applicable trade agreement. If the complained-against country is found to have violated an agreement and fails to remedy the problem, USTR is obligated to impose trade sanctions (unless USTR determines that this would be against the national interest).

Section 301 actions are not limited to situations in which a foreign country is engaging in acts that violate a trade agreement. Such actions also extend to "unreasonable" foreign trade practices that, even if not illegal, are "otherwise unfair and inequitable."[55] Unreasonable practices are expressly defined to include acts or practices that deny fair and equitable "provision of adequate and effective protection of intellectual property rights notwithstanding the fact that the foreign country may be in compliance with the specific obligations of the Agreement on Trade-Related Aspects of Intellectual Property Rights."[56] While a determination that a foreign trade practice is unlawful mandates (subject to exceptions) that USTR take action to remedy the situation, a determination that a practice is unreasonable leaves USTR with discretion regarding whether and what action to take.

From the standpoint of foreign countries that are Members of the WTO, it is a matter of concern that U.S. legislation expressly contemplates remedial action notwithstanding the lack of TRIPS Agreement violation. However, the United States might argue that some intellectual property issues fall outside the scope of the TRIPS Agreement, and that any remedial action it proposes will not necessarily contravene its WTO obligations.

Section 301, like the EU Trade Barriers Regulation (which post-dates it), provides a means for private enterprises and individuals to pursue redress of WTO-inconsistent measures (and measures inconsistent with other foreign trade agreements). Because the U.S. Congress commonly denies self-executing effect to trade agreements, private parties in the United States may not sue the U.S. government directly on the basis of rights that might be established by those agreements.

In 1988, Congress evidenced heightened attention to IPRs-related trade practices when it adopted, as part of the Omnibus Trade and Competitiveness Act, provisions referred to as "Special 301." Special 301, among other things, requires USTR to prepare an annual report regarding foreign IP-related practices and, as appropriate, identify the most serious violators of U.S. interests as "priority" countries. Priority countries are subject to an accelerated Section 301 process. While not provided for in Special 301 legislation, USTR from the outset of its implementation chose to establish a "priority watch list" and "watch list" to identify countries of particular concern. Placement on a "watch list" does not trigger the same statutory obligations for USTR as does a country's designation as a "priority" country. Following is part of USTR's 2010 Special 301 Report, which includes a brief description of USTR's Special 301

54. 19 U.S.C. §§2411 et seq.
55. 19 U.S.C. §2411(b) & (d).
56. 19 U.S.C. §2411(d)(3)(B)(i)(II).

mandate, and its 2010 discussion and identification of China and Russia as priority watch list countries.

---

## *Office of United States Trade Representative 2022 Special 301 Report*

### Executive Summary

The Special 301 Report (Report) is the result of an annual review of the state of intellectual property (IP) protection and enforcement in U.S. trading partners around the world, which the Office of the United States Trade Representative (USTR) conducts pursuant to Section 182 of the Trade Act of 1974, as amended (the Trade Act, 19 U.S.C. §2242). Congress amended the Trade Act in 1988 specifically "to provide for the development of an overall strategy to ensure adequate and effective protection of intellectual property rights and fair and equitable market access for United States persons that rely on protection of intellectual property rights." [1] In particular, Congress expressed its concern that "the absence of adequate and effective protection of United States intellectual property rights, and the denial of equitable market access, seriously impede the ability of the United States persons that rely on protection of intellectual property rights to export and operate overseas, thereby harming the economic interests of the United States."[2]

This Report provides an opportunity to put a spotlight on foreign countries and the laws, policies, and practices that fail to provide adequate and effective IP protection and enforcement for U.S. inventors, creators, brands, manufacturers, and service providers, which, in turn, harm American workers whose livelihoods are tied to America's innovation- and creativity-driven sectors. The Report identifies a wide range of concerns, including: (a) challenges with border and criminal enforcement against counterfeits, including in the online environment; (b) high levels of online and broadcast piracy, including through illicit streaming devices; (c) inadequacies in trade secret protection and enforcement in China, Russia, and elsewhere; (d) troubling "indigenous innovation" and forced technology transfer policies that may unfairly disadvantage U.S. right holders in markets abroad; and (e) other ongoing, systemic issues regarding IP protection and enforcement, as well as market access, in many trading partners around the world. Combating such unfair trade policies will encourage domestic investment in the United States, foster American innovation and creativity, and increase economic security for American workers and families.

A priority of this Administration is to craft trade policy in service of America's workers, including those in innovation- and creativity-driven export industries. The Report serves a critical function by identifying opportunities and challenges facing U.S. innovative and creative industries in foreign markets and by promoting job creation, economic development, and many other benefits that effective IP protection and enforcement support. The Report informs the public and our trading partners and seeks to be a positive catalyst for change. In addition, given the importance of innovation and IP in developing the advances necessary for fighting the ongoing COVID-19 crisis, this Administration is committed to trade policies that seek to save lives in this pandemic and ensure preparedness for the next one. USTR looks forward to working closely with the governments of the trading partners that are identified in this year's Report to address both emerging and continuing concerns, and to build on the positive results that many of these governments have achieved.

### The 2022 Special 301 List

The Special 301 Subcommittee received stakeholder input on more than 100 trading partners, but focused its review on those submissions that responded to the request set forth in the notice published in the *Federal Register* to identify whether a particular trading partner should be named as a Priority Foreign Country, placed on the Priority Watch List or Watch List, or not listed in the Report. Following extensive research and analysis, USTR has identified 27 trading partners as follows:

**Priority Watch List**
- Argentina
- Chile
- China
- India
- Indonesia
- Russia
- Venezuela

**Watch List**
- Algeria
- Barbados
- Bolivia
- Brazil
- Canada
- Colombia
- Dominican Republic
- Ecuador
- Egypt
- Guatemala
- Mexico
- Pakistan
- Paraguay
- Peru
- Thailand
- Trinidad and Tobago
- Turkey
- Turkmenistan
- Uzbekistan
- Vietnam

The Special 301 review of Ukraine has been suspended due to Russia's premeditated and unprovoked further invasion of Ukraine in February 2022.

### Out-Of-Cycle Reviews

An Out-of-Cycle Review is a tool that USTR uses to encourage progress on IP issues of concern. Out-of-Cycle Reviews provide an opportunity to address and remedy such issues through heightened engagement and cooperation with trading partners and other stakeholders. Out-of-Cycle Reviews focus on identified IP challenges in specific trading partner markets. Successful resolution of specific IP issues of concern can lead to a positive change in a trading partner's Special 301 status outside of the typical period for the annual review. Conversely, failure to address identified IP concerns, or further deterioration as to an IP-related concern within the specified Out-of-Cycle Review period, can lead to an adverse change in status.

In 2022, USTR will conduct an Out-of-Cycle Review of Bulgaria, which will consider the extent to which Bulgaria has addressed deficiencies in its investigation and prosecution of online piracy cases, particularly its failure to adopt evidence sampling in criminal cases. The Out-of-Cycle Review will assess whether Bulgaria has made any material progress on these issues.

USTR may conduct additional Out-of-Cycle Reviews of other trading partners as circumstances warrant or as requested by a trading partner.

. . .

**Frederick Abbott***

## *US Section 301, China, and Technology Transfer: Law and its Limitations Revisited (Again)*

ICTSD Opinion, 23 May 2018

. . .

China's use of law and policy instruments to "force" technology transfer from high income country enterprises, including those based in the US, has been an issue in international

* https://www.ictsd.org/opinion/us-section-301-china-and-technology-transfer-law-and-its-limitations-revisited.

economic law for more than 20 years. It was the subject of substantial negotiation during the process of China's accession to the WTO, and China made certain commitments in this regard in its Accession Protocol, and incorporated texts.

The US executive administration has pledged to reduce the US trade in goods deficit with China. United States action with respect to technology transfer may be tangentially related to that pledge. It appears more an attempt to restrain China's domestic technological advance. US strategic-military concerns are part of the equation. China's massive investments in science and technology are reducing the significance of imported technology as a factor in its progress. The US, Europe, and Japan may be able to affect the arc of China's emergence as a strategic technological competitor at the margin. Paradoxically, the US course of action may have the effect of encouraging China to increase the scale of its investments in R&D as it seeks to become more independent of foreign influence.

The legal situation under General Agreement on Tariffs and Trade (GATT) and WTO law with respect to technology transfers is not well-defined. Transfer of technology demands are principally made in two contexts. First, technology transfer may be demanded as a condition of purchase of products, imported or otherwise. Second, technology transfer may be demanded as a condition of approval of foreign direct investment.

The US issued a Request for Consultations (RFC) with China as a prelude to formally requesting the establishment of a dispute settlement panel at the WTO, though the US might refrain from requesting a panel pending the outcome of the current negotiations. The US makes some "not entirely implausible" claims in its RFC. The problem, however, is that while the US has identified several intellectual property (IP)-related practices that may affect investments in China, these appear to be minor matters from an economic standpoint, and not matters that go to the principal economic issues that the US is attempting to address through its threatening of trade sanctions. Put another way, there is a rather limited correlation with the allegations laid out in USTR's Section 301 findings regarding China's technology transfer, IP, and innovation-related practices. The Office of the USTR as much as concedes this point in electing to identify China's practices as unreasonable and discriminatory in the 301 findings, which makes them subject to discretionary measures, and at least in the US view (presumably) keeps them out of the purview of WTO dispute settlement.

The Chinese practices about which the US complains in the RFC concern mandatory indemnification by licensors for third-party patent infringement claims against licensees; prohibition against grant backs of technology improvements by licensees to licensors; and, mandating permission to licensees to continue using patented technologies after expiration of licenses. Each of these practices is said to apply to foreign licensors, but not to local Chinese companies. As noted above, on the scale of economic impact, these seem to be of limited significance.

The main allegations in the 301 findings are that the Chinese government, at the national and subnational levels, effectively compels foreign investors in China to transfer technology to domestic joint venture partners as a condition of approving inward investments, or in other contexts such as conditioning regulatory approvals. The Office of the USTR argues that to avoid complaints from foreign governments, the Chinese government pursues these practices largely in ways that do not leave a "paper trail," much in the nature of colluding co-conspirators in antitrust cases. Identifiable US corporate victims of the Chinese practices are unwilling to go on record with specific instances in which they have been affected by these practices, leaving it to industry group representatives to make the case without company-specific details, or at least company-specific details USTR maintains in confidence.

Another broad set of allegations in the 301 findings concerns allegations that China subsidises R&D in various key sectors, though this does not find its way into the RFC as a complaint against prohibited subsidisation. Since a substantial proportion of Chinese companies are state owned, this also potentially raises issues regarding state trading rules.

Finally, the Section 301 findings identify Chinese cyber piracy practices against US industry as unreasonable or discriminatory practices. The Office of the USTR says that these practices, though perhaps scaled back, continue notwithstanding Chinese government assurances they would cease. Such practices, at least in part, are undertaken through Chinese government agencies, which presumably make the pirated technology available to local Chinese companies.

A recent report prepared for the US-China Economic and Security Review Commission, established pursuant to US statute, suggests increasing concern with US federal procurement of Chinese-origin computer equipment, telecommunications equipment, and software which are said to lead to vulnerabilities in US security. An interesting aspect of the problem is that many of the exporters from China to the US are subsidiaries of US-based multinationals that have established production facilities in China. The report indicates that it is unrealistic to expect US-based enterprises to move manufacturing out of China to allay security concerns (because of the profitability of the Chinese market).

The retaliatory tariff measures that the US proposed, but now suspended, would clearly violate WTO norms. They would be inconsistent with most favoured nation (MFN) treatment under GATT Article I as they apply only to China. Almost certainly they would be inconsistent with US commitments on bound tariffs under GATT Article II. As the US tariff measures would be imposed without the benefit of authorisation by the WTO Dispute Settlement Body, they would be inconsistent with US obligations under the Dispute Settlement Understanding (DSU).

The Section 301 findings include a compilation by USTR of bilateral commitments said to have been made by China to the US within the framework of the US-China Joint Commission on Commerce and Trade (JCCT) and US-China Strategic & Economic Dialogue (S&ED). There is no suggestion made by USTR that these bilateral commitments—the legal status of which is not spelled out—are enforceable as a matter of WTO law or under some bilateral dispute settlement mechanism.

Even assuming the subject matter of the complaints by the US against China were within the scope of the WTO agreements, at this stage using the DSU as the mechanism to resolve those complaints raises additional questions. The WTO dispute settlement process is not designed to move expeditiously. From initiation to adoption of conforming measures, a dispute can readily be extended for 3.5 years without any meaningful adverse consequence to the losing party. The present US administration appears to have a short-term political outlook. A 3.5-year time horizon for what may be a modest outcome does not appear consistent with that outlook. Moreover, given the long-standing nature of the US complaints regarding China's practices, that perspective may not be entirely unreasonable in the circumstances. And, since WTO rules as drafted are unlikely to provide solutions to a number of the issues, the potential efficacy of WTO dispute settlement is questionable.

Not for the first time, we can turn to Professor Robert Hudec's argument regarding justified trade disobedience and ask whether the US would be acting from a "multilateral trade-responsible" standpoint by attempting to force a change in WTO rules that would address the technology issue. The question arises: is the US after new WTO norms as would be part of Robert Hudec's philosophical justification for disobedience?

A multilateral legal solution would seem to entail the negotiation of an investment agreement—inside or outside the WTO—that would address conditions placed on inward investment, such as technology transfer demands. Experience suggests that a broad multilateral investment agreement would be a difficult and long-term exercise. For this reason, the US is more likely to be able to achieve its objectives through a bilateral negotiation with China—though this is not to suggest whether the US will succeed.

It is noteworthy that bilateral and plurilateral trade and investment agreements more recently negotiated by the US, including the Transpacific Partnership (TPP), include provisions in the investment chapter that specifically address transfer of technology demands in a way that might encompass, at least in substantial part, the practices the US complains about with respect to China (for example Article 9.10(f) of the TPP final text). The US President concluded that the TPP was a terrible deal for the US and withdrew its signature, following which it was replaced by the Comprehensive and Progressive Agreement for Trans-Pacific Partnership (CPTPP). It will be of interest to see whether the forthcoming negotiations with China will generate a solution on technology transfer "less terrible" than the one in the TPP.

A significant element of the US 301 findings is a critique of China's strategic industrial and R&D policies as set out in a number of official documents, including most recently "Notice of the State Council on Issuing 'Made in China 2025'." These documents, according to USTR, target a number of key sectors regarding which China commits to devoting resources towards achieving technological leadership, local production, and global export capacity. These include, for example, artificial intelligence, advanced electric vehicles, aerospace, and biotechnology.

At one level, the dispute involves a basic confrontation between politico-economic ideologies. China is a top-down managed economy and political system which includes detailed planning and implementation of industrial policy. The US is at least nominally a "free market" economy in which the preponderance of business decisions is made by autonomous private entities.

Yet, of course, the characterisation of the US as a free market does not account for the relatively vast role that the government plays in effectively managing important parts of the economy by virtue of the very large federal budget and expenditures, including with respect to R&D that is directed towards the defence and pharmaceutical sectors, and subsidies for the energy and agricultural sectors, among other areas.

The USTR 301 findings are plain in stating that the main complaint of US-based multinational companies is that they should not be deprived of access to the large and growing Chinese market based on Chinese government regulatory policies and practices. The US companies implicitly acknowledge that they could choose to stay away from China, and that decisions to transfer technology in that regard involve exercise of "free will." China is not forcing these companies to choose China as an investment destination.

It is evident that China has substantial leverage in the present dialogue with the US. Non-technologically advanced investors, consider Starbucks for example, must be deeply concerned that the current tensions will spill over into anti-American sentiment that will change local consumer preferences. As noted earlier, a paradox of the action being taken currently by the US administration is that while a curtailment of US technology transfers to China may slow down China's advance towards technological parity with the US, it is also likely to result in even greater investment by the Chinese government in developing homegrown technological assets.

On another level, this entire set of issues is rooted in a "dark view" of international relations, including trade relations—a zero-sum game in which Chinese technological advances are at the expense of the US. Over the past 30 years, Chinese economic development has raised large numbers of people out of poverty and towards middle-class prosperity. Advances in technology made in China presumably will benefit individuals in the US, as well as globally. The question is where to strike the balance between encouraging Chinese technological advance while protecting the economic well-being of individuals in the US and elsewhere.

At the time China bargained for entry into the WTO its economy was in a much different circumstance than it is today. Seventeen years after its formal entry, China's economic posture in relation to the OECD and other developing countries is significantly different. To the extent that concessions were made to acknowledge the long path that China would need to take to become a largely developed country, those concessions would no longer appear to be necessary. It is reasonable for China's position vis-à-vis the OECD world to be rebalanced. This is in recognition of one of history's great economic success stories.

This brings us back (again) to Olivier Long's classic 1985 Law and its Limitations in the GATT Multilateral Trading System. Long, a former Director General of the GATT, argued that legal rules could not address all the complex issues raised within the international trading system, and that there was important room for political and economic diplomacy beyond those legal rules.

One of the driving ideas behind the Uruguay Round was that a comprehensive legal arrangement would move the organisation out of the realm of politics and diplomacy and further embed the rule of law. Yet even with successful conclusion and establishment of a more encompassing WTO, there was no pretence that the WTO agreements address every issue in the field of international trade. International investment is addressed only in limited ways.

There is still room for politics and diplomacy near and outside the boundaries of the framework of the WTO for matters that are unaddressed, or uncertainly addressed, by the norm-system. The "somewhat urgent" question is whether politics and diplomacy can resolve the tension between the US and China before the WTO legal system loses its relevance, and bilateralism becomes the "new normal." Although the future is famously difficult to predict, fragmentation of trade relations and reliance on power politics has proven problematic in the past.

## NOTES AND QUESTIONS

**1.** China agreed to address U.S. allegations of forced technology transfer and cyberpiracy in a so-called Phase 1 agreement, the "Economic and Trade Agreement between the Government of the United States of America and the Government of the People's Republic of China", dated January 15, 2020.[57] The terms accepted by China with respect to technology transfer, while similar to those incorporated in bilateral and regional trade and investment agreements previously negotiated with other countries by the United States, go beyond those agreements in expressly addressing the informal conditioning of investment approvals. China made significant commitments to the United States as well in respect to addressing cyberpiracy, including with respect to thresholds for initiating criminal enforcement, and placing substantial limits on requests for information from government authorities.

Because the WTO TRIPS Agreement requires that concessions granted with respect to higher levels of protection of IP be extended to all WTO Members on an MFN basis the commitments China has made to the United States pursuant to the Phase 1 Agreement will be extended to the EU and other WTO Members.

The Phase 1 Economic and Trade Agreement between the US and China bypassed WTO dispute settlement and illustrated from the US perspective the value of power-infused bilateral bargaining. As if to drive this point home, there is no "legalized" dispute settlement

57. https://ustr.gov/sites/default/files/files/agreements/phase%20one%20agreement/Economic_And_Trade_Agreement_Between_The_United_States_And_China_Text.pdf.

mechanism in the Phase 1 Agreement. Instead, the parties have agreed to establish a Bilateral Evaluation and Dispute Resolution Office composed of trade bureaucrats designated by each party. If a party has a complaint, it sends it to the trade bureaucrats of the other party for evaluation, following which there will be consultations. If those consultations do not yield a satisfactory result, the ultimate step of dispute settlement is an urgent meeting between the USTR and the designated Vice Premier of the PRC. The "final step" of resolution merits quoting: "If the Parties do not reach consensus on a response, the Complaining Party may resort to taking action based on facts provided during the consultations, including by suspending an obligation under this Agreement or by adopting a remedial measure in a proportionate way that it considers appropriate with the purpose of preventing the escalation of the situation and maintaining the normal bilateral trade relationship. The Party Complained Against can initiate an urgent meeting between the United States Trade Representative and the designated Vice Premier of the People's Republic of China before the effective date of the action to be taken by the Complaining Party. If the Party Complained Against considers that the action by the Complaining Party pursuant to this subparagraph was taken in good faith, the Party Complained Against may not adopt a counter-response, or otherwise challenge such action. If the Party Complained Against considers that the action of the Complaining Party was taken in bad faith, the remedy is to withdraw from this Agreement by providing written notice of withdrawal to the Complaining Party." Art. 7.4.4(b) China and the United States have thus agreed to turn the clock of dispute settlement back to the early days of GATT 1947 when trade disputes were resolved by diplomats meeting behind closed doors. If the thinking on either side is that this will encourage reinvigoration of the WTO, it is certainly a peculiar way to point in that direction. In other words, we will "encourage a return to multilateralism and legalization by embracing bilateralism, power politics and diplomacy".

**2.** As noted in the text excerpt by Abbott, the European Union shares concerns of the United States with respect to China's transfer of technology policies and practices. The European Union has initiated a work program that includes addressing gaps in WTO rules in this area. *See, e.g.*, European Commission, *WTO-EU's Proposals on WTO Modernization*, WK 8329/2018 INIT, 5 July 2018.

**3.** China has an advanced industrial and R&D infrastructure and is training large numbers of PhD scientists, and the government is actively financing R&D projects. By attempting to reduce Chinese access to advanced technologies, is the United States (or the European Union) merely strengthening the incentives for China to invest in local R&D and production? Is this going to provide more opportunities for U.S. and European business? It can be argued that if the United States and European Union intended to limit China's technological development, the time to do that was 1990, when China was just emerging from economic isolation. The reason they did not is that multinational business in the United States and the European Union saw tremendous opportunity in China's large and growing consumer market. That market is wealthier and more robust in 2023 than in 1990, and presents even more of a business opportunity.

**4.** U.S. bilateral trade pressure applied under Section 301 and Special 301 has been the source of political tension with foreign governments and nongovernmental organizations for many years, and the subject of numerous academic papers. The most thoughtful defense of Section 301 and U.S. action pursuant to it was written by Professor Bob Hudec during the GATT 1947 era: Robert E. Hudec, *Thinking About the New Section 301: Beyond Good and Evil*, in AGGRESSIVE UNILATERALISM: AMERICA'S 301 TRADE POLICY AND THE WORLD TRADING SYSTEM 113-22 (J. Bhagwati & H. Patrick eds., 1990). In his paper, Hudec argued that the GATT legal system included some significant gaps that governments were unwilling to address. Under certain circumstances, the United States was justified to engage in "disobedience" under the prevailing rules in order to force the system to change. Hudec posited five substantive guidelines for the use of extralegal GATT measures:

> "1. The objective of the disobedient act must be to secure recognition of the legal change that is consistent with the general objectives of the Agreement. . . .
>
> 2. Disobedience undertaken in support of a claim must be preceded by a good-faith effort to achieve the desired legal change by negotiation. This is a minimum condition of necessity.
>
> 3. Disobedience must be accompanied by an offer to continue negotiating in good faith, with a pledge to terminate the disobedient action upon satisfactory completion of such negotiations. . . .
>
> 4. The extent of the disobedience must be limited to that which is necessary to achieve the negotiated legal reform of the kind needed to solve the problem. . . .
>
> 5. Finally, governments acting out of a concern to improve GATT law must necessarily respect that law as fully as possible, even when disobeying it. Accordingly, they must except the power of the legal process to judge their disobedient behavior, and must accept the consequences imposed by law. . . ." (*Id.*, 137-38).

Hudec's defense of Section 301 was written before transformation of the GATT into the more comprehensive WTO legal system. Do you think Hudec's theory of justified disobedience retains its validity?

**5.** Up until quite recently, U.S. Special 301 reports were prepared almost wholly on the basis of data supplied by U.S. industry groups. In the past several years, USTR has been more encouraging of input from other stakeholder groups, including foreign industry groups, although the influence of that input on the annual reports seems to have been quite limited. USTR's Special 301 negotiating agenda is essentially established through consultation with U.S. industry groups. Of course, U.S. industry has a major stake in foreign IPRs policy. What other U.S. interest groups have a stake in that policy?

### *4. Civil Litigation and Extraterritorial Effects*

The most commonly used mechanism for enforcement of IPRs — following consultation and negotiation — is civil litigation. The holder of the IPR files a complaint with judicial or administrative authorities seeking, typically, an injunction to prevent an alleged infringer from continuing its activities. In addition, the IPRs holder usually seeks monetary damages and, as appropriate, forfeiture or destruction of infringing goods and the equipment used to make them. Up until now, almost all civil litigation to enforce IPRs has involved conduct within the territory of the country where the IPRs holder's rights are granted. This is because IPRs are granted with respect to specific national or regional territories and, generally speaking, do not establish rights in foreign territories.[58] Judgments may be enforced abroad on the basis of rules of international private law and the recognition of foreign rulings. Basically, the principle of territoriality applies. However, as we noted in Chapter 1, page 83, the U.S. Supreme Court recently permitted recovery for loss contract opportunities outside the United States based on patent infringement within the United States.[59] In Chapter 2 we also looked at the NTP

58. There are exceptions, for example, in the case of well-known trademarks.

59. *WesternGeco LLC v. ION Geophysical Corp.*, 138 S. Ct. 2129 (2018).

v. Research in Motion case, where the U.S. Court of Appeals for the Federal Circuit imposed liability for infringement of a U.S. software patent on the basis of processing activities taking place in Canada.[60] These decisions may be opening the door to further civil litigation based on activities taking place outside the country where the IPR is granted. The following decision by the U.S. Court of Appeals for the Eleventh Circuit, Babbit Electronics v. Dynascan, bases liability for U.S. trademark infringement on consumer confusion and injury in various Latin American markets. There are physical jurisdictional links with the United States, including the transit of infringing goods through a U.S. "free trade zone" (where goods transit the United States without passing through customs and enter the stream of commerce), as well as the presence of the parties to the dispute.[61]

The Babbit Electronics v. Dynascan decision is included here not only to illustrate the potential extraterritorial reach of U.S. trademark law, but also to show that the penalties for trademark infringement may be rather severe. It is a lesson in strong enforcement of IP law.

## *Babbit Electronics v. Dynascan*

38 F.3d 1161 (11th Cir. 1994)

Per Curiam . . .

### II. Conclusions of Law . . .

### B. Dynascan's Counterclaim . . .

#### 2. Trademark Infringement

Dynascan's trademark infringement claim, pursuant to 15 U.S.C. §1114(1)(a),[3] rests on the notion that a particular use of a registered trademark is likely to cause confusion. In this case, the registration of the trademarks is not an issue, because Dynascan presented certificates of registration for each of the "Cobra" trademarks owned by Dynascan. The Court must therefore determine whether Babbit's use of the Cobra trademark is likely to cause confusion in the minds of potential buyers as to the source, affiliation or sponsorship of the products. *Interstate Battery System v. Wright*, 811 F. Supp. 237, 241 (N.D. Tex. 1993).

In determining whether there is a likelihood of confusion, the Court may consider a variety of factors, including similarity of design, similarity of the products, identity of retail outlets and purchasers, similarity of advertising media, the defendant's intent and actual confusion. *Jaguar Cars Ltd. v. Skandrani*, 771 F. Supp. 1178, 1183 (S.D. Fla. 1991). Application of these elements to the facts of this case compels the conclusion that Babbit's sale of Cobra cordless telephones is likely to confuse the public into believing that Babbit's products are associated

60. *NTP v. Research in Motion*, 418 F.3d 1282 (Fed. Cir. 2005).

61. Babbit is a Florida corporation. Dynascan is a Delaware corporation.

3. Section 1114 provides, in pertinent part:

> (1) Any person who shall, without the consent of the registrant—
>
> (a) use in commerce any reproduction, counterfeit, copy or colorable imitation of a registered mark in connection with the sale, offering for sale, distribution, or advertising of any goods or services on or in connection with which such use is likely to cause confusion, or to cause mistake, or to deceive; or
>
> (b) reproduce, counterfeit, copy or colorably imitate a registered mark and apply such reproduction, counterfeit, copy or colorable imitation to labels, signs, prints, packages, wrappers, receptacles or advertisements intended to be used in commerce upon or in connection with the sale, offering for sale, distribution, or advertising of goods or services on or in connection with which such use is likely to cause confusion, or to cause mistake, or to deceive, shall be liable in a civil action by the registrant.

with Dynascan or that Dynascan sponsored, licensed or consented to the manufacture and sale of Babbit's products. The marks used by Babbit are identical to the Cobra trademarks owned by Dynascan, and the Model SA-660s telephones sold by Babbit containing a Cobra label are nearly identical to Dynascan's Model SA-620s cordless telephones.

In addition, although there is no evidence of actual confusion,[4] this Court has found that Babbit intentionally infringed upon Dynascan's trademark rights and intentionally breached the Agreement. . . .

In fact, a likelihood of confusion can be found as a matter of law if the defendant intended to derive benefit from the plaintiff's trademark. . . . Babbit intended to improve sales of MCE telephones by relabeling them with Cobra labels because Babbit was having difficulty selling MCE telephones. Based on the foregoing discussion, the Court concludes that there has been trademark infringement as determined by the likelihood of confusion analysis.

. . . Direct competition between the parties is not a prerequisite to relief under the Lanham Act. In fact, the Court would not expect to find substantial evidence demonstrating that Dynascan was in competition with Babbit in South America because Babbit was already selling Cobra telephones in that geographic territory with Dynascan's permission. Regardless of Dynascan's activities at the time of the infringement, its name continued to be a marketable commodity and it has the right to use it on other goods or to grant such a license to other companies. *Bowmar Instrument Co. v. Continental Microsystems, Inc.*, 497 F. Supp. 947, 208 U.S.P.Q. 496, 503 (S.D.N.Y. 1980).

As a corollary to this argument, Babbit contends that United States copyright laws and the Lanham Act do not apply to Babbit's sales of cordless telephones because the sales occurred outside of the United States. This argument is not compelling because this Court has already found that Lanham Act jurisdiction exists because Babbit imported cordless telephones into the United States to a free trade zone before shipping the products to South America. Babbit presses this argument, however, by presenting the Court with *Zenger-Miller, Inc. v. Training Team, GmbH*, 757 F. Supp. 1062 (N.D. Cal. 1991).

In *Zenger-Miller*, the court concluded that there was no subject matter jurisdiction over Lanham Act claims where all of the defendant's sales occurred in Germany. A close examination of the underlying rationale of *Zenger-Miller*, however, clearly supports this Court's conclusion that the Lanham Act can apply where sales occur outside of the United States. Specifically, the *Zenger-Miller* court found that the defendant was a foreign corporation and all negotiations leading to the contract in that case occurred abroad. In the instant case, Babbit is an American corporation, and the negotiations leading to the Agreement occurred primarily in the United States. In addition, the defendant in *Zenger-Miller* did not allege that any infringing activity took place in the United States. Babbit, however, imported labels and telephones into a free trade zone in the United States, and Babbit orchestrated sales from a Florida office.

In *Reebok Internat'l v. American Sales Corp.*, 11 U.S.P.Q.2D (BNA) 1229 [1989 WL 418625] (E.D. Wash. 1989), the court upheld the invocation of Lanham Act jurisdiction where the defendant, a California corporation, imported counterfeit shoes from Taiwan to a free trade zone in Los Angeles and then exported the goods to Belgium. The court noted that "the Lanham Act imposes upon this court the duty to protect the entire gamut of purchasers, including non-English speaking purchasers, in various countries throughout the world to which the defendants intend to export their products." *Id.* at 1231. Consequently, this Court concludes that it has jurisdiction to address the trademark infringement counterclaim, even though Babbit's sales of cordless telephones occurred outside of the United States. *See also*

4. "Evidence of confusion is not a prerequisite to a finding of likely confusion." *Jaguar Cars Ltd.*, 771 F. Supp. 1178, 1184, citing *E. Remy Martin & Co. v. Shaw-Ross Internat'l Imports, Inc.*, 756 F.2d 1525, 1529 (11th Cir. 1985).

*Ocean Garden, Inc. v. Marktrade Co., Inc.*, 953 F.2d 500, 505 (9th Cir. 1991) (Court held that "entry of infringing goods into a foreign trade zone is a sufficient act in commerce to trigger subject matter jurisdiction in federal courts under the Lanham Act.").

Babbit also argues that Dynascan has engaged in "naked licensing" and thereby forfeits all rights to the Cobra mark in the geographic and product markets where use of the mark has not been adequately protected. In this instance, there is substantial evidence that a number of counterfeiters were active in South America during the mid-1980s. "The existence of third party infringers, however, does not constitute an abandonment of a mark where the trademark owner does not consent to the use of the mark by these others but rather, vigorously pursues these third party infringers." *Visa International v. Bankcard Holders of America*, 211 U.S.P.Q. 28, 41 [1981 WL 40539] (N.D. [Cal.] 1981). In addition, the party seeking to prove abandonment must prove intent to abandon on the part of the trademark owner. *Id.* Although Dynascan did not act with particular vigor against third party infringers in South America, failure to institute legal action against an infringer is insufficient to establish abandonment of a trademark. *Playboy Enterprises v. P.K. Sorren Export Co.*, 546 F. Supp. 987, 996 (S.D. Fla. 1982). Babbit has utterly failed to prove that Dynascan intentionally abandoned its Cobra mark or ceased use of the Cobra trademark.

Finally, Babbit argues that there is no violation of the Lanham Act because the articles that are alleged to be counterfeits are actually genuine goods, produced in the same factory as the approved Cobra telephones. It is true that the unauthorized sale of a genuine trademarked product does not in itself constitute trademark infringement, but Babbit fails to appreciate that identical goods sold in an unauthorized manner are not necessarily genuine for purposes of the Lanham Act. *Hunting World, Inc. v. Reboans, Inc.*, 1992 U.S. Dist. LEXIS 21477, 24 U.S.P.Q.2D (BNA) 1844, 1849 [1992 WL 361741] (N.D. [Cal.] 1992), citing, *H.L. Hayden Co. v. Siemens Medical Systems, Inc.*, 879 F.2d 1005, 1023 (2nd Cir. 1989). . . . Although there is no evidence suggesting that the Model SA-660s cordless telephones are inferior to authorized Cobra products, inferiority is not a prerequisite to a finding of a Lanham Act violation. *Tanning Research Lab. v. Worldwide Import and Export*, 803 F. Supp. 606, 609 (E.D.N.Y. 1992). "Congress hardly intended to step through the looking glass into a world in which valid trademark owners were only protected from inartful counterfeiters." *Id.*

### 3. Counterfeiting

In order for Dynascan to prevail on its counterfeiting claim, it must demonstrate that Babbit infringed a registered trademark in violation of 15 U.S.C. §1114(1)(a), and it must prove that Babbit "intentionally used a mark, knowing such mark is a counterfeit mark." 15 U.S.C. §1117(b).[5]

The Court has determined that Babbit infringed registered marks in violation of 15 U.S.C. §1114(1)(a). The Court has also found that Babbit intentionally used the marks in question. "The analysis therefore focuses on whether [Babbit] used the marks knowing that they were counterfeit."[6]

---

5. Section 1117 provides, in pertinent part:

(b) Treble damages for use of counterfeit mark
In assessing damages under subsection (a) of this section, the court shall, unless the court finds extenuating circumstances, enter judgment for three times such profits or damages, whichever is greater, together with a reasonable attorney's fee, in the case of any violation of section 1114(1)(a) of this title or section 380 of Title 36 that consists of intentionally using a mark or designation, knowing such mark or designation is a counterfeit mark (as defined in section 1116(d) of this title), in connection with the sale, offering for sale, or distribution of goods or services.

6. A "counterfeit" mark means "a spurious mark which is identical with, or substantially indistinguishable from, a registered mark." 15 U.S.C. §1127.

In the Agreement, Babbit and Dynascan agreed that Babbit could use the Cobra trademark in connection with the distribution and sale of certain models of cordless telephones in South America, as long as Babbit ordered the products through Dynascan. . . . [I]t is clear that Babbit used Dynascan's trademarks knowing that they were counterfeit. Babbit is therefore liable for trademark counterfeiting.

### 4. Unfair Competition, False Designation & Dilution

Dynascan also presents an allegation of false designation of origin under Section 43(a) of the Lanham Act, 15 U.S.C. §1125(a), state law causes of action for dilution, pursuant to Fla. Stat. §495.151, and unfair and deceptive trade practices, pursuant to Fla. Stat. §501.204(1), and a common law cause of action for unfair competition. The same set of facts enabling Dynascan to prevail under Section 1114(a)(1) will result in recovery pursuant to Section 1125. *Marathon Mfg. Co. v. Enerlite Products Corp.*, 767 F.2d 214, 217 (5th Cir. 1985). This is because Section 1125(a) is broader than Section 1114 in that it covers false advertising or description whether or not it involves trademark infringement. . . . This Court's analysis is therefore equally conclusive of these issues.

Finally, Dynascan is entitled to relief under the state cause of action for dilution. *See Jaguar Cars Ltd. v. Skandrani*, 771 F. Supp. 1178, 1185 (S.D. Fla. 1991). Section 495.151 provides that any person using a mark is entitled to an injunction enjoining:

> Subsequent use by another of the same or similar mark if it appears to the court that there exists a likelihood of injury to business reputation or of dilution of the distinctive quality of the mark, notwithstanding the absence of competition between the parties or of confusion as to the source of goods or services.

Fla. Stat. §495.151. There is a strong likelihood of dilution in the present case because purchasers may associate Babbit's telephones with Dynascan telephones.[7]

## C. Damages and Injunctive Relief

Dynascan argues that it is entitled to a plethora of damages pursuant to the Lanham Act, including a permanent injunction, treble damages, attorney's fees and costs, and prejudgment interest.[8] The Lanham Act provides for recovery by a successful plaintiff of: "(1) defendants profits; (2) any damages sustained by the plaintiff; and (3) the costs of this action." 15 U.S.C. §1117. This recovery is cumulative, that is, the Court may award Dynascan both its damages and Babbit's profits. *Playboy Enterprises*, 546 F. Supp. at 997. There are, however, different standards for the awarding of each measure of damages.

---

7\. . . . The Court also notes that Dynascan has presented no case law, nor can the Court find any case law, suggesting that the Tariff Act of 1930, 19 U.S.C §1526, applies to a standard trademark infringement case. Although the plain language of the Tariff Act suggests that a party may not import trademarked merchandise into the United States without the consent of the trademark owner, this Court concludes that "there is no evidence that Congress intended such a sweeping scope to §1526(a)." *See Vivitar Corp. v. United States*, 595 [593] F. Supp. 420, 435 (Ct. Int'l Trade 1984) (Court held that "construing §1526 to apply when a foreign source of imports is related to, or the agent of, the American trademark owner could lead to results that Congress could not reasonably have intended when it enacted the section.").

8\. Babbit's sales of Model SA-660s cordless telephones bearing a Cobra trademark have infringed Dynascan's trademark registrations in violation of the Lanham Act, 15 U.S.C. §1114(1) and 15 U.S.C. §1125(a). Consequently, Dynascan is entitled to an injunction enjoining Babbit and its corporated affiliates and subsidiaries, officers, agents, servants, employees, attorneys and those in active concert and participation with them from the unauthorized use or employment in connection with buying, advertising, promoting, displaying, offering for sale or distributing of goods or merchandise containing or having attached or having in association therewith Dynascan's Cobra trademarks and trade name or colorable imitations thereof and specifically including cordless telephones manufactured by Hyundai or any related companies. 15 U.S.C. §1116(a). *See Jaguar Cars, Ltd.*, 771 F. Supp. at 1185.

### 1. Babbit's Profits

Where the defendant's infringement is deliberate and willful, as in this case, an accounting for profits is proper under a theory of unjust enrichment. *Maltina Corp. v. Cawy Bottling Co. Inc.*, 613 F.2d 582, 585 (5th Cir. 1980). This accounting serves to deter future infringement, and is thus appropriate even where the plaintiff is not in direct competition with the defendant. *Id.* In this instance, Babbit has demonstrated and the Court has found that Babbit's profits averaged 25% on all sales of Cobra products. Babbit's sales of infringing products to South America amounted to a total sum of $561,868.30. Babbit's profits on these sales, calculated consistent with Babbit's 25% profit margin, totaled $140,467.08.

### 2. Dynascan's Damages

In order to recover damages (apart from Babbit's profits), Dynascan must demonstrate that it suffered actual damages. *Id.* at 587. "The mark owners royalties are normally used as the measure of damages, but the plaintiff must prove both lost sales and that the loss was caused by defendants' actions." *Playboy Enterprises*, 546 F. Supp. at 998. Dynascan has not demonstrated that it would have made any of the sales that Babbit has made, but the Court concludes that it has demonstrated that Babbit would have purchased authentic Cobra telephones had they not acquired the counterfeit telephones. The Court draws this conclusion because Babbit was unable to sell its MCE labelled telephones, and the sales of Cobra telephones were still highly profitable, as demonstrated by the sale of the counterfeit telephones. Thus, Dynascan is entitled to an award of damages for Babbit's failure to pay the required five percent royalty on cordless telephone sales of $561,868.30. Consequently, Dynascan is entitled to damages totalling $28,093.42.[9]

### 3. Trebling of Damages

The Court may, in its discretion, reduce or enhance the resulting award up to three times the amount of profits or damages, whichever is greater, as justice shall require. 15 U.S.C. §1117(a). Such an award is discretionary, but it may not be punitive, and must be based on a showing of actual harm. *Donsco, Inc. v. Casper Corp.*, 587 F.2d 602 (3rd Cir. 1978). If the infringement is intentional, however, and the use of a counterfeit trademark has been proven, then §1117(b) governs, and the Court is required to treble damages and award attorney's fees unless the Court finds extenuating circumstances. *Chanel, Inc.*, 931 F.2d at 1476. *See also Louis Vuitton S.A. v. Lee*, 875 F.2d 584, 588 (7th Cir. 1989).

Dynascan has demonstrated and this Court has found that Babbit intentionally infringed the Cobra trademark and used a counterfeit Cobra trademark. Consequently, the Court finds that a trebling of damages is required. Pursuant to this conclusion, Dynascan is entitled to a trebling of Lanham Act damages from Babbit for lost profits in the amount of $421,401.24.

### 4. Costs

Dynascan is entitled to recover its costs. 15 U.S.C. §1117; Fed. R. Civ. P. 54(d). Dynascan is directed to submit a bill of costs to the Court within fifteen (15) calendar days of the date of this Order.

### 5. Attorney's Fees

In an exceptional case, the Court may award attorney's fees. 15 U.S.C. §1117. This is an exceptional case because Babbit intentionally arranged to obtain counterfeit goods from

9. Dynascan is also entitled to damages in the form of lost royalties pursuant to Babbit's breach of contract.

Hyundai, intentionally avoided contractual obligations, and intentionally passed off such goods as Cobra products. Consequently, attorney's fees are awarded to Dynascan.[10] Dynascan is directed to submit a detailed affidavit describing the work done, the time involved, and the amount claimed for each such item of work within fifteen (15) calendar days of the date of this Order.

#### 6. Prejudgment Interest

The Court may, in its discretion, award prejudgment interest on the total amount of the damages award. 15 U.S.C. §1117. For the reasons stated above, Dynascan is awarded prejudgment interest, beginning with the date that Dynascan filed its counterclaims, filed May 24, 1991, to the conclusion of the trial of this matter, November 13, 1992.

#### 7. Personal Guarantee of Damages Award

Dynascan has requested that all relief awarded in this case be applied jointly and severally to Defendants Babbit, Robert Steinmetz and Sol Steinmetz. Robert Steinmetz is President of Babbit and Sol Steinmetz is Chairman of Babbit. Both officers testified that they were personally involved in the unauthorized purchase and sale of Cobra products, even after receiving notification from Dynascan that the sale of any Model SA-660s cordless telephones was a violation of the Agreement and trademark statutes. . . . Robert Steinmetz and Sol Steinmetz are jointly and personally liable for their participation in Babbit's counterfeiting activities.

### III. Conclusion

For the preceding reasons, it is hereby

ORDERED AND ADJUDGED that judgment shall be entered in favor of Defendant Dynascan and against Plaintiff Babbit as to Babbit's Complaint, and in favor of Counter-plaintiff Dynascan and against Counter-defendant Babbit as to Dynascan's Counterclaim, by separate order, pursuant to Fed. R. Civ. P. 58.

## NOTES AND QUESTIONS

**1.** What if the cordless telephones at issue in *Babbit* had been shipped directly from the manufacturer/supplier in South Korea to Latin America and the "counterfeit" labels had been placed on the goods in Latin America? Could trademark infringement subject matter jurisdiction be predicated on the facts that the distribution and trademark licensing agreement was negotiated in the United States, that the domicile of the contracting parties is in the United States, and that sales were "orchestrated" from Florida? While this might involve sufficient contact with the forum state to establish jurisdiction over a breach of contract claim, should infringement of a U.S. registered trademark be predicated on so little contact with the forum? Can this decision be reconciled with the strong presumption against extraterritorial effect of U.S. law confirmed by the U.S. Supreme Court in *Microsoft v. AT&T*, excerpted in Chapter 1, section VII.D.1?

10. The Court notes that Dynascan is also entitled to attorney's fees pursuant to the Agreement. Specifically, Babbit's breach of the Agreement entitles Dynascan to attorney's fees pursuant to the personal guarantees executed by Robert and Sol Steinmetz in connection with the Agreement.

**2.** Note that the officers of Babbit are held personally liable for the damages in this case, despite the fact that they were acting on behalf of a corporation. The imposition of personal liability should act as an extraordinary deterrent to potential trademark infringers. Yet, do you think the court would have imposed personal liability on the officers of a major multinational corporation who directed their employees to breach a distribution contract and continue using a trademark without the permission of the trademark holder? Should it matter that Babbit is a closely held corporation?

### 5. *Criminal Enforcement*

Some of the most serious issues confronting the international intellectual property system are raised by the increased focus on criminal prosecution for infringement. There are legitimate law enforcement objectives in seeking to prevent trademark counterfeiting and copyright piracy from being used as mechanisms for financing broader criminal enterprises such as trafficking in narcotics and funding terrorist activities. Yet, there are serious risks involved in shifting responsibility for enforcing intellectual property laws to criminal enforcement authorities. First, the threat of criminal penalties may have a deterrent or "chilling" effect on the willingness of researchers to pursue innovation and on freedom of expression. Second, industry groups seeking to solidify their control over IPRs tend to view "balancing mechanisms" with suspicion, and seek to limit those mechanisms, including through the imposition of criminal liability. The U.S. Department of Justice Task Force on Intellectual Property, for example, has recommended that U.S. free trade agreements "restrict[] the ability of FTA partners to order compulsory licensing of patents."[62] This recommendation implies that compulsory licensing constitutes a form of theft or criminal activity, which is contrary to the letter and spirit of the Paris Convention, the TRIPS Agreement, and the WTO Doha Declaration on the TRIPS Agreement and Public Health. One of the more difficult policy problems confronting intellectual property lawyers and the international intellectual property system is achieving a socially appropriate balance between affording access to knowledge, on one hand, and providing fair compensation to innovators, on the other. The introduction of severe criminal penalties for IP violations may make achieving this balance more difficult.

The United States is moving increasingly in the direction of adopting criminal penalties for infringement of IPRs, and it is strongly encouraging other countries to follow its lead. The following is a list of the penalties established under U.S. law with respect to "IP" crimes and that may be sought by the U.S. Department of Justice in criminal enforcement proceedings.

---

## *Federal Criminal Laws Protecting Intellectual Property**

### Copyright

17 U.S.C. §506(a)(1)(A) [(formerly §506(a)(1))] & 18 U.S.C. §2319(b) *Copyright Infringement for Profit (Felony)*

Statutory maximum penalty of 5 years in prison and a $250,000 fine or twice the gain/loss for an individual first-time offender (10 years for second offense); $500,000 fine or twice the gain/loss for a corporate offender. Civil and criminal forfeiture available.

17 U.S.C. §506(a)(1)(B) [(formerly §506(a)(2))] & 18 U.S.C. §2319(c) *Large-Scale Copyright Infringement Without Profit Motive (Felony)*

62. U.S. Department of Justice, *Progress Report of the Department of Justice's Task Force on Intellectual Property*, June 2006, at 35.

* U.S. Department of Justice, *Progress Report of the Department of Justice's Task Force on Intellectual Property* 11-12, June 2006.

Statutory maximum penalty of 3 years in prison and $250,000 fine or twice the gain/loss for an individual first-time offender (6 years for second offense); $500,000 fine or twice gain/loss for corporate offender. Civil and criminal forfeiture available.

17 U.S.C. §506(a)(1)(C) & 18 U.S.C. §2319(d) *Distribution of Pre-Release Copyrighted Works or Material over Publicly-Accessible Computer Network*

If infringement is effected for commercial purpose: Statutory maximum penalty of 5 years in prison and a $250,000 fine or twice the gross gain/loss for an individual first-time offender (10 years for second offense); $500,000 fine or twice the gain/loss for a corporate offender. Civil and criminal forfeiture available.

If infringement is not effected for commercial purpose: Statutory maximum penalty of 3 years in prison and $250,000 fine or twice the gain/loss for an individual first-time offender (6 years for second offense); $500,000 fine or twice the gain/loss for a corporate offender. Civil and criminal forfeiture available.

17 U.S.C. §1204 *Technology to Circumvent Anti-Piracy Protections Digital Millennium Copyright Act ("DMCA")*

Statutory maximum penalty of 5 years in prison and a $500,000 fine or twice the gain/loss for an individual and corporate first-time offender. Statutory maximum penalty of 10 years in prison for a second offense and a $1 million fine or twice the gain/loss. No forfeiture available.

18 U.S.C. §2318 *Counterfeit/Illicit Labels and Counterfeit Documentation and Packaging for Copyrighted Works*

Statutory maximum penalty of 5 years in prison and a $250,000 fine or twice the gross gain/loss for an individual; $500,000 fine or twice the gain/loss for a corporate offender. Criminal and civil forfeiture available.

18 U.S.C. §2319A *Bootleg Recordings of Live Musical Performances*

Statutory maximum penalty of 5 years in prison and a $250,000 fine or twice the gain/loss for an individual first-time offender (10 years for second offense); $500,000 or twice the gain/loss for a corporate offender. Civil and criminal forfeiture available.

18 U.S.C. §2319B *Camcording*

Statutory maximum penalty of 3 years in prison and $250,000 fine or twice the gain/loss for an individual first-time offender (6 years for second offense); $500,000 fine or twice the gain/loss for a corporate offender. Criminal forfeiture available.

## Trademarks, Service Marks, and Certification Marks

### Counterfeit Trademarks, Service Marks, and Certification Marks

Statutory maximum penalty of 10 years in prison and a $2 million fine or twice the gain/loss for an individual first-time offender; $5 million fine or twice the gain/loss for corporate offender. For second-time offenders statutory maximum penalty of 20 years in prison and a $5 million fine or twice the gain/loss for an individual; $15 million fine or twice the gain/loss for corporate offender. Civil and criminal forfeiture available.

## Trade Secrets

### Economic Espionage to Benefit a Foreign Government

Statutory maximum of 15 years in prison and a $500,000 fine or twice the gain/loss for an individual offender, $10 million fine or twice the gain/loss for a corporate offender. Criminal forfeiture is available.

**Commercial Theft of Trade Secrets**

Statutory maximum penalty of 10 years in prison and a $250,000 fine or twice the gain/loss for an individual first-time offender (10 years for second offense); $5 million fine or twice the gain/loss for a corporate offender. Criminal forfeiture available.

## NOTES AND QUESTIONS

**1.** As noted in Chapter 5, on May 19, 2014, the United States Department of Justice announced the filing of criminal charges against five Chinese government officials for computer hacking, economic espionage, and other offenses directed at six American victims in the U.S. nuclear power, metals, and solar products industries. The charges included theft of trade secrets intended to benefit, among others, Chinese state-owned enterprises. These indictments of Chinese government officials raise the stakes in cross-border intellectual property disputes. No doubt the U.S. government considers its actions against the Chinese government officials justified and reasonably proportionate. But, this could be the beginning of a "tit-for-tat" exchange of criminal prosecutions, justifiable or not. Certainly the U.S. government considered the potential costs as well as benefits of bringing these charges. Whether that assessment was a sound one remains to be determined. It seems highly unlikely that the Chinese government will surrender its officials for criminal prosecution before the U.S. courts.

**2.** Note that there are no U.S. statutes that impose criminal liability for patent infringement. Recall that a substantial proportion of patents subject to challenge are found to be invalid. Recall also that major U.S. corporations frequently are involved in patent disputes. Might these factors explain why criminalization of patent infringement has not yet taken place? But see the following note regarding an EU proposal for criminalization of patent infringement. If such legislation were to be adopted in the European Union, would the United States again be facing a "protection gap"? Would IP-dependent industry groups urge Congress to criminalize patent infringement lest research and development teams move to Europe to take advantage of criminal prosecution of infringers?

**3.** The European Commission in July 2005 presented a proposal that would include criminalization of patent infringement. *See* Proposal for a European Parliament and Council Directive on criminal measures aimed at ensuring the enforcement of intellectual property rights and Proposal for a Council Framework Decision to strengthen the criminal law framework to combat intellectual property offences (SEC(2005)848) (presented by the Commission), Brussels, 12.7.2005, COM(2005)276 final, 2005/0127(COD), 2005/0128(CNS). This proposal did not gain traction in the legislative process and is no longer active.

**4.** In order to appreciate the trend toward stronger enforcement of IPRs, including through criminalization, it may be instructive to examine the April 2023 Annual Intellectual Property Report to Congress, developed by the Office of the U.S. Intellectual Property Enforcement Coordinator, https://www.whitehouse.gov/wp-content/uploads/2023/04/FY22-IPEC-Annual-Report_Final.pdf

## V. CIVIL LITIGATION AND THE ANTISUIT INJUNCTION PHENOMENON

A byproduct of the use of FRAND licensing negotiations (see discussion above regarding Section 337) for the determination of royalties to be paid in respect of standard-essential patents is multi-forum civil litigation. We know from earlier chapters of this book that patents are independent and that decisions by administrative authorities (including courts) in one country do not affect the validity of patents in other countries. As a general principle, the courts of one country cannot invalidate a patent maintained in another country. But this general rule does not extend to the question whether the royalty rates being charged for the licensing of parallel SEP are fair and reasonable. Conceptually, a court in one country may order an SEP patent owner to charge a certain royalty rate in another country, or globally where the patent owner owns patents, and it might enforce its order through a penalty in the jurisdiction where it has the power to enforce such an order. Assuming for the sake of argument that it might be expedient to have the FRAND royalty terms for an SEP license determined by a single court, what court should that be and where should it be situated? The absence of a determinative answer to that question underlies the recent emergence of anti-suit injunctions as an international litigation phenomenon.

**Giuseppe Colangelo and Valerio Torti**

## *Anti-Suit Injunctions and Geopolitics in Transnational SEPs Litigation*

14 European Journal of Legal Studies 45-84 (2023)

[P]arties have regularly failed to reach agreement on FRAND outcomes; hence a spate of cross-border litigation has arisen, often leading to inconsistent and conflicting rulings. However, some courts have claimed the authority to set global FRAND rates, thereby setting themselves up as global licensing tribunals determining the terms of worldwide FRAND licenses in the context of national proceedings. As a consequence, parties have been incentivised to litigate rather than to find negotiated solutions – and to look for the most convenient jurisdiction. Therefore, concerns have been raised about the risks related to a 'race to the courthouse' among litigants and a 'race to the bottom' among jurisdictions.2 Indeed, in setting global licensing terms courts may be interested in making themselves attractive venues for specific types of litigants (SEP holders rather than implementers), while parties are encouraged to bring suits in favourable jurisdictions as quickly as possible in order to exploit the advantages of being the first to strike.

As part of these forum shopping strategies, litigants are also increasingly eager to request (and courts appear prone to issue) anti-suit injunctions (ASIs), that is, orders restraining a party from pursuing foreign proceedings or enforcing a judgment obtained in foreign proceedings. ASIs may bring benefits by containing litigation costs and reducing the likelihood of inconsistent results across jurisdictions. However, rather than ending the game, the issuance of an ASI has resulted in a new form of unwelcome competition, with litigants and courts devising anti-anti suit injunctions (AASIs), which block a party from seeking or enforcing an ASI, anti-anti-anti suit injunctions (AAASIs), which prevent a party from obtaining an AASI to block another party from requesting or enforcing an ASI, and so on and so forth.

Although ASIs have existed in the context of transnational litigation since fifteenth-century England, SEP disputes have brought them into a new dimension. The present phenomenon reflects the global reach of markets for technology and the growing importance of SEPs as building blocks in the modern global economy, but also appears a natural fruit of the poison tree of FRAND determination. Furthermore, as the rise of the Internet of Things (IoT) and the evolution of many industries hinge on advanced mobile telecommunication standards (4G and 5G) to ensure interoperability and technical compatibility, SEP licensing has become a matter of geopolitics. Moreover, innovation in emerging technologies is crucially important to national security. For all these reasons, countries may have policy interests in preventing their companies' intellectual property rights from being adjudicated in foreign courts. Since the smooth implementation of mobile telecommunication standards is crucial to the economic potential of the IoT and United States (US) and European companies hold a significant amount of SEPs for these technologies, policymakers are worried that ASIs may represent a new and dangerous unfair practice adopted by Chinese companies, with the support of Chinese courts and authorities, to promote domestic economic interests and undervalue foreign patents by setting significantly lower FRAND rates. . . .

. . . [T]he US is among the jurisdictions where courts have sometimes issued ASIs (i.e. 'stays' of litigation) in the context of different transnational disputes, this does not mean that US courts have traditionally been willing to grant such an extra-territorial remedy in order to prevent parties from beginning or continuing proceedings before foreign tribunals. Instead, as Strong has noted, ASIs in the US should be understood as extraordinary remedies, particularly in the light of the established ('first to judgment') principle that 'parallel proceedings on the same *in personam* claim should ordinarily be allowed to proceed simultaneously, at least until judgment is reached in one, which can be pled as *res judicata* in the other'. This approach is supposed to avoid first-to-file strategies and the resulting 'race to the courthouse'.

. . . [I]n the CJEU's opinion, an ASI would be contrary to the general principle that every court in the EU determines whether it has jurisdiction to resolve disputes brought before it, and that 'in no case is a court of one Member State in a better position to determine whether the court of another Member State has jurisdiction'. In contrast, allowing EU national courts to grant ASIs would inevitably impair the mutual trust which Member States accord to one another's legal and judicial frameworks. Interference of this sort would not even be justified in extreme circumstances where an ASI is sought to prevent an abuse of process or a bad faith action by a litigant before the foreign authority.

. . .[T]he surge of ASIs and the risks related to their opportunistic use in the SEP landscape is linked to the role that certain national courts have come to play in setting themselves up as de facto global licensing tribunals. As the tendency of some courts to set high rates may attract patent holders to those jurisdictions, implementers may in turn be interested in challenging those results before courts in jurisdictions with an established reputation for being hostile to patent holders and prone to set low rates.

From this standpoint, the decisions by successive English courts in Unwired Planet v Huawei have triggered the global race to the courthouse. The High Court of Justice, under Mr Justice Birss, found that global portfolio licensing was common industry practice and offered efficiency benefits by saving transaction costs for licensors and licensees and obviating the need to determine a royalty rate on a patent-by-patent basis. Indeed, the patent portfolio at stake was 'sufficiently large and had sufficiently wide geographical scope that a licensor and licensee acting reasonably and on a willing basis would have agreed on a worldwide licence and would have regarded country-by-country licensing as madness'. Furthermore, Birss held that the approach supported did not contravene jurisdictional rules since the validity of patents would remain a matter falling within the exclusive jurisdiction of the judicial authorities of the territory where the patents subsist.

The UK Supreme Court ultimately upheld the ruling, confirming that national courts have the power to fix the conditions of a global FRAND license and grant an injunction to prevent infringements of SEPs . . .

Notably, by referring to some of the most significant jurisdictions (ie Germany, China and the US), the UK Supreme Court was able to identify a number of generally accepted principles or practices, recognising inter alia the lawfulness of: i) taking into account the usual negotiation practices in the relevant industries when setting the terms of a FRAND licence;

ii) determining a FRAND licence at a worldwide or international level in appropriate circumstances (eg when SEP holders have a sufficiently large and geographically diverse portfolio and the alleged infringers are activeglobally); and iii) granting injunctive relief against the infringement of SEPs if the implementer has refused to accept a FRAND licensing offer.

Moreover, the Court noted that the national nature of patents 'makes it very difficult, if not wholly impracticable, for a patent owner to protect an invention which is used in equipment manufactured in another country, sold in many countries and used by consumers globally'. Therefore, this attribute of patent law may invite holdout behaviour enabling implementers to deny patent holders' legitimate rights by avoiding paying them the proper price for the use of their inventions internationally. Finally, regarding the risk that this approach may favour forum shopping, conflicting judgments, and applications for ASIs, the Court argued that this would result from the policies of standard development organisations' (SDOs), which, though they allow

> FRAND worldwide licences when a SEP owner has a sufficiently large and geographically diverse portfolio and the implementer is active globally, do not provide for any international tribunal or forum to determine the terms of such licences.

. . .

It is worth noting that ASIs in SEP litigation were granted for the first time in the US, namely in Microsoft v Motorola, where a US district court concluded that resolving the US dispute would dispose of a German one. In the district court's view, the German action raised a number of serious concerns, from the risk of forum shopping and inconsistent judgements to duplicative or vexatious foreign litigation, which would undermine other equitable considerations by hampering, for instance, the US judge's ability to fairly adjudicate the FRAND dispute. Furthermore, the facts that both litigants were US corporations, the challenged conduct took place within the US, and the German action was filed after the U.S. action also contributed to overcoming any concern related to international comity. The Court of Appeal ultimately acknowledged the soundness of the district court's approach, confirming the willingness of US courts to grant ASIs.

. . .

Against this backdrop, interest in the role of ASIs in SEP litigation has been sparked by a sudden increase in the number of ASIs issued by Chinese courts. In particular, in 2020, four decisions were taken relating to applications for ASIs that signalled the courts' intention to set China as the jurisdiction of choice for global disputes. Three of the rulings were in favour of Chinese telecom companies.

. . .

The Supreme Court's judgement in Huawei was followed by the issuance of three other ASIs in Xiaomi v Inter Digital,65 OPPO v Sharp66 and Ericsson v Samsung, in which Chinese courts expanded the reach of Huawei by asserting their jurisdiction to set global FRAND rates and grant global injunctive relief barring legal action in any other country. Indeed, in upholding the decision in OPPO, the Supreme Court celebrated the emergence of China as a guide, rather than a follower, in setting international intellectual property rules.

. . .

In global SEP litigation, ASIs were soon followed by AASIs, which aim to prevent the opponent from seeking or enforcing an ASI. As a form of counter-ASI, an AASI seeks to preclude the blocking of an action before another court, thereby allowing the action to continue in parallel.

. . .

[T]he dynamics of ASIs and their countermeasures perfectly depict the evolution of the 'race to the court-house' and 'race to the bottom' phenomena that have engaged stakeholders and courts at the global level. Furthermore, these disputes have highlighted the increasingly central role played by the Chinese jurisdiction on the standard-setting stage, together with the clear divide between European common law (ie UK) and civil law (eg France and Germany) jurisdictions, with the latter reluctant to recognise the effectiveness of ASIs and more inclined to resist interference by foreign courts. More generally, the new wave of litigation has raised unresolved questions about international comity relations, conflicts of laws, and effective judicial protection, which have significantly amplified the already existing tensions among the players involved in SEP licensing. Indeed, if SEP owners have unfettered freedom to select the jurisdiction in which to bring an action for infringement, they will probably select the jurisdiction likely to settle FRAND terms most favourable to them. By the same token, if implementers have unfettered freedom to bring a claim in any jurisdiction for settlement of FRAND terms, they will select the country which is most favourable to them.99 Therefore, ASIs may have a pernicious impact on the protection of patent rights and on the proper functioning of standardisation processes.

. . .

Moreover, ASI wars are a new side effect of the FRAND mechanism. In the two decades since its adoption by the ICT standard-setting environment, this licensing framework has triggered a significant number of disputes related inter alia to the precise meaning and scope of FRAND licenses, the nature and legal implications of FRAND commitments, and the value chain level at which a SEP holder must grant FRAND licenses. Thus, focusing on the flaws of the FRAND model, rather than searching for answers from the comity principle, represents the optimal pathway.

In this regard, instead of waiting for complex international coordination, a prompt adjustment of SDO licensing policies seems desirable at this stage, also considering the increasing importance SEPs have been acquiring in other sectors, from automotives to health and energy. A moderate version of this approach could entail the inclusion in SDO policies of an arbitration clause according to which licensees and licensors – in the absence of consensus over the scope of a FRAND license – would be required to refer the matter to an arbitral panel rather than bring the case before a national court. A more drastic solution would abandon the much-debated FRAND mechanism and impose on SEP holders a duty to disclose ex ante the most restrictive licensing terms applied for a given essential patent.

## NOTES AND QUESTIONS

**1.** Now that the gates of anti-suit injunction have been opened, is there any reason why this phenomenon is likely to be limited to resolution of disputes regarding FRAND royalties and SEP patents? The current international system which has relies on countries respecting the independence and territoriality of other countries from a patent law perspective is showing some signs of wear and tear. Is a "judiciary war" a potential outgrowth of recent trade wars?

**2.** On February 18, 2022, the European Union initiated dispute settlement proceedings with China by requesting consultations regarding a series of measures authorizing Chinese courts to impose anti-suit injunctions. The EU specifically referred to five cases in which Chinese courts had imposed anti-suit injunctions based in part on a decision by China's Supreme People's Court in 2020 interpreting China's Civil Procedure Law. The EU alleged that China's measures and decisions are inconsistent with Article 1.1, first sentence, in conjunction with Articles 28.1-28.2, of the TRIPS Agreement; Article 41.1, second sentence, of the TRIPS Agreement; Article 1.1, first sentence, in conjunction with Article 44.1, of the TRIPS

Agreement, and; China's commitments in its Protocol of Accession. A WTO dispute settlement panel was appointed on March 28, 2023. This case is pending as of August 2023. Among elements of interest, the EU asserts that China has failed to comply with its obligations under Article 63.1 of the TRIPS Agreement to publish or make publicly available the court decisions to which the EU has referred, and under Article 63.3 of the TRIPS Agreement to provide the text of the cited decisions following an official request for information from the EU.

# TABLE OF CASES

*Principal cases are indicated by italics.*

# INDEX